BIBLIOGRAPHY OF CRIME AND CRIMINAL JUSTICE

1927-1931

59-966

BUREAU OF PUBLIC ADMINISTRATION
UNIVERSITY OF CALIFORNIA

BIBLIOGRAPHY OF CRIME AND CRIMINAL JUSTICE

1927-1931

COMPILED BY
DOROTHY CAMPBELL CULVER
Research Assistant

NEW YORK
THE H. W. WILSON COMPANY
1934

Published July 1934
Printed in the United States of America

FOREWORD

When in 1930 the Bureau of Public Administration of the University of California inaugurated a group of studies in Public Administration, each of which would involve a coordinated attack by different specialists on some governmental problem, the administration of criminal justice was selected as one of the projects and a number of studies in various phases of this problem have been carried on by the Bureau since that time. The research program of the Bureau also includes a series of bibliographies in various selected fields of public administration, which made a bibliography in the field of the administration of criminal justice serve a dual purpose.

Altho Kuhlman's *Guide to Material on Crime and Criminal Justice* covers the American and English materials published prior to 1927, the surprising increase of publications since that date has created a real need for a compilation of the numerous recent materials, including the addition of the more important foreign references.

The Bureau of Public Administration of the University of California accordingly presents this comprehensive bibliography of the literature of crime and the administration of criminal justice produced in America and abroad during the years 1927 to 1931 inclusive, and hopes that it will be helpful to the librarian, the official, and the public.

Samuel C. May
Director, Bureau of Public Administration
University of California

Berkeley, California
April 18, 1934

PREFACE

This volume is international in scope and includes materials published or in manuscript during the five-year period, 1927 to 1931, inclusive. The listing is not complete, as it would be impracticable to index all the fragmentary materials that have come into existence in this period; nor have all items been available for examination.

The system of classification has been based on that used by Kuhlman in his *Guide to Material on Crime and Criminal Justice,* but expansion in this field has necessitated many modifications, particularly in the Section on Police. There has been an attempt to fit the classification to the material rather than to fit the material to a preconceived plan. Tho the items are entered only once, and the classification of certain items may seem questionable, all items should be readily accessible thru the detailed subject index which follows the bibliography.

Annotations subjoined to items are informative and descriptive rather than critical, and are used to indicate hidden material or clarify obscure titles. Information given in brackets has been added for identification of author entries. In listing the items, the compiler endeavored to follow the original document, book or periodical in the spelling of names and discrepancies, particularly in the foreign names, will be due to transliterations and translations.

In compiling this bibliography, use has been made primarily of the collections and files of the Bureau of Public Administration and General Library of the University of California, but acknowledgment should also be made of the assistance rendered by the libraries of Stanford University, Northwestern, University of Illinois, Western Reserve and the California State Library in the loan of materials.

I wish to take this opportunity of expressing my appreciation of the understanding and kindly encouragement of Samuel C. May, Director of the Bureau of Public Administration.

It is a pleasure to express my gratitude to Viola Rohrs Avery for her unlimited interest and assistance thruout the preparation of this manuscript.

Grateful acknowledgment is made to August Vollmer for his helpful reading of the section on Police; to George Z. Patrick for his translations of Russian materials; to Thomas S. Dabagh for his assistance in setting up the system of classification; and to Carleton R. Ball for his valuable suggestions and constructive criticisms. To the staff of the Bureau of Public Administration I wish to express my appreciation of their friendly cooperation.

DOROTHY CAMPBELL CULVER

Berkeley, California
March 8, 1934

TABLE OF CONTENTS

LIST OF ERRATA

Page	No.	
2	39B	institit should read institut
59	2144	Mandoloni should read Mandolini
66		number 3402 should read 2402
67		numbers 2340, 2342, 2343 should read 2440, 2442, 2443
103		number 3751 omitted
112		number 4157 omitted
131	4905	Manual should read Manuel
133	4986	offcers should read officers
160	5950	Tkakore should read Thakore
182	6762	Rehfeld should read Rehfeldt
208	7768	Amadeo should read Amedeo
224		number 5338 should read 8338
229		number 6588 should read 8588
242		number 9119 omitted
		number 1927 should read 9127
253		numbers 9493 and 9496 omitted
263	9859	N. J. should read Conn.
	9887	Breckenridge should read Breckinridge
272		number 10321 should read 10221
311		number 11670 should read 11570
322	11975	Menschrenrechte should read Menschenrechte
323	11983	number 11893 should read 11983
	12653	Woman's should read Women's

LIST OF PERIODICAL ABBREVIATIONS

Abh aus d Ges d Kriminalpsychol: Abhandlungen aus dem Gesamt-gebiete der Kriminalpsychologie [Heidelberger Abhandlungen]; Berlin (Springer)
Acad d Sci Morales et Pol Compt Rend: Académie des sciences morales et politiques, Paris, Comptes Rendus
Acad Int Law Rec des Cours: Academy of international law, Hague, Recueil des cours
Acad Sci Belg Bul Cl Lett: Académie royale de Belgique, Bruxelles, Classe des lettres et des sciences morales et politiques, Bulletin
Accad Med-Chir di Torino Gior: R. Accademia medico-chirurgica di Torino, Giornale
Accountant: The Accountant, London
Accountants J: Accountants journal, London
Acta Obst et Gynec Scandinav: Acta Obstetrica et Gynecologia Scandinavica, Stockholm
Acta Psychiat et Neurol: Acta Psychiatrica et Neurologica, København
Adm Locale: Administration locale, Bruxelles. (Union internationale des villes)
Aerztl Monats: Aerztliche Monatsschrift. Zeitschrift für soziale Gesetzgebung und Verwaltung und für das Gesundheitswesen in Heer, Marine und Polizei, Berlin
Aerztl Sachverst-Zeit: Aerztliche Sachverständigen-Zeitung, Berlin
Ala L J: Alabama law journal, Tuscaloosa. (Alabama state bar association)
Alkoholfrage: Die Alkoholfrage. Vierteljahrsschrift für Erforschung der Wirkungen des Alkohols, Berlin
Allg ärztl Zeitsch f Psychotherap: Allgemeine ärztliche Zeitschrift für Psychotherapie und Psychische Hygiene, Leipzig
1930—titled: Zentralblatt für Psychotherapie und ihre Granzgebiete einschliesslich der medizinischen Psychologie und Psychischen Hygiene.
Allg statist Arch: Allgemeines statistisches Archiv, Jena
Allg Zeitsch f Psychiat: Allgemeine Zeitschrift für Psychiatrie und psychischgerichtliche Medizin, Berlin
Am Assn Stud Feeblemind Proc: American association for the study of the feebleminded, Proceedings
Am Bankers Assn J: American bankers association journal, New York
Am Bankruptcy R: American bankruptcy review, New York
Am B Assn J: American bar association journal, Baltimore
Am B Assn Rep: American bar association, Report, Baltimore
Am Childh: American childhood, Springfield, Mass.
Am City: American city, New York
Am County: American county, Taft, Calif.
Am Fed: American federationist, Washington, D.C.
Am Ind: American industries, New York
Am Inst Homeop J: American institute of homeopathy, Journal
Am J Dis Child: American journal of diseases of children, Chicago
Am J Hyg: American journal of hygiene, Baltimore
Am J Int L: American journal of international law, New York
Am J Nursing: American journal of nursing, New York
Am J Obst & Gynec: American journal of obstetrics and gynecology, St. Louis
Am J Orthopsychiat: American journal of orthopsychiatry, Menasha, Wis.
Am J Phys Anthrop: American journal of physical anthropology, Philadelphia
Am J Police Sci: American journal of police science, Chicago
Beginning July-August 1932 included in Journal of criminal law and criminology.
Am J Psychiat: American journal of psychiatry, Baltimore
Am J Pub Health: American journal of public health and the Nation's health, New York
Am J Sociol: American journal of sociology, Chicago
Am Jud Soc J: American judicature society, Journal, Chicago
Am L Inst Proc: American law institute, Proceedings
Am L R: American law review, Boston
Am L Sch R: American law school review, St. Paul, Minn.
Am Lab Leg R: American labor legislation review, New York
Am Lib Assn Bul: American library association, Bulletin, Chicago
Am Lib Assn Proc: American library association, Proceedings issued in Bulletin
Am M Assn J: American medical association, Journal, Chicago
Am Mag: American magazine, New York
Am Med: American medicine, Burlington, Vt.
Am Mercury: American mercury, New York

Am Munic: American municipalities, Marshalltown, Ia.
Am Orient Soc J: American oriental society journal, New Haven, Conn.
Am Pol Sci R: American political science review, Baltimore
Am Pris Assn Proc: American prison association, Proceedings, New York
Am R: American review of reviews, New York
Am Rd Builders Assn Proc: American road builders association, Summary proceedings, Cleveland, Ohio
Am Social Soc Proc: American sociological society, Papers and Proceedings, Chicago
Am Speech: American speech, Baltimore
Am Statist Assn J: American statistical association, Journal, Boston
Am Toy Mfr: American toy manufacturer
An de Univ de Chile: Anales de la Universidad de Chile, Santiago
Ann Am Acad: Annals of the American academy of political and social science, Philadelphia
Ann de Méd Lég: Annales de médecine légale, de criminologie et de police scientifique, Paris. (Société de médecine légale de France)
Ann della Univ Bari: Annali del Seminario giuridico-economico della R. Università di Bari
Ann della Univ Palermo: Annali del Seminario giuridico della R. Università di Palermo
Ann delle Univ Toscane: Annali delle Università Toscane, Pisa
Ann dell'Osped Psichiat di Messina: Annali dell'Ospedale psichiatrico di Messina
Ann dell'Osped Psichiat di Perugia: Annali dell'Ospedale psichiatrico di Perugia
Ann des Falsif et des Fraudes: Annales des falsifications et des fraudes, Paris
Ann des Mal Vén: Annales des maladies vénériennes, Paris
Ann di Clin Med: Annali di clinica medica, Palermo
Ann di Neurol: Annali di neurologia, Napoli
Ann Fac de Med de São Paulo: Annaes de Faculdade de medicina de São Paulo, Brazil
Ann Méd-Psychol: Annales médico-psychologiques, Paris
Ann Pol & Litt: Annales politiques et litteraires, Paris
Anthrop Anz: Anthropologischer Anzeiger, München
Arbeit: Arbeit; Zeitschrift für gewerkschaftspolitik und Wirtschaftskunde, Berlin. (Allgemeiner deutscher gewerkschaftsbund)
Arbeit u Beruf: Arbeit und Beruf, Bernau
Supersedes Arbeitsnachweis in Deutschland.
Arbeiterwohlfahrt: Arbeiterwohlfahrt, Berlin
Arbeitsrecht: Arbeitsrecht; Jahrbuch für das gesamte dienstrecht der Arbeiter, Angestellten und Beamten, Stuttgart
Arch Brasilerios: Archivos Brasilerios
Arch de Med, Cir y Espec: Archivos de medicina, cirugia y especialidades, Madrid
Arch de Méd des Enf: Archives de médecine des enfants, Paris
Arch de Med Leg: Archivo de medicina legal, Lisboa
Arch de Philos du Dr: Archives de philosophie du droit et de sociologie juridique, Paris
Arch di Antrop Crim: Archivio di antropologia criminale, psichiatria, medicina legale e scienze affini, Torino
Arch f d ges Psychol: Archiv für die gesamte Psychologie, Leipzig
Arch f Dermat u Syphilis: Archiv für Dermatologie und Syphilis, Prague
Includes Verhandlungen der deutschen dermatologischen Gesellschaft.
Arch f Frauenk: Archiv für Frauenkunde und Konstitutionsforschung, Leipzig
Arch f Gesch d Med: Sudhoffs Archiv für Geschichte der Medizin, Leipzig
Arch f Gynäk: Archiv für Gynäkologie, Berlin
Arch f Krim: Archiv für Kriminologie, Leipzig
Arch f Psychiat: Archiv für Psychiatrie und Nervenkrankheiten, Berlin
Arch f Rassen- u Gesell-Biol: Archiv für Rassen- und Gesellschafts-Biologie, einschliesslich Rassen- und Gesellschafts-Hygiene, München
Arch f Rechts u Wirtschaftsphilos: Archiv für Rechts- und Wirtschafts-Philosophie mit besonderer Berücksichtigung der Gesetzgebungsfragen, Berlin
Arch f Rechtspfl in Sachsen, Thür u Anhalt: Archiv für Rechtspflege in Sachsen, Thüringen und Anhalt, Leipzig
Arch f soz Hyg u Demog: Archiv für soziale Hygiene und Demographie, Berlin
Arch f Sozialwiss u Sozialpol: Archiv für Sozialwissenschaft und Sozialpolitik, Berlin
Arch f Strafr- u Strafproz: Archiv für Strafrecht und Strafprozess, Berlin
Arch Forum: Architectural forum, Boston
Arch Gen di Neurol, Psichiat e Psicoanal: Archivio generale di neurologia, psichiatria e psicoanalisi, Napoli
Arch Int Med: Archives of internal medicine, Chicago
Arch Ital di Psicol: Archivio italiano di psicologia, Torino
Arch Neurol & Psychiat: Archives of neurology and psychiatry, Chicago
Arch Path & Lab Med: Archives of pathology and laboratory medicine, Chicago; later titled: Archives of pathology

Arch Pediat: Archives of pediatrics, New York
Arch Psychol: Archives of psychology, New York
Arch Rec: Architectural record, New York
Ark B Assn Proc: Arkansas bar association, Proceedings
Ark M Soc J: Arkansas medical society, Journal, Little Rock
Ars Méd: Ars médica revista de medicina, cirugia y especialidades, Barcelona
Asia: Asia, New York
Asiatic R: Asiatic review, London
Assicurazioni Soc: Assicurazioni sociali, Roma
Assn of Dir Poor & Char & Correc Proc: Association of the directors of the poor and charities and correction of the state of Pennsylvania, Proceedings
Atlan M: Atlantic monthly, Concord, N.H.
Atlantica: Atlantica, Roma, New York
1-6 '23-'28 as Rivista d'Italia e d'America; 7(1) F '29 as Atlantis; no issues for Ja/F '30.
Atti d Real Acad d Sci Morali e Pol: Atti del Accademia di scienze morali e politiche della Società Reale di Napoli, Napoli
Atti d Real Ist Veneto di Sci, Lett ed Arti: Atti del reale Istituto Veneto di scienze, lettere ed arti, Venezia
Aus Hamburgs Verwaltung u Wirtschaft: Aus Hamburgs Verwaltung und Wirtschaft . . . Monatsschrift des Statistischen Landesamts
Austral For J: Australian forestry journal, Sydney
Austral L J: Australian law journal, Sydney
Australasian J Psychol: Australasian journal of psychology and philosophy, Sydney
Avenir Med: Avenir Medical, Lyons

Baltimore Munic J: Baltimore municipal journal, Baltimore
Bank N: Bank news, Kansas City, Mo.
Bankers M: Bankers monthly, Chicago
Bankers Mag: Bankers magazine, New York
Bayr Verwaltungsbl: Bayerische Verwaltungsblätter, München
Beitr z gerichtl Med: Beiträge zur gerichtlichen Medizin, Wien
Bereitschaft: Die Bereitschaft; Zeitschrift für menschenökonomie, Wohlfahrtspflege und soziale Technik, Wien
Berliner Wohlfahrtsbl: Berliner Wohlfahrtsblätter, Berlin
Betriebsräte-Zeitsch f Funktionäre d Metallind: Betriebsräte-Zeitschrift für Funktionäre der Metallindustrie, Berlin
Bi-M L R: Bi-monthly law review, Detroit
Bibl Nac de Crim y Cienc Afines Bol: Biblioteca nacional de criminologie y ciencias afines, Boletin, Buenos Aires
Bibliog Fascista: Bibliografia fascista, Roma
Bibliog Res Stud Educ: Bibliography of research studies in education
Birth Control R: Birth control review, New York
Bl d Deut Roten Kreuzes: Blätter des deutschen Roten Kreuzes, Berlin
Bl d Zentralleitung f Wohltätigk in Württ: Blätter der Zentralleitung für Wohltätigkeit in Württemberg, Stuttgart
Bl f Gefängniskunde: Blätter für Gefangniskunde, Heidelberg
Bl f Wohlfahrtspfl: Blätter für Wohlfahrtspflege, Dresden
Blackwood: Blackwood's magazine, Edinburgh, London
Bol de Crimin: Boletín de criminología, Lima. (Dirección general de prisiones, Lima, Peru)
Bol del Sindacato Fascista Avvocati: Il Bollettino del Sindacato Fascista avvocati e procuratori di Napoli, Napoli
Bol do Inst de Crimin: Boletim do Instituto de criminologia, Lisboa
Bookm: Bookman, London
Bost Med & Surg J: Boston medical and surgery journal *see* New England journal of medicine
Bost Univ L R: Boston university law review, Boston
Bradstreet's: Bradstreet's, New York
Brick & Clay Rec: Brick and clay record, Chicago
Brit J Educ Psychol: British journal of educational psychology
Brit J Inebriety: British journal of inebriety, London
Brit J M Psychol: British journal of medical psychology, London
Brit M J: British medical journal, London
Brooklyn: Brooklyn magazine, Brooklyn. (Chamber of commerce)
Bruxelles-Méd: Bruxelles-médical, Bruxelles
Bücherei u Bildungspfl: Bücherei und Bildungspflege, Leipzig
Buenos Aires Univ Nac R: Buenos Aires Universidad nacional, Revista, Buenos Aires
Bul de Dr Tchecoslovaque: Bulletin de droit tchecoslovaque, Praha
Bul Int de la Protec de l'Enf: Bulletin international de la protection de l'enfance, Bruxelles
Bul Méd [Paris]: Le bulletin médical, Paris

Bul St Inst [Iowa]: Bulletin of state institutions, Iowa
Bul Statist României: Buletinul Statistal României, Bucuresti
Burroughs Clearing House: Burroughs clearing house, Detroit
Bus W: Business week, Greenwich, Conn.

Calcutta R: Calcutta review, Calcutta
Calif & W Med: California and western medicine, San Francisco
Calif Conf Soc Wk Q Bul: California conference of social work, Quarterly bulletin
Calif Highw & Pub Wks: California highways and public works, Sacramento
Calif J Development: California journal of development, San Francisco
Calif L R: California law review, Berkeley
Calif Q Sec Educ: California quarterly of secondary education, Berkeley
Calif St B J: California state bar journal, San Francisco
Cambridge L J: Cambridge law journal, Cambridge
Can B Assn Proc: Canadian bar association, Proceedings
Can B R: Canadian bar review, Toronto
Can Forum: Canadian forum, Toronto
Can Gaz: Canadian gazette, London
Can M Assn J: Canadian medical association, Journal, Montreal
Can Mag: Canadian magazine of politics, science, art and literature, Toronto
Can Nat Comm Ment Hyg Bul: Canadian national commission on mental hygiene, Bulletin, Toronto
Can Police Bul: Canadian police bulletin, Toronto
Caridad: Caridad; revista de beneficencia y de bien social, Barcelona
Caritas: Caritas; Zeitschrift für Caritaswissenschaft und Caritasarbeit, Freiburg i. Br.
Case & Com: Case and comment, Rochester, N.Y.
Časop Lék Česk: Časopsis lékařuv českých. Orgán českého lékařstva
Published by Czechoslovakian Physicians in Prague, under Ministry of Schools and public education, Prague.
Časop pro Právni a Státní Vedu: Časopsis pro Právní a Státní Vedu
Cath Char R: Catholic charities review, New York
Cath Educ R: Catholic educational review, Washington
Cath World: Catholic world, New York
Cavalry J: Cavalry Journal, London
Cent: Century magazine, New York
Cent L J: Central law journal, St. Louis, Mo.
Cervello: Cervello; giornale di nevrologia, Napoli
Ceylon J Sci: Ceylon journal of science, Colombo, Ceylon
Chamber Comm St N Y Bul: Chamber of commerce of the state of New York, Bulletin
Chambers J: Chambers journal, Edinburgh
Chic Banker: Chicago banker, Chicago
Chic Sch J: Chicago schools journal, Chicago
Chief Constables Assn Can Proc: Chief constables association of Canada, Proceedings
Child [London]: Child, London
Child Welf: Child Welfare, Philadelphia
Childh Educ: Childhood education, Baltimore
China Critic: China critic, Shanghai
China Med J: China medical journal, Shanghai
China W R: China weekly review, Shanghai
Chinese Nation: Chinese nation, Shanghai
Chinese Soc & Pol Sci R: Chinese social and political science review, Peking
Chirurg: Chirurg; Zeitschrift für alle Gebiete der operativen Medizin, Berlin
Chosen M A J: Chosen medical association, Kaijo Imperial university, Journal, Kaijo
Chr Cent: Christian century, Chicago
Chr Q R: Church quarterly review, London
Christ u Wiss: Christentum und Wissenschaft, Leipzig
Chron Méd: La chronique médicale, Paris
City Club N Y Bul: City club of the city of New York, Bulletin
City Man Yrbk: City manager yearbook
Civic Alliance Bul: Civic alliance bulletin, Boston
Class J: Classical journal, Chicago
Class Philol: Classical philology, Chicago
Cleveland City Rec: Cleveland city record, Cleveland
Clin J: Clinical journal, London
Clin Med & Surg: Clinical medicine and surgery, Chicago
Cluj Med: Clujul medical, Bucuresti
Colegio de Abogados, Buenos Aires R: Colegio de abogados de Buenos Aires, Revista, Buenos Aires
Collier's: Collier's weekly, New York
Colo B Assn Rep: Colorado bar association, Report

Colo Med: Colorado medicine, Denver
Colo Munic: Colorado municipalities, Denver
Colo Univ Stud: Colorado university studies, Denver
Colum L R: Columbia law review, New York
Comm & Fin: Commerce and finance, New York
Comm & Fin Chron: Commercial and financial chronicle, New York
Comm L J: Commercial law journal, Chicago
Comm L Leag J: Commercial law league journal, Chicago
Comm Pénit Int Bul: Commission pénitentiaire internationale, Bulletin, Bern
Commerce [Chicago]: Commerce, Chicago. (Chicago association of commerce)
Commonweal: Commonweal, New York
Commonwealth Club Calif Tr: Commonwealth club of California, Transactions
Commonwealth R: Commonwealth review of the University of Oregon, Eugene
Communist [London]: Communist, London
Conf Gov'rs Proc: Conference of governors, Proceedings, Washington, D.C.
Conf Mayors N Y Proc: Conference of mayors and other municipal officials of the state of New York, Proceedings
Conf Jud Adm [Duluth]: Conference on judicial administration, Duluth
Conf Latino Am de Neurol, Psiquiat y Med Leg Actas: Conferencia latino-americano de neurologia, psiquiatria y medicina legal, Actas, Buenos Aires
Cong de Méd y Cir Nav y Mil de Chile: Congreso de médicina y cirugía naval y militar de Chile, Valparaiso
Congreg Q: Congregational quarterly, London
Cong Dig: Congressional digest, Washington, D.C.
Conn B J: Connecticut bar journal, Bridgeport
Conquista dello Stato: Conquista dello Stato
Cons Nac de Hig Bol: Consejo nacional de higiene, Boletín, Montevideo
Consensus: Consensus, Boston. (National economic league)
Const R: Constitutional review, Washington, D.C.
Contemp R: Contemporary review, London
Cornell L Q: Cornell law quarterly, Ithaca, N.Y.
Correction: Correction, Albany. (New York state department of correction)
Correspondant: Le Correspondant, Paris
Credit & Fin Man: Credit and financial management, New York
Credit M: Credit monthly, New York
Crim Just [Chicago]: Criminal justice, Chicago
Crim L J India: Criminal law journal of India, Lahore
Criminologist [Chicago]: Criminologist, Chicago
Criminologist [London]: Criminologist, London
Crón Méd [Lima]: La crónica médica, Lima
Crón Méd-Quir de la Habana: Crónica médico-quirúrgica de la Habana, Habana
Cuba Contemp: Cuba contemporanea, Habana
Cur Hist: Current history, New York
Czasopismo Sadowo-Lekarskie: Czasopismo sadowo-lekarskie, poswiecone medycynie, psychatrji sadoweij i kriminologji, Warszawa

Dakota L R: Dakota law review, Fargo
Danziger Statist Mitt: Danziger statistische Mitteilungen, Danzig
Dearborn Indep: Dearborn independent, Dearborn, Mich.
Dent Dig: Dental digest, Chicago
Dermat Wchnschr: Dermatologische Wochenschrift, Leipzig
Dermosifilografo: Dermosifilografo, Torino
Detective: Detective, Chicago
Deut Gesell z Bekämpf d Geschlechtskrankh, Mitt: Deutsche gesellschaft zur Bekämpfung der Geschlechtskrankheiten, Mitteilungen, Leipzig
Deut Juristen-Zeit: Deutsche Juristen-Zeitung, Berlin
Deut Med Wchnschr: Deutsche medizinische Wochenschrift, Leipzig
Deut Polizei-Arch: Deutsches Polizei-Archiv, Lübeck
Deut Richterzeit: Deutsche Richterzeitung, Berlin
Deut Rundsch: Deutsche Rundschau, Berlin
Deut Spiegel: Deutschen Spiegel, Berlin
Deut Statist Zentralbl: Deutsches statistisches Zentralblatt, Leipzig
Deut Volkstum: Deutsches Volkstum, Berlin
Deut Zeitsch f d ges gerichtl Med: Deutsche Zeitschrift für die gesamte gerichtliche Medizin, Berlin
Deut Zeitsch f Nervenh: Deutsche Zeitschrift für Nervenheilkunde, Leipzig
Deut Zeitsch f Wohlfahrtspfl: Deutsche Zeitschrift für Wohlfahrtspflege, Berlin
Deutschl Erneuerung: Deutschlands Erneuerung, München
Diag e Tecn di Lab: Diagnostica e tecnica di laboratorio, Napoli
Dickinson L R: Dickinson law review, Carlisle, Pa.
Dicta: Dicta, Denver

Dir del Lavoro: Il Diritto del Lavoro, Roma
Discovery: Discovery, London
Dizion Pen: Dizion. Pen.
Docket: Docket, Lebanon, Pa.
Dom Eng: Domestic engineering, Chicago
Drei: Drei, Stuttgart
Dr Aérien: Droit aérien, Paris

East Underw: Eastern underwriter, New York
Economist: Economist, London, Chicago
Ecrou: Ecrou, Bruxelles. (Fédération des fonctionnaires et émployés de prisons)
Edinb R: Edinburgh review, Edinburgh
Editorial Res Rep: Editorial research reports, Washington, D.C.
Educ: Education, Boston
Educ R: Educational review, New York
Eesti Statist: Eesti statistika, Tallinn
El Sch J: Elementary school journal, Chicago
Elec Ry J: Electric railway journal, New York
Elektrotech Zeitsch: Elektrotechnische Zeitschrift, Berlin
Empire R: Empire review, London
Encéphale: Encéphale, journal de neurologie et de psychiatrie, Paris
Endocrinology: Endocrinology, Los Angeles. (Association for the study of internal secretions)
Enfant: Enfant, Paris
Eng N: Engineering news-record, Chicago
Engl Hist R: English historical review, London
Engl R: English review, London
Ergebn d ges Med: Ergebnisse der gesamte Medizin, Berlin
Erziehung: Erziehung, Leipzig
Etudes Crimin: Etudes criminologiques, Paris
Eugen: Eugenics, New Haven, Conn.
Eugen N: Eugenical news, Cold Spring Harbor, Long Island, N.Y.
Eugen R: Eugenics review, London
Europa Orient: Europa orientale, Roma
Europäische R: Europäische revue, Berlin
Europe Nouv: Europe nouvelle, Paris

Family: The Family, New York
Filosofski Pregled: Filosofski pregled Rundschau für Philosophie, Sofia
First Friend: The first friend, Kansas City, Mo. (Society of the Friendless)
Fla M Assn J: Florida medical association, Journal, Jacksonville
Fla St B Assn L J: Florida state bar association law journal, Jacksonville
Foreign Language: Foreign language information service interpreter release, New York
Foro Ligure: Il Foro Ligure, Genova
Foro Umbro: Il Foro Umbro, Perugia
Fortn L J: Fortnightly law journal, Toronto
Fortn R [London]: Fortnightly review, London
Fortschr d Med: Fortschritte der Medizin, Berlin
Fortschr d Neurol, Psychiat: Fortschritte der Neurologie, Psychiatrie und ihrer Grenzgebiete, Leipzig
Fortschr d Zahnh: Fortschritte der Zahnheilkunde, Leipzig
Forum [N Y]: Forum, New York
Frankf Wohlfahrtsbl: Frankfurter Wohlfahrtsblätter
Frat Order Police J: Fraternal order of police journal, Pittsburgh, Pa.
Freie Wohlfahrtspfl: Freie Wohlfahrtspflege, Berlin

Ga B Assn Rep: Georgia bar association, Report
Ga L R: Georgia law review, Athens
Ga Lawyer: Georgia lawyer, Macon
Gas Age: Gas age-record, New York
Gas Logic: Gas logic, New York
Gaz Clin: Gazeta clinica, São Paulo
Gaz d Hôp: Gazette des hôpitaux civils et militaires, Paris
Gaz des Trib Libano-Syriens: Gazette des tribunaux libano-syriens, Beirut
Gazz Internaz Med-Chir: Gazzetta internazionale di medicina e chirurgia, Napoli
Gefängnisgesellsch f d Prov Sachsen & Anhalt Jahr: Gefängnisgesellschaft für die Provinz Sachsen und Anhalt, Jahrbuch, Halle
Gegenwart: Die gegenwart, Berlin
Gemeinde: Gemeinde. Monatsschrift für sozialdemokratische Kommunalpolitik, Wien
Genesis: Genesis. Rassegna di studi sessuali demografia ed eugenica, Roma

Geo L J: Georgetown law journal, Georgetown, D.C.
Gerarchia: Gerarchia; rivista politica, Milano
Gerichts-Zeit: Gerichts-Zeitung, Wien
Gerichtssaal: Der Gerichtssaal; Zeitschrift für Zivil- und Militärstrafrecht und Strafprozessrecht sowie der ergänzenden Disziplinen, Stuttgart
Gesellsch f Phys Anthrop Verh: Gesellschaft für Physische Anthropologie, Verhandlungen, Stuttgart
Gesetz u Recht: Gesetz und Recht, Berlin
Gesundh u Erziehg: Gesundheit und Erziehung, Leipzig
Gior di Psichiat Clin e Tecn Manic: Giornale di psichiatria clinica e tecnica manicomiale, Ferrara
Giuris delle Corti Regionali: Giurisprudenza delle Corti regionali, Bologna
Giustiz Pen: Giustizia penale; rivista critica di dottrina, giurisprudenza e legislazione, Roma
Giustiz Pen e la Proc Pen Ital: Giustizia penale e la procedura penale Italiana, Roma
Glasgow M J: Glasgow medical journal, Glasgow
Golden Bk: Golden book, New York
Good Govt: Good government, Washington, D.C.
Good Housekeeping: Good housekeeping, Holyoke, Mass.
Gov'tal Res Assn Proc: Governmental research association, Pittsburgh Proceedings
Previous to 1928 titled Governmental Conference of the United States and Canada.
Grade Teach: Grade teacher, Boston
Graphologie Sci: Graphologie scientifique
Greater Cleveland: Greater Cleveland, Cleveland
Grotius Soc: Grotius society, Problems of peace and war, London

Haagsch Maandbl: Haagsch Maandblad, 's Gravenhage
Hamburg Schr z Ges Strafrechtswiss: Hamburgische Schriften zur gesamten Strafrechtswissenschaft, Hamburg
Hamishpat: Hamishpat, Jerusalem
Hanseat Rechts- u Gerichts-Zeitsch: Hanseatische Rechts- und Gerichts-Zeitschrift
Harper's: Harper's magazine, New York
Harv Grad Mag: Harvard graduates magazine, Boston
Harv L R: Harvard law review, Cambridge, Mass.
Health & Empire: Health and empire, London
Health Bul: Health bulletin, North Carolina Board of Health, Raleigh
Heat & Ven: Heating and ventilating magazine, New York
Heating-Piping: Heating, piping and air conditioning, Chicago
Hereditas: Hereditas; genetiskt arkiv, Lund
Hilfe: Hilfe, Berlin
Hilfsschule: Hilfsschule, Haale
Hindustan R: Hindustan review, Allahabad, India
Hispan-Am Hist R: Hispanic-American historical review, Baltimore
Hogaku-Shirin: Hogaku-Shirin, Tokyo
Hokuyetsu Igakkai Zatshi: Hokuyetsu Igakkai Zatshi
Homiletic R: Homiletic review, New York
Hosp Soc Serv: Hospital social service, New York
Howard J: Howard journal, London
Huddersfield Chamber Comm J: Huddersfield chamber of commerce journal
Human Biol: Human biology, Baltimore
Hyg Ment: Hygiène mentale, Paris
Hygeia: Hygeia, Chicago

Id L J: Idaho law journal, Moscow
Id St B Proc: Idaho state bar, Proceedings
Ill Conf Pub Welf Proc: Illinois conference on public welfare, Proceedings
Ill J Comm: Illinois journal of commerce, Chicago
Ill L R: Illinois law review, Chicago
Ill Med J: Illinois medical journal, Springfield
Ill St B Assn Proc: Illinois state bar association, Proceedings
Illustration: L'Illustration, Paris
Imago: Imago, Leipzig
Ind Bul Char & Correc: Indiana bulletin of charities and correction, Indianapolis
Ind Eng: Industrial engineer, Chicago
Ind L J: Indiana law journal, Indianapolis
Ind Police N: Indiana police news, Kokomo, Ind.
Ind Psychotechn: Industrielle Psychotechnik, Berlin
Indep: Independent, New York
Index to Leg Per & L Lib J: Index to legal periodicals and Law library journal, New York
Indian J M Res: Indian journal of medical research, Calcutta

Indian M Gaz: Indian medical gazette, Calcutta
Indian M Rec: Indian medical record, Calcutta
Indian R: Indian review, Madras
Indianapolis M J: Indianapolis medical journal, Indianapolis
Inf Anorm: Infanzia anormale, Milano
Inf Serv: Information service, New York
Innere Mission im Evang Deut: Innere Mission im evangelischen Deutschland, München
Inst Gen Psychol Bul: Institut général psychologique, Bulletin général, Paris
Inst Hist Res Bul: Institute of historical research, Bulletin, London
Inst Int Am de Protec a la Infancia Bol: Instituto internacional americano de protección a la infancia, Boletin, Montevideo
Inst Int de Statist Bul: Institut international de statistique, Bulletin, Roma
Inst Intermed Int de la Haye Bul: Institut intermédiaire international de la Haye, Bulletin, The Hague
Inst Police Adm Proc: Institute of police administration, Proceedings
Instit Psiquiat Bol: Instituto psiquiatrico, Boletin, Rosario
Insur Field: Insurance field, Louisville, Ky.
Int Assn Chiefs Police Proc: International association of chiefs of police, Proceedings
Int Assn Identif Proc: International association for identification, Proceedings
Int Assn Identif, Calif Div Proc: International Association for identification, California division, Proceedings
Int Clin: International clinics, Philadelphia
Int J Ethics: International journal of ethics, Philadelphia
Int J Med & Surg: International journal of medicine and surgery and Surgical journal, Burlington, Vt.
Int J Psycho-Analysis: International journal of psycho-analysis, London
Int Krimin Verein Mitt: International Kriminalistische Vereinigung, Mitteilungen, Berlin
Int Nursing R: International nursing review, Geneva
Int Pict Police J: International pictorial police journal, Montreal
Int R Educ Cinematog: International review of educational cinematography, Rome
Int R Miss: International review of missions, Edinburgh
Int Zeitsch f Individualpsychol: Internationale Zeitschrift für Individualpsychologie, Leipzig
Internationale: Die Internationale, Berlin
Ia L R: Iowa law review, Iowa City
Ia St B Assn Proc: Iowa state bar association, Proceedings
Ia St Conf Soc Wk Proc: Iowa state conference of social work, Proceedings
Irish L T: Irish law times and Solicitors journal, Dublin
Iron Age: Iron age, Middletown, N.Y.
Ist Ital d Attuari Gior: Istituto italiano degli attuari, Giornale, Roma

J Abnorm & Soc Psychol: Journal of abnormal and social psychology, Princeton, N.J.
J Account: Journal of accountancy, New York
J Adult Educ: Journal of adult education, New York
J Am Inst Homeop: Journal of the American institute of homeopathy, Camden, N.J.
J Am Insur: Journal of American insurance, Chicago
J Ap Psychol: Journal of applied psychology, Worcester, Mass.
J Comp Leg: Journal of comparative legislation and international law, London
J Comp Psychol: Journal of comparative psychology, Baltimore
J Crim L & Crimin: Journal of criminal law and criminology, Chicago
J de Méd de Lyon: Journal de médecine de Lyon, Lyon
J de Méd de Paris: Journal de médecine de Paris, Paris
J de Neurol et de Psychiat: Journal de neurologie et de psychiatrie, Bruxelles
J Débats: Journal des débats politiques et littéraires, Paris
J Delin: Journal of delinquency, Whittier, Calif.
Continued as Journal of juvenile research.
J des Juges de Paix [Paris]: Journal des juges de paix, juges suppléants et greffiers de paix, Paris
J du Dr Int: Journal du droit international, Paris
J Econ: Journal des économistes, Paris
J Educ: Journal of education, Boston
J Educ Res: Journal of educational research, Bloomington, Ill.
J Educ Meth: Journal of educational method, Yonkers, N.Y.
J Educ Soc: Journal of educational sociology, New York
J f Psychol u Neurol: Journal für Psychologie und Neurologie, Leipzig
J Franklin Inst: Journal of the Franklin institute, Philadelphia
J Hered: Journal of heredity, Washington, D.C.
J Ind & Fin: Journal of industry and finance, Newark, N.J.
J Juv Res: Journal of juvenile research, Whittier, Calif.

J Med: Journal of medicine, Cincinnati
J Méd Fr: Journal médical français, Paris
J Ment Sci: Journal of mental science, London
J Mod Hist: Journal of modern history, Chicago
J Negro Hist: Journal of Negro history, Lancaster, Pa.
J Nerv & Ment Dis: Journal of nervous and mental disease, New York
J Neurol & Psychopath: Journal of neurology and psychopathology, London
J Nevropat i Psikhiat: Jurnal nevropatologii i psikhiatrii imeni, Moskva
J Orient Med: Journal of Oriental medicine, Darien, Manchuria
J Personnel Res: Journal of personnel research, Baltimore
J Philos Stud: Journal of philosophical studies, London
J Psycho-Asthenics: Journal of psycho-asthenics, Faribault, Minn.
J Soc Hyg: Journal of social hygiene, New York
J Soc Psychol: Journal of social psychology, Worcester, Mass.
J St Med [London]: Journal of state medicine, London
Jahrb d Charakterol: Jahrbuch der Charakterologie, Berlin
Jahrb d Köln Geschichtsver: Jahrbuch des Kölnischen Geschichtsvereins, Köln
Jahrb f Kultur u Gesch d Slaven: Jahrbücher für Kultur und Geschichte der Slaven, Breslau
Jahrb f Nationalökon u Statist: Jahrbücher für Nationalökonomie und Statistik, Jena
Jahrb f Psychiat u Neurol: Jahrbücher für Psychiatrie und Neurologie, Wien
Jahresk f ärztl Fortbild: Jahreskurse für ärztliche Fortbildung, München
Jahresk f jurist Fortbild: Jahreskurse für juristische Fortbildung, Berlin
Jap J Psychol: Japanese journal of psychology, Tokyo
Jap M World: Japan medical world, Tokyo
Jap W Chron: Japan (weekly) chronicle, Kobe
Jeugd en Beroep: Jeugd en Beroep; tijdschrift voor jeugdpsychologie voorlichting bij beroepskeuze en beroepsvorming, Purmerend
Jewish Soc Serv Q: Jewish social service quarterly, New York
Jogállam: Jogállam, Budapest
Jogtudományi Közlöny: Jogtudományi Közlöny
Jüdische Wohlfahrtspfl u Sozialpol: Juedische Wohlfahrtspflege und Sozialpolitik, Berlin
Jurid R: Juridical review, Edinburgh
Jurist Bl: Juristische Blätter, Wien
Jurist Rundsch: Juristische Rundschau, Berlin
Jurist Wchnschr: Juristische Wochenschrift, Berlin
Juristen-Zeit f d Geb d Tschecho-slowak: Juristen-Zeitung für das gebiet der Tschecho-slowakischen Republik, Brno
Just Peace: Justice of the peace and local government review, London
Justice: Justice, Chicago. (Sheriffs' and police officers' association of America)
Justiz: Die Justiz, Berlin

Kampf: Der Kampf: organ für gewerkschaftsbewegung und soziale Fragen, Berlin
Kampf [Wien]: Kampf, sozialdemokratische Monatsschrift, Wien
Kan M Soc J: Kansas medical society, Journal, Topeka
Kan Munic: Kansas municipalities, Lawrence
Kan Offic: Kansas official
Kan St B Assn Proc: Kansas state bar association, Proceedings
Kan Teach & W Sch J: Kansas teacher and Western school journal, Topeka
Kantstud: Kantstudien, Hamburg
Karitas: see Caritas
Ky L J: Kentucky law journal, Lexington
Ky St B Assn Proc: Kentucky state bar association, Proceedings, Louisville
Kirke og Kultur: Kirke og Kultur, Oslo
Klin Wchnschr: Klinische Wochenschrift, Berlin
Kölner Vjsh f Soz: Kölner Vierteljahrshefte fü Soziologie, Köln
Koloniale Stud: Koloniale Studiën, Weltevreden
Kommun Int: Kommunistische Internationale, Leningrad
Konzern Nachrichten: Konzern Nachrichten, Frankfurt a M. (H. Fuld & co. Telephon- u Telegraphenwerke)
Krasnaya Nov: Krasnaya nov; literaturno-khudozhestvennyi i nauchno-publitsisticheskii zhurnal, Moskva
Krimin Abh: Kriminalistische Abhandlungen, Leipzig, hrsg. von Franz Exner
Krimin Monatsh: Kriminalistische Monatshefte; Zeitschrift für die gesamte kriminalistische Wissenschaft und Praxis, Berlin
Krimin Probl: Kriminalistische Probleme, Berlin
Special suppl to Kriminalistische Monatshefte.
Kriminal-Arch: Kriminal-Archiv
Kriminol Abh: Kriminologische Abhandlungen, hrsg. von W. Gleispach. Wien (Springer)

Kwartalnik Hist: Kwartalnik historyczny, Lwów
Kwartalnik Statyst: Kwartalnik Statystyczny, Warszawa
Kyoiku Shinri Kenyu: Kyoiku Shinri Kenyu

L I D M: L. I. D. Monthly, New York. (League for industrial democracy)
L Inst J: Law institute journal, Melbourne
L J: Law journal, London
L Lib J: Law library journal, New York
L Notes: Law notes, London
L Q R: Law quarterly review, London
L Soc J: Law society journal, Boston
L Times: Law times, London
La St B Assn Proc: Louisiana state bar association, Proceedings
Lab M: Labour monthly, London
Lab Psicol Sperim Un Roma: Contributi psicologici del Laboratorio di psicologia sperimentale della R. Università di Roma
Labor: Labor, Washington, D.C.
Ladies Home J: Ladies home journal, Philadelphia
Lancet: Lancet, London
Law & Lab: Law and labor, New York
Lawyer & Banker: Lawyer and banker and Southern bench and bar review, San Francisco
Leg Aid R: Legal aid review, New York
Leipz Rechtswiss Stud: Leipziger Rechtswissenschaftliche Studien, Leipzig
Leipz Zeitsch f Deut Recht: Leipziger Zeitschrift für deutsches Recht, München
Lib: Libraries, Chicago
Lib J: Library journal, New York
Lib R [Scotland]: Library review, Dunfermline, Scot.
Life & Lab Bul: Life and labor bulletin, Chicago
Lincoln L R: Lincoln law review, Buffalo
Lit Dig: Literary digest, New York
Living Age: Living age, Boston
Lois Nouvelles: Lois nouvelles; revue de législation et de jurisprudence et revue des travaux législatifs, Paris
Long Island M J: Long Island medical journal, Brooklyn
Los Angeles B Assn Bul: Los Angeles bar association, Bulletin
Los Angeles Chron: Los Angeles chronicle, Los Angeles
Los Angeles Sch J: Los Angeles school journal, Los Angeles
Loyola L J: Loyola law journal, New Orleans

M Assn S Africa J: Medical association of South Africa, Journal, Cape Town
M Clin N Am: Medical clinics of North America, Philadelphia
M Herald, Phys Therapist: Medical herald, Physical therapist and Endocrine survey, Portland, Ore.
M J & Rec: Medical journal and record, New York
M J Austral: Medical journal of Australia, Glebe, N. S. W.
M Lab R: Monthly labor review, Washington, D.C.
M Press: Medical press and circular, London
M R of R: Medical review of reviews, New York
M Soc N J J: Medical society of New Jersey, Journal, Orange
M Times: Medical times, London
M Times [N Y]: Medical times, New York
M Times & Long Island M J: Medical times and Long Island medical journal, New York
M World: Medical world, New York
Maandbl v Ber en Reclasseer: Maandblad voor Berechting en Reclasseering van Volwassenen en Kinderen
McNaught's M: McNaught's monthly, New York
Madras M J: Madras medical journal, Madras
Mag Bus: Magazine of business, Chicago
Mag Hist: Magazine of History, Elken, W.Va.
Magistrato dell'Ordine: Il Magistrato dell' Ordine
Magyar Jogi Szemle: Magyar jogi szemle, Budapest
Manicomio: Manicomio, Nocera
Mann's Päd Mag: (Friedrich) Mann's Pädagogisches Magazin, Langensalza
Marquette L R: Marquette law review, Milwaukee
Marseille-Méd: Marseille-médical, Marseille
Mass Dept Correc Q: Massachusetts Department of Corrections, Quarterly, Boston
Mass L Q: Massachusetts law quarterly, Boston
Mater I Vsesoju Sez Izuch Poved Chelov: Materialy Imperial Vsesoju sez Izuchenii͡a Poveda Chelovedke

Matern & Child Welf: Maternity and child welfare, London
Md St B Assn Rep: Maryland state bar association, Report
Me M J: Maine medical journal, Portland
Me St B Assn Proc: Maine state bar association, Proceedings
Mech Eng: Mechanical engineering, New York
Mecklenb Zeitsch f Rechtspfl, Rechtswiss, Verwaltung: Mecklenburgische Zeitschrift für Rechtspflege, Rechtswissenschaft, Verwaltung, Wismar
Med Condotto: Il medico Condotto
Med Contem: A medicina contemporanea, Lisboa
Med Klin: Medizinische Klinik, Berlin
Med-Leg J: Medico-legal journal, New York
Med-Leg Soc Tr: Medico-legal society, Transactions, London
Med Welt: Die medizinische Welt, Berlin
Mededeel v d dienst d volksgezondh in Nederl-Indië: Mededeelingen van den dienst der volksgezondheid in Nederlandsch-Indië, Batavia
Medicina [Kaunas]: Medicina, Kaunas, Lithuania
Medizinal-Statist Nachr: Medizinalstatistische Nachrichten, Berlin
Mensch en Maatschappij: Mensch en Maatschappij, Groningen
Ment Health Bul: Mental health bulletin, Danville state hospital, Danville, Pa.
Ment Hyg: Mental hygiene, Albany
Ment Welf: Mental welfare, London
Mentor: Mentor, New York
Mercure Fr: Mercure de France, Paris
Metal Prog: Metal progress, Cleveland
Meth R: Methodist review
Metropolitan Life Insur Co Stat Bul: Metropolitan life insurance company, Statistical bulletin, New York
Mex Univ Nac R Mens: Mexico universidad nacional, Revista mensual, Mexico
Mfr Rec: Manufacturers record, Baltimore
Mich Assn Chiefs Police Proc: Michigan association of chiefs of police, Proceedings
Mich L R: Michigan law review, Ann Arbor, Mich.
Mich M Soc J: Michigan state medical society, Journal, Grand Rapids
Mich Munic R: Michigan municipal review, Ann Arbor
Mich St B J: Michigan state bar journal, Ann Arbor
Mid-W Banker: Mid-western banker, Milwaukee
Mil Surg: Military surgeon, Washington, D.C.
Mind: Mind
Minn L R: Minnesota law review, Minneapolis
Minn Munic: Minnesota municipalities, Minneapolis
Minn St Bd Con Q: Minnesota state board of control, Quarterly representing Minnesota education, philanthropic, correctional and penal institutions, St. Paul
Minn St Conf & Inst Soc Wk Proc: Minnesota state conference and institute of social work, Proceedings
Miss L J: Mississippi law journal, Jackson
Miss R World: Missionary review of the world
Miss St B Assn Rep: Mississippi state bar association, Reports
Mitt d Industrie- u Handelskammer, Berlin: Mitteilungen der Industrie- und Handelskammer zu Berlin, Schweidnitz
Mo B Assn Proc: Missouri bar association, Proceedings, Columbia
Mo B J: Missouri bar journal, Kansas City, Mo.
Mod Mex: Modern Mexico, New York
Mod Philol: Modern philology, Chicago
Mod R [Calcutta]: Modern review, Calcutta
Monats f Harnkrankh u Sex Hyg: Monatsschrift für Harnkrankheiten und Sexuelle Hygiene, Stuttgart
Monats f Kriminalpsychol u Strafrechtsref: Monatsschrift für Kriminalpsychologie und Strafrechtsreform, Heidelberg
Monats f Psychiat u Neurol: Monatsschrift für Psychiatrie und Neurologie, Berlin
Monatsbl d deut Reichsverb f Gerichtshilfe: Monatsblätter des deutschen Reichsverbands für Gerichtshilfe, Gefangenen- und Entlassenenfürsorge, Hamburg
Monde Nouv: Monde nouveau, Paris
Monist: Monist, Chicago
Monitore dei Tribunali [Milano]: Monitore dei Tribunali, Milano
Mont B Assn Proc: Montana bar association, Proceedings, Helena
Morgagni: Il morgagni, Milano
Moyen Âge: Moyen âge, Paris
München med Wchnschr: München medizinische Wochenschrift, München
Munic Index: Municipal index, New York
Munic R: Municipal review, London
Munic Ref Lib Notes: Municipal reference library notes, New York

Municipality: Municipality, Madison. (League of Wisconsin municipalities)
Mus Soc Arg Bol: Museo social Argentino, Boletín, Buenos Aires

N Am R: North American review, Boston
N C L R: North Carolina law review, Chapel Hill
N J B Assn Yrbk: New Jersey bar association, Yearbook
N J Conf Soc Wk Proc: New Jersey conference of social work, Proceedings, Newark
N J Dept Inst & Agencies Pub: New Jersey Department of institutions and agencies, Publications, Trenton
N J L J: New Jersey law journal, Somerville
N Mex St B Assn Proc: New Mexico state bar association, Proceedings
N Y Acad Med Bul: New York academy of medicine, Bulletin
N Y Conf Soc Wk Q Bul: New York (city) conference of social work, Quarterly bulletin, New York
N Y L R: New York law review, New York
N Y Pub Lib Bul: New York public library, Bulletin
N Y St Assn Chiefs Police Proc: New York state association of chiefs of police, Proceedings
N Y St Assn Judges Proc: New York state association of judges of county children's courts, Proceedings
N Y St Assn Magistrates Proc: New York state association of magistrates, Proceedings
N Y St B Assn Bul: New York state bar association, Bulletin
N Y St B Assn Proc: New York state bar association, Proceedings
N Y St Conf Prob Offic Proc: New York state conference of probation officers, Proceedings
N Y St Conf Soc Wk Q Bul: New York (state) conference on social work, Quarterly bulletin, Albany
N Y St Educ: New York state education, Albany
N Y Univ L R: New York university law review, New York
Naoukovi Zapiski Kievskogo Inst Naradnogo Gospod: Naoukovi Zapiski Kievskogo Institutul Naradnogo Gospod
Nat Assn Referees Bankruptcy J: National association of referees in bankruptcy, Journal, Winona, Minn.
Nat Conf Juv Agencies Proc: National conference of juvenile agencies, Proceedings
Nat Conf Soc Wk Proc: National conference of social work, Proceedings
Nat Council Educ [Can]: National council of education, Canada
Nat Leag Compul Educ Offic Proc: National league of compulsory education officials, Proceedings
Nat Munic R: National municipal review, New York
Nat Police Offic: National police officer, St. Louis, Mo.
Nat Prob Assn Proc: National probation association, Proceedings
Nat Repub: National republic, Washington, D.C.
Nat Res Council Bul: National research council, Bulletin, Washington, D.C.
Nat Retail Dryg Assn Proc: National retail drygoods association, Proceedings
Nat Soc Pen Inf N Y Bul: National society of penal information of New York, News bulletin, New York
Nat Underw: National underwriter, Chicago
Nation [N Y]: Nation, New York
Nation & Athen: Nation and Athenaeum, London
Nation's Bus: Nation's business, Washington, D.C.
Nation's Health: Nation's health, Chicago
Nation's Sch: Nation's schools, Chicago
Nation's Traffic: Nation's traffic, St. Louis
Natur & Gesell: Natur und Gesellschaft, Berlin
Nature [London]: Nature, weekly illustrated journal of science, London
Nature [Paris]: La Nature, Paris
Nature Mag: Nature magazine, Washington, D.C.
Nauchnoe Slovo: Nauchnoe Slovo, Moskva
Near East & India: Near East and India, London
Neb L Bul: Nebraska law bulletin, Lincoln
Neb St M J: Nebraska state medical journal, Omaha
Nederl Tijdschr v Geneesk: Nederlandsch tijdschrift voor geneeskunde, Amsterdam
Neighborhood: Neighborhood, Boston
Neue Bahnen: Neue Bahnen, Leipzig
Neue Generation: Neue Generation, Berlin
Neue Psychol Stud: Neue Psychologische Studien, Leipzig
Neue Rundsch: Neue Rundschau, Berlin
Neue Russland: Neue Russland, Berlin
New England J Med: New England journal of medicine, Boston

New Orleans M & Surg J: New Orleans medical and surgical journal, New Orleans
New Repub: New republic, New York
New Statesman: New statesman and Nation, London
9th Dist Banker: Ninth district banker, Minneapolis
19th Cent: Nineteenth century and after, London
Nord Hyg Tids: Nordisk hygiensk tidsskrift, København
Nord Kriminalteknisk Tidsk: Nordisk Kriminalteknisk Tidskrift, Stockholm
Nord Tids f Straf: Nordisk tidsskrift for strafferet, København
Northeast Phila Cham Comm Bul: Northeast Philadelphia chamber of commerce, Bulletin, Philadelphia
Northwest Police J: Northwest police journal, Seattle
Note e Riv di Psichiat: Note e Riviste di psichiatria, Pesaro
Notre Dame Law: Notre Dame lawyer, Notre Dame
Nuov Antol: Nuova antologia di lettere, scienze ed arti, Firenze
Nuov Dir: Nuovo Diritto, Roma
Nuov Riv di Clin ed Assis Psichiat: Nuova rivista di clinica ed assistenza psichiatria, Napoli
Nuov Stud di Dir Econ e Pol: Nuovi studi di diritto, economica e politica, Roma
Nyt Mag for Naturvidensk: Nyt magazin for naturvidenskaberne, Oslo

Oboz Psikhiat, Nevrol i Reflek: Obozrenie psikhiatrii, nevrologii i refleksologii, Leningrad
English title: Review of psychiatry, neurology and reflexology; abstracts in German.
Occup Therapy: Occupational therapy and rehabilitation, Baltimore
Odessky Med J: Odessky meditsinsky jurnal, Odessa
Öster Anwalts-Zeit: Öster Anwalts-Zeitung
Ohio Cit: Ohio citizen, Columbus
Ohio Soc Sci J: Ohio social science journal, Athens
Ohio St Police J: Ohio state police journal
Ohio St Univ Contrib Hist & Pol Sci: Ohio state university. Contributions in history and political science, Columbus
Ohio Welf Bul: Ohio welfare bulletin, Columbus
Okla Munic R: Oklahoma municipal review, Norman
Okla St B Assn Proc: Oklahoma state bar association, Proceedings
On Guard: On guard, New York
Opbouw: Opbouwen, Antwerp
Opportunity: Opportunity; journal of Negro life, New York
Ore L R: Oregon law review, Eugene
Organized Lab: Organized labor, San Francisco
Osp Maggiore: L'ospedale maggiore, Milano
Our Boston: Our Boston, Boston. (Women's municipal league of Boston)
Outl: Outlook, New York
Overland & Out West: Overland [monthly] and Out West, Los Angeles

P I M Assn J: Philippine Islands medical association, Journal, Manila
P L A M: Port of London authority monthly
Pa B Assn Q: Pennsylvania bar association, Quarterly
Pac Coast J Nursing: Pacific coast journal of nursing, San Francisco
Pac Munic: Pacific municipalities and counties, San Francisco
Pac Police Mag: Pacific police magazine, Los Angeles
Pac Purchasor: Pacific purchasor, San Francisco
Päd Hochschule: Pädagogische Hochschule wissenschaftl. Vierteljahrsschrift d. Badischen Lehrervereins
Palestra del Dir: Palestra del diritto, Ferrara
Pan-Am Union Bul: Pan American union, Bulletin, Washington, D.C.
Panel: The Panel, New York
Paper Tr J: Paper trade journal, New York
Parents' Mag: Parents' magazine, Jamaica, New York
Paris Méd: Paris médical, Paris
Peace Offic: Peace officer, Oklahoma City
Peace Offic Assn Calif Proc: Peace officers association of California, Proceedings
Pedag Sem: Pedagogical seminary, Worcester, Mass.
Pediatría Españ: La pediatría española, Madrid
Pen Affairs: Penal affairs, Philadelphia
Pensiero Giurid-Pen: Pensiero giuridico-penale, Messina
Phil L J: Philippine law journal, Manila
Phila Pris R: Philadelphia prison review, Philadelphia
Pittsburgh Rec: Pittsburgh record, Pittsburgh
Playground: Playground and recreation, New York
Pol Q: Political quarterly, London
Pol Sci Q: Political science quarterly, Boston

Pol Soc: Politica sociale, Roma
Police & Peace Offic: Police and peace officers
Police J [London]: Police journal, London
Police J [N Y]: Police journal, New York
Police J [St. Louis]: Police journal, St. Louis
Police Rep: Police reporter, Los Angeles
Police "13-13": Police "13-13", Chicago
Policeman: The policeman, Vancouver
Policewoman's Int Bul: Policewoman's international bulletin, Washington, D.C.
Policewoman's R: Policewoman's review
Policia e Justiça: Policia e Justiça
Policlinico: Policlinico, Roma
Polizei: Die polizei; Zeitschrift für polizeiwissenschaft dienst und wesen, Berlin
Polizei im Bild: Polizei im Bild, Dresden
Polizei-Arch: Deutsches Polizei-Archiv, Lübeck
Polizeibeamten-Bl: Polizeibeamten-Blatt, München
Polizeipraxis: Polizeipraxis, Berlin
Polska Gaz Lek: Polska Gazeta lekarska, Lwów
Pop Govt: Popular government, Chapel Hill, N.C.
Pop Mech: Popular mechanics magazine, Chicago
Pop Sci M: Popular science monthly, New York
Post-Grad M J: Post-graduate medical journal, London
Post Mag & Insur Monitor: Post magazine and insurance monitor, London
Praca i Opieka Spoleczna: Praca i Opieka spoleczna, Warszawa
Practitioner: Practitioner, London
Prager Juris Zeitsch: Prager juristische Zeitschrift, Praha
Pravo i zhizn': Pravo i zhizn', Moskva
Praxis: Praxis, Bern
Praxis d Berufssch: Praxis der Berufsschule, Leipzig
Prensa Méd Arg: Prensa médica argentina, Buenos Aires
Presse Méd: Presse médicale, Paris
Preuss Jahrb: Preussische Jahrbücher, Berlin
Ptr Ink: Printers' ink, New York
Pris Assn N Y Ann Rep: Prison association of New York, Annual Report
Pris J: Prison journal, Philadelphia
Probation: Probation, New York
Problemy Prestupnosti: Problemy prestupnosti, Moskva
Proc Pen Ital: Procedura penale Italiana, Roma
Profilak Med: Profilaktichna meditsina, Kharkov
Prog Méd: Le progrès médical, Paris
Prophylax Antivén: La prophylaxie antivénérienne, Paris
Prophyl Ment: Prophylaxie mentale, Paris
Przeglad Polski: Przeglad polski ustawodawstwa cywilnego i kriminalnego, Warszawa
Psyche [London]: Psyche, London
Psychiat en Neurol Bl: Psychiatrische en neurologische Bladen, Amsterdam
Psychiat-Neurol Wchnschr: Psychiatrisch-neurologische Wochenschrift, Halle
Psychiat Q: Psychiatric quarterly, Utica, N.Y.
Psychoanal Beweg: Psychoanalytische bewegung, Wien
Psychoanal R: Psychoanalytic review, Washington, D.C.
Psychol Bul: Psychological bulletin, Lancaster, Pa.
Psychol Clin: Psychological clinic, Philadelphia
Psychol et Vie: Psychologie et la vie, Paris
Psychol R: Psychological review, Princeton, N.J.
Psychol Rundsch: Psychologie Rundschau, Basel
Psychol u Med: Psychologie und Medizin, Berlin
Pub Adm: Public administration, London
Pub Affairs: Public affairs, Washington, D.C.
Pub Bus: Public business, Detroit. (Bureau of governmental research)
Pub Health: Public health, London
Pub Health Nurse: Public health nurse, New York
Pub Health Rep: Public health reports, Washington, D.C.
Pub Manage: Public management, Chicago
Pub Personnel Stud: Public personnel studies, Washington, D.C.
Pub Util: Public utilities fortnightly, Washington, D.C.
Pub W: Publishers' weekly, New York

Q R: Quarterly review, London
Queen's Q: Queen's quarterly, Kingston, Ontario
Quetzalcoatl: Quetzalcoatl, Mexico

R Anthrop: Revue anthropologique, Paris
R Arg de Cienc Pol: Revista Argentina de ciencias políticas, Buenos Aires
R Arg de Neurol, Psiquiat y Med Leg: Revista argentina de neurología, psiquiatría y medicina legal, Buenos Aires
R Belge de Police Adm & Jud: Revue belge de la police administrative et judiciaire, Bruxelles
R Bimestre Cubana: Revista bimestre Cubana, Habana
R Celtique: Revue Celtique, Paris
R Chilena: Revista Chilena, Santiago de Chile
R Crit de Lég et de Juris: Revue critique de législation et de jurisprudence, Paris
R d'Hyg: Revue d'hygiène, Paris
R de Cienc Soc: Revista de ciencias sociales, Mexico
R de Crimin e Med Leg: Revista de criminologia e medicina legal
R de Crimin, Psiquiat y Med Leg: Revista de criminología, psiquiatria y medicina legal, Buenos Aires
R de Cultura: Revista de cultura, Rio de Janeiro
R de Cultura Jurid: Revista de cultura juridica, Bahia
R de Derecho Pen: Revista de derecho penal, Buenos Aires
R de Drept Pen: Revista de drept penale si stiinta penitenciaria, Bucuresti
R de Dr Int et de Lég Comp: Revue de droit international et de legislation comparée, Bruxelles
R de Dr Pen et de Crimin: Revue de droit penal et de criminologie et Archives internationales de médecine légale, Bruxelles
R de Gendarm: Revue de la gendarmerie, Paris
R de Identif y Cienc Pen: Revista de identificación y ciencias penales, La Plata
R de Med [Rosario]: Revista de medicina, Rosario de Santa Fe, Arg.
R de Méd et d'Hyg Trop: Revue de médecine et d'hygiène tropicales, Paris
R de Med Leg de Cuba: Revista de medicina legal de Cuba, Habana
R de Méd Lég, de Psychiat Lég et de Crimin: Revue de médicine légale, de psychiatrie légale et de criminologie, Varsovie
R de Paris: Revue de Paris, Paris
R de Philol Fr: Revue de philologie française de littérature et d'histoire anciennes, Paris
R de l'Univ de Bruxelles: Revue de l'Université de Bruxelles, Bruxelles
R Deux Mondes: Revue des deux mondes, Paris
R Españ de Crimin: Revista española de criminologie
R Españ de Med y Cir: Revista española de medicina y cirugía, Barcelona
R Especialid: Revista de especialidades, Buenos Aires
R Fr de Dermat et de Vén: Revue française de dermatologie et de vénéréologie, Paris
R Fr de Psychanal: Revue française de psychanalyse, Paris
R Gen de Der y Juris: Revista general de derecho y jurisprudencia, Mexico
R Gén de Dr Int Pub: Revue générale de droit international public, Paris
R Gen de Leg y Juris: Revista general de legislación y jurisprudencia, Madrid
R Gén de Med et de Chir: Revue générale de médecine et de chirurgie de l'Afrique du Nord, Algiers
R Hist [Peru]: Revista histórica, Lima
R Int de Crimin: Revue internationale de criminalistique, Lyon
R Int de Dr Pén: Revue internationale de droit pénal, Paris
R Int de l'Enf: Revue internationale de l'enfant, Geneva
R Int de Soc: Revue internationale de sociologie, Paris
R Méd de Barcelona: Revista médica de Barcelona, Barcelona
R Méd de la Suisse Rom: Revue médicale de la Suisse Romande, Lausanne
R Mexicana de Der Pen: Revista Mexicana de derecho penal, Mexico
R Mondiale: Revue mondiale, Paris
R Pénitent de Pologne: Revue pénitentiaire de Pologne, Varsovie
R Pénitent et de Dr Pén: Revue pénitentiaire et de droit pénal, Paris
R Phil: Revue philosophique de la France et de l'étranger, Paris
R Pol & Litt: Revue politique & littéraire, Paris
R Polon de Leg Civile et Crim: Revue polonaise de législation civile et criminelle, Varsovie
R of R: Review of reviews, New York, London
R Polish L & Econ: Review of polish law and economics, Warsaw
R Sci: La revue scientifique de la France et de l'étranger, Paris
R Sci Pol: Revue des sciences politiques, Paris
R Univ [Universidad Mayor de San Marcos]: Revista universitaria, Universidad mayor de San Marcos
Radio N: Radio news, New York
Radiology: Radiology, St. Paul
Rassegna Bibliog delle Sci Giurid: Rassegna bibliografica delle scienze giuridiche, Napoli

Rassegna di Studi Psichiat: Rassegna di studi psichiatrici, Sienna
Rassegna di Stud Sess: Rassegna di studi sessuali, Roma
Rassegna Giurid: Rassegna giuridico, Salerno
Rassegna Int di Clin e Terap: Rassegna internazionale di clinica e terapia, Napoli
Rassegna Ital: Rassegna Italiana, Roma
Rassegna Pen: Rassegna penale; dizionario di dottrina, giurisprudenza e legislazione, Roma
Realist: Realist, London
Realtà: Realtà, Milano
Ref Shelf: Reference shelf, New York. (Wilson)
Reichs-Gesundheitsbl: Reichs-Gesundheitsblatt, Berlin
Rel Educ: Religious education, Chicago
Rice Inst Pam: Rice Institute, Pamphlet, Houston, Tex.
Riforma Med: La riforma medica, Napoli
Riga Zeitsch f Rechtswiss: Rigasche Zeitschrift für Rechtswissenschaft, Riga
Rinnovamento Med: Rinnovamento medico, Genoa
Riv Crit di Dir e Giuris: Rivista critica di diritto e giurisprudenza e cronache forensi, Roma
Riv d Dir Comm: Rivista del diritto commerciale e del diritto generale delle obbligazioni, Milano
Riv di Antrop: Rivista di antropologia, Roma
Riv di Cultura: Rivista di cultura, Roma
Riv di Dir e Proc Pen: Rivista di diritto e procedura penale, Milano
Riv di Dir Int: Rivista di diritto internazionale, Roma
Riv di Dir Peniten: Rivista di diritto penitenziario, Roma
Riv di Dir Proces Civile: Rivista di diritto processuale civile, Padova
Riv di Dir Pub Ammin in Italia: Rivista di diritto pubblico e della amministrazione in Italia, Roma
Riv di Psicol: Rivista di psicologia, Bologna
Riv di Soc: Rivista di sociologia, Milano
Riv Int di Filosofia del Dir: Rivista internationale di filosofia del diritto, Genoa
Riv Int di Sci Soc e Discip Ausil: Rivista internazionale di scienze sociale e discipline ausilarie, Roma
Riv Ital di Dir Pen: Rivista italiana di diritto penale, Padova
Riv Med: Rivista medica, Milano
Riv Pen di Dott, Legis e Giuris: Rivista penale di dottrina, legislazione e giurisprudenza, Firenze
Riv Sper di Freniat: Rivista sperimentale di freniatria e medicina, Reggio Emilia
Riverside Junior College, Occasional papers, Riverside, Calif.
Rocky Mo L R: Rocky Mountain law review, Boulder
Round Table: Round table, London
Roy Hist Soc Tr: Royal historical society, Transactions, London
Roy Med-Chir Soc Glasgow Tr: Royal medico-chirurgical society of Glasgow, Transactions, Glasgow
Roy Soc Can Proc: Royal society of Canada, Proceedings
Roy Soc Med Proc: Royal society of medicine, Proceedings, London
Roy Stat Soc J: Royal statistical society, Journal, London
Ruch Prawn i Ekon i Socjol: Ruch prawniczny i ekonomiczny i socjologiczny, Poznán
Rundsch f Kommunalbeamte: Rundschau für Kommunalbeamte, Berlin
Rural Am: Rural America, New York

S Atlan Q: South Atlantic quarterly, Durham, N.C.
S Calif L R: Southern California law review, Los Angeles
S D B Assn Rep: South Dakota bar association, Report, Sioux Falls
S M J: Southern medical journal, Nashville, Tenn.
S Workm: Southern workman, Hampton, Va.
Sachverständ-Zeit: Aerztliche Sachverständigenzeitung, Berlin
Safeguarding Am Against Fire: Safeguarding America against fire, New York
Safety Eng: Safety engineering, New York
St John's L R: St. John's law review, Brooklyn, N.Y.
St Louis L R: St. Louis law review, St. Louis
San Francisco Bus: San Francisco business, San Francisco
San Francisco Munic Rec: San Francisco municipal record, San Francisco
San Francisco Police & Peace Offic J: San Francisco police and peace officers journal, San Francisco
Sat Eve Post: Saturday evening post, Philadelphia
Sat R of Lit: Saturday review of literature, New York
Scalpel: Le Scalpel, Bruxelles
Sch & Soc: School and society, New York
Sch Exec Mag: School executive magazine, New York
Sch Life: School life, Washington, D.C.

Sch R: School review, Ithaca, N.Y.
Schweiz Arch f Neurol u Psychiat: Schweizer Archiv für Neurologie und Psychiatrie, Zürich
Schweiz Juristen-Zeit: Schweizerische Juristen-Zeitung, Zürich
Schweiz med Wchnschr: Schweizerische medizinische Wochenschrift, Basel
Schweiz Monats Zahnheilk: Schweizerische Monatschrift für Zahnheilkunde, Zürich
Schweiz Zeitsch f Gesundheitspfl: Schweizerische Zeitschrift für Gesundheitspflege, Zürich
Schweiz Zeitsch f Strafr: Schweizerische Zeitschrift für Strafrecht, Bern
Schweiz Ver f Straf- Gefängniswes u Schutzaufsicht Verh: Schweizerischen Vereins für Straf-, Gefängniswesen und Schutzaufsicht, Verhandlungen
Science: Science, New York
Sci Am: Scientific American, New York
Sci M: Scientific monthly, New York
Scot L R: Scottish law review and Sheriff court reports, Glasgow
Scots L T: Scots law times, Edinburgh
Scribners: Scribners magazine, New York
Scuola Pen Uman: Scuola penale umanista, Catania
Scuola Pen Unit: Scuola penale unitaria, Roma
Scuola Pos: Scuola Positiva; rivista di diritto e procedura penale, Milano
Selbstschutz: Selbstschutz, Berlin
Semana Méd: La semana médica, Buenos Aires
Shakaigaku-Zasshi: Shakaigaku-Zasshi, Tokyo
Shield: The Shield, London
Si-De-Ka Q: Si-De-Ka quarterly, Hammond, Ind.
Sierra Educ N: Sierra educational news, San Francisco
Siglo Méd: El siglo médico, Madrid
Smith Coll Stud Soc Wk: Smith college studies in social work, Northampton, Mass.
Soc & Ind R: Social and industrial review, Pretoria, S. Africa
Soc Arbeid: Socialt Arbeid, Oslo
Soc Chem Ind J: Society of chemical industry, Journal, London
Soc de Biol Compt Rend: Société de biologie, Comptes Rendus, Paris
Soc de Lég Comp Bul: Société de législation comparée, Bulletin, Paris
Soc de Obst y Ginec Bol: Sociedad de obstetrica y Ginecología de Buenos Aires, Boletin
Soc Forces: Social forces, Chapel Hill, N.C.
Soc Fr d'Hist de la Méd Bul: Société française d'histoire de la médecine, Bulletin, Paris
Soc Fr de Dermat et de Syphil Bul: Société française de dermatologie et de syphilographie, Bulletin, Paris
Soc Hyg N: Social hygiene news, New York
Soc Méd Ment Bul: Société de médecine mental de Belgique, Bulletin, Ghent
Soc Sci Monog: Social science monographs, New York. (Columbia university. Teachers college, Lincoln school)
Soc Serv R: Social service review, New York
Soc Welf [Toronto]: Social welfare, Toronto
Sociál R: Sociálni revue, Praha
Socialist R [London]: Socialist review, London
Sociol & Soc Res: Sociology and social research, Los Angeles
Sociol R: Sociological review, Manchester, Eng.
Sociol World: Sociological world, Peking
Sociologická R: Sociologická revue, Brno
Sol J: Solicitors journal and reporters weekly, London
Soviet Union R: Soviet union review, London
Sovrem Psikhonevrol: Sovremmennaya psikhonevrologia, Kiev
Sovyetskoe Pravo: Sovyetskoe pravo, Moskva
Soz Berufsarbeit: Soziale Berufsarbeit, Berlin
Soz Kultur: Soziale Kultur, Köln
Soz Praxis: Soziale Praxis, Berlin
Spectator [London]: Spectator, London
Spring 3100: Spring 3100, New York. (New York city police department)
Standard [N Y]: Standard, New York. (American ethical union)
Standard [Boston]: Standard, weekly insurance paper, Boston
Standardte: Standardte, Berlin
State Govt: State government, Denver
State Trooper: State trooper, Detroit
Statist Oboz: Statisticheskoe obozrenle, Moskva
Strafrechtl Abh: Strafrechtliche Abhandlungen. Breslau. (Schletter)
Strafvollzug: Strafvollzug, Berlin
Strasbourg-Méd: Strasbourg-médical, Strasbourg

Studi Econ e Giurid Univ Cagliari: Studi economici e giuridici, Università di Cagliari
Studi Senesi: Studi Senesi, Siena
Studi Urbinati: Studi urbinati, Urbino
Sunset: Sunset, San Francisco
Survey: Survey, New York
Svensk Juristt: Svensk Juristtidning, Stockholm
Svenska Läk-tidning: Svenska Läkartidningen, Stockholm
Sw R: Southwest review, Austin, Tex.
Sw Med: Southwestern medicine, Phoenix, Ariz.

Tagebuch: Tagebuch, Berlin
Tax Dig: Tax digest, Los Angeles
Tegen de Tuberc: Tegen de tuberculose, 's Gravenhage
Temple L Q: Temple law quarterly, Philadelphia
Tenn L R: Tennessee law review, Memphis
Tex B Assn Proc: Texas bar association, Proceedings
Tex L R: Texas law review, Austin
Tex St J Med: Texas state journal of medicine, Fort Worth
Thought: Thought, New York
Tids f Retsvidensk: Tidsskrift for Retsvidenskab, Oslo
Tijdschr v de Politie: Tijdschrift voor de politie, Zwolle
Tijdschr v h Onderwijs in d Aardrijkskunde: Tijdschrift voor het Onderwijs in de Aardrijkskunde, Rotterdam
Tijdschr v Strafr: Tijdschrift voor Strafrecht, Leyden
Tijdschr v Wetenschappelijke Graphologie: Tijdschrift voor Wetenschappelijke Graphologie, Amsterdam
Toledo City J: Toledo city journal, Toledo
Tr Sch Bul: Training school bulletin, Vineland, N.J.
Trans-Pac: Trans-Pacific, Tokyo
Travel: Travel, New York
Trust Co: Trust companies magazine, New York
Tulane L R: Tulane law review, New Orleans
"2-0" Police J: "2-0" Police journal, San Francisco

U S Bur Lab Stat Bul: U. S. Bureau of labor statistics, Bulletin, Washington, D.C.
U S Bur Standards Tech N Bul: U. S. Bureau of standards, Technical news bulletin, Washington, D.C.
U S Daily: United States daily, Washington, D.C.
U S L R: United States law review, New York
U S Vet Bur M Bull: U. S. Veteran's bureau, Medical bulletin, Washington, D.C.
Umschau: Umschau, Frankfurt a M.
Union Nova Scotia Munic Proc: Union of Nova Scotia municipalities, Proceedings, Halifax
United Empire: United empire, London
Univ Debaters' Ann: University debaters' annual, New York
Univ Cin L R: University of Cincinnati law review, Cincinnati
Univ Minn Bul: University of Minnesota, Bulletin, Minneapolis
Univ Mo Bul L Ser: University of Missouri bulletin, Law series, Columbia
Univ N C Ext Bul: University of North Carolina extension bulletin, Chapel Hill
Univ N C N Lett: University of North Carolina news letter, Chapel Hill
Univ N D Q J: University of North Dakota quarterly journal, Fargo
Univ Pa L R: University of Pennsylvania law review, Philadelphia
Univ Pittsburgh Bul: University of Pittsburgh, Bulletin, Pittsburgh
Univ S Calif L Lib Bul: University of Southern California, Law library bulletin, Los Angeles
Univ Va Rec Ext Ser: University of Virginia record extension series, Charlottesville
Upsala Läkaref Förh: Upsala läkareförening fördhandlingar, Upsala
Urol & Cutan R: Urologic and cutaneous review, St. Louis

Va L R: Virginia law review, Charlottesville
Va L Reg: Virginia law register, Charlottesville
Va Munic R: Virginia municipal review, Richmond
Va Q R: Virginia quarterly review, Charlottesville
Va St B Assn Rep: Virginia state bar association, Report, Richmond
Vererb u Geschlechtsleb: Vererbung und Geschlechtsleben, Stuttgart
Veröffentl a d Geb Heeres-San-Wes: Veröffentlichungen aus dem gebiete des Heeres-sanitätswesen, Berlin
Versich u Geldwirts: Versicherung und Geldwirtschaft, Berlin
Verslag Vergadering v h Indisch Genootschap:
Verwaltungsarch: Verwaltungsarchiv, Berlin
Vestnik: Vestnik, Praha

Vita e Pensiero: Vita e pensiero, Milano
Vita Ital: Vita Italiana, Roma
Vita Nova: Vita nova, Bologna
Vjsch f Wiss Päd: Vierteljahrsschrift für wissenschaftliche Pädagogik, Münster
Vjsch z Statist d Deut Reich: Vierteljahrsschrift zur Statistik des deutschen Reiches, Berlin
Volkswohlfahrt: Volkswohlfahrt, Berlin
Vrach Delo: Vrachebnoe delo, nauchnyi meditsinskii zhurnal, Kharkof
Vragen d Tijds: Vragen des tijds, Haarlem
Vt B Assn Proc: Vermont bar association, Proceedings
Vt Highw: Vermont highways, Montpelier

W Arch: Western architect, Minneapolis
W City: Western city, Los Angeles
W Underw & Insur Press: Weekly underwriter and the insurance press, New York
W Va B Assn Proc: West Virginia bar association, Proceedings
W Va L Q: West Virginia law quarterly and the bar, Morganston
W Va M J: West Virginia medical journal, Huntington, W. Va.
Wash L R: Washington law review, Seattle
Wash St B Assn Proc: Washington state bar association, Proceedings
Welf: Welfare see Welfare magazine
Welf Mag: Welfare magazine, Springfield, Ill.
Welt d Islams: Welt des Islams, Berlin
Weltbühne: Die Weltbühne, Berlin
Westerm Monatsh: Westermanns Monatshefte, Berlin
Wetensch Bl: Wetenschappelijke bladen, Haarlem
Wien klin Wchnschr: Wiener klinische Wochenschrift, Wien
Wien med Wchnschr: Wiener medizinische Wochenschrift, Wien
Wille u Werk: Wille und Werk, Berlin
Wilson Bul: Wilson bulletin, New York
Wirtsch u Statist: Wirtschaft und Statistik, Berlin
Wis L R: Wisconsin law review, Madison
Wis M J: Wisconsin medical journal, Milwaukee
Wis St B Assn Proc: Wisconsin state bar association, Proceedings
Woman Cit: Woman citizen, New York
Woman's City Club Bul [Chicago]: Woman's city club bulletin, Chicago
Woman's J: Woman's journal, New York
Woman's Leader [London]: Woman's leader and common cause, London
Workm Insur Ser: Workman's insurance series
World R: World review, Chicago
World Today: World today, New York
World Tomorrow: World tomorrow, New York
World Tr: World trade, Paris
World's Wk: World's work, New York
Württ Jahrb f Statist u Landeskunde: Württembergische jahrbücher für Statistik und Landeskunde, Stuttgart
Württ Statist Landesamt Mitt: Württembergisches Statistisches Landesamt, Mitteilungen, Stuttgart
Wyo St B Assn Proc: Wyoming state bar association, Proceedings

Yale L J: Yale law journal, New Haven, Conn.
Yiddisher Viss Instit Ekon-Statis. Sektzie Shr f Ekon u Statis

Zacchia: Zacchia, rassegna di studi medico-legali, Roma
Zeitsch d Bayer Statist Landesamts: Zeitschrift des Bayerischen statistischen Landesamts, München
Zeitsch d Savigny-Stift f Rechtsgesch: Zeitschrift der Savigny-Stiftung für Rechtsgeschichte, Weimar
Zeitsch des Bernischen Juristenvereins: Zeitschrift des Bernischen Juristenvereins
Zeitsch f ärztl Fortbild: Zeitschrift für ärztliche Fortbildung, Jena
Zeitsch f Ang Chem: Zeitschrift für Angewandte Chemie, Berlin
Zeitsch f Ang Psychol: Zeitschrift für Angewandte Psychologie, Leipzig
Zeitsch f Ausländ u Int Privatrecht: Zeitschrift für Ausländisches und Internationales Privatrecht, Berlin
Zeitsch f d freiw Gerichtsbark u d Gemeindeverwaltung in Württ: Zeitschrift für die freiwillige Gerichtsbarkeit und die Gemeindeverwaltung in Württemberg, Stuttgart
Zeitsch f d ges Anat: Zeitschrift für die gesamte Anatomie. Abteilung 1: Zeitschrift für Anatomie und Entwicklungsgeschichte, München
Zeitsch f d ges Neurol u Psychiat: Zeitschrift für gesamte Neurologie und Psychiatrie, Berlin
Zeitsch f d ges Staatswiss: Zeitschrift für die gesamte Staatswissenschaft, Tübingen

Zeitsch f d ges Strafrechtswiss: Zeitschrift für die gesamte Strafrechtswissenschaft, Berlin
Zeitsch f d ges Versicherungswiss: Zeitschrift für die gesamte Versicherungswissenschaft, Berlin
Zeitsch f Geburtsh u Gynäk: Zeitschrift für Geburtshülfe und Gynäkologie, Stuttgart
Zeitsch f Gewerbe-Hyg: Zeitschrift für Gewerbe-Hygiene, Unfall-Verhütung und Arbeiter-Wohlfahrts-Einrichtungen, Wien
Zeitsch f Hyg u Infektionskr: Zeitschrift für Hygiene und Infektions-krankheiten, Berlin
Zeitsch f Indukt Abstammungs- u Vererbungsl: Zeitschrift für induktive Abstammungs- und Vererbungslehre, Leipzig
Zeitsch f jüd Wohlfahrtspfl: Zeitschrift für jüdische Wohlfahrtspflege, Berlin
Zeitsch f Kinderforsch: Zeitschrift für Kinderforschung, Berlin
Zeitsch f Kinderschutz: Zeitschrift für Kinderschutz, Familien- und Berufsfürsorge, Wien
Zeitsch f Med-Beamte: Zeitschrift für Medizinalbeamte, Leipzig
Zeitsch f Menschenk: Zeitschrift für Menschenkunde, Heidelberg
Zeitsch f Ostrecht: Zeitschrift für Ostrecht, Berlin
Zeitsch f pädagog Psychol: Zeitschrift für pädagogische Psychologie, Leipzig
Zeitsch f Psychis Hyg: Zeitschrift für Psychische Hygiene, Berlin
Zeitsch f Psychoanal Päd: Zeitschrift für psychoanalytische Pädagogik, Wien
Zeitsch f Psychol: Zeitschrift für Psychologie, Leipzig
Zeitsch f Rassenphysiol: Zeitschrift für Rassenphysiologie, München
Zeitsch f Rechtspfl in Bayern: Zeitschrift für Rechtspflege in Bayern, München
Zeitsch f Rel-psychol: Zeitschrift für Religionspsychologie, Gütersloh
Zeitsch f Schulgesundhpflg: Zeitschrift für Schulgesundheitspflege und soziale Hygiene, Hamburg
Zeitsch f Schweiz Recht: Zeitschrift für Schweizerisches Recht, Basel
Zeitsch f Sexualwissensch: Zeitschrift für Sexualwissenschaft und Sexualpolitik, Berlin
Zeitsch f Tuberk: Zeitschrift für Tuberkulose, Leipzig
Zeitsch f Vergl Rechtswiss: Zeitschrift für Vergleichende Rechtswissenschaft, Stuttgart
Zeitsch f Völkerpsychol u Soz: Zeitschrift für Völkerpsychologie und Soziologie, Leipzig
Zeitsch f Völkerrecht: Zeitschrift für Völkerrecht, Breslau
Zeitwende: Zeitwende, München
Zentralbl f d jurist Praxis: Zentralblatt für die juristische Praxis, Wien
Zentralbl f Gynäk: Zentralblatt für Gynäkologie, Leipzig
Zentralbl f Handelsr: Zentralblatt für Handelsrecht, Berlin
Zentralbl f Jugendrecht u Jugendwohlfahrt: Zentralblatt für Jugendrecht und Jugendwohlfahrt, Berlin
Zentralbl f Psychotherap: Zentralblatt für Psychotherapie und ihre grenzgebiete einschliessliche der medizinischen Psychologie und psychischen Hygiene, Leipzig
Zentralst f d Gefängenenfürsorgewesen f d Prov Brandenburg
Zhur Nevropat i Psikhiat: Zhurnal nevropatologii i psikhiatrii, Moskva
Zürcher Taschenbuch: Zuercher taschenbuch, Zürich

CLASSIFICATION OUTLINE

CRIME AND CRIMINAL STATISTICS

OFFENDERS

ADMINISTRATION OF CRIMINAL JUSTICE

POLICE

CRIMINAL PROCEDURE

JUDICIAL ADMINISTRATION

PUNISHMENT

PROBATION

INSTITUTIONAL TREATMENT

PARDON, PAROLE AND INDETERMINATE SENTENCE

CRIME PREVENTION

BIBLIOGRAPHY

CRIME AND CRIMINAL STATISTICS

BIBLIOGRAPHIES

Bibliographies listed in this section are of a general nature. Specialized bibliographies are listed under appropriate headings.

Bibliography of recent periodical literature. Dakota L R 1: 41-2, 56-7, 95-7 Ja-Jl '27; 2: 179-81, 268-70, F-Je '28 1

Brown, Roy M. Recent contributions in the field of crime and criminal justice. Social forces 6: 645-8 Je '28 2

Cameron, John. Recent British books on crime. Scots L R 45: 191-7 Jl '29 3
Tr: Neuere britische kriminalistische Literatur. Monats f Kriminalpsychol u Strafrechtsref 20: 529-35 '29.

Crime and criminals, criminal law, crime commissions, criminal law cases. Univ S Calif L Lib Bul 1: 3-6 D '30 4

Criminology and trials. Catalogue no46, season 1927-28. Surrey Bookshop, Blackridge Road, Woking, England. 32p. 1927 5
1,055 titles.

Dabrowski, W[iktor] Grzywo. La bibliographie polonaise criminologiques et médico-légale en 1929. R de Med Lég, de Psychiat Lég et de Crimin pt 3: 162- '30 6

Eaton, Allen and Harrison, Shelby M. A bibliography of social surveys; reports of fact-finding studies made as a basis for social action; reports to January 1, 1928. 467p. N.Y. Russell Sage, 1930 7
Correction; crime and criminals; delinquency and correction; desertion; detention; gangs; illegitimacy; jails, juvenile courts, juvenile delinquency; penal institutions, police, prisons, prohibition, probation, parole, prostitution, sex delinquency, vagrants, vice, white slave traffic.

Fuchs, Wilhelm. Juristische Bücherkunde. Eine Einführung in die Bibliographische Technik und in den Bibliographischen Apparat der Rechts Staats und ihrer Hilfswissenschaften. 244p. Linz a. d. Donau, Franz Winkler, 1928 8
International bibliographical handbook in the legal and social sciences.

Gault, Robert H. Criminology. Psychol Bul 24: 692-707 D '27 9A
Review of 101 titles.

Headicar, B. M. and Fuller, C. comps. A London bibliography of the social sciences. 3v. London, London School of economics and political science, 1931 9B

Hentig, Hans von. Amerikanische kriminalwissenschaftliche Literatur. Monats f Kriminalpsychol u Strafrechtsref 21: 677-89 '30 10
Discussion of recent American publications in the field of criminology, 1929-30.

Iddings, Elizabeth S. Current research in law for the academic year 1929-1930. 298p. Baltimore, Johns Hopkins press, 1930 11
Crimes, criminal law and procedure, juvenile delinquency, public defenders, judicial councils, statistics, juries, evidence, jury trials, juvenile courts, etc.

Kuhlman, Augustus Frederick. A guide to material on crime and criminal justice. 633p. N.Y. Wilson, 1929 12
Criminology, administration of criminal justice, criminal law, police, judicial organization, criminal procedure, punishment, institutional treatment: prisons, jails and reformatories; pardon, parole, probation, juvenile court, crime prevention.

Los Angeles. Public library. Municipal reference library. The control of crime; selected list of recent books. 15p. Los Angeles, 1930 13

Neueste englische und französische literatur. Arch f Krim 80: 77-80 Ja 27 14

New York university law quarterly review. 7, 1929/30— 15
Each number has check-list of and index to current legal literature, covering magazine articles, books, documents, laws, etc.

Pittsburgh federation of social agencies. Bureau of social research. Bibliography of studies of social conditions in the Pittsburgh area, 1920-30. 85p. Pittsburgh, March 1931 16
Courts; boys clubs; juvenile delinquency; prisons; suicides.

Sallmayer'sche Buchhandlung. Verzeuchnis wissenschaftlicher und technischer Werke für Hörer des kriminalistischen Institutes der Bundes-Polizei-Direktion Wien. 61p. Wien, October 1930 17
Catalog of European titles on criminology and police science.

Sellin, Thorsten. Science of criminology: bibliography. J Crim L & Crimin 18: 147-58, 295-318, 451-84 My-N '27; 629-39, 118-58, 290-320, 456-508 F-N '28; 656-91 F '29 18

Students' dissertations of criminological interest. J Crim L & Crimin 10: 95-7 My '28 19

Stumberg, George Wilfred. Guide to the law and legal literature of France. 242p. Washington, Govt. Ptg. Off. 1931 20
Criminal law, criminal procedure, extradition.

Sutherland, E. H. Neue amerikanische kriminalwissenschaftliche Literatur. Monats f Kriminalpsychol u Strafrechtsref 19:228-36 Ap '28 21

United States. Library of Congress. Crime and criminal justice: a short list of books. 8p. (mim) Washington, April 11, 1930 22A

JOURNALS, PERIODICALS, ETC.

Journals listed here are of a general nature. Specialized journals are listed under appropriate headings.

Abhandlungen der Kriminalistischen Instituts an der Universität Berlin, hrsg von James Goldschmidt und Eduard Kohlrausch. s4, 1927- Berlin, Gruyter, 1927- 22B

Annales de médecine légale de criminologie et de police scientifique. Paris, 1, 1921- 23
Société de médecine légale de France.

Archiv für Kriminologie. Leipzig, 1, 1898- 24A

Arkhiv kriminologii i sudebnoi meditsiny. Kharkof, 1 pt2/3 1927- Russia (UKR SSR) Narodnii komisariiat iustitsii 24B
Title also in English: Archives of criminology and forensic medicine; in German: Archiv für criminologie und gerichtliche medizin; in Italian: Archivio di criminologia e medicina legale; in French: Archives de criminologie et de médecine légale.

Badisches Justizministerialblatt, herausgegeben vom Justizministerium. Karlsruhe, 1, 1911- 25

Boletim do Instituto de criminologia; revista de criminologia, antropologia, policia scientifica, psiquiatria e legislaçao. Lisboa, 12, 1930- 26A
Published under the direction of Rodolfo Xavier da Silva.

Boletin de criminología. Lima, 1, 1927/28- 26B
Organo de la Dirección general de prisiones, Lima, Peru.

Boletin de la Biblioteca nacional de criminología y ciencias afines. Buenos Aires, 1, July 1926- 3, 1929// 27

Criminologist. London, 1, 1927// 28

Etudes criminologiques. Paris, 1, 1926- 29
Institut de criminologie de l'Université de Paris. Beginning January 1932 merged with Revue pénitentiaire et de droit penal et Etudes criminologiques.

La Giustizia penale; rivista critica di dottrina, giurisprudenza, legislazione. Roma, 37, 1931- 30

Giustizia penale e la procedura penale italiana. Roma, 1, 1895- 31

Journal of criminal law and criminology. Chicago, 1, May 1910- American institute of criminal law and criminology 32
Official organ of American prison association and American society of military law. Includes American journal of police science 23 (2) Jl-Ag '32.

Journal of delinquency. Whittier, Calif. 1, 1916- California Bureau of juvenile research 33A
1929 and after titled Journal of juvenile research.

Journal of juvenile research. Whittier, Calif. 13, 1929- 33B
Previous to 1929 titled Journal of delinquency.

Journal of social hygiene. Baltimore, 1, 1914- 33C
American social hygiene association.

Jurisprudencia criminal. Madrid, 1, 1871- 34

Justiz. Berlin, 1, 1925- 35

Justizministerialblatt für das königreich Bayern. München, 1, 1863- 36

Justizministerialblatt für den Freistaat Sachsen. Dresden, 1, 1867- 37A

Kriminalistische Abhandlungen, herausgegeben von Franz Exner. Leipzig, 1, 1926- 37B

Kriminalistische Monatshefte, Zeitschrift für die gesamte kriminalistische Wissenschaft und Praxis. Berlin, 1, 1927- 38A

Kriminologische Abhandlungen, herausgegeben von Wenzeslaus Gleispach. Wien, 1, 1926- 38B

Literatur-Rundschau für Mitarbeiter in der Straffälligenfürsorge. Dresden, 1, 1929 [/30]- 38C

Il pensiero giuridico-penale; rivista internazionale di dottrina. Messina, 1, 1929- 39A

Problemy prestupnosti. 1, 1926- Russia (RSFSR) Gosudarstvennyi institit po izucheniiu prestupnosti i prestupnika 39B

Revista de criminologia, psiquiatra y medicina legale. Buenos Aires, 1, 1914- 40A
Organ of Instituto de criminologia de la penitenciaria nacional.

Revista de justiça. Lisboa, 13 (301) September 10, 1928- 40B

Revista de cultura juridica. Bahia, 1, 1929- 41

Revista de criminologia e medicina legal. São Paulo, 1, 1926- 42

Revista de estudios juridicos e sociaes. Rio de Janeiro, 1, 1930- 43
Centro academico de estudios juridicos e sociaes.

Revista de psiquiatria y neurologia. Habana, 1, 1929- 44

Revista española de criminologia y psiquiatria forense. Madrid, 1, 1929- 45

Revista judicial. Santa Marta, 1, 1888- 46

Revista judicial de la Republica de El Salvador. San Salvador, 1, 1892- 47

Revista juridica de Cataluña. Barcelona, 1, 1895- 48

Revista penal argentina. Buenos Aires, 1, 1922- Universidad nacional. Facultad de derecho y ciencias sociales. Centro de estudios penales, Buenos Aires 49

Revista penală. Bucuresti, 1, 1922- 50

Revue internationale de criminalistique. Lyon, 1, 1929- 51
Official organ of Académie internationale de criminalistique.

Revue pénitentiaire et de droit pénal. Paris, 1, 1877- 52
Bulletin de la Société générale des prisons et de legislation criminelle.

Rivista penale. Rassegna di dottrina-legislazione-giurisprudenza. Roma, 1, 1930- 53
Supersedes Rivista penale di dottrina, legislazione, e giurisprudenza.

Scuola penale umanista. Catania, 1, 1923- 54A

Scuola penale unitaria, revista crítica internationale de dottrina, giurisprudenza e legislazione. Roma, 1, 1927- 54B

ASSOCIATIONS, CONGRESSES, ETC.

Anti-gang rule league. J Crim L & Crimin 22: 147 My '31 55

Canadian conference on social work. Proceedings. 1, 1928- 56

Cleveland association for criminal justice. Quarterly bulletin. no1, 1927- 57A

Comité de patronage des enfants moralement abandonnés, des condamnés, vagabonds et malades mentaux de l'arrondissement de Tournai. Rapport sur l'activité de l'oeuvre en 1929. 32p. Tournai, 4, rue des Maux, au Siège social, 1929 57B

Lashly, A[rthur] V. Crime in Illinois is subject of careful study: plans of the Illinois association for criminal justice. Ill J Comm 21- Je '27 58

Minnesota state conference and Institute of social work. Proceedings. 1927-1930. Minneapolis, 1927-30 59
No conference in 1931.

National conference of juvenile agencies. Proceedings. 1, 1904- 60
Before 1921 titled National conference on the education of backward, truant, delinquent and dependent children.

National conference of social work. Proceedings. 1, 1874- 61

National institute on mercenary crime. Statement of principles, by Ernest D. McDougall, October 24, 1931. Chicago, 1931 62

Sachs, H. Kriminalist Kongressen i Karlsruhe, September 1927. Nord Tids f Straf 16: 214-19 Ap '28 63

Southern California academy of criminology. Committee on resolutions and recommendations. Report. J Delin 11: 210-11 S '27 64

Tschelzov-Bebutov, M. Mizchnarodne spilkouvania kriminalistiv ta nasha karna politika. Naoukovi zapiski Kievskogo inst. Narodnogo Gospod 8: 49-70 '27 65

PHILADELPHIA CRIMINAL JUSTICE ASSOCIATION

Meryweather, Thomas A. The Philadelphia criminal justice association. Panel 9: 18 Mr '31 66

Philadelphia criminal justice association. Annual reports. 1, 1930- 67

Philadelphia criminal justice association. [Quarterly] report. April 1-June 30, 1931 68

AMERICAN INSTITUTE

American law institute. J Comp Leg s3 10: 129-31 F '28 69

Bromberg, Frederick G. American law institute. Ala L J 3: 260-2 My '28 70

Burch, R. A. Activities of the American law institute. Kan St B Assn Rep 1929: 132-41 71

Goodrich, Herbert F. American law institute; address. Ill St B Assn Rep 1929: 253-67 72

Goodrich, Herbert F. American law institute adopts its first official draft. Am B Assn J 14: 245-9 My '28 73

Goodrich, Herbert F. The work of the American law institute. Ann Am Acad 136: 10-15 Mr '28 74

Harris, Rufus C. American law institute and the Louisiana law; address. La St B Assn Rep 29: 28-43 '29 75

Lewis, William Draper. American law institute; address. Fla St B Assn L J 3: 30-1 Ap '30 76

Lewis, William Draper. Work of the American law institute; address. Me St B Assn Proc 27: 30-41 '31 77

Parker, Emmett N. The American law institute. Wash L R 3: 124-32 Jl '28 78

Smith, Sidney. American law institute. Miss St B Assn Rep 1927: 98-105 79

Wickersham, George W. American law institute and its relation to the New York state bar. N Y St B Assn Proc 1927: 201-8 80

Wilson, Scott. American law institute. Me St B Assn Rep 25: 63-9 '27 81

INTERNATIONAL AKADEMIE FUR KRIMINALISTISCHE WISSENSCHAFTEN

Bischoff, A. and Türkel, Siegfried. L'Académie internationale de criminalistique; [Internationale Akademie für kriminalistische Wissenschaften]. R de Identif y Cienc Pen 5: 412-18 Mr '30 82

Extraits de statuts de l'Académie internationale de criminalistique. R de Identif y Cienc Pen 6: 150-6 My '30 83

Internationale Akademie für Kriminalistische Wissenschaften, [Proceedings]. R Int de Crimin 1: 483-503 N '29 84

Sitzungsbericht der Internationalen Akademie für kriminalistische Wissenschaften. Arch f Krim 85: 216-32 D '29 **85**

Status de l'Académie internationale de criminalistique. R Int de Crimin 2 (2): 84-101 '30 **86**

Türkel, Siegfried. Compte rendu officiel de la deuxième Assemblée générale de l'Académie internationale de criminalistique à Vienne, 8-10 Octobre 1930; rédaction française par Marc-A. Bischoff. R Int de Crimin 3 (6): 408-16; (7): 568-604 '31 **87**

Türkel, Siegfried. Sitzungsbericht der Internationalen Akademie für kriminalistische Wissenschaften (Académie internationale de criminalistique). Arch f Krim 85: 216-32 '29 **88**

INTERNATIONALEN KRIMINALISTISCHEN VEREINIGUNG

Foltin, Edgar, ed. Tagung der deutschen Landesgruppe zu Bonn vom 9-11 September 1926. (Mitteilungen der Internationalen Kriminalistischen Vereinigung, ns2: 21). 226p. Berlin, W. de Gruyter, 1927 **89**

Internationalen Kriminalistischen Vereinigung, Mitteilungen. ns 2 '27. Berlin, W. de Gruyter, 1927 **90**

Mittermaier, W. Nachwort zur Karlsruher Tagung der Deutschen Landesgruppe der Internationalen kriminalistischen Vereinigung. Monats f Kriminalpsychol u Strafrechtsref 18: 657-60 D '27 **91**

Die Tagung der Internationale kriminalistischen Vereinigung in Karlsruhe. Die Polizei 24: 466-7 O 5 '27 **92**

THE CRIME PROBLEM

Arbore, P. Il problema della criminalità quale appare vivendo coi criminali. Zacchia 8: 13-25 Ja '29 **93**

Asúa, Luis Jiménez de. *see* Jiménez de Asúa, Luis **94**

Barnes, Harry Elmer. Scientific treatment of crime. Cur Hist 27: 309-14 D '27 **95**

Baumes, Caleb H. Present-day crime problem. Docket 4: 3119-22 Ja '28 **96**

Best, Harry. Crime and the criminal law in the United States. 615p. N.Y. Macmillan, 1931 **97**

Parties to crime; responsibility for crime; classification of crimes; criminal procedure; criminal population in prison; forms of punishment; penal institutions; probation; measures for reduction of crime.

Bie, H. de. [The crime problem]. Maandbl v Ber en Reclass 6: 338-45 D '27 **98**

Brasol, Boris Leo. Elements of crime (psycho-social interpretation): with introductions by John H. Wigmore and William A. White. 433p. N.Y. Oxford, 1927 **99**

Causes of crime: economic; religion and family; education and press; crime and legislation and procedure; criminal responsibility; crime and mental disease; bibliog.

Brown, C. O. The crime menace, some of the causes and some of the remedies. Wyo St B Assn Proc 1927: 73-88 **100**

Burges, Austin E. Can the law cure crime? Cur Hist 27: 344-6 D '27 **101**

Business of crime. Commonweal 12: 623-4 O 22 '30 **102**

Butler, Rush C. The crime situation; address. Ill St B Assn Proc 1928: 155-65 **103**

Carr, A. S. Comyns. Civil liabilities arising from crime. Sol J 71: 551-3 Jl 9; 571-2 Jl 16 '27 **104**

Carver, Roy. The twin forces of opposition. Welf Mag 18: 741-4 Je '27 **105**

Author "doing time" in San Quentin, throws a side light on the crime question.

Cass, E. R. The crime problem. 13p. N.Y. American prison assn. 1928 **106**

Cass, E. R. Society's responsibility for crime. Pris Assn N Y Ann Rep 87: 79-96 '31 **107**

Chafee, Zechariah, jr. Complexities of crime. Outl 152: 341 Je 26 '29 **108**

Cochran, Herbert G. Old crime and new methods of dealing with it. Nat Prob Assn Proc 22: 62-88 '28 **109**

Collins, Cornelius F. Crime, a critical analysis. N Am R 226: 27-36 Jl '28 **110**

Commonwealth club of California. Delinquency studies. Trans 23(10A) D 11 '28 **111**

Costa, Fausto. Delitto e pena nella storia del pensiero umano. 291p. (Bibliot di scienze mod 101) Torino, Bocca, 1928 **112**

Coulter, Ernest Kent. Jews war on crime. Outl 158: 463-4 Ag 12 '31 **113**

Crime. Commonweal 14: 394 Ag 26 '31 **114**

Crime and the police. Just Peace 94: 215-16 Ap 5 '30 **115**

Crime under Volsteadism. Outl 159: 7 S 2 '31 **116**

Darrow, Clarence. Combatting crime. Forum 82: 271-5 N '29 **117**

Darrow, Clarence. Crime and its treatment; address. S D B Assn Rep 29: 110-27 '28 **118**

Darrow, Clarence. Crime and the alarmists (*In* Overton, Grant, ed. Mirrors of the year, 205-27. N.Y. Stokes, 1927) **119**

Darrow, Clarence. What to do about crime. Neb L Bul 6: 117-34 Jl '27 **120**

Davis, Jerome. Crime and the criminal (*In* Davis, Jerome and Barnes, Harry Elmer, eds. An introduction to sociology, 802-32. bibliog. 829-32. N.Y. Heath, 1927) **121**

Dewar, Frank D. Crime and the citizen. Los Angeles Chron 14: 15, 22 F 28 '31 **122**

Dexter, Robert Cloutman. Crime and punishment. (*In his* Social adjustment, 297-340. N.Y. Knopf, 1927) **123**

"Reference readings" at end of each chapter.

Doll, Edgar A. The control of crime. Sci M 26: 551-6 Je '28 **124**

Donohue, John Francis. Impediment of crime; an historical synopsis and commentary. (Canon law stud no69) 110p. Washington, D.C. Catholic University of America, 1931 **125**

Enright, Richard E. Our biggest business—crime. N Am R 228: 385-91 O '31 **126**

FitzGerald, C. J. Blame for crime. Commonweal 15: 157 D 9 '31 **127**

Gehlke, C. E. Crime. Am J Sociol 34: 157-71, 1108-15 Jl '28, My '29 **128**

Getting at the facts behind the city crime situation. Chr Cent 47: 908 Jl 23 '30 **129**

Giannitrapani, Alfredo. Vers la synthèse du problème pénal. R Int de Dr Pén 8: 76-99 '31 **130**
Recapitulation of the ideas which the author developed in his work *Psicoinfezione criminale.*

Gibbons, Peter M. A study in crime. Welf Mag 18:1029-35 Ag 27 **131**
The author is a former inmate of Massachusetts penitentiary.

Glueck, Sheldon. Perennial puzzle: crime. Survey 60: 332-4 Je 15 '28 **132**

Godwin, George Stanley. Cain; or, The future of crime. (Today and tomorrow ser) 108p. N.Y. Dutton, 1929 **133**

Gray, Archibald J. Delinquency. Australasian J Psychol 5: 265-76 '27 **134**

Gribben, S. H. Delinquency. M J Austral 2: 387-8 '27 **135**

Harris, Louis. Story of crime. 334p. Boston, Stratford, 1929 **136**

Healy, William. Anti-social behavior: delinquency and crime. (*In* Cowdrey, Edmund V. ed. Human biology and racial welfare, chap. xvi. N.Y. Hoeber, 1930) **137**

Healy, W[illiam]. Interpretation of delinquency trends. M R of R 36: 217-21 Mr '30 **138**

Hepbron, James M. Crime at home and abroad. Policewoman's Int Bul 5: 6-7 My '29; same title: Police J [N Y] 17: 13, 32 O '29 **139**

Hoopman, Sylvester V. Crime. Northwest Police J 5: 9 Mr '28 **140**

Houlton, Thomas L. Delinquency and crime. Neb St M J 13: 464-6 D '28 **141A**

Illinois bar association and Illinois association for criminal justice. Joint conference on crime. Report of proceedings, December 30, 1927. 24p. **141B**

International crimes. L Times 165: 461-2 My 26 '28 **142**

Is increase in crimes due to police laxity or prohibition? Med-Leg J 45: 67 My '28 **143**

Jevons, T. Seton. Crime. Lawyer & Banker 22: 24-9 Ja '29 **144A**

Jiménez de Asúa, Luis. Crónica del crimen. 272p. Madrid, Ed. de Historia Nueva, 1929 **144B**
Book of articles on crime: a double murder and robbery; history of judicial errors; motion pictures and crime; lynch law.

Josephs, N. Henry. Present-day crime problem. Docket 4: 3216-17 D '28 **145**

Kennedy, Hugh A. Studdert. First in crime and yet the spiritual leader of the world. Cent 113: 326-31 Ja '27 **146**

Kirchwey, George W. Delinquency. Minn St Conf & Inst Soc Wk Proc 37: 171-81 '29; same title: Minn St Bd Con Q 29: 38-47 S 13 '29 **147**

Krueger, Maynard C. Philadelphia grand jury reports on crime and corruption. Nat Munic R 18:347-8 My '29 **148**

Lane, Winthrop D. Science in pursuit of crime. Nation [N Y] 129: 770-2 D 25 '29 **149**

Lashly, Arthur [V]. Crime in the community as viewed by those interested in point of view of Illinois society of criminal justice. Ill Conf Pub Welf Proc 1927: 88-92 **150**

Lawes, Lewis E. Crime; a radio talk, December 2, 1928. Ind Bul Char & Correc (166): 9-11 Ja '29 **151**

Lawes, Lewis E. Sing Sing warden looks at the crime business. Police J [N Y] 17: 16-17 S '29 **152**

Levy, Newman. Crime situation. Harper's 154: 262-4 Ja '27 **153**

Lewisohn, Adolph. Problem of crime. Nation [N Y] 131: 526 N 12 '30 **154**

Lombardi, Giovanni. Civiltà e delitto. 432p. Napoli, La Toga, 1929 **155**

Lundquist, Gustav Adolph and Carver, Thomas Nixon. Rural criminality. (*In their* Principles of rural sociology, 197-201. Boston, Ginn, 1927) **156**
"References" at end of each chapter.

McMurray, Orrin K. Nip crime in the bud. Sunset 59: 12-15 Jl '27 **157**

Manich, Francisco. No protejamos las escuelas del crimen. Caridad 5: 3-5 Mr '30 **158**

Matheson, Duncan. About delinquency. Police J [N Y]: 16: 14, 32 N '28 **159**

Mayer, Si. The history of crime and criminals. Criminologist [Chicago] 5: 9-11, 25 Je '29 **160**

Meijer-Wichmann, Clara. Misdaad, Straf en Maatschappij. 206p. Utrecht, Erven J. Byleveld, 1931 **161**

Mezger, E[dmund]. Konstitutionelle und dynamische Verbrechensauffassung. Monats f Kriminalpsychol u Strafrechtsref 19: 385-400 Jl '28 **162**

Miller, Justin. The lawyer's part in the solution of the crime problem. Am B Assn Rep 51:534-40 '28 **163**

Mirto, Pietro. Le condizioni di individualizzazione del reato. 122p. Messína, Ind. Grafiche Meridionali, 1930 **164**

Mirto, Pietro. Saggio di una teoria generale del reato. v. 1. 204p. Messína, "La Serena," 1928 **165**

Monteiro, Mario. Do crime. 237p. Lisboa, Livraria Avelar Machodo, 1929 **166**

Murphy, Bradford J. Delinquency. Police J [N Y] 16: 28-9 Je; 28 32 Jl '29 **167**

Nagler, Johannes. Die Genesis des Verbrechens. Gefängnisgesellsch f d Prov Sachsen & Anhalt Jahr 47: 31-49 '31 **168**

National crime digest: diamond jubilee edition. S F Police & Peace Offic J 7 (14) D '29 **169**

Our new crime front. Outl 150: 1403 D 26 '28 **170**

Outevski, B. L'étude du criminel et de la criminalité. R Mondiale 190: 291-4 Ap 1 '29 171

Parks, Clayton J. Crime. Minn St Conf & Inst Soc Wk Proc 37: 221-4 '29 172
Address before Minnesota and Northwest association of policewomen.

Parsons, Philip Archibald. New conception and treatment of crime. Am City 36: 625-8 My '27 173

Patterson, R. C. jr. Crime and criminals. 5p. (mim) N. Y. Association of grand jurors, 1928 174

Picone-Chiodo, C. La conception spiritualiste et la sociologie criminelle; trad. de l'anglais par C. de Vesme. 191p. Paris, Ficker, 1929 175

Pierce, A. Russell. Crime loopholes. Forum 80: 476-7 S '28 176

Potts, W. A. Crime and delinquency. Police J [London] 2: 416-28 Jl '29 177

Potts, W. A. Delinquency. Roy Soc Med Proc [Sect Psychiat] 22: 13-16 Ja '29 178

Pound, R[oscoe]. Crime and the law. M Times & Long Island M J 59: 117-22 Mr '31 179

Proskauer, Joseph M. How shall we deal with crime? Harper's 159: 419-22 S '29 180

Reeve, Arthur Benjamin. Golden age of crime. 272p. N.Y. Mohawk, 1931 181

Reik, Theodor. Zwei analytische Werke über Verbrechen und Strafe. Imago 16 (1): 138-44 '30 182

Reuter, Edward Byron. Delinquency and crime. (*In his* The American race problem, 338-64. N.Y. Crowell, 1927) 183
"Readings" at end of each chapter.

Reynolds, Ralph Arthur. Delinquency: a possible new approach. Pac Coast J Nursing 26: 798-800 D '30 184

Richberg, Donald R. Crime, common and preferred. Minn L R 15: sup97-102 D '30 185

Roberts, Kenneth L. Watchdogs of crime. 12p. Chicago, Chicago crime com'n, 1927 186

Robinson, Louis N. Our crime problem. Nat Soc Pen Inf N Y Bul 2: 1-2 Je '31 187

Roosevelt, Franklin Delano. Cooperation of the governors on crime problems. Conf Gov'rs Proc 21: 22-32 '29 188

Roosevelt, Franklin D[elano]. States should solve crime problems. N Y St B Assn Bul 333-8 O '29 189

Salmon, André, London, George and Divoire, Fernand. Roman d'un crime. 206p. Paris, Les Editions des Portiques, 1929 190

Schmidt, Eugen. Das Verbrechen als Ausdrucksform sozialer Entmutigung. 80p. München, Schweitzer-Verl. 1931 191

Shulman, Harry M. Popular misconceptions regarding delinquency. Nat Prob Assn Proc 24: 94-103 '30 192

Snow, Francis. View of crime held by eminent Russian writers. Cur Hist 27: 342-3 D '27 193

Social service council of Canada. Social welfare: delinquency number. v10, no2 N '27 194

Solving the crime problem. Sch Exec Mag 50: 566 Ag '31 195

Sorokin, Pitrim A., Zimmerman, Carle C. and Galpin, Charles J. Rural social control and comparative rural-urban criminality, immorality and intemperance. (*In their* A systematic source book in rural sociology, 266-342. St. Paul, University of Minnesota press, 1931) 196

Stevens, E. Ray. Crime and criminal justice. J Crim L & Crimin 21: 325-9 N '30 197

Stewart, Mary L. Some aspects of delinquency. Minn St Bd Con Q 26: 4-10 F 15 '27 198

Stigmata of crime. Just Peace 93: 574-6 S 14 '29 199

Sullivan, John L. Science versus crime. Int Assn Chiefs Police Proc 1927: 28-30; same title: Police J [N Y] 15: 19-20 Ag '27 200

Sutherland, E[dwin] H. Crime and the conflict process. J Juv Res 13: 38-48 Ja '29 201

Tepley, Lee V. The psycho-biology of crime. Dicta 7: 3-11 D '29 202

United States. Congress. House. Committee on District of Columbia. False information regarding commission of crimes in District of Columbia, report to accompany H.R. 8558, March 10, 1928. 2p. Washington, Govt. Ptg. Off. 1928 (70th Cong. 1st sess. H.R. 876) 203

Waite, John Barker. What is being done about crime? Mich St B J 6: 100-4 Ja '27 204

War on crime. Nation [N Y] 129: 158 Ag 14 '29 205

Warren, Frank H. Crime—a complex or a crisis. Notre Dame Law 4: 147-7 D '28 206

Wassermann, Rudolf. 40 Jahre moderne Kriminalpolitik. Monats f Kriminalpsychol u Strafrechtsref 20: 207-12 Ap '29 207

What to do about crime. Neb L Bul 6: 117-34 Jl '27 208

White, R. Clyde. The Indianapolis Star's articles on crime. Ind Bul Char & Correc (177): 584-6 D '29 209

Wilson, Samuel B. The crime situation. Minn L R 12:54-66 '27 210

Woehlke, Walter V. Hurrah for crime. Sunset 58: 28-9 Ap '27 211

Wood, Arthur Evans. Crime. Am J Sociol 35: 1027-41 My '30 212

Wood, Arthur Evans. Crime and penology. Am J Sociol 36: 1017-29 My '31 213
Review of more important developments of the year, including publications.

Woodhull, Charles. Fashions in crime. Welf Mag 19: 883-90 S '28 214

BELGIUM

Belym, Léon. Die belgische Kriminalität. Monats f Kriminalpsychol u Strafrechtsref 22: 29-31 Ja '31 215

EUROPE

Woodhull, Charles. Overseas crime. Welf Mag 19: 1200-5, 1405-10 N, D '28 216

FEDERATED MALAY STATES

Hannigan, C. Crime in the Federated Malay States. Police J [London] 3: 213-25 Ap '30 217

FRANCE

Laurent, E. Criminal Paris of today. Criminologist [London] 1: 5-6 My 15 '27 218A

GERMANY

Tönnies, Ferdinand. Verbrechertum in Schleswig-Holstein. Arch f Sozialwiss u Sozialpol 61: 322-59 '29 218B

GREAT BRITAIN

Crime in England. Commonweal 15: 171-2 D 16 '31 219

Ingram, George. Hell's kitchen; the story of London's underworld as related by the notorious ex-burglar to De Witt Mackenzie. 312p. London, Jenkins, 1930 220

Troup, Edward. Crime in greater London. (*In* New survey of London life and labor, I: Forty years of change, 389-403, 1930) 221

HUNGARY

Pálosi, Ervin. Budapest kriminalitása és moralitása az 1909-1925 években. 108p. Budapest, Druckerei der Hauptstadt Budapest, 1927 222

INDIA

Fairweather, C. E. S. Crime in the port of Calcutta: with special reference to the cargo pilferage question. Police J [London] 3: 370-82 Jl '30 223

Gupta, Rama Prasas Das. Crime and punishment in ancient India. 2bks in 1. 69, 168p. Calcutta, Book co. 1930 224

Purser, W. C. B. Burma in transition. Int R Miss 17: 655-62 O '28 225

Walsh, Cecil. Crime in India; with an introduction on forensic difficulties and peculiarities. 287p. London, Benn, 1930 226

Walsh, Cecil. Indian village crimes with an introduction on police investigations and confessions. 230p. London, Benn, 1929 227

Walsh, Cecil. Moeurs criminelles de l'Inde; trad. par Maurice Gérin. 309p. Paris, Payot, 1930 228

ITALY

Manci, Filippo. Il problema della delinquenza in Sicilia. Scuola Pos ns8: 389-408 S '28 229

NETHERLANDS

Bonger, W. A. De criminaliteit van Nederland. Mensch & Maatschappij 6: 230-51 My '30 230

RHODESIA

Stephenson, A. Crime in northern Rhodesia. Police J [London] 3: 519-25 O '30 231

RUSSIA

[Gernet, M. N.] (M. N. Hernett). Prestupnostj sa granizei i v S.S.S.R. 186p. Moskva, "Sovietskoye Zakonodatelstvo," 1931 232

SYRIA

Ammoun, Fouad. Essai sur la criminalité en Syrie, au Liban, dans l'état des Alaouites et en Palestine anglaise. 495p. Paris, Giard, 1929 233

UNITED STATES

Adams, James Truslow. Our lawless heritage. Atlan M 142: 732-40 D '28 234

Calvert, E. Roy. Problem of crime in America. L Notes 34: 63-4 Jl '30 235

Crime in the United States. Round Table 20: 273-87 Mr '30 236

Dodd, William Edward. Habit of crime in the United States. Rice Inst Pam 16: 143-51 Jl '29 237

Duncan, J. G. Why America leads in crime. Peace Offic 5: 9, 17 Ap '27 238

McDougall, William. Crime in America. The psychological resolution of a sociological paradox. Forum 77: 518-23 Ap '27 239

M'Govern, Chauncey. Crime in the United States, its causes and its cures. Int Assn Identif, Cal Div Proc 16: 23-7 '31 240

Makarewicz, J. Ce que j'ai vu aux Etats-Unis; les impressions d'un criminaliste. R Int de Dr Pén 6 (2): 150-72 '29 241

Merz, Charles. Bigger and better murders. (*In his* The great American band-wagon, 71-87. N.Y. Day, 1928) 242

Owens, Collison. King crime: an English study of America's crime problem. 306p. London, Benn, 1931 243

Paterson, Alexander. United States way with crime. Pris Assn N Y Ann Rep 87: 47-55 '31 244

Sullivan, Edward Dean. I know you, Al. N Am R 228: 257-64 S '29 245

CALIFORNIA

Benesh, M. D. Crime and So. California. Los Angeles Chron 13: 15 N 29 '30 246

Crime in California. Police J [N Y] 16: 26-7 Jl; 23-4 S '28 247

Simmons, W. M. Present crime conditions in California. Commonwealth club Calif Tr 23: 211-14 Je 26 '28 248

ILLINOIS

Alcock, John H. Crime and the police; is Chicago the crime capital? What are the police doing about it? Police "13-13" 5: 3-5, 27 Ja '31 **249**

Boettiger, John. Jake Lingle; or, Chicago on the spot. 335p. N.Y. Dutton, 1931 **250**

Burns, Walter Noble. One-way ride; the red trail of Chicago gangland from prohibition to Jake Lingle. 313p. N.Y. Doubleday, 1931 **251**

Chamberlin, Henry Barrett. Figures show crime decrease in Chicago. Crim Just [Chicago] (55): 3, 5-7 F '28 **252**

Chicago crime. Welf Mag 18: 384-6 Mr '27 **253**

Crissey, Forrest. What price a city's reputation; an explanation of Chicago's unwarranted ill-fame and a suggestion for its correction. Commerce [Chicago] 22-4, 56, 58-9 Ag '31 **254**

Finnegan, R[ichard] J. Chicago not a breeder of crime. Ill Med J 52: 152-7 Ag '27 **255**

Finnegan, Richard J. The city of many main streets. Welf Mag 18: 863-71 Jl '27 **256**

Howe, Lawrence. Crime and the courts in Chicago. Nation [N Y] 131: 315-16 S 24 '30 **257**

McDermott, William F. Chicago strikes back. N Am R 232: 56-64 Jl '31 **258**

Sullivan, Edward Dean. Chicago surrenders; a sequel to Rattling the cup on Chicago crime. 239p. N.Y. Vanguard, 1930 **259**

Sullivan, Edward Dean. Rattling the cup on Chicago crime. 228p. N.Y. Vanguard, 1929 **260**
English title: Look at Chicago! 214p. London, Bles, 1930

INDIANA

Indiana state conference on social work. Indiana committee on delinquency. [Report, 1, October 14, 1928]. Ind Bul Char & Correc (165): 485-96 D '28 **261**

Indiana state conference on social work. Indiana committee on delinquency. [Report, 2, 1929]. Ind Bul Char & Correc (177): 571-2 D '29 **262**

Ogden, James M. Attitude of the Indiana bar towards the crime situation; address of the President. Ind L J 6: 3-15 O '30 **263**

Visher, S. S. Indiana county contrasts in criminality and insanity. Ind Bul Char & Correc (164): 446-8 N '28 **264**

MASSACHUSETTS

Gates, Charles A. and Simmons, Eva L. Crime in Massachusetts. Survey 60: 103-5 Ap 15 '28 **265**

MICHIGAN

Detroit. Bureau of governmental research. Crime in Detroit, 1916-1926. Pub Bus 4 (2) Mr 1 '27 **266**

NEW YORK

Crime in New York state. Correction 1: 6 N '31 **267**

New York (state). Crime commission. A study of crime conditions in the Red Hook district of Kings county. 78p. (mim) Albany, 1927 **268**

Patterson, Richard C. Opportunity knocks. On Guard 1:1-2, 4 Ap '31 **269**

TENNESSEE

Bruce, Andrew A. and Fitzgerald, Thomas S. A study of crime in the city of Memphis, Tenn. J Crim L & Crimin 19 pt2: 3-124 Ag '28 **270**

VIRGINIA

Virginia. Commission on crimes and prisons. Crimes and prisons: report of the Commission appointed to inquire into and make recommendations as to the solution of these problems. 8p. (Sen. doc. no7) Richmond, 1930; Supplement. 4p. January 13, 1930 **271**

PSYCHOLOGY AND CRIME

Alexander, F[ranz]. Psychische Hygiene und Kriminalität. Imago 17: 145-73 bibliog 172-3 '31 **272**

Bahr, M. A. Psychiatry in relation to crime. Si-De-Ka Q 12: 5-9 Ap '28 **273**

Branham, V. C. The reconciliation of the legal and psychiatric viewpoints of delinquency. Crim L J India 28: 1-17 Ja '27 **274**

Brill, A. A. Psychopathology of crime, its psychiatric and social implications. Am Inst Homeop J 22: 186-202 Mr '29 **275**

Brown, Sanger. A psychiatric view of crime and the criminal. Am Assn Stud Feeblemind Proc 52: 115-23 '28 **276**

Davis, Watson. Psychiatry and crime. Cur Hist 28: 829-30 Ag '28 **277**

Glueck, Sheldon. Mental hygiene and crime. Psychoanal R 19: 23-35 '31 **278**

Jastrow, Joseph. Psychology and crime. Nat Conf Soc Wk Proc 54: 157-68 '27 **279**

Martin, Walter B. Crime in the community as viewed by those interested in the mental hygiene program. Ill Conf Pub Welf Proc 1927: 92-100 **280**

Overholser, Winfred. Psychiatry and crime. Nat Prob Assn Proc 24: 36-46 '30 **281**

Overholser, Winfred. Some psychiatric aspects of crime. New England J Med 205: 441-6 Ag 27 '31 **282**

Porto Carrero, J. P. Concepto psicoanalítico de la pena. Conf Latino-Am de Neurol Psiquiat y Med Leg Actas 1: 395-412 '29 **283**

Schlesinger, Therese. Strafjustiz und Psychoanalyse. Der Kampf [Wien] 23: 34-40 Ja '30 **284**

White, William A. Need for cooperation between lawyers and psychiatrists in dealing with crime. Am B Assn J 13: 551-5 O '27; same title: Am J Psychiat 84: 493-506 N '27 **285**

MEDICAL ASPECTS OF CRIME

Ebaugh, Franklin G. Medical aspects of the crime situation. Colo Med 26: 47-55 F '29 **286**

Lurie, L. A. Medical aspects of crime. J Med 12: 469-74 N '31 **287**

Menninger, K. A. Crime as a medical problem. Tex St J Med 23: 20-3 My '27 **288**

National crime commission. Sub-committee on the medical aspects of crime. Report, December 18, 1930. 25p. (mim) N.Y. 1930 **289**

Provent, P. La répression des crimes de guerre et la médecine légale. Ann de Méd Lég 8: 95-103 F '28 **290**

Thayer, Walter N. jr. A doctor surveys the criminal problem. Am Pris Assn Proc 60: 196-207 '30; same title: Nat Soc Pen Inf N Y Bul 1: 5-8 D '30 **291**

SOCIAL ASPECTS OF CRIME

Binford, Jessie F. Crime in the community as viewed by those interested in community welfare, particularly from the point of view of protective and preventive agencies. Ill Conf Pub Welf Proc 1927: 100-4 **292**

Chingyueh, Y. [Sociological analysis of crimes in Peking]. Sociol World [Peking] 2: 32-77 Je '28 **293**

Lombardi, Giovanni. Dottrina sociologica del reato. 351p. Napoli, Libreria internazionale guida, 1931 **294**

Miller, Justin. Social aspects of crime. Sociol & Soc Res 13: 526-35 Jl '29 **295**

Picone-Chiodo. La teoria bio-sociologica del delitto. Riv di Soc 1: 273-81 '27 **296**

Prieto, Marcial Martinez. La actitud social frente al delito. 365p. bibliog 360-5. Santiago, Imp. Nascimento, 1931 **297**

Sutherland, E[dwin] H. Social aspects of crime. Crim L J India 29 pt1: 43-5 My '28 **298**

CRIME WAVES

Babson, Roger Ward. Crime waves. Child Welf 23: 597-8 Jl '29 **299**

Barnes, Harry Elmer. Battling the crime wave; applying sense and science to the repression of crime. 245p. Boston, Stratford, 1931 **300**

Bierstadt, Edward Hale. Our permanent crime wave. Harper's 156: 61-70 D '27 **301**

Defective police organization in the United States.

Burney, J. B. The crime wave. Int Assn Identif Proc 13: 105-7 '27 **302**

Burney, J. B. Crime waves. Int Assn Chiefs Police Proc 34: 37-40 '27 **303**

The cause of the crime wave; a reply. Am B Assn J 14: 103-7 F '28 **304**

Coe, Charles Francis. Cures for crime waves. Sat Eve Post 200: 24-5 Ap 14 '28 **305**

Coe, Charles Francis. Why crime waves? Sat Eve Post 200: 8-9 Mr 17 '28 **306**

Jenkins, W. Frank. Crime waves; address. Ga B Assn Rep 1929: 257-67 **307**

Kirchwey, George W. Breasting the crime wave. Survey 58: 69-71 Ap 15 '27 **308**

Steffens, Lincoln. How I made a crime wave. Bookm 68: 416-19 D '28 **309**

This winter's crime wave—fact or fancy? Wherein ten . . . western police chiefs set forth their views, giving the statistics for their cities. W City 7: 21-3 Ja '31 **310**

J. A. Greening, Berkeley; Wm. J. Quinn, San Francisco; Robert F. Reed, Denver; C. H. Kelley, Pasadena; L. V. Jenkins, Portland; J. M. Kirkley, Reno; Jos. E. Burbridge, Salt Lake City; Andy Robinson, Boise; Louis J. Forbes, Seattle; W. G. McClusky, Spokane.

Walston, I. B. Causes of the crime wave. Peace Offic 5: 9, 15 N '27 **311**

White, John Turner. Cause of the crime wave. Mo B Assn Proc 1927: 72-90; same title: Am B Assn J 13: 726-32 D '27. A reply. Am B Assn J 14: 103-7 F '28 **312**

CRIME COMMISSIONS

BIBLIOGRAPHY

Conner, Esther. Crime commissions and criminal procedure in the United States since 1920: a bibliography, January 1920-June 1927. J Crim L & Crimin 21: 129-44 My '30 **313**

GENERAL

Brucker, Wilbur M. Necessity for a state crime commission. Mich St B J 8: 139-51 F '29 **314**

The crime commission. Lawyer & Banker 20: 5-8 Ja '27 **315**

Cass, E. R. National crime commission conference. J Crim L & Crimin 18: 497-513 F '28 **316**

Crime commissions. J Crim L & Crimin 18: 120-1 My '27 **317**

Davis, Philip Richard. Crime curbs. Ill L R 22: 106-8 My '27 **318**

Death and disability rate of crime commissions. Am B Assn J 16: 770 D '30 **319**

Fox, Charles Edwin and Wales, B. Roger. Crime commissions—what they have done and what they can do. Am Pris Assn Proc 59: 124-45 '29 320

Hepbron, James M. Local crime commissions; their origin, purpose and accomplishments. Sci M 24: 426-31 '27 321

Morse, Wayne L. and Moley, Raymond. Crime commissions as an aid in the legal-social field. Ann Am Acad 145: 68-73 S '29 322

CALIFORNIA

California. Crime commission. Report, January 7, 1929. 101p. Sacramento, 1929 323

California. Crime commission. Report . . . 1931. 142p. Sacramento, 1931 324
Commission created by statute, 1927 ch.407, May 10.

California crime commission's successful legislative program. Am B Assn J 13: 300-1 Je '27 325

Fox, Chris B. Legislative program of California crime commission. Peace Offic Assn Calif Proc 9: 83-91 '29 326

Fox, Chris B. Recommendations of the California crime commission. Calif Conf Soc Wk Q Bul 12: 39-42 F '29 327

Johnston, James A. The work of the California crime commission. Nat Prob Assn Proc 23: 50-61 '29 328

Los Angeles crime committee. Results of investigations of the California crime commission. J Crim L & Crimin 22: 272-8 Jl '31 329

HAWAII

Hawaii. Governor's advisory committee on crime. Report . . . February 1931. 192p. Honolulu, 1931 330

ILLINOIS

Chicago. Crime commission. Criminal justice, no47, January 1927- 331
No. 1-46 as the Commission's Bulletin.

[Munger, R. F.] Methods of crime commission. Crim Just [Chicago] 9: 6 Ap '27 332

Survey of Chicago crime commission. Crim Just [Chicago] (58): 7-11 My '30 333

To make criminal justice more just; brief findings and recommendations of Chicago crime commission. Am City 39: 161 S '28 334

MARYLAND

Baltimore. Criminal justice commission. Annual reports, 5, 1927—9, 1931. [Baltimore 1927-31] 335

Baltimore. Criminal justice commission. Quarterly bulletin, September 30, 1927- 336

MICHIGAN

Detroit. Bureau of governmental research. Memorandum to Mr. Harvey Campbell, Detroit Board of commerce, re proposed crime commission. Bd of Directors Min 10-22 Ap 19 '28 337

Michigan. Crime commission. Report, 1930. 54p. Lansing, 1930 338

Michigan. Procedure commission. Report October 1928. 200p. (mim) [Lansing, 1928] 339

MINNESOTA

Cherry, Wilbur H. The recommendations of the Minnesota crime commission as viewed in 1930. Minn Munic 16: 10-14 Ja '31 340

Minnesota. Crime commission. Report, pt. 1, January 6, 1926. Minn L R 11: sup1-77 Ja '27 341

Moley, Raymond. The administration of criminal justice. Police J [N Y] 17: 16-17, 27 D '30 342
Comment on Crime commission report, 1927.

MONTANA

Montana. State crime commission. Report, November 29, 1930. 100p. [Helena, 1930] 343

NEW HAMPSHIRE

New Hampshire. Crime commission. Report. . . , [1929]. 8p. [Concord, 1929] 344

NEW JERSEY

New Jersey. Commission to investigate the subject of crime in New Jersey. Report of the Commission . . . appointed by Governor A. Harry Moore. 12p. Trenton, 1927 345

NEW YORK

Anderson, Nels. New York studies causes of crime. Survey 58: 206-7 My 15 '27 346

Branham, V. C. Symposium of remarks made at hearing given by New York state crime commission to psychiatrists and criminologists. Psychiat Q 2: 444-75 '28 347

Hoey, Jane M. Suggestions from the New York state crime studies. Nat Prob Assn Proc 23: 67-75 '29 348

New York Crime commission's report. Am B Assn J 13: 337-9 Je '27 349

New York (state). Crime commission. Reports, 1927-30. (Legislative document, (1927) no94; (1928) no23; (1929) no99: (1930) no98; Albany 1927-31 350
Caleb H. Baumes, chairman. Commission ceased to exist April 1931.
Contains reports of sub-committees; statistics; courts; penal institutions; adjustment of sentences; firearms legislation; psychiatric and expert testimony in criminal cases; causes and effects of crime.

New York (state). Crime commission. Special report to the Commission on the Proceedings of the Commission in Canada; [written by David S. Taylor] 10p. Albany, 1927 351

PENNSYLVANIA

Gray, James H. The Crime commission program. Assn of Dir Poor & Char & Correc Pa Proc 54: 109-17 '29 **352**

Pennsylvania. Commission appointed to study the laws, procedure, etc., relating to crime and criminals. Report to the General Assembly meeting, January 1, 1929. 118p. Philadelphia [1929] **353**

Pennsylvania. Crime commission. Report . . . on measures recommended to the 1929 Legislature . . . particularly stating the Legislative history of the recommendations by the Judicial Conference to the Crime commission. 67p. [Philadelphia] May 22, 1929 **354**

RHODE ISLAND

The recommendations of the Rhode Island Criminal law advisory commission. J Crim L & Crimin 19:269-71 Ag '28 **355**

Rhode Island. Criminal law advisory commission. Annual reports, 1, 1927—5, 1931. [Providence 1927-31] **356**
Commission created Ch 950, Laws 1927.

NATIONAL COMMISSION ON LAW OBSERVANCE AND ENFORCEMENT

Anderson plan. Chr Cent 48: 600-2 My 6 '31 **357**

Backstage in Washington. Outl 154: 218 F 5 '30 **358**

Committee rule or rumors. Commonweal 13: 118 D 3 '30 **359**

Death of a commission. Nation [N Y] 133: 55 Jl 15 '31 **360**

Farce goes on. Outl 155: 412-13 Jl 16 '30 **361**

Four aspects of the Wickersham report. New Repub 65: 311-13 F 4 '31 **362**

Franklin, Fabian. Nuggets from the Wickersham report with comments. 30p. N.Y. Riverside press, 1931 **363**

Hart, Albert Bushnell. Hoover commission begins law enforcement inquiry. Cur Hist 30: 683 Jl '29 **364**

Jackson, Gardner. Wickersham and his commission. Nation [N Y] 132: 63-4 Ja 21 '31 **365**

Kellogg, Arthur. Eleven Wickersham reports. Survey 65: 539 F 15 '31 **366**

Lane, Winthrop D. Crime and the Wickersham reports. Survey 67: 134-7 N 1 '31 **367**

McManus, Robert Cruise. Unhappy warrior; a portrait of G. W. Wickersham. Outl 156: 85-8 S 17 '30 **368**

M[orse], W[ayne] L. Hoover crime commission. Ore L R 9: 56 D '29 **369**

Murphy, William C. jr. Sphinx commission. Commonweal 10: 249-50 Jl 3 '29 **370**

National commission on law observance and enforcement; plans for a national study of law administration in the federal courts. Sch & Soc 33: 190 F 7 '31 **371**

Prohibition report of the law enforcement commission. Cur Hist 31: 985-92 F '30 **372**

Real and intangible costs; Wickersham report. Commonweal 13: 562-3 Mr 25 '31 **373**

Ryan, John A. The Wickersham report: a defense and a criticism. Cath Char R 15: 67-71 Mr '31 **374**

Strout, [Richard] L. Mr. Wickersham in retrospect. N Am R 232: 413-23 N '31 **375**

Strout, Richard Lee. Why are we lawless? The Wickersham commission and our legal chaos. Woman's J ns15: 12-14, 40 D '30 **376**

Wickersham, George W. The program of the Commission on law observance and enforcement. Am B Assn Rep 55: 212-36 '30; same title: Am B Assn J 16: 654-61 O '30 **377**

Wickersham report. Chr Cent 48: 159-61 F 4 '31; same title: Commonweal 13: 369-70 F 4 '31; New Repub 61: 237 Ja 22 '30; Outl 154: 174 Ja 29 '30; Woman's J ns16: 24 Mr '31 **378**

Wickershammers. Outl 155: 374 Jl 9 '30 **379**

Wolf, D. E. United States: [discussion of the Wickersham reports with text of its conclusions and recommendations]. Cur Hist 33: 911-15 Mr '31 **380**

COST OF CRIME

BIBLIOGRAPHY

New York (state). Library. Legislative reference section. List of references relating to law costs. 3p (typw) Albany, March 30, 1930 **381**

GENERAL

Administrative cost of crime. Univ N C N Lett 13: 1 Ag 17 '27 **382**

Barnhart, W. L. Cost of crime to electric railways each year is enormous. Elec Ry J 70: 579-80 O 8 '27 **383**

Baum, James E. Crime takes $12,000,000 toll from banks. J Am Insurance 17: 5-7 N '30 **384**

Circuit court costs [in Ireland]. Irish L T 65: 187-8 Ag 8 '31 **385**

The cost of evidence. Can B R 6: 388 My '28 **386**

Cost of police departments, criminal courts and correctional institutions. Am City 36: 363-4 Mr '27 **387**

Costs of prosecution of criminal offences, payment by private prosecutor. Just Peace 95: 153-4 Mr 7 '31 **388**

Dunlop, William C. The cost of administration of justice in municipalities. Union Nova Scotia Munic Proc 26: 70-5 '31 **389**

Economic costs of crime. Dakota L R 1: 63-4 Ap '27 **390**

Fairman, Charles and others. Report on the cost of administration of justice in the city of Pittsfield, Massachusetts. 66p. (mim) Williamstown, Mass. Williams College, Department of Political Science, 1931 **391**

Feldman, Herman. Prohibition and the high cost of crime. (*In his* Prohibition, its economic and industrial aspects, 351-67. N.Y. Appleton, c1927) **392**

Fifoot, C. H. S. Cost of litigation. Fortn R [London] 132: 59-69 Jl '29 **393**

Fogarty, E. J. Human cost of crime. Woman's City Club Bul [Chicago] 16: 174-6 Ja '27 **394**

Great Britain. Commissioner of police of the metropolis. Accounts showing the sums received and expended for the purposes of the metropolitan police and police courts between April 1, 1930 and March 31, 1931. 19p. [London] 1931 **395**

Gunther, John. The high cost of hoodlums. Harper's 159: 529-40 O '29; same title: Police J [N Y] 17: 9-13, 21 Ap '30 **396**
Discusses racketeering in Chicago and estimates annual per capita cost of racketeering to the residents of that city.

Harrison, Leonard V. Are we spending too much for government? VII: Expenditures for police service. Nat Munic R 16: 638-42 O '27 **397**

Hartkorn, August. Nation's loss by forgery in 1929—120 million. Police J [N Y] 17: 8-10 Ag '30 **398**

Healy, William. The devil's workshop where criminal ideas are hatched and young delinquents are spawned. Cent 120: 122-32 Winter '30 **399**

Holden, Charles R. What we pay for crime yearly. Woman's City Club Bul [Chicago] 16: 169-71 Ja '27 **400**

How the expenses of legal proceedings could be reduced. Sol J 73: 214, 229-30, 246-7, 261-2 Ap 6-27 '29 **401**

Johns Hopkins University. Institute of law. Expenditures of public money for the administration of justice in Ohio in 1929. (tentative draft; mim) Baltimore, 1931 **402**
Study of the cost of administration of justice in Ohio in 1929: covers both civil and criminal.

Loesch, Frank J. Crime and your balance sheet. Mag Bus 55: 405-6 Ap '29 **403**
Discusses the direct and indirect cost of racketeering in Chicago.

McLellan, Howard. High cost of nullification. R of R 81: 56-61 Ap '30 **404**

National commission on law observance and enforcement. Manual for studies of the cost of administration of criminal justice in American cities. 38p. Washington, 1930 **405**
Also reprinted as Appendix C in National commission on law observance and enforcement, Report on the cost of crime (no12).

National commission on law observance and enforcement. Report on the cost of administration of criminal justice in Rochester, New York. 38p. Prepared by the Rochester bureau of municipal research. Washington, 1931 **406**
Also reprinted as Appendix D in National commission on law observance and enforcement, Report on the cost of crime (no12).

National commission on law observance and enforcement. Report on the cost of crime. 657p. (No12) Washington, June 24, 1931 **407**
Dorr, Goldthwaite H. and Simpson, Sidney P. Introductory analysis of the cost of crime; Simpson, Sidney P. and Schmeckebier, Laurence F. The cost of administration of criminal justice by the federal government; Simpson, S. P. and Libby, John H. Published statistical material on state and municipal costs of administration of criminal justice; Simpson, S. P. The cost of state police forces; Simpson, S. P. The cost of penal and correctional institutions and parole agencies; Simpson, S. P., Franzen, Raymond H. and Hubbell, William B. The cost of administration of criminal justice in American cities; Simpson, S. P. and Waldecker, Sydney. Private expenditures for protection against crime; Simpson, S. P. Private losses due to criminal acts, Indirect losses to the community due to the existence of crime; bibliography.

Peirce, John M. Cost of prisons in California: prisoners cost California twelve million dollars in ten years. Tax Dig 8: 320-2 S '30 **408**

Prentiss, Mark O. Economic consequences of crime. Mfr Rec 91: 49-51 F 24 '27; same title: Northwest Phila Cham Comm Bul 27-32 Ap '27; Ref Shelf 6 (3): 43-8 Ag '29 **409**
Contains an estimate of total cost of crime, which is regarded as including all losses to individuals and the loss of productive labor of criminals, prisoners, and law enforcement officers reduced to monetary basis.

Put, E. La compression des dépenses dans l'administration des prisons. Ecrou 8: 70-4 Ja '27 **410**

Roscoe, E. S. The cost of litigation. 19th Cent 107: 86-92 Ja '30 **411**

St. Louis. Bureau of municipal research. What price crime? Mind your Business (87) Jl 16 '31 **412**

Scavarada, C. J. Efficiency aim of police expenditures. Mich Munic R 2: 161-4 S '29 **413**

United States. Bureau of the census. Financial statistics of cities having a population of over 30,000. 1925-1929. Washington, Govt. Ptg. Off. 1927-32 **414**
Court and police costs.

Vandegrift, Rolland A. Reducing governmental costs through state and local cooperation. Peace Offic Assn Calif Proc 11: 66-71 '31 **415**

Virginia. Governor. Communication . . . transmitting the report of the Commission appointed to consider the question of criminal costs in Virginia, December 19, 1931. 16p. Richmond, 1932 **416**

What the criminal costs and what to do about it. R of R 75: 431-44 Ap '27 **417**
Gives various estimates of losses to individuals due to crime, and quotes figures on police salaries.

STATISTICS OF CRIMES AND CRIMINALS

BIBLIOGRAPHY

Checklist of printed reports containing criminal statistics. *In* National commission on law observance and enforcement, Report on criminal statistics (no3) April 1, 1931, Appendix I **418**
Police, courts, children's courts, probation, penal institutions, jails, etc.

GENERAL

Bates, Sanford. Criminal records and statistics. J Crim L & Crimin 19: 8-14 My '28 **419**

B[ruinj]. Crimineele-justiteele-en kinderwetstatistiek. Maandbl v Ber en Reclaseer 6: 251-3, 281-4, 312-14 S-N '27 **420**

Carr-Saunders, A. M. Surveys. Current social statistics. Crime and punishment. Pol Q 1: 265-72 Ap '30 **421**
Crime statistics not comparable except in murder. Figures for England and Wales given.

Curious correlations in crime statistics. Am B Assn J 16: 769-70 D '30 **422**

Davies, Audrey M. Criminal statistics and the National commission [on law observance and enforcement] report. J Crim L & Crimin 22: 357-74 S '31 **423**

For uniform and accurate crime statistics. Am B Assn J 14:564-5 N '28 **424**

Frankel, Emil. Some suggestions for state action in securing standardized criminal statistics. J Delin 11: 277-8 D '27 **425**

Fuente, Hector M. de la and Ramos, Juan P. Registro nacional de reincidentes y de estadística criminal. R de Crimin, Psiquiat y Med Leg 16: 467-76 Jl '29 **426**

Gehlke, C. E. The problems of method in criminal statistics. Am Sociol Soc Proc 24: 239 '29 **427**

Gernet, M. Noveishie dannie o prestupnosti v Germanii, Anglii i ee koloniach. Problemy Prestupnosti 2: 248-64 '27 **428**

Gernet, M. Statistics of repressive struggle against criminality. Statist Oboz (3-4): 87-95 Mr '30 **429**

Gernet, M. Statistika gorodskoi i selskoi prestupnosti. Problemy Prestupnosti 2: 15-24 '27 **430**

Gilson, Albert I. What about crime records; a timely discussion on criminal statistics. Police J [N Y] 15: 6 My '28 **431**

Gumbel, E. J. Strafvollzugsstatistik. Justiz 5: 690-703, 738-58, 6: 21-42 Ag-O '30 **432**

Hacker, E. Internationale Kriminalstatistik. Monats f Kriminalpsychol u Strafrechtsref 22 (5-6): 269-79 '31; same title: 10p. Heidelberg, Carl Winters, 1931 **433**

Hentig, v. Versuch und Teilnahme. Beiträge zur Kriminalstatistik. Monats f Kriminalpsychol u Strafrechtsref 22: 231-4 '31 **434**

Labaree, Mary S. The purpose of statewide statistics in building the foundation for the prevention of delinquency. Nat Conf Soc Wk Proc 54: 498-502 '27 **435**

Leonard, Frank A. Criminal statistics. N Y St Assn Magistrates Proc 21: 12-22 '29 **436**

Locke, Arthur. Criminal statistics. Police J [London] 4: 188-96 Ap '31 **437**

Los Angeles. Police department. Statistical bureau. Criminal statistics. Police J [N Y] 16: 6, 7, 32 Jl '28 **438**

[Lowden, Frank O.] Criminal statistics and identification of criminals. J Crim L & Crimin 19: 36-48 My '28 **439**

Marsico, A. de. Sul bilancio della giustizia. 17p. Roma, Camera dei Deputati, 1928 **440**

May, Carl L. Survey of criminal statistics. J Delin 11: 279-93 D '27 **441**

Moley, Raymond. The collection of criminal statistics in the United States. Mich L R 26: 747-62 My '28 **442**

National commission on law observance and enforcement. Report on criminal statistics. 205p. (No3) Washington, 1931 **443**
Survey of criminal statistics in the U.S. by Sam B. Warner. A critique of federal criminal statistics by Morris Ploscowe.

National crime commission. Sub-committee on pardons, parole, probation, penal laws and institutional correction. Criminal statistics and identification of criminals: report. J Crim L & Crimin 19: pt1: 36-48 My '28 **444**

Nissen, Hartung. Forbrydelse og straff i statistikkens lys. Soc Arbeid 2 (3): 73-81 '28 **445**

Pigelet, Robert. Criminalité juvénile. (Tableau d'une année) 126p. Paris, Spes, 1927 **446**

Poelchau, Harald. Kriminalstatistik der Jugendlichen 1927 und 1928. Zeitsch f d ges Strafrechtswiss 51 (1): 84-115 '31 **447**

Robinson, Louis N. Criminal statistics and identification of criminals: a report submitted to the National crime commission by the Sub-committee on pardons, parole, probation, penal laws and institutional correction, December 5, 1927. N.Y. National crime com'n, 1927; same title: Nat Munic R 16: 769-77 D '27; J Crim L & Crimin 19 pt1: 34-68 My '28 **448**

Robinson, Louis N. Need for adequate criminal statistics. Am Statis Assn J 23: sup123-7 Mr '28 **449**

Roos, J. R. B. de. Consonnes et voyelles. Communication sur la statistique criminelle. Inst Int de Statist Bul 23 (2): 762-7 '28 **450**

Roos, J. R. B. de. Rapport de la Comission pour l'étude comparative des statistiques criminelles dans les divers pays. Inst Int de Statist Bul 24 (2): 567-8 '30 **451**

Rzepkiewicz, Stéphane. Observation sur la possibilité des comparisons des statistiques criminelles de divers pays. Inst Int de Statist Bul 23: 569-77 '30 **452**

Schiavo, Giovanni. What crime statistics show about the Italians. 30p. N.Y. Italian Historical Soc. 1930? **453**

Sellin, Thorsten. The basis of a crime index. J Crim L & Crimin 22: 326-56 S '31 **454**

Sellin, Thorsten. Die Grundlagen eines Kriminalitätsindex. Monats f Kriminalpsychol u Strafrechtsref 22: 577-97 '31 **455**

Smith, Bruce. Uniform crime statistics and their importance. Panel 9: 3-4, 7 Ja '31 **456**

Stephan, Otto. Kriminalistik. Polizei 25: 451-2 Jl 20 '28 **457**

Truesdell, L. E. Problem of collecting and standardizing statistics of crime in forty-eight sovereign states. Am Statis Assn J 23: sup128-35 Mr '28 **458**

Ueberschaer. Über die Ausgestaltung der Kriminalstatistik. Monats f Kriminalpsychol u Strafrechtsref 18: 129-31 Mr '27 **459**

United States. Bureau of the census. Instructions for compiling criminal statistics. A manual for the use of penal institutions, police departments, courts, prosecutors and parole and probation agencies. 64p. Washington, 1927 **460**

Upson, Lent D. Crime statistics as a police problem. Am Statist Assn J 23: sup 136-41 Mr '28 **461**

Verkko, V. Kriminalstatistiken och den verkliga brottsligheten. Nord Tids f Straf 18: 95-128 Ap '30 **462**

Vollmer, August. Criminal statistics. Int Assn Chiefs Police Proc 1927: 71-6; same title: Police J [NY] 15: 10-11 D '27 **463**

Vollmer, August. Statistics on criminality. Peace Offic 5: 7-8 N '27 **464**

Wassermann, Rudolf. Die Entwicklungsphasen der Kriminalstatistischen Forschung. 99p. (Krimin Abh hrsg v Franz Exner, Heft V) Leipzig, Ernst Wiegandt, 1927 **465**

Summary of the development of criminal statistical research from Quetelet to the present.

AUSTRALIA

Laughton, A. M. Victorian yearbook, 1930-31. Pt. IV: Law, crime, etc. p.91-112. Melbourne, Govt. Ptr. 1931 **466**

Courts, prison statistics, arrests, drunkenness, jails, police, etc.

Queensland. Statistics of the state of Queensland for the year 1930-31. Pt. V: Law, crime, etc. 57p. Brisbane, Govt. Ptr. [1931] **467**

South Australia. Statistical register . . . for the year 1930-31. Pt. I: Social (Administration, Justice, Education, Hospitals, Charities, etc.) Adelaide, Govt. Ptr 1932 **468**

AUSTRIA

Austria. Bundesministerium für Justiz. Kriminalistik für das Jahr 1925. 45p. Wien, 1927 **469**

Fischinger, Helmuth. Die österreichische Kriminal-Statistik 1926. Monats f Kriminalpsychol u Strafrechtsref 20: 433-6 Jl '29 **470**

Hentig, H[ans] von. Die Entwicklung der Kriminalität in Österreich seit 1882. Monats f Kriminalpsychol u Strafrechtsref 18: 640-1 N '27 **471**

Koppenfels, v. Die österreichische Kriminalstatistik 1928. Monats f Kriminalpsychol u Strafrechtsref 21: 625-8 '30 **472**

Siegel, Otto. Die Kriminalität in Österreich. Krimin Monatsh 4: 165 Jl '30 **473**

Vienna. Statistiches departement. Statistisches jahrbuch der Stadt Wien, nsl, 1929- **474**

Suspended 1914-28. Rechtspflege und offentliche Sicherheit.

BULGARIA

Bulgaria. Direction générale de la statistique. Annuaire statistique du royaume de Bulgarie, 23, 1931. 650p. Sofia, Imp. de l'état, 1931 **475**

Text in Bulgarian; title and table of contents in French and Bulgarian.
Judicial statistics, criminal statistics, suicides.

Bulgaria. Direction générale de la statistique. Statistique criminelle, crimes et délits et individus jugés, pendant l'année 1, 1910- Sofia, Imp. de l'état [1911?]- **476**

Text in Bulgarian; title and table of contents in French and Bulgarian.

CANADA

Canada. Bureau of statistics. Judicial statistics branch. Annual report of juvenile delinquents for the year ended 1926/27- Ottawa, Acland, 1927- **477**

Canada. Bureau of statistics. Judicial statistics branch. Annual report of statistics of criminal and other offences 52, 1926/27—54, 1928/29. Ottawa, 1929-30 **478**

Adult offenders, juvenile delinquency, court proceedings, police statistics, prison statistics, pardons and commutations.

Quebec. Department of the Secretary of the Province. Bureau of statistics. Statistical yearbook 14, 1927—17, 1930. Quebec, Proulx, 1927-30 **479**

Offenses, courts, police, coroners, penal institutions.

CHILE

Chile. Direccion general de estadística. Estadística anual: 2: Administración, justicia y educación, 1928- Santiago. Previous to 1928 *see* Anuario estadístico: 4: Justicia, policia y criminalidad s3, 1911-27// **480**

Cuba

Cuba. Comision nacional de estadistica y reformas economicas. Cuadros estadisticos que espresan el numero y otras circunstancias de delincuentes penados con privacion de libertad por los tribunales de la republica en el año 1928, y de los que habiendolo sido con multas sufren prision subsidiaria en defecto de su pago. (mim) Habana, [1929]
1929. (mim) [Habana, 1930]
1930. (mim) [Habana, 1931] **481**

Czechslovakia

Czechoslovakia. Office de la statistique. Aperçu statistique de la République Tchécoslovaque. 319p. Prague, 1930 **482**
Criminal statistics, court statistics, penal and police statistics.

Czechoslovakia. Office de la statistique. Manuel statistique de la République Tchécoslovaque, 3, 1928. 472p. Prague, 1928 **483**
Penal justice, courts, judges, lawyers, police, etc.

Danzig

Die Entwicklung der Kriminalität im Gebiet der Freien Stadt Danziger in den Jahren 1922 bis 1926. Danziger Statist Mitt 7 (11-12): 144-9 '28 **484**

Die Kriminalität der Freien Stadt Danzig in den Jahren, 1924 und 1925. Wirtsch u Statist 7: 260 Mr 1 '27 **485**

Muhl. Die Kriminalität der freien Stadt Danzig im Jahre 1926. Arch f Krim 80: 177-9 Mr '27 **486**

Denmark

Denmark. Statistiske departement. Annuaire statistique 1927-1931. København, 1927-31 **487**
Text in Danish and French. Statistics on criminal justice.

Denmark. Statistiske departement. Danmarks Retspleje i Aarene 1916-25. 200p. (Statistik Tabelvaerk, s5, B No8) København, Gyldendalske, 1931 **488**

Trommer, Harry. Zur Rückfallskriminalität in Dänemark. Monats f Kriminalpsychol u Strafrechtsref 21: 435-7 '30 **489**

Dutch East Indies

Dutch East Indies. Departement van Landbouw. Central Kantoor voor de statistiek. Indisch verslag, II, 1927-31. Batavia, 1927-31 **490**
English and Indian text; criminal statistics, court martial, dactyloscopy and prisons.

Egypt

Schneickert, Hans. Die Kriminalität in Aegypten. Krimin Monatsh 1: 173-5 Ag '27 **491**

Estonia

Estonia. Riigi statistika keskbüroo. Estonie de 1920-1930. Résumé retrospectif. 405p. Tallinn, 1931 **492**
Also edition in Estonian. Statistics of courts, prisons, crimes, alcohol, suicides, etc.

Reiman, H. Justice criminelle et civile de 1920-29. Eesti Statist 103: 313-28 Je '30 **493**

Finland

Finland. Bureau central de statistique. Annuaire statistique de Finlande ns26, 1928—28, 1930. Helsingfors, 1928-30 **494**
Text in French and Finnish.
Judicial, offense and penal statistics.

France

France. Ministère du travail, de l'hygiène de l'assistance et de la prévoyance sociales. Statistique générale de la France. Annuaire statistique 43, 1927-45, 1929. Paris, Imp. Nat. 1928-30 **495**
Statistics of courts, suicide, extradition, military law, and penal institutions.

Roesner. Die Kriminalität in Frankreich nach dem Kriege. Arch f Krim 86: 167-70 Ap '30 **496**

Germany

Aschaffenburg, Gustav. Kriminalstatistik für das Jahr 1924. Monats f Kriminalpsychol u Strafrechtsref 18: 150-5 Mr '27 **497**

Berlin. Statistisches Amt. Statistiches Jahrbuch der Stadt Berlin 3, 1927—7, 1931. Berlin, 1927-31 **498**
Statistics of administration of justice and police.

Deutsche Reichskriminalstatistik für 1924. Arch f Krim 80: 174-5 Mr '27 **499**

Die Entwicklung der Kriminalität im Deutschen Reich seit 1882. Arch f Krim 86: 248-62 Je '30 **500**

Fischinger, Helmuth. Deutsche Kriminalstatistik für das Jahr 1927. Monats f Kriminalpsychol u Strafrechtsref 21: 514-18 Ag '30 **501**

Fischinger, Helmuth. Entwicklung der Kriminalität im Deutschen Reich seit 1882. Monats f Kriminalpsychol u Strafrechtsref 19: 41-9 Ja '28 **502**

Fischinger, Helmuth. Kriminalstatistik für das Jahr 1924. Monats f Kriminalpsychol u Strafrechtsref 18: 150-3 '27 **503**

Francke. Die Jugendlichen in der Reichskriminalstatistik. Bl d Dt Roten Kreuzes 7 (2): 19-21 '28 **504**

Germany. Statistiches Reichsamt. Kriminalstatistik für das Jahr; Bearb. im Reichsjustizministerium und im Statistisches Reichsamt. Berlin, Hobbing
1918. 35p. (Statist d Dt Reich 342) 1927
1919. 36p. (Statist d Dt Reich 301) 1927
1920. 38p. (Statist d Dt Reich 346) 1928

Germany. Kriminalstatistik—*Continued*
1922. 44p. (Statistit d Dt Reich 354) 1928
1924. 53p. (Statist d Dt Reich 328) 1926
1925. 93p. (Statist d Dt Reich 335) 1927
1926. 119p. (Statist d Dt Reich 347) 1928
1927. 159p. (Statist d Dt Reich 370) 1930
1928. 195p. (Statist d Dt Reich 384) 1931 **505**

Germany. Statistisches Reichsamt. Statistisches Jahrbuch für das Deutsche Reich, 1927-1931. Berlin, 1927-31 **506**
Criminal statistics.

Hentig, Hans von. Die Kriminalität einer Grossstadt. Monats f Kriminalpsychol u Strafrechtsref 18: 41-5 Ja '27 **507**

Hentig, Hans von. Die Kriminalität einer Grossstadt, Augsburg, 1914-26. Monats f Kriminalpsychol u Strafrechtsref 18: 231-7 My '27 **508**

Kempner, R[obert]. Justizstatistik 1930. Monats f Kriminalpsychol u Strafrechtsref 22: 565-7 '31 **509**

Koppenfels, v. Die Kriminalität im Jahre 1925. Monats f Kriminalpsychol u Strafrechtsref 18: 55-7 '28 **510**

Die Kriminalität Deutschlands im Jahre 1925. Arch f Krim 81:54-60 Jl '27 **511**

Die Kriminalität Deutschlands im Jahr 1927. Arch f Krim 86: 230-44 Je '30 **512**

Die Kriminalität im Deutschen Reich im Jahre 1928. Krimin Monatsh 4: 138-9 Je '30 **513**

Die Kriminalität im Deutschen Reich im Jahre 1927. Wirtsch u Statist 9(8): 349-52 '29 **514**

Die Kriminalität in Bayern im 3. Vierteljahr 1926. Zeitsch d Bayer Statist Landesamts 59: 175-6 '27 **515**

Die Kriminalität in Bayern im Jahre 1926. Zeitsch d Bayer Statist Landesamts 59 (4): 606-11 '27 **516**

Die Kriminalität in Württemberg mit besonderer Berücksichtigung des Jahre 1928. Württ Statist Landesamt Mitt 2: 25-8 F 28 '30 **517**

Kriminalstatistik für das Jahr 1928. Arch f Krim 86: 244-8 Je '30 **518**

Roesner, E. Die Entwicklung der Kriminalität im Deutschen Reich seit 1882. Deut Juristen-Zeit 36: 935-8 Jl 15 '31 **519**

Tönnies, Ferdinand. Ortsherkunft von Verbrechern in Schleswig-Holstein. Deut Statist Zentralbl 21: 145-50 Ag '29 **520**

Trommer, Harry. Die Entwicklung der Kriminalität im Deutschen Reiche im Jahre 1926. Monats f Kriminalpsychol u Strafrechtsref 20: 421-8 '29 **521**

Vienna. Magistratsabteilung für Statistik. Statistisches Jahrbuch der Stadt Wien, 1929-1930. Wien, 1929-30 **522**
Rechtspflege und öffentliche Sicherheit.

Zur deutschen Justizstatistik für das Jahr 1925. Vjsch z Statist d Deut Reich 36 (2): 82 '27 **523**

Great Britain

C[raven], C[icely] M. Criminal statistics, 1925. Howard J 1: 115-19 '27 **524**
Chart.

Craven, Cicely M. Criminal statistics, 1926. Howard J 1: 237-41 '27 **525**

Craven, Cicely M. The criminal statistics: England and Wales, 1928. Howard J 3: 56-61 S '30 **526**

Crime in the metropolis. L Times 163: 536 Je 18 '27; same title: L Notes 31: 137-8 O '27 **527**

Criminal statistics. L Times 169: 532 Je 14 '30 **528**

Criminal statistics for year 1927. L Times 167: 299-300 Ap 13 '29; Just Peace 93: 263-4 Ap 27 '29 **529**

Criminal statistics, 1928. Just Peace 94: 403-4 Je 28 '30 **530**

Criminal statistics, 1929. Just Peace 95: 347 My 30 '31; Sol J 75: 397-8 Je 20 '31 **531**

Elkin, W. A. Criminal statistics: England and Wales, 1929. Howard J 3: 48-56 '31 **532**

Great Britain. Home office. Criminal statistics: England and Wales, 1928: crime, criminal proceedings and coroners investigations, 1928. 197p. (Cmd 3581) London, 1930 **533**

Great Britain. Home office. Criminal statistics: England and Wales, 1929. 197p. London, 1931 **534**

Great Britain. Home office. Criminal statistics relating to criminal proceedings, police, coroners, prisons and criminal lunatics for the year 1927. 229p. (Cmd 3301) London, 1929 **535**

Great Britain. Home office. Criminal statistics returns, 1927: instructions to police authorities for preparing annual returns of crime. 73p. London, 1927 **536**

H[entig], [Hans] v. Die englische Kriminalstatistik 1926. Monats f Kriminalpsychol u Strafrechtsref 20: 436-8 Jl '29 **537**

Greece

Greece. Genike statistike hyperesia. Annuaire statistique de la Grèce 1, 1930- Athenes, Imp. Nat. 1931- **538**
French and Greek text. Statistics on crime and criminals.

Hungary

Hacker, E. Die Kriminalität Ungarns in den Jahren 1921-1928. Monats f Kriminalpsychol u Strafrechtsref 21: 372-9 Je '30 **539**

Hacker, E. Kriminalstatistisches aus Ungarn. Monats f Kriminalpsychol u Strafrechtsref 22: 498-500 Ag '31 **540**
Comparison of crime statistics of 1928 and 1929.

India

India. Department of commercial intelligence and statistics. Statistical abstract for British India with statistics, where available, relating to certain Indian states from 1917/18 to 1926/27. Calcutta, 1928 541

Statistics of courts, police and prisons.

Italy

Italy. Istituto centrale di statistica. Annuario statistico Italiano s3 v1, 1927- Roma, 1927- 542

Penal statistics.

Italy. Ministero della giustizia e degli affari di culto. Statistica della criminalità per l'anno 1906- Notizie complementari alla statistica giuridiziaria penale, Roma, [1907?]- 543

Italy. Ministero della giustizia e degli affari di culto. Statistica giuridiziaria penale, 1863- Roma 544

Japan

H[entig, Hans] v. Japanische Kriminal- und Gefängnisstatistik. Monats f Kriminalpsychol u Strafrechtsref 22: 50-1 '31 545

Netherlands

Netherlands. Centraal bureau voor de statistiek. Crimineele Statistieken; Justieele Statistiek. (Sub series of Bijdragen tot de statistiek 1, 1900-) 's Gravenhage, Algemeene Landsdrukkerij 546

New Zealand

New Zealand. Census and statistics office. Report on the justice statistics of the Dominion of New Zealand for the years 1927-1930. Wellington, Govt. Ptr. 1928-31 547

Criminal cases in magistrates courts; criminal cases in supreme courts; prisons and prisoners; Borstal institutions; juvenile offenders; offenses of women; offenses by Maoris; drunkenness.

Norway

Norway. Statistike centralbureau. Annuaire statistique de la Norvège 46, 1926/27—50, 1930/31. Oslo, 1928-31 548

Statistics of justice. Norwegian and French text.

Peru

Delgado, Vicente H. Proyecto de organización de la estadistica criminal del Peru de los adultos de 18 años a mas de edad. 40p. Lima, "La Opinión Nacional," 1927 549

Peru. Department of treasury and commerce. Bureau of statistics. Statistical abstract of Peru 1929-30. Lima, 1931 550

Chapter on criminality statistics.

Poland

Poland. Office central de statistique de la Republique polonaise. Annuaire statistique . . . 1930. Varsovie, 1931 551

Justice et criminalité: administration de la justice, statistique pénitentiaire, criminalité.

Statystyka czynności sadów. Czynnósci sadów powszechnych w sprawach cywilnych i karnych 1927-1928. Kwartalnik Statist 8 (1): 99-138 '31 552

Portugal

Gonçalves, João. Estadística geral da criminalidade em Portugal no ano de 1930 (distrito judicial da relação de Lisboa). Bol do Inst de Crimin s8 15 (2): 445-51 '31 553

Rumania

Rumania. Ministère de l'industrie et du commerce. Institut de statistique générale de l'état. Annuaire statistique 1927- Bucuresti, 1928- 554

Judicial and penal statistictics. Rumanian and French text and title.

Scotland

Paterson, Mary. The Scottish criminal statistics, 1929, and the report of the Prisons department for Scotland, 1930. Howard J 3: 57 '31 555

Sweden

Sweden. Statistika Centralbyrån. Brottsligheten år 1923-1929. Stockholm, Norstedt, 1927-31 556

Sweden. Statistika Centralbyrån. Statistik årsbok för Sverige 14, 1927—18, 1931. Stockholm, 1927-31 557

Swedish and French text. Statistics of offenses; penal and judicial statistics.

Switzerland

Switzerland. Bureau fédéral de statistique. Annuaire statistique de la Suisse 1927-1930. Berne, 1928-31 558

German and French text. Statistics of prisons and administration of justice.

Switzerland. Bureau fédéral de statistique. Statistique de la criminalité en Suisse, 1929. 109p. Berne, 1931 559

Turkey

Turkey. Office central de statistique. Annuaire statistique 1, 1928- Ankara, 1929- 560

Text in Turkish. Statistics of judicial organization, 1927-30; Cour de Cassation 1924-30; statistics of offenses, 1927-30; prison population, 1926-30.

UNITED STATES

Registration of social statistics for the year 1928, 1929. Chicago, Joint committee of the Association of community chests and councils and the local community research committee of the University of Chicago, 1929-30 **561**

1928 by Helen Rankin Jeter and A. W. McMillen; 1929 by Helen Rankin Jeter, A. W. McMillen and A. R. Grffiths. Statistics of juvenile courts and probation, institutional care of delinquents.

GEORGIA

Criminal statistics. *In* Georgia. Department of public welfare, Report 1927/28: 22-31 **562**

ILLINOIS

Criminal and delinquent group [statistics]. *In* Illinois. Department of public welfare, Report of statistician 1927: 198-241; 1928: 101-23; 1930: 94-119; *also in* Illinois. Department of public welfare, Annual report 10, 1927: 359-77; 477-525; 11, 1928: 435-57, 559-600; 12, 1929: 348-71, 468, 475-521; 13, 1930: 486-511, 634-81 **563**

INDIANA

Adamson, Wendell. Some statistics of crime in Indiana. Ind Bul Char & Correc (177): 572-6 D '29 **564**

Indiana. Library and historical department. Legislative bureau. Criminal and civil statistics for the state of Indiana for the year 1929. 27p. [Indianapolis, 1930] **565**

IOWA

Burrows, Charles N. Criminal statistics in Iowa. 112p. (Stud in Soc Sci v9 no2) Iowa City, Iowa University, 1930 **566**

KANSAS

Kansas. State board of administration. Statistics relating to district courts, probate courts, poor farms, miscellaneous charity and mothers' pensions in Kansas, 1927- Topeka, 1927- **567**

Statistics of state penal institutions, juvenile courts, and county jails.

LOUISIANA

Steiner, J. F. Criminal statistics in Louisiana. Tulane L R 4: 234-6 F '30 **568**

NEW YORK

New York (state). Commissioner of correction. Summary and comment . . . on crime statistics for the year 1930. (Legislative doc (1931) no85A) [Albany, 1931] **569**

New York (state). Crime commission. Sub-commission on statistics

Report, February 28, 1928. 106p. Albany, 1928

Report, February 28, 1929. 25p. Albany, 1929

Report, December 28, 1929. 25p. Albany, 1930 **570**

Trommer, Harry. Die Kriminalität im Staate New York in dem Jahre 1918 bis 1927 nach den Statistiken seiner Gefängnisse. Zeitsch f d ges Strafrechtswiss 50 (6): 755-60 '30 **571**

NORTH CAROLINA

Williams, Lena Mae. Trends of crime rates in North Carolina 1900-30. Thesis (M.A.) University of North Carolina, 1931 **572**

OHIO

Ohio. Auditor of state. Comparative statistics of cities of Ohio, 1927, 1928, 1929. Columbus, 1929 **573**

Courts, corrections, police.

Ohio. Secretary of state. Annual reports, 1927- [Columbus] 1928- **574**

Social statistics: no. of commitments to industrial schools; Judicial statistics: fines, cost and forfeited recognizances in criminal courts; prosecutions and convictions.

RHODE ISLAND

Phelps, Harold A. Cycles of crime. J Crim L & Crimin 20: 107-21 My '29 **575**

STATISTICS OF OFFENSES

Albrecht, Hans. Der Selbstmord in Deutschland. Arch f Krim 80: 242-5 My '27 **576**

Alessio, G. Appunti sulla statistica della delinquenza omicida in Italia. Atti d Real Ist Veneto di Sci, Lett ed Arti 90: 525-50 '30-'31 **577**

Bandel, R. Der bevorzugte Rückgang der Selbstmordsterblichkeit während der alkoholknappen Zeit bei der nichtjüdischen männlichen Bevölkerung in Preussen. Zeitsch f Hyg u Infektionskr 111: 699-702 '30 **578**

Bandel, R. Selbstmord und Alkoholismus. München med Wchnschr 75: 1465-6 Ag 24 '28 **579**

Baum, James E. Re: Forgery statistics. 1p. (mim) N.Y. American bankers association, Protective department, 1931? **580**

Berg, A. Statistische Untersuchungen der von 1920 bis 1929 im Städtischen Krankenhaus Ullevaal in Oslo behandelten Aborte. Acta Obst et Gynec Scandinav 11: 68-83 '31 **581**

Bingler. Statistische Betrachtungen über den Selbstmord im Reichsheere in den Jahren 1921-1929. Veröffentl a d Geb Heeres-San-Wes (84): 74-88 '30 **582**

Boie, Maurine. An analysis of Negro crime statistics for Minneapolis for 1923, 1924 and 1925. Opportunity 6: 171-3 Je '28 **583**

Chicago. Municipal reference library. Number of auto thefts reported in 83 cities of the United States having a population of over 100,000 for the twelve months period ending December 31, 1930. 2p. Frederick Rex, comp. Chicago, 1931 **584**

Chicago. Municipal reference library. Number of known offenses reported in 81 cities of the United States having a population of over 100,000 for the nine months ending September 30, 1930. 2p. (mim) Chicago, 1930 **585**

Chicago. Municipal reference library. Number of murders reported in 76 cities of the United States having a population of over 100,000 for the nine months ending September 30, 1930. 2p. (mim) Frederick Rex, comp. Chicago, 1930 **586**

Concerning suicides in the city of Chicago. Crim Just [Chicago] 9: 15 Je '27 **587**

Crime in America. Just Peace 93: 294 My 11 '29 **588**

Donalies, G. Statistische Erhebungen an 3000 Fällen von vollendetem und versuchtem Selbstmord. Monats f Psychiat u Neurol 69: 380-96 Ag '28 **589**

Gallia, C. La sifilide è veramente in diminuzione? Dermosifilografo 3: 606-12 N '28 **590**

Garofalo, R. Osservazioni statistische sugli omicidii in Italia ed in alcune altre nazioni. Atti d Real Acad d Sci Morali e Pol 50: 278-88 '27 **591**

Gast, Peter. Die Mörder. 74p. Leipzig, Ernst Wiegandt, 1930 **592**

Statistical and topographical study of murder in Germany. Criminal statistics analyzed to show murder rates by years from 1882 to 1927.

Gernet, M. N. Prestupnost I Samouiistva Vo Vremia Voiny I Posle Neya. 270p. Moskva [Central Statistical Office] 1927 **593**

Gernet, M. (M. Hernett). Statistics of murders of children. Statist Oboz (2): 102-8 '28 **594**

[Gernet, M.] (M. Hernett). Die Statistik der Abtreibungen in Sowjet-Russland. Monats f Kriminalpsychol u Strafrechtsref 19: 236-9 Ap '28 **595**

Gordon, A. P. L. Statistics of totalisator betting; with discussion. Royal Stat Soc J 94:ptl 31-76 '31 **596**

Grünewald, Max. Über Selbstmordstatistik. Monats f Kriminalpsychol u Strafrechtsref 18: 41-5 Ja '27 **597**

Gumbel, E. J. Landesverrats-statistik. Justiz 3(4): 386-95 Ap '28 **598**

Heindl, R[obert]. Der Selbstmord in Sowjet-Russland 1922-1925. Arch f Krim 80: 252-3 My '27 **599**

Hentig, Hans v. Exhibitionisten-Statistik. Monats f Kriminalpsychol u Strafrechtsref 20: 327-31 Je '29 **600**

H[entig, Hans] v. Neuere Ergebnisse der Selbstmordstatistik. Monats f Kriminalpsychol u Strafrechtsref 19: 627-8 O '28 **601**

H[entig, Hans] v. Der Selbstmordversuch. Monats f Kriminalpsychol u Strafrechtsref 19: 626-7 O '28 **602**

H[entig, Hans] v. Statistik der Sittlichkeitsdelikte. Monats f Kriminalpsychol u Strafrechtsref 21: 691-3 '30 **603**

Hentig, Hans von. Über Brandursachen. Monats f Kriminalpsychol u Strafrechtsref 18: 203-5 Ap '27 **604**

H[entig, Hans] v. Über die Selbstmordneigung der Frau in Russland und Deutschland. Monats f Kriminalpsychol u Strafrechtsref 19: 624 O '28 **605**

Hentig, Hans von. Zunahme der Brande in Bayern. Monats f Kriminalpsychol u Strafrechtsref 18: 210-11 Ap '27 **606**

Hiramuna, Daisabro. Der Selbstmord in Japan. Arch f Krim 80: 246-51 My '27 **607**

Hoffman, F[rederick] L. Homicide record of 1930 in the United States. Am J Pub Health 21: 938-9 Ag '31 **608**

Hoffman, Frederick L. Homicide records for 1929. Am J Pub Health 20: 775 Jl '30 **609**

Hoffman, Frederick L. Murder and the death penalty. Cur Hist 28: 408-10 Je '28; same title: 3p. American league to abolish capital punishment, March 14, 1929 **610**

Hoffman, Frederick L. The suicide record for 1926. Spectator [N Y] 118: 8- Je 23 '27 **611**

Hoffman, Frederick L. The suicide record of 1930. Spectator [N Y] 126: 7-9 My 14 '31 **612**

Homicide death rates in the United States and Canada. Am J Pub Health 17: 753 Jl '27 **613**

John, Alfred. Die Rückfallsdiebe: Eine Untersuchung über Erscheinungsformen des Verbrechens. 96p. (Krimin Abh hrsg von Franz Exner, Heft IX) Leipzig, Ernst Wiegandt, 1929 **614**

Study of the recidivist thief; analysis of criminal statistics of Germany for purpose of determining the distribution of thefts by recidivists by years, 1882-1926, by sex, age, family status, occupation, etc.

Kolle, Kurt. Polizeistatistik der Sittlichkeitsvergehen. Zeitsch f Sexualwissensch 17: 457-63 '31 **615**

Koppenfels, v. Österreichische Abtreibungsstatistik für das Jahr 1924. Monats f Kriminalpsychol u Strafrechtsref 18: 645-6 N '27 **616**

Lacassagne, Jean and Pigeaud, H. Avortements grossesses et fonctions maternelles chez les prostituées. Ann des Mal Vén 25: 251-63 Ap '30 **617**

Lo Cascio, G. I suicidi per veleno in Italia dal 1898 al 1923. Ann di Clin Med 19 (Special no): 435-52 '29 **618**

Michels, Robert. Altes und Neues zum Problem der Moralstatistik. II. Arch f Sozialwiss u Sozialpol 57: 701-45 '27 **619**

Sexualkriminalistik und Prostitution, p710-23.

Michels, Robert. Sittlichkeit in Ziffern? Kritik der Moralstatistik. 229p. München, Duncker & Humblot, 1928 **620**

Question whether moral phenomena are capable of statistical measurement and analysis. Objective indices of morality are illegitimacy, sexual crimes, prostitution, etc.

Mord- und Totschlagstatistik in Preussen 1924. Arch f Krim 80: 175-6 Mr '27 **621**

Mord- und Totschlag in Preussen im Jahre 1925. Medizinalstatist Nachr 15 (3-4): 117-20 '28 **622**

Müller, Johannes. Moral und Moralstatistik. Allg Statist Arch 20 (3): 319-29 '30 **623**

Nippe. Über Kindesmord. Deut Zeitsch f d ges gerichtl Med 14: 44-53 S 3 '29 **624**

Novitzky, R. Crimes against property in the capitalist countries in 1913-26. Statist Oboz 8: 88-94 Ag '29 **625**

Peller, S. Studien zur Statistik des Abortus. Zentralbl f Gynäk 53: 2216-27 Ag 31 '29 **626**

Pietrusky, F. Zur Frage der kriminellen Fruchtabtreibung. Deut Zeitsch f d ges gerichtl Med 14: 54-61 S 3 '29 **627**

Poisoning statistics for 1928. Just Peace 93: 645 O 12 '29 **628**

Puppel, E. Der kriminelle Abort in Thüringen 1915-26. München med Wchnschr 76: 780-1 My 10 '29 **629**

Ratios of robberies, auto thefts listed for seventeen large cities. Insur Field (Fire ed) 59: 33 N 20 '30 **630**

Rehfeldt. Über den Selbstmord. Med Welt 3: 1205-9 Ag 24 '29 **631**

Roesner, [E.]. Die Prostitution in Wien in den Jahren 1913 bis 1926. Krimin Monatsh 2: 46 F '28 **632**

Roesner, [E.]. Die Selbstmorde im Deutschen Reiche im Jahre 1925. Arch f Krim 81: 257-8 D '27 **633**

R[oesner, E.]. Die Selbstmorde in der Schweiz im Jahre 1926. Arch f Krim 82: 64-5 Ja '28 **634**

Rubenovitch, P. Les mobiles du suicide. Prophyl Ment 5: 385-8 '31 **635A**
Statistics of suicide follow same law as psychopathies, showing recrudescence in spring and fall.

Russia (USSR). Tsentral'noe statisticheskoe upravlenie. Aborty v . . . gody 1, 1926-? **635B**

Russia (USSR). Tsentral'noe statisticheskoe upravlenie. Samoubiistva v SSSR 1, 1923/25- **635C**

Schwalbe, J. Zeitströmungen und Statistik. [Modernes Sexualleben und Selbstmorde]. Deut med Wchnschr 55: 1007-9 Je 14 '29 **636**

Die Selbstmorde im Deutschen Reich im Jahre 1927. Wirtsch u Statist 9: 968-71 D 1 '29 **637**

Suicide among Negroes in the United States. Metropolitan Life Insur Co Statist Bul 11: 4-5 S '30 **638**

[Table of homicide and robbery cases in Prussia, May 1, 1925-December 31, 1927, by district, showing complaints and clearings in totals and in percentages.] Polizei 24: 171 Ap 20 '27 **639**

Többen, H. Über Selbstmorde Jugendlicher. Deut Zeitsch f d ges gerichtl Med 14: 499-516 Ja 14 '30 **640**

Tönnies, Ferdinand and Jurkat, Ernst. Die schwere Kriminalität von Männern in Schleswig-Holstein in den Jahren 1899-1914. Zeitsch f Völkerpsychol u Soz 5: 26-39 Mr '29 **641**

United States. Bureau of the census. Homicide. *In* Mortality statistics, 1924: 70-2; 1929/30: 43-4. Washington, 1927-32 **642**
Homicide rates, 1915-24 by states and cities with more than 100,000 population in 1920.

United States. Bureau of the census. Suicide. *In* Mortality statistics, 1924: 69-70; 1929/30: 42-3. Washington, 1927-32 **643**

Weinberg, Siegfried. Die Abtreibungen in der neuesten Kriminalstatistik. Neue Generation 23: 201-2 Je '27 **644**

Weinberger, Hugo. Ein Ausschnitt aus der Sexualkriminalität der Grossstadt. Arch f Krim 89: 199-200 N '31 **645**

Zurkuhlen, H. Die Kriminalität in Vergangenheit und Gegenwart. Welch Verbrechen haben zu- und welche abgenommen? Jahrb f Nationalökon u Statist 135: 589-94 O '31 **646**

POLICE STATISTICS

Cross, Rhoda. The practical application of police statistics. Int Assn Identif, Cal Div Proc 16: 95-6 '31 **647**

Finland. Ministère de la justice. Statistique criminelle de Finlande pour l'année 1927-1929. Infractions dont la police a eu connaissance. Helsingfors, 1928-30 **648**
Title in Finnish and French; text in Finnish.

Harper. Police statistics. Peace Offic Assn Calif Proc 10: 14-18 '30 **649**

Jahresbericht der Kriminalpolizei von Elberfeld-Barmen für das Jahr 1926. Arch f Krim 80: 259-62 My '27 **650**

Jahresbericht der Kriminalpolizei von Elberfeld-Barmen für das Jahr 1927. Arch f Krim 82: 191-4 '28 **651**

Julier. Streiflichter aus der Polizeistatistik. Polizei 24: 448 S 20 '27 **652**

Die Kriminalpolizei in Nürnberg im Jahre 1928. Arch f Krim 86: 166-7 Ap '30 **653**

Mead, Bennett. Police statistics. Ann Am Acad 146: 75-95 N '29 **654**

Mourot. Statistique des résultats obtenus par le Gendarmerie en 1927. R de Gendarm 1: 175-83 Mr 15 '28 **655**

Police department statistics—places less than 5,000. Munic Index 1927: 609-15 **656**

Roesner, E. Die englische Polizeistatistik für das Jahr 1927. Arch f Krim 85: 166-71 O '29 **657**

South Dakota. State sheriff. Report of arrests . . . for the year ending December 31, 1929. 15p. [Pierre] 1929 **658**

Statistics of arrest. *In* Massachusetts. Commissioner of correction, Annual report 1927: 129-35; 1929: 109-15 **659**

Die Tätigkeit der Kölner Kriminalpolizei im Jahre 1927. Arch f Krim 83: 81-2 Jl '28 **660**

Die Tätigkeit der Kriminalpolizei in Breslau im Jahre 1927. Arch f Krim 82: 262-3 Je '28 **661**

Thüringische Kriminalstatistik für 1927. Krimin Monatsh 3: 115 My '28 **662**

Übersicht über die im Jahre 1927 in Preussen verübten und aufgeklärten Schwerverbrechen. Krimin Monatsh 2: 91 Ap '28 **663**

JUDICIAL STATISTICS

Alkoholstrafstatistik. Zeitsch d Bayer Statist Landesamts 60: 294 '28 **664**

Arnold, Thurman W. The collection of judicial statistics in West Virginia. W Va L Q 36: 184-90 F '30 **665**

Belgium. Ministère de la justice. Statistique judiciaire de la Belgique, ns 1920/21- Bruxelles **666**

Brown, Roy M. Aspects of crime and its treatment. Univ N C Ext Bul 10: 72-8 My '31 **667**
Study of reports of North Carolina superior courts, 1899-1929.

Canada. Bureau of statistics. Judicial statistics branch. Annual report 52, 1927—55, 1930. Ottawa, 1929-31 **668**
Offenses by adults; juvenile delinquency; court proceedings; police statistics; prison statistics; pardons and commutations.

Canada. Quebec (Province). Bureau of statistics. Statistiques judiciaires, 1914- Quebec, 1914- **669**
French and English texts.

Ching-Yü, C. [An analysis of crime statistics from the records of the Ministry of Justice, Peking]. Sociol World 2: 79-144 '28 **670**

Clark, Charles E. Present status of judicial statistics. Am Jud Soc J 14: 84-8 O '30 **671**

Criminal statistics, 1926. L Times 165: 299 Ap 7 '28 **672**

Criminal work of justices in 1925. Just Peace 91: 293 Ap 16 '27 **673**

Czernicki, Karol. Dzialalność sadów powszechnych w latach 1925-1928. Kwartalnik Statyst 8: 609-43 '31 **674**

Dühren, van. Kriminalstatistik der Jugendlichen 1925 und 1926. Zeitsch f d ges Strafrechtswiss 49: 255-90 '29 **675**

Finland. Ministère de la justice. Fonctionnement des tribunaux et des huissiers principaux de Finlande en 1925 et 1926- Helsingfors, 1929- **676**
Text in Finnish; title in French and Finnish.

Finland. Ministère de la justice. Statistique criminelle de Finlande pour l'année 1927- Accusés. Helsingfors, 1929- **677**
Text in Finnish; title in French and Finnish.

Frick. Die Kriminalität in Baden, 1926 und 1925. Monats f Kriminalpsychol u Strafrechtsref 19: 282-92 My '28 **678**

Georgia. Department of public welfare. Criminal court statistics (Studies 2-7). An analysis of the work of the Criminal court of Atlanta, the Superior court of Fulton county, the City court of Macon, the Superior court of Bibb county, the City court of Columbus, the Superior court of Muscogee county, 1916-1925; by Hugh N. Fuller. 126p. (mim) Atlanta [1929] **679**

Great Britain. Home office. Judicial statistics, England and Wales, 1927: criminal statistics. . . 229p. (Cmd 3301) London, H.M. Stationery office, 1929 **680**

Hentig, [Hans v]. Die deutsche Kriminalstatistik für des Jahr 1925. Monats f Kriminalpsychol u Strafrechtsref 19: 57-9 Ja '28 **681**

H[entig, Hans] v. Die Kriminalität Finnlands. Monats f Kriminalpsychol u Strafrechtsref 19: 620 O '28 **682**

Hotchkiss, Willis Livingston and Gehlke, Charles E. Uniform classifications for judicial criminal statistics: with particular reference to classification of dispositions: report to the Institute of law, Johns Hopkins University. 133p. Baltimore, Johns Hopkins press, 1931 **683**

Indiana. Library and historical department. Legislative bureau. Statistical report for the state of Indiana for the year ending 1927- [Indianapolis] **684**
Judicial statistics: circuit, superior, criminal and probate court statistics.

Kempner, [R.]. Preussische Justizstatistik. Monats f Kriminalpsychol u Strafrechtsref 19: 560-1 S '28 **685**

Kempner, R. Preussische Justizstatistik 1926. Monats f Kriminalpsychol u Strafrechtsref 18: 646-7 N '27 **686**

Kempner, R. Preussische Justiz-Statistik 1929. Monats f Kriminalpsychol u Strafrechtsref 21: 557-8 '30 **687**

Die Kriminalität Deutschlands im Jahre 1926. Arch f Krim 82: 181-90 Ap '28 **688**

Die Kriminalität im Deutschen Reich im Jahre 1925. Wirtsch u Statist 7: 257-60 Mr 1 '27 **689**

Die Kriminalität im Deutschen Reich im Jahre 1926. Wirtsch u Statist 8: 41-4 Ja '28 **690**

Die Kriminalität im Deutschen Reich im Jahre 1927. Wirtsch u Statist 9: 349-52 Ap '29 **691**

Die Kriminalität in Amsterdam im Jahre 1927. Arch f Krim 82: 261-2 Je '28 **692**

Die Kriminalität in Bayern im Jahre 1927. Zeitsch d Bayer Statist Landesamts 60: 293-4 '28 **693**

Die Kriminalität in Danzig im Jahre 1926. Wirtsch u Statist 8: 44 Ja '28 **694**

Die Kriminalität in Österreich im Jahre 1926. Wirtsch u Statist 8: 260 Ap '28 **695**

Lummus, Harry T. Statistics and successions in the supreme judicial court and the superior court, to January 1, 1930. Mass L Q 15: sup no2 My '30 **696**

Martin, Clarence R. (Statistics of the condition in the supreme court; address). Ind L J 4: 40-51 O '28 **697**

Maus, Isidore. L'application de la loi du 15 mai 1912 sur la protection de l'enfance de 1913 à 1927. R de Dr Pén et de Crimin 8: 1142-66 '28 **698**

Maus, Isidore. L'application de la loi du 15 mai 1912 sur la protection de l'enfance de 1912 à 1928. R de Dr Pén et de Crimin 9: 1072-88 '29 **699**

Maus, Isidore. L'application de la loi du 15 mai 1912 sur la protection de l'enfance de 1913 à 1925. R de Dr Pén et de Crimin 7: 221-35 F '27 **700**

Maus, Isidore and Delannoy, Alphonse. L'application de la loi du 15 mai 1912 sur la protection de l'enfance de 1920 à 1929. R de Dr Pén et de Crimin 10: 525-42 '30 **701**

Mexico. Departamento de la estadística nacional. Estadistica nacional, revista mensuel, 1, 1925- **702**
Judicial statistics listed each month.

Need for judicial statistics realized. Am Jud Soc J 14: 12-13 Je '30 **703**

New York (state.) Crime commission. Sub-commission on statistics. A statistical analysis of the criminal cases in the courts of the state of New York for the year 1925; by C. E. Gehlke and Raymond Moley. 80p. Albany, 1927 **704**

New York (state.) Supreme court. First judicial department. Judicial statistics of the work . . . in the First judicial department for the years 1927-1931. [New York, 1928-32] **705**

Nutt, Alice Scott. Juvenile court statistics. N Y St Conf Prob Offic Proc 20: 94-8 '27 **706**

Nutt, Alice Scott. National juvenile court statistics; progress in the reporting of juvenile statistics. Nat Prob Assn Proc 23: 119-30 '29 **707**

Nutt, Alice Scott. The value of uniform statistics in children's courts. N Y St Assn Judges Proc 5: 61-6 '27 **708**

Ohio. Judicial council. Judicial statistics. Interim statement, study of judicial administration in Ohio. 25p. (Bul no2) [Columbus, 1930] **709**

Roesner, E. Die Entwicklung der Kriminalität in Österreich. Arch f Krim 82: 255-61 Je '28 **710**

Roesner, E. Die Kriminalität in Baden, Thüringen und Hessen im Jahre 1926. Krimin Monatsh 2: 185-6, 211-12 Ag, S '28 **711**

Roesner, E. Die Kriminalität in Bayern und Württemberg im Jahre 1926. Krimin Monatsh 2: 70-1 Mr '28 **712**

Roesner, E. Die Kriminalität in Dänemark in den Jahren 1924 und 1925. Arch f Krim 82: 61-3 Ja '28 **713**

Roesner, E. Die Kriminalität in Danzig in den Jahren 1925 und 1926. Krimin Monatsh 3: 115-16 My '28 **714**

Roesner, E. Die Kriminalität in Österreich im Jahre 1926. Krimin Monatsh 2:210-11 S '28 **715**

Roesner, E. Die Kriminalität im Schweden im Jahre 1926. Krimin Monatsh 2: 233-4 O '28 **716**

Roesner, E. Die Kriminalität in Stockholm in den Jahren 1920-1925. Arch f Krim 82: 63-4 Ja '28 **717**

Rumania. Ministerul justitiei. Dare de seama asupra statisticei judiciare din vechiul regat si Basarabia pe anii 1919-1924. 82p. Bucuresti, 1929 **718**

Rumania. Ministerul justitiei. Statistica judiciară a României pe anii 1925-1928. 220p. Bucuresti, 1931 **719**

Scotland. Prisons department. Judicial statistics . . . criminal judicial statistics, 1925- **720**

Siam. Ministry of finance. Department of general statistics. Statistical yearbook of the Kingdom of Siam 12, 1926/27—15, 1929/30. Bangkok, 1927-31? **721**
English edition. Court statistics.

Sunderland, Edson R. Defects of English and American statistics. Am B Assn J 16: 773-5 D '30 **722**

Sweden. Statistika Centralbyrån. Domstolarnas och de exekutiva myndigheternas verksamhet åren 1927 och 1928; 1929 och 1930. Stockholm, 1930-32 **723**
Court statistics.

United States. Children's bureau. Juvenile court statistics, 1927; based on information supplied by 42 courts. 37p. (Pub no195) Washington, 1929 **724**

United States. Children's bureau. Juvenile court statistics, 1928; based on information supplied by 65 courts. 76p. (Pub no200) Washington, 1930 **725**

United States. Children's bureau. Juvenile court statistics, 1929; based on information supplied by 96 courts. Third annual report. 61p. (Pub no207) Washington, 1931 **726**

Warner, Sam Bass. Creating a plan for criminal court statistics. Am Jud Soc J 14: 88-93 O '30 **727**

Wilder, Francis S. Crime in the superior courts of North Carolina. Soc Forces 5: 423-7 Mr '27 **728**

Wisconsin. State board of control. Number of defendants appearing in courts in Wisconsin having criminal jurisdiction from 1922 to 1929, inclusive; disposition of defendants committed in courts having criminal jurisdiction in Wisconsin from 1922 to 1929 inclusive. 2p. 1930? **729**

Zur deutschen Justizstatistik für das Jahr 1926. Vjsch z Statist Deut Reich 37: 124-5 '28 **730**

PENAL STATISTICS

[Alabama. State prison inspector]. A comparative table of commitments to the county jails for the first six months of the last two fiscal years with some observations. 17p. Montgomery, August 28, 1930 **731**

Alsina, Eugenio E. Estadística penal. R de Identif y Cienc Pen 7: 229-52 N '30 **732**

Aschrott. Die preussische Gefängnisstatistik und die Reichskriminalstatistik. Deut Juristen-Zeit 32 (15): 1076-8 '27? **733**

California. Los Angeles county. Sheriff's department. County jail statistics for the fiscal year July 1, 1927/June 30, 1928. (mim) [Los Angeles, 1928] **734**

Canada. Quebec (Province). Bureau of statistics. Statistics of penal establishments (prisons, reformatory schools and industrial schools) for the year 1927- Quebec, Proulx, 1928- **735**
Text in French and English.

Cuba. Comision nacional de estadistica y reformas economicas. Cuadros estadisticos de los penados de ambos sexos que se encontraban condena en los establecimientos penales de la republica en 30 de Junio de 1927. (mim) Habana, 1927 736

Cuba. Comision nacional de estadistica y reformas economicas. Penados que se encontraban en las carceles de la republica y presidio nacional en 31 de Diciembre de 1927. (mim) Habana, 1928? 737

Deutsche Gefängnis-Statistik. Arch f Krim 84: 158-64 Ap '29 738

Ecuador. Penitenciaria nacional. Cuadros estadísticos. 38p. Quito, Talleres Tipográficos Nacionales, 1930 739

Finland. Ministère de la justice. Statistique criminelle de Finlande pour l'année 1927. Personnes subissant une peine. 143p. Helsingfors, 1930 740
Title in Finnish and French; text in Finnish.

France. Direction de l'administration pénitentiaire. Statistique pénitentiaire pour l'année. . . Exposé général de la situation des services et des divers établissements, 1, 1852- 741

Frankel, Emil and Heyer, Helen E. Adult offenders committed to New Jersey state institutions: a statistical summary for the fiscal year 1928-29. 38p. (mim) Trenton, New Jersey state department of institutions and agencies, May 1930 742

Frankel, Emil and Heyer, Helen E. Commitments to state institutions for adult offenders 1930: a statistical summary for the fiscal year 1929/30. 42p. (mim) Trenton, New Jersey state department of institutions and agencies, July 1931 743

Frankel, Emil and Heyer, Helen E. Juvenile delinquents enter state institutions—1930; statistical summary of admissions and discharges for the year ending June 30, 1930. (mim) 17p. Trenton, New Jersey state department of institutions and agencies, October 1931 744

Germany. Statistischen Reichsamt. Statistik des Gefängniswesens im Deutschen Reich. 16p. Berlin, Heymann, 1929 (Reichstag. 4. Wahlperiode 1928. Drucks 814) 745

[Gernet, Mikhail N.] (M. Hernett). Le mouvement de la population dans les lieux de réclusion de l'URSS. Statist Oboz 5: 104-11 My '28 746

Griesmeier, Josef. Die Statistik über die württembergischen Landesstrafanstalten in den Jahren 1926 und 1927. Württ Jahrb f Statist Landeskunde 1929: 167-208 '30 747

Guelton, Georges. Questions pénitentiaires et pénales. R Pénitent et de Dr Pén 55: 138-46 Ja '31 748

Guelton, Georges. Statistique pénale et statistique criminelle en Belgique. R Pénitent et de Dr Pén 51: 336-51 My '27; 54: 263-78 Ap '30 749

Gumbel, E. J. Probleme der Strafvollzugsstatistik. Arch f Sozialwiss u Sozialpol 64 (1): 122-35 '30 750

Italy. Direzione generale delle carceri. Statistica dei riformatori, 1922/23- Roma, Libr. dello Stato, 1927- 751

Italy. Direzione generale delle carceri. Statistica delle carceri, 1922/23- I. Stabilimenti di detenzione preventiva. II. Stabilimenti penali. Roma, Libr. dello Stato, 1927- 752

Kampmann, E[rik]. Meddelelser om dansk Faengselsvaesen 1927. Nord Tids f Straf 16: 271-82 Jl '28 753

Kampmann, Erik. Meddelelser om dansk Faengselsvaesen 1926. Nord Tids f Straf 15: 126-49 Ap '27 754

MacColl, H. H. Holland. Report on prisons and prison statistics, 1925-26. Howard J 2: 242-5 O '28 755

Maine. State auditor. Condensed statistical information relative to state institutions as of June 30, 1929: penal: Maine state prison; State reformatory for men; State reformatory for women; correctional: State school for boys; State school for girls. *In* Biennial report of State auditor 11, 1926/28—12, 1928/30 756

Massachusetts. Commissioner of correction. Statistics of prison population. *In* Annual report 1927: 126-9; 1929: 106-9 757

Mead, Bennett. Federal figures. Nat Soc Pen Inf N Y Bul 2: 3-4, 6 Ap '31 758

Minnesota. State board of control. [Statistics of institutions for delinquent children]. *In* Biennial report 14, 1927/28: 182-4; 15, 1929/30: 203-5 759

Missouri. State penitentiary, Jefferson City. Statistical report. *In* Biennial report of Department of penal institutions 1926/28: 29-149; 1928/30: 47-128 760

Netherlands. Centraal bureau voor de statistiek. Statistiek van het gevangeniswezen. *In* Bijdragen tot de statistiek 1, 1900- 761

Ohio. Department of public welfare. County jail statistics for year ending June 30, 1926. Ohio Welf Bul 3: 7 Je '27 762

Ohio. Department of public welfare. General county statistics, juvenile court, county jails. Ohio Welf Bul 6: 5, 7, 8-9 Ag '29 763

Ohio. Department of public welfare. Institution statistics. Annual report 6, 1927: 141B; 7, 1928: 78A 764

Ohio. Department of public welfare. Statistics of county jails for year ending December 31, 1929. Ohio Welf Bul 7: 6-7 N '30 765

Peru. Department of treasury and commerce. Bureau of statistics. Statistical abstract of Peru, 1927, 1928. Lima, 1928-29 766
Statistics of penal population.

[Prison statistics of Sweden]. Nord Tids f Straf 15: 73-80 '27 767

Prisoners in Pennsylvania, 1927; preliminary report. Prison J 8: 7- O '28 768

Prisons (statistics). Just Peace 91: 474 Je 18 '27 769

Prussia. Justizministerium. Statistik über die Gefangenenanstalten der Justizverwaltung in Preussen 1, 1902- Berlin 770

Die Reichskriminalstatistik für 1926. Bl f Gefängniskunde 60: 79-84 '29 **771A**

Russia (USSR). Tsentral'noe statisticheskoe upravlenie. Statistika osuzhdennykh 1, 1923/24-? **771B**

Sauthoff, Friedrich and Schulzke, Willy. Anleitung zur Aufstellung und Nachprüfung der Statistik über die Gefängenenanstalten der Justizverwaltung in Preussen. 23p. Berlin, Selbstverl d Verf, 1927 **772**

Schickert, Hans. Statistik der Todesstrafe in Baden 1851-1929. Monats f Kriminalpsychol u Strafrechtsref 21: 161-71 Mr '30 **773**

Schmidt. Strafvollzugsstatistik und Strafvollzugskritik. Justiz 6(3): 127-35 D '30 **774**

Spain. Ministerio de justicia. Dirección general de prisiones. Estadística penitenciaria, año de 1907- Madrid, Imp. de Jesús López, 1910?- **775**

Statistik über die Gefangenenanstalten der Justizverwaltung in Preussen für das Rechnungsjahr 1926 (1.4.1926-31.3.1927). Bl f Gefängniskunde 60: 84-92 '29 **776**

Statistiques des prisons hollandaises en 1925. Ecrou 8: 397-405 Jl '27 **777**

Sweden. Fångvårdsstyrelsen. Fångvården år 1927-1930. Stockholm, Kungl. Boktryckeriet, P. A. Norstedt & Söner, 1929-32 **778**

Trüdinger. Die Statistik über die württembergischen Strafanstalten in den Jahren 1924 und 1925. Württ Jahrb f Statist u Landeskunde 1927: 22-60 **779**

United States. Bureau of the census. The prisoner's antecedents: statistics concerning the previous life of offenders committed in 1923 to state and federal prisons and reformatories: supplement to "Prisoners," 1923. 77p. Washington, Govt. Ptg. Off. 1929 **780**

United States. Bureau of the census. Prisoners in state and federal prisons and reformatories, 1926: summary. 20p. Washington, Govt. Ptg. Off. 1929; same title: Pris Assn N Y Ann Rep 85: 117-38 '29 **781**

United States. Bureau of the census. Prisoners in state and federal prisons and reformatories, 1926: statistics of prisoners during the year, for state and federal penal institutions. 139p. Washington, Govt. Ptg. Off. 1929 **782**

United States. Bureau of the census. Prisoners in state and federal prisons and reformatories, 1927: statistics of prisoners received and discharged during the year for state and federal penal institutions. 127p. Washington, Govt. Ptg. Off. 1931 **783**

United States. Congress. House. Committee of the census. Collection of annual statistics relating to public institutions, report to accompany S. 1812 [to authorize collection of annual statistics relating to crime and to defective, dependent and delinquent classes], February 19, 1931. 2p. (71st Cong. 3d Sess. H.Rep. 2757) Washington, Govt. Ptg. Off. 1931 **784**

Virginia. State department of public welfare. Summary of jail statistics. *In* Annual report 18, 1927: 32; 19, 1928: 33; 20, 1929: 39 **785**

Wallén, K. [Swedish prison statistics, 1926]. Nord Tids f Straf 16: 94-103 Ja '28 **786**

Ward, H. Prussian prison statistics. Howard J 2: 226-7 O '28 **787**

We grow less lawless. Survey 62: 346 Je 15 '29 **788**

Figures showing decline in commitments.

Wisconsin. Board of control. Inmate population on May 31, 1930, October 31, 1931. (mim) (Bulletin 197, 215) **789**

OFFENDERS

CRIMINOLOGY

Alexander, Franz. Mental hygiene and criminology. Ment Hyg 14: 853-82 '30 **790**

[**The Anti-social** and their treatment]. M Press 175: 211-13 S 14 '27 **791**

Barnes, Harry Elmer. Psychiatry in the field of criminology as seen by the sociologist. Nat Soc Pen Inf N Y Bul 1: 5-6, 9-10 O '30 **792**

Belloni, G. A. Le droit naturel et la nouvelle école criminologique italienne. R Int de Dr Pén 7 (2): 194-203 '30 **793**

Beltrán, J. R. La psychanalyse en criminologie. R Fr de Psychanal 4: 487-507 '31; also: Psicoanálisis y delito. Semana Méd 2: 207-17 Jl 16 '31 **794**

Brasol, Boris. Anthropology and criminology. Am J Phys Anthrop 12: 339-46 O '28 **795**

Davis, George T. The study of criminology. Police J [N Y] 16: 16-18 F; 16-18 Mr; 29-30 Ap; 10-11 Je '29 **796**

Delitala, Giacomo. Il "fatto," nella teoria generale del reato. 218p. Padova, A. Milani, 1930 **797**

Desoille, Henri. L'occultisme contemporain en criminologie; considérations juridiques et médico-légales. Etudes Crimin 4: 145-56 My '29 **798**

Engelhardt, K. F. Klinische Kriminologie. Monats f Kriminalpsychol u Strafrechtsref 21: 532-5 Ag '30 **799**

Ferenczi, S. Psicoanálisis y criminología. R Med de Barcelona 11: 318-30 Ap '29; same title: R de Med [Rosario] 4: 312-33 N '29 **800**

Ferri, Enrico. Sociologia criminale. ed. 5. 2v. 552, 612p. Torino, Unione Tipografico-Editrice Torinese, 1930 **801**

[**Ferri, Enrico**]. Le visite scientifiche della Scuola di Applicazione giuridico-criminale. Scuola Pos ns7: 471-5 S '27 **802**

Grispigni, Filippo. Introduzione alla sociologia criminale. Oggetto e natura della sociologia criminale. Il metodo. Il concetto sociologico della criminalità. 192p. Torino, Unione Tipografico-Editrice Torinese, 1928 **803**

De Haan, P. B. Kriminologische stellingen. Maandbl v Ber en Reclasseer 6: 179-90 Jl '27 **804**

Haynes, Frederick Emory. Criminology. 417p. N.Y. McGraw-Hill, 1930 **805**
"Social responsibility for crime. . . Sociological approach for solution of crime problem."

Illinois. Division of criminology. Annual report in Department of public welfare, Annual report 10, 1927: 16-118; 11, 1928: 25-130; 12, 1929: 54-153; 13, 1930: 33-146 **806**
Includes reports of Institute for juvenile research, which are also published separately.

Kriminologie und Familienrecht. Allg Zeitsch f Psychiat 87: 222-7 '27 **807**
Brief resume of addresses at International congress for sexual research, 1926.

Krylenko, N. Die Kriminalpolitik der Sowjetmacht. 31p. Berlin, Verl. f. Lit. u. Pol. 1927 **808**

Leahy, S. R. Notes on certain abuses in the field of criminology. Psychiat Q 3: 462 '28 **809**

Lugiato, Luigi. Pazzi, squilibrati e delinquenti nelle opere dei letterati. v2 Bergamo, C. Conti, 1927 **810**

McKee, W. C. New methods in criminology. Brooklyn 10-11 My 5 '28 **811**

Mendonça, Joao. A orientação actual da criminologia. R de Cultura Jurid 1: 56-8 Ap '29 **812**

Mendoza, Salvador. The new Mexican system of criminology. J Crim L & Crimin 21: 15-25 My '30 **813**

Orebaugh, David A. The new criminology. Welf 19: 1038-46 O '28 **814**

Papillault, G. Galton y la biosociología. R de Identif y Cienc Pen 4: 217-29 Jl '29 **815**

Petrén, Alfred. Neues Kriminalistisches aus Schweden. Monats f Kriminalpsychol u Strafrechtsref 22: 265-9 My '31 **816**

Philipp, Lothar. Einführung in die kriminalistische Denklehre. 170p. Berlin, O. Walter, 1927 **817**

Picard, Octave. Essai de conciliation du libre-arbitre et de la théorie positive. R de Dr Pén et de Crimin 9: 109-33 '29 **818**

Provent, Paul. Freudisme et criminologie. Etudes Crimin 2: 52-4 My, 72-4 O '27; 3: 70-3 Mr '28 **819**

Röhrer, Carl. Zur Darstellung des sadistischen Typus in der älteren Malerei. Monats f Kriminalpsychol u Strafrechtsref 18: 377-80 Jl '27 **820**

Saldana y Garcia Rubio, Quintiliano. La criminologie nouvelle. 315p. Paris, Les Presses universitaires de France, 1929 **821**
Bibliography at end of each chapter.

Sanctis, S. de. El concepto de la alienación mental en la criminología. R de Crimin 14: 169-286 '27; Il concetto moderno di

Sanctis, S. de. El concepto, etc.—*Continued* alienazione mentale nella criminologia. Lab Psicol Sperim Univ Roma 5: 1-17 '22-'28 **822**

Sheinis, L. Problemi kriminologii i sotzialnoi psichologie. 229p. Paris, 1929? **823**

Solomon, M. Modern psychiatry and criminology. Ill Med J 60: 429-35 N '31 **824**

Stein, Emily A. A Russian experiment in criminology. Sch & Soc 28: 789-92 D 22 '28 **825**

Sutherland, E. H. Criminology, public opinion and the law. Nat Conf Soc Wk Proc 54: 168-75 '27 **826**

Sutherland, E. H. The person versus the act in criminology. Cornell L Q 14: 159-67 F '29 **827**

Tacy, Thomas O. New criminology. Lawyer & Banker 23: 236-41 S '30 **828**

Tél, Franz. Verbesserte sich der Mensch vom Urmenschen bis zum Heutigen? Arch f Krim 81: 235-48 D '27 **829**

Veratti, Nino. Sociologia e politica criminale (istituzioni di criminologia). 298p. Torino, Bocca, 1931 **830**

Wolf, Erik. Entwicklungen in der nordamerikanischen Kriminologie. Monats f Kriminalpsychol u Strafrechtsref 20: 661-70 '29 **831**

Wood, Arthur Evans. Program for criminological research. Am J Sociol 33: 431-43 N '27 **832**

Wyndham, Horace. Criminology. 105p. London, Cape, 1929? **833**

Znaniecki, Florian. The object matter of sociology. Am J Sociol 32: 529-84 Ja '27 **834**
Definition of scope of criminology, 575-7.

Znaniecki, Florian. Social research in criminology. Sociol & Soc Res 12: 307-22 Mr '28 **835**

BIOGRAPHIES OF CRIMINOLOGISTS

Abascal, Horacio. La obra científica de Israel Castellanos. R Bimestre Cubana 26: 100-209 S '30 **836**

Biografia y bibliografia de Ladislao Thót. R de Identif y Cienc Pen 1: 22-7 N '27 **837**

Bischoff, A. Le Professeur R.-A. Reiss. R Int de Crimin 1: 325-32 O '29 **838**
Prof. Reiss of the police school, Lausanne.

Chapman, John Jay. Osborne's place in historic criminology. Harvard Grad Mag 35: 599-605 Je '27 **839**

Dahl, F. Karl von Lilienthal. Nord Tids f Straf 16: 212-14 Ap '28 **840**

Donati, Mario. Note di un penalista dilettante. 143p. Milano, Casa Ed. Agnelli, 1928 **841**

East, W. N. Sir Horatio Bryan Donkin, M.A., M.D., Oxon, F.R.C.P. J Ment Sci 74: 1-12 Ja '28 **842**

Extracts from the writings of Fred C. Nelles. J Delin 11: 107-14 Je '27 **843**
Nelles is interested in rehabilitation of wayward children.

Fallows, Alice Katherine. Everybody's Bishop. Being the life and times of the Right Rev. Samuel Fallows, D.D. 461p. N. Y. Sears, 1927 **844**
Rev. Fallows gave 21 years of service to the state of Illinois in the reformatory field.

Gatti, Tancredi. Luis Jiménez de Asúa e il sistema "protettore." 34p. Città di Castello, "Leonardo da Vinci," 1930 **845**
Extr de la Giustizia penale, 36 (8).

Hegler, August, ed. Festgabe für Reinhard von Frank, zum 70 Geburtstag, 16. August 1930. 2v. Tübingen, J. C. B. Mohr, 1930 **846**

Herrero, A. Noticia sobre Lavater. R de Identif y Cienc Pen 1: 123-30 Ja '28 **847**

Locard, Edmond. R.-A. Reiss. R Int de Crimin 1: 333-6 O '29 **848**

Lyon, F. Emory. John L. Whitman—dreamer and doer. J Crim L & Crimin 18: 5-10 My '27 **849**

Moruzi, Jean. Vincenzo Lanza si doctrina sa penala 1869-1929. R de Drept Pen (1-2): 62- '30 **850**

A prince in Israel [Albert Hiatt Votaw]. Prison J 11: 9-11 Ap '31 **851**

Provent, Paul. Edmond Bayle, 28 Septembre 1879—16 Septembre 1929. Etudes Crimin 4: 285-6 N '29 **852**

Roux, J. A. Un criminaliste du milieu du xixe siècle. Etudes Crimin 2: 41-3 My '27 **853**
Bonneville de Marsangy.

S[asserath], S. Commemoration Jules LeJeune. R de Dr Pén et de Crimin 8: 463-5 My '28 **854**

Science and physical evidence. Northwest Police J 6: 8-10 Ap '29 **855**
L. S. May, criminologist, Seattle.

Tirone, U. ed. Alla memoria di Leonardo Bianchi. 22p. Benevento, "Le forche caudine," 1928 **856**

Vigneron, R. M. Bergeret et la criminologie. Mod Philol 26: 129-48 N '28 **857**

Zerboglio, Adolfo. Alessandro Stoppato. Pensiero Giurid Pen 3: 189-92 Jl '31 **858**

CESARE BECCARIA

Manci, F. I tempi e il pensiero di Cesare Beccaria. Scuola Pos ns8: 432-48 S '28 **859**

Saldana [y Garcia Rubio], Quintiliano. Le droit pénal de Beccaria et de son école. Etudes Crimin 2:61-7, 89-94 Jl, D '27 **860**

ENRICO FERRI

Altavilla. Enrico Ferri. R Int de Dr Pén 6 (2): 139-49 '29 **861**

Carton de Wiart. Enrico Ferri et Jules LeJeune; leur influence sur la réforme pénale en Belgique. R de Dr Pén et de Crimin 9: 157-62 '29 **862**

Collin, Fernand. Etude critique du système Ferri. R de Dr Pén et de Crimin 7: 434-52 Ap '27 **863**

Collin, Fernand. Le théorie pénale de Ferri. R de Dr Pén et de Crimin 7: 352-69 Mr '27 **864**
A chapter of Collin's book on Enrico Ferri et l'avant projet de code pénal italien de 1921.

Donnedieu de Vabres, H. Enrico Ferri. Etudes Crimin 4: 133-7 My '29; abstract: R de Dr Pén et de Crimin 9: 747-53 '29 865

Loudet, Osvaldo. Enrique Ferri y la ciencia penale. R de Crimin, Psiquiat y Med Leg [16] (93) Mr '29 866

Pozzolini, A. La sociologia criminale nella definitiva sistemazione del pensiero scientifico di Enrico Ferri. 17p. Messina, Giacomo d'Anna, 1930 867
Extr d'Il pensiero giuridico-penale, 2 (1).

Rappaport, Emil Stanislaw. Les deux faces de la carrière scientifique d'Enrico Ferri. R Pénitent de Pologne 4: 347-52 Jl '29 868

Santoro, Arturo. La sociologia criminale nel pensiero di Enrico Ferri. Scuola Pos 9: 289-93 Jl '29 869

Cesare Lombroso

Belloni, G. A. Cesare Lombroso e la criminologia italiana. Arch di antrop Crim 50: 333-41 My '30 870

Belloni, G. Andrea. Lombroso e la criminologia italiana. Riv di Cultura 16: 345-53 S '29 871

Moreno, A. Recordando á Cesare Lombroso. Bibl Nac de Crim y Cienc Afines Bol 2: 408-12 Ap '28 872

Juan Vucetich

Almandos, Luis Reyna. Jucio sobre Vucetich en Chile; comentario sobre la resoluciones de la Comisión de Reformas, 1929. R de Identif y Cienc Pen 6: 254-72 Jl '30 873

Almandos, Luis Reyna. Wells y Vucetich. R de Identif y Cienc Pen 3: 188-200 Ja '29 874

Quirós, Constancio Bernaldo de. En memoria de Juan Vucetich. R de Identif y Cienc Pen 5: 220-3 Ja '30 875

Silva, Rodolfo Xavier da. Juan Vucetich. R de Identif y Cienc Pen 6: 349-54 S '30 876

FACTORS INVOLVED IN MAKING OF OFFENDER

GENERAL

Azzalini, Mario. Sulla natura e genesi della criminalità. Scuola Pos 11: 437-53 O '31 877

Belgrano, R. O. Las verdaderas causas del aborto provocado en la mujer soltera. R de Crimin, Psiquiat y Med Leg 14: 504-7 Jl '27 878

Bonne, Georg. Das Verbrechen als Krankheit. 197p. München, Reinhardt, 1927 879

Brown, Fred. A practical study of some etiological factors in theft behavior. J Crim L & Crimin 22: 221-53 Jl '31 880

Butcher, William Lewis. A test of public opinion on causes of crime. Nat Conf Soc Wk Proc 54: 656-62 '27 881

Casselberry, Wm. S. Symptomatic factors in delinquency: a very abbreviated account of a study conducted at the Preston School of Industry, California. 8p. (mim) [Stanford, Stanford Univ. The Author, 1930] 882

Causes of crime. Can B R 5:285-7 Ap '27 883

Cincinnati. Bureau of municipal research. Crime and criminal justice. 3p. (Pam no4) Cincinnati, April 1928 884

Cocurullo, Baldassare. I moventi a delinquere. 298p. Napoli, Edit. "La Toga," 1927 885

Coutts, W. E. El delito imitativo. R de Crimin, Psiquiat y Med Leg 15: 160-5 Mr '28 886

Davenport, Walter. Making of a criminal. Collier's 85: 12-13 Je 7 '30 887

Dosenheimer, E. Die Ursachen der Verbrechen und ihre Bekämpfung. Natur & Gesell 14: 25-8 '27 888

Fenton, Jessie Chase. Why children go wrong. Parents' Mag 6: 22-3 Je '31 889

Franken. Kurze Betrachtung über Ursache, Beweggrund und Zweck mit Bezug auf die verbrecherische Tat. Monats f Kriminalpsychol u Strafrechtsref 21: 207-11 Ap '30 890

Gleispach, W. Die Erforschung der Verbrechensursachen. Zeitsch f d ges Strafrechtswiss 48: 99-148 '28 891

Grover, J. P. Burglar's apology. Scribner's 84: 739-43 D '28 892

Gruhle, Hans W. Die Erforschung der Verbrechensursachen. Monats f Kriminalpsychol u Strafrechtsref 19: 257-68 My '28 893

Indiana. State conference on social work. Committee on delinquency. Subcommittee on causes of crime. Report. Ind Bul Char & Correc (165): 496-502 D '28 894

Jastrow, Joseph. How misery breeds crime. N Am R 229: 305-11 Mr '30 895

Kirchwey, George W. What makes criminals. Cur Hist 27: 315-19 D '27 896

Knoles, Tully C. The fundamental cause for the high rate of crime among the population in the United States. Int Assn Identif, Calif Div Proc 12: 43-7 '27 897

Koosis, Abraham. A survey of present day theories as to the causation of delinquency. 100p. Thesis (M.A.) University of California, 1931 898

Korn. Über die Erforschung von Verbrechensursachen. Allg Zeitsch f Psychiat 92: 525-8 '29 899

Leoncini, F. La pericolosità criminale nelle sue cause e nelle sue manifestazioni. Gazz Internaz Med-Chir 37: 337-50 Je 15 '29 900

Lilly, Joseph. What makes a criminal? Outl 154: 181-3 Ja 29 '30 901

Lowell, James R. What causes lawlessness? Police J [N Y] 16: 34-6 Ap '29 902

McAdoo, William. Causes and mechanisms of prevalent crime. Sci M 24: 415-20 My '27 903

Myers, Garry Cleveland. A proposed program for studying the causes of crime. J Juv Res 12: 122-3 Je '28 904

National commission on law observance and enforcement. Report on the causes of crime. 2v. (No13) Washington, June 26, 1931 905

I: Report of Henry W. Anderson; Some causative factors in criminality, by Morris Ploscowe; Work and law observance, by Mary van Kleeck, Emma A. Winslow, and Ira deA. Reid. II: Social factors in juvenile delinquency; a study of the community, the family, and the gang in relation to delinquent behavior, by Clifford R. Shaw and Henry D. McKay.

Patrizi, M. L. Addizioni al "Dopo Lombroso." Ancora sullo monogenesi psicologia del delitto. 271p. Milano, Soc Ed. Libraria, 1930 906

Patrizi, M. L. Il dinamismo dei bisogni e la criminalità. 34p. Bologna, Stab. Poligraf. Riuniti, 1928 907

Removable cause of crime. L Notes 31: 121 O '27 908

Rojas, Nerio. Discusión sobre un delito por celos. R de Crimin Psiquiat y Med Leg 17: 268-72 My '30; same title: R Especialid 5: 543-9 Je '30 909

Root, William T. The causes of crime. Pittsburgh Rec 5: 41-8 D '30 910

Rossi, E. Natura delle reazioni antisociali. Manicomio 40: 33-40 '27 911

Simon, Carleton. Basic causes of crime. N Y St Assn Chiefs Police Proc 29: 11-21 '29; same title: Police J [N Y] 16: 27-31 Ag '29 912

Slawson, John. Causal relations in delinquency research. Am Sociol Soc Proc 22: 169-73 '28 913

Tarnowski, Hans. Die systematische Bedeutung der adäquaten Kausalitätstheorie für den Aufbau des Verbrechensbegriffs. 340p. (Abh d Krimin Inst an d Univ Berlin 4:1, hrsg v James Goldschmidt u Eduard Kohlrausch) Berlin, deGruyter, 1927 914

Tiebout, H. M. Delinquency: problems in the causation of stealing. Am J Psychiat 9: 817-26 '30 915

Wulffen, E. Das Verbrechen als Ausdruck. Fortschr d Med 49: 223, 263 Mr 20, Ap 3 '31 916

AGE AND CRIME

Devon, James. Age and crime. Police J [London] 3: 118-26 Ja '30 917

Hacker, Erwin. Der kriminalätiologische Einfluss des Alters bei der Einwanderung. Monats f Kriminalpsychol u Strafrechtsref 19: 600-4 O '28 918

ALCOHOLISM AND CRIME

Alcoholism and suicide in Illinois. J Crim L & Crimin 22: 613-14 N '31 919

Arenaza, C. de. El alcoholismo y la delincuencia infantil. Semana Méd 1: 1115-19 My 5 '27 920

Bandel, Rudolf. Statistik des Alkoholismus in Deutschland 1927 bis 1930 nach den Erhebungen der Heil- und Pflegeanstalten für Geisteskranke und der Trinkerfürsorgestellen. Alkoholfrage 27 (6): 230-4 '31 921

Benjamin, Dora and Fränkel, Fritz. Alkoholismus und Kriminalität. Monats f Kriminalpsychol u Strafrechtsref 21: 705-13 D '30 922

Beltran, J. R. Alcoholismo y delincuencia. Conf Latino Am de Neurol Psiquiat y Med Leg Actas 2: 944-56 '29; same title: Semana Méd 2: 770-5 S 12 '29 923

Channing, Alice. Alcoholism among parents of juvenile delinquents. Soc Serv R 1: 357-83 S '27 924

Figures from records of Judge Baker foundation.

Chapman, Cecil. Alcoholism and crime. Brit J Inebriety 26: 9-11 Jl '28 925

Grünewald, Max. Alkohol und Verbrechen. Monats f Kriminalpsychol u Strafrechtsref 18: 682-6 D '27 926

Is drunkenness an excuse for a crime? Just Peace 92:535 Ag 11 '28 927

Krassusky, V. S. Effect of alcohol on crime. Odessky Med J 4: 144-6 '29 928

Lassally, Oswald. Strafbare Handlungen in selbstverschuldeter Trunkenheit. Monats f Kriminalpsychol u Strafrechtsref 18: 100-3 F '27 929

Legrain. Les crimes de l'enfance et l'alcohol. Enfant 35: 207-15 O '28 930

Leppmann, Friedrich. Zur Begutachtung der Alkoholdelikte. Krimin Monatsh 2: 51-4 Mr '28 931

Moser, K. Zur Frage der sogenannt "selbstverschuldeten" Trunkenheit und ihrer Bedeutung für die Alkoholkriminalität und Trinkerfürsorge. Arch f Psychiat 86: 382-426 '29 932

Ostmann. Über sogenannte normale Kriminalität der Alkoholkranken. Monats f Kriminalpsychol u Strafrechtsref 19: 351-2 Je '28 933

Ross, Roderick. Intemperance and crime in Scotland. Police J [London] 2: 109-20 Ja '29 934

Schmölders, G. Soziale Missstände und Alkoholverbrauch. Ein Beitrag zur statistischen Ursachenforschung. Allg Statist Arch 17: 258-66 '27 935

Segalov, T. D. Piania draki v gorode i derevne. Problemy Prestupnosti 2: 88-99 '27 936

Thomas, Ernest. The verdict of science on alcohol; the consensus of informed opinion on the physiological and psychological effects of alcohol. 29p. [Toronto], Social service council of Canada, Committee on research, April 1928 937

Trommer, Harry. Alkohol und Kriminalität in Dänemark in den Jahren 1922 bis 1926. Monats f Kriminalpsychol u Strafrechtsref 20: 542-3 '29 **938**

Vivian, Margaret. Alcoholism and drug addiction. Brit J Inebriety 24: 129-31 Ja '27 **939**

Weymann. Alkoholmissbrauch und Kriminalität. Alkoholfrage 27: 73-83 '31 **940**

DRUGS AND CRIME

Darrow, Chester W. Psychological effects of drugs. Psychol Bul 26: 527-45 Ag '29 **941**

Dupouy, Roger. La question de l'opium et les stupéfiants. R Int de Crimin 2 (3): 221-34 '30 **942**

Fraeb, Walter Martin. Die Strafe und Zivilrechtliche Stellungnahme Gegen den Rauschgiftmissbrauch. 235p. Leipzig, G. Thieme, 1927 **943**
Narcotic problem as attacked by the German penal code.

Künzel and Ömig. Über Missbrauch von Rauschgiften. Allg Zeitsch f Psychiat 85: 498-501 F '27 **944**

Lambert, Alexander. Narcotic addiction. Report of the mayor's committee to Hon. Richard C. Patterson, jr., commissioner of correction. Am Med Assn J 93: 1297-1301 O 26 '29 **945**

Lambert, June, comp. Laws of the United States and the states of North Dakota and Ohio which require that the quantity of any narcotic drug in patent medicine shall be stated on the labels. 5p. Albany, New York (state) Library. Legislative reference section, December 1927 **946**

Meyer, E. Die forensische Bedeutung des Morphinismus. Arch f Psychiat 81: 500-21 '27 **947**

Newman, F. L. The drug traffic in the Punjab. Police J [London] 3: 89-102 Ja '30 **948**

Rollings, E. J. The narcotic problem. Mich Assn Chiefs Police Proc 6: 41-5 '29 **949**

Salinger, Fritz. Falsche Selbstbezichtigung im Kokainrausch. Arch f Krim 86: 15-22 F '30 **950**

Sharman, C. H. L. The narcotic problem. 16p. Toronto, Social service council of Canada, April 1928 **951**

Shinkarenko, V. I. Hashish smoking in the underworld in Krassnodar (Soviet Russia). Sovrem Psikhonevrol 10: 269-78 '30 **952**

Simon, Carleton. Exploding some narcotic theories. Police J [N Y] 15: 21, 30 N '27 **953**

Stanley, Eugene. Marihuana as a developer of criminals. Am J Police Sci 2: 252-61 bibliog (p257-61) My '31 **954**

Stowe, Lyman Beecher. The halo of heroin. Forum 83: 346-50 Je '30 **955**

Tereshkovich, A. M. [Narcomania and criminality]. Sovrem Psikhonevrol 4 (2): 147-9 '27 **956**

Terry, Charles E. and Pellen, Mildred. The opium problem. 1042p. N. Y. Bureau of social hygiene, and the Committee on drug addiction, 1928 **957**

Todarelli, Thomas J. Is the narcotic evil growing? Police J [N Y] 17: 19, 21 Jl '30 **958**

United States. Library of Congress. Drug habit and traffic: references supplementing mimeographed list, May 1, 1926. 18p. (mim) [Washington] June 12, 1929 **959**

Verna, F. Profilo clinico, giuridico e sociale del cocainismo. Giustiz Pen 34: col 732-62 Je 30 '28 **960**

Woods, Arthur. Dangerous drugs: the world fight against illicit trade in narcotics. 123p. New Haven, Yale Univ. press, 1931 **961**

ECONOMIC CONDITIONS AND CRIME

Calverton, V. F. Economic factors in criminality. Cur Hist 27: 335-8 D '27 **962**

Chingyueh, Yen. Crime and economic conditions in China. Howard J 3: 28-31 S '30 **963**

Esslinger, Fritz. Zusammenhänge zwischen Teuerung und Kriminalität. 95p. Diss. München. Heilbronn, 1927 **964**

Hentig, Hans von. Die Anpassung des Verbrechens an die Deflation. Monats f Kriminalpsychol u Strafrechtsref 18: 51-2 Ja '27 **965**

Höpler, E. Wirtschaftskrisen und Kriminalität. Arch f Krim 87: 15-27, 129-32, 193-213 Ag-D '30 **966**
Crime and economic conditions in Austria.

Koppenfels, S. v. Zur Gestaltung der Kriminalität in Sachsen seit der Inflation. Monats f Kriminalpsychol u Strafrechtsref 18: 437-8 Ag '27 **967**

Mayer, Joseph. Crime in the commercial field. Sci M 24: 420-5 My '27 **968**

Nelken, S[igmund]. Verbrechen und Versicherung. ed.2. 226p. Berlin, Verband öffentlicher Feuerversicherungsanstalten in Deutschland, 1928 **969**

Neymark, Edward. Wplyw bezrobocia na przestepczość. Praca i Opieka Spoleczna 11: 323-8 Jl '31 **970**

Robb, C. F. How the A B C of employment reduces crime losses. Bankers' M 43: 46-8 D '27 **971**

Roesner, Ernst. Der Einfluss von Wirtschaftslage, Alkohol und Jahreszeit auf die Kriminalität. Zentralst f d Gefängenenfürsorgewesen f d Prov Brandenburg Ber '30 **972**

Rozengart, Eugène. Le crime comme produit social et économique. 182p. Paris, Marcel Rivière, 1929 **973**

Wood, Charles W. American industry and crime: a new angle of this problem. Welf Mag 18: 1219-25 S '27 **974**

Woytinsky, Wladimir. Kriminalität und Lebensmittelpreise. Zeitsch f d ges Strafrechtswiss 49 (7-8): 647-75 '29 975

Woytinsky, Wladimir. Lebensmittelpreise, Beschäftigungsgrad und Kriminalität. Arch f Sozialwiss u Sozialpol 61 (1): 21-62 '29 976

Child Labor

Reise, O. Die Not der erwerbslosen Jugend. R Int de l'Enf 11: 354-67 Ap '31 977

Unemployment

Yoder, Dale. Some probable effects of unemployment insurance upon delinquency. J Juv Res 15: 260-7 O '31 978

ENVIRONMENT AND CRIME

Additon, Henrietta. Environment as it relates to delinquency. J Soc Hyg 14: 471-9 '28 979

Boorman, William Ryland. Delinquency areas: another viewpoint. Rel Educ 26: 858-63 '31 980

Breuling, F. Immunität und Republik. 46p. Stuttgart, Kohlhammer, 1927 981

Faure, Maurice. Influence des taches solaires sur les suicides, les crimes et les accidents. Gaz d Hôp 104: 1250-3 Ag 19 '31; same title: Strasbourg-Méd 91: 652-5 N 5 '31 982

Gleispach, W. Die Kriminalität der Jahreswende. Schweiz Zeitsch f Strafr 43: 113-30 '29 983

Grosse. Der Einfluss der Grossstadt auf die Kriminalität der Jugendlichen. Polizei 24: 260-1, 329-33 Je 5, Jl 5 '27 984

Grout, Edward Harold. Burglary risks in relation to society, law and insurance. 311p. London, Pitman, 1927 985

Hacker, Erwin. Budapest hatása a kriminalitásra. 70p. Budapest, Budapest Székesfövaros Statisztikai Hivatala, 1931 986

Hacker, [E.]. Kriminalität und Jahreszeit. Monats f Kriminalpsychol u Strafrechtsref 22: 424-6 Jl '31 987

Hentig, Hans von. Die Jahreszeitliche Periodizität der weiblichen Selbstmörder. Monats f Kriminalpsychol u Strafrechtsref 18: 434-7 Ag '27 988

Hentig, Hans von. Die soziale Grossstadt und das kriminelle Land (Ein kriminalstatistischer Vergleich von Wien und Tirol). Monats f Kriminalpsychol u Strafrechtsref 18: 440-2 Ag '27 989

Ishii, S. Weather and emotional crimes. Jap J Psychol 2: 64-86 '27 990

Jones, Dollye. Environment and juvenile delinquency. 140p. Thesis (M. A.) University of California, 1929 991
Bibliog 138-40.

Luxenburger, H. Anlage und Umwelt beim Verbrecher. Allg Zeitsch f Psychiat 92: 411-39 F 10 '29 992

Mezger, Edmund. Anlage und Umwelt als Verbrechensursache. Monats f Kriminalpsychol u Strafrechtsref 19: 141-7 Mr '28 993

New York (state). Crime commission. Sub-commission on causes and effects of crime. A study of environmental factors in juvenile delinquency. 93p. Albany, 1928 994
Study in Manhattan Borough, New York.

Norbury, Frank P. Seasonal climatic curves. Their relation to neuropsychiatry. Welf Mag 18: 356-70 Mr '27 995

Pisa, F. Crime e seus factores. Gaz Clin 26: 251 N '28 996

Reinhardt, James M. and Harper, Fowler Vincent. Comparison of environmental factors of delinquent and non-delinquent boys. J Juv Res 15: 271-7 O '31 997
Study of 40 delinquent and 40 non-delinquent boys in Grand Forks, N. D.

Salvemini, Gaetano. The reign of the bludgeon. Survey 57: 695-8 Mr 1 '27 998

Schuppe, Franz. Die Kriminalität der Wochentage. Krimin Monatsh 4: 248-50 N '30 999

Seif, Leonard. The environmental background of juvenile delinquency. Arch Neurol & Psychiat 24: 921-9 N '30 1000

HEREDITY AND CRIME

D'Alfonso, N. R. L'eredità psicologia (Genio, delinquenza, follìa). ed. 2. 63p. Milano, Albrighi, Segati, 1928 1002

Bernard, L. L. Heredity and environmental factors in human behavior. Monist 37: 161-82 Ap '27 1003

Bernhardt, Rudolf. Studien über erbliche Belastung bei Vermögensverbrechen. 49p. (Krimin Abh no12, hrsg von Exner). Leipzig, Wiegand, 1930 1004

Bleuler, E. Der geborene Verbrecher. Vererb u Geschlechtsleb 3: 93-100 '30 1005

Coughlin, J. D. Heredity as a cause of crime. Int Assn Chiefs Police Proc 1927: 33-5 1006

Creutz, W. Der Einfluss der "erblichen Belastung" und der "Umwelt" bei Kriminellen. Allg Zeitsch f Psychiat 95: 73-106 Je 12 '31 1007

Crime and heredity. Eugen R 19: 229-30 O '27 1008

Crux, J. and Haeger, F. Das Kind des Verbrechers. Arch f Krim 88: 126-32 Mr '31 1009

Davenport, Charles B. Crime, heredity and environment. J Hered 19: 307-13 '28 1010

Dehnow, F. Was kann die Gesetzgebung für die Vererbungshygiene tun? Arch f Krim 87: 41-52 Ag '30 1011

Fetscher, R. Vererbung und Kriminalität. Allg Zeitsch f Psychiat 85: 483-4 F '27; same title: Deut Zeitsch f Wohlfahrtspfl 4: 450-3 D '28; Vererb u Geschlechtsleb 2: 3-10 '28 1012

Fitzpatrick, F. Heredity as related to crime and progress. Int Assn Chiefs Police Proc 36: 135-41 '29; same title: Police J [N Y] 17: 13-15, 32 S '29 1013

Friedman, H. M. The heredity factor in mental conditions. M Times [N Y] 55: 224-6, 243 O '27 **1014**

Grünewald, Max. Die kriminellen Anlagen und ihre Erblichkeit. Fortschr d Med 46: 791 Ag 10 '28; same title: Neue Generation 25: 168-71 Ap '29 **1015**

Hapke, E. Über die Bedeutung des Anlagefaktors im verbrecherischen Charakter. Zeitsch f ang Psychol 33: 1-60 Ap '29 **1016**

Holub, Arthur. Kriminelle Anlagen und Erblichkeit? Neue Generation 26: 22-4 Ja '30 **1017**

McKenna, George M. Are inherited mental or emotional defects the principal cause of criminal delinquency? Dakota L R 1: 2-14 Ap '27 **1018**

Manouvrier, Léonce. L'inneïté criminelle. Inst Gén Psychol Bul 28: 175-91 '28 **1019**

Poffenberger, Albert Theodor. Applied psychology. 586p. N.Y. Appleton, 1927 **1020**

Chapters on heredity, subjective and environmental influences on efficiency; psychology and the law; psychological approach in prevention of crime.

Popenoe, Paul. Heredity and behavior. Eugen 2: 3-13 S '29 **1021**

Rüdin, Ernst. Wege und Ziele der biologischen Erforschung der Rechtsbrecher mit besonderer Berücksichtigung der Erbbiologie. Monats f Kriminalpsychol u Strafrechtsref 22: 129-35 Mr '31 **1022**

Sanctis, Sante de. Criminalità latente e realizzazioni criminali. Scuola Pos 10: 289-97 Jl '30 **1023**

Simon, Carleton. The influence of heredity and environment upon crime. Police J [N Y] 18: 13, 23 D '31 **1024**

INTELLIGENCE AND CRIME

Castellano, Mario. Se esista una correlazione tra intellegenza comportamento e condotta morale. Riv di Psicol 23: 6-12 '27 **1025**

Doll, Edgar A. Relation of intelligence to criminality. J Soc Psychol 1: 527-31 N '30 **1026**

Erickson, Milton Hyland. A study of the relationship between intelligence and crime. Med-Leg J 45: 114-28, 135-54 bibliog (p153-4) Jl, O '28; same title: J Crim L & Crimin 19: 592-635 F '29 **1027**

Goddard, Henry H. Levels of intelligence and the prediction of delinquency. J Juv Res 13: 262-5 O '29 **1028**

White, Ralph and Fenton, Norman. Aspects of delinquency and superior mentality. J Juv Res 15: 101-7 '31 **1029**

MENTAL ABNORMALITIES AND CRIME

Aichenvald, L. I. Kriminal' naîa psikhopatologiîa. 108p. Leningrad, Prakticheskaîa Meditsina, 1928 **1030**

Altavilla, Enrico. Dalla monomania omicida alla delinquenza per tendenza. Scuola Pos 11: 193-206 My '31 **1031**

Altavilla, Enrico. De la monomanie homicide a la délinquance par tendance. R Int de Dr Pén 8: 225-43 '31 **1032**

Benon, R. La persécution homicide chez la femme. Ann de Méd Lég 8: 162-73 Ap '28 **1033**

Bermann, G. Neuropata alcoholizado que comete un homicidio. R de Crimin, Psiquiat y Med Leg 14: 764-8 N '27 **1034**

Birnbaum, [Karl]. Die kriminalistische Bedeutung der Hysterie. Krimin Monatsh 1: 79-81 Ap '27 **1035**

Bugaiski, I. P. [The psychopathology of hooliganism in connection with the question of the determination of the conduct of the mentally diseased]. Zhur Nevropatol i Psikhiat (1): 71-84 '27 **1036**

Calasans, José Julio de. "Violencia carnal" e alienação. R de Cultura Jurid 1: 401-6 Jl '29 **1037**

Carp, E. A. D. E. Die Analyse einer besonderen Form vom Sadismus. Psychiat en Neurol Bl 31: 403-15 N '27 **1038**

Criminality and mental deficiency. M J Austral 581-2 Ap 16 '27 **1039**

De la emoción violenta. R de Identif y Cienc Pen 1: 211-27 Ja '28 **1040**

Drouet, P. L. and Hamel, J. Les psychopathies hérédosyphilitiques de l'enfance et de l'adolescence et leur rôle dans la criminalité juvénile. Prophylax Antivén 1: 257-92 My '29 **1041**

East, W. Norwood. Mental inefficiency and adolescent crime. Lancet 221: 166, 221 Jl 18, 25 '31 **1042**

Fairfield, Letitia. Women mental defectives and crime; practical study. Lancet 220: 109-13 Ja 10 '31 **1043**

Fleck. Über die psychischen Folgezustände nach Encephalitis epidemica bei Jugendlichen. Arch f Psychiat 79: 723-85 F '27 **1044**

Frank, Benjamin. Mental level as a factor in crime. J Juv Res 15: 192-7 Jl '31 **1045**

Study of 401 cases admitted to New Jersey Reformatory, Rahway.

Gelma, Eugène. Psychose périodique de délinquance à répétition. 27p. Strasbourg, Les Ed. Univ. de Strasbourg, 1928 **1046**

Gonzales Deleito, F. Notas de psiquiatría militar. Psicosis y presuntos delitos y faltas. R Españ de Med y Cir 13: 484-9 S '30 **1047**

Greeff, Et. de and Louvain, S. A. P. Un vagabond délirant méconnu pendant trente années (contribution à l'étude de la délinquance des Schizophrènes). R de Dr Pén et de Crimin 7: 1004-14 '27 **1048**

Hamilton, Engla B. Mentality and delinquency. Educ 49: 331-45 F '29 **1049**

Healy, William. The mental factors in crime. Ment Hyg 12: 761-7 O '28 **1050**

Heine. Beitrag zur Frage des sogenannten menstruellen Irreseins und dessen forensischer Bedeutung. Aerztl Sachverst-Zeit 33: 218-21, 229-36 Ag 15, S 1 '27 **1051**

D'Hollander and de Greeff. Les crimes, actes d'affranchissement du moi, prodromes d'états schizophréniques. J de Neurol & de Psychiat 29: 397-417 Jl '29 1052

Holters. Eine Psychopathin fingiert ein Verbrechen. Krimin Monatsh 3: 129-31 Je '28 1053

Kankeleit, O. Kriminalität und Psychotherapie. Allg ärztl Zeitsch f Psychotherap 1: 229-30 '28 1054

Karpman, Ben. Impulsive neuroses and crime: a critical review. J Crim L & Crimin 19: 575-91 F '28 1055

Kolle, K. Forensische Bedeutung der sogenannten schizophrenen Reaktion. Deut Zeitsch f d ges gerichtl Med 10: 498-513 S '27 1056

Laignel-Lavastine. Vols impulsifs à l'étalage chez une déprimée périodique. Ann de Méd Lég 7: 436-40 O '27 1057

Laignel-Lavastine and Fay, H. M. L'étiologie de la "folie morale." Paris Méd 2: 170-2 Ag 24 '29 1058

Lavrentieff, N. N. Mental diseases and sexual crimes. J Nevropat i Psikhiat 21: 59-74 '28 1059

Leroy, Louis. Public attitude toward mental defectives and their relationship to crime. Int Assn Identif Proc 13: 64-74 '27 1060

Levi Bianchini, M. Insufficienza evolutiva dell'ego affettivo come fattore di una psicosi depressiva e di criminalità psicopatica (Sindrome psicopatica da scompenso affetivo). Arch Gen di Neurol, Psichiat e Psicoanal 10: 262-72 Ja 30 '30 1061

Levy, Samuel D. Retarded tenth. N Am R 227: 229-35 F '29 1062

Meagher, J[ohn] F. W. Adolescent mentality and crime. Long Island M J 21: 706-12 D '27 1063

Meagher, John F. W. Senile psychoses, dementia, forensic considerations. Med-Leg J 48: 35-49 Mr '31 1064

Montague, Helen. The causes of delinquency in mentally defective boys. Am Assn Stud Feeblemind Proc 35: 104-13 '30 1065

Study in Children's court, N.Y.C.

Nogues, E.; Pietranera, P., and Beltran, J. R. Tentiva de homicidio por emoción violenta de un paranoico-hiperemotivo. R de Crimin, Psiquiat y Med Leg 14: 496-501 Jl '27 1066

Osnato, Michael. Problem of mental disease and delinquency in adolescent. J Nerv & Ment Dis 74: 11-33 Jl '31 1067

Ostmann. Landstreichen und Betteln bei geistig Abnormen. Monats f Kriminalpsychol u Strafrechtsref 19: 677-9 N '28 1068

Parhon, C. I. Constitutia somato psichica si raporturile ei ou criminologia. R de Drept Pen (3-4): 123- '30 1069

Puyn, H. Beiträge zur Psychopathologie von Mord und Totschlag. Allg Zeitsch f Psychiat 93: 66-98 '30 1070

Raven, Alice. Murder and suicide as marks of an abnormal mind. Sociol R 21: 315-33 '29 1071

Revault d'Allonnes, G. Las hetero-impulsiones. R de Crimin Psiquiat y Med Leg 14: 462-70 Jl '27 1072

Rojas, N. Capacidad de los debiles de espiritu. R de Crimin Psiquiat y Med Leg 14: 322-35 My '27 1073

Rojas, N.; Esteves, J. A.; Nogues, J. G. and Delpiano, J. Capacidad y debilidad de espiritu. R de Crimin Psiquiat y Med Leg 14: 482-6 Jl '27 1074

Sacerdote, A. Studio catamnestico di un imbecille omicida per sadismo. Arch di Antrop Crim 47: 616-28 S '27 1075

Salinger, F. and Jacobsen, H. Psychische Störungen nach Strangulationsversuch. Zeitsch f d ges Neurol u Psychiat 110: 372-92 '27 1076

Sanctis, Sante de. El concepto moderno de la alienacion mental en la criminologia. R de Crimin Psiquiat y Med Leg 14: 269-86 My '27 1077

Sanctis, Sante de. Il concetto moderno di alienazione mentale nella criminologia. Scuola Pos ns7: 27-41 Ja '27 1078

Serrani, L. La patologia mentale e la delinquenza minorile. Riv di Sociol 1: 282-8 '27 1079

Sierra, A. M. Estudio acerca de un antigui pero siempre renovado problema de psicofisiologia. R de Crimin Psiquiat y Med Leg 15: 267-77 My '28 1080

Sorel, E.; Riser, and Sorel, R. Tumeur cérébrale, troubles mentaux, vol pathologique. Ann de Méd Lég 7: 433-6 O '27 1081

Stocking, Leonard. Science versus cells. J Juv Res 14:157-64 Jl '30 1082

Strassmann, G. Die Beurteilung krimineller Handlungen von Altersschwachsinnigen. Deut Zeitsch f d ges gerichtl Med 10: 346-59 Ag 16 '27 1083

Strother, F. The cause of crime: defective brain. Phila Pris R 4: 5-8, 29-30 Jl '28 1084

Di Tullio, B. Sul furto patologico. Zacchia 6: 100-8 Jl '28 1085

Vermeylen, G. Vol morbide au cours d'un état mélancolique. J de Neurol et de Psychiat 27: 300-5 My '27 1086

Wall, Willem van de. Seeing our job through: predispostions of crime in relation to prevention. Am Pris Assn Proc 59: 265-78 '29 1087

What was Cain's I. Q.? Survey 63: 86 O 15 '28 1088

Willey, G. F. Mental health and delinquency. Ment Health Bul 6(3) '28 1089

Wyman, B. L. Crime and delinquency in relation to mental disorders. S M J 21: 25-9 Ja '28 1090

Feeblemindedness

Erickson, Milton H. Some aspects of abandonment, feeble-mindedness and crime. Am J Sociol 36: 758-69 Mr '31 1091

Feeble-minded offenders. Sol J 71: 749 O 1 '27 **1092**

Richmond, Frank C. The criminal feeble-minded. J Crim L & Crimin 21: 537-52 bibliog(p551-2) F '31 **1093**

Solomon, M. The moron problem. Clin Med & Surg 34: 501-7 Jl '27 **1094**

Unsworth, H. R. Relationship of feeble-mindedness to criminality. New Orleans M & Surg J 82: 156-60 S '29 **1095**

Insanity

Campbell, Katherine J. Crime and dementia praecox: a study of the criminal insane to determine the possible relation of crime and dementia praecox. Welf Mag 19: 799-805 Je '28 **1096**

Cisternas, Ramón and Laurnagaray, José M. Consideraciones sobre la simulación de la locura en los delincuentes. R de Crimin Psiquiat y Med Leg 18: 562-74 S '31 **1097**
Study at the Lucio Meléndez clinics, 1899-1930; 97 cases: 52 foreign, 44 Argentine, and 1 unknown.

Dávila, G. F. and Bambarén, C. A. Alienación mental y delincuencia. (Informe de psiquiatría forense). Crón Méd 45: 232-8 Ag '28 **1098**

East, W. N. Crime and insanity. Post-Grad M J 5: 172-4 Jl '30 **1099**

Génil-Perrin. La criminalité paranoïaque. Etudes Crimin 5: 70-82 Mr '30 **1100**

Hopwood, J. Stanley. Child murder and insanity. J Ment Sci 73: 95-108 Ja '27 **1101**

Jacobs, Charles M. Why crime and insanity. Med-Leg J 45: 4-19 Ja '28 **1102**

Lidbetter, E. J. Insanity and detention. Eugen R 18: 312-21 Ja '27 **1103**
Report of Royal commission on lunacy and mental disorder.

Loudet, O. Constitución paranóica y criminalidad. R de Crimin Psiquiat y Med Leg 17: 129-37 Mr '30; same title: R Especialid 5: 550-60 Je '30 **1104**

Minogue, S. J. Crime and insanity. M J Austral sup12: 384 N 12; sup 13: 385 N 19 '27 **1105**

Parasuram, G. R. Crime and insanity. Madras M J 10: 147-71 O '28 **1106**

Parasuram, G. R. Crime and insanity in India. J Ment Sci 77: 365-74 Ap '31 **1107**
Study of 175 cases in Madras government mental hospital.

Pighini, Giacomo. Kriminalität und Dementia Praecox. Monats f Kriminalpsychol u Strafrechtsref 18: 193-6 Ap '27 **1108**

Raven, Alice. A contribution towards a psychological conception of insanity and its relation to crime. Sociol R 20: 274-92 O '28 **1109**

Révész, Bela. Zur Psychologie der Moral Insanity. Zeitsch f d ges Neurol u Psychiat 108: 178-217 Ap '27 **1110**

Stephen, Harry L. Insanity and crime. Police J [London] 2: 218-24 Ap '29 **1111**

PHYSICAL ABNORMALITIES AND CRIME

Adler, Herman. Biological and pathological aspects of behavior disorders. Am J Psychiat 84: 507-16 N '27; reprint: 9p. (sB no113) Chicago, Institute for juvenile research, November 1927 **1112**

Ameghino, A. and Fernandez, H. Delito y constitución individual. R Arg de Neurol, Psiquiat y Med Leg 1: 87-99 Ja '27 **1113**

Bambaren, C. A. and Vargas Prada, L. Epilepsia y delincuencia. Crón Méd 46: 52-7 F '29 **1114**

Bambaren, C. A. and Vargas Prada, L. Observaciones de clinica criminológica. Crón Méd 47: 297-304 O '30 **1115**

Benon, R. Encéphalite léthargique et vols. Ann de Méd Lég 7: 132-8 Mr '27 **1116**

De Block. Fracture du crâne, syndrome et compression cérébrale et manifestations epileptoides méconnues chez un meurtrier. R de Dr Pén et de Crimin 8: 711-18 Jl '28 **1117**

Ciampi, L. and Bosch, G. Las toxi-infecciones y la delincuencia infanto-juvenil. Inst Psiquiat Bol 2: 148-52 '30 **1118**

Cicala, Salvatore. Malattie celtiche e reati veneri. Scuola Pos ns7: 225-39 My '27 **1119**

Coutts, W. E. De las razones biológicas y juridicas para considerar el contagio como delito. Conf Latino Am de Neurol, Psiquiat y Med Leg Actas 2: 670-6 '29 **1120**

Décsi, Karl. Beitrag zur forensischen Bedeutung der pathologischen Rauschzustände. Psychiat-Neurol Wchnschr 29: 38-9 Ja 8 '27 **1121**

East, W. Norwood. The relation of the skull, brain, and crime; Henderson trust lecture. 28p. Edinburgh, Oliver & Boyd, 1928 **1122**

Emerson, Charles P. Relation of health to poverty and crime. Hosp Soc Serv 22: 5-18 Jl '30 **1123**

Eyrich, Max. Die Folgezustände der epidemischen Gehirnentzündung in ihren Beziehungen zu Asozialität und Kriminalität. Bl f Gefängniskunde 60 (2): 192-7 '29 **1124**

Finke. Krankheit als Verbrechensursache. Strafvollzug 21: 264-72 S '31 **1125**

Forman, George H. Teeth, their relation to criminals. On Guard 1: 4 S '31 **1126**

Fribourg-Blanc, A. Les réactions antisociales au cours de l'encéphalite épidémique. Ann de Méd Lég 8: 281-354 Jl '28 **1127**

Gajardo, Samuel. La génesis biológica del delito y la delincuencia de menores. 101p. bibliog 3-4. Santiago, Imp. Nascimento, 1928 **1128**

Henry, Guy A. Defective eyesight and delinquency. J Soc Hyg 13: 312- My '27 **1129**

Hentig, Hans von. Die biologischen Grundlagen der Jugendkriminalität. Monats f Kriminalpsychol u Strafrechtsref 19:705-20 D '28 **1130**

Hentig, Hans von. Fortpflanzungsphasen und Zurechnungsfähigkeit. Monats f Kriminalpsychol u Strafrechtsref 21: 149-60 Mr '30 **1131**

Physical changes are accompanied by psychical changes which affect the individual's social relations.

Hentig, H[ans] v. Die Kriminellen Tendenzen der Blinden. Schweiz Zeitsch f Strafr 40: 32-48 '27 **1132**

Hollander, B[ernard]. The criminal from brain disease. Criminologist [London] 1: 3-4 My 15 '27 **1133**

Ill-health as a factor in crime. Sol J 72: 277 Ap 28 '28 **1134**

Krasusky, W. S. Erfahrungen durch das Vergleichsstudium der Konstitutionseigenheiten bei normalen Kindern, jugendlichen Rechtsübertretern und psychisch kranken Kindern. Monats f Kriminalpsychol u Strafrechtsref 20: 76-85 F '29 **1135**

Leppman, Friedrich. Weibliche Generationsphasen und Kriminalität. Arch f Frauenk 14: 292-321 S '28 **1136**

[McIlroy, Louise]. The influence of parturition upon insanity and crime. L J [London] ns65: 214-15 Mr 10 '28 **1137**

Miller, Emanuel. Types of mind and body. 95p. N. Y. Norton, 1927 **1138**

Mönkemöller. Enzephalitis und Verbrechen. Psychiat-Neurol Wchnschr 31: 398-402 Ag 10 '29 **1139**

Morselli, E. La teoria sulle costituzione e l'opera di Cesare Lombroso. Arch di Antrop Crim 47: 851-2 S '27 **1140**

Ovanessoff, A. G. Postencephalitic psychic changes and criminality. Sovrem Psikhonevrol 10: 147-58 '30 **1141**

Perelmann, A. and Blinkow, S. Über einige Faktoren, welche die Verteilung der Körperbautypen bei den Schizophrenen, Kriminellen und Geistig-Gesunden beeinflussen (Zum Problem: Körperbau und Charakter). Arch f Psychiat 86: 501-24 '29 **1142**

Richmond, Frank C. Venereal disease and delinquency. Med-Leg J 44: 135-6 S '27 **1143**

Rothman, Philip E. Delinquency and disease. J Delin 11: 294-5 D '27 **1144**

Saporito, F. Tubercolosi i criminalità. Scuola Pos 37: 118-25 '29 **1145**

Seelig, E. Die psycho-diagnostische Ausdrucksregistrierung und ihre Verwendung in der Kriminologie. Psychol u Med 2: 210-14 '27 **1146**

Di Tullio, Benigno. Anlage und Kriminalität. Zeitsch f d ges Strafrechtswiss 50: 492-8 '30 **1147**

VanNuys, W. C. Epilepsy and delinquency. Ind Bul Char & Correc (180): 95-8 Mr '30 **1148**

Vervaeck. Les affections chroniques du nez et des sinus peuvent-elles déterminer des réactions psychiques et quelles est leur importance au point de médico-légal? Ann de Méd Lég 8: 90-5 F '28 **1149**

Vidoni, Giuseppe. Osservazioni su la costituzione somatica nei giovani anormali. Riv Sper di Freniat 50: 426-41 F '27 **1150**

Wood, T. D. Health and delinquency. Health Bul [North Carolina] 42: 12-16 Ap '27 **1151**

Endocrinology

Bauer, Julius. Innere sekretion; ihre physiologie, pathologie und klinik. 479p. bibliog 466-7. Berlin, Springer, 1927 **1153**

Bayer, Gustav and Velden, Reinhard von den, eds. Klinisches lehrbuch der Inkretologie und Inkretotherapie. 423p. Leipzig, Thieme, 1927 **1154**

"Literatur" at ends of chapters.

Berman, Louis. The glands regulating personality; a study of the glands of internal secretion in relation to the types of human nature. ed.2. 341p. N. Y. Macmillan, 1928 **1155**

Brownstein, Simon W. Battling with the gods: the bio-chemical basis of crime. Welf 18: 1413-29 N '27 **1156**

Chaneton, J. Adolfo. Neuva jurisprudencia sobre homicidio causado por extorsión inmoral continua y por factores endocrinos. R de Identif y Cienc Pen 5: 273-90 Ja '30 **1157**

Cobb, Ivo Geikie. The glands of destiny; a study of the personality. 295p. bibliog 288-90. London, W. Heineman, 1927 **1158**

Conti, E. Endocrinologia e criminalità. Scuola Pos ns7: 412-16 S '27 **1159**

Endocrine survey. Glendale, Calif. O '23-D '29// **1160**

Merged into Medical herald and physiotherapist.

Endocrinologia e patologia costituzionale. Roma, ns 1, 1926- **1161**

Endocrinology. Los Angeles, 1, 1917- **1162**

Bulletin of the Association for the study of internal secretions.

Endokrinologie; zentralblatt für das gebiet der innern Sekretion und Konstitutionsforschung. Leipzig, 1, 1928- **1163**

Faggioli, R. El porvenir de los criminales natos. Semana Méd 1: 1266-7 My 7 '31 **1164**

Foà, Carlo and Pende, Nicola. La fisiologia e la clinica degli increti. 180p. Milano, Istituto biochimico italiano [1927] **1165**

Guyer, Michael Frederic. The internal secretions and human well-being. Science ns 74 (1911): 159-66 Ag 14 '31 **1166**

Harding, John R. The endocrines in penal therapy. Am Pris Assn Proc 59: 256-64 '29; same title: M J & Rec 130: 610-13 D 4 '29 **1167**

Held, William. Sex glands and the whole man. Med-Leg J 44: 141-50 S '27 **1168**

Hunt, H. Lyons. Gland dysfunction and the criminal. Police J [N Y] 17: 20-1, 25 O '30 **1169**

Hunt, H. L[yons]. Relation of endocrine glands to crime. M R of R 33: 267-79 Je '27 **1170A**

Jiménez de Asúa, Luis. Libertad de amar y derecho a morir; ensayos de un criminalista sobre eugenisia, eutanasia, endocrinologia. 269p. Madrid, Historia nueva, 1928 **1170B**
"Notas" (including bibliog): 227-60.

Parhon, C. I. Constitutia somato-psichica si raporturile ei ou criminologia [endocrino e delinquenza]. R de Drept Pen (9-10): 465- '30 **1171**

Ray, Marie Beynon. Gland-made criminals. World's Wk 59: 49-50 Je '30 **1172**

Revue française d'endocrinologie. Paris, 1, 1923- **1173**

Ruiz-Funes, Mariano. Criminalidad y endocrinologia. 36p. Habana, Imp. y Lib. el Universo, 1928; same title: R Bimestre Cubana 24: 481-512 Jl '28 **1174**

Ruiz-Funes, Mariano. La criminalidad y las secreciones internas. Discurso leido en la Sesion de Apertura del Curso Academico 1927-28, Universidad Literaria de Murcia. 155p. Murcia, Imp. Sucesores de Nogués, 1927 **1175**

Ruiz-Funes, M[ariano]. Criminalità e endocrinologia. Riv di Psicol 24: 73-97 Ap '28 **1176**

Ruiz-Funes, Mariano. Endocrinologia y criminalidad. 352p. Madrid, Javier Morata, 1929 **1177**

Ruiz-Funes, Mariano. L'imputabilità parziale. 12p. Torino, Bocca, 1929; same title: Arch di Antrop Crim 50: 15 '30 **1178**
Endocrine basis of partial responsibility.

Schlapp, Max Gustav and Smith, Edward Henry. The new criminology; a consideration of the chemical causation of abnormal behavior. 325p. N.Y. Boni & Liveright, 1928 **1179**

Stockard, Charles Rupert. The physical basis of personality. 320p. bibliog 306-16. N.Y. W. W. Norton [c1931] **1180**

SEX AND CRIME

Burt, Cyril. Causes of sex delinquency in girls. J Soc Hyg 13: 109-14 F '27 **1181**

Ceillier, A. De l'influence des maladies vénériennes et des perturbations de la fonction sexuelle dans la genèse de l'impulsion exhibitionniste. Ann de Méd Lég 7: 190-2 Ap '27 **1182**

Does respectability demand vice? Chr Cent 48: 296-8 Mr 4 '31 **1183**

Galet. Recherches sur la délinquance sexuelle. Scalpel 80: 84-5 '27 **1184**

Gelma, E. Abus sexuel d'une jeune fils de 26 ans élève d'une école de Beaux-Arts et débile mentale. Ann de Méd Lég 8: 522-3 O '28 **1185**

Held, William. Sex and crime. Am Med 33: 216-19, 290-4 Ap, My '27; same title: Med-Leg J 44: 115-19 Jl '27 **1186**

Hirschfeld, Magnus. Geschlecht und Verbrechen. Bearb von Jakob Richard Spinner. 410p. Leipzig, Schneider, 1931 **1187**

Hoffmann, Walter and Stern, W[ilhelm]. Sittlichkeitsvergehen an höheren Schulen und ihre disziplinare Behandlung. 141p. Leipzig, Quelle & Meyer, 1928 **1188**

Johnson, Bascom. Social hygiene problems. N Y St Assn Magistrates Proc 20: 29-35 '28 **1189**

Kleinschmidt. Ein Fall von Sexualmord. Krimin Monatsh 2: 2-6 Ja '28 **1190**

Law and sex. Sol J 73: 590 S 14 '29 **1191**

Lind, W. A. T. The sex instinct and its disorders. M J Austral 14: 182-5 Ag 6 '27 **1192**

Lyhs, A. Geschlechtsleben und Kriminalität. 48p. Berlin, Deut. Polizeibuchhandl. u. Verlag, 1927 **1193**

MacWilliams, G. Sex perversion and its relation to crime. Detective 42: 3 Mr; 2 Ap; 2 Je '27 **1194**

Reuter, Fritz. Zwei interessante Fälle von Tötung aus sexuellen motiv. Deut Zeitsch f d ges gerichtl Med 9: 182-92 Ja '27 **1195**

Scheuer, O. F. Bibliographie der Sexualwissenschaft. Zeitsch f Sexualwissensch 14: 121-8, 234-40, 359-67, 469-76 Je '27-Mr '28; 15: 214-24, 436-48, 511-12, 593-7 Jl '28-Mr '29 **1196**

Schläger. Die Behandlung von Geschlechtskrankheiten. Krimin Monatsh 4: 44-5 F '30 **1197**

Sears, Florence and Witmer, Helen. Some possible motives in the sexual delinquency of children of adequate intelligence. Smith Coll Stud Soc Wk 2: 1-45 S '31 **1198**
Study of 40 cases referred to Illinois Institute for juvenile research because of sexual activity.

Strasser, C. Zur Psychotherapie der Sexualanomalien. Zeitsch f d ges Neurol u Psychiat 110: 528-48 '27 **1199**

ILLEGITIMACY

Canadian council on child welfare. Legislation, as of date January 1, 1929: Canada and her provinces; affecting the status and protection of the child of unmarried parents; comparative summary: [chart of legislative procedure]. 30p. (Pub nos46-46A) 1929 **1200**

Connecticut child welfare association. Study of children born out of wedlock in Connecticut. 48p. New Haven, The Association, 1927 **1201**

Cornas, Marie-Louise. La situation des enfants illégitimes à Lausanne. 18p. Zürich, Gutzwiller, 1930 **1202**

Donahue, A. Madorah. Children of illegitimate birth whose mothers have kept their custody. 105p. (Pub no190) Washington, U. S. Children's bureau, 1928 **1203**

Felber, Franz. Die Unehelichen im steirischen Gebirge. Zeitsch f Kinderschutz 22: 172-6 N '30 **1204**

Fleischer, Ludwig. Über das Schicksal der 1891-1905 in Düsseldorf geborenen unehelichen Kinder und ihrer Mütter. 26p. (Veröff. aus d. Gebiete d. Medizinalverwaltung 34, 7) Berlin, Schoetz, 1931 **1205**

Graham, Robert Blackwood Whidder and Read, Frederick. The law relating to corroboration in criminal and illegitimacy proceedings. Toronto, Carswell, 1928 **1206**

Hanauer. Uneheliche Geburten bei den Juden. Jahrb f Nationalökon u Statist s3 77: 902-11 Je '30 1207

Hecke, Wilhelm. Die Unehelichen in Österreich. Jahrb f Nationalökon u Statist s3 77: 572-91 Ap '30 1208

Illegitimacy in Europe. J Soc Hyg 13: 242-4 Ap '27 1209

Kenney, J. J. Illegitimacy under the Children's code. Marquette L R 14: 26-9 D '29 1210

League of Nations. Advisory commission for the protection and welfare of children and young people. Child welfare committee. Study of the position of the illegitimate child, based on the information communicated by governments. 107p. Geneva, 1929 (1929.IV.5) 1211

Liebhold, Trude. Die Reform der Rechtsstellung des unehelichen Kindes als Problem der Rechtsangleichung mit Österreich. 136p. (Heidelberger rechtswiss. Abh 11) Heidelberg, Winter, 1930 1212

Lowe, C. The intelligence and social background of the unmarried mother. Ment Hyg 11: 783-94 '27 1213
Study of 344 unmarried mothers.

McClure, W. E. and Goldberg, Bronett. Intelligence of unmarried mothers. Psychol Clin 18: 119-27 My '29; 20: 154-7 O '31 1214

Myers, Earl D. Provision for the illegitimate child in Germany. Soc Serv R 5: 258-75 Je '31 1215

Preston, Clarence R. Good care of unmarried mothers as an important phase of preventive and protective work. J Soc Hyg 17: 94-8 F '31 1216

Prettenhofer, Emerich. Die Rechtsstellung des unehelichen Kindes in den Kulturstaaten. Soz Praxis 39: 1175-80 D 11 '30 1217

Rentrop, Ernst. Die unehelichen Kinder. 135p. (Beitr z Jugendhilfe 12) Berlin, Heymann, 1931 1218

Schumacher, H. C. The unmarried mother: a socio-psychiatric viewpoint. Ment Hyg 11:775-82 '27 1219

Skeehan, Elizabeth Anne. The unmarried mother. 85p. Thesis (M. A.) University of Pittsburgh, 1930 1220

Smill, Eva. Unmarried mothers. Family 9: 240-2 N '28 1221

Stück, Hans. Das Recht der unehelichen Kinder im 19. Jahrhundert unter Berücksichtigung der in diese zeit fallenden Reformbestrebungen. 69p. Jena, Neuenhan, 1931 1222

Tamforde, Hans. Das Recht des unehelichen Kindes und seiner Mutter im In- und Ausland. Neu Bearb von Friedrich Diefenbach und Heinrich Webler. 3. vollst. umgearb.Aufl. 246p. Berlin, Heymann, 1930 1223

Die Unehelichen Geburten im hamburgischen Staat 1905 bis 1929. Aus Hamburgs Verwaltung u Wirtschaft 8: 105-9 Je 15 '31 1224

Prostitution

Acuna, Chile. Women for sale. 201p. N.Y. Godwin, 1931 1225

Albrecht, Hans. Die Prostitution in Berlin. Monats f Kriminalpsychol u Strafrechtsref 21: 171-8 Mr '30 1226

Albrecht, Hans. Die weibliche Prostitution in Berlin. Freie Wohlfahrtspfl 4: 514-19 F '30 1227

Anstice, E. H. Licensed prostitution in Japan: complete abolition versus regulation. Chinese Nation 2: 287-8 Ag 12 '31 1228

Bénech, J. Bilan de la syphilis chez les prostituées. Ann des Mal Vén 26: 721-7 O '31 1229

Bénech, J. Causes de la prostitution. Prophylax Antivén 1: 712-33 D '29 1230

Bizard, L. Au sujet de la syphilis. Bul Méd [Paris] 45: 93-5 F 14 '31 1231
Syphilis in prostitutes in Paris.

Bizard, Léon. L'extension de la prostitution; ses causes et ses remèdies. Acad d Sci Morales et Pol Compt Rend 90: 147-63 Ja '30; same title: Prophylax Antivén 2: 758-61 D '30 1232

Bowler, Alida C. Social factors promoting prostitution. J Soc Hyg 17: 477-81 N '31 1233

Brian-Chaninov, N. La prostitution dans l'Union Sovietique. Mercure Fr 228: 589-99 Je 15 '31 1234

Clemenceau, G. La prostitution. Prophylax Antivén 2: 1-9 Ja '30 1235

Dewalt, D. C. Clandestine prostitution. Tex St J Med 25: 656-8 F '30 1236

Documents pour servir à l'histoire de la réglementation de la prostitution en France. Prophylax Antivén 2: 539-60 S '30 1237

Gougerot, H. and Burnier. L'accroissement continu de la syphilis. Prophylax Antivén 1: 231-4 Ap '29 1238

Hannich, W. Werkstätten und Fabriken als Keimstätten von Prostitution und Geschlechtskrankheiten. Zeitsch f Gewerbe-Hyg 34: 24, 40 F 15, 29 '28 1239

Kirchhoff, Auguste. Kultur und Prostitution. Neue Generation 23: 115-23 Ap '27 1240

Lacassagne, Jean and Pigeaud, H. Avortements grossesses et fonctions maternelles chez les prostituées. Ann des Mal Vén 25: 251-63 Ap '30 1241

Lacroix, Paul. The history of prostitution; translated by Samuel Putnam. 2v. N.Y. Covici Friede, 1931 1242

Lai, D. G. and Chang, T. S. Syphilis and prostitution in Kiangsu; preliminary report. China Med J 44: 558-63 Je '30 1243

Landesco, John. The exploitation of prostitution. (*In* Illinois association for criminal justice, Illinois crime survey, 845-63, 1929) 1244

Lombroso, C. and Ferrero, G. La donna delinquente, la prostituta e la donna normale. ed. 5. 502p. Torino, Bocca, 1927 1245

Luisi, P. Algunas consideraciones sobre prostitución y enfermedades venéreas. Cons Nac de Hig Bol 25: 410-43 Je '31 **1246**

Martell, P. Zur Geschichte der Prostitution der Stadt Berlin. Zeitsch f Sexualwissensch 16: 133-45 My 22 '29 **1247**

Minami, S. and Loewenstein, G. Prostitution und Geschlechtskrankheiten in Japan. Deut Gesell z Bekämpf d Geschlechtskrankh Mitt 25: 41-50 My 1 '27 **1248**

Pan, Quentin. Browbeating prostitution? China Critic 1: 313-16 S 13 '28 **1249**

Picton, Werner. Male prostitution in Berlin. Howard J 3: 89-92 '31 **1250**

Rabut, R. Morale et prostitution. Prophylax Antivén 3: 570-6 S '31 **1251**

Richard, Gaston. Urbanisme et prostitution. R Int de Soc 38: 327-31 My '30 **1252**

Robinson, William Josephus. The oldest profession in the world: prostitution, its underlying causes, its treatment and its future. 100p. N.Y. Eugenics pub. co. 1929 **1253**

Roeschmann. Die Prostitutionsfrage. Deut Med Wchnschr 55: 2146-8 D 20 '29 **1254**

Schemnitz, R. Prostituzione e tubercolosi. Gazz Internaz Med-Chir 37: 163, 191, 219, 263, 291 '29 **1255**

Schidlof, Berthold. Prostitution und Mädchenhandel. Eine zeitgeschichtl. Untersuchung. 326p. (Neue Studien z Geschichte d sexuellen Verirrungen, 1) Leipzig, Lykeion, 1931 **1256**

Scoseria, J. La prostitución clandestina en los cabarets. Cons Nac de Hig Bol 24: 467-72 O '29 **1257**

Scott, Franz, ed. Die Prostitution. ed. 4 96p. Leipzig, Asa-Verl. 1930 **1258**

Vidoni, Giuseppe. Prostitutas y prostitución. 168p. Madrid, Morata, 1930 **1259**

Villavicencio, V. Otros aspectos de la prostitucion Peruana. Bol de Crimin [1] (7): 565-78 '28 **1260**

Voina, A. La prostitución y las enfermedades venereas en Rumania. Crón Méd-Quir de la Habana 56: 363 Ag '30 **1261**

Traffic in Women

Everett, Ray H. International traffic in women and children. J Soc Hyg 13: 269-88 My '27 **1262**

Johnson, Bascom. International traffic in women and children; the inquiry of the Special body of experts on Traffic in women and children appointed by the Council of the League of Nations. J Soc Hyg 14: 65-75 '28; same title: Police J [N Y] 16: 4-5 Mr '29 **1263**

Kundt, E. Mädchenhandel und Bordelle. Deut Gesell z Bekämpf d Geschlechtskrankh Mitt 27: 83-6 Mr '29 **1264**

League of Nations. Advisory commission for the protection and welfare of children and young people. Traffic in women and children committee. Minutes, 1, 1922- Boston, World Peace Foundation **1265**

L.N. Committee no.IV (Social Questions) publications contain much valuable material on traffic in women.

Londres, Albert. Road to Buenos Ayres; translated by Eric Sutton. 251p. N.Y. Boni & Liveright, 1928 **1266**

Maus, Isidore. L'enquête de la Société des Nations sur la traite des femmes et des enfants. R de Dr Pén et de Crimin 8: 366-80, 477-87 '28 **1267**

Owen, Frank. Fighting the traffic in women. World Tomorrow 11: 79-80 F '28 **1268**

Riddell, William Renwick. A half-told story of real white slavery in the seventeenth century. J Crim L & Crimin 21: 247-56 Ag '30 **1269**

Schlanbusch. Auslandreisen weiblicher Artisten als besondere Form des Mädchenhandels. Krimin Monatsh 5: 2-4 Ja '31 **1270**

Schneider, Fritz. Der Mädchenhandel und seine Bekämpfung, insbesondere nach schweizerischem Recht. 239p. Aarau, Verl. H. R. Sauerländer, 1929 **1271**

United States. Library of Congress. White slave act: a list of bibliographical references. 6p. (typw) [Washington] January 17, 1930 **1272**

Vice Commissions

Lewis, Leslie. Survey of a vice district in the Middle West. J Soc Hyg 13: 93-6 F '27 **1273**

New York (city.) Committee of fourteen. Annual reports, 1927-30 **1274**

Committee disbanded in 1932.

Sumner, J. S. The New York society for the suppression of vice. Pub W 117: 2516-18 My 17 '30 **1275**

Three views of a years work; by Charles E. Miner, Kate J. Adams, and Albert W. Palmer. J Soc Hyg 14: 139-47 Mr '28 **1276**

Addresses delivered at annual meeting of Chicago, Committee of fifteen, 1928.

SOCIAL CONDITIONS AND CRIME

Avé-Lallemant. Die persönlichen und sozialen Verhältnisse des Gaunertums. Krimin Monatsh 1: 122-6 Je '27 **1277**

Brown, L. Guy. Social causes and cures for delinquency. Nat Prob Assn Proc 24: 9-30 '30 **1278**

Bruce, H. Addington. If we really would lessen crime. Cent 117: 471-8 '29 **1279**

Burling, Lancaster D. Stages of evolution and relation to crime. Sci M 24: 431-9 '27 **1280**

Coatsworth, E. Motor-car as a crime breeder. Can B R 6: 253-6 Ap '28 **1281**

Frede. Hinrichtung als Mordsuggestion. Monats f Kriminalpsychol u Strafrechtsref 19: 252-3 Ap '28 **1282**

H[erzog], A[lfred] W. Disrespect for law and the increase of crime; editorial. Med-Leg J 47: 65-7 My '30 **1283**

Lawless America. R of R 80: 64-5 Jl '29 **1284**

Lind, Andrew W. Some ecological patterns of community disorganization in Honolulu. Am J Sociol 36: 206-20 '30 **1285**

Mendum, Gladys. Conditions breeding delinquency in rural communities. Nat Conf Soc Wk Proc 54: 143-51 '27 **1286**

Motor car as crime factor. Am B Assn J 15: 326 Je '29 **1287**

Moxon, Cavendish. Antisocial attitudes, their formation and reformation. Ment Hyg 13: 542-9 Je '29 **1288**

Nelken, S[igmund]. Publikum und Verbrechen. 184p. Berlin, R. Mosse, 1928 **1289**

Neumann, Henry. The revolt of modern youth. Standard [Am Ethical Union] 13: 167-74 F '27 **1290**

Shaw, Clifford R. Delinquency and the social situation. Rel Educ 24: 409-17 My '29; same title: Ind Bul Char & Correc (180): 98-107 Mr '30 **1291**

Thrasher, Frederic M. The group factor; an element to be reckoned with in the causation and treatment of juvenile delinquency. Welf Mag 18: 141-7, 314-18 F, Mr '27 **1292**

Van Waters, Miriam. Why Hickman hangs. Survey 61: 20-3, 252-3 O 1, N 15 '28 **1293**

Cultural Conflicts

Allport, Floyd H. Culture conflict and delinquency: II: Culture conflict versus the individual as factors in delinquency. Soc Forces 9: 493-7 Je '31 **1294**

Brandl, Franz. Weltanschauung und Kriminalität. Zeitsch f Rel-Psychol 3: 26-56 '30 **1295**

Handman, Max Sylvius. Nationality and delinquency: the Mexicans in Texas. Nat Conf Soc Wk Proc 1930: 133-45 **1296**

Hentig, Hans von. Inveterationserscheinungen bei europaïschen Bevölkerungsgruppen und ihre kriminologische Bedeutung. Monats f Kriminalpsychol u Strafrechtsref 18: 30-3 Ja '27 **1297**

Lellep, Constantin. Der Einfluss der Rasse auf die Kriminalität der Esten. Monats f Kriminalpsychol u Strafrechtsref 18: 144-50 bibliog [p150] Mr '27 **1298**

Meyer, E. Der Einfluss der Kultur auf das Menschengeschlecht. Deut Med Wchnschr 52: 1-2 Ja 1 '27 **1299**

Miner, John Rice. Nativity and parentage of population of United States and homicide rate. Human Biol 1: 274-8 My '29 **1300**

Santee, J. F. Nationality and crime in the United States. Educ 50: 261-70 Ja '30 **1301**

Todd, T. Wingate. Culture conflict and delinquency: III: Culture conflict and physical inadequacy as bases for misconduct. Soc Forces 9: 497-9 Je '31 **1302**

Wassermann, Rudolf. Die Kriminalität der Juden. Monats f Kriminalpsychol u Strafrechtsref 19: 461-74 Ag '28 **1303**

Williams, Tom A. Racial factors in delinquency. Med-Leg J 47: 114-17 S '30 **1304**

Wirth, Louis. Culture conflict and delinquency: I: Culture conflict and misconduct. Soc Forces 9: 484-92 Je '31 **1305**

Young, Pauline V[islick]. Jim's mother; study in conflict of cultures. Survey 59: 506-8 Ja 15 '28 **1306**

Young, Pauline V[islick]. Jim's own story. Survey 59: 777-8 Mr 15 '28 **1307**

IMMIGRATION

Alien and crime. New Repub 68: 59 S 2 '31 **1308**

Bowler, Alida C. Law enforcement and the alien: recent statistics on crime and the foreign born. Nat Conf Soc Wk Proc 1931: 479-94 **1309**

Carpenter, Niles and Haenszel, William M. Migratoriness and criminality in Buffalo Soc Forces 9: 254-5 D '30 **1310**

Fairchild, Henry Pratt. Immigration and crime. Eugen N 15: 5-7 Ja '30 **1311**
Address before Galton Society, New York, December 6, 1929.

Hacker, Ervin. Criminality and immigration. J Crim L & Crimin 20: 428-38 N '29 **1312**

Hacker, Ervin. Kriminalitás és Bevándorlás. 270p. Budapest, Dunántúl Egyltemi nyomdája Pécsett, 1929 **1313**

Hacker, Erwin. Kriminalität und Einwanderung. Bl f Gefängniskunde 59: 25-31 '28 **1314**

Kirchwey, George W. Crime among the foreign born. Minn St Conf & Inst Soc Wk Proc 37: 195-9 '29 **1315**

Miller, Joseph. Foreign born parentage and social maladjustment. Psychol Clin 19: 19-25 Mr '30 **1316**

National commission on law observance and enforcement. Report on crime and the foreign born. 416p. (No10) Washington, June 24, 1931 **1317**
Abbott, Edith. The problem of crime and the foreign born; Bowler, Alida C. Recent statistics on crime and the foreign born; Taylor, Paul S. The problem of the Mexican; Handman, Max S. Preliminary report on nationality and delinquency: the Mexican in Texas; Warnshuis, Paul L. Crime and criminal justice among the Mexicans of Illinois; Steiner, Jesse F. Crime and the foreign born: New Orleans; Taylor, Paul S. Crime and the foreign born: San Francisco; Taylor, Paul S. Crime and the foreign born: Stockton, Calif.

Orebaugh, David A. Crime, degeneracy and immigration; their interrelations and interreactions. 272p. Boston, Badger, 1929 **1318**

Sutherland, E. H. Is there undue crime among immigrants? Nat Conf Soc Wk Proc 54: 572-9 '27 **1319**

THE NEGRO

Brearley, H. C. The Negro and homicide. Soc Forces 9: 247-53 D '30 **1320**

Cantor, Nathaniel. Crime and the Negro. J Negro Hist 16: 61-6 Ja '31 **1321**

Griggs, Sutton. The Negro today. Nat Prob Assn Proc 1928: 352-60 **1322**

Reid, Ira DeA. Social conditions of the Negro in the Hill district of Pittsburgh. 117p. Pittsburgh, General committee on the Hill survey, 1930 **1323**

Recommendations and factual data resulting from a survey of the 3d and 5th wards, Pittsburgh, made June-September 1929, including delinquency, prostitution, juvenile delinquency, parole, courts, etc.

Rucker, Alvin Maceo. The social and economic status of Negro boys discharged from Thorn Hill school. 6p. (typw) Pittsburgh, Federation of social agencies, 1930 **1324**

Sellin, Thorsten. The Negro criminal. Ann Am Acad 140: 52-64 N '28 **1325**

Sellin, Thorsten. El Negro criminal. Una nota estadística. R de Identif y Cienc Pen 5: 115-33 N '29 **1326**

Wall, Peter T. Criminality among Negroes in Chicago: its causes and results. Thesis (M.A.) Northwestern university, 1927 **1327**

Washington, Forrester B. Negro survey of Pennsylvania. 97p. Harrisburg, Pennsylvania Department of welfare, 1927 **1328**

Chap. x: crime among the Negroes in Pa.; table showing disposition of 3,842 Negro arrests, 1924; table showing Negro population of institutions, 1924-1919-1914.

Work, Monroe N. comp. A bibliography of the Negro in Africa and America. 698p. N.Y. Wilson, 1928 **1329**

Items on Ku Klux Klan; Negro and crime; convict systems and Negro; Negro juvenile delinquency; Negro and lynching.

Education

Bagley, William Chandler. Education, crime and social progress. 165p. N. Y. Macmillan, 1931 **1330**

Banks, William. Crime and education in Canada. Police J [London] 3: 176-84 Ap '30 **1331**

Dearborn, Frances. What does honesty mean to third and fourth grade children? A study in citizenship. J Educ Meth 6: 205-12 Ja '27 **1332**

Education, environment and the criminal. Nature 126: 45-7 Jl 12 '30 **1333**

Die erzieherische Beeinflussung straffälliger Jugendlicher. 68p. Berlin, F. A. Herbig, 1927 **1334**

Forbes, A. W. Is education responsible for the crime wave? Educ 48: 487-91 Ap '28 **1335**

Johnson, Eleanor Hope. School maladjustment and behavior. Ment Hyg 11: 558-69 Jl '27 **1336**

Johnson, F. E. Crime and education. Homiletic R 96: 280-1 O '28 **1337**

Kendall, Carlton. Does American education produce criminals? Overland & Out West ns89: 7-8 N '31 **1338**

Krawczyk, Monica. Over-age! Educ 51: 462-6 Ap '31 **1339**

McAndrew, William. Westchester jury jolts the schools. Sch & Soc 32: 771-5 D 6 '30 **1340**

McDonald, S. Education and crime. Chief Constables Assn Can Proc 24: 35-9 '28 **1341**

Mercer, Mary L. School maladjustment as a factor in juvenile delinquency. J Juv Res 14: 41-2 Ja '30 **1342**

Myers, Garry Cleveland. Crime and the schools. Sch Exec Mag 50: 557-8 Ag '31 **1343**

Owens, Albert A. Behavior-problem boys and the curriculum. J Educ 111: 151-3 F 10 '30 **1344**

Palmquist, T. R. School's responsibility in the problem of crime. Kan Teach & W Sch J 30: 7-16 N '29 **1345**

Parkinson, William D. Problems for research: schooling and crime. J Educ 110: 408-9 N 11 '29 **1346**

Sacher, Frederick R. The relation of our educational system to delinquency. N Y St Assn Magistrates Proc 22: 50-8 '30 **1347**

Storey, George J. Crime, education, and the man from Mars. Pac Police Mag 6: 7, 21, 27 Je '29 **1348**

Stryker, Sue B. Undergrading as a cause for delinquency—report of a case. Sch & Soc 26: 821-2 D 24 '27 **1349**

Home Conditions

Armstrong, Clairette P. Why boys desert their homes. 236p. Thesis (Ph.D.) New York university, 1931 **1350**

Case study of conditions in lives of boys in N.Y.C. who desert their homes.

Beisser, Paul T. The social workers' problem—unsatisfactory and inadequate matrimonial and parental relationship. Nat Conf Juv Agencies Proc 27: 77-85 '30 **1351**

Blanchard, Phyllis. The family situation and personality development. Ment Hyg 11: 15-22 Ja '27 **1352**

Blanchard, Phyllis and Paynter, Richard H. Socio-psychological status of children from marginal families. Family 8: 3-10 Mr '27 **1353**

Brinton, Hugh P. jr. Family and child welfare in Pennsylvania, 1921-1926. 42p. Philadelphia, Committee on philanthropic labor, 1927 **1354**

Caldwell, Morris Gilmore. The economic status of families of delinquent boys in Wisconsin. Am J Sociol 37: 231-9 S '31 **1355**

Study of 492 cases at Wisconsin Industrial School, Waukesha, Wis.

Caldwell, Morris Gilmore. Home conditions of institutional delinquent boys in Wisconsin. Soc Forces 8: 390-7 Mr '30 **1356**

Cowan, Lillian S. Environmental conflicts in the family and social life of the modern child. Nat Conf Soc Wk Proc 1927: 291-4 **1357**

Crosby, Sarah B. A study of Alameda county delinquent boys with special emphasis upon the group coming from broken homes. J Juv Res 13: 220-30 Jl '29 **1358**

Duffy, Alice E. The modern home. Minn St Conf & Inst Soc Wk Proc 37: 228-37 '29 1359

Address before Minnesota and northwest association of policewomen.

Family's failure in flood of crime. Va L Reg ns12: 731-4 Ap '27 1360

Goodenough, Florence and Leahy, Alice M. The effect of certain family relationships upon the development of personality. Pedag Sem 34: 45-71 Mr '27 1361

Harper, Roland M. Divorce and crime on Prince Edward Island. Eugen 3: 182-91 My '30 1362

Khalfin, V. Zhilischnii vopros i imushchestvennaya prestupnost v gorodakh RSFSR. Problemy Prestupnosti (4): 19-23 '29 1363

Lombroso, Gina. Les crimes contre les parents et l'influence de la femme. R de Dr Pén et de Crimin 7: 737-41 Jl '27 1364

McKinney, D. Domestic differences. Chief Constables Assn Can Proc 25: 122-6 '29 1365

Miller, Ruth Scott. Divorce and child crime. Ladies Home J 44: 26 Mr '27 1366

Moulton, Bryant E. Some causes of delinquency in relation to family attitudes. Am J Orthopsychiat 1: 173-7 Ja '31 1367

Mowrer, Ernest R. Family disorganization. 317p. Chicago, Univ. of Chicago press, 1927 1368

Study of desertion, divorce and non-support in Chicago.

Postma, H. De samenstelling van het gezin in verband met het anti-sociaal gedrag van het meisje. Mensch & Maatschappij 7: 258-74 My '31 1369

Study of 1,691 girls in institutions for female juvenile delinquents in Netherlands.

Quiroga, Roberto Solis. La familia anti-social y la delincuencia juvenil. R Mexicana de Der Pen 1: 61-70 Jl '30 1370

Study of 2,291 juvenile delinquents before juvenile court of Mexico City, 1927-29.

Schneickert, Hans. Ehe und Kriminalität. Krimin Monatsh 1: 157-8 Jl '27 1371

Schumacher, Henry C. Environmental conflicts in the family and social life of the modern child. Nat Conf Soc Wk Proc 1927: 281-6; same title: Hosp Soc Serv 16: 299-306 O '27 1372

Theodorowitsch, M. Schilistnijo Usslowija i Prestupnost. (Wohnverhältnisse und Kriminalität). Abdruck aus der Serie: "Studienüber die Kriminalität im Nordkaukasus." Arbeiten des Medico-kriminologischen Instituts zu Rostow am Don, Heft 3-4. Rostow am Don, 1928 1373

Wolff, Gottlieb. Der Einfluss der Ehe auf die Kriminalität des Mannes. 42p. Diss. Leipzig. Berlin, Ebering, 1927 1374

Study covers 1908-17.

NEGLECT

Bappert, J. Die Beziehung der Verwahrlosung zur jeweiligen Gemeinschaftsform. Ein Versuch zur rechten Begriffsbestimmung der Verwahrlosung. Freie Wohlfahrtspfl 1: 193-203 '27 1375

Franceschi, Gustavo J. La familia en el abandono y la delincuencia infantil. Museo Soc Arg Bol 19: 461-70 O '31 1376

Heller, D. Th. Extreme Verwahrlosungsfälle aus einwandfreiem Milieu. Monats f Kriminalpsychol u Strafrechtsref 19: 117-21 F '28 1377

Krawczyk, Monica D. Relation of neglect to delinquency, case presentation II. Minn St Conf & Inst Soc Wk Proc 36: 155-62 '28 1378

McNamara, Frances. Relation of community neglect to delinquency. Minn St Conf & Inst Soc Wk Proc 35: 206-8 '27 1379

McNamara, Marie. Relation of neglect to delinquency, case presentation I. Minn St Conf & Inst Soc Wk Proc 36: 140-51 '28 1380

Leisure

Hoffer, C. Russell. Leisure and delinquency. Rural Am 5: 3 My '27 1381

Laziness as a cause of crime. Organized Lab 29 (35): 112 S 1 '28 1382

McGovern, John T. More athletics, fewer crimes. Playground 21: 84-7 My '27 1383

Platt, Charles. Leisure and crime. Playground 21: 142-6 Je '27 1384

MOTION PICTURES

Aguirre, E. El factor cinematográfico en la delincuencia infantil. Bol de Crimin 2: 245-54 '29 1385

Crime and the cinema in the United States. Int R Educ Cinematog 1: 303-414 S '29 1386

Fleming, Peter. Cinema: more crime. Spectator [London] 147: 292 S 5 '31 1387

Hellwig, Albert. Cinematógrafo y criminología. R de Crimin, Psiquiat y Med Leg 17: 224-37 Mr '30 1388

Jacquillard, R. La cinématographe et l'enfance criminelle. R Int de l'Enf 9: 32-40 Jl '30 1389

Jiménez de Asúa, Luis. Cinematógrafo y delincuencia. R de Crimin, Psiquiat y Med Leg 16: 377-84 My '29 1390

Joy, Jason S. Motion pictures and crime. Inst Police Adm Proc [1]: 42-50 '29 1391

Lorentz, Pare. Moral racketeering in the movies. Scribner's 88: 256-62 S '30 1392

Pitkin, Walter Boughton. Screen crime vs. press crime. Outl 158: 398-9 Jl 29 '31 1393

Roubinovitch, J. and Schiff, P. Tentative d'homicide par un débile sous l'influence d'une suggestion obsédante d'origine cinématographique. Hyg Ment 22: 156-8 D '27 1394

Simon, Carleton. Crime and the motion picture. Police J [N Y] 16: 20-1, 28 Jl '28 1395

Thót, László. El cinematógrafo y la criminalidad juvenil. 34p. Lima, Imp. A. J. Rivas Berrio, 1927; also: Rev Univ [Universidad mayor de San Marcos] 2: [983]-1016 '26 **1396**

RECREATION

Butcher, William Lewis. What are and what should be the relations of recreation to delinquency: community causes of crime. N Y St Conf Prob Offic Proc 21: 209-22 '28 **1397**

A crime incubation center is uncovered by survey. Am City 43: 144 D '30 **1398**
Indianapolis recreation survey.

Hammer, Lee F. The relation of public recreation to delinquency. Am City 40: 119-20 Ja '29; same title: Munic R 25: 101-2 Mr '29 **1399**

Sullenger, Thomas Earl. Determinants of delinquency in the play group. Playground 24: 431-4 N '30 **1400**

Thrasher, Frederic M. The scientific approach to recreation and delinquency. N Y St Conf Prob Offic Proc 21: 222-32 '28 **1401**

Mysticism

Costedoat, André. La criminalité mystique dans les sociétés modernes; discussion du rapport. Ann de Méd Lég 10: 125- Mr '30; 11: 1-14 Ja '31 **1402**

Dalla Volta, Amedeo. Superstizione e criminalità sessuale. Rassegna di Stud Sess 9: 157-66 '29 **1403**

Hellwig, Albert. Okkultismus und Verbrechen. Eine Einführung in die kriminalistischen Probleme des Okkultismus für Polizeibeamte, Richter, Staatsanwälte, Psychiater und Sachverständige. 408p. Berlin, Langenscheidt, 1929 **1404**

Kirk, R. T. F. Crime and superstitution in India. Edin R 247: 245-61 Ap '28 **1405**

Peacock, F. Witchcraft and its effect on crime in East Africa. Police J [London] 2: 121-31 '29 **1406**

Roe, H. R. Superstition and crime in India. Police J [London] 3: 1-10 Ja '30 **1407**

Newspapers and Literature

Behr, Detloff von. Statistiches zum Thema Pornographie. Zeitsch f Sexualwissensch 14: 167-78 Ag '27 **1408**

Bent, Silas. Newspapermen—partners in crime? Scribner's 88: 520-6 N '30 **1409**

Bent, Silas. The press and crime. *In* Ballyhoo; the voice of the press, 190-7. N.Y. Boni, 1927 **1410**

Bent, Silas. Scarlet journalism. Scribner's 84: 563-9 N '28 **1411**

Cole, Virginia Lee. Newspaper and crime. 84p. (Bul v28 no4 Journalism ser no44) Columbia, Univ. of Missouri, 1927 **1412**

Crime and publicity. New Statesman & Nation 1: 380 My 9 '31 **1413**

Crime news in the press. Science ns73: supl4 Ja 23 '31 **1414**

Dewey, Ernest A. Crime and the press. Commonweal 15: 231-3 D 30 '31 **1415**

Dorland, W. A. Newman. Influence of the newspaper; a plea for better journalism. Welf Mag 18: 557-69 My '27 **1416**

Further study in newspaper practice; with texts of Chicago tribune editorial. Chr Cent 46: 736-8, 756-7 Je 5 '29 **1417**

Gault, Robert H. An observation on publicity *re* notorious crimes. J Crim L & Crimin 18: 495-6 F '28 **1418**

Harris, Frank. The presentation of crime in the newspaper. Thesis (Ph.D.) University of Minnesota, 1931 **1419**
An examination of 3 Minneapolis newspapers for years 1890, 1905, and 1921.

Harris, Frank. The selective factor in the presentation of crime news. Am Sociol Soc Proc 25: 163-6 '30 **1420**
Study of Minneapolis newspapers.

Hellwig, Albert. Ein Beitrag zur Frage der Gerichtsberichterstattung. Monats f Kriminalpsychol u Strafrechtsref 21: 321-3 '30 **1421**

Herschfield, Alex S. The newspaper moron. Welf Mag 18: 435-7 Ap '27 **1422**

Highfill, Robert D. The effects of news of crime and scandal upon the public opinion. Am L R 62: 13-93 Ja '28 **1423**

Hoffmann, Walter. Schundliteratur und Schundfilm. Ein Beitrag zur Psychologie des Jugendlichen. Zeitsch f pädagog Psychol 28: 284-95 Je '27 **1424**

Holmes, Joseph L. Crime and the press. J Crim L & Crimin 20: 6-59, 246-93 My, Ag '29 **1425**

Hutchinson, P. Aurora killing; a study in newspaper practice. Chr Cent 46: 641-7 My 15 '29 **1426**

Justice endangered by sensational press. Am Jud Soc J 11: 50-2 Ag '27 **1427**

Kelchner, Mathilde and Lau, Ernst. Die Berliner Jugend und die Kriminalliteratur. Eine Untersuchung auf Grund von Aufsätzen Jugendlicher. 110p. (Beihefte Zeitschrift f ang Psychol 42) Leipzig, Barth, 1928 **1428**

Kline, Chester M. The press, police and crime. Inst Police Adm Proc [1]: 50-4 '29 **1429**

M., J. P. Press reports of judicial proceedings. Notre Dame Law 3: 39-41 O '27 **1430**

Martens, Kurt. Psychopathie und strafrechtliche Bedeutung unzüchtiger Abbildungen. Zeitsch f Sexualwissensch 18: 17-23 My 30 '31 **1431**

Martin, Kingsley. Crime and the newspapers. Pol Q 2: 428-32 Jl '31 **1432**

Mayo, Morrow. Glorifying the criminal. Commonweal 14: 438-9, 462-4 S 9, 16 '31 **1433**

Newspaper criminals in Chicago. Nation [N Y] 131: 88-9 Jl 23 '30 **1434**

Newspaper publication of sex crimes. Police J [N Y] 16: 10-11 O '28 **1435**

Newspapers and the cult of crime. Can B R 6: 205 Mr '28 **1436**

Newspapers as breeders of criminals. Educ R 75: 186 Ap '28 **1437**

Perrin, Frank L. Publicity and crime. Am Pris Assn Proc 59: 145-52 '29; same title: Nat Prob Assn Proc 1930: 248-50 **1438**

The press and crime. Sol J 73: 653 O 12 '29 **1439**

Prudhomme, H. La liberté de diffusion des idées et des opinions en Roumanie. R Pénitent et de Dr Pén 51: 295-320 My '27 **1440**

Relation of daily press to crime and the administration of justice. Am B Assn J 13: 390-7 Jl '27 **1441**

Rice, Thomas S. How to make crime news constructive. Police J [N Y] 16: 12-14 Mr '29 **1442**

Rice, Thomas S. Increase in "torch murders" not due to publishing crime news. Police J [N Y] 17: 5 S '29 **1443**

S[asserath], S. Moins de publicité. R de Dr Pén et de Crimin 8: 183-4 F '28 **1444**

Sherriff, Andrew R. Cooperation of press and bar to date. Am B Assn J 13: 130-2 Mr '27 **1445**

Taft, Charles P. 2d. So this is justice! See what newspapers and juries have done to it. World's Wk 56: 95-8 My '28 **1446**

A Veteran Journalist. Newspaper criminals in Chicago. Nation [N Y] 131: 88-9 Jl 23 '30 **1447**
Jake Lingle and others.

Watts, Harvey M. The fourth estate and court procedure as a public show. J Crim L & Crimin 19: 15-29 My '28 **1448**

Wilkinson, Lupton A. Divine rights of newspapers. N Am R 230: 610-16 N '30 **1449**

Williams, A. F. Crime and the press; address. Kan St B Assn Proc 1929: 113-19 **1450**

Religion

Bates, Sanford. Crime and Christianity. Ind Bul Char & Correc (165): 503-14 D '28 **1451**

Hacker, Ervin. Der Einfluss der Konfession auf die Kriminalität in Ungarn. 45p. Miskolc, Jun, Judvig & Janovits, 1930 **1452**

Miner, John R. Church membership and commitments of prisoners. Human Biol 3: 429-36 S '31 **1453**

Thümmel, W. Das neue Strafgesetzbuch und die Religions-vergehen. 37p. Tübingen, Mohr, 1927 **1454**

Thümmel, W. Der Religionsschutz durch das Strafrecht. ed. 2. 68p. Jena, Frommansche, 1927 **1455**

Social Heritage in Groups and Families

Clay, William M. and Wilcox, E. Mead. Five generations of an inferior family. J Hered 18: 121-3 Mr '27 **1456**

Leyen, Ruth von der. Darstellung einer "Verbrecher-familie." Zeitsch f Kinderforsch 37: 220-82 Ag '30 **1457**

Moran, Frederick A. Is there a unit cause for crime? The Gay family vs. Society. Cath Char 11: 125-8 Ap '27 **1458**

Urbanization

Thompson, John Giffin. The moral consequences of urbanization. *In his* Urbanization, its effects on government and society, 479-508. N.Y. Dutton, 1927 **1459**
Intemperance, vice and immorality, crime and criminality, the divorce problem.

Watts, Reginald E. The influence of population density on crime. Am Statist Assn J 26: 11-20 Mr '31 **1460**
Study of crime in Canada, 1891 to 1929.

Young, Pauline Vislick. Urbanization as a factor in juvenile delinquency. Am Sociol Soc Proc 24: 162-6 '29 **1461**

War

Calbirac, G. Les répercussions de la Grande Guerre sur la criminalité en France. Etudes Crimin 3: 62-70 Mr '28 **1462**

Constantin, A. Observations relatives à l'influence de la guerre sur la criminalité et la moralité. Ann de Méd Lég 10: 89-124 Mr '30 **1463**

Escande de Messieres. Les facteurs de la criminalité d'après-guerre. Marseille-Méd 1: 701-15 My 25 '29 **1464**

Exner, Franz. Krieg und Kriminalität in Österreich. Mit einem Beitrag über die Kriminalität der Militärpersonen von Georg Lelewer. 219p. Wien, Hölder-Pichler-Tempsky, 1927; also published in English by Yale university press, New Haven, 1927 **1465**

Hacker, E. L'influence de la guerre mondiale sur la criminalité. R Int de Dr Pén 4: 68-94; English transl by Fitz-Gerald 95-109 Ja '27 **1466**

Kantorowicz, Hermann. Ein vergessener Tatestand: die Kriegshetze. Justiz 3 (2): 149-56 '27 **1467**

Liepmann, Moritz. Krieg und Kriminalität in Deutschland. 197p. bibliog 171-97. Stuttgart, Deutsche Verlags-Anstalt, 1930 **1468**

May, Carl L. The ex-service man and our crime problem. 7p. [California legionnaire, Reprint] 1931? **1469**

Pella, Vespasien V. La criminalité de la guerre et les illusions de la paix. R Int de Dr Pén 8: 65-75 '31 **1470**

Schulz, Erich. Die Kriegsverbrechen; eine international-strafrechtliche Studie über die Strafanspruchs- und Rechtswidrigkeitslehre, unter berücksichtigung der Schuld- und Irrtumslehre. 132p. bibliog v-xi. Berlin-Hohenschönhauser, Lakal-blatt-Verl. 1928 **1471**

Solnar, Vladimir. La guerre mondiale et la criminalité en Tchécoslovaquie. R de Dr Pén et de Crimin 9: 858-91 Ag '29; same title: 36p. Louvain, Imp. Pierre Mafrans, 1929 **1472**

Ströbel, Heinrich. Krieg, Soziale Not und Verbrechen. Betriebsräte-Zeitsch f Functionäre d Metallind 8 (16): 487-91 '27 1473

Trommer, Harry. Urkundenfalschung und Betrug im Weltkrieg. Eine Kriminologische Untersuchung. 190p. (Krimin Abh no6 hrsg von Franz Exner) Leipzig, Ernst Wiegandt, 1928 1474

Wieczorek, Viktor. Die Sittlichkeitskriminalität nach dem Kriege. 60p. Diss. Leipzig. Leipzig, A. Schmidt, 1931 1475

OFFENDERS

GENERAL

Adler, Alfred. The individual criminal and his cure. 18p. N.Y. National committee on prisons and prison labor, 1930 1476

Ammoun, Fouad. La Syrie criminelle: essai sur la criminalité en Syrie, au Liban, dans l'Etat des Alaouites et en Palestine anglaise. 495p. Paris, Giard, 1929 1477
Comprehensive outline of the penal institutions and crime and criminals.

Angeloni, G. C. Un paese di criminali sulla via della redenzione. Scuola Pos ns8: 365-9 Jl '28 1478

Anossow, J. J. Tat und Täter. Monats f Kriminalpsychol u Strafrechtsref 22: 537-46 S '31 1479

Arthur, Herbert. All the sinners. 285p. London, Long, 1931 1480

Bedford, Scott E. Social adjustment of delinquents. *In his* Readings in urban sociology, 788-801. N.Y. Appleton, 1927 1481
Chicago municipal court, by Herbert Hailey; Feeblemindedness and delinquency, by Harry Olson; Work of the N Y Psychopathic laboratory, by Louis E. Bisch; Probation in Boston, by Wilfred Bolster; A study of 100 immoral women [Boston], by V. V. Anderson; Convictions for prostitution in N Y Women's court, by Frederic Whitin; Follow-up work for women offenders, by Katherine Bement Davis; Discharged prisoners, by J. E. Sanford.

Bermann, G. El juicio pericial y el de peligrosidad. Semana Méd 1: 785-94 Ap 4 '29 1482

Binford, Jessie F. Understanding the delinquent. Nat Prob Assn Proc 25: 19-29 '31 1483

Brand, Lillian. Delinquents at wholesale. Atlan M 146: 348-53 S '30 1484

Brockway, A. Fenner. A new way with crime. 164p. London, Williams & Norgate, 1929 1485
Juvenile offender: in court, treatment, Borstal; adult offender: in court, imprisonment, death penalty.

Butler, Amos W. The individual treatment of the offender. J Crim L & Crimin 19: 220-30 Ag '28 1486

Buttersack. Wie schützen wir uns vor Verbrechern? Umschau 31: 269-71 Ap 2 '27 1487

Carnevale, Emanuele. L'investigazione obiettiva nel persono criminale. 23p. Città di Castello, Unione artigrafiche, 1928 1488
Extr de Rivista penale, LIV.

Cicala, Salvatore. Delinquenti e pena. 36p. Catania, Viaggi-Campio, 1927 1489
Extr du Foro pénale, 1927.

Coatsworth, Emerson. Handling the criminals in Ontario. Munic R 28-30 Ja '27 1490

Cooley, Edwin J. The genesis of the criminal. Am Pris Assn Proc 59: 13-28 '29 1491

Criminals "by privilege." Just Peace 94: 755-6 D 6 '30 1492

Down with the crooks. Sci Am 145: 13 Jl '31 1493

Farnell, Frederic J. The state, the psychotic and the criminal. J Nerv & Ment Dis 72: 34-45 Jl '30 1494

Finke, Hanns. Der Rechtsbrecher im Lichte der Erziehung. Kritisch aufbauende Gedanken aus d. Praxis für die Änderung des Strafvollzugs. 77p. (Forschungen u. Werke z. Erziehungswiss. no15, hrsg von Prof. Petersen) Weimar, Böhlau, 1931 1495

The first offender looks at crime. Fla St B Assn L J 4: 134-6 Je '30 1496

First offenders. L Notes 31: 142 N '27 1497

Gardner, Arthur R. L. The criminal. I: The habits of the hardened offender. 19th Cent 106: 277-86, 423-30 Ag, S '29 1498

Gardner, Arthur R. L. Criminal: sheep in wolves clothing. 19th Cent 106: 567-74 O '29 1499

Gardner, Arthur R. L. Prisoner at the bar. 223p. London, Allan, 1931 1500
Criminals, prisons, criminal law, criminal courts.

Gardner, Arthur R. L. Science approaches the lawbreaker. Howard J 2: 203-7 O '28 1501

Gefängnisgesellschaft für die Provinz Sachsen und Anhalt. Die Unerziehbaren. Jahrbuch 43, 1927. 119p. Halle (Saale), Selbstverlag, 1927 1502

Geisert, Henry A. The criminal: a study. 466p. St. Louis, Herder bk co. 1930 1503
Bibliog. 453-5. Approved by Catholic church.

Glueck, Sheldon and Glueck, Eleanor T. 500 criminal careers. 365p. N.Y. Knopf, 1930 1504
Study of 510 men who left Massachusetts reformatory.

Gómez, E. Acerca de la anormalidad del delinquente. Bibl Nac de Crim y Cienc Afines Bol 2: 381-3 Ap '28 1505

Gosline, H. I. The pathologist looks at the criminal. Eugen 2: 14-20 S '29 1506

Guthrie. Is the criminal a weakling? Chief Constables Assn Can Proc 25: 90-101 '29 1507

Harper, William J. The offender, the offense and punishment. N Y St Assn Magistrates Proc 22: 30-5 '30 1508

Haynes, F. E. The individual delinquent. J Crim L & Crimin 18: 65-74 My '28 1509

Healy, William. The delinquent as an individual. Nat Prob Assn Proc 1930: 31-5 1510

Heintz, Michael G. A refuge for American criminals. J Crim L & Crimin 18: 331-6 N '27 **1511**

Hoey, Jane M. Understanding the delinquent: society in relation to the child. Nat Conf Soc Wk Proc 1931: 87-96 **1512**

Johnston, William. Law protects the criminal. Good Housekeeping 84: 20-1 Mr '27 **1513**

Jones, George W. What happens to the convicted offender? N Y St Assn Magistrates Proc 21: 99-106 '29 **1514**

Kavanagh, Marcus A. The criminal and his allies. 433p. Indianapolis, Bobbs-Merrill, 1928; same title: Justice 1: 9-10, 12 O; 11-13 N; 8-14 D '28 **1515**

Kirchwey, George W. The criminal and society. Minn St Conf & Inst Soc Wk Proc 37: 21-8 '29; same title: Minn St Bd Con Q 29: 60-7 S 13 '29 **1516**

Kochko, A. de. Scènes du monde criminel russe; trad. du russe par Hippolyte de Witte. 373p. Paris, Payot, 1929 **1517**

Kohs, Samuel C. What science has taught us regarding the criminal. J Delin 11: 170-80 S '27 **1518**

Krassnushkin, E[ugenii] K[onstantinovich]. Der Verbrecher. Monats f Kriminalpsychol u Strafrechtsref 18: 65-89 F '27 **1519**

Study of 2,601 delinquents from reports of Moskauer Kabinetts zum Studium des Verbrechers und der Kriminalität.

Krassnushkin, Eugenii Konstantinovich and Feinberg, Tsetsiliíà Mirovna, eds. [Murders and murderers; symposium]. 375p. Moskva, Kabinet i klinika po izucheniíù i prestupnosti, 1928 **1520**

Kreiner, Mrs. Israel A. The adult offender from the point of view of a case-working agency. Minn St Conf & Inst Soc Wk Proc 38: 126-30 '30 **1521**

Kutz, Fred B. Coddling the criminal. Peace Offic Assn Calif Proc 10: 20-3 '30 **1522**

Leppmann, F. Die Kriminalität Misshandelter. Monats f Kriminalpsychol u Strafrechtsref 21: 101-2 '30 **1523**

Loesch, Frank J. The criminal and his allies. Neb L Bul 9: 88-96 Jl '30 **1524**

Logan, Malcolm. Glorifying the criminal. Scribner's 90: 43-6 Jl '31 **1525**

Montagnes, James. How Canada deals with its criminals. N Am R 231: 264-8 Mr '31 **1526**

Morrison, A. C. L. Society, the offender and the reformatory agencies, a brief general survey. Just Peace 94: 555-7 S 6 '30 **1527**

Müller, Johannes. Schutzaufsicht für Erwachsene. Monats f Kriminalpsychol u Strafrechtsref 20: 90-9 F '29 **1528**

Naegele, O. Kriminalität und Justiz. Int Zeitsch f Individualpsychol 5: 350-7 '31 **1529**

Nelson, Victor F. The code of the crook. Welf Mag 19: 343-7 Mr '28 **1530**

Neumiller, Charles. The problem of crime and the problem of criminals. Int Assn Identif, Calif Div Proc 12: 15-20 '27 **1531**

Our "criminals." Just Peace 94: 777-8 D 13 '30 **1532**

Overholser, Winfred. Sizing up the criminal. Mass Dept Correc Q 3: 1- Ap '27 **1533**

Paterson, Alexander. The apprentice to crime. Police J [London] 1: 139-48 Ja '28 **1534**

England, Burma, Ceylon.

Picard, Octave. A propos du projet de loi de défense sociale: [anormaux, recidivistes]. R de Dr Pén et de Crimin 9: 694-703 '29 **1535**

Pierce, David H. Training the criminal. Welf Mag 19: 907-8 '28 **1536**

Podolsky, E. Vivisection of capital criminals for advancement of knowledge in medicine. Ill Med J 52: 414-17 N '27 **1537**

Pozzolini, Alfredo. L'organizzazione giuridica internazionale della difesa sociale contra lo delinquenza. 15p. Messina, Giacomo d'Anna, 1929 **1538**

Extr. Il pensiero giuridico penale.

Purroy, David. On the lam. Am Mercury 14: 475-83 Ag '28 **1539**

Ritter, Pierre Henri. Die Apologie des Verbrechers. 30p. Duisburg, Deutscher Brücke-Verl. 1931 **1540**

Römer. Die kriminalpolizeiliche Erfassung und Überwachung bemerkenswerter Verbrecher. Krimin Monatsh 4: 268-71 D '30 **1541**

Rolle, C. M. E possibile una cura del criminale? Osp Maggiore 15: 216-23 Jl 31 '27 **1542**

Roughead, William. Bad companions; with an introduction by Hugh Walpole. 301p. London, Duffield, 1931 **1543**

St. John, Arthur. A new way with criminals. Sociol R 21: 233-40 Jl '29 **1544**

Selling, Lowell Sinn. Restlessness in a delinquent group. Psychol Clin 20: 92-3 My '31 **1545**

Sempill, C. I. The criminal in Kenya colony. Police J [London] 2: 557-70 O '29 **1546**

Shaw, Clifford Robe and Moore, Maurice E. The natural history of a delinquent career. 280p. Chicago, Univ. of Chicago press, 1931 **1547**

Social defectives. Sol J 72: 562 Ag 25 '28 **1548**

Stern, Leon. Treatment of adult offenders and children by the courts of Berks county, Pennsylvania. 53p. Philadelphia, Pennsylvania committee on penal affairs, 1928 **1549**

Stern, Leon. Treatment of adult offenders and children in Luzerne county, Pennsylvania. 98p. Philadelphia, Pennsylvania committee on penal affairs, 1929 **1550**

Tejera y Garcia, Diego Vicente. El matonismo como figura delictuosa. 62p. Habana, Imp. Casa "Soles," 1927 **1551**

Tönnies, Ferdinand. Uneheliche und Verwaiste Verbrecher. Studien über Verbrechertum in Schleswig-Holstein. 48p. (Krimin Abh no17) Leipzig, Ernst Wiegandt, 1930 **1552**

Tucker, F. St. G. Booth. The Salvation Army and the Indian criminal. Police J [London] 1: 578-93 O '28 **1553**

Utevski, B. S. [Crimes and criminals of Western Europe]. 150p. Moskva, Narkomvnudel, 1929 **1554**

Van Waters, Miriam. Why we hang the "Hickmans"; do you know? Northwest Police J 7: 19, 59-60 D '29 **1555**

Vasaly, Chas. E. Paths of the handicapped: of the delinquent men. Minn St Bd Con Q 29: 28-32 S 13 '29 **1556**

Victorio, R[amon]. The adult offender and the community; address, First annual conference of social work, November 4, 1927. [Manila, Bureau of prisons] 1927 **1557**

Watson, Frederick. Century of gunmen; a study in lawlessness. 295p. London, Nicholson & Watson, 1931 **1558**

Wedge, F. R. A study of delinquent and criminal groups. Police J [N Y] 14: 21-4 Ja, 25 F, 12-14 Mr '27 **1559**

Wulffen, Erich. Sexualspiegel von Kunst und Verbrechen. 444p. Dresden, Aretz, 1928 **1560**

CLASSIFICATION OF OFFENDERS

Aschaffenburg, G[ustav]. Einheitlichkeit der Sicherungsmassnahmen. Monats f Kriminalpsychol u Strafrechtsref 22: 257-65 My '31 **1561**

Metelmann, Karl. Zum Problem der Einteilung der Verbrecher nach psychologischen Gesichtspunkten. Monats f Kriminalpsychol u Strafrechtsref 22: 725-30 D '31 **1562**

Pozzolini, Alfredo. La classificazione dei reati, la classificazione dei delinquenti e la loro reciproca integrazione. 21p. Pisa, Pacini, 1929 **1563**
Extr: Scuola positiva ns9: 1929.

Tullio, B. di. A proposito della classificazione dei delinquenti. Arch di Antrop Crim 50: 1494 '30 **1564**

CLASSES OF OFFENDERS

JUVENILE

GENERAL

"Age limits" in juvenile delinquency. Probation 8: 7 Ap '30 **1565**

Albertson, J. Lester. The slot machine racket—maker of juvenile criminals. Panel 9: 6-7 Ja '31 **1566**

Allen, Frederick H. Psychic factors in juvenile delinquency. Ment Hyg 11: 764-74 O '27; same title: 8p. (typw) Philadelphia, All-Philadelphia conference on social work, 1927 **1567**

Allen, Perry T. The unrestrained youth of today. Int Assn Identif Proc 13: 85-94 '27 **1568**

Alpert, Augusta. Delinquent children. New Repub 59: 105-6 Je 12 '29 **1569**

Alzina Melis, J. La delincuencia y la frenastenia. Ars Méd 6: 361-7 O '30 **1570**

Amending the Children Act. Just Peace 94: 439-40 Jl 12 '30 **1571**

Anders. Charakterveränderung und Kriminalität bei postencephalitischen Jugendlichen. Arch f Psychiat 81 (5): 756-7 '27; same title: Allg Zeitsch f Psychiat 18: 174-5 '28 **1572**

Appelget, Norma. Unadjusted child: bibliography. Educ 48: 273-90 Ja '28 **1573**

Are criminals made in childhood? Just Peace 94: 819 D 27 '30 **1574**

Arenaza, Carlos de. La infancia y sus problemas. Infancia abandonada y delincuente. Museo Soc Arg Bol 19: 273-7 Jl '31 **1575**

Astredo, J. C. Not all boys and girls are bad. Pac Munic 43: 111 Mr '29 **1576**

Atkinson, Edith M. Juvenile problems. Int Assn Identif Proc 16: 193-6 '30 **1577**

Atkinson, H. A. Juvenile delinquency. Nat Council Educ [Can] Education and leisure, 257-68 **1578**

Bahr, Max A. Some psychiatric problems in juvenile delinquency. Indianapolis M J 31: 305-9 N '28 **1579**

Beckham, Albert Sidney. Juvenile delinquency and the Negro. Opportunity 9: 300-2 O '31 **1580**

Bedford, Scott E. W. How can children behave if parents misbehave? J Crim L & Crimin 18: 568-73 F '28 **1581**

Bentley, Herbert. Child offenders and industrial schools. Child 17: 169-71 Mr '27 **1582**

Blanchard, Phyllis Mary. Juvenile delinquency. *In her* The child and society: an introduction to the social psychology of the child, 296-308. N.Y. Longmans, 1928 **1583**

Bleidt. Unsere Arbeit an der verwahrlosten und verbrecherischen Jugend! Schweiz Ver f Straf- Gefängniswes u Schutzaufsicht Verh ns8: 117-41 '28 **1584**

Bonar, J. J. "Protection and training": the Scottish young offenders' report. Howard J 2: 227-30 O '28 **1585**

Bondy, Curt. Zur Frage der Erziehbarkeit. Zeitsch f d ges Strafrechtswiss 48 (4): 329-34 '28 **1586**

Bradway, John S. The legal approach to the problem of juvenile delinquency. S Calif L R 2: 128-38 D '28 **1587**

Bridges, K. M. Banham. Factors contributing to juvenile delinquency. J Crim L & Crimin 17: 531-80 bibliog (p577-80) F '27 **1588**

Brill, Marion S. Motivation of conduct disorders in boys. J Delin 11: 5-22 Mr '27 **1589**

Brown, L. Guy. The problems of juvenile delinquency and dependency. Nat Conf Juv Agencies Proc 27: 53-65 '30; same title: J Juv Res 15: 155-68 Jl '31 **1590**

Bryan, W. C. The youthful criminal. Chief Constables' Assn Can Proc 25: 116-22 '29 **1591**

Bushong, R. E. Diagnosing for juvenile delinquency. Wis M J 27: 312-13 Jl '28 **1592**

Butcher, William Lewis. The challenge of the boy and what to do about it. N Y St Prob Offic Proc 20: 149-55 '27 1593

Cadilhac, P. E. Un problème social: l'enfance du carrefour. Illustration 180: 255-60 O 24 '31 1594

Carp, E. A. D. E. Observations on criminal tendencies in children. Nederl Tijdschr v Geneesk 2: 5693-700 D 7 '29 1595

Catching them young. Sol J 73: 507 Ag 3 '29 1596

Causes and remedies of juvenile delinquency. J Soc Hyg 13: 52 Ja '27 1597

Ceillier, A. Délits de nécessité et délits par imprévoyance chez l'enfant. Utilité d'éviter la prison préventive aux enfants dont l'intention délicteuse n'est pas suffisamment établie. Ann de Méd Lég 10: 715-28 D '30 1598

Child criminals. Sol J 73: 357 Je 8 '29 1599

Children who went wrong. Survey 57: 644-5 F 15 '27 1600

Close, O. H. The adjustment of older delinquent boys. Nat Prob Assn Proc 1929: 62-6 1601

Costas, Saturnino. Los menores ante la nueva ciencia penal y la legislacion. R de Crimin, Psiquiat y Med Leg 15: 446-53 Jl '28 1602

Curry, John A. Youth and crime. N Y St Assn Chiefs Police Proc 30: 39 '30 1603

Dahlstrom, Sigurd. "Is the young criminal a continuation of the neglected child?" J Juv Res 12: 97-121 Je '28 1604

Delgado, Vicente H. Delincuencia de menores. Museo Soc Arg Bol 18: 335-7 Je '30 1605

Derrick, Calvin. The problems of problem children. Nat Conf Juv Agencies Proc 24: 62-70 '27 1606

Detroit. Department of health. City wide housing study and its relation to juvenile delinquency, major crime and important health problems. City Health 13: 7-8 Jl '29 1607

Dexter, Robert Cloutman. The delinquent child. *In his* Social adjustment, 123-37. N.Y. Knopf, 1927 1608

Dobbs, Harrison A. The first offender in delinquency. Neighborhood 4: 202-12 S '31 1609

Dobbs, Harrison A. Off beaten paths with the problem boy. Nat Prob Assn Proc 22: 216-24 '28 1610

Dobbs, Harrison A. [Social case work responsibilities in meeting problems of children]. Nat Conf Juv Agencies Proc 27: 11-21 '30 1611

DuBois, Charlotte A. Potential citizens. Homiletic R 101: 483-4 Je '31 1612

Dugan, Daniel J. Juvenile delinquency. N Y St Assn Judges Proc 5: 74-8 '27 1613

Dunkelberger, G[eorge] F. What is the explanation of increased juvenile delinquency. J Educ Soc 1: 421-3 Mr '28 1614

Eliot, Thomas D. Saving school children from the hand of the law. Nation's Sch 6: 29-32 Ag '30 1615

Engelbach, W. Infantile defectiveness. M Clin N Am 11: 381-98 S '27 1616

Ettinger, Clayton James. Radial pattern in an urban community—a study in human ecology. 96p. Thesis, Univ. of Pittsburgh, 1929 1617

Study of juvenile delinquency records.

Faber, P. C. [The distribution of the ages of juvenile offenders 1909-1927]. Maandbl v Ber en Reclasser 7: 215-17 Jl '28 1618

Fagan, Bernard J. The conflict of youth. N Y St Conf Prob Offic Proc 21: 198-204 '28 1619

Farnell, Frederic J. Children as state wards. J Nerv & Ment Dis 73: 20-9 Ja '31 1620

Fenton, Jessie C. Delinquent boys individualized. Sierra Educ N 27: 34-41 S '31 1621

Fesler, Bert. Juvenile crime. Int Assn Chiefs Police Proc 37: 68-70 '30 1622

Fischer, Edmund. Über die Stellung des Kindes zum Diebstahl. Zeitsch f pädagog Psychol 29: 295-300 Je '28 1623

Francke, Herbert. Jugendkriminalität. Zeitsch f Kinderforsch 36: 72-9 Ja 18 '30 1624

Fuchs, Daniel. Where Al Capone grew up. New Repub 68: 95-7 S 9 '31 1625

Fulton, J. T. Paths of the handicapped: of the delinquent boy. Minn St Bd Con Q 29: 13-15 S 13 '29 1626

Gage, Charles A. The challenge of youth delinquency. Police "13-13" 4: 6-7 D '29 1627

Gajardo, Samuel. El problema de la delincuencia de menores. An de Univ de Chile s2A 6: 805-30 '28 1628

Gardner, O. Max. Our youthful criminals. Conf Gov'rs Proc 1929: 37-45 1629

Gordon, Ronald Grey. Autolycus; or, The future for miscreant youth. 94p. London, Routledge, 1928 1630

Gregor, A. Die psychische Struktur Verwahrloster auf verschiedenen Altersstufen. Zeitsch f Kinderforsch 35: 22-64 Ja 30 '29 1631

Griboedov, A. S. [Paths to crime (Difficult children)]. 115p. Leningrad, Rabochi Sud, 1928 1632

Grimberg, Leizer E. Emotion and delinquency; a clinical study of five hundred criminals in the making. 147p. N.Y. Bretano's, 1928 1633

Gross, Nathan. The youth problem. Police "13-13" 4: 13, 48 O '29 1634

Guilford, P. W. Juvenile delinquency. Minn St Bd Con Q 28: 7-13 My 7 '29 1635

Hall, Gertrude E. Misfits; causes and cures for delinquency. Grade Teach 47: 688 My '30 1636

Hamilton-Pearson, E. A. Child delinquency. Lancet 213: 1312-13 D 17 '27 1637

Harper, Fowler Vincent and Reinhardt, James M. Four relationship status of a group of delinquent boys. J Crim L & Crimin 21: 379-92 N '30 1638

Harris, J. W. The unadjusted boy. Int Assn Identif, Calif Div Proc 12: 36-42 '27 1639

Hartog, J. Misdadig aangelegde kinderen en beroepskeuze. Jeugd en Beroep 3: 272-4 '30 1640

Hartwell, S. W. Mental hygiene and the delinquent child. Nat Prob Assn Proc 25: 3-13 '31 1641

Healy, William; Bronner, Augusta Fox; Baylor, Edith M. H., and Murphy, J. Prentice. Reconstructing behavior in youth; a study of problem children in foster families. 325p. (Judge Baker foundation. Pub no5) N.Y. Knopf, 1929 1642

Herrle, Theo. Psychologie und Sittlichkeitsvergehen auf der Schule. Zeitsch f pädagog Psychol 30: 433-44 O '29 1643

Heuyer, G. L'examen médico-psychologiques des enfants délinquants. Prophyl Ment 3: 298-304 '27 1644

Heuyer, G. and Serin. La delinquance infantile et juvénile. J Méd Fr 18: 227-40 Je '29 1645

Hickson, W. J. Can science detect future criminal in child? Si-De-Ka Q 19: 95-106 Ja '27 1646

Hill, T. R. The problem of juvenile behavior disorders in chronic epidemic encephalitis. J Neurol & Psychopath 9: 1-10 Jl '28 1647

Hörst, Wilhelm. Fürsorgeerziehung krimineller Jugendlicher über 16 Jahre in England. Zentralbl f Jugendrecht u Jugendwohlfahrt 21: 301-5, 351-6 D '29, Ja '30 1648

Hoey, Jane M. Society in relation to the child. Nat Prob Assn Proc 25: 30-9 '31 1649

How bad boys behave; thirty-three behavior traits. Survey 65: 440 Ja 15 '31 1650

Howard league for penal reform. Treatment of young offenders: being the report of a representative conference convened by the . . . League, October 27, 1927. 35p. 1651

Innes, A. Mitchell. Society and the young criminal. Socialist R 2: 22-30 My '30 1652

Jail and the child. Probation 8: 1-2 Ap '30 1653

Johnson, Andrew G. Treatment of delinquent boys. Nat Leag Compul Educ Offic Proc 20: 73-8 '30 1654

Juvenile. Chicago. 1, 1900- 1655
Published in interest of handicapped children. [Children's charities, inc.]

Juvenile crime and juvenile courts. Just Peace 92: 704 O 27 '28 1656

Juvenile delinquency and the cinema. Just Peace 92: 426 Je 23 '28 1657

The juvenile offender. 4p. (Social workers' booklists, no2) Baltimore, Enoch Pratt Free Library, 1927 1658

Juvenile offenders of yesterday and to-day. Nation's Sch 4: 78 Ag '29 1659

Kahlbaum. Hinausgeschobene Volljährigkeit als Schutz- und Heilmittel bei drohender Verwahrlosung Jugendlicher. Monats f Psychiat u Neurol 66: 44-51 S '27 1660

Killick, Victor W. Suggestions for parental administration calculated to reduce juvenile delinquency. J Delin 11: 194-205 S '27 1661
Car stealing in Los Angeles county.

Klein, Melanie. Criminal tendencies in normal children. Brit J M Psychol 7: 177-92 Jl '27 1662

Krebs, Albert. Die Stellung des Minderjährigen im amtlichen Entwurf eines Strafvollzugsgesetzes. Zentralbl f Jugendrecht u Jugendwohlfahrt 19 (5): 115-21 '27 1663

Die Kriminalität der Jugendlichen. Arch f Krim 80: 177 Mr '27 1664

Lafora, Gonzalo R. Juvenile delinquency and mental deficiency; translated by Ernest H. Templin. J Delin 11: 53-7 Mr '27 1665

Lambert, June, comp. Digest of the laws of the various states fixing the age when a child becomes amenable to the criminal law. 11p. Albany, New York (state) Library, Legislative reference section, March 30, 1930 1666

Lampel, Peter Martin. Jugen in Not. Berichte von Fürsorgezöglingen. 240p. Berlin, Spath, 1928 1667

Lenroot, Katharine F. Youth and the law. Am Pris Assn Proc 60: 176-88 '30 1668

Levin, Max. The young offender. Hygeia 8: 515-17 Je '30 1669

Longenbaugh, May M. Parties of the third part. Survey 57: 500-1 Ja 15 '27 1670

Luzuriaga, Lorenzo. Juvenile delinquency and mental deficiency; in behalf of the health of Spanish children; translated by Ernest H. Templin. J Delin 11: 223-6 S '27 1671

Lyon, F. Emory. Problems of boyhood. Welf Mag 19: 645-51 My '28 1672

McChristie, Mary E. What is success and what is failure? Nat Prob Assn Proc 22: 242-50 '28 1673

McClure, W. E. Characteristics of problem children based on judgments of teachers. J Juv Res 13: 124-40 Ap '29 1674

McFadden, Elizabeth. Are some boys born bad? Parents' Mag 4: 29 Ap '29 1675

McGrath, William A. Baby bandit. Survey 66: 95 Ap 15 '31 1676

McIver, Joseph. The juvenile delinquent. Am M Assn J 89: 1598-1600 N 5 '27 1677

Mackaye, Milton. Youthful killers. Outl 151: 3-6 Ja 2 '29 1678

MacMurchy, Helen. [Place of the social worker in juvenile delinquency]. Nat Conf Juv Agencies Proc 27: 21-7 '30 1679

MacNeill, N. M. "Good and bad children." Arch Pediat 44: 437-41 Jl '27 1680

Magistrates and young offenders. L Times 164: 310 O 22 '27 1681

Minor offenders and the dock. Sol J 71: 415-16 My 28 '27 1682

Moley, Raymond. The relationship of juvenile to adult delinquency. Nat Conf Soc Wk Proc 1930: 81-6; same title: Nat Prob Assn Proc 1930: 131-6 1683

Morrison, A. C. L. Juvenile offenders. Just Peace 94: 542-3 Ag 30 '30 1684

Murphy, J. Prentice. Adjustments of the delinquent child. Nat Prob Assn Proc 1930: 4-8 1685A

Naegele, Otto. Der Erziehungsgedanke im Jugendrecht. Beiträge zur kriminalpädagogischen Reform. 123p. Leipzig, Ernst Oldenburg [1927] **1685B**

National commission on law observance and enforcement. Report on the child offender in the federal system of justice. 175p. (No6) Washington, May 28, 1931 **1686**

Jail detention of federal child offenders; administration of federal system of justice in relation to child offenders; penal and correctional institutions; juvenile court legislation.

Nebel, R. W. The juvenile offender. Int Assn Chiefs Police Proc 37: 172-7 '30 **1687**

Neill, Alexander S. The problem child. 256p. N.Y. McBride, 1927 **1688**

Criminality in the child, 199-206.

Neilson, N. P. The relation of school health, physical education and recreation to juvenile research. J Juv Res 14: 176-80 Jl '30 **1689**

New York (city). Municipal reference library. Adolescent offenders: their study and treatment (age 12-21): a selected list from material published since 1915. 3p. (mim) October 11, 1927 **1690**

Oseretzky, N. Die minderjährigen Rechtsbrecher. (Nach den Materialien des Moskauer Arbeitzhauses). Zeitsch f Kinderforsch 34: 53-74 '28 **1691**

Owens, Albert Alexander. Behavior-problem boy; a socio-educational survey. 188p. Thesis, Univ. of Pennsylvania, 1929

Pacareo, Orencio. Delincuencia infantil y remedios. 31p. Madrid, Magisterio Español [1927] **1693**

Palluch, Josef. Die sittliche Einsicht männlicher schulentlassener Fürsorgezöglinge in ihren Beziehungen zum sittlichen Verhalten sowie zur allgemeinen intellektuellen Entwicklung. Zeitsch f ang Psychol 30 (1-3): 1-80 '28 **1694**

Parker, Edwin. Loose screws. Int Assn Identif Proc 16: 75-7 '30 **1695**

Pierce, Paul R. Maladjustments of adolescents. Sch R 37: 679-86 N '29 **1696**

Polwarth. The young offender. Police J [London] 2: 51-61 Ja '29 **1697**

Potter, Ellen C. Have we progressed? Has the last hundred years witnessed progress in dealing with delinquency? Welf Mag 18: 302-10 Mr '27 **1698**

Prior, G. P. U. Some physical causes of juvenile delinquency. M J Austral 2: 602-5 O 29 '27 **1699**

Problem boys. Sch R 38: 327-9 My '30 **1700**

Problem of the young criminal. World's Wk 59: 23 Je '30 **1701**

Quinn, John R. Juvenile delinquency. Los Angeles Chron 14: 6-7 N 30 '31 **1702**

Rackham, C. D. Treatment of young offenders. Woman's Leader 19: 88 Ap 22 '27 **1703**

Read, George M. The wayward minor. Nat Prob Assn Proc 1930: 191-9 **1704**

Reca, Telma. Influencia del medio familiar en la delincuencia infantil. Museo Soc Arg Bol 19: 187-93 Ap '31 **1705**

Reckless, Walter Cade. Six boys in trouble. 150p. Ann Arbor, Mich. Edwards bros. 1929 **1706**

Reinhar[d]t, James M. Juvenile delinquency in a town of 18,000. Dakota L R 2: 233-40 Je '28 **1707**

Reinhardt, James M. A note on juvenile delinquency. Dakota L R 2: 81-4 F '28 **1708**

Reinhardt, James M. and Harper, Fowler Vincent. Social and ethical judgments of two groups of boys—delinquent and non-delinquent. J Crim L & Crimin 21: 364-78 N '30 **1709**

Reining. Die Fürsorgeerziehung im Jugendstrafverfahren. Zentralbl f Jugendrecht u Jugendwohlfahrt 19: 6-8 '27 **1710**

Reinold, K. Zur Entwicklung des Jugendstrafrechtes. Juristen-Zeit f d Geb d Tschecho-slowak 8: 161-4 '27 **1711**

Rights of juveniles to constitutional guarantees in delinquency proceedings. Colum L R 27: 968-74 D '27 **1712**

Robinson, Bruce B. Problems of community management of non-institutionalized feebleminded and delinquent in the public schools. Nat Conf Soc Wk Proc 1928: 367-72 **1713**

Rosenow, E. and Whyte, A. H. Ordinal position of problem children. Am J Orthopsychiat 1: 430-4 Jl '31 **1714**

Rosner, R. Moralprüfungen bei Jugendlichen. Allg Zeitsch f Psychiat 86: 91-101 Mr '27 **1715**

Roubinovitch; Boncourt, O., and Heyer. Examen neuro-psychiatrique des enfants délinquants. Ann de Méd Lég 7: 442-8 O '27 **1716**

Roubinovitch, J. L'examen systematique des enfants délinquants. Prophyl Ment 3: 295-8 '27 **1717**

Russell Sage Foundation. Library. A bibliography of juvenile delinquency. (Second supplement). 4p. (Bul no101) N.Y. June 1930 **1718**

St. Antoine, H. E. Juvenile delinquency. Hosp Soc Serv 20: 287-300 O '29 **1719**

Sanders, Wiley B. Recent contributions in the field of juvenile delinquency, child welfare, and family case work. Soc Forces 6: 648-53 Je '28 **1720**

Sayles, Mary Buell. Problem child at home. 342p. N.Y. Commonwealth fund, 1928 **1721**

"Suggestions for reading" 331-3.

Scheidemann, Norma Valentine. Delinquent children. *In her* Psychology of exceptional children, 430-74. Boston, Houghton, 1931 **1722**

Scott, Robert H. Growing citizens and our laws. Los Angeles B Assn J 6: 154-6 Ja 15 '31 **1723**

Scott, Robert H. Juvenile delinquency and the schools. Tax Dig 7: 60 F '29 **1724**

Shaw, Clifford R[obe]. Correlation of rate of juvenile delinquency with certain indices of community organization and disorganization [in Chicago]. Am Sociol Soc Proc 22: 174-9 '27 **1725**

Shaw, Clifford Robe, ed. Jack-roller; a delinquent boy's own story. 205p. Chicago, Univ. of Chicago press, 1930 **1726**

Shaw, Clifford R[obe]. What the delinquent boy's own story reveals. Rel Educ 26: 163-9 F '31 **1727**

Shaw, Clifford R[obe] and Myers, Earl D. The juvenile delinquent. *In* Illinois association for criminal justice, Illinois crime survey, 645-735, 1929 **1728**

Shaw, Clifford R[obe]; Zorbaugh, Frederick; McKay, Henry D., and Cottrell, Leonard S. Delinquency areas; a study of the geographic distribution of school truants, juvenile delinquents, and adult offenders in Chicago. 214p. (Behavior research fund, Monographs) Chicago, Univ. of Chicago press, 1930 **1729**

Shelly, Patrick J. The wayward minor. Nat Prob Assn Proc 1930: 200-8 **1730**

Shelly, Patrick J. Wayward minors. N Y St Assn Magistrates Proc 19: 107-13 '27 **1731**

Sherwood, Henry Noble. Youth and crime. Sch & Soc 25: 527-32 My 7 '27 **1732**

Shrubsall, F. C. Notes on investigation and treatment of "difficult" children in the United States of America. Ment Welf 8: 41-8 Ap 15 '27 **1733**

Sieradzki, W. Child criminal. Polska Gaz Lek 8: 348-51 My 12 '29 **1734**

Sletto, Raymond. The relationship between sibling's position and juvenile delinquency. Thesis (M.A.) University of Minnesota, 1931 **1735**

Sobre la infancia abandonada y delincuente. R de Crimin Psiquiat y Med Leg [16] (99): 343- '30 **1736**

Some problems of the school child. Cath Educ R 27: 426-36 S '29 **1737**

Steeves, C. A. Juvenile offenders. Chief Constables Assn Can Proc 25: 17-21 '29 **1738**

Stephen, Harry. Young offenders; review of Report of the departmental committee on treatment of young offenders. Edin R 246: 320-30 O '27 **1739**

Stern, E. Jugendpsychologie und Jugendkriminalität. Allg ärztl Zeitsch f Psychotherap 1: 412-25 '28 **1740**

Stewart, M[ary] L. Some aspects of delinquency. Minn St Bd Con Q 26: 4-10 F 15 '27 **1741**

Stratton, George Malcolm. Black beast in our education? Sci M 29: 546-50 D '29 **1742**

Sullenger, T[homas] Earl. The newsboy as a juvenile delinquent. J Juv Res 15: 215-19 Jl '31 **1743**

Study of 119 "downtown" boys in Omaha.

Sullenger, T[homas] Earl. Relation of juvenile delinquency to outdoor relief. Sociol & Soc Res 15: 255-62 Ja '31 **1744**

Sullenger, Thomas Earl. Social determinants in juvenile delinquency. Thesis (Ph.D.) University of Missouri, 1930; same title: 87p. Omaha, Neb. Douglas ptg. co. 1930 **1745**

Tandy, Elizabeth C. Trends in juvenile delinquency and child labor. Am Statist Assn J 24 sup180-1 Mr '29 **1746**

Teodorescu, J. Los congresos y el problema de la delincuencia de los menores. Bibl Nac de Crim y Cienc Afines Bol 2: 400-7 Ap '28 **1747**

Thomas, William I. The child in America; behavior problems and programs. 583p. N. Y. Knopf, 1928 **1748**

Tobias, Norman. A study of syphilis among one thousand cases of juvenile delinquency. J Juv Res 12: 188-92 Je '28 **1749**

Study at House of detention, St. Louis.

Truxall, A[ndrew] G[ehr]. Attempts to evaluate recreation in relation to juvenile delinquency. *In his* Outdoor recreation legislation and its effectiveness. . . , 119-66. (Studies in history, economics and public law no311) N. Y. Columbia univ press, 1929 **1750**

Tyson, Dorothy Kinzer. A study of certain behavior traits of young delinquent boys. J Juv Res 14: 280-9 O '30 **1751**

United States. Bureau of the census. Juvenile delinquents. *In its* Children under institutional care, 1923, 260-381. Washington, 1927 **1752**

United States. Office of education. Library division. Problem and delinquent children [bibliography]. Bibliog Res Stud Educ 1929-30: 406-10 **1753**

Van Doninck, A. Stigmates de dégénérescence chez les anormaux débiles. R de Dr Pén et de Crimin 8: 826-40 Ag '28 **1754**

Van Waters, Miriam. Parents on probation. 347p. N. Y. New Republic, 1927 **1755**

Vanden Bergh, Leonard John. Public schools versus delinquent youth. 224p. Los Angeles, Clark pub. co. 1929 **1756**

Verdun, Henri. La participation médicale au relèvement de l'enfance coupable. Ann de Méd Lég 11: 501-16 Je '31 **1757**

Vidoni, G. [The life of the child during the scholastic period with a consideration of criminality in minors.] Ann dell'Osped Psichiat di Messina (1-2) '28 **1758**

Vidoni, G. Tra i problemi della delinquenza minorile. Rinnovamento Med 9: 3-11 '30 **1759**

Vignes, H. Medical examination of delinquent children: Heuyer Institution in Paris. Matern & Child Welf 11: 281-3 S '27 **1760**

Warner, Charles H. Undue publicity given to juvenile delinquents. N Y St Assn Judges Proc 6: 38-50 '28 **1761**

Weatherly, L. A. Juvenile psychologic delinquencies. Lancet 215: 1130-2 '28 **1762**

Weiss, Hans. The placing of delinquent children in private foster homes. R Int de l'Enf (71-2): 275-87 N '31 **1763**

Wembridge, Eleanor Rowland. Were they insane? Outl 153: 90-1 S 18 '29 **1764**

Wets, Paul. L'observation de l'enfant de justice. R de Dr Pén et de Crimin 10: 1-16 '30 **1765**

Whipp, Frank D. Juvenile delinquency law; some suggested changes. Welf Mag 18: 354-5 Mr '27 **1766**

Whitley, Robert L. The observation of the problem boy. J Educ Soc 3: 326-40 F '30 1767

Wile, Ira S. Behavior difficulties in children. Ment Hyg 11: 38-52 Ja '27 1768

Wile, Ira S. Behavior problems of children with special reference to delinquency. Am J Dis Child 40: 1076-88 N '30 1769

Wile, Ira S. Conduct disorders of children. Am M Assn J 88: 1222-7 Ap 16 '27 1770

Wile, Ira S. The delinquent child and the delinquent community. Hosp Soc Serv 18: 41-8 Jl '28 1771

Wile, Ira S. Some medical phases of child behavior. M J & Rec 125: 613-18, 674-5 My 4, 18 '27 1772

Williams, Herbert D. Experiment in self-directed education. Sch & Soc 31: 715-18 My 24 '30 1773

Willson, G. M. Adaptation of treatment to cause in male juvenile delinquency. J Crim L & Crimin 18: 207-17 Ag '27 1774

Wolfe, W. Béran. The psychopathology of the juvenile delinquent. Int Zeitsch f Individualpsychol 6 (2): 121-9 '28; same title: J Delin 11: 159-69 S '27 1775

Yoshimasu, S. Moral sentiment of juvenile delinquent. Jap J Psychol 6: 75-94 '31 1776

Young, E[rle] F[iske] and Young, P[auline] V[islick], comps. Juvenile delinquency: selected readings. 93p. (mim) Los Angeles, Western Education service, 1928 1777

Young offenders and prison. Sol J 73: 306 My 18 '29 1778

Young sexual offenders. Just Peace 94: 721 N 22 '30 1779

Zimmerle. Strafverfügungen gegen Jugendliche. Zeitsch f d feeiw Gerichtsbark u d Gemeindeverwaltung in Württ 69: 201-12 '27 1780

Argentina

Bermann, G. El problema médicosocial de los menores retardados. Semana Méd 1: 786-92 Mr 27 '30 1781

Belgium

Wets, Paul. L'enfant de justice. Quinze années d'application de la loi sur la protection de l'enfance. 508p. Bruxelles, Association internationale pour la protection de l'enfance, 1928 1782
Juvenile delinquency in Belgium; detention homes for children; causes of juvenile delinquency.

Bohemia

Einhorn, Ulrich. Kriminalität der Jugendlichen in Böhmen, Mähren und Schlesien. Prager Juris Zeitsch 11: 19-24 Ja 1 '31 1783

Canada

Canadian council on child and family welfare. Study outlines of some child welfare problems in the Canadian field. Ottawa, 1927 1784

Canadian council on child and family welfare. Delinquency section. Youth in revolt; study of youthful offenders in Canadian penitentiaries. 30p. (C.C.C.F.W. Public no48A ed.2) Toronto, 1931 1785

Colombia

Bejarano, Jorge. La delincuencia infantil en Colombia y la profilaxis del crimen. Instit Int Am de Protec a la Infancia Bol 3: 262-93 O '29 1786

Czechoslovakia

Steiner, Robert. Der tschechoslowakische Entwurf über die Jugendstrafgerichtsbarkeit. Monats f Kriminalpsychol u Strafrechtsref 22: 151-61 Mr '31 1787

France

Juvenile delinquency in France. Sch & Soc 26: 802 D 24 '27 1788

Paul-Boncour, G[eorges]. Les causes de la criminalité juvénile parisienne. (Enquête médical et psychosociologique). Prog Méd 44: 1413-21 Ag 24 '29 1789

Paul-Boncour, Georges. Une récente enquête sur la criminalité infantile et juvénile à Paris. Etudes Crimin 4: 65-72 Mr '29 1790

Germany

Liszt, Elsa v. Die Kriminalität der Jugendlichen in Berlin in den Jahren 1926 und 1927. Zeitsch f d ges Strafrechtswiss 50: 505-23 '30 1791

Great Britain

Blouw, H. C. V. De behandeling van de jeudige misdadigers in Engeland. 74p. Haarlem, Dr. Warnier, jr. 1928 1792

Craven, Cicely M. The young offenders' report. Howard J 2: 100-6 '27 1793
Report of the Departmental committee on the treatment of young offenders.

Fuller, E. Juvenile offenders in England; a historical survey. R Int de l'Enf 3: 420-34 '27 1794

Great Britain. Department of state. Report of the Departmental committee on the treatment of young offenders. 139p. (Cmd 2831) London, H. M. Stationery office, 1927 1795

Hatton, S. F. London's bad boys. 203p. London, Chapman, 1931 1796

Mesurier, L. Le. Boys in trouble. 284p. London, Murray, 1931 1797

Holland

Juvenile delinquency in Holland. Just Peace 92: 496 Jl 21 '28 1798

India

Chatterjee, Mohinimohan. Juvenile offenders in Calcutta. Calcutta R 34: 417-21 '30 **1799**

Italy

Petraccone, G. Il problema sociale e giuridico della delinquenza dei minorenni con speciale riguardo al nuovo codice penale. Riv di Dir Peniten 1: 732-48 '30 **1800**

Veratti, N. Della delinquenza minorile. Scuola Pos 11: 374-82 Ag '31 **1801**

Japan

Maruyama, R. Studies on delinquent children. Kyoiku Shinri Kenkyu 4(4) '29 **1802**

Poland

Neymark, Edward.. Des mineurs en Pologne. R de Dr Pén et de Crimin 8: 152-61 F '28 **1803**

Portugal

Legislaçao sôbre menores delinqüentes. 359p. Lisboa, Reformatório Central de Lisboa, 1930 **1804**

Collection of all Portuguese laws and decrees dealing with juvenile delinquency, 1871-1930.

Russia

Child vagrancy in Russia. Sch & Soc 28: 262-3 S 1 '28 **1805**

Weissenberg, S. Die Verwahrlosung der Jugend in Sowjetrussland. Zeitsch f Sexualwissensch 15: 225-53 S 4 '28 **1806**

Spain

Heras, Josè de Las. La juventud delincuente en España y su tratamiento reformador. 150p. Alcalà de Henares, Imp. de la Escuela Ind. de Jòvenes, 1927 **1807**

Study of juvenile delinquents with special reference to the reformatory school at Henares.

Switzerland

Fiala, H. Der Regierungsentwurf. Bundesgesetz über die Behandlung junger Rechtsbrecher. Jurist Bl 57: 140-6 '28 **1808**

Thormann, P. Entwurf eines Gesetzes betreffend die Jugendstrafrechtspflege für den Kanton Bern (vom 30. März 1921) nebst Erlaüterungen. Schweiz Zeitsch f Strafr 40: 257-96 '27 **1809A**

Union of South Africa

Gray, G. D. Juvenile crime in the Union. Police J [N Y] 18: 21, 27 Ja '31 **1809B**

United States

California

Ball, Robert Jaudon. A survey of 146 committed delinquents in San Francisco. J Juv Res 12: 241-3 S '28 **1810**

California. Commission for the study of problem children. Report, January 1929. 64p. bibliog 54-64. Sacramento, 1929 Report January 1931. 88p. bibliog 70-88. Sacramento, 1931 **1811**

Mangold, George B. and Hardy, Sophie. Juvenile delinquency. *In their* Building a better San Jose: a social survey, 127-38. San Jose, Calif. Community Chest, 1930 **1812**

Mangold, George B. and Thompson, S. Lucille. [Juvenile delinquency]. *In their* Community welfare in San Diego, 118-29. San Diego, Calif. Community Welfare Council, 1930 **1813**

Nelles, Fred C. Californa's commission for the study of problem children. J Delin 11: 1-4 Mr '27 **1814**

Scudder, Kenyon J. Report of the California commission for the study of problem children. Calif Conf Soc Wk Q Bul 12: 37-8 F '29 **1815**

Slaughter, E. M. The trend of juvenile delinquency in Los Angeles. Pac Police Mag 6: 5, 23 Je '29 **1816**

Colorado

City club of Denver. Juvenile delinquency in Denver, August 1, 1930. 23p. (Pam no21) [Denver, 1930] **1817**

Ebaugh, Franklin G. and others. Studies in juvenile delinquency in Colorado. I: One hundred boys. Univ Colo Stud 18: 9-28 Ag '30 **1818**

Study of boys committed to the State industrial school at Golden.

Georgia

Work with delinquent children. *In* Georgia. Department of public welfare, Report 1927-1928: 82-97 **1819**

Illinois

Burke, Dorothy Williams. Youth and crime: a study of the prevalence and treatment of delinquency among boys over juvenile court age in Chicago. 205p. (Pub no196) Washington, U. S. Children's bureau, 1930 **1820**

Study of 82 boys, 1915-1925.

Chicago. Police department. Boy's employment bureau. Police "13-13" 4: 35 S '29 **1821**

Cottrell, Leonard Slater. Juvenile delinquency among the Negro groups of Chicago. Thesis (Ph.D.) University of Chicago, 1929 **1823**

Hanna, Francis D. Murder by juveniles in Chicago. Crim Just [Chicago] (48): 10-11 F '27 **1824**

IOWA

Iowa. Board of control of state institutions. Compilation of the laws of Iowa relating to children, 1927. 53p. Des Moines, 1927 **1825**

MAINE

United States. Children's bureau. Juvenile delinquency in Maine. 90p. (Pub no201) Washington, 1930 **1826**

MICHIGAN

Pilidies, A. P. Detroit where boys were bad. R of Rs 79: 69-71 Je '29 **1827**

NEW JERSEY

New Jersey. Juvenile and probation study commission. Report, authorized by Joint resolution no2, approved March 28, 1927. 40p. Trenton, February 17, 1928 **1828**

United States. Children's bureau. Child welfare in New Jersey: Pt.4: Local provision for dependent and delinquent children in relation to the state's program. 76p. (Pub no180) Washington, 1927 **1829**

NEW YORK

Joint committee on Negro child study in New York city. Study of delinquent and neglected Negro children before the New York city children's court 1925; the Committee in cooperation with the department of research of the National urban league and the Women's city club of New York. 48p. N. Y. 110-2d ave. 1927 **1830**

New York (state). Crime commission. Sub-commission on causes and effects of crime. From truancy to crime—a study of 251 adolescents. 139p. Albany, 1928 **1831**

New York (state). Crime commission. Sub-commission on causes and effects of crime. Individual studies of 145 offenders. 128p. Albany, 1928 **1832**

New York (state). Crime commission. Sub-commission on causes and effects of crime. A study of delinquency in a district of Kings county. 57p. Albany, 1927 **1833**

New York (state). Crime commission. Sub-commission on causes and effects of crime. A study of delinquency in two rural counties. 48p. Albany, 1927 **1834**

New York (state). Crime commission. Sub-commission on causes and effects of crime. A study of problem boys and their brothers. 408p. Albany, 1929 **1835**

Offenses committed by continuation school boys in New York state. Sch & Soc 29: 799-800 Je 22 '29 **1836**

Survey of child crime [by the sub-committee of the Baumes crime commission of New York state on causes and effects of crime]. Inf Serv 2-3 Je 1 '28 **1837**

NORTH DAKOTA

Harper, Fowler V. and Reinhardt, James M. Juvenile delinquency, a study of environmental factors in the city of Grand Forks, North Dakota. Univ N D Q J 21: 26-32 D '30 **1838**
Analysis of 40 cases of juvenile delinquency.

OKLAHOMA

Stoner, Worthy E. Oklahoma plan; a proposed enactment . . . to . . . decrease crime . . . during the age of adolescence. 31p. Oklahoma City, Okla. Salesman co. 1929 **1839**

OREGON

Chamberlin, Clara Wilkins. Survey of juvenile delinquency in Portland from September 1, 1929 to June 1, 1930. Commonwealth R 13: 160-75 Jl '31 **1840**

Roach, William L. Record of juvenile delinquency in Benton county, Oregon (1907-1929). J Juv Res 14: 34-40 Ja '30 **1841**

PENNSYLVANIA

Moss, Margaret Steel. Care of juvenile delinquents in Pennsylvania. 21p. (Bul no29 rev. ed.) Harrisburg, Pennsylvania, Department of welfare, Bureau of children, April 17, 1929 **1842**

United States. Children's bureau. Care of juvenile offenders. *In* Child-welfare conditions and resources in seven Pennsylvania counties, by Neva R. Deardorff, 82-160. (Pub no176) Washington, 1927 **1843**

TENNESSEE

Hiller, Francis H. The treatment of juvenile offenders in Nashville, Tennessee; report of a survey. 72p. N. Y. National probation association, April 1931 **1844**

TEXAS

Dallas county, Tex. Juvenile board. Report . . . and case analyses by Child guidance clinic from January 1, 1925 to January 1, 1927. 72p. Dallas, Juvenile board, 1927 **1845**

UTAH

Beeley, Arthur Lawton. Boys and girls in Salt Lake City; the results of a survey made for the Rotary club and the Business and professional women's club of Salt Lake City. 220p. (Pub of Dept of sociology & social technology) Salt Lake City, University of Utah, 1929 **1846**

WISCONSIN

Caldwell, Morris Gilmore. Juvenile delinquency in Wisconsin. J Juv Res 14: 87-95 Ap '30 **1847**

GIRL DELINQUENTS

Ball, Lucy D. The delinquent girl—and music. Welf Mag 18: 93-7 Ja '27 1849

Bellot, E. Das verwahrloste Mädchen. Int Zeitsch f Individualpsychol 6: 130-40 '28 1850

Courthial, Andrée. Social diagnosis in a girls' service agency. Family 11: 251-3 D '30 1851

Duffy, Alice. The missing girl. Minn St Conf & Inst Soc Wk Proc 36: 241-52 '28 1852

Address before Association of policewomen of Minnesota and Northwest.

Milliken, Rhoda J. The missing girl. Nat Prob Assn Proc 1928: 225-31; same title: Policewoman's Int Bul 4: 6-8 Jl '28; Police J [N Y] 16: 15, 31 N '28 1853

Patterson, Inez B. Paths of the handicapped: of the delinquent girl. Minn St Bd Con Q 29: 16-17 S 13 '29 1854

Roberts, Beth. Zaida, chronic runaway. Survey 62: 568-71 S 1 '29 1855

Wembridge, Eleanor Rowland. Girls gone wrong. Am Mercury 23: 200-8 Je '31 1856

Wiethold, F. Sadismus bei weiblichen Jugendlichen. Deut Zeitsch f d ges gerichtl Med 11: 329-39 Je 5 '28 1857

PRE-DELINQUENTS

Crosby, Joyce. When should a pre-delinquent child be removed from his own home? Minn St Conf & Inst Soc Wk Proc 37: 118-23 '29 1858

Driver, Mary F. The place of the boarding home for the pre-delinquent. Minn St Conf & Inst Soc Wk Proc 37: 127-33 '29 1859

Glenn, Laurence A. A description and definition of the pre-delinquent child. Minn St Conf & Inst Soc Wk Proc 37: 116-18 '29 1860

Jones, Blanche. When is a child a pre-delinquent? Minn St Conf & Inst Soc Wk Proc 37: 108-12 '29 1861

McDonald, Marie. When is a child pre-delinquent? Minn St Conf & Inst Soc Wk Proc 37: 112-16 '29 1862

Sanctis, Sante de. Il problema assistenziale dei predelinquenti. Scuola Pos 337-48 Ag '31 1863

Schumacher, Henry C. The place of the boarding home for the pre-delinquent child. Minn St Conf & Inst Soc Wk Proc 37: 123-7 '29 1864

West, Max W. An experiment in treatment of the pre-delinquent boy. Nat Prob Assn Proc 1928: 206-15 1865

TRUANTS

Bender, John Frederick. The functions of courts in enforcing school-attendance laws. 187p. (Contrib to Educ no262) N. Y. Columbia univ. Teachers college, 1927 1866

McElwee, Edna Willis. A study of truants and retardation. J Juv Res 15: 209-14 Jl '31 1867

Mead, Laura L. Report on the survey of truancy for the year 1929-1930. Commonwealth R 13: 245-65 N '31 1868

New York (state). Crime commission. Sub-commission on causes and effects of crime. A study of 201 truants in the New York city schools. 20p. Albany, 1927 1869

Thót, Ladislao. La inasistencia escolar y la criminalidad de los niños. Instit Int Am de Protec a la Infancia Bol 3: 681-90 Ap '30; same title: R de Crimin, Psiquiat y Med Leg 18: 10-16 Ja '31 1870

Williams, Herbert D. Truancy and delinquency. J Ap Psychol 11: 276-88 Ag '27 1871

GANGS (BOY)

McLellan, Howard. Boys, gangs, and crime. R of R 79: 54-9 Mr '29 1872

Miller, Mildred E. The "cops" adopt the "gang." Welf Mag 19: 169-74 F '28 1873

Thrasher, Frederic M. The boy and his gang. Nat Prob Assn Prob 1930: 113-24 1874

Thrasher, Frederic M. Gang; a study of 1,313 gangs in Chicago. 571p. Chicago, Univ. of Chicago press, 1927 1875

POLITICAL

Barthès, Léon. Les condamnés politiques au Mont-Saint-Michel. 32p. Chartres, Imp. Lainé & Tantea, 1929 1876

Beffel, John Nicholas. Political prisoners, 1931. Nation [N Y] 132: 475-6 Ap 29 '31 1877

International committee for political prisoners. Memorandum and report—August 1931. 4p. (mim) N.Y. [1931] 1878

International committee for political prisoners. Venezuela, land of oil and tyranny. 11p. N.Y. February 1931 1879

Langle, Emilio. La teoria de la política criminal. 253p. Madrid, Reus, 1927 1880

Political internments in Italy. Living Age 332: 577-81 Ap 1 '27 1881

Thót, Ladislao. Estudios de política criminal practica norteamericana. R Arg de Cienc Pol 34: 153-222 Ap '27 1882

Thot, Ladislao. Política criminal Norteamericana; sentencias indeterminadas; sistema de palabra; sistema de perdón; delincuentes menores. R de Identif y Cienc Pen 3: 401-39 Mr '29 1883

Thót, Ladislao. La politica criminale. Giustiz Pen 37: col 22-31, 222-32, 342-55, 476-85, 605-20 Ja-My '31 1884

Walling, William English. Terrorism under the Cuban dictatorship; an exposure of facts suppressed by the press. 11p. N. Y. International committee for political prisoners, May 1930 1885

Professional

Adamic, Louis. Dynamite; the story of class violence in America. 437p. N. Y. Viking press, 1931 **1886**
Present-day racketeering and its relation to the conflict between labor and capital.

Adamic, Louis. Racketeers. New Repub 65: 210-12 Ja 7 '31 **1887**

Adamic, Louis. Racketeers and organized labor. Harper's 161: 404-16 S '30 **1888**
Brief history of labor racketeering, tracing back to the Molly Maguires, and from them back to the 19th century landlord feuds in Ireland.

Asbury, Herbert. Gangs of New York; an informal history of the underworld. 382p. N.Y. Knopf, 1928 **1889**

Bennett, James O'Donnell. Chicago gang land; the true story of Chicago crime. 87p. (Chicago tribune pub no35) Chicago, Chicago tribune, 1928 **1890**

Bolitho, William. The gangster traumatism. Survey 63: 661-5, 688 Mr 1 '30 **1891**

Bolitho, William. The psychosis of the gang. Survey 63: 501-6 F 1 '30; same title: R of R 81: 86-8 Mr '30 **1892**

Booth, Ernest. Ladies of the mob. Am Mercury 12: 399-407 D '27 **1893**

Bundesen, Herman N. The gang murders; beer war slayings in Chicago. Police "13-13" 4: 3, 20 My '29 **1894**

Business and the racketeers. R of R 83: 72-3 My '31 **1895**

Carey, Arthur A. Business men at arms; rise of gang warfare. Collier's 85: 10-11 F 15 '30 **1896**

Chicago gang wars in pictures; X marks the spot. 64p. Rockford, Ill. Spot pub co. 502 Manufacturers bank bldg. 1930 **1897**

Chicago's gang leaders and gangsters: some data concerning the present status of the "public enemies." Crim Just [Chicago] (59): 1, 55 D '30 **1898**

Chicago's gang wars. Outl 152: 132-3 My 22 '29 **1899**

Conboy, Martin. Organized crime as a business and its bearing upon the administration of criminal law. N Y Univ L R 7: 339-51 D '29 **1900**

Crowther, Samuel. Invisible government; organized crime hides under the cloak of bootlegging. Ladies Home J 48: 20 Ap '31 **1901**

Crowther, Samuel. Invisible government; what racketeering costs the home. Ladies Home J 48: 3 F '31 **1902**

The dinner of the racketeers; a review by one of the guests. Welf Mag 18: 184-90 F '27 **1903**

Duffus, R. L. The function of the racketeer. New Repub 58: 166-8 Mr 27 '29 **1904**

Farrar, Irene. Racketeering: an interesting brief of the origin and present activity of racketeering; it can thrive only under political protection. Kan Munic 17: 13-17 Ag '31 **1905**

Ferri, E[nrico]. La lotta contro la mafia in Sicilia. Scuola Pos ns8: 289-96 Jl '28 **1906**

Gang crimes, the possible remedies. L Notes 32: 102-3 S '28 **1907**

Gangland and its foundation; views of a sixteen-year-old gangster. Survey 64: 511 S 15 '30 **1908**

Gangster. Nation [N Y] 129: 31-2 Jl 10 '29 **1909**

Glueck, Sheldon. The gang phenomenon. Soc Serv R 1: 557-66 D '27 **1910**

Government by the gangster. New Repub 67: 329-30 Ag 12 '31 **1911**

Gowen, Emmett, ed. True exposé of racketeers and their methods. 96p. N.Y. Popular bk. corp. 1930 **1912**

Grey, Jack. New underworld. Outl 151: 443-6 Mr 20 '29 **1913**

Grinnell, Flint. Eight types of "white collared bandits." Chic Banker 13- Ap 13 '29 **1914**

Grünewald, M. Moralische Minderwertigkeit, Berufsverbrechertum und Nachkommenschaft. Fortschr d Med 46: 843-4 Ag 24 '28 **1915**

Hanna, Francis D. Professional racketeer in new graft. Crim Just [Chicago] 9: 6-7 S '27 **1916**

Hart, Albert Bushnell. The modern Mafia. Cur Hist 34: 409-11 Je '31 **1917**

Heindl, Robert. Der Berufsverbrecher; ein Beitrag zur Strafrechtsreform. (ed. 6 1928) ed. 7 Berlin, R. Heise, 1929 **1918**

Hellstern, Erwin P. Kriminalitätsverhältnisse und deren Ursachen bei Schwerverbrechern. Arch f Psychiat 82: 719-43 '28 **1919**

H[entig, Hans] von. Beitrag zur Frage des Berufsverbrechers. Monats f Kriminalpsychol u Strafrechtsref 22: 371-5 '31 **1920**

Holitscher, Arthur. Wiedersehn mit Amerika. Neue Rundsch 41 pt1: 71-106, 188-222, 354-8 Ja-Mr '30 **1921**

Hostetter, Gordon L. and Beesley, Thomas Quinn. It's a racket! 299p. Chicago, Les Quin Books Inc. 1929 **1922**
Includes glossary of hoodlum language; sup1: Business by bombs: list of bombs set in Chicago area, October 11, 1927-January 15, 1929; sup2: There's a law against it: sections of Illinois statutes under which rackets may be prosecuted; sup3: Contract by which Dental laboratories assn. of Chicago agreed to resist a racket; sup4: For the cost of crime—eleven billion dollars! address by George E. Q. Johnson; sup5: The injunction as a defense against rackets, by Dudley Taylor.

Hunt, Lewis W. The rise of a racketeer; portrait of Alphonse Capone. Outl 156: 574-6 D 10 '30 **1923**

Keulers, P. H. Der Berufsverbrecher. Deut Richterzeit 19 (5): 183-6 My '27 **1924**

Landesco, John. Gang life and organized crime in Chicago. Am B Assn Rep 55: 579-93 '30 **1925**

Landesco, John. Organized crime in Chicago. *In* Illinois association for criminal justice, Illinois crime survey, 815-1091, 1929 **1926**

Lashly, Arthur V. Professional criminal and organized crime; with a symposium on the effects of prohibition. 37p. Chicago, American bar assn. 1928 **1927**

Lewis, Lloyd. Chicago's booze war. New Repub 58: 88-90 Mr 13 '29 1928
Lima, Estacio de. Haverá maior temibilidade no criminoso profissional? R de Cultura Jurid 1: 464-7 Jl '29 1929
Lippmann, Walter. The underworld: a stultified conscience. Forum 85: 1-4 Ja '31 1930
Lloyd, George. War on gangs dries Chicago; Chicago gangdom's rise. Int Pict Pol J 15-21 Ap '29 1931
Lynd, Robert (Y. Y. pseud). Business man a hero. New Statesman 35: 616-17 Ag 23 '30 1932
McCarthy, Katherine O'Shea. Racketeering: a contribution to a bibliography. J Crim L & Crimin 22: 578-86 N '31 1933
McConaughy, John. From Cain to Capone; racketeering down the ages. 336p. N.Y. Bretano's, 1931 1934
McGrath, William. Who are the gangsters? Cath Char R 14: 132-6 My '30 1935
Mackaye, Milton. Milwaukee gangless. 8p. (Pub no3) N.Y. New York Committee of one thousand, 25 E. 26 st. 1931 1936
Markey, Morris. Gangs. Atlan M 141: 296-305 Mr '28 1937
Moley, Raymond. Crime as a profession. Cur Hist 30: 999-1006 S '29 1938
Morain, Alfred. The underworld of Paris. 320p. N.Y. Dutton, 1931 1939
New king of racketeers. New Repub 68: 195 O 7 '31 1940
On outlawing gangsters. Rocky Mo L R 3: 151-2 F '31 1941
Orlov, Vladimïr Grigor'evich. Underworld and Soviet; transl. by Mona Heath. 273p. N.Y. Dial press, 1931 1942
Memoirs of a Russian judge.
Page, James A. Organized crime and suggested remedies. Mo B J 1: 5 My '30 1943
Parsons, Floyd W. Better people as well as better machines. Gas Age 65: 863-4 Je 7 '30 1944
Parsons, James. Are criminals to rule the United States? First Friend 26 (2-3): 3 '31 1945
Pasley, Fred D. Muscling in. N.Y. Ives Washburn, 1931 1946
The "lowdown" on the gangster's increasing control of legitimate business.
Racketeering. Economist 111: 753-5 O 25 '30 1947
Racketeering as it is done in New York. Am Ind 30: 17-27 D '29 1948
Racketeering drives. Outl 156: 530 D 3 '30 1949
Rackets of Chicago. New Statesman 35: 110-12 My 3 '30 1950
Rackets of New York. New Statesman 36: 262-4 D 6 '30 1951
Reinhardt, Charles Gilbert and Coolbaugh, Kenneth. Employment rackets. Sat Eve Post 203: 25 N 8 '30 1952
Rice, Thomas S. "No quarter to gangsters." Police J [N Y] 18: 5, 16 Ag '31 1953
Schnurmacher. Yo! ho! ho! and the jolly racketeers! Comm & Fin 18: 11-13 Ja 21 '29 1954
Shepherd, William G. What's the racket. Collier's 87: 10-11 Ap 11 '31 1955
Smith, Bruce. Business can whip the racketeer. Nation's Bus 19: 27-30 Ap '31 1956
Sollima, Pasquale. I delinquenti di professione. Scuola Pos 37: 225-31 '29 1957
Stabilization through racketeering. New Repub 68: 183 S 30 '31 1958
States and the racketeers. World's Wk 60: 18 F '31 1959
Non extension of federal laws to cover racketeering.
Sullivan, Edward Dean. Racketeers—after repeal; the racket threat under prohibition repeal. Police "13-13" 5: 5-7, 74 Ag '30 1960
Terrett, Courtenay. Only saps work; a ballyhoo for racketeering. 235p. N.Y. Vanguard, 1930 1961
Uncle Sam takes his cut; undeclared incomes of gangsters and racketeers. Collier's 87: 66 My 23 '31 1962
War on the underworld. Outl 151: 372 Mr 6 '29 1963
Whitaker, Ulrich. Finance company racket. Am Mercury 23: 433-9 Ag '31 1964
Willemse, Cornelius W. Detective vs. gangster; the fight on gangdom. Police "13-13" 6: 3-6, 16-17, 20 Mr '31 1965
Worthington, George E. New York's underworld. Panel 8: 5, 9 N '30 1966
Worthington, George E. The underworld on top? Chamber Comm St N Y Bul 22: 450-7 Mr '31 1967

International

Boutet, Frederick. International criminals past and present; translated by W. Mostyn. 192p. London, Hutchinson, 1930 1968
Politis, Nicolas. La criminalité internationale. R Pol & Litt 65: 232-6 Ap 16 '27 1969

Transient

Robb, W. L. The transient criminal. Police "13-13" 5: 16-18 Mr '30 1970
Roberts, A. J. The problem of the transient criminal. Police J [N Y] 17: 14-15, 32 O '29 1971
Roberts, A. J. The problem of the transient criminal and how to deal with it. Int Assn Chiefs Police Proc 36: 31-6 '29 1972
Rogers, William A. The roving criminal. Justice 1: 57-60 D '28 1973

Women

Aikman, Duncan. Ladies and lawlessness. Harper's 158: 312-19 F '29 1974
Binford, Jessie. Police and women offenders. Policewoman's Int Bul 3: 2-3 N '27 1975
Bishop, Cecil. Women and crime. 295p. London, Chatto, 1931 1976
Braungard, Marion. Cultivating a wild rose. Psychol Clin 18: 282-90 F '30 1977
Butler, Charlotte Sperry. Women delinquents: their custodial care. Welf Mag 18: 438-40 Ap '27 1978

Capital offenses by women. L Times 171: 440-1 My 23 '31 1979

Carey, Arthur A. Women overdo it. Collier's 86: 12-13 Ag 16 '30 1980

Castellanos, Israel. La delincuencia femenina en Cuba; estadísticas judiciales, penitenciarias y clínicas; gráficas criminológicas. v. 1, 3. bibliog 117-22. Habana, Imp. "Ojeda," 1929 1981
v.2, unpubl.

Celebrated criminal women. Justice 1: 77-80 O '28 1982

Chesterton, Ada E. (Jones) (Mrs. Cecil Edward Chesterton) (John Keith Prothero, pseud). Women of the underworld. London, Stanley Paul, 1930 1983

Comstock, Harriet J. The woman offender in Illinois. Welf 18: 311-13 Mr '27 1984

Hodder, Jessie D. The problem of the woman offender. Mass Dept Correc Q 3: 3 Ap '27 1985

Krille, Hans. Weibliche Kriminalität und Ehe. 64p. (Krimin Abh no15) Leipzig, Ernst Wiegandt, 1931 1986

Ladu, Lena and Garrison, K. C. A study of emotional instability and intelligence of women in the penal institutions of North Carolina. Soc Forces 10: 209-16 D '31 1987

Lombroso-Ferrero, G. I delitti femminili e le nuove professioni della donna. Arch di Antrop Crim 50: 839-42 N '30 1988

McAdoo, William. Young women and crime. Ladies Home J 44: 32 N '27 1989

MacGill, Helen Gregory. A woman delinquent. Police J [N Y] 18: 25 Ja '31 1990

Monahan, Florence. Paths of the handicapped: of the delinquent women. Minn St Bd Con Q 29: 27-8 S 13 '29 1991

Morel, G. Les tueuses d'enfants. 122p. Nancy, Rigot & Cie. 1927 1992

Neville, Marion. Ladies of the gang: a study in feminine deportment: underworld specie. Police "13-13" 5: 10-11 My '30 1993

Neville, Marion. Our laws and the ladies; does justice discriminate against sex? Police "13-13" 4: 16-17, 77 My '29 1994

O'Donnell, Elliott. Women bluebeards. 286p. London, Stanley Paul, 1930 1995

Swiller, Yvonne-Marie. Déficiences morales féminines. Etudes Crimin 5: 188-93 Je '30 1996

Williamson, William Henry. Annals of crime; some extraordinary women. 285p. London, Routledge, 1930 1997

Wyndham, Horace. Feminine frailty. 352p. London, Benn, 1929 1998

Murderers

Bridgman, Olga. Four young murderers. J Juv Res 13: 90-6 Ap '29 1999

Cooper, Courtney Ryley. Worst of us: murderers. Collier's 87: 19 F 28 '31 2000

Frenkel, Helene. Der Mörder der nicht aus Gewinnsucht handelt. Monats f Kriminalpsychol u Strafrechtsref 20: 207-17 O '29 2001

Lucas, N. Innocent murderers? Criminologist [London] 1: 10-11 My 15 '27 2002

Merz, Charles. Bigger and better murders. Harper's 155: 338-43 Ag '27 2003

Bandits, etc.

Bigger and better bandits. Collier's 83: 66 Ap 13 '29 2004

Eberlein, K. K. Berühmte räuberfrauen. Westerm Monatsh 149: 270-2 N '30 2005

Elwenspoek, C. Räuberhistorien und historische räuber. Westerm Monatsh 146: 75-80 Mr '29 2006

Fighting pirates in China. Pop Mech 47: 194-7 F '27 2007

Glasgow, George. Bias Bay pirates [China]. Contemp R 132: 522-4 O '27 2008

Hotson, Leslie. Pirates in parchment. Atlan M 140: 208-15 Ag '27 2009

Van Cise, Philip S. The bandit of 1928—what makes him possible. Police J [N Y] 16: 22-3, 25 S '28 2010

Waddell, Georgiana. Hi-jackers of the high seas. Nat Repub 17: 24-5 Mr '30 2011

Others

Baum, James E. Stepping ahead of the bank crook. 7p. N.Y. American bankers association, Protective department, 1931? 2012

Butt-Thompson, F. W. The criminal native secret societies of the west coast of Africa. Police J [London] 4: 263-72 Ap '31 2013

Ceillier, A. Os epilépticos delinqüêntes e criminosos—Sua responsibilidade; Sua assistência. Bol do Inst de Crimin s7 12 (1): 231-55 '30 2014

[Clark, W. D.]. Old-time yeggman disappearing. Spectator [London] 125: 43 D 18 '30 2015

Fricke, Charles W. Narcotic peddlers as a police problem. Peace Offic Assn Calif Proc 8: 21-5 '28 2016

Grey, Jack. Safe makers and safe breakers. Outl 152: 609-11 Ag 14 '29; same title: R of R 80: 101-2 O '29 2017

Hollins, S. T. The criminal tribes of Northern India. Police J [London] 3: 277-88 Ap '30 2018

Locard, E[dmond]. Evolution of the motor bandit. Criminologist [London] 1: 11-12 My 15 '27 2019

Mills, M. Bombers and window-smashers. Police "13-13" 2: 10-11 Jl '27 2020

O'Connor, John James. Broadway racketeers. 255p. N.Y. Liveright, 1928 2021

Onaert, R. H. The problem of the armed criminal in Singapore. Police J [London] 3: 425-34 Jl '30 2022

Preaching burglar of Tokio. Living Age 336: 120-1 Ap '29 2023

Semerau, Alfred and Zeidler, Paul Gerhard. Die grossen Diebe. 338p. Wittenberg, Ziemsen, 1927 2024

Tozer, Basil John. Confidence crooks and blackmailers; their ways and methods. 236p. London, Laurie, 1929 2025

Vollmer, August. The hold-up man. "2-0" Police J 6: 7- Ap '28; same title: Police J [N Y] 16: 16-17 O '28 2026

CRIMINAL ANTHROPOLOGY

Amaldi, P. Verso più ampi orizzonti dell'antropologia criminale. Riv Sper di Freniat 54: 567-91 S 30 '30 **2027**

Archivio di antropologia criminale, psichiatria, medicina legale e scienze affini. Torino, 1, 1880- **2028**
Official organ of Italian association of legal medicine and Seminary of criminal anthropology and penal law.

Arquivo de Repartiçào de antropologia criminal, psicologia experimental e identifiçào civil do Porto. fasc 1, March 1931- **2029**
Director: Prof. Pires de Lima, Araujo e Sobrinho, 50 L. de S. Domingos Porto (Oporto).

Ashton-Wolfe, H. Facial characteristics of the criminal. Criminologist [Chicago] 5: 33-4 Je '29 **2030**

Balthazard, V. Organisation de services d'anthropologie criminelle dans les prisons. Paris Méd 2: 457-60 N 23 '29; same title: Arch di Antrop Crim 50: 843-9 '30 **2031**

Bertillon, A. and Chervin, A. Anthropologie métrique. Conseils pratique aux missionnaires scientifiques sur la manière de mesurer, de photographier et de décrire des sujets vivants et des pièces anatomiques. Anthropométrie. 234p. Paris, Gamber, 1931? **2032**

Brasol, Boris [Leo]. Anthropology and crime. Am J Phys Anthrop 12: 339-46 O '28 **2033**

Carrara, Mario. Le devenir de l'anthropologie criminelle. R de Dr Pén et de Crimin 10: 661-9 bibliog (p668-9) '30 **2034**

Castellanos, Israel. La constitucion en el Laboratorio de Antropología penitenciaria. 11p. Habana, Imp. y libreria "La Propagandista," 1930 **2035**

Castellanos, Israel. Los estigmas somaticos de la degeneration. Su appreciacion en las razas de color. 17p. Habana, Imp. y Libreria "La Propagandista," 1927 **2036**

Corrêa, A.-A. Mendes. A nova antropologia criminal. Porto, Imp. Portuguesa, 1931 **2037**

El curso de antropologia criminal del doctor Vervaeck. Bibl Nac de Crim y Cienc Afines Bol 1: 226-31 Ja 27 **2048**

Gómez Robleda, José. Algunas consideraciones sobre antropología criminal. Quetzalcoatl 1: 8-10 S '30 **2049**

Greeff, Etienne de. La notion de responsabilité en anthropologie criminelle. R de Dr Pén et de Crimin 11: 445-60 My '31 **2050**

Gualdi, V. Ricerche cliniche anatomiche e anthropometriche su d'una anomalia di conformazione ereditaria e familiare del naso e sui suoi rapporti con le affezioni delle vie lacrimali. Arch di Antrop Crim 51: 217-52 '31 **2051**

Hacker. Kriminalanthropologische Forschungen und Datensammlungen der Gegenwart. Monats f Kriminalpsychol u Strafrechtsref 20: 37-8 '29 **2052**

Hartenstein, H. Das Verbrecheralbum. R Int de Crimin 2(3): 201-5 '30 **2053**

Hentig, Hans von. Physiognomik in Sprichwort. Arch f Krim 80: 136-44 Mr '27 **2054**

Herrero, Antonio. Contribución al estudio de la individualización humana; Síntesis de la antroponimia de Alberto Dauzat. R de Identif y Cienc Pen 8: 164-82 My '31 **2055**

Kleinschmidt. Problematik in der Kriminalistik. Krimin Monatsh 4: 103-6 My '30 **2056**
Correlation between anatomical configuration and criminal behavior.

Lange, Johannes. Verbrechen als Schicksal. Studien an kriminellen Zwillingen. 96p. Leipzig, G. Thieme, 1929
Tr: Crime and destiny; translated by Charlotte (Franken) Haldane. 250p. Revisions for American ed. by Eugene William Löhrke. N. Y. Boni, 1930
Tr: Crime as destiny; translated by Charlotte (Franken) Haldane. 200p. London, Allen & Unwin, 1931 **2057**
Study of 13 pairs of twins, one brother or one sister of which was a criminal.

Lindenau, Heinrich. Physionomik und Kriminalistik. Arch f Krim 80: 171-3 Mr '27 **2058**

Loewenstein, Georg. Ein Beitrag zur Physiognomik des Verbrechers. Krimin Monatsh 1: 270-5 D '27 **2059**

Lucifero, Falcone. Antropologia, biologia e delinquenza minorile. Scuola Pos ns11: 212-21 My '31 **2060**

Mohr, G. J. and Gunlach, R. H. Further study of relation between physique and performance in criminals. J Abnorm & Soc Psychol 24: 91-103 Ap '29 **2061**

Ottolenghi. L'interpretazione antropologica biografica del Cartellino Segnaletico. R Int de Crimin 2 (2): 103-7 '30 **2062**

Ramos, Juan P. La escuela de Enrico Ferri en la republica Argentina. Buenos Aires Univ R 8: 5-22 Ja '29 **2063**

Saldana, Quintiliano. L'anthropologie criminelle intégrale. Pensiero Giurid-Pen 1: 189-201 Ap '29 **2064**

Saporito, Filippo. L'antropologia criminale e i suoi maggiori sviluppi. Arch di Antrop Crim 50: 25-33 Ja '30 **2065**

Türkel, Siegfried. Beiträge zur Kriminalistischen Symptomatologie und Technik. 173p. Graz, Moser, 1931 **2066**

Tullio, B di. Die Kriminalanthropologie und das neue italienische Strafgesetzbuch. Monats f Kriminalpsychol u Strafrechtsref 22: 342-6 My '31 **2067**

Tullio, B. di. Manuale di antropologia e psicologia criminale applicata alla pedagogia emendativa, alla polizia ed al diritto penale e penitenziario. 367p. Roma, Anonima Romana Editoriale, 1931 **2068**

Wimmer, A. Zur Kriminalität der Encephalitiker. Acta Psychiat & Neurol 5: 23-43 '30 **2069**

CRIMINAL LANGUAGE

Aebischer, Paul. Un argot de malfaiteurs parlé dans le canton de Fribourg à la fin du XVIIe siècle. R de Philol Fr 42 (1): 106-17 '30 **2070**

Ashton-Wolfe, H. Languages and the criminal. Criminologist [London] 1: 8-9 My 15 '27 **2071**

Beath, Paul Robert. More crook words. Am Speech 6: 131-4 D '30 **2072**

Booth, Ernest. Language of the underworld. Am Mercury 14: 78-81 My '28 **2073**

Brown, W. F. Thieves and their argot. Police J [London] 4: 500-5 O '31 **2074**

Burke, James P. The argot of the racketeers. Am Mercury 21: 454-8 D '30; same title: Am J Police Sci 2: 419-27 S '31 **2075**

Dussort, Antoine. Existe-t-il un argot propre aux criminels? R Int de Crimin 2 (10): 758-65 '30 **2076**

Esnault, Gaston. La moderna gyria. R Int de Crimin 2 (4): 244-61 '30 **2077**

Finerty, James J. Criminalese. Justice 1: 59-61 O; 29-30 N; 19-20, 35 D '28 **2078**
Dictionary of the slang of criminals.

Gill, Merle Avery. Underworld slang. 30p. Kansas City, Mo. South Side printing co. 1929 **2079**

Giuseppe, S. Considerazioni sul gergo della galera con speciale riguardo al gergo della galera palermitana. Arch di Antrop Crim 47: 467-73 Jl '27 **2080**
Changes in prison slang, 1882-1927.

Grodenski, J. M. Bemerkungen zur Gaunersprache. Arch f Krim 81: 169-72 S '27 **2081**

Herbertz, R. Das Verbrechen im Spiegel der Sprache. Psychol Rundsch 2: 302-7 '31 **2082**

Irwin, Godfrey, ed. American tramp and underworld slang; words and phrases used by hoboes, tramps, migratory workers and those on the fringes of society, with their uses and origins; with a number of tramp songs. 264p. London, Scholartis press, 1931 **2083**

Kinkel. Die Gaunersprache. Polizei 25: 116-17, 143-4, 165-6 F 20-Mr 20 '28 **2084**

Lacassagne, Jean. L'argot du "milieu." 316p. Paris, A. Michel, 1928 **2085**

Martinez, Benjamin A. Jerga carcelaria, "Calo." 16p. Mexico, 1930 **2086**

Martinez, Benjamin A. Lenguaje carcelario (Caló). R de Identif y Cienc Pen 6: 35-53 My '30; same title: R Int de Crimin 3 (1): 6-25 '31 **2087**

Maurer, David W. The argot of the underworld. Am Speech 7: 99-118 D '31 **2088**
Material for this article obtained from prisoners and officials of Ohio state Penitentiary.

Niceforo, Alfredo. La personalité et le langage. Le parler des hommes médiocres, la conversation, le style personnel. Riv di Psicol 26: 1-21 Ja '30 **2089**

Prétrozinne. Une langue internationale des malfaiteurs. R Int de Crimin 1: 531-44 N '29 **2090**

Streicher, Hubert. Die graphischen Gaunerzinken. 82p. (Krimin Abh no5 hrsg von W. Gleispach) Wien, Springer, 1928 **2091**
Study of graphic symbols of the itinerant criminal classes. Historical data *re* vagrancy in Austria and Germany.

Wilstach, J. New words and phrases common among racketeers. Sat R of Lit 7: 978 Jl 18 '31 **2092**

Wittich, Engelbert. Beitrag zur Kenntnis der Sprache der süddeutschen Zigeuner. Arch f Krim 81: 61-2 Jl '27 **2093**

TATTOOING

Grangeversannes, J. M. Quelques tatouages de guerre. R Int de Crimin 2 (1): 42-8 '30 **2094**

Herber, J. Le détatouage des empiriques; les causes du détatouage. Le détatouage et ses procédés. La jurisprudence et le détatouage. R Int de Crimin 3 (6): 417-60 '31 **2095**

Herber, J. Tatouage crapuleux. R Int de Crimin 1: 266-75 bibliog (p274-5) S '29 **2096**

Herber, J. Tatouages curatifs au Maroc. R Int de Crimin 2 (6): 446-56 '30 **2097**

Lacassagne, Jean; Rousset, J., and Carmer, R. Le tatouage thérapeutique; essai d'étude critique. R Int de Crimin 1: 563-619 bibliog (p614-19) D '29 **2098**

Un nouveau procédé de détatouage. R Int de Crimin 2 (6): 472-4 '30; same title: Soc Fr de Dermat et de Syphil Bul (4): 442- Ap '30 **2099**

Probst, J. H. Les tatouages traditionnels des indigènes algériens. R Int de Crimin 2 (3): 206-14; (5): 342-51 '30 **2100**

Rodriguez, Santana. Le tatouage. Arch de Med Leg 2 (4) '23-'28 **2101**

Solowjewa, M. W. Die Tatuierung der Jugendlichen Verbrecher. Arch f Krim 87: 214-19 D '30 **2102**

Sudomir, A. and Zeranskaya, P. Acerca del tatuaje en los delincuentes. R de Crimin, Psiquiat y Med Leg 17: 100-6 Ja '30 **2103**

Sudomir, A. and Zeranskaja, P. Die psychologie der Tätowierung bei Verbrechern. Arch f Krim 85: 14-22 Ag '29 **2104**

Yoshimasu, S. Über die Tätowierung der Verbrecher. Jap J Psychol 5: 583-604 '30 **2105**

CRIMINAL TYPES

Daly, F. C. Some types of the Indian hereditary criminal. Police J [London] 1: 105-17 Ja '28 **2106**

Delfino, Victor. Sur deux projets du gouvernement Argentin: "L'état dangereux des délinquants" et: "L'état dangereux sans délit." R de Dr Pen et de Crimin 10: 573-83 Je '30 **2107**

Ferri, Enrico. La fonction juridique de l'état de danger chez le criminel. R Int de Dr Pén 4: 53-67 Ja '27 **2108**

Holler, Ernst. Ein jugendlicher Mördertyp. Bl f Gefängniskunde 61: 60-76 '30 **2109**

Luz, Euvaldo. Criminoso occasional. R de Cultura Jurid 1: 152-3 Ap '29 **2110**

Napolitano, Alberto Rafael and Davide, Juan. El proyecto de estado peligroso de 1924. R de Crimin, Psiquiat y Med Leg 18: 707-28 N '31 **2111**

Poznychew, S. Verbrechertypen, Klassifikation der Verbrecher. Monats f Kriminalpsychol u Strafrechtsref 19: 65-98 F '28 **2112**

Proyecto de ley sobre el "estado peligroso" sin delito. R de Crimin, Psiquiat y Med Leg 15: 291-301 My '28 **2113**

Schneider, Kurt. Typenbildungen in der Kriminalistik. Monats f Kriminalpsychol u Strafrechtsref 21: 332-7 Je '29 **2114**

Soler, Sebastian. Exposicion y crética de la teoria del estado peligroso. ed.2. corr & aug. 240p. Buenos Aires, Lavalle, 1929 **2115**

Vecchio, Giuseppe Del. La criminalità negli "Sports." 274p. Torino, Bocca, 1927 **2116**

Born or Instinctive

Altavilla, Enrico. Imbecilli morali e delinquenti per tendenza. 17p. Roma, Tip. dell Littorio, 1930 **2117**
Extr de Rivista penale 1(2) F '30.

Carrara, M. A proposito del trattamento del delinquente per tendenza. Scuola Pos 38: 101-8 '30; same title: Arch di Antrop Crim 50: 739-48 S '30 **2118**

Corberi. Sulla perversione istintiva. Inf Anorm 22: 155-60 '30 **2119**

Donnedieu de Vabres, H. De délinquant par tendance instinctive dans les projets de code pénal italien. Etudes Crimin 5: 97-102, 225-9 Ap, N '30 **2120**

Donnedieu de Vabres, H. El delincuente por tendencia instintiva en los proyectos des código penal italiano. R de Crimin, Psiquiat y Med Leg 18: 84-93, 202-10 Ja, Mr '31 **2121**

Funkhouser, Ralph M. Remarks concerning stigmata. Med-Leg J 44: 70-5 My '27 **2122**

Lattes, L[eone]. Il "delinquente per istintiva tendenza" nel progetto italiano di C. P. Arch di Antrop Crim 47:899-904 N '27 **2123**

Lattes, Leone. A proposito del delinquente per tendenza. Arch di Antrop Crim 50: 927-30 N '30 **2124**

Ottolenghi, S. Il delinquente per istintiva tendenza nel Progetto Rocco e l'antropologia criminale. Scuola Pos 37: 501-15 '29; same title: Zacchia 7:1- Ja '28; also 20p. Roma, Tip. S. Ana, 1928 **2125**

Perrando, G. G. Sulla figura del delinquente per istintiva tendenza. Nuov Dir (9): 497- '30; same title: 8p. Roma, "Il Nuovo Diritto," 1930 **2126**

Rasmus, Kurt. Zum Problem des geborenen Verbrechers. 79p. Inaug.-Diss. Bonn, 1929 **2127**

Sacerdote, A. Progetto preliminare di un nuovo codice penale in rapporto all'antropologia criminale. Il "delinquente nato" lombrosiano entra nella legislazione penale. Arch di Antrop Crim 47: 857-60 S '27 **2128**

Trossarelli, Alberto. Il delinquente per tendenza dal progetto preliminare al progetto definitivo del nuovo codice penale. Rassegna di Studi Psichiat 19 fasc 2: 293- '30 **2129**

Mental Defectives

Alexander, Franz. Neurotic criminal. M R of R 36: 205-16 Mr '30 **2130**

Bates, Sanford. Practical problems of the defective delinquent. Am Assn Stud Feeblemind Proc 52: 110-14 '28 **2131**

Battey, P. B. and Thayer, Walter N. jr. The defective delinquent. Am Assn Stud Feeblemind Proc 53: 69-81 '29 **2132**

Branham, V. C. Notes on the classification of defective delinquents. Psychiat Q 1: 59-69 Ja '27 **2133**

Curtis, H. C. Constitutional psychopaths and criminal law. Kan M Soc J 28: 179-82 Je '28 **2134**

Daly, W. H. The defective adult delinquent. Ind Bul Char & Correc (180): 93-4 Mr '30 **2135**

Duschewno-boljnyje prawonaruschiteli i prinuditeljnoje letschenije. (Geisteskranke Delinquenten und Zwangstherapie). 112p. Sammelheft des Staatsinstituts zur Erforschung der Kriminalität und des Kriminellen. Moskau, Verlag von Kommissariats für Inneres, 1929 **2136**

Giannitrapani, Alfredo. Psicoinfezione criminale. 432p. Palermo, Remo Sandon, 1930 **2137**

Greeff, Etienne De. Normaux et débiles mentaux. R de Dr Pén et de Crimin 8: 793-826 Ag '28 **2138**

Illinois. Department of public welfare. Laws of Illinois concerning insane, feebleminded and epileptics. . . . 146p. [Springfield, 1927?] **2139**
Laws *re* criminal insane.

Kahn, Eugen. Psychopathic personalities; translated from German by H. Flanders Dunbar. 521p. New Haven, Yale univ. press, 1931 **2140**

Karpman, Ben. Psychotherapy and the criminal insane. Psychiat Q 3: 370-83 Jl '29 **2141**

Lorand, A. S. Crime in fantasy and dreams and the neurotic criminal. Psychoanal R 17: 183-94 Ap '30 **2142**

Loudet; Noguès; Pietranera; Delpiano, and Isla. Jucio de peligrosidad en un exalienado delincuente. R de Crimin, Psiquiat y Med Leg 16 (100) Jl '30 **2143**

Mandoloni, Hernani. Los fanaticos criminales. R de Crimin, Psiquiat y Med Leg 15: 521-6 S '28 **2144**

d'Ormea, A. Sindromi degenerative e sindromi patologiche negli alienati e nei criminali. II: Pseudologia fantastica e simulazione. Arch di Antrop Crim 48: 517-21 '28 **2145**

Palmer, Leo J. The defective delinquent as a state problem. Psychiat Q 1: 91-5 Ja '27 **2146**
Proportion of defectives in correctional institutions.

Pescor, M. J. The psychoneurotic delinquent. Med-Leg J 47: 12-32 Ja '30; same title: Madras M J 12: 258 '30; 13: 51 '31 **2147**

Richmond, Frank C. Neurosyphilitic criminal insane; criteria of cure—a medico-legal problem. Med Leg J 46: 32-6 Ja; 32-6 Mr '29 **2148**

Shaw, F. C. Types of criminal insane. Psychiat Q 4: 458-65 '30 **2149**

Singer, H. Douglas. The deranged or defective delinquent. Ill Assn Crim Just, Ill Crime Survey 737-810, 1929 **2150**

Turner, J. S. Criminally insane; discussion of etiologic factors and need for state hospital. Tex St J Med 26: 255-8 Jl '30 **2151**

Wallace, George L. Are the feeble-minded criminals? Ment Hyg 13: 93-8 Ja '29 **2152**

Wiersma, D. Frequency and rôle of nervous temperament in criminal psychopaths. Psychiat en Neurol Bl 35: 440-51 Jl '31 **2153**

Wildenskov, H. O. 15 Aars Erfaring med de forbryderiske Aandssvage paa Livø. Nord Tids f Straf 15: 1-9 Ja '27 **2154**

Recidivists

Alfred, John. Die Rückfallsdiebe: eine Untersuchung über Erscheinungsformen des Verbrechens. 94p. (Krimin Abh no9, hrsg von Franz Exner). Leipzig, Wiegandt, 1929 **2155**

Almquist, V. Svensk lagstiftning om förvaring av förminskat tillräkneliga och internering av återfallsförbrytare. Nord Tids f Straf 15: 322-31 O '27 **2156**

Armstrong, Richard H. Problems in crime. Va L Reg ns 12: 541-7 Ja '27 **2157**

Beger, Fritz. Die Rückfälligen Betrüger. 79p. (Krimin Abh no7, hrsg von Franz Exner) Leipzig, Wiegandt, 1929 **2158**

Canadian council on child welfare. Recidivist group and custodial care. Pub no37) Ottawa, Ont. The Council, 1928 **2159**

Chicago, Ill. Municipal reference library. Notes on recommendations by crime commissions relative to placing professional criminals, chronic repeaters charged with felonies, persons committing or attempting robbery with a gun or other deadly weapon, and offenders having a long criminal record under high bail bonds or sureties. 5p. (typw) Chicago, October 18, 1930 **2160**

Cornil, Léon. La loi de défense sociale à l'égard des anormaux et des délinquants d'habitude. Discours prononcé par le procureur général à l'audience solennelle de rentrée de la Cour d'appel de Bruxelles le 15 septembre 1930. 112p. Bruxelles, Cour d'Appel, 1930 **2161**

Cornil, Léon. La loi de défense sociale a l'égard des anormaux et des délinquants d'habitude du 9 avril 1930. R de Dr Pén et de Crimin 10: 837-79, 1019-69 '30 **2162**

Doby, Walter F. The enforcement of law against the habitual criminal. Int Assn Chiefs Police Proc 36: 143-5 '29 **2163**

Dondina, Mario. La legge belga di difesa in confronto degli anormali e dei delinquenti abituali. Scuola Pos 11: 111-16 Mr '31 **2164**

Eimbeck, Carl V. Some recent methods of harassing the habitual criminal. St. Louis L R 16: 148-62 F '31 **2165**

Elson, Sam. Habitual criminal acts and the ex post facto clause. St Louis L R 14: 414-22 Jl '29 **2166**

Fourth offender prosecutions in New York city in 1927. Ref Shelf 6 (3): 70-9 Ag '29 **2167**

Fourth offenders. Sol J 73: 305-6 My 18 '29 **2168**

Freudenthal, Berthold. Kann man Verbrecher bessern? Amerikanish-Englische Reiseindrücke. 14p. Reprint. Frankfurter Zeitung, December 30, 1927 **2169**

Gévay-Wolff, Ferdinand, jr. Der internationale Kampf gegen die unverbesserlichen Rückfälligen. 63p. Budapest, Verl. Sigmund Politzer & Söhne, 1931 **2170**
(in ungarischer Sprach erschienen in)

Gomez, C. de Maria. Note sul delinquente abituale. Scuola Pos 38: 449-51 '30 **2171**

Grüllich. Der Gewohnheitsverbrecher nach dem Entwurfe des neuen Strafgesetzbuchs. Monats f Kriminalpsychol u Strafrechtsref 18: 671-8 D '27 **2172**

Habitual criminal. L J [London] 72: 119-20, 131-2 Ag 22, 29 '31 **2173**

Hallheimer, Julius. Justice by formula; who is an habitual criminal and what is a felony? Cent 117: 232-40 D '28 **2174**

[Kelley], Charles H. The habitual criminal. Inst Police Adm Proc 81-3 '29 **2175**

Kirchwey, George W. The elimination from the community of the psychopathic recidivist. J Juv Res 13: 266-9 O '29; same title: Psychiat Q 3: 453-6 '28 **2176**

Knowles, C. M. The problem of the old offender. Police J [London] 4: 506-21 O '31 **2177**

The law of the tyrant; (editorial). Lawyer & Banker 22: 2-3 Ja '29 **2178**

McCuaig, J. A. Royce. Modern tendencies in habitual criminal legislation. Cornell L Q 15: 62-83 D '29 **2179**

McLellan, H. Life for habitual criminals. Burroughs Clearing House 11: 25-7 F '27 **2180**

Mansueti, Cesare. L'istituto di polizia e la recidiva. ed. 2. 46p. Clusone, D. Guidici, 1927 **2181**

Michel, R[udolf]. Il delinquente d'abitudine psicopatico. Arch di Antrop Crim 49: 808-29 N '29 **2182**
Study of 400 criminals in Karlau penitentiary, 300 of whom were habituals.

Michel, Rudolf. Der psychopathische Gewohnheitsverbrecher. Bl f Gefängniskunde 60 (3): 377-401 '29 2183

Michigan's new habitual criminal act hits hard at the underworld. State Trooper 8: 19 N '27 2184

Murphy, Vernon F. Limitation of the Baumes fourth offender laws. St John's L R 4: 325-7 My '30 2185

Nelson, W. Recidivism in juvenile court under psychiatric guidance. S M J 22: 793-802 S '29 2186

Petrén, Alfred. Die neue schwedische Gesetzgebung betreffs rückfälliger Verbrecher und vermindert zurechnungsfähiger Verbrecher. Monats f Kriminalpsychol u Strafrechtsref 19: 513-20 S '28 2187

Projet de loi de défense sociale à l'égard des anormaux et des délinquants d'habitude. R de Dr Pén et de Crimin 10: 408-14 '30 2188

Santangelo, G[iuseppe]. Il delinquente per tendenza nel nuovo codice penale dal punto di vista psichiatrico e medicolegale. Ann dell'Osped Psichiat di Perugia 25: 189 Jl '31 2189

Schepper, J. M. J. Hoe staat het met de recidive in Nederlandsch-Indië? Koloniale Stud 13: 400-10 D '29 2190

Schurich, Joachim. Lebensläufe vielfach rückfälliger Verbrecher. 160p. (Krimin Abh no10, hrsg von Franz Exner) Leipzig, Wiengandt, 1930 2191

The second offender. L Notes 32: 45 Je '28 2192

[**The suspended** sentence, probation, imprisonment and treatment of habitual and professional criminals]. Maandbl v Ber en Reclasseer 7: 44-68 Ja '28 2193

Di Tullio, B. Il temperamento ossessivo nella genesi di alcune forme di criminalità recidiva specifica. Zacchia 6: 38-42 Ja '27 2194

Villamor, Ignacio. Habitual delinquency. Phil L J 9: 49-59 Ag '29 2195

Vollmer, August. The recidivist from the point of view of the police official. J Delin 11: 72-87 Je '27 2196

V[oorhees], T[heodore]. Habitual-criminal statutes and the proposed Pennsylvania act. Univ Pa L R 77: 798-803 Ap '29 2197

Wiart, H. Carton de. Rapport sur le traitement des récidivistes, et des délinquants d'habitude. R de Dr Pén et de Crimin 7: 206-8 F '27 2198

SEXUAL

Beck, Walter. Zuhälter X. Monats f Kriminalpsychol u Strafrechtsref 19: 49-50 Ja '28 2199

Beck, Walter. Zuhälter Y. Monats f Kriminalpsychol u Strafrechtsref 19: 598-600 O '28 2200

Beck, Walter. Zuhälter Z. Monats f Kriminalpsychol u Strafrechtsref 19: 749-52 '28 2201

Beloussow. Ein homosexueller männlicher Prostituierter. Problemy Prestupnosti 2: 309-20 '28 2202

Bermann, G. Sobre una "prostituta nata." Conf Latino-Am de Neurol, Psiquiat y Med Leg Actas 2: 711-25 '29; also: Sur une "prostituée née." Ann de Méd Lég (8): 582-5 '30 2203

Boeters, G. Ein homosexueller Kraftwagenfuhrer. Monats f Kriminalpsychol u Strafrechtsref 22: 734-9 '31 2204

Boeters, [G.]. Ein Lehrer als Exhibitionist. Monats f Kriminalpsychol u Strafrechtsref 22: 214-17 '31 2205

Borms, V. Tayart de. La prostitution masculine. R Belge de Police Adm & Jud livraison 138 Mr '31 2206

Götz, Berndt. Über weiblichen Exhibitionismus. Monats f Kriminalpsychol u Strafrechtsref 20: 162-6 '29 2207

Guckenheimer. Über die Zuhälterfrage. Deut Gesell z Bekämpf d Geschlechtskrankh Mitt 28: 41-54 F '30 2208

Guckenheimer. Das Zuhältertum in Hamburg. Monats f Kriminalpsychol u Strafrechtsref 19: 479-82 Ag '28 2209

Gummersbach. Der Zuhälter in der schweren Kriminalität. Monats f Kriminalpsychol u Strafrechtsref 19: 679-85 N '28 2210

Gumpertz, Karl. Ein postencephalitischer Sittlichkeitsverbrecher. Zeitsch f Sexualwissensch 17: 53-5 My 5 '30 2211

Heindl, R[obert]. Erpresser. Vererb u Geschlechtsleb (4): 233-7 '27-'28 2212

Hentig, Hans v. Eigenartige Formen der Zuhälterei. Zeitsch f Sexualwissensch 14: 129-35 Jl '27 2213

Johnson, Bascom. Attitudes of governments toward foreign prostitutes. J Soc Hyg 14: 129-38 Mr '28 2214

Julier. Der Zuhälter. Polizeiliche Erfahrungen. Monats f Kriminalpsychol u Strafrechtsref 18: 696-7 D '27 2215

Kern, Elga. Wie sie Dazu Kamen. 35 Lebensfragmente Bordellierter Mädchen. 182p. München, Ernst Reinhardt, 1928 2216

Study of prostitutes of Baden under state control.

Luz, Walter. Zum Problem der Zuhälterei. Monats f Kriminalpsychol u Strafrechtsref 19: 491-2 '28 2217

Menzel. Zur Zuhälterfrage. Monats f Kriminalpsychol u Strafrechtsref 19: 482-5 Ag '28 2218

Pollitz. Die strafrechtliche Behandlung des Zuhälters im zukünftigen Strafgesetz. Monats f Kriminalpsychol u Strafrechtsref 17: 595-7 '27 2219

Raecke. Zur Zuhälterfrage. Monats f Kriminalpsychol u Strafrechtsref 19: 59-60 Ja '28 2220

Reitman, Ben L. The second oldest profession. 286p. N.Y. Vanguard, 1931 2221

Study of the prostitute's "business manager."

Rojas, Nerio and Gonzàles, Juan M. E. Obsesion impulsiva exhibicionista. R de Crimin, Psiquiat y Med Leg 15: 380-9 Jl '28 2222

Schweizer, O. Das Zuhältertum in der Stadt Zürich. Monats f Kriminalpsychol u Strafrechtsref 19: 170-1 Mr '28 2223

Strewe. Der Exhibitionist. Krimin Monatsh 4: 34-7 F '30 2224

Weinberger, [Hugo]. Prostitution und Kriminalität. Krimin Monatsh 2: 57-9 Mr '28 2225

Weinberger, Hugo. Verbrecher und Dirne. Arch f Krim 81: 33-7 Jl '27 2226

Weissenrieder, Otto. Zur Frage der Zuhälterei. Mitteilungen aus der Strafvollzugspraxis. Monats f Kriminalpsychol u Strafrechtsref 18: 635-9 N '27 2227

Wulffen, Erich i.e. Wolf Hasso Erich. Sexualverbrecher. ed. 11 727p. Berlin, Langenscheidt, 1928 2228

Wulffen, Erich. Das Weib als Sexualverbrecherin. ed. 3 408p. Hamburg, Hanseat. Rechts u Wirtschaftsverl. 1931 2229

Vagrants

[Anderson, Nels]. The milk and honey route; a handbook for hobos, by Dean Stiff [pseud.] With a comprehensive and unexpurgated glossary. 219p. bibliog 218-19. N.Y. Vanguard, 1931 2230

Crime and vagrancy; the new Chicago scheme for combatting vagrants and gangsters. Police "13-13" 5: 11-12 Ag '30 2231

Gilmore, Harland W. Types of begging. Sociol & Soc Res 14: 562-6 Jl '30 2232

Kerr, Lennox. Back door guests; decorations by James C. Reid. 275p. N.Y. Bodds, 1930 2233

Koch, E. von and others. Lösdrivaren och samhället. Inlägg i en aktuell samhällsfråga. 87p. Stockholm, Norstedt, 1927 2234

Martin, Esther. The tramp and vagrant problem. Assn of Dir Poor & Char & Correc Proc 52: 73-4 '27 2235

Nathorst-Böös, E. jr. Det svenska förslaget till ny lösdrivarelagstiftning. Några kritiska reflektioner. Nord Tids f Straf 15: 19-35 Ja '27 2236

Néron, G. Le vagabondage infantile; étude statistique de 250 cas. Hyg Ment 24: 214-22 '28 2237

Norton, Kay. Beggars. Welf Mag 19: 348-51 Mr '28 2238

Nyman, H. Lösdrivarlagstiftningen i Sverige. Nord Tids f Straf 16: 53-73 Ja '28 2239

Problem of the tramp. Just Peace 94: 810-11 D 27 '30 2240

Rodin, D. P. Jizdrinskie nishchie. Problemy Prestupnosti 2: 76-87 '27 2241

Rogues and vagabonds, incorrigible rogues. Just Peace 92: 727-8 N 10 '28 2242

Smith, George. Rogues and vagabonds. Chief Constables' Assn Can Proc 25: 67-74 '29 2243

Tully, Jim. Beggars of life. 336p. N.Y. Garden City pub co. 1928 2244

Willard, Eugene Bertram. Psychopathic vagrancy. Welf Mag 19: 565-73 '28 2245

Witten, George. Outlaw trails; a Yankee hobo soldier of the queen. 252p. N.Y. Minton, 1929 2246

CRIMINAL BIOLOGY

Blinkov, S. Zur Frage nach dem Körperbau des Verbrechers. Monats f Kriminalpsychol u Strafrechtsref 20: 212-16 Ap '29 2247

Böhmer, Kurt. Untersuchungen über den körperbau des Verbrechers. Monats f Kriminalpsychol u Strafrechtsref 19: 193-209 Ap '28 2248

Canuto, Giorgio. La distribuzione dei gruppi sanguigni nei criminali piemontesi. Arch di Antrop Crim 48: 687-704 Jl '28 2249

Castellanos, Israel. La talla de los delincuentes en Cuba. 179p. Habana, Imp. A. Dorrbecker, 1927 2250

Erickson, Milton H. Marriage and propagation among criminals. Med-Leg J 46: 25-31 Mr '29; same title: J Soc Hyg 15: 464-75 N '29 2251

Erkens, Josefine. Kriminalbiologie und Kriminalpolizei. Monats f Kriminalpsychol u Strafrechtsref 22: 491-8 Ag '31 2252

Eyrich, Max. Kriminal-biologische und psychologische Untersuchungen an Mördern und Totschlägern. Bl f Gefängniskunde 61: 247-61 '30 2253
Study of murderers entering Ludwigsburg prison, 1924-1928.

Fetscher, R. Kriminalbiologische Erfahrungen an Sexualverbrechern. 1: Statistische Analyse der Ausgangsfälle und ihrer Verwandtschaft. Zeitsch f Sexualwissensch 17: 356-63 D '30 2254
Study of 818 heterosexual males sentenced in Saxony for sexual offenses.

Fetscher, R. Kriminalbiologische Erfahrungen an Sexualverbrechern. 2: Das Schriftbild der Sexualverbrecher. Zeitsch f Sexualwissensch 18: 265-74 O 26 '31 2255

Gefängnisgesellschaft für die Provinz Sachsen und Anhalt. Kriminalbiologie und Individualpsychologie. Jahrbuch, 45, 1929. 116p. Halle (Saale), Selbstverlag, 1930 2256

Gruhle, H[ans] W. Der biologische Typus des Verbrechers. Päd Hochschule 1: 45-52 '30? 2257

Gruhle, Hans W. Kriminalbiologie und Kriminalpraxis. Krimin Monatsh 2: 241-2 N '28 2258

Haldane, J. B. S. Scientific Calvinism. Harper's 159: 551-8 O '29 2259

Hellstern, Erwin P. Kriminalbiologische Untersuchungen bei Strafgefangenen. Zeitsch f d ges Neurol u Psychiat 108: 261-73 Ap '27 2260

Hellstern, Erwin P. Kriminalbiologische Untersuchungsergebnisse bei Schwerverbrechern. Deut Zeitsch f d ges gerichtl Med 11: 301-16 Ap 28 '28 2261

Hoffmann. Die erbbiologische Persönlichkeitsforschung und ihre Bedeutung in der Kriminalbiologie. Bl f Gefängniskunde 58: 308-21 '27 2262

Kalmann, Heinrich. Kriminalbiologie. Zeitsch f Sexualwissensch 14: 143-6 Jl '27 2263

Kalmann, Heinrich. Die kriminalbiologische Untersuchung der Täterpersönlichkeit und ihr Wert für die polizeilichen Vorerhebungen. Monats f Kriminalpsychol u Strafrechtsref 22: 175-83 Mr '31 2264

Klare, Hans. Das kriminalbiologische Gutachten im Strafprozess. 143p. (Strafrechtl Abh no277) Breslau, Schletter, 1930 2265

Kolle, Kurt. Zur Biologie des Zuhälters. Monats f Kriminalpsychol u Strafrechtsref 19: 488-91 Ag '28 2266

Koppenfels, v. Zur Frage der Ausbildung in Kriminalbiologie. Monats f Kriminalpsychol u Strafrechtsref 20: 160-2 '29 2267

Kriminalbiologischen Gesellschaft. Mitteilungen, Band I-III. Graz, Moser, 1928-31 2268

Lenz, Adolf. Die Bedeutung der Kriminalbiologie. Arch f Krim 88: 218-30 My '31 2269

Lenz, Adolf. Grundriss der Kriminalbiologie; Werden und Wesen der Persönlichkeit des Täters nach Untersuchungen an Sträflingen. 252p. Wien, Julius Springer, 1927 2270

Lungwitz, Hans. Zur Psychobiologie des Verbrechers. Arch f Krim 81: 207-15 D '27 2271

Mezger, E. and Lenz, Adolf. Die Bedeutung der Kriminalbiologie. Monats f Kriminalpsychol u Strafrechtsref 22: 43-7 Ja '31 2272

Palmieri, V. M. Ricerche di biologia criminale. Nuov Riv di Clin ed Assis Psichiat 5: 155-77 '28 2273

Palmieri, V. M. Die Verteilung der morphologisch-konstitutionellen Typen unter den geisteskranken Verbrechern. Deut Zeitsch f d ges gerichtl Med 12: 592-601 D 10 '28 2274

Reiter, H. Grundsätzliche Bemerkungen zum gegenwärtigen Stande der Kriminalbiologie. Monats f Kriminalpsychol u Strafrechtsref 22: 78-84 F '31 2275

Riedl, Martin. Ein Beitrag zur Frage der Fortpflanzung von Verbrechern. Arch f Rassen- u Gesell-Biol 25: 257-67 O '31 2276

Riffel, Paul. Die kriminalbiologische Untersuchung von Strafgefangenen und Fürsorgezöglingen in Baden. Bl f Gefängniskunde 61: 262-7 '30 2277

Rodríguez Cabo, Mathilde. Braves apuntes sobre la biologia criminal. R Mexicana d Der Pen 1: 7-20 Jl '30 2278

Rohden, F[riedrich] v. Kriminalbiologische Untersuchungen an gesunden und geisteskranken Verbrechern. Deut Zeitsch f d ges gerichtl Med 10: 621-33 '27 2279

Rohden, F[riedrich] von. Lombrosos Bedeutung für die moderne Kriminalbiologie. Arch f Psychiat 92: 140-54 '30 2280

Rohden, F[riedrich] von. Probleme, Aufgaben und Ziele der Kriminalbiologie. Monats f Psychiat u Neurol 80: 15-33 Ag '31 2281

Sabrazès, J. Observations microscopiques sur la moelle costale d'un supplicié. Soc de Biol Compt Rend 96: 792 Mr 25 '27 2282

Schlör, Walter. Biologie und Strafrecht. Umschau 31: 561-4 Jl 9 '27 2283

Seelig, Ernst. Das Typenproblem in der kriminalbiologie. J f Psychol & Neurol 42: 515-26 Je '31 2284

Skorpil, R. Kriminalbiologie, Jugendgerichtsbarkeit und das kommende Strafrechtswesen für Erwachsene. Psychol Rundsch 2: 265-70 '30 2285

Tullio, B. di. La costituzione delinquenziale nella etiologia e terapia del delitto. 204p. Roma, Anonima Romana Editoriale, 1929 2286

Vassileff, B. H. L'alto grado di movimento immunitario antitubercolare nell'uomo delinquente. Arch di Antrop Crim 50: sup1626-30 '30 2287

Viernstein, Theodor. Der kriminalbiologische Dienst in den bayerischen Strafanstalten. Arch f Rassen- u Gesell-Biol 19: 34-53 bibliog (p53) F '27 2288

Villinger, Werner. Kriminalbiologie. Fortschr d Neurol, Psychiat 1: 493-513 N '29; 2: 489-505 N '30 2289

Weddige. Die kriminalbiologischen Untersuchungen an preussischen Gefangenenanstalten. Krimin Monatsh 4: 222-3 O '30 2290

CRIMINAL PSYCHOLOGY

Abhandlungen aus dem Gesamtgebiete der Kriminalpsychologie (Heidelberger Abhandlungen), hrsg. von Karl v. Lilienthal, H. W. Gruhle, G. Radbruch, S[igm] Schott, K[arl] Wilmanns. Berlin, Springer, 1, 1912- 2291

Adler, Alfred. The criminal pattern of life. Police J [N Y] 17: 8-11, 22-3 Mr '30 2292

Adler, Alfred. The roots of the criminal pattern. Police J [N Y] 17: 5-7, 24 Ap '30 2293

Alexander, Franz and Staub, Hugo. The criminal, the judge, and the public: a psychological analysis; translated from the German by Gregory Zilboorg. 238p. N.Y. Macmillan, 1931 2294

Alexander, Franz and Staub, Hugo. Der Verbrecher und seine Richter; ein psychoanalytischer Einblick in die Welt der Paragraphen. 125p. Wien, Internationaler Psychoanalytischer Verl. 1929 2295

Aschaffenburg, Gustav. Der Einfluss Kraepelins auf die Kriminalpsychologie und Kriminalpolitik. Arch f Psychiat 87 (1): 87-95 Ap 25 '29 2296

Aschaffenburg, Gustav. Kriminalpsychologie Seminare. Monats f Kriminalpsychologie u Strafrechtsref 19: 546-9 '28 2297

Belloni, G. A. Criminologia postlombrosiana (la monagenesi psicologia del delitto). 12p. Roma, 1930 2298
Extr: Rivista di cultura fasc12 '30.

Bernfeld, Siegfried. Die Tantalussituation; Bemerkungen zum "kriminellen Uber-Ich." Imago 17: 253-67 '31 2299

Big brother and big sister federation, inc. A study in the attitudes of delinquents. 4p. (mim) N. Y. 425 5th ave. May 1, 1931 2300

Birnbaum, Karl. Kriminalpsychopathologie und psychobiologische verbrecherkunde. ed.2 304p. Berlin, Springer, 1931 2301

Birnbaum, Karl. Psychologie der Rauschsüchtigen. Krimin Monatsh 4: 73-6 Ap '30 2302

Bjerre, [Sören] Andreas. Psychology of murder; a study in criminal psychology; translated from the Swedish by Ernest Classen. 164p. N. Y. Longmans, 1927 2303
Based . . . on investigations conducted in the Central prison at Långholman, Stockholm.

Bohne. Individualpsychologische Betrachtungen zu den Kapitalverbrechen der letzten Zeit. Deut Juristen-Zeit 33 (22): 1502-7 N 15 '28 2304

Bohne, G. Individualpsychologische Beurteilung krimineller Persönlichkeiten. Int Zeitsch f Individualpsychol 5: 330-45 '31 2305

Bonaparte, Marie. Der Fall Lefebvre; Psychoanalyse einer Mörderin. Imago 15: 16-62 '29 2306

Branham, V. C. The psychology of the minor offender. N Y St Assn Magistrates Proc 22: 36-42 '30 2307

Brodsky, Paul. Strafjustiz und Individualpsychologie. Kampf [Wien] 24: 225-30 My '31 2308

Brusilovski, A. E. [The fundamental problems of criminal psychology in penology]. Mater I Vsesoju Sez Izuch Poved Chelov 1930: 119-21 2309

Budzinski, Wilhelm. Der überzeugungsverbrecher. 54p. Leipzig, Noske, 1931 2310

Buerschaper. Die innere Tatseite beim Glücksspiel mit Geldspielautomaten. Arch f Krim 83: 228-33 N '28 2311

Canella, Mario F. Umanità criminale. Riv di Psicol 26: 314-30 '30 2312

Courthial, Andree. Emotional differences of delinquent and non-delinquent girls of normal intelligence. 102p. (Arch of Psychol 133) N. Y. Columbia Univ. 1931 2313

Crichton-Miller, H. Psychology of suicide. Brit M J 2: 239-41 Ag 8 '31 2314

Criminologists by criminals; what the crook thinks of his enemy, the policeman. Policeman 1: 3-4 D '29 2315

Doná, Gaetano. La delinquenza negli affari, secondo la psicologia criminale e la polizia guidiziaria. 203p. Torino, Bocca, 1928 2316

Ferri, Enrico. Dante et la psychologie criminelle à propos du comte Ugolino; translation by Gino Cutore di San Carlo. R de Dr Pén et de Crimin 8: 305-21 Ap '28 2317
Conférence à Rome, à la Casa di Dante, 27 mai 1927. Le texte italien a paru dans l'Eloquenza, 17 année, fasc 8-10.

Florian, Eugenio. La teoria psicologica della diffamazione. Studio sociologico-giuridico. ed.2 300p. Torino, Bocca, 1927 2318

Frank, Reinhard. Del danno ideologico del reato. Riv Ital di Dir Pen 3: 25-35 Ja '31 2319

Freudenthal, Dorothea. Zur Täterpsychologie. Krimin Monatsh 3: 77-9 Ap '29 2320

Fromm, Erich. Zur Psychologie des Verbrechers und der strafenden Gesellschaft. Imago 17: 226-51 '31 2321

Fürst, Bruno; Hirschfeld, Magnus; Riese, Walther and Steinschneider, A. M. Der Fall Wiechmann. Zur Psychologie und Soziologie des Familienmordes. 165p. Hrsg von Hertha und Walther Riese. Stuttgart, Püttmann, 1928 2322

Galant, Johann Susmann. Zur Psychologie der verwahrlosten Kinder. Monats f Kriminalpsychol u Strafrechtsref 20: 343-51 '29 2323

Gerland. Der Überzeugungsverbrecher in der Reichstagsvorlage des Strafgesetzbuches. Deut Juristen-Zeit 32: 1514-18 '27 2324

[Gernet, Mikhail] (Michael Hernett). Die Gedankenwelt im Kerker. Bl f Gefängniskunde 59: 10-24 '28 2325

Gibson, Katherine. The psychology of crime. Int Assn Identif Proc 13: 94-8 '27; same title: Peace Offic 5: 18, 19 O '27 2326

Glasenapp, G. Il carettere secondario (Osservazioni di psicologia criminale). Scuola Pos 10: 371-7 Ag '30 2327

Grossmann, A. Zur Psychologie und dynamischen Situation eines Mordes. Schweiz med Wchnschr 59: 1405-10 D 28 '29 2328

Gruhle, Hans W. Aufgaben der Kriminalpsychologie. Zeitsch f d ges Strafrechtswiss 51 (4): 469-80 '31; translation by T. Plazinski: J Crim L & Crimin 22: 506-16 N '31 2329

Gummersbach. Begnadigte Mörder. Drei Beiträge zur Psychologie des Mördes. I. Übersicht—Personalien—Zeit der Tat. II. Über Beweggrund, Ursache und Zweck. III. Die Frau als Mörderin. Monats f Kriminalpsychol u Strafrechtsref 21: 25-34, 727-35 '30; 22: 35-42 '31 2330

H., [R.]. Kriminalpsychologische Praxis. Psychol Rundsch 3: 56-8 '31 2331

H., R. Kriminalpsychologische Praxis. Brandstiftung. Psychol Rundsch 3: 90-3 '31 2332

H., R. Kriminalpsychologische Praxis. Zürcher Vorbedacht und deutsche Überlegung. Psychol Rundsch 2: 379-81 '31 2333

Hänsel, M. R. Tiefenpsychologie und strafrechtliche Willensfreiheit. Monats f Psychiat u Neurol 65: 61-7 Je '27 2334

Hárnick, J. Zur Psychologie des Zopfabschneiders. Zeitsch f Sexualwissensch 14: 451-4 Mr '28 2335

Hegemann, H. Kriminalpsychologie und Psychoanalyse. Krimin Monatsh 5: 241-7 N '31 2336

Heller, Theodor. Über Psychologie und Psychopathologie des Jugendlichen. 91p. Wien, Julius Springer, 1927 2337

Hellwig, Albert. Kriminalistisch bedeutsamer sexueller Aberglaube. Zeitsch f Sexualwissensch 18: 131-6 Je '31 2338

Hentig, H[ans] v. Justizirrtum und Kriminalpsychologie. Monats f Kriminalpsychol u Strafrechtsref 19: 60-2 Ja '28 2339

Herbertz, [R]. Aus der kriminalpsychologischen Praxis. Psychol Rundsch 1: 308-11 '29; 341-4, 373-6 '30 2340

Herbertz, R. Ausschaltung des "Vergeltungsprinzips." Psychol Rundsch 1: 308-10 '29 2341

Herbertz, R. Ein einzigartiger Fall von "fixer Idee" eines Verbrechers. Krimin Monatsh 3: 8-10 Ja '29 2342

Herbertz, R. Gedanken eines "Lebenslänglichen." Psychol Rundsch 1: 310-11 '29 2343

Herbertz, R. Kriminalpsychologische Praxis. Psychol Rundsch 2: 119-21 '30 2344

Herbertz, R. Schuldig oder unschuldig? Betrachtungen eines Kriminalpsychologen zum Delmenhorster Justizirrtum. Krimin Monatsh 4: 54-6 Mr '30; same title: Psychol Rundsch 1: 393-6 '30 2345

Herbertz, R. Vom Leugnen. Psychol Rundsch 1: 217-22 '29 2346

Herbertz, R. Was ist Kriminalpsychologie? Psychol Rundsch 1: 5-12 '29 2347

Hesnard, A. and Laforgue, R. Les processus d'autopunition en psychologie des névroses et des psychoses, en psychologie criminelle et en pathologie générale. R Fr de Psychanal 4: 2-84 '30 2348

Heygster, Hans. Zur Frage der Selbstbezichtigung. Monats f Kriminalpsychol u Strafrechtsref 22: 338-42 My '31 2349

Huebsch, Daniel Adolph. Murder complex; a psychoanalytic study. 95p. Cleveland, Ohio, 5518 Euclid ave. The Author, 1927 2350

Ilkov, Al. Mozhe li nakaztelniyat sŭd da pronikne v dushata na prestŭpnika? Filosofski Pregled 3 (2): 182-5 '31 2351

Jacobi, Erich. Zur Psychopathologie des Familienmordes. Arch f Psychiat 83: 501-32 '28 2352

Kallman, F. Zur Psychopathologie des abergläuberischen Verbrechers. Monats f Psychiat u Neurol 72: 37-60 Ap '29 2353

Karpman, Ben. Criminality, the superego and the sense of guilt. Psychoanal R 17: 280-96 Ap '30 2354

Kinberg, Olof. Aktuella Kriminalitetsproblem I Psykologisk Belysning. 382p. Stockholm, Bokförlaget Natur och Kultur, 1930 2355

Kingsford, A. Beresford. The comparative psychology of murder by poisoning. Police J [London] 2: 607-18 O '29 2356

Kleist, F. "Th. K." Zur Psychologie eines jugendlichen Kriminellen. Int Zeitsch f Individualpsychol 6: 108-16 '28 2357

Kley. Zur Psychologie des Mordes. Krimin Monatsh 1: 113-15, 158-61, 181-5 My-Ag '27 2358

Köhler, F. Kriminalpsychologische Probleme zum Mordprozess Dr. Bröcker. Aerztl Sachverst-Zeit 33: 200-10 Ag 1 '27 2359

Kössler, Maximilian. Ein kriminalpsychologisches Experiment aus der Praxis. Monats f Kriminalpsychol u Strafrechtsref 20: 239-40 '29 2360

Krassnuschkin, E. K. Beitrag zur psychiatrischen Charakterologie der Verbrecher. Monats f Kriminalpsychol u Strafrechtsref 18: 561-90 O '27 2361

Landesco, John. Psychology of the gangster; an analysis of the hoodlum's moral defense. Police "13-13" 5: 3-5, 35 My '30 2362

Leary, John [J]. Psychology of criminology. Int Assn Identif Proc 13: 20-7 '27; same title: Peace Offic 5: 11-14 N '27 2363

Lesemann, G. Vor welche Aufgaben stellt uns die Kriminalität unserer Hilfsschüler. Hilfsschule 1: 308-22 '28 2364

Lipmann, Otto and Plaut, Paul, eds. Die Lüge in psychologischer, philosophischer, juristischer, pädagogischer, historischer, soziologischer, sprach- und literaturwissenschaftlicher und entwicklungsgeschichtlicher Betrachtung. 567p. Leipzig, Barth, 1927 2365

Löwy, Malwine. Die Jugendliche Minderwertigkeit und die Einstellung zum eigenen Delikt. Monats f Kriminalpsychol u Strafrechtsref 22: 720-5 D '31 2366

Louttit, C. M. comp. Bibliography of bibliographies on psychology, 1900-1927. Nat Res Council Bul (65) N '28 2367
Criminal psychology: items 49, 347, 352, 459, 607, 625, 656, 681, 744-9, 750, 852.

Luz, Walter. Ursachen und Bekämpfung des Verbrechens im Urteil des Verbrechers. Ein Beitrag zur Psychologie des Verbrechers und Verbrechens und zur Reform der Verbrechensbekämpfung. 274p. Heidelberg, Carl Winter, 1928 2368

Maass. Erinnerungsfälschung als Form der Haftpsychose. Allg Zeitsch f Psychiat 92: 517-18 '29 2369

Maass. Selbstanklagen und pathologische Geständnisse. Allg Zeitsch f Psychiat 92: 515-17 '29 2370

Mahrer, M. Quando noi morti ci destiamo. Contributo alla fisio-psicologia del suicidio. Arch di Antrop Crim 50: 161-96 Mr '30 2371

Mauerhofer, R. Kriminalpsychologie. Psychol Rundsch 3: 174-6 '31 2372

Meagher, John F. W. Malingering in criminals; its forensic psychiatric significance. Med Leg J 45: 78-86 My '28 2373

Michaëlis, Edgar. Vom "Verbrecher aus Schuldbewusstsein." Zeitsch f Kinderforsch 34: 132-43 Mr 20 '28 2374

Mittermaier, W. Kriminalpsychologisches Praktikum. Monats f Kriminalpsychol u Strafrechtsref 20: 545 '29 2375

Monatsschrift für Kriminalpsychologie und Strafrechtsreform. Heidelberg. 1, April 1904- 2376

Mönkemöller. Psychologie des Eisenbahnattentates. Arch f Krim 83: 21-65 Jl '28 2377

Morandi, A. Risposte caratteristiche di delinquenti. Zacchia 6: 43-4 '27 2378

Nóvoa Santos, R[oberto]. El instinto de la muerte. 184p. Madrid, J. Morata, 1927 2379

Oertel. Zur Psychologie eines Mörders. Arch f Krim 83: 222-7 N '28 2380

The overt act of a criminal mind. Just Peace 91: 707-8 S 24 '27 2381

Patrizi, M. L. La criminalità della specie. Riv di Psicol 24: 133-46 Jl '28 2382

Pt 1a of chap. 4 (La delinquenza dell' individuo e quella della specie) of Addizioni al "Dopo Lombroso."

Penso, Girolamo. Lo studio psicologico del delinquente. 21p. Messina. Giacomo d'Anna, 1931 2383

Extr: Il pensiero giuridico-penale 3 (1)

Pilsudski, Jósef. La psychologie du prisonnier. R Pénitent de Pologne 4: 3-22 English transl (p23-41) Ja '29 2384

Plaut, Paul. Zur Psychologie der Notzucht und ihre forensische Begutachtung. Krimin Monatsh 4: 106-10 My '30 2385

Pozzolini, A. L'elemento psicologico del delitti colposi. 10p. Pisa, Pacini Mariotti, 1930 2386

Extr: Ann delle Univ Toscane 14 (1)

The problem of the criminal mind; (editorial). J Abnorm & Soc Psychol 23: 1-3 Ap '28 2387

Rabinowicz, Leon. Le crime passionel. Collection des études de psychologie sociale. 250p. Paris, Rivière, 1931; same title: R de Dr Pén et de Crimin 10: 1223-35 '30 2388

Rehm, O. Arbeiten aus dem Gebiete der Kriminal- und Sozialpsychologie. Zeitsch f Völkerpsychol u Soz 5: 446-63 D '29 2389

Summary of 30 articles from Monats f Kriminalpsychol u Strafrechtsref on the problem of criminality and suicide from various standpoints, including race, mental abnormality and personality types.

Rehm, [O.]. Zur Kriminalpsychologie. Aus der rechts- und Kriminalpsychologischen Literatur. Zeitsch f Völkerpsychol u Soz 4: 70-6 Mr '28 2390

Renda, Sebastiano Emilio. Note critiche sull'elemento psichico del reato colposo. 49p. Catania, Scuola tipografica salesiana, 1929 2391

Sanders, Hans Theodor. Zur Psychologie des Giftmordes durch Aerzte. Die Fälle: Dr. Richter und Dr. Broicher. Arch f Krim 86: 33-55 F '30 2392

Scheinmann, Hans. Psychologie der männlichen Kokotte. Zeitsch f Sexualwissensch 16 (3): 206-10 Jl '29 2393

Schlesinger, E. Hat der Verbrecher Gemeinschaftsgefühl? Int Zeitsch f Individualpsychol 5: 345-50 '31 2394

Schlör, [Walter]. Zur Psychologie des Taschen- und Warenhausdiebstahls. Umschau 31: 347-8 Ap 30 '27 2395

Schmitz, Oscar A. H. Zur Psychologie des Zuchthäuslers. Zeitsch f Menschenk 7 (3): 91-5 S '31 2396

Schneickert, Hans. Über Verbrecherhumor. Krimin Monatsh 1: 276-9 D '27 2397

Seelig, E. Die Psychosexuelle Struktur des Zuhälters. Monats f Kriminalpsychol u Strafrechtsref 20: 169-73 Mr '29 2398

Seidler, R.; Goldberger, E., and Friedmann, A. Der Diebstahl als Entmutigungserscheinung. Int Zeitsch f Individualpsychol 6: 68-70 '28 2399

Sieverts, Rudolf. Die Wirkungen der Freiheitsstrafe und Untersuchungshaft auf die Psyche der Gefangenen. Phänomenologische Studien an literarischen Selbstzeugnissen ehemaliger Häftlinge. 187p. (Hamburg Schr z Ges Strafrechtswiss no14, hrsg von M. Liepmann). Mannheim, J. Bensheimer, 1929 2400

Autobiographies of 45 prisoners analysed.

Sighele, Scipio. La coppia criminale; psicologia degli amori morbosi. ed.3. rev. 251p. (Piccola biblioteca di scienze moderne 165) Torino, Bocca, 1927 2401

Stephan, Otto. Überzeugungstaten. Polizeibeamten-Bl 10 (2): 9-10 '27 3402

Tasker, Robert Joyce. A man is hanged. Am Mercury 11: 162-70 Je '27 2403

Description of a convict's feeling when another prisoner is being hung.

Tersiev, N. Die Bewertung ihrer Taten seitens der verurteilten Mörder. Monats f Kriminalpsychol u Strafrechtsref 21: 198-207 Ap '30 2404

Többen, [Heinrich]. Beitrag zur Psychologie des Hoch- und Landesverrats. Deut Zeitsch f d ges gerichtl Med 9: 202-11 Ja 15 '27 2405

Többen, Heinrich. Neuere Beobachtungen über die Psychologie der zu lebenslänglicher Zuchthausstrafe verurteilten oder begnadigten Verbrecher. 194p. bibliog 192. Leipzig, Deuticke, 1927 2406

Truelle. Un cas curieux de psychologie criminelle. Etudes Crimin 4: 227-34 Jl '29 2407

Türkel, S[iegfried]. Verbrecher-Aberglaube. Krimin Monatsh 2: 112-13 My '28 2408

Wächter. Die Bedeutung der Phantasie für die Tätigkeit des Kriminalisten. Krimin Monatsh 4: 217-22 O '30 2409

Wembridge, Eleanor Rowland. Emotion in the court room. Am Mercury 17: 48-53 My '29 2410

Weygandt, W. Über krankhafte Selbstbeschuldigung. Monats f Kriminalpsychol u Strafrechtsref 19: 17-29 Ja '28 2411

Witte, H. J. Criminal psychology. M Times [N Y] 56: 143, 163 '28 2412

Wolf, Erik. Verbrechen aus Überzeugung. 32p. (Recht u Staat in Geschichte u Gegenwart. 52) Tübingen, Mohr, 1927 2413

Wolff, Friedrich. Der Fall Neckermann. Ein Beitrag zur Psychologie des Lustmordes. Monats f Kriminalpsychol u Strafrechtsref 21: 212-26 Ap '30 2414

Woworski. Die Arsenmorde in Steiermark (Ein Beitrag zur Psychologie des Dorfverbrechens). Monats f Kriminalpsychol u Strafrechtsref 21: 536-45 '30 2415

Ziehen, T. Charakterologische Studien an Verbrechern. Jahrb d Charakterol 4: 195-209 '27; 5: 375-94 '28 2416

Criminal Telepathy

Dangel, Richard. Pseudotelepathie und Kriminalistik. Arch f Krim 86 (1): 23-33 F '30 2417

Hellwig, Albert. Betrugsverfahren gegen Kriminaltelepathen. Arch f Krim 84: 15-48 Ja '29 2418

Hellwig, A[lbert]. Der Beweiswert der Kriminaltelepathie. Schweiz Zeitsch f Strafr 42: 212-40 '29 2419

Hellwig, Albert. Der gegenwärtige Stand der Kriminaltelepathie. Monats f Kriminalpsychol u Strafrechtsref 20: 17-29 '29 2420

Hellwig, Albert. Gibt es nachweisbar echte Fälle von Kriminaltelepathie? Eine Betrachtung zum Insterburger Okkultistenprozess. Krimin Monatsh 2: 121-3 Je '28 2421

Hellwig A[lbert]. Die Kriminaltelepathie vom Standpunkt der forensischen Psychologie. Allg Zeitsch f Psychiat 92: 503-5 '29 2422

Hellwig, A[lbert]. Zum Streit um die Kriminaltelepathie. Zeitsch f Med-Beamte 42: 287-93 Jl 1 '29 2423

Hellwig, Albert. Zur Frage der Kriminaltelepathie: Die Begründung des Urteils des Schöffengerichts Bernburg gegen den Lehrer Drost mit Anmerkungen. Arch f Krim 81: 102-40 S '27; same title: Monats f Kriminalpsychol u Strafrechtsref 18: 631-5 N '27; also: 41p. Leipzig, Vogel, 1927 2424

CRIMINAL PERSONALITY

Adler, A. Die kriminelle Persönlichkeit und ihre Heilung. Int Zeitsch f Individualpsychol 5: 321-8 '31 2425

Almaraz, José. Como puede conocerse la personalidad del acusado. R Mexicana d Der Pen 1: 21-48 Jl '30 2426

Bekhterev, Y. Y. [A study of the personality of prisoners]. 72p. Moskva, Narkomvnudel, 1928 2427

Brennecke, Hans. Die Erforschung der Persönlichkeit des Gefangenen; ihre Methode und ihre Auswirkung im Strafvollzug. Monats f Kriminalpsychol u Strafrechtsref 21: 655-68 N '30 2428

Burdick, C. M. The importance of knowing the personality make-up of the criminal. Psychiat Q 3: 456-8 '28 2429

Ferri, Enrico. A character study and life history of Violet Gibson, who attempted the life of Benito Mussolini. J Crim L & Crimin 19: 211-19 Ag '28 2430A

Ferri, Enrico. La personalité de Mlle. Violet Gibson qui, le 7 avril 1926, blessa par un coup de revolver Benito Mussolini. R Int de Dr Pén 4: 230-9, English transl 240-51, by Mary Hint Cassola, '27; same title: trad par Gino Cutore di San Carlo. R de Dr Pén et de Crimin 7: 475-85 '27 2430B

Fuchs-Kamp, Adelheid. Lebensschicksal und Persönlichkeit ehemaliger fürsorgezöglinge. 172p. (Abh aus dem Gesamtgebiete der Kriminalpsychol no6) Berlin, Springer, 1929 2431

Study of 65 cases at Flehinger Reformatory.

Harris, Mary B. Personality in prison. Am Pris Assn Proc 59: 292-301 '29 2432

Jorgulesco, Ric. Les recherches sur la personalité du délinquant empêchent-elles le reclassement? 30p. Bucuresti, 1930 2433

Kalmann, Heinrich. Neue Wege zur Erforschung der kriminellen Persönlichkeit. Zeitsch f Menschenk 3: 145-56 S '27 2434

Kogan, I. M. Verwendung des Assoziationsexperimentes bei der Erforschung der Persönlichkeit des Verbrechers. Zeitsch f d ges Neurol u Psychiat 116: 199-213 '28 2435

Leibbrand, Werner. Die "überwertige Idee" in der Kriminalistik. Arch f Krim 81: 230-4 D '27 2436

Lenz, Adolf. Der Anteil der Sexualität am Aufbau der kriminellen Persönlichkeit. Zeitsch f Sexualwissensch 14: 1-6 Ap '27 2437

Lenz, Adolf; Seelig, E.; Kalmann, H.; Müller, D. G., and Torkorn, A. Mörder. Die Untersuchung der Persönlichkeit als Beitrag zur Kriminalbiologischen Kasuistik und Methodik. 106p. Graz, Moser, 1931 2438

Leppmann, F. Bericht über eine kriminelle Persönlichkeit. Zeitsch f Kinderforsch 37: 175-84 '30 2439

Nimkoff, Meyer F. Personality problems of beggars. Sociol & Soc Res 12: 431-42 My '28 2340

Rittenbruch, Wolfgang. Die Erforschung der Persönlichkeit des Gefangenen. Monats f Kriminalpsychol u Strafrechtsref 22: 32-5 '31 2441

Schneider, Kurt. Studien über Persönlichkeit und Schicksal eingeschriebener Prostituierter. Kölner Vjsh f Soz 6: 274-8 '27 2342

Stearns, Albert Warren. The personality of criminals. 158p. Boston, Beacon press, 1931 2343

Thomas, Will. Die strafrechtliche Bedeutung der sogenannten Integrierten Persönlichkeitstypen von E. R. Jaensch. Zeitsch f ang Psychol 35: 1-75 Mr '30 2444

PERSONAL DOCUMENTS

Arrow, Charles. Rogues and others. 244p. London, Duckworth, 1929 **2445**

Ashton-Wolfe, Harry. Crime of violence and revenge. 359p. N. Y. Houghton, 1929 **2446**
Stories of 12 bandits and criminals in Mexico, Italy, Paris, etc.

Ashton-Wolfe, Harry. Warped in the making; crimes of love and hate. 323p. Boston, Houghton, 1928 **2447**

Barry, Philip Beaufoy. Twenty human monsters in purple and rags, from Caligula to Landru, A.D. 12-1922. 286p. [London] Jarrolds, 1929 **2448**

Benjamin, Lewis S. and Hargreaves, R. eds. Famous duels and assassinations. 288p. London, Jarrolds, 1929 **2449**

Birkenhead, Frederick Edwin Smith. The adventures of Ralph Rashleigh; a penal exile in Australia, 1825-1844. London, Cape, 1930 **2450**

Black, Jack. Burglar looks at laws and codes. Harper's 160: 306-13 F '30 **2451**

Black, Jack. Two crimes of 1928. New Repub 57: 293-5 Ja 30 '29 **2452**

Brock, James. Die Leiche im Reisekorbe, ein rätselhafter Mord. Arch f Krim 85: 23-9, 160-5 Ag, O '29 **2453**

Burns, Walter Noble. Saga of Billy the Kid. 322p. N.Y. Garden city pub co. 1928 **2454**

Byloff, Fritz. Der Tod im Koffer. Arch f Krim 84: 224-33 My '29 **2455**

Clarke, Donald Henderson. In the reign of Rothstein. 306p. N.Y. Vanguard, 1929 **2456**

Davenport, Walter. Morgan, Blackbeard and Kidd. Mentor 15: 1-13 Ap '27 **2457**

Dearden, Harold. The mind of the murderer. 288p. London, Bles, 1930 **2458**
Account of 20 cases, illustrating the author's thesis that the concept of instinct is basic to the understanding of murder.

Dilnot, George. Celebrated crimes. 256p. London, Paul, 1929 **2459**

Dvorak, R. W. In re Leon Simon, Louis Asher et al. Story of a forger, a professional bondsman and the intricacies of a case in the Municipal court of Chicago. Crim Just [Chicago] 9: 3-4 Mr '27 **2460**

Engelhardt, L. Legenden um einen unbekannten Täter. (Jack the Ripper) Ein Beitrag zur Frage der Kriminal-Hellseherei. Arch f Krim 87: 28-40 Ag '30 **2461**

Espina, Antonio. Luis candelas; el bandido de Madrid. 263p. Madrid, Espasa-Calpe, 1929 **2462**

Fanning, Peter. Great crimes of the west. 292p. San Francisco, 951 Eddy st. The Author, 1929 **2463**

Finger, Charles Joseph. Romantic rascals. 251p. N.Y. McBride, 1927 **2464**

Forgy, Martha Lee. "Mike" Letcher. Welf Mag 18: 1211-14 S '27 **2465**

French, Joseph Lewis, ed. Gallery of old rogues. 285p. N.Y. King, 1931 **2466**

French, Joseph Lewis. Gray shadows. 276p. N.Y. Century, 1931 **2467**

Garrett, Pat F. Authentic life of Billy the Kid; edited by Maurice Garland Fulton. 233p. N.Y. Macmillan, 1927 **2468**
First published in Santa Fe in 1882.

Gelli, Jacopo. Banditi, briganti e brigantesse nell' ottocento. 250p. Firenze, R. Bemporad, 1931 **2469**

Gerould, Katherine Fullerton. Jessica and Al Capone. Harper's 163: 93-7 Je '31 **2470**

Gide, André Paul Guillaume. L'affaire Redureau, suivie de faits divers. ed. 12. 222p. Paris, Gallimard, 1930 **2471**

Glasscock, Carl Burgess. Bandits and the Southern Pacific. 294p. N.Y. Stokes, 1929 **2472**

Goddefroy, E. Die Phönix-Park-Affaire. Arch f Krim 86: 189-98 Je '30 **2473**

Gollomb, Joseph. Master highwaymen. 312p. N.Y. Macaulay, 1927 **2474**

Gollomb, Joseph. Spies. 286p. London, Hutchinson, 1928 **2475**

Gordon, Charles George. Crooks of the underworld. 256p. London, Bles, 1929 **2476**

Greenwood, William de Redman (Maitland Crichton, Thornton Hall, Guy Russell, pseuds). Guilty or not guilty? stories of fifty sensational crimes in many countries. 288p. London, Hutchinson, 1931 **2477**

Hatch, William John. Land pirates of India; an account of the Kuravers, a remarkable tribe of hereditary criminals, their extraordinary skill as thieves, cattle-lifters and highwaymen, etc., and their manners and customs. 272p. N.Y. Lippincott, 1928 **2478**

Haworth, Peter, ed. Classic crimes in history and fiction. 286p. N.Y. Appleton, 1927 **2479**
Published in London, 1927 under title: Before Scotland Yard.

Hayward, Arthur Lawrence, ed. Lives of the most remarkable criminals, who have been condemned and executed for murder, the highway, housebreaking, street robberies, coining or other offenses; collected from original papers and authentic memoirs and published in 1735. 640p. N.Y. Dodd, 1927 **2480**

He shot himself; Saul Black's criminal record. Credit & Fin Management 33: 20-1 S '31 **2481**

Head, Richard and Kirkman, Francis. English rogue described in the life of Meriton Latroon. 660p. N. Y. Dodd, 1928 **2482**

Herbertz. Die Familientragödie in Glackau. Krimin Monatsh 1: 279-80 D '27 **2483**

Howard, Harvey James. Ten weeks with the Chinese bandits. new ed. 272p. N.Y. Dodd, 1930 **2484**

Jeffries, Graham Montague (Bruce Graeme, pseud). Passion, murder and mystery. 287p. London, Hutchinson [1928] **2485**

Judges, Arthur Valentine, ed. Elizabethan underworld: a collection of Tudor and early Stuart tracts and ballads, telling of the lives and misdoings of vagabonds, thieves, etc., and giving some account of the operation of the criminal law. 543p. London, Routledge, 1930 **2486**

Kah, Philippe. Aux enfers du crime; causes célèbres. 310p. Lille, Mercure de Flandre, 1931 **2487**
11 notable crimes and their trials; popular presentation.

Kingston, Charles. Enemies of society. London, Stanley Paul, 1930 **2488**

Kingston, Charles. Lawbreakers. 280p. London, Lane, 1930 **2489**

Kingston, Charles. Rogues and adventuresses. 238p. London, Lane, 1928 **2490**

Laurence, John. Extraordinary crimes. 242p. London, Low, 1931 **2491**

Lives of highwaymen, pirates, and robbers. Golden Bk 13: 72 Ja '31 **2492**

Logan, Guy B. H. Great murder mysteries. 288p. London, Paul, 1931 **2493**

Logan, Guy B. H. Guilty or not guilty? Stories of celebrated crimes. 288p. London, Duffield, 1929 **2494**

Logan, Guy B. H. Masters of crime: a study of multiple murders. 288p. London, Paul, 1930 **2495**

Logan, Guy B. H. Rope, knife, and chair. Studies of English, French and American crimes. 280p. London, Paul, 1930 **2496**

McAdoo, William. The procession to Tyburn: crime and punishment in the eighteenth century. 306p. N. Y. Boni, 1927 **2497**
Series of 17 records of criminal cases from a work of 3 vols published by an anonymous law student in 1804.

Mackenzie, Frederick Arthur. Twentieth century crimes. 273p. Boston, Little, 1927 **2498**

Mackenzie, Frederick Arthur. World-famous crimes. 293p. London, Bles [1927] **2499**
Leopold and Loeb; Henri Landru; Stockholm dynamite murder; Rasputin; Steinie Morrison, etc.

Marquis, Don. As crook sees crook. Sat Eve Post 201: 14-15 O 27 '28 **2500**

Mitchell, E. V. ed. The Newgate calendar; memoirs of the most notorious characters who have been convicted of outrages on the laws of England. 264p. London, Lane, 1928 **2501**

Overton, Grant. He says crime can't win; Jack Black's story. Mentor 15: 60 F '27 **2502**

Pearson, Edmund Lester. Five murders; with a final note on the Borden case. 299p. N.Y. Doubleday, 1928 **2503**

Poynter, James William. Forgotten crimes. 284p. London, Selwyn & Blount, 1928 **2504**

Raine, William MacLeod. Famous sheriffs and western outlaws. 295p. N. Y. Doubleday, 1929 **2505**

Sabin, Edwin Legrand. Wild men of the wild west. 363p. N.Y. Crowell, 1929 **2506**

Smalley, David E. Stumbling. N.Y. Barse & co. 1929? **2507**
Medico-legal study of a condemned and sentenced criminal.

Smith, Edward Henry. Famous American poison mysteries. 340p. London, Hurst & Blackett, 1927 **2508**

Smith, Edward Henry. Mysteries of the missing. 317p. N.Y. Dial, 1927 **2509**

Speer, W. Harold. Secret history of great crimes. 110p. London, Stockwell, 1929 **2510**

Stevens, C. L. McCluer. Famous crimes and criminals. ed. 2. 264p. London, Paul, 1929 **2511**

Stevens, C. L. McCluer. From clue to dock. 256p. N.Y. Duffield, 1927 **2512**

Stuart, Hix Cook. Notorious Ashley gang; a saga of the king and queen of the Everglades. 80p. Stuart, Fla. St. Lucie ptg. co. [1928] **2513**

Sutherland, Sidney. Ten real murder mysteries. 347p. London, Putnam, 1929 **2514**

Villiers, Elizabeth. Riddles of crime. 250p. London, W. Laurie, 1928 **2515**

Villiers, Elizabeth. Stand and deliver; the romantic adventures of certain gentlemen of the high toby, their times, their associates, friends and victims. 256p. London, Paul, 1929 **2516**

Walsh, Cecil Henry. The Agra double murder. 254p. London, Benn, 1929 **2517**

Wells, L. A. History of regicides in New England. N.Y. Hitchcock, 1927 **2518**

Wire, G. E. Index of celebrated cases, crimes, criminals, detectives, escapes, homicides, mysteries, swindles, trials, etc., described in general books (not in volumes specifically devoted to the particular case or person). J Crim L & Crimin 21: 339-63 N '30 **2519**

Wyndham, Horace. Crime on the continent. 316p. Boston, Little, 1928 **2520**

CASE HISTORIES

Alexander, F. Der Doppelmord eines 19 jährigen. Psychoanal Beweg 2: 80-93 '30 **2521**

Alker, Ernst. Prophetin und Verbrecherin (ein psychologisches Rätsel). Monats f Kriminalpsychol u Strafrechtsref 20: 129-37 '29 **2522**

Allen, Glenna M. The rankly incorrigible boy. Nat Prob Assn Proc 25: 127-43 '31 **2523**

Almandos, Luis Reyna. Causas célebres de doble personalidad. R de Identif y Cienc Pen 2: 154-73 Jl '28 **2524**

Almandos, Luis Reyna; Aguirre, Barreiro; Ramos; Villanueva, Molla, and Buzzo y Houssay. El proceso Ray; causa y hora de la muerte del doctor Carloa A. Ray. R de Identif y Cienc Pen 2: 275-314 S '28 **2525**

Aus dem Lebenslauf eines sechszehnjährigen Raubmörders. Schweiz Zeitsch f Strafr 42: 277-96 '29 **2526**

Bäyer, W. von. Ein Fall von psychopathischer Selbstbezichtigung. Zeitsch f d ges Neurol u Psychiat 135: 779-93 '31 2527

Barlow, Howard [L.]. The Hatch murder case. Int Assn Identif, Calif Div Proc 16: 27-30 '31 2528

Bell, Marjorie. Juvenile case no. 1: John of Oregon. Nat Prob Assn Proc 24: 281-6 '30 2529

Bermbach. Der Fall Bröcker Oberreuter. Aerztl Sachverst-Zeit 33: 179-82 Jl 1 '27 2530

Bernhard, H. Über jugendliche Brandstifter. Aerztl Sachverst-Zeit 36: 51-60 '30 2531

De Block, L. Un escroc pathologique. J de Neurol et de Psychiat 29: 595-605 '29 2532

Brown, S. Clement. Some case studies of delinquent girls described as leaders. Brit J Educ Psychol 1 pt2: 162-79 Je '31 2533

Investigation in Los Angeles county, Calif.

Dehnow, F. Zusammenfassendes zum Fall Haarmann. Vererb u Geschlechtsleb (3): 176-85 '27 2534

Dieckhöfer, Clemens. Über einen Fall von grundloser Selbstbeschuldigung. Monats f Kriminalpsychol u Strafrechtsref 20: 321-6 '29 2535

Dietl, Hugo. Ein meuchlerischer Raubmord in Tirol. Krimin Monatsh 4: 154-7 Jl '30 2536

Dyrenfurth. Karl Böttcher und seine Verbrechen. Aerztl Sachverst-Zeit 33: 317-30 '27 2537

Eliasberg, W. and Hirschberg, M. Ein "Fall" von Notdiebstahl. Monats f Kriminalpsychol u Strafrechtsref 18: 661-70 D '27 2538

Engelhardt, Leopold. Der Gardien de la Paix Prévost. Ein Beitrag zur Aetiologie des Mördes. Arch f Krim 89: 177-90 N '31 2539

Ezekiels, Jeannette. Adult case no 3: a non-support case. Nat Prob Assn Proc 24: 272-80 '30 2540

Feis, O. Verhandlungen über einen Fall sexueller Perversion aus dem Jahre 1776. Arch f Gesch d Med 19: 293-7 Jl '27 2541

Frank, Leonhard. The cause of the crime; translated from German by Cyrus Brooks. 118p. London, Davis, 1928 2542

Friedersdorff. Brandstiftung aus psychologischen und pathologischen Ursachen. Krimin Monatsh 4: 271-2 D '30 2543

Gennat. Die Düsseldorfer Sexualverbrechen. Krimin Monatsh 4: 2-7, 27-32, 49-54, 79-85 Ja-Ap '30 2544

Gennat. Der Kürtenprozess (Düsseldorfer Sexual-Verbrechen). Krimin Monatsh 5: 108-11, 130-3 My, Je '31 2545

Goddefroy, E. Le comptable infidèle; enquête à propos d'un cachet postal. R Int de Crimin 2(5): 352-6 '30 2546

Goldwyn, Jacob. Impulses to incendiarism and theft. A case report. Am J Psychiat 9: 1093-9 My '30 2547

Hacker, W. A. Some case histories in juvenile delinquency. Ind Bul Char & Correc (177): 576-84 D '29 2548

Hapke, E. Lebenslauf eines jungen Zuchthausgefangenen. Zeitsch f Kinderforsch 37: 208-20 '30 2549

Hartwell, Samuel W. Fifty-five "bad" boys. 359p. N.Y. Knopf, 1931 2550

Hellwig, A. Zwei Fälle von Tötung in schlaftrunkenem Zustande. Zeitsch f d ges Neurol u Psychiat 126: 262-71 '30 2551

Hentig, H. v. Bemerkung zum Fälle Bröcker. Aerztl Sachverst-Zeit 33: 265-7 O 1 '27 2552

Herbertz. Der Juwelenräuber Spruch und seine Tat. Krimin Monatsh 1: 105-8 My '27 2553

Hirschberg. Ein Fall von sexuellem Infantilismus. Monats f Kriminalpsychol u Strafrechtsref 22: 412-18 '31 2554

Hussa, R. Ein Mordgeständnis, ausgelöst durch eine Haftpsychose. Ein Beitrag zur Beurteilung der Selbstbeschuldigungen. Arch f Krim 89: 117-25 S '31 2555

Hussa, R. Ein seltener Fall von Selbstbeschädigung. Monats f Kriminalpsychol u Strafrechtsref 22: 500-2 Ag '31 2556

Jacobi, H. Ein jugendlicher Verbrecher. Individualpsychologische Betrachtung zum Fall Willy Hintze. Int Zeitsch f Individualpsychol 6: 117-20 '28 2557

Joint committee on methods of preventing delinquency. Three problem children: narratives from the case-records of a child guidance clinic. 142p. (Pub no2) N. Y. Commonwealth Fund, 1924. (corr pub) London, Allen, 1931 2558

Jones, Abram Nicholls. Adult case no 2: Successes and failures in Rochester. Nat Prob Assn Proc 24: 263-71 '30 2559

Kempner, Robert. Das "Sittlichkeitsvergehen" des Schuhmachers Gramm.—Erst 1 1/2 Jahre Gefängnis—jetzt Freispruch und 20000 RM Entschädigung. Krimin Monatsh 5: 121-5 Je '31 2560

Kinberg, O. En ovanlig lagbrytare. Svenska Läk-tidning 5: 129-44 '30 2561

Knobloch, Edward. Die Ermordung der Margit Vörösmarty. Arch f Krim 86: 131-44 Ap '30 2562

Kolle, Kurt. Der Fall Völler. Ein Beitrag zur Psychopathologie des Mörders und zur Strafrechtsreform. Monats f Kriminalpsychol u Strafrechtsref 21: 226-36 Ap '30 2563

Loewenfeld, Philipp. Der Fall Jungmann. Monats f Kriminalpsychol u Strafrechtsref 20: 734-51 '29 2564

Longstreth, T. Morris. Murder at Belly Butte. Police J [London] 4: 68-82 Ja '31 2565

Longstreth, T. Morris and Vernon, Henry. The unquestioned alibi. Police J [London] 4: 406-17 Jl '31 2566

McKenna, Henry C. Adult case no 1: the boy who did not like work. Nat Prob Assn Proc 24: 260-2 '30 2567

Marcuse, Max. Ein Fall von "Kleptomanie." Monats f Kriminalpsychol u Strafrechtsref 19: 401-15 Jl '28 2568

Markowin, J. W. and Brailowsky, Victor. Der Fall Waldanow. Monats f Kriminalpsychol 19: 549-57 '28 2569

Mommsen, Theodor. Das Kriminalrätsel einer pseudonymen Schenkung. Krimin Monatsh 5: 53-6 Mr '31 2570

Moon, Marjorie M. Juvenile case no 4: Arthur of New York state. Nat Prob Assn Proc 24: 297-300 '30 2571

O'Mara, Edward J. Juvenile case no 2: the boy from a drunken home. Nat Prob Assn Proc 24: 287-8 '30 2572

Otto. Zwei "Unglücksfälle." Krimin Monatsh 4: 177-81 Ag '30 2573

P., A. M. Jack Sheppard; legendary and real. Police J [London] 1: 148-68 '28 2574

Petrova, Anna. Ein Fall von Verstümmelung des Gatten. Monats f Kriminalpsychol u Strafrechtsref 18: 177-93 '27 2575

Petzet, Wolfgang. Stand der Untersuchung im Falle Kaspar Hauser (Überblick über die Literatur der letzten Jahre). Monats f Kriminalpsychol u Strafrechtsref 19: 436-41 '28 2576

Plaut, Paul. Ein dreizehnjährige Kindesmörderin. Krimin Monatsh 5: 221-4 O '31 2577

Post, H. and Tumlirz, O. Eine junge Diebin. *In* Die Jugendlichen und ihre Erzieher. II. Mann's Päd Mag (1314): 38-44 '30 2578

Prada, L. V. and Bambaren, C. A. Constitucion psicopatica y delincuencia. Bol de Crimin 2: 7-14 '29 2579

Purdunn, Charles A. Benny. Welf Mag 18: 799-805 Je '27 2580

Rector, Leonora. Juvenile case no3: James of Arkansas. Nat Prob Assn Proc 24: 289-96 '30 2581

Roehrer, Karl. Eine lesbische Schwindlerin (Adele Spitzeder 1869-72). Monats f Kriminalpsychol u Strafrechtsref 20: 101-13 '29 2582

Rojas, N. Un crimen medioeval en la actualidad. R Especialid 6: 1303-10 N '31 2583

Scanlan, Mary F. The "W" family's domestic problems. Nat Prob Assn Proc 25: 122-6 '31 2584

Schmidt, Otto. Ein Beitrag zur Frage von Mord oder Selbstmord: Der Fall von H. . . . Arch f Krim 85: 185-96 D '29 2585

Spatz, H. Bemerkung zu . . . "Ein Fall von Notdiebstahl." Monats f Kriminalpsychol u Strafrechtsref 19: 415-17 Jl '28 2586

Stooss, C. Der Fall Marek. Monats f Kriminalpsychol u Strafrechtsref 18: 429-34 Ag '27 2587

Strewe. Zur Kasuistik sexual-pathologischer Kriminalfälle. Krimin Monatsh 4: 280-1 '30 2588

T., L. Forger of soviet documents. Nation [N Y] 125: 213-15 Ag 31 '27 2589

Tubbs, Eston V. A study of five problem cases. Psychol Clin 17: 249-69 '29 2590
Cases of Institute for juvenile research, Chicago.

Vértes, T. Der Weg zum Verbrechen. Int Zeitsch f Individualpsychol 5: 403-6 '31 2591

Villavicencio, V. M. El caso de un delincuente pederasta. Bol de Crimin 3: 235-50 '30 2592

Wilson, C. E. Adult case no 1: The builder. Nat Prob Assn Proc 23: 145-7 '29 2593

BIOGRAPHIES, AUTOBIOGRAPHIES AND CONFESSIONS

Ahearn, Danny (pseud). The confessions of a gunman. 254p. London, Routledge, 1930; same under title: How to commit a murder. 254p. N.Y. Washburn, 1930 2594

Allen, Trevor. Underworld: the biography of Charles Brooks, criminal. 299p. London, Fronto, 1931 2595

Booth, Ernest. Stealing through life. 308p. N.Y. Knopf, 1929 2596

Booth, Ernest. We rob a bank. Am Mercury 12: 1-11 S '27 2597

Callahan, Jack. Man's grim justice; my life outside the law. 296p. N.Y. Sears, 1928 2598

Cederholm, Boris. In the clutches of the Tcheka; translated by F. H. Lyon. 349p. Boston, Houghton, 1929 2599

Coffey, John. Thief's progress—autobiography. Outl 154: 203-6, 252-5, 301-4, 342-6, 379-82, 421-4, 460-3, 500-3, 538-41, 581-4, 620-2, 661-3 F 5-Ap 23 '30 2600

Crowe, Patrick T. Spreading evil, Pat Crowe's autobiography. 331p. N.Y. Branwell co. [1927] 2601

Guerin, Eddie. Crime: the autobiography of a crook. 319p. London, Murray, 1928; same under title: I was a bandit. 334p. N.Y. Doubleday, 1929 2602

Hodgetts, Edward Arthur Brayley. Vidocq: a master of crime. 318p. London, Selwyn, 1929 2603

Jacoby, H. Wie ich zum Verbrecher wurde. Int Zeitsch f Individualpsychol 5: 389-95 '31 2604

Körber, Lenka von. Meine Erlebnisse unter Strafgefangenen. 150p. Stuttgart, Hädecke, 1928 2605

O'Dare, Kain. Philosophy of the dusk. 247p. N.Y. Century, 1929 2606

Pasley, Fred D. Al Capone: the biography of a selfmade man. 355p. N.Y. Washburn, 1930 2607

Schucht, Elisabeth. Gezeichnete. Meine Erlebnisse unter Gefangenen und Strafentlassenen. 134p. Hamburg, Agentur des Rauhen Hauses, 1930 2608

Sharpe, May Churchill. Chicago May: her story. 336p. N.Y. Macmillan, 1928 2609

Tozer, Basil John. Story of a terrible life; the amazing career of a notorious procuress. 242p. London, Lowie, 1928: London, Stratford, 1929 2610

Tufts, Henry. The autobiography of a criminal, Henry Tufts; edited, with an introduction by Edmund Pearson. 357p. N.Y. Duffield, 1930 2611

STUDIES OF AND METHODS OF STUDYING OFFENDERS

STUDIES

Baker, Harry J.; Decker, Fred J., and Hill, Arthur S. Study of juvenile theft. J Educ Res 20: 81-7 S '29 **2612**

Beane, James C. A survey of three hundred delinquent girls [abstract of M. A. thesis, Indiana Univ., unpubl.]. J Juv Res 15: 198-208 Jl '31 **2613**

Bridges, J. W. A study of a group of delinquent girls. Pedag Sem 34: 187-204 Je '27 **2614**

Brooke, Margaret C. Results of examination of 91 girls at a state institution. Psychol Clin 17: 22-8 Mr '28 **2615**

Brugger, C. Versuch einer Geisteskrankenzählung in Thüringen. Zeitsch f d ges Neurol u Psychiat 133: 352-90 '31 **2616**
Classification and statistical survey of psychotics and criminal psychotics in Thuringia.

Bunbury, Doris Elizabeth. Juvenile delinquency in girls in Colorado. Colo Univ Stud 18 (4): 215-29 N '31 **2617**
Study of 100 girls, 11-19 years, of State industrial school for girls, Mt. Morrison.

Calhoon, C. H. A follow-up study of 100 normal and 100 subnormal delinquent boys. J Juv Res 12: 236-40 S '28; same title: Thesis (Ph.D.) Ohio State Univ. 1930 **2618**

Cushing, Hazel M. and Ruch, G. M. An investigation of character traits in delinquent girls. J Ap Psychol 11: 1-7 F '27 **2619**
Study made at State training school, Mitchellville, Iowa.

Elowson, Margaret L. A study of delinquent girls in Cook county. Thesis (M.A.) University of Chicago, 1931 **2620**

Gordon, R. G.; Thomas, R. E., and Greenall, E. G. Study of tendency towards delinquency of backward children. Brit M J (3610): 490-1 Mr 15 '30 **2621**

King, Anna Elizabeth. Changing the delinquent attitude; a study of effective treatment in the cases of forty-four delinquent girls. 80p. Cleveland, Ohio, Western Reserve university, 1927 **2622**

Kolakoski, Louis. A comparative social psychological study of Polish prisoners of Western penitentiary. 120p. (typw) Thesis (M.A.) University of Pittsburgh, 1930 **2623**
Study of 53 Polish immigrant male prisoners and of 38 native born males of Polish parentage compared with 845 native white males.

Levy, John. A mental hygiene study of juvenile delinquency; its causes and treatment. 47p. Brooklyn, Juvenile protective association, 1931? **2624**

Martin, Walter B. Behavior studies of criminals. 13p. (Ser C no130) Chicago, Institute for juvenile research, December 1927; same title: Welf Mag 18: 1581-91 D '27 **2625**
Statistics of inmates of Joliet penitentiary.

Murray, Verl. A comparative study of play information and athletic achievement in delinquent and non-delinquent boys. J Juv Res 15: 111-20 Ap '31 **2626**
Study of Whittier state school and Monrovia-Arcadia-Duarte high school.

Oberdörffer, Paula. Von der Wertwelt der Gefährdeten. 207p. Paderborn, Schöningh, 1928 **2627**
Study of 278 girls, 17-21 years, committed to Catholic reformatory institutions in the Rhine valley.

Overholser, Winfred. Psychiatric examinations of prisoners in Massachusetts. Psychiat Q 3: 469-70 '28 **2628**

Overholser, Winfred. Psychiatric studies of jail prisoners in Massachusetts. Am Assn Stud Feeblemind Proc 51: 202-17 bibliog (p215-17) '27 **2629**

Root, William T. A psychological and educational survey of 1916 prisoners in the Western penitentiary of Pennsylvania. 246p. Pittsburgh, Western Penitentiary, 1927 **2630**

Study of juvenile delinquency. Sch & Soc 27: 13 Ja 7 '28 **2631**

Study of problem boys and their brothers. J Educ Soc 3: 242-6 D '29 **2632**

Willey, Gordon F. The mental handicaps of delinquents; a preliminary study of the neuropsychiatric findings in over 1700 white male reformatory prisoners. Am Assn Stud Feebleminded Proc 53: 100-11 '29 **2633**
Study at Pennsylvania Industrial reformatory.

Zeleny, L. D. A comparative study of the investigations of the intelligence of criminals. Thesis (Ph.D.) University of Minnesota, 1931 **2634**

METHODS OF STUDY

Almandos, Luis Reyna. Documentación oficial del Museo Vucetich. Informe anual de la Dirección (1929). R de Identif y Cienc Pen 5: 161-72 N '29 **2635**

Almaraz, José. La creacion y el funcionamiento del consejo supremo de defensa y prevencion social de Mexico. R Int de Dr Pén 8: 105-14 Fr transl (p115-24) '31 **2636**

Arbore, Pasquale. Il trattamento profilattico della criminalità. Scuola Pos 11: 222-6 My '31 **2637**
Proposal of central institute where detailed life history and anthropometric data for each delinquent would be available.

Ball, Robert Jaudon. The correspondence method in follow-up studies of delinquent boys. J Juv Res 14: 107-13 Ap '30 **2638**

Balthazard, Victor. Projet de création d'un Laboratoire d'anthropologie criminelle. Arch di Antrop Crim 50 (6): 843-9 N '30 **2639**

Barnard, H. E. The White House conference study of the delinquent child. Am Pris Assn Proc 60: 80-90 '30 2640

Bekhterev, G. [The experimental penitentiary institute.] Sovyetskoe pravo 6(24): 119-24 '27 2641

Bermann, G. Direcciones para el estudio de menores abandonados y delincuentes. Conf Latino-Am de Neurol, Psiquiat y Med Leg Actas 2: 303-16 '29; same title: R Arg de Neurol, Psiquiat y Med Leg 3: 18-32 Ja '29 2642

Blacque-Belair. Proposition de résolution concernant l'examen des détenus et des condamnés, ainsi que la création d'annexes psychiatriques des prisons et de laboratoires d'anthropologie criminelle. Hyg Ment 26: 32-52 F '31 2643

Blacque-Belair and Ceillier, [André]. Exposé du projet de résolution invitant le gouvernement a créer des annexes psychiatriques, dans les prisons et les laboratoires d'anthropologie criminelle. Ann de Méd Lég 11: 99-114 discussion (p164-85) F, Mr '31 2644

Brasol, Boris. Criminalistic institutes on the continent of Europe. R Int de Crimin 3 (8): 610-16 '31 2645

Brasol, Boris. Institute of scientific criminology. Am J Police Sci 1: 100-6 Ja '30 2646

Brown, Sanger. The care of mental defectives in New York state. Psychiat Q 1: 146-59 Ap '27 2647

Criminal research laboratories.

Brown, Sanger. A psychiatric view of crime and the criminal. Am Assn Stud Feeblemind Proc 52: 115-23 '28 2648

Brown, Sanger. The value of psychiatric examination of court cases not actually insane. Psychiat Q 3: 448-50 '28 2649

Bryan, W. A. Psychiatry in Massachusetts courts. New England J Med 201: 1049-51 N 21 '29 2650

Ceillier, A[ndré]. Exposé d'un projet de loi concernant la création d'annexes psychiatriques dans les prisons, de laboratoires d'anthropologie criminelle et de maisons d'observation pour enfants vagabonds. Hyg Ment 26: 29-31 F '31 2651

Chicago academy of criminology. J Crim L & Crimin 22: 446 S '31 2652

Edwin H. Sutherland, President.

Claps, Albert. Les laboratoires de police et la justice. R Belge de Police Adm & Jud livraison 139 Ap '31 2653

Claude, H. L'expertise psychiatriques et les annexes psychiatriques des prisons. Hyg Ment 22: 149-55 D '27 2654

Consultatiebureaux voor moeilijke kinderen in Amerika. Maandbl v Ber en Reclasseer 6: 40-4, 67-70 F, Mr '27 2655

Crimino-biological research bureaus in the Prussian prisons. J Crim L & Crimin 22: 156 My '31 2656

Decree of July 29, 1930, established laboratories in prisons of Berlin (the detention jail), Breslau, Munster, Cologne, Wittlich, Frankfurt, Goldnow, Rheinbach, Halle.

Cuba. President. Decree . . . establishing the Central laboratory for penitentiary anthropology. 13p. Habana, Imp. de Rambla, 1928 2657

English, Spanish and French text.

Derome, Wilfrid. The laboratory of legal medicine and technical police of Montreal. Am J Police Sci 1: 216-23 Mr '30 2658

Durea, Mervin A. Psychological study and social follow-up. Tr Sch Bul 24: 49-59 '27 2659

Dyche, William Andrew. Science in the detection of crime; Scientific crime detection laboratory of Northwestern university. R of R 85: 52-4 Ja '31 2660

L'Ecole des sciences criminelles de l'université de Louvain. R de Dr Pén et de Crimin 10: 149-60 '30 2661

Finke. Biologische Zentralstellen im Dienste der Kriminalpolitik. Strafvollzug 21: 49-52 '31 2662

Finzi, Marcello. Das Kriminal Museum von Lyon. Arch f Krim 87 (2-3): 125-8 N '30 2663

Gamio, Manuel. Comentarios sobre la investigación sociológica de los delincuentes. R Mexicana de Der Pen 1: 49-60 Jl '30 2664

[Gernet, Mikhail] (M. Hernett). Das Staatsinstitut zur Erforschung der Kriminalität und des Verbrechers in Moskau. Monats f Kriminalpsychol u Strafrechtsref 19: 112-17 '28 2665

Giardini, G. I. Crime, causes and criminals. Pedag Sem 34: 144-68 Mr '27 2666

Work of the Department of Psychology, Western state penitentiary, Pennsylvania.

Glueck, Sheldon. Psychiatric examination of persons accused of crime. Yale L J 36: 632-48 Mr '27; same title: Ment Hyg 11: 287-323 Ap '27 2667

Goddard, Calvin H. Crime detection laboratory; the American experiment with a European police institution. Police "13-13" 5: 3-7 O '30 2668

Goddard, Calvin H. Medico-legal significance of Scientific crime detection laboratory of Northwestern university. Mil Surg 67: 759-66 D '30 2669

Goddard, Calvin H. The police scientific laboratory and its purpose. Int Assn Identif Proc 16: 182-6 '30 2670

Goddard, Calvin H. Scientific crime detection laboratories in Europe. Am J Police Sci 1: 13-37, 125-55 Ja, Mr '30 2671

Goddard, Calvin [H.] The scientific crime detection laboratory. Int Assn Chiefs Police Proc 37: 49-55 '30 2672

Gompert, Frank B. The research laboratory and its function in criminal investigation. Peace Offic Assn Calif Proc 11: 77-80 '31; same title: Int Assn Identif, Calif Div Proc 16: 62-8 '31 2673

Harvard university. Institute of criminal law. [Announcement] 1931-32. 13p. (Official register 28 (30) Je 18 '31) 2674

Haviland, C. F. Psychiatric examinations as a routine court procedure. Psychiat Q 3: 444-7 '28 2675

Helot, Henry. The laboratory of legal medicine and crime detection of Algiers. Am J Police Sci 2: 171-3 Mr '31 2676

Heuyer, G. and Abramson, J. Le profil mental dans l'examen des jeunes délinquants. Hyg Ment 26: 117-20 '31 2677

Heuyer, G.; Roudinesco, and Néron, M. L'examen médico-psychologique des enfants délinquants avant le passage devant le Tribunal des mineurs de Paris. R Int de l'Enf 10:223-38 O '30 2678

Ingrao, V. C. Sull'importanza pratica dell' esame psicoantropologico degli imputati. Arch di Antrop Crim 49: 838 '29 2679

Institute for juvenile research [Chicago]. Welf Mag 18: 889-91 Jl '27 2680
7 plates and organization chart.

Kalmann, Heinrich. Inwieweit erfüllt die Reform des Fahndungswesens in Österreich Heindls Vorschlag eines "Verbrecher-Clearing-House." Arch f Krim 86: 145-63 Ap '30 2681

Kamenetzki, Paul. Über die Tätigkeit des Psychiaters im Moskauer Gefängniswesen. Monats f Kriminalpsychol u Strafrechtsref 21: 193-7 Ap '30 2682

Kanger, A. Die kriminaltechnische Ausbildung der Juristen an der Lettländischen Universität. Arch f Krim 87: 178-82 N '30 2683

Un laboratoire de criminalistique à Lattaquié. R Int de Crimin 3 (8): 635-9 '31 2684

Legrand, E. A propos des annexes psychiâtriques des prisons. R de Dr Pén et de Crimin 7: 675-7 Je '27 2685

Locard, Edmond. Laboratoire de police et instruction criminelle. R Int de Crimin 2 (10): 766-9 '30 2686

Los Angeles school of criminology. J Crim L & Crimin 22: 444 S '31 2687

Loudet, O. El valor probatorio y legal de la pericias psiquiátricas. R de Crimin, Psiquiat y Med Leg 16: 529-35 S '29; same title: R Especialid 4: 1207-15 O '29 2688

Luria, A. R. Die Methode der abbildenden Motorik in der Tatbestandsdiagnostik. Zeitsch f ang Psychol 35: 139-83 Mr '30 2689

McFadden, Elizabeth. Dey's all got debbils. Parents' Mag 4: 22-3 O '29 2690
Institute of juvenile research, Chicago.

Martin, E. and Mouret, V. La création à Lyon d'un centre d'examen médico-légal et d'orientation professionnelle des enfants anormaux et délinquants. J de Méd de Lyon 11: 651-67 N 20 '30 2691

Mezger, Edmund. Ein kriminologisches Institut an der Universität Marburg. Bl f Gefängniskunde 60: 3-7 '29 2692

Michal, Clara. The scientific vs. the superficial attitude toward the offender. J Crim L & Crimin 19: 49-63 My '28 2693

Moore, J. W. Examination of prisoners before trial. Psychiat Q 3: 451-2 '28 2694

Nippe. Die gerichtsärztlichen Institute und die kriminalistisch-technische Tätigkeit an ihnen. Deut Zeitsch f d ges gerichtl Med 14: 411-27 D 10 '29 2695

Ohio. Bureau of juvenile research, Columbus. Annual reports *in* Annual report of Department of public welfare 6, 1926/27: 447-54; 7, 1927/28: 419-28 2696

O'Neill, Arthur A. A plea for the complete medical, psychological and psychiatric examination of all persons accused of crime. Int Assn Chiefs Police Proc 1927: 156-61 2697

Overholser, Winfred. Practical operation of Massachusetts law providing for psychiatric examination of certain persons accused of crime. Mass L Q 13: 35-51 Ag '28 2698

Overholser, Winfred. Psychiatry and the courts in Massachusetts. J Crim L & Crimin 19: 75-83 My '28 2699

Overholser, Winfred. Psychiatry and the Massachusetts courts as now related. Soc Forces 8: 77-87 S '29 2700

Overholser, Winfred. Use of psychiatric facilities in courts and penal institutions throughout the United States: a survey of progress. Nat Conf Soc Wk Proc 55: 143-50 '28; same title: Ment Hyg 13: 800-8 O '29 2701

Overholser, Winfred. The value of psychiatry; address January 10, 1929. Prison J 9: 1-4 Ja '29 2702

Park, Robert E. Murder and the case study method. Am J Sociol 36: 447-54 N '30 2703

Petrzilka, Werner. Persönlichkeitsforschung und Differenzierung im Strafvollzug; eine kriminalpolitische Betrachtung. 184p. Hamburg, Friederichsen, De Gruyter, 1930 2704
Account of two most prominent European methods of studying prisoners, those of Bavaria and Belgium.

Reorganización del Museo Vucetich. R de Identif y Cienc Pen 2: 376-91 S '28 2705

Richmond, Frank C. First biennial report of psychiatric field service of the State board of control of Wisconsin. Med-Leg J 44: 43-54 Mr '27 2706

Rockefeller foundation. Division of medical education. Methods and problems of medical education. 386p. N.Y. 1928 2707
Views and plans and description of institutes of legal medicine of the world.

Roubinovitch, [Jacques]. Sur l'organisation nouvelle du service médico-psychologique pour les mineurs de la prison de Fresnes. Ann de Méd Lég 11: 161-3 Mr '31 2708

Russia (RSFSR). Gosudarstevennyi institut po izucheniiu prestupnosti prestupnika. Problemy prestupnosti, 1, 1926- 2709
Edited by E. Shirvindt and others; Russian state institute for the study of criminality and the criminal, brought into existence by a decree of the People's Commissariat of the Interior, July 1925. Publishes annually, *Problems of crime.*

Scientific crime detection laboratory. Some figures from the annual report of the director, December 1, 1929 to December 1, 1930. Am J Police Sci 1: 615-20 N '30 2710

Sellin, Thorsten. The study of the criminal in Europe. Pris J 11: 24-6 Ap '31 2711

Shaw, Albert. Research in law and justice. R of R 83: 36-43 My '31 2712
Johns Hopkins Institute of law.

Shirvindt, E. O metode izuchenia prestupnosti i mer borde s nei v SSSR. Problemy Prestupnosti 2: 3-14 '27 2713

Simmons, Eva L. Psychiatric signposts. Survey 60: 104-5 Ap 15 '28 2714
Massachusetts experiment in psychiatric study of penal and correctional institution inmates.

Spasokukotskii, N. Deyatelnost Gosudarstvennogo instituta po izucheniu prestupnosti i prestupnika. Problemy Prestupnosti 2: 233-47 '27 2715

Stephens, Earl. The scientific laboratory. Int Assn Identif Proc 16: 87-8 '30 2716

Sutherland, Edwin H. The prison as a criminological laboratory. Ann Am Acad 157: 131-6 S '31 2717

Türkel, Siegfried. Criminalistic institutes and laboratories; translated from German. Ann Am Acad 146: 199-204 N '29 2718

United States. Congress. House. Committee on judiciary. To establish laboratory for study of criminal, dependent and defective classes, hearings on H.R. 10655, May 19, 1930. 18p. Washington, 1930 (Serial no10) 2719

Vega, Francisco González de la. Al Consejo supremo de defensa y prevención social. R Mexicana de Der Pen 1 (1): 87- '30 2720

Verhaeghe, D. Organisation générale. Rapport á l'administration municipale. Ann de Méd Lég 7: 124-31 Mr '27 2721
Institute of forensic and social medicine, Lille, Belgium.

Vervaeck, [Louis]. Les avantages des annexes psychiatriques des prisons au point de vue pénal et pénitentiaire. R de Dr Pén et de Crimin 7: 259-69 Mr '27 2722

Vervaeck, L[ouis]. La création de colonies psychiatriques pour buveurs et toxicomanes. R de Dr Pén et de Crimin 7: 1126-30 N '27 2723

Vervaeck, Louis. L'organisation du service anthropologique dans les prisons cubaines. R de Dr Pén et de Crimin 9: 1099-1101 '29 2724

Vervaeck, L[ouis]. Las ventajas de los anexos psiquiátricos de las prisiones desde el punto de vista penal y penitenciario. R de Crim Psiquiat y Med Leg 14: 287-309 My '27 2725

Vozzi, Roberto. Museo criminale. 52p. Roma [Ministry of Justice] 1931 2726
Description of criminological museum in the Carceri Nuove in Rome.

Vseukraïnśkyj Kabinet dlja Rozslidiv zlocynnosty [All-ukrainischen Kabinetts für die Erforschung des Verbrechers und der Kriminalität]. Rostow am Don. Isutschenie prestupnosti i penitenziarnaia praktika [Erforschung der Kriminalität und Strafvollzugspraxis]. 181p. (Abh v2) Odessa, 1928 2727
Chalezky, A. M. Zur Psychologie des Rowdytums (Hooliganerie). Eine psychologisch-psychoanalytische Studie.
Fränkel, Helene. Mörder aus Gewinnsucht.
Nemirowsky, E. J. Gewohnheitsverbrecher, Berufsverbrecher und das neue Strafgesetzbuch.
Kogan, J. M. Über die Tätowierung der Verbrecher.
Woiewoda, M. J. Die Rowdys in den Erziehungstalten und ihre Behandlung.
Krassusky, V. S. and Makarowsky, D. B. Verwahrlosten-Gemeinschaften und einzelgehende Verwahrloste.
Fränkel, Helene and Chalezky, A. M. Zur Technik der Verbrechensforschung.

Waldo, Alice. Technique involved in making a legal-social investigation. Ann Am Acad 145: 105-13 S '29 2728

Warstadt, A. Vergleichende kriminalbiologische Studien an Gefangenen. Zeitsch f d ges Neurol u Psychiat 120: 178-235 '29 2729

Weigel, John C. El instituto de investigacion juvenil, la extension de sus servicеs—a todo el estado. 16p. Reprint. Vida Nueva [Habana] 25: F '30 2730

Weigel, John C. The state-wide service of the Institute. 11p. (Series C no105) Chicago. Institute for juvenile research, May 1927 2731

Whitley, Robert L. Interviewing the problem boy. J Educ Soc 5: 89-100 O '31 2732

Williams, F. E. Delinquency. *In* The Medical department of the U. S. Army in the world war. X: Neuropsychiatry, 131-8. Washington, Govt. Ptg. Off. 1929 2733
Psychological and psychiatric work at U.S. Disciplinary barracks, Fort Leavenworth, Kansas.

Wisconsin. State board of control. Psychiatric field service. Biennial report, 2, 1926/28 *in* Biennial reports of State board of control, 19, 1926/28: 103-19; 20, 1928/30: 10-21 2734
Appendix I: Classification of delinquents.

Young, Pauline V[islick] and Young, Erle F. Getting at the boy himself: through the personal interview. Soc Forces 6: 408-15 Mr '28 2735

Zaki, Mohamed. Relations du Laboratoire de police avec les magistrats et le médecin legiste. R Int de Crimin 2(2): 121-30 '30 2736

Zaki, Mohamed. Le rôle des laboratoires de police technique au point de vue de la police judiciaire et de l'instruction préparatoire. Lyon, J. Desvigne, 1929 2737

Znaniecki, Florian. Criminological research. Sociol & Soc Res 12: 411-13 My '28 2738
Plan for contest to get prisoners to write autobiographies and then study the authors to determine criminal tendencies.

Clinical Methods

Anderson, Harold H. Les cliniques psychologiques pour l'enfance aux États-Unis et l'oeuvre du Dr. Healy. Paris, Delachaux & Niestlé, 1929 2739

Baskett, George T. Some impressions gained by experience in conducting a community mental health clinic. Assn of Dir Poor & Char & Correc Proc 55: 97-103 '30 2740

Bernan, N. A. Anormali minores. Scuola Pos 39: 130-6 '31 2741
Analysis of the work of Wilmanns, director of psychiatric clinic of Heidelberg.

Branham, V. C. Need for additional clinic service. Psychiat Q 3: 470-2 '28 2742
N Y Mental hygiene commission recommended clinic in connection with Magistrates' court.

Branham, V. C. The relation of the clinic to the court. N Y St Conf Prob Offic Proc 20: 98-105 '27 2743

Brinker, Dorothy and Fenton, Norman. The visiting child guidance clinic and the community. 10p. (Bul ns no3) Sacramento, California. Bureau of juvenile research, July 1930 2744

Brinker, Dorothy and Fenton, Norman. The visiting child guidance clinic of the California Bureau of juvenile research. Manual for community workers. 12p. (Bureau of juvenile research, Bul no5 Ag '31) Berkeley, 1931 2745

Brown, Muriel W. The relation of the mental hygiene clinic to children's court work. N Y St Conf Prob Offic Proc 21: 121-9 '28 2746

Brown, Sanger. Child guidance clinics. Hosp Soc Serv 15: 149-52 F '27 2747

Burt, Cyril. The psychological clinic. Howard J 2: 290-4 Je '29 2748

Close, O. H. The child guidance clinic. Commonwealth Club Calif Tr 23: 397-404 D 11 '28 2749

Collins, Cornelius F. New York court requests psychiatric service clinic for criminals; supplemental memorandum. J Crim L & Crimin 19: 337-43 N '28 2750

Commonwealth club of California. Clinics for the pre-delinquent. Tr 25 (2) Ap 8 '30 2751

Coulter, Charles Wellsley. The place of the sociologist in a clinic for delinquents. Nat Conf Juv Agencies Proc 24: 51-61 '27; same title: J Delin 11: 267-76 D '27 2752

Fellows, J. A. Detroit's crime clinic. Nation [N Y] 130: 568-70 My 14 '30 2753

Fenton, Norman. The experience of the travelling child guidance clinic of the California Bureau of juvenile research. Calif Q Sec Educ 401-8 Je '30 2754

Fenton, Norman. The visiting child guidance clinic of the California bureau of juvenile research. 7p. (Bul ns no2) Sacramento, California Bureau of juvenile research, January 1930 2755

del Greco, F. L'indirizzo clinico e psicologico-concreto nello studio dei criminali. Arch Gen di Neurol, Psichiat e Psicoanal 11: 286-95 O 15 '30 2756

Hapke. Zur klinischen Methode im kriminalwissenschaftlichen Unterricht. Monats f Kriminalpsychol u Strafrechtsref 22: 604-28 O '31 2757

Jarrett, Mary C. Mental clinics; an account of their development in the United States. 57p. N. Y. National committee for mental hygiene, 1927 2758

Karpman, Ben. Psychoses in criminals. Clinical studies in the psychopathology of crime. J Nerv & Ment Dis 67: 224-47, 355-74, 478-88, 599-608 '27; 68: 39-54 '28; 70: 622-41 '29 2759

Kendel, Fanny Robson. Child guidance clinic and the family. Am Childh 14: 24-7 N '28 2760

Kirkland, Isabelle M. The Springfield clinic: history and procedure of a visiting clinic from the Institute for juvenile research. Welf Mag 19: 367-72 Mr '28 2761

Lichtenstein, Perry M. Are crime clinics a necessity? Police J [N Y] 17: 4-5, 32 Ja '30 2762

McCord, Elizabeth. Child guidance clinics and the child caring agencies: the value of psychiatric approach for all children's case workers. Nat Conf Soc Wk Proc 55: 110-16 '28 2763

Martin, Walter B. The child guidance clinic. Welf Mag 18: 1192-8 S '27 2764

Orgel, S. Z. The handling of the delinquent and abnormal child in European clinics. Arch Pediat 44: 521-8 Ag '27 2765

Pennsylvania. Department of welfare. Bureau of mental health. Mental health clinics. 8p. (Bul no28, rev March 1929) [Harrisburg, 1929] 2766

Plant, J. S. The psychiatric clinic and the juvenile court. Nat Prob Assn Proc 23: 195-201 '29 2767

Plant, J. S. The relationship of the psychiatric clinic to the juvenile court. Ment Hyg 13: 708-18 O '29 2768

Potts, W. A. A state psychological clinic in Australia. Howard J 2: 295 Je '29 2769

Rademacher, Grace Corwin. Clinic's contribution. Childh Educ 4: 121-7 N '27 2770

Reckless, Walter C. A sociological clinic for the study of juvenile delinquency. Am Sociol Soc Proc 22: 187-94 '27 2771

Sapir, Jean. A morning in the clinic. Observations at the Institute of juvenile research. Welf Mag 18: 319-30 Mr '27; same title: 14p. (Ser C no112) Chicago, Institute for juvenile research, September 1928 2772

Schwartz, Louis Adrian. Aims of a clinic for juvenile research. J Crim L & Crimin 22: 266-72 Jl '31 2773

Stevenson, George S. When is a community ready for a child guidance clinic. Ment Hyg 12: 492-503 Jl '28 2774

Taylor, Graham R. The Commonwealth fund child guidance program. J Juv Res 12: 249-53 S '28 2775

Truitt, Ralph Chess Purnell; Lowrey, Lawson G.; Hoffman, Chas. W.; Connor, William L.; Taylor, Ethel, and Kendel, Fanny Robson. Child guidance clinic and the community; a group of papers written from the viewpoints of the clinic, the juvenile court, the school, the child welfare agency, and the parent. 106p. N.Y. Commonwealth fund, 1928 2776

United States. Children's bureau. List of psychiatric clinics for children in the United States. 28p. (Pub no191) Washington, Govt. Ptg. Off. 1929 2777

TESTING

Asher, E. J. and Haven, S. E. The reactions of state correctional school and public school boys to the questions of an emotional inventory. J Juv Res 14: 96-106 Ap '30 2778

Atkinson, Mary C. A study of infants of feeble-minded delinquent females. Am Assn Stud Feeble-mind Proc 51: 110-28 '27 2779

Kuhlmann-Binet I.Q.'s and Gesell ratings for 25 borderline and feeble-minded delinquent mothers.

Ball, Robert Jaudon. Some psychological aspects of the prisoner with special reference to introversion-extroversion and emotional instability. 52p. Thesis (M.A.) University of California, 1930 2780

Bronner, Augusta Fox; Healy, William; Lowe, Gladys M., and Shimberg, Myra E. Manual of individual mental tests and testing. 287p. (Pub no4) Judge Baker foundation, 1927 2781

Cox, John F. Differences between Negro and native white convicts tested with the Stanford-Binet and retested with reorganized form of this scale. 64p. (typw) Thesis (M.A.) University of Pittsburgh, 1930 2782

32 Negroes and 39 native whites tested on re-grouped scale and results compared with 1000 Negroes and whites previously tested.

Eccles, August K. The performance of delinquent boys on the Healy completion test II. Tr Sch Bul 28: 61-9 Je '31 2783

Erickson, Milton H. and Pescor, M. J. The application of the Pressey X-O tests to delinquents. Med-Leg J 47: 75-87 bibliog (p86-7) My '30 2784

An investigation of emotions.

Ernst, John Lewis. An analysis of the religious and ethical habits of a group of convicts. (typw) Thesis (Ph.D.) University of Pittsburgh, 1930; abstract: Univ Pittsburgh Bul 27: 47-53 N 15 '30 2785

Specialized testing of 100 convicts at Western penitentiary, Pennsylvania.

Grohmann. Versuche über Willensübungen Gefangener. Monats f Kriminalpsychol u Strafrechtsref 19: 604-7 O '28 2786

Grove, William R. An experimental study of the Kent-Shakow industrial farm board series (applied to penitentiary inmates). (typw). Thesis (M.A.) University of Pittsburgh, 1931 2787

Study of Western penitentiary, Pennsylvania.

Hackbusch, Florentine. A study of 258 inmates of the Pennsylvania industrial reformatory whose I.Q.'s on the Terman group test fall below 75. . . . Am Assn Stud Feeblemind Proc 53: 33-51 bibliog (p50-1) '29 2788

Harris, Mary B. I supposed I was stupid. Survey 61: 235-7 '28 2789

Psychological examination, education and vocational training of the Federal industrial institution for women in West Virginia.

Kline, George M. Mental examination of offenders. Ind Bul Char & Correc (180): 107-11 Mr '30 2790

Limburg, Charles C. A preliminary study of personality tests: male criminals. (typw) Thesis (M.A.) University of Pittsburgh, 1930 2791

26 male prisoners tested.

McCullough, Robert S. The use of standardized tests at the Indiana boys' school. Ind Bul Char & Correc (191-2): 252-5 Mr '31 2792

Manifold, Stanley Shaffer. The relationship between brain capacity and the intelligence of 204 native white American male convicts at the Pennsylvania Western penitentiary. 36p. (typw) Thesis (M.A.) University of Pittsburgh, 1930 2793

Nakamura, R. and Shikiba, R. The second report of psychological studies of criminals—a study of intelligence. Hokuyetsu Igakkai Zatshi 44 (1) '29 2794

Mental tests given 163 criminals at psychological laboratory, Tokyo imperial university.

Pescor, M. J. Application of the Woodworth-Cady questionnaire to juvenile delinquents. Med-Leg J 48: 74-8 My '31 2795

Poull, Louise E. and Montgomery, Ruth P. Porteus maze test as a discriminative measure in delinquency. J Ap Psychol 13: 145-51 Ap '29 2796

Richmond, F[rank] C. An exceptional case. Med-Leg J 47: 43-9 Mr '30 2797

Explanation of examination (mental and physical) given to inmates, delinquents, parolees, etc.

Richmond, Frank C. Mental examination of fourteen year old parricide. Med-Leg J 47: 6-12 Ja '30 2798

Richmond, Frank C. Mental testing and measuring. Med-Leg J 44: 65-70 My '27 2799

Schneider, Josef. Intelligenzprüfungen an Strafgefangenen. Monats f Kriminalpsychol u Strafrechtsref 22: 472-81 Ag '31 2800

Investigations at Butzbach and Saarbrücken prisons.

Small, Sidney Herschel and Terman, Lewis M. Testing for the crime germ in the child. Sunset 60: 24-5 My '28 2801

Snyder, Marguerite Atwater. A comparison of mental traits and attitudes of delinquent boys and girls. J Juv Res 15: 181-91 Jl '31 2802

Tests of 100 girls and 100 boys committed to Pennsylvania training school.

Thomas, Coronal. Results of the Sims socio-economic rating scale when given to delinquent and non-delinquent juveniles. Am J Orthopsychiat 1: 527-39 O '31 2803

Study of 205 delinquents and 375 non-delinquents in the region of Detroit, Michigan.

Wiegmann, Otto. Beiträge zur Methodologie der Intelligenzprüfung. Untersuchungen an kriminellen und nichtkriminellen Jugendlichen. Zeitsch f ang Psychol 32: 1-101 Ja '29 2804

Wiegmann, Otto. Vergleichende Test-Untersuchungen an kriminellen und nichtkriminellen Jugendlichen. Zeitsch f pädagog Psychol 30: 246-9 '29 2805

Wolfer, L. Die experimentelle Psychologie im Dienste der Rechtsprechung. München med Wchnschr 78: 1569-70 S 11 '31 2806

ADMINISTRATION OF CRIMINAL JUSTICE

Addams, Jane. Efforts to humanize justice. Survey 63: 275-8 D 1 '29 2807

Administration of justice. Consensus 13: 1-65 Je '28 2808

Alexander, F[ranz] and Staub, H[ugo]. Der Kampf ums Recht. Psychoanal Beweg 1: 117-22 '29 2809

Alger, George W. The irritating efficacy of English criminal justice. Atlan M 142 (2): 218-26 Ag '28; same title: Calif St B J 3 pt1: 45-9 S '28 2810

Alsberg, Max. Zur Lage der Strafrechtspflege. Die Lehren eines Praktischen Falles. Arch f Krim 82: 99-138 Ap '28 2811

Appearance of justice; (editorial). Lawyer & Banker 22: 263-4 S '29 2812

Aumann, Francis R. Municipal administration of justice. *In* State historical society of Iowa, Applied history series v6: Municipal government and administration in Iowa 2: 145-221 '30 2813

Bacq, Jean. Beccaria: "Des délits et des peines." R de Dr Pén et de Crimin 7: 521-34 My '27 2814

Barton, R. F. White man's law among Filipino tribesmen. Asia 30: 410-16 Je '30 2815

Baumbach. Der Bankerott der Strafjustiz. Deut Juristen Zeit 33: 38-43 '28 2816

Bentini, Genuzio. Arringhe penali. 200p. Milano-Sesto S. Giovanni, Madella & C. 1927 2817

Bentwich, Norman. Law and justice in Russia. Howard J 3: 62-4 '31 2818

Bergman, H. A. A brief outline of some of the principal differences between the Canadian and American systems of the administration of justice. Dakota L R 3: 187-206 D '30 2819

Bonner, Robert Johnson and Smith, G. E. Administration of justice from Homer to Aristotle. 399p. Chicago, Univ of Chicago press, 1930 2820

Bradway, John S. ed. Progress in the law: a discussion of some of the tendencies of the law and the administration of justice tending constantly to adapt law to the changing conditions of our modern social and economic life. Ann Am Acad 136 (225) Mr '28 2821

Pt. IV: Progress in criminal courts.

Bringing criminal justice up to date. Pub Affairs 9: 5-6 Ag '27 2822

Bush, Samuel T. Is the bar responsible for the administration of justice? Comm L J 36: 129-33 Mr '31 2823

Butler, Charles C. The administration of criminal justice. Police J [N Y] 16: 26, 32 Ag; 26-9, 31 S '29 2824

Caloyanni, Megalos A. La justice pénale internationale. R de Dr Pén et de Crimin 7: 139-45 F '27; same title: R Pénitent de Pologne Ja-Ap '29; also: 24p. Paris, Sirey, 1929 2825

Car, Stanislaw. Les problèmes de la justice. R Pénitent de Pologne [5]: 17-31 '30 2826

Carr, N. A. Administration of justice. Accountants J 47: 215-23 Jl '29 2827

Conwell, James. Administration of justice in two great nations. Justice 1: 56-8 O '28 2828

Ireland and U.S.

Creyssel, Paul. Propos sur la justice. R Int de Crimin 2(3): 198-200 '30 2829

Criminal justice acts. Being the Criminal justice administration act, 1924, and the Criminal justice acts, 1925 and 1926. With explanatory notes by A. Lieck and A. C. L. Morrison. ed. 2. 344p. London, Stevens, 1927 2830

Davidson, T. Whitfield. A business administration of justice. Am Jud Soc J 11: 40-9 Ag '27 2831

Edwards, J. Glenn. Ministry of justice in France. N C L R 8: 328-34 Ap '30 2832

Enslow, Chas. A. Is justice blind? Lawyer & Banker 20: 90-100 Mr '27; same title: Va L Reg ns13: 81-96 Je '27 2833

Feibelman, Herbert U. More justice, less law, less crime. Fla St B Assn L J 3: 19-21 D '29 2834

Flaws in administration of justice. Va L R ns12: 741-2 Ap '27 2835

France. Ministère de la justice. Compte general de l'administration de la justice criminelle. . . 1924- Paris, Imp. Nat. 1928- 2836

Fritz, R. Some contrasts between American and German administration of justice. Docket 3: 3097-8 N '27 2837

Fritze, Ulrich. Unabhängigkeit der Rechtspflege. Deut Rundsch 58 (3): 169-84 D '31 2838

Fromm, F. Der Staat als Erzieher [zur Psychologie der Strafjustiz]. Zeitsch f Psychoanal Päd 4: 5-9 '30 2839

Fuller, Hugh N. Criminal justice in Virginia. 195p. N.Y. Century, 1931 2840

Glueck, Sheldon. Predictability in the administration of criminal justice. Harv L R 42: 297-329 Ja '29; same title: Ment Hyg 13: 687-707 O '29 2841

Glueck, Sheldon. Significant transformations in the administration of criminal justice. Ment Hyg 14: 280-306 Ap '30 2842

Graves, W. Brooke, ed. Public opinion and the administration of justice. *In his* Readings in public opinion, 1059-1103. N.Y. Appleton, 1928 2843

Hacker, Ervin. Die künftigen Aufgaben und Ziele der Strafrechtswissenschaft, insbesondere der Kriminalätiologie, der Pönologie und der Gefängniskunde. Bl f Gefängniskunde 61: 197-208 '30 2844

Hajje, Antoine. Histoire de la justice seigneuriale en France. 186p. (Thèse, Paris) Paris, Boccard, 1927 2845

Hall, Jerome. Social science as an aid to administration of the criminal law. Dakota L R 3: 285-98 Ap '31 2846

Hardy, Georges. La justice indigène au Maroc. Europe Nouv 14: 1220-1 S 5 '31 2847

Harvey, Cyril Pearce. Solon; or The price of justice. 103p. London, Paul, Trench, Trubner, 1931 2848

Hentig, H[ans] v. Der abgeschaffte Laienrichter. Monats f Kriminalpsychol u Strafrechtsref 18: 643-4 N '27 2849

Howard, Pendleton. Criminal justice in England: a study in law administration. 451p. N.Y. Macmillan, 1931 2850
English executive and management of prosecutions; movement for public prosecution; director of public prosecutions; police and prosecutions; criminal courts; summary jurisdiction and trial on indictment.

Howard, Pendleton. Some characteristics and tendencies of English criminal justice. Minn L R 47: 525-45 Ap '31 2851

Hughes, Charles Evans. Progress in administration of justice. N Y St B Assn Proc 52: 545-53 '29 2852

Johnson, Gerald White. How does the law work? World's Wk 59: 63-5 D '30 2853

Justice in British Columbia. Am Jud Soc J 13: 84-7 O '29 2854

Justice is breaking down. Outl 156: 370-1 N 5 '30 2855

Kelso, Robert Wilson. Science of public welfare. 428p. N.Y. Holt, 1928 2856
Care and treatment of lawbreakers; government and the criminal; jail and the workhouse; evolution of system of correction; delinquent children; juvenile court.

Knight, William D. To facilitate the administration of justice. Ill St B Assn Proc 1929: 269-85 2857

Die Kriminalität in Frankreich nach dem Kriege. Arch f Krim 86: 167-70 Ap '30 2858

Krücke. Die Übertragung der Justizverwaltung auf das Reich. Justiz 3: 482-8 '28 2859

Levie, Wm. Elder. [The administration of justice]. Jurid R 39: 191-208 Je '27 2860

Lucchini, Luigi. L'avvenire del processo penale. Riv Pen 105: 400-3 My '27 2861

Lucht, Friedrich Wilhelm. Strafrechtspflege in Sachsen-Weimar-Eisenbach unter Carl August. Beiträge zur Geschichte der deutschen Strafrechtspflege; herausgegeben von Max Grünhut und Eberhard Schmidt. 112p. (no1) Berlin, Gruyter, 1929 2862

Lucifero, Falcone. La difesa penale avanti le Preture. Scuola Pos ns7: 211-24 My '27 2863

Miltner, Charles C. Legal versus moral justice. Notre Dame Law 6: 451-7 My '31 2864

Moley, Raymond. How criminal justice works. Nat Conf Soc Wk Proc 56: 172-81 '29 2865

Namysłowski, Władysław. Die Teilnahme der Bevölkerung an der Rechtsprechung in den mittelalterlichen kroatischen und serbischen Ländern. Jahrb f Kultur u Gesch d Slaven ns3 (3): 345-64 '27 2866

National economic league. The administration of criminal justice. Vote of a special committee of the National economic league on the most important questions concerning the administration of criminal justice, with comments by members of the special committee. Consensus 13 (1): 1-65 Je '28 2867

Nelson, Frederic. North Carolina justice. New Repub 60: 314-16 N 6 '29 2868

Neymark, Edward. Le développement des sciences pénales en Pologne ressuscitée (1918-1928). R de Dr Pén et de Crimin 9: 162-7 '29 2869

Nowak, J. L'organisation de justice criminelle en Pologne. J Débats 35 pt2: 593-5 O 12 '28 2870

Olson, Floyd B. Efficient criminal justice. Nat Prob Assn Proc 25: 241-8 '31 2871

Outline of a plan for a state Department of criminal justice in California. J Crim L & Crimin 19: 271-2 Ag '28 2872

Overholser, Winfred. Psychiatry as an aid to the administration of criminal justice. Ann Am Acad 145: 23-30 S '29 2873

Overholser, Winfred. The role of psychiatry in the administration of criminal justice. Am M Assn J 93: 830-4 S 14 '29 2874

Palmer, Ben W. May the judge sleep? Am L R 61: 321-35 My '27 2875

Party of the third part; (editorial). Am B Assn J 13: 446-7 Ag '27 2876

LePaulle, Pierre. Administration of justice in the United States. Docket 4: 3192-5 O '28 2877

Péritch, J. Idée d'individualité et idée de collectivité en matière pénale. Etudes Crimin 3 (4-5): 129-31 S '28 2878

Perkins, Rollin M. The great American game: our sporting theory of criminal justice. Harper's 155: 750-8 N '27 2879

Plummer, Clyde. Administration of criminal justice. Int Assn Identif, Calif Div Proc 15: 36-9 '30 2880

Porrero, C. R. Sobre jurisprudencia penal. R Gen de Leg y Juris 76: 257-63 Mr '27 2881

Portland city club. Some suggestions for improving the administration of justice in Oregon. Ore L R 10: 161-7 F '31 2882

Porto Rico. Governor. Annual reports, 27, 1927- Washington 2883
Department of justice: court statistics; penal institutions; reform school; pardons; insular police; attorney general report.

Pound, Roscoe. Criminal justice in America. 226p. N.Y. Holt, 1930 2884

Pound, Roscoe. Le problème de la justice criminelle. R de Dr Pén et de Crimin 7: 715-37 '27 2885
Address before Institute of public affairs, Los Angeles, U.C.L.A., July 6, 1926; translated by Ada Sand and Paul Cornil.

Pound, Roscoe. What can law schools do for criminal justice? Ia L R 12: 105-13 F '27; same title: Am L Sch R 6: 127-32 My '27 2886

Prompt administration of justice; (editorial). Ky L J 17: 371-2 My '29 2887

Radbruch, Gustav. Der Mensch im Recht. 18p. Tübingen, Mohr, 1927 2888

Riddell, William Renwick. By-gone phases of criminal justice in England. J Crim L & Crimin 22: 517-35 N '31 2889

Robinson, James J. Enactments of the 1927 general assembly for the improvement of the administration of criminal justice in Indiana. Ind L J 2: 552-6 Ap '27 2890

Rosenberry, Marvin B. Upholding the law and administering justice. Wis L R 4: 209-16 Jl '27 2891

Rosenfeld. "Der Bankerott der Strafjustiz." Justiz 3: 225-32 '28 2892

Rumpf, [Otto], ed. Strafprozess. 187p. (Danziger Rechtsbibliothek v8) Berlin, Stilke, 1927 2893

Saada, Raoul. Essai sur l'oeuvre de justice française en Tunisie. 300p. Paris, Libr. Gén. de Dr. et de Jurispr. 1928 2894

Saldaña, Quintiliano. La justice pénale internationale. 202p. Paris, Hachette, 1927; same title: Acad Int Law Rec des Cours 1925 V. 10: 223-429 '27 2895

S[asserath], S. La justice répressive en Russie Soviétique. R de Dr Pén et de Crimin 7: 1211-17 D '27 2896

Schiffer, D. Fünfzig Jahre Reichsjustizministerium. Gesetz u Recht 28: 17-20 Ja 15 '27 2897

Schlosky. Der Verbrauch der Strafklage. Arch f Strafr u Strafproz 71: 285-95, 327-36 O, N '27 2898

S[eale], H[arry]. Criminal justice. Ala L J 2: 32-5 Ja '27 2899

Senn, Félix. De la justice et du droit; explication de la définition traditionnelle de la justice, suive d'une étude sur la distinction du Ius naturale et du Ius Gentium. 96p. Paris, Sirey, 1927 2900

Simms, John F. Speed in the administration of justice. Am B Assn J 16: 290-2 My '30 2901

Sims, Henry Upson. The responsibility of the bar for the administration of justice. Am B Assn J 16: 361-2 Je '30 2902

Sloovere, Collard de; Van Parys; Henry, A.; Altavilla; Glaser, Stéphane; Teodoresco, Julien; Vabriesco, Georges, and Moruzi, J. De la poursuite pénale par des associations. R Int de Dr Pén 6: 474-522 '29 2903

Stokvis, Benno J. Ein Justizirrtum in Holland. Monats f Kriminalpsychol u Strafrechtsref 21: 105-10 '30 2904

Stone, Seymour H. Is the administration of criminal law in Great Britain preferable to that practised in the commonwealth of Massachusetts? J Crim L & Crimin 19: 237-43 Ag '28 2905

Sullenger, T. Earl. Popular attitudes toward the administration of criminal justice. J Crim L & Crimin 20: 500-18 F '30 2906

Sweet, Joseph G. First and most essential reform in the administration of justice. Calif St B J 1: 182-5, 194-6 Ap '27 2907

Toller, Ernst. Justiz, erlebnisse. 146p. Berlin, E. Laubsche, 1927 2908

Walsworth, Roscoe. "To establish justice." Comm L League J 35: 204 Ap '30 2909

White man's justice. Nation [N Y] 129: 102 Jl 24 '29 2910

Wickersham, George W. Shortcomings of the administration of justice—causes and remedies. N Y St B Assn Bul 2: 294-9 My '30 2911

Windolph, F. Lyman. Country justice. Atlan M 147: 451-8 Ap '31 2912

Zexiados, Jean B. La justice pénale chez les Soviets. 107p. Salonique, A. Bolone et Ph. Zexopoulos, 1931 2913
In Greek.

SURVEYS OF ADMINISTRATION

Bettman, Alfred. The relationship of crime surveys to the administration of criminal justice. Gov'tal Res Assn Proc 62-9 '29 2914

Bettman, Alfred. What the criminal justice surveys show. Nat Conf Soc Wk Proc 54: 50-60 '27 2915

Bruce, Andrew A. The administration of criminal justice in Illinois: a summary of the crime survey of the Illinois association for criminal justice. J Crim L & Crimin 19 (4) pt2 F '29 2916

Frankfurter, Felix. Surveys of criminal justice. Nat Conf Soc Wk Proc 1930: 63-9 2917

Hanna, Francis D. Putting hands on the clock of justice: one study of a six year survey by the Chicago crime commission as to the administration of criminal justice. Crim Just [Chicago] 1-4 Ap '27 2918

Illinois association for criminal justice completes crime survey. Am B Assn J 15: 426-8 Jl '29 2919

Kuhlman, Augustus Frederick. Survey of research in crime and criminal justice [bibliography]. J Crim L & Crimin 18: 123-5 My '27 2920

Landesco, John. Observations on a survey of organized crime in Chicago. 14p. (mim) Charlottesville, Va. Institute of public affairs, August 6, 1929 2921

Lashly, Arthur V. The Illinois crime survey. J Crim L & Crimin 20: 588-605 F '30 2922

Miller, Justin. Getting away with murder; the Illinois crime survey penetrates the underworld. Survey 62: 399, 418 Jl 1 '29 2923

Moley, Raymond. Problems of a scientific survey of criminal justice. Am Pol Sci R 21: 401-2 My '27 2924

Morse, Wayne L. and Beattie, Ronald H. Survey of the administration of criminal justice in Oregon. Commonwealth R 12: 329-72 Ja '31 2925

Pfiffner, John M. Activities and results of crime surveys. Am Pol Sci R 23: 930-55 N '29 2926

PUBLIC OPINION

Bent, Silas. Death and the newspapers. New Repub 53: 274-5 Ja 25 '28 2927

Carter, J. F. C. The press and the police. Police J [London] 3: 509-18 O '30 2928

Delius, H. Justiz und Presse. Gesetz u Recht 28: 161-6 Je 1 '27 2929

How should a criminal trial be reported in a newspaper? Am B Assn J 15: 196-8 Ap '29 2930

Miller, Justin. Public opinion and crime. S Atlan Q 30: 141-54 Ap '31; same title: R of R 83: 71-2 Je '31 2931

Morbid publicity. Commonweal 14: 482 S 23 '31 2932

New York (state). Crime commission. Sub-commission on causes and effects of crime. A study of the relation of the daily press to crime and the administration of justice. 24p. Albany, 1927 2933

Public opinion of the treatment of crime. Just Peace 93: 813 D 21 '29 2934

Rice, Thomas S. The importance of publishing crime news. Panel 9: 31 My '31 2935

Rowell, Chester H. Changing the public attitude toward crime. Nat Prob Assn Proc 1929: 34-42 2936

Sherriff, Andrew R. Newspapers and the courts. Comm L Leag J 35: 286-91 Je '30 2937

Terrett, Courtenay. Hangman's holiday. Outl 148: 166-7 F 1 '28 2938

Yankwich, Leon R. Sensationalism in crime news. The newspaper and the administration of justice. Los Angeles B Assn Bul 5: 291-5 Je 19 '30 2939

Young, Stark. Nose bleed. New Repub 68: 97-9 S 9 '31 2940
Publicity given to crime.

LEGAL AID

Abuse of legal aid, false declaration. Sol J 73: 4-6 Je 22 '29 2941

Abuse of poor persons rules. L Times 171: 348 Ap 25 '31 2942

Abuse of poor persons' system. Sol J 73: 519 Ag 10 '29 2943

Albertsworth, E. F. A university legal clinic for injured industrial workers. Am B Assn J 16: 26-9 Ja '30 2944

American bar association. Standing committee on legal aid work. Report. Am B Assn Rep 55: 460-4 '30 2945

Association of the bar of the city of New York and Welfare council of New York city. Report of Joint committee for the study of legal aid, with foreword by John W. Davis. 156p. N.Y. 1928 2946

Banton, Joab H. The prisoner at the bar. Leg Aid R 26: 7-9 Ap '28 2947
Work of voluntary defenders committee.

Barth. Gerichtshilfe. Deut Spiegel 7: 22-5 Ja 3 '30 2948

Being the "poor man's lawyer" has its difficulties. Leg Aid R 26: 1-3 Ja '28 2949

Bozi, Alfred. Die soziale Gerichtshilfe als Rechtseinrichtung. Monats f Kriminalpsychol u Strafrechtsref 19: 658-62 N '28 2950

Bradway, John S. Administrative problems of the legal aid clinic. S Calif L R 4: 103-14 D '30 2951

Bradway, John S. Beginning of the legal clinic of the University of Southern California. S Calif L R 2: 252-76 F '29 2952

Bradway, John S. Establishment and extension of state associations of legal aid organizations. Family 10: 24-7 Mr '29 2953

Bradway, John S. ed. Law and social welfare; a preliminary study of the interrelationship between these two fields of human activity. Ann Am Acad 145 ptl S '29 2954

Bradway, John S. Law and social work. Leg Aid R 25: 1-6 Ap '27 2955

Bradway, John S. Law laboratories: how the legal aid clinic trains budding lawyers. Survey 66: 250-2 Je 1 '31 2956

Bradway, John S. The legal aid clinic—a means of coordinating the legal profession. Univ Pa L R 79: 549-70 Mr '31 2957

Bradway, John S. Population and the administration of justice. Ann Am Acad 145: 37-49 S '29 2958

Bradway, John S. Problems in the adjustment between legal aid organizations and social agencies. Leg Aid R 26: 1-6 O '28 2959

Bradway, John S. Public or private legal aid work? Pub Manage 13: 371-2 N '31 2960

Bradway, John S. and Wheaton, Carl. Legal aid organizations and their connections with law schools and students. Am B Assn J 16: 453-4 Jl '30 2961

Campbell, Le Roy. The work of the Voluntary defenders committee of the Legal aid society of New York. Leg Aid R 25: 1-8 O '27 2962

Cobb, W. Bruce. Legal-social field in practice—the field in a large city. Ann Am Acad 145: 130-6 S '29 2963

Cohn, Max. Gerichtshilfe und Verteidigung. Jurist Wchnschr 58 (4): 232-5 Ja 26 '29 2964

Conclusions and recommendations of legal aid committee. M Lab R 27: 73-6 Jl '28 2965

Report of joint committee for the study of legal aid of the Associations of the Bar of the city of New York and Welfare Council of New York city, 1928.

Deschauer, R. Die Bedeutung der Gerichtshilfe für die richterliche Rechtsfindung. Frankf Wohlfahrtsbl ns11 (2): 17-22 My '29 2966

Douglass, Mildred M. Legal aid bureau of Dallas. Tex B Assn Proc 1928: 79-84 2967

Dudley, T. E. The Harvard legal aid bureau. Am B Assn J 17: 692-4 O '31 2968

Edinburgh legal dispensary. Scots L T 63-4 Ap 20 '29 2969

Friedländer, Walter. Strafrechtsreform und soziale Gerichtshilfe. Arbeiterwohlfahrt 6 (8): 233-5 Ap 15 '31 2970

Gentz, Werner. Aufgaben und Aufbau der Gerichtshilfe. Zeitsch f d ges Strafrechtswiss 50 (2): 235-48 '30 2971

Great Britain. Committee on legal aid for the poor. Final report, January 1928. 19p. (Cmd 3016) London, 1928 2972

Haeckel, Heinrich. Die Gerichtshilfe im Entwurf des Einführungsgesetzes zum Allgemeinen Deutschen Strafgesetzbuch und zum Strafvollzugsgesetzes. Deut Zeitsch f Wohlfahrtspfl 7 (4): 201-7 Jl '31 2973

Hartung, Fritz. Soziale Gerichtshilfe. Zeitsch f d ges Strafrechtswiss 50 (2): 208-30 '30 2974

Hertz, Wilhelm. Gerichtshilfe für Erwachsene. Zeitsch f d ges Strafrechtswiss 50 (2): 230-5 '30 2975

Horovitz, Samuel B. Boston plan of legal aid in compensation cases; with discussion. U S Bur Lab Stat Bul (456): 25-49 '28 2976

Horovitz, Samuel B. Need for specialization in legal aid cases. Ann Am Acad 145: 62-7 S '29 2977

Howard league conference: poor prisoners' defence. L Times 167: 182-3 Mr 2 '29; same title: Sol J 73: 175 Mr 16 '29 2978

Howard league for penal reform. Legal aid for poor prisoners. Howard J 2: supl-18 Je '29 2979

Hunter, Joel D. Field occupied jointly by law and social service. Ann Am Acad 145: 7-11 S '29 2980

Jones, James Edmund. Legal aid for the poor. Can B R 9: 271-6 Ap '31 2981

Justice. Boston, 1929- Boston legal aid society 2982

Kobrak. Zum Streit um die Soziale Gerichtshilfe. Deut Zeitsch f Wohlfahrtspfl 5 (4): 221-8 Jl '29 2983

League of Nations. Legal aid for the poor. 472p. Geneva, 1927 (1927. V. 27) 2984

Section on the U.S. contains summary of all state and federal laws on assignment of counsel, waiver of court costs, etc.

Legal aid and the poor. L Times 165: 97 F 4 '28; same title: L J [London] ns65: 125-7 F 11 '28 2985

Legal aid and workmen's compensation. M Lab R 26: 776-7 Ap '28 2986

Legal aid in criminal cases. Am Jud Soc J 11: 29-30 Je '27 2987

Legal aid review. New York, 1, 1903- Legal aid society 2988

Legal aid societies in the United States. Foreign Language 5: 102-7 My 14 '28 2989

Legal aid society of New York. Annual report of the president, treasurer and attorney: 54, 1929- 2990

Legal aid vs. ambulance chasing. Panel 6: 5-6 Mr '28 2991

Legal aid work in the United States. U S Bur Lab Stat Bul (439): 383-8 Je '27 2992

McGee, Leonard. "If you could know what I know-." Leg Aid R 27: 7-12 O '29 2993

Legal aid society of New York.

Maguire, John MacArthur. The lance of justice: a semi-centennial history of the Legal aid society, 1876-1926. 305p. Cambridge, Harvard univ press, 1928 2994

Mailänder. Die Gerichtshilfe für Erwachsene in Württemberg. Bl d Zentralleitung f Wohltätigk in Württ 8: 119-20 Ag '29 2995

Members of National association of legal aid organizations. M Lab R 27: 199-200 Jl '28 2996

Meyer, Charlotte. Entwicklung und Probleme der Berliner sozialen Gerichtshilfe. Berliner Wohlfahrtsbl 5 (24): 201-6 D 8 '29 2997

Meyer, Charlotte. Geschichtliche und Grundsätzliches über soziale Gerichtshilfe. Zeitsch f jüd Wohlfahrtspfl 1 (3): 125-36 My '29 2998

Meyer, Charlotte. Vorschläge zur Eingliederung der Sozialen Gerichtshilfe in die Strafrechtspflege nach einem Entwurf der Vereinigung für Jugendgerichte und Jugendgerichtshilfen. Bl f Wohlfahrtspfl 11: 47-50 F '31 2999

Michel. Fünf Jahre Gerichtshilfe. Arbeiterwohlfahrt 5 (24): 751-4; 6: 7-16 D 15 '30, Ja 1 '31 3000

Michel. Stand der Gerichtshilfe für Erwachsene. Soz Praxis 38 (20): 496-501 My 16 '29 3001

Mittermaier, Wolfgang. Grundgedanken der Gerichtshilfe. Justiz 6 (1): 3-10 O '30 3002

Mollenhauer, Wilhelm. Soziale Gerichtshilfe. Bl d Deut Roten Kruezes 8 (9): 23-9 S '29 3003

Muthesius. Bemerkungen zur den Beratungen der Internationalen kriminalistischen Vereinigung über die soziale Gerichtshilfe. Soz Praxis 38 (26): 625-9 Je 27 '29 **3004**

National association of legal aid organizations. Records of proceedings 6, 1928—9, 1931. Philadelphia, [1928-31] **3005**

National association of legal aid organizations. Reports of committees, 1927/28-1930/31. Philadelphia, 1928-31 **3006**

Nölting, Lilli. Die Gerichtshilfearbeit der A. W. Frankfurt a.M. Arbeiterwohlfahrt 5 (10): 314-16 My 15 '30 **3007**

Noetzel. Die Gerichtshilfe an Erwachsenen vom Standpunkt der Fürsorge. Bl f Wohlfahrtspfl 8 (3): 76-83 '28? **3008**

Norton, William J. Problem of financing legal-social work. Ann Am Acad 145: 143-9 S '29 **3009**

The Pennsylvania association of legal aid organization: a new type of legal aid machinery. Leg Aid R 25: 1-6 Ja '27 **3010**

Pfefferkorn, Hugo. Gerichtshilfe. 136p. Berlin, Heymanns, 1930 **3011**

Pfeiffer, Timothy Newell. Legal aid service in the criminal courts. Ann Am Acad 145: 50-4 S '29 **3012**

Pirsig, Maynard E. Legal clinic of the University of Minnesota law school and the principles underlying its operation. Leg Aid R 25: 9-14 Ja '27 **3013**

Poor man's lawyer. Survey 60: 92-3 Ap 15 '28 **3014**

"Poor persons" in the law courts. Q R [London] 502: 235-46 O '29 **3015**

Report on work of legal aid organizations in 1929. M Lab R 31: 926-8 O '30 **3016**

Raggendorf, Wilhelm. Der Stand der sozialen Gerichtshilfe in Preussen und die Mitarbeit der freien Liebstätigkeit. Caritas ns8: 167-75 My '29 **3017**

Ruben, Ernst. Die soziale Gerichtshilfe, eine Aufgabe der Gemeinde. Gemeinde 6 (14): 639-43 Jl '29 **3018**

Russell Sage foundation, New York. Library. Legal aid. 4p. (Bul no91) N.Y. 1928 **3019**

Schramm, Gustav L. Legal aid. Assn of Dir Poor & Char & Correc Proc 54: 54-9 '29 **3020**

Seuffert, S. Help the poor litigants; Society of Our Lady of Good Counsel, London. Cath World 129: 351-2 Je '29 **3021**

Sickel. Vorbeugende Wohlfahrtspflege durch Rechtshilfe. Rundsch f Kommunalbeamte 35 (5): 71-3 F 2 '29 **3022**

Silverman, George H. Legal aid society of Cincinnati. Univ Cin L R 3: 165-9 Mr '29 **3023**

Smith, Reginald H. "Before the law all men are equal." Am Fed 36: 537-42 My '29 **3024**

Smith, Reginald Heber. Justice for every man. Leg Aid R 27 (2) Ap '29 **3025**

Smith, Reginald H[eber] and Bradway, John S. Legal aid and the bar. Tenn L R 5: 223-6 Je '27 **3026**

Starke. Welche Bedeutung korm die soziale Gerichtshilfe für die Feststellung der psychischen Grenzzustande haben? Monats f Kriminalpsychol u Strafrechtsref 21: 178-82 Mr '30 **3027**

Starke and Neumann. Soziale Gerichtshilfe und Tatsachenfestellung. Jurist Wchnschr 58 (20): 1438-45 My 18 '29 **3028**

Thormann, Ph. Die Rechtshülfe der Kantone auf dem Gebiet des Strafrechts. Zeitsch f Schweiz Recht ns47: 1a-60a '28 **3029**

Ulrich, Friedrich. Die Soziale Gerichtshilfe und ihre Einordnung in das neue Strafrecht. Innere Mission im evang Deut 26: 328-36 N '31 **3030**

Ulrich, Friedrich, ed. Soziale Gerichtshilfe. 43p. (D. evang. Wohlfahrtsdienst 20). Berlin, Wichern-Verl. 1929 **3031**

Van Schaick, George S. Handicap of poverty in litigation. Cornell L Q 12: 460-6 Je '27 **3032**

Wardwell, Allen. The legal aid worker looks at the "field". Ann Am Acad 145: 12-16 S '29 **3033**

Wardwell, Allen. Work of the Legal aid society of the city of New York and its relation to the New York state bar association; with discussion. N Y St B Assn Proc 1927: 134-43 **3034**

Welfare council of New York city. Legal aid guide for social workers. 19p. N.Y. 1929 **3035**

Wismer, Otto G. Legal aid organization: "Lobbyists for the poor." Ann Am Acad 136: 172-6 Mr '28 **3036**

Wright, E. Blackwood. Law and the poor man. 19th Cent 110: 75-81 Jl '31 **3037**

Wüllner. Die soziale Gerichtshilfe als Aufgabe der freien Wohlfahrtspflege. Freie Wohlfahrtspfl 4 (3): 102-9; (4): 175-86 Je, Jl '29 **3038**

POLICE

BIBLIOGRAPHY

Bibliography on police and penology. Munic Index 1929: 648, 636, 656 3039

Bibliography on police departments and on penal and correctional institutions. Munic Index 1927: 598 3040

Bibliography on police departments and penal and correctional institutions. Munic Index 1928: 600-1 3041

Books and periodicals on police science and allied subjects. Am J Police Sci 1: 525-7 S '30 3042

Books on police science. Am J Police Sci 1: 108-11, 229-30 Ja, Mr '30 3043

California. University. Bureau of public administration. Police administration: bibliography. 4p. (typw) Berkeley, November 21, 1928 3044

Cumming, John. A select book list for students of police administration. Police J [London] 4: 386-97 Jl '31 3045

Louwage, F. E. Bibliographie [police and crime]. R Belge de Police Adm & Jud livraison 124 D '29 3046

McGoldrick, Joseph. A brief booklist for police departments. Munic Index 1930: 681 3047

Vollmer, August. Bibliography on police organization and administration, criminal identification and investigation. Am J Police Sci 2: 76-9 Ja '31 3048

GENERAL

Abegg, Wilhelm. Verwaltungsreform und Polizei. Polizei 25: 186-90 Ap 10 '28 3049

D'Almeras, Henri. Un policier sous le Consulat. R Mondiale 178: 122-30 Jl 15 '27
Mehée de Latouche. 3050

Anderson, John. The police. Pub Adm 7: 192-202 Ap '29 3051

Barry, A. G. Police problems in the light of modern science. Am Sociol Soc Proc 24: 159-60 '29 3052

Bedford, Scott E. W. ed. Police protection. *In his* Readings in urban sociology, 323-36. N.Y. Appleton, 1927 3053
Woods, Arthur. Graft in the police department; Woods, Arthur. Political influence and the police; Cleveland Foundation. Police training school; Koester, Frank. Signaling system in German cities; O'Brien, Martin. A model police record department; Police dogs; Smith, Bruce. The police and citizens should get together; Peto, D. O. G. Qualifications of a policewoman; Van Winkle, Mina C. Need, handicaps and duties of policewomen; Wells, Alice Stebbins. Training of policewomen.

Bell, J. R. Organization and operation of a police department. Va Munic R 4: 247-50 Ag '27 3054

Bernauer, [Willi]. Polizei unter besonderer Berücksichtigung der Wahlzeit. 37p. Darmstadt, Hessisches Polizeiamt, 1928 3055

Blok, P. R. Reorganisatie der politie. Tijdschr v d politie 1 (11): 177-85 Je 13 '28 3056

Böhme, [Albrecht]. Kriminalpolizei und Landjägerei. Grossstadtische Kriminalpolizei und Landgendarmerie von Böhme; Landgendarmerie der Gegenwart von Joachim. Krimin Monatsh 5 (9): 201-5 S '31 3057

Böhme, A[lbrecht]. Sittenpolizeiliche Rechtsfragen der Gegenwart. Polizei 25: 503-6, 537-40 Ag 20, S 5 '28 3058

Böhme, Albrecht. Grossstädtische Kriminalpolizei und Landgendarmerie. Krimin Monatsh 5 (2): 26-30 F '31 3059

Boxler, Eugen. Wirtschaftspolizei. 455p. Lübeck, Polizei-Verl. 1928 3060

Brownlow, Louis. Police and the causes of crime. Am City 36: 797-8 Je '27 3061

Cahalane, Cornelius F. American and European police problems. Police J [N Y] 16: 13, 29 D '28 3062

Conrady. Einheit der polizei. Polizei 25: 201-21 Ap 10 '28 3063

Cooper, E. F. Policing border counties. Peace Offic Assn Calif Proc 9: 56-9 '29 3064

Davis, M. N. Let the police have the breaks rather than the criminals. Am City 44: 102 Mr '31 3065

Davison, A. E. Patrolling cities from the air: a forecast. Am City 45: 95-6 Jl '31 3066

Delius. Die Polizei als Strafgesetzgeber und Strafrichter. Gegenwart 57: 222-5 O '28 3067

Deville, Sainte-Claire. L'enquête historique et la recherche policière. R Int de Crimin 2 (3): 164-97 '30 3068

Dosi, Giuseppe. The international value of the police. Police J [N Y] 17: 3-4, 22 My '30 3069

Dunsany. Policeman's prophecy. Fortn R 133: 14-18 Ja '30 3070

Edy, John N. Police administration. Pub Manage 9: 166-7 Mr '27 3071

Estey, J. W. Police and their work. Chief Constables Assn Can Proc 24: 59-63 '28 3072

Eustatziu, Sebastien S. La grande lutte du siècle. 111p. Lyon, Société anonyme de l'Imp. A. Rey, 1929 3073

The feasibility of state control as a test of the scope of the federal "police power." Colum L R 29: 321-8 Mr '29 3074

Friedensburg. Wirtschaft und Polizei. Leipzig, Glöckner, 1927 (Heft 4 von Ernest Schulze herausgegeben Sammlung "Wirtschaftspolitische Zeitfragen") 3075

Friedrichs, K. Polizeiliche Strafverfügungen im Lichte des Allgemeinen Rechtes. Arch f Strafr u Strafproz 71: 281-5, 321-7 O, N '27 3076

Gay, W[illy]. Eisenbahnverwaltung oder Kriminalpolizei. Polizei 25: 335-7 My 20 '29 3077

Gay, Willy. Die Neuordnung des Fahndungswesens. Krimin Monatsh 2: 79-82 Ap '28 3078

Gleason, Joseph M. Evolution of the police system. Peace Offic Assn Calif Proc 9: 28-36 '29; same title: Police & Peace Offic 1: 12-13 My '30 3079

Goines, L. A. The small town police department. Municipality 25: 7- Ja '30 3080

Grzesinski, A[lbert]. Die Bedeutung der Polizei für den Staatsgedanken. Polizei 25 (7): 185-6 Ap 10 '28 3081

Grzesinski, A[lbert]. Das Neue Polizeibeamten-Gesetz. Polizei 24: 97-9 Mr 5 '27 3082

Hensen. Die Modernisierung der Gemeindepolizei. Polizei 28 (14): 321-8 Jl 20 '31 3083

Higgins, James W. The theft of automobiles as it relates to the police. Int Assn Chiefs Police Proc 35: 38-43 '28 3084

Hirschfeld, H[ans Emil] and Vetter, Karl, eds. Tausend Bilder. Grosse Polizei-Ausstellung. 257p. Berlin, Gersbach, 1927 3085

Holtby, Winifred. Sex and the policeman. Nation & Athen 43: 391-2 Je 23 '28 3086

Ignatius, Gustav. Till frågen om Kriminalpolisens organisation. Nord Kriminalteknisk Tidsk 1 (3) '31 3087

Instael, C. Politiebewaakten. Ecrou 8: 47-50 Ja '27 3088

International police and detective directory, 1928; compiled by General efficiency co. 267p. San Francisco, 136 McAllister st. 1928 3089

International world police. Am City 45: 94 D '31 3099

Kelley, C. H. The Wickersham report. Peace Offic Assn Calif Proc 11: 86-9 '31 3100

Kennedy, Raymond E. Practical and scientific policing. 180p. Baltimore, 1013 Munsey bldg. 1930 3101

Klausener, [Erich]. Der Fall Hussmann und die Kriminalpolizei. Polizei 25: 701-3 N 20 '28 3102

Klausener, [Erich]. Tagesfragen der Polizei. Polizei 25: 375-9, 403-6 Je 20, Jl 5 '28 3103

Klausener, [Erich]; Kerstiens, Christian, and Kempner, Rob. Das Polizeiverwaltungsgesetz vom 1.6.1931 nebst Quellenmaterial und kurzen Erläuterungen. ed. 3. 311p. Berlin, C. A. Weller, 1931 3104

Kleinow. Die kommunale Polizei. Polizei 25: 218-20 Ap 10 '28 3105

Kleinschmidt. Modernisierung des kriminalpolizeilichen Bürobetriebes. Krimin Monatsh 2: 89-90 Ap '28 3106

Koch, D. "Die Polizei." 25 Jahre im Dienste der Polizei. Polizei 25: 171-8 Ap 10 '28 3107

Landeskriminalpolizei. (Vorschriften f d staatl Polizei Preussens no32). 96p. Berlin, Kameradschaft, 1928 3108

Leonard, Donald S. The police problem. Mich Assn Chiefs Police Proc 6: 81-5 '29 3109

Los Angeles. Bureau of budget and efficiency. Comparison of police and fire departments: Chicago, Boston, San Francisco, Los Angeles, Milwaukee, Detroit, and Philadelphia, January 1929. 25p. (mim) [Los Angeles, 1929] 3110

McGoldrick, Joseph. Important problems of police department organization and administration. Munic Index 1930: 672-80 3111

Mead, Lucia Ames. Armies and police. Educ 51: 176-9 N '30 3112

Menna, Eugenio. Polizia urbana e rurale. Toscana, Sancasciano Val di Pesa, 1929 3113

Muhr. Der polizeiliche Notstand. Polizei 25: 476-80 Ag 5 '28 3114

Mulert. Wandlung der Polizeibegriffe im modernen Staat. Polizei 25: 444-6 Jl 20 '28 3115

National commission on law observance and enforcement. Report on police: police conditions in the United States; a report . . . by David G. Monroe and Earle W. Garrett under the direction of August Vollmer. 140p. (No14) Washington, June 26, 1931 3116
The police executive; personnel: selection, training; communication and equipment; records; crime prevention; police service and the state.

One police force for whole country. Just Peace 91: 103-4 F 12 '27 3117

Our police failure. Nation [N Y] 133: 173-4 Ag 19 '31 3118

Paetsch, [H]. Verkehn und Technik bei der Polizei in 25 Jahren. Polizei 25: 247-50 Ap 10 '28 3119

Police advocacy. Sol J 73: 699 O 19 '29 3120

Police and witnesses. Sol J 74: 681 O 18 '30 3121

Policing in the 90's and now. Am City 44: 140 Ja '31 3122

A question of police methods. L Notes 34: 144-5 N '30 3123

Ridley, Clarence E. Measuring municipal government: suggested standards for measuring the results of fire, health, police and public works departments. 88p. (Pub no4) N.Y. Municipal administration service, 1927 3124

Riege. Einiges über den Zweck des Studiums fremder Polizeien. Polizei 25: 631-3 O 5 '28 3125

Riege. Die Polizei aller Länder in Wort und Bild. 415p. Dresden, Metro-Verl. 1928 3126

Rioux, Geo. H. Police problems of today. Int Assn Chiefs Police Proc 1927: 115-19 3127

Rittau, Martin. Justizbeamte bei der Kriminalpolizei. Krimin Monatsh 2: 151-3 Jl '28 3128

Le rôle de la police dans la société moderne. Adm Locale (55): 1101-4 Jl '30 3129

Rosanoff, Aaron J. Mental hygiene, the police and crime. Inst Police Adm Proc 1929: 103-7 3130

Ruocco, F. Il nuovo diritto di polizia. Manuale teorico pratico. ed. 2. 156p. Roma, Mantellate, 1927 3131

Saracini, Emilio. Nuova pratica di polizia amministrativa. ed. 5 enl. by G. Caruso and G. Candia. 506p. Napoli, Elpis, 1929 3132

Scavarada, C. J. Economy in police administration. Mich Assn Chiefs Police Proc 6: 57-62 '29 3133

Schmitz, Hans. Das internationale Verbrechertum und seine Bekämpfung. 116p. Diss.-Univ. Köln. Köln, Scharmitzel, 1927 3134

Sellin, Thorsten, ed. Police and the crime problem. Ann Am Acad 146 (235) N '29 3135

Smith, Bruce. Municipal police administration. Ann Am Acad 146: 1-27 N '29; same title: Police J [N Y] 17: 11-14, 24 F; 15-18, 24 Mr; 14-15, 22-3 Ap '30 3136

Smith, George. Keep the criminal out. Chief Constables Assn Can Proc 24: 74-83 '28 3137

Smith, R. A. Police control. Can B R 6: 521-4 S '28 3138

Sound moral support the first essential of efficient police work. Am City 39: 100 Jl '28; same title: Police J [N Y] 16: 25, 36 Ap '29 3139

Stobbe. Woher kommt die Bezeichnung "Polizei"? Polizei 24: 405 Ag 20 '27 3140

Stone, Donald C. Can police effectiveness be measured? Pub Manage 12: 465-71 S '30 3141

A study of police departments. Toledo City J 14 (30) Jl 27 '29 3142

Sullivan, John L. The question of police publicity. Police J [N Y] 16: 3, 32 D '28 3143

Troup, Edward. Police administration, local and national. Police J [London] 1: 5-18 Ja '28 3144

Van den Bergh, E. Das Polizeibeamtengesetz. Polizei 24: 356-8 Jl 20 '27 3145

Van den Bergh, E. 25 Jahre Polizeibeamtenrecht. Polizei 25: 197-8 Ap 10 '28 3146

Vohl. Police des étrangers. 92p. Paris, Charles-Lavauzelle, 1930 3147

Vollmer, August. Outline of a course in police organization and administration. Am J Police Sci 2: 70-5 Ja '31 3148

Vollmer, August. Police organization and administration; with discussion. Pub Manage 10: 140-52 Mr '28 3149

Vollmer, August. Police progress in practice and principles. Int Assn Identif Proc 16: 54-6 '30 3150

Vollmer, August. Police progress in practice and theory. Am City 43: 111-12 S '30 3151

Wagner, Hans. Kriminalpolizei und Buchführung. Krimin Monatsh 5 (6): 125-7 Je '31 3152

Walker, John Otey. Fiction is a police curse—what are the facts? Am City 41: 85-8 Ag '29 3153

Weiss, [B.]. 25 Jahre Kriminalpolizei. Polizei 25: 209-14 Ap 10 '28 3154

Wickersham report on police. Am J Police Sci 2: 337-48 Jl '31 3155

Withdrawing police charges. Sol J 74:649 O 4 '30 3156

Zaaijer, H. R. de. Reorganisatie der politie. Tijdschr v d politie 1 (15): 261-7 Ag 17 '28 3157

ALGERIA

Baulard. La gendarmerie de l'Algérie. R de Gendarm 2 (11-14) S 15 '29-Mr 15 '30 3158

ARGENTINA

Rouquette de Fonvielle, A. La meilleure police du monde. Ann Pol & Litt 93: 242 S 1 '29 3159

AUSTRALIA

MacKenzie, A. H. A review of police system and methods in Victoria, Australia. Northwest Police J 6: 14-15, 56-61 My '29 3160

Manton, Philip. Police of Australia. Police & Peace Offic 8: 38 My '30 3161

Mitchell, James. The New South Wales police: a retrospect. Police J [London] 2: 477-84 Jl '29 3162

New South Wales. Police department. Annual report, 1927-30. Sydney, Govt. Ptr. 1928-31 3163
Criminal statistics: arrests.

South Australia. Police department. Report of the Commissioner, 1921- 3164

Tasmania. Police department. Report, 1924/25- 3165

Western Australia. Police department. Report of the Commissioner, 1896/97- 3166

AUSTRIA

Bibl, Viktor. Die Wiener Polizei. Eine Kulturhistorische Studie. 387p. Leipzig, Stein-Verl. 1927 3167

Dressler, Oscar. The Austrian police; translation. Police J [London] 2 (3): 437-52 Jl '29 3168

Schober, H. Polizei und öffentliche Sicherheit in Österreich. Arch f Krim 83: 89-93 S '28 3169

Tätigkeit der Wiener Kriminalpolizei 1927. Arch f Krim 85: 172-81 O '29 3170

Vienna. Polizeidirektion. Jahrbuch der Polizeidirektion in Wien, mit statistischen Daten aus dem Jahre 1927-1931. Wien, 1929-32 3171

BELGIUM

[Anglo-Belgian]. The Belgian police. Police J [London] 1: 443-57 '28 **3172**

BORNEO

Adams, W. C. The constabulary of North Borneo. Police J [London] 2: 310-15 Ap '29 **3173**

BRAZIL

[Cruz, Mario Bastos and Alvarenga, Octavio E. de]. Policia do estado de São Paulo. Laboratorio de policia technica. Album illustré. São Paulo, 1929 **3174**

Pinho, Madureira de. Orientacâo e pratica da policia na Bahia. 322p. Bahia, 1930 **3175**

Silva, Rodolfo Xavier da. A polícia técnica e a organisação policial no estado de São Paulo. Bol do Inst de Crimin s7 12 (1): 257-308 '30 **3176**

CANADA

British Columbia. Department of attorney-general. Report of the Superintendent of provincial police for the years 1927-1930. Victoria, 1928-31 **3177**
Criminal statistics, Finger print bureau, Conduct and discipline.

Canada. Royal Canadian mounted police. Annual report, 1927-31. Ottawa, Kings Ptr. 1928-32 **3178**

Edmonton. Police department. Annual reports, 1928/29—1929/30. [Edmonton, 1929-30] **3179**
Personnel: health, discipline, pension, salaries; Detective department; Offenses committed; Coroners report; Bureau of identification.

Forbin, Victor. La gendarmerie du pôle nord. R Deux Mondes 59: 402-30 S 15 '30; same title: R de Gendarm 4 (20) Mr 15 '31 **3180**
Royal Canadian mounted police.

Hamilton, C. F. The Royal Canadian mounted police. Police J [London] 1: 641-56 '28 **3181**

Lee, Herbert Patrick. Policing the top of the world. London, Lane, 1928 **3182**
Royal Canadian mounted police.

Liggett, Walter W. Pioneers of justice: the story of the Royal Canadian mounted police. 249p. N.Y. Macaulay, 1930 **3183**

Longstreth, T. Morris. The silent forces: scenes from the life of the Mounted police of Canada. London, Allan, 1928 **3184**

Longstreth, T. Morris. Some geographical difficulties of the R.C.M.P. Police J [London] 2: 37-50 Ja '29 **3185**

MacBeth, R. G. Canada's famous mounted police. Policeman 1: 11-13 N '29 **3186**

Ottawa. Police department. Annual reports, 1927-30. Ottawa, 1928-30 **3187**
Arrests, cases in police court, occupations of prisoners arrested, statistical statement.

Panet, E. de B. The investigation department of the Canadian Pacific railway. Police J [London] 4: 33-43 Ja '31 **3188**

Rules and regulations for the government and guidance of the Royal Canadian mounted police force of Canada. 152p. Can Gaz sup Ag 11 '28 **3189**

Starnes, Cortlandt. A federal police force. Am Pris Assn Proc 59: 309-17 '29 **3190**
Royal Canadian mounted police.

Starnes, Cortlandt. [Police in Canada]. Chief Constables' Assn Can Proc 24: 130-9 '28 **3191**

Windsor, Ont. Chief constable. Annual report, 1930. [Windsor, 1931] **3192**

CHILE

Rodríguez, Alejandro Peralta and Sánchez, Arturo Venegas. Album histórico de la policía de Chile. Santiago de Chile, 1927 **3193**

CHINA

Bourne, K. M. The Shanghai municipal police: Chinese uniform branch. Police J [London] 2: 26-36 Ja '29 **3194**

Bruce, C. D. Shanghai. The international settlement and its municipal police force. Police J [London] 1: 128-38 Ja '28 **3195**

Buchler, Walter. The police in China. Just Peace 92: 254-5 Ap 14 '28 **3196**

Parsons. A Pacific police pilgrimage. Chief Constables' Assn Can Proc 24: 93-100 '28 **3197**
Shanghai and Hong Kong, Philippine Islands, Australia and New Zealand, Fiji and Hawaii.

CUBA

Quintana, Eduardo L. Moreno. Policia y delincuentes. 246p. Habana, 1927 **3198**

CYPRUS

Gallagher, A. E. The development of the police in Cyprus. Police J [London] 1: 470-4 '28 **3199**

DENMARK

A "close-up" of Denmark; a travelogue in Copenhagen. Northwest Police J 5: 8-9 Ap '28 **3200**

Hansen, Andreas. The police of Denmark. Police J [N Y] 14: 1-10 F '27 **3201**

Mensen, Valdemar H. The Danish police forces. Police J [London] 1: 240-55 '28 **3202**

DUTCH EAST INDIA

Hoorweg, A. The Dutch East Indian police. Police J [London] 2: 579-95 O '29 **3203**

ECUADOR

Ecuador. Ministerio de lo interior. Informe del Ministerio . . . a la nacion, 1926-28, 1930-31. Quito, 1928-31 3204
Police, courts, jails.

EGYPT

La police en Egypte, en Australie, aux Indes anglaises, à Porto-Rico, en Californie à Madagascar, en Pologne, à Saint Louis (U.S.A.). Polizei im Bild (7) Ag '29 3205

Policing Cairo, Egypt. Northwest Police J 5: 9-10 F '28 3206

White, Ibrahim. La police judiciare en Égypte; étude de droit criminel comparé. 136p. Paris, Chauny & Quinsac, 1927 3207

FEDERATED MALAY STATES

Pennefather-Evans, J. P. Policing the Federated Malay states. Police J [London] 2: 406-15 Jl '29 3208

FIJI ISLANDS

Police indigène des îles Fidji. Polizei im Bild 3 (11) D '29 3209

FRANCE

Arnaud, Emile. La police municipale et rurale et les gardes champêtres. 621p. Paris, Jouve, 1928 3210

Ashton-Wolfe, Harry. The invisible web; strange tales of the French sûreté. 289p. N.Y. Stokes, 1929 3211

France. Ministère de l'intérieur. Direction de la Sûreté générale. Liste alphabetique des individus qui ont été l'objet de mandats de justice, insérée au Bulletin hebdomadaire de police criminelle, du no1 au no1105 inclus, et qui n'ont pas été signalés comme ayant cessé d'être recherchés au 31 décembre 1928. 479p. Melun, Imp. Adm. 1929 3212

Garcia Mercadal, J. La policía de París (Desde Luis XIII a la revolutión). 370p. Madrid, G. Hernández y Galo Sáez, 1928 3213

Groen, H. A. The French police organization: the varied and heavy functions of the prefecture de police. Police J [N Y] 16: 4-5 Je '29 3214

Guitet, Vanquelin Pierre. French police: its evolution from its source to the present day. Police J [London] 1: 605-20 O '28 3215

Kiehl. Faut-il donner la qualité d'officier de police judiciaire auxiliaire du Procureur de la République aux commandmants des Brigades départmentales de la gendarmerie. Etudes Crimin 5: 185-7 Je '30 3216

Lauwick, H. La nouvelle police des routes par la gendarmerie en automobile. Illustration 86 pt2: 70-1 Jl 21 '28 3217

Monsarrat, G. Police municipale et rurale traité formulaire théorique et pratique. 540p. Paris, Pub Adm. 1929 3218

Sanford, Thomas. Reforming Paris police system. Police J [N Y] 16: 3 N '28 3219

Service sanitaire de la police coloniale française à Madagascar. Polizei im Bild (10) N '29 3220

GERMANY

Barck, [Lothar]. Die Bilanz der Berliner Grossen Polizeiausstellung für Baden. Polizei 24: 401-2 Ag 20 '27 3221

Barck, [Lothar]. Das Neue Polizeibeamtenrecht in Baden. Polizei 25: 353-5 Je 5 '28 3222

Bartels, L. Die "7. Preussische Polizeiwoche" zu Köln a Rhein. Polizei 25: 406-8, 446-51 Jl 5, 20 '28 3223

Bavaria. Polizeidirektion. Bayerisches polizeiblatt, 1, 1866- 3224

Blankenstein, Werner. Die Preussische Landjägerei im Wandel der Zeiten. Mit zahlreichen Abbildungen und 2 bunten Tafeln von Herbert Knötegl. 275p. Im Selbstverl. des Verfassers, 1931 3225

Böhme. Zur reichseinheitlichen Reform des Polizeirechts. Deut Juristen-Zeit 32 (22): 1528-31 '27 3226

Finke. Neuordnung des Polizeiverordnungsrechtes in Thüringen. Polizei 25: 42-3 Ja 20 '28 3227

Friedensburg, F. Die Polizeidirektion in Niedermöllrich Bezirk Kassel. Polizei 24: 472-5 O 5 '27 3228

Gay, Willy. Die Preussische Landeskriminalpolizei. 87p. Berlin, Kameradschaft, 1928 3229

Geissel. Die Berliner Kriminalberatungsstelle. Krimin Monatsh 4: 86-8 Ap '30 3230

Graeser. Fünf Jahre Landeskriminalpolizei in Preussen. Krimin Monatsh 4: 122-5 Je '30 3231

Grüttner, Edwin Bruno. Preussisches Polizeirecht im Rahmen des neuen Polizeiverwaltungsgesetzes vom 1. Juni 1931. 94p. [Leipzig, G. Brauns] 1931 3232

Grzesinski. Das Polizeivordnungswesen in Preussen. Polizei 25: 1-5 Ja 5 '28 3233

Kerstiens. Die Reform des Polizeirechts in Preussen. Verwaltungsarchiv 36 (2): 206-23 Ap '31 3234

Klausener. Die Organisation der preussischen Polizei. Ein Rückblick. Polizei 25: 190-7 Ap 10 '28 3235

Kötzschke, Richard and Thiele, Walter. Die Geschichte der Dresdner staats polizei zu ihrem 75 jahrigen Bestehen. 54p. Dresden, H. Hackarath, 1928 3236

Die Kriminalpolizeiliche Nachrichtenzentrale in Preussen. Krimin Monatsh 2: 162-3 Jl '28 3237

Kuphal, E. Das Polizeiwesen der Reichsstadt Köln im Spiegel der Grossen Morgensprache. Jahrb d Köln Geschichtsver 1928: 81-100 3238

Latuske. The organization of the police of Prussia. Northwest Police J 6-7, 40, 53-4 D '31 3239

Mayer, Hans. Die Polizeigewalt in Hessen. 86p. Mainz, Diemer, 1931 3240

Melcher. Die Organisation der staatlichen Polizei an der Ruhr. Polizei 24: 375-82 Ag 5 '27 3241

Menzel. Reformmöglichkeiten bei der Preussischen Polizei. Polizei 25: 31-3 Ja 20 '28 3242

Meyer, Otto. Die kriminalpolizeiliche Tätigkeit von Reichsbahnbehörden. Monats f Kriminalpsychol u Strafrechtsref 21: 669-76 '30 3243

Öhler, H[elmuth] and Albrecht, Wilh[elm]. Preussisches allgemeines Polizeirecht. ed.6. 173p. (Handbuch d Polizei v1) Berlin, Hirschfeld, 1930 3244

Palitzsch. Die Organisation des kriminalistischen Nachrichtendienstes in Sachsen. Krimin Monatsh 2: 27-30 F '28 3245

Philipp, L. Die modernste polizei. Westerm Monatsh 142: 667-72 Ag '27 3246

Preussische Polizeiwoche zu Magdeburg vom 15. bis 20. Oktober 1928. Polizei 25: 706 N 20 '28 3247

Reuss. Das Polizeirecht Thüringens. Polizei 25: 96-9 F 20 '28 3248

Riege, Paul. The German police. Police J [N Y] 17: 5-7, 22 Ag '30 3249

Riege, Paul. The Prussian police. Police J [London] 2: 225-46 Ap '29 3250

Schmitt, [Hermann]. Polizeistrafgesetzbuch für Bayern. Mit Erläuterungen und Nebengesetzen. ed. 8 261p. 1927; ed. 9 277p. München, C. K. Beck, 1930 3251

Verwaltungsbericht das Polizeipräsidiums Leipzig vom 1 Oktober 1922—31. Dezember 1927. 74p. Leipzig, 1928 3252

Wiegand. Die Preussische Landjägerei in den letzten 25 Jahren. Polizei 25: 203-9 Ap 10 '28 3253

Württemburg. Polizeipräsidium. Tagesbericht 1, 1917- 3254

Zschockelt. Organisationsänderung der Kriminalpolizei in Sachsen. Krimin Monatsh 5: 217-18 O '31 3255

GOLD COAST

Gold Coast. Police department. Reports, 1929/30- 3256

GREAT BRITAIN

Adam, Hargrave L. C.I.D., behind the scenes at Scotland Yard. 248p. London, Sampson Low [1931] 3257

Baggallay, E. P. Burrell. The Metropolitan mounted police. Police J [London] 3: 185-200 Ap '30 3258

Benjamin, Harold. The internal police administration of England. Police J [London] 4:438-60, 598-622 Jl, O '31 3259

Birmingham. Official handbook, 1929/30, 1930/31. Birmingham, 1930-31 3260
Police and fire, 1929/30: 152-6; 1930/31: 168-72.

Biron, Chartres. Public and police: a magistrate's view. Police J [London] 3: 164-75 Ap '30 3261

Blumenfeld, David L. Scotland Yard; fashions in fighting crime. Frat Order Police J 12: 12, 27, 31 My '29 3262

Cumming, John. The police services of the empire: unity amid diversity. United Empire 21: 538-45 O '30 3263

Dilnot, George. The story of Scotland Yard. 340p. London, Bles, 1927 3264

Dixon, A. L. The English police system. Ann Am Acad 146: 177-92 N '29 3265

Faralicq, G. Scotland Yard. R de Gendarm 2 (11) S 15 '29 3266

Great Britain. Commissioner of police of the metropolis. Report for the year 1926- London, H.M. Stationery Off. 1927- 3267

Great Britain. Inspectors of constabulary. Police (counties and boroughs, England and Wales) reports for the year ended September 29, 1926- London, H.M. Stationery Off. 1927- 3268

Great Britain. Metropolitan police fund. Accounts of . . . fund showing the sums received and expended for the purposes of metropolitan police and police courts, April 1, 1926-March 31, 1927- London, 1927- 3269

Great Britain. St. Helens county borough police force. Reports . . . of inquiry, March and April 1927 and November 1927. 38p. (Cmd 3103) London, H. M. Stationery Off. 1928 3270

Law, Alfred. Police patrol systems: practice in an English county. Police J [London] 2: 280-96 Ap '29 3271

Lieck, Albert Henry. Justice and police in England. 152p. London, Butterworth, 1929 3272

Liverpool and its police system. Northwest Police J 7: 18-19 My '30 3273

London's police peril. Can B R 6: 461-3 Je '28 3274

Louwage. Scotland Yard and the metropolitan police (article bibliographique). R Belge de Police Adm & Jud (120) Ag '29 3275

Moriarty, Cecil Charles Hudson. Police procedure and administration. 287p. London, Butterworth, 1930 3276
English police service, training of a constable, beat or patrol duty, detection of crime, summary jurisdiction, summary trial, extradition, public prosecutor, constables, pensions.

Moylan, J[ohn] F[itzgerald]. Police reform before Peel: the Fieldings and the Bow street police. Police J [London] 2: 150-64 Ja '29 3277

Moylan, John Fitzgerald. Scotland Yard and the metropolitan police. 331p. N.Y. Putnam, 1929 3278

Police systems. Munic R [London] 1: 391-2 O '30 3279

Prothero, Margaret. The history of the criminal investigation department at Scotland Yard from earliest times until today. 319p. London, Herbert Jenkins [1931] 3280

Reay, W. T. The Metropolitan special constabulary; the war force—the reserve. Police J [London] 1: 317-34 '28 3281

Schoner, Joseph. Le policier londonien. R Belge de Police Adm & Jud (123) N '29 3282

Stark, John. The police of the city of London. Police J [London] 4: 5-16, 197-210 Ja, Ap '31 3283

Stewart, David A. On law and order—and bobbies. Policeman 1: 16-17 N '29 3284

Trubshaw, W. The Lancashire constabulary: eighty years ago and today. Police J [London] 1: 487-98 '28 3285

Turnbull, Hugh S. The police of the city of London. Police J [London] 4: 5-16 Ja '31 3286

Webster, David. The English police system. Police J [London] 2: 571-95 O '29 3287

Webster, W. H. A. The Port of London authority's police. P L A M 99-103 F '31 3288

Wright, Sydney Fowler. Police and public. ed. 2. rev. 140p. London, Wright, 1929 3289

GREECE

Forbes, C. A. Peripoloi at Sicyon. Class Philol 25: 75-7 Ja '30 3290

HOLLAND

Cohen, Leo A. A. Dutch police systems. Police J [N Y] 15: 3, 9, 30 Jl '27 3291

The land of tulips: [Holland police]. Northwest Police J 7: 14-15 Ap '30 3292

HUNGARY

Dorning, Heinrich. The Hungarian state police. Police J [London] 2: 62-77 Ja '29 3293

INDIA

Assam. [Police department]. Report on police administration. Shillong, 1927- 3294

Bengal. Police department. Report on the police administration. Calcutta, 1912- 3295

Bihar and Orissa. Police administration. Report, Patna, 1927- 3296

Bombay. Police department. Police reports of the Bombay presidency including Sind. Bombay, 1874- 3297

Burma. Police department. Report on police administration. Rangoon, 1867- 3298

Central provinces and Berar. Police department. Report on the police administration. Nagpur, 1886- 3299

Coorg. [Police, criminal courts and trials conducted, jails (Mercara)] *In* Report on the administration of Coorg, 1926-27- Bengalore, 1927- 3300

Dowbiggin, H. L. The Ceylon police and its development. Police J [London] 1: 203-17 '28 3301

Forgotten frontier force; the Punjab frontier force. Engl R 52: 69-72 Ja '31 3302

Galloway, F. W. Adventuring with India's native police. Travel 49: 31-3 Jl '27 3303

Madras presidency. Police department. Reports, 1927-30. Madras, 1928-31 3304
Police: strength, education, discipline, cost, special police; statistics of crime; detection and prevention: prosecutions, habitual criminals, fingerprinting.

North West frontier province. Report on the police administration, Peshawar, 1916- 3305

Peters, C. R. Mounted police in India: the United Provinces M. P. Police J [London] 4: 100-6 Ja '31 3306

Punjab. Police department. Report on the police administration. Lahore, 1869- 3307

United provinces of Agra and Oudh. Police department. Reports, 1927/28- Lucknow, 1929- 3308

Young, J. W. The Burma military police. Police J [London] 1: 374-91 '28 3309

IRAQ

Wilson, A. T. The Iraq police: a notable example of administrative adaptability. Police J [London] 1: 31-8 '28 3310

With the British air patrol in Iraq. World's Wk 56: 435-40 Ag '28 3311

ITALY

Dosi, Giuseppe. The Fascisti police in Italy. Police J [N Y] 18: 3-4, 21 D '31 3312

Reynolds, P. K. The police in ancient Rome. Police J [London] 1: 432-42 '28 3313

[Tiberinus]. The royal carabiniers of Italy. Police J [London] 1: 48-61 '28 3314

JAMAICA

Jamaica. Police department. Report *in* Annual general report of Jamaica, 1927: 107-25; 1928: 107-24; 1929: 152-70; 1930: 165-83. Kingston 3315

JAPAN

Buchler, Walter. The Japanese police. Just Peace 92: 336 My 19 '28 3316

Japanese police methods praised. Trans-Pac 18: 13 Je 12 '30 3317

Wildes, Harry Emerson. The Japanese police. J Crim L & Crimin 19: 390-8 N '28 3318

LATVIA

The Latvian police and their activities: the youngest European police force. Police J [London] 4: 232-41 Ap '31 3319

MAURITIUS

Rountree, F. R. G. The Mauritius police force. Police J [London] 3: 50-62 Ja '30 3320

PALESTINE

Heath, A. J. Kingsley. The Palestine police force under the mandate. Police J [London] 1: 78-88 '28 3321

PAPUA

Murray, I. H. P. The armed constabulary of Papua. Police J [London] 4: 571-82 O '31 3322

PERSIA

Dargahi, Mohammed Khan. . . . Persia's police. Northwest Police J 6: 20-1, 43 Je '29 3323

Thiele. The Persian police. Police J [N Y] 15: 4, 32 Ap '28 3324

PHILIPPINE ISLANDS

Murphy, William. The police of Manila, P.I. Northwest Police J 5: 6-7 F '28 3325

White, John Roberts. Bullets and bolos; fifteen years in the Philippine Islands. 348p. N.Y. Century, 1928 3326

RHODESIA

Adam, J. H. Stanley. The British South Africa police in Southern Rhodesia; history, present organization and work. Police J [London] 1: 553-67 '28 3327

Hole, H. Marshall. The police forces of Southern Rhodesia. Police J [London] 3: 435-46 Jl '30 3328

Rhodesia, Southern. Police commission. Report on the British South African police, 1923-? 3329

ST. VINCENT

St. Vincent. Police department. Report of the chief of police, 1924-? 3330

SCOTLAND

Great Britain. Inspector of constabulary for Scotland. Annual reports 69, 1926- London, H.M. Stationery Off. 1927- 3331

Rait, R. S. Scottish police in early times. Police J [London] 3: 79-88 Ja '30 3332

Ross, Donald A. Scottish police administration in town and country. Police J [London] 3: 412-24 Jl '30 3333

Ross, Roderick. The Edinburgh city police. Police J [London] 3: 498-508 O '30 3334

Ross, Roderick. Who's who in Edinburgh. Northwest Police J 7: 14-15 Mr '30 3335

Steuart, James. The city of Edinburgh's special constabulary. Police J [London] 2: 485-91 Jl '29 3336

SIAM

Forty, C. H. A sketch of Siam's gendarmerie. Police J [London] 4: 425-37 Jl '31 3337

SIERRA LEONE

Sierra Leone. Police department. Annual report of the police force, 1928- 3338

SPAIN

Bermejo Cerezo, Pedro. Derecho administrativo y legislación de policia. 324p. Madrid, Voluntad [1928] 3339

Sanjurjo, José. The Spanish civil guard. Police J [London] 4: 368-80, 531-42 Jl, O '31 3340

STRAITS SETTLEMENTS

Straits Settlements. Police department. Annual report on the police force and on the state of crime, 1927- 3341

SWEDEN

Stoneman, William H. The police of Stockholm. Police "13-13" 4: 10-11, 87 My '29 3342

SWITZERLAND

Schlatter, Arnold. Das materielle Strafrecht des aargauischen Zuchtpolizeigesetzes. 182p. (Abh zum Schweizerischen Recht ns no39) Bern, Stämpfli, 1929 3343

Schneeberger, V. A Swiss travelog. Northwest Police J 7: 13, 62-4 Ja '30 3344

Switzerland. Justiz- und polizeidepartment. Bericht . . . über seine geschäftsführung . . ., 1853- 3345

Switzerland. Zentralpolizeibureau. Moniteur suisse de police, 1, 1905- 3346

Switzerland. Zentralpolizeibureau. Schweizerischer polizeianzeiger, 1, 1905- 3347

Zurich (canton). Direktion der polizei. Jahresbericht . . . über ihre geschäftsführung, 1912- 3348A

UNION OF SOUTH AFRICA

Clarke, W. T. Natal mounted police. Police J [London] 4: 337-50 Jl '31 3348B

Cooper, F. W. The police force of South Africa. Police J [London] 2: 247-65 Ap '29 3348C

Quirk, W. H. Special police problems in the Union of South Africa. Police J [London] 1: 284-90 '28 3348D

Union of South Africa. Police department. Report by the Commissioner. Pretoria, 1911- 3348E

UNITED STATES

Crawley, Frederick J. Observations on American police systems. J Crim L & Crimin 20: 167-78 Ag '29 3349

Feng, Yukon. Progress of American police administration. 92p. bibliog [93]. University of Michigan, 1931 3350

Paetsch, H. Die amerikanische Polizei. Polizei 25: 39-42 Ja '28 3351

CALIFORNIA

Burbank, Calif. Police department. Police annual, 6, 1927 [Burbank, 1928] 3352

Denton, R. B. Pasadena, Calif., police department leads. Pac Munic 44: 293-4 Ag '30 3353

Los Angeles. Bureau of budget and efficiency. Police and fire studies. (typw) June 7, 1930 3354

Los Angeles. Police department. Annual report, 1926/27—1930/31. [Los Angeles, 1927-31] 3355

Personnel, radio communication division, detective division, record and identification division, crime prevention divison, arrests.

Niblick, Jack. Policing the richest oil city in the world [Signal Hill, Calif.]. Peace Offic Assn Calif Proc 10: 99-100 '30 3356

Pasadena. Police department. Recapitulation and yearly report, 1928, 1930. [Pasadena, 1929-31] 3357

Quinn, William [J.]. Police department's responsibility to business discussed by Chief Quinn. Pac Purchasor 13: 23-4 N '31 3358

Roller, Anna. Vollmer and his college cops. Survey 62: 304-7 Je 1 '29 3359

Santa Monica. Department of public safety. Division of police. Annual [report] 6, 1928 3360

South Gate. Department of public safety. Division of police. Police annual, 1927, 1928 3361

Stockton. Police department. Annual reports, December 31, 1927 3362

Arrests, occupations of offenders, statistics.

COLORADO

Denver. Police department. Annual reports, 1927-1930. [Denver, 1928-32] 3363

Personnel statistics, detective division, Bureau of identification and records, vice division, city jail, police radio division.

CONNECTICUT

Bridgeport. Board of police commissioners. Annual reports contained in "Municipal Register" 1928: 97-115; 1929: 113-29; 1930: 256-73 3364

New Haven. Department of police service. Annual reports, 1928-1929 [New Haven, 1929-30] 3365

Personnel: offenses; Bureau of criminal identification; detective bureau; police matron; police signal service.

New London. Division of police. Annual reports *in* Annual report of City manager 1927: 16; 1928: 15-16 3366

Waterbury. Police department. Annual reports, 1927-1928 [Waterbury, 1928-29] 3367

Statistics, arrests, etc.

DELAWARE

Wilmington. Superintendent of police. Annual report, 1926/27 3368

Statistics, arrests, occupations of offenders.

DISTRICT OF COLUMBIA

District of Columbia. Metropolitan police department. Compilation of laws dealing with the organization, rules and regulations, powers, discipline, and other matters pertaining to the Metropolitan police department, compiled and arranged by L. I. H. Edwards. 43p. Washington, Govt. Ptg. Off. 1928 3369

District of Columbia. Metropolitan police department. Daily bulletin, February 15, 1929- 3370

District of Columbia. Metropolitan police department. Police regulations of the District of Columbia, amended to November 9, 1929. 230p. Washington, Govt. Ptg. Off. 1929 3371

District of Columbia. Metropolitan police department. Report of the major and superintendent of the metropolitan police, 1926/27-1929/30. Washington, Govt. Ptg. Off. 1927-30 3372

United States. Congress. Senate. Committee on District of Columbia. Woman's Bureau in Metropolitan police department of District of Columbia, report to accompany S.4174, April 23, 1928. 3p. Washington, 1928 (70th Cong. 1st sess. S. Rep. 874) 3373

FLORIDA

Jacksonville. Police department. Annual report, 1929 [Jacksonville, 1930] 3374

Personnel: distribution, salary; offenses by months; criminal identification bureau; homicides; suicides; detective bureau; woman's bureau; pension.

GEORGIA

Brunswick. Police department. Report *in* Annual report of the city of Brunswick, 1927 [Brunswick, 1928] 3375

ILLINOIS

Alcock, John H. Crime and the police. Is Chicago the crime capital? What are the police doing about it? Police "13-13" 3-5, 27 Ja '31 3376

Basuino, F. M. jr. Police protection in in Cicero, Ill. Police J [N Y] 14: 4-6 Je '27 3377

Chamberlin, Henry Barrett. To survey the Chicago police department; scientific study to be made as the result of a crime commission report. Crim Just [Chicago] 11 (57): 8-11 Mr '29 3378

Chicago. Citizens' police committee. Chicago police problems. 281p. Chicago, University of Chicago press, 1931 3379

Chicago. Citizens' police committee. Reorganization plan for the Chicago police department. 23p. (Rep no4) Chicago, February 1, 1930 3380

Chicago. Police department. Annual report, 1927-31. Chicago 1928-32 3381
Statistics, arrests, charges preferred in municipal courts, convictions in municipal courts.

Chicago. University. Police conference. Proceedings, November 20, 1930 (typw) 58p. 3382
[Association of law enforcement officers of America]

Croucher, Ollie W. Evanston police. Police J [N Y] 14: 17-21 Ap '27 3383

DeLacy, Charles. The reorganization plan; a review of the changes to be made in the Chicago police structure. Police "13-13" 4: 3-4, 37-9 N '31 3384

Hanna, Francis D. Chicago's police department. Crim Just [Chicago] 9: 14 Jl '27 3385

A program for police improvement in Chicago. Am City 44: 133-4 My '31 3386

Smith, Bruce. The human side: an answer to a criticism of the Chicago police survey. Police "13-13" 4: 3-4 D '31 3387

To survey the Chicago police department. Crim Just [Chicago] (56): 8-11 Mr '29 3388

Vollmer, August. The police [in Chicago]. *In* Illinois association for criminal justice, Illinois crime survey, 357-72, 1929 3389

INDIANA

Gary. Police department. Bulletin, v1 no1 November 13, 1930- 3390

McCormick, J. S. Facing criminal influx; Evansville is ready. Police J [N Y] 14: 11-16 Ap '27 3391

Perry, A. G. Efficient police administration at East Chicago, Indiana. Police J [N Y] 14: 11-12 My '27 3392

Stern, A. B. Michigan City, Ind. Police J [N Y] 14: 22-5 Ap '27 3393

IOWA

Brown, Roy Edward. The municipal administration of police and fire departments in Iowa. 311p. Thesis (Ph.D.) University of Iowa, 1929 3394

KANSAS

Kansas City, Kan. Police department. Annual reports, 1929-31 [Kansas City, 1930-32] 3395
Distribution of force; personnel; offenses known to the police; disposition of cases handled; criminal complaints and arrests; misdemeanor complaints and arrests; Bureau of identification; motor equipment; raiding squad; parole officer.

KENTUCKY

Louisville. Police department. Annual reports, 1926/27—1929/30 [Louisville, 1927-30] 3396
Personnel; police training school; Bureau of detectives; Bureau of records and identification; homicides by month, by hour of day, by method, sex and color; manslaughter; communications.

MARYLAND

Baltimore. Police commissioner. Report . . . to . . . the Governor of Maryland, 1927-1931 [Baltimore, 1928-32] 3397
Statistics of offenses, arrests, juvenile cases, criminal court case dispositions, work of policewoman; bureau of identification; patrol boats.

Record of Baltimore police dates back to the stirring days of the "night watch." Baltimore Munic J 5-6 S 27 '29 3398

MASSACHUSETTS

Adams. Police department. Annual reports, 1928-30. Adams, 1929-31 3399
Monthly statistics of arrests.

Boston. Police commissioner. Annual reports 22, 1927—26, 1931. Boston, 1927-31 (Pub doc 49) 3400
Arrests, uniform crime record reporting, Bureau of criminal investigation, Bureau of records, plant and equipment, personnel, homicide division, identification division, signal service.

Brookline. Chief of police. Annual reports, 1928-31. Boston, 1929-32 3401
Detective bureau, police signal system.

Carter, P. J. The police force of Adams, Massachusetts. Police J [N Y] 14: 12-Ag '27 3402

Cambridge. Chief of police. Annual reports, 1926/27-1929/30 [Cambridge, 1927-30] 3403
Statistics of offenses and arrests; report of policewoman.

Holyoke. Department of police. Annual reports, 1926/27—1929/30 [Holyoke, 1927-30] 3404
Arrests, signal system, female department, detective bureau, policewoman.

Lowell. Police department. Annual reports, 1927-1930 [Lowell, 1928-31] 3405
Statistics: arrests; monthly report of lock-up; report of police matron of arrests of women; criminal bureau of investigation; signal system; police women's report.

Newton. Police department. Annual reports, 1927-30 [Newton, 1928-31] 3406
Offenses, statistics, etc.

Perry, Ross A. Our harbor police. Our Boston 3: 15-20 Mr '28 3407

Pittsfield. Police department. Annual report, 1930. Pittsfield, 1931 3408
Includes reports, 1925-1930. Arrests, disposition of cases.

Springfield. Police commission. Annual report, 1927/28-1929/30 3409
Offenses, arrests, Detective bureau, criminal identification, policewoman, vice squad, juvenile cases.

Worcester. Chief of police. Annual reports *in* Report of Mayor, City documents 3410

MICHIGAN

Allen Park. Police department. Report *in* Municipal activities, 1928-30, village of Allen Park [Allen Park, 1931] **3411**

Detroit. Police department. Annual reports 62, 1927—66, 1931. Detroit, 1928-32 **3412**

Reports also in Annual report of Common council. Statistics of personnel; offenses known to police; criminal investigation division; arrests; robberies; women's division; habitual criminal squad.

Detroit. Police department. Woman's division. Annual report, 1928. (mim) [Detroit 1929] **3413**

The Detroit police department radio system. Am J Police Sci 1: 456-65 S '30 **3414**

MINNESOTA

Minneapolis. Department of police. Annual report, 1927 [Minneapolis 1928] **3415**

No annual reports for 1928-30.
Bureau of identification, Bureau of policewomen.

MISSOURI

Kansas City. Police department. Annual reports, 1929/30—1930/31 **3416**

No reports publ 1927 and 1928.

Matscheck, Walter. Kansas City studies its police department. Nat Mun R 28: 453-7 Jl '29 **3417**

Study by Kansas City Public Service Institute under direction of August Vollmer.

Matscheck, Walter. The police budget controversy in Kansas City. Pub Manage 12: 579-80 D '30 **3418**

Police de Saint-Louis. Polizei im Bild 4 (2) F '30 **3419**

St. Louis. Board of police commissioners. Annual reports 66, 1926/27—70, 1930/31. St. Louis 1927-31 **3420**

Police training school, policewoman's division, communication system, retirement system, personnel, salary, distribution of force, offenses, arrests, criminal identification.

Vollmer, August. Survey of the metropolitan police department of Kansas City, Missouri. 165p. Kansas City, Kansas City Chamber of commerce, March 1929 **3421**

NEW JERSEY

Elizabeth. Police department. Annual report . . . for the fiscal year ending December 31, 1931. (mim) [Elizabeth 1932] **3422**

Personnel statistics, offenses.

New Jersey. State league of municipalities. Bureau of municipal information. Size and character of police force in New Jersey municipalities in 1927. 2p. (mim) (Rep no188) 1927 **3423**

Paterson. Chief of police. Annual reports, 1927-1928. Paterson, 1928-29 **3424**

Reports for 1929 and 1930 not printed.

Polices de New-Jersey et de Tokio. Polizei im Bild 4 (1) Ja '30 **3425**

Stillman, W. M. Police power in New Jersey. N J L J 50: 205-8 Jl '27 **3426**

Treworgy, Lloyd J. Police force of Summit, New Jersey. Police J [N Y] 15: 12, 24 Ap '28 **3427**

NEW YORK

Buffalo. Municipal research bureau. Police department; a memorandum on the organization and work of the uniformed force of the Buffalo police department with suggestions for increased patrol efficiency. 15p. (Munic Res Bul no13) Buffalo, April 1928 **3428**

Buffalo. Police department. Annual reports 54, 1927—57, 1930. Buffalo, 1927-30 **3429**

Statistics: personnel, salary, scale and distribution of force; police training school; radio communication; arson and narcotic squad; gambling and vice; policewomen; offenses; burglaries; robberies; homicides.

Burns, R. Vernon. History of the New York police department. Police J [N Y] 18: 16-17, 21 Jl; 11-13, 27 Ag; 15-16, 20 S; 16, 27 N; 16-17 D '31 **3430**

Centenary of the metropolitan police, 1829-1929. Police J [London] 2: 353-4 Jl '29 **3431**

Gates, Alfred. An interview with the chief of police of Rochester, N.Y. Nat Munic R 19: 242-8 Ap '30 **3432**

McGoldrick, Joseph. Commissioner Whalen's spectacular police career. Am City 42: 154-7 Je '30 **3433**

McGoldrick, Joseph. A policeman's lot: an appraisal of Grover Whalen's *tour de force* as police commissioner of New York city. Nat Munic R 19: 391-7 Je '30 **3434**

New York (city). Police department. Annual reports, 1927-1931. New York, 1927-31 **3435**

Arrests, police academy.

New York (state). Crime commission. Sub-commission on police.
Report, January 17, 1927. 43p. Albany, 1927
Report, February 28, 1928. 7p. Albany, 1928
Report, February 28, 1929. 8p. Albany, 1929 **3436**

Rochester. Department of public safety. Police bureau. Annual reports, 1927-1930 [Rochester, 1928-31] **3437**

Detective bureau; crime conditions; burglaries, non-support cases; policewoman; arrests; Bureau of identification.

Whalen creates secret police to prevent crime: fifty men . . . to run down gangs. Int Pict Police J 47, 49 Je '29 **3438**

Whalenism. Nation [N Y] 130: 350 Mr 26 '30 **3439**

OHIO

Akron. Police department. Annual reports, 1927-1931. (mim) **3440**

Reports not for distribution.

Cincinnati. Bureau of governmental research. Regional police survey for southwestern Ohio and northern Kentucky including the counties of Hamilton, Butler, Warren, Clermont, Campbell, and Kenton. 35p. (mim) (Rep no26) December 1, 1930 **3441**

Cincinnati. Department of safety. Division of police. Annual report 44, 1929—45, 1930 [Cincinnati] 1930-31 **3442**

Police training school; radio; signal system; Bureau of records; statistics of personnel; salary scale and distribution of force; offenses known to the police; detective bureau; criminal identification bureau. Annual reports summarized in Municipal Activities, city of Cincinnati. 1927: 102-6; 1928: 104-7; 1929: 73-8.

Cleveland. Police department. Annual reports, 1927-1928 **3443**

Columbus. Department of public safety. Division of police. Annual report *in* City clerk, City bulletin, suppl. **3444**

Dayton. Department of public safety. Division of police. Report *in* Annual report of the city of Dayton, 1927-1928 [Dayton, 1928-29] **3445**

Arrests, Bureau of crime prevention, Bureau of policewomen.

Oglesby, R. C. The Middleton, Ohio, police force. Police J [N Y] 15: 20-2 Ap '28 **3446**

Painesville. Police department. Annual report *in* Annual report of City Manager, 1928: 22-5; 1929: 14-15 **3447**

Police administration in Cleveland: an efficient organization. Greater Cleveland 3 (33) My 9 '28 **3448**

Smith, Bruce. A regional police plan for Cincinnati and its environs. 28p. N.Y. Institute of public administration, December 15, 1931 **3449**

Springfield. Police department. Annual report, 1931. (mim) [Springfield, 1932] **3450**

Personnel, salary, distribution of force, complaints and arrests.

Stone, Donald C. Cincinnati surveys its police. Nat Munic R 17: 157-62 Mr '28 **3451**

Toledo's police in 1929. Toledo City J 15 (20) My 17 '30 **3452**

Oregon

Portland. Police department. Bureau of records. Annual reports, 1927/28—1929/30 [Portland, 1928-30] **3453**

Expenses, Division of records, arrests, Women's protective division.

Oklahoma

Police department statistics: survey discloses important facts regarding police departments of 33 Oklahoma municipalities. Okla Munic R 3: 233 Ag '29 **3454**

Pennsylvania

Philadelphia police investigation. Good Govt 46: 10 F '29 **3455**

South Carolina

Charleston. Police department. Annual report *in* Yearbook of the city of Charleston, 1928: 154-7; 1929: 149-54 **3456**

Personnel, Detective bureau, Bureau of identification, city prisoners, equipment, signal system, Woman's bureau, amount of fines, number of arrests.

Texas

Austin. Police department. Report *in* Annual report of the City Manager, 1927: 33-4; 1928: 79-80; 1929: 75-7; 1930: 37-40; 1931: 33-6 **3457**

Detective division, Bureau of identification.

Beaumont. Police department. Annual report, December 31, 1931 [Beaumont, 1932] **3458**

Houston. Police department. Annual reports, 1927-1930. Houston, 1928-31 **3459**

Utah

Salt Lake City. Police department. Annual reports, 1927-1930 [Salt Lake City 1928-31] **3460**

Crime statistics; crimes—males, females, occupations of persons arrested, nationality of offenders; Detective bureau.

Virginia

Roanoke. Department of police. Review of the department of police, 1928 . . . with a report of the Superintendent of police, 1922-1928. 133p. [Roanoke, 1928] **3461**

Later reports *in* Annual report of city of Roanoke.

Washington

Seattle. Police department. Annual reports, 1929-1931. (mim) [Seattle, 1930-32] **3462**

Spokane. Chief of police. Annual reports, 1928-1930 [Spokane, 1929-31] **3463**

With the Spokane police. Northwest Police J 7: 83, 85 Jl '30 **3464**

Wisconsin

Milwaukee. Chief of police. Annual report, 1930. (mim) [Milwaukee, 1931]; *also in* Annual report of Common council, 1927: 9-10, 29-30; 1928: 13, 33-5; 1929: 16-17, 44-6 **3465**

COOPERATION WITH OTHER AGENCIES

Burke, John J. Closer welding of various police units. Int Assn Identif Proc 13: 56-9 '27 **3470**

Doran, James M. The police and prohibition enforcement; can there be municipal co-operation? Police "13-13" 5: 3-4 Mr '30 **3471**

French, Harry E. The educational advantage of exchanging detectives between police departments. Int Assn Chiefs Police Proc 36: 113-14 '29 **3472**

Glaister, John. The medical profession and the police. Police J [London] 3: 201-12 Ap '30 **3473**

National crime commission. Relation of the police and the courts to the crime problem; a report submitted to the Commission by the sub-committee on pardons, parole, penal laws and institutional correction. 37p. N.Y. 1928; excerpts: Am City 38: 84-6 Ap '28 **3474**

Newton, Chris H. Relationship between the police of Canada and the United States. Int Assn Chiefs Police Proc 37: 45-9 '30 **3475**

O'Brien, Daniel J. Cooperation between the law enforcement officers of the United States and Canada. Police J [N Y] 16: 27-8 S '28 **3476**

O'Brien, Daniel J. Police cooperation between U. S. and Canada. "2-0" Police J 6: 5-6 Jl '28 **3477**

Rassow, Ernst. Die Stellung der Kriminalpolizei im Strafprozessualen Ermittelungsverfahren und ihr Verhältnis zur Justiz. Polizei 25: 440-4, 483-6 Jl 20, Ag 5 '28 **3478**

Sargent, Albert J. Getting police cooperation. Nat Prob Assn Proc 1930: 245-7 **3479**

Shute, A. G. Co-operation and co-ordination of effort between police departments. Chief Constables Assn Can Proc 26: 23-8 '30 **3480**

Stoeckel, Robbins B. The relation between state administrators of motor vehicles and police. Police J [N Y] 16: 23-5 Ap '29 **3481**

Tenner, F. Zur Frage der zwischenstaatlichen Zusammenarbeit gegen das Verbrechertum. Arch f Krim 89: 46-51 Jl '31 **3482**

Tillard, J. N. Cooperation in police work. Int Assn Chiefs Police Proc 36: 108-10 '29 **3483**

Van Houten, M. C. The international co-operation of criminal police: its history and aims. Police J [London] 3: 482-97 O '30 **3484**

Wallace, Carl J. Cooperation. Int Assn Identif, Calif Div Proc 14: 34-6 '29 **3485**

POLICE AND THE PROSECUTOR

Alspaugh, F. R. Relationship between the prosecuting attorney's office and the police department. Mich Assn Chiefs Police Proc 6: 63-6 '29 **3486**

Böhme, Albrecht. Neue Wege der Kriminalpolizei. Verschmelzung von Staatsanwaltschaft und Kriminalpolizei. Arch f Krim 89: 129-38 S '31 **3487**

Boykin, John A. The relationship between the police department and the prosecuting attorney. Int Assn Chiefs Police Proc 36: 92-6 '29 **3488**

Coon, William H. Police work from the viewpoint of the district attorney. N Y St Assn Chiefs Police Proc 29: 70-4 '29 **3489**

Dehler, Wilhelm. Die Stellung der Polizei zu Staatsanwaltschaft und Untersuchungsrichter. 59p. Lübeck, Deutscher Polizeiverl. 1930 **3490**

Hartung, F. Untersuchungsrichter und Polizei. Polizei 24: 23-7 Ja 20 '27 **3491**

Kelley, C. H. Co-operation between police, sheriffs and district attorneys. Peace Offic Assn Calif Proc 10: 85-7 '30 **3492**

Main, Harold W. Cooperation between police magistrates, police and prosecuting officers in the administration of the criminal law. N Y St Assn Magistrates Proc 21: 48-54 '29 **3493**

Renner. Staatsanwaltschaft und Kriminalpolizei. Deut Juristen-Zeit 32: 1580-3 '27 **3494**

Warren, Earl. Cooperation between police and district attorneys. Police J [N Y] 15: 14, 30 My '28 **3495**

POLICE AND THE PUBLIC

Basuino, Francis M. The policeman and the public. Police J [N Y] 16: 18 N '28 **3496**

Brockman, Phil. H. Selling the police to the public. Police J [N Y] 16: 10-11, 32 F '29 **3497**

Fort, T. Hicks. Creating a better spirit of cooperation between police and public. Police J [N Y] 17: 10-11, 32 S '29 **3498**

Fort, T. Hicks. How to create a better spirit of cooperation between the police and the public. Int Assn Chiefs Police Proc 36: 103-8 '29 **3499**

Funck, Richard M. Relation between the police officer and the public. Int Assn Chiefs Police Proc 37: 100-3 '30 **3500**

Funston, William H. The relations of the press and police. Police J [N Y] 16: 26, 31 S '28 **3501**

Hagemann. Ein Beitrag zu dem Thema: Kriminalpolizei und Presse. Krimin Monatsh 1: 98-100 My '27 **3502**

Kline, Chester M. The press, police and crime. Inst Police Adm Proc 50-4 '29 **3503**

Miller, Justin. Public opinion, police and crime. Inst Police Adm Proc 55-69 '29 **3504**

O'Neill, Francis P. Cooperation between reporters and the police. Police J [N Y] 15: 23 S '27 **3505**

Peake, John. The cooperation between the police and the public in the detection and prosecution of crime. Police J [London] 3: 383-411 Jl '30 **3506**

Pick, Frank. The police and the public. Howard J 3: 18-22 S '30 **3507**

The police and the public. Sol J 72: 344-5 My 26 '28 **3508**

Tripp, H. Alker. Police and public: a new test of police quality. Police J [London] 1: 529-39 '28 **3509**

Waite, John Barker. Distrust of police officers by the public and the remedy. Int Assn Chiefs Police Proc 1927: 228-31 **3510**

Waite, John Barker. Why people distrust the police and the remedy. Police J [N Y] 15: 16-17 O '27 **3511**

POLICE AND SOCIAL SERVICE GROUPS

Bowler, Alida C. The social worker and the police. Inst Police Adm Proc 34-42 '29 **3512**

Erkens, Josephine. Kriminalpolizei und soziale Gerichtshilfe. Krimin Monatsh 2: 193-6 S '28 **3513**

Ottolenghi, S. Coordinazione dell'assistenza alla delinquenza fra le istituzione filantropiche e le funzioni delle autorità di publica sicurezza. Zacchia 6: 91-9 Jl '28 **3514**

Police and legal aid. Sol J 74: 113 F 22 '30 **3515**

ASSOCIATIONS, CONGRESSES, ETC.

Bee, R. V. The twenty-seventh annual convention of the New York state association of chiefs of police. Police J [N Y] 15: 14-15 S '27 **3516**

Boltze. Internationaler Kongress für Frauenpolizei 1932. Krimin Monatsh 5: 89-90 Ap '31 **3517**

Branthwaite, J. M. The genesis, aims and scope of the police federation system of England and Wales. Police J [London] 1: 19-30 Ja '28 **3518**

Chief constables' association of Canada. Proceedings 23, 1927—27, 1931. Sec.-Treas. Chris H. Newton, Winnipeg, Man. **3519**

Constitution of the International association of policewomen. Policewoman's Int Bul 5: 3-4 Ap '29 **3520**

Convenio internacional de policía (1905). R de Identif y Cienc Pen 4: 318-70 S '29 **3521**

Dresdner Tagung der Deutsche Kriminalpolizeiliche Kommission vom 14.-16. Juni 1928. 55p. Dresden, 1928 **3522**

Geschaftsbericht der Freien Vereinigung für Polizei und Kriminalwissenschaft über das Geschäftsjahr 1926. Polizei 25: 9-10 Ja 5 '28 **3523**

Gilson, Albert I. New England association of chiefs of police. . . . . Police J [N Y] 16: 16, 31 N '28 **3524**

Hildesheim, Peinemann. Zur Kongressionierung des Detektivgewerbes. Selbstschutz 2 (9) O '30 **3525**

Institute of police administration. Proceedings [1], 1929. Riverside Junior Coll, Occasional papers v5 no1 Mr 5 '30 **3526**

International police conference. Proceedings, 1931. New York, [1931] **3527**

No sessions of conference, 1926-1930.

Iowa association of chiefs of police. Annual proceedings 23, 1931: summary. 6p. (typw) Sec., Otto Karbusicky, 612 11th ave. Cedar Rapids, 1931 **3528**

Previous proceedings not available.

Kleinow. Konferenz der Polizei-Oberbeamten des rheinwestf. Industriegebiets zu Dortmund-Wambel am 15. November 1927. Polizei 25: 11-12 Ja 5 '28 **3529**

Krauss, E. G. Aims and achievements of the State police chiefs association of Ohio. Ohio St Police J (Convention no) 3- Je '31 **3530**

Massachusetts chiefs of police association. Minutes of meetings, February 2, 1928—December 3, 1931. (typw) Brookline, Mass. H. Allen Rutherford, Sec. [1931] **3531**

Massachusetts police association. Reports of annual conventions, 1927-1931. Newton, Mass. John H. Shaughnessy, Sec. **3532**

Massachusetts police mutual aid association convenes and reports with above association.

Michigan association of chiefs of police. Proceedings 5, 1928—6, 1929 **3533**

No proceedings issued for 1930 and 1931.

O'Reilly, Joseph J. New York state police conference. Police J [N Y] 16: 7 O '28 **3534**

L'Organisation du Bureau international [de police]. R Int de Crimin 3 (4): 299-312 '31 **3535**

Palitzsch. Die dritte Tagung der Deutschen kriminalpolizeilichen Kommission. Krimin Monatsh 2: 146-51 Jl '28 **3536**

Raymond, Frank. The Wisconsin association of chiefs of police convention. Police J [N Y] 15: 16-17 N '27 **3537**

Sheriffs and police officers' association. Official guide and directory and bulletin, 1931-32. 307p. Chicago, 188 W. Randolph st. 1931 **3538**

State police chiefs association of Ohio, Inc. Minutes of convention, 1930. Ohio St Police J (Convention no) 25, 27 Je '31 **3539**

Texas. Chiefs of police and city marshalls union. Proceedings 29, 1927- **3540**

Virginia. League of municipalities. Police executives association. Official program: . . . annual convention 24, 1929 **3541**

Wood, S. A. The police mutual assurance society. Police J [London] 4: 242-9 Ap '31 **3542**

PEACE OFFICERS' ASSOCIATION OF THE STATE OF CALIFORNIA

California sheriffs association *see* Peace Officers association of the state of California **3543**

Peace officers' association of the state of California. Program [of] annual convention, September 17, 1929. 330p. **3544**

Peace officers' association of the state of California. Proceedings, 1928-31 **3545**

Veale, R. R. Sheriffs' association and its accomplishments. Peace Offic Assn Calif Proc 9: 36-40 '29 **3546**

Women peace officers association of California. Yearbook, 1928-1929. Los Angeles, City Hall, 1929 **3547**

INTERNATIONAL ASSOCIATION OF CHIEFS OF POLICE

Basuino, F. M. The International association of chiefs of police. Police J [N Y] 14: 16-19 Je '27 3548

International association of chiefs of police. Advisory board bulletin 3, April 1927—5, November 1927. Sec., George Black, Wilmington, Del. 3549

International association of chiefs of police. Proceedings, 1927-1930. Sec., George Black, Wilmington, Del. 1927-30 3550

Tillard, J. N. The history of the formation of the I.A.C.P. Police J [N Y] 16: 6, 21 Mr '29 3551

Upson, Lent D. The International association of chiefs of police and other American police organizations. Ann Am Acad 146: 121-7 N '27 3552

INTERNATIONAL CRIMINAL POLICE COMMISSION

Cohen, Leo A. A. Convention of the International Criminal police commission. Police J [N Y] 15: 16-17, 32 S '27 3553

Dressler, D. The International criminal police commission. Police J [N Y] 18: 7-9 Ag; 9-10, 23 S; 7, 24 N '31 3554

Ducloux, Louis. La Commission internationale de police criminelle. R de Gendarm 4 (20) Mr 15 '31 3555

International criminal police commission. Resolutions passed by the . . . Commission . . . at the 5th ordinary meeting at Berne, September 10-12, 1928. 7p. 3556
German and English text.

International criminal police commission. Resolutions passed by the . . . Commission . . . at the 4th ordinary meeting at Amsterdam, July 6-8, 1927. 4p. 3557
German and English text.

International criminal police commission. Resolutions passed by the . . . Commission . . . at the 7th ordinary meeting at Antwerp, September 24, 30, 1930. 2p. 3558

International criminal police commission. Resolutions adopted by the . . . Commission . . . during the 8th ordinary meeting, at Paris, September 28-30, 1931. 5p. 3559

International police congress, III. Antwerp. The organization of the International bureau. 5p. (no21) September 25-30, 1930 3560

International police congress, III. Antwerp. Resolutions of . . . the Congress, September 25-30, 1930. 4p. 3561

Internationalen kriminalpolizeilichen Kommission. Die 6. Tagung. Krimin Monatsh 4: 25-7 F '30 3562

Klaiber. Die 5. Tagung der Internationalen Kriminalpolizeilichen Kommission. Krimin Monatsh 2: 218-21 O '28 3563

Louwage, F. E. IIIe Congrès international de police criminelle et VIIIe session de la Commission internationale de police criminelle (C.I.P.C.). R de Dr Pén et de Crimin 11: 184-98 F '31 3564

Palitzsch. Die 5. Tagung der Internationalen Kriminal polizeilichen Kommission. Polizei 25: 654-6 O 20 '28 3565

Palitzsch. Die Internationale Kriminalpolizeiliche Kommission in Amsterdam. Polizei 24: 383-4 Ag 5 '27 3566

Résolutions du IIIe Congrès internationale de police à Anvers (25-30 septembre 1930). R Int de Crimin 3 (3): 222-32 '31 3567

Schober, J. Internationale Zusammenarbeit der Kriminalpolizei. Der Antwerpener Polizeikongress. Arch f Krim 87: 88-100 N '30 3568

Weiss. Der "III Internationale Polizeikongress." Krimin Monatsh 4: 226-8 O '30 3569

PERIODICALS

A. H. T. A. weekly news [Anti-Horse-Thief Association]. St. Paul, Kan. 1927- 3570

American bankers association, Journal, sec2: Protective department, monthly bulletin, illustrated, issued for identification of bank criminals 3571
This is not available to libraries, only to those in banking circles.

American journal of police science. Chicago, v1 no1 January-February 1930- Scientific crime detection laboratory, Northwestern university 3572
Included in Journal of criminal law and criminology, 23 (2) Jl-Ag '32.

Boletin de estadistica y jurisprudencia de la policia de la capital. Buenos Aires, 1928- Imprenta y encuadernación de la policia, Buenos Aires 3573

Der Born; Zeitschrift für die Ausbildung den Aufstieg und die Versorgung des Polizeibeamten. Dresden, 2, 1926/27- 3574

The Buzzer. Wichita, 1, 1929- Wichita, Kansas, Square deal police department 3575

The California state highway patrolman. Los Angeles. 1, August 1930- Public service bureau of Los Angeles, 253 So. Broadway 3576

Canadian police bulletin. Toronto, 13, 1927- Chief constables association of Canada 3577

Criminologist. Chicago, v5 no6, June 1929- O'Sullivan pub. house, Inc., Chicago 3578

Detective. Chicago, 1927- 3579
Official journal of the police authorities and sheriffs of the United States.

Der Deutsche Schäferhund. 5, 1926- Deutscher Schäferhund Verband, Eisenach, Germany. 3580

Deutsches Kriminalpolizeiblatt. daily. 3, 1930- Polizei Präsidium, Landeskriminalpolizeiamt, Berlin 3581

Finger print magazine. Chicago, July 1919- Finger print pub. assn. Chicago 3582

Fraternal order of police official journal. Pittsburgh, Pa. monthly. 12, 1929- Grand Lodge fraternal order of police 3583

Gaceta policial. Santiago de Chile (7-10) 1927- 3584

Graphologie scientifique. 1, 1926- 3585
Organe officiel de la Société de graphologie.

Hanseatisches Polizei-archiv. Lübeck. 1, 1925- 3586

Illinois police officer. St. Louis, 1930- 3587

Indiana police news. 1, 1929- Indiana association of chiefs of police, R. H. Benson, Kokomo, Ind. 3588

International association of policewomen bulletin. nos1-31, 1925-27 3589
Continued by Policewomen's international bulletin.

International pictorial police journal. Montreal, April 1929- 3590

The Investigator. 3 (7) March 1927- F. Dalton O'Sullivan, editor, Chicago-Clark bldg. Chicago 3591

Justice. Chicago, 1, 1928- Sheriffs' and police officer's association of America 3592

Kugel und Schrot. Berlin, 35, 1930- 3593
Zeitschrift der deutschen Versuchsanstalt für Handfeuerwaffen und Deutscher Kartell für Jagd und Sport Schiessen.

Lightnin'. Chicago, 4, 1931- Chicago, N. Winchester ave. Elmer L. Williams 3594

Main "7810". Seattle, 1, 1924- Seattle, Washington, Police department 3595

Mikrokosmos. Stuttgart, 1906- Franck'sche Verlagshandlung, Stuttgart, Germany 3596

National counterfeiter detector. New York, 1907- 3598

National police gazette. New York, September 1845- 3599
Titled Police gazette. v138 no2768 Ag '30.

National police officer. St. Louis, 1, 1929- Chiefs of police of Missouri and sheriffs' and peace officers association of Missouri 3600

Nordisk Kriminalteknis Tidskrift. Stockholm, 1, January 1931- Stockholm, Bryggaregaten 4, Harry Söderman 3601

Northwest police journal. Seattle, 5, 1927- 3602
Official publication of the Northwest association of sheriffs and police, Washington state sheriffs and peace officers association, Oregon state sheriffs association, Idaho sheriffs and police association, Montana sheriffs and police officers association, Washington relief and prison association, Washington state highway patrol, Oregon state highway patrol and Idaho highway traffic patrol.

Pacific police magazine. Los Angeles, 1, 1925- 3603
International detective chiefs association official journal; formerly, Pacific police chronicle.

The Peace officer. Oklahoma City, Okla. 5, 1927- Peace officer pub. co. 718 Insurance bldg. Oklahoma City, Okla. 3604

Peace officer and police reporter. Los Angeles, 1, 1929- Peace officers association of Los Angeles county 3605

Philippine Islands. Philippine constabulary. Bulletin, no1, January 25, 1927- Manila (mim) 3606

Police department bulletin. Gary, Indiana. 1, November 13, 1930- Gary, Indiana, Police department 3607

Police journal. London. 1, January 1928- 3608

Police journal. New York. 1, 1922- 3609
Official journal of National committee on police welfare.

Police news. Detroit. 1, June 1928- Detroit, Michigan, Police department 3610

Police reporter. Los Angeles. 1, 1929- Los Angeles, 1006 West Manchester ave. 3611

Police review. Hagerstown, Md. 4, January 1925- 3612
Official publication of National association of policemen.

Police review and parade gossip. London. 1, 1893- (British constabulary) 3613

Police "13-13". Chicago, 1917- Chicago, Ill. Police department 3614

The Policeman. Vancouver. 1, August 1929- 3615
Vancouver, B.C. Police book publ.

Policewoman's international bulletin. 3, 1927- 3616
Formerly International association of policewomen bulletin.

Policia cubana. Habana. 5, 1925- 3617

Policia e justiça. Pernambuco. 2 (7) May 1930- Ramos de Freitas, Dir. Rua Conde de Iraja 634 3618

Policía española. Madrid. 37 (1261) March 2, 1929- Revista profesional y cientifica de vigilancia y seguridad. Madrid 3619

Polizei; zeitschrift für Polizei wissenschaft, dienst und wesen. Berlin. 1, 1904- 3620
Includes current suppl: Archiv für polizeirecht, 1923-

Polizei im Bild. Berlin. 2, 1928- 3621

Polizei Württembergisches. Stuttgart. 1, 1928- Württ. Polizeifachschule, Stuttgart, Kohlhammer 3622

Polizeifachkunde. Zeitschrift für die Ausbildung den Aufstieg und die Versorgung des Polizeibeamten. Dresden, 1920- 3623

Polizeioffizier; zeitschrift des Reichsverbandes Deutscher polizeioffiziere. Berlin. 1, 1922- Vereinigung der polizeioffiziere Preuzens 3624

Polizeipraxis. Berlin, 1925- 3625

Polizeiwissen. Dresden. 1, 1929- 3626
Monatszeitschrift d. Verbandes d. Sächs. Schutzpolizei.

Polizeiwissen. Leipzig, 1928- Polizeiobert a. D. Weickert 3627

Progreso; revista de identificación científica. Santiago. 1, 1928- 3628
Organo oficiel del Servicio de identificación de la República de Chile.

Revista de identificación y ciencias penales. La Plata. 1, 1927- Universidad nacional de la Plata, Argentine 3629

Revista de los Carabineros de Chile. Santiago. 1(9) April 15, 1928- 3630

Revista de policia. Quito, Ecuador. 1, January 1927- 3631

Revista de policía. Buenos Aires. 31 (732) December 16, 1928- 3632
Organo de los interesses generales de la institución policial. Directores: Leopoldo C. López y Samuel C. Ruffet.

Revue belge de la police administrative et judiciaire. Bruxelles. 1, 1880- 3633

Revue de la gendarmerie. Paris. 1, January 15, 1928- Charles-Lavauzelle, Boulevard Saint-Germain, 124 3634

Schweizerisches Polizeiblatt. Luzern, 1920- 3635

Der Selbstschutz. Monatsschrift für Kriminalistik und Kriminalistische Praxis. Berlin. 1, 1929- 3636
Fachorgan für Kriminalistischen Selbstschutz und für die Selbstschutz-Betriebe. Lothar Philipp, ed.

Sheriffs and police review. St. Paul, 1927- International sheriffs and police association, St. Paul, 333 University ave. 3637

State trooper. Detroit. 1, 1919- 3638
Detroit, Michigan, state police journal.

Tijdschrift voor de politie. Rotterdam. 1, April 1928- 3639

Tijdschrift voor Wetenschappelijke Graphologie. Amsterdam. 1. 1929/30- 3640

[Douglas] "2-0": police journal. San Francisco, 6, 1928- San Francisco, Calif. Police department 3641
Later entitled: San Francisco police and peace officers journal of the state of California.

Uniform crime reports. 1, January 1930- 3642
v1 no1-7 January-July 1930 published by International association of chiefs of police; v1 no[8] August 1930- published by U.S. Department of justice, National division of identification and information.

Van Every, Edward. Sins of America as "exposed" by the Police Gazette. 297p. N.Y. Stokes, 1931 3643
National police gazette.

Verbandsblatt der Thüringer Polizeibeamten. Weimar, 1903- 3644

The vigilant. Norfolk, Va. 1, July 1927- 3645

Western police review. Sacramento. 1, April 1925- Sacramento, Calif. Northern California detective bureau 3646

Young, Donald. Police journalism in the United States. Ann Am Acad 146: 128-34 N '29 3647

NON-OFFICIAL ORGANIZATIONS: VIGILANTES

Bergenroth, Gustav. The first vigilance committee in California. Mag Hist 38 (3) extra no151: 143-9 '29 3648
Appears in the Memoir of Gustav Bergenroth, but its first appearance and that from which this was copied was in *Household Words*, edited by Dickens, November 15, 1856.

Birney, Hoffman. Vigilantes. . . a chronicle of the rise and fall of the Plummer gang of outlaws in and about Virginia City, Montana, in the early 60's. . . 346p. Philadelphia, Pennsylvania Pub. co. [1929] 3649

Dowd, W. J. Vigilance committees. Forum 85: sup28 My '31 3650

McLellan, Howard. Corn belt vigilantes and what they do to the friendless bank robber. World's Wk 56: 639-47 O '28 3651

Shepherd, William G. Vigilantes take charge. Collier's 83: 8-9 Ap 20 '29 3652

EQUIPMENT

Paetsch, [H.]. Technische Ausrüstung der amerikanischen Polizei. Polizei 25: 113-15, 141-2 F 20, Mr 5 '28 3653

Salmony, A. Der Kohlenoxyd Schnellbestimmungs-Apparat in der Kriminalistik. Krimin Monatsh 5: 187-8 Ag '31 3654

[Vollmer, August]. Adequate equipment and efficient personnel essential for success in police administration. Am City 38: 111-12 Je '28 3655

BUILDINGS, STATIONS, ETC.

Bartelsmeyer, E. H. New headquarters and gymnasium occupied by St. Louis police department. Am City 40: 105-7 Je '29 3656

Ely, John H. and Ely, Wilson C. Planning and construction of police headquarters. Arch Forum 55:371-80 S '31 3657

Forty-second district police station, Philadelphia, Pa., views and plans. Arch Rec 61: 329-33 Ap '27 3658

Hart, Hastings H. A plan for a model police station. Am Pris Assn Proc 60: 165-9 '30 3659

Ohnesorge. Neubauten für die Schutzpolizei in Bremen und Bremerhaven. Polizei 24: 419-24 S 5 '27 3660

Police department headquarters, Boston. Arch Forum 46: 539-44 Je '27 3661

Police headquarters building, Cleveland, Ohio, views and plan. Arch Rec 61: 141-3 F '27 3662

St. Louis. Board of police commissioners. A detailed description of the new police headquarters buildings in St. Louis, containing data concerning their plan, construction and costs. 32p. St. Louis, Mo. 1928 3663

Trench, G. Mackenzie. Metropolitan police buildings [London]. Police J [London] 2: 91-108 Ja '29 3664

PERSONAL EQUIPMENT

Newton, [Chris] H. Is a bullet-proof vest bullet proof? Chief Constables' Assn Can Proc 26: 55-7 '30 3665

O'Brien, John. Handy-kit equipment for crime detection to be used by New York police. Am City 40: 156 My '29 3666

Preuss, J. Eine verbesserte Handfessel. Krimin Monatsh 4: 41-2 F '30 3667

Singleton, Robert. The law's strong arm. Am J Police Sci 2: 382-7 S '31 3668
Historical sketch of various types of police uniforms.

MOTOR EQUIPMENT

Beating the motorized criminal with swifter motors. Lit Dig 95: 71-5 N 12 '27 3669

Belknap, Harry. New police boat for patrol service in Boston harbor. Am City 44: 132 Ap '31 3670

Motor vehicle equipment for police departments. Municipality 25: 43-4 Mr '30 3671

Schmidt, H. Der Kraftwagen bei der Polizei. Polizei 25: 25-6 Ja 5 '28 3672

INSTRUMENTS

General

Gay, Willy. Ein Apparat zur Identifizierung von Fingerabdrücken. Krimin Monatsh 5: 113-15 My '31 3673

Karsten, A. Ein neuer Reproduktionsautomat für kriminalistische Zwecke. Arch f Krim 89: 57-9 Jl '31 3674

Locard, Edmond. Deux appareils de laboratoires pour les recherches de criminalistique: 1, le graphoscope; 2, l'hastoscope. R Int de Crimin 1 (1-3): 113-17 '29 3675

Graphoscope for written documents, Hastoscope for bullets.

Nelken. Das "Tresoroskop". Krimin Monatsh 3: 155-6 Jl '29 3676

Simonin, Camille. Micrographie parkinsonienne et analyse graphométrique. Y a-t-il chez le parkinsonien micrographique désorganisation ou simple pertubation de l'automatisme graphique? R Int de Crimin 3 (1): 31-7 '31 3677

Simonin, Camille. Procédés géometrique et graphique de photographie métrique judiciaire. R Int de Crimin 2 (2): 131-43 '30 3678

Werner, Otto. Empfindliche Galvanometer für gleich- und Wechselstrom. 208p. bibliog. 196-205. Berlin, Gruyter, 1928 3679

Lamps

Heger-Gilbert. Note sur la spectroscopie à l'épimiscroscope et la spectrographie des objects illuminés à la lumière de Wood. Ann de Méd Lég 9 (10) O '29 3680

Müller, Helmut. Ein neues Gerät für Untersuchungen im ultra-violett-filtrierten Licht. Krimin Monatsh 5: 260-1 N '31 3681

Preuss, Von J. Eine neue Quecksilberdampflampe für kriminalistische Untersuchungen. Arch f Krim 84: 241-3 My '29 3682

Preuss, Von J. Eine neuartige tragbare Analysen-Quarzlampe für Kriminaltechnische Untersuchungen. Krimin Monatsh 4: 67 Mr '30 3683

Salmony, A. Ein Fortschritt in der Analysen-Quarzlampen-Apparatur. Krimin Monatsh 4: 235 O '30 3684

Microscopic

Brüning, A. Entlastung des Beschuldigten durch wissenschaftliche Nachprüfung seiner Aussage. Arch f Krim 89: 146 '31 3685

Importance of microscope and microchemical investigations.

Brunner, E. Das Mikroskop im Dienste der Schriftuntersuchung. Zeitsch f Menschenk 3: 338-49 '28 3686

Foster, L. V. Microscope for the examination and photography of paper. Paper Tr J 85: 47 O 13 '27 3687

Pacini, August J. The ultra-violet detective; uses of the ultra-violet microscope in crime detection. Am J Police Sci 1: 237-45 My '30; same title: Police "13-13" 5: 3-5, 45 Jl '30 3688

Salisbury, George R. The fourth degree. Nat Police Offic 2: 1 D '30 3689

Schaeffer, Edwin. Über die Prüfung von Farbresten mit der Ultra-lamoe im Zusammenhang mit einer mikroskopischen Untersuchung zum Zwecke der Aufdeckung eines Diebstahls. Arch f Krim 86: 68-73 F '30 3690

Schneider, Albert. Compound microscope in detective work. Am J Police Sci 2: 30-44 Ja '31 3691

Teale, Edwin Way. Microscope detectives. Pop Sci 119: 34-6 D '31 3692

The use of optical instruments in criminal investigation. Int Assn Identif Proc 16: 142-5 '30 3693

Prepared by Bausch & Lomb co. Rochester, N.Y.

Welsh, Rex. Police chemistry and microscopy in crime detection. Inst Police Adm Proc 28-33 '29 3694

Photographic

Brüning, A. Eine einfache Tatort- und Stereokamera. Arch f Krim 85: 155-9 O '29 3695

Brüning, A. Eine neue Fingerabdruck- und Reproduktionskamera. Arch f Krim 86: 67-8 F '30 3696

Detektivkameras. Krimin Monatsh 2: 20 Ja '28 3697

Merkel. Die technische Ausrüstung der Lichtbildanstalt einer Landeskriminalpolizeistelle. Polizei 24: 435-6, 481-2 S 5, O 5 '27 3698

The photographic department of the Liverpool city police. Police J [London] 2: 534-45 O '29 3699

Türkel, Siegfried. Eine Lampe für mikrophotographische Aufnahmen in kriminalistischen Laboratorien. Arch f Krim 81: 160-2 S '27 3700

WEAPONS

Basuino, Francis M. The policeman's weapons; radio address. Police J [N Y] 17: 20 D '30 3701

Machine guns and radio . . . for Seattle police. Northwest Police J 6:10 F '29 3702

Police revolvers. Policeman 1: 22-3 Ag '29 **3703**

Schwartzkopf, H. Norman. Revolvers and marksmanship the best insurance for policemen. Int Assn Chiefs Police Proc 37: 55-8 '30 **3704**

Tear Gas

Burglary protection versus fire protection; possible effects upon firemen of tear gas apparatus installed to thwart hold-ups. W Underw & Insur Press 123: 1031-2 N 1 '30 **3705**

Use of tear gas by police department. Am City 57: 326 S '27 **3706**

Whitney, Charles A. Tear gas protective devices. N Y St Assn Chiefs Police Proc 28: 45-51 '28 **3707**

Young, John W. Experiences of police departments with tear gas. Police J [N Y] 15: 30-1 Mr '28 **3708**

Young, John W. Various experiences of police departments with tear gas. Int Assn Chiefs Police Proc 1927: 205-8 **3709**

COMMUNICATION

General

American telephone and telegraph company. Long lines commercial department. Communication systems of the police departments of the United States. 55p. N.Y. November 22, 1930 **3710**

Becker, Burton F. California sheriff sets up code alarm system. Am City 42: 156 Ja '30 **3711**

Belknap, Harry. New flashing police signals, Boston, Mass. Am City 44: 128 Je '31 **3712**

Brown, Fred T. Protection against crime. Calif J Development 19: 13, 24 Ap '29 **3713**

Chicago, Ill. City council. Committee on gas, oil and electric light. Police-signal systems in certain cities. 32p. Chicago, 1928 **3714**

Crawley, Frederick James. Decentralization and the police box system. Police J [London] 1: 118-27 '28 **3715**

Hansley, H. A. [History of communication]. Peace Offic Assn Calif Proc 11: 50-9 '31 **3716**

Köllner. Kriminalpolizeilicher Nachrichtendienst innerhalb der Landjägerei. Krimin Monatsh 5: 35-6 F '31 **3717**

New York telephone company. Coordinating police communication system; proposed layout developed at the request of New York state association of chiefs of police. 7p. tables. N.Y. 1931? **3718**

Parsons, T. W. S. Experiments in radiotelegraphy. Chief Constables' Assn Can Proc 25: 57-62 '29 **3719**

Parsons, Thomas W. S. Wireless telegraphy for police purposes; British Columbia practice. Police J [London] 3: 103-10 Ja '30 **3720**

Rae, Frank B. Police call system protects city banks. W City 7: 13, 47 Ag '31 **3721**

Tenner. Der "Internationale Polizei-Telegraphen-code" (Polcod). Krimin Monatsh 1: 241-4 N '27 **3722**

Voit. Der internationale Kriminalfunkverkehr. Krimin Monatsh 4: 10-11 Ja '30 **3723**

Wade, Clem F. Police television; possibilities for police use of television broadcasting. Police "13-13" 5: 4 D '30 **3724**

Alarms

Blut, W. Eine alarmeinrichtung mit überwachungstromkreisen aus halbeitermaterial. Elektrotech Zeitsch 48: 837-41 Je 16 '27 **3725**

Feagin, F. The system of alarms installed in New York city. N Y St Assn Chiefs Police Proc 28: 61-3 '28 **3726**

Gradenwitz, A. Sensitive relays without magnets. Sci Am 136: 254-5 Ap '27 **3727**
Burglar alarms.

Hyde, Raymond K. Policing electrically; guarding automatically against fire and theft. Ind Eng 88: 520-3 O '30 **3728**

Kierdorff, G. P. De politie-alarm-centrale te 's-Gravenhage. Tijds v d politie 1(20): 369-76 O 3 '28 **3729**

Shaw, D. A. Electrical protection for banks. Arch Forum 48: 927-32 Je '28 **3730**

Weatherbe, R. W. Modern police alarm and signal systems. City Man Yrbk 1931: 181-5 **3731**

Radio

Barkley, Wm. J. Radio goes man-hunting. Sci Am 144: 246-7 Ap '31 **3732**

Catching crooks red-handed by police radio broadcast. Lit Dig 104: 45-7 Ja 16 '30 **3733**

Cox, Kenneth R. The police radio; what the radio will mean to Chicago's police service. Police "13-13" 4: 3-5, 38 F '30 **3734**

Davis, Clyde B. Radio turns crook-catcher. Nation's Bus 18: 100- Mr '30 **3735**

Denver police radio station goes on air. W City 7: 15-16 D '31 **3736**

The Detroit police department radio systems. Am J Police Sci 1: 456-65 S '30 **3737**

Eaton, Geo. F. Radio in police work. Chief Constables' Assn Can Proc 26: 45-7 '30 **3738**

The first year of police radio. . . . Toledo City J 16: 521-2 N 14 '31 **3739**

Geiger, C. W. Equip Berkeley police cars with radio sets. Am City 41: 154 N '29 **3740**

Glasgow, Roy S. Police radio tends to discourage crime, St. Louis, Mo. Am City 43: 152 D '30 **3741**

[Green, Fred W.]. Michigan claims right to operate radio for police. Pub Util 5: 505 Ap 17 '30 **3742**

Grunow, John. Radio to the front; Detroit adopts it. Police "13-13" 4: 22-4 My '29 3743

Hawtrey, F. T. Organization of a motor radio patrol and communication system. Peace Offic Assn Calif Proc 11: 40-3 '31 3744

Hilliard, William. The radio division; the supervisor's report on the Chicago police radio. Police "13-13" 6-7, 35 Je '31 3745

Invisible man hunter. Pop Mech 51: 712-16 My '29 3746

Kaufman, Samuel. How the police are using the radio third degree. Radio N 13: 105-6 Ag '31 3747

Kent, Roscoe. Catching the criminal by police radio. Am City 45: 106 N '31 3748

Kent, Roscoe. Radio in police signal work. Colo Munic 205-8 D '31 3749

McCormick, John A. A historical summary of radio station WMDZ; Indianapolis police, introducing Robert L. Batts. Northwest Police J 10-11 N '31 3750

MacDonald, J. R. Radio equipped police department. Int Assn Identif, Calif Div Proc 15: 62-4 '30

Noack, F. Die Polizei wird das Bildfunkverfahren Lorenz-Korn verwenden. Umschau 32: 236-8 Mr 17 '28 3752

Olander, Oscar G. State-wide broadcasting system promotes crime control [Michigan]. Am City 44: 92-4 F '31 3753

Park, Kenneth C. Michigan. . . "crime" radio. State Trooper 11: 5-6, 19-21 Je '30 3754

Park, Kenneth C. Michigan. . . installation of. . . state-wide radio hook-up. State Trooper 11: 13-14 Jl '30 3755

Park, Kenneth C. Michigan visions a nation-wide radio hook-up to catch criminals. State Trooper 12: 13-14 N '30 3756

Peters, Ralph L. Cops don headphones. Radio N 11: 716-18 F '30 3757

Peters, Ralph L. Manhunts by radio. Radio N 12: 136-8 Ag '30 3758

Peters, Ralph L. New arm of the law. Radio N 11: 826-7 Mr '30 3759

Peters, Ralph L. Police radio routs racketeers; a year's experience with Detroit's radio police cars. Radio N 11: 400-3 N '29 3760

Peters, Ralph L. Radio blocks the getaway. Am Bankers Assn J 21: 1198- Je '29 3761

Peters, Ralph L. Radio revolutionizes police work. Am City 42: 151-2 F '30 3762

Peters, Ralph L. Radio waves vs. crime waves; progress and development of the police radio. Police "13-13" 5: 5-8, 42 Jl '30 3763

Peters, Ralph L. Split-second arrests. Sat Eve Post 202: 68-70 D 7 '29 3764

Police radio system KGPA; Seattle's radio equipped "prowler cars." Northwest Police J 14, 54 D '31 3765

Quinn, William J. Radio used to capture criminals. Pac Munic 45: 372-3 Ag '31 3766

Quinn, William J. San Francisco finds radio great aid in crime detection. Pac Munic 45: 125-6 Mr '31 3767

Quinn, William J. Value of police radio in detection of criminals. San Francisco Munic Rec 5: 9-12 Jl '31 3768

Roche, James. Experiments prove radio's worth in broadcasting orders to police. Calif Highw & Pub Wks 9: 6 Jl '31 3769

Rutledge, William P. "Radio in police work." Mich Assn Chiefs Police Proc 6: 22-31 '29 3770

Rutledge, William P. Radio's growing place in police work. Int Assn Chiefs Police Proc 37: 58-63 '30 3771

Shenefield, H. T. How the radio aids police work [in Toledo]. Nat Munic R 20: 267-71 My '31 3772

Shute, A. G. Radio and police work. Chief Constables' Assn Can Proc 24: 88-92 '28 3773

Squires, J. E. Radio polices a western city. Radio N 9: 1223- My '28 3774

Wiley, Ralph W. Radio, teletype and police signal systems. San Francisco Munic Rec 5: 7-8 Jl '31 3775

Wiley, Ralph W. San Francisco installs complete fire and police broadcasting system. Pac Munic 45: 169-70 Ap '31 3776

Telephone, Teletype and Telegraph

Abbott, F. W. Printing telegraphs for police communications. Police J [London] 4: 398-405 Jl '31 3777

Blakeslee, Harvey. What Portland thinks of the teletype. Northwest Police J 4 N '27 3778

Brandenburg, F. C. Teletype system. Int Assn Identif, Calif Div Proc 16: 101-3 '31 3779

Chicago, Ill. Bureau of fire alarm and police telegraph. Report *in* Annual report of Department of gas and electricity 31, 1927: 44-5; 32, 1928: 42-7; 33, 1929: 47-9; 34, 1930: 43-5 3780

Columbus, Ohio. Department of public safety. Division of fire and police telegraph. Annual report *in* City clerk, City bulletin, Supplement 3781

Discouraging news for criminals in Westchester county. Am City 42: 150 Ap '30 3782

County-wide telephone typewriter system.

Harker, J. H. The invisible arm. Police J [London] 4: 590-7 O '31 3783

Harrel, R. Frank. Teletypewriter aids in police work. Am City 44: 81-4 Je '31 3784

Maps showing network of installations.

Hart, W. C. The telephone-teletype. Int Assn Chiefs Police Proc 1927: 88-91 3785

Henrici, S. Die Strafverfolgungsbehörden und der gesetzliche Schutz des Telegraphen- und Fernsprechgeheimnisses unter Berücksichtigung der drahtlosen Telegraphie und Telephonie. Krimin Monatsh 1: 221-7 O '27 **3786**

McCoy, J. W. Using the teletypewriter to catch criminals; this modern service is the "Seven-leagued boots" of the law enforcement officers. Kan Munic 16-18 Ap '31 **3787**

Morrill, Clarence S. Practical use of statewide telephone-typewriter system. Peace Offic Assn Calif Proc 11: 20-1 '31 **3788**

Murnane, J. E. How the teletype aids New Jersey police work. Nat Munic R 20:192-6 Ap '31 **3789**

Peace officers association of California. Report of Committee to investigate and report on the advisability of establishing immediate inter-communication between cities in California by teletype system. Proceedings 8: 30-49 '28 **3790**

Rhoades, B. K. The telephone typewriter as an aid to police work. N Y St Assn Chiefs Police Proc 29: 75-8 '29 **3791**

Richmond, Va. Fire alarm and police telegraph bureau. Annual reports in Annual reports of Mayor **3792**

Ristow, A. Telephonie oder Telegraphie in Polizeifunkverkehr. Polizei 24: 482, 504 O 5, 20 '27 **3793**

Robinson, F. E. The use of wireless telegraphy and telephony for police purposes. Police J [London] 3: 226-34 Ap '30 **3794**

Sienang, Richard. Die Fernsprechanlage der Gross-Berliner Polizeiverwaltung. Konzern Nachrichten 3 (18): 463-91 '28 **3795**

Timmerman, L. Stephen. New police alarm system. Police J [N Y] 16:19-20 N '28 **3796**

New York city police department telephone-typewriter system.

Toler, W. A. Statewide cooperation in identification of criminals. Va Munic R 4: 68-70 Mr '27 **3797**

Wilson, Fred J. Catching the crook: how teletype-equipped police and sheriff's department of the Pacific coast use science in war against crime. Pac Munic 43:518-21 D '29 **3798**

Wilson, Fred J. Teletype: is it a success? Northwest Police J 6: 11-13 S '29 **3799**

MANUALS, RULES, ETC.

Bose, C[arl] and Fellmann, P[aul]. Der Schriftverkehr des Polizeibeamten. 79, 78p. Berlin, Deutsche Polizeibuchh, 1931 **3800**

Chandler, George Fletcher. The policeman's manual; a standard guide to the latest methods and duties of American police. rev. ed. N.Y. Funk & Wagnalls, 1930 **3801**

Fricke, Charles W. Peace officers manual; containing the police manual adopted and used by the Los Angeles police department; methods of investigation; a discussion of the law and procedure in criminal cases; rules of evidence, etc. ed.8. 70p. Los Angeles, Los Angeles review, 1931 **3802**

Gallery, Michael J. Winning his star: guide to every policeman or other peace officer, such as marshal, sheriff, constable, bailiff, guard, warden, jailer, private detective, prohibition agent, constabulary, etc., with a view of passing the civil service examination. 218p. Milwaukee, Caspar, 1929 **3803**

Galrup, James F. comp. California police officers' manual, 1931. ed.2. Oakland, Calif., A. V. Lake & co. 1931 **3804**

Goddefroy, E. Manuel de police technique. 313p. Bruxelles, Ferdinand Larcier, 1931 **3805**

A handy guide to the police forces of the British empire. ed.11. London, "Police Review" pub. co. 1928 **3806**

Lorenz, Gustav A. Book of instructions for the police force of the city of Cincinnati. 802p. Cincinnati, Police department, 1929 **3807**

Luca, G. de. Manuale di polizia ferroviaria. 92p. Asti, V. Morrico, 1927 **3808**

Meynieux, Et. Guide-formulaire de la gendarmerie dans l'exercice de ses fonctions de police judiciaire civile et militaire. Contenant plus de 400 formules de procès-verbaux appropriés à toutes les circonstances et répondant à tous les besoins. ed.26. Paris, Charles-Lavauzelle, 1930 **3809**

Moriarty, Cecil Charles Hudson. Police law; an arrangement of law and regulations for the use of police officers. 337p. London, Butterworth, 1929 **3810**

Nemitz. Französisches Lehrbuch für Polizeibeamte. Köln, Bukum-Verl. 1930 **3811**

New York (city). Police department. Manual of procedure, by Grover A. Whalen. 260p. New York, 1929 **3812**

Pessoa, Alberto. Guia de tecnica policial. 183p. Coimbra, Imp. da Universidade, 1929 **3813**

Puttkamer, Ernst W. A manual of criminal law and criminal procedure for police. rev. ed. 100p. Chicago, Chicago university press, 1931 **3814**

Rogers, Arthur Wyckoff and Magone, Clifford R. Police officers' manual with forms of charges and outlines of evidence for criminal offences. 256p. Toronto, Carswell, 1931 **3815**

Schmitt, Gustav. Waffentechnisches Unterrichtsbuch für den Polizeibeamten. ed.13. 306p. Berlin, Eisenschmidt, 1931 **3816**

Sheriffs and police officers' association of America. The policeman's handbook of law, especially designed for police officers. 160p. 1928? **3817**

Sir Howard Vincent's police code. ed.17. 351p. London, Butterworth, 1930? 3818

Söderman, Harry and Fontell, Ernst. Handbok I Kriminalteknik. 675p. Stockholm, Wahlström and Widstrand, 1930 3819

Manual of police technique; organization of detective bureaus of Germany, England, France, Italy; psychology of oral testimony; forensic experts; crime investigation; personal identification.

United States. Office of public buildings and public parks of the national capital. Manual for the United States park police. 78p. Washington, June 16, 1927 3820

Vallette, Lucien. Nouveau guide pratique des gardes champêtres des communes et des gardes particuliers. 196p. Paris, Garnier, 1929 3821

Voutta, [Heinrich]. Kraftfahrzeugverkehr für Kraftfahr- und Polizeibeamte. ed.4. rev. 128p. Berlin, Deutsche Polizeibuchh. 1931 3822

Württembergisches Polizeihandbuch. Herausgegeben von der Württemb. Polizeifachschule beim Polizei präsidium Stuttgart. Stuttgart, W. Kohlhammer, 1927-28 3823

PERSONNEL

GENERAL

Atkins, J. B. "A policeman's lot is not a happy one." Indep 121: 15-17 Jl 7 '28 3824

Basuino, Francis M. The policeman's job. Police J [N Y] 16: 13 N '28 3825

Basuino, Francis M. Put the policeman on a business basis. Police J [London] 16: 2-4 Jl '28 3826

Bismarck, E. Versetzungen und Abordnungen von Polizeioffizieren. Polizei 25: 33-9 Ja 20 '28 3827

Borland, Charles B. Fundamentals of police service. Pub Manage 11: 229-40 Mr '29 3828

Brooks, George. Those stupid policemen. Scribner's 81: 261-9 Mr '27 3829

Bucquoy. La gendarmerie d'élite de la garde impériale (1801-1915). R de Gendarm (16) Jl 15 '30 3830

Burbridge, Jos. E. Athletics in the police department. Int Assn Chiefs Police Proc 1927: 48-50; same title: Police J [N Y] 15: 12- N '27 3831

[Carlson, Samuel A.]. Policeman's lot is not a happy one. Am City 38: 83 Ap '28 3832

Certain acute problems of police departments. Am City 45: 75-6 S '31 3833

Excerpts of Wickersham report on police.

Clark, N. M. What color are your wife's eyes? Interview with A. Vollmer. Am Mercury 112: 42-4 N '31 3834

Coatsworth, Emerson. Police efficiency. Chief Constables' Assn Can Proc 24: 120-7 '28 3835

Coatsworth, Emerson. Police efficiency; address. Can B R 7: 169-74 Mr '29 3836

Davis, J. Edgar. Moral fiber in modern times. Peace Offic Assn Calif Proc 10: 47-52 '30 3837

Davis, James E. Police organization to cope with organized crime. Int Police Adm Proc 70-81 '29 3838

Dierske, L. Die Beurteilung der Polizei-Offiziere. 37p. Berlin, Kameradschaft, 1928 3839

Directory of police and traffic officials. Munic Index 1928: 598-9 3840

The efficiency and bravery of the police. Am City 39: 21 S '28 3841

English policeman. Just Peace 93: 277 My 4 '29 3842

Finlinson, Jack. Ideals of the police profession. Int Assn Identif, Calif Div Proc 15: 43-6 '30 3843

Fundamentals of police service. Police J [N Y] 16: 9-10, 29 D '28 3844

Gerk, Joseph A. Higher type police service. Int Assn Chiefs Police Proc 36: 40-3 '29; same title: Police J [N Y] 17: 22-3 S '29 3845

Harding, T. Swann. If only policemen could sing. N Am R 231: 251-6 Mr '31 3846

Johnson, Gerald W. Policeman's bed of roses. Harper's 162: 735-9 My '31 3847

Kilmer, Theron W. The policeman—his health and hygiene. N Y St Assn Chiefs Police Proc 30: 25-8 '30 3848

Kilmer, Theron W. The policeman—his health and hygiene. Police J [N Y] 17: 12, 28 D '30 3849

Langeluttig, Albert. Federal police. Ann Am Acad 146: 41-54 N '29 3850

Lélu. L'évolution de la gendarmerie. R de Gendarm 2 (11) S 15; (12) N 15 '29; 3 (13) Ja 15 '30 3851

Louwage, F. E. Le guépéou. R Belge de Police Adm & Jud (120) F '30 3852

McLellan, Howard. Our inefficient police. N Am R 227:219-28 F '29 3853

Marshall, Donald L. Necessary fundamentals to elevate police work. Peace Offic Assn Calif Proc 9: 49-51 '29 3854

Matheson, Duncan. The modern policeman. Chambers J pt198: 367-8 Je '27 3855

Matheson, Duncan. The "science" bogey; an attack on the fallacy of the "scientific policeman." Police "13-13" 5: 11-12 N '30 3856

[Mencken, H. L.]. Cops and their art. Am Mercury 22: 161-3 F '31 3857

O'Reilly, Joseph J. A sidelight on the New York policeman. Police J [N Y] 15: 5, 31 D '27 3858

Peterson, Leroy. The police and boys' work. Welf 19: 38-60 Ja '28 3859

Philipp, Lothar. Polizei und privater Selbstschutz. Krimin Monatsh 3: 150-2 Jl '29 3860

The police force. L Notes 32: 182 Ja '29 3861

Police from B. C. to A. D.: tracing the genealogy of the policeman. Policeman 1: 17 D '29 3862

Police functions best performed by men and by women police officers. Am City 38: 109-10 My '28 3863

Police patrol systems: 1, Practice in an English county, by Alfred Law; 2, Hours of duty in a crown colony, by J. D. Aitken. Police J [London] 2: 280-96 Ap '29 3864

Police surgeons as police witnesses. Just Peace 94: 709, 741 N 15, 29 '30 3865

Robberson, C. F. A police chief. Peace Offic Assn Calif Proc 10: 27-31 '30 3866

Sanders, G. E. Maintaining police traditions. Chief Constables' Assn Can Proc 24: 83-7 '28 3867

Sinclair, Donald C. A bluenose magistrate's impressions of police forces in general. Chief Constables' Assn Can Proc 25: 24-31 '29 3868

Size of police departments compared with population figures. Am City 43: 23 O '30 3869

Smith, D. C. Police recreation. Va Munic R 4: 323-5 O '27 3870

Street, Arthur L. H. European cities traffic policemen. Am City 41: 104-5 D '29 3871

Sylvester, Richard. The efficiency of the police. Police J [N Y] 15: 24-5 Je '28 3872

Tielhet, Darwin L. All cops are grafters. Outl 157:590-7 Ap 29 '31 3873

Vollmer, August. The scientific policeman. Am J Police Sci 1: 8-12 Ja '30 3874

Vollmer, August. The scientific policeman; introducing a new type of crime fighter. Police "13-13" 5: 5-6, 50 Je '30 3875

Weaver, Elvin D. Courtesy an asset to all police departments. N Y St Assn Chiefs Police Proc 30: 45-6 '30 3876

Weinberg, Harry E. The scientific policeman; a definition of the expert law enforcement officer. Police "13-13" 5: 15-16 Ag '30 3877

Weinberger, Hugo and Walitschek, Anton. Polizeirecht, sein Wesen, seine Grundlagen und gesetzliche Erfassung. 84p. Wien, Beyer, 1927 3878

Wiard, Seth. The army and the policeman. Am J Police Sci 1: 481-6 S '30 3879

Wilcox, Uthai Vincent. The American policeman: city government depends upon the intelligence, the memory, the justice and the adaptability of its policemen. Welf Mag 19: 289-95 Mr '28 3880

Wilkinson, J. R. The world's most scientific police officer: August Vollmer, Chief of police, Berkeley, California. Int Pict Police J 30, 32 My '29 3881

Wykoff, Marguerite. Policeman in Cincinnati. 44p. (Vocational pam no9) Cincinnati, Cincinnati public schools, 216 E. 9 st. 1929 3882

DISCIPLINE

Chase, Don M. Police, law-keepers or law-breakers? World Tomorrow 13: 127-9 Mr '30 3883

Criminal law—defenses—entrapment. S Calif L R 2: 283-94 F '29 3884

Davenport, Walter and Levine, Emmanuel H. Why cops go wrong. Collier's 85: 10-11 My 31 '30 3885

Entrapment as a defense to criminal prosecution. Harv L R 44: 109-13 N '30 3886

Entrapment by government officials. Colum L R 28: 1067-75 D '28 3887

Hopkins, Ernest Jerome. Our lawless police; an indictment of modern police methods of investigation. Police "13-13" 3-4 O '31 3888

Hopkins, Ernest Jerome. Our lawless police; a study of the unlawful enforcement of the law. 392p. N.Y. Viking press, 1931 3889

Study of violence, illegal detention, third degree, and perjury practiced by the police.

Hopkins, Ernest Jerome. The war theory of crime control. New Repub 68: 288-90 O 28 '31 3890

Police use violence to cure crime.

Miller, Wm. Discipline and esprit-de-corps. Chief Constables' Assn Can Proc 25: 62-6 '29 3891

Official lawlessness. L Notes 33: 201 F '30 3892

Official ruthlessness. World Tomorrow 12: 56 F '29 3893

Police discipline. Just Peace 91: 746-7 O 8 '27 3894

Recent cases dealing with police officers. Irish L T 65: 169-70 Jl 18 '31 3895

St. John, Milton. Notes on drinking with cops. Outl 158: 238-9 Je 24 '31 3896

Stone, Donald C. The control and the discipline of police forces. Ann Am Acad 146: 63-73 N '29 3897

When the police are lawless; reply to E. J. Hopkins. Commonweal 14: 413-14 S 2 '31 3898

Wilson, O. W. Police discipline. Int Assn Chiefs Police Proc 36: 122-5 '29 3899

FUNCTIONS: POWERS, DUTIES, LIABILITIES

Amelung. Soll der Chef der Kriminalpolizei Volljurist sein? Krimin Monatsh 5: 219-21 O '31 3900

The authority of peace officers to require the use of property of private persons in the enforcement of the criminal law. Colum L R 29: 637-43 My '29 3901

Behr, Detloff von. Interessiert der Bettler den Kriminalpolizisten? Monats f Kriminalpsychol u Strafrechtsref 22: 559-65 '31 3902

Bowler, Alida C. A police department's social hygiene activities. J Soc Hyg 15: 528-37 D '29 3903

Burke, J. Frank. Relation of law enforcement work and the law of patriotism. Peace Offic Assn Calif Proc 8: 26-30 '28 3904

Contrôle des bohémiens par la gendarmerie française. Polizei im Bild (10) N '29 3905

Cowburn, A. Douglas. The metropolitan policeman as coroner's officer. Police J [London] 2: 397-405 Jl '29 3906

Damages claimed for unlawful imprisonment, county court and police duty. Just Peace 93: 693 N 2 '29 3907

Davis, James E. Should police officers carry firearms when not on duty? Int Assn Chiefs Police Proc 36: 29-31 '29; same title: Police J [N Y] 16: 8-9 Jl '29 3908

Delehanty, M. J. What a New York city police sergeant must know. Panel 9: 54-5 N '31 3909

Delius. Die Polizei als Hilfsorgan des Arrest- und einstweilige Verfügungs-Richters. Leipz Zeitsch f Deut Recht 25: 273-7 Mr 1 '31 3910

Desloovère, Ph. A propos des récentes modifications à la police des chemins de fer. R Belge de Police Adm & Jud (136) Ja '31 3911

Dewez, Em. De la police des audiences. R Belge de Police Adm & Jud (120) Jl '29 3912

Dowson, O. F. The position of police authorities as to acts done by or to constables. Just Peace 92: 663-4, 679-80, 695-6, 710-11 O 13-N 3 '28 3913

Duty of the police to call witnesses. Just Peace 95: 35 Ja 17 '31 3914

Erkens, J. Die Aufgaben der Polizei aus dem Gesetz zur Bekämpfung der Geschlechtskrankheiten. Polizei 24: 428-9 S 5 '27 3915

Fuster and Perreau. Surveillance de la fréquentation scolaire par gendarmerie. R de Gendarm 3 (14) Mr 15 '30 3916

Great Britain. Royal commission on police powers and procedure. Report, March 16, 1929. 161p. (Cmd 3297). London, H. M. Stationery Off. 1929 3917

Powers of police, police investigation of crimes, duties of police *re* street offences, betting, lotteries, etc.; director of public prosecutions, women police, misconduct of police.

Guillaume. Zur Anwendung polizeilicher Zwangsmittel. Polizei 24: 543-5 N 20 '27 3918

Haertel. Kriminalpolizei und Alkoholfrage. Krimin Monatsh 3: 171-3 Ag '28 3919

Heiland. Polizeiliche Unterlagen zur Begutachtung der Alkoholdelikte. Krimin Monatsh 3: 173-4 Ag '29 3920

Heimannsberg. Schutzmannschaft-Sicherheitswehr - Sicherheitspolizei - Schutzpolizei. Polizei 25: 200-1 Ap 10 '28 3921

Holters. Kriminalpolizei und Geschlechtskrankengesetz in der Praxis. Krimin Monatsh 5: 224-7 O '31 3922

Hurley, Thomas F. The officer and the prisoner. Policeman 1: 12, 15 Ag '29 3923

Jorgensen, S. J. Answering emergency calls. Northwest Police J 6: 6-7 Mr '29 3924

Jorgensen, S. J. Prowler car duty. Northwest Police J 6: 8-9 F '29 3925

Kerstiens. Vereinfachungen beim Erlass von polizeilichen Strafverfügungen. Polizei 25: 480-3, 511-14 Ag 5, 20 '28 3926

Lieck, Albert and Morrison, A. C. L. False imprisonment by police officers. Just Peace 92:57-9 Ja 28 '28 3927

McNitt, Rollin L. Extension of police powers. Am Munic 52: 26-30 F '28 3928

Marienfeld. Landjäger und Hellseher. Krimin Monatsh 5: 36-8 F '31 3929

Melcher. Stellung der Polizei gegenüber der Prostitution nach dem Geschlechtskrankengesetz. Krimin Monatsh 4: 97-101 My '30 3930

Muhl. Das Recht der Polizeibeamten zur Personalienfestellung. Krimin Monatsh 2: 236-7 O '28 3931

New York state conference of mayors and other city officials. State bureau of municipal information. Powers of policemen. 22p (typw) (Rep no1105) December 10, 1929 3932

Peppin, Jack Calvin. Comments on constitutional law: police power. 74p. Thesis (J.D.) University of California, 1930 3933

Peter. Die Aufgaben der Polizei bei der Bekämpfung unzüchtiger Schriften, Abbildungen und Darstellungen. Arch f Krim 83: 67-71 Jl '28 3934

Picard and Kiehl. Le gendarmerie doit-elle intervenir en matière de répression des fraudes et des falsifications? Etudes Crimin 5: 1-5 Ja '30 3935

Pierce, Wilbur S. The position of peace officers in relation to handling of crime. Peace Offic Assn Calif Proc 9: 119-21 '29 3936

Police executing process. Just Peace 93: 163 Mr 16 '29 3937

Police liability for false imprisonment. Just Peace 95: 207 Mr 28 '31 3938

Police liability for unlawful acts done to detect crime or arrest criminals. Sol J 73: 359-60 Je 8 '29 3939

Police power and the citizen. Economist 108: 672 Mr 30 '29 3940

Police powers and procedure. Just Peace 93: 199, 215-16, 247-8, 279-80, 295-6 Mr 30-My 11 '28 3941

Police powers to bail. Just Peace 92: 547 Ag 18 '28 3942

Police seizures of property. Just Peace 95: 98-101 F 14 '31 3943

Policeman as a community adviser. Am City 38: 93 F '28 3944

Powers of the police. Sol J 73: 812 D 7 '29 3945

Questioning an accused person. Just Peace 92: 743-4, 758-9 N 17, 24 '28 3946

Rapacz, Max P. Protection of officers who act under unconstitutional statutes. Minn L R 11: 585-604 Je '27 3947

Report of the Royal commission on police powers. Sol J 73: 199, 245-6 Mr 30, Ap 20 '29; same title: L Times 167: 258, 322-4, 342, 344 Mr 30-Ap 27 '29 3948

Rinehart, John C. Tracing people—lost, stolen and strayed away. Am City 41: 114 O' 29; same title: Police J [N Y] 17: 3- N '29 3949

Sherril, C. O. Duties of a policeman. Pub Manage 10: 334-6 Ap '28 3950

Should police officers carry firearms when off duty? Am City 41: 122 S '29 3951

Sirks. Die Polizei und die Rauschgiftfrage. Krimin Monatsh 5: 6-11 Ja '31 3952

Smith, J. P. Psychology applied by the police officer. Detective 42:2- S '27 3953

Smith, J. P. Psychology applied by the police officer. Int Assn Identif Proc 13: 130-3 '27 3954

Sullivan, John J. The police officer as a witness. Northwest Police J 6: 15 Ag '29 3955

Taylor, Clarence P. Police handling of crowds at special events, processions and fires. Am City 42: 149-50 Mr '30 3956

Taylor, Clarence P. The policeman and the traffic offender. Am City 43: 171-3 S '30 3957

Vaughan, George C. Additional duties imposed on the police. Police J [London] 3: 334-41 Jl '30 3958

Vulterini, E. Diritto di caccia e bracconaggio nella Venezia Giulia. Riv Pen di Dott, Legis e Giuris 105: 276-84 Mr '27 3959

Weinberg, Harry E. Drafting the citizen; the law on the commandeering of private automobiles. Police "13-13" 5: 8, 25 Ja '31 3960

Werber, E. K. Die Geschlechtsasozialen und ihre polizeiliche Behandlung. Deut Gesell z Bekämpf d Geschlechtskrankh Mitt 25 (1): 2-7 '27 3961

POLITICS

Butler, Smedley D. Making war on the gangs; a plan to take the police out of politics. Forum 85: 134-41 Mr '31 3962

Marsh, H. W. Independent civil service commission only defense against politics. Nat Munic R 16: 721-3 N '27 3963

Meijer, D. H. Politie en politiek. Koloniale Stud 15: 578-610 O '31 3964

Merriam, Charles E. The police, crime and politics. Ann Am Acad 146: 115-20 N '29 3965

PENSIONS

Cincinnati. Bureau of governmental research. Report on an actuarial investigation of the police relief fund of the city of Cincinnati, as of May 1, 1930. 40p. (mim) (Rep no24) Cincinnati, Ohio, October 1930 3966

Conyngton, Mary A. Public service retirement systems, United States, Canada, and Europe. U S Bur Lab Statist Bul (477): 119-25, 131-3, 134-70 Ja '29 3967

Metcalf, C. S. Report [to the Cleveland city council] relative to proposed pension plan of the police and fire divisions. Cleveland City Rec 15: 1076-8 S 5 '28 3968

O'Reilly, Joseph J. A defense of the police pension system of New York. Police J [N Y] 15: 16-17 Ja '28 3969

O'Reilly, Joseph J. A plea for the existing police and fire pensions. Police J [N Y] 15: 12-13 F '28 3970

O'Reilly, Joseph J. Police pensions; radio address. Police J [N Y] 15: 15 D '27 3971

Philadelphia. Chamber of commerce. Report on the police pension fund. 9p. February 1927 3972

Police pensions. Am City 36: 48 Ja '27 3973

Policeman's pension. Just Peace 93: 562 S 7 '29 3974

Retirement systems for police and firemen. Am City 40: 173 Ja '29 3975

Retirement systems for police and firemen. U S Bur Lab Statist Bul (477): 118-70 '29 3976

Robinson, R. Police pensions. Chief Constables' Assn Can Proc 26: 15-18 '30 3977

United States. Bureau of labor statistics. Retirement systems for police and firemen. M Lab R 27: 24-39 O '28 3978

SALARIES

Beyer, William C. and Toerring, Helen C. The policeman's hire. Ann Am Acad 146: 135-46 N '29 3979

Compensation and hours of police officers in Virginia municipalities. Va Munic R 5: 78-80 Ap '28 3980

Crandall, Esther. Salaries of policemen and firemen in 35 cities, 1928. 5p. (Statist ser no1) N.Y. Municipal administration service, 1928; same title: Nat Munic R 17: 268-79 My '28 3981

Dunlap, A. Higher salaries for identification experts. Detective 42: 3- Ag '27 3982

Greenman, E. D. Police and firemen's salaries in New York state cities. Am City 44: 145 My '31 3983

Harriman, Celia. Personnel and salaries of police departments in Wisconsin cities, 1929. 16p. (mim) (Information rep no74) Madison, Wisconsin university, Extension division, November 1928 3984

Lewis, Lorna L. Personnel, salary and working conditions in police departments, cities of over 30,000 population in the United States. 83p. (mim) Madison, Wisconsin information bureau, 1928 3985

[Municipal administration service]. Policemen's salaries, hours . . . in 49 cities. Am City 42: 108-9 Ap '30 3986

New Jersey state league of municipalities. Bureau of municipal information. 1927 policemen's salaries in New Jersey municipalities. 3p. (mim) Trenton, 1927 3987

O'Reilly, Joseph J. An appeal for an 8-hour working day. Police J [N Y] 15: 5 N '27 3988

O'Reilly, Joseph J. The new wage law for police and firemen. Police J [N Y] 15: 3 Mr '28 3989

Police and firemen's salaries in New York state cities. Am City 44: 145 My '31 3990

Policemen's salaries, hours, etc. in 49 cities. Am City 42: 108-9 Ap '30 3991

Salaries in the police departments of the principal cities. M Lab R 30: 118-38 Ja '30 3992

Salaries of police chiefs in Wisconsin cities. Am City 42: 123 Mr '30 3993

Table of police and firemen's salaries. Mich Munic R 24 F '30 3994

United States. Congress. House. Committee on District of Columbia. Salary increases for policemen and firemen in the District of Columbia: hearings on the bill H.R. 5713, January 31, 1930. 73p. Washington, 1930 (71st Cong. 2d sess) 3995

Wages of enforcement. New Repub 58: 187 Ap 3 '29 3996

SELECTION AND PROMOTION

Baker, G. B. The selection and training of recruits and promotion of officers. Chief Constables' Assn Can Proc 26: 65-6 '30 3997

Berkeley, Calif. Police department. Application questionnaire. 8p. (mim) Berkeley, January 25, 1930? 3998

Bureau of public personnel administration. Partially standardized tests for policewomen. Pub Personnel Stud 5: 259-74 '27 3999

Dickson, Samuel J. The qualifications for policemen. Police J [N Y] 16: 19, 32 Ja '29 4000

Drew, James T. What are the attributes of a good policeman. Peace Offic Assn Calif Proc 10: 38-9 '30 4001

Garrett, E. W. How police heads are appointed in three countries: [United States, Canada and England]. Panel 9: 21-3 Mr '31 4002

Measurement of the intelligence of policemen. Science ns65: sup10-12 Ap 1 '27 4003

Merrill, Maud. Intelligence of policemen. J Personnel Res 5: 11-15 Ap '27 4004

Moriarty, Cecil C. H. The police recruit. Police J [London] 2: 453-66 Jl '29 4005

National crime commission's report on the abstract intelligence of police officers. Pub Personnel Stud 5: 74-80 Ap '28 4006

New York state conference of mayors and other municipal officials. Bureau of training and research. Model plan for the selection of patrolmen. 20p. (Pub no8) Albany, 1931 4007

Nolting, Orin F. Important considerations in the selection of patrolmen. Am City 40: 124-5 Ap '29 4008

Nolting, Orin F. The selection of patrolmen [Syracuse, N Y]. Police J [N Y] 16: 19-20 Je '29 4009

O'Rourke, L. J. The use of scientific tests in the selection and promotion of police. Ann Am Acad 146: 147-59 N '29 4010

Osborn, C. M. Kenosha's merit system for policemen. Pub Manage 9:440-1 My '27 4011

Partially standardized promotion tests for police sergeant. Pub Personnel Stud 5: 51-65 Mr '27 4012

The perfect policeman. Just Peace 92: 435-6 Je 30 '28 4013

Physical tests for policemen. Am City 44: 23 Mr '31 4014

Qualifications of patrolmen. Pub Manage 13: 100-5 Mr '31 4015

Selecting and training police officers. Pub Personnel Stud 7: 182-3 D '29 4016

The selection of patrolmen in Syracuse. Pub Personnel Stud 7: 54-6 Ap '29 4017

A suggested method for the selection of patrolmen. Pub Manage 13: 105-7 Mr '31 4018

Syracuse, N.Y. Municipal research commission. The selection of patrolmen in Syracuse, New York. 48p. (mim) January 1929 4019

Telford, Fred. Tests for selecting police sergeants. Am City 36: 665-7 My '27 4020

Thompson, Hollis R. and Greening, J. A. Berkeley seeks patrolmen rather than depend on voluntary applications. Pub Manage 13: 102-4 Mr '31 4021

Viteles, Morris S. Psychological methods in the selection of policemen in Europe. Ann Am Acad 146: 160-5 N '29 4022

Walker, W. G. Politics versus civil service and efficiency; or, should chiefs be appointed subject to civil service regulations? Police J [N Y] 15: 20-1 Jl '27 4023

West, E. A. Requirements for a modern police officer. Peace Offic Assn Calif Proc 10: 77-9 '30 4024

Wiewiorowski. Röntgenserienuntersuchungen bei der Schutzpolizei. Aerztl Monats (7): 193-215 Jl '29 4025

TRAINING AND EDUCATION

Barck. Die Organisation des Fernunterrichts für den Sicherheitsdienst. Krimin Monatsh 1: 147-8 Jl '27 4026

Barck. Das Polizeiinstitut in Berlin. Monats f Kriminalpsychol u Strafrechtsref 19: 109-12 F '28 4027

Barck. Die Schulausbildung der Gendarmerie. Krimin Monatsh 4: 241-2 N '30 4028

Barry, A. G. Courses for Kenosha policemen. Municipality 23: 3-6 Ja '28 4029

Barry, A. G. Courses for Wisconsin's policemen. Pub Manage 10: 67-70 F '28; same title: Police J [N Y] 15: 25-6 Ap '28 4030

Barry, A. G. Needs and goals for police training. J Crim L & Crimin 22: 171-95 Jl '31 4031

Barry, A. G. Selected list of references for police school. Am J Police Sci 2: 454-9 S '31 4032

Bartels, L. Die freie Fortbildung der Poliziebeamten. Polizei 25: 223-5 Ap 10 '28 4033

Basuino, Francis M. The police training school in St. Louis, Mo. Police J [N Y] 15: 5 My '28 4034

Bildungswoche für Polizeibeamte der Provinz Oberschlesien. Polizei 24: 495-6 O 20 '27 4035

Booth, Bates. Courses for policemen at the University of Southern California. Am J Police Sci 2: 349-51 Jl '31 4036

Borgerhoff, Th. Le dixième anniversaire de l'école de criminologie et de police scientifique. R Int de Crimin 3 (5): 379-400 '31 4037

Boyesen, R. R. Los Angeles police training school. Police J [N Y] 14: 11- Mr '27 4038

Brereton, George H. San Jose state college police school. Int Assn Identif, Calif Div Proc 16: 98-100 '31 4039

Bundesen, Herman N. The New York police college. Police "13-13" 5: 9-12 Mr '30 4040

Cahalane, Cornelius F. The need for and benefits to be derived from police training. Int Assn Chiefs Police Proc 36: 87-92 '29 4041

Cahalane, Cornelius F. Police training. Ann Am Acad 146: 166-9 N '29 4042

Cahalane, Cornelius F. Training of police. N Y St Assn Chiefs Police Proc 28: 38-41 '28 4043

Carroll, Abner A. Training of policemen; discussion. Mich Assn Chiefs Police Proc 6: 15-22 '29 4044

Clifton, C. C. A school to combat crime. Am Bankers Assn J 20: 471- D '27 4045

Colleges for cops. Policeman 1: 22 S '29 4046

Course of study at the University of Paris Institute of criminology; translated by L. Kaempfer. Am J Police Sci 2: 528-31 N '31 4047
Reprint of Annales de médecine légale 11 (9) inside of front cover N '31.

Cross, William I. Departmental training of policemen. Mich Assn Chiefs Police Proc 6: 12-14 '29 4048

Degenhardt. Das preussische Polizeischulwesen. Polizei 25:220-3 Ap 10 '28 4049

Degner. Warum soll der Kriminalbeamte Sport treiben? Polizei 25: 43-6 Ja 20 '28 4050

Demoll. Lehrmittel bei der Polizeischule. Polizei 24: 230-2 My 20 '27 4051

Dengler, Harry M. Correspondence study lessons on criminal investigation. (mim) Washington, U. S. Bureau of prohibition, May 15, 1930 4052

Dengler, Harry M. Training of prohibition enforcement officers in the United States. Am J Police Sci 2: 45-51 Ja '31 4053

Ecole de police au Congo belge. Polizei im Bild (10) N '29 4054

Fairbairn, William Ewart. Scientific self-defense. 165p. N.Y. Appleton, 1931 4055
Methods of dealing with armed and unarmed assailants.

Finlinson, J. J. Police training schools. City Man Yrbk 1931:160-5 4056

La Fontaine. Lichtbildwettbewerb der Beamten des badischen staatlichen Sicherheitsdienstes bei der Badischen Polizeischule. Krimin Monatsh 4: 203-5 S '30 4057

For your notebook: a typical program for "short course" on law enforcement in Iowa. Justice 1: 25, 35 D '28 4058
Iowa state sheriffs' association.

Funston, William H. Educational problems of a police force. Int Assn Chiefs Police Proc 1927: 44-7; summary: Raising educational standards for police. Am City 37: 370 S '27 4059

Funston, William H. Police education. Police J [N Y] 15: 15-16 Jl '27 4060

Gauditz. Was ich von der Polizeischule für Leibesübungen mit heimbrachte. Polizei 25: 681-2 N 5 '28 4061

Gilbert. Über Drill und Erziehung in der Polizei. Polizei 25: 529-31 S 5 '28 4062

G[illard], J[ules]. L'Ecole des sciences criminelles de l'Université de Louvain. R de Dr Pén et de Crimin 10: 149-60 F '30 4063

[Goddard, Calvin]. Outline of teaching program for a course in methods of scientific crime detection. Am J Police Sci 2: 67-9 Ja '31 4064

Gossage, Ralph E. Bibliography of police training and police schools. 4p. (typw) N.Y. Municipal reference library, January 27, 1930 4065

Grenzow, Daisy B. Training to be a policeman. World R 8: 59 F 25 '29 4066

Hall-Dallwood, J. Police training and education. Police J [London] 2: 636-42 O '29 4067

Harrell, C. A. Police school developed from local material. Am City 43: 158 N '30 4068

Heimannsberg. Prüfungen auf der Polizeischule. Polizei 25: 704-5 N 20 '28 4069

Herr, Fred A. A police traffic school conducted for every uniformed man. Nation's Traffic 2: 9 Ja '29 4070

Hildebrand, E. Bildungsfragen der Polizeibeamten. Polizei 24: 460-2, 484-5 S 20, O 5 '27 4071

Hodgetts, Cal. Should all police officers be qualified in first aid? Chief Constables' Assn Can Proc 24: 106-13 '28 4072

Hopkins, Albert A. Policemen are made, not born. Sci Am 142: 286-9 Ap '30 4073
New York police college.

Hopkins, P. F. Police training necessary. Am Munic 54: 15-18 F '30 4074

Horst, Albert. Der Dienstvorgesetzte als Lehrer. 223p. Berlin, Gersbach & Sohn, 1927 4075

Hunter, John. Glasgow police training school. Police J [London] 4: 83-99 Ja '31 4076

L'Institut de police scientifique de Lausanne. R Int de Crimin 1: 317-20 S '29 4077

The Institute of police science at the University of Lausanne [Switzerland]. Am J Police Sci 1: 474-80 S '30 4078
Institut de police scientifique, Université de Lausanne.

Instruction for the control of mobs by non-lethal chemicals. 29p. (mim) (Chemical warfare school mim no233). Edgewood arsenal, Md., Duplication plant, Chemical warfare school, 1931 4079

Italy. Ministero dell'interno. Bollettino della Scuola superiore di polizia e dei servizi tecnici annessi (Scuola di policia scientifica), 7 fascl8—9 fasc20 '28-'30. Roma, Istituto poligrafico dello stato libreria, 1929-31 4080

Jahresbericht des Polizeiinstituts. Polizei 25: 419-21 Jl 5 '28 4081

Le jiu-jitsu à l'Ecole de police de Lodz. Polizei im Bild 3 (11) D '29 4082

Jorgensen, S. J. "Come along" holds: jiu-jitsu for policemen. Northwest Police J 6: 13, 74-7 Jl '29 4083

Kleinschmidt, F. Wissenschaft und Praxis. Deut Zeitsch f d ges gerichtl Med 10: 249-52 Ag '27 4084

Klemm. Die erste Thüringische Polizeiwoche. Polizei 24: 402-5 Ag 20 '27 4085

Koch. Augewandtes Schiessen. Polizei 25: 6-7 Ja 5 '28 4086

Langenscheidt. Der 4. Polizeimajors-Anwärterlehrgang. Polizei 25: 337-8, 360 My 20, Je 5 '28 4087

League of Kansas municipalities. Police training school. Outline of instruction, police training school, June 1-6, 1931, Wichita, Kansas. 191p. (mim) 1931 4088

LeValley, Victor R. Hartford police go to school. Police J [N Y] 15: 28-9, 32 F '28 4089

Longfellow, Wilbur Edmund. New emphasis in life saving and first aid in police department training. Am City 37: 643-6 N '27 4090

Los Angeles, Calif. Police department. Report of conference with the executive heads and unit commanders of the. . . Department conducted. . . October 23-November 25, 1931 by the Division of vocational education, Los Angeles city schools. 45p. (mim) [Los Angeles] 1931 4091

McDonagh, Martin J. B. Police school graduates. State Trooper 8: 13-14 Ap '27 4092

May, Samuel C. Schools of instruction. Peace Offic Assn Calif Proc 9: 80-1 '29 4093

Merkel, W. Abschluss des ersten Weiterbildungslehrganges für obere Verwaltungspolizeibeamte beim Polizeiinstitut in Berlin. Polizei 25: 20-1, 53-4 Ja 5, 20 '28 4094

Metzger, E. Ein kriminologisches Institut an der Universität Marburg. Polizei 25: 226-8 Ap 10 '28 4095

Michigan hopes to expand the scope of state police training school. State Trooper 12: 21-2 F '31 4096

Moore, Albert B. Education of policemen. N Y St Assn Chiefs Police Proc 28: 56-7 '28 4097

Moore, Albert B. Police training in New York state, 1928-1929. N Y St Assn Chiefs Police Proc 29: 27-31 '29 4098

Moriarty, Cecil C. H. The making of an English policeman. Police J [London] 2: 1-9 Ja '29 4099

Morris, R. W. Police training. N Y St Assn Chiefs Police Proc 30: 31-3 '30 4100

New York (city). Police department. Police college. School of horsemanship for the year 1930. 12p. N.Y. 1929 4101

New York (city). Police department. Police college. School of aviation for the year 1930. 23p. N.Y. c1929 4102

New York (city). Police department. Police college. School of detectives; course in criminology for the year 1930. 48p. N.Y. 1929 4103

New York (city). Police department. Police college. School of motor transport. 39p. N.Y. [1929] 4104

New York (city). Police department. Recruits' training school. Syllabus. 98p. N.Y. [1929] 4105

New York municipalities promote police training system. Am City 39: 153 Jl '28 4106

New York state conference of mayors and other city officials. State bureau of municipal information. Police training facilities in New York state. 3p. (typw) (Rep no2417) Albany, May 1, 1928 4107

[New York state conference of mayors and other municipal officials and the New York state association of police chiefs]. Institute for police chiefs of New York state. 11p. (mim) [Albany] 1931 4108

Niles, Harry M. The primary course in the education and training of the police officer. Police J [London] 2: 529-33 O '29 4109

Nine police training schools being established in New York state. Am City 39: 107 N '29 4110

Nolte, Wilhelm. Psychologie für Polizeibeamte. Ein Abriss. 132p. Berlin, Bali-Verl. 1928 4111

O'Connell, John J. The police academy, city of New York. Spring 3100 23-5 D '31 4112

O'Sullivan, F. Dalton. Curriculum for a proposed police school. . . Criminologist [Chicago] 5: 24-5 Je '29 4113

O'Sullivan, F. Dalton. [Scientific course in police procedure—secret service and crime investigation]. Criminologist [Chicago] 5: 17-19 Je '29 4114

Pepin, R. D. Training "rookie" patrolmen. State Trooper 8: 25-6 Mr '27 4115

Philipp, Lothar. Vorschlag zur Einrichtung eines Kriminalpolizei-Instituts. Krimin Monatsh 1: 206-10 S '27 4116

Police and fire training schools. Toledo City J 13 (35) S 1 '28 4117

Police officers go to school [Colorado and Kansas]. Pub Manage 13: 271 Ag '31 4118

Police school dean urges adequate training and salaries. Am City 44: 133 Ap '31 4119

The police school of the University of Chicago. Police "13-13" 4: 15-16 D '29 4120

Police school offers courses at Williamette university, Oregon. Pac Munic 45: 31-2 Ja '31 4121

Police training, the Birmingham police school. Just Peace 92: 750 N 17 '28 4122

Police training schools. Munic Ref Lib Notes 14: 114-15 S 5 '28 4123

Police training schools being established in New York state and New Jersey. Am City 39: 107 N '28 4124

Police training schools placed on permanent basis in New York state. Am City 40: 128 Ap '29 4125

A policeman's university [New York]. Northwest Police J 7: 13, 94-8 Je '30 4126

Die preussischen Ausbildungs vorschriften. Polizei 25: 641, 665 O 5, 20 '28 4127

Quinn, Wm. J. Schooling police officers. Peace Offic Assn Calif Proc 11: 46-50 '31 4128

Ragsdale, George T. The police continuation school of Louisville, Kentucky. Police J [N Y] 16: 22 Je '29 4129

Ragsdale, George T. The police training school. Ann Am Acad 146: 170-6 N '29; same title: Police J [N Y] 17: 15-16, 24 My '30 4130

Ragsdale, George T. The training of policemen. Police J [N Y] 14: 59-60 F '27 4131

Raising educational standards for police. Am City 37: 370 S '27 4132

Randall, Martha. Portland police school. Policewoman's Int Bul 4 (36): 5-6 F '28 4133

Rausch. "Eine kritische Betrachtung über das Polizeibildungswesen in Preussen." Polizei 25: 707-8 N 20 '28 4134

Rechter, Gustave de. The school of criminology and of scientific police of Belgium. Ann Am Acad 146: 193-8 N '29 4135

Rodgers, Don. Michigan giving recruit troopers intensive training under new system. State Trooper 12: 9-10 Ag '31 4136

Roediger, W. Das Sinnbild (Denkbild) im Polizeifachunterricht. Polizei 25: 506-8 Ag 20 '28 4137

Rutledge, W. P. comp. Detroit police department training school for police service. 119p. Revised by Charles Rhodes. Detroit, Police department, 1929 4138

Ryan, Paul C. Massachusetts police chief wants school of police training. State Trooper 12: 7-8 Mr '31 4139

Schaewen, E. v. Wirtschaft und Recht. Betrachtungen über Ziele und Wege des Unterrichts in den Wirtschaftswissenschaften im Rahmen der Ausbildung der Polizeibeamten. Polizei 24: 198-200 My 5 '27 4140

Schelle, P. Die Schiessausbildung der Polizei-Verwaltungsbeamten. Polizei 24: 556 N 20 '27 4141

Schools for the man-hunters. Pop Mech 52: 418-23 S '29 4142

Schunck, E. Aufgabenstellung im polizeilichen Fachunterricht. Polizei 25: 679-80 N 5 '28 4143

Sempill, C. I. The making of an East African policeman. Police J [London] 1: 669-81 '28 4144

Sheriffs' and police officers' association. Efficiency course for law enforcement officers. Chicago, 139 N. Clark st. 1931 4145

Shute, A. G. Advanced training for police officers. Chief Constables' Assn Can Proc 25: 40-4 '29 4146

Smith, Harold D. Discussion of a training school for policemen. Mich Assn Chiefs Police Proc 6: 66-8 '29 4147

Snook, R. A. State police school successful. State Trooper 10: 13-14 Mr '29 4148

Snook, R. A. Will young recruits make good? How they're trained in New Jersey. State Trooper 10: 15, 17 N '28 4149

Sowers, D. C. Training schools for police officers. Colo Munic 6: 21-4 F '30 4150

Stumpf. Stand der Ausbildungsfrage in Hessen. Bl f Gefängniskunde 60: 38-45 '29 4151

Stutsman, J. O. A uniform, a club and a gun—or a profession. Pris J 11: 4-11 Ja '31 4152

Training for Wisconsin policemen. Municipality 26: 209 O '31 4153

The training of detectives in Sweden. J Crim L & Crimin 22: 292 Jl '31 4154

Training the policeman. Sol J 74: 747 N 8 '30 4155

Türkel, Siegfried. Die Kriminologische Ausbildung des höheren Polizeibeamten, des Strafrichters und des Staatsanwaltes. R Int de Crimin 1: 337-57 O '29 4156

Two new courses, one in police training and one in scientific methods of crime detection. Am J Police Sci 2: 532-7 N '31

Scientific crime detection laboratory, Northwestern university.

United States. Department of war. Office of the chemical officer. Headquarters Hawaiian department. Chemical warfare training memorandum: information and suggestions for the control of mobs by the use of non-lethal chemical agents. 29p. (mim) Oct. 1, 1931 4158

Uzzell, Thos. H. Training the New York police. Police "13-13" 4: 8-12, 62 O '29 4159

Van den Bergh. Das Polizei-Institut in Berlin. Polizei 24: 487-9 O 20 '27 4160

Vienna. Police department. Criminalistic institute. Prospectus and information leaflets regarding scope and activities. 1929? 4161

Whalen, Grover. "Enter to learn—go forth to serve": the New York police college is based on that fundamental. Police J [N Y] 17: 3-7, 23 Mr '30 4162

Whalen, Grover. The New York police college. Police J [London] 3: 342-58 Jl '30 4163

Wiegand. Die kriminalistische Fortbildung der Landjägerbeamten. Krimin Monatsh 2: 217-18 O '28 4164

Wiese. Praktische Schiessausbildung der Polizei. Polizei 25: 675-9 N 5 '28 4165

Williamette university. College of law. Police school. Lectures given at Second annual school, March 9-14, 1931. 75p. (mim) 4166

Police department organization, police records, crime prevention, criminal evidence, search and seizure, criminal psychology.

Williams, Eustis. The "cop" invades the class room; Chicago university offers novel course in which policemen are students. Welf Mag 19: 823-7 Je '28 4167

Wilson, O. W. Picking and training police and traffic officers. Am City 42: 115-18 My '30 4168

Wilson, O. W. The Wichita [Kansas] police school: a discussion of the methods used in training policemen together with the curriculum. Kan Munic 11-13 Je '30 4169

Wisconsin. University. University extension division. The first annual Wisconsin police course, Madison, Wisconsin, October 26-29, 1931; in cooperation with the League of Wisconsin municipalities, Wisconsin police chiefs' association, Milwaukee police department. [Madison 1931] 4170

Woods, Arthur. Some aspects of training for police service. Police J [London] 2: 355-66 Jl '29 4171

Target Practice

Anuschat, Erich. Pistolen- und Revolverschiessen im Polizei- und Sicherheitsdienst. 60p. Berlin, Gerstmann, 1928 4172

Cox, Dan. Training peace officers in the use of firearms. Peace Offic Assn Calif Proc 10: 97-8 '30 4173

Delius. Der Waffengebrauch. Polizei 25: 119-21, 150-1 Mr 5, 20 '28 4174

Fitzgerald, J. Henry. Target practice. N Y St Assn Chiefs Police Proc 29: 34-40 '29 4175

Frazer, Wm. D. Pistol practice is vital. Northwest Police J 7: 11-12 My '30 4176

Goddard, Calvin. Police pistol practice. Am J Police Sci 1: 353-7, 444-55 Jl, S '30 4178

Hallanan, W. M. The importance of regular target practice. Peace Offic Assn Calif Proc 10: 95-7 '30 4179

Jones, Roy D. Gunfighting police doom gangsters. Pop Mech 54: 452-7 S '30 4180

Jorgensen, S. J. Gun disarming. Northwest Police J 6: 12-13 Ap '29 4181

Jorgensen, S. J. Quick on the draw; easy on the trigger. Northwest Police J 6: 8-9 Ja '29 4182

Jorgensen, S. J. "Shaking down" the gunman; an expert tells policemen how to protect themselves. Northwest Police J 5: 8-9 D '28 4183

Pollard, Hugh B. C. The pistol in practice. Police J [London] 4: 522-30 O '31 4184

Roche, Austin J. Care and use of firearms by policemen. Nat Police Offic 2: 1-2 N; 3 D '30 4185

Shoot above the waist. New Repub 68: 60 S 3 '31 4186

Stop reckless shooting. Outl 149: 141 My 23 '28 4187

POLICE OTHER THAN MUNICIPAL

SHERIFFS AND CONSTABLES

Brower, Floyd. The sheriff's pay-check. Northwest Police J 5: 26-7, 31, 37-8 F '28 4188

The chief constable in court. Just Peace 92: 744 N 17 '28 4189

Cress, Gerald. A sheriff tries crime prevention. J Crim L & Crimin 22: 422-9 S '31 4190

Dewar, Frank D. The Sheriff's department in emergencies. Los Angeles Chron 14: 12 My 29 '31 4191

Dickinson, William Croft, ed. The sheriff court book of Fife, 1515-1522; transcribed and edited. 440p. Edinburgh, Constable, for Scottish historical society, 1928 4192

Fitzgerald, William J. San Francisco sheriff's duties. "2-0" Police J 7: 5-6 N '28 4193

Giauque, Florien. Ohio constable's guide; a manual for constables, marshals, and other ministerial officers in Ohio. ed.9. rev. 279p. Cincinnati, Anderson, 1931 4194

Gregg, Benjamin Moore and Lightburn, J. E. Police constable's guide to his daily work (and what he ought to know about criminal law and police practice). ed.5. enl. 475p. London, E. Wilson, 1929 4195

Karraker, Cyrus Harrell. The seventeenth-century sheriff: a comparative study of the sheriff in England and the Chesapeake colonies, 1607-1689. 219p. Chapel Hill, University of North Carolina press, 1930 4196

Killick, Victor W. A glimpse at the sheriff's office. Tax Dig 6: 304-8 S '28 4197

Los Angeles county. Bureau of efficiency. Survey of the sheriff's department of the county of Los Angeles, California, 1929. 221p. [Los Angeles] 1929 4198

Police organization, Bureau of records, constabulary, detention camps, discipline, education, personnel, contact office, county jail, office of sheriff, modus operandi system, photographic unit, sheriffs substations.

Los Angeles county. Sheriff's department. Annual reports, 1928-1930. Los Angeles, 1928-30 4199

Bureau of records and identification, jail, detention camps, prisoners classified by crimes and occupations; Sheriff relief association.

Michigan university. William L. Clements library of American history. Eighteenth century documents relating to the royal forests, the sheriffs and smuggling. 328p. (Univ of Mich pub, Hist & Pol Sci v7) N.Y. Macmillan, 1928 **4200**

Moley, Raymond. The sheriff and the constable. Ann Am Acad 146: 28-33 N '29 **4201**

P., A. M. The old-time constable as portrayed by the dramatists. Police J [London] 2: 656-73 O '29 **4202**

Parish constables and high constables. Just Peace 93: 344 Je 1 '29 **4203**

Raine, William MacLeod. Famous sheriffs and western outlaws. 294p. N.Y. Doubleday, 1929 **4204**

Roster of counties, county seats and sheriffs of the United States. Peace Offic 5: 11-24 S '27 **4205**

South Dakota. State sheriff. Annual report. 10, 1926/27. Pierre [1927] **4206**

Toronto. Chief constable. Annual report, 1927-1931. Toronto, 1928-32 **4207**
Offenses, statistics of crimes, warrants, police patrol signals.

Traeger, Wm. I. Burglary and robbery matters. Los Angeles Chron 14: 12, 14 S 16 '31 **4208**
Burglary-robbery detail of sheriff's office.

Traeger, Wm. I. Crime and criminals. Los Angeles Chron 14: 12, 14 O 30 '31 **4209**

Traeger, Wm. I. Sheriff's Bureau of records and identification. Los Angeles Chron 14: 11 D 23 '31 **4210**

Traeger, Wm. I. Sheriff's office administration. Los Angeles Chron 14: 12 Ap 30 '31 **4211**

Traeger, W[m.] I. What constitutes an ideal sheriff's department. Los Angeles Chron 14: 15, 22 Ja 31 '31 **4212**

SPECIAL POLICE

Commonwealth club of California. Rural police. Trans 23 (6): 209-40 Je 26 '28 **4213**

How fire police function in New York communities [36 towns]. Am City 40: 139 Je '29 **4214**

Larrieu. Service de maréchaussée aux armées. R de Gendarm 1: 163-74 Mr 15 '28 **4215**

McKinley, Charles. Special police patrol in Portland, Oregon. Nat Munic R 18: 509-12 Ag '29 **4216**

Smith, Bruce. Rural police protection. *In* Illinois association for criminal justice, Illinois crime survey, 337-51, 1929 **4217**

Wachenfeld. Politische Polizei. Krimin Monatsh 2: 38-40 F '28 **4218**

PRIVATE

Childs, Marquis W. Muscle men. Scribner's 89: 203-5 F '31 **4219**

Green, Leon. The private police; the significance of private participation in law enforcement. Police "13-13" 5: 3-5 N '30 **4220**

Haager, J. H. Relationship of private detective agencies to police departments. Int Assn Chiefs Police Proc 34: 76-8 '27 **4221**

McLellan, Howard. Shadow business. N Am R 230: 29-35 Jl '30 **4222**

Private police should go. World Tomorrow 12: 150-1 Ap '29 **4223**

Rice, Thomas S. Private detective agencies aid local police departments. Police J [N Y] 18: 8, 17 My '31 **4224**

Shaloo, Jeremiah P. The private police of Pennsylvania. Ann Am Acad 146: 55-62 N '29 **4225**

SECRET SERVICE

Aston, George Grey (George Southcote, pseud). Secret service. 348p. London, Faber, 1930 **4226**

Baldwin, Roger N. Liberty under the soviets. Nation [N Y] 125: 505-7 N 9 '27 **4227**

Brady, Edward Mark. Ireland's secret service in England. 160p. Dublin, Talbot press, 1928 **4228**

Brunovsky, Vladimir. The methods of the Ogpu. 255p. N.Y. Harper, 1931 **4229**

Bywater, Hector C. and Ferraby, H. C. Strange intelligence. 299p. N.Y. Long & Smith, 1931 **4230**
Naval investigations of the British secret service before and during the Great War.

Chamberlin, William Henry. Liberty in the soviet state; gay-pay-oo, or political police. Atlan M 144: 544-54 O '29 **4231**

Feldman, Ben. Secret service man; an intimate sketch of the Captain of federal secret agents [Captain Thomas Callaghan]. Police "13-13" 5: 7-9 Je '30 **4232**

Gylden, Yves. Note sur l'espionomanie. R Int de Crimin 1: 669-76 D '29 **4233**

Hahn, J. E. Intelligence service within the Canadian corps, 1914-18. 263p. Toronto, Macmillan, 1930 **4234**

Jenssen, Carla. I spy; the true story of a woman secret service agent. 282p. N.Y. Dodd, 1930 **4235**

Jung, H. A. From a 1930 spy hunter: reply to R. Wohlforth with rejoinder. New Repub 62: 101-2 Mr 12 '30 **4236**

Kaledin, Viktor K. F-l-a-s-h- D 13. 325p. N.Y. Coward-McCann, 1930 **4237**

Keyes, Harold C. Tales of the secret service. 272p. N.Y. 33 W. 42 st. The Author, 1927 **4238**

Lucieto, Charles. On special missions; translated from French. 280p. N.Y. McBride, 1927 **4239**

Lüdecke, Winfried. Secrets of espionage; tales of the secret service. 250p. N.Y. Lippincott, 1929; same with title: Behind the scenes of espionage. London, Harrap, 1929 **4240**

McLellan, Howard. Spying on the reds. N Am R 230: 419-25 O '30 **4241**

Moran, William H. How police departments can aid the secret service. Int Assn Chiefs Police Proc 34: 101-3 '27; same title: Police J [N Y] 16: 5 Jl '28 **4242**

Rowan, Richard Wilmer. Spy and counterspy; the development of modern espionage. 322p. N.Y. Viking press, 1928 **4243**

The Russian secret police, by J. R. Police J [London] 2: 492-502 Jl '29 **4244**

Vasil'ev, Alekseĭ Tikhonovich. The Ochrana; the Russian secret police. Edited with an introduction by René Fülöp-Miller. 305p. Philadelphia, Lippincott, 1930 **4245**

Wohlforth, R. Spy-hunters: 1930. New Repub 61: 271-3 Ja 28 '30 **4246**
American vigilant intelligence federation.

STATE POLICE

Adams, Lynn G. The state police. Ann Am Acad 146: 34-40 N '29 **4247**

Beavers, James L. Should state and city police cooperate. Int Assn Chiefs Police Proc 36: 100-3 '29 **4248**

Burney, H. C. [The state police]. State Trooper 8: 15 My '27 **4249**

Chamber of commerce of the United States. State police and state highway patrols. 79p. (typw) Washington, 1931 **4250**

French, J. W. Trooper on the highway: he is the best argument there is in favor of de-localizing public protection. . . J Ind & Fin 8-10 Ap '31 **4251**

Günther, W. Von der Neugestaltung des Bürowesens in der staatlichen Polizei. Polizei 24: 318-22 Jl 5 '27 **4252**

Lambert, June, comp. Digest of the laws of the various states relating to state police. 13p. (Photostat) Albany, New York, New York (state) Library, Legislative reference section, June 29, 1929 **4253**

Leonard, Donald S. Relationship and cooperation between state and municipal police. Int Assn Chiefs Police Proc 37: 111-18 '30 **4254**

Leonard, Donald S. State and municipal police; points on which police forces of the state and city may coordinate. Police "13-13" 5: 8-10 S '30 **4255**

Mayo, Katherine. Standard-bearers; true stories of law and order. 324p. N.Y. Houghton, 1930 **4256**

Olander, Oscar G. Municipal or state police? Police "13-13" 4: 10-11 D '29 **4257**

Olander, Oscar G. Should state and city police be centralized under one control? State Trooper 10: 13-14, 20-1 My '29 **4258**

[Olander], Oscar G. Should state and city police be under one control? Int Assn Chiefs Police Proc 36: 130-5 '29 **4259**

Shartel, Stratton. What is state police: what will it do; what will it cost. Bank N 5-7 F 1 '29 **4260**

Smith, Bruce. The state police. *In* Crawford, Finla Goff. Readings in American government, 625-32. N.Y. Knopf, 1927 **4261**

Smith, Bruce. The state police: an American experiment in rural protection. Police J [London] 3: 20-9 Ja '30 **4262**

CALIFORNIA

Peace officers association of the state of California. Report of Committee on state police. Proc 8: 52-5 '28 **4263**

COLORADO

Warren, Frederick S. Colorado legislative committee urges state police organization. State Trooper 12: 13-14 D '30 **4264**

CONNECTICUT

Connecticut. State police department. Report, 1926/27—1929/30. Hartford, 1928-31 **4265**

INDIANA

Indiana. State police bureau. Report *in* Indiana Yearbook, 1927: 30-1; 1928: 33-4; 1929: 12-15; 1930: 8-15; 1931: 7-10 **4266**

MAINE

Maine. State highway police department. Report, 1929/30—1930/31. (mim) Augusta, 1930-31 **4267**

MASSACHUSETTS

Beaupre, Charles T. . . . Work of the Massachusetts state police patrol. State Trooper 12: 7-8 Ja '31 **4268**

Massachusetts. Commissioner of public safety. Annual reports, 1928/29—1929/30. Boston, 1930-31 **4269**

MICHIGAN

Michigan. Department of public safety. Information pertaining to the Department of public safety. 27p. Lansing, 1930 **4270**

Michigan. Department of public safety. Reports, 1926/27—1930/31 [Lansing, 1928-31] **4271**

Park, Kenneth C. District organization, to give Michigan greater protection by its troopers. State Trooper 13: 1-2 D '31 **4272**

Park, Kenneth C. Michigan force makes cooperation important factor of its activities. State Trooper 13: 5-6 O '31 4273

Park, Kenneth C. Michigan, with an enlarged force, prepared for more adequate patrol of rural regions. State Trooper 13: 5-6 N '31 4274

Park, Kenneth C. Standardization plan is now being laid out for Michigan state police. State Trooper 12: 5-6 Ag '31 4275

Park, Kenneth C. Uniform crime reporting system will aid Michigan state police. State Trooper 12: 5-6 Jl '31 4276

Rodgers, Don. Revised rules and regulations of Michigan state police department. State Trooper 11: 13-14 Ap '30 4277

MINNESOTA

Minnesota. Commission on criminal apprehension. Research committee. State organizations for the apprehension of criminals. 187p. Minneapolis, 1931 4278

NEVADA

Nevada. State police. Biennial report of the superintendent of Nevada state police and warden of State penitentiary, 1927/28. Carson City, 1929 4279

NEW HAMPSHIRE

New Hampshire. State police commission. Report of State police commission to the Legislature, January session, 1931. 15p. [Concord, 1931]; *also in* New Hampshire, House of representatives, Journal, Tuesday, January 20, 1931 4280

NEW JERSEY

New Jersey. Department of state police. Annual reports 6, 1927—10, 1931. Trenton, 1927-31 4281

New Jersey. Department of state police. New Jersey police academy. 29p. [Trenton, 1928] 4282

New Jersey state police to conduct training school for municipal and county police officers. Am City 39: 107 N '28 4283

NEW YORK (STATE)

New York (state). Executive department. Division of state police. Annual reports of the New York state troopers, 1927- Albany, 1928- 4284
Previous reports published by Department of state police.

New York (state). Executive department. Division of state police. New York state troopers manual, compiled by the New York state school for police. ed.5. 275p. Albany, July 1, 1930 4285

OREGON

Oregon. Department of state police. Annual reports [1] August 1, 1931/July 31, 1932. (typw) [Salem 1932] 4286

Oregon. Department of state police. Manual. 16p. Salem, 1931 4287

PENNSYLVANIA

Pennsylvania. Department of police. Biennial reports, 1927/28—1929/30. [Harrisburg, 1928-30] 4288

They get their man. New Repub 60: 188-9 O 9 '29 4289

RHODE ISLAND

Rhode Island. Department of state police. Annual reports, 2, 1927- [Providence] 1927- 4290

WEST VIRGINIA

West Virginia. Department of public safety. State police. Biennial report 6, 1928/30 [Charleston] 1930 4291

WOMEN POLICE

Allard, Paul. Weibliche Polizei im Strassendienst. Deut Gesell z Bekämpf d Geschlechtskrankh Mitt 25 (6): 59-60 '27 4292

Allen, Mary S. How women police work. Hosp Soc Serv 17: 591-5 Je '28 4293

Barck. The development of women police in Germany. Policewoman's R 1: 9-10 Je '27 4294

Barck. Polizeifürsorge und weibliche Polizei in Baden. Krimin Monatsh 2: 6-8 Ja '28 4295

Barck, Lothar. Ziele und Aufgaben der weiblichen Polizei in Deutschland. 143p. Lübeck, Polizei-Verl. 1928 4296

Binford, Jessie F. Policewomen and women offenders. Police J [N Y] 15: 14 D '27 4297

Boole, Barbara. Bibliography on policewomen. Policewomen's Int Bul 5: 3-4 Mr '29 4298

Brownlow, Louis. The city and the citizen. Policewoman's Int Bul 3: 12 Ag; 2 O; 8 N '27 4299

Brownlow, Louis. The effectiveness of the policewoman. Policewoman's Int Bul 4:8 Ag '28 4300

Brownlow, Louis. The effectiveness of the policewoman. Police J [N Y] 16: 19 D '28 4301

Brownlow, Louis. How women got into police work. Policewoman's Int Bul 4: 8 F '28 4302

Brownlow, Louis. The policewoman and the woman criminal. Nat Munic R 16: 467-8 Jl '27 4303

Brownlow, Louis. The policewoman's sphere. Nat Munic R 17: 136-8 Mr '28 4304

Brownlow, Louis. Policewomen work quietly but very effectively. Policewoman's Int Bul 4: 8 Ja '28 4305

Buwalda, Imra. Policewomen on the Pacific coast. Woman Cit ns11: 34 Mr '27; same title: Police J [N Y] 14: 5 Ap '27 4306

Carelli, A[ugusto]. La polizia femminile e i suoi compiti sociali. 6p. Roma, "Difesa Sociale," January 1927 4307

Clark, Jane Perry. The policewoman and deportation. Woman Cit ns12: 34 Je '27 4308

Curley, Marguerite O. Women in police work. Peace Offic Assn Calif Proc 11: 44-5 '31 4309

Davis, Mrs. J. C. Woman's work in a police department. Policewoman's Int Bul 5: 9 Je '29 4310

Davis, Mrs. J. C. Woman's work in the police department. Int Assn Chiefs Police Proc 36: 125-6 '29 4311

Effective policewomen; study program. Woman's J ns16: 43 My '31 4312

Gerk, Joseph A. Police women. Int Assn Chiefs Police Proc 37: 158-61 '30 4313

Gloderer, G. Die Polizeifürsorge in Baden. Polizei 24: 75-6 F 20 '27 4314

Guilford, Paul W. Policewomen and the juvenile court. Minn St Conf & Inst Soc Wk Proc 37: 224-7 '29 4315
Minnesota and northwest association of policewomen.

Hutzel, Eleanore L. The policewoman. Ann Am Acad 146: 104-14 N '29 4316

Hutzel, Eleanore L. Women's division in a police department. Int Assn Chiefs Police Proc 1927: 222-4 4317

Hutzel, Eleanore L. The work of a police woman. Am Pris Assn Proc 1927: 72-7 4318

Johnson, Mrs. E. Women police—the present situation in Scotland. Woman's Leader 21: 364 D 27 '29 4319

Johnson, Willard. Municipal mother: Elizabeth Lossing, Berkeley, California. Sunset 62: 25 Ap '29 4320

Johnston, Helen Berry. The policewoman and public recreation. Int Assn Policewomen Bul (27): 5-7 Ja '27; same title: Inst Police Adm Proc 1929: 95-9 4321

Kraus-Fessel, Meta. Frauen in Polizeidienst. Neue Generation 23: 46-9 F '27 4322

League of Nations. Traffic in women and children committee. The employment of women in the police. 13p. Geneva, 1927 4323

Loo, Florence S. Woman police in the San Francisco bay region. Thesis (M.A.) University of California, 1931 4324

Los Angeles. Department of the public library. Municipal reference library. Suggested reading for women peace officers. 3p. Los Angeles, 1930 4325

Lossing, Elizabeth. The functions of a policewoman. City Man Yrbk 1931: 155-60 4326

McMullen, Frances Drewry. Policewoman's beat. Woman's J ns14: 7-9 Mr '29 4327

McShane, Bessie. The policewoman; the status of the woman in police work. Police "13-13" 5: 13, 29 O '30 4328

Mangold, George B. and Thompson, S. Lucille. Policewomen. *In their* Community welfare in San Diego, 183-4. San Diego, Community welfare council, 1930 4329

Matthes, C. Zwei Jahre Dresdner Polizei. [Frauen im Polizeidienst]. Soz Berufsarbeit 9: 105-6 D '29 4330

Meikel, Theresa. Legal preparation of cases for court by policewomen. Policewoman's Int Bul 5: 5-6 Je '29 4331

Minnesota and northwest association of policewomen. The policewoman—a protective and preventive agent. Minn St Conf & Inst Soc Wk Proc 35: 258-64 1927 4332

[Owings, Chloe. Report of Committee on the qualifications of policewomen]. Policewoman's Int Bul 3: 9-10 Ag '27 4333

[Peto, D. O. G.]. Women police—the need for statutory regulations and training. Woman's Leader 21: 391-2 Ja 17 '30 4334

Peto, D. O. G. Women police, the stabilization of an essential service. Health & Empire 2: 23-9 Mr '27 4335

Pigeon, Helen D. How Berkeley helps its policewoman. Police J [N Y] 14: 5-6 My '27 4336

Pigeon, Helen D. One thousand sponsors. Woman Cit ns11: 34 My '27 4337

Pigeon, Helen D. Policewomen and public recreation. Am City 37: 448-50 O '27 4338

Pigeon, Helen D. Policewomen in the United States. J Crim L & Crimin 18: 372-7 N '27 4339

Pigeon, Helen D. Sponsoring the policewoman. Policewoman's Int Bul 3: 5-6 O '27 4340

Pigeon, Helen D. Woman's era in the police department. Ann Am Acad 143: 249-54 My '29 4341

Police féminine de Londres et de Dresden. Polizei im Bild (6) Jl '29 4342

The police woman and her duties. Police Rep 1: 17-22 Ag '29 4343
Reprint from Welfare Magazine.

Roszelle, M. Why the curfew ordinance. Police J [N Y] 14: 62- F '27; same title: Int Assn Policewomen Bul (28): 6-7 F '27 4344

Sadler, Ann. The ideal policewoman [Mina Van Winkle]. Welf Mag 19: 638-45 My '28 4345

Sadler, Ann. The ideal policewoman and her duties [Mina Van Winkle]. Criminologist [Chicago] 5: 12-13, 25, 37 Je '29 4346

Sesqui policewomen. Women Cit ns11: 34 F '27 4347

Sullivan, Mary A. Activities of the New York policewomen. Police J [N Y] 14: 33, 63 Ja '27 4348

Sullivan, Mary A. The woman police officer. Spring 3100 7-8 D '31 4349

Tancred, Edith. Women police abroad. Police J [London] 4: 175-87 Ap '31 4350

Tancred, Edith. Women police in Great Britain. Policewoman's Int Bul 5: 2-3 My '29; same title: Police J [N Y] 17: 12, 17 S '29 4351

Tancred, Edith. Women police—the present position. Woman's Leader 21: 347-8, 355-6 D 13, 20 '29 4352

Telford, Fred. The qualifications required for policewomen. Police J [N Y] 16: 25-7 F '29 4353

Telford, Fred. The qualifications required for policewomen and the development of tests for measuring such qualifications. Policewoman's Int Bul 4: 3, 5-6 Ag '28 4354

Topping, Ruth. Counselors-at-large. Woman Cit ns11: 34 Ap '27 4355

Tripp, H. Alker. Women police. 19th Cent 107: 815-24 Je '30 4356

United States. Congress. House. Committee on District of Columbia. To establish Woman's Bureau in metropolitan police department [of District of Columbia], report to accompany H. R. 6664, March 9, 1928. 8p. Washington, 1928 (70th Cong. 1st sess. H. Rep. 868) 4357

Vollmer, August. Meet the lady cop. Survey 63: 702-3 Mr 15 '30 4358

Waite, Edward F. Policewomen and the court. Minn St Conf & Inst Soc Wk Proc 35: 264-9 '27 4359
Minnesota and northwest association of policewomen.

Walker, George B. The relationship of policewomen and social service as viewed from the sidelines. Minn St Conf & Inst Soc Wk Proc 38: 163-6 '30 4360
Minnesota and northwest association of policewomen.

Wieking, Frederike. Die praktische Tätigkeit der weiblichen Polizei. Krimin Monatsh 2: 108-9 My '28 4361

Winter, Alice Ames. The policewoman of policewomen [Mina Van Winkle]. Policewoman's Int Bul 3: 12 O '27 4362

Women police abroad [U. S. and Scandinavia]. Police J [London] 4: 175-87 Ap '31 4363

PERSONAL DOCUMENTS

Adventures in criminology: series of true detective stories. I: The Presley murder. II: The Dovery murder. Northwest Police J 6: 10, 64-5 My; 17, 106-8 Je '29 4364

Breakenridge, William M. Helldorado; bringing the law to the mesquite. 256p. Boston, Houghton, 1928 4365

Carey, Arthur A. On the track of murder; introduction by Howard McLellan. 286p. London, Jarrolds, 1930 4366

Carey, Arthur A. and McLellan, Howard. Memoirs of a murder man. 326p. N.Y. Doubleday, 1930 4367

Carlin, Francis. Reminiscences of an ex-detective. 256p. N.Y. Doran, 1927 4368

Cassellari, René. Dramas of French crime; being the exploits of the celebrated detective. 288p. London, Hutchinson, 1930 4369

Dilnot, George. Triumphs of detection. 276p. Boston, Houghton, 1929 4370

Divall, Tom. Scoundrels and scallywags and some honest men. 230p. London, Benn, 1930 4371

Dunn, H. H. True stories of the man hunters. Pop Mech 49: 595-9 Ap 1 '28 4372

Ferrier, J. Kenneth. Crooks and crime. 314p. Philadelphia, Lippincott, 1927 4373

Fiaschetti, Michael. You gotta be rough; the adventures of Detective Fiaschetti of the Italian squad as told to Prosper Buranelli. 308p. N.Y. Doubleday, 1930; same with title: The man they couldn't escape. 286p. London, Selwyn, 1930 4374

Gollomb, Joseph. Master man-hunters. N.Y. Gold Label book, 1931 4375

Gollomb, Joseph. The war on crime. Am J Police Sci 2: 262-7 My '31 4376
Detectives of London, New York, Paris, Berlin, Vienna.

Gough, W. C. From Kew Observatory to Scotland Yard; 28 years of crime investigation. 284p. London, Hurst, 1927 4377

Heller, Leo. Mein interessantester Fall. Aus den Erlebnissen Berliner Kriminalkommissarie. 102p. Berlin, Siwinna, 1927 4378

Henderson, George C. House detective talks. Sunset 60: 30-2 My '28 4379

History of William J. Burns. Nation [N Y] 125: 561 N 23 '27 4380

Lépine, Louis. Mes souvenirs. 276p. Paris, Payot, 1929 4381

Memoirs of Vidocq [The famous Chef de Sureté, 1820]. 319p. London, Cassel's, 1928 4382

Nor Nalla, pseud. Yellow sleuth; being the autobiography of Nor Nalla (detective sergeant, Federated Malay states police). 288p. London, Hutchinson, 1931 4383

Richert, J. Gust. Detektiven i romanen och verkligheten. Stockholm, Ahlén & Akerlund, 1928 4384

Rowan, Richard Wilmer. The Pinkertons: a detective dynasty. 350p. Boston, Little, Brown, 1931 4385

Smith, Horace Herbert. Crooks of the Waldorf, being the story of Joe Smith, master detective. 256p. London, J. Long, 1930 4386

Stevens, H. L. The autobiography of a border policeman. 320p. London, Wetherby, 1927 4387

Strange and mysterious crimes; revealing twenty true detective mysteries. 326p. N.Y. Macfadden, 1929 4388

Wensley, Frederick Porter. Forty years of Scotland Yard: the record of a lifetime's service in the criminal investigation department. 312p. N.Y. Doubleday, 1931 4389

Willemse, Cornelius William. Behind the green lights. 364p. N.Y. Knopf, 1931 4390

Author's experiences during 25 years of service in the police department, N.Y.C., 12 of them as captain of detectives.

Woodhall, Edwin T. Detective and secret service days. 282p. London, Jarrolds, 1929 4391

RECORDS AND REPORTS

California. Department of penology. Division of criminal identification and investigation. Guide for use in compiling crime records by modus operandi. 12p. Sacramento, 1930 4392

Carstensen, Adolph. Criminal records. Int Assn Identif, Calif Div Proc 15: 9-11 '30 4393

Cincinnati. Bureau of municipal research. Record system for the Cincinnati police department. 100p. (Rep no10) Cincinnati, March 1928 4394

Cross, Homer B. Development of the record and identification system of the Los Angeles police department. Pac Police Mag 6: 7-8 My '29 4395

Doyle, Harry A. Standardization of criminal complaints. Int Assn Identif, Calif Div Proc 15: 20-2 '30 4396

Helping police departments to compile and report crime statistics intelligently. Am City 42: 163-5 Ja '30 4397

Ho, Ping Yin. Study of police record systems. Thesis (M.A.) University of California, 1928 4398

International association of chiefs of police. Guide for preparing annual police reports, tentative draft. 24p. December 1928; 36p. 1929 4399

International association of chiefs of police. Manual of police records as installed in Pasadena, California, and applicable to cities of 25,000 to 150,000 population, August 1931. 37p. (mim) 1931 4400

International association of chiefs of police. Committee on uniform crime records. Consolidated daily report; standard form. 2p. chart. July 30, 1931 4401

International association of chiefs of police. Consolidated monthly report; standard form. 3p. chart. July 1931 4402

International association of chiefs of police. Uniform classification of major offenses. 55p. June 1928 4403

International association of chiefs of police. Uniform crime reporting: a complete manual for police. 464p. 1929 4404

Jamison, W. C. Crime record systems. Illinois association for criminal justice, Illinois crime survey, 579-91, 1929 4405

Jenkins, L. V. Police bureau records. Int Assn Chiefs Police Proc 34: 40-3 '27 4406

Kittredge, Perry. Cross-indexing the criminal; central clearing house for criminal records. Indep 121: 273-4 S 22 '28 4407

Knoles, Fred A. The functions of the Los Angeles police statistical bureau. Tax Dig 6: 170-2 My '28 4408

Knoles, Fred A. The statistical bureau—a police necessity. J Crim L & Crimin 19: 383-9 N '28 4409

Lieck, Albert. Criminal records. Sol J 71: 200-1, 220 Mr 12, 19 '27 4410

Many cities adopt uniform crime reporting systems. Pub Manage 12: 94 Mr '30 4411

Modern police records. Pac Munic 45: 441 S '31 4412

New crime reporting system became effective January 1, 1930. Pub Manage 12: 56 F '30 4413

Niles, Harry M. Portland, Oregon, standardizes police records. Pac Munic 45: 134-5 Mr '31 4414

Niles, Harry M. Standardized records. Policewoman's Int Bul 4: 2-3, 5 Ja '28; same title: Police J [N Y] 15: 26 My '28 4415

Raitzin, A. Los informes médicos policiales. R Especialid 3: 530-5 S '28 4416

Rutledge, William P. Progress report of the Committee on uniform records. J Crim L & Crimin 19: 378-82 N '28 4417

Rutledge, William P. Standardization of police crime records. Int Assn Chiefs Police Proc 1927: 131-3 4418

Salaw, H. Kartothek oder Buchregister? Krimin Monatsh 2: 18-19 Ja '28 4419

Smith, Bruce. Police record keeping and reporting. City Man Yrbk 1931: 148-55 4420

Stone, Donald C. Uniform crime reporting. Police J [N Y] 18: 16-17 Ja '31 4421

Timmerman, L. S. The annual police report. Ann Am Acad 146: 96-103 N '29 4422

A uniform classification of major offenses by the Committee on uniform crime records of the International association of chiefs of police. Police J [N Y] 16: 3 O '28 4423

Uniform crime reporting installed at Pasadena and Berkeley. W City 7: 32-4 S '31 4424

Upson, Lent D. The "squeal book": the facts. . . about the number and character of crimes lie buried in the "squeal book" of the police departments. Nat Munic R 16: 695-9 N '27 4425

Welch, Guy C. Centralization of police information. Peace Offic Assn Calif Proc 10: 87-91 '30 4426

Wheeler, Chas. A. Records and systems as aids to apprehension of criminals. Int Assn Chiefs Police Proc 36: 145-9 '29 4427

CRIMINAL INVESTIGATION

Ammoun, Fouad. La méthode criminalistique et son application en Syrie et au Liban. Gaz des Trib Libano-Syriens 3: 1083-7 Mr '28 4428

Bayle, Edmond. Une affaire criminelle; vue au laboratoire. Etudes Crimin 2: 3-8 Ja '27 4429

Deville, Paul Sainte-Claire. L'enquête historique et la recherche policière. R Int de Crimin 2: 164-97 '30 4430

Heindl, Robert. The technique of criminal investigation in Germany. Ann Am Acad 146: 223-36 N '29 4431

Larson, John A. Psychology in criminal investigation. Ann Am Acad 146: 258-68 N '29; same title: Police J [N Y] 17: 16-20, 21 Ag '30 4432

Locard, Edmond. Die Kriminaluntersuchung und ihre wissenschaftlichen Methoden; bearbeitet von Willy Finke. 230p. Berlin, Kameradschaft Verl. 1930 4433

Louwage, F. E. Willkürliche Untersuchungsmethoden der Kriminalpolizei. Krimin Monatsh 5: 218-19 O '31 4434

Ogle. Hints on investigation of crime, etc. 24p. London, "Police Review," 1930 4435

Söderman, Harry. Science and criminal investigation. Ann Am Acad 146: 237-48 N '29 4436

Tenner, [Friedrich]. Kriminalistik. Krimin Monatsh 5: 79-81 Ap '31 4437

Tenner, Fr[iedrich]. Kriminalistik in Merkblättern. München, Bayerischer Kommunalschriften Verl. 1930 4438

Tenner, [Friedrich]. Kriminaltaktische Grundsätze. Krimin Monatsh 4: 265-8 D '30 4439

POLICE TECHNIQUE

Ahlemann, H. R. Ein Fall von besonders schwerer Leuchtgasexplosion. Arch f Krim 83: 301-5 N '28 4440

Arco, George von and Herzberg, Alexander. Die Bisskysche Diagnoskopie. 32p. Stuttgart, Püttmann, 1927 4441

Atwell, George C. Homicide procedure. N Y St Assn Chiefs Police Proc 29: 78-80 '29 4442

Barck. Neue Technik der Verbrechensbekämpfung. Polizei-Arch 6: 137-9 '27 4443

Behr, Detloff von. Kriminalpolizist und Feder. Krimin Monatsh 5: 274-7 D '31 4444

Beyer, Georg. Glücks- und Geschicklichkeitsapparate. Krimin Monatsh 2: 274-6 D '28 4445

Bischoff. Les méthodes scientifiques de recherche en matière d'incendie. R Int de Crimin 1 (1-3): 45-65 '29; translation: Methodes scientificos de pesquisas nos casas de incendio. Policia e Justiça 2 (7) My '30 4446

Bogdan, G. Deux cas de strangulation criminelle. Survie-guérison. Ann de Méd Lég 8: 132-3 Mr '28 4447

Chavigny. Baillon et ligotage. R Int de Crimin 2(2): 108-20 '30 4448

Chavigny. La collerette d'essuyage. Ann de Méd Lég 8: 126-7 Mr '28 4449

Elster, Botho and Jilski, Herbert. Polizei-Tatik. 185p. Berlin, Kameradschaft, 1928 4450

Feistle. Fahndungserfolg mit Hilfe der Presse. Krimin Monatsh 1: 89-90 Ap '27 4451

Flatau. Hypnose zur Aufklärung von Verbrechen. Krimin Monatsh 2: 33-5 F '28 4452

Freitas, Ramos de. Ensaios de policia technica. 310p. Recife, Libraria Universal, 1929 4453

Gennat. Die Bearbeitung von Mordsachen. Krimin Monatsh 1: 81-3 Ap '27 4454

Goodwin, John C. Crook pie. 319p. London, Alston Rivers, 1927 4455

Gottlieb, Theodor; Haschamova, Bogdana; Maurer, Robert; Meder, Joseph; Penn, Karl; Petertil, Eduard, and Türkel, Siegfried. Fälschungen. Beiträge zur Phänomenologie, Symptomalogie und Diagnostik; Herausgegeben von Siegfried Türkel. 93p. Graz, Moser, 1930 4456

Grass. Flugzeuge im Dienste der Kriminalpolizei bei der Aufklärung von Verbrechen. Krimin Monatsh 5: 208-9 S '30 4457

Grünewald, Max. Die Untersuchung von Eisenbahnzugzusammenstössen. Monats f Kriminalpsychol u Strafrechtsref 18: 197-200 Ap '27 4458

Hazard, Robert. And the cops got their man, including the taxi driver. Scribner's 90:511-13 N '31 4459

Heiland, Gerhard. Aufklärung einer schweren Mordtat nach sieben Jahren. Krimin Monatsh 1: 266-9 D '27 4460

Die Hellseherin beider Mordaufklärung. Krimin Monatsh 2: 182-3 Ag '28 4461

Hellwig, Albert. Die "Hellseher" bei der Aufklärung der Düsseldorfer Mordtaten. Krimin Monatsh 5: 171-3 Ag '31 4462

Hellwig, Albert. Vernehmungstechnik und Protokollierungstechnik in ihrer Bedeutung für den Ausgang des Strafverfahrens. Krimin Monatsh 4: 7-9 Ja '30 4463

Hellwig, A[lbert]. Zur Psychologie der polizeilichen Vernehmungstechnik und ihrer Würdigung durch den Richter. Polizei 25: 72-3 F 5 '28 4464

Hentig, Hans v. Das gezeichnete Geständnis. Monats f Kriminalpsychol u Strafrechtsref 18: 514-26 S '27 4465

Hermann. Die Iserlohner Hellseher-Experimente. Krimin Monatsh 2: 221-4 O '28 4466

Hesselink, W. F. Photographische Verwertung von Schädelverletzungen. Arch f Krim 84: 207-10 My '29 4467

Hildebrand, Heinrich. Die Leichenerscheinungen. Arch f Krim 82: 1-23 Ja '28 4468

Hiller, Marie Louise. Kriminalistik und Kunstfälschung. Krimin Monatsh 4: 223-6 O '30 4469

Hoepler, E. Mord durch Starkstrom. Arch f Krim 88: 199-206 My '31 4470

Jebens. Der Landjägereibeamte als Kriminalbeamter. Polizei 24: 429-30 S 5 '27 4471

Julier. Die Anwendung militärischer Kampfgrundsätze in der Kriminalistik. Krimin Monatsh 1: 154-7 Jl '27 4472

Julier. Die polizeiliche Untersuchung von Kraftfahrzeugunfällen. 51p. München, Schweitzer Verl. 1929 4473

Julier. Die Untersuchung von Kraftfahrzeugunfällen. Krimin Monatsh 2: 224-9 O '28 4474

Klauer, H. Die Elektrizität als Brandursache. Krimin Monatsh 5: 127-30 Je '31 4475

Kley, [Jakob Karl]. Ein Beitrag zur Psychologie der Aussage in Bildern. Krimin Monatsh 3: 149-50 Jl '29 4476

Kley, J[akob] K[arl] and Schneickert, Hans. Die Kriminalpolizei. ed.2. rev. 2v. 528,300p. Lübeck, Deut. Polizei-Verl. 1927 4477

Knobloch, Eduard. Fingierten Raubüberfall mit Tötung des Täters. Arch f Krim 87: 116-24 N '30 4478

Kockel, Heinz. Das falsche Bergonzi-Cello. Arch f Krim 83: 271-3 N '28 4479

Kockel, Heinz. Mordversuch mit metallischem Quecksilber. Arch f Krim 83: 309-11 N '28 4480

Kockel, [Heinz], and Timm. Nachweis des Petroleums bei Brandstiftungen. Krimin Monatsh 2: 123-35 Je '28 4481

Kopp. Erpresserfang. Krimin Monatsh 2: 196-8 S '28 4482

Kreusch, Max von. Die Bedeutung der Mimik und Physiognomik für den Kriminalisten. Krimin Monatsh 1: 58-62 Mr '27 4483

Krüger, O. F. Begriff und Grenzen der kriminalistischen Kombination. Krimin Monatsh 1: 126-9 Je '27 4484

Lehnerdt, G. Auf der Verbrecherjagd. Wie die Kriminalpolizei arbeitet. Gesetz u Recht 28: 49-54, 67-73, 84-6 F 15-Mr 15 '27 4485

Lerich, L. Identification d'un assassin à l'aide d'un éclat de bois, d'une vis et de deux douilles de cartouches de chasse. R Int de Crimin 3(4): 261-6 '31 4486

Lipik, E. and Salaw, H. Lehren der jüngsten Berliner Bluttat. Krimin Monatsh 2: 85-7 Ap '28 4487

Liszt, E. v. "Kriminalistischer Blick" im täglichen Leben. Krimin Monatsh 2: 106-8 My '28 4488

Locard, Edmond. Die Verwendung der Daktyloskopie bei dem Nachweiss der Echtheit von Altertümern. Krimin Monatsh 2: 229-31 O '28 4489

McDaniel, Ruel. Wisconsin gets her man. N Am R 227: 744-51 Je '29 4490

Mezger, Otto and Frankle, Paul. Ermittlung eines Poststempels. Arch f Krim 82: 271-2 Je '28 4491

Mezger, O[tto] and Heess, W. Zur Identifizierung loser paginierter Blätter. Arch f Krim 84: 171-7 Ap '29 4492

Miranda-Pinto, O. De l'importance d'une bonne observation sur les lieux du crime. R Int de Crimin 1: 398-9 O '29 4493

Moser, Hans. Nachweis von Falschmünzerei. Arch f Krim 84: 56-8 Ja '29 4494

Moser, Hans and Mezger, Otto. Nachweis einer Münzfälschung. Arch f Krim 82: 197-9 Ap '28 4495

Muehlberger, C. W. The scientific estimation of alcoholic intoxication. Am J Police Sci 1: 206-15 Mr '30 4496

Müller, Johannes. Geschäftsbücher verraten einen Mörder. Krimin Monatsh 5: 209-11 S '31 4497

Müller, R. Die kriminalpolizeiliche Bearbeitung von Banksachen. Polizei 24: 426-8, 444-5, 467-8 S 5-O 5 '27 4498

Nebe. Kriminalpolizei und Rauschgifte. Krimin Monatsh 3: 59-61, 81-5 Mr, Ap '29 4499

Neves, J. Alberto Pereira de Azevedo. Médecine légale et police criminelle (France, Belgique, Allemagne, Autriche et Italie). 374p. Lisboa, Imp. Nac. 1931 4500

Nippe. Kriminalistisch bemerkenswerte Querschlägerverletzungen. Deut Zeitsch f d ges gerichtl Med 10: 54-7 Jl '27 4501

Palitzsch. Der Raubmord an dem Rentenempfänger Todt. Arch f Krim 83: 215-21 N '28 4502

Pines, C. Clifton. The story of alcohol. Am J Police Sci 2: 500-8 N '31 4503

Provent, P. À propos d'un cas supposé d'empoissement par la strychnine. Ann de Méd Lég 8: 11-19 Ja '28 4504

Quintin, Paul. Les fraudes et falsifications des vins. R de Dr Pén et de Crimin 9: 1136-44 '29 4505

Raestrup. Sublimathaltige Pralinen. Arch f Krim 83: 286-7 N '28 4506

De Rechter, [G.]. Application de procédées physiques à l'expertise des tableaux. R de Dr Pén et de Crimin 8: 1-7 Ja '28 4507

Renaux; Decraene, and Firket, J. Rapport sur les propositions à soumettre par la "Société de Médecine légale de Belgique" pour le diagnostic de l'ivresse. R de Dr Pén et de Crimin 7: 597-606 Je '27 4508

Rhine, Albert A. Fortune tellers, spiritualistic mediums and pseudo psychologists exposed. Police J [N Y] 16: 12, 19 Jl '28 4509

Rhine, Albert A. Spiritualists, mediums, and fortune tellers exposed by magician police officers. Int Assn Chiefs Police Proc 1927: 239-41 4510

Römer, [M.] Die Bedeutung der Personalakten für die Kriminalpolizei. Krimin Monatsh 2: 176-80 Ag '28 4511

Römer, M. Bettler, Landstreicher und Kriminalpolizei. Krimin Monatsh 3: 129-34 Je '29 4512

Rozumek, E. Was muss eine Chiffriermaschine leisten? Polizei 24: 369-71 Jl 20 '27 4513

Rubner, J. Das Zeichnung des Täters, ein Überführungsmittel. Krimin Monatsh 2: 198-202 S '28 4514

Schnarke, D. Der Reichswasserschutz. Seine Wesen und sein Wirkungskreis. Krimin Monatsh 2: 37-8 F '28 4515

Schneickert, Hans. Die Kriminalpolizei. Bd.II: Kriminaltaktik und Kriminaltechnik. ed.2. 300p. 1927; ed. 3. 350p. Lübeck, Deutscher Polizeiverl. 1929 4516

Schröder. Strassen- und Häuserkampf. Polizei 24: 489-91, 518-20, 548-51 O 20-N 20 '27 4517

Schultz. Von Spielern und Falschspielern. Polizei 24: 7- '27 4518

Schulz. Der Kriminalbeamte als Porträtmaler. Krimin Monatsh 2: 61-2 Mr '28 4519

Schwarzacher, W. Beiträge zum Mechanismus des Erhängenstodes. Deut Zeitsch f d ges gerichtl Med 11: 145-53 '28 4520

Strauch, [Kurt]. Kriminalärztliches zu tödlichen Stichverletzungen. Krimin Monatsh 2: 97-101 My '28 4521

Thiemann. Polizei und Gnadensachen. Polizei 24: 327-8 Jl 5 '27 4522

Timm, [F.]. Über Brandstiftungen. Arch f Krim 83: 306-8 N '28 4523

Timm, F. Über Brandstiftungen und ihren Nachweis. Arch f Krim 81: 193-206 D '27 4524

Van der Giesen, A. H. "Streng verhoor." Tijdschr v d Politie 1: 127-32 My 23 '28 4525

Vilma, M. Sui caratteri microscopici tra ferite cutanee in vita e ferite postmortali negli annegati. Arch di Antrop Crim 47: 474-96 Jl '27 4526

Weimann, Waldemar. Selbstfesselung und Selbstknebelung. Arch f Krim 85: 70-88 bibliog (p87-8) Ag '29 4527

Zwei Wiener Mordfälle. Arch f Krim 82: 264-70 '28 4528

CORONER

Abatement of inquest where person charged with homicide. Sol J 71: 130 F 12 '27 4529

Committals for trial by coroners. Just Peace 93: 514 Ag 10 '29 4530

The coroner and the commandments. Sol J 74: 759-60 N 15 '30 4531

A coroner dissociates himself from his jury. Sol J 73: 773 N 23 '29 4532

Coroners [legislation]. L Times 168: 326-7 O 26 '29 4533

The Coroners amendment act, 1926. Sol J 71: 381-2 My 14 '27 4534

Coroners' inquests. Sol J 73: 82-3 F 9 '29; same title: L Times 168: 293-4 O 19 '29 4535

Coroners' juries and their verdicts. Sol J 72: 108-9 F 18 '28 4536

Coroners' powers; exclusion of solicitors and counsel. L Times 171: 267-78 Mr 28 '31 4537

Davison, W. H. Coroner and medical officer of health. Pub Health 43: 287-94 Je '30 4538

Declining status of inquests. L Times 168: 190-1 S 14 '29 4539

Difficulties of coroners. Sol J 72: 601-2 S 15 '28 4540

Disagreement of coroner's jury. Sol J 72: 92 F 11 '28 4541

District of Columbia. Coroner. Report *in* Annual report of Commissioners of the District of Columbia 4542

Hektoen, Ludvig. The coroner [in Cook county]. *In* Illinois association for criminal justice, Illinois crime survey 377-88, 1929 4543

Howard-Watson, J. A. Modern changes in ancient coroner's law. L Times 164: 244-5 O 1 '27; same title: Sol J 71: 825-7 O 22 '27 4544

Inquests and publicity, coroner and the law, public inquiry greatest safeguard. Just Peace 94: 58 Ja 25 '30 4545

The law as to coroners. M Press ns123: 209 Mr 16 '27 4546

Leary, T. Early American experience under coroner laws. New England J Med 200: 759-66 Ap 11 '29 4547

Leary, T. Medical examiner system [coroner]. Am M Assn J 89: 579-83 Ag 20 '27 4548

Ottaway, T. The law and practice relating to coroners. 120p. London, Butterworth, 1927 4549

San Diego county, Calif. Coroner. Report. . . January 1/December 31, 1931. (mim) [San Diego, 1932] 4550

San Francisco. City and county. Coroner. Yearly report, January 1/December 31, 1931. (mim) [San Francisco, 1932] 4551

Schultz, Oscar T. Our antiquated coroner system. Hygeia 8: 908-12 O '30 4552

Schultz, Oscar T. and Morgan, E. M. The coroner and the medical examiner. Nat Res Council Bul (64): 1-101 Jl '28 4553

Surridge, C. W. W. Relationship of coroner and medical profession. Lancet 217: 838-9 O 19 '29 4554

Verdicts of coroners' juries. Sol J 73: 18 Ja 12 '29 4555

Weinmann, George H. Compendium of the statute law of coroners and medical examiners in the United States. Nat Res Council Bul (83): 1-240 '31 4556

Woodward, William C. The coroner's office: its proposed abolition. Am B Assn Rep 54:548-63 '29 4557

Zisch, P. J. National association of coroners. Med-Leg J 47: 72-4 My '30 4558

Zisch, P. J. Paraphrase and synopsis of "our antiquated coroner system." Med-Leg J 47: 146-9 N '30 4559

CORPSES, AUTOPSIES

Alexander, J. Cultural medicine. Embalming, and its medical and legal aspects. M Times & Long Island M J 59: 184, 217, 251 My-Jl '31 4560

Böhmer, K. Identifikation nach Verbrennung. Deut Zeitsch f d ges gerichtl Med 18: 250-69 D 19 '31 4561

Bokarius, N. S. Narujni Osmotr Troupa na miestie Proisshestvia ili Obnarujenia. 188p. Kharkoff, Medico-Legal Institute, 1929 4562

Carboneschi, C. L. Marcha y técnica a seguir en una pericia toxicológica. Semana Méd 2: 887-91 S 17 '31 4563

Collin, Pierre. Le droit à l'autopsie. Etudes historique, médico-légale et administrative. 107p. Paris, Legrand, 1927 4564

Thèse de médecine de Paris, 1927.

Domingues, Aurelio. L'identité des cadavres. R Int de Crimin 2 (3): 218-20 '30 4565

Duvoir. La vérification des décès et l'identification des cadavres. Ann de Méd Lég 11: 360-75 Ap '31 4566

Finding of a body in cases of murder. Fortn L J 1:31 S 1 '31 4567

Gompert, Frank B. Dead bodies. Los Angeles Chron 13: 14, 22 S 30; 14 O 30 '30 4568

Kleinvogel. Leichenerscheinungen. Kriminal Monatsh 5: 136-9 Je '31 4569

Merkel, H. Diagnostische Feststellungsmöglichkeiten bei verbrannten und verkohlten menschlichen Leichen. Deut Zeitsch f d ges gerichtl Med 18: 232-49 D 19 '31 4570

Müller, F. W. Augenschein, Leichenschau und Leichenöffnung. Krimin Monatsh 5: 134-5 Je '31 4571

Müller, Helmut. Schematische Darstellung des Verfahrens bei Ermittelung Vermisster und Feststellung unbekannter Toten. Krimin Monatsh 4: 39-40 F '30 4572

Nippe. Die kriminalistischen Gesichtspunkte der gerichtlichen Sektion. Deut Zeitsch f d ges gerichtl Med 18: 103-20 D 18 '31 4573

Pfreimbter, Richard. Leichenöffnungen und Rechtspflege. Krimin Monatsh 1: 100-2 My '27 4574

Ross, Joan Margaret. Post-mortem appearances. ed.2. 226p. N.Y. Oxford, 1928 4575

Schultz, Oscar T. The law of the dead human body. Arch Path & Lab Med 9: 1220-41 Je '30 4576

Tenner. Vermisste und unbekannte Tote. Polizei 24: 553-5 N 20 '27 4577

Warneyer, O. Zur Obduktionsfrage. Chirurg 3: 497-501 Je 1 '31 4578

Weimann, Waldemar. Befunde und Identifizierung einer Wasserleiche. Arch f Krim 87:225-30 D '30 4579

Weinmann, George H. A survey of the law concerning dead human bodies. Nat Res Council Bul (73): 1-199 '29 4580

THIRD DEGREE

Ageloff, Hilda. Third degree. New Repub 56: 321-4 N 7 '28 4581

American Torquemadas. New Repub 62: 113-14 Mr 19 '30 4582

Cardozo on the third degree. Outl 156: 450 N 19 '30 4583

Chafee, Zechariah, jr. Remedies for the third degree. Atlan M 148: 621-30 N '31 4584

Finlinson, Jack. The third degree. Inst Police Adm Proc 1929: 83-8 4585

French views on the "third degree." Just Peace 93: 734 N 23 '29 4586

Herzog, Alfred W. The third degree and Dr. House's truth serum. Med-Leg J 44: 34-6 Mr '27 4587

In the driftway. Nation [N Y] 129: 719-20 D 11 '29 4588

Irvine, Frank. Third degree and the privilege against self-incrimination. Cornell L Q 13: 211-18 F '28; same title: L Notes 32: 27-30 My '28 4589

Is third degree ever necessary? Police officials give their views. . . . W City 7: 27-8 S '31 4590

Chas. H. Kelley, L. V. Jenkins, August Vollmer, M. D. Guy, and J. Finlinson.

Keeping the law officer within the law. Chr Cent 47: 1076 S 10 '30 4591

Lane, L. J. Third degree. Outl 157: 40 Ja 7 '31 4592

Lavine, Emanuel H. The third degree, a detailed and appalling exposé of police brutality. 248p. N.Y. Vanguard, 1930 4593

Lie-detecting. Outl 153: 533 D 4 '29 4594

Maxwell, Cliff. Crook and the bull. N Am R 228: 641-8 D '29 4595

Murphy, Charles J. V. Third degree; another side of our crime problem. Outl 151: 522-6 Ap 3 '29 4596

Origin of the term "third degree." Just Peace 94: 562 S 13 '30 4597

Sedgwick, A. C. Third degree and crime. Nation [N Y] 124: 666-7 Je 15 '27 4598

Shall police torture go? Nation [N Y] 126: 579 My 23 '28 4599

The third degree. L Notes 32: 202 F '29; same title: Harv L R 43: 617-23 F '30; Med-Leg J 47: 49-54 Mr '30; Outl 156: 447 N 19 '30; Outl 158: 485 Ag 19 '31; U S L R 65: 584-9 N '31 4600

The "third degree" in America. Just Peace 91: 847 N 5 '27 4601

Untermyer, Samuel. Third degree; reform through the Continental system. Nation [N Y] 133: 600 D 2 '31 4602

Villard, Oswald Garrison. Official lawlessness; third degree and the crime wave. Harper's 155: 605-14 O '27 4603

DETECTION

Alberti, [H. W.]. Sporen op de plaats des misdrijfs. Tijdschr v d Politie 1 (23): 413-17 O 24 '28 4604

Beatty, John D. The science of crime detection. Frat Order Police J 12: 9, 43 Ag '29 4605

Bova, P. Ricerche metapsichiche ed investigazione del delitto. Scuola Pos 11: 367-73 Ag '31 4606

Cramp, Arthur J. The Bureau of investigation of the American medical association. Am J Police Sci 2: 285-9 Jl '31 4607

Crawley, F. J. The difference between official and fictional investigation of crime. Police J [N Y] 18: 20-1, 23 Mr '31 **4608**

Crime detection by clairvoyance. Just Peace 91: 667 S 10 '27 **4609**

Ghosal, R. M. Science and detection in Burma. Police J [London] 2: 619-35 O '29 **4610**

Hallgren, Eric. Ett fall från det praktiska detektivarbetet. Nord Kriminalteknisk Tidsk 1 (3) '31 **4611**

Hesselink, W. F. Ein verräterisches Eichenblattstückchen. Arch f Krim 80: 55-6 Ja '27 **4612**

Hiserman, O. M. Invisible informers. Peace Offic Assn Calif Proc 9: 121-4 '29 **4613**

Luria, A. R. [Psychology in the detection of crime]. Nauchnoe Slovo (3): 79-104 '28 **4614**

Mimin, Pierre. Le constat criminel (règles légales et règles techniques). 283p. Paris, Godde, 1930 **4615**

Minnesota. Commission on criminal apprehension. Report . . . December 31, 1930. 24p. [St. Paul] 1930 **4616**

"Municipal murder maps" effectively used. Am City 39: 87 O '28 **4617**

O'Sullivan, Frank Dalton (Don Sullington, pseud). Crime detection. 667p. Chicago, O'Sullivan pub. house, 1928 **4618**

Peace officers association of the state of California. Report of Committee on homicides. Proc 8: 88-93 '28 **4619**

Publicity and crime detection. Just Peace 95: 82 F 7 '31 **4620**

Reid, Alexander H. The detection and apprehension of criminals; address before the Committee on crime and criminal justice of the Wisconsin conference on social work, 1930. 4p. Madison, Kilgore ptg. co. 1930 **4621**

Rhodes, Henry T. F. Some persons unknown; being an account of scientific detection. 268p. London, Murray, 1931 **4622**
Poisons; dust; fingerprints; camera; ultraviolet rays; microscope; blood; criminal psychology.

Rioux, Geo. H. Criminal enquiry. Chief Constables' Assn Can Proc 24: 51-8 '28 **4623**

Schober. Internationale Zusammenarbeit der Kriminalpolizei. Arch f Krim 83: 12-20 Jl '28 **4624**

Schrader, Hart. Being thorough in your search for and examination of evidence. Int Assn Identif, Calif Div Proc 16: 42-5 '31 **4625**

Sellers, J. Clark. Physical clues and the law. Int Assn Identif, Calif Div Proc 12: 67-80 '27 **4626**

Simon, Carleton. Observation and its importance to the police. Police J [N Y] 18: 10-15 N '31 **4627**
Address before New York state association of chiefs of police.

Singleton, Seth. "How we catch the criminal." Police J [St. Louis] 16:1-3 N 12 '27 **4628**

[Smith, Charles Sidney]. Railroad detective work. 47p. La Crosse, Wis. 232 S. 11 st. The Author, 1927 **4629**

White, Leslie T. Bureau of investigation, District Attorney's office of Los Angeles. Int Assn Identif, Calif Div Proc 14: 38-9 '29 **4630**

Williams, E. C. The part the surveyor plays in the investigation of crime and police work. Int Assn Identif, Calif Div Proc 15: 15-16 '30 **4631**

Yakimov, Y. N. [The detection of criminals]. 56p. Moskva, Narkomvnudel, 1928 **4632**

Detectives

Bayle, E. The scientific detective. Am J Police Sci 2: 158-70 Mr '31 **4633**

Crawley, F. J. The technique of investigation of the English detective. Ann Am Acad 146: 219-22 N '29 **4634**

Dilnot, George. Great detectives and their methods. 271p. Boston, Houghton, 1928 **4635**

Hiserman, [O. M.]. The detective in a small town. Peace Offic Assn Calif Proc 10: 72-5 '30 **4636**

Matheson, Duncan. The technique of the American detective. Ann Am Acad 146: 214-17 N '29 **4637**

Mitchell, C. Ainsworth. Scientific detective and the expert witness. rev. and enl. ed. 242p. London, Heffer, 1931 **4638**
Originally issued in 1923 as "The expert witness."

New York's Scotland Yard; Governor Roosevelt suggests a state bureau of expert detectives. Outl 151: 337 F 27 '29 **4639**

Post, Melville Davison. The man hunters. London, Hutchinson, 1928 **4640**
Methods of detective police in Europe and U.S. based on collection of typical cases.

Teale, Edwin Way. Now, real detectives beat Sherlock Holmes. Pop Sci 119: 13-15 Ag '31 **4641**

Wartenberg. Der Detektiv und das Kind. Selbstschutz 2 (4) Ap '30 **4642**

Modus Operandi

Ball. Betrug-heute Hochkonjunktur. Polizei 25: 28-9 Ja 5 '28 **4643**

Barth, E. Bordell und bordellartige Betriebe. Polizei 24: 520-2 N 5 '27 **4644**

Benassi, G. Infanticidio per decapitazione. Arch d Antrop Crim 48: 221-40 Mr '28 **4645**

Berg, J[oseph]. Un cas d'escroquerie. R de Dr Pén et de Crimin 8: 257-8 Mr '28 **4646**

Bünger. Neuzeitliche Methoden Berliner Geldschrankeinbrecher. Krimin Monatsh 2: 82-5 Ap '28 **4647**

Burns, William J. Weapons of the crook Justice 1: 68-9 O '28 **4648**

Cochrane, J. A. How the layer-down works. Detective 42: 11 Ja '27 **4649**

Cochrane, J. A. Professional check crook gangs a menace to business men. Detective 42: 8 Mr; 3 Ap '27 4650

Dalla Volta, A. Omicidio doloso per investimento di autoveicolo. Arch di Antrop Crim 48: 553-9 My '28 4651

Deschauer, R. Methodischer Blindenschwindel. Krimin Monatsh 4: 101-3 My '30 4652

Fecker. Gedanken zur Beurteilung von Geschicklichkeitsspielen. Polizei 24: 324-5 Jl 5 '27 4653

Fleischer. Verbrechensperseveranz. Krimin Monatsh 2: 64-5 Mr '28 4654

Gardner, Arthur R. The art of crime. 254p. London, Allen, 1931 4655

Popular presentation of the modus operandi.

Grempe. Der Wert moderner Panzerschränke bei Geldschrank-Einbrüchen. Krimin Monatsh 2: 25-7 F '28 4656

Hann, K. Beitrag zur Lehre vom Kindesmord. Deut Zeitsch f d ges gerichtl Med 10: 58-69 Jl '27 4657

Heberda, A. Kriminelle Leichenzerstückelung. Deut Zeitsch f d ges gerichtl Med 10: 242-8 Ag '27 4658

Kappelmeyer, Otto. Elektrische Fernkräfte im Dienste des Verbrechers. Krimin Monatsh 2: 171-6 Ag '28 4659

Kley. Wer ist der Fälscher? Krimin Monatsh 2: 15-17, 65-7 Ja, Mr '28 4660

Kriminaltechnik. Krimin Monatsh 2: 20 Ja '28 4661

Lehnerdt, G. Taschendiebe. Gesetz u Recht 28: 241-4 Ag 15 '27 4662

Locard, Edmund. Die kriminelle Verkleidung. Krimin Monatsh 1: 275-6 D '27 4663

Mandolini, H. El crimen científico. R de Crimin, Psiquiat y Med Leg 14: 159-63 Mr '27 4664

Marsh-Smith, R. N. The detection of burglary in India. Police J [London] 2: 78-90 '29 4665

Gayer system of crime detection thru modus operandi.

Modus operandi bureau opened [in New York state department of correction, Division of criminal identification]. Correction 1: 5 O '31 4666

Moll, Albert. Nötigung zur Unzucht durch Hypnose. Zeitsch f Sexualwissensch 15: 108-16 Je '28 4667

Mordversuch mittels angeblicher Hypnose. Arch f Krim 82: 159-64 Ap '28 4668

Parsons, T. S. How they do it in Australia. Can Police Bul 13: 8 D '28 4669

Pelz, A. Einiges von den "Erfolgen" einer Hellseherin im Memelgebiet. Polizei 24: 325-7 Jl 5 '27 4670

Polke. Erpressung. Polizei 25: 349-50, 370-1 My 20, Je 5 '28 4671

Possehl, Ulrich. Moderne Betrüger. 115p. Berlin-Charlottenburg, Bali-Verl. 1928 4672

Possehl, Ulrich. Zum Einsponbetrugsprozess. Krimin Monatsh 2: 206-7 S '28 4673

Prati, M. Sulla morte improvvisa da gaz illuminante. Arch di Antrop Crim 47: 1007-16 N '27 4674

Riege, P. Bauer, Bauernfänger und Polizist. Polizei 24:438-40 S 15 '27 4675

Ritchie, David. Modus operandi. Chief Constables' Assn Can Proc 24: 39-50 '28 4676

Roehrer, Carl. Die Urkundenfälschung des Veit Stoss. Monats f Kriminalpsychol u Strafrechtsref 19: 245-8 Ap '28 4677

Seifert, O. Einiges über Darlehns-Vermittlungsschwindel. Polizei 25: 358-9, 383-4 Je 5, 20 '28 4678

Thompson, C. J. S. Poisoned clothes. Criminologist [London] 1: 13-14 My 15 '27 4679

Türkel, Siegfried. Prähistorische Fälschungen. 79p. Graz, Moser, 1928 4680

Vogel. Die Brandstiftung unter besonderer Berücksichtigung der sogenannten "Zeitzündung." Polizei 24: 101-3, 122-3 Mr 5, 20 '27 4681

Weide. Die spanische Gräfin. Ein Beitrag zur Geschichte des Heiratsschwindels. Arch f Krim 82: 24-7 '28 4682

Police Dogs

Andros, Butler and Eustis, Dorothy Harrison. Dogs on patrol. Sat Eve Post 203: 16-17 Jl 5 '30 4683

Arundel, Reginald. The police dog: his selection and training. Police J [London] 1: 423-31 '28 4684

Ash, Edward C. Wolf in the Alsatian. Spectator [London] 139: 415-16 S 17 '27 4685

Cecil-Gurney, P. L. Police dog training. Police J [London] 3: 526-34 O '30 4686

Champod. L'emploi des chiens de police par la gendarmerie vaudoise. R de Gendarm 4 (21) My '31 4687

Cofer, Kermit R. Bloodhound evidence in Mississippi. Miss L J 2: 247-50 N '29 4688

Courtney, W. L. Alsatian's defense. Spectator [London] 138: 478-9 Mr 19 '27 4689

Dressage des chiens de police à Berlin. Polizei im Bild (6) Jl '29 4690

Eustis, Dorothy Harrison. Dog's life. Sat Eve Post 201: 38-40 Ag 18 '28 4691

Eustis, Dorothy Harrison. L'élevage et le dressage des chiens de police à Fortunate Fields. R de Gendarm 4 (21) My '31 4692

Galzow. Der Suchhund im kriminalistischen Ermittlungsdienst. Krimin Monatsh 3: 132-3 Je '28 4693

Kollet, Fred. Training the police dog. ed. 4. rev. and enl. 57p. Chicago, Judy publ. 1927 4694

Music of hound in a Texas convict hunt. Lit Dig 102: 38-40 Ag 17 '29 4695

Police dogs for patrol duty. Correction 1: 1, 3-4 O '31 4696

Police dogs guard German railroads. Pop Sci 119: 41 S '31 4697

Reiss. Der Schutzhund im Dienste der Gendarmerie, insbesondere bei der Verbrecherbekämpfung. Krimin Monatsh 5: 59-60 Mr '31 4698

Richardson, E. H. Bloodhounds as mantrackers. Criminologist [London] 1: 14-15 My 15 '27 4699

Rine, Josephine Z. Doberman pinschers. Nature Mag 13. 387 Je '29 4700

Roger, N. L'école des chiens. Illustration 88 ptl: 317-18 Mr 8 '30 4701

Schoenherr, H. Der Wach- und Polizeihund als Beweismittel vor Gericht. Krimin Monatsh 1: 108-12 My '27 4702

Thomson, [J. G. P. A.]. De Politiehond. Tijdschr v d Politie 1 (16): 305-7, (17): 321-3 S 5, 12 '28 4703

Villiers, I. P. de. Dogs as detectives in South Africa. Police J [London] 2: 188-92 Ap '29 4704

Scientific Methods of Detection

Brunskill, Frank W. Science as an aid to law enforcement. Int Assn Chiefs Police Proc 34: 31-3 '27; same title: Police J [N Y] 15: 13-14 Mr '28 4705

Catton, Joseph. The medical aspect of police work. Peace Offic 5: 4-8 D '27 4706

Catton, Joseph. Some medical aspects of police work. Int Assn Chiefs Police Proc 34: 208-22 '27 4707

Derome, Wilfrid. Quantitative determination of alcohol in the human organism. Am J Police Sci 1: 515-20 bibliog (p520) S '30 4708

Dunlap, Al. Science versus practical common sense in crime detection. Am J Police Sci 2: 322-7 Jl '31 4709

Goddard, Calvin. Employment of scientific laboratory methods in the detection of crime: address. Am B Assn Rep 55: 567-74 '30 4710

Goddard, Calvin. Scientific methods of crime detection. Int Assn Identif, Calif Div Proc 16: 18-23 '31 4711

Harper, Hugh D. Scientific criminology. Int Assn Identif Proc 13: 59-62 '27 4712

Leonard, Donald S. Modern police methods; just how much can science be of aid to the police? Police "13-13" 5: 3,33 D '30 4713

Loadholtes, J. W. Science as an aid to handcuffs. Int Assn Identif Proc 16: 108-9 '30 4714

Magrath, George B[urgess]. Medical science and the police; with special reference to the investigations of deaths and the interpretation of wounds. Police "13-13" 4: 9, 13, 44 Ja '30 4715

Magrath, George Burgess. Medical science in the service of the state, with special reference to the investigation of deaths. Ann Am Acad 146: 249-57 N '29 4716

Methods of scientific crime detection as infringements of personal rights. Harv L R 44: 842-6 Mr '31 4717

Miloslavich, Edward L. Modern methods of scientific criminology in detection of crime. Marquette L R 14: 51-8 F '30; same title: Med-Leg J 47: 124-5 S '30 4718

Montagnes, James. How science helps Canada's mounted police. Pop Mech 56: 84-7 Jl '31 4719

Pinker, Ray H. A review of the scientific methods for determining alcoholic intoxication. Int Assn Identif, Calif Div Proc 16: 97-8 '31 4720

Reynolds, Ruth. Six factors in the detection of crime. Police J [N Y] 17: 26, 31 O '29 4721

Laboratory method of inquiry.

Sawyer, F. T. Use science to defeat crime! Int Pict Police J 41-5 Je '29 4722

Schultz, Oscar T. Medical science and criminal justice; abstract, address before Academy of medicine of Cincinnati, February 9, 1931. J Med Jl '31, Reprint 4723

Science helps police in detection of crime [in France]. Police J [N Y] 15: 24 S '27 4724

Taylor, Joseph F. Scientific methods of crime detection. Int Assn Identif, Calif Div Proc 16: 32-4 '31 4725

Watzek, Ferdinand. Technique in scientific criminal investigation. Int Assn Identif Proc 16: 159-62 '30 4726

CHEMICAL ANALYSIS

Heindl, Robert. Chemie und Photographie im Dienst der Verbrechensaufklärung. Arch f Krim 87: 3-14 Ag '30 4727

Jeserich, Rudolf. Chemie und Photographie im Dienste der Verbrechensaufklärung. 258p. Berlin, Georg Stilke, 1930 4728

Krause, William. Chemistry in its relation to criminal evidence. Int Assn Identif Proc 13: 75-9 '27 4729

Leffman, Henry. Chemistry as an aid in the detection of crime. Am J Police Sci 2: 375-81 S '31 4730

Lucas, A. Forensic chemistry and scientific criminal investigation. ed.2. 324p. London, Arnold, 1931 4731

Stains, documents, dust, dirt, explosives, fibres, string and rope, fingerprints, fires and insurance fraud, firearms, poisons, microscopy, photography and ultra-violet ray, tobacco.

Park, Kenneth C. Chemist as detective. State Trooper 8: 5-6 F '27 4732

Praessler, Robert T. Chemistry and its application to police work. Int Assn Identif Proc 16: 96-108 '30 4733

Rhodes, Henry T. F. Forensic chemistry: past, present and future. Police J [London] 3: 359-69 Jl '30 4734

Rhodes, Henry T. F. The nature of chemical evidence and its place in the detection of crime. Police J [London] 1: 657-68 O '28 4735

Rogers, L. Joselyn. Application of chemistry to the detection of crime. Soc Chem Ind J 49: 951 N 7 '30 4736

Teale, Edwin Way. Hidden crime clues bared by chemists magic. Pop Sci 119: 22-4 N '31 **4737**

Walton, Robert P. comp. Starches, 1811-1925; a list of references dealing with the chemistry and technology of starches, dextrins and amylases. N Y Pub Lib Bul 31: 12-34, 97-140, 178-221, 411-41, 464-523, 572-617, 639-90, 718-87 Ja-S '27 **4738**

Weduwen, A. J. der. Chemische strijdmiddelen in dienst van de politie. Tijdschr v d politie 1 (14): 238-41 Jl 21 '28 **4739**

Welsh, Rex. Modern chemistry as an exact science when used in the detection and conviction of the criminal. Int Assn Identif, Calif Div Proc 16: 82-4 '31 **4740**

CRYPTOGRAPHY

Bohne, G. Dechiffrierung eines Kassibers. Krimin Monatsh 2: 269-71 D '28 **4741**

Gylden, Yves. Le chiffre des Nihilistes. R Int de Crimin 2 (9): 690-6 '30 **4742**

Gylden, Yves. Le chiffre particulier de Louis XVI et de Marie-Antoinette lors de la fuite de Varennes. R Int de Crimin 3 (3): 248-56 '31 **4743**

Gylden, Yves. Chifferbyråernas insatser i väldskriget till lands. 139p. Stockholm, Militärlitteraturföreningens fôrlag, 1931 **4744**

Gylden, Yves. Histoire du décryptement. R Int de Crimin 2 (5): 363-80 '30 **4745**

Gylden, Yves. De quelques systèmes de chiffres synthétiques. R Int de Crimin 1: 358-73 O '29 **4746**

Hooker, C[harles] W. R. The deciphering of cryptograms. Police J [London] 1: 621-33 '28 **4747**

Hooker, Charles W. R. The Jules Verne cipher. Police J [London] 4: 107-19 Ja '31 **4748**

Kingman, Robert. Mirror writing; the modern survival of primitive functions. Welf Mag 19: 496-505 Ap '28 **4749**

Philipp, Lothar. Geheimschriften und ihre Entzifferung. Westerm Monatsh 74: 285-90 '30 **4750**

Probst, J. H. Expertise et analyse graphometrique des écritures sémitiques. R Int de Crimin 2 (10): 726-37 '30 **4751**

Un système cryptographique mentionné par Fridérici. R Int de Crimin 2 (6): 480 '30 **4752**
Fridérici, Cryptographia oder Geheime Correspondentz, 268 (1684).

Türkel, Siegfried. Chiffrieren mit Geräten und Maschinen. Eine Einführung in die Kryptographie. 94p. Graz, Moser, 1927 **4753**

Türkel, Siegfried. Kryptographische Parerga (vom Chiffrieren und Dechiffrieren). Kasuistisches aus der kriminalistischen Praxis. Wissenschaftlicher Leiter der Kriminalistischen Institutes der Polizeidirektion, Wien. 63p. Graz, Moser, 1929 **4754**

Yardley, Herbert O. The American black chamber. 375p. Indianapolis, Bobbs-Merrill, 1931 **4755**

CLOTH, HAIRS AND WOOLS

Barnes, H. C. The identification of cloth in criminal investigation. Police J [London] 4: 44-59 Ja '31 **4756**

Bialoszabski. [Méthode biochemique de Kostjakoff pour l'examen cheveux]. Czasopismo Sadowo-Lekarskie 3 (3) '30 **4757**

Glaister, John. A study of hairs and wools. 187p. Cairo, Misr Press, 1931 **4758**
1061 photomicrographs of hairs selected from the mammalian group of animals, 28 per cent of which represents study of human hair.

Mitchell, C. Ainsworth. Circumstantial evidence from hairs and fibres. R Int de Crimin 2 (9): 678-89 '30; same title: Am J Police Sci 1: 594-602 N '30 **4759**

DIRT AND DUST

Kockel, Heinz. Über den Wert der Untersuchung von Fingernagelschmutz. Arch f Krim 82: 209-14 bibliog (p214) Ap '28 **4760**

Kraft, B. Neues zur Kotuntersuchung in Kriminalfällen. Arch f Krim 84: 211-15 My '29 **4761**

Locard, Edmond. L'analyse des poussières en criminalistique. R Int de Crimin 1: 176-249 bibliog (p249) S '29; translation: Analysis of dust traces, by D. J. Larson. Am J Police Sci 1: 276-98, 401-18, 496-514 My-S '30 **4762**
Translated into English by the Adam brothers under title: "Criminal investigation."

Locard, Edmond. Dust and its analysis. An aid to criminal investigation. Police J [London] 1: 177-92 Ap '28 **4763**

Schatz, W. Hilfs-Indizien. Krimin Monatsh 3: 200-2 S '29; translation: Dirt scraped from shoes, as a means of identification; by Jeannie Van Toch. Am J Police Sci 1: 55-9 Ja '30 **4764**

Soderman, Harry. Un appareil nouveau pour recueillir par aspiration les poussières des vêtements portés par le criminel. R Int de Crimin 3 (5): 373-8 '31 **4765**

DECEPTION TESTS

Adler, Herman M. and Larson, John A. Deception and self-deception. J Abnorm & Soc Psychol 22: 364-71 bibliog (p371) Ja '28 **4766**

Chappell, Matthew N. Blood pressure in deception. Arch Psychol (105): 1-39 Ap '29 **4767**

Crosland, Harold Randolph. The psychological methods of word-association and reaction-time as tests of deception. 104p. bibliog 101-4. (University of Oregon Publ, Psychol ser v1 no1) Eugene, 1929 **4768**

Crosland, Harold R. and Beck, Lester F. Objective measurements of emotion: 1, The relative efficiency of visual and acoustical presentations of stimulus-words in the association-reaction test. 2, The relative efficiency of visual and two auditory methods of presenting the word-stimuli in an experiment which combines the association, reaction-time technique with the psychogalvanic technique; 3, The relation (correlation) obtaining between reaction-time data and psychogalvanic data in a combination experiment and comprising the word association, reaction-time and psychogalvanic techniques; 4, general bibliography. (University of Oregon Publ, Psychol ser v1 no3) Eugene, 1931 **4769**

Do "lie-detectors" work? Northwest Police J 7: 12-13 N '29 **4770**

House, Robert E. The use of scopolamine in criminology. Am J Police Sci 2: 328-36 Jl '31 **4771**

Keeler, Leonarde. "The canary murder case"; the use of the deception test to determine guilt. Am J Police Sci 1: 381-6 Jl '30 **4772**

Keeler, Leonarde. [Deception tests and the lie detector]. Int Assn Identif Proc 16: 186-93 '30 **4773**

Keeler, Leonarde. A method for detecting deception. Am J Police Sci 1: 38-57 Ja '30 **4774**

Larson, John A. The polygraph and deception; the use of this mechanical device in cases of deception as tested at the Institute for juvenile research. Welf Mag 18: 646-69 bibliog (p668-9) My '27 **4775**

Larson, John A.; Haney, George W., and Rouse, Kenneth. Present status of the problem: use of deception tests in judicial procedure and the investigation of the validity and reliability of the so-called "lie detector" technique. 36p. (typw) [Chicago, Institute for juvenile research] 1930 **4776**

McCormick, Charles T. Deception tests and the law of evidence. Calif L R 15: 484-504 bibliog (p503-4) S '27; same title: Am J Police Sci 2:388-408 bibliog (p407-8) S '31 **4777**

Mussati, Cesare L. Ricerche sulla diagnosi pneumografica delle testimonianze col metodo Benussi—1. Testimonianze a colorito personale. Arch Ital di Psicol 8: 25-50 F 10 '30 **4778**

Possibilities of lie detector in insurance shown. Nat Underw 35: 39 Mr 19 '31 **4779**

Spencer, Carlton E. Methods of detecting guilt: word association, reaction-time method. Ore L R 8: 158-66 F '29 **4780**

Trunk, H. Zur Kennzeichnung krimineller Persönlichkeiten vermittels der Ewaldschen Charakterstrukturformeln. Zeitsch f d ges Neurol u Psychiat 131: 375-91 '30 **4781**

Truth serum demonstrated. Peace Offic 5: 16, 21 Ap '27 **4782**

Truth serum tests. J Crim L & Crimin *22*: 291 Jl '31 **4783**

Twilight sleep induced by morphine and scopolamine.

GLASS

Chavigny. L'identification des verres dans les accidents d'automobiles. R Int de Crimin 2 (8): 566-9 '30 **4784**

Malaval, René. L'identification des verres dans les accidents d'automobiles. R Int de Crimin 2 (6): 437-45 '30 **4785**

Matwejeff, S. N. Kriminalistische Untersuchung zerbrochener Fensterscheiben. Arch f Krim 86: 100-10 Ap '30; translation and reprint: Criminal investigation of broken window panes. Am J Police Sci 2: 148-57 Mr '31 **4786**

METALLOGRAPHIC ANALYSIS

Mathews, J. H. Metallographic analysis in crime detection. Am J Police Sci 1: 439-55 S '30 **4787**

Metallurgical detective story. Metal Prog 19: 94-8 Je '31 **4788**

Simonin, C. L'examen métallographique des balles de plomb. Ann de Méd Lég 9: 183- Ap '29 **4789**

RADIOGRAPHY

Black ray valuable police aid. Police J [N Y] 17: 12-13 My '30 **4790**

Castellanos, I. Los rayos X en la técnica policial. R de Crimin, Psiquiat y Med Leg 14: 84-96 Ja '27 **4791**

Danckwortt, P. W. Lumineszenz-Analyse in filtriertem, ultraviolettem Licht. Ein Hilfsbuch mit der Analysenlampe. 147p. Leipzig, Akademische Verlagsgesellschaft, 1928 **4792**

Evans, W. S. Roentgen findings as evidence in medico-legal cases. Mich M Soc J 30: 329-39 My '31 **4793**

Gerngross, O. Ultraviolettlicht als Erkennugsmittel: Die Verwendung von Fluoreszenzerscheinungen zu diagnostischen Zwecken. Arch f Krim 81: 13-21 Jl '27 **4794**

Glimm, E. and Schroeder, H. Nachweis von Banknotenfälschungen durch ultraviolette Strahlen. Arch f Krim 83: 1-11 Jl '28 **4795**

Goodman, Herman N. Detection by violet rays; more possible police uses for filtered ultraviolet light. Police "13-13" 5: 8-10, 73 Ag '30 **4796**

Goodman, Herman [N.]. Medico-legal uses of filtered ultra-violet or black light. Am J Police Sci 1: 260-71 My '30 **4797**

Goodman, Herman N. Ultraviolet light in crime detection. Police J [N Y] 18: 12, 25 Mr '31 **4798**

Goodman, Herman [N.]. Uses of ultraviolet light in criminal investigation. Police J [London] 4: 225-31 Ap '31 **4799**

Hulsebosch, C. J. van Ledden. La aplicación de los rayos ultra-violetas en la justicia. R de Crimin, Psiquiat y Med Leg 14: 650-5 S '27 **4800**

Identification by X-ray photographs of the nasal sinuses. Science ns74: sup10 O '31 4801

Kögel, G[ustav]. Typen der Fluoreszenz- und Ultraviolett-photographie. Arch f Krim 80: 81-9 Mr '27 4802

Kögel, G[ustav]. Über eine neue technische Anwendung der Kathodenstrahlen in der Kriminalistik. Arch f Krim 86: 94-9 Ap '30 4803

Kögel, G[ustav]. Die unsichtbaren Strahlen im Dienste der Kriminalistik. Photographie radierter Schriften. 183p. Graz, Moser, 1928 4804

Pacini, August J. Ultraviolet spectographic detection of mercury. Am J Police Sci 1: 387-95 bibliog (p395) Jl '30 4805

Scott, Orlando F. Roentgenograms and their chronologic legal recognition. Ill L R 24: 674-9 F '30 4806

Simonin, C. Quelques applications de la lumière de Wood au dépistage des faux documents. Ann de Méd Lég 11: 87-8 F '31 4807

Söderman, Harry. Les rayons ultra-violets et la criminalistique. R Int de Crimin 1: 509-12 N '29 4808

Symons, C. T. The fluorescence test: ultraviolet light in scientific criminal investigation. Police J [London] 3: 235-43 Ap '30 4809

Teale, Edwin Way. Weird unseen rays trap master crooks. Pop Sci 119: 36-8 O '31 4810

X-ray photographs furnish new means of identification. Sci Am 138: 57 Ja '28 4811

STAINS

Bentini, Genuzio. Le macchie sulla toga. 114p. Napoli, Morano, 1927 4812

How body stains betray criminals. Pop Mech 57: 98-101 Ja '31 4813

Hudson, Alfred A. The examination of seminal stains. Policeman 1: 13-15 S '29 4814

Hudson, Alfred A. Seminal stain detection. Police J [N Y] 16: 20-1 Mr '29 4815

Niederland. Bedeutung und Nachweis von Samenspuren in der Kriminalistik. Krimin Monatsh 5: 100-4 My '31 4816

Schwarzacher, W. Altersbestimmungen von Blutspuren. Deut Zeitsch f d ges gerichtl Med 15 (2): 119- Ap 8 '30; translation: Determination of age of bloodstains. Am J Police Sci 1: 374-80 bibliog (p379-80) Jl '30 4817

Simonin, C. Contribution a l'identification médico-légale des taches par la photographie par transparence. Ann de Méd Lég 11:85-6 F '31 4818

Simonin, C. La valeur médico-légale de l'examen des taches de sperme à la lumière de Wood. Ann de Méd Lég 9: 60-2 F '29 4819

Blood Stains, Tests and Groups

Ahlemann, Hans Robert. Blut und Rost. Arch f Krim 83: 311-12 N '28 4820

Böhmer, K. Die Blutgruppen als Beweismittel. Krimin Monatsh 3: 145-7, 174-8 Jl, Ag '29 4821

Böhmer, K. Blutgruppen und Verbrechen. Deut Zeitsch f d ges gerichtl Med 9: 426-30 Mr '27 4822

Boldrini, B. Un nuovo procedimento per la preparazione dei cristalli di Teichmann. Riforma Med 46: 139 Ja 27 '30 4823

Cattaneo, Luis. Las catalasas en la identificación de la sangre. R de Crimin, Psiquiat y Med Leg (98): 159- '30 4824

East, W. Norwood. Heredity and crime. Blood tests and inheritance in law. Eugen R 20: 169-72 O '28 4825

Elias, Rudolf. Der Blutprobenbeweis, seine Zulässigkeit und Erzwingbarkeit. 34p. bibliog vi-viii. Diss. Breslau, 1931 4826

Fan, Leung. Une nouvelle méthode de détermination de l'origine du sang par les cristaux de Strzyzowski. R Int de Crimin 3 (10): 738-41 '31 4827

Foerster, A. Blutgruppen und Verbrecher. Deut Zeitsch f d ges gerichtl Med 11: 487-90 Jl 28 '28 4828

Folomina, W. Isohämoagglutinationsgruppen bei Verbrechern. Arch f Krim 84: 145-8 Ap '29 4829

Frenkel. Das Blutgruppen-Untersuchungsverfahren vor dem Schwurgericht. Zeitsch f d ges Strafrechtswiss 48: 671-6 '28 4830

Fujiwara, K. Einige Erfahrungen mit der Blutgruppenbestimmung an Flecken in Kriminalfällen. Deut Zeitsch f d ges gerichtl Med 15: 470-7 Jl 10 '30 4831

Furuhata, T. Vaterschaftsnachweis durch Blutgruppendiagnose bereits vor 700 Jahren. Arch f Krim 82: 190 '28 4832

Gaude, G. L'expertise des taches de sang. R Int de Crimin 3 (1): 38-43 '31 4833

Glaister, John. Some results of recent medico-legal research in the examination of bloodstains and hairs. Police J [London] 1: 62-77 Ja '28 4834

Gompert, Frank B. Blood and blood chemistry. Los Angeles Chron 13: 14, 22 N 29 '30 4835

Gundel, M. Blutgruppen-Untersuchungen bei Strafgefangenen. Deut Zeitsch f d ges gerichtl Med 11:99-119 '28 4836

Hellwig, Albert. Meineidsverhütung durch Blutsgruppenprobe. Krimin Monatsh 3: 75-7 Ap '29 4837

Hennemann, W. Über Blutgruppenbestimmungen an Strafgefangenen. Deut Zeitsch f d ges gerichtl Med 16: 126-38 N 5 '30 4838

Hesselink, W. F. Blutspuren in der kriminalistischen praxis. Zeitsch f Ang Chem 44: 653-5 Ag 1 '31 4839

Hooker, Sanford B. and Boyd, William C. The chances of establishing non-paternity by blood-grouping tests. J Crim L & Crimin 20: 360-3 N '29; same title: Am J Police Sci 1:121-4 Mr '30 4840

Hudson, Alfred. Blood examination as an aid to identify criminals. Police J [N Y] 15: 10-11 Ap '28 4841

Hudson, Alfred. Microscopical examinations of blood stains. Police J [N Y] 16: 20-1 F '29 4842

Ishihashi, M. Blood types of criminals. Shakaigaku-zasshi (509) '29 **4843**
Study of 500 criminals at Niigata criminal court.

Jankovich, Ladislaus. Helyes-e a vércsoportmeghatározás alkalmazása az igazságszolgáltatásban? Magyar Jogi Szemle 12 (7): 334-44 '31 **4844**

Kössler, Maximilian. Die Blutprobe als Beweismittel in Vaterschaftsstreitigkeiten. Arch f Krim 81: 141-59 S '27 **4845**

Koller, S. Statistische Untersuchungen zur Theorie der Blutgruppen und zu ihrer Anwendung vor Gericht. Zeitsch f Rassenphysiol 3: 121-83 Ap 1 '31 **4846**

Latour, Cesar Juarros y Tolosa. Grupos sanguineos y delincuencia (le sang de group II prédominerait chez les criminels contre la propriété et le sang de group I chez les anormaux sexuels). R Españ de Crimin (11) Jl '29 **4847**

Lee, Blewett. Blood tests for paternity. Med-Leg J 44: 57-61 Mr '27 **4848**

Lénárt, George. A vérsoportvizsgálotok szerepe az igazságszolgáltatásban. Jogtudományi Közlöny 64: 74-5 Ap 15 '29 **4849**

Leonhard. Die Bedeutung der Blutgruppenuntersuchung im Straf- und Zivilprozess. Deut Juristen-Zeit 34: 135-9 Ja 15 '29 **4850**

Locard, Jacques. La détermination du sang par le leucovert malachite (réactif de Médinger). R Int de Crimin 3 (9): 713-15 '31 **4851**

Lüdicke, Klaus. Der gegenwärtige Stand der Blutgruppenuntersuchung und ihre Anwendbarkeit im Unterhaltsprozess. 25p. bibliog v-xii. Diss. Breslau, 1931 **4852**

Medinger, Pierre. Contribution au diagnostic de traces minimes de sang; 20 ans d'expérience avec le réactif leuco-vert-malachite. R Int de Crimin 3 (7): 493-506 '31 **4853**

Nicoletti, Ferdinando. La cristallizzazione dell'emoglobina nelle varie età dell'uomo. Arch di Antrop Crim 50 (3): 386- My '30 **4854**

Palmieri, V. M. Die Verteilung der Blutgruppen unter geisteskranken Verbrechern. Deut Zeitsch f d ges gerichtl Med 12: 506-12 O 30 '28 **4855**

Pichon, S. and Sannié, C. Influence du Ph dans la détermination de l'origine humaine du sang par la réaction des sérums préciptitants. Ann de Méd Lég 11: 733-6 D '31 **4856**

Raestrup. Blutgruppenzugehörigkeit und Recht. Arch f Krim 83: 278-81 N '28 **4857**

Rehfeldt, Paul. Blutgruppenuntersuchungen in der kriminalistischen Praxis. Krimin Monatsh 1: 175-8 Ag '27 **4858**

Rivière, R. D. de la and Kossovitch, N. La question des "groupes sanguons" en médecine légale. Ann de Méd Lég 7: 390-9 Jl '27 **4859**

Romanese, R. Tecnia per la dimostrazione di macchie di sangue su lame arrugginite. Arch di Antrop Crim 50: 1620-3 '30 **4860**

Salaw. Fortschritte auf dem Gebiet der Blutgruppenforschung. Krimin Monatsh 5: 157-8 Jl '31 **4861**

Schiff, F. Die Blutgruppen und ihre Anwendung vor Gericht. Deut Zeitsch f d ges gerichtl Med 9: 369-401 Mr '27 **4862**

Schiff, F.; Leonard, Heim, and Scheurlen, Oppe. Die Bedeutung der Blutgruppenuntersuchung im Zivil- und Strafrecht. Monats f Kriminalpsychol u Strafrechtsref 20: 152-60 '29 **4863**

Schiff, Fritz. Die Technik der Blutgruppenuntersuchung für Kliniker und Gerichtsärzte. Nebst Berücksichtigung ihrer Anwendung in der Anthropologie und der Vererbungs- und Konstitutionsforschung. ed.2. Berlin, Springer, 1929 **4864**

Schmidt, A. Blutgruppenbestimmungen an Strafgefangenen. Deut Zeitsch f d ges gerichtl Med 13: 373-6 Je 4 '29 **4865**

Serebrianikoff, P. Technic and medicolegal importance of determination of blood groups through blood stains. Odessky Med J 2: 87-93 Ja '27 **4866**

Serebrianikoff, P. and Leitschick, M. Zur Frage der Herstellung und Verwendung von Serumglobulinpulver für Blutgruppenbestimmung. Deut Zeitsch f d ges gerichtl Med 15 (2): 125- Ap 8 '30 **4867**

Simonin, C. Le diagnostic médico-légal d'une tache de sang. Strasbourg-méd 89: 288-91 Je 5 '29 **4868**

Siracusa, Vittorio. Sull'applicazione pratica dei metodi per la diagnosi individuale del sangue. Arch di Antrop Crim 47: 307-39 My '27 **4869**

Snyder, Laurence H[asbrouck]. Blood grouping and its practical applications. Arch Path & Lab Med 4: 215-57 '27 **4870**

Snyder, Laurence Hasbrouck. Blood grouping in relation to clinical and legal medicine. 153p. bibliog 136-49. Baltimore, Williams & Wilkins, 1929 **4871**

Snyder, Laurence H[asbrouck]. The medico-legal application of hereditary human characters, with especial reference to the blood groups. Am M Assn J 88: 562-3 F 19 '27 **4872**

Soerono, M. Simple method for staining blood films on large scale. Mededeel v d dienst d volksgezondh in Nederl-Indië 20: 122 '31 **4873**

Teale, Edwin Way. How modern sleuths read murder clues in blood. Pop Sci 119: 18-20 S '31 **4874**

Über Blutgruppenuntersuchung und ihre gerichtliche Bedeutung. Arch f Krim 80: 173-4 Mr '27 **4875**

Ujlaki, Géza. A vérvizsgálat bizonyitási értéke, különösen a gyermektartási perben. Magyar Jogi Szemle 10: 383-402 D '29 **4876**

Werneburg. Die praktische Bedeutung der Blutgruppenuntersuchung. Krimin Monatsh 2: 180-1 Ag '28 **4877**

TOXICOLOGY

Autenrieth, Wilhelm. Detection of poisons; transl by William H. Warren. 6th

American ed. from 5th German ed. rev. Philadelphia, Blakiston, 1928 **4878**

Cloetta, M.; St. Faust, E.; Flury, F.; Hubener, E., and Zangger, H. Lehrbuch der Toxikologie. Berlin, Julius Springer, 1928 **4879**

Dettling, J. Zum exakten Nachweis des chemischen Unfalles. Schweiz med Wchnschr 61: 1138-40 N 28 '31 **4880**

Driver, John Edmund and Trease, G. E. Chemistry of crude drugs; an elementary textbook for students of pharmacognosy. 159p. N.Y. Longmans, 1928 **4881**

Dutt, N. B. Commercial drugs of India. 256p. [Calcutta] Thacker, 1928 **4882**

Frets, Gerrit Pieter. Alcohol and the other germ poisons. 179p. bibliog 151-74. 's Gravenhage, Nijhoff, 1931 **4883**

Lewin, Louis. Gifte und Vergiftungen. ed. 4. 1087p. Berlin, Stilke, 1929 **4884**

McCrae, J. Toxicology. J Med Assn S Africa 4: 197-8 Ap 12 '30 **4885**

Meixner, K. Die Erkennung von Vergiftungen an der Leiche. München med Wchnschr 78: 1750-3 O 9 '31 **4886**

Trumper, Max. Memoranda of toxicology; partly based on Tanner's Memoranda of poisons. ed.2. 214p. [Philadelphia] Blakiston, 1929 **4887**

Underhill, Frank Pell. Toxicology; or, The effect of poison. ed.2. rev. and enl. 311p. [Philadelphia] Blakiston, 1928 **4888**

Wilcox, W. Recent advances in toxicology and forensic medicine. M Press 175: 365-9 N 2 '27 **4889**

Willcox, William. Toxicology and crime. Police J [London] 1: 98-104 Ja '28 **4890**

IDENTIFICATION

Almandos, Luis Reyna. Bases fundamentales del programa de identificación. R de Identif y Cienc Pen 3: 307-24 Mr '29 **4891**

Almandos, Luis Reyna. Ciencia y derecho de identidad; su existencia y definición. R de Identif y Cienc Pen 4: 151-70 Jl '29 **4892**

Almandos, L[uis] Reyna. Identificación del recien nacido. R Int de Crimin 2 (1): 15-22 '30 **4893**

Almandos, Luis Reyna. Juan Vucetich y la gratitud argentina. R de Identif y Cienc Pen 2: 149-53 Jl '28 **4894**

Almandos, Luis Reyna. Legislación del derecho de identidad. Discusión legislativa del primer proyecto de ley de identidad civil y criminal. (Registro general de identificación, 1909-1910). R de Identif y Cienc Pen 5: 5-84 N '29 **4895**

Almandos, Luis Reyna. Das naturalización de la cédula de identidad. R de Identif y Cienc Pen 1: 78-87 N '27 **4896**

Almandos, Luis Reyna. Union internacional de identificación. R de Identif y Cienc Pen 6: 394-402 S '30; same article: Union internationale d'identification. R Int de Crimin 3 (10): 728-37 '31 **4897**

Argiuvos do Instituto medico-legal e do gabinete de identificaçao (3) D '31 **4898**
Direçao de Leonidio Ribeiro e Miguel Salles. Rio de Janeiro, Imp. Nac.

Balbino-Rego, Antonio. Les services d'identification au Portugal. R Int de Crimin 1: 381-2 O '29 **4899**

Batchelor, Chester A. Legal procedure: identifications of persons and evidentiary articles. Northwest Police J 6: 11, 61-3 My '29 **4900**

Berardi, Domingo A. Pericía caligráfica (causa criminal por homicidio de Carlos A. Ray). R de Identif y Cienc Pen 1: 268-89 Mr '28 **4901**

Berland, Lucien. Utilisation possible de la Soie des Araignées pour l'identification des criminels. R Int de Crimin 1 (1-3): 39-44 '29 **4902**

Carmody, Charles C. Identification of criminals by scientific methods. Mich Assn Chiefs Police Proc 6: 48-50 '29 **4903**

Castellanos, Israel. Personal identification; what it is and what it should be. Int Assn Identif Proc 13: 108-13 '27 **4904**

Chanetón, J. A.; Ríos, Eduardo; Ureta, Manual, and Facio, Julio M. El Instituto Vucetich y la nueva carrera de peritos identificadores. R de Identif y Cienc Pen 2: 67-70 My '28 **4905**

Chavigny, P. Identification internationale des disparus. Ann de Méd Lég 10 (1) Ja '30 **4906**

Chavigny, P. Les petits procédés d'identification (le boitier de la montre). Ann de Méd Lég 7: 82-3 F '27 **4907**

La ciencia y el derecho de identidad en el Brasil. Programma do curso de Sciencias juridicas e sociaes. Theoria e pratica do processo criminal. R de Identif y Cienc Pen 7: 218-22 N '30 **4908**

Conto, César and Isaza, Emiliano. Contribución al estudio de la individualización human. Origen y significado de los nombres. R de Identif y Cienc Pen 2: 230-45 Jl '28 **4909**

Dangers of identification. Sol J 73: 165 Mr 16 '29 **4910**

De l'identité en Belgique. R Belge de Police Adm & Jud 51: 2- Ja '30 **4911**

Documentos para la historia de la identidad; Herschel y Faulds, precursores de la dactiloscopia. R de Identif y Cienc Pen 6: 240-53 Jl '30 **4912**

Doepner, Herman. The differentiation of human identities. Int Assn Identif, Calif Div Proc 16: 14-16 '31 **4913**

Domingues, Aurelio. Manual pratico de identificaçao (Systema de Vucetich). 90p. Recife, Ediçao do autor, 1929 **4914**

Evidence of identification. Sol J 73: 393 Je 22 '29 **4915**

Ellis, Robert. Identification work extended. Peace Offic 5: 11, 37 Ag '27 **4916**

Forest, Henry P. de. Bibliography of personal identification. Int Assn Identif Proc 16: 162-71 '30 **4917**

Foster, Edward. Identification by wire. Chief Constables' Assn Can Proc 25: 54-6 '29 **4918**

Goffin, L. De l'identité en Belgique. R Belge de Police Adm & Jud (125) Ja '30 4919

Gorphe, F. Comment apprécier les reconnaissances d'identité. Etudes Crimin 4 (11): 287-93 N '29 4920

Heindl, Robert and Gorphe F. Wie bei der Anfertigung von Steckbriefen und bei Gegenüberstellungen zum Zweck der Identifizierung zu verfahren ist. Arch f Krim 89: 60-74 Jl '31 4921

Herrero, Antonio. Breve síntesis histórica de la identificación. R de Identif y Cienc Pen 1: 243-67, 2: 35-63, 3: 23-62 Mr-D '28 4922

Homenaje de los identificadores de Chile a Vucetich. R de Identif y Cienc Pen 4: 378-85 S '29 4923

Hoover, J[ohn] Edgar. Criminal identification. Ann Am Acad 146: 205-13 N '29; same title: Am J Police Sci 2: 8-19 Ja '31 4924

International association for identification. Proceedings. 13, 1927—16, 1930. Sec.-Treas. Leroy Goodwin, Youngstown, Ohio, 1928-31 4925

Jerlov, Emil. Projet de système de classification plantaire chez les nouveaux-nés. R Int de Crimin 2 (9): 662-77 '30 4926

Jörgensen, Hakon. Das Fernidentifizierungssystem. Krimin Monatsh 1: 146-7 Jl '27 4927

Kockel, H. Identifizierung von Werkzeugeindrücken. Arch f Krim 83: 288-91 N '28 4928

[Miguez, E. J. and Almandos, Luis Reyna]. De los peritos identificadores. R de Identif y Cienc Pen 1: 28-49 N '27 4929

Morrill, Clarence S. Speculative identification. Int Assn Identif, Calif Div Proc 12: 49-55 '27 4930

Müller, H. Der Erkennungsdienst bei der Polizeidirektion Heidelberg. Arch f Krim 80: 103-9 Mr '27 4931

D'Onofrio, Andrés. Una institución indispensable. El registro general de identificacion. R de Identif y Cienc Pen 1: 62-75 N '27 4932

Ortube, Celestino. Transmisión y archivo de señas particulares. R de Identif y Cienc Pen 3: 63-9 N '28 4933

Ottolenghi, S. L'atto di ricognizione e i confronti. Zacchia 6: 10-18 '27 4934

Ottolenghi, S. Ricognizioni e confronti ai fini dell'identificazione giudiziaria. Policlinico 34: 902 '27 4935

Park, Kenneth C. New style of identification cards for criminals. State Trooper 11: 5-6, 19 S '29 4936

Pita, Arturo Marcos. Requisitos legales de la cédula de identidad. R de Identif y Cienc Pen 4: 195-216 bibliog (p216) Jl '29 4937

De Rechter, G. and Mage, J. Considérations sur une méthode d'identification des objets. Son application a un cas particulier. R de Dr Pén et de Crimin 7: 269-77 Mr '27 4938

La réorganisation du Service de l'Identité judiciaire à Paris. R Int de Crimin 2 (6): 470-1 '30 4939

Rogers, William A. Identification in industry. Justice 1: 28-9 D '28 4940

Schaffer, E. The distant identification system. Int Assn Chiefs Police Proc 1927: 146-51 4941

Schneickert, Hans. Das Erkennungsdienst in Kairo. Krimin Monatsh 1: 102-5 My '27 4942

Sellers, J. Clark. Scientific identification. Inst Police Adm Proc 1929: 9-17 4943

Sorrentino, Ugo. Accertamento di identita personale. R Int de Crimin 1 (1-3): 99-112 '29 4944

Urgent need for greater efficiency in criminal identification. Am City 38: 116-17 Mr '28 4945

Valenzuela, Gilberto Llanos. La identificación civil en Chile. Fusión de los servicios del Registro civil e identificación. R de Identif y Cienc Pen 8: 146-56 My '31 4946

Voit. Die Nachrichtentechnik im Dienste der Berliner Polizei. Polizei 25: 142 Mr 5 '28 4947

Vucetich, Juan. Convención internacional de identificación. R de Identif y Cienc Pen 4: 313-18 S '29 4948

Vucetich, Juan. Cuales eran los fines del Registro general de identificación (determinación de la personalidad humana). R de Identif y Cienc Pen 3: 10-22 N '28 4949

Vucetich, Juan. Fragmento de la historia sintética de la identificación (1920). R de Identif y Cienc Pen 1: 96-100 N '27 4950

Vucetich, Juan. Historia sintética de la identificación. R de Identif y Cienc Pen 6: 177-239, 355-93; 7: 5-110 Jl-N '30; 8: 5-121 My '31 4951

Bureaus of Identification

Almandos, Luis Reyna. Proyecto de registro nacional de identificación para la república Argentina (codificación del derecho de identidad). R de Identif y Cienc Pen 7: 155-81 N '30 4952

Almandos, Luis Reyna. Registro nacional de identificación para la República Argentina. R de Crimin, Psiquiat y Med Leg 18: 182-94, 210-18 Mr, Ap '31 4953

Bureau internationale d'identification a distance. R Int de Crimin 1: 144-7 Jl '29 4954

Buskirk, Eugene Van. The identification division of the Bureau of investigation, Department of justice. N Y St Assn Chiefs Police Proc 29: 45-8 '29 4955

California. State bureau of criminal identification and investigation. Biennial reports, 1926/28. Sacramento, 1928 4956

California. State division of criminal identification and investigation. Report . . . for the biennial period ending June 30, 1930. 18p. Sacramento, 1930 4957

Correa, Edgard Simoes. Estatistica dos Archivos dactyloscopicos do Gabinete de identificaçào da policia do Districto federal (Brazil). R de Identif y Cienc Pen 4: 80-96 My '29 4958

Cuba. Gabinete nacional de identificación. Boletin. 1 (4). Habana 4959

Cuba. Gabinete nacional de identificación. Reglamento del Gabinete nacional de identificación. 19p. Habana, Imp. y Paleria de Rambla, 1927 (Graceta oficial, S 15 '27) 4960

DeVore, Glen M. Valuation of a Bureau of identification. Int Assn Identif, Calif Div Proc 14:18-21 '29 4961

Ericson, Hugo. The State bureau of identification [Michigan]. Mich Assn Chiefs Police Proc 6: 51-3 '29 4962

Das Erkennungsamt der Wiener Polizeidirektion. Arch f Krim 82: 65-7 Ja '28 4963

The federal finger print bureau. L Notes 31: 255- Mr '28 4964

Hoover, J[ohn] Edgar. The benefits to be derived through cooperation with the Bureau of investigation of the United States Department of justice. Int Assn Chiefs Police Proc 36: 73-9 '29 4965

Hoover, J[ohn] Edgar. Investigations as benefited by the co-operative exchange of data with the Bureau of investigation of the United States Department of justice. Int Assn Chiefs Police Proc 37: 40-5 '30 4966

Hoover, J[ohn] Edgar. Investigations; how the United States Department of justice assists police forces. Police "13-13" 5: 3-5, 38 S '30 4967

Hoover, J[ohn] Edgar. The national bureau of criminal identification. Police "13-13" 4: 12-14, 89 D '29 4968

Hoover, J[ohn] Edgar. National division of identification and information. Am J Police Sci 2: 241-51 My '31 4969

Hoover, J[ohn] Edgar. Report of the Division of identification and information of the Bureau of investigation of the United States Department of justice. Int Assn Chiefs Police Proc 1927: 144-6 4970

Hoover, J[ohn] Edgar. The value of a national bureau of identification. Northwest Police J 7: 13-14, 56-8 F '30 4971

Hoover, J[ohn] Edgar. What the federal bureau of investigation has done for the police of the nation. Police J [N Y] 17: 24-5, 32 N '29 4972

Hoover, J[ohn] Edgar. The work of the Bureau of identification. Am J Police Sci 2: 101-7 Mr '31 4973

Indiana. Bureau of criminal identification and investigation. [Reports] *in* Indiana Yearbook 1927: 35-40; 1928: 26-31; 1929: 15-19; 1930: 15-18; 1931: 10-12 4974

Low, Walter. The value of the Identification bureau to the Board of public utilities. Int Assn Identif, Calif Div Proc 14: 36-8 '29 4975

Macy, W. J. Bureau of identification and records, a public relations agency. Int Assn Identif Proc 16: 91-2 '30 4976

Michigan. [Bureau of criminal identification]. Report *in* Report of Department of public safety 4977

Das moderne Meldeamt. Polizei 25: 131 Mr 5 '28 4978

Morrill, Clarence [S.]. Functions of the division of criminal identification and investigation. Int Assn Identif, Calif Div Proc 15: 51-3 '30 4979

Morrill, C[larence] S. New methods of combating crime. Cur Hist 29: 107-10 O '28 4980

Neal, Ann, comp. State bureaus of criminal identification: a digest of state laws. 19p. (Photostat) Madison, Wisconsin Legislative reference library, September 30, 1930? 4981

New Jersey identification bureau. State Trooper 8: 27-8 Je '27 4982

Ohio. State bureau of criminal identification and investigation. Annual reports, July 1, 1926/June 30, 1927; July 1, 1927/December 31, 1928; January 1/December 31, 1929 4983

Resume: *in* Annual report of Department of public welfare 6, 1926/27: 91-4; 7, 1927/28: 59-65; 8, 1929: 114-19.

Park, Kenneth C. Michigan criminal identification bureau. State Trooper 11: 9-10, 21-2 Mr '30 4984

Parsons, Clara L. The work of the Bureau of criminal identification. N Y St Assn Magistrates Proc 20: 35-48 '28 4985

Peace offcers association of the state of California. Committee on special investigators of the State bureau of criminal identification and investigation. Report. Proc 8: 702- '28 4986

Scavarada, C. J. All departments should support Bureau of identification at Washington. Int Assn Chiefs Police Proc 1929: 96-100 4987

Service d'identification du bureau suisse de police centrale. R Int de Crimin 3 (3): 233-5 '31 4988

Snook, R. A. Identification bureau and teletype system . . . in New Jersey. State Trooper 12: 7-8 N '30 4989

Snook, R. A. N[ew] J[ersey] legislature passes bills for identification bureau and teletype. State Trooper 11: 13-14 My '30 4990

Tulk, Sam W. The value of a state bureau to peace officers. Int Assn Identif Proc 16: 81-2 '30 4991

United States. Congress. House. Committee on judiciary. Establishment of Division of identification and information, report to accompany H. R. 11802, February 8, 1929. 1p. Washington, 1929 (70th Cong. 2d sess. H. Rep. 2431) 4992

Valenzuela, Gilberto Llanos. La identificación civil en Chile; fusión de los servicos del Registro civil e identificación. R de Identif y Cienc Pen 8: 146-56 My '31 4993

Vucetich, Juan. Proyecto de ley de registro general de identificación. 272p. La Plata, Taller de Imp. Oficiales, 1929 4994

Warren, **Earl.** Scope and functions of state bureau of criminal identification. Peace Offic Assn Calif Proc 9: 65-9 '29 4995

Forensic Ballistics

A acção dos projectis de armas de fogo sobre as vestes. [50p.] São Paulo, 1928 4996

Thesis submitted to the Faculty of medicine, São Paulo.

Askins, Charles. Modern shot guns and loads. Marshallton, Del. Small arms tech. pub. co. 1927 4997

Bayle, E. L'identification de la charge meurtrière dans le cas d'attentats par fusil de chasse. R de Gendarm 1: 150-62 Mr 15 '28 4998

Bergé, M. Les trajets de balles dans les vêtements. R Int de Crimin 1: 513-20 N '29 4999

Berntheisel; Chavigny, and Laborde. Identification de balles de revolver. R Int de Crimin 1: 383-9 O '29 5000

Berntheisel; Chavigny, and Laborde. Une expertise d'identification de balles de revolver. Strasbourg méd 89: 185-7 Ap 20 '29 5001

Brüning, A. Waffen und munition als Beweismittel. Krimin Monatsh 3: 31-4 F '29 5002

Buxton, Joseph T. jr. Science of ballistics: judicial applications. L Notes 34: 24-8 My '30; same title: Am J Police Sci 2: 211-19 My '31 5003

Campbell, Harry. Explosives and combustibles. N Y St Assn Chiefs Police Proc 28: 16-20 '28 5004

Cassidy, Henry E. Ballistics forensically applied. J Crim L & Crimin 20: 439-47 N '30 5005

Chavigny, P. Etude médico-légale critique sur les brulûres imputées aux coups de feu. 58p. Strasbourg, Les Editions Universitaires de Strasbourg, 1929? 5006

Churchill, Robert. The forensic examination of firearms and projectiles. Police J [London] 2: 367-79 Jl '29 5007

Couraly, F. Les armes de chasse et leur tir. 344p. Paris, Emile Nourry, 1931 5008

Crossman, E[dward] C. Forensic ballistics. Detective 42: 3 Je '27 5009

Crossman, Edward C. Science turns detective [identification of firearms]. Sci Am 136: 18-21 Ja '27 5010

Crossman, Edward C. Some ????? not in the programme; being a discussion of some of the queer angles of the experience of a ballistic expert. Am J Police Sci 1: 313-24 My '30 5011

Dérome, Wilfrid. Expertise en armes à feu. Montreal, Privately printed, 1929 5012

Dyrenfurth, and Weimann, W. Über Nachweis und Fixierung von Nahschussspuren. Deut Zeitsch f d ges gerichtl Med 11: 288-90 '28 5013

Ferreira; Flaminio, and Arnaldo. A distancia e a dirrecçâa dos tiros determinadas por exames procedidos nas vestes da victima. Policia e Justiça 2 (7) My '30 5014

Fingerprinting the guns of crime. Pop Mech 56: 914-17 D '31 5015

Fleischer. Füllbleistifte als Waffen. Kriminal Monatsh 5: 235-6 O '31 5016

[Goddard, Calvin]. Books on arms, ammunition and firearm identification. Am J Police Sci 2: 84-7 Ja '31 5017

Goddard, C[alvin]. Forensic ballistics; illustrated lecture on identification of bullets and firearms in homicide cases, with special emphasis on part played by medical profession. M Times [N Y] 57: 183-9 Jl '29 5018

Goddard, Calvin. Method of bullet identification. Int Assn Identif Proc 13: 46-55 '27 5019

Goddard, Calvin H. Scientific identification of firearms and bullets. Peace Offic 5: 7, 24 Ja '27 5020

Goddard, Calvin H. Scientific identification of firearms and bullets. Pac Police Mag 6: 9-10, 22-5 My '29 5021

Goddard, Calvin [H.]. The Valentine day massacre: a study in ammunition-tracing. Am J Police Sci 1: 60-78 Ja '30 5022

Gorman, Stanley F. Scientific criminology; how bullets and firearms are matched for identification. Sci Am 143: 265-7, 456-7 O, D '30 5023

Graff, G. Welche Festellungen sind nach Schussverletzungen kriminalistisch besonders wichtig? Krimin Monatsh 1: 129-38 Je '27 5024

Gunprinting. Policeman 1: 17-19 Ag '29 5025

Gunther, C. O. Markings on bullets and shells fired from small arms. Mech Eng 52: 107-13, 1065-9 F, D '30 5026

Hall, A. L. The missile and the weapon. Am J Police Sci 2: 311-21 Jl '31 5027

Hasslacher, Fritz. Die Bestimmung des Pistolensystems aus verfeuerten Hülsen und Geschossen. Arch f Krim 89: 3-32, 93-116 Jl, S '31 5028

Hulst, J. P. L. Eigenaardigheden van schoten. Tijdschr v d Politie 1(7): 105-10 My 16 '28 5029

Journée and Piédelièvre. Pénétration des plombs de chasse et des chevrotines dans le corps humain. Ann de Méd Lég 8: 225-31 My '28 5030

Journée and Piédelièvre. Le transport des crosses par les balles cylindroconiques. Ann de Méd Lég 8: 129-31 Mr '28 5031

Kockel, Heinz. Schusskuriosa. Arch f Krim 82: 41-4 Ja '28 5032

Kraft, B. Apparatus used in forensic ballistics. Am J Police Sci 2: 409-18 S '31 5033

Kraft, B. A central registry office for forensic firearms identification. Am J Police Sci 2: 268-9 My '31 5034

Kraft, B. Critical review of forensic ballistics. Am J Police Sci 2: 52-66, 125-42 Ja, Mr '31 5035

Kraft, B. Hilfsapparaturen für die gerichtliche Schussuntersuchung. Arch f Krim 88: 211-17 My '31 5036

Kraft, B. Kritisches zur gerichtlichen Schussuntersuchung. Arch f Krim 87: 133-77 N '30 5037

Kraft, B. Über den Wert einer Waffenidentifizierungszentrale. Krimin Monatsh 5: 60-1 Mr '31 5038

Lerich, L. Quelques cas d'identification de malfaiteurs d'après des bourres ou d'après des projectiles. R Int de Crimin 3 (7): 511-14 '31 5039

Maingard, J. Méthode improvisée pour l'identification photographique des projectiles et des douilles de revolver. Ann de Méd Lég 11: 674-91 bibliog (p691) N '31 5040

Matwejeff, S. N. Zur Identifizierung der Selbstladepistolen. Deut Zeitsch f d ges gerichtl Med 13: 461-8 Jl 20 '29 5041

Mezger, Otto. Über die Entwicklung schiesstechnischer Untersuchungen im Dienste der Justiz. 20p. Berlin, Springer, 1929 5042

Mezger, [Otto] and Fränkle, [P.]. Geschoss- und Pulverladung. Arch f Krim 82: 58-9 '28 5043

Mezger, [Otto] and Heess, [Walter]. Die Bestimmung des Zeitpunktes, wann eine Waffe das letztemal beschossen und eine Patrone verfeuert wurde. Arch f Krim 87: 239-42 D '30 5044

Mezger, Otto; Heess, Walter, and Hasslacher, Fritz. Determination of the type of pistol employed from an examination of fired bullets and shells. Am J Police Sci 2: 473-99 N '31 5045

Moxley, Spencer. Forensic ballistics. Int Assn Identif, Calif Div Proc 15: 14-15 '30 5046

Müller, Gustav. Schuss- oder Steinwurf? (Ist bei einem Steinwurf ein Substanzverlust möglich?) Arch f Krim 87: 234-6 D '30 5047

Nippe. Die kriminalistische Bedeutung der Erkennung absoluter und relativer Nahschüsse. Krimin Monatsh 1: 148-51 Jl '27 5048

O'Neil, Morris B. Scientific bullet identification and results obtained. Int Assn Identif Proc 16: 116-21 '30 5049

Park, Kenneth C. Michigan adopts new type of criminal identification—forensic ballistics. State Trooper 12: 5-6, 19-20 D '30 5050

Piédelièvre, [R.]. Les empreintes des vêtements relevées sur les balles de plomb. Etudes Crimin 2 (3): 43-4 My '27 5051

Piédelièvre, R. and Simonin, C. Medicolegal study of residue in barrel of firearms; translated by Alma Rosenthal. Am J Police Sci 1: 299-301 My '30; same article: Ann de Méd Lég 9: 537-88 O '29 5052

Pirwitz. Ein Beitrag zur Untersuchung von abgeschossenen Patronenhülsen. Krimin Monatsh 5: 248-51 N '31 5053

Porta, Carlo Felice. Sopra un nuovo reattivo dei nitrati e sul valore comparativo delle diverse reazioni nelle polveri da sparo. Arch di Antrop Crim 50: 213- Mr '30 5054

Porta, C[arlo] F[elice]. Über den Wert Schwefelnachweises zur Erkennung von Schwarzpulver. Deut Zeitsch f d ges gerichtl Med 17:237-32 Jl 18 '31 5055

Raestrup. Mord durch Pistolenschuss. Deut Zeitsch f d ges gerichtl Med 14: 62-70 S 3 '29 5056

De Rechter, G. and Mage, J. Considerations sur une méthode d'identification des objets. Son application à un cas particulier. R de Dr Pén et de Crimin 7: 269-77 Mr '27 5057

Ruggles, Colden. The use of pistols by criminals. Northwest Police J 7: 14-15 Ja '30 5058

Schrader, G. Zur Bestimmung des Gewehrkalibers an aufgefundenen groben Schroten. Arch f Krim 87: 244-9 D '30 5059

Simonin, C. Traces laissées dans les vêtements par les coups de feu tirés de près. Tatouage en cocarde. Ann de Méd Lég 8: 261-7 Je '28 5060

Smith, Sydney. The identification of firearms and projectiles as illustrated by the case of the murder of Sir Lee Stack Pasha. Police J [London] 1: 411-22 '28 5061

Smith, Sydney. Injuries from firearms. Am J Police Sci 1: 603-14 N '30 5062

Smith, Sydney. Investigation of firearm injuries. Clin J 60: 361, 379 Ag 5, 12 '31 5063

Söderman, Harry. L'expertise des armes à feu courtes. 166p. Lyon, J. Desvigne & Fils, 1928 5064

Süskin, N. Militärische Feuerwaffen, von Verbrechern für ihre Spezialzwecke umgeändert. Arch f Krim 86: 111-25 Ap '30; translation: Military firearms adapted by criminals to suit their purposes. Am J Police Sci 1: 549-64 N '30 5065

Sullington, Don. Ballistics a new science. Criminologist [Chicago] 5: 32, 42 Je '29 5066

Tangen, E. Spring guns. Am J Police Sci 1: 307-12 My '30 5067

Tyrrell, John F. Documentary ballistics. Am J Police Sci 2: 108-24 Mr '31 5068

Waite, C. E. Forensic ballistics. Detective 42: 2-3 O '27 5069

Waizenegger. Zur Frage der Zentralisierung der Waffenidentifizierung. Krimin Monatsh 5: 112-13 My '31 5070

Weimann, W. Zur Wirkung und gerichtsärztlichen Beurteilung der Scheintodspistolen. Arch f Krim 80: 40-8 Ja '27 5071

Werkgartner, A. Schürfungs- und Stanzverletzungen der Haut am Einschuss durch die Mündung der Waffe. Deut Zeitsch f d ges gerichtl Med 11: 154-68 '28 5072

Wiard, Seth. Application of ballistics in legal cases. Am J Police Sci 2: 174-8 Mr '31 5073

Wiard, Seth. Ballistics as applied to police science. Am J Police Sci 1: 538-41 N '30 5074

Forensic Dentistry

Braschwitz, R. Kriminalistik und Zahnheilkunde. Krimin Monatsh 2: 104-5 My '28 5075

Clue to a murder in which a single tooth is the key to the solution of the mystery. Police "13-13" 5: 6-7, 34 S '30 5076

Guébel. De l'identification par l'estampillage des pièces de prothèse dentaire. Ann de Méd Lég 11: 751-2 D '31 5077

Klein, Alexander. Die Identifizierung durch die Zähne bei Brandkatastrophen. Schweiz Monats Zahnheilk 39: 607-28 '29; translation: Forensic value of teeth in identification of fire victims, by Alma Rosenthal. Am J Police Sci 1: 325 My '30 5078

Merkel. Berufsmerkmale am menschlichen Gebiss. Krimin Monatsh 4: 253-4 N '30 5079

Rehfeldt. Das Zahngebiss als Mittel zur Wiedererkennung von Leichen. Krimin Monatsh 2: 87-8 Ap '28 5080

Saint-Cyr. Recherche de l'identité par l'examen de la bouche et des dents. R Gén de Méd et de Chir de l'Afrique (77) Ap '29 5081

Thomas. Zahnreparatur als Mittel zur Identifizierung. Krimin Monatsh 4: 276-7 D '30 5082

Weissenstein, S. Die Identitätsstanze zur Agnoszierung Lebender und Toter. Schweiz Monats Zahnheilk 41: 612-14 Je '31 5083

Identification Parades

Bailey, Louis M. 16mm. movies as a police aid in the detection and conviction of criminals. Police J [N Y] 18: 3-5, 21 Jl '31 5084

Gorphe, F. Comment procéder aux confrontations d'identité. R Int de Crimin 1: 165-75 S '29; translation: Showing prisoners to witnesses for identification. Am J Police Sci 1: 79-88 Ja '30 5085

Identification parade. Sol J 71: 669 Ag 27 '27 5086

Krosnick, David A. Movietone goes to court. Survey 63: 290-1 D 1 '29; same title: Am J Police Sci 1: 521-4 S '30 5087

Instruments

Kockel, R. Identifizierung von Werkzeugeindrücken. Arch f Krim 83: 288-94 O '28 5088

May, Luke S. The identification of knives, tools and instruments a positive science. Am J Police Sci 1: 246-59 My '30 5089

May, Luke S. The tools of the crime; the identification of instruments and tools as a police science. Police "13-13" 5: 6-8 N '30 5090

Mezger, O.; Hasslacher, F. and Heess, W. Bohr- und Sägespuren. Arch f Krim 85: 197-201 D '29 5091

Rechter, Gustave de. Affaire de Beernem; identification du marteau ayant servi d'instrument du crime. R de Dr Pén et de Crimin 9: 1121-36 '29 5092

Rechter, Gustave de. Identification de la hache (couperet) qui a servi a sectionner de jeunes arbres (acte de vandalisme). R de Dr Pén et de Crimin 9: 39-45 '29 5093

Schatz, W. Hilfs-Indizien. Krimin Monatsh 2: 271-4 D '28 5094
Knife cuts on a rope.

Masks and Molds

Barck. Das Moulageverfahren. Krimin Monatsh 3: 134 Je '29 5095

Death-masks to trap crooks; negacoll plastic modelling material for making death-masks for the living. Lit Dig 105: 38 My 10 '30 5096

Goddefroy, E. Sur un nouveau procédé de moulage pour relever les traces d'effraction et mouler des tranchants d'outils. R Int de Crimin 3(3): 173-80 '31; translation: A process of "moulage" for reproducing marks indicative of forcible entry and molding those left by tools, by L. J. Kaempfer. Am J Police Sci 3: 42-6 Ja '32 5097

[Hulsebosch, C. J. Van Ledden]. Een nieuwe wijze van vormafdrukken. Tijdschr v d politie 1 (34): 614-16 Ja 9 '29 5098

Mullner, Hans. Das Müllnersche Abformverfahren. Krimin Monatsh 4 (12): 272-6 '30; translation: La méthode de moulage Mullner. R Int de Crimin 3 (6): 461-8 '31 5099

Poller, Alphonse. Mein Abformverfahren im Dienste der Kriminalistik. Krimin Monatsh 1: 230-4, 254-7 O, N '27 5100

Poller, Alphonse. Das Pollersche Verfahren zum Abformen an Lebenden und Toten sowie an Gegenständen. 216p. Wien, Urban & Schwarzenberg, 1931 5101

Rodgers, Don. Moulage process in identification work added to Michigan system. State Trooper 12: 17-18 Mr '31 5102

Tracks and Traces

Belgique. Ministère de la justice. Instructions concernant le relevé des marques particulières. R Int de Crimin 1: 432-41 O '29 5103

Chavigny. Les traces des véhicules. R Int de Crimin 1 (1-3): 9-38 '29; translation: Tracks of vehicles. Am J Police Sci 1: 156-77 Mr '30 5104

Fingerprinting autos; imprints of automobile tires. Sci Am 142:33 Ja '30 5105

Mezger, O. and Heess, W. Überführung durch Knieabdrücke. Arch f Krim 87: 249-50 D '30 5106

Mezger, Otto; Hasslacher, Fritz, and Fränkle, Paul. Schartenspurennachweis bei Baumbeschädigungen. Arch f Krim 80: 7-31 Ja '27; translation: Identification of marks made on trees. Am J Police Sci 1: 358-65 Jl '30 5107

Nelken, S. Spuren an Schlössern. Arch f Krim 84: 105-13 Ap '29 5108

Plessen. Fahrradspuren. Krimin Monatsh 5: 228-30 O '31 5109

Timm, F. Beiträge zum mikrochemischen Spurennachweis. Arch f Krim 81: 26-32 Jl '27 5110

Weimann, W. Radspuren an Überfahrenen und ihre kriminalistische Bedeutung. Arch f Krim 80: 1-6 Ja '27 5111

PHOTOGRAPHY

Eichberg. Photogrammetrie im Dienste der praktischen Kriminalistik. Krimin Monatsh 2: 53-7 Mr '28 5112

Folmer Graflex company, Rochester. The need of standardization of photographs of criminals. Int Assn Identif Proc 16: 138-42 '30 5113

Friedrichs, Karl. Das Recht der Personenaufnahme. Krimin Monatsh 1: 265-6 D '27 5114

Gaude, G[aston]. La photographie des objets colorés dans l'enquête criminelle. Etudes Crimin 5: 272-3 S '30 5115

Gaude, G[aston]. La photographie des objets colorés en criminalistique. R Int de Crimin 3 (4): 267-77 '31 5116

Identification by photograph. Crim L J India 28: 53-4 My '27 5117

Jürgens, Ernst. Photographische Aufnahmen im Ultraviolett und Ultrarot. Krimin Monatsh 5: 173-8 Ag '31 5118

Maingard, J. La photographie dans les expertises médico-légales aux colonies. Ann de Méd Lég 11: 765-82 D '31 5119

Mukherjee, S. N. Finger print photography in medical jurisprudence. Indian M Rec 50: 58-60 F '30 5120

Ortube, Celestino. Valor de la fotografía en los documentos de identidad. 28p. La Plata, Mario Sciocco y Co. 1927 5121

Reeves, Hal. Catching crooks by camera. Northwest Police J 5: 14, 55-6 N '28 5122

Saal. Das Polizeiliche bildwesen. Polizei 25: 607-9 S 20 '28 5123

Söderman, Harry. Brottets Värld hur Förbrytare Avslöjas med Kamera och Mikroskop. 211p. Stockholm, Wahlström & Widstrand, 1927 5124

Stewart, Alonzo. Special investigation at the scene of the crime; or, The photographer. Int Assn Identif, Calif Div Proc 15: 16-20 '30 5125

X-ray photographs furnish new means of identification. Sci Am 138:57 Ja '28 5126

TELEPHOTOGRAPHY

Baum, James E. Electricity now pursues the criminal. Am Bankers Assn J 21: 899-900 Mr '29 5127

Farrow. Telephotography. Int Assn Identif, Calif Div Proc 15: 56-8 '30 5128

Gradenwitz, A. La téléphotographie en Allemagne; le système Korn-Lorenz et ses applications policières. Nature [Paris] 56 pt2: 12-14 Jl 1 '28 5129

Korn, Artur. Die Bildtelegraphie im Dienste der Kriminalpolizei. Krimin Monatsh 1:7-9 Ja '27 5130

Korn, Arthur. Die Bildtelegraphie im Dienste der Polizei. 95p. Graz, Moser, 1927 5131

SIGNALETICS

Almandos, Luis Reyna. Bertillón y Vucetich: Juzados por la Academia de ciencias de Paris. R de Identif y Cienc Pen 2: 5-34 My '28 5132

Casati, A. I fatti cicatriziali dell'apparato respirato come segni personali di riconoscimento. Arch di Antrop Crim 51: 494-8 My '31 5133

Claps, Albert. Les plis de flexion de la main. Leur valeur identificatrice. R Int de Crimin 3 (7): 515-20 '31 5134

Collin, F. Une nouvelle enquête anthropometrique. R de Dr Pén et de Crimin 7: 218-20 F '27 5135

Culbert, William Ledlie and Law, Frederick M. Identification by comparison of roentgenograms of nasal accessory sinuses and mastoid processes. Am M Assn J 88: 1634-6 My 21 '27 5136

Dorpe, van den and Lefebvre, G. Le dossier anthropologique. Ecrou 12: 425-41 O '31 5137

Evidence of birthmarks, bruises, scars. U S L R 64: 172-3 Ap '30 5138

Heindl, Robert. Der wichtigste Bestandteil des Signalements nebst genauer Darstellung des Bertillonschen Portrait parlé. Arch f Krim 80: 208-38 My '27 5139

Isnard, A. Déformations. Facteur déformant. Espèces. Graphologie Sci (40) O '30 5140

Jannoni-Sebastianini, G. Faccette articolari dei condili occipitali e cavità. Zacchia 6: 10-37 '27 5141

Nuremberg, M. F. Skin identification. Int Assn Identif Proc 16: 34-6 '31 5142

Oppenheim, M. Die Schädigungen der Haut durch Arbeit und Beruf als kriminalistische Erkennungsmittel. Arch f Krim 88: 133-46 Mr '31 5143

Ottolenghi, Salvatore. L'interpretazione antropologica biografica del cartellino segnalitico. R Int de Crimin 2 (2): 103-7 '30 5144

Parsons, Clara L. Bertillon measurements. Correction 1: 7-8 N '31 5145

"Science of facial resemblances" as applied in courts. N Y L R 5: 196-7 My '27 5146

Simonin, C. Les réactions biologiques appliquées à l'identification médico-légales des muscles. Ann de Méd Lég 11: 32-7 Ja '31 5147

Simonsen, S. How vestiges (other) than fingerprints lead to the detection of criminals. Police J [N Y] 14: 26 My '27 **5148**

Simpson, F. E. and Flesher, R. E. Radium in the removal of "birth marks." Clin Med & Surg 34: 605-7 Ag '27 **5149**

Türkel, Siegfried. Das Auge als Identifizierungsgrundlage. Unter Berücksichtigung von Blascheks Photofundoskopie. Ein Kapitel aus der Geschichte der Erkenntnislehre. 51p. Graz, Moser, 1927 **5150**

Valadares, M. Carte d'identité au Portugal. R de Dr Pén et de Crimin 8: 267-9 Mr '28 **5151**

Venters, Carl V. Evidence of birthmarks, bruises, scars. L Notes 35: 10-13 Ap '31 **5152**

Vogel, O. Die Personenbeschreibung. Ein Wegweiser zum richtigen Sehen und Beschreiben der Person für Polizei-, Justiz-, Landjägerei-, Zoll-, und insbesondere Passund Fahndungsbeamte. Bearbeitet unter Benutzung des beim Preussischen Landeskriminalpolizeiamt vorhandenen Materials. 130p. Berlin, A. W. Hayn's Erben, 1931 **5153**

Wilkinson, J. R. Why amputations should be classified and cross indexed by all police departments. Int Pict Police J 34-6 My '29 **5154**

Gems and Precious Stones

Emmons, R. C. The identification of gems and precious stones. Am J Police Sci 1: 542-8 N '30 **5155**

Johnsen. Das Zentralinstitut für Edelsteinforschung. Arch f Krim 81: 1-8 Jl '27 **5156**

Michel, Hermann. Neuere Methoden zur Untersuchung und Identifizierung von Edelsteinen und Perlen. Arch f Krim 88: 249-51 My '31 **5157**

Moresby, Walter H. The discrimination and testing of precious stones and pearls. Police J [London] 1: 475-86 '28 **5158**

Söderman, H. L'identification des pierres précieuses. Une méthode préventive de la technique policière. Avenir Méd 25: 141-7 My '28 **5159**

Graphology

Bührig, Wilh. Zur Geschichte der Graphologie. Zeitsch f Menschenk 4: 219-33 N '28 **5160**

Bührig, Wilh. Mit de Geschiedenis der graphologie. Tijdschr v Wetenschappelijke Graphologie (4) O '30 **5161**

Coimbra, Francisco. La valeur de la methode de Locard dans les faux par surcharge. R Int de Crimin 2 (3): 215-17 '30 **5162**

Crépieux-Jamin, J. A B C de la graphologie. 2v. Paris, Alcan, 1930 **5163**

Cuissinat, J. Pour connaître l'homme par son écriture. Etude des états et des déformations graphiques, base rationnelle de l'expertise en écritures et de la graphologie. 150p. Saint-Didier-en-Donjon, Chez l'auteur, 1931 **5164**

Destable, Jacques. La graphométrie dans l'expertise des écritures. Etudes Crimin 5: 305-10 D '30 **5165**

Dreyfus-Nirtz, A. Graphothérapie. Graphologique Sci (40) O '30 **5166**

Exner, F. Graphologie und Strafrecht. Monats f Kriminalpsychol u Strafrechtsref 22: 104-6 '31 **5167**

Fan, Leung Yui. L'expertise des faux en écriture chinoise. R Int de Crimin 2 (8): 597-612 '30 **5168**

Goddefroy, E. Sur la valeur de la méthode pour le trait postécrit dans les cas de faux par surcharge. R Int de Crimin 2 (8): 592-6 '30 **5169**

Guiral, Maggie. La valeur de la preuve dans l'expertise des écritures. 111p. Thèse pour le doctorat de droit, Lyon, 1927 **5170**

Hentig, [Hans von]. Grenzen der Graphologie. Monats f Kriminalpsychol u Strafrechtsref 19: 445-6 Jl '28 **5171**

Jacoby, Hans. De Oorzaak van verkeerde graphologische Diagnosen. Tijdschr v Wetenschappelijke Graphologie 2 (3) Jl '30 **5172**

Klages, Ludwig. Graphologisches Lesebuch. Hundert Gutachten aus der Praxis. 218p. Leipzig, Ambrosius Barth, 1930 **5173**

Locard, Edmond. L'analyse graphométrique. Etudes Crimin 4 (12): 325-6 D '29 **5174**

Meloun, J. Neue Ergebnisse graphologischer Forschungen. Umschau 33: 489-93 Je 22 '29 **5175**

Mezger, O.; Hasslacher, Fr., and Heess, Walter. Entzifferung der Schrifteindrücke auf Schreibunterlagen. Arch f Krim 86: 73-4 F '30 **5176**

Mitchell, C. Ainsworth. Estimating the age of writing. Discovery 10: 117-19 Ap '29; same title: Sci Am 141: 28-9 Jl '29 **5177**

Moll, Albert. Eine Nachprüfung der Graphometrie. Arch f Krim 84: 149-51 Ap '29 **5178**

Müller, B. Erfahrungen mit dem photographischen Verfahren von Burinsky zur Darstellung unsichtbarer bzw. schlecht sichtbarer Schriften. Krimin Monatsh 2: 203-4 S '28 **5179**

Pellat, E. S. Les lois de l'écriture. 64p. Paris, Vuilbert, 1927 **5180**

Pulver, Max. De Groote van het Schrift. Tijdschr v Wetenschappelijke Graphologie 3 (1) Ja '31 **5181**

Pulver, Max. Symbolik der Handschrift. 291p. Zürich, Orell Füssli, 1931 **5182**

Rechter, G[ustave] de. Application de la micrographie et de la photo-micrographie à l'expertise en écritures. R de Dr Pén et de Crimin 7: 145-54 F '27 **5183**

Rougemont, E. de. L'analyse et la synthèse en graphologie. 48p. Paris, Rivière, 1930 5184

Rougemont, E. de. Les difficultés et les progrès de l'expertise en écriture. 60p. Paris, Rivière, 1930 5185

Rougemont, E. de. Het Waarde-Begrip in de Graphologie. Tijdschr v Wetenschappelijke Graphologie 2 (3) Jl '30 5186

Sampson, A. R. Graphology in police work. Northwest Police J 5: 11, 57, 59 My '28 5187

Sampson, A. R. The value of graphology. Northwest Police J 5: 37-40 Ja '28 5188

Saudek, Robert. Experimentelle Graphologie. Arch f Krim 83: 103-95 S '28 5189

Saudek, Robert. Methods of graphology. Brit J M Psychol 7: 221-58 Jl '27 5190

Schenck, C. M. Observations on graphology. Nederl Tijdschr v Geneesk 74: 2522-41 My 17 '30 5191

Schneickert, Hans. Locards Graphometrie. Arch f Krim 83: 101-2 S '28 5192

Schrijver. De Grondslagen der wetenschappelijke Graphologie. Tijdschr v Wetenschappelijke Graphologie (4) O '29 5193

Söderman, Harry. Die moderne Graphometrie. Eine objektive Methode für Schriftexpertisen. Arch f Krim 82: 165-77 Ap '28 5194

Spanjaard, L. De verantwoordelijkheid van den Grapholoog naar nederlandsch Recht. Tijdschr v Wetenschappelijke Graphologie 3 (1) Ja '31 5195

Stengel-Buchheim, I. Uber die Verwendbarkeit graphologischer Untersuchungen in der Psychopathologie des Kindesalters. Zeitsch f Menschenk 5: 303 Ja '30 5196

Streletski, Camille. Graphologie du praticien. 132p. Paris, Doin, 1927 5197

Streletski, Camille. Le cinéma et la graphologie. Graphologie Sci (40) O '30 5198

Teale, Edwin Way. Science is bloodhound at heels of forger. Pop Sci 118: 26-7 Mr '31 5199

DOCUMENTS

Abstoss. Eine beachtenswerte Urkundenfälschung. Krimin Monatsh 5: 161-2 Jl '31 5200

Brüning, August. Die Urkundenfälschung und das zu ihrem Nachweis erforderliche Beweismaterial. Krimin Monatsh 4: 193-7 S '30 5201

Cazzaniga, Antonio. Probativa coincidenza di indizi in una questione di alterazione di documento. R Int de Crimin 3 (7): 521-31 '31 5202

Claps, Albert. Un procédé de détermination de la date relative de deux textes. R Int de Crimin 2 (10): 741-5 '30 5203

DuPuy, William Atheraton. With intent to deceive; exposing forged documents. World's Wk 59: 61-3 O '30 5204

Duyster, M. Untersuchung von gefälschten Dokumenten. Prüfung der Strichkreuzungen. Arch f Krim 82: 200 Ap '28 5205

Heindl, R[obert]. Zur Diagnose der Urkundenfälschung. Was Staatsanwälte, Untersuchungsrichter und Polizeibeamte beim Vorliegen dubioser Bleistiftschriften beachten sollen. Arch f Krim 82: 81-95 Ap '28 5206

Jacobsen, J. Hartvig. Dokument forbrydelserne. 391p. bibliog [383]-91. København, A. Busck, 1927 5207

Jobez, Robert. L'expertise en écriture des documents chinois. 42p. Tientsin, Chihli press, 1930 5208

Lévy, E. and Guiral, M[aggie]. L'expertise des documents écrits dans le droit actuel. R Int de Crimin 1: 504-8 N '29 5209

Locard, Edmond. Anonieme brieven. Tijdschr v d Politie 1(3): 41-7 Ap 18 '28 5210

Locard, Edmond. L'expertise des faux timbres poste. R Int de Crimin 2 (7): 496-520 '30 5211

Locard, Edmond. Die Untersuchung falscher Briefmarken. Krimin Monatsh 3: 271-4 D '29 5212

Locard, Edmond. La valeur de la preuve dans l'expertise des documents écrits. R Int de Crimin 3 (8): 617-22 '31 5213

Mezger, [O.] and Fränkle, [P.]. Nachweis einer Urkundenfälschung. Arch f Krim 82: 59-61 '28 5214

Michaud, Félix. Additions et intercalations frauduleuses. R Int de Crimin 2 (7): 486-95 '30 5215

Osborn, Albert Sherman. Questioned documents; with an introduction by John Henry Wigmore; with citations of discussions of the facts and the law of questioned documents from many sources. ed.2. 1028p. bibliog 985-1004. Albany, Boyd ptg. co. 1929 5216

Pellat, E. Solange. L'expertise des pièces anonymes. Etudes Crimin 4: 205-9 Jl '29 5217

Probst, J. H. Expertise et analyse graphométrique des écritures sémitiques. R Int de Crimin 2 (10): 726-37 '30 5218

Quigley, Marjorie. [Questioned documents]. Calif S B J 1: 135, 157, 179, 203, 225, 248 Ja-Je '27 5219

Quirke, Arthur J. Forged, anonymous and suspect documents. London, Routledge, 1930 5220

Römer, S. Demonstrationen bei Schriftgutachten. Zeitsch f Menschenk 2: 55-7 '27 5221

Ruenes, Rafael Fernández. Clasificación y archivo de escritura manuscrita. R de Identif y Cienc Pen 7: 114-24 N '30 5222

Ruenes, Rafael Fernández. La falsificación de documentos y la fotografia. R de Identif y Cienc Pen 5: 224-31 Ja '30 5223

Ruenes, Rafael Fernández. Investigación fotográfica de documentos. R de Identif y Cienc Pen 6: 54-6 My '30 5224

Schneickert, Hans. Urkundenfälschungen durch Ausschneiden echter Schriftteile. Krimin Monatsh 2: 35-7 F '28 5225

Schneickert, Hans. Valschheid in geschriften, voorheen en thans. Tijdschr v d Politie 1(13): 217-25 Je 27 '28 5226

Shearman, J. C. Document identification in trial courts. Neb L Bul 6: 103-15 Jl '27 5227

Stein, Elbridge. Dates in documents. Am L R 61: 90-8 Ja '27 5228

Türkel, Siegfried. Fälschungen. Beiträge zur Phänomenologie, Symptomatologie und Diagnostik. 93p. Graz, Moser, 1930 5229

Türkel, Siegfried. Die gefälschten Berichte über eine angebliche Umschiffung Afrikas unter Necho auf zwei Skarabäen. (Zur Kasuistik des Raritätenbetruges). Arch f Krim 80: 180-4 Mr '27 5230

HANDWRITING

Becker, Minna. De Ontwikkeling van het Schrift. Tijdschr v Wetenschappelijke Graphologie (4) O '29 5231

Buckley, James. Classifying handwriting; a simple and adequate method for small police bureaus. Northwest Police J 6: 8, 42 Mr '29 5232

California Sherlock who traps criminals with their own pens. Lit Dig 102: 49-52 Ag 17 '29 5233

Chambon, Joannès. L'écriture de main gauche chez les rééduqués. R Int de Crimin 2 (5): 334-41 '30 5234

Chevassus, Amand. L'analyse graphométrique appliquée à une cause célèbre. Le "bordereau" est-il de Dreyfus ou d'Esterhazy? R Int de Crimin 1: 374-80 bibliog (p379-80) O '29 5235

Delhougne, A. Donkere lijnen in het Handschrift. Tijdschr v Wetenschappelijke Graphologie 2 (3) Jl '30 5236

Delhougne, A. Hysterie und Schriftexpertise. Zeitsch f Menschenk 3: 93-106 Jl '27 5237

Ellis, Bobby. Handwriting. Int Assn Identif Proc 16: 92-6 '30 5238

Fane, Edward. Forged signatures can be detected. Police J [N Y] 17: 15, 18-19, 23 O '30 5239

Goldbladt, H. Graphologische Betrachtungen. Psychol u Med 3: 81-8 '28 5240

Handwriting tests in court. Just Peace 91: 542 Jl 16 '27 5241

Hartkorn, August. The extraneous stroke: how psychology helped the handwriting expert. Police J [N Y] 18: 11-12, 27 Je '31 5242

Klages, Ludwig. Die psychologischen Hilfsmittel der Schriftvergleichung. Monats f Kriminalpsychol u Strafrechtsref 20: 417-21 '29 5243

Lee, Clarence Dunlap and Abbey, R. A. Classification and identification of handwriting. 113p. Toronto, Carswell, 1931 5244

Linker, Gertrud. Over spanningsverschijnselen in het Handschrift. Tijdschr v Wetenschappelijke Graphologie 3 (2) Ap '31 5245

Locard, Edmond. L'écriture de main gauche. R Int de Crimin 2 (5): 324-33 bibliog (p333) '30 5246

Locard, Edmond. Les faux sur découpage. R de Dr Pén et de Crimin 7: 742-58 Jl '27 5247

Michaud, F[élix]. Ce qu'il faut connaître de l'homme par l'écriture. 158p. Paris, Boivin, 1930 5248

Michaud, F[élix]. L'expertise en écritures et la méthode statistique. R Scient 64: 658-61 N 13 '27 5249

Michaud, Félix. Sur l'interprétation des différences dans l'identification des documents écrits. R Int de Crimin 3 (7): 488-92 '31 5250

Montgomery, Paul. Convincing a jury; tricks of handwriting. Can Mag 75: 12 My '31 5251

Müller, B. Studien über schriftverstellung. Deut Zeitsch f d ges gerichtl Med 15: 102- Mr '30 5252

Newell, George. Is there a crook fist: a study of criminal handwriting. Outl 147: 174-6 O 12 '27 5253

Nutt, Howard. Cooperation of investigating officers with the handwriting expert. Inst Assn Identif, Calif Div Proc 16: 39-41 '31 5254

Philipp, Lothar. Der Schriftindizienbeweis. Arch f Krim 81: 251-7 D '27 5255

Potapow, S. M. Zur systematischen Registrierung von Verbrecherhandschriften. Arch f Krim 80: 36-9 Ja '27 5256

Saudek, Robert. Experimentelle Graphologie. 348p. Berlin, Pan-Verl. 1929 5257

Saudek, Robert. Experiments with handwriting. 407p. N.Y. William Morrow, 1929 5258

Schneickert, Hans. Die Begutachtung von Unterschriftsfälschungen. Krimin Monatsh 1: 9-11 Ja '27 5259

Seelig, Ernst. Anleitung zur Durchführung des Identitätsnachweises durch vergleichende Handschriftenuntersuchungen. 17p. Graz, Moser, 1929 5260

Sellers, J. Clark. Standardization of handwriting investigation and expert testimony. Int Assn Identif, Calif Div Proc 15: 46-50 '30 5261

Stein, Elbridge W. Handwriting, typewriting and document expert testimony tested by its convincingness. J Crim L & Crimin 21: 330-8 N '30 5262

Steinitzer, H. Graphologie und Verbrechertum. Zeitsch f Menschenk 5: 180-8 S '29 5263

Tyrrell, J. F. The forged signature and how to detect it. Mid-W Banker 10-12 N '31 5264

Ward, W. Signature, or cipher? Europe's new proposal to curb the international crook. Burroughs Clearing House 12: 15-16 Ag '28 5265

Webb, W. M. Handwriting as a help to identification. Police J [London] 1: 297-305 Ap '28 5266

Wieser, Roda. Die Verbrecher Handschrift; hrsg. von W. Gleispach. (Krimin Abh no6) Wien, Springer, 1930 5267

Wood, Jay Fordyce. The Loeb-Leopold case from the standpoint of the handwriting, pen printing and typewriting expert. Am J Police Sci 1: 339-53 Jl '30 5268

INK, PEN, PENCIL AND PAPER

Brun, Henri. Recherche du "Corrector" sur les documents effacès avec ce produit. R Int de Crimin 2 (6): 432-3 '30 5269

Goddefroy, E. De l'identification de la plume en matière d'expertise dans certain cas particuliers. R Int de Crimin 2 (10): 746-50 '30 5270

Goddefroy, E. De l'identification des traces produits par l'écriture au crayon. R Int de Crimin 1: 390-7 O '29 5271

Hulsebosch, C. J. van Ledden. Der Nachweis junger Tintenschrift. Arch f Krim 80: 239-41 My '27 5272

Mezger and Fränkle. Beobachtung von Schneid- und Gummierungsfehlern an Briefumschlägen. Arch f Krim 81: 81-5 S '27 5273

Mezger and Heess. Freilegung einer mit Tusche übermalten Tintenschrift. Arch f Krim 83: 76-7 Jl '28 5274

Mezger, O.; Hasslacher, F. and Heess, W. Beiträge zur Kenntnis der Bleistiftschrift. Arch f Krim 85: 131-40 O '29 5275

Müller, Helmut. Das Sichtbarmachen einer mit sympathetischer Tinte geschriebenen Schrift. Krimin Monatsh 4: 277-8 D '30 5276

Pines, Charles C. The story of ink. Am J Police Sci 2: 290-301 bibliog (p301) Jl '31 5277

Proof of age of ink by experts. L Notes 31: 83-4 Ag '27 5278

Rechter, G. de and Laet, M. de. Recherches sur la permanence d'écrits faits au moyen de diverses encres du commerce. (Application de la photographie en lumière ultra-violette). R de Dr Pén et de Crimin 7: 886-8 Ag '27 5279

Türkel, Siegfried. Atlas der Bleistiftschrift. 48p. Graz, Moser, 1927 5280

Türkel, Siegfried. Entzifferung von mit Bleistift durchstrichenen Bleistiftschriften. Arch f Krim 82: 95-8 Ap '28 5281

Türkel, Siegfried. Technische Bemerkungen zur Farbuntersuchung von Tintenflecken. Arch f Krim 85: 246-8 D '29 5282

SECRET WRITINGS

Kytka, T. Description of methods by which secret communications may be prepared and of the procedures employed to render them visible. Am J Police Sci 1: 326-31 My '30 5283

Langen, B. Geheimschrift und unsichtbare Schrift. Med Klin 26: 1323-5 S 5 '30 5284

TYPEWRITING

Bureau of standards and typewriting identification. L Notes 33: 121-2 O '29 5285

Chavigny. La machine a écrire et les expertises dactylographiques. R Int de Crimin 3 (9): 648-703 '31 5286

Disputed typewriting. L Notes 34: 184 Ja '31 5287

Grempe, Max. Urkunden-Fälschungen mit Schreibmaschinen. Krimin Monatsh 2: 250-2 N '28 5288

Locard, Edmond. L'imitation typographique. R Int de Crimin 1(1-3): 75-81 bibliog (p81) '29 5289

Osborn, Albert S. Typewriting in courts of law. R Int de Crimin 2 (1): 23-9 '30 5290

Paddock, Paul. True stories of the manhunters; telltale typewriters. Pop Mech 49: 418-21 Mr '28 5291

Schmidt, Gero. Die kriminalistische Bedeutung von Maschinenschriften. Arch f Krim 83: 292-300 N '28 5292

Sorrentino, Ugo. Methodologia della perizia segnaletica applicata nei confronti de scritture a machina. R Int de Crimin 2 (7): 521-44 '30 5293

Souder, Wilmer. Identification of typewriters and guns by precision methods of comparison and measurement. U S Bur Standards Tech N Bul (147): 61-3 Jl '29; same title: J Franklin Inst 208: 283-7 Ag '29 5294

Stein, Elbridge W. Typewriting as evidence. Lawyer & Banker 21: 176-82 My '28 5295

Türkel, Siegfried. Die Begutachtung von Schreibmaschinenschriften, die mittels Wachsmatrizen vervielfältigt wurden. Arch f Krim 88: 252-4 My '31 5296

DERMATOGLYPHICS

NOSE, PAW AND HAND

Bettmann, S. Über Dermatogramme und ihre Verwertung. Arch f Dermat u Syphilis 153: 637-48 '27 5297

Claps, Albert. Les empreintes labiales. R Int de Crimin 3 (9): 707-12 '31 5298

Cummins, Harold and Midlo, Charles. Dermatoglyphics in Jews. Am J Phys Anthrop 10 (1): 91-113 '27 5299

Goddefroy, E. Les empreintes de pattes de chien comme moyen d'identification. R Int de Crimin 1: 521-30 N '29 5300

Marelli, Carlos A. Impresión plantar rarísima en el hombre, que es normal en los primates. R de Identif y Cienc Pen 4: 171-4 Jl '29 5301

Miranda-Pinto, Osvaldo. Contribution à la morphologie comparée des empreintes. 140p. Lyon, Desvigne, 1930 5302

Miranda-Pinto, Osvaldo. Les crêtes papillaires dans la série animale. R Int de Crimin 2(6): 406-31 '30 5303

Miranda-Pinto, Osvaldo. L'empreinte en arc chez le chimpanzé. R Int de Crimin 2(7): 545-6 '30 5304

Miranda-Pinto, [Osvaldo]. La morphologie comparée des crêtes papillaires. 135p. Lyon, Desvigne, 1930 5305

Müller, B. Die Lehre von der Erblichkeit des Reliefs der Hohlhand und der Fingerbeeren vom gerichtlich-medizinischen Standpunkt aus. Deut Zeitsch f d ges gerichtl Med 17: 407-25 O 12 '31 5306

Ortube, Celestino. Clasificación palmer y clave para la transmisión de la identidad (memoria presentada al Museo Vucetich). R de Identif y Cienc Pen 2: 64-6 My '28 5307

Sabatini, A. Su di un nuovo metodo di presa della impronte palmari e plantari. Riv di Antrop 28: 509-14 '28-'29 5308

Schrader, G. Dermatographische Untersuchungen an Leichen. (Unter besonderer Berücksichtigung der Todeszeitbestimmung). Deut Zeitsch f d ges gerichtl Med 16: 256-71 Ja 28 '31 5309

Serres, José R. La identificación de los animales por las impresiones nasales. R de Identif y Cienc Pen 6: 30-4 My '30 5310

FOOTPRINTS

Bauernfeind. Fussspurensicherung. Streuverfahren oder Gussverfahren? Krimin Monatsh 4: 149-51 Jl '30 5311

Derome, Wilfrid. The resource of technical police. Police J [N Y] 17: 15, 32 N '29 5312

Gnepper, H. Fussspurensicherung mit Pausrahmen. Krimin Monatsh 4: 234-5 O '30 5313

Karpfen, Fritz. Fährten im Schnee. Arch f Krim 81: 216-19 D '27 5314

Kleinschmidt. Verwertung von Fussspuren. Krimin Monatsh 4: 88 Ap '30 5315

Locard, Edmond. Nature et substratum des empreintes de pas. R de Identif y Cienc Pen 3: 201-7 Ja '29; translation: Naturaleza y substratum de las huellas de pasos. R de Identif y Cienc Pen 3: 391-7 Mr '29 5316

Manwaring, G. Personal identification from foot-prints. Ceylon J Sci 2 pt1: 1-6 Mr 16 '27 5317

Montgomery, Robert B. Classification of footprints. J Crim L & Crimin 18: 105-10 My '27 5318

Müller, J. Spurensicherung durch Gips. Polizei 25: 8 Ja 5 '28 5319

Timmer, H. Value of footprints. Nederl Tijdschr v Geneesk 2: 5313-16 N 9 '29 5320

FINGERPRINTS (DACTYLOSCOPY)

Aguilera, Federico Olóriz. Dactiloscopia. R de Identif y Cienc Pen 5: 375-411 Mr '30 5321

Almandos, Luis Reyna. Anormalidades dactiloscópicas. R de Identif y Cienc Pen 6: 405-7 S '30 5322

Almandos, Luis Reyna. Dactiloscopia Argentina; su historia e influencia en la legislación. R de Identif y Cienc Pen 8: 363-516 My '31 5323

Almandos, Luis Reyna. La dactiloscopia y la pintur antigua. R de Identif y Cienc Pen 5: 217-19 Ja '30 5324

Almandos, L[uis] Reyna. Elementos diferenciales de la impresión digital. R de Identif y Cienc Pen 7: 111-13 N '30 5325

Almandos, Luis Reyna. Fichas antiguas del sistema Vucetich. R de Identif y Cienc Pen 8: 122-45 My '31 5326

Almandos, Luis Reyna. Fichas dactiloscópicas de delincuentes célebres. R de Identif y Cienc Pen 1: 88-9 N '27 5327

Almandos, Luis Reyna. Identificación dactiloscópica de recién nacidos en los Estados Unidos. R de Identif y Cienc Pen 5: 346-9 Mr '30 5328

Almandos, Luis Reyna. Identificación dactiloscópica del recién nacido. R de Identif y Cienc Pen 4: 371-5 S '29 5329

Almandos, Luis Reyna. Identificación dactiloscópica internacional. R de Identif y Cienc Pen 4: 301-12 S '29 5330

Almandos, Luis Reyna. La identificación dactiloscópica y el código civil. R de Identif y Cienc Pen 7: 145-54 N '30 5331

Almandos, Luis Reyna. Las líneas blancas dactiloscópicas. R de Identif y Cienc Pen 6: 5-14 My '30 5332

Almandos, Luis Reyna. Las lineas blancas dactiloscopicas. R Int de Crimin 2 (9): 652-61 '30 5333

Almandos, Luis Reyna. Mutabilidad de la líneas blancas dactiloscópicas. R de Identif y Cienc Pen 6: 403-4 S '30 5334

Almandos, Luis Reyna. La prueba dactiloscópica en materia civil; primer caso judicial de identificación civil "post mortem." R de Identif y Cienc Pen 2: 351-60 S '28 5335

Almandos, Luis Reyna. Teratología dactiloscópica. R de Identif y Cienc Pen 1: 76-7, 321-5 '27 5336

Almandos, Luis Reyna. Teratología dactiloscópica. Forma anormal de verticilo. R de Identif y Cienc Pen 2: 246-7 Jl '28 5337

Almandos, Luis Reyna. Teratología dactiloscópica. Un caso de adéltica dactiloscópica. R de Identif y Cienc Pen 1: 321-5 Mr '28 5338

Almandos, Luis Reyna. Vucetich y Galton (génesis de la dactiloscopia). R de Identif y Cienc Pen 5: 173-211 bibliog (p210-11) Ja '30 5339

Baeza, Roberto Vega and Artigas, Carlos Salcedo. Dactiloscopia. R de Identif y Cienc Pen 3: 271-9 Ja '29 5340

Barlow, Howard [L.]. The standardization of all angles of fingerprint investigation. Int Assn Identif, Calif Div Proc 15: 27-9 '30 5341

Barlow, Howard [L.]. What finger prints have done for the Los Angeles police department. Int Assn Identif Proc 16: 171-5 '30 5342

Benassi, Giorgio. A propos des empreintes digitales chez l'homme et les singes. R Int de Crimin 2 (8): 589-91 '30 5343

Benincasa, Vicente. Legislación dactiloscópica. R de Identif y Cienc Pen 4: 189-94 Jl '29 5344

Berg. Interessante Abnormitäten beim Fingerabdruckverfahren. Krimin Monatsh 5: 13-16 Ja '31 5345

Berque, S. S. Finger prints. Police J [N Y] 14: 32-6 F '27 5346

Bettmann, S. Ueber Papillarleistenzeichnungen am menschlichen Daumenballen. Zeitsch f d ges Anat 96: 427-52 N 25 '31 5347

Bettmann, S. Verwendung der Dermatogramme in der Gerichtlichen Medizin. Deut Zeitsch f d ges gerichtl Med 15: 1-15 Mr 14 '30 5348

Biggs, E. R. Outline history of finger prints. Northwest Police J 6: 36-41 Ag '29 5349

Bonnevie, Kristine. Die ersten Entwicklungsstadien der Papillarmuster der menschlichen Fingerballen. Nyt Mag Naturvidensk 65: 19-56 '27 5350

Bonnevie, K[ristine]. Papillar-muster und psychische Eigenschaften. Hereditas 9: 180-92 '27 5351

Bonnevie, K[ristine]. Was lehrt die Embryologie der Papillarmuster über ihre Bedeutung als Rassen- und Familiencharakter? Zeitsch f indukt Abstammungs- u Vererbungsl 59: 1-60 '31 5352

Bregenzer. Mordaufklärung durch Fingerspur. Krimin Monatsh 4: 228-30 O '30 5353

Breull, G. Die praktische Auswirkung des Fingerabdrucksverfahrens. Polizei 24: 525-6 N 5 '27 5354

Cabezas, D. La dactiloscopia al alcance de Todos. 50p. Valparaiso, Imp. Victoria, 1927 5355

Cabrera, Angel. La dactiloscopia entre los beduinos. R de Identif y Cienc Pen 4: 376-7 S '29 5356

Caldwell, Harry. Erroneous newspaper and magazine articles relating to fingerprints and the duplication and forgery of fingerprints. Int Assn Identif, Calif Div Proc 12: 63-7 '27 5357

Cañás, Manuel T. Valor probatorio de la dactiloscopia. Tesis para optar al grado de doctor en ciencias jurídicas y sociales. R de Identif y Cienc Pen 6: 57-95 bibliog (p94-5) My '30 5358

Castellanos, Israel. The value received by fingerprinting the inmates of an insane asylum. Int Assn Identif Proc 16: 121-7 '30 5359

Catching crooks by fingerprints. Toledo City J 13 (39) S 29 '28 5360

Chevassus, A. Les empreintes digitales contre les aveux. R Int de Crimin 1: 263-5 S '29 5361

Cooke, Thomas G. Finger prints, secret service, crime detection. 79p. Chicago, 1920 Sunnyside ave. The Author, 1930 5362

La dactiloscopia en Chile. R de Identif y Cienc Pen 1: 288-92 Mr '28 5363

Daktyloskopisches Fehlgutachten. Krimin Monatsh 2: 109 My '28 5364

Duffaux, Marius. Contribution à la statistique dactyloscopique chez les chinois et chez les prostituées chinoises. R Int de Crimin 3 (4): 278-81 '31 5365

Duffaux, Marius. Les empreintes digitales chez les chinois. Contribution à l'ethnologie dactyloscopique. R Int de Crimin 3 (1): 44-6 '31 5366

Duffaux, Marius. Les formules dactyloscopiques réelles. R Int de Crimin 1: 620-8 D '29 5367

Finger print records of criminals. L Notes 32: 25 My '28 5368

Finger-prints. U S L R 65: 185-7 Ap '31 5369

The fingerprints of identical twins. Lancet 212: 300-1 '27 5370

Foster, Edward. Finger prints. Chief Constables' Assn Can Proc 24: 64-70 '28 5371

Furuhata, T. The difference of the index of fingerprints according to race. Jap M World 7: 162-5 '27 5372

Gay. Die praktische Auswirkung des Fingerabdrucksverfahrens. Polizei 25: 20-2 F 5 '28 5373

Giraud, Georges and Henquel, Eugène. Un fichier des suspects par mains séparées. R Int de Crimin 2 (4): 262-8 '30 5374
Services de police scientifiques, Algérie.

Gonçalves, Ribeiro. Da identificação scientifica pelas impressões digitaes. R de Cultura Jurid 1: 113-39 Ap '29 5375

Guevara, Carlos Pantoja L. de. La dactiloscopia y la legislacion moderna. 234p. Santiago de Chile, 1929 5376

Hardcastle, Selina Winifred. Biography of Sir Wm. J. Herschel. Int Assn Identif, Calif Div Proc 16: 37-9 '31 5377

Hasslacher. Kann aus dem Verlauf der Hautlinien eines einzelnen Fingerabdrucks auf die Herkunft desselben von einer rechten oder linken Hand geschlossen werden. Arch f Krim 85: 93-6 Ag '29 5378

Heiland, Gerhard. Der Ramsdorfer Mord. Ein Lehrreicher Erfolg des Fingerabdrucksverfahrens. Krimin Monatsh 1: 171-3 Ag '27 5379

Heindl, [Robert]. Die Fingerabdrücke als Ueberführungsmittel. Krimin Monatsh 1: 74-5 Ap '27 5380

Heindl, R[obert]. System und Praxis der Daktyloskopie und der sonstigen technischen Methoden der Kriminalpolizei. ed.3. rev. and enl. 780p. Berlin, Gruyter, 1927 5381

Hellstern, E. P. Fingerabdruckverfahren und Blutgruppenbestimmung im Strafvollzug. Reichs-Gesundheitsbl 2: 711-13, 724-6 '27 5382

Herrero, Antonio. Sobre dactiloscopia española; cartas del doctor Federico Olóriz Aguilera a Vucetich. R de Identif y Cienc Pen 4: 97-105 My '29 5383

Herrman, Louis. Finger patterns. Am J Police Sci 2: 306-10 Jl '31; same title: New Statesman 2: 191-3 Ag 15 '31 5384

Hildebrand, W. N. The fingerprint expert. Int Assn Identif, Calif Div Proc 15: 22-4 '30 5385

Infallible finger prints. Sol J 73: 458 Jl 13 '29 5386

L, **Julio Larraín.** Legislación dactiloscópica de Chile. Fusión de los servicios de identificación y registro civil (codificación del derecho de identidad). R de Identif y Cienc Pen 7: 182-215 N '30 **5387**

L, **Julio Larraín.** Proyecto de clave dactiloscópica. R de Identif y Cienc Pen 4: 175-88 Jl '29 **5388**

Legislación dactiloscópica [Ecuador]. R de Identif y Cienc Pen 1: 228-31 Ja '28 **5389**

Locard, Edmond. L'histoire de la dactyloscopie. R Int de Crimin 2 (4): 269-91 bibliog (p290-1) '30 **5390**

Locard, Edmond. Historia de la dactiloscopia; trad. del francés por Ataulfo Pérez Aznar. R de Identif y Cienc Pen 5: 353-74 bibliog (p374) Mr '30 **5391**

Locard, Edmond. Traité de criminalistique. Les empreintes et les traces dans l'enquête criminelle. 2v 998p. Lyon, Desvigne, 1931 **5392**

Miranda-Pinto, Osvaldo. La determination du doigt dans les recherches dactyloscopiques. R Int de Crimin 2 (1): 30-5 '30 **5393**

Morrill, Clarence. Food for thought. Int Assn Identif Proc 16: 70-1 '30 **5394**

Mueller, B. Untersuchungen über die Erblichkeit von Fingerbeerenmustern unter besonderer Berücksichtigung rechtlicher Fragestellungen. Zeitsch f indukt Abstammungs- u Vererbungsl 56: 302-82 '30 **5395**

Palitzsch. Gibt es gleichartige oder so ähnliche Papillarlinienmuster dass die Beweiskraft der Polizeidaktyloskopie erschüttert wird? Polizei 42: 165-6 Ap 20 '27 **5396**

Parks, John. Why universal fingerprinting should be enacted. Int Assn Identif Proc 16: 89-91 '30 **5397**

Pozzo, F. Dactyloscopie. Système d'identification. Arch de Méd des Enf 32: 372-6 Je '29 **5398**

Rechter, [Gustave] de. De quelques critiques récentes formulées contre la dactyloscopie. R de Dr Pén et de Crimin 7: 939-43 Ag '27 **5399**

Refusing finger prints. Sol J 73: 825 D 14 '29 **5400**

Renoe, A. J. Modification and extension to the Henry system. 24p. (mim) Washington, U. S. Bureau of investigation, Division of identification, 1927 **5401**

Renoe, A. J. Modification and extension to the Henry system. Police J [N Y] 16: 26-7 Ja '29 **5402**

Renoe, A. J. Modification and extension of the Henry system. Int Assn Identif Proc 16: 148-59 '30 **5403**

Rodgers, Don. Michigan department has 600,000 fingerprints and records filed. State Trooper 11: 13-14 O '29 **5404**

Rusticucci, Luigi. L'impronta digitale nell'anagrafe civile e criminale. 236p. Bologna, Capelli, 1927 **5405**

Sagredo, José L. de. Dactiloscopia civil. 224p. bibliog 223-4. Barcelona, Graphos S.A. 1928 **5406**

Sagredo, José L. de. Dactiloscopia; sistema de identificación. 95p. Barcelona, Imp. de la Casa P. de Caridad, 1931 **5407**

Sagredo, José L. de. Tablas del dactilograma adaptadas al método de dactiloscopia. 11p. Barcelona, Imp. de la Casa P. de Caridad, 1930? **5408**

Sandbury, Fred. History of fingerprints in the Hall-Mills murder case. Int Assn Identif, Calif Div Proc 16: 58-62 '31 **5409**

Sava, Valentin. Dactiloscopia in serviciul Justitiei. R de Drept Pen (7-8): 350-'30 **5410**

[Schrader], Hart. The value of the signature of an arrested man upon the fingerprint card. Int Assn Identif, Calif Div Proc 12: 56-8 '27 **5411**

Silva, Rodolfo Xavier da. A dactiloscopia em Moçambique. Bol do Inst de Crimin s8 15 (2): 437-43 '31 **5412**

Simmonds, W. L. Finger prints. Justice 1: 22-3 N, 26-7 D '28 **5413**

State laws respecting finger-printing and identification photographs. Int Assn Identif Proc 16: 145-8 '30 **5414**

Stewart, R. G. Do fingerprints fail. Northwest Police J 5: 31 Mr '28 **5415**

Sveen, Reidar. Det nye mono daktyloskopiske system ved Scotland Yard. Nord Kriminalteknisk Tidsk 1(1) '31 **5416**

Taking finger-prints. Sol J 73: 688 O 26 '29 **5417**

Taylor, J. H. The Navy's finger print system. Int Assn Identif Proc 16: 73-5 '30 **5418**

United States. Bureau of investigation. How to take finger prints. 8p. Washington, Govt. Ptg. Off. Jl 1 '31 **5419**

Valadares, Manuel. Anomalies dactyloscopiques. R de Identif y Cienc Pen 8: 157-8 My '31 **5420**

Viotti, Manuel. Dactyloscopia e anthropología. R de Identif y Cienc Pen 7: 125-30 N '30 **5421**

Viotti, Manuel. Dactyloscopie et anthropologie. R Int de Crimin 3 (10): 742-8 '31 **5422**

Virchow, H. Das Manuar oder die Verteilung der Fingerleistenmuster bei verschiedenen Rassen. Gesellsch f Phys Anthrop Verh 5: 49-59 '31 **5423**

Vucetich, Juan. Conferencia sobre el sistema dactiloscópico. R de Identif y Cienc Pen 4: 27-79 My '29 **5424**

Vucetich, Juan. Documentos para la historia de la legislación dactiloscópica; carta de Vucetich al legislador Adolfo Dickman (1916). R de Identif y Cienc Pen 2: 361-75 S '28 **5425**

Weinberg, Harry E. Universal fingerprinting; the record of an experiment with the aging fingerprint. Police "13-13" 5: 11-12 O '30 **5426**

Wentworth, Bert. Impossibility of duplicating fingerprints. Police J [N Y] 17: 17, 24 Ap '30 **5427**

Why we need universal fingerprinting. Peace Offic 5: 12, 24 Ap '27 **5428**

Wigle. Why a vagrant should be fingerprinted. Chief Constables Assn Can Proc 26: 57-62 '30 5429

Wilkinson, J[ames] R. Finger prints in the dark continent: . . . compulsory finger print registration in British East Africa. . . . Int Pict Police J 29- Je '29 5430

Wilkinson, James R. Sir Edward Richard Henry, Baronet. Int Pict Police J 21-5 Je '29 5431

Wilkinson, James R. Would the adoption of universal fingerprinting of the people be beneficial? Int Assn Chiefs Police Proc 1927: 179-81 5432

Wossidlo, Otto. Das Recht der polizeilichen Daktyloskopie und Photographie. 70p. Diss. Erlanger, 1930. Hamm, E. Griesbsch, 1930 5433

Classification

Almandos, Luis Reyna. Identificación dactiloscópica de los primates (nuevos elementos de clasificación y nomenclatura). R de Identif y Cienc Pen 4: 5-13 My '29 5434

Almandos, Luis Reyna. El problema de la subclasificación dactiloscópica. R de Identif y Cienc Pen 1: 293-310 Mr '28 5435

Barlow, H. L. The classification of finger prints. Pac Police Mag 6: 11-12 My '29 5436

Berque, S. S. Fingerprints: a set of simplified lessons in their taking, classification, and use in police work. Police J [N Y] 14: 19-20 Ja '27 5437

Henry, Edward Richard. Classification and uses of finger prints. ed.6. 142p. London, H. M. Stationery Off. 1928 5438

Martínez, Benjamín A. Subclasificación aplicable al Vucetichismo. R de Identif y Cienc Pen 5: 327-45 Mr '30 5439

Martinez, Benjamin A. Subclasificacion aplicable al Vucetichismo. R Int de Crimin 2 (8): 570-88 '30 5440

Miranda-Pinto, [Osvaldo]. Une nouvelle méthode de classement dactyloscopique et ses applications. R Int de Crimin 1 (1-3): 82-98 '29; translation: Un nuevo método de clasificación dactiloscópica y sus aplicaciones, by Léon Brailovsky. R de Identif y Cienc Pen 6: 15-29 My '30 5441

Schneickert, Hans. Probleme der Fingerabdruck-Klassifizierung. Monats f Kriminalpsychol y Strafrechtsref 18: 37-41 Ja '27 5442

Sicouley, Alberto. Sistema de subclasificación dactiloscópica. R de Identif y Cienc Pen 1: 178-210 bibliog (p210) Ja '28 5443

As Evidence

Altmann, Victor. Dactyloscopy as a proof in criminal process. Police J [N Y] 16: 21 Ag '29 5444

Barlow, H. L. Where fingerprints have figured in securing convictions in the courts. Int Assn Identif, Calif Div Proc 12: 59-63 '27 5445

Dangers of finger-print testimony. L Notes 30: 182-3 Ja '27 5446

Finger printing held to be legal. Am County 13: 17 S '31 5447

Kelley, Walter. Fingerprints as evidence of identity. Univ Cin L R 5: 201-12 Mr '31 5448

Kidd, A[lexander] M[arsden]. Is it legal to take fingerprints and photographs of persons charged with crime, under the California law? Peace Offic Assn Calif Proc 9: 40-6 '29 5449

Muhl. Eine interessante Gerichtsentscheidung über das zwangsweise Herstellen von Fingerabdrücken. Arch f Krim 82: 194-6 '28 5450

Shaw, John Arthur. Fingerprints for the lawyer. Temple L Q 4: 227-53 My '30 5451

Shaw, John Arthur. The lawyer and the finger-print. Case & Com 34: 11-12 S '28 5452

Sufficiency of finger prints alone to sustain conviction. Am B Assn J 17: 72-3 F '31 5453

Identification

Almandos, L. R. Las nueve bases fundamentales de la identificación dactiloscópica. R de Identif y Cienc Pen 1: 92-5 N '27 5454

Barlow, H. L. Identification by fingerprints. Inst Police Adm Proc 17-28 '29 5455

Bonnevie, K. Lassen sich die Papillarmuster der Fingerbeere für Vaterschaftsfragen praktisch verwerten? Zentralbl f Gynäk 1927: 539-43 5456

Fan, Leung. Identification d'un cas d'empreinte digitale roulée anormale. R Int de Crimin 3 (9): 704-6 '31 5457

Heindl, Robert. Die erste deutsche Arbeit über das Fingerabdruckverfahren als polizeiliches Identifizierungsmittel. Ein bisher verschollenes, unveröffentliches Manuskript. Arch f Krim 85: 30-69 Ag '29 5458

Lauer, A. and Poll, H. Der Vaterschatsnachweis mit Hilfe der Papillarmuster der Fingerbeeren. Krimin Monatsh 3: 217-21 O '29; translation: Tracing paternity through fingerprints. Am J Police Sci 1: 92-9 Ja '30 5459

Quertier, A. Quelques cas d'identification par les empreintes digitales. R Int de Crimin 2 (1): 49-57 '30 5460

Schaffer, E. Empreintes digitales et frontières. Identification à distance. Transmissions télégraphiques d'images. Multiplication des empreintes digitales. R Int de Crimin 1 (1-3): 70-4 '29 5461

The science of fingerprint identification. Am J Police Sci 2: 302-5 bibliog (p305) Jl '31 5462

Sommerfeld. Identizifierung eines unbekannten Toten auf Grund daktyloskopischer Vergleichungen. Krimin Monatsh 5: 232-3 O '31 **5463**

Wentworth, Bert. About finger-prints identification. R Int de Crimin 1 (1-3): 66-9 '29 **5464**

Single Fingerprint

Almandos, L. R. Identificación monodactilar. R de Crimin, Psiquiat y Med Leg 14: 129-43 Mr '27 **5465**

Barlow, H. L. Classifying and filing single finger prints. Pac Police Mag 6: 13, 25, 27 Je '29 **5466**

Battley, Henry. Single finger prints; a new and practical method of classifying and filing single finger prints and fragmentary impressions. 98p. New Haven, Yale, 1931 **5467**

Heindl, R. Monodaktyloskopie: Zwei Vorschläge für Einzenfingerabdruckregistraturen. Arch f Krim 82: 239-54 '28 **5468**

Heinrich, Edward O. Battley fingerprint system. Int Assn Identif, Calif Div Proc 16: 53-8 '31 **5469**

Jaycox, Thomas S. Classification of single fingerprints. 30p. Wichita, Kan. Police department, 1931 **5470**

Larson, John A. Single fingerprint system. Toronto, Carswell, 1931 **5471**

Larson, John [A.]. Single finger prints. Police J [N Y] 18: 10, 24 Mr '31 **5472**

Pérez, Salustiano. Adopción del sello digital en los actos jurídicos. R de Identif y Cienc Pen 5: 350-2 Mr '30 **5473**

Sagredo, José L. de. La policía. Sistema de identificación monodactilar. 68p. Barcelona, Industrias Gráficas, 1927 **5474**

Transmission

Almandos, Luis Reyna. Radiofotografía de impresiones digitales (Transmisión dactiloscópica de Buenos Aires a Berlin). R de Identif y Cienc Pen 5: 212-16 Ja '30 **5475**

A[lmandos], L[uis] R[eyna]. Teledactiloscopia. Sistema propuesto por Francisco L. Romay. R de Identif y·Cienc Pen 2: 248-54 Jl '28 **5476**

Ottolenghi, Salvador. Le prime impronte digitale trasmesse telegraficamente. R de Identif y Cienc Pen 7: 131-44 N '30 **5477**

Romay, F[rancisco] L. Teledactiloscopia. R de Crimin, Psiquiat y Med Leg 15: 168-88 Mr '28 **5478**

Methods of Securing

Bauernfeind. Neuer Taschen-Fingerabdruckapparat. Arch f Krim 81: 9-12 Jl '27 **5479**

Bettmann and Lutz, G. Zur Anwendung der Dermato-Photographie. Arch f Krim 81: 22-5 Jl '27 **5480**

Claps, Albert. Considérations sur la découverte d'empreintes digitales sur un verre à vin dans un cas de vol. R Int de Crimin 3 (1): 26-30 '31 **5481**

Claps, A[lbert]. Un procédé simple de relevé d'empreintes digitales sur le lieu d'un crime, son transport et ses utilisations. R Int de Crimin 3 (2): 136-9 '31 **5482**

The dactiloscopic press; new invention takes prints of both hands at once. Police J [N Y] 17: 16 Jl '30 **5483**

Ehrhardt, S. Die Verwendung einer wasserlöslichen Farbe für daktyloskopische Abdrucke. Anthrop Anz 8: 143 '31 **5484**

Ferreira, A. Amado. Das impressões digitaes nas fructas e nas folhas das plantas. Ann Fac de med de São Paulo 5: 307-9 '30 **5485**

Fischer, Eugen. Ein neues Verfahren der Daktyloskopie. Anthrop Anz 5: 49-51 '28 **5486**

Friedemann, Adolf. Zwei neue einfache Hand-(Finger-) Abdruckverfahren ohne Druckerschwärze für anthropologische Zwecke. Arch f Krim 84: 234-7 bibliog (p237) My '29 **5487**

Great Britain. Registry of criminals. Instruction in the method of taking finger prints: with a memorandum on the working of the finger print system of identification. 18p. London, H. M. Stationery Off. 1928 **5488**

Hoover, J[ohn] Edgar. Taking fingerprints; the mechanics of registering and filing finger impressions. Police "13-13" 7-9 D '31 **5489**

How to take fingerprints. Am City 38: 117-19 Mr '28 **5490**

Kuhne, Frederick. The finger print instructor. N.Y. Munn & co. 1927 **5491**

Leung. Une méthode nouvelle de transfert des empreintes. R Int de Crimin 2(10): 738-40 '30; translation: New method for transferring fingerprint traces. Am J Police Sci 2: 183 Mr '31 **5492**

Leung and Claps. De l'utilisation des empreintes digitales transférées. Un nouveau type de fichier. R Int de Crimin 3(4): 257-60 '31 **5493**

Mezger, [Otto] and Fränkle, [Paul]. Wiedersichtbarmachen eines mit Tinte hergestellten Fingerabdrucks, der nachträglich mit Federstrichen aus einer Tinte gleicher Art ausgestrichen worden war. Arch f Krim 83: 74-5 Jl '28 **5494**

Popp, G. Chemische Hervorrufung und Fixierung latenter Fingerspuren. Zeitsch f Ang Chem 41: 1005-7 S 8 '28; same title: Krimin Monatsh 5: 5-6 Ja '31 **5495**

Richardson, Phil M. The art of lifting finger-prints. Police J [N Y] 16: 20 D '28 **5496**

Schmidt, Otto. Über die topographische Verlagerung korrespondierender Punkte im daktyloskopischen Bilde. Arch f Krim 84: 48-55 bibliog (p55) Ja '29 **5497**

Simonin, C. Simplification de l'expertise dactyloscopique par photographie par transparence. Ann de Méd Lég 11: 85-6 F '31 **5498**

Watzek, Ferdinand. Criminalistic technique in the treatment of finger and palm print traces and their value as circumstantial evidence. Am J Police Sci 1: 366-73, 466-73, 565-74 Jl-D '30 **5499**

Zirpins, W. Die gebräuchlichsten Methoden zur Sichtbarmachung latenter Fingerabdrücke. Deut Zeitsch f d ges gerichtl Med 10: 372-6 Ag '27 **5500**

CRIMINAL LAW

GENERAL

Administration of the criminal law is a disgrace. Va L Reg ns12: 723-8 Ap '27 5501

Alimena, Francesco. Se l'azione penale possa concepirsi come un'attivita obbligatoria dello stato. Riv Pen di Dott, Legis e Giuris 108: 483-510 D '28 5502

American prison association. Report of Committee on criminal law and statistics. Proc 60: 118-24 '30 5503

Andrade, A. de. Sobre el ilícito penal. R de Crimin, Psiquiat y Med Leg 14: 182-200 Mr '27 5504

D'Antonio, F. Le dottrine di Bergson e il diritto penale. Riv Pen di Dott, Legis e Giuris 107: 110-38 Ja '28; translation: Las doctrinas de Bergson y el derecho penal. R de Crimin, Psiquiat y Med Leg 15: 206-21, 330-42 Mr, My '28 5505

Archer, Gleason Leonard. Laws that safeguard society. 382p. Boston, Suffolk law school press, 1931 5506

Aumann, F. R. Where to with criminal equity? Am L R 62: 355-76 My '28 5507

Barbey, Alec. De l'application internationale de la règle "non bis in idem" en matière répressive. 272p. Lausanne, La Concorde, 1930 5508

Battaglini, Giulio. La concilazione fra Stato e Chiesa nei suoi riflessi penale. Riv Ital di Dir Pen (5): 418-22 '29 5509

Battaglini, G[iulio]. Sull'efficacia delle leggi penali straniere. Riv Ital di Dir Pen 1: 7-12 '29 5510

Battaglini, Giulio. La questione delle fonti specialmente in rapporto al diritto penale. Riv Int di Filosofia del Diritto 10 (4-5): 528-43 Jl '30; extr: 18p. Roma, Rivista internazional di filosofia del diritto, 1930 5511

Baumgarten, A. Die Gesamtpersönlichkeit im Licht der Jurisprudenz und der Rechtsphilosophie. Schweiz Zeitsch f Strafr 40: 58-82 '27 5512

Beale, Joseph H[enry]. Justification for injury. Harv L R 41: 553-63 Mr '28 5513

Beale, Joseph Henry and Margold, Nathan Ross. A selection of cases and other authorities upon criminal law. ed.4. 1145p. Cambridge, Harvard univ. press, 1928 5514

Bédour, Jean. Les accidents du travail et la loi pénale. 198p. These, Paris, 1930. Paris, Perrin, 1930 5515

Beling, Ernst. Grundzüge des Strafrechts. ed.11 rev. 139p. Tübingen, Mohr, 1930 5516

Beling, Ernst. Il significato del principio: "nulla poena sine lege poenali" nella determinazione dei concetti fondamentali di diritto penale; translated by Ernesto Vito. Giustiz Pen 37 (3) pt1: 319-29 Mr '31 5517

Benedetti, Isidoro de. El proyecto de ley de 1928 sobre "Estado peligroso sin delito." R de Crimin, Psiquiat y Med Leg 18: 22-60 Ja '31 5518

Benvenuto, Giuseppe. Le due scuole penali. Rassegna Pen (7-8): 663-71 '29 5519

Beratung des Entwurfs des Strafgesetzbuchs. Jurist Wchnschr 56: 2735-84 '27 5520

Berg, Joseph. Doctrine et application du code pénal. R de Dr Pén et de Crimin 8: 417-33 My '28 5521

B[ertrand], E. Encore le projet de loi de défense sociale. Ecrou 8: 365-73 Jl '27 5522

Bettiol, Giuseppe. L'efficacia della consuetudine nel diritto penale. 56p. (Pub. della Università Cattolica del Sacro Cuore, s2 v32) Milano, "Vita e Pensiero," 1931 5523

Beya, Putnoki. Becsület-védelmi irányok a büntetojagbau (les modalités de la défense de l'honneur dans le droit pénal). 79p. Miskolc, Magyar Jövö nyomdaüzem ès lapkiadóvallalat r.-t. 1927 5524

Bianchi, V. Positivismo e progetto di codice penale. Scuola Pos 9: 17-20 Ja '29 5525

Biondolillo, G. Imputato detenuto e giudizio contumaciale. Riv Pen di Dott, Legis e Giuris 105: 91-2 Ja '27 5526

Biondolillo, G. Intorno alla citazione direttissima. Riv Pen di Dott, Legis e Giuris 105: 285-6 Mr '27 5527

Biondolillo, G. Ordine di cattura e prescrizione della condanna penale. Riv Pen di Dott, Legis e Giuris 105: 466-7 My '27 5528

Bisthoven, R. Janssens de. L'application de la loi de défense sociale du 9 avril 1930 aux poursuites fiscales. R de Dr Pén et de Crimin (1): 1-9 '31 5529

Blanc, Eugene, jr. Preliminary analysis for the formulation of a philosophy of criminal law. St John's L R 2: 177-87 My '28 5530

Borja, Francisco Pérez. Apuntes para el estudio del código penal. 3v. Quito, Tip. de la Escuela de Artes y Oficias, 1927-30 5531

Bovio, C. L'evoluzione del diritto penale come funzione superiore dello spirito. Riv Pen di Dott, Legis e Giuris 105: 497-501 Je '27 5532

Braas, Ad. Traité élémentaire de droit pénal. ed.2. 290p. Liège, Vaillant-Carmance, 1928 5533

Braffort, Louis. Essai de contribution à l'évolution du droit pénal. 63p. Bruxelles, Ferd. Larcier, 1929 5534

Brassloff, Stephan. Die Rechtssicherheit. Eine Studie aus dem Gebiete der allgemeinen Rechtslehre. 143p. Wien, Moritz Perles, 1928 5535

Brichetti, Giovanni. L'atto invalido nella storia del diritto penale. Riv Pen di Dott, Legis e Giuris (6): 501-7 '29 5536

Bürk, Albert. Über das Wesen der Idealkonkurrenz. Eine strafrechtliche Untersuchung. . . [Austria]. 104p. Stuttgart, Hofer in Komm. 1927 5537

Buerschaper, Hans. Soziale Strafrechtspflege. 140p. Leipzig, F. C. W. Vogel, 1929 5538

Bustamente, Antonio S. de; Aloisi, and Ammoun, Fouad. Pour quels délits convient-il d'admettre la compétence universelle? R Int de Dr Pén 8: 295-9, 300-17, 318-31 '31 5539

Calker, Fritz v. Strafrechtlicher Grundriss zu Vorlesungen und Leitfaden zum Studium. ed.3 rev. 186p. München, Schweitzer, 1927 5540

Campbell, F. H. Science and the law. L Inst J [Melbourne] 2: 73 Je '28 5541

Cardone, Domenico Antonio. Le reazioni collettive e la genesi del diritto penale. 90p. Torino, G. B. Paravia, 1927 5542

Carnevale, Emanuele. Diritto criminale unitario nel nuovo codice penale. 77p. Roma, Mantellate, 1931 5543

Carrara, Mario. Biologia e diritto. Riv di Diritto Peniten (3): 573-82 '30 5544

Carta, Stanislao. Concorso di aggravanti e di qualifiche nel delitto di lesioni personali volontarie. Giustiz Pen (44): 1920-4 '28 5545

Cass, E. R. Legislation in 1926. J Crim L & Crimin 18: 92-9 My '28 5546

Cassinelli, Bruno. L'avvenire del diritto penale. 156p. (Collez. Omnia 20) Roma, Paolo Cremonese, 1928 5547

Cassinelli, Bruno. Il nuovo codice penale. 700p. Roma, Paolo Cremonese, 1931 5548

Cavanaugh, Frank. The joke of our criminal code. Cath Char R 11: 84-5 Mr '27 5549

Cecchi, O[rfeo]. L'innocente nel procedimento penale. 22p. Salerno, Ed. Cron. Forensi, 1927 5550

Celetano, Federico. L'esistenza ed il contenuto del diritto penale amministrativo. Rassegna Pen (1-2): 11-24 '29 5551

Cermesoni, Fernando. Legislación del nombres. R de Identif y Cienc Pen 3: 325-90 bibliog (p389-90) Mr '29 5552

Cevolotto, M[ario]. Le sanzioni penali nel progetto di codice procedura civile. Scuola Pos ns7: 508-29 N '27 5553

Chamberlain, Joseph P. Criminal legislation for 1928. Am B Assn J 15: 339-42 Je '29 5554

Chamberlain, Joseph P. Criminal statutes in 1929. Am B Assn J 16: 100-3 F '30 5555

Chamberlain, Joseph P. Criminal statutes in 1930. Am B Assn J 17: 219-22 Ap '31 5556

Checchi, O[ttorino]. Il nuovo codice di pubblica sicurezza. 270p. Empoli, R. Noccioli, 1927 5557

Chiarappa, Sabino. Il testo unico delle leggi di pubblica sicurezza. 138p. Pesaro, La Poligrafica, 1927 5558

Chiossone, Julio. Anotaciones al libro primero del código penal. 179p. Mérida, Venezuela, 1929 5559

Coates, Albert. Criminal law and criminology. N C L R 7: 150-61 F '29 5560

Cornil, Léon. La mesure de sureté envisagée objectivement. R de Dr Pén et de Crimin 9: 825-57 Ag '29 5561

Cornil, Léon. Le rôle de la jurisprudence et celui de la loi dans l'évolution du droit pénal contemporain. R de l'Univ Bruxelles 32 (2): 149-67 D '26-Ja '27; same title: R de Dr Pén et de Crimin 7: 635-64 Je '27; also separate: 34p. Bruxelles, Imp. Médicale et Scientifique, 1927 5562

Criminal law and police court practice. Sol J 73: 181-2, 211-12, 227-8, 243, 259-60, 275-6, 291, 307, 339, 375-6 Mr 23-Je 15 '29 5563

Criminal law and practice. Sol J 75: 383, 399, 415 Je 13-27 '31 5564

The criminal law in civil cases. Dickinson L R 31: 185-7 Ap '27 5565

Criminal law in 1930. L Times 171: 23-5 Ja 10 '31 5566

Dalcke, Albert. Strafrecht und Strafprozess. Eine Sammlung der wichtigsten, das Strafrecht und das Strafverfahren betreffenden Gesetze. ed.19. 1927. ed.20. Berlin, Müller, 1928 5567

Damsté, P. H. Onze hedendaagsche strafrechtspolitiek. Tijdschr v Strafr 37: 141-50 '27 5568

Derby, Augustin, ed. Cases on criminal law. ed.3. 865p. Indianapolis, Bobbs-Merrill, 1930 5569

Diniz, Almachio. O experimentalismo juridico da jurisprudencia. R de Cultura Jurid 1: 381-7 Jl '29 5570

The distinction between mala prohibita and mala in se in criminal law. Colum L R 30: 74-86 Ja '30 5571

Doleschall, Alfred. Strafrecht im Völkerrecht (Zur Frage der internationalen Strafgerichtsbarkeit). 94p. Budapest, Eggenberger, 1930 5572
(in ungarischer Sprache erschienen)

Dongoroz, Vintilëo. Drept penal. 221p. Bucuresti, "Curierul judiciar," 1929 5573

Donnedieu de Vabres, H. [F. A.]. La justice pénale d'aujourd'hui 220p. Paris, Colin, 1929 5574

Donnedieu de Vabres, H. F. A. Les principes modernes du droit pénal international. 470p. Paris, Sirey, 1928 5575
Bibliographical footnotes.

Dronke, Ernst. Ehe und Strafrecht. 20p. Berlin, F. Vahlen, 1930 5576

Drost, Heinrich. Das Problem einer Individualisierung des Strafrechts. (Recht und Staat in Geschichte und Gegenwart 73). 23p. Tübingen, Mohr, 1930 **5577**

E., U. P. ed. Le leggi per la difesa dello stato. 20p. Mortara, Barbè, 1927 **5578**

Effertz, Josef. Die strafrechtliche Behandlung des Rückfalls. 222p. (Strafrechtl Abh no218, von Lilienthal) Breslau, Schletter, 1927 **5579**

Egloffstein, Leo von. Die Unterbringung in Trinkerheilanstalten nach dem künftigen Strafrecht. Bl f Gefängniskunde 59: 216-20 '28 **5580**

Elliott, Mabel A. Conflicting penal theories in statutory criminal law. 274p. Chicago, University of Chicago press, 1931 **5581**

Thesis (Ph.D.) Northwestern University, 1929.

Elliott, Mabel A. Conflicting penal theory in statutory criminal legislation since 1900. Am Sociol Soc Proc 24: 65-73 '29 **5582**

Engisch, Karl. Die Kausalität als Merkmal der strafrechtlichen Tatbestände. (Beiträge zur strafrechtswissenschaft, ns no 1) 87p. Tübingen, Mohr, 1931 **5583**

Esmond, Burton D. The new crime laws. N Y St Assn Magistrates Proc 20: 63-76 '28 **5584**

Falck, C[arl]. Die Berichterstattung in Strafsachen und der Entwurf des Strafgesetzbuches. Justiz 3: 186-95 '27 **5585**

Ferrari, U. Il concetto giuridico e i caratteri della verità penale nel diritto sostantivo. Riv Pen di Dott, Legis e Giuris 107: 402-24 My '28 **5586**

Ferrari, U. La verità nel diritto penale sostantivo. 159p. Milano, Scient. 1928 **5587**

Ferri, Enrico. Il metodo di studio e di insegnamento nel diritto criminale. *In* Scritti della Facoltà Giuridica di Roma in onore di Antonio Salandra, 39-42. Milano, Vallardi, 1929 **5588**

Finger, A. Kritische Bemerkungen zur Lehre vom Tatbestand und der Rechtswidrigkeit. Gerichtssaal 97: 385-400 '28 **5589**

Fischer, M. Der neue Strafgesetzbuch-Entwurf. Psychiatneurol Wchnschr 29: 253-5 My 21 '27 **5590**

Florian, Eugenio. Diritto e procedura penale negli Atti Lateranensi. Scuola Pos (8-9): 337-9 '29 **5591**

Florian, Eugenio. Principî di diritto processuale penale. 384p. Torino, Giappichelli, 1927 **5592**

Foignet, René and Dupont, Émile. Manuel élémentaire de droit criminel. Suivi d'un résumé en tableaux synoptiques et d'un recueil méthodique des principales questions d'examen. ed.10. 525p. Paris, Rousseau, 1930 **5593**

Fragoso, Fernando. Derecho penal de marina. 184p. Madrid, Reus, 1928 **5594**

Frank, Reinhard. Strafrechtliche Fälle für Übungen an Universitäten und bei Justizbehörden. ed.8 rev. 56p. Giessen, Töpelmann, 1927 **5595**

Fréjaville, Marcel. L'absolution en droit pénal. Etudes Crimin 4 (9-10): 256-70 '29 **5596**

Fuchs, E. Zur Bekämpfung der strafrechtlichen Begriffsjurisprudenz. Leipz Zeitsch f Deut Recht 22: 17-31 '28 **5597**

Fulci, Lodovici. I cardini del nuovo progetto di codice penale. 108p. Calabria, A. Morabito, 1927 **5598**

Gabrieli, Francesco P. Progetto preliminare di un nuovo codice penale. Giustiz Pen (44): 1992-2003 '28 **5599**

Gatti, Tancredi. L'elemento subbiettivo del reato nella più antica legge criminale conosciuta. R de Identif y Cien Pen 5: 260-72 Ja '30 **5600**

Gefängnisgesellschaft für die Provinz Sachsen und Anhalt. Strafrecht und Moral. Jahrbuch, 44, 1928. Halle (Saale), Selbstverlag, 1929 **5601**

Gentz, Werner. Wohlfahrtspflegerische und fürsorgerische Gesichtspunkte in Allgemeinen Teil des Entwurfs zum Strafgesetzbuch. Deut Zeitsch f Wohlfahrtspfl 3 (3): 117-28 '27 **5602**

Giesen, A-. H. v. D. Het Ontwerp van Wet betreffende de Bewaring. Tijdschr v d Politie 1(4): 57-64 Ap 25 '28 **5603**

Givanovitch, Thomas. Les problèmes fondamentaux du droit criminal. I. Infraction. II. Delinquant. III. Sanction criminelle. 227p. Paris, Rousseau, 1929 **5604**

Givanovitch, Thomas. La situation du désistement volontaire dans le système du droit criminel. R Int de Dr Pén 4: 187-210 '27 **5605**

Givanovitch, Thomas. Systèmatique de l'argumentation contre le système bipartite du droit criminel en faveur du système tripartite. R Int de Dr Pén 5: 99-115 '28 **5606**

Glaser, Stefano. L'idea di giustizia nel diritto penale. Riv Int del Filosofia del Diritto 9 (4): 769-87 N '29 **5607**

Glueck, Sheldon. Principles of a rational penal code. Harv L R 41: 453-82 F '28; same title: Ment Hyg 13: 1-32 Ja '29 **5608**

Göring, M. H. Kritik an den Entwürfen zu einem Bewahrungsgesetz. Monats f Kriminalpsychol u Strafrechtsref 18: 33-6 bibliog (p36) Ja '27 **5609**

G[oldman], A. [A.]. "Conviction"—what constitutes. Ill L R 25: 939-42 Ap '31 **5610**

Goldschmidt, James. Rechtsfälle aus dem Strafrecht. ed.3. 1930. 86p. Berlin, Springer, 1927 **5611**

Gottschling, E. Die rechtliche Seite der Verurteilung Jesu Christi. Deut Richterzeit 20: 209-11 '28 **5612**

Goyet, Francisque. Précis de droit pénal spécial. Supplément 1930. [382]p. Paris, Sirey, 1930? **5613**

Gramatica, Filippo. La irrazionalità della colpa nel diritto penale. Il Foro Ligure (2-3): 69-88 '29; separate: 36p. Genova, "Circolo di cultura giuridica," 1929 **5614**

Grau, [Hans]. Automobil-Strafrecht. ed. 2. 187p. Berlin, Lind, 1930 **5615**

Graven, Jean. Essai sur l'évolution du droit pénal valaisan jusqu'à l'invasion française de 1789. 539p. Lausanne, Pache-Varidel, 1927 5616

Green, Leon. Recent steps in law administration. Am Jud Soc J 14: 113-16 D '30 5617

Gregori, Isaïa. La dottrina dello stato e la scienza del diritto penale. 49p. Messina, Giacoma, 1931 5618
Extr: Il pensiero giuridico penal 2 (3-4)

Grünhut, Max. Artikel "Kriminalpolitik" im Handwörterbuch der Rechtswissenschaft, herausgegeben von Fritz Stier-Somlo und Alexander Elster. 885p. (v5) Berlin, Gruyter, 1928 5619

Guckenheimer. Strafrecht und Verwaltung. Verwaltungsarch 35 (3): 276-91 Jl '30 5620

Guevara, Guillermo B. Commentaries on the revised penal code. Manila, Philippine Educ. Co. 1931 5621

Guevara, G[uillermo] B. Essentials of criminal law and criminology. 255p. Manila, Oriental Print. 1928 5622

Guilhot, Jacques. De l'application du droit pénal en matière d'enregistrement. Etudes Crimin 4: 38-45, 82-90, 113-23, 157-61, 188-90 F-Je '29; same: 105p. Paris, Sirey, 1929 5623

Häberlin. Alte und neue Ziele und Wege im Strafrecht. Schweiz Ver f Straf-Gegängniswes u Schutzaufsicht Verh 8: 4-21 '28 5624

Haeckel, Heinrich. Die Zusammenarbeit von Strafrechtspflege und Straffälligenfürsorge im geltenden Recht und nach den Strafgesetzentwürfen. Berliner Wohlfahrtsbl 7(6): 41-3; (7): 49-50 Mr 15, 29 '31 5625

Hagemann. Zwischen den Gesetzen. Krimin Monatsh 4: 1-2 Ja '30 5626

Hallam, O. Crime legislation. 9th Dist Banker 21- Je 1 '27 5627

Haller, Marguerite. A propos du nouveau code disciplinaire et pénal de la Marine Marchande. 23p. Paris, Librairie Générale de Droit et de Jurisprudence, 1930 5628

Hammond, T. C. Concerning penal laws. 186p. London, Thynne, 1930 5629
Reprint from Church of Ireland Gazette.

DeHartog, L. S. G. Aanteekening bij artikel 326 wetboek van strafrecht. Tijdschr v Strafr 37: 133-400 '27 5630

Heimberger, Josef. Strafrecht. 177p. Berlin, Späth & Linde, 1931 5631

Hencke, A. Die pflichten des Kraftfahrers im Lichte der neueren höheren Rechtssprechung. 103p. Berlin, Klasing, 1928 5632

Henckel, Hans (Henkel). Der Gefahrbegriff im Strafrecht. 83p. (Strafrechtl Abh no270). Breslau, Schletter, 1930 5633

Hentig, H[ans] v. Der Konflikt zwischen Rechtssicherheit und der Freiheit richterlichen Ermessens. Justiz 2: 553-9 '27 5634

Hesseltine, Norman T. Laws helping criminals. Bost Univ L R 10: 524-6 N '30 5635

Hill, Arthur W. Comment on recent decisions concerning torts, automobiles, business trusts, criminal law and evidence. 64p. Thesis (J.D.) University of California, 1930 5636

Hinderling, H. Eine ungelöste Kausalitätsfrage. Schweiz Zeitsch f Strafr 41: 117-46 '28 5637

Hitchler, Walter Harrison. Criminal law in civil cases. Dickinson L R 31: 185-204 Ap '27 5638

Hörler, Franz Otto. Das Wesen der Strafe. Grundlegung zu einer Strafrechtserneuerung. 288p. Basel, Zbinden & Hügin, 1927 5639

Hofmann, Fritz. Die normativen Elemente des besonderen und allgemeinen Tatbestands im Strafrecht. 52p. (Strafrechtl Abh no272) Breslau, Schletter, 1930 5640

Holmes, Harold C. Comments on criminal law and torts. 25p. Thesis (J.D.) University of California, 1928 5641

Hugueney, Louis. Commentaire de la loi du 3 décembre 1926. Lois Nouvelles 46 (4): 65-80 F '27 5642

Humphreys, Travers. Some modern criminal legislation. Sol J 71: 5-6, 28 Ja 1, 8 '27 5643

Husband and wife in the criminal law. Just Peace 91: 662-4 S 10 '27 5644

Hyde, Robert Edward. Handbook on criminal law and criminal procedure. 192p. Cleveland, Ohio, 728 Leader bldg. The Author, 1929 5645

Irk, Albert. Die heutige Lage des Strafrechts. Monats f Kriminalpsychol u Strafrechtsref 21: 449-52 '30 5646

Isoldi, V. Del responsabile civile nel giudizio penale. Riv Pen di Dott, Legis e Giuris 105: 386-9 Ap '27 5647

Jiménez de Asúa, Luis. Mangelnde Rechtswidrigkeit. (Dogmatische Bemerkungen zu einem Strafrechtsfall). Monats f Kriminalpsychol u Strafrechtsref 18: 526-30 S '27 5648

Jiménez de Asúa, Luis. Programma de derecho penal. 215p. Madrid, Libreria General de Victoriana Suárez, 1927 5649

Junckerstorff, K[urt]. Die Durchbildung der eigentlichen Dogmatik im Sinne des Postulats der Individualisierung des Strafrechts. Eine rechtsvergleichende Studie. Zeitsch f Vergl Rechtswiss 45: 150-60 '29 5650

Junckerstorff, Kurt. Kritisches zum Bewahrungsgesetz-Entwurf. Monats f Kriminalpsychol u Strafrechtsref 21: 724-7 '30 5651

Keedy, Edwin Roulette, ed. Cases on the administration of the criminal law, selected and arranged. 586p. Indianapolis, Bobbs-Merrill, 1928 5652

Keeton, W. Page. Criminal law appeal-bills of exception. Tex L R 9: 248-54 F '31 5653

Kelley, Henry Smith. Treatise on criminal law and practice for use in all courts under the code system, adapted especially to the law and evidence relating to crimes defined by the statutes of Missouri, Kansas, and Oklahoma, with forms and precedents for indictments. ed.4. rev. & enl. by Jay M. Lee. 1310p. [Kansas City] Vernon, 1928 5654

Kenny, Courtney Stanhope. Outline of criminal law based on lectures delivered in the University of Cambridge. ed.13. 555p. London, Cambridge Univ. Press, 1929 5655

Kidd, Alexander Marsden. (Readings and cases on criminal law). 559p. (ms) Berkeley, The Author, 1929? 5656

Kiser, Donald J. comp. Outlines of criminal law. 135p. N.Y. American Law Bk. co. 1928 5657

Kley. Die geistig Armen und das Strafgesetz. Hilfsschule 20: 7-14 '27 5658

Kley. Zukunftsrecht und Kriminalistik. Krimin Monatsh 1: 2-3 Ja '27 5659

Kohlrausch. Kriminalpolitische Rückschritte im Strafgesetzentwurf. Deut Juristen-Zeit 32: 1365-9 '27 5660

Kohlrausch, Eduard, ed. Strafgesetzbuch. Textausgabe mit Anmerkungen und Sachregister. ed.29 562p. Berlin, Gruyter, 1930 5661

Krabbe, Oluf Haraldsen. Tillaeg til Noter til Strafferetten. 6p. København, Gad, 1927 5662

Kruglewski, Alexander. Das Strafrecht als Kulturfaktor. Grundlegung einer psychologischen Theorie des Strafrechts. 204p. Riga, G. Löffler, 1927 5663

Laborde-Lacoste. De la protection par la loi pénale française des appellations d'origine étrangère et plus specialement des appellations "Porto" et "Madère." 11p. Paris, Godde, 1927 5664

Lal, R. Law of crimes. ed.11. 150p. Calcutta, M. C. Sarkar, 1928 5665

Lang. Rationalisierung im Strafrecht. Hanseat Rechts- u Gerichts-Zeitsch 11: 193-212 '28 5666

Lanza, Vincenzo. Istituzioni di diritto penale. 288p. Catania, Scuola Penale Umanista, 1927 5667

Lanza, V[incenzo]. Sistema generale umanista del diritto penale. Scuola Pen Uman (4): 248-52 '28 5668

Lanza, Vincenzo. Unmanesimo e diritto penale. ed.2. 333p. Catania, Vincenzo Muglia, 1929 5669

Larenz, Karl. Hegels Zurechnungslehre und der Begriff der objektiven Zurechnung. 109p. Lucka i Th., R. Berger, 1927 5670

Liberati, Fernando. Nozioni di diritto penale. 120p. Amelia, Pastura-Petrignani, 1927 5671

Liepmann, H. R. Kriminal- und Administrativdelikt. Prager Juris Zeitsch 7: 475-8 '27 5672

Lilienthal, K[arl] von. Strafen und sichernde Massnahmen in der Reichstagsvorlage. Zeitsch f d ges Strafrechtswiss 48: 300-5 '28 5673

Lilienthal, K[arl von]. Strafrecht und Medizin. Deut Juristen-Zeit 32: 1229-31 '27 5674

Lisi, G. C. Le idee penali di G. B. Vico. Scuola Pos ns8: 200-11 My '28 5675

Liszt, Franz von. Tratado de derecho penal. Traducio de la vigésima edición alemana por Luis Jiménez de Asúa y adicionada con el derecho penal español por Quintiliano Saldaña. Madrid, Reus, 1927 5676

Lobdell, Hugh L. Criminal law—automobiles—manslaughter—failure to stop at highway intersection. N C L R 9: 66-8 D '30 5677

Loi portant révision du code disciplinaire et pénal pour la marine marchande et la pêche maritime. R de Dr Pén et de Crimin 8: 989-1001 N '28 5678

Lombardi, Giovanni. Le leggi penali di repressione e prevenzione nel loro clima sociale e politico (a proposito di pericolosità e misure di sicurezza). Pensiero Giurid Pen 3: 212-32 Jl '31 5679

Los Angeles bar association. Committee on criminal law and procedure. Report, December 30, 1931. 5p. (typw) [Los Angeles, 1931] 5680

Lucas, Hermann. Anleitung zur strafrechtlichen Praxis; ein Beitrag zur Ausbildung unserer jungen Juristen und ein Ratgeber für Praktiker. 2v. Berlin, Liebmann, 1931 5681

Lucchini, L. Reato e danno. Riv Pen di Dott, Legis e Giuris 107: 185-8 Mr '28 5682

M., J. P. Criminal law and the public. Notre Dame Law 3: 92-4 D '27 5683

Macedo, Miguel. Historia sinoptica del derecho penal. R Gen de Derecho u Juris 1: 415-32 Jl '30 5684

Magnol, Joseph and Solnar, Vladimir. Est-il désirable d'avoir, à côté du code pénal et du code de procédure pénal, un code d'exécution des peines? R Int de Dr Pén 8: 348-58, 359-68 '31 5685

Makowski, W. Les transformations du droit penal. R de Dr Pén et de Crimin 9: 341-74 '29; separate: 34p. Louvain, Pierre Mafrans, 1929 5686

Mamroth, H. Rationalisierung des Strafrechts. Leipz Zeitsch f Deut Recht 25: 29-33 Ja 1 '31 5687

Manfredini, M[ario]. Diritto penale esecutivo. 48p. Ascoli Piceno, Tossi, 1927 5688

Masaveu, Jaime. Nuevo derecho penal. Obra ajustada al programa de 6 de marzo de 1929 para las oposiciones a ingreso en la Escuela de policía. 318p. Madrid, Reus, 1929 5689

Massari, Eduardo. Le dottrine generali del diritto penale; corso di lezioni universitarie. 351p. Napoli, Jovene, 1930 5690

Mauro, G. B. de. Pene e misure di sicurezza nella riforma dei codici penali dei vari Stati. 15p. Kharkow, 1927 **5691**

Mehring, Karl. Inwieweit ist praktischer Einfluss Montesqieus und Voltaires auf die strafrechtliche Tätigkeit Friedrichs des Grossen anzunehmen bezw. nachzuweisen? 58p. Breslau, Schletter, 1928 **5692**

Merkel, Paul. Grundriss des Strafrechts. 263p. Bonn, Röhrscheid, 1927 **5693**

Mezger, Edmund. Lehrbuch des Strafrechts. 528p. München, Duncker, 1931 **5694**

Mezger, Edmund. Moderne Strafrechtsprobleme rede bei der Reichsgrundlungscheier der Universität Marburg am 18: Januar 1927. 34p. (Marburger Akademische Reden no43) Marburg, 1927 **5695**

Milani, Mario. Il diritto nel processo di Gesù: Studio di diritto penale sul Vangelo. 46p. Pavia, Tip. Cooperativa, 1927 **5696**

Milhaud, Léon. La loi du 22 août 1929. Le projet complémentaire du 17 décembre 1929. Le rétablissement des tribunaux. Conséquences pour les juges de paix. J des Juges de Paix 26: 124- Ap '30 **5697**

Miller, Justin. The scientific development of criminal law. Am B Assn Rep 1929: 529-47 **5698**

Mirto, P. La teoria fenomenista dell'imputabilità. Riv Pen di Dott, Legis e Giuris 107: 377-401 My '28 **5699**

Mittermaier, W. Einige Grundgedanken einer neuen Strafgesetzgebung. Justiz 2 (6): 543-53 '27 **5700**

Mittermaier, W. Strafrechtliche Systematik. Monats f Kriminalpsychol u Strafrechtsref 21: 452-4 Ag '30 **5701**

Modern law and the offender. Just Peace 91: 344 My 7 '27 **5702**

Moley, Raymond. Some tendencies in criminal law administration. Pol Sci Q 42: 497-523 D '27 **5703**

De Monté Ver Loren, J. P. De ontwikkeling van het bewijs in strafzaken naar oud-Hollandsch en Zeeuwsch recht. Tijdschr v Strafr 37: 267-315 '27 **5704**

Moore, W. J. The evolution of criminal law as viewed by a constable. Police J [London] 3: 254-61 Ap '30 **5705**

Morrison, A. C. L. Some principles of the criminal law. Just Peace 94: 152-4, 172-3 Mr 8, 15 '30 **5706**

Morse, Wayne L. The social scientist and the criminal law. Commonwealth R 12: 3-10 Mr '30 **5707**

Obornicker, Alfred. Kritische Betrachtungen zum allgemeinen Teil des Strafgesetzentwurfs. Justiz 2 (6): 579-90 '27 **5708**

Ossorio, Angel. La justicia poder. 195p. Madrid, Pueyo, 1927 **5709**

Pagano, Antonio. Volontà psicologica e volontà giuridica in diritto penale. *In* Scritti in onore di Enrico Ferri per il cinquantesimo anno di suo insegnamento universitario, 323-6. Torino, "Sociale Torinese," 1928 **5710**

Palazzo, Gennaro Alfredo. Territorialità della legge penale. Scuola Pos ns7: 530-7 N '27 **5711**

Parys, Jean Van. Faut-il soustraire aux jurisdictions ordinaires pour les confier à des arbitres, les jugements de délits d'atteintes portées à l'honneur ou à la considération des personnes? R Int de Dr Pén 8: 337-42 '31 **5712**

Pella, Vespasiano V. La criminalidad colectiva de los Estados y el derecho penal del porvenir; traducción de Jerónimo Mallo. 590p. Madrid, Aguilar, 1930 **5713**

Penal statutes and their effect on contracts and civil rights. Just Peace 91: 562-4 Jl 23 '27 **5714**

[Penso], Girolamo. La "claque" dans le droit pénal et dans le droit civil; traduit par Gino Cutore di San Carlo. R de Dr Pén et de Crimin 10: 1185-95 D '30 **5715**

Penso, Girolamo. Metodologia della scienza giuridico-penale nella concezione integrale. Pensiero Giurid Pen 1: 115-52 Ap '29 **5716**

Penso, Girolamo. L'unitarismo nell'internazionalizzazione del diritto penale. Bol del Sindacato Fascista Avvocati (3): 1 '29 **5717**

Petrocelli, Biagio. La illeceità penale della violenza sportiva. Contributo alla teoria generale delle cause di esclusione della illeceità penale. Riv Crit di Dir e Giuris (7-12): 242-70 '28 **5718**

Petters, Walter. Praktische Strafrechtsfälle mit Lösungen. ed.2. 212p. Mannheim, Bensheimer, 1928 **5719**

Pinto, Manfredo. Il desegno preliminare del nuovo codice penals. Studi Urbinati (3-4): 5-11 '29 **5720**

Ploscowe, Morris. Examen de quelques dispositions relatives aux motifs et au caractère dans les codes pénaux modernes. R de Dr Pén et de Crimin 10: 321-38 Ap '30 **5721**

Potts, Charles S. Criminal law, what's wrong with it? 32p. (Dallas Morning news, Reprints no1) Dallas, 1929 **5722**

Pozzolini, Alfredo. I casi di giustificazione comme causa di esclusione del reato nella legislazione italiana. *In* Scritti in onore di Enrico Ferri per il cinquantesimo anno di suo insegnamento universitario, 381-6. Torino, "Sociale Torinese," 1928 **5723**

Projet de loi de défense sociale à l'égard des anormaux, des délinquants d'habitude et de l'adolescence coupable. R de Dr Pén et de Crimin 7: 213-20 F '27 **5724**

Proteus. Intorno ad un articolo del progetto del nuovo codice penale. Rassegna di Stud Sess 7: 211-15 Ag '27 **5725**

Quevedo, Antonico. Cuestiones penales. 158p. Quito, Imp. de la Univ. Central, 1927 **5726**
Report on Congrès international de droit pénal de Bruxelles de 1926.

Rabinowicz, L[eon]. La crise et l'avenir du droit pénal. 44p. Paris, Rivière, 1928 **5727**

Rabinowicz, L[eon]. Mesures de sureté. Étude de politique criminelle. 176p. Paris, Rivière, 1928 **5728**

Rabinowicz, Leon. Il problema della misure di sicurezza e l'evoluzione moderna del diritto penale. *In* Scritti in onore di Enrico Ferri per il cinquantesimo anno di suo insegnamento universitario, 387-94. Torino, "Sociale Torinese," 1928 **5729**

Radbruch, Gustav. Abbau des Strafrechts. Bemerkungen über den Entwurf 1925 mit Anmerkungen über den Entwurf 1927. Justiz 2 (6): 537-43 '27 **5730**

Raggi, Luigi. Della legge penale e della sua applicazione. 127p. (Università Cattolica del Sacro Cuore. Pub. s2: Scienze Giuridiche v15) Milano, Vita e Pensiero [1927] **5731**

Rappaport, Emil Stanislaw. Le problème du droit pénal interétatique. Przeglad Polski 2: 25- '30 **5732**

Rappaport, Emil Stanislaw. Projekt Wstepny Ustawy o Wykroczeniach, na podstawie opinij bieglych sedziów: Konrada Berezowskiego i Jósefa Rosenzweiga. 320p. Warszawa, 1929 **5733**

Reitmeyer, T. Die historische Entwicklung der Notstandslehre. 154p. München, Salesian. Offizin, 1927 **5734**

Retroactive effect of judicial change of existing law in criminal proceedings. Colum L R 28: 963-8 N '28 **5735**

Ribeiro, Carlos. A "mulher publica" perante o codigo penal (§1. art. 268). R de Cultura Jurid 1: 388-94 Jl '29 **5736**

Roberts, Owen J. [The administration of criminal law]. Am L Inst Proc 5: 472-6 '27 **5737**

Robinson, James J. Criminal law and its administration; a manual of legal principles and administrative practice governing criminal cases. 44p. Bloomington, Ind. Indiana university, School of law, 1928 **5738**

Robinson, James J. Recent legislation concerning crime. Fla St B Assn L J 4: 392-402 Ja '31 **5739**

Robinson, James J. Report on progress of criminal law referendum. Ind L J 2: 316-21 Ja '27 **5740**

Rocco, Arturo. Le misure di sicurezza e gli altri mezzi di tutela giuridica. 43p. Roma, Mantellate, 1930 **5741**
Extr: Rivista di Diritto Penitenziairio, 6 '30; same title: Palestra di Diritto (12) D '30.

Sachocki, C. La responsabilité de l'Allemagne du fait des confiscations pénales opérées en territoire polonais pendant la guerre. R Gén de Dr Int Pub s3 2: 411-32 Je '28 **5742**

Salmoria, F. Il nuovo codice penale e la opportunità pel medico di considerare le sorprese del rischio professionale. Policlinico (sez prat) 38: 1802-3 N 30 '31 **5743**

Saltelli, Carlo and Falco, Enrico Romano-di. Commento teorico-pratico del nuovo codice penale. 896p. Roma, Mantellate, 1930 **5744**

Santoro, Arturo. Sulla pretesa plurimità dell'azione penale: contributo alla dottrina dell'unità. *In* Scritti in onore di Enrico Ferri per il cinquantesimo anno di suo insegnamento universitario, 443-51. Torino "Sociale Torinese," 1928 **5745**

Sasserath, Simon. De la qualification concernant l'application de l'article 240 du Code pénal. R de Dr Pén et de Crimin 8: 727-9 Jl '28 **5746**

Sayre, Francis Bowes. A selection of cases on criminal law; with an introduction by Roscoe Pound. 1135p. Rochester, N.Y. Lawyers Cooperative pub. co. 1927 **5747**

Schaffstein, Friedrich. Die allgemeinen Lehren vom Verbrechen in ihrer Entwicklung durch die Wissenschaft des gemeinen Strafrechts. 221p. Berlin, Springer, 1930 **5748**

Scharfmesser, H. Die strafbare Handlung nach den jüngsten Entwürfen eines österreichischen und deutschen Strafgesetzes. Öster Anwaltszeit 4: 398-401 '27 **5749**

Schultz. Kasuistik im Strafrecht. Deut Richterzeit 20: 108-10 '28 **5750**

Schumacher, Oskar. Um das Wesen der Strafrechtsschuld. Eine Auseinandersetzung mit modernen Schuldgedanken. 135p. (Hamburg Schr z Ges Strafrechtswiss no10) Mannheim, Bensheimer, 1927 **5751**

Schwinge, Erich. Teleologische Begriffsbildung im Strafrecht. 72p. (Bonner Rechtswiss Abh 14) Bonn, Ludwig Röhrschneid, 1930 **5752**

Seelig, E. Der allgemeine Strafbemessungsgrundsatz. Zentralbl f d jurist Praxis 46: 809-20 '28 **5753**

Shepherd, Harold and Sears, Kenneth. Judicial decisions on criminal law and procedure. J Crim L & Crimin 21: 598-606 F '31 **5754**

Siebert, Wolfgang. Der strafrechtliche Besitzbegriff, besonders in der Rechtssprechung des Reichsgerichts. 126p. (Strafrechtl Abh no235) Breslau, Schletter, 1928 **5755**

Smith, Reginald Heber. Laws under the microscope. Ann Am Acad 145: 55-61 S '29 **5756**

Sohier, A. Le droit pénal des colonies. R Int de Dr Pén 4: 177-86 '27 **5757**

Solberg, P. C. and Cros, Guy C[harles]. Le droit et la doctrine de la justice. 178p. Paris, Alcan, 1930 **5758**

Soler, S. El delito continuado ante nuestro derecho. Bibl Nac de Crim y Cienc Afines Bol 2: 386-95 '28 **5759**

Sperber, Hugo. Die Lüge im Strafrecht. 63p. Wien, Zahn & Diamant, 1927 **5760**

Spirito, Ugo. La concezione tecnico-giuridica del diritto penale. Nuov Stud di Dir Econ & Pol (1): 26-45 '29 **5761**

Spirito, Ugo. La determinazione tecnico-giuridico delle misure di sicurezza e la nuova scienza del diritto penale. Extr: Nuovi Stud di Dir Econ e Pol Mr '31 **5762**

Sternberg, Theodor. Einführung in die Rechtswissenschaft. I: Methoden-und Quellenlehre. ed.2 rev. 190p. Berlin, Gruyter, 1927 5763

Stjernberg, Nils. Straffrättsliga studier. 151p. Uppsala, Almquist & Wicksell, 1928 5764

Stooss, Carl. Strafrechtliche Systematik. Schweiz Zeitsch f Strafr 44: 160-85 '30 5765

Stricker, Walter. Der neue Strafgesetzentwurf. Kritische Bemerkungen. Jurist Bl 56 (21): 323-7; (22): 340-3 '27 5766

Swancara, Frank. Medieval theology in modern criminal law. J Crim L & Crimin 20: 489-99 F '30 5767

Swanson, John A. Progress in administration of criminal law. Ill St B Assn Proc 1931: 308-18 5768

Syed, Guffar. Elements of the criminal law. ltd. ed. 61p. Ajmer, Rajputana, India, Vedic Yantralaya, 1930 5769

Taranto, Giovanni. Il valore probatorio della scrittura in materia penale. Magistrato dell'Ordine (2): 21-2 '29 5770

Tedeschi, A. Osservazioni in tema di sequestro assicurativo penale. 11p. Padova, C.E.D.A.M. 1927 5771

Tesar, Ottokar. Die Überwindung des Naturrechts in der Dogmatik des Strafrechts. 227p. Halle, Niemeyer, 1928 5772

Thot, Ladislao. La aplicación judicial de la ley penal (crinología penal). R de Identif y Cienc Pen 7: 253-332 N '30 5773

Thot, Ladislao. La ciencia jurídico-penal Romana. R de Identif y Cienc Pen 5: 232-59 Ja '30 5774

Thot, Ladislao. Codificación penal moderna. R de Identif y Cienc Pen 2: 174-96 Jl '28 5775

Thót, L[adislao]. Il diritto penale angloamericano. Giustiz Pen 34: 393-411, 913-25, 1009-23, 1233-44 Ap 15-N 30 '28 5776

Thot, Ladislao. Estudios históricos de derecho penal oriental: derecho Anamita, Mongol y Cambodgiano. R de Identif y Cienc Pen 6: 284-325 Jl '30 5777

Thot, Ladislao. Estudios históricos de derecho penal oriental: Historia del derecho penal egipcio, armenio, afgano y tibetano. R de Identif y Cienc Pen 8: 250-86 My '31 5778

Thót, Ladislau. A evolução historica do direito penal. Bol do Inst de Crimin s8 15 (2): 361-436 '31 5779

Thót, László. Historia de las Antiguas Institutiones de derecho penal. 503p. Buenos Aires, Talleres gráficos argentinos L. J. Rosso [1927] 5780

Thot, Ladislao. Sul diritto penale latinoamericano. *In* Scritti in onore di Enrico Ferri per il cinquantesimo anno di suo insegnamento universitario, 487-509. Torino, "Sociale Torinese," 1928 5781

Thyrén, Johan C[arl] W[ilhelm]. Forberedande utkast till Strafflag:
Speciella delen 7. 7p. Lund, Gleerupska Unio, 1928
Speciella delen 8. 26p. Lund, Gleerupska Unio, 1929
Speciella delen 10. 34p. Lund, Gleerupska Unio, 1930
5782

Tolomei, Alberto Domenico. Il pentimento nel diritto penale. 311p. Torino, Bocca, 1927 5783

Di Tullio, Benigno. Il fattore essenziale specifico della criminalità. *In* Scritti in onore di Enrico Ferri per il cinquantesimo anno di suo insegnamento universitario, 177-85. Torino, "Sociale Torinese," 1928 5784

Ueberhorst. Der neue Sinn des Strafrechts. Gegenwart 57: 127-30 Je '28 5785

Vaccaro, Michelangelo. Il diritto penale. Critica e sistemazione di essa. 195p. Torino, Bocca, 1927 5786

A critique of penal law which in reality is a critique of the positive school in general and Enrico Ferri in particular.

Vaccaro, Mickelangelo. Pour une nouvelle organisation scientifique du droit pénal; traduit de l'italien par J. Gaure. R Int de Dr Pén 5: 308-26 '28 5787

Vannini, Ottorino. Attività esecutiva e attività preparatoria. Riv Ital di Dir Pen (3): 233-42 '29 5788

Vannini, Ottorino. Le condizioni estrinseche di punibilità nelle struttura del reato. (A proposito degli art. 47 e 185 del progetto preliminare). Studi Senesi (1-2): 32-58 '29 5789

Vannini, Ottorino. L'elemento soggettivo del reato nel progetto del nuovo codice penale. Studi Senesi (2-3): 111-44 '30 5790

Vannini, O[ttorino]. Riconstruzione sintetica della dottrina del reato. Studi Senesi 41: 80-120, 181-221, 273-316 '27 5791

Vecchio, Giorgio del. Lezioni di filosofia del diritto. 351p. Città di Castello, Leonardo da Vinci, 1930 5792

Vieites, Moises A. Como debe ser la llamada ley penal. 384p. [Habana, Comision de justicia y codigos, 1929] 5793

Vieites, Moises [A.]. Est-il désirable d'avoir, à côté du code pénal et du code de procédure pénale, un code pénal d'exécution des peines? R Int de Dr Pén 8: 344-8 '31 5794

Vieites, Moises A. Triple aspect de l'état dangereux de l'homme vis-à-vis de la loi pénale. R Int de Dr Pén 5: 416-24 '28 5795

Vieites, Moises A. Triplice aspetto dello stato pericoloso di fronte alla legge penale. Scuola Pen Unit (3-4): 184-8 '29 5796

Wegner, Arthur. Jugendrecht. Ein Lehrbuch zur Einführung. 219p. Berlin, Gruyter, 1928 5797

Werner, John. Outline of criminal law and procedure based on the New York penal law and code of criminal procedure. 86p. N.Y. Central bk co. 1930 5798

Whitman, Charles S. [Address on problems of law and procedure]. Am B Assn J 13: 491-9 S '27 5799

Whitman, Charles S. Protecting ourselves against crime. Mich St B Assn J 6: 212-21 Ap '27 5800

Wilhelm, Charles P. Ratiocination of criminal law. Lawyer & Banker ns21: 183-5 My '28 5801

Wolter, L. Die Krise der Rechtswidrigkeitslehre. Zeitsch f d ges Strafrechtswiss 48: 32-48 '28 5802

Wroblewski, Bronislaw. Principes fondamentaux de la politique pénale. Etudes Crimin 5: 84-91, 110-23 Mr, Ap '30 5803

Wroblewski, Bronislaw. Rationalisation téléo-évolutive des peines. R de Dr Pén et de Crimin 8: 434-42 My '28 5804

Zeiler, A. Die "Unterbrechung" des Ursachenzusammenhangs. Zeitsch f d ges Strafrechtswiss 49: 235-40 '29 5805

Zimmerl, Leopold. Aufbau des Strafrechtssystems. 339p. Tübingen, Mohr, 1930 5806

Zimmerl, Leopold. Juristisch bedeutsame, für den Täter unwichtige Tatumstände. Monats f Kriminalpsychol u Strafrechtsref 19: 449-56 Ag '28 5807

Zimmerl, Leopold. Strafrechtliche Arbeitsmethode de lege ferenda. 354p. Berlin, Gruyter, 1931 5808

Zimmerl, Leopold. Zur Lehre vom Tatbestand. Übersehene und vernachlässigte Probleme. 162p. (Strafrechtl Abh no237) Breslau, Schletter, 1928 5809

AFGHANISTAN

Beck, Sebastian. Das Afghanische Strafgesetzbuch vom Jahre 1924 mit dem Zusatz vom Jahre 1925. Aus dem Persischen übersetzt und mit einer allgemeinen Einleitung in die Afghanische Strafgesetzgebung versehen. 157p. Berlin, Deutsche Gesellschaft für Islamkunde, 1928; same title: Welt d Islams 11: 67-157 '28 5810

ARGENTINA

García, Eduardo Augusto. El código penal de 1922 ante a la constitución. Buenos Aires, Univ Nac R 8: 74-86 Ja '29 5811

Jiménez de Asúa, Luis. El nuevo código penal argentino y los recientes proyectos complementarios ante las modernas direciones del derecho penal. 379p. Madrid, Reus, 1928 5812

Peco, José. El sistema del Art.41 del código penal. R de Crimin, Psiquiat y Med Leg 17: 594-603 S '30 5813

Ramos, J. P. La teoría del "estado peligroso" en la legislación penal argentina. R de Crimin, Psiquiat y Med Leg 14: 448-61 Jl '27 5814

Ruiz-Funes, Mariano. Il proyecto de ley argentino sobre el estado peligroso. 32p. Madrid, Reus, 1928 5815

Thót, Ladislao. Législation pénale et politique criminelle dans la république Argentine. R de Dr Pén et de Crimin 10: 205-18 '30 5816

AUSTRIA

Altmann, Ludwig; Jacob, Siegfried, and Weiser, Max. Die österreichische Strafgesetzgebung nach dem Stande vom 30. Juni 1927. ed.6. 1057p. Wien, Staatsdruckerei, 1927 5817

Altmann, Ludwig; Jacob, Siegfried, and Weiser, Max. Sammlung oberstgerichtlicher Entscheidungen zum österreichischen Strafrecht. ed.2 rev. & enl. 688p. (Handausgabe österr. Gesetze u Verordnungen no206A) Wien, Staatsdruckerei, 1927 5818

Benda, Richard and Lichem, Arnold. Die österreichische Strafgesetzgebung nach dem Stande bis Ende Juni 1929. 668p. Graz, Leykam-Verl. 1929 5819

Kadečka, Ferdinand, ed. Der österreichische Strafgesetzentwurf vom Jahre 1927. 132p. 1927. ed.2. 167p. Wien, Manz, 1931 5820

Loening. Gleiches Strafrecht in Oesterreich und Deutschland. Gesetz u Recht 28: 177-9 Je 15 '27 5821

Rittler, T[heodore]. Das österreichische Strafgesetzbuch von 1852 als Spiegel und Chronik seiner Zeit. Schweiz Zeitsch f Strafr 40: 83-96 '27 5822

Rittler, Theodore. Le projet de code pénal austro-allemand de 1927 et la défense de l'individu contre l'arbitraire du juge. R Polon de Leg Civile et Crim 2: 3- '30 5823

Thót, L. Historia del derecho penal Austriaco. R Arg de Cienc Pol 36: 88-123 Ap '28 5824

BELGIUM

Defroidmont, J. H. Recherches pour l'application de la loi sur les jeux. R de Dr Pén et de Crimin 7: 318-34 '27 5825

Delattre, Edmondo. Recherches sur le droit pénal à Cambrai et dans le Cambrésis au Moyen-Age. 266p. Lille, René Giard, 1929 5826

Goedseels, Jos. M. C. H. Commentaire du code pénal Belge. 885p. Bruxelles, Hauchamps, 1928 5827

Lagacos, Elie L. La défense sociale à l'égard des anormaux, des délinquants d'habitude et de l'adolescence coupable (un projet de loi belge). 143p. Athènes, Imp. de la prison-école Avéroff, 1930 5828

Vervaeck, L. Le projet belge de loi de défense sociale. R de Dr Pén et de Crimin 7: 193-206 F '27 5829

Wets, P. Note sur le projet de législation sociale et sur la proposition de modification de la loi du 15 mai 1912. R de Dr Pén et de Crimin 7: 208-13 '27 5830

BRAZIL

Araujo, Edgar Altino de. De um novo codigo penal, à luz da Clinica Criminologica. R de Cultura Jurid 1: 33-8 Ap '29 5831

Britto, Lemos. Succincte exposition sur l'évolution pénale au Brésil. 36p. Rio-de-Janeiro, 1930 5832

Jiménez de Asúa, Luis. Un viaje al Brasil; impressiones de un conferenciante, segeudas de un estudio sobre el derecho penal brasileño. 167p. Madrid, Reus, 1929 5833

Pereira, Virgilio de Sá. Proyecto de código penal Brasileiro. Exposição de motivos sobre a parte geral. Rio-de-Janeiro, 1930 5834

Thot, Ladislao. Codificación penal moderna [Brazil and Chile]. R de Identif y Cienc Pen 4: 408-34 S '28 5835

Viotti, Manuel. Código penal Brazileiro; manual do jury. R de Identif y Cienc Pen 5: 419-28; 6: 273-83 Mr, Jl '30 5836

CANADA

Banks, William. Canada's effective criminal law system. Cur Hist 28: 405-7 Je '28 5837

Brown, C. R. Bibliography of Quebec or Lower Canada laws. Index to Leg Per & L Lib J 19: 90-109 Ja '27 5838

Popple, Arthur Ernest, ed. Snow's criminal code of Canada. ed.4. 785p. Toronto, Carswell, 1928 5839

Riddell, William Renwick. Administration of criminal law in the far north of Canada. J Crim L & Crimin 20: 294-302 Ag '29 5840

CHILE

Calón, Eugenio Cuello. El proyecto del código penal chileno. R Gen de Leg y Juris (1): 5- '30 5841

Chile. Ministerio de justicia. Proyecto de código penal Chileno. Santiago, 1929 5842

Proyecto de código penal para la república de Chile. R de Derecho Pen (1): 57- '30 5843

Riquelme, Rafael Fontecilla. La pena (los problemas modernos y sus influencias en el nuevo derecho penal chileno). 434p. Santiago, Imp. "Cisneros," 1931 5844

CHINA

Escarra, Jean. Code pénal de la république de Chine, promulgué le 10 Mars 1928, traduit du chinois, avec une introduction. 214p. Paris, Giard, 1930 5845

Escarra, Jean. Le droit pénal chinois et les codes de 1928. R Pénitent et de Dr Pén 53: 193-244 Je '29; extr: Le code pénal chinois de 1928. R de Dr Pén et de Crimin 10: 549-63 '30 5846

Riasanovsky, V. A. Influence of Chinese law upon Mongolian law. Chinese Soc & Pol Sci R 15: 402-21 O '31 5847

Steinwallner, Bruno. Chinesische Strafrechtsreform. Monats f Kriminalpsychol u Strafrechtsref 22: 597-604 O '31 5848

Steinwallner, Bruno. Das neue chinesische Sexualstrafrecht. Zeitsch f Sexualwiss 18 (3): 199-203 Ag '31 5849

Yueng-li, Liang. New criminal code. China W R 46: 61-2 S 8 '28 5850

CUBA

Gatti, Tancredi. Il nuovo progretto di codice penale cubano. Giustiz Pen (10): 305-19 '29 5851

Neymark, Edward. L'idée Ferri dans le projet de code criminel cubain. R Pénitent de Pologne 4 (3-4): 353-69 Jl '29 5852

Ortiz, Fernando. Projet du code criminel cubain. 193p. Paris, Godde, 1927 5853

Ortiz, Fernando. Proyecto de código criminal cubano. R de Crimin, Psiquiat y Med Leg 14: 118-24, 231-56, 345-53 Ja-My '27; resume: Bibl Nac de Crim y Cienc Afines Bol 1(3): 244-50 Ja '27 5854

Ortiz, Fernando. Projecto de código criminal Cubano (livro primeiro ou parte geral). Relatório oficial; versão portuguẽsa de R. Xavier da Silva. Bol do Inst de Crimin s7 12(1): 60-222 '30 5855

Vieites, Moises A. Projet de code pénal; traduit de l'espangol par Calixto Whitmarsh. 165p. Paris, Rousseau, 1928 5856

CZECHOSLOVAKIA

Eigl, Hans. Der tschechoslowakische Entwurf eines Gesetzes über die Jugendstrafgerichtsbarkeit. Zentralbl f Jugendrecht u Jugendwohlfahrt 22: 14-19 Ap '30 5857

Eppinger, H. Das čechoslovakische Gesetz über die Tilgung der Verurteilung. Zeitsch f Ostrecht 5: 405-10 Je '31 5858

Exposé des motifs de l'avant projet de code pénal Tchech-Slovaque (se rapportant aux mesures de sûreté). R de Dr Pén et de Crimin 8: 611-16 '28 5859

Gabrieli, Francesco P. Il progretto di codice penale cecoslovacco. Giustiz Pen (44): 2022-4 '28 5860

Osservazioni critiche intorno al "Avant projet de code penal Tchécoslovaque 1926," traduzione in francese edita da l'Association Tchécoslovaque de droit pénal. (Prague, "Orbis," 1927)

Ruiz-Funez, Mariano. El anteproyecto penal Checoeslovaco. 64p. Madrid, Reus, 1929 5861

Solnar, Vladimir. Chronique Tchécoslovaque. R de Dr Pén et de Crimin 8: 606-11 Je '28 5862

Solnar, Vladimiro. La legislazione penale in Cecoslovacchia (anni 1919-1929). 21p. Roma, Istituto di Studi Legislativi, 1930 5863

Extr: Annuario di diritto comparato e di studi legislativi 6 ptl (1): 427- '30.

Thot, Ladislao. El nuevo anteproyecto del código penal Checoeslovaco. R de Identif y Cienc Pen 4: 252-64 Jl '29 5864

Weber, Hellmuth v. Grundriss des tschechoslowakischen Strafrechtes. 114p. Reichenberg, Gebr. Stiepel, 1929 5865

DENMARK

Ebeling, C. Strafvollzug in Dänemark. Monats f Kriminalpsychol u Strafrechtsref 22: 385-90 Jl '31 5866

Geill, Christ. Den danske Lov af 11.4.1925 om Sikkerhedsforanstaltninger mod visse Personer, der udsaetter Retssikkerheden for Fare-fra retspsykiatrisk Standpunkt. Nord Tids f Straf 1928: 301-58 5867

Goos, Carl. Den danske strafferets specielle del [1916]. v3 København, Gad, 1927 5868

EUROPE

Jiménez de Asúa, Luis. El nuevo derecho penal. Escuelas y códigos del presente y del porvenir. 241p. Madrid, Paez, 1929 5869

Junckerstorff, Kurt. Principal characteristics of legal policy in the recent European drafts of penal codes: a comparative study. Univ Pa L R 77: 498-503 F '29; same title: J Comp Leg 11: 204-8 N '29 5870

FRANCE

Ardant, Marcel. Les jurisdictions criminelles dans les colonies françaises. 324p. Paris, Presses Univ. de France, 1930 5871

Carpentier, A. and Etienne. Code d'instruction criminelle et code pénal. 920p. Paris, Sirey, 1927 5872

Crabitès, Pierre. Napoleon Bonaparte and the French criminal code. Am B Assn J 15: 469-72 Ag '29 5873

Cuche, Paul. Précis de droit criminel. ed.2. 445p. 1927. ed.3. 455p. Paris, Dalloz, 1929 5874

Dupont, Pierre. Les monitoires. Etudes Crimin 5: 161-75, 250-63 Je, S '30 5875

Garraud, Pierre and Laborde-Lacoste, Marcel. Précis élémentaire de droit pénal (conforme au programme des examens de capacité). 517p. Paris, Sirey, 1930 5876

Hugueney, Louis. Variations sur l'article 10 du Code d'instruction criminelle. Etudes Crimin 2: 1-3 Ja '27 5877

Lapie, P. O. The *partie civile* in the criminal law of France. J Comp Leg 10: 33-45 F '28 5878

Mouvement législatif criminel en France du 1er Janvier 1926 au 31 Décembre 1927: index alphabétique des textes concernant le droit criminel et la procédure pénale applicables a la métropole. Etudes Crimin 3: 30-7 Ja '28 5879

Roux, J. A. Cours de droit criminel français. ed.2 rev. & augm. 2v. Paris, Sirey, 1927 5880

Tchernoff, J. Les syndicats financiers et l'article 419 du code pénal. J Econ 87: 54-61 Ap '27 5881

Vidal, Georges. Cours de droit criminel et de science pénitentiaire. ed.7 by Joseph Magnol. 576p. Paris, Rousseau, 1927 5882

GERMANY

Allfeld, Philipp. Lehrbuch des deutschen Strafrechts. ed.8 by Hugo Meyer. 35p. Leipzig, Deichert, 1928 5883

Alsberg, Max. Der Versicherungsbetrug im Entwurf zu einem neuen Strafgesetzbuch. Versich u Geldwirts ns4 (8): 61-3 '28 5884

Baumgarten, Edwin. Die Geburtsstunde des modernen deutschen Strafrechts. Zeitsch f d ges Strafrechtswiss 49 (1-2): 1-31 '29 5885

Beck, Alexander. Das Unrechtsbewusstsein in den deutschen Strafgesetzentwürfen. 54p. Breslau, Schletter, 1927 5886

Bernau, A. Dottrine penali nella Germania attuale. Scuola Pos 39: 22-30 '31 5887

Brons. Die Sprache der Reichstagsvorlage. Monats f Kriminalpsychol u Strafrechtsref 18: 622-5 N '27 5888

Brunner, Heinrich. Deutsche Rechtsgeschichte. v2 ed.2 by C. v. Schwerin. 934p. München, Duncker & Humblot, 1927 5889

Bruns, Hans-Jürgen. Können die organe juristischer personen, die im interesse ihrer körperschaffen rechtsgüter dritter verletzen, bestraft werden? 112p. bibliog [vii]-x. (Strafrechtl Abh no295) Breslau, Schletter, 1931 5890

Doerr, Friedrich. Strafgesetzbuch für das Deutsche Reich nebst Einführungsgesetz und ergänzenden Gesetzen, insbesondere auch dem Militärstrafgesetzbuch. ed.4. 259p. München, J. Schweitzer, 1927 5891

Eberding, Walter. Gesundheitswesen und Medizinalpolitik im Entwurfe eines allgemeinen deutschen Strafgesetzbuches nebst amtliche Begründung und kritische Stellungnahme. 117p. Eckernförde, Schwensen, 1927 5892

Ebermayer, Ludwig; Lobe, Adolf, and Rosenberg, Werner. Das Reichs-strafgesetzbuch. ed.4. 1282p. Berlin, Gruyter, 1929 5893

Entwurf eines allgemeinen deutschen Strafgesetzbuches. Mitt d Industrie- u Handelskammer, Berlin 25: 782-5 '27 5894

Finger, August. Die Reichstagsvorlage des Amtlichen Entwurfs eines Allgemeinen Deutschen StGB. Gerichtssaal 95 (1-5): 106-41 '27 5895

Frank, Reinhard. Kommentar zum Strafgesetzbuch für das Deutsche Reich nebst den Ausführungsgesetzen. 262p. Tübingen, Mohr, 1930 5896

Frank, Reinhard. Das Strafgesetzbuch für das Deutsche Reich. ed.17. 1927. ed. 18. Tübingen, Mohr, 1928 5897

Frosali, Raoul Alberto. Orientazione dei recenti progetti per un codice penale generale germanico. *In* Scritti in onore di Enrico Ferri per il cinquantesimo anno di suo insegnamento universitario, 215-21. Torino, "Sociale Torinese," 1928 5898

Gerland, H. B. German draft penal code and its place in the history of penal law. J Comp Leg s3 11: 19-33 F '29 5899

Germany. Laws, statutes, etc. Entwurf eines allgemeinen deutschen Strafgesetzbuchs. 212, 134, 46p. (No.3390. Der reichsminister der justiz Reichstag III. Wahlperiode 1924/27) Berlin, Heymann, 1927 **5900**

Germany. Laws, statutes, etc. Entwurf eines strafvollzugsgesetzes vom 9.9.1927. 139p. (No.3628) Berlin, Heymann, 1927 **5901**

Grünhut, Max. Der amtliche Entwurf eines Reichsstrafvollzugsgesetzes. Deut Richterzeit 19: 325-8 S '27 **5902**

Halle, Felix. Das neue Strafgesetzbuch gegen das deutsche und österreichische Proletariat. 32p. Berlin, Mopr, 1927 **5903**

Halle, Felix. Die politische Bedeutung des deutschen Strafgesetzentwurfs von 1927. Kommun Int 8 (50): 2455-64 '27 **5904**

Hampe, Theodor. Die Nürnberger Malefizbücher als Quellen der reichstädtischen Sittengeschichte vom 14. bis zum 18. Jahrhundert. 102p. Bamberg, Buchner, 1927 **5905**

Hentig, [Hans] v. Il progetto del codice penale germanico. Giustiz Pen 37: 7-11, 200-3 Ja, F '31 **5906**

Hentig, [Hans] v. Il progetto tedesco di codice penale; trad. Ascarelli. Giustiz Pen 37: 337-42 Mr '31 **5907**

Hippel, Robert. Deutsches Strafrecht. II: Das Verbrechen: Allgemeine lehren. 584p. Berlin, Springer, 1930 **5908**

Kahl, William. Strafrechtseinheit zwischen Deutschland und Österreich. Jurist Wchnschr 56 (47): 2658-63 '27 **5909**

Keinath, Erich. Die Unterbrechung der Verjährung im Strafrechte unter Berücksichtigung der deutschen und ausländischer Strafgesetzentwurfe. 55p. bibliog 4-6. Diss. Universität zu Erlangen, 1930 **5910**

Kneissl, Karl, ed. Das Strafgesetz vom 27. Mai 1852, mit den Entscheidungen des Obersten Gerichtes in Brünn, sowie mit wichtigen Entscheidungen des ehemaligen Obersten Gerichts und Kassationshofes in Wien. 1328p. Reichenberg, Verl. von Gebrüder Stiepel, 1927 **5911**

Köhler, Aug[ust]. Strafrechtliche Bestimmungen grundlegender Art in neueren Entwürfen und Gesetzen. 33p. Erlangen, Palm & Enke, 1929 **5912**

Krell, Otto. Gedanken eines Laien zum Entwurf eines Allgemeinen deutschen Strafgesetzbuches. 13p. Charlottenburg, Fänger, 1927 **5913**

Lindner, Willy. Das künftige Landesstrafrecht. 66p. bibliog vi-vii. Diss. Erlangen, 1931. Kallmünz, Michael Lassleben, 1931 **5914**

Liszt, Franz von and Delaquis, Ernst. Strafgesetzbuch für das Deutsche Reich mit Nebengesetzen. ed.27 by Eduard Kohlrausch. 602p. Berlin, Gruyter, 1927 **5915**

Liszt, Franz von and Schmidt, Eberhard. Lehrbuch des deutschen Strafrechts. ed. 25 by Eberhard Schmidt. 976p. Berlin, Gruyter, 1927 **5916**

Littauer, Hans Alfred. Der Alkohol im deutschen Strafrecht der Gegenwart und Zukunft unter besondere Berücksichtigung der . . . Entwürfe eines allgemeinen deutschen Strafgesetzbuches. 102p. Berlin-Dahlem, "Auf der Wacht," 1927 **5917**

Maier, Lothar. Der Rechtsirrtum nach geltendem Recht und den Entwürfen zu einem deutschen Strafgesetzbuch. 95p. bibliog 91-5. Diss. Universität zu Erlangen, 1931. Kulmbach, G. Schuhmann, 1931 **5918**

Nagler, J[ohannes]. Die Strafzumessung nach dem amtlichen Entwurf eines allgemeinen deutschen Strafgesetzbuches. Gerichtssaal 95: 83-111 '27 **5919**

Olshausen, Justus vom. Kommentar zum Strafgesetzbuch für das Deutsche Reich. ed.11 revised by Karl Lorenz, Hans Freiesleben, Emil Niethammer, Karl Kirchner, and Georg Gutjahr. 2v. 2,299p. Berlin, Vahlen, 1927 **5920**

Rottmüller, J. Das neugeschaffene Delikt der dauernden Entziehung von Sachen nach no304 des amtlichen entwurfs eines Allgemeinen Deutschen Strafgesetzbuches von 1925. 54p. München, M. Müller, 1927 **5921**

Rudert; Eichler; Hänel; Krahl; Pfützner; Reiss; Selle, and **Oppe.** [Discussion of the proposed German penal code from a psychiatric point of view]. Allg Zeitsch f Psychiat 85: 487-508 F '27 **5922**

Schäfer, Leopold. Deutsche Strafgesetzentwürfe von 1909/1927. Synoptische Gegenüberstellung der deutschen und österreichischen Strafgesetzentwürfe und des geltenden deutschen Strafrechts. 333p. Mannheim, Bensheimer, 1927 **5923**

Schmitt, Hermann, ed. Polizeistrafgesetzbuch für Bayern. new ed. 8. 261p. München, Beck, 1927 **5924**

Schmitt, Hermann. Strafgesetzbuch für das Deutsche Reich. ed. 14 rev. 487p. München, Beck, 1927 **5925**

Schotte, Walther. Irrungen und wirrungen. Preuss Jahrb 207: 97-9 Ja '27 **5926**

Schultze, Ernst. Der Reichstagsentwurf eines allgemeinen deutschen Strafgesetzbuchs vom Standpunkt des Psychiaters. Arch f Psychiat 82: 1-42 O '27 **5927**

Schultze, E[rnst]. Die Reichstagsvorlage eines Allgemeinen Deutschen Strafgesetzbuchs vom Standpunkte des Psychiaters. Allg Zeitsch f Psychiat 88: 321-3 '28 **5928**

Stammler, Rudolf. Deutsches Rechtsleben in alter und neuer Zeit. I: Deutsches Rechtsleben in alten Reich. 515p. Berlin-Charlottenburg, Pan-Verl. 1928 **5929**

Stenglein, [Melchior]. Kommentar zu den strafrechtlichen nebengesetzen des Deutschen Reiches. ed.5 by Ebermayer, Conrad, Feisenberger and Schneidewin. 1600p. Berlin, Otto Liebmann, 1928 **5930**

Thót, L. Historia del derecho penal alemán. R Arg de Cienc Pol 35: 170-232 O '27 **5931**

Torp, Carl. De ny tyske Straffeloosforslag af 1927. Tids f Retsvidensk 7(3-4): 323-47 '28 **5932**

Ukshe, S. Ugolovnopravovie voprose v germanskom reichstag v 1925/1926. Problemy Prestupnosti 2: 308-22 '27 **5933**

Ullmann, Johannes Gottfried. Das Strafrecht der Städte der Mark Meissen, der Oberlausitz, des Pleissner-, Oster- und Vogtlandes während des Mittelalters. 100p. (Leipziger Rechtswissensch. Studien no34) Leipzig, Weicher, 1928 **5934**

Weisbart. Die Wirtschaft und der Entwurf eines allgemeinen deutschen Strafgesetzbuches. Mitt d Industrie- u Handelskammer, Berlin 25: 925-7 '27 **5935**

Wittman, Josef. Die Verjährung nach den Entwürfen zu einem deutschen Strafgesetzbuch, verglichen mit dem geltenden Recht. 70p. bibliog v-vi. Diss. Universität zu Erlangen, 1930. Kallmünz, Michael Lassleben, 1931 **5936**

Wolf, Erik. Die Wertung der Rechtsgüter im Reichsstrafgesetzbuch und ihre Unwertung durch die Reform. Justiz 3(2): 105-19 '27 **5937**

GREAT BRITAIN

Effect of the Great war on English criminal law and procedure. Sol J 71: 593-4 Jl 23 '27 **5938**

The English criminal code; editorial. Notre Dame Law 4: 465-8 Ap '29 **5939**

[Indiana. State library]. Topic for debate: resolved that a criminal code similar in procedure to the criminal code of Great Britain should be adopted throughout the United States. 10p. (mim) [Indianapolis, 1928] **5940**

Montmorency, James Edward Geoffrey. The legal system of England. 80p. London, Benn, 1928 **5941**

Thót, L. Historia del derecho penal inglés. R Arg de Cienc Pol 35: 437-75 Ja '28 **5942**

GREECE

Calhoun, George Miller. The growth of criminal law in ancient Greece. 149p. Berkeley, University of California press, 1927 **5943**

Venturas, Demetrius G. Entwurf eines griechischen Strafgesetzbuches Übersetzt und Eingeleitet. 123p. (Samml. ausserdt. Strafgesetzbücher. no47) Berlin, Gruyter, 1928 **5944**

HAWAII

Thot, Ladislao. Le droit pénal hawaïen. Soc de Lég Comp, Bul (7-9): 393- '28 **5945**

HUNGARY

Auer, G. Neue Gesetzesbestimmungen im ungarischen Strafrecht. Deut Juristen-Zeit 33 (8): 564-7 '28 **5946**

Baranyay, Karl. Magyar büntetöjogtörtenet. 225p. Miskolc, Druckerei Magyar Jövö, 1928 **5947**

Irk, Albert. Ungarisches Strafrecht. 348p. Pécs-Fünfkirchen, Druckerei Dunantul, 1928 **5948**

INDIA

Gour, Hari Singh. The penal law of British India. ed.4. 2v. London, Butterworth, 1928 **5949**

Ranchhoddas, Ratanial and Tkakore, D. K. Criminal procedure code (India). 637p. London, Sweet, 1930 **5950**

ITALY

Altavilla, Enrico. Lineamenti di diritto penale, commento teorico-pratico della parte generale del nuovo codice penale. 298p. Napoli, Alberto Morano, 1931 **5951**

Altavilla, Enrico. Projet d'un nouveau code pénal vu par un positiviste; traduit de l'Italien par M. F. Champeaux. R Int de Dr Pén 6(1): 47-65 '29 **5952**

Battaglini, Giulio. Principii di diritto penale in rapporto alla nuova legislazione. Questioni preliminari. 266p. bibliog [241]-9. Milano, Istituto Editoriale Scientifico, 1929 **5953**

Berenini, A. Il nuovo codice penale. Misure di sicurezza e categorie di delinquenti. Arch di Antrop Crim 51 (1-2): 316 Ja '31 **5954**

Bianchi, Vincenzo. Positivismo e progetto di codice penale. Scuola Pos (1-2): 17-20 '29 **5955**

Brasiello, Teucro. Il nuovo codice penale. La parte generale. 188p. Napoli, A. Morano, 1931 **5956**

Brunello, Bruno. Il nuovo diritto penale. Vita Nova (7): 601-11 '29 **5957**

Bruni, Alessandro. Questioni di diritto e procedura penale. 95p. Firenze, O. Gozini, 1929? **5958**

Bruno, A. ed. Codice penale del regno d'Italia . . . aggiuntevi la nuova legge di pubblica sicurezza e la legge sulla pena di morte. 532p. Firenze, G. Barbèra, 1927 **5959**

Bunge, Karl. Italienischer Vorentwurf zu einem neuen Strafgesetzbuch. 224p. (Sammlung ausserdeutscher Strafgesetzbücher no48) Berlin, Gruyter, 1928 **5960**

Calzia, Pintor Mario. La riforma della giustizia criminale e il progetto preliminare di un nuovo codice penale. Arch di Antrop Crim (6): 997-1029 '29 **5961**

Carnevale, Emanuele. L'unita nella lotta contro il delitto nel progetto di codice penale italiano. 29p. Roma, Istituto di studi legislativi, 1930 **5962**
Extr: Annuario di diritto comparato e di studi legislativi 6 pt1: 31- '30.

Carrara, Mario. L'elemento antropologico nel nuovo codice penale. Scuola Pos 11: 97-110 Mr '31 **5963**

Cicala, Salvatore. Il progetto per il nuovo codice penale. Conquista dello Stato (11-12): 5 '28 **5964**

Cuboni, Guglielmo. Dell'opportunità di un nuovo codice penale italiano. *In* Scritti in onore di Enrico Ferri per il cinquantesimo anno di suo insegnamento universitario, 115-20. Torino, "Sociale Torinese," 1928 5965

Dahm, Georg. Das Strafrecht Italiens im ausgehenden Mittelalter. 555p. (Beiträge zur Geschichte der Deutschen Strafrechtspflege no3) Berlin, Gruyter, 1931 5966

Dematteis, F. Il nuovo codice penale ed il suo orientamento scientifico. Giuris delle Corti Regionali (parte penale) (2) pt2a: 33- '31 5967

Dondina, Mario. Le "actiones liberae in causa" e la loro sistemazione nel nuovo codice penale. Scuola Pos 11: 233-53 My '31 5968

Falco, Enrico Romano-di. Gli elementi politici e sociologici del progetto definitivo di codice penale. Riv Ital di Dir Pen 2: 434-61 My '30 5969

Ferri, Enrico. Principii di diritto criminale. Delinquente e delitto nella scienza, legislazione, giurisprudenza in ordine al codice penale vigente, progetto 1921, progetto 1927. 847p. Torino, Tip. ed. Torinese, 1928 5970

Filitti, I. C. and Suchianu, D. Î. Contributi la istoria justitiei penale in principatele române. R de Drept Pen 41-108 Ja '28 5971

Franchi, L. Cinque codice: codice civile; codice di procedura civile; codice di commercio; codice penale; codice di procedura penale. new ed. 344p. Milano, Ulrico Hoepli, 1929? 5972

Franchi, L. Codice penale e codice di procedura penale. ed.8 rev. 311p. Milano, Ulrico Hoepli, 1927 5973

Gabrieli, Francesco P. Esposizione dei principî direttivi e spiegazione pratica del nuovo codice penale italiano. Giustiz Pen 37 pt1: 329-37, 458-75 Mr, Ap '31 5974

Gabriéli, F[rancesco] P. Le projet préliminare du nouveau code d'instruction criminelle italien (juin 1929). Etudes Crimin 4: 273-7, 312-14, 338-9 S-D '29; 5: 13-16, 50-4, 277-80, 312-17 Ja-D '30 5975

Galimberti, Tancredi. Remoti precedenti legislativi italiani delle norme sulla pericolosità. Scuola Pos 11: 529-55 D '31 5976

Goldschmidt, James. Errore e colpa nel progetto di codice penale tedesco e italiano. Pensiero Giurid-Pen 1: 217-23 Ap '29 5977

Great Britain. Foreign Office. Penal code of the kingdom of Italy, as approved by royal decree of October 19, 1930. 218p. London, H. M. Stationery Off. 1931 5978

Gregoraci, G. La definitiva interpretazione dell'art. 76 codice penale. Riv Pen di Dott, Legis e Giuris 105: 567-71 Je '27 5979

Herschmann, Heinrich. Der Vorentwurf zu einem italienischen Strafgesetz (1927) vom forensisch-psychiatrischen Standpunkt aus betrachtet. Arch f Psychiat 87(3): 416-54 '29 5980

Jannitti-Piromallo, Eugenio. Elementi di diritto criminale coordinati con la nuova legislazione. v1. 325p. Roma, "Foro Italiano," 1930 5981

Jovane, Enrico. La colpa penale nel progetto Rocco. Rassegna Giurid (1-2): 4- '30 5982

Jovane, E[nrico]. L'elemento subbiettivo del reato nel progetto Rocco. Scuola Pos 7: 505-7 '27 5983

Maas Geesteranus, Henry G. J. La rèforme pénale en Italie. Étude sur le nouveau projet préliminaire. 166p. bibliog footnotes. Paris, Sirey, 1929 5984

Manci, F. L' "animus diffamandi" nella dottrina e nel codice penale italiano. Riv Pen di Dott, Legis e Giuris 107: 189-223 Mr '28 5985

Mangini, R.; Gabrieli, F. P. and Cosentino, U. Codice penale illustrato con i labori preparatori. 583p. Roma, Carlo Colombo, 1930 5986

Manzini, Vincenzo. Istituzioni di diritto penale italiano. ed.3 rev. 498p. Padova, A. Milani, 1927 5987

Martini, D. de. La disciplina giuridica dei sindacati, l'istituzione della Magistratura del lavoro ed il divieto di sciopero e di serrata nella nuova legislazione italiana. Giustiz Pen 33: 576-632 '27 5988

Massari, Eduardo. Lineamenti del processo penale italiano. ed.2 rev. & enl. 304p. Napoli, N. Jovene, 1928 5989

Massari, Edoardo. Le origini e la elaborazione della riforma penale fascista. Vita Italiana (192-3): 1-7 '29 5990

Massini, I. C. La pericolosità criminosa nella nuova legislazione, il problema tecnico e dei tecnici. Arch di Antrop Crim 50: 1571 '30 5991

Maugini, Ruffo. Profili politici del progetto definitivo di un nuovo codice penale. Gerarchia (11): 879-84 '29 5992

De Mauro, Giambattista. Il diritto penale dello stato dello Città del Vaticano. Riv Pen di Dott, Legis e Giuris 110: 181-8 S '29 5993

De Montmorency, J. E. G. New Italian penal codes. Contemp R 140: 793-7 D '31 5994

Musillami, Giovanni. Il cumulo materiale delle pene del progetto del nuovo codice penale. Riv Pen di Dott, Legis e Giuris (8): 871- '30 5995

Osservazioni intorno al "Progetto preliminare di un nuovo codice penale (Agosto 1927. Anno V)." 212p. Milano, "Vita e Pensiero," 1927 5996

Péritch, J. M. Base fondamentale du nouveau code pénal italien (art. 85, 202 c.p.). Pensiero Giurid-Pen 3: 240-6 Jl '31 5997

Il progetto Rocco di codice penale italiano. Scuola Pos ns7: 465-71 S '27 5998

Ratesco, Const. G. La réforme pénale en Italie et à Cuba; a propos du livre de M. H. S. J. Maas Geesteranus. Etudes Crimin 4: 322-5 D '29; separate: 11p. Paris, Sirey, 1930 5999

Rende, Domenico. Il nuovo sistema penale nel progetto Rocco: la valutazione critica del sistema. Riv Int di Filosofia del Dir 8(1): 55-67 '28; 9(1): 81-114 '29 6000

Rota, S. Le disposizioni de progetto del nuovo codice penale. 80p. Napoli, Casa Ed. Majo, 1927 6001

Salmoria, F. Percosse e lesioni nell' applicazione del nuovo codice penale. Policlinico (sez prat) 38: 1494-6 O 5 '31 6002

Santoro, Arturo. Le nuove figure di reato nella legislazione sindacale italiano. Scuola Pos ns7: 1-26 Ja '27 6003

Saporito, Filippo. L'apport de la biologie au code pénal qui va être rédigé en Italie. Arch di Antrop Crim 47: 449-62 Jl '27; same title: Ann de Méd Lég 7: 430-3 O '27 6004

Saunders, S. E. The new penal code in Italy. L Times 165: 307-9 Ap 7 '28 6005

Signorini, V. and Gatta, L. Della nuova legge di pubblica sicurezza. 557p. Torino, E. Arduini, 1928 6006

Spirito, Ugo. Commenti al progetto del nuovo codice penale. Bibliog Fascista (1-2): 10-13 '28 6007

Spirito, Ugo. Il nuovo diritto penale. 143p. Venezia, "La nuova Italia" [1928] 6008

Thót, Ladislao. Geschiedenis van het italiaansche Strafrecht en strafrechtelijke letterkunde tot de eerste nationale Kodifikatie. Tijdschr v Strafr 37: 60-112 '27 6009

Thot, Ladislao. Nuevo proyecto preliminar del código penal italiano. R de Identif y Cienc Pen 2: 315-50 S '28 6010

Valsecchi, Wolfango. Atlanto del diritto penale italiano. 40p. Siena, Sordomuti, 1927 6011

Visscher, F. de. La formule paricidas esto et les origines de la jurisdiction criminelle à Rome. Acad Sci Belg Bul Cl Lett s13 5(6): 298-332 '27 6012

Zenni, F. Sul progetto del nuovo codice di procedura penale. Riv Ital di Dir Pen 2: 3-8, 105-22, 225-40 Ja-Mr '30 6013

JAPAN

Kusano, Hyoichiro; Sugiura, Tadao, and Bartelt, Fritz, eds. Japanische Strafgesetze. Schwurgerichtsordnung vom 18. April 1923. 55p. (Sammlung ausserdeutscher Strafgesetzbücher 44) Berlin, Gruyter, 1927 6014

Motoji, Shinkuma. [Treatise on the penal law of Japan.] ed.40. 2v. [Tokyo, Ministry of Justice, Director of criminal affairs, 1928] 6015
In Japanese.

Thot, Ladislao. Estudios históricos del derecho penal oriental: historia del derecho penal japonés. R de Identif y Cienc Pen 8: 187-249 My '31 6016

JUGOSLAVIA

Péritch, J. Jugoslavische Strafrechtsliteratur 1926-28. Monats f Kriminalpsychol u Strafrechtsref 20: 292-7, 351-7, 523-5 '29 6017

Péritch, J. Die Wiederaufnahme des Strafverfahrens nach der neuen jugoslavischen StPO. vom 16. Februar 1929. Monats f Kriminalpsychol u Strafrechtsref 21: 576-91 bibliog(p591) O '30 6018A

Thot, Ladislao. El proyecto del código penal yugeoslavo. R de Identif y Cienc Pen 3: 96-113 N '28 6018B

MEXICO

Almaraz, José. Codice penale messicano. Arch di Antrop Crim 51 (1-2) Ja '31 6019

Almaraz, José. Las escuelas básicas del código penal de 1872 y del vigente. R de Cienc Soc (1): 36- '30 6020

Almaraz, José. Exposición de motivos del codigo penal de 1929. 200p. Mexico, D.F. 1931 6021

Almaraz, José. Le innovazioni e le nuove tendenze del codice penale messicano. Giustiz Pen 37: 11-21 Ja '31 6022

Almaraz, José. New penal legislation in Mexico. *In* Herring, Hubert Clinton and Terrill, Katharine, eds. The genius of Mexico, 208-17. N.Y. Committee on cultural relations with Latin America, 1931 6023

Angel Ceniceros, José. El nuevo código penal mexicano; glosa sintética. Mex Univ Nac R Mens 3: 141-51 D '31 6024

La colaboración judicial y la nueva legislación penal. R Mexicana d Der Pen 1: 74-90 Jl '30 6025

Mendoza, Salvador. Mexico's bold experiment in the new criminal code. Cur Hist 31: 107-11 O '29 6026

Mendoza, Salvador. El nuevo codigo penal de México. Hispan-Am Hist R 10: 299-312 Ag '30 6027

The Mexican criminal code. L Notes 33: 142 N '29 6028

Rippy, J. Fred. The new penal code of Mexico. Hispan-Am Hist R 10: 295-8 Ag '30 6029

Thot, Ladislao. Codificación penal moderna. El nuevo código penal Mejicano. R de Identif y Cienc Pen 4: 84-114 N '29 6030

NETHERLANDS

Delierneux, Adolphe. Le projet de loi néerlandais de défense sociale. R de Dr Pén et de Crimin 10: 160-5 '30 6031
"Nederlandsche Vereeniging voor Strafrechtspraak."

Hartog, L. J. C. den. Het geval Loewenstein en de Nederlandsche Strafwet. Tijdschr v de Politie 1(26): 461-6 N 14 '28 6032

Swinderen, O[ncko] Q[iurijn] van. Esquisse du droit pénal actuel dans les Pays-Bas et à l'étranger. v12, 13. Groningue, Noordhoff, 1928 6033

Weber, Franz. Die holländischen Psychopathen-Gesetze. Bl f Gefängniskunde 60: 65-9 '29 6034

NETHERLANDS EAST INDIES

Neytzell de Wilde, A. De rechtsbedeeling der Indische bevolkingsgroepen in ontwikkeling en verwikkeling. Verslag Vergadering v h Indisch Genootschap 84-107 O '31 6035

PARAGUAY

González, Teodosio. Derecho penal; tratado bajo el doble aspecto científico y legislativo; contiene la explicación y comentario del código penal paraguayo. 3v. La Colomona S.A., Asunción, 1928 6036

PERSIA

Thot, Ladislao. Derecho penal Persa; historia del derecho penal Oriental. R de Identif y Cienc Pen 6: 418-53 S '30 6037

PERU

Altavilla, Enrique. Del proyecto italiano al peruano para un nuevo código penal. R de Derecho Pen (1): 8- '30 6038

Contursi, Lisi Gaetano. Il progetto di codice penale peruviano. Scuola Pos (5-6): 269-73 '29 6039

Cornejo, A. Gustavo. Proyecto de codigo penal présenté par la Commission parlementaire. 172p. Lima, Minerva, 1928 6040

Gatti, Tancredi. Il nuovo progetto di codice penale Peruviano. Giustiz Pen (44): 2024-38 '28 6041

PHILIPPINE ISLANDS

Gilmore, Eugene A. Administration of criminal law in the Philippines. Phil L J 9: 30-7 Jl '29 6042

Prudhomme, Henri. L'avant-projet du code pénal philippin. R Int de Dr Pén 4: 275-320 '27 6043

POLAND

Glaser, Stéphane. Les travaux de la Commission de codification en Pologne. R de Dr Pén et de Crimin 8: 113-29 '28 6044
Extr de la conférence faite à Bruxelles, January 23, 1928, à l'Union belge de droit penal.

Makowski, Waclaw. Uwagi w sprawie koniecznych zmian i uzupelnień cześci ogònej projektu kodesku karnego. Ruch Prawn i Ekon i Socjol 9: 245-62 Jl '29 6045

Neymark, Edward. Chronique de Pologne: Commission de codification—projet de code de procédure pénale . . . projet de code pénal—conseil juridique. R de Dr Pén et de Crimin 7: 99-109 '27 6046

[Poland]. Komisja Kodyfikacyjna Rzeczypospolitej Polskiej. Sekcja Prawa Karnego. Projekt Czesci Szczególnej Kodesku Karnego. 110p. (Tom IV. Zeszyt 3) Lwów, 1929 6047

Rappaport, E. S. Le champ d'application de la loi pénale quant au temps dans les avant-projets de codes pénaux polonais et italiens. 8p. Messina, Giacomo d'Anna, 1929 6048
Extr: Il Pensiero Giuridico-Penale 1(4) O '30.

Rappaport, Emile-Stanislas. Le nouveau système de codification de la législation criminelle. R Int de Dr Pén 8: 34-64 bibliog (p63-4) '31 6049

Rappaport, E[mile-]Stanislas. Le problème de la codification des contraventions dans la législation polonaise. R Int de Dr Pén 7(2): 129-50 '30 6050

PORTUGAL

Gatti, Tancredi. Il nuovo codice di procedura penale portoghese. 14p. Lisboa, Tip. la penitenciaria, 1930 6051

Santos, Alfredo Ary dos. Pretextos para discussão em redor do código penal Português. Bol do Inst de Crimin s8 15(2): 315-36 '31 6052

RUMANIA

Ionescu-Muscel, Petre. Sur le droit pénal en Roumanie. R Dr Pén et de Crimin 10: 54-9 '30 6053

Radulesco, Jean. Le projet de code pénal roumain. 62p. Agen, Imp. Moderne, 1929 6054
Extr: Bulletin de la Société de législation comparée, October-December 1928.

Thot, Ladislao. El proyecto de código penal Rumano. R de Identif y Cienc Pen 4: 106-36 My '29 6055

Thot, [Ladislao]. El proyecto de codigo penal Rumano. Polizei im Bild (8) S '29 6056

RUSSIA

Anossof, I. L'analogia nel diritto penale soviettico. Scuola Pos 38: 444-8 '30 6057

Anossow, J. J. Religion und Strafrecht in USSR. Monats f Kriminalpsychol u Strafrechtsref 22: 299-309 My '31 6058

Anossow, J. J. Der Verbrechensbegriff im Strafkodex RSFSR. Monats f Kriminalpsychol u Strafrechtsref 21: 422-9 '30 6059

Cicala, Salvatore. La legislazione penale della Russia bolscevica. 22p. Catania, Viaggi-Campio, 1927 6060

Codice penale della Republica Sovietista Federativa Socialista Russa (R.S.F.S.R.) Scuola Pos ns7: 434-43 S '27 6061

Conforto, Giorgio. I principi della rielaborazione del codice penale della R.S.F.S.R. Europa Orient 11: 173-201 My '31 6062
Translation of a report submitted by Krilenko during meeting at Commissariat of Justice, May 1928.

Duranty, W. Soviet criminal jurisprudence. Dickinson L R 34: 114-17 Ja '30 6063

Ferri, Enrico. Das Strafrecht Sowjetrusslands. Justiz 3(4): 311-14 '28 6064

Gallas, Wilhelm. Kriminalpolitik und Strafrechtssystematik unter besonderer Berücksichtigung des sowjet-russischen Rechts. 88p. (Abh d Krimin Inst an d Univ Berlin s4 2(1) '31) Berlin, Gruyter, 1931 6065

Gallas, Wilhelm, transl. Strafgesetzbuch (Ugolownyj Kodex) der Russischen Sozialistischen Föderativen Sowjet-Republik (R.S.F.S.R.) vom 22. November 1926 mit den Änderungen bis zum 1. August 1930. 68p. Berlin, Gruyter, 1931 6066

Gatti, Tancredi. Il codice sovietico. Giustiz Pen (44): 2003-12 '28 6067

[Gernet, Mikhail Nikolaevich] (M. N. Hernett) and Trainin, A. N. Ugolowny Kodeks. Moskva, Prawo i Shisn, 1927 6068

Grodsinsky. El nuevo código penal de la Rusia soviética precedido de un estudio preliminar; traducción directa de los manuscritos alemanes por Luis Jiménez de Asúa en colaboración con José Arturo Rodriguez Muñoz. 44p. Madrid, Reus, 1927 6069

Grodzinskij. Das neue Strafgesetzbuch der Sovětukraine. Zeitsch f Ostrecht 2: 177-89 '28 6070

Jiménez de Asúa, Luis. La ley penal de Rusia. Phila Pris R 3: 37-8 S '27 6071

Krylenko, N. Criminal law in the Soviet Union. Communist [London] 2: 173-80 N '27 6072

Kufaeff, B. Die Gesetzgebung für minderjährige Verbrecher in Sowjet-Russland. Zentralbl f Jugendrecht u Jugendwohlfahrt 21: 199-208 '29 6073

Maurach, Reinhart. Das russische Strafgesetzbuch. Zeitsch f d ges Strafrechtswiss 47 (4): 362-71 '27 6074

Maurach, Reinhart. Das Sovetstrafrecht, 1919-1931. Zeitsch f Ostrecht 5: 410-32 Je '31 6075

Maurach, Reinhart. System des russischen Strafrechts. 207p. (Osteuropa-Inst. in Breslau. Quellen u. Studien. Abt. Recht ns5) Berlin, Sack, 1928 6076

Müller. Die Entwicklung des sowjetrussischen Strafrechts: Zwei neue Strafgesetzentwürfe. Monats f Kriminalpsychol u Strafrechtsref 21: 647-54 N '30 6077

Napolitano, T. Evoluzione del diritto penale sovietico dall'ottobre 17 ai giorni nostri. Giustiz Pen 37 (8) Ag '31 6078

Pernis, C. Le nuove teorie penali della Russia sovietica. Scuola Pos 39: 1-22 '31 6079

Rácz, Georg. Ein Grundriss des neuesten Sowjetstrafrechts. 54p. Budapest, Sigmund Politzer & Söhne, 1931 6080
(in ungarischer Sprache erschienen in)

[Ruiz-]Funes, M[ariano]. El derecho penal de los Soviets. R de Crimin, Psiquiat y Med Leg 14: 49-82, 164-81, 336-44 Ja-My '27 6081

Schwartzkopf, Heinz. Das Strafrecht Sowjet-Russlands. 88p. (Strafrechtl Abh no250) Breslau, Schletter, 1929 6082

Sovjetruslands Strafferet. Nord Tids f Straf 15: 41-66 Ja '27 6083

Thót, L. Historia del derecho penal ruso y baltico. R Arg de Cienc Pol 34: 535-62 Jl '27 6084

Valkhoff, J. De rechtsontwikkeling in Sovjet-Rusland gedurende de afgelopen tien jahren (November 1917-November 1927). Mensch & Maatschappij 4: 1-7 Ja 1 '28 6085

Weissenberg, S. Das neue russische Strafgesetz. Arch f Rassen- u Gesell-Biol 20: 334-6 My 15 '28 6086

Zelitch, Judah. Soviet administration of criminal law. 418p. Philadelphia, University of Pennsylvania press, 1931 6087

SCOTLAND

Macdonald, John Hay Athole. A practical treatise on the criminal law of Scotland. ed.4. 713p. Edinburgh, W. Green, 1929 6088

SIAM

Thot, Ladislao. Estudios históricos de derecho penal oriental: derecho Siamés y Coreano. R de Identif y Cienc Pen 7: 333-65 N '30 6089

SPAIN

Anton Oneca, José. Derecho penal. 191p. Madrid, Reus, 1929 6090

Cadalso, Fernando. Le nouveau code pénal et les systèmes modernes en Espagne. 38p. Faculté de Droit de l'Université de Toulouse, 1929 6091

Calón, Eugenio Cuello. Código penal du 8 de septiembre de 1928. 532p. Barcelona, Libreria Bosch, 1929 6092

Calón, Eugenio Cuello. El nuevo código penal español. 327p. Barcelona, Libreria Bosch, 1929 6093

Calón, Eugenio Cuello. El nuevo código penal español. R Int de Dr Pén 6: 173-92 Fr transl by R. Roger (p193-213) '29 6094

Corsanego, Camillo. Il nuovo codice penale spagnolo. R Int di Sci Soc e Discip Ausil 3(1): 24-30 '29 6095

Frosali, Alberto. Sul nuovo codice penale spagnuolo. Scuola Pos (8-9): 336-78 '29; extr: 15p. Milano, Vallardi, 1930 6096

Gatti, Tancredi. Il nuovo codice spagnolo 1° gennaio 1929. Giustiz Pen (32): 1109-20; (36-7): 1246-66 '29 6097

Goicoechea, José Guallart L. de. Le nouveau code pénal espagnol. Inst Intermed Int de la Haye Bul 210-23 O '29 6098

Goicoechea, José Guallart L. de. El nuevo código penal español. 17p. Zaragoza, Tip. la Académica, 1929 6099

Jiménez de Asúa, Luis. Die Strafgesetzgebung der spanischen Republik. Monats f Kriminalpsychol u Strafrechtsref 22: 641-63 N '31 6100

Jiménez de Asúa, Luis and Anton Oneca, José. Derecho penal conforn al código de 1928. pt. I, 633p. Madrid, Reus, 1929 6101

Jiménez de Asúa, Luis; Cardo y Crespo, Tomas and Rodriguez Muñoz, José Arturo. Casos de derecho penal. 170p. Madrid, Huelves, 1929 6102

Lafora, G. R. La peligrosidad y las medidas de seguridad en el nuevo código penal español. Siglo Med 84: 46, 74, 102, 130 Jl 13-Ag 10 '29 6103

Lafora, Gonzalo R. Psychiatry in the new Spanish penal code. R Gen de Leg y Juris 154: 386-459 Ap '29 6104

Magnol, Joseph and De Moulins, Charles, transl. Le code pénal espagnol du septembre 1928; suivi du décret-loi du 3 février 1929 sur les tribunaux tutélaires pour mineurs et des règlements pénitentiaires. 609p. Paris, Rousseau, 1931 6105

Perreau, E. H. Les médecins et pharmaciens et le nouveau code pénal espagnol. Paris Méd (annexe) 1: i-iii Je 13 '31 6106

Thot, Ladislao. Codificación penal moderna. El nuevo código penal de España y proyectos de Grecia y Colombia. R de Identif y Cienc Pen 5: 429-69 Mr '30 6107

Viada y Vilaseca, Salvador. Codigo penal reformado de 1870. ed.5. v5, 574p. Madrid, Hernández, 1927 6108

De Villaverde, José María. La psiquiatría en el nuevo codigo penal Español. R de Crimin, Psiquiat y Med Leg 16: 363-9 My '29 6109

SWEDEN

Hammarlöw, Uno Anton. Das Strafensystem in Vorentwurf zu einem schedischen Strafgesetzbuche; mit besonderer Berücksichtigung des Entwurfes zu einem schweiz. Strafgesetzbuch vom 23 Juli 1928. 91p. Inaug.-diss. Bern, 1927. Bern, Hallwag, 1927 6110

Heimer, Einar Henrik. Svensk rättsvetenskap. I. Professuren i straffrätt och juridisk encyclopedi vid Lunds universitet. 28p. Lund, Torekov, 1928 6111

Kinberg, Olof. Les lois suédoises de défense sociale contre les anormaux criminels et les délinquants d'habitude. R Int de Dr Pén 8: 154-71 '31 6112

SWITZERLAND

Bleuler, Eugen. Zum eidgenössischen Strafgesetzbuch. Schweiz Zeitsch f Strafr 42: 366-73 '29 6113

Bürgi, Wolf. Die Lehre von der adäquaten Verursachung und ihre Bedeutung in der schweizerischen Rechtsprechung. 121p. (Abh z. Schweizer. Recht ns no28) Bern, Stämpfli, 1927 6114

Burckardt, W. Le droit fédéral suisse; traduit de l'allemand par Georges Bovet. 2v. Paris, Alcan, 1931? 6115

E. Il progetto del codice penale svizzero. Giustiz Pen (44): 2013-22 '28 6116

Gautschi, G. Zur Schweigepflicht des Arztes, speziell im Hinblick auf den Entwurf eines neuen zürcherischen Medizinalgesetzes und unter Berücksichtigung des eidgenössischen Strafrechtsentwurfes. Schweiz med Wchnschr 61: 775-84 Ag 8 '31 6117

Lang, Otto. Die Unzulänglichkeit des Kantonalen Strafrechtes. Schweiz Zeitsch f Strafr 44: 433-51 '30 6118

Milazzo, Gioachino. Diritto penale svizzero. Riv Ital di Dir Pen (3): 257-75 '29 6119

Pfenninger, H[ans] F[elix]. Bedingte Verurteilung oder bedingter Strafvollzug im schweizerischen Strafrecht. 35p. Zürich, Schulthess, 1928 6120

Pfenninger, H[ans] F[elix]. Das zürcherische Jugendstrafrecht. 168p. Zürich, Schulthess, 1928 6121

Stämpfli. Die Eisenbahngefährdung nach der schweizerischen Rechtssprechung. Schweiz Juristen-Zeit 24: 337-42 '28 6122

Stämpfli. Das schweizerische Strafgesetzbuch vor dem Nationalrat. Monats f Kriminalpsychol u Strafrechtsref 19: 226-8 Ap '28 6123

Stämpfli. Die Wiederaufnahme in neueren schweizerischen Gesetzen und Entwürden. Monats f Kriminalpsychol u Strafrechtsref 21: 493-501 '30 6124

Thót, Ladislao. [Historia] del derecho penal suizo y holandés. R Arg de Cienc Pol 36: 353-94 Jl 12 '28 6125

Wyss, Oscar. Der Rückfall in den kantonalen Strafgesetzbüchern und in den Vorentwürfen zu einem schweizerischen Strafgesetzbuch. 111p. Bern, Haupt, 1927 6126

Zeller, Heinrich, ed. Das Strafgesetzbuch für den Kanton Zürich. ed.2. 391p. Zürich, Orell Füssli, 1928 6127

TURKEY

Bianchedi, Camillo. Note sul codice penale Turco. Scuola Pos (5-6): 243-61 '29 6128

La literatura penal Turca. R de Identif y Cienc Pen 3: 294-7 Ja '29 6129

Ziemke, Kurt. Das Türkische Strafgesetzbuch vom 1. März 1926. 138p. Berlin, Gruyter, 1927 6130

UNITED STATES

Administration of criminal law in the United States. L Q R 43: 315-17 Jl '27 **6131**

America's first criminal code, established at Jamestown, Va. in 1611. Golden Bk 11: 58 Mr '30 **6132**

Atwell, William Hawley. Treatise on federal criminal law and procedure with forms of indictment and writ of error, and the federal penal code. ed.4. 1116p. St. Louis, Thomas Law Bk. Co. 1929 **6133**

Clark, William Lawrence. A treatise on the law of crimes. ed.3. 794p. Chicago, Callaghan & co. 1927 **6134**

Criminal law in the United States. Can B R 5: 618-19 O '27 **6135**

Good, E. E. A brief survey of the criminal law and procedure in America. Neb L Bul 6: 91-101 Jl '27 **6136**

Hopkins, James Love. The new federal penal code. 1370p. Cincinnati, W. H. Anderson co. 1928 **6137**

Rey, Charles. La commission américaine d'uniformité des lois d'États. 140p. Paris, Giard, 1927 **6138**

ALABAMA

Davis, Harwell G. Administration of criminal laws. Ala L J 2: 99-113 Mr '27 **6139**

CALIFORNIA

California. Crime commission. Laws relating to crime and administration of criminal law, passed by California legislature in 1929. 109p. Sacramento, 1929 **6140**

[Clowdsley, Forsythe Charles]. California criminal code commission. Int Assn Identif, Calif Div Proc 12: 26-35 '27 **6141**

Fricke, Charles William. California criminal law. 261p. Los Angeles, Los Angeles Review, 1927 **6142**

Fricke, Charles W[illiam]. Crime laws of California. J Delin 12: 42-7 Mr '28 **6143**

Fricke, Charles W[illiam]. The new California crime laws, their effect as shown by a five months trial. J Juv Res 12: 42-7 Mr '28 **6144**

Fricke, Charles W[illiam]. The 1927 statutes relating to crime and punishment. Los Angeles B Assn Bul 3: 5-12 S 15 '27 **6145**

Fricke, Charles W[illiam]. Some of the important changes in the California criminal law. J Delin 11: 184-8 S '27 **6146**

Kidd, A[lexander] M[arsden]. California legislation in regard to crime for 1929. Calif L R 17: 537-52 Jl '29 **6147**

Paddock, George A. Ask modern laws to fight crime: California and Minnesota are seeking to remedy present conditions which impede the progress of justice. Crim Just [Chicago] 9: 13 Mr '27 **6148**

Parma, Rosamond and Armstrong, Elizabeth. Codes and statutes of California: a bibliography. L Lib J 22: 41-56 Ap '29 **6149**

CONNECTICUT

Clark, Charles E. Some of the facts of law administration in Connecticut. Conn B J 3: 161-9 Jl '29 **6150**

Keeler, John E. Administration of criminal law in Connecticut. Conn B J 1: 75-86 Ap '27 **6151**

ILLINOIS

Clark, Harold J. Crime measures in the legislature. Review of some of the bills concerning criminal justice now pending before the General Assembly of Illinois. Crim Just [Chic] 9: 12-13 F '27 **6152**

Smith, June C. Illinois criminal digest. ed.3. 870p. Chicago, B. J. Smith & co. 1928 **6153**

INDIANA

Ewbank, Louis Blasdel. Indiana criminal law; a treatise on criminal procedure, pleading, evidence and instructions and the law of public offenses, with full set of forms. ed.2. 1507p. [N.Y.] Bobbs, 1929 **6154**

Kettleborough, Charles. Changes in the criminal laws. Ind Bul Char & Correc (168): 98-101 Mr '29 **6155**

[Report of the Committees on criminal jurisprudence and on legislation of the Indiana state bar association]. Ind L J 3: 29-38 O '27 **6156**

IOWA

Patton, O. K. Continuous code revision in Iowa, the code of 1927. Ia L R 13: 1-46 D '27 **6157**

KANSAS

Bennett, E. C. The Kansas Baumes law. Kan St B Assn Proc 1927: 154-64 **6158**

KENTUCKY

Roberson, J. M. Roberson's new Kentucky criminal law and procedure: both statute and common law. ed.2. 2219p. Cincinnati, Anderson, 1927 **6159**

LOUISIANA

Marr, Robert H. comp. Criminal statutes of Louisiana. 662p. New Orleans, Hansell, 1929 **6160**

Marr, R[obert] H. Necessity of criminal code for Louisiana. Tulane L R 4: 18-26 D '29 **6161**

Moore, Elon H. The Livingston code. J Crim L & Crimin 19: 344-66 bibliog (p363-6) N '28 **6162**

Ogden, Percy T. Forms in criminal proceedings, under code of criminal procedure of Louisiana. 169p. Crowley, La. The Author, 1929 **6163**

MASSACHUSETTS

Stone, Seymour H. Is the administration of criminal law in Great Britain preferable to that practised in the commonwealth of Massachusetts? J Crim L & Crimin 19: 237-43 Ag '28 **6164**

MICHIGAN

Michigan's new criminal code. Am B Assn J 13: 679-80 D '27 **6165**

Report of the Committee on legislation and law reform of the Michigan state bar association. Mich St B J 6: 105-16 Ja '27 **6166**

MISSOURI

Grimm, J. H. Developments in the criminal law of Missouri. St Louis L R 15: 47-60 D '29 **6167**

NEW YORK

Banton, Joab H. The Baumes law. Pris J 7: 17-19 O '27 **6168**

[Battle, Raymond A.]. Constitutionality and mandatory nature of the Baumes law. St John's L R 3: 135-9 D '28 **6169**

Baumes, Caleb H. The Baumes laws. N Y St Assn Magistrates Proc 19: 66-79 '27 **6170**

Baumes law again. Outl 154: 338 F 26 '30 **6171**

Cass, E. R. New York legislation in 1926: a move to suppress crime. Welf Mag 18: 207-13 F '27 **6172**

City club of New York. "Blue laws and fool laws." 11p. (Pam no14) N.Y. April 1931 **6173**

Summarizes sections of penal law of New York state held to be obsolete, nullified or unenforceable.

Civic welfare alliance. Baumes laws: texts of the principal Baumes law. (Bul no522) Boston, January 1927 **6174**

Clark, Harold J. Protecting society from the criminal. Crim Just [Chic] (50): 7 Ap '27 **6175**

Baumes laws in New York.

Cressman, L. S. New York's bludgeon law; Baumes laws. R of R 77: 77-80 Ja '28 **6176**

Dayton, Joseph E. Recent legislation for the repression of crime in New York and other states. Pris Assn N Y Ann Rep 85: 83-116 '29 **6177**

Fitzpatrick, J. T. ed. Penal law and the code of procedure of the state of New York. ed.19. 1205p. Albany, Bender, 1927 **6178**

Gilbert, F. B. Criminal law and practice of the state of New York: consisting of the penal law, the code of criminal procedure, the inferior criminal courts act, parole commission law for first class cities, and children's court acts of New York state, New York city and Buffalo, exhaustively annotated. ed.13 by J. T. Fitzpatrick. N.Y. Bender, 1930 **6179**

Howe, John I. The Baumes laws; the results of New York's radical criminal code revision. Police "13-13" 5: 15-16 Jl '30 **6180**

Johnsen, Julia Emily, comp. Baumes law. 189p. (Ref Shelf v6 no3) N.Y. Wilson, 1929 **6181**

McLellan, Howard. A panic in crookdom. R of R 75: 155-7 F '27 **6182**

McLellan, Howard. Rough on crime in New York: sharp teeth in new criminal laws of the state are setting a fashion for legislatures. Burroughs Clearing House 11: 10-12 Ja '27 **6183**

Mr. Baumes defends fourth offender act. Am B Assn J 15: 257-8 My '29 **6184**

New York (state). Crime commission. Crime law, 1928. 36p. Albany, 1928
Crime laws, 1929. 22p. Albany, 1929
Crime laws advocated by the Joint Legislative committee on the coordination of civil and criminal practice acts, 1926 and Crime commission, 1927, 1928, 1929 and 1930. 163p. Albany, 1930 **6185**

New York (state). Legislature. Joint legislative committee. The crime laws advocated by the . . . committee on the coordination of civil and criminal practice acts of 1926 and Crime commission of New York state. 65p. Newburgh, N.Y. Senator C. W. Baumes, 1927 **6186**

Oppression and defense. Commonweal 10: 371-2 Ag 14 '29 **6187**

Overbeck, A. von. Aus der neuesten Strafgesetzgebung des Staates Neuyork. Gerichtssaal 94: 393-5 '27 **6188**

Porter, H. F. J. Practical results of the Baumes law. Panel 5: 3 F '27 **6189**

Rowe, Leonard. Habitual criminal legislation—the Baumes law—conviction. Univ Cin L R 4: 479-81 N '30 **6190**

United States. Library of Congress. Baumes laws: a bibliographical list. 5p. Washington, February 1, 1928 **6191**

OKLAHOMA

Durham, W. F. ed. The criminal laws of the state of Oklahoma. 567p. Guthrie, Okla. Co-operative pub. co. 1928 **6192**

Shive, R. J. comp. Shive's criminal digest. 662p. Oklahoma City, Harlow pub co. 1928 **6193**

Pennsylvania

Pennsylvania. Committee on penal affairs. Pending legislation for 1929. Penal Affairs (19) Ja '29 **6194**

Pennsylvania. Conference on the criminal law. Reports of committees appointed by Judicial section of 1928 conference on criminal law submitted to the members of the 1929 conference for advance study. 41p. Philadelphia, 1929 **6195**

Pennsylvania. Conference on the criminal law. Judicial section. Report of 1928 Conference on the criminal law. 38p. Philadelphia, 1928 **6196**

Pennsylvania prison society. Committee on legislation. A proposed legislative program for Pennsylvania. Pris J 11: 15-20 Ja '31 **6197**

County jails, prison farms, parole, salaries of sheriffs, capital punishment.

Texas

Report of the Committee on criminal law and procedure. Tex B Assn Proc 46: 145-50 '27 **6198**

Virginia

Scott, Arthur Pearson. Criminal law in colonial Virginia. 335p. bibliog 324-9. Chicago, University of Chicago press, 1930 **6199**

System of courts; criminal procedure; offenses against government; against justice; against the person; against property; against religion; against public morals; felony trials.

Wisconsin

Sanborn, John B. Wisconsin legislation of 1927. Wis L R 4: 349-61 Ja '28 **6200**

Steel, Ida Helen. Index of the laws of Wisconsin relating to children compiled from the 1927 statutes. 17p. (Information Bul no1) Madison, University of Wisconsin, Bureau of economics and sociology, May 1, 1928 **6201**

Laws re: contributing to delinquency; county industrial schools; delinquent children; detention home; jail; juvenile courts; kidnapping; probation; sex offenses; state industrial schools; truants and vagrants.

INTERNATIONAL CRIMINAL LAW

[Caloyanni, Megalos A.]. Het internationale strafrecht. Wetensch Bl 4: 52-8 '28 **6203**

Caloyanni, Megalos A. L'unification du droit pénal international aux Conférences internationales de Varsovie et de Rome. 34p. Agen, Imp. Moderne, 1929 **6204**

Canonne, G. Essai de droit pénal international. L'Affaire du "Lotus". 345p. Paris, Sirey, 1929. (Biblioth. de l'Inst. de Criminologie et de sciences pénales de Toulouse no4) **6205**

Carnevale, Emanuele. Diritto internazionale e diritto criminale. Pensiero Giurid-Pen 1: 153-88 Ap '29; separate: 34p. Messina, Giacomo d'Anna, 1929 **6206**

Cortina, José Manuel. El misticisme en el derecho internacional. 20p. Habana, Imp. El Siglo XX, 1929 **6207**

Donnedieu de Vabres, Henry Félic Auguste. L'action publique et l'action civile dans les rapports de droit pénal international. 102p. (Hague. Acad. Intern. Law. Recueil des Cours, 1929, I, 26: 207-309) Paris, Hachette, 1930 **6208**

Gichtel, Hermann. Das internationale Strafrecht nach den Entwürfen eines Allgemeinen Deutschen Strafgesetzbuchs und eines Einführungsgesetzes dazu im Vergleich zum geltenden Recht. 111p. München, 1931. Inaug.-Diss. Erlangen **6209**

Marsico, A. de. Principî informatori del diritto penale internazionale. Ann della Univ di Bari 1928-29: 23-81 **6210**

Mauro, G. B. de. Diritto penale dell-avvenire e giustizia penale internazionale. 18p. Città di Castello, 1929 **6211**

Mendelsohn-Bartholdy, [A.]. Internationales Strafrecht und Politik. Deut Juristen-Zeit 33 (1): 53-7 '28 **6212**

Neymark, Edward. L'importanza della cooperazione internazionale nel dominio del diritto penale. Pensiero Giurid-Pen 1(4) O '29; same under title: L'importance de la cooperation internationale dans le domaine du droit penal. R de Identif y Cienc Pen 6: 120-33 My '30 **6213**

Piacentini, Mario. L'internazionalizzazione del diritto penale. Giustiz Pen 37 (5) pt1: 585-605 My '31 **6214**

Zygmunt, Cybichowski. Międzynarodowe prawo karne. Kompetencja sadów do ścigania przestępstw zagranicznych. Warszawa, 1927 **6215**

BIBLIOGRAPHY

Articles on foreign law published in recent law journals. Am B Assn J 13: 232-5 Ap '27 **6216**

Beale, Joseph Henry, comp. A bibliography of early English law books. 304p. Cambridge, Harvard University press, 1927 **6217**

[Bibliography of criminal law]. Index to Leg Per & L Lib J 18: 86-92 1926-27; 20: 28-31, 126-8, 215-17 Ap-O '27 **6218**

Calhoun, George Miller and Delamere, Catherine. A working bibliography of Greek law. 144p. Cambridge, Harvard University press, 1927 **6219**

Evers, G. A. Strafrechtlijke bibliographie. Binnenlandsch overzicht 1926. Tijdschr v Strafr 37: 113-32, 360-98, 485-515 '27
Bibliography of about 500 items. 6220

Grandin, A. Bibliographie générale des sciences juridiques, politiques, économiques et sociales de 1800 à 1925-26; suppl. 1-4. Paris, Sirey, 1931 6221
Section: "droit pénal."

Periodicals

Criminal law journal of India. Lahore, 1, 1904- 6222

Criminal law reporter. Parvatipur, 1, 1911- 6223

Criminal law review. Madras, 1, 1913- 6224

Criminal lawyer. Parvatipur, 1, May 1928-
Not publ N-D 1928. 6225

Przeglad Polski utsawodawstwa cywilnego i kryminalnego. Warszawa, 1, 1928- 6226
French title: Revue polonaise de législation civile et criminelle.

Revista Cubana de derecho. Sección jurisprudencia. Materia penal. Habana, 1, 1929- 6227

Revista de derecho penal. Buenos Aires, 1, Ap 30 1929- 6228

Revista de direito civil, commercial e criminal. Rio de Janeiro, 1906- 6229

Revista de drept penal si Stünti penitenciara. Bucuresti 6230
Organe officiel du Cercle d'études pénales et de police scientifique.

Revista Mexicana de derecho penal. Mexico, 1, 1930- 6231
Organo del Consejo supremo de defensa y prevencion social.

Revue de droit international privé et de droit pénal international. Paris, 1, 1905- 6232

Revue de droit penal et de criminologie et Archives internationales de médecine légale. Bruxelles, ns v1, 1921- 6233
Organes des administrations de la législation pénale, des prisons et de la Bienfaisance, de l'Ecole de criminologie et de police scientifique et de la Société de médecine légale de Belgique.

Revue internationale de droit pénal. Paris, 1, 1924- Association internationale de droit pénal 6234
Suppl to Revue pénitentiaire et de droit pénal.

Rivista italiana di diritto penale. Padova, 1, 1929- 6235

Rivista penale di dottrina, legislazione e giurisprudenza. Firenze, ns1, 1874- 6236

Scuola positiva; rivista di diritto e procedura penale. Milano, ns1, 1921- 6237

Vestnik Ceskoslowenské spolec nosti pro pravo trestni. Praha, 2 (1-2) 1926- 6238
Bulletin de l'Association tchécoslovaque de droit pénal.

ASSOCIATIONS, CONGRESSES, ETC.

Aloisi, U. Relazione sull'attività svolta dalla Delegazione italiana al Congresso [di diritto penale] di Bucarest. Riv di Diritto Peniten 1: 612-27 '30 6239

Carton de Wiart, H. and Roux, J. A. Actes du Premier Congrès international de droit pénal (Bruxelles, 1926). 690p. Paris, Lib. des Juris-Classeurs, 1927 6240

Commission chargée de la rédaction d'un projet de code pénal international. Procès-verbaux des travaux. R Int de Dr Pén 8: 191-224 '31 6241

Commission chargée de la rédaction d'un projet de code répressif international. Procès-verbaux. R Int de Dr Pén 7: 253-309 '30 6242
Commission: Megalos A. Caloyanni; H. Donnedieu de Vabres; A. Mercier; E.-S. Rappaport; J.-A. Roux; Q. Saldana.

Conférence internationale de codification pénal. Rome (1928) Textes des résolutions votées par la Conférence. R Int de Dr Pén 5: 253-60 '28; same title: R de Dr Pén et de Crimin 8: 574-605 '28 6243

Conférence internationale de représentants des commissions de codification pénale. Varsovie (1927) Texte des résolutions adoptées par la Conférence. R Int de Dr Pén 5: 13-18 English transl (p19-24) '28 6244

Conférence internationale d'unification du droit pénal. Varsovie (1927) Actes de la Conférence . . . publiées sous la direction du E. S. Rappaport et Vespasien V. Pella. 186p. Paris, Sirey, 1929 6245

Conférence internationale pour la codification du droit pénal. II. Documents et résolutions. Etudes Crimin 3(3): 90-4 My '28 6246

Conférence internationale pour l'unification du droit pénal. III (1930). Actes, publiées par Simon Sancrable. 198p. Bruxelles, Office de publicité, 1931; summary: R de Dr Pén et de Crimin 10: 728-57 '30 6247

Congrès international de droit pénal. Bucarest, Octobre 1929. R de Dr Pén et de Crimin 9: 911-28 '29 6248

Congrès international de droit pénal. Bucarest, 6-11 Octobre 1929: voeux adoptés. R Int de Dr Pén 7: 2-14 '30 6249

Congrès international de droit pénal. [Rapports présentés au Congrès de Palerme]. R Int de Dr Pén 8: 296-457 '31 6250

Donnedieu de Vabres, H. Le 2e Congrès international de droit pénal. Etudes Crimin 4(12): 317-21 D '29 6251

Ferri, Enrico. La criminologia italiana nei Congressi internazionali di Bruxelles e di Vienna. Nuov Antol 251: 205-15 Ja 16 '27 6252

Ferri, Enrico. La criminologie italienne aux Congrès internationaux de Bruxelles et de Vienne; traduit de l'italien par L.-O. Roux. R Int de Dr Pén 4: 135-56 English transl (p156-76) '27 6253

Garofalo, Raffaele. La solidarietà delle nazioni nella lotta contro il delitto. Congressi internazionali per la unificazione del diritto penale. Nuov Antol s7 275 (1412): 139-45 Ja 16 '31 6254

Glaser, Stephan. La conférence de Rome: IIe Conférence internationale des représentants des commissions de codification pénale. Etudes Crimin 3(3): 87-90 My '28 6255

Kiefé, R. Notes sur le Congrès international de droit pénal de Bruxelles (Juillet 1926). R Pénitent et de Dr Pén 51: 237-61 My '27 6256

Laplaza, Francisco P. El Congreso internacional de derecho penal de Bucarest. R de Crimin, Psiquiat y Med Leg 17: 603-13 S '30 6257

Makowski, W. La conférence de Varsovie. Etudes Crimin 3: 1-2 Ja '28 6258

Mayer, H. Ordentliche Tagung der Deutschen Strafrechtlichen Gesellschaft am 30 und 31 März 1928. Gerichtssaal 97: 1-19 '28 6259

Neymark, Edward. Les 2me Congrès international de droit penal. R de Identif y Cienc Pen 4: 386-407 S '29 6260

Pascalis, R. Congrès national de droit pénal colonial, Paris, 20 et 30 septembre 1931. R de Dr Pén et de Crimin 11: 1065-74 '31 6261

Ramos, Juan P. Conferencias sobre el derecho penale (Conférences faites à l'Université de Rome du 10 au 23 janvier 1929). 117p. Buenos-Aires, Imp. de la Universidad, 1929 6262

R[oux], J.-A. Le IIe conférence internationale de codification pénale, Rome, 21-25 mai, 1928. R Int de Dr Pén 5: 248-52 '28 6263

R[oux], J.-A. La troisième conférence internationale d'unification du droit pénal. R Int de Dr Pén 7: 338-46 '30 6264

Sasserath, S. Groupe belge de l'Association. R Int de Dr Pén 5: 389-95 '28 6265
Union belge de droit pénal. List of members.

Sasserath, Simon. Union belge de droit pénal. R Int de Dr Pén 7: 335-7 '30 6266

Simon, Jules. Le Congrès de droit pénal de Carlsruhe. R de Dr Pén et de Crimin 10: 60-6 '30 6267

Statut du Bureau international pour l'unification du droit pénal. R Int de Dr Pén 6: 6-11 '29 6268

PSYCHOLOGY, PSYCHIATRY AND CRIMINAL LAW

Bohne. Die strafrechtliche Verwertbarkeit der Psychoanalyse. Deut Juristen-Zeit 32(13): 919-23 '27 6269

Bouman, K. H. De strafrechte, de psychiate en hun gemeenschappelijke taak. Mensch & Maatschappij 4 (1) '28 6270

Coenen, Hans. Strafrecht und Psychoanalyse. 96p. (Strafrechtl. Abh. hrsg. von Bennecke no261) Breslau, Schletter, 1929 6271

Glueck, Sheldon. Psychiatry and the criminal law. Va L R 14: 155-81 Ja '28; same title: Ment Hyg 12: 569-95 Jl '28 6272

Hellwig, Albert. Psychoanalyse und Strafrechtspflege. Jurist Rundsch 60(21): 1430-2 My 23 '31 6273

Henderson, D. K. Psychiatry and the criminal law. Psychiat Q 4: 103-17 Ja '30 6274

Juarros y Ortega, C. La psiquiatría en el nuevo código penal. Siglo Méd 83: 429-35 Mr 9 '29 6275

Morse, Wayne L. Contributions of psychology and psychiatry to the criminal law. Thesis (J.D.) Columbia university, 1931? 6276

Overholser, W[infred]. The place of psychiatry in the administration of criminal law. New England J Med 201: 479-84 '29 6277

Overholser, Winfred. What immediate practical contribution can psychiatry make to criminal law administration? Am B Assn Rep 55: 594-613 '30 6278

Psychiatry, psychiatrists and the law. Mass L Q 13: 28-34 Ag '28 6279

Schultze, E. Stellungnahme des Psychiaters zu dem Reichstagsentwurf eines Strafvollzugsgesetzes. Arch f Psychiat 82: 194-231 '27 6280

Staub, Hugo. Psychoanalyse und Strafrecht. Imago 17: 194-216 '31 6281

Strasser, Charlot. Psychiatrie und Strafrecht. 266p. Zürich, Polygraphischer Verl. 1927 6282

Terman, Lewis M. Psychology and the law. Los Angeles B Assn Bul 6: 142-3, 145-6, 148-51, 153 Ja 15 '31 6283

Vallejo Nágera, A. La psiquiatría en el código penal. Siglo Méd 83: 570-7 Ap 13 '29 6284

Vogelsang, Heinz. Psychologie und Strafvollzug. Monats f Kriminalpsychol u Strafrechtsref 22: 418-22 Jl '31 6285

NATURE AND ELEMENTS OF CRIME AND DEFENSES

CLASSIFICATION OF OFFENSES

Cincinnati. Bureau of governmental research. An analysis of 11,180 misdemeanor cases. 21p. (mim) (Rep no19) Cincinnati, January 1930. Summary. 11p. (Pam no6) December 1929 6286

Cincinnati. Bureau of municipal research. What happens to felony cases in Cincinnati? 15p. (Pam no5) Cincinnati, May 1928 6287

Cotter, John I. Why are drug peddlers not felons? Police J [N Y] 16: 12-13, 22 Je '29 6288

Davies, Audrey M. The uniform classification of offenses. Am B Assn J 17: 215-19 Ap '31 6289

Gehlke, C. E. Recorded felonies: an analysis and general survey. *In* Illinois association for criminal justice, Illinois crime survey, 31-103, 1929 6290

Is a summary offence a misdemeanor? Just Peace 92: 363 My 26 '28 6291

Lanier, Alexander S. Line of demarcation between felonies and misdemeanors as marked out by statute and the federal courts. Va L Reg ns12: 524-9 Ja '27 6292

Mere failures to report felony not a crime. U S L R 63: 621-2 D '29 6293

The petty offense category and trial by jury. Yale L J 40: 1303-9 Je '31 6294

United States. Congress. House. Committee on judiciary. Defining petty offenses and providing penalties therefor, report to accompany H. R. 10341. Washington, 1930 (71st Cong. 2d sess. H. Rep.1699) 6295

Winfield, Percy H. Nuisance as a tort. Cambridge L J 4: 189-206 '31 6296

EXTRATERRITORIALITY

Buzea, N. Règle de droit pénal et des applications extraterritoriales (contribution à l'éclaircissement de la notion du droit international pénal). R Int de Dr Pén 8: 126-46 '31 6297

Keeton, George William. The development of extraterritoriality in China. 2v. bibliog 399-402 N.Y. Longmans, 1928 6298

Lawson, Eric. Extra-territoriality as viewed by a police officer. Police J [London] 3: 40-9 Ja '30 6299

Lehmann, Helmuth. Exterritorialität und Strafverfolgung. Krimin Monatsh 2: 101-4 My '28 6300

CRIMINAL INTENT

Absence of motive. Just Peace 91: 561-2 Jl 23 '27 6301

Angioni, M. La volontarietà del fatto nei reati. 220p. Torino, Bocca, 1928 6302

Barnes, John Winthrop. The elimination of act and intent as elements of crime. 62p. Thesis, University of Southern California, 1929 6303

Crimes involving moral turpitude. Harv L R 43: 117-21 N '29 6304

Criminal intent. L Notes 29: 223 Mr '28 6305

Dost. Die Motive zur Eisenbahn-Transportgefährdung. Krimin Monatsh 5: 193-8 S '31 6306

Fulci, Lodovici. L'intenzione nei singoli reati. 2v. 316, 258p. Messina, Ed. La Sicilia, 1927 6307

Gatti, T[ancredi]. I moventi del reato nella scienza del diritto penale. Preliminari a un indirizzo bio-psicologico. 44p. Ferrara, Ugo Grossi, 1927 6308

Hitchler, Walter Harrison. Motive as an essential element of crime. Dickinson L R 35: 105-18 Mr '31 6309

Hosenfeld, Leo G. Criminal intent generally and as applied to crimes mala in se and crimes mala prohibita. St John's L R 6: 137-42 D '31 6310

Klee, K. Vorsatz und Triebhaftigkeit der Handlung. Zeitsch f d ges Strafrechtswiss 48: 1-10 '28 6311

Koch, Erich. Die unbeabsichtigte schwere Körper-Verletzung im geltenden Recht und nach den Reformvorschlägen. 63p. bibliog. Diss. Universität zu Erlangen, 1930. Kulmbach, G. Schuhmann, 1931 6312

Meagher, J. F. W. Question of premeditation; case of Caruso, murderer of Doctor Pendola. Long Island M J 21: 517-26 S '27 6313

Moral turpitude and the eighteenth amendment. Ia L R 17: 76-81 N '31 6314

Motives. Sol J 72: 145 Mr 3 '28 6315

Ploscowe, Friedrich. An examination of some dispositions relating to motives and character in modern European penal codes. J Crim L & Crimin 21: 26-40 My '30 6316

Shepherd, William G. What's moral turpitude? Collier's 87: 20-1 My 9 '31 6317

Vocke, G. Vorsatz und Fahrlässigkeit vom psychologischen Gesichtspunkt. Zeitsch f d ges Strafrechtswiss 48: 269-90 '28 6318

Weihofen, Henry. Partial insanity and criminal intent. Ill L R 24: 505-27 Ja '30; same title: Med-Leg J 47: 87-104 My '30 6319

PREMEDITATION

Costa, Stefano. Contributo alla dottrina della premeditazione. Scuola Pos ns8: 124-33 Mr '28 6320

Engisch, Karl. Untersuchungen über Vorsatz und Fahrlässigkeit im Strafrecht. 493p. Berlin, Otto Liebmann, 1930 6321

Gaitan, Jorge Eliecer. Criterio positivo della premeditazione. Scuola Pos ns8: 212-29 My '28 6322

Manci, Filippo. Note sulla premeditazione. Scuola Pos ns11: 291-306 Jl '31 6323

Rocco, Amedeo. Esame critico della premeditazione. ed.2. 103p. Lanciano, G. Carabba, 1927 6324

CRIMINAL ATTEMPT

Alimena, F. La questione dei mezzi inidonei nel tentativo (Contributo alla teoria del conato criminoso). 163p. Roma, Società editrice del Foro ital. 1930 6325

Arnold, Thurman W. Criminal attempts—the rise and fall of an abstraction. Yale L J 40: 53-80 N '30 6326

Curran, John W. Criminal and non-criminal attempts. Geo L J 19: 185-202 Ja '31 6327

Kadecka, Ferdinand. Versuch einer Revision des Versuchsbegriffes. (Eine Untersuchung de lege ferenda). Monats f Kriminalpsychol u Strafrechtsref 20: 129-41 Mr '29 6328

Rittler, Theodor. Zu Kadeckas Versuch einer Revision des Versuchsbegriffes. Monats f Kriminalpsychol u Strafrechtsref 19: 520-6 '28 6329

Sayre, F[rancis] B[owes]. Criminal attempts. Harv L R 41: 821-59 My '28; same title: Crim L J India 29 pt1: 59-65 Jl '28 6330

Strahorn, John S. jr. Effect of impossibility on criminal attempts. Univ Pa L R 78: 962-98 Je '30 6331

ACT

Allen, Carleton Kemp. The nature of a crime. J Comp Leg 13: 1-25 F '31 6332

Antolisei, Francesco. L'azione e l'evento nel reato. 148p. Milano, Spoleto, 1928 6333

Augioni, M. Le circonstanze del reato aggravanti e attenuanti communi. Studi Econ e Giurid, Univ Cagliari 16: 177-234 '28 6334

Batchelor, Chester A. Corpus delicti. Northwest Police J 6: 12-13 F '29 6335

Battaglini, Giulio. Il luogo e il tempo del commesso reato. Riv Ital di Dir Pen (11): 805-10 '29 6336

Besson, André. Le délit impossible. R Crit de Lég et de Juris 49: 332- '29; extract: 42p. Paris, Libr. gén. de droit et jurisprudence, 1929 6337

Bretschneider and Raestrup. Auf frischer Tat ertappt. Arch f Krim 83: 234-41 N '28 6338

Delitala, Giacomo. In tema de reato continuato. Riv Ital di Dir Pen (2): 192-204 '29 6339

Delphino, Aldo. Il mezzo e le modalità dell'azione criminosa. Scuola Pos 9: 138-54 Mr '29 6340

Freudenthal, Berthold. Vom Werte des allgemeinen Verbrechenstatbestandes. Zeitsch f d ges Strafrechtswiss 48: 290-300 '28 6341

Gregoraci, Giuseppe. Del reato continuato e del concorso di reati. *In* Scritti in onore di Enrico Ferri per il cinquantesimo anno di suo insegnamento universitario, 229-38. Torino, "Sociale Torinese," 1928 6342

His, Rudolph. Geschichte des deutschen Strafrechts bis zum Karolina. 188p. Berlin, R. Oldenbourg, 1929 6343

Honig, Richard. Straflose Vor- und Nachtat. 116p. Leipzig, Deichert, 1927 6344

Marsich, P. Gli elementi costitutivi e i presupposti del reato. Riv Pen di Dott, Legis e Giuris 195: 105-21 F '27 6345

Nagler, J. Das Verbrechen der Menge. Gerichtssaal 95: 157-218 '27 6346

Ranieri, Silvio. L'azione penale. Contributo alla teoria dell'azione nel diritto processuale penale. 156p. Milano, Ist. Ed. Scient. 1928 6347
"Indice degli autori" [155]-6.

[Ranieri], Silvio. Gli aspetti del reato: il reato come azione. Riv Pen di Dott, Legis e Giuris 105: 404-22, 502-11 My, Je '27 6348

Ranieri, Silvio. Gli aspetti del reato: reato come azione colpevole. Riv Pen di Dott, Legis e Giuris (4-5): 305-21 '29 6349

Vannini, O. Il concetto del reato nel progetto preliminare del nuovo codice penale. Studi Senesi 1928: 331-6 6350

Del Vecchio, Giuseppe. Il soggetto attivo e passivo del reato nel diritto e nella procedura. 233p. Milano, Ettore Sormani, 1929 6351

Viotti, Manuel. Dos crimes justificaveis. R de Identif y Cienc Pen 6: 408-17 S '30 6352

GUILT

Abraham, Hans Fritz. Friedrich Nietzsches Bedeutung für die Rechtsentwicklung der Gegenwart, Schuld und Strafe. Jurist Rundsch (5): 57-61; (6): 74-8 '28 6353

Allegra, Giuliano. Il problema della "modificabilità dell'accusa" secondo de leggi del giudizio razionale. Riv Pen di Dott, Legis e Giuris (7-8): 33-40 '29 6354

Berg, Otto. Der gegenwärtige Stand der Schuldlehre im Strafrecht. 89p. (Strafrechtl Abh no220) Breslau, Schletter, 1927 6355

Dohna, Graf zu. Rechtswidrigkeit und Schuld nach der Reichstagsvorlage. Leipz Zeitsch f Deut Recht 21: 978-84 '27 6356

Harboe, N[icolai]. Les conditions subjectives de la culpabilité. 147p. Oslo, I. Kommission Hos Jacob Dybwad, 1930 6357

Hirschberg. Die Lüge als Schuldbeweis. Monats f Kriminalpsychol u Strafrechtsref 20: 337-43 '29 6358

Hirschberg, Rudolf. Schuldbegriff und adäquate Kausalität, eine Untersuchung über das Zurechnungsproblem. 112p. Breslau, Schletter, 1928 6359

Kaufmann, Felix. Die philosophischen Grundprobleme der Lehre von der Strafrechtsschuld. 138p. (Wiener Staats- u. Rechts-wissenschaftliche Studien v11) Leipzig, Deuticke, 1929 6360

Köhler, A. Die Schuld als Grundlage des Strafrechts. Gerichtssaal 95: 433-68 '27; 96-188 '28 6361

Land, Erich. System der äusseren Strafbarkeitsbedingungen. Ein Beitrag zur Lehre von Tatbestand. 81p. bibliog [vii]-ix (Strafrechtl Abh no229) Breslau, Schletter, 1927 6362

Lorenz, Max. Die dreiteilung der Schuldformen und ihre Auswertung in den tschechoslowakischen Strafgesetzvorentwürfen von 1926. 177p. Prag, H. Mercy, 1930 6363

Mahrer, Herbert, Die Bedingungen der Strafbarkeit. 57p. Diss. Universität zu Breslau, 1930. bibliog vii-viii 6364
Marcuse, M. Schuld und Zurechnungsfähigkeit. Zeitsch f Sexualwissensch 14: 428-30 F '28 6365
Neukötter, Heinrich. Die Strafbarkeit des Konkubinats. 61p. (Strafrechtl Abh no273) Breslau, Schletter, 1930 6366
Radbruch, Gustav. Zur Psychologie der strafrechtlichen Schuldformen. Monats f Kriminalpsychol u Strafrechtsref 19: 296-300 My '28 6367
Schaffstein, Friedrich. Die Behandlung der Schuldarten im ausländischen Strafrecht seit 1908. 73p. (Strafrechtl Abh no 232) Breslau, Schletter, 1928 6368
Stienen. Über Schuld und Strafgesetz. Monats f Kriminalpsychol u Strafrechtsref 18: 337-57 Jl '27 6369
Tzortzopulos, C. Die Schuld und ihre Arten. Gerichtssaal 97: 227-34 '28 6370
Vannini, O. Sul concetto unitario di colpevolezza. Studi Senesi 1927: 222-5 6371
Wolf, Erik. Strafrechtliche Schuldlehre. I: Die gegenwärtige Lage der theoretischen Voraussetzungen und der methodologischen Struktur der strafrechtlichen Schuldlehre. 179p. Mannheim, J. Bensheimer, 1928 6372
Zeidler, Carl F. Guilty or not guilty? Marquette L R 15: 164-7 Ap '31 6373

DEFENSES

Alternative defenses. Just Peace 92: 286 Ap 28 '28 6374
Burgardt, Lothar. Die Verteidigung im Entwurf einer Strafprozessordnung im Vergleich zum neuen italienischen Recht. 56p. bibliog vii-viii. Diss. Universität zu Erlangen, 1931. Leipzig, Robert Noske, 1931 6375
Defences good and bad. Sol J 72: 476 Jl 14 '28 6376
Diaz, Emilio C. Exceso en la defensa. R de Derecho Pen 1(1) Ap 30 '29 6377
Duty to retreat and self-defence. Just Peace 91: 860 N 12 '27 6378
Glaser, Stefan. "Ignorantia juris" dans le droit pénal. R de Dr Pén et de Crimin 11: 133-9 F '31 6379
Glaser, Stefan. Ignorantia juris w pravic karnem (ignorantia juris dans le droit pénal). 48p. Krakowie, Iklad Glówny W Księgarui Léona Frommera, 1931 6380
In Polish, with résumé in French.
Heimberger. Die Notwehr im Strafgesetzentwurf von 1927. Deut Juristen-Zeit 32: 1378-81 '27 6381
Hewitt, Harrison. A note on the defense of persons guilty of crime. Conn B J 1: 139-45 Ap '27 6382
Hilton, O. N. Pre-natal influence as a defense. Case & Com 33: 136-7 N '27 6383
Hitchler, W[alter] H[arrison]. Necessity as a defence in criminal cases. Dickinson L R 33: 138-49 Mr '29 6384
"Ignorantia juris non excusat." Sol J 71: 613-14 Jl 30 '27 6385
Medical defences. Just Peace 93: 458 Jl 20 '29 6386
Paoli, G[iulio]. Sulla legittima difesa. La fuga. Riv Pen di Dott, Legis e Giuris 105: 295-321 Ap '27 6387
Ray, Roy Robert. Truth: a defense to libel. Minn L R 16: 43-69 D '31 6388
Rosenthal, Alfred. Notwehr und der Geist des neuen Strafrechts. Deut Juristen-Zeit 33: 146-50 '28 6389
Schmidt. Der Begriff der "Notwehr" im Strafgesetzentwurf von 1927. Polizeipraxis, 123-4 '28 6390
Self-defense. Sol J 74: 98 F 15 '30 6391
Yankwich, Leon R. Defenses in the law of libel. Los Angeles B Assn Bul 2: 5-8 Je 2 '27 6392

CRIMINAL RESPONSIBILITY

Alsberg, Max. Die verminderte Zurechnungsfähigkeit. Krimin Monatsh 3: 221-2 O '29 6393
Altavilla, E. Imputabilità penale e capacità civile. Pensiero Giurid-Pen 2: 97- '30 6394
Aschaffenburg, Gustav. Erfolgshaftung und Versuchsstrafe. Monats f Kriminalpsychol u Strafrechtsref 18: 502-13 S '27 6395
Azzalini, Mario. Responsabilità morale e reattivita sociale. Scuola Pos 139:51 Mr '31 6396
Badr, Aziz. L'influence du consentement de la victime sur la responsabilité pénale. 304p. Paris, Libr. Gén. et Dr. et de Juris. 1928 6397
Battaglini, Giulio. Responsabilità penale delle persone giuridiche? Riv Ital di Dir Pen 2: 661-71 Ag '30; same: Responsabilité pénale des personnes juridiques? R Int de Dr Pén 7: 347-58 '30 6398
Belloni, Giulio-Andrea. La responsabilité légale dans l'évolution du droit pénal italien. Etudes Crimin 4: 270-3 S '29 6399
Bernhard, H. Beitrag zur Frage der Haftunfähigkeit. Aerztl Sachverst-Zeit 34: 97 Ap 1 '28 6400
Bosch, R. El examen médicolegal de los criminales antes de la condena para establecer su grado de imputabilidad. Conf Latino Am de Neurol, Psiquiat y Med Leg Actas 2: 215-22 '29 6401
Brasiello, Teucro. I limiti della responsabilità per danni. 250p. Napoli, Morano, 1927 6402
Brassaud, P. A. La solidarité légale en droit pénal. Interprétation et application de l'art. 55 du code pénal. 108p. Paris, Sirey, 1927 6403
Brennan, Daniel J. Weighing responsibility. Nat Prob Assn Proc 1930: 239-44 6404

Bruni, Alessandro. La responsabilità penale nella scienza. 58p. Tivoli, Mantero, 1927 6405

Ceillier, A. La responsabilité pénale des épileptiques et leur assistance. Ann de Méd Lég 9: 338-97 Je '29 6406

Cicala, Salvatore. De la responsabilité pénale des personnes juridiques, au point de vue du droit pénal interne. R Int de Dr Pén 6: 260-74 '29 6407

Cicala, Salvatore. Sulla responsabilità penale delle persone giuridiche dal punto di vista punitivo interno. Rassegna Pen (7-8): 628-38 '29 6408

Cohin, Marco R. L'abstention fautive en droit civil et pénal. (Etude sur la responsabilité). 308p. Paris, Sirey, 1929 6409

Compulsion and coercion. Sol J 71: 7-8 Ja 1 '27 6410

Criminal liability in legal history. L Times 163: 78-80 Ja 22 '27; L Notes 31: 32-5 My '27 6411

Delbez, Louis. La responsabilité internationale pour crime commis sur le territoire d'un état et dirigés contre la sureté d'un état étranger. R Gén de Dr Int Pub 37: 461-75 Jl '30 6412

Dumas, Jacques. De la responsabilité internationale des états à raison de crimes ou de délits, commis sur leurs territoires au préjudice d'étrangers. R Int de Dr Pén 6: 109-218 '29; translation: International responsibility of states by reason of offenses committed on their territory against aliens, by M. A. Caloyanni. R Int de Dr Pén 7: 359-74 '30 6413

Dumas, Jacques. De la responsabilité internationale des états à raison de crimes ou de delits commis sur leur territoire, au préjudice d'étrangers. 462p. Paris, Sirey, 1930 6414

Eccentric criminals. Sol J 73: 458 Jl 13 '29 6415

Edgerton, Henry W. Corporate criminal responsibility. Yale L J 36: 827-44 Ap '27 6416

Estabrooks, G. H. Moral responsibility in the light of certain psychological facts. Ment Hyg 12: 768-71 O '28 6417

Ettinger, Mieczyslaw. Responsabilité pénale des personnes morales. R Int de Dr Pén 6: 274-86 '29 6418

The extension of criminal liability. Sol J 72: 702-3 O 20 '28 6419

Farrar, C. B. Criteria of responsibility. Am Pris Assn Proc 59: 343-9 '29; same title: J Crim L & Crimin 21: 438-45 N '30 6420

Ferri, E[nrico]. Il principio di responsabilità legale nel nuovo codice penale Russo (1927) e nel progetto per Cuba (1926). Scuola Pos ns7: 385-400 S '27 6421

Ferri, Enrico. Le principe de responsabilité légale dans le nouveau code pénal russe (1927) et dans le projet de code pénal pour Cuba (1926). R Int de Dr Pén 5: 34-49; English transl by R. Geoffrey-Fitz-Gerald (p50-67) '28 6422

Garraud, P[ierre]. Le régime pénal des sociétés à responsabilité limitée. 16p. Paris, Godde, 1928 6423

Giaquinto, Adolfo. Risponsabilità degli enti per le contravvenzioni dei rappresentanti e dipendenti. Riv di Dir Pub Ammin in Italia 23: 117-26 Mr '31 6424
Articles 196 and 197 of Italian penal code contain norms of civil responsibility for indirect and subsidiary delicts.

Gordon, A. Morbid impulse, criminal act and mental responsibility. M Times [N Y] 58: 354-6 D '30 6425

Green, Leon. Rationale of proximate cause. 216p. Kansas City, Vernon, 1927 6426

Gregoraci, G. La circolare del ministro Rocco ed il problema della imputabilità nei reati passionali. Scuola Pos 10: 353-9 Ag '30; separate: 10p. Milano, Vallardi, 1930 6427

Grünewald, Max. Sind tödlich Verletzte noch handlungsfähig? Monats f Kriminalpsychol u Strafrechtsref 19: 540-4 S '28 6428

Gunsburg, Niko and Mommaert, Raymond. La responsabilité pénale des personnes morales privées. R Int de Dr Pén 6: 219-33 '29; same title: R de Dr Pén et de Crimin 9: 647-60 '29 6429

Haferland, Fritz. Die strafrechtliche Verantwortlichkeit des Verteidigers. Eine forensische Studie. 102p. Berlin, Pulvermacher, 1929 6430

Herschmann, H. Forensisch-Kriminalistisches. Wien med Wchnschr 77: 249-52 F 19 '27 6431

Hickson, William J. The criminal in everyday life. Med-Leg J 45: 183-7 N '28 6432
Reprint from Good Health Magazine, September 1928.

Junckerstorff, K. Das Problem der Ursachenanalyse bei der Beeinträchtigung der Zurechnungsfähigkeit im kommenden Strafrecht. Monats f Kriminalpsychol u Strafrechtsref 19: 98-100 F '28 6433

Kadečka, Ferdinand. Verkappte Zufallshaftung. Monats f Kriminalpsychol u Strafrechtsref 22: 65-78 F '31 6434

Kantorowicz, Manfred. Unechtes Unterlassungs- und unbewusstes Fahrlässigkeitsdelikt. 54p. (Strafrechtl Abh no297) Breslau, Schletter, 1931 6435

Kimura, K. Keÿi sekinin ni kansuru kihanshugi no hihan. Hogaku-Shirin 30: 79-97 S '28 6436

Kjerschow. Opportunitetsprincipet og dets anvendelse saerlig i norsk strafferetspleie. Nord Tids f Straf 16: 123-55 Ap '28 6437

Lee, Frederic P. Corporate criminal liability. Colum L R 28: 1-28, 181-200 Ja, F '28 6438

Lomberg, Robert. Die Lehre von der verminderten Zurechnungsfähigkeit. 156p. Diss. Göttingen. Bremen, 1930 6439

Longhi, Silvio. Problem di responsabilità criminale. Rassegna Pen (11-12): 1025-6 '29 6440

Longhi, Silvio. Responsabilité pénale des personnes juridiques. R Int de Dr Pén 6: 246-59 '29 6441

Maguire, John MacArthur and Epstein, Charles S. S. Rules of evidence in preliminary controversies as to responsibility. Yale L J 36: 1101-25 Je '27 6442

Martinez, José Augustin. La responsabilité pénale des personnes morales. R Int de Dr Pén 6: 234-9 '29 6443

Mercier, Charles. Criminal responsibility. 256p. N.Y. Physicians & Surgeons bk. co. 1927 6444

Miller, Justin and Dean, Gordon. Civil and criminal liability of physicians for sterilization operations. Med-Leg J 47: 120-4 S '30 6445

Miller, Justin and Dean, Gordon. Liability of physicians for sterilization operations. Am B Assn J 16: 158-61 Mr '30 6446

Monakow, C. v. Recht, Verbrechen und Zurechnungsfähigkeit in biologischer Beleuchtung. Schweiz Arch f Neurol u Psychiat 22: 181-226 '28 6447

Paoli, Giulio. La imputabilità difronte alla responsabilità nel nuovo codice penale. Riv Ital di Dir Pen 3: 44-51 Ja '31 6448

Patricolo, Maio G. Imputabilità penale e responsabilità morale. 191p. Roma, Laziale A. Marchesi, 1929? 6449

Petrén, A. Importance of new legislation for treatment of so-called diminished responsibility in criminals. Upsala Läkaref Förh 33: 413-97 Ap 2 '28 6450

Piacentini, Mario. Per una più efficace repressione e prevenzione della delinquenza, occorre diminuire il coefficiente della impunità. *In* Scritti in onore di Enrico Ferri per il cinquantesimo anno di suo insegnamento universitario, 365-71. Torino, "Sociale Torinese," 1928 6451

Ploscowe, Morris. La responsabilité pénale des personnes morales dans la jurisprudence Anglo-Américaine. Etudes Crimin 4: 48-53 F '29; same title: R de Dr Pén et de Crimin 9: 424-31 '29 6452

Porot, A. La responsabilité pénale des sourds-muets. J de Neurol et de Psychiat 30: 796-8 '30 6453

Porro, Augusto. I limiti della responsabilità per danni. Monitore dei Tribunali [Milano] (2): 80 '29 6454

Radulesco, Jean. La responsabilité pénale des personnes morales. R Int de Dr Pén 6: 286-306 '29 6455

Richmond, Frank C. Why justice sometimes miscarries. Med-Leg J 45: 69-73 My '28 6456

Roeder, H. Das Problem der strafrechtlichen Zurechnung bei Massenverbrechen. Gerichts-Zeit 79: 193-7 '28 6457

Rojas, N. Responsabilidad médica. R Arg de Neurol, Psiquiat y Med Leg 1: 259-66 My '27 6458

Roux, J.-A. La responsabilité pénale des personnes morales. R Int de Dr Pén 6: 239-46 '29 6459

Royo Villanova y Morales, Ricardo. La responsabilidad médica y el nuevo código penal. 205p. Madrid, Morata, 1930 6460

Ryckere, R. de. De la responsabilité pénale et civile du pilote. R de Dr Pén et de Crimin 7: 855-82 Ag '27 6461

Saldaña[y Garcia Rubio], Quintiliano. Capacidad criminal de las personas sociales. 143p. Madrid, Reus, 1928 6462

Sayre, Francis Bowes. Criminal responsibility for the acts of another. Harv L R 43: 689-723 Mr '30 6463

Schneider, K. Charakterfehler und ihre Beziehungen zur geminderten Zurechnungsfähigkeit. Allg Zeitsch f Psychiat 92: 513-15 '29 6464

Somnambulism and crime. Just Peace 93: 765-6 D 7 '29 6465

Stebbins, A. K. Legal responsibility for criminal acts. Univ Pa L R 76: 704-18 Ap '28 6466

Taussig, L. Le problème de la responsabilité pénale au point de vue médicale dans l'avant-project du code pénale tchécoslovaque. R Int de Dr Pén 7: 380-2 '30 6467

Tejera y Garcia, Diego Vicente. Las circunstancias agravantes y las ideas modernas. 23p. Habana, Talleres Graficos de Cuba Intelectual, 1927 6468

Thilo, E. De la réparation du tort moral en cas de faute concomitante de la victime. Schweiz Juristen-Zeit 24: 309-12 '28 6469

Traeger, L. Die Einwilligung des Verletzten und andere Unrechtausschliessungsgründe im zukünftigen Strafgesetz. Gerichtssaal 44: 112-76 '27 6470

Trasimeni, Roberto. Capisaldi della dottrina penale (meditazioni ed appunti). 220p. Spoleto, Panetto e Petrelli, 1927 6471

Über die Strafbarkeit der Sportverletzung. Monats f Kriminalpsychol u Strafrechtsref 22: 481-8 Ag '31 6472

Valenzuela Matte, A. De la responsabilidad civil del delito y del cuasidelito. 84p. Santiago, Imp. A. Prat, 1927 6473

Valeur, Robert. La responsabilité pénale des personnes morales dans les droits français et anglo-américains. 256p. Paris, Giard, 1931? 6474

Viotti, Manuel. Le délit et les passions. Quelques notes légères sur la question de "l'irresponsabilité" des criminels passionnés. R Int de Crimin 3(3): 181-7 '31 6475

Waller, Willard. A deterministic view of criminal responsibility. J Crim L & Crimin 20: 88-101 My '29 6476

Weber, C. O. Pseudo-science and the problem of criminal responsibility. J Crim L & Crimin 19: 181-95 Ag '28 6477

Weimann, Waldemar. Zur Frage der Handlungsfähigkeit Kopfverletzter. Arch f Krim 82: 178-80 '28 6478

Wiewiorska, Helene. La responsabilité pénale des personnes morales. R Polon de Leg Civile et Crim 2: 57- '30 6479

Wilson, Edward E. The responsibility for crime. Opportunity 7: 95-7 Mr '29 6480

Winn, C. R. N. The criminal responsibility of corporations. Cambridge L J 3(3): 298-317 '29 6481

Woods, Anderson. An utilitarian test for criminal responsibility. J Crim L & Crimin 18: 191-6 Ag '28 6482

Woodward, James W. Psychological aspects of the question of moral responsibility. J Crim L & Crimin 21: 267-96 Ag '30 6483

NEGLIGENCE

B[urke], H[yle] G. Violation of statute or ordinance—negligence per se or evidence of negligence? Nebraska rule. Neb L Bul 9: 448-53 My '31 6484

Graf, Ludwig. Die Bestrafung der Fahrlässigkeit (nach dem Entwurf eines Allgemeinen Deutschen Strafgesetzbuchs von 1927). 84p. bibliog 82-3. Inaug.-diss. Universität zu Erlangen, 1931. München, Max Schick, 1931 6485

Green, Leon. Contributory negligence and proximate cause. N C L R 6: 3-33 D '27 6486

Levy, N. Peculiarities of negligence and criminal law practice. Panel 5: 1-2 N '27 6487

Mohrmann, Gottlieb. Die neueren Ansichten über das Wesen der Fahrlässigkeit im Strafrecht. 86p. (Strafrechtl Abh no265) Breslau, Schletter, 1929 6488

Schmidt, H. Festellung der Verantwortlichkeit bei Fahrlässigkeitsdelikten. Prager Juris Zeitsch 8: 65-76 '28 6489

Schwarz, Wilhelm. Die Kausalität bei den sogenannten Begehungsdelikten durch Unterlassung. 115p. (Strafrechtl Abh no254) Breslau, Schletter, 1929 6490

Seavey, Warren A. Negligence—subjective or objective? Harv L R 41: 1-28 N '27 6491

ALCOHOLISM

Eliasberg, W. Bemerkungen zur forensischen Begutachtung von Alkoholdelikten. München med Wchnschr 77: 2221 D 26 '30 6492

Falsen, C. Straffansvar for beruselse og for handlinger foretatt i drukkenskap. Nord Tids f Straf 15: 107-21 Ap '27 6493

Llewellyn-Jones, F. Drunkenness and civil and criminal responsibility. Just Peace 92: 89 F 4 '28; L Times 165: 108-9 F 4 '28; Sol J 72: 104 F 11 '28 6494

Moll, A. Sexualverbrechen und Trunksucht. Med Welt 3: 21 Ja 5 '29 6495

HYPNOTISM

Blum, E. Hypnose im Strafverfahren. Allg Zeitsch f Psychiat 89: 241-63 N 30 '28 6496

Feisenberger; [Vorkastner], and Lange. Hypnotismus und Verbrechen. Monats f Kriminalpsychol u Strafrechtsref 21: 349-55 Je '30 6497

Goldmann, Otto. Selbstmord infolge Hypnose. Arch f Krim 86: 81-6 Ap '30 6498

Hartenstein, Horst. Verbrechen durch Hypnose. R Int de Crimin 2(5): 357-62 '30 6499

Heyer, G. R. Hypnose und Notzucht. Zeitsch f Sexualwissensch 15 (1): 1-8 Ap '28 6500

Die Hypnose als Mittel zur Aufklärung strafbarer Handlungen. Arch f Krim 87: 262-5 '30 6501

Ivers, Hellmut. Die Hypnose im deutschen Strafrecht. 108p. (Krimin Abh no3) Leipzig, Wiegandt, 1927 6502

John, K. Zum Problem "Hypnose und Verbrechen." Deut Zeitsch f d ges gerichtl Med 9: 603-17 Ap '27 6503

Lucas, Werner. Der Hypnotismus in seinen Beziehungen zum deutschen Strafrecht und Strafprozess. 97p. Berlin, Dümmler, 1930 6504

Meyer-Estorf. Verbrechen in Hypnose? Deut Zeitsch f d ges gerichtl Med 11: 295-300 '28 6505

Moll, Albert. Hypnose und Verbrechen. Krimin Probl 2(2): 17-36 Mr '28 6506

Mord und Abtreibung durch Hypnose. Arch f Krim 87: 255-6 '30 6507

Schlieper, H. Ist Notzucht mittels Suggestion oder Hypnose möglich. Krimin Monatsh 3: 244-6 N '29 6508

Selbstmord und Verbrechen infolge Hypnose? Arch f Krim 87: 254-5 '30 6509

Speer, E. Hypnose verbrechen. Allg ärztl Zeitsch f Psychotherap 1: 329-37 '28 6510

Verbrechen durch Hypnotisierte? Arch f Krim 87: 259-60 '30 6511

Young, Paul Campbell. A general review of the literature on hypnotism. Psychol Bul 24: 540-60 '27 6512

MENTAL ABNORMALITY

Abril, A. M. Importancia medico-legal de la paranoia. Crón Méd-Quir de la Habana 57: 229-33 Je '31 6513

Battaglini, G. Sull'azione civile per risarcimento di danno contro l'imputato assolto per totale infermità di mente. 10p. Milano, "Vita e Pensiero," n.d. 6514

B[ean], A[rthur] W. Mental deficiency as reducing the degree of the offense. Univ Pa L R 79: 209-13 D '30 6515

Boos, Wolfgang. Die strafrechtliche Behandlung der vermindert Zurechnungsfähigen nach den Entwürfen zu einem deutschen Strafgesetzbuch. 63p. bibliog [iv-xiv] Inaug.-diss. Freiburg i Br. 1931 6516

Bumke, Oswald. Lehrbuch der Geisteskrankheiten. 806p. ed.3. München, J. F. Bergmann, 1929 6517
Der Geisteskranke im Strafrecht, 179-84.

Eliot, Thomas Dawes. Mental disorder and the criminal law. Welf Mag 18: 703-10 My '27 6518

Flesch, Max. Sind Psychopathen zurechnungsfähig? (Eine Frage zum Mordprozess Hopp). Monats f Kriminalpsychol u Strafrechtsref 20: 732-4 D '29 6519

Garofalo, Raffaele. La irresponsabilità per vizio di mente sul nuovo codice penale. 8p. Napoli, San Giovanni, 1931 6520

Griffin, W. R. Criminal responsibility of the mentally deficient. S M J 20: 918-23 D '27 6521

Herschmann, Heinrich. Über die sog. verminderte Zurechnungsfähigkeit (v.Zfgkt) und die sichernden Massnahmen in den deutschen und österreichischen Strafgesetzentwürfen vom Jahre 1927. Arch f Psychiat 82 (3): 331-8 '27 6522

Herzog, Alfred W. Should mental or physical age rule as to criminal responsibility. Med-Leg J 46: 98-100 S '29 6523

Jolly, Ph. Das neue spanische Strafgesetzbuch vom Standpunkt des Psychiaters. Arch f Psychiat 88(1): 98-113 Ag 1 '29 6524

Lautier, J. Délire et responsabilité pénale. Ann Méd-Psychol 86: 409-14 '28 6525

Luxenburger, Hans. Die sogenannte verminderte Zurechnungsfähigkeit. Monats f Kriminalpsychol u Strafrechtsref 19: 304-13 My '28 6526

Luxenburger, H[ans]. Verminderte Zurechnungsfähigkeit oder Zurechnungsfähigkeit mit minderer Schuld? Psychiatneurol Wchnschr 30: 507-12 '28 6527

McCarty, Dwight G. Mental defectives and the criminal law. Ia L R 14: 401-19 Je '29; same title: Comm L Leag J 35: 671-9 N '30; reprint: 12p. Chicago, Municipal Reference Library, 1930 6528

Mezger, E. Vermindert Zurechnungsfähige und Gewohnheitsverbrecher. Gerichtssaal 96: 69-90 '28 6529

Mezger, Edmund. Psychoanalyse und strafrechtliche Schuld. Schweiz Zeitsch f Strafr 44: 185-93 '30 6530

Moser, Kurt. Zur strafrechtlichen Beurteilung der chronischen epidemischen encephalitis (Economo). Arch f Psychiat 91(5): 741-9 '30 6531

Overbeck, A. von. Zur Frage der verminderten Zurechnungsfähigkeit. Schweiz Zeitsch f Strafr 40: 49-57 '27 6532

Overholser, Winfred. Massachusetts statute for ascertaining the mental condition of persons coming before the courts of the Commonwealth, in the light of recent decisions. Mass L Q 16: 26-34 My '31 6533

Pound, Roscoe. Science and legal procedure. Am J Psychiat ns8: 33-51 Jl '28 6534

Raecke. Die verminderte Zurechnungsfähigkeit. Monats f Kriminalpsychol u Strafrechtsref 19: 300-4 My '28 6535

[Raw, Nathan]. Medico-legal problems of lunacy. L Times 165: 106-7 F 4 '28; L J [London]ns65: 123-4 F 11 '28 6536

Richmond, Frank C. The criminal feebleminded. Med-Leg J 48: 10-21 Ja '31 6537

Riese, Walther and Rothbarth, Otto. Zur Rechtsprechung des Reichsgerichts in der Frage der Zurechnungsfähigkeit. Monats f Kriminalpsychol u Strafrechtsref 22: 730-4 '31 6538

Stertz, G. Encephalitische Wesensveränderung und Mord. Gutachten über die Zurechnungsfähigkeit. Monats f Kriminalpsychol u Strafrechtsref 22: 320-32 '31 6539

Sträussler, E. Haftpsychosen, Simulation, Hysterie. Wien med Wchnschr 80: 329-34 Mr 1 '30 6540

Trossarelli, A. L'alienista revisore di perizia individuale nella procedura vigente e nel progetto Rocco pel nuovo codice di procedura penale. Rassegna di Studi Psichiat 18: 737-54 N '29 6541

Vervaeck, L.; Laignel-Lavastine, and others. La responsabilité pénale des épileptiques. Ann de Méd Lég 10: 1-24 Ja '30 6542

Wilmanns. Verminderte Zurechnungsfähigkeit. Allg Zeitsch f Psychiat 92: 518-25 '29 6543

Wilmanns and Alsberg. Die verminderte Zurechnungsfähigkeit. Monats f Kriminalpsychol u Strafrechtsref 19: 293-6 My '28 6544

Wilmanns, Karl. Die sogenannte verminderte Zurechnungsfähigkeit als zentrales Problem der Entwürfe zu einem deutschen Strafgesetzbuch. 422p. Berlin, Springer, 1927 6545

Wimmer, A. Die forensische Verwertung des spätluischen Humoralsyndroms. Deut Zeitsch f Nervh 117-19: 760-75 '31 6546

Insanity Defense

Beltrán, J. R. El crimen en los alienados. Semana Méd 1: 1389-92 My 21 '31 6547

Brand, James T. The insanity defense. Oregon L R 9: 309-31 Ap '30 6548

Claude, H. Legal aspects of general paralysis of insane. Int J Med & Surg 42: 386-8 Ag '29 6549

Cushman, Clara R. Do alienists disagree? Is insanity plea bunk? Ment Hyg 13: 449-61 Jl '29 6550

[East, W. Norwood]. Insanity in law and medicine. L J [London] ns65: 143-5 F 18 '28 6551

Franke, Georg. Weitere psychiatrische Schicksale des Falles D. der Arbeit: "Beiträge zur Simulationsfrage." Arch f Psychiat 89 (1): 113-16 '29 6552

Fribourg-Blanc, A. Les fausses simulations en médecine légale psychiatrique. Encéphale 26: 473-5 Je '31 6553

Hewart. Criminal law and insanity. Brit M J (3489): 949-50 N 19 '27 6554

Insanity and criminal responsibility. L Times 169: 138 F 15 '30 6555

Insanity as a defense in crime: University of Montana versus College of the Pacific. Univ Debaters' Ann 1928-29: 281-327 6556

Insanity as defence in law. Sol J 73: 857-8 D 28 '29 6557

Irwell, Lawrence. What constitutes insanity? Med-Leg J 44: 137-41 S '27 6558

Issue of insanity in criminal trials. Just Peace 94: 404-5 Je 28 '30 6559

Kefauver, Estes. Insanity as a defense in criminal proceedings. Tenn L R 8: 26-38 D '29 6560

Logan, Malcolm. Demobilizing the alienists. N Am R 227: 117-21 Ja '29 6561

Loudet, O. Sobresimulación de la locura en una alienada delincuente. R de Crimin, Psiquiat y Med Leg 17: 3-12 Ja '30; same title: Semana Méd 2: 948-52 S 25 '30 6562

McCarthy, D. J. and Maeder, LeRoy. Insanity and the law. Ann Am Acad 136: 129-35 Mr '28 **6563**

Mack, Cliffort W. The plea of insanity in criminal cases. Police J [N Y] 16: 15, 19 Jl '28 **6564**

Mackaye, Milton. Insanity: another legal fiction. Outl 151: 203-6 F 6 '29 **6565**

Mackaye, Milton. Legal fiction of insanity. Lawyer & Banker 22: 147-50 My '29 **6566**

Meagher, John F. W. Insanity and crime; the question of premeditation and a fabricated defense. Med-Leg J 44: 75-87 My; 12-14 Jl '27 **6567**

Meredith, William C. J. Insanity as a criminal defence. Montreal, Burton's, 1931 **6568**

Moore, Joseph W. Insanity as a defense for crime. Am J Psychiat 8: 263-7 S '28 **6569**

Neisser, C. Gegen die Nichtverantwortlichkeit der Geisteskranken. Allg Zeitsch f Psychiat 93: 213-20 '30 **6570**

Overholser, Winfred. Insanity pleas in court procedure. Cur Hist 32: 942-6 Ag '30 **6571**

Overholser, Winfred. Sanity of the criminal. Hygeia 7: 1096-9 N '29 **6572**

Parkes, Norman. Case of pathological drunkenness as insanity defence at murder trial. L Times 164: 441-2 D 3 '27 **6573**

Phelps, Edith M. ed. Insanity as a defense in crime. Univ Debaters' Ann 1928-29: 281-327 **6574**

Raitzin, Alexander. Los alienados ante el derecho penal. R de Crimin, Psiquiat y Med Leg 15: 1-25 Ja '28 **6575**

Regulation of expert testimony as to insanity in criminal cases. Yale L J 38: 368-76 Ja '29 **6576**

Richmond, Frank C. The criminal insane. Med-Leg J 45: 170-2 N '28 **6577**

Rojas, N. Concepto médicolegal sobre la alienación mental. Conf Latino Am de Neurol, Psiquiat y Med Leg Actas 1: 170-84 '29 **6578**

Rojas, N. Definición médico-legal del alienado. R de Crimin, Psiquiat y Med Leg 14: 545-53 S '27 **6579**

Rojas, N. Peritos de parte en los juicos de insanía. R Especialid 6: 403-12 Jl '31 **6580**

Romano, Michael A. Insanity defense in homicide cases. Crim Just [Chicago] (48): 7, 15 F '27 **6581**

Separate trial of issue of insanity. L Notes 31: 44-5 Je '27 **6582**

Shepherd, Harold. Plea of insanity under the 1927 amendments to the California penal code. S Calif L R 3: 1-9 O '29 **6583**

Sher, Alfred. Growth of the plea of insanity as defense to crime. Bi-M L R 13: 141-53 Mr '30 **6584**

Smoot, George A. The law of insanity. 635p. Kansas City, Vernon law bk co. 1929 **6585**

Sutcliffe, Eric. Plea of not guilty by reason of insanity: Cal. Penal code secs. 1016, 1026, 1027. Calif L R 19: 174-83 Ja '31 **6586**

Trial of the issue of sanity. L Notes 32: 122-3 O '28 **6587**

Turano, Anthony M. Insanity and the law. Am Mercury 19: 487-95 Ap '30 **6588**

Turner, J. S. Need of reform in medical jurisprudence as it relates to proof of insanity. Tex St J Med 25: 720-4 Mr '30 **6589**

Weintraub, David. Our insanity law; the criminal's haven. Tex L R 8: 249-51 F '30 **6590**

White, A. Moresby. Legal insanity in criminal cases. J Crim L & Crimin 18: 165-74 Ag '27 **6591**

White, William Anson. Outlines of psychiatry. ed.12. 445p. Washington, D.C. Nervous and mental disease pub. co. 1929 **6592**

Williams, Edward Huntington. The insanity plea. 169p. Baltimore, Williams & Wilkins, 1931 **6593**

Wilson, Howard B. Insanity plea. Am L R 62: 579-90 Jl '28 **6594**

PARTIES TO OFFENSE

Accessories and the death penalty. Sol J 75: 20 Ja 10 '31 **6595**

Co-defendants in criminal charges. Just Peace 93: 165-6 Mr 16 '29 **6596**

Common enterprise in crime. Just Peace 93: 535-6, 759 Ag 24, N 30 '29 **6597**

Connivance not aiding and abetting. Just Peace 91: 767 O 15 '27 **6598**

Covitt, L. D. Comments on accessory before the fact under Florida statutes. Fla St B Assn L J 4: 17-21 My '30 **6599**

The doctrine of "acting in concert." Sol J 72: 163 Mr 10 '28 **6600**

Fabisinski, L. L. Indictment for substantive felony of accessory before the fact under Florida statutes. Fla St B Assn L J 4: 147-53 Ag '30 **6601**

Palazzo, G. A. Chiamata di correo e discolpa del compartecipe. Riv Pen di Dott, Legis e Giuris 107: 139-45 Ja '28 **6602**

Sears, Kenneth C. Principals and accessories, some modern problems. Ill L R 25: 845-55 Mr '31 **6603**

Six of one and half-dozen of the other. Sol J 74: 825 D 13 '30 **6604**

PARTICIPATION

Bettiol, Giuseppe. Sulla natura accessoria della partecipazione delittuosa nel codice vigente e nel progetto Rocco. Riv Ital di Dir Pen 2: 417-34 My '30 **6605**

Cordóva, E. De la participación criminal. R Gén de Leg y Juris 76: 54-89 Ja '27 6606

Dahm, Georg. Täterschaft und Teilnahme im Amtlichen Entwurf eines allgemeinen deutschen Strafgesetzbuches. 143p. (Strafrechtl Abh no224) Breslau, Schletter, 1927 6607

Damrau, Siegfried. Hehlerei und Vortat. 55p. bibliog v-ix. Inaug.-diss. Königsberg. Breslau, Schletter, 1928 6608

Levori, Emilio. La partecipazione al reato nel nuovo codice penale. Riv Pen di Dott, Legis e Giuris (7): 746-58 Jl '30 6609

Ludwig, Wilhelm. Die Lehre von der Teilnahme und ihre Behandlung im Amtlichen eines allgemeinen deutschen Strafgesetzbuches. 58p. (Strafrecht Abh no 223) Breslau, Schletter, 1927 6610

Oetker, F. Teilnahme am Verbrechen. Gerichtssaal 44: 1-29 '27 6611

Participation in criminal negligence. Irish L T 65: 115-17 My 16 '31 6612

Wolf, Paul. Betrachtungen über die mittelbare Täterschaft. 235p. (Strafrechtl Abh no225) Breslau, Schletter, 1927 6613

Zimmerl, Leopold. Grundsätzliches zur Teilnahmelehre. Zeitsch f d ges Strafrechtswiss 49: 39-54 '29 6614

SPECIFIC OFFENSES

AGAINST PERSONS

Altavilla, Enrico. Delitti contro la persona. ed.3. 482p. Milano, Vallardi, 1928 6615

Tejera y Garcia, Diego Vicente. Delitos cometidos con ocasion del ejercicio de los derechos individuales garantizados por la Constitución. 588p. Habana, Imp. y Papelaria de Rambla, 1930 6616

Tejera y Garcia, Diego Vicente. Delito de lesiones. Memoria. 310p. Habana, Imp. y Papelaria de Rambla, 1931 6617

HOMICIDE

Altavilla, Enrico. Analisi psicologica e giuridica del consenso dell'offeso nell'omicidio. *In* Scritti in onore di Enrico Ferri per il cinquantesimo anno di suo insegnamento universitario, 17-35. Torino, "Sociale Torinese," 1928 6618

Blume, Gustav. Der Fall Laube. Ein Beitrag zur Irrengesetzgebung. Arch f Krim 80: 145-59, 254-8 Mr, My '27; 81: 38-52 Jl '27 6619

Brearley, H. C. Firearms and homicide. Sociol & Soc Res 15: 456-62 My '31 6620

Brearley, H. C. Homicide in South Carolina: a regional study. Soc Forces 8: 218-21 D '29 6621

Dublin, Louis I. and others. The components of death curves. An analysis of life table deaths by causes. Am J Hyg 7: 299-333 My '27 6622
Homicides and suicides.

Dullea, Charles W. "Homicide." Int Assn Chiefs Police Proc 36: 22-8 '29 6623

Falchi, Giuseppino Ferruccio. L'omicidio in Alberto da Gandino e nella tradizione romana. 94p. Treviso, Vianello, 1927 6624

Gabrieli, Francesco P. L'omicidio e la lesione personale del consenziente. Giustiz Pen (44): 1991-2 '28 6625

Glisson, W. F. Homicide as distinguished from murder. Peace Offic 5: 16-18 Jl '27 6626

Homicidal crime in Canada. Can B R 6: 79-80 Ja '28 6627

Lévy-Valensi, J. Les crimes passionnels (l'homicide passionnel). Ann de Méd Lég 11: 193-285 Ap '31; discussion by Louis Vervaeck. Ann de Méd Lég 11: 637-56 N '31 6628

Maffei, G. B. Omicidio colposo con pistola da macellazione. Arch di Antrop Crim 50 (3): 400-27 My '30 6629

Miner, John R. Church membership and the homicide rate. Human Biol 1: 562-4 '29 6630

Pitman, Olind H. When homicide committed to prevent commission of crimes is justifiable. Tex L R 6: 184-9 F '28; same title: Am L R 62: 265-71 Mr '28 6631

The right to kill. Sol J 73: 758-9 N 16 '29; Irish L T 63: 305 D 21 '29 6632

Rogers, Berto. Right of officer to shoot and kill fleeing felon. L Notes 34: 66-70 Jl '30 6633

Servais, Jean. Le meurte par omission. R de Dr Pén et de Crimin 7: 999-1003 N '27 6634

The "unwritten law." Sol J 71: 257-8 Ap 2 '27 6635

Valsecchi, Wolfango. L'omicidio e la lesione personale nei giuochi sportivi a forma di combattimento. 24p. Roma, Tip. del Littorio, 1930 6636
Extr: Rivista Penale (5-6) My-Je '30.

Visco, Antonio. L'omicidio e la lesione personale del consenziente. 217p. Milano, Scient. 1929 6637

MURDER AND MANSLAUGHTER

Brailovskiĭ, Viktor Vladimirovich. Opyt bio-sotsial'nozo issledovaniíà. (Trudy Sev.-Kavkaz. Assotsiatsii Nauch.-Issledovat. Inst-Tov. no71. Inst-t. Eksperimental'noi, klinich i Sots. Meditsiny Pri S.-Kav. Gos Un-te Vyp 11) Rostov, Donskaia Pravda, 1929 6638

Calvert, E. Roy. Murder and the death penalty. Nation [N Y] 129: 405-7 O 16 '29; same title: 12p. London, National Council for the Abolition of the Death Penalty, 1928 6639

Caprino, Antonello. Il "diritto di uccidere." Pol Soc (7-8): 771-2 '29 6640

Donlon, Edward J. Felony murder and the Jones law. St John's L R 4: 93-9 D '29 6641

Douthwaite, Louis Charles. Mass murder. 288p. London, Long, 1928; 313p. N. Y. Holt, 1929 6642

Eichberg. Mord oder Selbstmord. Krimin Monatsh 1: 84-7 Ap '27 6643

Elwenspoek, Curt. Mord und Totschlag. ed.4. 272p. Stuttgart, Dieck & co. 1931 6644

Hearne, J[ulian] G. jr. Murder, distinction between first and second degree, inconsistency in some West Virginia cases. W Va L Q 35: 287-90 Ap '29 6645

Hentig, Hans v. Die Repression des Mordes in Österreich. Monats f Kriminalpsychol u Strafrechtsref 19: 676-7 N '28 6646

Involuntary manslaughter. L Soc J 1: 6-11 My '29 6647

Italy puts teeth in murder laws. Fla St B Assn L J 3: 47 F '30 6648

Lang. Mord und Todesstrafe in Hamburg. Monats f Kriminalpsychol u Strafrechtsref 21: 129-48 Mr '30 6649

Manns, G. Derevenskie oubiastva i oubiatsi. Problemy Prestupnosti 2: 25-40 '27 6650

Marenholtz. Mord oder Selbstmord? Arch f Krim 84: 1-6 Ja '29 6651

Marx, A. M. Bemerkenswerte Fälle von Tötung kleiner Kinder. Deut Zeitsch f d ges gerichtl Med 12: 427-39 O 30 '28 6652

Marx, Anton Maria. Mord in hysterischen Dämmerzustand. Arch f Krim 85: 202-15 D '29 6653

Murder by acceleration of death. L Notes 31: 217 F '28 6654

Petrova, A. E. [A case of murder during the period of sexual maturation]. Zhur Nevropatol i Psikhiat 21 (5-6): 701-17 '28 6655

Phelps, Harold A. Rhode Island's threat against murder. J Crim L & Crimin 18: 552-67 F '28 6656

Raven, Alice. A theory of murder. Sociol R 22: 108-18 Ap '30 6657

Raymond, Jesse Andrews. What constitutes murder in Texas? Tex L R 8: 391-8 Ap '30 6658

Reuter, F. Mord oder Totschlag durch Halsdurchschneidung. Deut Zeitsch f d ges gerichtl Med 10: 279-87 Ag '27 6659

Reuter, F. Zweifacher Mord und Simulation einer Geistesstörung. Wien klin Wchnschr 40: 18-20 Ja 6 '27 6660

Schneble. Ein interessanter Beitrag zum Problem "Mord oder Selbstmord." Krimin Monatsh 2: 153-7 Jl '28 6661

Stern, Max. A study of unsolved murders in Wisconsin from 1924-1928. J Crim L & Crimin 21: 513-36 F '31 6662

Visco, Antonio; Zerboglio, Adolfo and Vannini, Ottorino. L'omicidio mediante ordigni meccanici posti a defesi della proprietà. Nuov Dir (7-8): 411-35 '29 6663

EUTHANASIA

Carinci, Nicola. Quinto: non uccidere; l'eutanàsia ossìa l'omicidio pietoso. 27p. Chiavari, Artigianelli, 1927 6664

Jiménez de Asúa, Luis. Eutanasia y homicidio por compasión. 77p. Montevideo, Imp. Nacional, 1927 6665

Kauschansky, D. M. Die Tötung auf Verlangen aus Mitleid in vergleichender Strafgesetzgebung. Rechtliche Verantwortung. Monats f Kriminalpsychol u Strafrechtsref 20: 286-90 '29 6666

Mercy murders once more; euthanasia. Commonweal 12: 293 Jl 16 '30 6667

Millard, Charles Killick. Case for euthanasia. Fortn R 136: 701-18 D '31 6668A

Millard, Charles Killick. Euthanasia: a plea for the legislation of voluntary euthanasia under certain conditions. 44p. London, Daniel, 1931 6668B

Miricka, August. L'homicide sur la demand de la victime et l'homicide par pitié suivant le projet de code pénal tchécoslovaque. Bul de Dr Tchécoslovaque 3(1): 1-17 My '30 6669

Moraes, E. de. El homicidio por altruismo o compasion. R de Crimin, Psiquiat y Med Leg 14: 502-4 Jl '27 6670

Murder of mercy. L Notes 33: 163 D '29 6671

Staiti, Domenico. Pena di morte ed eutanasia. Scuola Pos (5-6): 214-24 '29 6672

Vecchio, Giuseppe del. Morte benefica: l'eutanasia. 163p. Torino, Bocca, 1928 6673

INFANTICIDE

Falcone, Pompeo. L'infanticidio in Cina. Arch di Antrop Crim 48: 665-78 Jl '28 6674

Gelikhovski, S. M. and Soloveva, M. V. [The casuistics of child murders]. Zhur Nevropatol i Psikhiat (5-6): 673-81 '28 6675

Infanticide. L Times 165: 565 Je 30 '28; 166: 53 Jl 21 '28 6676

Infanticide or murder. Sol J 73: 772 N 23 '29 6677

Krusinger. Kindsmord? Arch f Krim 80: 32-5 Ja '27 6678

Lima, Estacio de. Infanticidio. Cabe á justiça publica a prova da existencia do crime. R de Cultura Jurid 1: 158-63 Ap '29 6679

Popoff, N. W. L'infanticide en Russie sous le rapport juridique et eugénétique. Ann de Méd Lég 8: 532-44 N '28 6680

Puntel, A. A. Infanticidio. Semana Méd 1: 786-92 Mr 19 '31 6681

Schestakowa. Die Tötung des Neugeborenen durch die Mutter. Problemy Prestupnosti 3: 154-63 '28 6682

Schmidt, Gero. Kindstötung in der Geburt. Arch f Krim 83: 260-5 bibliog (p265) N '28 6683

Scolari, E. G. Infanticidio per esposizione al freddo ed avvelenamento con la chimica. Arch di Antrop Crim 49: 1044-56 '28 6684

Smith, Sydney. A case of homicidal strangulation of a foetus by the umbilical cord. Lancet 213: 755-6 O 8 '27 6685

Sorel, E. Deux cas d'infanticide avant respiration. Ann de Méd Lég 8: 515-17 O '28 6686

PARRICIDE, ETC.

Gotz, Berndt. Vatermord und kultische Vatertötung. Monats f Kriminalpsychol u Strafrechtsref 21: 618-19 O '30 6687

Hentig, Hans von. Drei Vatermord-Fälle. Monats f Kriminalpsychol u Strafrechtsref 21: 613-18 O '30 6688

Hentig, H[ans] von. Zur Problematik des Familienmords. Monats f Kriminalpsychol u Strafrechtsref 20: 180-2 '29 6689

Peco, José. El uxoricidio por adulterio. 621p. Buenos Aires, Valerio Abeledo, 1929 6690

Polke. Ein Gattenmord. Arch f Krim 85: 141-54 O '29 6691

Reps, A. Zum Problem des Vatermordes. Monats f Kriminalpsychol u Strafrechtsref 22: 166-75 '31 6692

SUICIDE

Aisenscitat, J. Le cause del suicidio. Morgagni 13: 608-17 '31 6693

Albrecht, Hans. Selbstmord und Wirtschaftskrise. Monats f Kriminalpsychol u Strafrechtsref 22: 567-9 S '31 6694

Alvárez Villamil, V. El suicidio infantil. Sus causas. Su patogenia. Sus remedios y su clasificación como hecho moral. Pediatría Españ 18: 8-13 Ja '29 6695

Anzures, P. Analytical study of cases of suicide. P I M Assn J 7: 235-42 Jl '27 6696

Aswell, Edward C. Student suicide. Is it a disease or a symptom? Forum 77: 696-703 My '27 6697

Bayet, Albert. Le suicide et la morale. 823p. Paris, Alcan, 1927 6698

Beeley, Arthur L. Juvenile suicide. Soc Sci 3: 35-49 Mr '29 6699

Bennewitz, Carl. Die Selbstmordsterblichkeit deutscher Lebensversicherter. Zeitsch f d ges Versicherungswiss 31: 68-83 Ja '31 6700

Bermann, G. Der Selbstmord als Rache. Monats f Psychiat u Neurol 77: 297-309 N '30 6701

Bernfeld, S. Selbstmord. Zeitsch f Psychoanal Päd 3: 355-63 '29 6702

Blasi, Giuseppe di. Indagine sul suicidio. 76p. Palermo, M. Montaina, 1927 6703

Bochkor, Adamo. Suicidio mediante combinazione fluoridrica. Arch di Antrop Crim 50: 570-2 '30 6704

Bond, Hubert. Suicide from sociological aspect. Brit M J 2: 234-9 Ag 8 '31 6705

Bonger, W. A. Zelfmoord als maatschappelijk verschijnsel. Mensch en Maatschappij 5: 281-303 '29 6706

Brokhansky, N. La frequenza e le cause del suicidio in Russia. Arch di Antrop Crim 47: 366-77 '27 6707
In 1923 359 cases were investigated by special commission.

Brukhanskiĭ, Nikolaĭ Pavlovich. Ocherki po sotsial'noĭ psikhopatologiĭ. 72p. Moskva, Mospoligraf, 1928 6708

Caldas, M. Examen médico-psicológico de los predispuestos al suicidio. Conf Latino Am de Neurol, Psiquiat y Med Leg Actas 2: 35-61 '29 6709

Canuto, Giorgio. Suicidio per scannamento con un trinciapelli dopo tentativo di avvelenamento. Arch di Antrop Crim 50: 34-42 Ja '30 6710

Carrara, M. Un caso di suicidio simulante un omicidio. Arch di Antrop Crim 48: 415-46 My '28 6711

Cavan, Ruth Shonle. Suicide. 359p. Chicago, University of Chicago press, 1928 6712

Cirès, Mihail. Le crime et le suicide. 55p. Lyon, Desvigne, 1931; extr: R Int de Crimin 3(7): 507-10 '31 6713

Cleaver, J. H. Prevention of suicide. M Herald, Phys Therapist 49: 47, 95 '30 6714

Courbon, P. Le suicide par logique démentielle et les autres espèces de suicides des aliénés. Soc Méd Ment Bul 20: 99-101 '27 6715

Dabrowski, Wiktor Grzywo. Le suicide à Varsovie en 1929. Czasopismo Sadowo-Lekarskie 3(2): 111- '30 6716

Dabrowski, Wiktor Grzywo. Suicide ou meurte? Czasopismo Sadowo-Lekarskie 3(2): 65- '30 6717

Donne, John. Biathanatos. Reproduced from the first edition with a bibliographical note by J. William Hebel. 218p. N.Y. Facsimile Text Society, 1930 6718

Dreikurs, R. Zur Frage der Selbstmordprophylaxe. Allg Zeitsch f Psychiat 93: 98-115 '30 6719

Dublineau, J. Suicide et folie. Prophyl Ment 6: 42-9 '29 6720

Durkheim, Emilio. El suicidio. Estudio de sociologia; traducción y estudio preliminar sobre etiologia del suicidio en España, por Mariano Ruiz-Funes. 450p. Madrid, Reus, 1928 6721

East, W. N. Suicide from medico-legal aspect. Brit M J (3683): 241-2 Ag 8 '31 6722

Federn, P. Selbstmordprophylaxe in der Analyse. Zeitsch f Psychoanal Päd 3: 379-89 '29 6723

Feichtinger, Georg. Wie entstehen Schülerselbstmorde? 6 aufgezeichnete Fälle. 50p. Leipzig, W. Schwabe, 1928 6724

Franck, E. Der physiologische Selbstmord. Aerztl Sachverst-Zeit 36: 333-6 '30 6725

Frankl, V. Selbstmordprophylaxe and Jugendberatung. München med Wchnschr 76: 1675-6 O 4 '29 6726

Frenay, Adolph Dominic. The suicide problem in the United States. 200p. bibliog 173-80. Boston, Badger, 1927 6727
Statistical study based on publications of U.S. Bureau of census, Division of vital statistics, and other federal, state and municipal records and publications.

Friedjung, Josef K. Das Kind als Selbstmörder. Bereitschaft 10: 83-5 My '30 6728

Füllkrug, Gerhard. Der Selbstmord in der Kriegs- und Nachkriegszeit. Eine Moralstatistische Untersuchung. 136p. Bahn, Schwerin in Meckl. 1927 6729

Gargas, S. Le suicide aux Pay-Bas. Arch di Antrop Crim 50: 673-88 S '30 6730

Gargas, S. Zelfmoord in Nederland. Opbouw 11: 162-78 '28 6731

Gonçalves, João. Tuberculose, loucura e suicidio. Bol do Inst de Crimin s7 12(1): 1-59 '30 6732

Gordon, R. G. Certain personality problems in relation to mental illness with special reference to suicide and homicide. Brit J M Psychol 9: 60-6 My 14 '29 6733

Gottschick. Selbstmord als Unfallfolge. Arch f Krim 83: 266-70 N '28 6734

Guttman, M. J. Der zelbst-mord ba Yidden un zeine sibos. Yiddisher Viss Insti Ekon-Statis Sektzie Shr f Ekon u Statis 1: 117-21 '28 6735

Hachlaender, F. Aerzte und Lehrer über Schülerselbstmorde. Zeitsch f Psychoanal Päd 1: 188-91 '27 6736

Halbwachs, Maurice. Les causes du suicide. 500p. Paris, Alcan, 1930 6737

Halbwachs, M[aurice]. Le suicide et les maladies mentales. R Phil 108: 321-60 N '29 6738

Hanauer, W. Der Selbstmord bei den Frauen. Deut Med Wchnschr 53: 1231 Jl 15 '27 6739

Heiberg, P. Suicide among Danish city population, 1905-1925. Nord Hyg Tidsskr 9: 33-6 '28 6740

Hentig, H[ans] v. Selbstmord nach Sonnenstich. Monats f Kriminalpsychol u Strafrechtsref 19: 626-7 O '28 6741

Hoffman, Frederick L. Suicide problems, with an introduction. 270p. Newark, N.J. Prudential Insurance co. 1927 6742

Hook, Sidney. Ethics of suicide. Int J Ethics 37: 173-88 Ja '27 6743

Hsue-chuan, Shen. Causes of suicide among the youth of China. China W R 56: 122 Mr 28 '31 6744

Hübner. Selbstmord oder "zufälliges Erhängen" aus sexuellen Motiven. Aerztl Sachverst-Zeit 33: 134-6 My 15 '27 6745

Julier. Zweifelhafte Selbstmorde. Arch f Krim 84: 114-17 Ap '29 6746

Kempf, Edward J. The meaning of suicide. New Repub 50: 324-7 My 11 '27 6747

Kuhr, Elfriede. Das Selbstmordproblem in der Lebensversicherung. Zeitsch f d ges Versicherungswiss 31: 49-68 Ja '31 6748

Laignel-Lavastine and Desaille, H. Tentative de meurte et suicide provoqués par l'attitude ironique d'une hébéphrénique. Ann de Méd Lég 8: 176-9 Ap '28 6749

Leuthold, H. Eine Schülerin denkt an Selbstmord. Zeitsch f Psychoanal Päd 3: 436-8 '29 6750

Lynd, Robert (Y. Y. pseud). Suicide. New Statesman 32: 659-61 Mr 2 '29 6751

Meng, H. Gespräche mit einer Mutter über Selbstmord. Zeitsch f Psychoanal Päd 3: 344-55 '29 6752

Menninger, K. A. Suicides. Kansas M Soc J 28: 6-10 Ja '28 6753

Meyer, E. Zur Verhütung des Selbstmordes, insbesondere der Jugendlichen. München med Wchnschr 76: 1459-60 Ag 30 '29 6754

Mühl, A. M. America's greatest problem; study of over 500 cases [of suicide] in San Diego[1911-1927]. Psychoanal R 14: 317-25 Jl '27 6755

Oliveira, X. de. De la profilaxis del suicidio. Arch Brasilerios '27 6756

Oppler, W. Die Zunahme der Suicidversuche und ihre Gründe. Arch f Psychiat 82: 95-109 O '27; same title: Allg Zeitsch f Psychiat 88: 175-7 '28 6757

Polke. Mord oder Selbstmord? Polizei 24: 509-11 O 20 '27 6758

Pressler. Le suicide chez les enfants. Thèse, Strasbourg, 1928-29 6759

Provent, P. Le suicide "post aggressional." Ann de Méd Lég 8: 232-9 My '28 6760

Ramos, Arthur. Os suicidios de crianças (ensaio psychologico). R de Cultura Jurid 1: 101-12 bibliog(p111-12) Ap '29 6761

Rehfeld. Zum Selbstmordproblem. Krimin Probl 3(3): 1-60 '29 6762

Roalfe, Wm. R. The psychology of suicide. J Abnorm & Soc Psychol 23: 59-67 Ap '28 6763

Romanelli, Ilarione. La mortalità per suicidio tra gli assicurati dell'Istituto Nazionale delle Assicurazioni nel decennio 1920-1929. Ist Ital d Attuari Gior 2: 177-84 Ap '31 6764

Rosselet, E. Suicide par smothering (étouffement). Ann de Méd Lég 7: 222-6 My '27 6765

Rost, Hans. Bibliographie des Selbstmords. 392p. Augsburg, Literar Institut v. Haas & Grabherr, 1927 6766

Ruiz-Funes, Mariano. El suicidio y el homicidio en España. R Int de Dr Pén 5: 195-206 '28 6767

Ruiz-Funes, Mariano and Roger, René. Le suicide et l'homicide en Espagne. R Int de Dr Pén 5: 182-94 '28 6768

Sadger, J. Ein Beitrag zum Problem des Selbstmords. Zeitsch f Psychoanal Päd 3: 422-6 '29 6769

Sandberg, M. Der Selbstmord im schweizerischen Strafgesetzentwurf. Schweiz Juristen-Zeit 23: 279-81 '27 6770

Schackwitz, Alex. Selbstmordursachen. Deut Zeitsch f d ges gerichtl Med 10: 312-21 Ag '27 6771

Schletter, E. Zur Psychologie des Selbstmordes. Int Zeitsch f Individualpsychol 7: 7-14 '29 6772

Schmid, Calvin Fisher. Suicides in Seattle, 1914-1925. 93p. Seattle, University of Washington press, 1928 6773

Schmid, Calvin F[isher]. Suicides in Seattle, Washington, and Pittsburgh, Pennsylvania: a comparative study. 141p. Thesis (Ph.D.) University of Pittsburgh, 1930; summary: Univ Pittsburgh Bul 27: 149-57 N 15 '30 6774

Die Selbstmorde im Deutschen Reich in Jahre 1929. Wirtsch u Statist 11: 510-11 Jl '31 6775

Sérin, Suzanne. Les suicides d'enfants. Hyg Ment 22: 33-7 Mr '27 6776

Shaw, C. G. Why the wave of student suicides? McNaught's M 7: 104-6 Ap '27 6777

Shonle, Ruth. Who commits suicide? Survey 58: 200-1 My 15 '27 6778

Simon. Selbstmord bei einem Amputierten und die Beziehungen von Selbstmord und Sexualleben. Aerztl Sachverst-Zeit 35: 311-17 '29 6779

Simon, Alfred. Selbstmord und Kriegsgefangenschaft. Aerztl Sachverst-Zeit 33: 60-5 Mr 1 '27 6780

Stearns, A. W. Suicide. New England J Med 204: 9-11 Ja 1 '31 6781

A student suicide. Bost Med & Surg J 196: 491 '27 6782

Suicide in Germany. Lancet 213: 140 Jl 16 '27 6783

Suicides in the city of New York, 1900-1925. Bost Med & Surg J 196: 74 '27 6784

Tönnies, Ferdinand. Der Selbstmord in Schleswig-Holstein. Eine statistische sociologische Studie. 71p. (Schriften der baltischen Kommission zu Kiel v7. Veröffentlichen der schleswig-holsteinischen Universitäts-Gesellschaft no9) Breslau, Hirt, 1927 6785

Toulouse, E. Le suicide. Prophyl Ment 6: 91-6 '29 6786

Vidoni, G. Contributo allo studio del suicidio specialmente in riguardo all'età ed al sesso. Gior di Psichiat Clin e Tecn Manic 55: 1-34 '27 6787

Vivaldo, J. C. and Barrancos, A. Suicidio y demencia precoz. R Arg de Neurol, Psiquiat y Med Leg 1: 408-18 Jl '27 6788

Whitmire, C. L. Suicidal attempts of psychotic patients. U S Vet Bur M Bul 6: 309-16 Ap '30 6789

Wright, Maurice B. Sociological factors which influence the suicide rate. Psyche 12: 52-61 O '31 6790

DUELLING

Duelling in German universities. L Notes 33: 136 O '29 6791

Eickhoff, Fritz. Die Beteiligung Dritter am Zwei-kampf nach geltenden deutschen Strafrecht und den Entwürfen zu einem Allgemeinen Deutschen Strafgesetzbuch aus den Jahren 1925 und 1927 unter Berücksichtigung ausländischen Rechtes. 73p. Inaug.-diss. Erlangen, 1931. bibliog i-iii. Kulmbach, Schuhmann, 1931 6792

Kurz, Josef. Der zweikampf nach geltenden recht. 95p. Inaug.-diss. Tübingen. bibliog 8-10. Göppingen, Illig, 1928 6793

Lennartz, Josef. Die Strafbarkeit des Zweikampfes und der Mensur. Ein Beitrag zur Strafrechtsreform. 109p. Diss. Köln, 1929. Köln-Kalk, Welzel, 1929 6794

Masson, Jean. Le duel et la loi pénale. 119p. Thèse, Dijon, 1930. Paris, Berger-Levrault, 1930 6795

Nagler, J. Ist die Schlägermensur als Zweikampf Strafbar. Gerichtssaal 44: 78-82 '27 6796

Penso, Girolamo. La repressione del duello. Riv Pen di Dott, Legis e Giuris 108: 174-87 Ag '28 6797

Seitz, Don Carlos. Famous American duels; with some account of the causes that led up to them and the men engaged. 345p. N.Y. Crowell, 1929 6798

POISONING

Byloff, Fritz. Die Arsenmorde in Steiermark. Monats f Kriminalpsychol u Strafrechtsref 21: 1-14 Ja '30 6799

Cox, E. C. The successors of the Thugs in India. Police J [London] 1: 229-39 '28
Dhatura poisoning. 6800

F., T. E. Criminal law, prosecution for poisoning not resulting in fatality. Mich L R 29: 87-93 N '30 6801

Pavlica, F. Criminal poisoning with barium. Časop Lék Česk 70: 1237-8 S 4 '31 6802

Reuter, F. Über Giftmordversuch. Deut Zeitsch f d ges gerichtl Med 9: 431-41 Mr '27 6803

ASSAULT

Concurrent jurisdiction in assault. Sol J 72: 44 Ja 21 '28 6804

Indecent assault, non-appearance of person assaulted. Just Peace 93: 358-9 Je 8 '29 6805

Straub, Ralph. Action for threatening or abusive language. L Notes 33: 65-8 Jl '29 6806

AGAINST CHILDREN

Benvenuto, G. La corruzione de minorenni nel progetto Rocco. Scuola Pos ns8: 246-52 My '28 6807

Credner, L. Zwei Fälle von Kindermisshandlung. Int Zeitsch f Individualpsychol 6: 155-63 '28 6808

Feisenberger. Kindermisshandlung. Deut Richterzeit 19: 457-9 '27 6809

Fietta, Gerolamo. Della corruzione di minorenni. 94p. Verona, Operaia, 1929 6810

Kindermisshandlungen. Vorschläge zur Strafrechtsreform; ausgearb. v. d. Deutschen Vereinigung für Jugendgerichte, Berlin. 20p. Berlin, Deut. Arch. f Jugendwohlfahrt, 1928 6811

Loewenstein, G. Ueber Kinderprostitution. Deut Gesell z Bekämpf d Geschlechtskrankh Mitt 27: 354-66 O '29 6812

Loquercio, Lorenzo. Della corruzione dei minorenni. Riv Pen di Dott, Legis e Giuris 109: 440-5 Ap '29 6813
Comments on Art. 533 of Rocco project of law.

Manfredini, Mario. La corruzione di minorenni e la corruzione morale. Scuola Pos 38: 298-303 '30 6814

Mattern. Kindermisshandlungen. Monats f Kriminalpsychol u Strafrechtsref 19: 269-72 My '28 6815

Nisot, Pierre. L'age et le consentement de la victime en matière d'infractions contre les moeurs perpetrées envers des filles mineures. 155p. Renaix, J. Leherte-Courtain [1927] 6816

Pollack, Vera. Der strafrechtliche Schutz des Kindes. Nach dem geltenden Reichsstrafgesetzbuch und nach dem Entwurf eines Allgemeinen Deutschen Strafgesetzbuches von 1927. 131p. (Strafrechtl Abh no267) Breslau, Schletter, 1929 6817

Siegert. Misshandlung Jugendlicher. Krimin Monatsh 4(4): 76-7 Ap '30 6818

Tejera y Garcia, Diego Vicente. Protección de la niñez contra los trabajos inadecuados. 14p. Matanzas, Casa Imp. "Soles," 1927 6819

Tejera y Garcia, Diego Vicente. Protecciones generales para los niños que deben figurar en el codigo penal. 15p. Matanzas, Imp. Estrada, 1927 6820

Többen, Heinrich. Die Jugendverwahrlosung und ihre Bekämpfung. ed.2 rev. 988p. Münster, Aschendorff, 1927 6821

Trommer, Harry. Unzucht mit Kindern unter Missbrauch eines Abhängigkeitsverhältnisses. Arch f Krim 85: 223-9 D '29 6822

Wackerbauer, Hans. Die Kindsmisshandlung nach dem geltenden Recht und Entwürfen. 56p. bibliog 55-6. Diss. Erlangen, 1930 6823

AGAINST FAMILY RELATIONSHIPS

Henry, André. La sanction des devoirs de famille par la législation pénale. Etudes Crimin 4(4): 103-12 Ap '29 6824

Manfredini, M[ario]. L'assistenza famigliare nel diritto penale. Scuola Pos 38: 37-51 '30 6825

De Sanctis, S. L'assistenza famigliare nel diritto penale. Scuola Pos 38: 28-97 '30 6826

BIGAMY

Bigamy based on common law marriage. L Notes 33: 143 N '29 6827

Casual wedding witnesses. Sol J 73: 474-5 Jl 20 '29 6828

[Doherty, C. J.]. Extra-territorial bigamy. Can B R 8: 251-68 Ap '30 6829

Is belief in prior marriage a defence to bigamy? L Times 167: 44-6 Ja '29 6830

Our marriage laws and bigamy. L Times 166: 94-6 Ag 4 '28 6831

Penso, Girolamo. Questioni civili e penali nel reato di bigamia. 12p. Torino, "Sociale Torinese," 1928 6832
Extr: Giurisprudenza italiana 80(2).

Venters, Carl V. Effect of mistake as to termination of former marriage in bigamy prosecution. L Notes 34: 124-7 O '30 6833

Viglino, C. Il tentativo nel delitto di bigamia. Riv Pen di Dott, Legis e Giuris 107: 343-6 Mr '28 6834

DESERTION, ABANDONMENT, ETC.

Casanova, Pierre. L'abandon de famille en droit pénal français. 128p. Montpellier, Société méridionale de publications périodiques, 1931 6835

Chonez, Robert. L'abandon de famille (Loi du 7 février 1924, modifiée par la loi du 3 avril 1928). 260p. Paris, Godde, 1929 6836

Constant, Jean. L'abandon de famille. 79p. Bruxelles, F. Larcier, 1928 6837

Dechambre, Jean. L'abandon de famille. Sanction pénale d'une obligation civile (Lois des 7 février 1924 et 3 avril 1928). 130p. Thèse, Paris, 1929. bibliog 125-7. Paris, Les presses modernes, 1929 6838

Goyet, Francisque. Le délit d'abandon de famille après la loi de 3 avril 1928. Lois Nouvelles 47(12): pt1: 281-305 Jl '28 6839

Hugo, Jean Brackers d'. L'abandon de famille en droit international privé. Lois Nouvelles 46 (9): 143-4 My '27 6840

Hugueney, Louis. La législation française sur l'abandon de famille et son application possible aux familles polonaises. R Pénitent de Pologne 4(1-2): 124-32 Ja '29 6841

Livinec, J. Le délit d'abandon de famille (loi du 7 février 1924). 70p. Thèse, Rennes, 1928 6842

Mangold, George B. and Thompson, S. Lucille. Desertion and failure to provide. *In their* Community welfare in San Diego, 73-9. San Diego, Community Welfare Council, 1930 6843

Manitoba, Can. Department of health and public welfare. Report on the problem of family desertion in Manitoba by the Welfare supervision board, Manitoba. 32p. (Rep7) Winnipeg, April 1931 6844

Poittevin, G. le. La prescription en matière de désertion et d'insoumission. Etudes Crimin 4(6): 169-76 Je '29 6845

Saillard, Henry. De l'abandon de famille. 80p. Paris, Godde, 1930 6846

Shelly, Patrick J. Desertion and its consequences. N Y St Conf Prob Offic Proc 21: 114-19 '28 6847

SEXUAL OFFENSES

Beltrán, Juan Ramón. El crimen sexual. R de Crimin, Psiquiat, y Med Leg 18: 165-81 Mr '31 6848

[Bertrand, E.]. La "criminalité sexuelle." R de Dr Pén et de Crimin 8: 74-5 Ja '28 6849

Busch, Hans. Forensisch-psychiatrische Beiträge zur Frage des sexuellen Missbrauchs geistig minderwertiger Personen. Allg Zeitsch f Psychiat 94: 299-346 F 13 '31 6850

Capgras, J. Crimes et délires passionels. Ann Méd-psychol 85: 32-47 Ja '27 6851

Le crime passionnel. R Pénitent et de Dr Pén 55: 224-55 Jl '31 6852

Falchi, Giuseppino Ferruccio. I reati sessuali. 125p. Catania, Zuccarello, 1927 6853

Falchi, G[iuseppino] F[erruccio]. I reati sessuali secondo il progetto di un nuovo codice penale. Scuola Pen Uman 5: 79-80 '27 6854

Grassi, Ugo. La violenza carnale nel progetto Rocco di codice penale. Scuola Pos (7) ptl: 312- '30 6855

Hardtloff, Hans. Unzucht im Codex. 69p. Seeshaupt, Wolf, 1927 6856

Hiller, Kurt. Forderungen zum Sexualstrafrecht. Neue Generation 26(5-6): 109-16 My '30 6857

Klee, K. Der neue Kuppeleibegriff in der Praxis. Krimin Monatsh 2: 76-9 Ap '28 6858

Linsert, Richard. §297, "Unzucht zwischen Männern." Unter Mitwirkung von Magnus Hirschfeld, Gotthold Lehnerdt, Max Hodann, Peter Martin Lampel. 130p. Berlin, Neuer Deut. Verl. 1929 6859

Manci, Filippo. Il delitto passionale. 230p. Torino, Bocca, 1928 6860

Manci, Filippo. Reati sessuali, violenza carnale, atti di libidine, corruzione di minorenni, ratto, lenocinio, azione penale. 358p. Torino, Bocca, 1927 6861

Marcuse, Max. Ammerkungen zu dem Problem: Sexualtrieb und Strafrecht. Zeitsch f Sexualwiss 14: 211-15 S '27 6862

Mittermaier, Wolfgang. Strafbare Handlungen gegen die geschlechtliche Sittlichkeit im Entwurf eines Allgemeinen deutschen '27. Justiz 3(2): 176-82 '27 6863

Munk, Marie. Der strafrechtliche Schutz der Geschlechtslehre der Frau. Neue Generation 23 (1): 9-12 '27 6864

Nacktheit als Verbrechen. Der Kampf um §184 StrGB im Lüneburger Nacktkulturprozess. 245p. Egestorf Bez. Hamburg, R. Lauer, 1927 6865

Oseretzky, N. J. Die Sexualkriminalität der Minderjährigen. Monats f Kriminalpsychol u Strafrechtsref 20: 705-32 D '29 6866

Paul-Boncour, Georges. Sur l'homosexualité juvénile, ses types, sa genèse. Etudes Crimin 4: 33-7 F '29 6867

Plaut, Paul. Die Sexualbestimmungen im neuen deutschen Strafgesetzentwurf. Krimin Monatsh 3: 56-9 Mr '29 6868

Prochaska, E. Die Sittlichkeitsdelikte nach dem tschechoslowakischen Strafgesetzentwurf. Juristen-Zeit f d Geb d Tschechoslowak 8: 173-4 '27 6869

Reiterer, Karl. Aus alten Kriminalprotokollen. Beiträge zur Kenntnis des Geschlechtslebens in den Alpen. Zeitsch f Sexualwissensch 16: 581-92 Mr 15 '30 6870

Records of criminal cases involving sex offenses, 1612-1815.

Rojas, N. El delito pasional. Semana Méd 2: 609-16 Ag 28 '30 6871

Sex offence anomalies. Sol J 72: 293 My 5 '28 6872

Sittlichkeitsverbrechen an Hypnotisierten. Arch f Krim 87: 256-69 '30 6873

Staehelin, J. Zum Bekämpfung der Sexualdelikte. Schweiz Zeitsch f Strafr 41: 16-38 '28 6874

Suchanek, Viktor. Kinder und Jugendliche im neuesten Strafgesetzentwurf (1927). Zeitsch f Kinderschutz 19 (11): 167-71; (12): 189-92 '27 6875

Truelle, and Provent, Paul. Une affaire de castration; à propos d'un crime passionel commis par un homosexuel. Etudes Crimin 5: 33-44, 131-8 F, Ap '30 6876

V[ervaeck], L[ouis]. La répression des délits passionels. R de Dr Pén et de Crimin 10: 430-1 '30 6877

Reprint and literal translation of circular of 8-10-1929 no2237 of Rocco, "Les délits passionels et la procédure pénale" *in* Revista de criminologia, psiquiatria y medicine legal (96) November-December 1929.

Weinberger, Hugo. Sittlichkeit und Strafrecht. Krimin Monatsh 3: 125-9 Je '29 6878

Zmiev, B. Prestuplenia v oblasti polovich otnoshenii v gorode i v derevne. Problemy Prestupnosti 2: 41-50 '27 6879

Social Diseases

Adler, Waldemar. Reichsgesetz zur Bekämpfung der Geschlechtskrankheiten. 177p. München, C. H. Beck, 1929 6880

Beckaert, H. Le délit de contamination vénérienne. R de Dr Pén et de Crimin 10: 879-91, 1070-6, 1167-84 '30 6881

Dini, M. Il delitto di contagio venereo. Rassenga Bibliog delle Sci Giurid (4): 632-4 '29 6882

Elster, Alexander. Gesetz zur Bekämpfung der Geschlechtskrankheiten und preussische Ausfürungsverordnung dazu. Zeitsch f d ges Strafrechtswiss 48: 418-23 '28 6883

Eppstein, M. Strafgesetzentwurf und soziale Hygiene. Arbeiterwohlfahrt 2: 737-45 '27 6884

Finger, A. Das Gesetz vom 18 Februar 1927 zur Bekämpfung von Geschlechtskrankheiten. Gerichtssaal 94: 347-77 '27 6885

Gesetz zur Bekämpfung der Geschlechtskrankheiten vom 18. Februar 1927. Kriminin Monatsh 1: suppl Ap '27 6886

Halle, Felix. Geschlechtsleben und Strafrecht. 228p. Berlin, Mopr-Verl. 1931 6887

Hellwig, Albert. Gesetz zur Bekämpfung der Geschlechtskrankheiten. 480p. München, J. Schweitzer, 1928 6888

Jiménez de Asúa, Luis. Il delitto di contagio venereo. Studio e proposte. 79p. Torino, Bocca, 1928 6889

La loi allemande sur la lutte contre les maladies vénériennes. R de Dr Pén et de Crimin 8: 75-90 Ja '28 6890

Mittermaier, W. Gesetz zur Bekämpfung der Geschlechtskrankheiten. Zeitsch f Sexualwissensch 14: 178-82 Ag '27 6891

Paolucci, Raffaele. Le malattie sociali e il nuovo codice penale. Assicurazioni Soc 5(6): 23-32 N '29 6892

Pinho, Pericles Madureira. O delicto de contagio venéreo. R de Cultura Jurid 1: 201-8 Ap '29 6893

Roeschman, H. Das Gesetz zur Bekämpfung der Geschlechtskrankheiten in seiner Auswirkung. Arch f soz Hyg u Demog 2: 335-61 '27 6894

Schäfer, Leopold and Lehmann, Rudolf. Gesetz zur Bekämpfung der Geschlechtskrankheiten vom 18. Februar 1927. 340p. Mannheim, J. Bensheimer, 1927 6895

Schultz. Geschicklichkeits- oder Glücksspielautomaten? Krimin Monatsh 5(8): 178-81 Ag '31 6896

Schuppe. Die Geschlechtliche Ansteckung als strafbare Handlung. Krimin Monatsh 1: 90-1 Ap '27 6897

Siciliani, M. La lotta contro le malattie trasmissibili ed il delitto di contagio. Gazz internaz Med-Chir 39: 779-87 D 15 '31 6898

Struve, W. Das Gesetz zur Bekämpfung der Geschlechtskrankheiten, sein Werden und sein Wirken. Monats f Harnkrankh u Sex Hyg 1: 208-23 '27 6899

Rape

Benassi, Giorgio. I reato di violenza carnale ed affini sui minorenni e sui deficenti. Note e Riv di Psichiat 17: 97-120 Ja '29 6900

Brock, James. Klage auf Notzucht als entshuldigende Ausrede. Arch f Krim 82: 45-57 Ja '28 6901

Brock, J[ames]. Notzucht und Notzuchtsversuch. Deut Zeitsch f d ges gerichtl Med 9: 739-57 My 30 '27 6902

Lilienthal, Karl. Die Sittlichkeitsverbrechen im Entwurf eines schweizerischen Strafgesetzbuches von 1918 im Vergleich zum geltenden und werdenden deutschen Recht. Schweiz Zeitsch f Strafr 40(4): 333-46 '27 6903

Maronda, E. I. El rapto. R de Crimin, Psiquiat y Med Leg 14: 287-309 My '27 6904

Peschke, Kurt and Plaut, Paul. Notzuchtsdelikte, ihre forensische Bedeutung und Begutachtung. 97p. (Abh aus dem Geb der Psychotherapie und Medizinischen, hrsg von A. Moll and P. Plaut). Stuttgart, Enke, 1930 6905

Porta, F. P. El delito de rapto. Cuba Contemp 43: 105-19 F '27 6906

Tejera y Garcia, Diego Vicente. El rapto. ed. 2. 130p. Madrid, Reus, 1928 6907

Théry, José. Le cambriolage sexual. Mercure Fr 207: 36-55 O 1 '28 6908

Wisconsin. Legislative reference library. Penalties for forcible and statutory rape (carnal abuse of children) in the several states. 13p. (typw) Madison, May 1, 1928 6909

Abortion

Albert, W. Die latente Infektion der Uterushöhle und der §218 des Strafgesetzbuches. Zentralbl f Gynäk 55: 2796-2800 S 19 '31 6910

Bogdan, Georges. La définition et la législation actuelles de l'avortement criminel. Ann de Méd Lég 9: 169-71 Ap '29 6911

Bohác, A. Results of legal abortions in Soviet Russia. Statist Oboz 12: 57-60 F '31 6912

Bok, E. J. Medische Abortus provocatus en Strafrecht. Mensch en Maatschappij 4: 323-7 Jl '28 6913

Burk, S. B. Development of law of criminal abortion. M Times [N Y] 57: 153, 168 Je '29 6914

Burkard, O. Künstliche Schwangerschaftsunterbrechung und Gesetzgebung. Aerztl Sachverst-Zeit 33: 215-18 Ag 15 '27 6915

Cazeneuve, P. Où en sommes-nous de l'effort législatif pour la répression des avortements criminels? Ann de Méd Lég 8: 360-8 Jl '28 6916

Chalfin, V. Istreblenie ploda (abort) v Moskve i Moskovskoi gub. Problemy Prestupnosti 2: 140-211 '27 6917

Child destruction. Just Peace 93: 401 Je 22 '29 6918

Clément, Gustave. Thou shalt not kill: a doctor's brief for the unborn child; transl. from 4th French ed. 152p. Philadelphia, Reilly, 1930 6919

Commichau, R. Ein Beitrag zur Abortfrage. Zeitsch f Geburtsh u Gynäk 94: 174-84 '28 6920

Costa, Stefano. I delitti contro la vita nascente. Foro Ligure (2-3): 62-9 '29 6921

Credé-Hörder, Karl A. (Karl Credé, pseud). Volk in Not! Das Unheil des Abtreibungsparagraphen. 86p. Dresden, Reissner, 1927 6922

Dörr, Heinz. Die ärztliche schwangerschaftsunterbrechung nach geltendem und künftigen recht. Zugleich ein beitrag zu den beiden kernproblemen des Strafrechts. 90p. bibliog vii-xvi (Strafrechtl Abh no251) Breslau, Schletter, 1929 6923

Fairbairn, John S. Abortion. Med-Leg Soc Tr 21: 40-8, 61-71 '28 6924

Fairbairn, John S. An address on abortion. Lancet 212: 217-19 Ja 29 '27 6925

Fedotova, E. Abortions and the struggle against their legalization. Profilak Med 6: 80-5 Jl '27 6926

Ficklen, E. A. Criminal abortion. New Orleans M & Surg J 79: 883-93 Je '27 6927

Fürth, Henriette. Die Schwangerschaftsunterbrechung und das Strafgesetz. Arch f Sozialwiss u Sozialpol 57: 176-93 F '27 6928

Glaser, Stephan. L'avortement criminel; quelques remarques sur l'avortement criminel au point de vue du droit pénal. Etudes Crimin 2(4-5): 75-6 Jl '27 6929

Glaser, Stefan. Kilka Uwag o Spedzenin plodu ze Stanowiska prawa Karnego. 60p. Warszawa, 1927 6930
Résumé en français.

Gleispach, W. Das Verbrechen gegen das keimende Leben im geltenden und künftigen Strafrechte. Zeitsch f Kinderschutz 20: 1-4, 19-23 '28 6931

Goldberg, Erich. Ein Spezialgesetz zur Legalisierung der Schwangerschaftsunterbrechung? Zeitsch f Sexualwissensch 18: 330-5 O '31 6932

Goldbergas, T. Lithuanian legislation concerning medical abortions. Medicina 10: 609-20 S '29 6933

Grotjahn and Lönne. Über die Zunahme der Fruchtabtreibungen vom Standpunkt der Volksgesundheit und Rassenhygiene. Arch f Krim 80: 59-62 Ja '27 6934

Halle, Felix. Abtreibung und Geburtenregelung im geltenden und vorgeschlagenen deutschen Strafrecht. 33p. Berlin, Mopr-Verl. 1930 6935

Hoche, Ludwig and Brandenburg, Hermann. Der Kampf gegen die Abtreibungsseuche. 47p. Leipzig, Thieme, 1927 6936

Hüssy, P. Russische Erfahrungen mit der Abtreibung. Praxis 19 (38) S 16 '30 6937

Johnson, W. O. Two years résumé of abortions in Louisville city hospital. Am J Obst & Gynec 22: 778-82 N '31 6938

Kahn, Morris H. The legalization of abortion. Am Med ns22: 175-83 Mr '27 6939

Karlin, M. Acht Jahre Abortfreiheit in Russland (USSR). Arch f Frauenk 16: 12-29 Mr '30 6940

Kauschansky, D. M. Die Legalisierung des Abortes. Eine soziale, forensisch-medizinische und kriminalpolitische Studie. Zeitsch f Sexualwissensch 17: 393-407 F 5 '31 6941

Kipper, F. Ein Beitrag zur Abtreibung und Kindestötung. Med Klin 23: 327, 366 Mr 4, 11 '27 6942

Kolle. Psychiatrisches zur Frage der Schwangerschaftsunterbrechung. Monats f Kriminalpsychol u Strafrechtsref 22: 226-31 '31 6943

Krassilnikian, Serge. Russische Erfahrungen mit der Freigabe der Abtreibung—eine Lehre für Deutschland. 79p. Berlin, Emil Ebering, 1930 6944

Lebjedewa, W. Soviet Russia fights abortion. Birth Control R 15: 137-8 My '31 6945

Levit, I. B. Beitrag zur Statistik des Aborts als einer sozialen Frage. Zentralbl f Gynäk 53: 804-7 Mr 30 '29 6946

Liepmann, W[ilhelm]. Die Abtreibung. Eine medizinisch-soziologische Studie in bildlicher Darstellungen für Ärzte, Juristen und Soziologen. 24p. Berlin, Urban & Schwarzenberg, 1927 6947

Liepmann, W[ilhelm]. Gerichtsarzt und Gynäkologie. München Med Wchnschr 77: 231-2 F 7 '30 6948

Lobe; Pankow, and Sellheim, Hugo. Strafbare und straflose Schwangerschaftsunterbrechung. Monats f Kriminalpsychol u Strafrechtsref 19: 611-19 O '28 6949

Lustig, W. Die Schwangerschaftsunterbrechung und die Unfruchtbarmachung im Lichte des geltenden und des in Aussicht genommenen Strafrechts. Klin Wchnschr 6: 1437-40 Jl 23 '27 6950

Luxenburger. Über die Zunahme der Fruchtabtreibung vom Standpunkt der Volksgesundheit und Rassenhygiene. Monats f Kriminalpsychol u Strafrechtsref 18:326-8 '27 6951

Lynch, G. Roche. Some problems in medico-legal practice. L Times 165: 218-19 Mr 10 '28; same title: J St Med 410-20 Jl '28 6952

M., C. Attempt to procure abortion, misdirection, Criminal code section 1014, new trial. Can B R 5: 702-6 N '27 6953

Magid, M. Zur vergleichenden Statistik des legalisierten und des nichtlegalisierten Abortus. Zentralbl f Gynäk 54: 1939-47 Ag 2 '30 6954

Miltner, T. von. Die Gesetzgebung der Kulturvölker zum Problem der Fruchtabtreibung. Arch f Gynäk 142: 133-51 '30 6955

Mittermaier, W. Die Abtreibung in tschechoslovakischen Strafgesetzentwurf. Zeitsch f Sexualwissensch 13: 337 Ja '27 6956

Mittermaier, W. Die Fruchtabtreibung. Zeitsch f Sexualwissensch 14: 20-1 Ap '27 6957

Müller-Hess and Hey. Die kriminelle Abtreibung. Jahresk f ärztl Fortbild 18: 1-11 S '27 6958

Muret, M. M. La question de l'avortement et le nouveau code pénal vaudois. R Méd de la Suisse Rom 50: 689-99 O 25 '30 6959

Naujoks, H. Die Freigabe des künstlichen Abortes in Sowjetrussland und in Deutschland. Deut Med Wchnschr 53: 400-3 Mr 4 '27 6960

Negelein. Abtreibung als Mittel der Bevölkerungsregulierung. Krimin Monatsh 4: 125-9 Je '30 6961

Neukamp. Der Kampf um §218 des Deutschen Reichsstrafgesetzbuches. Deut Med Wchnschr 57: 1422-4 Ag 14 '31 6962

Niedermeyer, A. Der §218 und die Reform des Strafgesetzbuches. Arch f Frauenk 13: 281-303 '27 6963

Nippe. Zum Problem der kriminellen Fruchtabtreibung. Gerichtssaal 95: 1-41 '27 6964

Oetker, F. Die legislative Behandlung der Abtreibung. Gerichtssaal 95(1-5): 1-41 '27 6965

Pérez, M. L. El problema del aborto criminal en la república Rusa de los soviets. Semana Méd 2: 682-5 S 5 '29 6966

Riddell. Ethical, legal and medical aspects of abortion. Lancet 212: 219-23 Ja 29 '27 6967

Rodecurt, M. Die negativen Auswirkungen des §218. Zentralbl f Gynäk 55: 3069-71 O 17 '31 6968

Rojas, N[erio]. El aborto legal en la Argentina. Soc de Obst y Ginec Bol 9: 448-62 N 18 '30 6969

Rojas, Nerio. Concepto médico-legal del aborto. R de Crimin Psiquiat y Med Leg 17: 385-91 Jl '30; same title: R de Med [Rosario] 6: 121-7 Ap '31 6970

Roubakine, A. Avortement. Problème sociale, et sa solution dans l'Union des Républiques Socialistes Soviétiques. Ann de Méd Lég 9: 153-68 Ap '29 6971

Schrader, E. Wie könnte durch das Gesetz unerlaubte Schwangerschaftsunterbrechung bekämpft werden? Arch f soz Hyg u Demog 2: 165-7 Ja '27 6972

Spilsbury, B. Criminal abortion. Brit M J 2: 946-7 N 21 '31; same title: Lancet 1134 N 21 '31 6973

Strassmann, G. Über die Schwangerschaftsunterbrechung und die Unfruchtsbarmachung im Lichte des geltenden und des in Aussicht genommenen Strafrechts. Klin Wchnschr 6: 1805 S 17 '27 6974

Ulbrich, Martin. Der Mord der Ungeborenen des deutschen Volkes grösste Sünde. 46p. Schwelm in W., Meiners, 1927 6975

Verkhratsky, S. Immediate and remote results of legal abortions in villages in Russia. Vrach Delo 14: 17-22 Ja 31 '31 6976

Wildenskov, H. O. Bør Fosterfordrivelse hos Aandssvage vaere tilladt? Nord Tids f Straf 15: 122-5 Ap '27 6977

Zwaan, J. P. K. de. Abortus provocatus in den Indischen Archipel. Mensch en Maatschappij 4: 33-50, 127-44 Ja, Mr '28 6978

Prostitution

Adler, Rudel S. Die Juden Argentiniens im Kampfe gegen Prostitution und Zuhaltertum. Jüdische Wohlfahrtspfl u Sozialpol 1: 296-302 '30 6979

Albrecht, Hans. Prostitution und Bordellwesen in Hamburg. Monats f Kriminalpsychol u Strafrechtsref 21: 628-30 '30 6980

Catlin, G. E. G. Moral offenses and the criminal law. Outl 60: 807-9 D 17 '27 6981

Great Britain. Home Office. Report of the street offense committee. 49p. (Cmd 3231) London, H. M. Stationery Off. 1928 6982

Helperin, S. E. [Prostitution]. ed.2. 32p. Moskva, Okhrana Materinstva i Mladenchestva, 1927 6983

Marshall, Constance. Racketeering in vice: scandals in the vice repress in New York have started a civic housecleaning that offers points to other cities. Woman's J 18-19 My '31 6984

Maus, Isidore. Le devoir des honnètes gens en face du problème de la prostitution. R de Dr Pén et de Crimin 10: 78-88 '30 6985

Menzel. Bordell und bordellartige Betriebe. Arch f Strafr u Strafproz 72: 121-30 Ap '28 6986

Miner, Charles E. Commercialized prostitution: are we winning the fight against it? Welf Mag 19: 283-8 Mr '28 6987

Urban, Alfred. Staat und Prostitution in Hamburg vom Beginn der Reglementierung bis zur Aufhebung der Kasernierung. 145p. Hamburg, Conrad Behre, 1927 6988

Adultery

Admissions of adultery. Sol J 72: 127 F 25 '28 6989

Conducing to adultery. Sol J 71: 766 O 8 '27 6990

Coutts, W. E. El adulterio. R de Crimin, Psiquiat y Med Leg 14: 689-717 N '27 6991

Effect of misconduct of both parties. Just Peace 91: 945 D 10 '27 6992

King, P. D. Questions tending to prove adultery. Austral L J 5: 46-50 Je '31 6993

Maxwell, Ian R. The discretionary bar. Austral L J 4: 251-3 D '30 6994

Occo, M. L'assenza in rapporto ai delitti d'adulterio e di bigamia. Riv Pen di Dott, Legis e Giuris 105: 177-81 F '27 6995

Pagani, Piero. Adulterio e legittima difesa. Scuola Pos (8-9): 422-8 '29 6996

Tejera y Garcia, Diego Vicente. El adulterio. 362p. Habana, Imp. de Rambla, 1928 6997

AGAINST PROPERTY

Borettini, Adelmo. I reati d'investimento e di eccessiva velocità. Riv Ital di Dir Pen (1): 13-17; (2): 117-36 '29 6998

Busdorf, Otto. Wilddieberei und Förstermorde. ed.2. 220p. Berlin, Kameradschaft, 1928 6999

Cigolini, Francesco. Per una maggiore estensione del diritto di querela nei delitti contro il patrimonio. Riv Pen di Dott, Legis e Giuris 108: 85-9 Jl '28 7000

Cullen, Vincent. Crimes against banks and how they are perpetrated. Trust Co 50: 367-70 Mr '30 7001

Deisenberger. Strafrechtliche Verantwortlichkeit bei kaufmännischen Sonderstraften. Zentralbl f Handelsr 3: 132-4 '28 7002

Fischer, E. Kind und Eigentumsvergehen. Zeitsch f pädagog Psychol 29: 384-7 Jl '28 7003

Jauffret, Alfred. La vente à tempérament des valeurs mobilières devant la loi pénale. Etudes Crimin 2(6): 95-110 N '27 7004

Schier, Norbert. Historische Entwicklung der durch Zueignung beganenen Verbrechen gegen das Eigentum. 113p. Jur. Diss. Erlangen, 1927 7005

Seesemann, H. Strafbare Verfügung über die unter Eigentumsvorbehalt gekaufte Ware. Deut Richterzeit 19: 424-6 '27 7006

Stelling. Die Strafbarkeit der Jagdausübung bei Nichtigkeit des Jagdpachtvertrages. Arch f Strafr u Strafproz 71: 244-9 Jl '27 7007

Weber, H. Die Vermögensverbrechen nach dem Entwurf von 1927. Gerichtssaal 95: 236-47 '27 7008

Burglary

Constructive breaking and entering. Just Peace 92: 107 F 11 '28 7009

Crooks, Ezra B. Law enforcement and burglary insurance. J Crim L & Crimin 18: 180-90 Ag '27 7010

Griffin, William T. Burglary. Peace Offic 5: 27-30 My '27 7011

Griffin, William T. Store burglary. Peace Offic 5: 12-14 Je '27 7012

McIntosh, Andrew C. Intoxicating liquor as subject of burglary or larceny. L Notes 34: 81-4 Ag '30 7013

Scott, J. A. Burglary in an Indian province. Police J [London] 1: 457-69 '28 7014

Theft

Brown, Fred. An historical and clinical study of criminality with special reference to theft. J Crim L & Crimin 21: 400-37 bibliog (p435-7) N '30 7015

Edelson, William. Larceny generically and the office of a bill of particulars in respect to an indictment. St John's L R 5: 64-7 D '30 7016

Haley, J. Evetts. Horse thieves. Sw R 15: 317-32 Spring '30 7017

Hanna, Francis D. Automobiles as a factor in crime: motor cars valued at $9,000,000 were stolen in 1926 [Chicago]. Crim Just [Chicago] 4-6 F '27 7018

Higgins, James W. The stolen car problem. N Y St Assn Chiefs Police Proc 28: 64-6 '28 7019

Higgins, James W. The theft and recovery of automobiles. Int Assn Chiefs Police Proc 1927: 83-7; same title: Detective 42:2- Je '27 7020

Hughes, William. Cargo pilferage and dock thefts at Liverpool. Police J [London] 4: 351-67 Jl '31 7021

Jackson, John H. What's happening to the car stealing racket? J Am Insur 7: 7-9 Jl '30 7022

Larceny by finding. Just Peace 92: 8 Ja 7 '28 7023

Lucovnik, H. Ein spät entdeckter Raubmord. Arch f Krim 80: 205-7 My '27 7024

National crime commission. [Report of committee to study and report on practical steps which could be taken to efficiently combat motor vehicle thefts and frauds]. 18p. (mim) May 25, 1930? 7025

National crime commission. [Report of the Special committee on automobile thefts and frauds]. 25p. (mim) 1931? 7026

Palopoli, Nicola. L'abiegeato in relazione alla delinquenza associata: mafia e malandrinaggio. Giustiz Pen 34: 1023-42, 1244-58 S 8, N 30 '28; separate: 69p. Città di Castello, Leonardo da Vinci, 1928 7027

Raviart, G.; Vullien, R., and Nayrac, P. Le vol pathologique. Ann de Méd Lég 7: 309-27 Je '27 7028

Riddle, E. M. Stealing as a form of aggressive behavior. J Abnorm & Soc Psychol 22: 40-51, 157-69 '27 7029

Rouquier, A. Le vol pathologique dans le milieu militaire. Ann de Méd Lég 7: 440-2 O '27 7030

The science of shoplifting. Police "13-13" 4: 5-7 My '29 7031

Shop-lifting. Sol J 72: 126 F 25 '28 7032

"Sleepy sickness" and kleptomania. Just Peace 91: 489 Je 25 '27 7033

Stephan, Otto. Der Taschendiebstahl im künftigen Strafrecht. Zeitsch f d ges Strafrechtswiss 48: 723-6 '28 7034

Receiving Stolen Goods

Appleton, Robert. Feigned omissions of fences. Police J [N Y] 16: 9, 31 S '28 7035

[Appleton, Robert]. The "fence." Panel 5: 5-6 O '27 7036

Association of grand jurors of New York county. Prison committee. Criminal receivers in the United States (social and economic problems of the "fence"—the source of organized crime and creator of criminals.) Submitted to the New York state crime commission, National crime commission, National commissioners on uniform state laws, National trade relations committee of the Chamber of commerce of the United States of America, and Association of casualty and surety executives. 82p. (mim) N.Y. c1927 (Pub 17); same: 143p. N. Y. Putnam, 1928 7037

Chamberlain, Joseph P. Anti-fence legislation. Am B Assn J 14: 517-20 O '28 7038

Mattuck, Maxwell S. The "fence" system: a powerful aid to the credit crook. Credit M 29: 16-17 D '27 7039

Mattuck, M[axwell] S. The need for a new law against "fences." Panel 5: 2 Ap '27 7040

Mattuck, Maxwell S. Our privileged criminal class. Northwest Police J 7: 13 My '30 7041

The New Jersey "fence" law. L Notes 32: 64 Jl '28 7042
Proposed measures against "fences." L Notes 31: 144 N '27 7043
The receiver's explanation. Just Peace 95: 481-2 Jl 25 '31 7044
Skillman, W. McKay. The "fence." Mich L R 26: 303-5 Ja '28 7045
Weiss, Herbert. Die Hehler. 52p. (Krimin Abh no13). Leipzig, Wiegandt, 1931 7046
What about the "fence"? Northwest Police J 5: 8-9 N '28 7047

Embezzlement

Angelotti, Dante. Le appropriazioni indebite nel sistema del diritto vigente e nella nuova legislazione penale. 472p. bibliog [xv]-xviii. Napoli, Jovene, 1930 7048
Bulatov, S. Rostrate i otchetnost. Problemy Prestupnosti 2: 130-58 '27 7049
Lobenberg, Alfred. Die Unterschlagung an vertretbaren Sachen. 59p. bibliog 7-10. Diss. Erlangen, 1930. Münster, Fahle, 1931 7050

Forgery

Barnhart, W. L. Last year's amazing forgeries. Burroughs Clearing House 11: 14-16 Mr; 12-13 Ap; 22-3 My '27 7051
Becker, Rudolf. Die privilegierten Urkundendelikte der §§277-280 R.Str.GB. Eine systematische Darstellung unter vergleichender Berücksichtigung neuerer Entwürfe. 51p. bibliog vi-x. Diss. Erlangen, 1931. Warendorf, Karl Darpe, 1931 7052
Cheque-raising. L Inst J [Melbourne] 2: 53 My '28 7053
Cochrane, J. A. The different sorts of check crimes; an explanation of the terms. Detective 42: 8 F '27 7054
Forged deeds. L Times 163: 201 Mr 5 '27 7055
Friedmann, O. Die Urkundenfälschung nach dem amtlichen Entwürf . . . von 1925. 96p. Würzburg, Memminger, 1927 7056
Gebhardt, and Nelken, S. Der Scheckschwindel und seine Bakämpfung. Arch f Krim 82: 215-30 Ap '28 7057
Gutjahr, G. Landesverräterische Fälschung. Jurist Rundsch 93-6 '28 7058
Kern, E[duard]. Die Urkundenfälschung nach dem Strafgesetzentwurf von 1927. Gerichtssaal 95: 219-34 '27 7059
Klett, Hans. Die Fälschung und Benutzung von Legitimationspapieren §363 StGB. 38p. bibliog 3-5. Diss. Erlangen, 1931. Erlange, Karl Döres, 1931 7060
Kossler, M. Zum Tatbestande der Urkundenfälschung im Strafgesetzentwurf 1927. Jurist Bl 57: 93-5 '28 7061
Osborn, A. S. Science and the law and difficulties in proving forgery. Va L R 16: 451-69 Mr '30 7062
Quigley, Marjorie. Our navy costs less than forgeries. Lawyer & Banker ns20: 397-401 N '27 7063
West, George. Forgery: bills of exchange and cheques. Accountant 84: 516-17 Ap 18 '31 7064
Wilson, P. W. Forgeries that have made history. Cur Hist 33: 187-94 N '30 7065

Fraud

Allard, Paul. Comment on nous vole. L'ère de la fraude, de la triche, de la contrefaçon. 226p. Paris, Les Editions de France, 1930 7066
Allen, Carleton Kemp. Mistaken identity. L Q R 44: 72-7 Ja '28 7067
Application of the "fraud" rule in unfair competition. Colum L R 29: 44-52 Ja '29 7068
Arnold, Earl C. Availability of duress and fraud upon the principal as defenses to the surety and guarantor. Univ of Pa L R 77: 23-51 N '28 7069
Attalla, Teodoro. Il dolo nel peculato. Rassegna Pen (1-2): 26-31 '29 7070
Better business bureau of New York city. Stamping out the "tipster sheets": a record of work done against stock-swindlers, and a report of other activities. . . February 28, 1929. 19p. N. Y. 1929 7071
Better business bureau of New York city. The wages of swindling: reporting results of cooperation from November 1, 1926 to January 31, 1927. 9p. N. Y. 1927 7072
Bizière, Pierre. La clause d'intérêt fixe et le délit de distribution de dividendes fictifs. Etudes Crimin 5: 5-10 Ja '30 7073
Bohlen, Francis H. Misrepresentation as deceit, negligence, or warranty. Harv L R 42: 733-47 Ap '29 7074
Bolitho, William. Natural history of graft. Survey 64: 138-40 My 1 '30 7075
Bosc, Jean and Toubeau, Maxime. La répression des fraudes commerciales, commentaire de la loi du 21 juillet 1929. Lois Nouvelles 49(1): 5-26 Ja '30 7076
Brunyate, John. Fraud and the statutes of limitations. Cambridge L J 4(2): 174-88 '31 7077
Contursi, Lisi Gaetano. La pericolosità nella truffa. Scuola Pos (5-6): 220-1 '29 7078
Daly, F. C. Common swindles of India. Police J [London] 4: 250-62 Ap '31 7079
Demontés, E. Émission d'un chèque sans provision en règlement d'une dette de jeu. Etudes Crimin 3: 102-7 My '28 7080
Desbois, Henri. La notion de fraude à la loi et la jurisprudence française. 301p. Paris, Dalloz, 1927 7081
Domingues, Aurelio. Contre les faux passeports. R Int de Crimin 6: 434-6 '30 7082

Drexler, Karl. Betrug durch Unterdrückung von Tatsachen. 71p. bibliog iii-v. Diss. Erlangen, 1931. Kallmünz, Michael Lassleben, 1931 7083

Egelhofer, William F. Credit and commercial fraud. Lawyer & Banker 21: 27-9 Ja '28 7084

Ehrenzweig. Der Versicherungsbetrug im Entwurf des reichs-deutsch-österreichischen Strafgesetzbuchs. Versich u Geldwirts 4: 77-80 '28 7085

Erich. Betrug bei Krediteröffnungsgeschöften (Kreditbetrug) so wei bei deren Versicherung und Rückversicherung. Arch f Straf u Strafproz 72: 321-44 N '28 7086

Escobedo, Gennaro. Studî sul reato di truffa. 230p. Città di Castello, "Leonardo da Vinci," 1928 7087

Flad, W. Unechte Kriminalität. Krimin Monatsh 5: 270-4 D '31 7088

Frasca, Charles B. Stock swindlers and their methods. 209p. N. Y. Frasca, 1931 7089

Frauds other than by false pretenses. Just Peace 94: 455-6 Jl 19 '30 7090

Freeman, G. R. Miscellany of frauds and defalcations. 23p. London, Gee, 1931; same title: Accountant 84: 747-54 Je 6 '31 7091

Friedrich, Kurt. Die Vermögensbeschädigung als Merkmal des Betrugsbestandes (§263 R.St.G.B.) 66p. Jur. Diss. Marburg, 1927. Estner, Deutsch-Eylau, 1927 7092

Glenn, Garrard. The law of fraudulent conveyances. 774p. N. Y. Baker, Voorhis, 1931 7093

Goldschmidt, J. Beiträge zur Lehre vom Kreditbetrug. Zeitsch f d ges Strafrechtswiss 47: 149-66 '27 7094

Green, L. Deceit. Va L R 16: 749-70 Je '30 7095

Gregori, Isaja. I reati di truffa e di insolvenza fraudolenta nel nuovo codice penale. Pensiero Giurid-Pen 3: 280-314 Jl '31 7096

Grinnell, Flint. The better business bureau. Am J Police Sci 2: 195-201 My '31 7097

Hellwig, Albert. Betrügerische Ausnutzung spiritischer Leichtgläubigkeit. Arch f Krim 86: 220-7 Je '30 7098

Jacobi, Rudolf. Die mittelbare täterschaft als konstitutives Tatbestandselement bei den Vermögensbeschädigungsdelikten des Strafgesetzbuches und der Strafgesetzentwurfe. 111p. bibliog 105-9. Inaug.-diss. Königsberg, 1928 7099

James, Kennaway. Princes of false finance. London, Long, 1929 7100

Kastner, Heinz. Der versicherungsbetrug (§265 StGB.) 61p. bibliog 7-11. Inaug.-diss. Tübingen, 1928 7101

Kerr, William Z. The statute of frauds. Wash St B Assn Proc 39: 71-8 '27 7102

Law, Margaret Lathrop. Legality, life and loot. Indep 119: 111-13 Jl 30 '27 7103

Ligeropoulo, Alexandre. Le problème de la fraude à la loi. Etude de droit privé interne et international, de droit fiscal, pénal et comparé. 365p. Paris, Sirey, 1928 7104

Manci, Filippo. La truffa nel codice penale italiano. Studio teorico-pratico. 195p. (Nuova collezione di opere giuridiche no257) Torino, Bocca, 1929 7105

Meli, V. Zum Betrugsbegriff. Schweiz Juristen-Zeit 24: 321-3 '28 7106

Monier, F.; Chesney, F., and Roux, E. Traité théorique et pratique des fraudes et falsifications; ed.2 by F. Chesney and E. Roux. 828p. Paris, Sirey, 1927 7107

Morrish, R. Confidence tricksters. Police J [London] 4: 543-52 O '31 7108

Morrish, R. Fraud in various forms. Police J [London] 3: 589-600 O '30 7109

Obtaining credit by fraud, elements of the offence. Sol J 71: 794 O 15 '27 7110

Page, W. H. The effect of failure to comply with the Wisconsin statute of frauds. Wis L R 4: 323-48 Ja '28 7111

Parsell, Richard H. Arbitration of fraud in inducement of contract. Cornell L Q 12: 351-60 Ap '27 7112

Pearce, Edward Holroyd. Passing off: the law as to imitation and deception in trade. 156p. London, Solicitor's Law Stationery Society, 1928 7113

Pozzolini, A. La cambiale falsa a copertura di un credito reale. 12p. Pisa, Mariotti-Pacini, 1927 7114

Promise to cause another to give real estate mortgage is within statute of frauds. N Y L R 5: 250-2 Jl '27 7115

Rojas, M. A. Falsedad en documentos públicos y privados. 40p. Bogota, Ed. Colombia, 1927 7116

Rosier, C. La fraude fiscale et l'histoire. J Econ 91: 34-46 Jl '28 7117

Saillard, Henri. De abus de confiance art. 408 du code pénal. 375p. Paris, Librarie des Juris-Classeurs, 1929 7118

S[asserath], S. Émission de chèque sans provision. R de Dr Pén et de Crimin 8: 733-4 Jl '28 7119

The state of frauds. Cent L J 100: 171-2 Mr 11 '27 7120

Stevenson, John. Fraudulent conversion: a new aspect of prevention and detection. Police J [London] 4: 381-5 Jl '31 7121

Stoddard, William Leavitt. Financial racketeering, and how to stop it. 217p. N. Y. Harper, 1931 7122

Virenque, Louis and Bonn, Albert. Traité pratique des fraudes et falsifications et des appellations d'origine. 604p. Paris, Sirey, 1931 7123

Vold, Lauriz. Conflicting interests and bulk sales statutes. Notre Dame Law 6: 284-99 Mr '31 7124

Warren, Joseph. Fraud, undue influence and mistake in wills. Harv L R 41: 309-39 Ja '28 7125

Wassermann, Rudolf. Die strafrechtliche Verfolgbarkeit des sogenannten "Kreditschwindels" im deutschen recht der Gegenwart und Zukunft. Monats f Kriminalpsychol u Strafrechtsref 18: 89-95 F '27 7126

Willis, Hugh Evander. The statute of frauds; a legal anachronism. Ind L J 3: 427-43, 528-43 Mr, Ap '28 7127

Blackmail and Extortion

Bechtel, H. Die Erpressung durch Androhung rechtmassiger Handlungen. 80p. Kassel, Werner, 1927 7128

Blackmailers and the law. Sol J 71: 439-40 Je 4 '27 7129

"Demanding with menaces." Sol J 74: 225 Ap 12 '30 7130

[Goodhart, A. L.]. Blackmail and consideration in contracts. L Q R 44: 436-49 O '28 7131

Kuhn, Georg. Erpressung bei Naturalobligationen. 38p. bibliog vii-xii. Diss. Breslau, 1930 7132

Stamping out blackmail. Sol J 75: 67-8 Ja 31 '31 7133

Counterfeiting

Baber, Julian T. Keeping up with counterfeiters. Bankers Mag 122: 469-76 Ap '31 7134

Baber, Julian T. New styles in counterfeiting. World's Wk 55: 625-7 Ap '28 7135

Broekhoff, K. H. The League of Nations and the suppression of currency counterfeiting. Police J [London] 2: 10-25 Ja '29 7136

La coopération des états dans la lutte contre le faux monnayage. R de Dr Pén et de Crimin 9: 314-24 '29 7137

Garner, J. W. International convention for repression of counterfeiting. Am J Int L 24: 135-9 Ja '30 7138

Henderson, George C. You're bound to lose. Sunset 59: 26-8 Ag '27 7139

Pella, Vespasian V. La coopération des états dans la lutte contre le faux monnayage. Rapport et projet de convention présenté à la Société des Nations. 143p. Paris, A.Pedone, 1928 7140

Suppressing the counterfeiter: conference, Geneva, 1929. Commonweal 9: 705 Ap 24 '29 7141

Zaucke. Über Falschgeldvertrieb und seine Bekämpfung. Krimin Monatsh 5: 155-6 Jl '31 7142

Bankruptcy

Bartsch. Die Bekämpfung der Konkursdelikte. Krimin Monatsh 4:200-3 S '30 7143

Braham, V. G. Fraudulent preferences. Austral L J 3: 211-13 N '29 7144

Brilton, W. E. Cases on the law of bankruptcy, including the law of fraudulent conveyances. 769p. St. Paul, West pub. co. 1928 7145

Dohna, Graf zu. Die Behandlung der Verbrechenskonkurenz im künftigen Strafrecht. Monats f Kriminalpsychol u Strafrechtsref 22: 408-11 '31 7146

Faretra, Mario. Sulla costituzione di parte civile del creditore concordatario nel giudizio penale per bancarotta semplice. Proc Pen Ital (1-2): 49-55 '29 7147

Manci, Filippo. La bancarotta e il nuovo codice di commercio. Scuola Pos ns7: 193-210 My '27 7148

Pagani, P. La pena nei case gravi di bancarotta fraudolenta. 17p. Roma, Sinossi Giuridica, 1927 7149

Palazzo, G. Alfredo. L'insolvenza fraudolenta. *In* Scritti in onore di Enrico Ferri nel cinquantesimo anno di suo insegnamento universitario. Torino "Sociale Torinese," 1928 7150

Taormina, Vincenzo. L'estinzione dell'azione penale per bancarotta semplice. Rassegna Pen (3-4): 226-32 '29 7151

Verna, F. L'ordine di cattura nei reati di bancarotta. Proc Pen Ital 13: 560-6 S 1 '27 7152

Corporate Securities

Ashby, Forrest B. The operation of the blue-sky laws. Temple L Q 1: 103-17 My '27 7153

Bitker, Bruno V. Blue sky law in Wisconsin. Marquette L R 15: 158-62 Ap '31 7154

Champion, Marjorie D. Blue sky laws: corporate securities act; effect of failure to comply. Calif L R 18: 149-59 Ja '30 7155

Dalton, John E. California corporate securities act: its legislative, administrative and financial aspects. Calif L R 18: 115-35, 255-66, 373-99 Ja-My '30 7156

Gross, Jerome A. and Brown, Richard W. Administrative powers under blue sky laws. St Louis L R 16: 141-8 F '31 7157

Simpson, Laurence P. The New York blue sky law and the uniform act. N Y Univ L Q R 8: 265-76 Mr '31 7158

Statutory regulation of investment trusts. Harv L R 44: 117-20 N '30 7159

Thormodsgard, O. H. Middle West blue sky legislation. Dakota L R 1: 138-42 O '27 7160

Wham, Benjamin. Rights under blue sky laws. Am B Assn J 15: 310-13 My '29 7161

Usury

Atzeri-Vacca, Francesco. Osservazioni all'art.663 del progetto del nuovo codice penale sulla usura punibile. Riv Ital di Dir Pen (3): 243-56 '29 7162

Campbell, Sybil. Usury and annuities of the eighteenth century. L Q R 44: 473-91 O '28 7163

Cassimatis, Grégoire. L'usure en droit pénal. R Int de Dr Pén 8: 172-86 '31 7164

Cicala, Salvatore. Il delitto di usura (étude sociologique et juridique). 259p. Milano, Ist. Edit. Scientifico, 1929 7165

Coffin, William Tristam. Usury in California. Calif L R 16: 281-97, 387-424 My, Jl '28 7166

Costa, Stefano. Dell'usura come reato. Riv Pen di Dott, Legis e Giuris 109: 21-43 Ja '29 7167

D[aniel], T. F[ranklin]. Usury and the conflict of laws. Va L R 14: 570-4 My '28 7168

Delporte, Noel F. Call loans and the usury laws. St Louis L R 16: 163-7 F '31 7169

Effect of the state and national banking acts on the usury laws of New York. Colum L R 29: 977-85 N '29 7170

Ferrari, Francesco Antonio. L'usura del diritto, nella storia, nell'arte. 302p. Napoli, La Toga, 1928 7171

Griesinger, Robert Arnold. Der Wucher nach geltendem deutschen Strafrecht und in den Entwürfen zu einem Allgemeinen Deutschen Strafgesetzbuch. 53p. bibliog 4-6. Inaug.-diss. Tübingen, 1931. Tübingen, Eugen Göbel, 1931 7172

Grohmann, H. Raumwucher. Prager Juris Zeitsch 8: 163-7 '28 7173

Häussler, Arthur. Die Stellung des Sachwuchers im deutschen Wucherstrafrecht. 43p. Inaug.-diss. Erlangen. München, E. Huber, 1931 7174

McConlogue, Raymond B. Usury. S Calif L R 1: 253-67 Mr '28 7175

Romero, Jose E. Should the usury law be reformed? Phil L J 9: 116-20 S '29 7176

Wassermann, Rudolf. Wucher mit Räuman. Zeitsch f d ges Strafrechtswiss 48(1): 28-32 '28 7177

Arson

Besson, André. Le recours des voisins en cas d'incendie et la loi du 7 novembre 1922. R Crit de Lég et de Juris 47: 303- '27 7178

Böhlhoff. Brandstiftung und deren Bekämpfung. Polizei 24: 171-2 Ap 20 '27 7179

Brandstiftung und Brandversicherungsbetrug im Entwurf eines allgemeinen deutschen Strafgesetzbuches. Leipz Zeitsch f Deut Recht 21: 989-95 '27 7180

Christie, T. Criminal lunatics and crime of arson; 100 cases. Brit M J 1: 162-3 Ja 25 '30 7181

The crime of crimes. Safeguarding Am Against Fire 10: 1-7 Jl, 5-6 Ag '27 7182

Ewald, Hans. Die Brandstiftung und ihre Bekämpfung. 161p. (Wirtschaft und Recht der Versicherung ns3 no3) Berlin [Verband Öffentl. Feuerversicherungsanestalten in Deutschland] 1927 7183

Gallois, C. Les incendies de forêts. Leurs dévastations et leurs causes. Les lois qui les punissent ou les préviennent méthodes d'évaluation de leurs dommages. R Int de Crimin 3(5): 328-72 '31 7184

Grassberger, Roland. Die Brandlegungskriminalität. Eine Untersuchung über ihre Ausdehnung Bedingungen und Bekämpfung. 253p. bibliog 247-50. (Kriminol Abh no4, hrsg von W. Gleispach) Wien, Springer, 1928 7185

Hitchler, W[alter] H[arrison]. Arson as affected by the act of April 25, 1929, P. L. 767. Dickinson L R 34: 131-4 Ja '30 7186

Long, Percy B. California's new law of arson. Peace Offic Assn Calif Proc 9: 59-64 '29 7187

A model arson law. Spectator [N Y] 118: 31 F 24 '27 7188

Nelken. Brandstiftung und Zeugenaussagen. Krimin Monatsh 5: 65-6 '31 7189

Renner, Georg. Brandstiftung und Staatsanwalt. Arch f Krim 84: 216-23 My '29 7190

S[klar], J[ohn]. Arson, statutory change of common law requisites. Mich L R 25: 450-4 F '27 7191

Süe, Gabriel. Les incendies de forêts. R Int de Crimin 1: 250-62 S '29 7192

Venters, Carl V. Unfinished dwelling as subject of arson. L Notes 34: 209-10 F '31 7193

Vogel, O. Brandstiftungen und ihre Bekämpfung. ed.2. 150p. Verlin-Charlottenburg, Bali-Verl. 1929 7194

AGAINST PUBLIC PEACE AND ORDER

Brunker, Albert R. Thwarting official crime and corruption in Chicago. Nat Munic R 18: 663-9 N '29 7195

Disorderly public meetings. Sol J 72: 126-8 F 24 '28 7196

Hofmann, Albert. Die gemeingefährlichen Delikte nach Reichsstrafgesetzbuch, nach den neuen Strafgesetzentwürfen, insbesondere nach Entwurf 1927. 92p. bibliog 5-7. Inaug.-diss. Tübingen. Stuttgart, Stuttgarter Buchdruckerei-Gesellschaft [1931] 7197

Lebret, Jean. De la corruption d'employés. Etudes Crimin 3: 107-16 My '28; same title: 30p. Paris, Sirey, 1929 7198

Lee, Howard B. Radicalism and the constitution. W Va B Assn Proc 1930: 273-94 7199

Ley Polaca sobre competencia desleal. R de Identif y Cienc Pen 3: 398-400 Mr '29 7200

Mazeaud, Léon. Le délit d'altération des prix. Loi du 3 décembre 1926 modifiant les articles 419, 420, 421 du code pénal. 144p. Paris, Dalloz, 1927 7201

M[osely], C[harles] F. Criminal law, bombing. St Louis L R 16: 72-3 D '30 7202

Palumbo, Filippo. I delitti contro l'economia pubblica nel progetto preliminare del nuovo codice penale. Rassegna Pen (11-12): 1027-37 '29 7203

Petrocelli, Biagio. I delitti contro l'economia pubblica, l'industria e il commercio nel nuovo codice penale. Dir del Lavoro (11-12): 731-3 '29 7204

Prevention of corruption. L Times 169: 264 Mr 22 '30 7205

Sandulli, Nicola. La dottrina generale dei delitti contro l'economia pubblica, l'industria e il commercio. 130p. Napoli, Siem, 1928 7206

Carrying Weapons

Constant, Jean. Avant projet présenté à l'Union belge de droit pénal sur la fabrication, le commerce et le port des armes. R de Dr Pén et de Crimin 10: 991-1010 Ag '30; extract: 20p. Louvain, Imp. Pierre Mafrans, 1930 7207

Decourt. La règlementation de la vente des armes prohibées. R Int de Crimin 3(3): 209-11 '31 7208

Delius. Besitz und Führen von Waffen nach jetzigem und kunftigem Recht. Leipz Zeitsch f Deut Recht 22: 793-803 '28 7209

Driver, M. B. Issuing of gun permits. Peace Office Assn Calif Proc 11: 24-9 '31 7210

Finlinson, J. California gun law. Peace Offic Assn Calif Proc 10: 55-9 '30 7211

Fitzgerald, J. Henry. Fire arms and their uses. N Y St Assn Chiefs Police Proc 28: 41-4 '28 7212

Frederick, Karl T. Pistol regulation: its principles and history. Am J Police Sci 2: 440-51 S '31 7213

Goddard, Calvin. The pistol bogey; a criticism of legislation against firearms ownership. Police "13-13" 5: 11-13, 47 D '30 7214

Goddard, Calvin. This pistol bogey. Am J Police Sci 1: 178-92 Mr '30 7215

Hoche, Werner. Schusswaffengesetz. Das Gesetz über Schusswaffen und Munition nebst der Ausführungsverordnung und den einschlägigen Vorschriften. Berlin, Franz Vahlen, 1928 7216

Imlay, Charles V. Uniform firearms act reaffirmed. Am B Assn J 16: 799-801 D '30 7217

Koch, [Ernst]. Waffenrecht. 45p. Berlin, Deutsche Polizeibuchh. 1931 7218

Kraft, B. Zur Frage "Waffenerkennungsdienst." Krimin Monatsh 5: 278-80 D '31 7219

Kunze, Fritz. Das Waffenrecht im Deutschen Reich. 104p. Berlin, P. Parey, 1928 7220

McKenna, Daniel J. Right to keep and bear arms. Marquette L R 12: 138-49 F '28 7221

National crime commission. Address to the Committee on firearms regulation, January 28, 1927, by Ogden L. Mills. 3p. N.Y. 1927 7222

National crime commission. Draft of an act to regulate the sale, possession and use of firearms, silencers and noxious gases. 7p. N.Y. 1927 7223

New York (state). Crime commission. Special report to the Commission on firearms legislation, 1930. 15p. Albany, 1930 7224

New York (state). Crime commission. Special report to the Commission on firearms legislation and psychiatric and expert testimony in criminal cases. 22p. Albany, 1928
Special report. 19p. Albany, 1929 7225

Pistol laws. L Notes 31: 84-5 Ag '27; 32: 4-5 Ap '28 7226

Rogers, William A. Putting teeth in the gun laws. Justice 1: 34-5 D '28 7227

Salewski, A. Zum jetzigen und künftigen Waffenrecht. Polizei 25: 280-4 Ap 10 '28 7228

Starnes, Cortlandt. Firearms. Chief Constables Assn Can Proc 25: 104-9 '29 7229

Uniform state laws prohibiting the importation of revolvers, the recent federal law. N Y L R 5: 277-9 Jl '27 7230

War on organized gun running for killers. Pop Mech 56: 896 D '31 7231

Weinberg, Harry E. Stack arms! A defense of legislation against private firearms ownership. Police "13-13" 5: 14-15, 42 D '30 7232

Libel

Allegra, Giuliano. Il criterio distintivo fra ingiuria e diffamazione nel nuovo progetto di codice penale. Rassegna Pen (9-10): 853-64 '29 7233

Brend, W. A. Medical communications and the law of libel and slander. Practitioner 119: 280-7 N '27 7234

Communication of libel to stenographer or other employe as publication. N Y L R 6: 43-7 Mr '28 7235

Davis, Stephen B. Libel and slander by radio. Case & Com 34: 67-71 Je '28 7236

Defamation and the typewriter. L Times 170: 259-60 O 4 '30 7237

Escobedo, Gennaro. Diffamazione in seguito a lesione personale. Giustiz Pen (35): 1194-6 '29 7238

Gatley, Clement. The law and practice of libel and slander. ed.2. 1039p. London, Sweet & Maxwell, 1929 7239

Hallen, John E. Character and belief necessary for the conditional privilege in defamation. Ill L R 25: 865-76 Ap '31 7240

Hallen, John E. Fair comment. Tex L R 8: 41-100 D '29 7241

Hallen, John E. The Texas libel laws. Tex L R 5: 335-59 Je '27 7242

Harper, Fowler V. Ethical basis of the law of defamation. Dakota L R 1: 73-81 Jl '27 7243

Harrington, J. R. Truth as complete defence in action for libel. Notre Dame Law 4: 436-42 Ap '29 7244

Imputation of outlawed crime. N Y L R 5: 46-7 F '27 7245

Law of libel amendment. Sol J 71: 222-3 Mr 19 '27 7246

Libel by portrait. Sol J 72: 38-9 Ja 21 '28 7247

Libel on an editor. Sol J 73: 25 Ap 13 '29 7248

Libels upon prisoners. Just Peace 93: 310 My 18 '29 7249

Lonardo, F. Diffamazione con unica frase e con pluralità di offesi. 23p. Campobasso, Quartieri, 1930 7250

Malice in law of defamation. L Q R 53: 12-13 Ja '27 7251

Pester, Martin. Der Schutz des Privatlebens gegen Indiskretion im gegenwärtigen und künftigen Strafrecht unter besonderer Berücksichtigung der Sensationspresse. 138p. (Strafrechtl Abh no282) Breslau, Schletter, 1931 7252

Poittevin, G. le. Le projet de loi sur la diffamation. Etudes Crimin 4(12): 327-30 D '29 7253

Riquelme, Rafael Fontecilla. Le jury d'honneur et le délit de diffamation; traduit de l'espagnol par M. Daniel Fredes. R Int de Dr Pén 8: 342-4 '31 7254

Robinson, L. F. S. Exemplary damages for defamation. Austral L J 3: 250-2, 292-4 D '29, Ja '30 7255

Rossi, Paolo. Ingiuria e diffamazione nel progetto di codice penale. Foro Ligure (4-5): 123-32 '29 7256

Roth, Ernst W. Die materiellrechtliche und prozessuale Bedeutung des Indiskretionsdelikts (§ 285, Abs 4 des Strafgesetzentwurfs von 1925). 61p. (Strafrechtl Abh no219) Breslau, Schletter, 1927 7257

Sackett, Henry Woodward. The law of libel: what every newspaper man is expected to know about it; how to guard against libel suits. 23p. N.Y. Columbia university press, 1929 7258

Schuind, Gaston. Les jurys d'honneur et le délit de diffamation. R Int de Dr Pén 8: 331-7 '31; same title: R de Pén et de Crimin 11: 1036-41 '31 7259

United press associations. Synopsis of law of libel. 12p. N.Y. 1929 7260

Wettach, Robert H. Recent developments in newspaper libel. Minn L R 13: 21-38 D '28; same title: N C L R 7: 3-20 D '28 7261

Yankwich, Leon R. Libel and the newspaper. Los Angeles B Assn Bul 3: 9-11 N 17 '27 7262

RIOT

Betz, Joseph. Der Landfriedensbruch nach dem geltenden Recht und den Entwürfen. 74p. bibliog 7-8. Diss. Erlangen, 1930. Ingolstadr, Ludwig Stadelmeier, 1930 7263

Büttner, Robert. Die Meuterei im geltenden Strafrecht und in der Seemannsordnung (Unter Berücksichtigung der neueren und neuesten Entwürfe) 92p. bibliog 5-7. Diss. Erlangen, 1930 7264

Parsons, T. W. S. Riot. Chief Constables' Assn Can Proc 26: 12-15 '30 7265

LYNCHING

All honor to the women of Georgia. Chr Cent 48: 123 Ja 28 '31 7266

Black shirts and lynching. World Tomorrow 13: 437-8 N '30 7267

Bond, Horace M. What lies behind lynching. Nation [N Y] 128: 370-1 Mr 27 '29 7268

Boyer, Richard Owen. Texas bankers and lynch law. Sw R 13: 150-4 Winter '28 7269

Butler, Hilton. Lynch law in action. New Repub 67: 256-8 Jl 22 '31 7270

Chadbourn, James H. Plan for survey of lynching and the judicial process. N C L R 9: 330-6 Ap '31 7271

Churches and lynchings. Chr Cent 48: 429 Ap 1 '31 7272

Coercing courts by mob violence. L Notes 31: 181 Ja '28 7273

Commission to investigate lynching. Nation [N Y] 131: 337 O 1 '30 7274

Davis, Horace B. A substitute for lynching. Nation [N Y] 130: 12-14 Ja 1 '30 7275

Dyer, L. C. and George C. Constitutionality of federal anti-lynching bill. St Louis L R 13: 186-99 My '28 7276

Eleazer, R. B. Southern women against the mob. S Workm 60: 126-31 Mr '31 7277

Ethridge, Willie Snow. Southern women attack lynching. Nation [N Y] 131: 647 D 10 '30 7278

Garnett, B. P. Mob disturbances in the United States. Editorial Res Rep 701-18 O 20 '31 7279

Johnson, James Weldon. The practice of lynching. Cent 115: 65-70 N '27 7280

Kastler, Norman M. The control of race relations in the community [lynching]. Am Sociol Soc Proc 23: 336-7 '29; same title: Opportunity 7: 207-9 Jl '29 7281

Löwer, Albrecht. Das Wesen des Massenverbrechens. Eines rechtswissenschaftliche Untersuchung. 125p. Freiburg i.B. J. Bielefeld, 1927 7282

Lunt, Dudley Cammett. American inquisition. Scribner's 89: 56-65 Ja '31 7283

Lynch law in 1930. Survey 65: 69 O 15 '30 7284

Lynching [for the year 1930]. J Crim L & Crimin 22: 151 My '31 7285
Figures compiled by Tuskegee Institute of Alabama.

Lynching again on the increase. Chr Cent 48: 5 Ja 7 '31 7286

Lynching record [in the first six months of 1931]. J Crim L & Crimin 22: 448 S '31 7287

Lynching the innocent. Nation [N Y] 133: 561 N 25 '31 7288

Lynchings. Outl 156: 489 N 26 '30 7289

Maryland has a lynching. Outl 159: 521 D 23 '31 7290

Missouri mob murder. Outl 157: 123 Ja 28 '31 7291

Mob murder, Sherman, Texas. Outl 155: 96 My 21 '30 7292

Nearing, Scott. Lynch law. *In his* Black America, 197-212. N.Y. Vanguard, 1929 7293

North Carolina slips. Outl 156: 14 S 3 '30 7294

Odum, Howard W. Lynchings, fears, and folkways. Nation [N Y] 133: 719-20 D 30 '31 7295

Peet, H. W. Why more lynchings? Spectator [N Y] 146: 104-5 Ja 24 '31 7296

Pickens, Williams. Aftermath of a lynching. Nation [N Y] 132: 406-7 Ap 15 '31 7297

Reilly, Louis W. Lynching: a national crime. Cath World 127: 396-403 Jl '28 7298

Reuter, Edward Byron. Crimes against the Negro. *In his* The American race problem: a study of the Negro, 365-92. N.Y. Crowell, 1927 7299

Shame to Mississippi. Nation [N Y] 128: 62 Ja 16 '29 7300

Southern women speak out. World Tomorrow 13: 487 D '30 7301

Thornton, William. Southern comment on lynching. Nation [N Y] 131: 444 O 23 '30 7302

Tribble, Edwin. Impeaching Judge Lynch. New Repub 67: 226-7 Jl 15 '31 7303

Wembridge, Eleanor Rowland. Negroes in custody. Am Mercury 21: 76-82 S '30 7304

White, Walter. Investigate lynchings. Am Mercury 16: 77-84 Ja '29 7305

White, Walter Francis. Rope and faggot: a biography of Judge Lynch. 289p. bibliog 269-72. N.Y. Knopf, 1929 7306

Women and the lynch law. Commonweal 13: 171-2 D 17 '30 7307

Work, M. N. Lynchings in the United States since 1885. Miss R World 54: 620 Ag '31 7308

Young, Erle Fiske. The relation of lynching to the size of political areas. Sociol & Soc Res 12: 348-53 Mr '28 7309

Bribery

Bribery and secret commissions. Scot L R 44: 45-51 F '28 7310

Bronaugh, Minor. Right of government to bribes paid public officers. L Notes 33: 145-9 N '29 7311

Commercial bribery. Colum L R 28: 799-805 Je '28 7312

Flynn, John Thomas. Graft in business. 318p. N.Y. Vanguard press, 1931 7313

Kurzendorfer, Ludwig. "Die Bestechung nach §§332, 333 R. St. G. B. und ihre Weiterentwicklung" in den Entwürfen. 68p. bibliog 63-6. Diss. Erlangen, 1930. München, S. Wegele, 1931 7314

The police and confiscated money. Sol J 73: 489 Jl 27 '29 7315

Prevention of bribery. J Comp Leg s3 10: 128-9 F '28; same title: Just Peace 91: 772 O 15 '27 7316

Receiving and giving bribes. L Soc J 2: 50-2 My '30 7317

Two centuries of bribery. Just Peace 93: 346-7 Je 1 '29 7318

Strikes, etc.

Bianchedi, Camillo. Note sul delitto di sciopero nei pubblici servizi. Scuola Pos ns8: 140-53 Mr '28 7319

Meister, O. Strafgesetz und Arbeitsmarkt. Arbeit u Beruf 7: 71-7 '28 7320

Nevoigt, Rudolf. Der strafrechtliche Schutz der Arbeitskraft. 161p. (Strafrechtl Abh no228, hrsg von Lilienthal) Breslau, Schletter, 1927 7321

Potthoff, Heinz. Der Strafrechtliche Schutz der Arbeitskraft. Leipz Zeitsch f Deut Recht 22: 1224-31 '28 7322

Silberschmidt, W. Der strafrechtliche Schutz der Arbeitskraft. Leipz Zeitsch f Deut Recht 22: 1209-24 '28 7323

Spinelli, Giuseppe. I reati contro l'ordine del lavoro. 151p. Roma, Ed. del Diritto del Lavoro, 1928 7324

Weinberg, S. Der strafrechtliche Schutz der Arbeitskraft und der Strafgesetzentwurf. Arbeit 4: 524-31 '27 7325

Zimmermann, Hans. Die strafbaren Aufforderungen nach §110 St.G.B. und nach §169 des amtlichen Entwurfes von 1927 unter besonderer Berücksichtigung der Aufforderung zum Streik. 46p. bibliog vii-viii. Diss. Erlangen, 1930 7326

"Hooliganism"

Bugaiski, I. P. [The clinic and psychopathology of hooliganism]. Oboz Psikhiat, Nevrol i Reflek (1): 56-68 '27 7327

Bugaiski, I. P. [Psychic abnormalities and hooliganism]. Krasnaya Nov (1): 165-94 '27 7328

Chuliganstwo i Prestuplenie. 176p. [Leningrad, Verl. Raboczi Ssud] 1927 7329
Veröffentlichungen des kriminologischen Institutes am Leningradschen Gouvernementsgericht.

Chuliganstwo i Chuligany. 172p. [Moskau, Verl. des Volkskommissariats für Inneres] 1929 7330
Sammelwerk des Staatsinstituts für Erforschung der Kriminalität.

Grossman, I. [Hooliganism]. Sovrem Psikhonevrol 4(5-6): 417-21 '27 7331

Lobatsch, I. M. Über den Charakter des Hooliganwesens. Zeitsch f d ges gerichtl Med 12: 361-79 S 4 '28 7332

AGAINST PUBLIC HEALTH

Agrelo, R. Situación penal y civil de los toxicómanos (morfina). Semana Méd 1: 191-5 Ja 15 '31 7333

Costa, S. Nè frode in commercio, nè delitto contro la pubblica alimentazione. Riv Pen di Dott, Legis e Giuris 107: 557-61 My '28 7334

Fraeb, Walter Martin and Wolff, Paul. Die straf- und zivilrechtliche Stellungnahme gegen den Rauschgiftmissbrauch mit Abänderungsvorlichlägen zur strafrechtsreform, zum BGB. und zum Opiumgesetz. 235p. Leipzig, Georg Thieme, 1927 7335

Gallois, C. La pollution des rivières dommages et réparations. R Int de Crimin 3(2): 88-112 '31 7336

Karpman, Benjamin. Laws that cause crime [Harrison anti-narcotic act]. Am Mercury 23: 74-82 My '31 7337

Mitchell, C. Ainsworth. Food adulteration and its prevention. Police J [London] 2: 546-56 O '29 7338

AGAINST PUBLIC MORALS

Arnaud, Pierre. Réforme de la législation relative à l'outrage aux bonnes moeurs. 125p. Paris, Rousseau, 1927 7339

Barth, Max. Sittlichkeit und Strafrecht. Neue Generation 23: 352-4 N '27 7340

Borciani, Alberto. Le offese all'onore. 376p. Torino, Un. Tip. ed. Torinese, 1928 7341

Ebermayer. Sittlichkeit und Strafrecht. Deut Med Wchnschr 53: 1828 O 21 '27 7342

Exner, Franz. Strafrecht und Moral. Gefängnisgesellsch f d Prov Sachsen & Anhalt Jahr 44: 21-32 '28 7343

Haesaert, J. P. Etiologie de la répression des outrages publics aux bonnes moeurs. 216p. Bruxelles, L'Eglantine, 1931 7344

Haesaert, J. P. Evolution de la jurisprudence belge en matière d'outrages publics aux moeurs (art.385 du code pénal). R de Dr Pén et de Crimin 7: 1155-73 D '27 7345

Hugueney, L. La protection pénale des malades mentaux contre les attentats aux moeurs. Ann de Méd Lég 7: 229-34 My '27 7346

Kartell für Reform des Sexualstrafrechts. Sittlichkeit und Strafrecht. Gegenentwurf zu den Strafbestimmungen des Amtlichen Entwurfs eines Allgemeinen Deutschen Strafgesetzbuchs über geschlechtsliche und mit den Geschlechtsleben im Zusammenhang stehende Handlungen nebst Begründung. 99p. Berlin-Hessenwinkel, Neue Gesellschaft, 1927 7347

Köhler, A. Die Sittlichkeitsdelikte des Strafgesetzentwurf von 1927. Gerichtssaal 96: 360-96 '28 7348

Lassally, Oswald. Sittlichkeit und Strafrecht. Eine Betrachtung zum Strafgesetzentwurf. Monats f Kriminalpsychol u Strafrechtsref 22: 467-72 Ag '31 7349

Lenz, Hubert. Verbrechen und Vergehen wider die Sittlichkeit. Ein kritischer Beitrag zur Strafrechtsreform. 72p. Trier, Verl. der Paulinus-Druckerei G. m. b. H. 1928 7350

Liszt, E. Ehrenschutz. Zentralbl f d jurist Praxis 46: 715-24 '28 7351

Mauro, G. B. de. Incendio di navi e baratteria. Riv Pen di Dott, Legis e Giuris 105: 162-76, 268-75 F, Mr '27 7352

Public indecencies. Just Peace 91: 618-19 Ag 20 '27 7353

Putnoki, B. Becsület-védelni irányok a büntelòjagban. 79p. Miscolc, Mag. jövö nyomdaüzem, 1927 7354

Sandulli, Alfredo. I delitti nell'arte: ingiuria, diffamazione e oltraggio al pudore. 278p. Napoli, A. Morano, 1927 7355

Sandulli, Alfredo. L'opera d'arte nel nuovo codice. Scuola Pos (10-11) pt1: 469- '30 7356

Schultz. Sittlichkeit und Strafrecht. Deut Richterzeit 19: 422-4 '27 7357

Wilden, Adolf. Die Kriminalität der Sittlichkeitsdelikte seit 1910. Eine kriminalsoziologische Untersuchung. 38p. Diss. Königsberg, 1928 7358

Blasphemy

D'Antonio, F. Il reato di bestemmia nella legislazione delle due Sicilie. Scuola Pos ns7: 250-8 My '27 7359

Blasphemy. Sol J 74: 111-12 F 22 '30; same title: L Times 169: 125 F 8 '30; L Notes 34: 99-100 Ag '30 7360

Nokes, Gerald Dacre. A history of the crime of blasphemy. 178p. London, Sweet & Maxwell, 1928 7361

Seditious and blasphemous teaching. L Times 163: 302 Ap 2 '27 7362

Tentolini, Ottorino. La bestemmia negli statuti e negli stati parmensi e nella legislazione italiana. 35p. Colorno (Parma) Mutilati, 1928 7363

Obscenity

Alsberg, Max. Das schund- und schmutzgesetz. Preuss Jahrb 207: 86-93 Ja '27 7364

Brown, Agnes M. comp. Obscene literature: digest of laws enacted in the various states relating to the possession, circulation, and sale of obscene literature. 22p. (71st Cong. 2d sess. Sen Doc 54) Washington, Library of congress, 1929 7365

Conrad. Zur Strafrechtlichen Stellung der Mitglieder von Filmprüfungsstellen. Deut Juristen-Zeit 32: 1145-9 '27 7366

Ernst, Morris L[eopold] and Seagle, William. To the pure: a study of obscenity and the censor. 336p. N.Y. Viking press, 1928 7367

Kalbenbeyer, Erwin Guido. Zur Zensurfrage. Deut Volkstum 11: 761-6 O '29 7368

Kern, E. Das Gesetz zur Bewahrung der Jugend vor Schund- und Schmutzschriften vom 18. Dez. 1926. Gerichtssaal 94: 378-82 '27 7369

Kormann, Erich. Die Verbreitung unzüchtiger Schriften. 64p. bibliog 5-6. Diss. Erlangen, 1931. Nürnberg, Benedikt Hilz, 1931 7370

Mortier, Georges de. De la répression des écrits, figures ou images contraires aux bonnes moeurs projetées par le film. R de Dr Pén et de Crimin 8: 1025-9 N '28 7371

Neilson, William Allen. The theory of censorship. Atlan M 145: 13-16 Ja '30 7372

Peter. Weitere kriminalistische Erfahrungen mit dem Schund- und Schmutzgesetz in Leipzig. Krimin Monatsh 5: 135-6 Je '31 7373

Schroeder, Theodore. May it please the court. Med-Leg J 48: 89-95 My '31 7374

Seeger, E. Das Gesetz gegen Schund- und Schmutzschriften. Gesetz u Recht 28: 20-3 Ja 15 '27 7375

Standards of decency. Sol J 74: 711 N 1 '30 7376

State laws relating to obscene literature: a digest of legislative enactments covering publication and dissemination of obscene books, periodicals and pictures. Cong Dig 9: 41-3 F '30 7377

Wel, C. (pseud). Das verbotene Buch. Meine sensationellen Erlebnisse mit der Internationalen Liga freier Menschen. 224p. Hannover, P. Witte, 1929 7378

GAMBLING

Adler, Felix. Moral effect of gambling. 8p. American Ethical Union, 1929 7379

Betting. L Times 163: 207 Mr 5 '27 7380

Betting and the totalisator. L Times 165: 252 Mr 24 '28 7381

Betting certificates, liability of "runners." Just Peace 91: 840 N 5 '27 7382

Betting duty regulation, ultra vires. Just Peace 93: 137-8 Mr 2 '29 7383

Defects of the gaming laws. Sol J 74: 271-2 My 3 '30 7384

Failure of betting prosecution. Just Peace 93: 464 Jl 20 '29 7385

Gaming—the law and its administration. Just Peace 93: 19-30 Ja 12 '29 7386

The gaming laws. L Times 164: 345 N 5 '27 7387

Illegal betting and licenses. L Times 164: 78 Jl 30 '27 7388

McLellan, Howard. Four billions in easy money. N Am R 228: 609-15 N '29 7389

Magistrate's protest against betting laws. Just Peace 91: 528 Jl 9 '27 7390

Manufacturing criminals. Sat R of Lit 151: 144-5 Ja 31 '31 7391

Neal, Ann, comp. Abatement of gambling as a nuisance: digest of state laws providing for the abatement of gambling as a nuisance. 7p. Madison, Wisconsin Legislative reference library, March 1929 7392

Roehler, W. Die strafbaren Handlungen betreffend das Glücksspiel. 129p. Jena, 1927 7393

The slot machine racket and juvenile criminals. Am City 44: 135 Ap '31 7394

Weiser, Erich. Begriff, Wesen und Formen des strafbaren Glücksspiels. 98p. Leipzig, Weicher, 1930 7395

DRUNKENNESS

Barbier, P. Le délit alcoolique. Répression et prévention. Etude criminologique. 199p. Thèse, Paris, 1930 7396

Drunkenness as an offence or an ingredient of an offence. Austral L J 4: 378-80 Ap '31 7397

Fischer, Max. Der Alkoholmissbrauch. (D. kommende Geschlecht. 4,3) 72p. Berlin, Dümmler, 1929 7398

Flaig, J. Der Alkohol im Entwurf eines Strafvollzugsgesetzes. Alkoholfrage 23: 288-90 '27 7399

Goytre, Giovanni. L'ubbriachezza ed il codice penale. Med Condotto (1): 5-6 '28 7400

Junckerstorff, K. Strafrechtsreform und Alkoholmissbrauch. Arch f Strafr u Strafproz 71: 361-73 D '27 7401

Kilmer, Theron Wendell. The drunken driver; address before New York state association of chiefs of police, July 27-29, 1931. 5p. (mim) 7402

Kinberg, Olaf. La loi suèdoise relative au traitement des alcooliques. R Int de Dr Pén 8: 271-89 '31 7403

Lafora, G. R. El problema del alcoholismo en el nuevo código penal español. Arch de Med, Cir y Espec 31: 73-8 Jl 27 '29; same title: R de Crimin, Psiquiat y Med Leg 17: 462-71 Jl '30 7404

Mimin, Pierre. Les bouilleurs de cru devant la loi pénale. Les délits, les preuves, les peines. 289p. Paris, Sirey, 1931 7405

Mitton, R. D. The drunken driver and how to curb this menace. Chief Constables' Assn Can Proc 26: 47-51 '30 7406

A question of definition. Just Peace 95: 162 Mr 14 '31 7407

Stooss, Carl. Schuldhaftes Sichbetrinken. Monats f Kriminalpsychol u Strafrechtsref 19: 345-6 Je '28 7408

Thot, Ladislao. La embriaguez, la vagancia, la mendicidad, y la ociosidad en el derecho penal. R de Identif y Cienc Pen 1: 166-77 Ja '28 7409

Ventrella, Leone. L'ubriachezza. Scuola Pos ns 11: 36-8 Ja '31 7410

Wilson, Gordon. The definition of drunkenness. Police J [London] 1: 594-604 '28 7411

Vagrancy

Bignold, Hugh Barron. Police offenses acts and the vagrancy acts. ed.4. Toronto, Carswell, 1928 **7412**

Cicala, S. Mendicità, vagabondaggio ed ozio nel diritto pubblico italiano ed estero. Scuola Pos 38: 109-28 '30 **7413**

Grzegorzewski, Ziemowit. La lutte contre la mendicité et le vagabondage. R Penitent de Pologne (5-6): 165-206 '30 **7414**

Human various. Just Peace 94: 216-17 Ap 5 '30 **7415**

Incorrigible rogues—right of appeal from conviction. Just Peace 94: 456-7 Jl 19 '30 **7416**

Mattern, G.. Betteleidelikte. Monats f Kriminalpsychol u Strafrechtsref 20: 411-17 '29 **7417**

Rackstraw, J. W. Vagrancy and petty crime. Howard J 2: 352-5 Je '29 **7418**

Heresy, Occultism, Religious Offenses, etc.

Campolongo, Francesco. I delitti contro la religione e la pietà dei defunti. 240p. Napoli, A. Morano, 1930 **7419**

Campolongo, Francesco. Le dottrine dell' Abate Giovacchino e il delitto di eresìa. 47p. Benevento, Tip. de Martini, 1928. ed.2. 48p. Napoli, F. Giannini, 1929 **7420**

Ceillier, A. La criminalité mystique dans les sociétés modernes. Ann de Méd Lég 11: 1-14 Ja '31 **7421**

Cicala, Salvatore. L'esercizio dell'occultismo come reato. Riv di Dir e Proc Pen (5-6): 230-45 '28; same title: Scuola Pos ns8: 230-45 My '28; separate: 18p. Milano, Vallardi, 1928 **7422**

Daniel, Gerhard. Il vilipendio della religione nel prog. di cod. pen. italiano. Scuola Pos (8-9): ptla: 348- '30 **7423**

Hellwig, A. Hellsehen als strafbare Gaukelei. Arch f Strafr u Strafproz 71: 124-30 Ap '27 **7424**

Hugendubel, K. Die Religionsverbrechen nach §§215, 216 des Entwurfs von 1919... 47p. Ansbach, Brügel, 1927 **7425**

Institoris, Henricus. Malleus maleficarum; transl with introductory bibliography and notes by Montague Summers. 272p. London, J. Rodker, 1928 **7426**

Schorn, H. Religion und Strafrecht. Deut Richterzeit 20: 12-15 '28 **7427**

Press Laws

Exhenry, A. Le droit de réponse en matière de presse dans les législations d'Europe: Suisse, France, Allemagne, Italie, Iougoslavie. 96p. Thèse, Berne, 1929 **7428**

Hafter, Ernst. Umfang des Pressdelikts und strafrechtliche Sonderstellung der Presse. Schweiz Zeitsch f Strafr 40: 134-50 '27 **7429**

Jørgensen, T. G. Om presselovens revision. Nord Tids f Straf 16: 223-45 Jl '28 **7430**

Kevelaer, Wilhelm. Beiträge zum Pressstrafrecht unter besonderer Berücksichtigung der pressrechtlichen Verantwortlichkeit des Verlegers. 43p. Diss. Erlangen, 1931. Hagen, Erich Ose, 1931 **7431**

Ludwig, C. Presse und Strafjustiz. Schweiz Zeitsch f Strafr 41: 301-4 '28 **7432**

Perraud-Charmantier, André. Le droit de réponse en matière de presse; étude critique de législation et de juriprudence. 512p. Paris, Godde, 1930 **7433**

[Potulicki,] M. La cuestion de los delitos de la prensa. R de Crimin, Psiquiat y Med Leg 15:306-10 My '28 **7434**

Potulicki, Michel. Le régime de la presse (étude de législation pénale comparée). 211p. Paris, Sirey, 1929 **7435**

Schreder, Adolf. Die Wahrnehmung berechtigter Interessen mit besonderer Berücksichtigung der Presse. 38p. bibliog v-vi. Diss. Erlangen, 1931. Mayen, Louis Schreder, 1931 **7436**

AGAINST GOVERNMENT

Bourquin, Maurice. Crimes et délits contre la sûreté des états étrangers. Acad Int Law Rec des Cours 16: 117-246 '27 **7437**

Chicca, G. Il concetto classico del reato politico. Scuola Pos ns7: 417-22 S '27 **7438**

Finkey, Franz v. A politikai büncselekmény és a büntetötörvénykönyv. 34p. Budapest, 1927 **7439**

Fraeb, W. M. Unrichtige Parteibezeichnung und Prozessieren unter falschen Nahmen. Gerichtssaal 97: 235-356, 436-79 '28 **7440**

Longhi, Silvio. Reati di antifascismo commessi all'estero. Rassegna Pen (1-2): 1-5 '29 **7441**

Loquercio, L. Abuso del diritto come reato. 24p. Catania, "La Stampa," 1927 **7442**

Lorenz. Inwiefern verlangt das politische Delikt eine besondere Stellung in der Strafgesetzgebung? Deut Juristen-Zeit 34: 596-600 My 1 '29 **7443**

Manfredini, Mario. Dei delitti contro l'amministrazione della giustizia. ed.3 rev. v5 476p. Milano, Vallardi, 1927 **7444**

De Marsico, Alfredo. I delitti contro lo Stato nell'evoluzione del diritto publico. Scuola Pos ns7: 97-126 Mr '27; same title: Ann della Univ Bari 1: 1-41 '27 **7445**

Martini, Demetrio de. I reati commessi in territorî di capitolazioni. Giustiz Pen 37(2) ptl: 204-21 F '31 **7446**

Morasch, Georg. Die strafrechtliche behandlung des sogenannten über zeugungsverbrechers. 64p. bibliog 5-6. Diss. Tübingen. Stuttgart, Find, 1928 **7447**

Pella, Vespasien V. La répression des crimes contre la personalité de l'état. Acad Int Law Rec des Cours 3: 671-837 bibliog(p673-5) '30 **7448**

Rappaport, Emil Stanislaw. Propagande de la guerre d'aggression comme délit du droit de gens. R Pénitent de Pologne 4(3-4): 310-24 English transl (p341-6) Jl '29 7449

Rodière, René. Le délit politique. 296p. Paris, Rousseau, 1931 7450

Sagone, Giuseppe. Pour une répression efficace du délit politique. R Int de Dr Pén 7: 310-28 '30 7451

Stinson, J. Whitla. Some consideration governing title VI of the espionage act. Pa L R 77: 369-81 Ja '29 7452

Trasimeni, Roberto. Il delitto politico. 69p. Spoleto, Panetto e Petrelli, 1927 7453

Vecchio, G. del. Gli attentati contro la sede del partito nazionale fascista. Scuola Pos ns8: 101-15 Mr '28 7454

Züblin, Georg. Die Falschwerbung und das Delikt der Annahme unerlaubten fremden Militärdienstes nach schweizerischem Recht. 113p. Aarau, Sauerländer, 1928 7455

Obstructing Justice

Appel, Alfred. Publications tending to obstruct justice: right of review. Cornell L Q 12: 374-9 Ap '27 7456

Obstructing the course of justice. Sol J 74: 31 Ja 18 '30 7457

Obstruction of police. Just Peace 94: 667 O 25 '30 7458

Preventing the detection of offences. Irish L T 65: 49-50 F 28 '31 7459

Publications tending to interfere with the administration of justice. Minn L R 15: 442-53 Mr '31 7460

Perjury

Berg, J[oseph]. Subornation de témoins et faux témoignage. Une lacune de code pénal. R de Dr Pén et de Crimin 8: 177-81 F '28 7461

Bromley, Dorothy Dunbar. Perjury rampant. Harper's 163: 37-47 Je '31 7462

C[iplet], M. Law of perjury in Pennsylvania. Temple L Q 4: 71-6 D '29 7463

Colvin, Ewing D. Who tells the truth? Northwest Police J 6: 12, 117-18 Je '29 7464

Committals for perjury by justices. Just Peace 91: 69-70 Ja 29 '27 7465

Elpern, George S. Distintegration of justice by tampering with witnesses and testimony. Police J [N Y] 16: 8-10 Ja '29 7466

Goldschmidt, F. Eidesverletzung und Eidesüberschätzung. Justiz 3: 172-5 '27 7467

Hirschberg. Ein aufgedecktes Meineidskomplott. Arch f Krim 84: 81-104 Ap '29 7468

Is perjury increasing. L Notes 33: 165-6 D '29 7469

Jiménez de Asúa, Luis. Le délit de subornation (à propos d'un décret du gouvernement espagnol) traduit par Jules Gillard. R de Dr Pén et de Crimin 8: 566-74 Je '28 7470

Kössler, M. Zu den Bestimmungen des Strafgesetzentwurfes über Meineid und falsche Aussage. Gerichts-Zeit 79: 89-91 '28 7471

Koffka, Else. Die Bestrafung der falschen uneidlichen Zeugenaussage. Zeitsch f d ges Strafrechtswiss 48: 10-28 '28 7472

Kühn, Fritz. Der fahrlässige Falscheid nach geltendem Recht und den Entwürfen. 62p. bibliog vii-x. Diss. Erlangen, 1930 7473

Mackaye, M. Perjury in the modern manner. Outl 152: 162-6 My 27 '29 7474

Mullins, Claud. Perjury. Q R 256: 223-35 Ap '31 7475

[Perjury]. L Notes 30: 223-4 Mr '27 7476

Perjury in judicial proceedings. U S L R 64: 1-6 Ja '30 7477

Perjury in police courts. Sol J 71: 903 N 26 '27 7478

Prevention of perjury. L Notes 32: 81 Ag '28 7479

Ratzenhofer, G. Gegen die Bestrafung des fahrlässigen Falscheides. Gerichts-Zeit 79: 91-2 '28 7480

Rice, Thomas S. Brazen perjury makes false swearing act necessary. Panel 9: 53 N '31 7481

Robinson, C. L. A drag-net for perjurers. Panel 6: 6-7 D '28 7482

Toy, Harry S. Michigan law on alibi and insanity defences reduces perjury. Panel 9: 52 N '31 7483

Tuttle, Charles H. Perjury: a crime or a privilege. Cent 115: 1-12 N '27 7484

Ufenast, Walter. Das falsche Zeugnis in rechtsvergleichender Darstellung. 102p. Aarau, Sauerländer, 1927 7485

Weinberg, Harry E. Perjury and the witness; some aspects of the problem of the false-swearing witness. Police "13-13" 5: 13-14 S '30 7486

Contempt of Court

Attitude of judges toward contempt. L Notes 33: 83-4 Ag '29 7487

Bowron, Fletcher. Contempt of court. Los Angeles B Assn Bul 3: 5-11 My 3 '28 7488

Brinkman, O. H. Contempt of court. Geo L J 18: 287-98 My '30 7489

Butler, Paul M. Contempt and executive power to pardon. Notre Dame Law 4: 443-7, 548-56 Ap, My '29 7490

Cann, George T. Charge of contempt. Ga Lawyer 1: 91, 102-3 S '30 7491

Chused, Joseph J. Public comment as contempt of court. St Louis L R 16: 24-48 D '30 7492

Comment after trial. Sol J 75: 179 Mr 14 '31 7493

Committal for contempt. Sol J 75: 109 F 14 '31 7494

Contempt of court. Sol J 72: 790-1 N 24 '28; 73: 844-5 D 21 '29 7495

Contempt of court. Just Peace 95: 313-14 My 16 '31 7496

Contempt of court by publication of photograph of accused. Just Peace 91: 262-3 Ap 9 '27 7497

Contempt, power of governor to pardon. Mich St B J 10: 174-5 Ja '31 7498

Contempt procedure. Am Jud Soc J 10: 186-91 Ap '27 7499

Cordes, Joseph E. Contempt proceedings in Wisconsin. Marquette L R 13: 150-60 Ap '29 7500

Curtis, Charles P. jr. and Richard C. The story of a motion in the law of criminal contempt. Harv L R 41: 51-68 N '27 7501

Executive pardons of contempts of court. Ia L R 14: 447-53 Je '29 7502

Faught, Albert Smith. Contempt of federal courts. Am B Assn J 13: 636-7 N '27 7503

Fox, John Charles. The history of contempt of court, the form of trial and the mode of punishment. 252p. Oxford, Clarendon press, 1927 7504

"Gross and outrageous" contempt. Just Peace 94: 470 Jl 26 '30 7505

Hulse, Jim F. Procedure in contempt cases. Tex L R 7: 274-83 F '29 7506

Johnston, Henry A. Jury shadowing as contempt of court. U S L R 63: 511-22 O '29 7507

Jurisdiction of a court to punish criminal contempts committed in another state. Univ Pa L R 76: 984-8 Je '28 7508

Lardner, Rice. Executive pardon for contempt of court. Rocky Mo L R 2: 137-52 Ap '30 7509

Laski, Harold J. Procedure for constructive contempt in England. Harv L R 41: 1031-43 Je '28 7510

Nelles, Walter. The summary power to punish for contempt. Colum L R 31: 956-74 Je '31 7511

Nelles, Walter and King, Carol Weiss. Contempt by publication in the United States. Colum L R 28: 401-31, 525-62 Ap '28 7512

Newspaper cameras and contempt. Va L Reg ns13: 119-22 Je '27 7513

The privilege of the press and contempt of court. Va L R ns13: 117-19 Je '27 7514

R[eady], F[rancis] T. Pardon for contempt. Notre Dame Law 5: 31-3 O '29 7515

Riddell, William Renwick. The state trials and contempt of court. Can B R 4: 463-8 S '27 7516

Rogers, Waldo. Trial by jury in contempt cases. Rocky Mo L R 2: 115-21 F '30 7517

Russell, Charles G. Review of contempt judgments on habeas corpus proceedings. Tex L R 8: 105-11 D '29 7518

Shull, Charles W. Congressional investigations and contempts. U S L R 63: 326-9 Jl '29 7519

S[iegel], G[eorge] L. A newspaper publication as criminal contempt. Ill L R 25: 202-4 Je '30 7520

Venters, Carl V. Criticism of decision or opinion, of case then terminated, as contempt. L Notes 34: 190-3 Ja '31 7521

Willis, Hugh Evander. Punishment for contempt of court. Ind L J 2: 309-14 Ja '27 7522

Yankwich, Leon R. Judges and the law of contempt. Am Fed 37: 552-4 My '30 7523

Yankwich, Leon R. The newspaper and the law of contempt. Los Angeles B Assn Bul 2: 10-16 Ap 7 '27 7524

Yankwich, Leon R. Use and abuse of contempt commitments. U S L R 65: 481-95 S '31 7525

TREASON

Bell. Der Landesverrat im neuen Strafgesetzbuch. Jurist Wchnschr 58: 1770-5 Je 15 '29 7526

Frind, Josef Walter. Der Landesverrat im deutschen Strafrecht unter bes. Berücks. der Entwürfe. 128p. (Strafrechtl Abh no298) Breslau, Schletter, 1931 7527

Gutjahr, [Georg]. Diplomatischer Landesverrat im Bundesstaat Österreich. Zeitsch f d ges Strafrechtswiss 49: 210-34 '29 7528

Gutjahr, Georg. Diplomatischer Landesverrat innerhalb des Bundesstaats. 30p. Berlin, Vahlen, 1928 7529

Gutjahr, G[eorg]. Fahrlässiger Landesverrat. Jurist Rundsch 17-19 '28 7530

Gutjahr, [Georg]. Landesverräterische Waffenhilfe. Zeitsch f d ges Strafrechtswiss 49: 185-210 '29 7531

Jörns. Landesverrat. Deut Richterzeit 20: 105-8 '28 7532

Kiessel, Georg. Die Bestimmungen über Hochverrat in den Entwürfen zum neuen Strafgesetzbuch im Vergleich mit dem geltenden Recht unter Berücksichtigung des Republikschutzgesetzes vom 25. März 1930. 55p. bibliog 54-5. Diss. Erlangen, 1931. Erlangen, Döres, 1931 7533

Löwenthal. Der Landesverrat im Strafgesetzentwurf. Justiz 3: 120-42 '27 7534

Radbruch, G. Der Landesverrat im Strafgesetzentwurf. Justiz 3: 103-10 '27 7535

Schneider, Alfred. Die Strafbestimmungen des Republikschutzgesetzes. 75p. bibliog 5-8. Diss. Erlangen, 1930 7536

Wegner, A. Über Hochverrat. Justiz 3: 147-8 '27 7537

Zelt, Max. Der militärische Landesverrat nach geltendem deutschen Strafrecht und den Entwürfen zum Strafgesetzbuch. 79p. bibliog 78-9. Diss. Erlangen, 1930. München, Wegele, 1930 7538

SYNDICALISM

Azzariti, Gaetano. L'associazione sindicale come parte civile nel processo penale. Dir del Lavoro (12): 733-40 '28 7539

American civil liberties union. A strike is criminal syndicalism—in California. 11p. New York, March 1931 7540

Buck, Caldwell. The new syndicalism in France. Am Fed 38: 972-8 Ag '31 7541

California. Governor. Case of Charlotte A. Whitney. 14p. Sacramento, 1927 7542

California. Governor. The pardon of Charlotte Anita Whitney. 15p. Sacramento, 1927 7543

Capobianco, Giuseppe Leonida. Syndicalismo e diritto. 128p. Milano, Société Edit. Libraria, 1929 7544

Chafee, Zechariah, jr. Criminal syndicalism and the supreme court. *In his* The inquiring mind. 276p. N. Y. Harcourt [1928] 7545

Constitutionality of California's criminal syndicalism act upheld. Cong Dig 6: 210-12 Je '27 7546

Criminal syndicalism laws tested. Inf Serv 6: 3-4 Je 4 '27 7547

Decision on the application of the Kansas criminal syndicalism act. Cong Dig 6: 212- Je '27 7548

Gendel, Martin. Criminal law: criminal syndicalism: red flag history: history of enforcement in California. Calif L R 19: 64-9 N '30 7549

Laidler, Harry Wellington. Syndicalism. *In his* A history of socialist thought, 348-92. N. Y. Crowell, 1927 7550

National Supreme court decisions. Bradstreets 55: 345 My 21 '27 7551

Nettlau, M. Lebende Probleme der Anarchie und der [argentinische anarchistische] Kongress von Santa Fé. Internationale 3(2): 25-32 D '29 7552

Petition before United States Supreme court for rehearing of conclusions affecting criminal syndicalism act. Comm & Fin Chron 124: 3727 Je 25 '27 7553

Supreme court and criminal syndicalism. Comm & Fin Chron 124: 2966-8, 3157-60 My 21, 28 '27 7554

Syndicalism and the Supreme court. Outl 146: 100 My 25 '27 7555

Turano, F. I reati e le pene nella legislazione sindacale. 265p. Roma, Libr. del Littorio, 1927 7556

Whitaker, Robert. Repealing a vicious law. Chr Cent 48: 1213 S 30 '31 7557

MISCELLANEOUS

Brisard. Condamnation du chirurgien dans un cas de syncope chloroformique mortelle. Ann de Méd Lég 7: 207-12 Ap '27 7558

Crimes known to the police in Denmark. J Crim L & Crimin 22: 617-18 N '31 7559

Deransart, A. Repertoire alphabétique des crimes, délits, contraventions. ed.3 rev. 676p. Paris, Librarie des Juris-Classeurs, 1929 7560

Ebermayer and Fischer, Herwart. Bekämpfung des Kurpfuschertums de lege lata et de lege ferenda. Monats f Kriminalpsychol u Strafrechtsref 19: 165-6 Mr '28 7561

Fragnaud, Léopold. Répertoire formulaire des contraventions de simple police et des infractions correctionnelles. ed.8. 97p. Paris, Annales de justices de paix, 1927 7562

Glaser, Stefan. Les délits a distance. R de Dr Pén et de Crimin 9: 453-7 '29 7563
Résumé d'une dissertation qui a paru en Pologne, dans l'Annuaire juridique de Wilno, Rocznik Prawniczy Wilensku, 1929. 62p.

Hippel, R. v. Über Urkundenunterdrückung. Rechtswidrigheit und Schuld. Jurist Wchnschr 56: 3038-41 '27 7564

Jovane, E. In tema di truffo agli emigranti. Scuola Pos ns7: 159-60 Mr '27 7565

Kellner, Oskar. Die Gläubiger- und Schuldnerbegünstigung §241, 242 K.O. 104p. (Strafrechtliche Abh no233) Breslau, Schletter, 1928 7566

Klodt, H. Bildet §17 Abs. 1 Satz 1 der Verordnung über Kraftfahrzeugverkehr vom 5. Dezember 1925 in der Fassung vom 28. Juli 1926 eine selbständige Strafnorm? Arch f Strafr u Strafproz 72: 94-6 Mr '28 7567

Leonhard, F. Gefängnis für Kunstfehler. Zeitsch f ärztl Fortbild 25: 265 '28 7568

Marcetus, K. Die Bedeutung des Gesetzes zur Änderung des Telegraphengesetzes vom 3.12.27 (RGBl.S.311ff) für das Strafrecht. Zeitsch f d ges Strafrechtswiss 49: 290-305 '29 7569

Marfels, T. Das Verbrechen vorsätzlicher Lebensgefährtung. 104p. Leipzig, 1927 7570

Mueller, B. Missbräuchliche Wiederverwendung bereits entwerteter Gerichtskostenmarken. Arch f Krim 87: 103-15 N '30 7571

Neukamp. Berufsgeheimnis und Kurpfuscherei. Deut Med Wchnschr 53: 1828-9 O 21 '27 7572

Neukamp. Kurpfuscherei, Berufsgeheimnis, Rechtsangleichung und Strafgesetzentwurf. Deut Med Wchnschr 54: 281 '28 7573

Oppenheimer, L. Das ärztliche Recht und der Entwurf zu einem Allgemeinen Deutschen Strafgesetzbuch. Schweiz Juristen-Zeit 25: 36-40 '28 7574

Palazzo, G. Alfredo. Obbligo di cura medico-chirurgica e sanzione penale. 4p. Bologna, Stab. polig. Riuniti, 1928 7575
Extr: Il Diritto Sanitario no3.

Sabatini, Guglielmo. Delle contravvenzione. ed.3. 415p. Milano, Vallardi, 1927 7576

Sagone, Giuseppe. Il delitto internazionale. 136p. Palermo, Corselli, 1927 7577

Sasserath, Simon. Les faux certificats médicaux (Article 204 du code pénal). R de Dr Pén et de Crimin 8: 321-7 Ap '28 7578

Schleich, Botho. Die gefährliche Körperverletzung und die Misshandlung Pflegebefohlener des § 223a StGB. Eine rechtshistorische und rechtsvergleichende kritische Studie unter Berücksichtigung der Reformbewegung des 20. Jahrhunderts. 144p. Breslau, Schletter, 1928 7579

Seidlmayer. Der Arzt und der Entwurf zum Strafgesetzbuch. Allg Zeitsch f Psychiat 87: 146-54 '27 7580

Seinemeyer. Automobildiebstähle und deren Verhütung. Krimin Monatsh 5: 11-13 Ja '31 7581

Spano, Francesco. Il tentativo nel reato di emigrazione clandestina determinato da motivi di lavoro. Nuov Dir (6): 361-3 '29 7582

Stokvis, Benno Jules. Rond het misdrijf van frauduleusen invoer. 248p. bibliog. footnotes. Amsterdam, Koloniale boekcentrale, 1928 7583

Thót, L. La reincidencia. R de Identif y Cienc Pen 1: 12-22 N '27 7584

Van Voorhis, John S. A pocket digest of crimes and criminal procedure. 122p. Philadelphia, Leary, 1927. ed.19. 124p. 1930 7585

Volkmann, K. Crimes et délits à bord des aéronefs en droit international. Dr Aérien (1): 26- '31 7586

Warner, Sam Bass. Crimes known to the police: an index of crime? Harv L R 45: 307-34 D '31 7587

Zappulli. Ancora sull'interpretazione del no.20 dell'art.55 del codice pénal. Riv Pen di Dott, Legis e Giuris 17: 335-42 Mr '28 7588

REFORM OF CRIMINAL LAW

À propos du projet de loi sur l'adolescence coupable. R de Dr Pén et de Crimin 8: 729-31 Jl '28 7589

Abbott, Edwin M. The need for uniform reciprocal criminal laws. Am B Assn Rep 54: 583-8 '29; same title: J Crim L & Crimin 20: 582-7 F '30 7590

Baldassari, A. Il diritto penale internazionale nel progetto preliminare di un nuovo codice penale. Riv di Dir Int s3 7: 293-337 Jl '28 7591

Benson, Carville D. jr. The people and law reform. Minn L R 13: 687-701 Je '29 7592

Broglio, Rolf Paul. Der strafrechtliche Notstand im Lichte der Strafrechtsreform. 76p. Bonn, Röhrscheid, 1928 7593

Byrer, Harry H. Some suggested changes in our criminal law and procedure. W Va B Assn Proc 1930: 194-202 7594

Carnevale, E. Il momento scientifico attuale e la riforma della legislazione penale. 14p. Napoli, F. Raggi, 1927 7595

Chalupný, Emanuel. Reforma trestního práva s hlediska sociologického. Sociologická R 2: 441-61 '31 7596

Cicala, S. La conferenza di Roma per l'unificazione del diritto penale. Scuola Pos ns8: 376-84 Jl '28 7597

Cicala, S. Per una migliore disciplina della ingiurie sulla persona. Scuola Pos ns8: 409-26 S '28 7598

Conférence internationale des représentants des commissions de codification pénale. 94p. Roma, Provved. Gen. dello Stato, Libr. 1928 7599

Conti, U. Sul progetto preliminare di un nuovo codice penale. Schweiz Zeitsch f Strafr 41: 56-79 '28; separate: 42p. Bern, Stampfli, 1928 7600

Djermekov, Dusan. Les moments psychologiques dans la science pénale et la réforme du droit criminel. Etudes Crimin 3(6): 189-92 N '28 7601

Dohna, Graf zu. Der Stand des Streits um die Strafrechtsreform. Deut Juristen-Zeit 33: 43-7 '28 7602

Donnedieu de Vabres, H. Le droit pénal international devant le congrès de Varsovie. Etudes Crimin 3: 3-10 Ja '28 7603

Dürr. Zur Reform des Strafprozesses. Deut Juristen-Zeit 33: 1434-9 N 1 '28 7604

Ebermayer. Zur Strafrechtsreform. Jurist Rundsch 1-4 '28 7605

Eggleston, F. W. Legislative reform. L Inst J [Melbourne] 2: 74-5 Je '28 7606

Fischer, H. Das Strafvollzugsgesetz in ärtzlicher Beurteilung. Deut Zeitsch f d ges gerichtl Med 14: 520-44 Ja 14 '30 7607

Fuchs, Ernst. Strafrechtsscholastik und neues Strafgesetzbuch. Justiz 3(3): 238-65 '28 7608

Glaser, Stefan. Beccaria et son influence sur la réforme du droit pénal. R Int de Dr Pén 5: 425-40 '28 7609

Hecht, H. Bemerkungen zum besonderen Teile des Strafgesetzentwurfs. Gerichts-Zeit 78: 337-42 '27 7610

Illès, Marcel de. Le problème de l'unification du droit pénal et la défense internationale contre le crime. R Int de Dr Pén 8: 147-53 '31 7611

Jiménez de Asúa, Luis. Bases para una nueva legislación penal. R de Crimin, Psquiat y Med Leg 14: 417-21 Jl '27 7612

Kahl, Wilhelm. Politik gegen Strafrechtsreform. Jurist Wchnschr 60(14): 913-14 Ap 4 '31 7613

Kastner, O. Der Strafgesetzentwurf. Gerichts-Zeit 79: 24-6, 33-9 '28 7614

Kastner, O. Der Strafgesetzentwurf und die anwaltliche Wirksamkeit. Öster Anwalts-Zeit 5: 110-12 '28 7615

Kastner, O. Voraussetzungen der Strafgesetzreform. Jurist Bl 57: 195-7 '28 7616

Kern, Eduard. Zur Strafrechtsreform. 62p. Mannheim, Bensheimer, 1927 7617

Kohlrausch, Eduard. Rede des professor dr. Eduard Kohlrausch über strafrechtsreform. 26p. Berlin, Druck der Preussischen druckerei- und Verl.-aktiengesellschaft, 1927 7618

Lang. Der Stand der Strafrechtsreform. Leipz Zeitsch f Deut Recht 22: 433-40 '28 7619

Lehmann, R. Der Stand der Strafrechtsreform. Deut Richterzeit 20: 149-53 '28 7620

Lévitt, Albert. A proposed code of international criminal law. 16p. N. Y. The Arbitrator, 1928; same title: R Int de Dr Pén 6: 18-32 French transl by R. Geoffrey Fitz-Gerald (p33-46) '29; resume: R de Dr Pén et de Crimin 9: 771-8 '29 7621

Mar, P. Von Jugend, Schund und Schmitz. Weltbühne 24: 89-92 '28 7622

Massari, Edoardo. La riforma del codice penale nel pensiero del giornalismo politico. Bol del Sindacato Fascista Avvocati (2): 1 '28 7623

Mezger, Edmund. Kriminologische Grundlagen von Strafe und Sicherung im Strafgesetzentwurf 1927. Zeitsch f d des Strafrechtswiss 49: 171-85 '29 7624

Miller, Justin. Activities of bar associations and legislatures in connection with criminal law reform. Am B Assn Rep 1927: 452-76; same title: J Crim L & Crimin 18: 378-83 N '27 7625

Mittermaier. Der Stand der Strafrechtsreformen im Auslande. Deut Juristen-Zeit 36(14): 921-6 Jl 15 '31 7626

Moschini, Arturo. Considerazioni sopra la pratica presente penale. Scuola Pos ns8: 429-31 S '28 7627

The need of uniform crime laws. Police J [N Y] 17: 4-5 N '29 7628

Pella, Vespasien V. Vers l'unification du droit pénal par la création d'un Institut international auprès de la Société des Nations. Etudes Crimin 3: 49-56 Mr '28 7629

Potthoff, Heinz. Beiträge zur Strafrechtsreform. Arbeitsrecht 15: 4-14 '28 7630

Rappaport, Emil Stanislaw. Conférence de Varsovie. R Int de Dr Pén 5: 25-30 '28 7631

Rappaport, Emile Stanislaw. L'enseignement de la Conférence de Varsovie. R de Dr Pén et de Crimin 8: 8-12 Ja '28 7632

Rappaport, Emil Stanislaw. Le problème de l'unification internationale du droit pénal. R Pénitent de Pologne 4: 86-123 Ja '29 7633

Résolutions adoptées au congrès de Varsovie. Etudes Crimin 3: 10-11 Ja '28 7634

Reynolds, A. S. Needed changes in the penal law. N Y St Assn Magistrates Proc 19: 79-85 '27 7635

Roethe, E. Zur Strafrechtsreform. Standarte 3: 3-5 '28 7636

Roux, J.-A. La conférence de Varsovie. R Int de Dr Pén 5: 1-6 English transl (p7-12) '28 7637

Roux, J.-A. La IIe conférence international de Rome. R Int de Dr Pén 5: 248-52 '28

Sagone, Giuseppe. Pour un droit pénal international; traduit de l'italien par L.-O. Roux. R Int de Dr Pén 5: 363-82 '28 7639

Schetter. Die Wiederaufnahme der Strafrechtsreformarbeit. Deut Juristen-Zeit 36(5): 329-32 Mr 1 '31 7640

Schmidt, Eberhard. Strafrechtsreform und Kulturkrise. 23p. (Recht und Staat in Geschichte und Gegenwart no79) Tübingen, Mohr, 1931 7641

Schultz. Das Zusammentreffen mehrerer Gesetzesverletzungen nach jetzigem und nach künftigem Strafrecht. Jurist Rundsch 64-6 '28 7642

Schwarzer, Kurt. Probleme zur Reform des Unehelichenrechts. 39p. bibliog vi-viii. Diss. Breslau, 1931 7643

Sims, Henry Upson. The relation of constitutional limitations to the reform of the law. Am B Assn J 16: 613-18 O '30 7644

[Stickel, F. G.]. Crime revision. N J L J 51: 103-6 Ap '28 7645

Texte des résolutions adoptées par la Conférence internationale des représentants des commissions de codification pénale tenue à Varsovie (Novembre 1927). R Int de Dr Pén 5: 13-18 English transl (p19-24) '28 7646

Textes des résolutions votées par la conférence de Rome. R Int de Dr Pén 5: 253-60 '28 7647

The Warsaw conference. L J [London] ns66: 92-3 Ag 11 '28 7648

Weissenstein, R. Die Ehrenbeleidigung im Strafgesetzentwurf. Eine dogmatische Untersuchung. Öster Anwalts-Zeit 5: 52-6, 65-70 '28 7649

Winfield, Percy H. Law reform. L Q R 44: 289-304 Jl '28 7650

Wroblewski, Bronislaw. Ujednostajnonie prawa karnego. Wilno, 1929 7651
Published in L'Annuaire juridique de Wilno.

Wroblewski, Bronislaw. Unification du droit pénal. Etudes Crimin 4: 245-55, 294-307 S, N '29 7652

ARGENTINA

Ruiz-Funes, M. El proyecto de ley argentino sobre el estado peligroso. R Gen de Leg y Juris 152: 563-80 My '28; same title: R de Crimin, Psiquiat y Med Leg 15: 422-45 Jl '28; separate: 32p. Madrid, Reus, 1928 7653

AUSTRIA

Baltinester, G. Der Strafgesetzentwurf vom Jahre 1927 und die österreichische Rechtsanwaltschaft. Öster Anwalts-Zeit 5: 86-93 '28 7654

Dinghoffer, F. Österreichische Rechtsgedanken im Entwurf. Jurist Wchnschr 57: 385-90 '28 7655

Kraszna, Hermann. La riforma del diritto penale in Austria; trad.Ascarelli. Giustiz Pen 37 (3) pt1: 438-42 Mr '31 7656

Rittler, T. Der österreichische Strafgesetz-Entwurf vom Jahre 1927. Zentralbl f d jurist Praxis 46: 1-17 '28 7657

Schnek, F. Der österreichische Strafgesetzentwurf. Gerichts-Zeit 79: 2-5, 17-23 '28 7658

Türkel, Siegfried. Das Ärzterecht nach dem österreichischen Strafgesetzentwurfe. Gerichts-Zeit 79: 49-59 '28; separate: 37p. Wien, Manz, 1928 7659

BRAZIL

Gatti, T. Il nuovo progetto di codice penale Brasiliano. Scuola Pos ns8: 323-31 Jl '28 7660

CZECHOSLOVAKIA

Ruiz-Funes, Mariano. El anteproyecto penal checoeslovaco. R Gen de Leg y Juris 153:327-86 O '28; separate: 84p. Madrid, Reus, 1929 7661

S[asserath], S. L'avant projet de code-pénal Tchécoslovaque. R de Dr Pén et de Crimin 8: 487-505 My '28 7662

Schnek, F. Die Verbrechensbekämpfung im cechoslovakischen Strafgesetzentwurf. Zentralbl f d Jurist Praxis 45: 180-90 '27 7663

Torp, C. De čechoslovakiske Straffelsforslag af 1926. Nord Tids f Straf 15: 307-21 O '27 7664

DENMARK

Bergendal, Ragnar. Danmarks strafflagsreform. Svensk Juristt 15(6): 519-37 N '30 7665

Krabbe, Oluf. Strafrechtsreform in Dänemark. Zeitsch f d ges Strafrechtswiss 48: 335-8 '28 7666

Lucas, F. Entwurfe eines dänischen Strafgesetzbuches. Monats f Kriminalpsychol u Strafrechtsref 19: 577-97 O '28 7667

Lucas, F. Das neue dänische Strafgesetzbuches. Monats f Kriminalpsychol u Strafrechtsref 21: 641-6 N '30 7668

FRANCE

Weinkauff. Die französische Justizreform von 1926-1929. Jurist Rundsch (20): 221-8 O 15 '29 7669

GERMANY

Alsberg, Max. Die Sittlichkeitsdelikte im Strafgesetzentwurf. Arch f Krim 83: 94-100 S '28 7670

Bell. Strafrechtsreform und Reichstagsausschuss. Jurist Wchnschr 57: 778-82 '28 7671

Calon, E. C. El proyecto de código penal alemán de 1927. R Gen de Leg y Juris 76: 508-49 '28 7672

Delaquis, E. Gebt dem Bunde, was des Bundes ist! Bemerkungen zu den Beratungen über den Strafgesetzentwurf im Nationalrat. Schweiz Zeitsch f Strafr 41: 1-16 '28 7673

Dinghoffer, F. Die Ergebnisse der ersten beiden deutsch-österreichischen Strafrechts-Konferenzen. Wille u Werk 3: 496-8 '28 7674

Forster. Der neue Entwurf des allgemeinen Deutschen Strafgesetzbuches vom ärztlichen Standpunkte. Monats f Kriminalpsychol u Strafrechtsref 19: 476-9 Ag '28 7675

Gleispach, W. Die Bemessung der Strafe nach dem deutschen Strafgesetzentwurf. Arch f Rechts u Wirtschaftsphilos 21: 184-212 '28 7676

Gruhle, Hans W. Gedanken zur Beratung der Strafrechtsreform im Reichstag am 21. und 22. Juni 1927. Monats f Kriminalpsychol u Strafrechtsref 18: 465-7 S '27 7677

Hanssen, Kurt Walter. Der begriff urkunde im amtlichen Entwurf eines allgemeinen deutschen Strafgesetzbuches. 130p. (Strafrechtl Abh no234, hrsg von Schoetensack). Inaug.-diss. Heidelberg, 1928. bibliog v-x. Breslau, Schletter, 1928 7678

Honig, Richard. Der gegenwärtige stand der Strafrechtsreform. Krimin Monatsh 3: 1-4 Ja '29 7679

Hufner. Zur Auslegung des §11 des Gesetzes über die Presse, der Entwurfe des neuen Strafgesetzbuches und die Presse. Leipz Zeitsch f Deut Recht 22: 585-97 '28 7680

Kahl, W. Die deutsche Strafrechtsreform. Hoffnungen und Zweifel. Gesetz u Recht 28: 257-60 '27 7681

Klee, K. Inwieweit enthält die Reichstagsvorlage 1927 gegenüber dem Amtlichen Entwurfe des neuen Strafgesetzbuches von 1925 Verbesserungen und inwieweit Verschlechterungen? Arch f Strafr u Strafproz 72: 2-8 Ja '28 7682

Obornicker, Alfred. Die Beschlüsse des Reichstagsausschusses für Strafrechtsreform. Justiz 3(3): 232-7 '28 7683

Radin, Max. The proposed German penal code. Calif L R 15: 378-80 Jl '27 7684

Schmidt, R. Die Stellung der Strafrechtsreform innerhalb der Gesamtentwicklung des modernen deutschen Rechts. Gerichtssaal 96: 1-36 '28 7685

Schürff. Die Strafrechtsvereinheitlichung. Arch f Krim 88: 105-9 Mr '31 7686

Siehr, C[arl]. Die deutsche Strafrechtsreform. Jurist Wchnschr 56: 1971-4 '27 7687

Solomonescu, G. Un nou proect de cod penal german. R de Drept Pen 109-17 Ja '28 7688

Strassmann, G. Die ärztlich wichtigen Bestimmungen des deutschen Strafgesetzentwurfes in der Reichsratsfassung 1927. Med Klin 23: 1560-1, 1597-9 O 7, 14 '27 7689

GREAT BRITAIN

Liublinskii, P. Proyekt izmenenii v ugolovnom zakonodatelstve Anglii. Problemy Prestupnosti 2: 299-307 '27 7690

S., H. W. Parliament and penal reform. Howard J 2: 124-7 '27 7691

GREECE

Constantinidis, P. transl. Le nouveau projet de code pénal hellénique. R de Dr Pén et de Crimin 7: 335-51 Mr '27; same title: 17p. Paris, Godde, 1928 7692

Constantinidis, P. Rapport sur le projet du code pénal grec. 35p. Paris, Godde, 1928 7693

Ferri, E[nrico]. Il progetto (1924) di codice penal per la Grecia. Scuola Pos ns7: 431-4 S '27 7694

Hugueney, Louis. Le projet de code pénal grec. R de Dr Pén et de Crimin 8: 876-9 Ag '28 7695

Ténékidès, C. G. Le projet du nouveau code pénal hellénique et le droit des gens. R Int de Dr Pén 5: 165-81 '28 7696

ITALY

Altavilla, E[nrico]. Il progetto di un nuovo codice penale nella visione di un positivista. 18p. Spoleto, Panetto e Petrelli, 1928 7697
Extr: Revista critica di diritto e giurisprudenza e cronache forensi.

Altavilla, Enrico. La subbiettivazione del diritto penale nel progetto Rocco. 17p. Milano, Vallardi, 1928 7698
Extr: Scuola Positiva and Rivista di Diritto e procedura penale.

Assante, C. "Dei delitti contro il patrimonio" del nuovo codice penale. Giustiz Pen 34: 309-26 Ja 22 '28 7699

Benvenuto, Giuseppe. Il ratto consensuale nel progetto di codice penale. Scuola Pos ns8: 134-7 Mr '28 7700

Bunge. Der Fortgang der italienischen Strafrechtsreform. Deut Juristen-Zeit 36(5): 332-7 Mr 1 '31 7701

Bunge. Die Reform des italienischen Strafrechts. Deut Juristen-Zeit 33: 138-43 '28 7702

Bunge, Karl. Italienischer Vorentwurf zu einem neuen Strafgesetzbuch. 224p. (Sammlung ausserdeutscher Strafgesetzbücher no48) Berlin, Gruyter, 1928 7703

C., F. A. La reforma del codigo penal italiano. Bibl Nac de Crim y Cienc Afines Bol 1: 278-94 Ja '27 7704

Caldara-Russo, G. Il consenso dell'offeso secondo il progetto di un nuovo codice penale e il suicidio come reato. Scuola Pen Uman 5: 102-11 '27 7705

Carezzano, Paolo. Il ricovero degli alienati criminali secondo il nuovo progetto di codice penale italiano. Arch di Antrop Crim 48: 259-63 Mr '28 7706

Carnevale, E. Sul progetto preliminare d'un nuovo codice penale. Ann della Univ Palermo 13: 313-42 '29; extract: 32p. Palermo, "Boccone del Povero," 1928 7707

C[arrara], M. Appunti sul progetto del nuovo codice penale. Arch di Antrop Crim 47: 1027-32 N '27 7708

Casabianca, M. de. Le nouveau code pénal italien. R Pénitent de Dr Pén 54: 396-426 S '30 7709

Casabianca, M. and others. Derniers travaux sur le code pénal italien. Sa promulgation. R Pénitent de Dr Pén 54: 427-52 S '30 7710

Casabianca, Pierre de. Les mineurs dans le nouveau code pénal italien. R Pénitent de Dr Pén 54: 452-83 S '30 7711

Catalano, Emanuele. La riforma penale e i suoi riflessi educativi. 258p. (Bibliot. di scienze soc. e polit. no84) Palermo, Sandron, 1930 7712

Cecchi, Orfeo. Gli odierni progressi della scienza criminale in Italia e la riforma del codice penale. 42p. Roma, Tip. del Littorio, 1929 7713
Extr: Rivista Penale.

Cecchi, Orfeo. Sul progetto preliminare del nuovo codice penale. Pregi e difetti. Riv Pen di Dott, Legis e Giuris 158-73 Ag '28 7714

Conti, Ugo. Sul progetto preliminare di un nuovo codice penale italiano. Schweiz Zeitsch f Strafr 41: 147-64 '28 7715

Conti, Ugo. Sul progetto preliminare di un nuovo codice di procedura penale italiano. Schweiz Zeitsch f Strafr 44: 194-208 '30 7716

Corte di Cassazione del Regno. Relazione sul progetto preliminare del nuovo codice penale. Giustiz Pen 34: 1-56 Ja 8 '28 7717

Coscia, S. La più importante riforma nel codice Mussolini. 30p. Roma, 1928 7718

Costa, S. Progetto di un nuovo codice penale. Sul reato tentato. Riv Pen di Dott, Legis e Giuris 107: 553-6 My '28 7719

Criscuoli, V. Il reato di boicottagio nel progetto di un nuovo codice penale. Scuola Pen Uman 5: 91-101 '27 7720

Dalma, G. Osservazioni sul progetto del nuovo codice penale nelle suo attinenze colla psichiatria. Note e Riv di Psichiat 59: 315-28 '30 7721

Delitala, G. Reato continuato e cosa giudicata nel codice penale vigente e nel progetto di codice penale. Scuola Pos ns8: 116-23 Mr '28 7722

Dongoroz, Vintila. Observatiuni asupra proiectului de Cod penal Român. 161p. Bucuresti, "Curierul Judiciar," 1928 7723

Enea, G. M. A. Progetto di un nuovo codice penale. L'elemento economico nella codificazione della pena. Riv Pen di Dott, Legis e Giuris 107: 541-52 My '28 7724

Ferri, Enrico. Le nouveau projet de code pénal italien. R Int de Dr Pén 5: 400-15 '28 7725

Ferri, E[nrico]. Il progetto Rocco di codice penale. Scuola Pos ns7: 481-94 N '27 7726

Ferri, Enrico and Grispigni, Filippo. Pareri sul progetto preliminare di un nuovo codice penale italiano. Riv Int di Filosofia del Dir 8(2): 225-39 Mr '28 7727

Florian, Eugenio. L'insegnamento universitario del diritto e della procedura penale in relazione al progetto Rocco. Scuola Pos ns8: 138-9 Mr '28 7728

Fürth, H. Die fascistische Reform des italienischen Strafrechtes. Jurist Bl 57: 3-7 '28 7729

Gabrieli, Francesco P. Esposizione dei principii direttivi e spiegazione pratica del nuovo codice penale italiano. Giustiz Pen 37: 2-7 Ja '31 7730

Galimberti, Tancredi. Pene e misure di sicurezza nel progetto Rocco. Scuola Pos (10-11) pt1: 433- '30; extract: 13p. Milano, Vallardi, 1930 7731

Gismondi, [Antonio]. I concetti fondamentali del progetto di un nuovo codice penale italiano. Giustiz Pen 33: 632-5 '27 7732

Giudice, Arturo del. Il progetto del nuovo codice penale italiano. 188p. Napoli, Ed. La Toga, 1928 7733

Gregoraci, Giuseppe. Sommarie osservazioni critiche al progetto preliminare del nuovo codice penale italiano presentato alla commissione ministeriale. Giustiz Pen 34: 84-125 Ja 22 '28 7734

Hentig, Hans v. Der italienische Strafgesetzentwurf vom Jahre V. Monats f Kriminalpsychol u Strafrechtsref 19: 1-8 Ja '28 7735

Hugueney, Louis. Le projet de code pénal fasciste. Etudes Crimin 3: 41-9 Mr '28 7736

Italy. Ministero della giustizia e degli affari di culto. Avant-projet d'un nouveau code pénal italien, October 1927. 410p. Roma, Provveditorato generale dello stato libreria, 1928 7737

Italy. Ministero della giustizia e degli affari di culto. Codice penale. 132p. Roma, Istituto poligrafico dello stato libreria, 1930 7738

Italy. Ministero della giustizia e degli affari di culto. Lavori preparatori del codice penale e del codice di procedura penale. 4v. Roma, Provveditorato generale dello stato libreria, 1927-29 7739

Italy. Ministero della giustizia e degli affari di culto. Progetto preliminare di un nuovo codice penale. 298p. Roma, Tip. delle Mantellate, 1927 7740

Jacobsen, J. H. Forbrydelsens Retsfølger efter det italienske Straffelovsudkast af 1921. Nord Tids f Straf 16: 107-22 Ap '28 7741

Jannaccone, C. Le norme fondamentali non indifferenti del progetto preliminare del nuovo codice penale italiano. 16p. Forli, Valbonesi, 1927 7742

Jannitti Piromallo, Alfredo. Il nuovo codice penale italiano nel progetto preliminare. 582p. bibliog footnotes. Milano, Istituto Editoriale Scientifico, 1928 7743

Jolly, P. Der vorläufige entwurf eines neuen italienischen strafgesetzbuches. J f Psychol u Neurol 37: 131-42 Ag '28 7744

Lanza. Sul progetto preliminare di un nuovo codice penale. Scuola Pen Uman 5: 69-78 '27 7745

Longhi, Silvio. Anticipazioni della riforma penale. 286p. (Bibliot. di cultura polit. no13) Milano, Treves, 1931 7746

Maas Geesteranus, Henry G. J. La réforme pénale en Italie: étude sur le nouveau projet préliminare. 166p. bibliog footnotes. Paris, Sirey, 1929 7747

Mangini, R. La teoria dell' "errore" nel progetto preliminare di un nuovo codice penale. Giustiz Pen 34: 412-20 Ap 15 '28 7748

Marsich, P. La riforma del codice penale. Rassegna Ital 21: 19-26 Ja '28 7749

Mazzarino, G. I moventi a delinquere nel progetto Rocco e la intensità del dolo. Scuola Pen Uman 5: 112-15 '27 7750

Melli, R. Brevi appunti sul primo libro del progetto di codice penale. 26p. Ferrara, "Estense," 1927 7751

Meloni, Giuseppe. L'elemento psicologico del reato secondo il progetto di un nuovo codice penale. 61p. Napoli, Tip. del Progresso, 1930 7752
Extr: "La Corte d'Appello" 30 (1-2).

Miceli, F. Reato supposto erroneamente e reato impossibile nel progetto del nuovo codice penale. Scuola Pen Uman 5: 116-18 '27 7753

Montesano, G. Il progetto Rocco di nuovo codice penale nei riguardi de la psichiatria. Nuov Riv di Clin ed Assis Psichiat 6: 201-21 '30 7754

Moruzi, Jean. Infractinnile contra onoraei in nouva legistatie penale italiana. 73p. Bucuresti, Imp. Penitenciaruli Vacaresti, 1931 7755

Paoli, G. Il concorso dell'offeso nel progetto preliminare dell'on Rocco. Scuola Pos ns8: 297-312 Jl '28 7756

Paoli, G. and others. Voto a S.E. il Ministro della giustizia sul progetto preliminare di un nuovo codice penale. 40p. Firenze, Vallechi, 1928 7757

Penso, Girolamo. Studi sul progetto preliminare di un nuovo codice penale italiano. 149p. bibliog footnotes. Milano, Istituto Editoriale Scientifico, 1929 7758

Penso, Girolamo. La "tendenza criminosa" e il progetto definitivo di un nuovo codice penale italiano. 24p. Messina, Giacomo d'Anna, 1929 7759
Extr: Il pensiero giuridico-penal 1(4).

Pili, E. Relazione sul progetto preliminare di un nuovo codice penale. 52p. Sassari, Tip. Operaia, 1928 7760

Pozzolini, Alfredo. Il concorso di piu persona in un reato secondo il progetto preliminare 1927 di codice penale italiano; prelezione al corso di istituzioni di diritto penale. 15p. Pisa, Pacini-Mariotti, 1928 7761

Pozzolini, Alfredo. L'exceptio veritatis nei delitti contro l'onore nel nuovo diritto penale italiano. 37p. Pisa, Pacini Mariotti, 1931 7762

Pozzolini, Alfredo. La fisionomia scientifica della riforma della legislazione penale italiana. Scuola Pos (5-6): 223- '30; extract: 15p. Pisa, Pacini Mariotti, 1930 7763

Pozzolini, A[lfredo]. Osservazioni sul libro primo del progetto preliminare di codice penale italiano. 62p. Pisa, Pacini Mariotti, 1928 7764

Rende, D[omenico]. La difesa della moralità e del buon costume nel progetto del codice penale fascista. Giustiz Pen 34: 326-9 Ja 22 '28; [translation]: La defensa de la moralidad y de las buenas costumbres en el proyecto del codigo penal fascista. R de Crimin, Psiquiat y Med Leg 15: 302-5 My '28 7765

Rocco, Alfredo. Bases de la reforma penal fascista. R de Crimin, Psiquiat y Med Leg 17: 69-85 Ja '30 7766

Rocco, Alfredo. La réforme pénale fasciste. R Pénitent de Pologne 4: 353-69 Jl '29 7767

Rocco, Amadeo. Il fondamento psicologico del progetto del nuovo codice penale italiano. 62p. Lanciano, G. Carabba, 1928 7768

Sauer, W. Der italienische Strafgesetzvorentwurf von 1927. Gerichtssaal 97: 193-226 '28 7769

Savinelli, Luigi. La giustizia penale in Italia. Realtà 56-64 Jl '29 7770

Tallarigo, C. Le riforme e le innovazioni della parte generale. Riv Pen di Dott, Legis e Giuris 107: 307-34 Mr '28 7771

Teisen, Axel. The Italian project for a new criminal code. Am B Assn J 13: 213-16 Ap '27 7772

JAPAN

Kusano, H. Die Vorschläge der Kommission "Rinji-Hosei-Shingikwai" zur Reform des japanischen Strafgesetzbuchs. Zeitsch f d ges Strafrechtswiss 48: 70-91 '28 7773

Makino, E. Gendai Hosei no hattatsu ni okeru keiko kaisei no igi. Hogaku-Shirin 30: 1-21 S, 1-25 O, 1-27 N '28 7774

POLAND

Rappaport, Emile Stanislas. Les travaux de la commission de codification en Pologne. Re de Dr Pén et de Crimin 8: 113-22 F '28 7775

RUMANIA

Muxel, P. J. Il progetto di codice penale rumeno del 1928. Scuola Pos ns8: 257-9 My '28 7776

RUSSIA

Gleispach, W. Das neue Sowjetstrafgesetzbuch. Schweiz Zeitsch f Strafr 41: 334-55 '28 7777

SCANDINAVIA

Thót, Ladislao. La riforma penale negli stati Scandinavi con riferimento alla storia e alla letteratura. Giustiz Pen 33: 209-21, 545-8, 881-904 '27; 34: 57-83 Ja 22 '28 7778

SPAIN

Jiménez de Asúa, Luis. Die Reform des spanischen Strafgesetzbuches. Monats f Kriminalpsychol u Strafrechtsref 18: 1-12 Ja '27 7779

Jiménez de Asúa, Luis. Die reform des Strafrechts in den Ländern spanischer Kultur. Monats f Kriminalpsychol u Strafrechtsref 20: 257-78 My '29 7780

El nuevo codigo penal español y las bases sobre que descansa la reforma penal que se ha hecho. Phila Pris R 4: 39-41 N '28 7781

SWITZERLAND

Farbstein, D. [The draft of the new penal code in Switzerland]. Hamishpat 3: 1-8, 49-54 '28 7782

Farbstein, D. Der Entwurf des eidg. Strafgesetzbuches nach den Vorschlägen der nationalrätlichen Kommission. Schweiz Juristen-Zeit 24: 225-30, 241-7 '28 7783

Le Fort, J. Le projet de code pénal suisse et la lutte contre la Bolchévisme. Schweiz Zeitsch f Strafr 41: 38-54 '28 7784

Logoz, P[aul]. Pour l'unification du droit pénal suisse. Schweiz Zeitsch f Strafr 41: 195-211 '28 7785

Logoz, Paul. Le projet de code pénal suisse. 57p. Bern, F. Pochon-Jen, 1928 7786

Rauber, Hermann. Die Strafrechtsrevision im Kanton Aargau. Schweiz Zeitsch f Strafr 44: 474-85 '30 7787

Seiler, A. Strafe und Strafvollzug im Lichte der schweizerischen Strafrechtsreform. Schweiz Ver f Straf- Gefängniswes u Schutzaufsicht Verh ns9: 3-19 '29 7788

Silbernagel, Alfred. Das schweizerische Jugendstrafrecht vor dem Nationalrat. Schweiz Juristen-Zeit 24: 257-66, 273-80, 292-5 '28 7789

TURKEY

Hudson, Manley O. Law reform in Turkey. Am B Assn J 13: 5-8 Ja '27 7790

Thót, Ladislao. Codificación penal moderna. El proyecto de Noruega y el código de Turquía. R de Identif y Cienc Pen 2: 174-96 Jl '28 7791

UNITED STATES

Criminal code revision. Pris J 7: 12-14 O '27 7792

Hargest, William M. The effort to harmonize laws in the United States. Ann Am Acad 136: 31-6 Mr '28 7793

O'Malley, William Lee. Criminal law, proposal for reform in Illinois. Notre Dame Law 6: 119-22 N '30 7794

CRIMINAL PROCEDURE

GENERAL

D'Agostino, G. L'unità fondamentale del processo civile e penale. 94p. Nicastro, Bevilacqua, 1928 **7795**

American law institute. Code of criminal procedure. 179p. Philadelphia, June 15, 1930 **7796**

American law institute. Code of criminal procedure: tentative draft no.1: submitted by the council to the members for discussion at the sixth annual meeting [Washington] April, 1928. 509p. Philadelphia, 1928 **7797**

American law institute. Code of criminal procedure: tentative draft no.2; submitted by the council to the members for discussion at the seventh annual meeting [Washington] May 1929. 318p. Philadelphia, 1929 **7798**

American law institute completes model code of criminal procedure. Am B Assn J 16: 351-60, 398-402 Je '30 **7799**

The background of criminal procedure. L Notes 31: 223 Mr '28 **7800**

Batchelor, Chester A. Legal procedure—the charge. Northwest Police J 6: 16, 46, 92-3 S '29 **7801**

Bernau, Arrigo. Il progetto tedesco sulla esecuzione. (Regolamento giuridico e sistema penale). Scuola Pos (5-6): 262-8 '29 **7802**

Black, William Harman. How to conduct a criminal case; a simple, understandable story of what happens from an arrest to a final sentence or discharge. 394p. N.Y. Prentice-Hall, 1929 **7803**

Bonisconti, Vincenzo. L'istituto dell'ammonizione tentativo d'una costruzione sistematica. Rassegna Pen (9-10): 865-78 '29 **7804**

Breyhan, C. Niederschlagung und Prozessrecht. Arch f Strafr und Strafproz 71: 11-17 Ja '27 **7805**

Bumke, Erwin. Gerichtsverfassungsgesetz und Strafprozessordnung mit Nebengesetzten. ed.2. 284p. Berlin, Vahlen, 1927 **7806**

Carnelutti, Francesco. Controlli della esecuzione penale. Riv di Dir Proces Civile (3): 213-17 '29 **7807**

Cherry, Wilbur H. American law institute code of criminal procedure. Minn L R 15: 370-4 F '31 **7808**

Civil and criminal proceedings: which first? Just Peace 93: 458 Jl 20 '29 **7809**

Constantinescu, N. Jac. Procedura penala, dupa ultima doctrina si jurisprudenta. 328p. Bucuresti, "Curierul Judicar," 1930 **7810**

Conti, Ugo. Giudice penale unico o collegiale? Riv Pen di Dott, Legis e Giuris (11): 409-17 '29 **7811**

Criminal procedure: bibliography. Univ S Calif L Lib Bul 2: 3-4 D '31 **7812**

Doerr, Friedrich. Strafprozessordnung nebst Gerichtsverfassungsgesetz. ed.12 369p. München, C. H. Beck, 1930 **7813**

Dohna, Alexander Graf zu. Das Strafprozessrecht. ed.3 rev. 281p. Berlin, Heymanns, 1929 **7814**

Falchi, Giuseppino Ferruccio. La concezione umanista del diritto processuale penale. 318p. Catania, "Zuccarello i Izzi," 1929 **7815**

Ferri, Enrico. Lezioni di diritto e procedura penale [1925-27]. 2v. Roma, A. Sampaolesi [1928] **7816**

Finzi, Marcello. Avviamento allo studio della procedura penale mediante lettura e illustrazione di processi. Anno academico 1926-27. 389p. Padova, A. Milani, 1927 **7817**

Finzi, Marcello. Ernst Beling e la teoria del "Tatbestand." Giustiz Pen 37 (3) pt1: 313-18 Mr '31 **7818**

Finzi, Marcello. Intorno al metodo di insegnamento della procedura penale. 13p. Modena, Univ. degli Studi, 1927 **7819**

Glaser, Stefan. Wstep do nauki procesur karnego. 311p. Warszawa, Nakladem Gazety Administracji i Policji Pánstwowej, 1928 **7820**

Hélie, Faustin. Pratique criminelle des cours et tribunaux. ed.4 rev. by M. J. Depeiges. 2v. Code penal. 1080p. Paris, Godde, 1928 **7821**

Hibschman, Harry. When animals were criminals. Forum 84: 177-82 S '30 **7822**

Hughes, William Joseph. Federal practice, jurisdiction and procedure, civil and criminal, with forms. 14v. St. Paul, West pub. co. 1931 **7823**

Hutchins, Everett O. Criminal procedure. Police "13-13" 5: 12-13, 33 Jl, 21-3, 58 Ag '30 **7824**

Kiesow, Wilhelm. Strafprozessordnung und Gerichtsverfassungsgesetz mit den Nebengesetzen. ed.6. 398p. Mannheim, 1930 **7825**

Kohlrausch, Eduard, ed. Strafprozessordnung und Gerichtsverfassungsgesetz. ed. 22. 510p. Berlin, Gruyter, 1930 **7826**

Leonardi, Nino. Se il processo penale costituisca rapporto giuridico. Riv Pen di Dott, Legis e Giuris (10): 365-93 '29 **7827**

Logoz, P. Notes sur quelques problèmes de procédure pénale à propos de divers projets récents. Schweiz Zeitsch f Strafr 40: 3-31, 113-33 '27 7828

Loomis, Frank D. My pickpockets day in court. N Am R 228: 499-507 O '29 7829
Account of delays, technical aids to the criminal, and finally the jury which let the man go free.

McAdoo, William G. Criminal procedure and crime and a foreword about the magistrates' courts. N Y Univ L R 5: 111-20 Ap '28 7830

Maiorano, Paolo. La identificazione e gli avvertimenti di querela. Rassegna Pen (7-8): 639-62 '29 7831

Manzini, Vincenzo. Istituzioni di diritto processuale penale secondo il nuovo codice di procedura penale. ed.4. 343p. Padova, A. Milani, 1931 7832

Mayer, Edgar. Über die Wiederaufnahme des Verfahrens im Strafprozess. Geltendes und künftiges Recht. 78p. (Strafrechtl Abhl, hrsg von August Schoetensack) Breslau, Schletter, 1931 7833

Meukel, Leonhard. Der zwischenstaatliche Rechtsverkehr in Zivil- und Strafsachen. 321p. München, Beck, 1929 7834

Miller, Justin. General progress in criminal procedure. Ann Am Acad 136: 112-18 Mr '28 7835

Moruzi, I. Principüle directive ale procesului penal. R de Drept Pen 55-71 Mr '28 7836

Munch-Petersen, H. The law of procedure from a social point of view. N C L R 5: 321-31 Je '27; same title: Minn L R 11: 623-34 Je '27 7837

National commission on law observance and enforcement. Report on criminal procedure. 51p. (No8) Washington, June 9, 1931 7838

National crime commission. Outline of a code of criminal procedure. 11p. (mim) 1927 7839

Page, George T. Improvements in procedure and practice. Am B Assn J 15: 282-3 My '29 7840

Palopoli, Nicola. La difesa nel procedimento penale. 50p. Città di Castello, Unione artigrafiche, 1928 7841
Extr: Il Foro Umbro 12 (9-12).

Polansky, N. N. Etudes sur la théorie générale de la procédura pénale. 127p. Moscou, 1928 7842
In Russian language.

Reid, Erle H. Code of criminal procedure of the American law institute. Wyo St B Assn Proc 1930: 11-29 7843

Riddell, William Renwick. Criminal procedure seven centuries ago. Ill L R 22: 520-8 Ja '28 7844

Il principio della obbligatorietà del processo penale. Scuola Pen Unit (2): 81-9 '29 7845

Ritter. Praktische Strafprozessfälle mit Lösungen. 200p. Mannheim, Bensheimer, 1931 7846

Salvioli, G[abriele]. Storia della procedura civile e criminale. pt.2. 815p. Milano, Hoepli, 1927 7847

Schmidt, Richard and Weber, Hellmuth. Strafprozess. ed.5. Tübingen, Mohr, 1927 7848

Schwarz. Taschenkommentar der Strafprozessordnung. 629p. Berlin, Liebmann, 1929 7849

Smith, H. E. Humorous interludes in criminal case. Police J [London] 4: 557-70 O '31 7850

Strafprozessrecht. (Württembergisches Polizeihandbuch no5) 162p. Stuttgart, Kohlhammer, 1927 7851

Strogovich, M. S. Ratzionalizatzia ugolovnogo protzessa. Vestnik (3): 11-21 Jl '27 7852

Vouk, G. Strafprocesrecht en samenleving. 30p. Batavia, G. Kolff, 1928 7853

Werder, Hans. Die Grundgedanken der Lehre vom Rechtsgeschäft im Strafprozess. 147p. (Strafrechtl Abh no256) Breslau, Schletter, 1929 7854

Werthauer, Johannes. Die Privatklage Kommentar zu Strafprozessordnung. 174p. Berlin, Stilke, 1930 7855

Who shall control criminal procedure? Am Jud Soc J 13: 107-10 D '28 7856

Wilke. Nochmals: Polizeiliche Vorladungen. Krimin Monatsh 5: 183-4 Ag '31 7857

Windolph, F. Lyman. Defending a bad cause. Atlan M 139: 482-8 Ap '27 7858

Withdrawal of criminal charge. Sol J 73: 99 F 16 '29 7859

AUSTRIA

Lissbauer, Karl and Suchomel, Hugo. Die österreichischen Strafprozessgesetze mit einer Übersicht über die Rechtsprechung des Obersten Gerichtshofes. Nach dem Stande des Gesetzgebung vom 15. September 1928. 1162p. Wien, Verl. der österr. Staatsdruckerei, 1929 7860

EGYPT

Percival, John. Egyptian criminal procedure comparatively treated. Police J [London] 3: 30-9 Ja '30 7861

FRANCE

Aubenas, Roger. Note sur quelques formulaires notariaux et styles de procédure civile et criminelle tirés des archives de Provence et du comtat Venaissin (1294-1539). Moyen Âge 41: 195-200 Jl '31 7862

Wright, A. C. French criminal procedure. L Q R 44: 324-43 Jl '28; 45: 92-117 Ja '29 7863

GERMANY

Beling, Ernst Ludwig. Deutsches reichsstrafprozessrecht mit einschluss des Strafgerichtsverfassungsrechts. 568p. Leipzig, Gruyter, 1928 **7864**

Brandt, Arthur, ed. Die Strafprozessnovelle vom 27. Dezember 1926. 91p. Berlin, Sack, 1927 **7865**

Frede, Lothar. Strafrechtspflege in Thüringen. Sammlung der landesrechtlichen Bestimmungen. 334p. Weimar, Panse g.m.b.h. 1928 **7866**

Gerland, Heinrich. Der deutsche Strafprozess. Eine systematische Darstellung. 526p. Mannheim, Bensheimer, 1927 **7867**

Liu, Keetsin. Der Begriff der Identität der Tat im geltenden deutschen Strafprozessrecht. 96p. (Strafrechtl Abhl no221) Breslau, Schletter, 1927 **7868**

Löwe, Ewald Karl August Erdmann. Die Strafprozessordnung für das Deutsche Reich vom 22.3. 1924, nebst dem Gerichtsverfassungsgesetz. Kommentar. ed. 17 by Werner Rosenberg. 1244p. Berlin, Gruyter, 1927 **7869**

Rasch. Neue Entscheidungen des Reichsgerichts auf dem Gebiete des Strafverfahrens. Arch f Strafr u Strafproz 72: 14-24, 242-51 Ja, Jl '28 **7870**

Schwarz, Otto. Strafprozessordnung mit Gerichtsverfassungsgesetz und den wichtigsten Nebengesetzen. 615p. Berlin, Otto Liebmann, 1929 **7871**

GREAT BRITAIN

Phelps, Edith M. ed. British criminal procedure. Univ Debaters' Ann 15: 71-129 '28-'29 **7872**

Sabonadière, A. Criminal procedure before magistrates in England and Wales and India. J Comp Leg s3 11: 52-67 F '29 **7873**

Seitz, Emile E. Les principes directeurs de la procédure criminelle de l'Angleterre. 340p. (Collect. d'études théoriques et pratiques de droit d'étranger, de droit comparé et de droit int. 13) Paris, Rousseau, 1928 **7874**

Urch, Erwin J. Modern English and ancient Roman criminal procedure. U S L R 63: 451-60 S '29 **7875**

HUNGARY

Dombováry, Géza. Beiträge zur Geschichte des Strafprozess und des Gefängniswesens der ungarischen Komitate im 19. Jahrhundert. 78p. Budapest, 1931 **7876**
In ungarischer Sprache erschienen in.

Irk, Albert. Grundriss des ungarischen Strafprozessrechts. 300p. Pécs, Dunantel, 1931 **7877**
In ungarischer Sprache erschienen in.

ITALY

Assante, Carlo. "Dell'istruzione" nel progetto del nuovo codice di procedura penale. Foro Ligure (6-7): 157-70 '29 **7878**

Delitala, Giacomo. Il divieto della reformatio in pejus nel processo penale. 216p. Milano, "Vita e Pensiero," 1927 **7879**

Florian, Eugenio. Pensieri sul progetto del Cod. di Proc. Pen. Scuola Pos (8-9): 340-4 '29 **7880**

Gabrieli, F. P. Il progetto preliminare di un nuovo codice di procedura penale. Proc Pen Ital (13): 401-24 '29 **7881**

Gregoraci, Giuseppe. Sommario osservazioni critiche al progetto preliminare di un nuovo codice di procedura penale. 33p. Città di Castello, Unione artigrafiche [1929] **7882**

Guidice, Arturo del. Relazione della Commissione per l'esame del progetto preliminare di un nuovo codice di procedura penale. 45p. Napoli, Vesuvio, 1929 **7883**

Longhi, Silvio. Ciò che sarà la nuova procedura penale. Pol Soc (4-5): 485-8 '29 **7884**

Meloni, Giuseppe. Relazione della commissione incaricata dalla Facolta di giurisprudenza di examinare il progetto preliminare di un nuovo codice di procedura penale. 116p. Napoli, Achille Cimmaruta, 1929 **7885**

Il progetto Rocco di codice di procedura penale. Scuola Pen Unit (3-4): 161-83 '29 **7886**

MEXICO

Mendoza, Salvador. Recent tendencies in Mexican criminal procedure. Pan-Am Union Bul 64: 433-9 My '30; same title: Mod Mex 16-19 Je '30; translation: Les récentes tendances de la procédure criminelle Mexicaine. Etudes Crimin 5: 274-7 S '30; Las recientes tendencias del procedimiento en lo criminel en Méjico. R de Crimin, Psiquiat y Med Leg 18: 75-83 Ja '31 **7887**

NETHERLANDS

Blok, A. J. and Besier, L. Ch. Het Nederlandsche strafprozes. 264p. Haarlem, Willink & Zoon, 1927 **7888**

NEW SOUTH WALES

Hamilton, Hugh Montgomerie and Addison, G. C. eds. Criminal law procedure, New South Wales, containing the Crimes act, 1900, the Criminal appeal act, 1912, and other statutes. ed.3 by C. E. Weigall and G. C. Addison. 693p. Sydney, Law bk. co. of Australasia, 1930 **7889**

PALESTINE

Kaiserman, J. [Notes on the criminal procedure in Palestine]. Hamishpat 2: 66-9 Jl '27 **7890**

Kermack, Stuart Grace. Handbook of law of criminal procedure in Palestine. 158p. [Palestine] Tarbuth, 1928 7891

POLAND

Glaser, Stefan. Strafrecht und Strafprozessrecht. Das neue allgemeine Strafprozessrecht. R Polish L & Econ 2: 107-13 '30 7892

Glaser, Stefan. Zarys Polskiego procesu Karnego. 330p. Warszawa, Nakladem Gazety Administracji i Policji Pänstwowez, 1929 7893

Mogilnicki, Alessandro. L'apello e la cassazione nel nuovo codice polacco di procedura penale. Pensiero Giurid-Pen 1: 210-16 Ap '29 7894

Neymark, Edward. Le nouveau code de procédure pénale. R de Dr Pén et de Crimin 9: 515-28 '29 7895

Per un codice d'esecuzione penale in Polonia. Riv di Dir Peniten 1: 1324-8 '30 7896

RUSSIA

Russia (RSFSR). Laws, statutes, etc. Ugolovno-protsessual'-nyĭ kodeks, January 1927- 7897

Russia (UKR SSR). Laws, statutes, etc. Kriminal'noprotsesual'niĭ kodeks, ed.1, 1927- 7898

Official pocket edition in Ukrainian incorporating changes to date of issue.

SCOTLAND

Gibb, Andrew Dewar. Scottish criminal procedure comparatively considered. Police J [London] 1: 540-52 O '28 7899

UNITED STATES

Beamer, George N. Criminal procedure in the United States and England. Notre Dame Law 4: 388-91 Mr '29 7900

Longsdorf, George Foster. Cyclopedia of federal procedure, civil and criminal. 7v Chicago, Callaghan & co. 1928-29 7901

Montgomery, Charles Carroll. A manual of federal jurisdiction and procedure: with statutes, rules and forms. ed.3 by Berkeley Reynolds Davids. 1511p. San Francisco, Bancroft, 1927 7902

O'Connor, Larry. Origin and effect of technicality upon American criminal procedure. Notre Dame Law 5: 22-5 O '29 7903

CALIFORNIA

Yankwich, Leon R. The other side of the shield. J Delin 11: 189-93 S '27 7904

"Omnibus" indictment scheme; ¾s jury system; notice of defense of alibi; comment of judges on facts.

COLORADO

Allen, Henry Covert. Colorado justice procedure for lawyers, justices of the peace, constables, police magistrates, town marshals, county judges, sheriffs, and all persons interested in justice court practice. ed.2 rev. by William H. Courtright. 848p. Denver, W. H. Courtright pub. co. 1930 7905

CONNECTICUT

Beach, John K. Observations on Connecticut procedure. Conn B J 1: 15-24 Ja '27 7906

ILLINOIS

Harno, Albert J. Recent criminal cases in Illinois. Ill L R 22: 1-21 My '27 7907

LOUISIANA

Adams, St. Clair, comp. Code of criminal procedure of the state of Louisiana; regulating Louisiana criminal practice and procedure. 169p. New Orleans, Hansell, 1929 7908

Louisiana. Criminal code commission. The code of criminal procedure for the state of Louisiana. 146p. Baton Rouge, 1928 7909

MASSACHUSETTS

Lyons, Daniel Michael and Manning, J. P. Criminal procedure in Massachusetts courts. 210p. Brattleboro, Vt. Hildreth, 1930 7910

MICHIGAN

Haggerty, John S. Code of criminal procedure, 1927. 94p. Lansing, Mich. 1927 7911

Michigan. Commission of inquiry into criminal procedure. Report of the Commission. 24p. Lansing, 1927 7912

Michigan. Commission of inquiry into criminal procedure. Schedule submitted by Commission. 28p. Lansing, 1927 7913

MINNESOTA

Hallam, Oscar. The essentials—Minnesota's experiment. Am B Assn Rep 1927: 452-76; same title: J Crim L & Crimin 18: 337-45 N '27 7914

NEBRASKA

Orfield, Lester B. Should Nebraska adopt the model code of criminal procedure. Neb L Bul 9: 146-91 N '30 **7915**

NEW YORK (STATE)

Cahill, James Christopher. New York code of criminal procedure: containing the Code of criminal procedure, Inferior criminal courts act of the city of New York, Children's court act of the state of New York, and Children's court act of the city of New York, . . . as amended to and including the 1928 session of the Legislature. 430p. Chicago, Callaghan & co. 1928 **7916**

New York (state). Laws, statutes, etc. Code of criminal procedure of the state of New York, including 1930 amendments. 149p. 1930 **7917**

NORTH CAROLINA

Coates, Albert. The codification of criminal procedure in North Carolina. N C L R 10: 57-60 D '30 **7918**

OHIO

Weygandt, Carl V. Weygandt's Ohio charges. Cleveland, Howard Hayes, William bldg. 1927 **7919**

TEXAS

Vernon's annotated civil and criminal statutes of the state of Texas, revision of 1925: general index and tables, including tables of session laws, 1923-1925, tables of corresponding articles in revised statutes 1911 and Vernon's former compilations. 628p. Kansas City, Mo. Vernon law bk co. 1927 **7920**

CRIMINAL TRIAL COLLECTIONS

Adam, George L. Treason and tragedy; an account of French war trials. 254p. London, Cape, 1929 **7921**

Aurand, Ammon Monroe. Account of the witch murder trial, York, Pa., January 7-9, 1929: Commonwealth of Pennsylvania vs. John Blymyer, et al. 31p. [Harrisburg, Pa.] Aurand press, 1929 **7922**

Berlinicke, Harry Robert. Trail of the trial, and other essays. 58p. N.Y. The Author, 551-5th ave. 1927 **7923**

Bierstadt, Edward Hale. Curious trials and criminal cases from Socrates to Scopes. 366p. N.Y. Coward-McCann, 1928 **7924**

Birkenhead, Frederick Edwin Smith. Famous trials of history. 319p. N.Y. Garden city pub. co. 1927 **7925**

Birkenhead, Frederick Edwin Smith. More famous trials. 298p. Toronto, Doubleday, 1929 **7926**

Blundell, Robert Henderson and Seaton, Reginald Ethelbert, eds. Trial of Jean Pierre Vaquier. 208p. London, W. Hodge, 1929 **7927**

Boguet, Henri. Examen of witches drawn from various trials of many of this sect in the district of Saint Oyan de Joux, commonly known as Saint Claude, in the county of Burgundy; including the procedure necessary to a judge in trials for witchcraft; transl. by E. Allen Ashwin; edited by Montague Summers. 328p. N.Y. McKee, 1929 **7928**

Borrow, George, ed. Celebrated trials and remarkable cases of criminal jurisprudence from the earliest records to the year 1825, re-edited, abridged and annotated by Edward Hale Bierstadt. ed. 2. 2v. N.Y. Payson & Clarke, 1928 **7929**

Chudleigh, Elizabeth, countess of Bristol, calling herself duchess of Kingston. Trial of the Duchess of Kingston; edited by Lewis Melville. 328p. N.Y. Day, 1928 **7930**

Curtis, J. Mysterious murder of Maria Marten at Polstead in Suffolk (reprinted from the edition of 1828). 300p. London, Scribner, 1928 **7931**

Dilnot, George, ed. Trial of the detectives. 302p. N.Y. Scribner, 1928 **7932**

Dobarro, Vicente L. Causas criminales; defensa en un proceso por infanticidio. R de Identif y Cienc Pen 3: 253-70 Ja '29 **7933**

Ewen, Cecil Henry L'Estrange, ed. Witch hunting and witch trials; the indictments for witchcraft from the records of 1373 assizes held for the home circuit A.D. 1559-1736. 345p. N.Y. Dial press, 1930 **7934**

Hall, John, ed. Trial of Adelaide Bartlett (1886). 402p. London, Hodge, 1927 **7935**

Hall, John Richard, ed. Trial of Abraham Thornton. 183p. N.Y. Day, 1927 **7936**

Harry, Gérard. Peltzer case. 243p. N.Y. Scribner, 1928 **7937**

Hays, Arthur Garfield. Let freedom ring. 341p. N.Y. Dodd, 1928 **7938**

Hicks, Frederick Charles. Human jettison; a sea tale from the law. 414p. St. Paul, Minn., West, 1927 **7939**

Irving, Henry Brodribb, ed. Trial of Mrs. Maybrick. 354p. N.Y. Day, 1927 **7940**

Jesse, Fryniwyd Tennyson (Mrs. H. M. Harwood) ed. Trial of Madeleine Smith (1857). 413p. new ed. London, Hodge, 1927 **7941**

Kavanagh, Marcus A. You be the judge. 316p. Chicago, Reilly & Lee [1929] **7942**
26 cases with decisions.

Kingston, Charles. Dramatic days at old Bailey. 332p. London, Paul, 1929 7943

Macdonnell, John. Historical trials; edited by R. W. Lee. 234p. London, Oxford, 1927 7944

Mahon, Patrick Herbert. Trial of Patrick Mahon, with an introduction by Edgar Wallace. 286p. N.Y. Scribner, 1928 7945

Minot, George E. Murder will out. 291p. Boston, Marshall Jones [1928] 7946
Description of 29 famous murder cases.

Moulton, H. Fletcher, ed. The trial of Alexander Campbell Mason. 309p. London, Bles, 1930 7947

Normanton, Helena. Trial of Alfred Arthur Rouse. 316p. Toronto, Canada law bk. co. 1931 7948

Normanton, Helena. The trial of Norman Thorne. 367p. London, Bles, 1930? 7949

Parry, Edward Abbott. The persecution of Mary Stewart; the queen's cause: a study in criminology. 363p. N.Y. Scribners [1931] 7950

Parry, Leonard Arthur. Some famous medical trials. 326p. N.Y. Scribner, 1928 7951

Robert, H. Les grands procès de l'histoire. 256p. Paris, Payot, 1928 7952

Roughead, William, ed. Trial of Oscar Slater. 306p. N.Y. Day, 1927 7953

Roughead, William. What is your verdict? 318p. London, Faber [1931] 7954

Shore, W. Teignmouth. Trial of Frederick Guy Browne and William Henry Kennedy. 218p. Edinburgh, William Hodge, 1929; London, Hodge, 1930 7955

Soulié, Maurice. Les procès célèbres de l'Espagne. 256p. Paris, Payot, 1931 7956

Street, Cecil John Charles (John Rhode, pseud). Case of Constance Kent. 278p. London, Scribner, 1928 7957

Tenney, Horace K. Trial of Mary Queen of Scots. Am B Assn J 17: 285-91 My '31 7958

Twyman, Harold William. The best laid schemes. 318p. London, Harold Shaylor, 1931 7959
Popular account of recent celebrated criminal cases.

Webster, John White. Trial of Professor John White Webster; with an introduction by George Dilnot. 275p. N.Y. Scribner, 1928 7960

Wyndham, Horace Cowley. Crimes in high life; some society causes célèbres. 322p. N.Y. Dodd, 1927; English title: Judicial dramas; some society causes célèbres. 322p. London, Unwin, 1927 7961

Young, Alexander Bell Filson, ed. Trial of Herbert Rowse Armstrong. 396p. N.Y. Day, 1927 7962

DUE PROCESS

Brown, Ray A. Due process of law, police power, and the supreme court. Harv L R 40: 943-68 My '27 7963

Constitutional law—due process—forfeiture of automobile seized while carrying prohibitive liquors. Va L R 15: 54-8 N '28 7964

Dissimilarities in content between the two due process clauses of the federal constitution. Colum L R 29: 624-30 My '29 7965

Fellman, David. Due process of law in Nebraska: history and underlying conceptions. Neb L Bul 9: 223-77 N '30 7966

Judicial errors, unfair trials and the fourteenth amendment. Harv L R 44: 447-51 Ja '31 7967

K[eane], V[incent] J. Further developments in due process. St John's L R 3: 244-7 My '29 7968

Manson, Richard E. Due process, limitations on judicial process. Tex L R 9: 422-9 Ap '31 7969

Wire, G. E. Massachusetts homicide trial according to due process of law. Am L R 63: 86-117 Ja '29 7970

ARREST AND DETENTION

Alpha. Die Wirkung der Untersuchungs- und der Strafhaft. Monats f Kriminalpsychol u Strafrechtsref 21: 296-9 My '30 7971

Arrest. Am L Inst Proc 5: 361-4 '27 7972

Arrest without a warrant in Iowa. Ia L R 16: 434-6 Ap '31 7973

Arrest without a warrant, power of conservation officer to arrest. Mich St B J 9: 126 Ja '30 7974

Arrests by magistrates. Just Peace 93: 198 Mr 30 '29 7975

Batchelor, Chester A. Legal procedure—the arrest. Northwest Police J 6: 13, 113-16 Je '29 7976

Bohlen, Francis H. and Shulman, Harry. Arrest with and without warrant. Univ Pa L R 75: 485-504 Ap '27 7977

Bohlen, Francis H. and Shulman, Harry. The effect of subsequent misconduct upon a lawful arrest. Colum L R 28: 841-58 N '28 7978

Castorkis, D. E. L'arrestation provisoire. Etude de droit pénal international pour l'élaboration d'un traité-type d'extradition. 24p. Paris, Sirey, 1928 **7979**
Extr: Revue de droit international privé 23(1): 65- '28.

Creydt, Oscar A. El derecho de expulsión, ante el derecho internacional, constitucional, administrativo y penal. 178p. Asunción, 1927 **7980**

Dangl, R. Die Unterbringung der unzurechnungsfähigen und der vermindert zurechnungsfähigen kriminellen. Jahrb f Psychiat u Neurol 46: 66-75 Je 6 '28 **7981**

Delaquis, Ernst. Die Verfahrung von Gewohnheitsverbrechern nach den kantonalen Rechten der Schweiz. Monats f Kriminalpsychol u Strafrechtsref 18: 468-75 S '27 **7982**

Directiva para los oficiales y sargentos que desempeñan las funciones de alcaides. 70p. Santiago, Dir. Gen. de Tall. Fiscales de prisiones, 1927 **7983**

Dullea, Charles W. Arrests for outside counties. Peace Office Assn Calif Proc 11: 75-7 '31 **7984**

Dullea, Charles W. The procedure to be followed in making an arrest in a felony case. Peace Offic Assn Calif Proc 10: 106-7 '30 **7985**

Enquête sur les garantis contre l'abus de la détention préventive. Comm Pénit Int Bul ns4: 1-144 S '28 **7986**

Ethridge, Geo. H. Law of arrest. Miss L J 3: 79-96 N '30 **7987**

Felsart, Adolf and Phönix, C. Das "ABC" des Angeklagten. 107p. Berlin, Linser, 1928 **7988**

Fisher, Irving. [Arrests for intoxication in certain cities and towns of the United States of America]. 4p. New Haven, The Author, 1927 **7989**

Franklin, Thomas H. When may a police officer slay in making an arrest? Am B Assn J 17: 675-6 O '31 **7990**

Hawley, John Gardner. Law of arrest on criminal charges. new edition by M. J. Parsons and H. H. Lewis. Chicago, Flood co. 1930 **7991**

Herschmann, H. Die Unterbringung der unzurechnungsfähigen und vermindert zurechnungsfähigen Rechtsbrecher. Jahrb f Psychiat u Neurol 46: 66-75 Je 6 '28 **7992**

Hoefer, Friedrich. Bewährungsfrist vor dem Urteil. 90p. (Abh der Kriminalistische s4 v2 no3) Berlin, Gruyter, 1931 **7993**

Hürlimann, Peter. Die Haftung für den aus der Einlösung falscher und verfälschter Checks entstandenen Schaden. 166p. Diss. Univ. Zürich. Zürich, Füssli, 1927 **7994**

Hurley, Thomas F. Use of force in making arrests. Policeman 1: 9-11 S '29 **7995**

Kluge. Betrachtungen zum Verwahrungsgesetzentwurf. Monats f Kriminalpsychol u Strafrechtsref 19: 456-60 '28 **7996**

Lassally. Beschlagnahmen und Durchsuchungen bei Abgeordneten. Deut Polizei-Arch 7: 627- '28 **7997**

Leser, Albert. Die Rechtlosigkeit der Untersuchungsgefangenen. Monats f Kriminalpsychol u Strafrechtsref 20: 655-61 N '29 **7998**

Lobe, Adolf and Alsberg, Max. Die Untersuchungshaft. Kommentar zum 9. Abschnitt des 1. Buches der Strafprozessordnung in der Fassung von 27. Dez. 1926. 95p. Berlin, Heymann, 1927 **7999**

Loewenstein, G. Kritische Bemerkungen zum Bewahrungsproblem vom ärztlichen und juristischen Standpunkt. Arch f soz Hyg u Demog 2: 317-23 '27 **8000**

McIntosh, Andrew C. Right of officer to arrest without warrant one using abusive language toward him or making assault on him. L Notes 33: 210-14 F '30 **8001**

Murray, Alex J. Arrest on telegram. Chief Constables Assn Can Proc 25: 85-90 '29 **8002**

Oehler. Polizeiliche Vorladungen. Krimin Monatsh 5: 104-7 My '31 **8003**

Oetker. Die Anrechnung von Untersuchungshaft. Gerichtssaal 96: 321-59 '28 **8004**

Pearson, Karl G. The right to kill in making arrests. Mich L R 28: 957-76 Je '30 **8005**

Peschke, K. Das neue Untersuchungshaft-Verfahren. Gesetz u Recht 28: 33-7 F 1 '27 **8006**

Picard, Charles. De l'exercice du droit d'arrestation par la gendarmerie. Etudes Crimin 3: 150-8, 193-208 S, N '28 **8007**

Powers of arrest. Just Peace 91: 727-8 O 1 '27 **8008**

Rechter, Alfred. Die Sicherungsverwahrung nach den Entwürfen (Reichstagsvorlagen) eines Strafgesetzbuches und eines Strafvollzugsgesetzes von 1927. 123p. Inaug.-diss. Tübingen. Grossenhain i.Sa. G. Weigel, 1928 **8009**

Right of arrest. Just Peace 92: 526 Ag 4 '28 **8010**

Runge, K. Die Einziehung. Arch f Strafr u Strafproz 72: 24-33, 97-102 Ja, Mr '28 **8011**

Schütz. Die Haftfähigkeit bei Untersuchungs- und Strafgefangenen. Deut Zeitsch f d ges gerichtl Med 9: 730-8 '27 **8012**

Shepherd, Arthur B. Right of self-defense by an officer who kills while attempting an illegal arrest. L Notes 35: 29-31 My '31 **8013**

South Dakota. State sheriff's department. Report of arrests . . . for the year ending December 31, 1929. Pierre [1930] **8014**

Stevens, W. H. N. The law of arrest. 181p. Columbus, Ohio, The Author, c1930 **8015**

Stirum, O. E. G. Graff van Limburg. Onmisbare elementen in processen-verbaal wegens overtredigen. Tijdschr v d Politie 1(8): 121-6; (16): 297-304 My 23, S 5 '28 **8016**

Strube. Zum Vollzug der Untersuchungshaft. Deut Richterzeit 20: 61-3 '28 **8017**

Survey of arrests in 88 cities over ten-year period. Spectator [London] 125: 35 Jl 31 '30 **8018**

Troitzsch. Glossen zum Haftrecht nach der Novelle vom 27. Dezember 1926. Mecklenb Zeitsch f Rechtspfl, Rechtswiss Verwaltung 44: 185-92 '28 **8019**

Über Haft-Wirkungen. Selbstbeobachtungen. Monats f Kriminalpsychol u Strafrechtsref 18: 688-94 D '27 **8020**

United States. Congress. House. Committee on District of Columbia. Provide for detention of fugitives apprehended in District of Columbia, report to accompany H. R. 8915, March 10, 1928. 1p. Washington, 1928 (70th Cong. 1st sess. H. Rep. 877) **8021**

Van der Aa, J. Simon. Enquête sur les garanties contre l'abus de la détention préventive. 144p. (Comm Pénit Int Bul ns no4 S '28) Bern, Stämpfli, 1928 **8022**

Waite, John Barker. Some inadequacies in the law of arrest. Mich L R 29: 448-68 F '31 **8023**

Weiss, E. C. Arrestment: a comparative sketch [in German law]. L Q R 43: 493-8 O '27 **8024**

Wood, Arthur Evans. A study of arrests in Detroit, 1913 to 1929. J Crim L & Crimin 21: 168-200 Ag '30 **8025**

Wunderer, C. Die neuen Vorschriften über die Untersuchungshaft. Leipz Zeitsch f Deut Recht 21: 129-41 Mr '27 **8026**

SEARCH AND SEIZURE

Admissibility of evidence obtained by illegal search and seizure. Case & Com 34: 8 Ja '28 **8027**

[Ailes, Edgar Holt]. Injunction against search by police officers. Mich L R 25: 892-7 Je '27 **8028**

Andrews, Lewis M. Historical survey of the law of searches and seizure. L Notes 34: 42-8 Je '30 **8029**

Baker, J. Newton. Searches and seizures under the national prohibition act. Geo L J 16: 415-37 Je '28 **8030**

Batchelor, Chester A. Search and seizure: legal rules for searching residences of accused persons after lawful arrest. Northwest Police J 7: 13 Mr '30 **8031**

Campbell, Hugh Brown. Tests of legality of searches and seizures in North Carolina and federal courts. N C L R 10: 79-82 D '31 **8032**

Cornelius, Asher L. Search and seizure without a warrant as well as under a search warrant. ed.2. Indianapolis, Bobbs-Merrill, 1931? **8033**

Ehrlich. Fahndungsnachweis. Polizei 25: 127-30 Mr 5 '28 **8034**

Ely, Ben, jr. Federal constitutional limitations on search by state authority. St Louis L R 12: 159-74 Ap '27 **8035**

Enforcing prohibition under the federal rule on unreasonable searches. Yale L J 36: 988-97 My '27 **8036**

Fraenkel, Osmond K. Recent developments in the law of search and seizure. Minn L R 13: 1-20 D '28 **8037**

Huffine, Sherman. Constitutionality of a search and seizure, without a warrant, of an automobile—reasonable cause—anonymous tips. Wash L R 5: 73-5 Ap '30 **8038**

Kachel. Der Grenzfahndungsdienst in Baden. Polizei 24: 323-4 Jl 5 '27 **8039**

Kriminalpolizeiliches Fahndungswesen. Kriminal-Arch (1): 1-14 Ap '28 **8040**

Lehr, Milron A. The law of searches and seizures incident to the enforcement of amendment 18 to the United States constitution. Tenn L R 7: 84-106 F '29 **8041**

Offerhaus, J. Beperkte opsporingsbevoegheid en procesverbaal. Tijdschr v d Politie 1 (15): 269-76 Ag 17 '28 **8042**

Police officer's right of search. Sol J 72: 791 N 24 '28 **8043**

Right of search. Just Peace 94: 642, 674 O 18, N 1 '30 **8044**

Roberts, Glenn D. Does the search and seizure clause hinder the proper administration of criminal justice? Wis L R 5: 195-208 Je '29 **8045**

Searches and seizures—admissibility of evidence procured by tapping telephone wires. Va L R 15: 62-8 N '28 **8046**

The Supreme court and unreasonable searches. Yale L J 38: 77-81 N '28 **8047**

W[aite], J[ohn] B[arker]. Search and seizure—wire tapping—judicial method. Mich L R 27: 78-84 N '28 **8048**

Waiver of constitutional privilege against unlawful searches and seizures. Ia L R 13: 342-4 Ap '28 **8049**

Wilford, Isham Marion. Extent of lawful search incident to arrest. Rocky Mo L R 2: 111-15 F '30 **8050**

Willis, Hugh E. Unreasonable searches and seizures. Ind L J 4: 311-20 F '29 **8051**

Wilson, Howard B. Search and seizure under national prohibition. Const R 12: 189-98 O '28 **8052**

Wood, John E. F. The scope of the constitutional immunity against searches and seizures. W Va L Q 34: 1-29, 137-55 D '27, F '28 **8053**

PRELIMINARY EXAMINATION

Alvendia, Carmelino G. Law on preliminary investigation. Phil L J 10: 335-44 F '31 8054

Champdavoine, L. De la nouvelle législation quant à l'exercise de l'article 70 du code d'instruction criminelle. Lois Nouvelles 50 (14): 227-9 Ag '31 8055

Cornil, Léon. De la nécessité de rendre a l'instruction préparatoire en matière pénale, le caractère légal qu'elle a perdu. R de Dr Pén et de Crimin 11: 809-27 '31 8056

Garraud, René and Pierre. Traité théorique et pratique d'instruction criminelle et de procédure pénale. v5, 762p. v6, 490p. Paris, Sirey, 1928 8057

The "invisible" prisoner. Just Peace 93: 653-4 O 19 '29 8058

Miller, Justin. The preliminary hearing. Am B Assn J 15: 414-17 Jl '29 8059

Pinna, Gonario. L'interrogatorio dell'imputato e le attribuzioni della polizia giuridizaria. Scuola Pos (5-6): 232-42 '29 8060

Preliminary enquiry and trial in absence of accused. Sol J 73: 738 N 9 '29 8061

Preliminary hearings in camerâ. Sol J 75: 323 My 16 '31 8062

Preliminary inquiries and proceedings in camerâ. L Times 171: 450-2 My 30 '31 8063

Roux, J. A. L'instruction contradictoire. R de Dr Pén et de Crimin 8: 664-78 Jl '28 8064

Sunderland, Edson R. Pre-trial procedure for eliminating, disclosing and restricting issues. Conf Jud Adm [Duluth] Proc 1930: 13-20 8065

Vigouroux, P. De la preuve scientifique dans l'instruction criminelle préalable. 242p. Nîmes, Chastanier & Almeras, 1931 8066

BAIL

The administration of bail. Yale L J 41: 293-300 D '31 8067

Bail bonds. Spectator [N Y] 118: 19 Mr 3 '27 8068

Bail bonds of surety companies. Sol J 72: 589-90 S 8 '28 8069

Bail by corporations. Just Peace 92: 222 Mr 31 '28 8070

Bail by the police. Sol J 73: 134 Mr 2 '29 8071

Bail pending appeal. L Notes 32: 24 My '28 8072

Bailbondsmen, "fences," and certain lawyers. Panel 5:4 Je '27 8073

Beeley, Arthur Lawton. The bail system in Chicago. 189p. Chicago, University of Chicago press, 1927 8074

Broyles, Nash R. A historic bail-bond. Ga B Assn Proc 1930: 257-60 8075

Cobb, W. Bruce. Bondsmen fatten on needless bail. Panel 9: 39 S '31 8076

C[onder], R[obert] W[endell]. Bail after conviction. Mich L R 25: 646-54 Ap '27 8077

Dvorak, R. W. Defeating justice with worthless bonds. Crim Just [Chicago] 9: 1-3 S '27 8078

Dvorak, R. W. How Arthur Defoe plays with justice. Story of a farcical bond system which enables a defendant charged with forgery to remain at liberty. Crim Just [Chicago] 9: 1-3 F '27 8079

Elliott, William Frederick. Treatise on the law of bailments and carriers. ed.2 rev. 620p. Indianapolis, Bobbs, 1929 8080

Feldman, Ben. The bond fugitive; the problem of the bailjumper and how he is to be thwarted. Police "13-13" 5: 9, 32 My '30 8081

Gannett, Lewis S. Skipping bail. Nation [N Y] 131: 437 O 22 '30 8082

Goddard, Edward Charles. Outlines of the law of bailments and carriers. ed.2 by C. E. Cullen. 504p. Chicago, Callaghan & co. 1928 8083

Hanna, Francis D. To check municipal court bail bonds. Crim Just [Chicago] 9: 12-13 Ap '27 8084

Holbrook, W. Sumner, jr. Bail in criminal cases: need for legislative revision. Los Angeles B Assn Bul 6: 89-92 N 13 '30 8085

Involuntary bailees. Sol J 75: 126 F 21 '31 8086

Nugent, Robert M. Bail bond bureau proves its usefulness in first year. Panel 9: 56 N '31 8087

Principles guiding the court in admission to bail. Irish L T 62: 165-6 Jl 14 '28 8088

Scott, Hugh D. jr. Law of bailments, with special reference to Pennsylvania. 559p. Philadelphia, Cyrus M. Dixon, 1931 8089

Simpson, George W. Bail and bondsmen. N Y St Assn Magistrates Proc 19: 28-37 '27 8090

To make criminal bail bonds effective. Crim Just [Chicago] 9: 1-3 Je '27 8091

United States. Congress. House. Committee on the judiciary. Issuance and execution of warrants in criminal cases and to authorize bail: hearing, February 9, 1928, on H.R.9784. 21p. Washington, 1928 (70th Cong. 1st sess.) 8092

Waite, John Barker. Code of criminal procedure: problem of bail. Am B Assn J 15: 71-5 F '29 8093

EXTRADITION AND RENDITION

Adinolfi, Salvatore. Estradizione dei nazionali. Scuola Pos ns7: 239-41 My '27 8094

Adinolfi, Salvatore. L'extradition résumé du rapport fait au groupe italien de l'Association internationale de droit pénal. R Int de Dr Pén 5: 441-6 '28 8095

Association of grand jurors of New York county. Interstate exchange of witnesses and interstate extradition; presented by Gov. Franklin D. Roosevelt . . . to the Governor's conference, New London, July 1929. 31p. New York, 1929 8096

Baldassari, Aldo. L'estradizione nella nuova legislazione penale italiana. Riv di Dir Int 23(1): 3-31 8097

Balestra, D. Il diritto d'estradizione nei rapporti italo-svizzeri. 146p. Lugano, A. Arnold, 1927 8098

Barth. Das Auslieferungsgesetz. Deut Spiegel 4: 2165-8 '27 8099

Bayly, Edward. [Extradition]. Int Assn Chiefs Police Proc 1927: 171-4 8100

Bumke, E. Zum Entwurf eines Deutschen Auslieferungsgesetzes. Ein Wort der Einführung. Zeitsch f d ges Strafrechtswiss 48: 425-7 '28 8101

Calòn, E. Cuello. Extradition des criminels politiques. R de Dr Pén et de Crimin 8: 653-63 Jl '28 8102

Calòn, E. Cuello. L'extradition des nationaux. R de Dr Pén et de Crimin 8: 641-52 Jl '28 8103

Calòn, Eugenio Cuello. Les principes de l'extradition. R Pénitent de Pologne 4: 169-98 Ja '29 8104

Castorkis, D.-E. Le droit extraditionnel et les conventions d'extradition avec la Grèce. R Gén de Dr Int Pub 36: 225-65 '29 8105

Conti, Ugo. Estradizione e delinquenza politica. 14p. Città di Castello, Tip. Unione artigrafiche, 1927 8106
Extr: Revista penale 106(4).

Corbaz, Roger. Le crime politique et la jurisprudence du tribunal fédéral suisse en matière d'extradition. 182p. Diss. Lausanne. Lausanne, Vaney-Burnier, 1927 8107

Craven, Cicely M. Extradition—the case of fugitive criminals from French Guiana. Howard J 3: 33-5 '31 8108

Crehan, James. How to extradite. Northwest Police J 6: 12 Jl '29 8109

Delaquis, E. Unzulänglichkeiten im internationalen Auslieferungsrecht der Gegenwart. Schweiz Zeitsch f Strafr 40: 154-73 '27 8110

Delaquis, Ernst. Aus der Praxis des Auslieferungsverkehrs zwischen der Schweiz und dem Deutschen Reich. Zeitsch f d ges Strafrechtswiss 48: 475-87 '28 8111

Doerner. Auslieferungsgesetz und Polizei. Krimin Monatsh 4: 174-7 Ag '30 8112

Donnedieu de Vabres, H. La nouvelle loi relative à l'extradition des étrangers. Etudes Crimin 2(2): 21-3 Mr '27 8113

Donnedieu de Vabres, H. De la réciprocité en matière d'extradition d'après la loi française du 10 mars 1927 et le nouveau projet allemand. R Gén de Dr Int Pub s3 2: 553-70 S '28 8114

Donnedieu de Vabres, H. Les tendances actuelles du droit extraditionnel d'après la loi française du 10 mars 1927 et le projet de loi allemand sur l'extradition. R Int de Dr Pén 5: 327-62 '28 8115

Drucker, Abraham. A proposed correction of the Illinois statute to facilitate extradition. Ill L R 26: 168-80 Je '31 8116

Elpern, George S. Important phases of the law of interstate extradition. L Notes 33: 188-90 Ja '30 8117

Entwurf eines Deutschen Auslieferungsgesetzes. Zeitsch f d ges Strafrechtswiss 48: 509-22 '28 8118

Escape from Devil's Island. Sol J 75: 89 F 7 '31 8119

Extradition and interstate exchange of witnesses. Am B Assn J 15: 664-5 N '29 8120

Extradition law reform. Sol J 74: 130-1 Mr 1 '30 8121

Grimm, Melitta. Das Auslieferungswesen im Recht des Deutschen Bundes. Zeitsch f d ges Strafrechtswiss 48: 448-66 '28 8122

Guthrie, George S. Extradition in Canada: from a Canadian police point of view. Police J [London] 1: 193-202 Ap '28 8123

Hardy, Russell. Removal of federal offenders. 107p. Washington, D.C. Byrne, 1929 8124

Hastings, Harold W. How to achieve uniformity in extradition. Panel 8: 3 N '30 8125

Joël, Günther. Wirkungen der Spezialität der Auslieferung im deutschen Strafverfahren. Zeitsch f d ges Strafrechtswiss 48: 487-509 '28 8126

Kraus, H. Observations concernant les tendances de l'évolution du droit international de l'extradition. R de Dr Int et de Lég Comp s3 8: 161-81 '27 8127

Larsen, Leroy L. Extradition. Northwest Police J 6: 16-17 My '29 8128

Lederle, A. Die Gegenseitigkeit im Auslieferungsrecht und der Entwurf eines Deutschen Auslieferungsgesetzes. Zeitsch f d ges Strafrechtswiss 48: 466-75 '28 8129

Levie, Howard S. Uniform criminal extradition act. Lawyer & Banker 23: 87-90 Mr '30 8130

Medalie, George Z. Interstate exchange of witnesses in criminal cases. Police J [N Y] 16: 22-5 Ag '29 8131

Medalie, G[eorge] Z. Inter-state exchange of witnesses in criminal cases. L Notes 33: 166-70 D '29 8132

Mettgenberg, W. Das erst Verbot der Auslieferung politischer Verbrecher. Zeitsch f Völkerrecht 14: 237-47 '27 8133

Mettgenberg, Wolfgang. Der Entwurf des Deutschen Auslieferungsgesetzes. Zeitsch f d ges Strafrechtswiss 48: 427-48 '28 8134

Meyer. Die Bekämpfung des internationalen Verbrechertums im Rahmen des Auslieferungsgesetzes. Krimin Monatsh 4: 77-9 Ap '30 8135

O'Hearn, W. J. Extradition. Can B R 8: 175-83 Mr '30 8136

Optional extradition. Sol J 73: 701 O 26 '29 8137

Pente, Julius I. Principles of international extradition in Latin America. Mich L R 28: 665-722 Ap '30 8138

Le Poittevin, G. La loi française sur l'extradition. R de Dr Pén et de Crimin 7: 903-18 Ag '27 8139

Rhenanus, J. H. Die französische Auslieferungsforderung aus Anlass des Zweibrücher Zwischenfalle. Gerichtssaal 97: 400-3 '28 8140

Saint-Aubin. L'extradition des étrangers. R Gén de Dr Int Pub s3 2: 10-31 Ja '28 8141

Shivers, Lyda Gordon. Interstate rendition, was it meant to be obligatory? Miss L J 2: 240-4 N '29 8142

Sims, Henry Upson. Uniform extradition act—history and present status. Panel 8: 7-8 N '30 8143

Topf, Erich. Die Neugestaltung des französischen Auslieferungsrechts. Zeitsch f d ges Strafrechtswiss 48: 630-71 '28 8144

Travers, Maurice. L'entr'aide répressive internationale et la loi française du 10 mars 1927. 772p. Paris, Sirey, 1928 8145

Travers, Maurice. La loi française d'extradition du 10 mars 1927. J du Dr Int 54: 595-610 My '27 8146

Wolgast, Ernst. Die Auslieferungsgesetze Norwegens, Schwedens, und Finnlands. 487p. (Sammlung ausserdeutscher Strafgesetzbücher no45) Berlin, Gruyter, 1928 8147

PROSECUTION

[Baldwin, Simeon E.]. Criminal prosecutions in America. Am B Assn J 13: 651-2 N '27 8148

Bodkin, Archibald H. The prosecution of offenders: English practice. Police J [London] 1: 353-60 '28 8149

Boeters. Strafverfolgungsaufschub nach erfolgter Kastration. Krimin Monatsh 5: 184-6 Ag '31 8150

Bovio, Corso. L'accusa e la difesa nel nuovo codice di procedura penale. Riv Ital di Dir Pen 2: 725-33 O '30 8151

Child, Richard Washburn. Criminals, prosecution, et al. Sat Eve Post 202: 20-1 My 3 '30 8152

Cleveland association for criminal justice. "Theoretical" prosecutions. (Spec Bul no30) Cleveland, July 20, 1928 8153

Dunning, Leonard. Discretion in prosecution. Police J [London] 1: 39-47 Ja '28 8154

Grant, Donald. The prosecution of misdemeanors. N Y St Assn Magistrates Proc 21: 54-72 '29 8155

Grebe. Verfolgung oder Nichtverfolgung von Übertretungen nach §153 Abs 1 St.PO. Arch f Strafr u Strafproz 72: 81-90 Mr '28 8156

Howard, Pendleton. Criminal prosecution in England. Colum L R 29: 715-47 Ja '29; 30: 12-59 Ja '30 8157

Krabbe, Oluf H. Über Verjährung der Strafverfolgung. Zeitsch f d ges Strafrechtswiss 49: 54-9 '29 8158

Moley, Raymond. Politics and criminal prosecution. 241p. New York, Minton, 1929 8159

National commission on law observance and enforcement. Report on prosecution. 337p. (No4) Washington, 1931 8160
Public prosecutor; Public defender; Grand jury; Criminal justice surveys analysis, by Alfred Bettman; Bibliography of prosecution, including references to grand jury, legal aid, public defender and related subjects, by Julian Leavitt.

Pearce, Edwin. Prosecution of lesser offense as bar to prosecution for greater on new trial. L Notes 31: 47-50 Je '27 8161

Perreau, Bernard. A propos d'une pratique judiciaire illégale. R Crit de Lég et de Juris 50: 441-50 Jl '30 8162

The prosecution of offenders: South Africa. Police J [London] 2: 380-6 Jl '29 8163

Rice, Thomas S. The proper prosecution of sex offenses. Police J [N Y] 16: 15, 32 F '29 8164

Stephen, James F. Private prosecutions. Sol J 74: 362-3 Je 7 '30 8165

PLEADING

Ames, Alden, ed. California cases on pleading and practice. 505p. Chicago, Callaghan, 1930 8166

Archbold, John Frederick. Archbold's pleading, evidence and practice in criminal cases, by John Jervis. ed.27 by Robert Ernest Roos. 1609p. London, Sweet & Maxwell, 1927 8167

Carmody, Francis X. The effect on trial by jury of certain reforms in pleading. N Y Univ L R 4: 104-13 Ap '27 8168

Carmody, Francis Xavier. New York practice [pleading]. 806p. 1928; 912p. 1929; 1088p. N. Y. Boardman, 1931 8169

Carson, James Milton. A treatise on common law pleading, practice and procedure in the state of Florida. 1412p. Cincinnati, W. H. Anderson co. 1927 **8170**

Clark, Charles Edward. Cases on pleading and procedure. v1 St. Paul, West pub. co. 1930 **8171**

Clark, Charles E[dward]. Should pleadings be filed promptly? Conn B J 3: 69-79 Ap '29 **8172**

Clark, Charles E[dward] and Yerion, Ruth A. Amendment and aider of leadings. Minn L R 12: 97-138 Ja '28 **8173**

Harrison, W. B. Notes on Alabama pleading. Ala L J 4: 24-30 N '28 **8174**

Ingram, William A. Georgia pleading and practice; the prosecution of the cause in the trial court. 816p. Charlottesville, Va. Michie co. 1927 **8175**

Kiser, Donald J. Outlines of pleading. 89p. N. Y. American law bk. co. 1927 **8176**

Lynch, Lawrence R. Pleading and practice under the revised code. W Va B Assn Proc 1930: 170-88 **8177**

McBaine, J[ames] P[atterson]. Recent pleading reforms in California. Calif L R 16: 363-86 Jl '28 **8178**

Medina, Harold Raymond. Summary of the law of pleading, practice and evidence, in the state of New York. ed.8. 187p. New York, 165 Broadway, The Author, 1931 **8179**

Ross, G. W. C. Minnesota pleading as "fact pleading." Minn L R 13: 348-60 Mr '29 **8180**

Yankwich, Leon R. The limitations of pleading reform. Los Angeles B Assn Bul 6: 255-6 Ap 16 '31 **8181**

Yankwich, Leon R. The theory of a pleading in California. N Y Univ L Q R 8: 285-97 D '30 **8182**

JEOPARDY

Autrefois convict. Sol J 72: 457 Jl 7 '28 **8183**

Ewbank, Ernest W. jr. Former jeopardy—tests for identity of offense. N C L R 10: 73-5 D '31 **8184**

Former jeopardy in relation to offenses continuing thru several counties. Ia L R 16: 261-4 F '31 **8185**

Kneier, Charles M. Prosecution under state law and municipal ordinance as double jeopardy. Cornell L Q 16: 201-11 F '31 **8186**

Pearce, Edwin. Conviction of lesser offense as bar to prosecution for greater on new trial. L Notes 31: 47-50 Je '27 **8187**

Prosecution of crime limitation in Scotland. Sol J 72: 539 Ag 11 '28 **8188**

Reitzel, C[laude] E. Double jeopardy in sale of narcotics. N C L R 9: 312-15 Ap '31 **8189**

Successive prosecutions based on the same evidence as double jeopardy. Yale L J 40: 462-9 Ja '31 **8190**

INDICTMENT AND INFORMATION

Cranston, Leslie A. Brief on forms of Illinois indictments. 447p. Du Quoin, Ill. Cranston & co. 1930 **8191**

Duplicity in indictment. Sol J 72: 260 Ap 21 '28 **8192**

Green, Frederick. Constitutional law, waiver of indictment, election to be tried on information. Ill L R 24: 319-25 N '29 **8193**

Grounds for setting aside an indictment in Iowa. Ia L R 14: 500 Je '29 **8194**

Hannan, A. J. Election by informant in summary jurisdiction. Austral L J 4: 356-60 Mr '31 **8195**

Joinder of charges in indictment. Just Peace 95: 435-6 Jl 11 '31 **8196**

Moley, Raymond. The initiation of criminal prosecutions by indictment or information. Mich L R 29: 403-41 F '31 **8197**

Comparison of 4 states using indictments with 4 states using informations.

Moley, Raymond. The use of the information in criminal cases. Am B Assn J 17: 292-4 My '31 **8198**

Number of counts in an indictment. Just Peace 95: 208 Mr 28 '31 **8199**

Perkins, Rollin M. Abridged indictments and information. Ia L R 12: 209-34, 355-92 Ap, Je '27 **8200**

Perkins, Rollin M. Short form of indictment. Ia L R 14: 129-60 F '29 **8201**

Perkins, Rollin M. The "short indictment act." Ia L R 14: 385-400 Je '29 **8202**

Perkins, Rollin M. Short indictments and informations. Am B Assn J 15: 292-6 My '29 **8203**

Perkins, Rollin M. The trial information in Iowa. Ia L R 13: 264-91 Ap '28 **8204**

Potts, C. S. Need of simplified form of indictment. St Louis L R 12: 281-3 Je '27 **8205**

Riddell, William Renwick. Settlement of an appeal as a bar to an indictment at the common law in the county of Gloucester, 1221. J Crim L & Crimin 20: 565-7 F '30 **8206**

Ryan, Sylvester. Bronx county's legal device to make gangsters talk. Panel 9: 36 My '31 **8207**

Charge of obstructing justice and so indicting on conspiracy charge.

Voluntary bill of indictment. Sol J 73: 260 Ap 27 '29 **8208**

JURISDICTION AND VENUE

Allen, Eleanor Wyllys. Position of foreign states before Belgian courts. 40p. (Harvard university and Radcliffe college. Bureau of international research, Publications) N. Y. Macmillan, 1929 8209

Allen, Eleanor Wyllys. Position of foreign states before French courts. 42p. (Harvard university and Radcliffe college. Bureau of international research, Publications) N. Y. Macmillan 1929 8210

Allen, Eleanor Wyllys. Position of foreign states before German courts. 51p. (Harvard university and Radcliffe college. Bureau of international research, Publications) N.Y. Macmillan, 1928 8211

Allen, Ward. Mississippi's compact with Arkansas. Miss L J 2: 428-33 My '30 8212

Berge, Wendell. Criminal jurisdiction and the territorial principle. Mich L R 30: 238-69 D '31 8213

Bunn, Charles Wilson. Brief survey of the jurisdiction and practice of the courts of the United States. ed.3. 169p. St. Paul, West, 1927 8214

Cofer, Kermit R. Local prejudice as ground for change of venue of criminal prosecutions. Miss L J 2: 464-6 My '30 8215

Committing prisoner for trial to wrong court, a point under the Criminal justice act. Just Peace 92: 462 Jl 7 '28 8216

Crail, Joe, jr. Jurisdiction over crimes committed in the air. S Calif L R 2: 483-90 Je '29 8217

Cruppi, Jean. Les jurisdictions criminelles et l'échevinage. Etudes Crimin 4: 97-103 Ap '29 8218

Desprez, Jean. Des particularités de l'action civile devant les jurisdictions criminelles. Etudes Crimin 4: 216-27 Jl '29 8219

Dodd, Walter Farleigh and Edmunds, P. D. Appellate jurisdiction and practice in the courts of Illinois. 1160p. Chicago, Callaghan, 1929 8220

Heintz, Michael G. Removal of defendants from one federal district to another for trial. Univ Cin L R 2: 423-8 N '28 8221

Jurisdiction as to offences on board ship. L Times 164: 296-8 O 15 '27 8222

Jurisdiction under the Criminal justice act. Just Peace 91: 858 N 12 '27 8223

Justices and extended jurisdiction. L Times 165: 158-9 F 25 '28 8224

Justices and reduction of charges. L Times 164: 403-4 N 26 '27 8225

Justices' jurisdiction in assault. Just Peace 94: 326-7 My 24 '30; 95: 487-8 Ag 1 '31 8226

Medina, Harold R. Conclusiveness of rulings on jurisdiction. Colum L R 31: 238-63 F '31 8227

Ranieri, Silvio. La giurisdizione penale. 175p. bibliog footnotes. Milano, Istituto editoriale scientifico, 1930 8228

Reducing the charge. Sol J 71: 886 N 19 '27 8229

Reduction of charges at petty sessions. Sol J 72: 276-7 Ap 28 '28; same title: L Times 165: 412 My 12 '28 8230

Van Bergh, Joseph Alvin. Jurisdiction of the court of appeals of the state of New York. 443p. N. Y. Baker, Voorhis, 1928 8231

DELAY

Clark, N. M. Milwaukee courts move fast. World's Wk 59: 78-80 O '30 8232

Cohalan, Daniel F. Inefficiency of trial counsel as contributing to calendar congestion. N Y L R 6: 383-9, 456-7 N, D '28 8233

Congestion of trial calendars [in New York state]. L Notes 31: 81 Ag '27 8234

Cox, Louis S. Congestion in the superior court. Boston Univ L R 11: 155-63 Ap '31 8235

Curtis, Wilbur C. Master calendar system of municipal court for handling criminal cases [in Los Angeles]. Los Angeles B Assn Bul 6: 283-4 My 21 '31 8236

Dearborn, Henry, jr. Illustrating a delay of justice. Crim Just [Chicago] 9: 14 F '27 8237

Delay in "prosecution." Just Peace 91: 848 N 5 '27 8238

Delay in trials. L Soc J 2: 13 Ag '30 8239

Farrand, George E. The "Blazing car" case: an example of speedy justice in the London criminal court. Los Angeles B Assn Bul 6: 319 Je 19 '31 8240

Friedman, Leo. Some causes of delay of criminal justice. Calif St B J 1: 173-6 Mr '27 8241

Hutchinson, Arthur H. Why not try a criminal case in four months? Case & Com 36: 2-4 Autumn '30 8242

Law's delay; Sacco-Vanzetti case. Outl 146: 530-1 Ag 24 '27 8243

Lunt, Dudley Cammett. Swifter and saner justice. World's Wk 59: 39-42 Je '30 8244

McAdoo, William. The law's delays and the crime situation. Chamber Comm St N Y Bul 18: 40-6 Ja '27 8245

Morrill, Fred B. Farmer Jones goes to law. Am Mercury 22: 219-22 F '31 8246

Peterson, Fred H. Concerning the law's delays. L Notes 31: 230-2 Mr '27 8247

Reviriego, Emilio. El problema de la morosidad en la justicia. Colegio de Abogados Buenos Aires R 7: 651-9 N '29 8248

Ridgely, C. V. The law's delays—some procedural changes. Ind L J 5: 448-52 Mr '30 8249

Root, Elihu. [The law's delay]. *In* Crawford, F. G. Readings in American government, 655-60. N. Y. Knopf, 1927 8250

Smith, R. H. The law's delay in criminal courts. Pittsburgh Rec 12-17 F '30 8251

Sturges, Wesley A. Law's delays, lawyers' delays and forwarded cases. Minn L R 12: 351-77 Mr '28 8252

Sutherland, W. R. comp. A debate handbook on the law's delay and the trial jury. 310p. Lexington, University of Kentucky, 1929 8253

T., G. C. Punishment after five years' dalliance since sentence. Can B R 5: 145-6 F '27 8254

Welch, J. R. Congestion—a suggested remedy. Calif St B Assn Proc 1928: 100-4 8255

Wrestling with calendar congestion. Am B Assn J 13: 487-9 S '27 8256

Z[eidler], C[arl] F. The law's delay. Marquette L R 15: 44-6 D '30 8257

PLEAS

Evidence of withdrawn plea of guilty. N Y L R 5: 329-31 S '27 8258

Herzog, Alfred W. Bargaining by the District Attorney for pleas of guilty. Med-Leg J 47: 4-5 Ja '30 8259

Jadd, Henry. Plea of guilty as evidence. Lincoln L R 1: 1-3 Ja '28 8260

P[ackel], I[srael]. Withdrawal of the plea of guilty. Univ Pa L R 79: 484-91 F '31 8261

Special pleas of affirmative defences by defendant in criminal cases. Yale L J 38: 650-7 Mr '29 8262

What is a plea of guilty? Sol J 75: 163, 179 Mr 7, 14 '31 8263

TRIAL

Altschul, J. Sind Feme und Folter wirklich vollständig abgeschafft? Öster Anwalts-Zeit 4: 356-8 '27 8264

Berardelli, Adolfo. Arringhe penali. 273p. Torino, Bocca, 1928 8265

Bretzfeld. Der Antrag auf gerichtliche Entscheidung §172 StPO. Zeitsch f Rechtspfl in Bayern 24: 133-5, 149-50 '28 8266

Buckner, Emory R. The trial of cases. Am B Assn J 15: 271-5 My '29 8267

Capobianco, Giuseppe Leonida. L'accusation et la défense dans le procès pénal. Napoli, "Vésuvis," 1929 8268
Extr: Eco Forense.

Caution on committal for trial. Sol J 73: 324-5 My 25 '29 8269

Chamberlain, Harry O. Pitfalls in trial practice. Ind L J 2: 673-82 Je '27 8270

The Cleveland system of assigning cases. Am B Assn J 16: 805-8 D '30 8271

The court and undefended prisoners. Sol J 71: 886 N 19 '27 8272

Donovan, Joseph Wesley. Modern jury trials and advocates; containing condensed cases, with sketches and speeches of American advocates; the art of winning cases and manner of counsel described. ed.5 rev. & enl. 740p. N. Y. Jennings co. 1927 8273

English procedure in trials and appeals. Am Jud Soc J 13: 117-21 D '29 8274

Folk, Ernest H. Appeal and error—trial before court without jury—presumptions as to fact not found by trial court. Tex L R 8: 545-53 Je '30 8275

Foster, Roger S. Place of trial, interstate application of intrastate methods of adjustment. Harv L R 44: 41-64 N '30 8276

Garrett, George P. Public trials. Am L R 42: 1-12 Ja '28 8277

Goldberg, W. Abraham. Felony trials in Michigan counties. J Crim L & Crimin 22: 566-75 N '31 8278

H., F. E. Conduct of English criminal trial. Can B R 5: 124-6 F '27 8279

Hale, Quincy H. Pre-trial procedure in Wisconsin. Minn L R 15: 491-500 Mr '31 8280

Hayes, Paul. The trials to convict. Peace Offic Assn Calif Proc 10: 34-7 '30 8281

Hewes, Thomas. English procedure in trials and appeals. Conn B J 3: 13-24 Ja '29; same title: Am Jud Soc J 13: 117-21 D '29 8282

Johnson, Frank E. Municipal court trials and practice: an outline for law students and beginners, to which is added the Municipal court code and the municipal court rules. 152p. N. Y. Baker, 1927 8283

Judge or justice. Sol J 73: 323 My 25 '29 8284

Kessler, August. Die Vorbereitung der öffentlichen Klage im Strafverfahren. 136p. (Würzburger Abh z deutscher und ausländ. Prozessrecht no17) Leipzig, Hirschfeld, 1928 8285

Leser. Welche praktische Bedeutung haben die Berichte der sozialen Gerichtshilfe für die Urteilsfindung. Monats f Kriminalpsychol u Strafrechtsref 19: 29-31 Ja '28 8286

Longenecker, Rolla Rudolph. Some hints on the trial of a lawsuit. 314p. N. Y. Lawyers co-op. 1927 8287

Ludwig, C. Aus der baselstädtischen Rechtsprechung. Schweiz Zeitsch f Strafr 41: 273-85 '28 8288

Maier, M. Soll man die Berichte der sozialen Gerichtshilfe verlesen? Monats f Kriminalpsychol u Strafrechtsref 19: 356-7 Je '28 8289

Massachusetts practice of avoiding unnecessary murder trials of insane prisoners, judged from without. Mass L Q 16: 95-6 Ja '31 **8290**

Misdirection and failure to direct. Just Peace 94: 487-8 Ag 2 '30 **8291**

Pappenheim, M. Über die Anfänge des germanischen Gottesurteils. Zeitsch d Savigny-Stift f Rechtsgesch (Germ Abt) 48: 136-75 '28 **8292**

Preston, Robert Lee. Remus trial, with some observations on the jury system. 16p. Leesburg, Va. The Author, 1928 **8293**

Re-trial extraordinary. Sol J 73: 619 S 28 '29 **8294**

Roberts, Owen J. Trial procedure: past, present and future. N Y St B Assn Proc 1929: 241-58; same title: Am B Assn J 15: 667-72 N '29 **8295**

Sensational trials and tabloid journalism—newspaper bias. Va L Reg ns13: 422-6 N '27 **8296**

Shumaker, W. A. Public trial of sensational cases. L Notes 30: 225-7 Mr '27 **8297**

Smith, J. Joseph. The assignment of cases for trial. Am Jud Soc J 12: 15-17 Ap '28 **8298**

Sunderland, E. R. The problem of trying issues. Am Jud Soc J 10: 165-71 Ap, 11: 20-8 Je '27 **8299**

Vážný, František. [The problem of reporting trials in the law courts]. Časopsis pro Právní a Státní Vědu (5-7): 157-62 '29 **8300**

Weiss, Samuel. How to try a case: giving practical illustrations and cases. 347p. N. Y. Baker, 1930 **8301**

OATH

Administering the oath. L Notes 34: 118 S '30 **8302**

Boehringer, Margrit. Die Eidesreform im Strafprozess und Strafrecht. 203p. Berlin, Gruyter, 1931 **8303**

Binding oaths. Just Peace 94: 35-6 Ja 18 '30 **8304**

Curtis, Wilbur C. The truth: has the oath of witnesses to speak the truth become meaningless? Los Angeles B Assn Bul 6: 363, 365 Ag 20 '31 **8305**

Flad, Wolfgang. Eid und Eidesverletzung in Frankreich. Monats f Kriminalpsychol u Strafrechtsref 21: 519-26 '30 **8306**

Forms of oaths in court. L Notes 32: 98 Ag '28 **8307**

Gieser, W. Eidesmündigkeit Jugendlicher. Deut Richterzeit 19: 463-4 '27 **8308**

Hegler, August. Die Eidesreform. 86p. (Tübinger Abh zum öffentlichen Recht 23) Stuttgart, Ferdinand Enke, 1930 **8309**

Leonhardt, Curt. Beitrag zur psychologischen Beweisführung in Ansehung existenzstreitiger Vorgänge. Die Eidesbelehrung im Dienste der Beweisführung. Arch f d ges Psychol 78: 95-102 D '30 **8310**

Lücking. Die Zwangshandlung des Eidesrechts. Mit Berücksichtigung des Entwurfes 1927. Gerichtssaal 96: 49-68 '28 **8311**

Nygard, Finn. Edene stilling i Norge. Kirke og Kultur 38 (10): 551-66 '31 **8312**

The oath. Just Peace 91: 938-9 D 10 '27 **8313**

Oath or affirmation? Sol J 72: 587 S 8 '28 **8314**

Oaths and orientals. L Times 170: 266 O 4 '30 **8315**

Price, Ira M. Oath in court procedure in early Babylonia and the Old Testament. Am Orient Soc J 49: 22-9 Mr '29 **8316**

Shumaker, W. A. Judicial oaths. L Notes 32: 85-7 Ag '28 **8317**

WRITS

Albuquerque, Pires E. O habeas-corpus e a reforma constitucional. R de Cultura Jurid 1: 141-7 Ap '29 **8318**

"Certiorari denied." L Notes 32: 105 S '28 **8319**

Compter, Herman E. Effect of statute abolishing writ of error in federal procedure. Cornell L Q 14: 222-8 F '29 **8320**

Curran, Edward T. The courageous judge. Lawyer & Banker 20: 402-6 N '27 **8321**

Dobie, Armistead M. Habeas corpus in the federal courts. Va L R 13: 433-60 Ap '27 **8322**

Folsom, F. G. Necessity for writs of error and motions for new trial for a review in Colorado. Rocky Mo L R 2: 99-104 F '30 **8323**

Fraga, Alberico. O habeas corpus e a reforma constitucional. R de Cultura Jurid 1: 53-5 Ap '29 **8324**

Golds, Harold D. Use of the writ of habeas corpus to obtain release of a prisoner after conviction under an unconstitutional statute. Bi-M L R 14: 161-70 Ja '31 **8325**

Habeas corpus. Sol J 74: 762-3 N 15 '30 **8326**

H[ayes], L[auffer] T. Federal courts, act of Congress abolishing writs of error. Va L R 14: 565-7 My '28 **8327**

Jones, Walter B. Law of habeas corpus in Alabama. Ala L J 3: 155-85 Mr '28 **8328**

Meyer, Harold G. Successive applications for habeas corpus. L J [London] ns66: 107-8 Ag 18 '28 **8329**

Moore, Frank D. Right of review by certiorari in the Supreme court. Geo L J 17: 307-13 Je '29 **8330**

Murphy, John B. The rise and growth of the writ of habeas corpus. Loyola L J 8: 23-9 Ja '27 **8331**

Palacios, Alfredo L. and Caminos, Carlos N. Derecho de Asilo y hábeas corpus; caso de Maciá y Gassol. R de Identif y Cienc Pen 2: 71-136 My '28 **8332**

Payne, Philip M. The abolition of writs of error in the federal courts. Va L R 15: 305-20 F '29 **8333**

Peacock, James Craig. Purpose of certiorari in supreme court practice and effect of denial or allowance. Am B Assn J 15: 681-4 N '29 8334

Review of orders in habeas corpus proceedings. Harv L R 41: 902-5 My '28 8335

S[anborn], J[ohn] B. Writ of error abolished in federal courts. Wis L R 4: 440-1 Ap '28 8336

Sears, Kenneth C. Judicial abuse of habeas corpus. Ill L R 24: 566-9 Ja '30 8337

Successive applications for habeas corpus. L Times 165: 531 Je 23 '28 5338

Viamonte, C. S. El habeas corpus. La libertad y su garantía. 233p. Buenos Aires, V. Abeledo, 1927 8339

ARRAIGNMENT

Lücking, F. Alternative Anklage und Verurteilung. Arch f Strafr u Strafproz 71: 161-5 My '27 8340

Tejera y Garcia, Diego Vicente. La denuncia y las ideas modernas. 43p. Matanzas, "Soles," 1928 8341

DEFENDANT'S RIGHTS, LIABILITIES, PRIVILEGES, ETC.

Absent defendants. Sol J 72: 602 S 15 '28 8342

Bernstein, B. R. Separate trials for defendants jointly indicted. St John's L R 4: 256-60 My '30 8343

Boiarsky, Mose E. Right of the accused in a criminal case not to be compelled to be a witness against himself. W Va L Q 35: 27-45, 126-45 D '28, F '29 8344

City club of New York. Why delinquent public officers escape; a loop-hole in the law. 10p. N.Y. 1928 8345
Claim of immunity from self-incrimination.

Controlling the defendant. Just Peace 92: 23-4 Ja 14 '28 8346

Cooper, H. H. Privilege of non-incrimination. Const R 12: 157-70 Jl '28 8347

Corwin, Edward S. The supreme court's construction of the self-incrimination clause. Mich L R 29:1-27, 191-207 N, D '30 8348

Counsel and defendants; admission of attorneys to visit client held in prison. Pris Assn N Y Ann Rep 84: 87-92 '28 8349

Grant, J. A. C. Self-incrimination in the modern American law. Temple L Q 5: 368-403 Ap '31 8350

Joint trial in criminal cases. L Notes 31: 43 Je '27 8351

Littleton, Martin W. The defendant's rights to change appearance. Panel 9: 27, 34 My '31 8352

McGoldrick, Joseph. Public officers and official investigations. Am City 43: 119-20 N '30 8353
Suggestion that guarantee against self-incrimination and double jeopardy be denied delinquent public officers.

Privilege of counsel. Sol J 71: 183-4 Mr 5 '27 8354

Privilege of non-resident criminal defendants from service of civil process. Harv L R 43: 802-5 Mr '30 8355

Saranoff, Nicolas. Convient-il de considérer l'accusé comme un témoin dans sa propre cause? R Int de Dr Pén 8: 438-43 '31 8356

Self-incrimination. Sol J 72: 144-5 Mr 3 '28 8357

Silence as an accused person. Just Peace 95: 163 Mr 14 '31 8358

Silence as evidence of guilt. L J [London] 72: 143-4 S 5 '31 8359

Summary trial of indictable offenses: giving the accused the option. Just Peace 91: 503 Jl 2 '27 8360

Waiver of the privilege against self-incrimination by public officers. Colum L R 30: 1160-5 D '30 8361

Wartels, Gabriel and Pollitt, Basil H. Critical comment on privilege against self-incrimination. Ky L J 18: 18-30 N '29 8362

TRIAL WITHOUT JURY

Bundick, George R. Trial without jury. Case & Com 36: 26 Winter '30 8363

Ervin, Spencer. Trial without jury in criminal cases. Am Jud Soc J 15: 71-2 O '31 8364

Frank, Eli. Trying criminal cases without juries in Maryland. Va L R 17: 253-62 Ja '31 8365

Grant, J. A. C. Felony trials without a jury. Am Pol Sci R 25: 980-95 N '31 8366

TRIAL BY JURY

d'Amélio. Faut-il admettre, en matière criminelle, le système du jury ou celui de l'échevinage? R Int de Dr Pén 8: 388-401 '31 8367

Anderson, Paul Y. Twelve good men and true. Nation [N Y] 124: 8-10 Ja 5 '27 8368

Bailey, J. Kenton. Jury trial no burden in Louisiana. Am Jud Soc J 13: 47-9 Ag '29 8369

Burr, A. G. Progress in trial by jury. Ann Am Acad 136: 75-81 Mr '28 8370

Campolongo. La giuria. Scuola Pos ns7: 557-60 N '27 8371

Cicala, Salvatore. La giuria e il nuovo stato. 228p. bibliog 223-5. Milano, Istituto editoriale scientifico, 1929 8372

Clapperton, D. W. Some thoughts on the usefulness of trial by jury. Can B R 5: 478-82 S '27 8373

Coatsworth, Emerson. Trial by jury. Can B R 5: 650-3 N '27 8374

Communications to jurors. L Times 163: 269 Mr 26 '27; same title: L Notes 31: 97 Ag '27 8375

Connecticut. Judicial council. A handbook for jurors. 16p. [Hartford] 1930 8376

A critic of the jury system. Lancet 213: 820-1 O 15 '27 8377

Dalgety, George S. The new juryman thinks aloud. Am Jud Soc J 15: 56-60 Ag '31 8378

Dell, Robert. Killing no murder. Nation & Athen 44: 483-5 Ja 5 '29 8379
Indictment of French jury system.

Edmunds, Sterling E. Trial by jury or by judge? Am Mercury 16: 438-44 Ap '29 8380

The effect of the constitutional provision that the jury is to determine law. Minn L R 11: 472-4 Ap '27 8381

Fifoot, C. H. S. Trial by jury. Fortn R 135: 12-22 Ja '31 8382

The French jury. Sol J 73: 17-18 Ja 12 '29 8383

Glaser, S. Le suicide de jury. Etudes Crimin 3: 19-23 Ja '28 8384

Green, A. Leon. Jury trial and the appellate court. Ill St B Assn Proc 1930: 261-77 8385

Green, Leon. A new development in jury trial: functions of judge and jury still present some far-reaching and difficult problems of criminal procedure. Am B Assn J 13: 715-20 D '27 8386

Guiral, Maggie. La question du jury. R Int de Crimin 1: 309-17 S '29 8387

Hanna, Francis D. Jury service in the municipal court. Crim Just [Chicago] 1-2 My '27 8388

Harris, Silas A. Is the jury vanishing? N Y Univ L Q R 7: 657-73 Mr '30; same title: Conn B J 4: 73-94 Ap '30 8389

Harrison, G. On juries in Hawaii. Woman's J ns14: 29 D '29 8390

Hazard, Leland. Ballyhoo, juries and judges. Mo B J 1: 9-10 Ap '30 8391

History of trial by jury: the jury system in the United States; modern movement for jury reform. Cong Dig 8(11) N '29 8392

Hogan, George M. The strangled judge [American system of jury trial]. Am Jud Soc J 14: 116-25 D '30 8393

Howard, Pendleton. Trial by jury. Cent 117: 683-90 Ap '29 8394

Jordon, G. Ray. Churchmen and jury men. Chr Cent 46: 86-7 S 25 '29 8395

A judicial requiem. L Notes 34: 202-3 F '31 8396

Juries in criminal cases. Sol J 73: 608-9 S 21 '29 8397

A jury of less than twelve. Sol J 71: 988-9 D 31 '27 8398

Jury service in Cleveland. Am Jud Soc J 15: 8-10 Je '31 8399

Jury shadowing. U S L R 63: 345-6 Jl '29 8400

Jury specialization. Sol J 73: 605 S 21 '29 8401

[The jury system]. L Notes 31: 222 Mr '27 8402

Kössler. Das Schwurgerichtsproblem in Österreich. Deut Juristen-Zeit 32: 1586-9 '27 8403

Lepaulle, Pierre. Jury, democracy and efficiency. Forum 80:49-55 Jl '28 8404

Leseur, James A. The jury system. N Y Assn Magistrates Proc 19: 8-15 '27 8405

Leyton, Patrick and Rickett, Arthur Compton. Gentlemen of the jury. 312p. London, H. Jenkins [1927] 8406

[Lynch, Humphrey J.]. "Trying" mental cases by jury. Ment Hyg 5:5 Je '27 8407

Maas Geesteranus, H. J. Observations sur la crise du jury. Etudes Crimin 5: 65-9 Mr '30 8408

Martin, George W. Twelve men in a box. Forum 79: 863-7 Je '28 8409

Mason, Gregory. Shall we hang the jury. World's Wk 57: 57-65 N '28 8410

Maxman, George. The Pennsylvania requirement of trial by jury in criminal cases compared with the law of other jurisdictions. Univ Pa L R 76: 727-35 Ap '28 8411

Megaarden, Theodor. Current criticisms of trial by jury. L Notes 33: 123-6 O '29 8412

Moley, Raymond. The vanishing jury. S Calif L R 2: 97-127 D '28 8413
Excessive use of *nolles*, bargaining, etc.

More criticism of the jury system. Can B R 9: 427-8 Je '31 8414

Mornet, A[ndré]. Le jury criminel. Etudes Crimin 4: 138-45 My '29 8415

Moschzisker, Robert von. Trial by jury; a brief review of its origin, development and merits and practical discussions on actual conduct of jury trials. ed.2 rev.& enl. 489p. Philadelphia, Geo. T. Bisel co. 1930 8416

Mullins, Claud. The curse of trial by jury. Q R 255: 17-28 Jl '30 8417

Napier, Rodger. Murder by jury: a layman's inquiry. 48p. (Criterion misc. no32) London, Faber, 1931 8418

Non-unanimous juries. Lawyer & Banker 22: 200-1 Jl '29 8419

Norton, Thomas James. What a jury is. Va L R 16: 261-70 Ja '30 8420

Oakley, Imogen B. Sentimental juries. N Am R 229: 286-94 Mr '30 8421

Olsen, Albert. Extent to which affidavits of jurors will be considered for purpose of setting aside their own verdict. Wash L R 4: 78-83 My '29 8422

Oppenheim, S. Chesterfield. Attack on the jury. New Repub 61: 219-21 Ja 15 '30 8423

Origin of trial by jury. Just Peace 93: 552 Ag 31 '29 8424

Parsons, V. L. Strangers in the jury room. Can B R 7: 161-8 Mr '29 8425

Perreau, Bernard. Faut-il admettre, en matière criminelle, le système du jury ou celui de l'échevinage? R Int de Dr Pén 8: 368-77 '31 8426

Peters, Glenn D. Invading the province of the jury. Ind L J 2: 539-45 Ap '27 8427

Poumeyrol. Etude sur le jury d'assises. R Int de Crimin 3(3): 205-8 '31 8428

Pound, Roscoe and Plucknett, Theodore F. T. Readings on the history and system of the common law. ed.3 rev. 731p. Rochester, Lawyers coop. 1927 8429
Jury, p134-77.

Powell, George M. Juries. Fla St B Assn L J 3: 14-19 N '29 8430

Practice of discharging the jury. Irish L T 64: 133-4 Je 7 '30 8431

Pugh, J. A. Notes on the English jury system. Scots L T 49-53 Mr 5 '27 8432

Riddell, William Renwick. Thanking the jury—and the reverse. Am B Assn J 13: 289-91 My '28; same title: L Times 165: 567-8 Je 30 '28 8433

Robinson, Louis N. The revolt of the jury. J Crim L & Crimin 18: 100-4 My '28 8434

Robira, John J. ed. Robira's compiled laws of Louisiana relating to police juries. 355p. New Orleans, Montgomery-Andree, 1927 8435

Rolfsen. Lagmannsretten i Straffsaker. Nord Tids f Straf 16: 74-88 Ja '28 8436

Sebille, B. Trial by jury an ineffective survival. Crim L J India 28 pt1: 17-23 F '27 8437

Reprint from American law review.

Shadowing the jury. Sol J 73: 653 O 12 '29 8438

Shea, John. Defense of the jury system. Notre Dame Law 4: 543-7 My '29 8439

Shelton, Thomas W. Federal juries. Lawyer & Banker 24: 94-101 Mr '31 8440

Sidelights on jury trial. Am Jud Soc J 13: 124-5 D '30 8441

Smith, Robert J. The jury system. Mo B J 2: 12-13, 15-16 Mr '31 8442

Stalmaster, Irvin. Jury system. 119p. Omaha, National Bank, The Author, 1930 8443

Stalmaster, Irvin. What price jury trials? 143p. Stratford, 1931 8444

Sutliffe, Robert Stewart. Impressions of an average juryman. 114p. N. Y. Banks law pub co. 1931 8445

Toulemon, André. Histoire du jury en France. R Int de Crimin 2(8): 613-25 '30 8446

Toulemon, André. La question du jury. 295p. Paris, Sirey, 1930; same title: Etudes Crimin 5: 123-31 Ap '30 8447

Trial by jury. Editorial Res Rep 1-22 Mr '30 8448

Tuttle, Charles H. The jury system. Northwest Police J 7: 17, 94 Ap '30 8449

Weiss, K. Ein Vorschlag zur Schwurgerichtsreform. Öster Anwalt-Zeit 4: 373-4 '27 8450

Wherry, William M. Study of the organization of litigation and of the jury trial in the supreme court of New York county. N Y Univ L Q R 8: 396-427, 640-73 Mr, Je '31 8451

White man's court. New Repub 64: 86 S 10 '30 8452

Bibliography

Detroit. Public library. Civics division. The jury system, a list of references. 14p. [Detroit] 1929 8453

Johnsen, Julia E. comp. Jury system. 176p. (Ref Shelf v5 no6) N.Y. Wilson, 1928 8454

Phelps, Edith M. ed. Jury system. Univ Debaters' Ann 1928-29: 329-85 8455

United States. Library of Congress. The jury system: a bibliographical list. 17p. [Washington] December 5, 1927 8456

United States. Library of Congress. The jury system: a bibliographical list. 21p. (mim) [Washington] September 5, 1929 8457

United States. Library of Congress. The jury system: a bibliographical list. 23p. (mim) [Washington] June 24, 1931 8458

Challenges to Jurors

Challenging jurors. Just Peace 93: 621-2 O 5 '29 8459

Challenging the jury. Sol J 73: 619 S 28 '29 8460

Challenging women jurors. Sol J 74: 510 Ag 2 '30 8461

Hill, Arthur W. jr. Right of counsel to question prospective jurors with view to exercising challenge: construction of penal code section 1078. Calif L R 18: 70-5 N '29 8462

Jury—Peremptory challenges. Univ Pa L R 76: 105-6 N '27 8463

Examination of Jurors

Moore, Roger D. Voir dire examination of jurors. I: The English practice; II: The federal practice. Geo L J 16: 435-53 Je '28; 17: 13-38 N '28 8464

Instructions to Jury

Carlin, Leo. Relation between separate instructions to the jury. W Va L Q 36: 313-18 Je '30 8465

Corcoran, George F. comp. Nebraska instructions to juries. 3v Chicago, Callaghan, 1930 8466

Disregard by jury of erroneous instructions. N Y L R 6: 351-3 O '28 8467

Folsom, F. G. Necessity for exceptions to instructions. Rocky Mo L R 1: 102-7 F '29 8468

W[ood], A[rthur] [Richard]. Crimes, charge to jury. Mich L R 25: 443-5 F '27 8469

Interrogatories

Harbert, Arlos Jackson. Special interrogatories. W Va L Q 35: 359-63 Je '29 8470

Linn, William B. Special interrogatories to juries in Pennsylvania. Temple L Q 4: 3-25 D '29 8471

Powers of Jury

Sauer, Karl. Rechte und Pflichten der Schöffen und Geschworenen. ed.2. 90p. Berlin, Simon, 1927 **8472**

Toulemon, André. La question du jury. La séparation du fait et du droit. Etudes Crimin 5: 123-31 Ap '30 **8473**

Reform

Abolish the jury? Just Peace 95: 82 F 7 '31 **8474**

A[rnold], T[hurman] W. Should the jury system be abolished? W Va L Q 35: 277-9 Ap '29 **8475**

Corbin, Harold H. The jury on trial. Am B Assn J 14: 507-12 O '28 **8476**

Coulon, Marcel. Une enquête sur la réforme du jury. Mercure Fr 217: 161-7 Ja 1 '30 **8477**

Cruppi, Jean. La question du jury: une solution. R de Paris 36: 781-97 F 15 '29; same title: R de Dr Pén et de Crimin 9: 781-91 '29 **8478**

Dilkes, James A. Should the jury system pass? St John's L R 3: 30-41 D '29 **8479**

Donley, Robert T. Trial by jury in civil cases—a proposed reform. Am Jud Soc J 13: 16-24 Je '29 **8480**

Elder, Robert H. Trial by jury: is it passing? Am L Sch R 6: 290-300 My '28 **8481**

F[ite], J[ulian] B. Changes in the jury. Va L R 17: 497-501 Mr '31 **8482**

Forgues, E. Faut-il supprimer le jury? R Pénitent et de Dr Pén 53: 262-9 Je '29 **8483**

Galloway, George B. Trial by jury: defects and proposed remedies. Editorial Res Rep 845-64 O 23 '29 **8484**

Giudice, Arturo del. Il giuri in Italia; abolizione o riforma? 56p. Napoli, N. Nappa, 1928 **8485**

H[entig]. Die Reform des Schwurgerichts in Frankreich. Monats f Kriminalpsychol u Strafrechtsref 20: 117-20 '29 **8486**

Herschmann, H. Schwurgerichtskrise und forensische Psychiatrie. Beitr z gerichtl Med 9: 56-68 '29 **8487**

Labriola, T. Su la riforma della giuría. Corr. dei Tribun (Napoli) March 15, 1927 **8488**

Linn, William B. Changes in trial by jury. Temple L Q 3: 3-16 N '28 **8489**

Long, Thomas G. Should trial by jury be abolished? Am Jud Soc J 14: 162-4 F '31 **8490**

Monnet, Albert. Entre jurés. Contribution à l'enquête sur la réforme du jury. 30p. Paris, Van Oest, 1930 **8491**

Perkins, Rollin M. Proposed jury changes in criminal cases. Ia L R 16: 20-52 D '30 **8492**

Poe, Edgar A. and Littleton, Martin W. Should the criminal jury be abolished? Forum 80: 661-73 N '28 **8493**

Proposed legislation for jury reform in New York. Colum L R 30: 721-8 My '30 **8494**

Richardson, I. T. The jury and methods of increasing its efficiency. Kan St B Assn Proc 1927: 136-41; same title: Am B Assn J 14: 410-12 Jl '28 **8495**

Sasserath, Simon. La réforme du jury. 12p. Bruxelles, Ferdinand Larcier, 1928 **8496**
Extr: Journal des Tribunaux.

Should our jury system be modified? [Pro and con discussion]. Cong Dig 8: 257-80 N '29 **8497**

Stern, Samuel R. First judicial reform: [an argument for abolishing trial by jury]. Ore L R 9: 3-22 D '29 **8498**

Substitute for jury trial proposed. Am Jud Soc J 10: 157-9 F '27 **8499**

Sweet, Joseph G. The jury on trial. Am B Assn J 15: 241-3 Ap '29 **8500**

Toulemon, André. Une ligue pour la réforme du jury. Etudes Crimin 5: 282-8 D '30 **8501**

Weaver, Elvin D. Is the present jury system satisfactory? N Y St Assn Chiefs Police Proc 38: 54-5 '28 **8502**

Weinberg, Harry E. Trial by jury: is it an obsolete and impractical institution? Police "13-13" 5: 9-11, 38 Jl '30 **8503**

Wigmore, John H. A program for the trial of jury trial. Am Jud Soc J 12: 166-71 Ap '29 **8504**

Wilkin, Robert N. The jury: reformation, not abolition. Am Jud Soc J 13: 154-6 F '30 **8505**

Wilkin, Robert N. The jury: some reforms by reversion. Am B Assn J 13: 50-1 Ja '27 **8506**

Right to Jury Trial

C[arlin], L[eo]. The right to trial by jury in West Virginia. W Va L Q 33: 183-92 F '27 **8507**

Claim to trial by jury. Sol J 73: 199 Mr 30 '29 **8508**

Giving the option of trial by jury. Just Peace 93: 563 S 7 '29 **8509**

H[enderson], G[eorge] W. Right to trial by jury in criminal cases—denial of the right—decrease in number of substitutions of jurors. S Calif L R 4: 303-10 Ap '31 **8510**

Selection of Jurors

Baltimore's jury selecting plan. Am Jud Soc J 12: 53 Ag '28 **8511**

Better jurors. L Notes 32: 114 N '28 **8512**

Buckley, Leer. Jury selection in Kentucky. Ky L J 18: 272-80 Mr '30 **8513**

Buttz, C. W. Selecting a petit jury. Dakota L R 2: 467-71 D '29 **8514**

Coe, John M. What preconceived opinion disqualifies a juror? Fla St B Assn L J 3: 22-3 D '29 **8515**

Disqualification of juror by kinship. Sol J 74: 555-6 Ag 23 '30 **8516**

Grant, J. A. C. Methods of jury selection. Am Pol Sci R 24: 117-34 F '30 **8517**

Hannan, W. E. comp. Compilation and digest of the laws of the various states relating to qualification of jurors. 72p. (Photostat) Albany, New York (state) Library. Legislative reference section, 1929 **8518**

Hannan, W. E. comp. Compilation of the laws of the various states relating to alternate jurors. 16p. Albany, New York (state) Library. Legislative reference section, 1928 **8519**

Hannan, W. E. comp. Statutory provisions of New York state relating to commission of jurors and to qualifications and length of service of jurors. 20p. Albany, New York (state) Library. Legislative reference section, 1927 **8520**

Jury qualifications and exemptions. Panel 5:4 Ja '27 **8521**

Oetker, F. Vorsitz im Schwurgericht und Eignung zur Schuldbeurteilung. Zeitsch f Psychol 112: 243-56 '29 **8522**

Rosenwald, Robert E. Exemptions from jury service and challenges for cause in Missouri. St Louis L R 15: 230-66, 361-89 Ap, Je '30 **8523**

Samford, Thos. D. How to pick a jury. Ala St B Assn Proc 1928: 135-47 **8524**

Tanney, Joseph P. Reflections of a juror: mixed feelings on being summoned for jury duty. Am B Assn J 14: 337-40 Je '28 **8525**

Waiver of Trial by Jury

Aronson, Robert L. Would a statute providing for the waiver of a jury in felony cases be constitutional in Missouri? St Louis L R 14: 34-47 D '28 **8526**

Durgan, Walter T. Waiver of jury trial in felony cases. Ore L R 10: 366-74 Je '31 **8527**

Elpern, George S. Waiver of jury trial in criminal cases. Panel 9: 9-10 Ja '31 **8528**

Goldberg, W. Abraham. Optional waiver of jury in felony trials in recorder's court, Detroit, Michigan. J Crim L & Crimin 21: 41-121 My '30 **8529**

Goldberg, W. Abraham. Waiver of jury in felony trials. Mich L R 28: 163-78 D '29 **8530**

Oppenheim, S. Chesterfield. Waiver of jury trial in criminal cases. Mich L R 25: 695-9 My '27 **8531**

Smith, William A. Waiver of trial by jury in criminal cases. Univ Cin L R 4: 80-5 Ja '30 **8532**

Waiver of jury trial in criminal cases; reasons for waiving jury trial. L Notes 31: 122 O '27 **8533**

Waiver of trial by jury. Am B Assn J 16: 372-3 Je '30 **8534**

Women as Jurors

Baumes, Caleb. Efficiency of women jurors. U S Daily 4(248): 2848 D 21 '29 **8535**

Day, R. H. Ohio's experience with women in juries. 8p. Washington, National league of women voters, 1929 **8536**

Grossman, E. M. and McNulty, George A. Right of women to serve on juries in Missouri. St Louis L R 12: 138-44 F '27 **8537**

Hannan, W. E. comp. Compilation and digest of the laws of the various states relating to women as jurors. 35p. Albany, New York (state) Library. Legislative reference section, 1929 **8538**

Hicks, Julia Margaret, comp. Women jurors. 35p. Washington, National league of women voters, 1928 **8539**

Little, Roger F. Shall women serve on juries in Illinois. Ill St B Assn Proc 1930: 278-84 **8540**

Sawyer, H. H. Women as jurrors. Am Mercury 15: 139-44 O '28 **8541**

Women and juries. L Times 168: 237 O 5 '29 **8542**

Women and jury service. M Press ns123: 188-9 Mr 9 '27 **8543**

Women as jurors. L Notes 32: 124 O '28 **8544**

EVIDENCE

Admissibility of statements by agent as evidence against his principal. Harv L R 43: 936-40 Ap '30 **8545**

Anossof, J. J. Le prove penali nel diritto sovietico. Scuola Pos ns11: 125-9 Mr '31 **8546**

Articles found, used as evidence. Sol J 74: 225 Ap 12 '30 **8547**

Batchelor, Chester A. Suppression of evidence. Northwest Police J 6: 12-13 Ja '29 **8548**

Bates, Samuel O. Evidence. Int Assn Identif Proc 13: 79-84 '27 **8549**

Bayle and Amy. Sur un perfectionnement apporté à la technique de l'analyse spectrale. Application à l'exercise judiciaire. Ann de Méd Lég 8: 525-31 N '28 **8550**

Bibliography of evidence. Univ S Calif L Lib Bul 1: 2-3 S '30 **8551**

Birdseye, Storey. Degrees of secondary evidence. Wash L R 6: 21-33 F '31 **8552**

Byrne, John Elliott. Manual of federal evidence. 721p. Chicago, National law bk. co. 1928 **8553**

Caffrey, Edwin Charles. Cases on evidence in civil and criminal cases. 664p. Newark, New Jersey law sch. press, 1928 **8554**

Chitty, Willes. Affidavit of document. Irish L T 61: 71-2 Mr 19 '27 **8555**

Commonwealth fund. Legal research committee. The law of evidence. 98p. New Haven, Yale univ. press, 1927 **8556**

Coroner's verdict as evidence. Sol J 73: 651 O 12 '29 **8557**

The corpse as evidence of murder. Sol J 73: 619 S 28 '29 **8558**

Cowling, Robert. Evidence. Post Mag & Insur Monitor 92: 1496 Jl 25 '31 **8559**

The defence of drunkenness, a point of evidence. Sol J 72:74 F 4 '28 **8560**

D[ent], D[aniel] M[iller]. Some observations on origin and application of res ipsa loquitur. Temple L Q 2: 378-82 Jl '28 **8561**

E[mery], W[illiam] M. Evidence—other crimes. Mich L R 29: 473-81 F '31 **8562**

Evidence in receiving. Sol J 73: 407 Je 29 '29 **8563**

Evidence of identity. Just Peace 91: 502-3 Jl 2 '27 **8564**

Evidence of similar acts. Sol J 71: 380-1 My 14 '27 **8565**

Evidence of statements made in presence of a party. Harv L R 43: 289-93 D '29 **8566**

Evidence that "must be accepted." Sol J 75: 197 Mr 21 '31 **8567**

Forcing accused to give evidence. Sol J 71: 592 Jl 23 '27 **8568**

Ford, Edmond John. Massachusetts evidence and trials. 4v. Chicago, Callaghan, 1931 **8569**

Ford, Edmond John. A treatise on trial evidence in Massachusetts. 244p. Boston, Hildreth, 1927 **8570**

Fricke, Charles W. Criminal investigation; the investigation of criminal cases, the securing of evidence and its proper presentation in court. 241p. Los Angeles, O. W. Smith, 1930 **8571**

Gallego, Manuel V. Philippine law of evidence; containing a concise statement of the rules in civil and criminal trials, based upon the statutory provisions, with annotations embracing opinions and comments of leading American and English authors of evidence, amplified by decisions of the Supreme court of the United States and of the Philippine Islands. 507p. Manila, Oriental commercial co. 1927 **8572**

Gober, George Fletcher. Gober's Georgia evidence: being a presentation of the law of evidence as enforced in Georgia from the code and decisions of the higher courts. 1158p. Athens, Ga. The Author, 1928 **8573**

Hanna, William S. Ohio trial evidence. 1607p. Indianapolis, Bobbs-Merrill, 1931 **8574**

Hellwig, A. Ueber die Technik von Gegenüberstellungen zur Festellung der Personengleichkeit. Zeitsch f ang Psychol 34: 213-43 N '29 **8575**

Hesseltine, Norman T. Laws helping criminals. Bost Univ L R 10: 524-6 N '30 **8576**

Hewitt, E. P. Evidence in criminal cases. Sol J 71: 111-12 F 5 '27 **8577**

Holman, W. A. Evidence in conspiracy cases. Austral L J 4: 247-51 D '30 **8578**

Hutchins, Robert M. and Slesinger, Donald. Some observations on the law of evidence. Colum L R 28: 432-40 Ap '28; same title: Harv L R 41: 860-73 My '28; Yale L J 37: 1017-28 Je '28 **8579**

Hutchins, Robert M. and Slesinger, Donald. Some observations on the law of evidence: state of mind to prove an act. Yale L J 38: 283-98 Ja '29 **8580**

Interrogation of prisoner. Sol J 71: 686 S 3 '27 **8581**

King's evidence. Just Peace 91: 571-2 Jl 23 '27 **8582**

Kiser, Donald J. comp. Outlines of evidence. 83p. N. Y. American law bk. co. 1927 **8583**

Leach, W. Barton. State law of evidence in the federal courts. Harv L R 43: 554-85 F '30 **8584**

Lockhart, Walter Samuel. Handbook of the law of evidence for North Carolina. ed.2 rev. 540p. Cincinnati, Anderson, 1931 **8585**

Long, Stanley B. Judicial control over sufficiency of evidence in jury trials. Wash L R 4: 117-38 Ag '29 **8586**

McDade, Thomas M. Best evidence rule, oral proof of contents of writings. St John's L R 5: 229-33 My '31 **8587**

McNeill, John Abraham and Weaver, Jess C. The law of evidence in civil and criminal cases in Illinois. ed.2. 3v. Chicago, Callaghan, 1927 **6588**

Maguire, John MacArthur and Epstein, Charles S. S. Preliminary questions of fact in determining the admissibility of evidence. Harv L R 40: 392-430 Ja '27 **8589**

Maguire, John MacArthur and Epstein, Charles S. S. Rules of evidence in preliminary controversies as to responsibility. Yale L J 36: 1101-25 Je '27 **8590**

Melcher, Webster A. Compulsory chemical testing of adversary's documents. Lawyer & Banker 21: 108-16 Mr '28 **8591**

Morgan, Edmund Morris; Chafee, Zechariah, jr., and Gifford, Ralph W. The law of evidence; some proposals for its reform. 98p. New Haven, Yale univ. press, 1927 **8592**

Morren, John. Criminal procedure and law of evidence in Scotland. 177p. Edinburgh, Hodge, 1928 **8593**

Newbolt, Francis. Evidence. Police J [London] 1: 568-77 '28 **8594**

Nichols, Clark Asahel. Applied evidence: an encyclopedic treatment of the proof of facts in evidence based on the statutes and decisions of the states of Arizona, California, Colorado, Idaho, Kansas, Montana, Nevada, New Mexico, Oklahoma, Oregon, Utah, Washington and Wyoming. 5v. Chicago, Callaghan, 1928 **8595**

Out of his own mouth convict. Sol J 73: 756 N 16 '29 **8596**

Philo-Judex. Motion to strike out the evidence. Va L R 17: 299-302 Ja '31 **8597**

Phipson, Sidney Lovell. Manual of the law of evidence. ed.4. 308p. Toronto, Carswell, 1928 **8598**

Police evidence and the public. Sol J 71: 795-6 O 15 '27 **8599**

Police questions to suspects. Sol J 74: 541 Ag 16 '30 **8600**

Prisoners' statements to police officers. Just Peace 92: 98-9 F 11 '28 **8601**

Quigley, Marjorie. Care of documents. Va L Reg ns13: 435-6 N '27 **8602**

Reconstructing the crime. Just Peace 91: 502 Jl 2 '27 8603

Refusal of suspected person to aid investigation. L Notes 31: 142 N '27 8604

Richardson, William Payson. Law of evidence. ed.4. 571p. Brooklyn, Brooklyn law bk. co. 1931 8605

Richardson, William Payson; Cady, Edwin Welling and Frankham, Markley. Selected cases in evidence. 1098p. N. Y. 305 Washington st. The Author, 1927 8606

Roscoe, Henry. Roscoe's digest of the law of evidence, and the practice in criminal cases. ed.15 by Anthony Hawke. 1283p. London, Stevens, 1928 8607

Shaw, G. M. Admissibility of non-testimonial evidence extorted from accused before and at the trial. N C L R 5: 333-40 Je '27 8608

Spencer, Edward W. Use of extraneous or unproved writings in cross-examination in questioned document cases, with some digressions. Marquette L R 13: 129-49 Ap '29 8609

Stein, Elbridge W. Science in the courtroom. Crim L J India 28 pt1: 27-31 F '27 8610

Taggart, Henry C. The securing and preservation of evidence. Police J [N Y] 17: 30-1 N '29 8611

Taking a statement. Just Peace 92: 792 D 8 '28 8612

Tyler, Morris. Finding of facts in Connecticut. Conn B J 4: 265-75 O '30 8613

Unreliable evidence. Sol J 72: 293 My 5 '28 8614

Völcker, Hans. Die Ablehnung von Beweisanträgen im Strafprozess. 47p. Bonn, Bonner univ.-Buchdr. 1931 8615

Winstanley, Herbert. The limitations of evidence. Police J [London] 2: 177-87 Ap '29 8616

Privileged Communications

Ahlemann, H. R. Kasuistische Mitteilungen. Arch f Krim 83: 274-7 N '28 8617

Polanski, N. N. Das private Wissen des Anwalts. Zeitsch f d ges Strafrechtswiss 51: 116-28 '31 8618

Pollitt, Basil H. and Rotalo, Joseph M. Confidential communications between attorney and client. Geo L J 18: 53-9 N '29 8619

Riddell. An address on the law and ethics of medical confidences. Lancet 213: 4-8 Jl 2 '27 8620

Presumptions

B., J. W. Power of the legislature to create presumptions and prima facie evidence. Calif L R 17: 565-75 Jl '29 8621

Brosman, Paul. Statutory presumption. Tulane L R 5: 178-210 F '31 8622

Chamberlain, Joseph P. Presumptions as first aid to the district attorney. Am B Assn J 14: 287-9 My '28 8623

Glenn, J. Frazier, jr. Constitutionality of statutory presumptions. N C L R 8: 50-5 D '29 8624

McCormick, Charles T. Charges on presumptions and burden of proof. N C L R 5: 291-310 Je '27 8625

Morgan, Edmund M. Some observations concerning presumptions. Harv L R 44: 906-34 Ap '31 8626

Presumptions. L Times 168: 143 Ag 24 '29 8627

Presumptions, burden of proof, and the conflict of laws. Harv L R 43: 1134-7 My '30 8628

Presumptions of guilt. L Notes 32: 82-3 Ag '28 8629

Statutory presumptions as devices to facilitate proof of crimes. Colum L R 28: 489-95 Ap '28 8630

Stauffacher, Caspar R. Statutory presumptions of guilt. St Louis L R 15: 181-7 F '30 8631

Windeyer, W. J. V. Presumption of sanity and the burden of proof of insanity. Austral L J 3: 328-32 F '30 8632

Ballistic

Goddard, Calvin. Firearms as evidence. Am J Police Sci 2: 3-7 Ja '31 8633

Serhant, Joseph E. The admissibility of ballistics in evidence. Am J Police Sci 2: 202-10 My '31 8634

Tangen, Ed. The Schopflin case. Am J Police Sci 2: 518-27 N '31 8635

Reputation and Character

Bates, Ruth E. Reputation of the victim on the issue of self-defense in Missouri. St Louis L R 14: 259-76 Ap '29 8636

Catterall, Ralph T. Character evidence in Virginia. Va L R 15: 34-50 N '28 8637

Cripe, Joseph. Character evidence in criminal cases. Ind L J 3: 706-17 Je '28 8638

Evidence of general reputation. N Y L R 5: 287-90 Ag '27 8639

Prevention of crimes act, when is "character" evidence. Just Peace 93: 541 Ag 24 '29 8640

Prisoner's character. Sol J 73: 619 S 28 '29 8641

Circumstantial

Brennan, T. C. Circumstantial evidence. Austral L J 4: 106-10 Ag '30 8642

Courtney, W. B. Circumstantial evidence. Collier's 87: 10-11 My 16 '31 8643

Foley, Thomas P. Circumstantial evidence, what is its value? Ill M J 54: 73-6 Jl '28; same title: Med-Leg J 47: 110-14 S '30 8644

Herschmann, Heinrich. Über psychiatrische und psychologische Sachverständigentätigkeit im Indizienprozess. Monats f Kriminalpsychol u Strafrechtsref 22: 351-62 My '31 8645

M'Kechnie, Hector. Circumstantial evidence. Scot L R 46: 160-2 My '30 8646

Mitchell, C. Ainsworth. Science as applied to circumstantial evidence. Police J [London] 1: 256-67 Ap '28 8647

Troeltsch. Zur Problematik des Indizienbeweises. Arch f Krim 80: 119-35 Mr '27 8648

Watzek, Ferdinand. Searching for and recording circumstantial evidence. Am J Police Sci 1: 272-5 My '30 8649

Wentzel, Karl. Das Schriftindizienbeweis. 47p. Berlin, Berger, 1927 8650

Admissions and Declarations

Admissibility of dying declarations. Ia L R 16: 530-4 Je '31 8651

D[ubin], J[oseph] S. Admission in evidence of book alleged to be obscene. S Calif L R 4: 225-36 F '31 8652

Fisk, Otis H. Judicial admissions. Univ Cin L R 1: 57-72 Ja '27 8653

Harper, Ellahue A. Admissibility of declarations of corporate agents. Univ Pa L R 76: 1-18 N '27 8654

Harper, Ellahue A. Scope of dying declarations, restoration of original scope. Dickinson L R 33: 168-76 Mr '29 8655

M'Kechnie, Hector. Notes on death-bed and dying declarations. Jurid R 41: 126-43, 238-59 Je, S '29 8656

Morgan, Edmund M. Rationale of vicarious admissions. Harv L R 42: 461-82 F '29 8657

Other Offenses

Evidence of a prisoner's other offences. Just Peace 94: 267-8, 282-3 Ap 26, My 3 '30 8658

Macklem, Carol. Evidence of other crimes in murder trials. Dickinson L R 35: 235-40 My '31 8659

Illegally Obtained

Bronaugh, Minor. Wire tapping evidence. L Notes 32: 65-7 Jl '28 8660

Evidence obtained by unlawful search. L Notes 31: 62-3 Jl '27 8661

Gemmell, Lynn. Use of evidence illegally obtained. Dakota L R 2: 160-3 Ap '28 8662

H[ines], R[ichard] K. jr. Admissibility of evidence procured by tapping telephone wires. Va L R 15: 62-8 N '28 8663

Howard, Robert L. Admissibility of evidence obtained by wire tapping. Univ Mo Bul L Ser 40: 13-21 D '28 8664

Wire tapping. L Notes 32: 183 Ja '29 8665

Corroboration

Corroboration. Irish L T 62: 235-6 S 29 '28 8666

Corroboration by silence. Sol J 72: 635 S 29 '28 8667

Corroboration in affiliation cases. Just Peace 95: 219-20 Ap 4 '31 8668

Corroboration of accomplices. L Times 164: 345-6 N 5 '27; same title: L Notes 31: 198 Ja '28 8669

Corroboration of police evidence. Sol J 71: 148 F 19 '27 8670

Burden of Proof

Daniele, Luigi. L'assoluzione per "insufficienza di prove." Rassegna Pen (9-10): 379-84 '29 8671

Davis, M. Philip. Burden of proof: California alien land laws. Calif L R 19: 295-303 Mr '31 8672

Effect of unnecessary affirmative pleading upon the burden of proof. Yale L J 39: 117-22 N '29 8673

Fisk, Otis H. Burden of proof. Univ Cin L R 1: 257-87 My '27 8674

Fisk, Otis Harrison. Fundamentals of the law of proof in judicial proceedings. 217p. Cincinnati, Anderson, 1928 8675

Groom, Littleton. Proof of crime in civil proceeding. Minn L R 13: 556-91 My '29 8676

White, Albert A. and Evans, Giles L. Burden of proving contributory negligence. Tenn L R 5: 76-91 F '27 8677

Wigmore, John Henry. The principles of judicial proof; or, The process of proof as given by logic, psychology and general experience and illustrated in judicial trials. ed.2. 1056p. Boston, Little, Brown, 1931 8678

Confessions

Booth, Bates. Confessions, and methods employed in procuring them. S Calif L R 4: 83-102 D '30 8679

Cautions and confessions. Just Peace 94: 49-50 Ja 25 '30 8680

Composto, Frank. Preliminary examination to determine competency of confession as evidence. St John's L R 5: 308-14 My '31 8681

Confessions of convicts. Mass L Q 12: 29-34 Ag '27 8682

Confessions of third parties. Just Peace 94: 235-6 Ap 12 '30 8683

Extracting confessions by machinery. Sol J 73: 807 D 7 '29 8684

Finlinson, J. The California public, the California peace officer and Senate bill number 666. Peace Offic Assn Calif Proc 9: 68-73 '29 8685
Admissibility as evidence of confessions.

Forced confessions. Lawyer & Banker 20: 9-12 Ja '27 8686

Grassberger, R. Ein falsches Mordgeständnis. Monats f Kriminalpsychol u Strafrechtsref 19: 239-45 Ap '28 8687

Heindl, R. Ein gezeichnetes Geständnis. Arch f Krim 80: 90-102 Mr '27 8688

Peschke, Kurt. Ein Geständnis. Arch f Krim 86: 87-93 Ap '30 8689

The "talkie" confession. L Notes 33: 203 F '30 8690

"Talkie" confessions. U S L R 64: 227-8 My '30 8691

Wimmer, August. Gestehen und Leugnen im Strafprozess. Zeitsch f d ges Strafrechtswiss 50: 538-96 '30 8692

With unclean hands. New Repub 59: 166-7 Jl 3 '29 8693

Family Relations

Hutchins, Robert M. and Slesinger, Donald. Some observations on the law of evidence: family relations. Minn L R 13: 675-86 Je '29 8694

Man giving evidence against daughter when wife charged with aiding and abetting. Just Peace 91: 731-2 O 1 '27 8695

Former Testimony

Hale, William G. The Missouri law relative to use of testimony given at former trial. St Louis L R 14: 375-93 Jl '29 8696

Hale, William G. Use by witness of his prior testimony for purpose of refreshing recollection. St Louis L R 15: 137-50 F '30 8697

H[oback], F[rederick] L. Admissibility of prior statements to corroborate testimony. Va L R 17: 696-8 My '31 8698

Prior consistent statements. Yale L J 36: 1162-6 Je '27 8699

Depositions

C[oleman], S. B. Admissibility of depositions or former testimony of witnesses, rule in Virginia. Va L R 14: 673-5 Je '28 8700

Court deposition challenge. Sol J 73: 721 N 2 '29 8701

Dying depositions: Russell Gurney's act. Sol J 73: 490 Jl 27 '29 8702

The judge's depositions. Sol J 73: 823 D 14 '29 8703

Jurat. Depositions of witnesses for the defence, signing by examining justices. Just Peace 94: 729 N 22 '30 8704

Right of prosecution to put in deposition of accused. Just Peace 93: 116 F 23 '29 8705

Taking depositions. Just Peace 94: 251 Ap 19 '30 8706

By Experiment

Admissibility of evidence obtained by experiment. Minn L R 12: 416-17 '28 8707

Sarber, John Delbert. The use of experiment in the introduction of evidence. 78p. Thesis (J.D.) University of California, 1927 8708

Photographs

Photographs in evidence. Sol J 71: 197-8 Mr 12 '27 8709

Quigley, Marjorie. Photographs at trials. Va L Reg ns13: 379-80 O '27 8710

Motion Pictures

The cinema in court. Sol J 72: 57-8 Ja 28 '28 8711

H[erzog], A[lfred] W. Talking motion pictures as evidence. Med-Leg J 48: 2-3 Ja '31 8712

A "talkie" as evidence. Sol J 73: 754 N 16 '29 8713

Parol

Chadbourn, James H. and McCormick, Charles T. The parol evidence rule in North Carolina. N C L R 9: 151-76 F '31 8714

G[lassman], W[illiam]. New Jersey rule of admissibility of parol-evidence to show written instrument a "sham." Univ Pa L R 75: 261-6 Ja '27 8715

Harrison, Earl G. Admissibility of parol evidence to alter recital of consideration. Temple L Q 2: 217-31 Ap '28 8716

Mechem, Frank L. Implied and oral warranties and the parol evidence rule. Minn L R 12: 209-24 F '28 8717

Puchner, Irving. Application of parol evidence rule under Wisconsin fraud and warranty cases. Marquette L R 15: 205-10 Je '31 8718

Urquico, Joseph. Parol evidence rule. Notre Dame Law 5: 303-15 Mr '30 8719

Williston, Samuel. Parol evidence rule; forbearance as consideration. Pa B Assn Q 1930: 1-4 8720

Forensic Psychology

Altavilla, Enrico. La psicologia giudiziaria. ed.2. 671p. Torino, Editrice Torinese, 1927 8721

Barnhoorn, J. A. J. Übersicht über die holländische psychiatrisch-juridische Literatur seit 1925. Monats f Kriminalpsychol u Strafrechtsref 21: 355-63 '30 8722

Bonhoeffer; Albrecht, H., and Beitzke, H. Bemerkungen zu Schorns Aufsatz. Monats f Kriminalpsychol u Strafrechtsref 19: 433-6 Jl '28 8723

Boriani, G. Rendiconto del corso di psicologia sperimentale giudiziaria tenuto nell'anno 1928 alla Scuola d'Applicazione giuridico-criminale. Scuola Pos ns8: 313-22 Jl '28 8724

Brailovski, V. V. [When is a psychiatrist needed in a criminal proceeding?] Pravo i zhizh' [6] (6-7): 109-13 '27 8725

Brandam, J. Error judicial e impericia psiquiatrica. R Arg de Neurol, Psiquiat y Med Leg 1: 474-7 S '27 8726

[Brown, William; Bosanquet, S. R. C; Fry, S. M[arjorie], and Smith, Hamblin]. Psychology and the law. Howard J 2: 135-46 '27 8727

Brukhanski, N. Sudebnaja psichiatrija. 439p. Moskva, Sabaschinkow, 1928 8728

Bryan, Douglas. A dream of forensic interest. Int J Psycho-Analysis 9: 247-55 Ap '28 8729

Buerschaper, Hans. Die Arbeitsscheu und ihre forensische Bedeutung. Monats f Kriminalpsychol u Strafrechtsref 22: 391-401 '31 8730

Burtt, Harold Ernest. Legal psychology. 467p. N. Y. Prentice-Hall, 1931 8731

Suggestion and hypnotism; methods of obtaining and evaluating testimony; confessions; association reaction and crime; breathing and crime detection; blood pressure and minor methods; mentally disordered criminal; mentally defective criminal; predelinquency; eugenics; punishments; drugs; suggestion and imitation; education and crime prevention.

Cimbal. Die forensisch-psychologische Bedeutung des paranymphalen Geschlechtsverkehrs. Monats f Kriminalpsychol u Strafrechtsref 20: 32-7 '29 8732

Cleric, G. F. von. Zur forensischen Würdigung der Suggestivfragen. Schweiz Zeitsch f Strafr 43: 223-64 '29 8733

Connolly, Thomas J. D. Plea for forensic psychology. Scot L R 46: 145-53 My '30 8734

Cutinelli, Francesco. Psicologia delle corti d'assise. Trani, Paganelli, 1928 8735

De psychiater en de voorlichting van den Rechter. Maandbl v Ber en Reclasseer 7: 254-69 S '28 8736

Djermekov, Dusan. La psychologie du procès criminel. Etudes Crimin 4: 330-5 D '29 8737

East, W. W. Some problems in forensic psychiatry. J St Med [London] 36: 205-21 Ap '28 8738

East, William Norwood. An introduction to forensic psychiatry in the criminal courts. 381p. London, Churchill, 1927 8739

Edlin, G. Rechtlich-psychiatrische Grenzfragen. Monats f Kriminalpsychol u Strafrechtsref 18: 301-16 Je '27 8740

Eliasberg, W. and Jankau, V. Zur forensischen Bedeutung des Assoziations experimentes. Zeitsch f d ges Strafrechtswiss 51: 191-8 '31 8741

Fernberger, Samuel W. Can an emotion be accurately judged by its facial expression alone? J Crim L & Crimin 20: 554-64 F '30 8742

Ferrari, G. C. Psychologie der Juristen. Zeitsch f ang Psychol 36: 209-14 '30 8743

Ferrari, U. La ricerca della verità nel processo penale. Riv Pen di Dott, Legis e Giuris 105: 5-23 Ja '27 8744

Ferrari, U. La verità penale e la sua ricerca nel diritto processuale italiano. 418p. Milano, Ist. Edit.Scient. 1927 8745

Fiore, Umberto. La psicologia giudiziaria. Scuola Pos ns7: 135-43 Mr '27 8746

Fränkel, F. Zur Psychologie des ärztlichen Gutachtens. Zeitsch f d ges Neurol u Psychiat 110: 223-34 '27 8747

Friedländer, A. A. Gesetz und Gefühl. Eine forensische-psychologische Betrachtung. Monats f Kriminalpsychol u Strafrechtsref 20: 406-11 '29 8748

Gordon, Alfred. Amnesia from a medico-legal standpoint. J Crim L & Crimin 19: 563-74 F '29 8749

Gorphe, F. L'utilisation de la psychologie dans la découverte de la verité en justice. Psychol et Vie 5: 248-51 '31 8750

Gruhle, Hans W. and Beringer, Kurt. Gerichtliche Psychiatrie und Kriminalpsychologie. Zeitsch f d ges Strafrechtswiss 50: 428-42 '30 8751

Hellwig, A. Forensische Psychologie und Strafrechtspflege. Gerichtssaal 97: 357-84 '28 8752

Hellwig, Albert. Psychologie und Vernehmungstechnik bei Tatbestandsermittlungen. Eine Einführung in der forensischen Psychologie für Polizeibeamte Richter, Staatsanwalte, Sachverständige und Laienrichter. 318p. Berlin, Langenscheidt, 1927 8753

H[entig, Hans]. Zur Psychologie der Ausrede. Monats f Kriminalpsychol u Strafrechtsref 19: 620-1 O '28 8754

Herschmann, H. Zur forensisch-psychiatrischen Beurteilung krankhafter Triebhandlungen. Arch f Psychiat 91: 750-66 '30 8755

Hirschberg. Zur Psychologie des Wiederaufnahme-Verfahrens. Monats f Kriminalpsychol u Strafrechtsref 21: 395-412 '30 8756

Hirschfeld, R. ed. Jahresbericht neurologie und psychiatrie; bibliographisches Jahresregister des Zentralblattes für die gesamte Neurologie und Psychiatrie. 599p. Berlin, Springer, 1929 8757

Criminal psychology; psychology of evidence; suicide; self-mutilation; sex pathology; forensic psychiatry.

Hübner, A. Die kriminalistische Bedeutung des Schlafes. Arch f Krim 81: 86-101 S '27 8758

Hutchins, Robert M. and Slesinger, Donald. Legal psychology. Psychol R 36: 13-26 Ja '29 8759

Hutchins, Robert M. and Slesinger, Donald. Some observations on the law of evidence—consciousness of guilt. Univ Pa L R 77: 725-40 Ap '29 8760

Lippert, E. Bibliographie der deutscher und ausländischen Literatur des Jahres 1926 über Psychologie, ihre Hilfwissenschaften und Grenzgebiete. Deutscher Teil. Zeitsch f Psychol 104: 369-473 N '27 8761

Luria, A. [Experimental psychology in court-trial inquests]. Sovyetskoe pravo (2): 84-100 '27 8762

McCarty, Dwight Gaylord. Psychology for the lawyer. 723p. N. Y. Prentice-Hall, 1929 8763

Mager, Harold. Deception; study in forensic psychology. J Abnorm & Soc Psychol 26: 183-98 Jl '31 8764

Maier, Hans W. Rechtliche-psychiatrische Grenzfragen. Bemerkungen zu dem Aufsatz von Dr. G. Edlin. Monats f Kriminalpsychol u Strafrechtsref 18: 316-22 Je '27 8765

Marbe, Karl. Ein experimentelles Gerichtsgutachten über Intelligenz und Glaubwürdigkeit eines erwachsenen Mädchens. Arch f Krim 85: 1-13 Ag '29 8766

Meggendorfer, F. Gerichtliche Psychiatrie. Fortschr d Neurol, Psychiat 2: 285-301 '30 8767

Michel, Rudolf. Lehrbuch der Forensischen Psychiatrie. 274p. Berlin, Urban & Schwarzenberg, 1931 8768

Mönkemöller, Otto. Psychologie und Psychopathologie der Aussage. 451p. (Bibliothek der Kriminalistik. Einzeldarstellungen der Strafrechtswissenschaft und ihrer Hilfswissenschaften, hrsg. von Aschaffenburg & Kriegsmann, v4) Heidelberg, Carl Winter, 1930 8769

Moll, Albert. Eine notwendige Kritik der forensischen Aussagepsychologie Sterns. Krimin Monatsh 1: 76-9 Ap '27 8770

Moll, Albert. Über die Aussagepsychologie Sterns. Zeitsch f Sexualwissensch 14: 109-16, 143 Je, Jl '27 8771

Pittock, H. J. Legal psychiatry. U S Vet Bur M Bul 7: 1050-2 N '31 8772

Plaut, P. Beiträge zur forensischen Psychologie. Zeitsch f ang Psychol 38: 510-23 '31 8773

Plaut, Paul. Forensische Psychologie. Krimin Monatsh 1: 36-7 Ja '27 8774

Plaut, Paul. Der Psychologie im Vorverfahren von Sittlichkeitsprozessen. Arch f Krim 82: 231-8 Je '28 8775

Pollitz. Mordversuch. Ein Beitrag zur Zeugenaussage und zum Geständnis. Monats f Kriminalpsychol u Strafrechtsref 18: 694-6 D '27 8776

Ruiz Maya, M. Psiquiatría penal y civil. 975p. Madrid, Plus Ultra, 1931 8777

Schilder, Paul and Gruhle, Hans W. Die Psychoanalyse in der Rechtsprechung. Monats f Kriminalpsychol u Strafrechtsref 19: 474-6 Ag '28 8778

Schneider, C. Hat die Psychoanalyse eine praktische forensische Bedeutung? Monats f Kriminalpsychol u Strafrechtsref 19: 321-44 Je '28 8779

Seelig, E. Die Registrierung unwillkürlicher Ausdrucksbewegungen als forensisch-psychodiagnostische Methode. Zeitsch f ang Psychol 28: 45-84 Ja '27 8780

Slade, J. A. Law and psychology. J Abnorm & Soc Psychol 24: 212-16 Jl '29 8781

Slesinger, Donald and Pilpel, E. Marion. Legal psychology. Psychol Bul 26: 677-92 D '29 8782

Smith, M. Hamblin. The value of psychology in court work. Police J [London] 1: 402-10 '28 8783

Stern, William. Mehr Psychologie im Vorverfahren von Sittlichkeitsprozessen! Betrachtungen zu zwei Freispruchfällen. Monats f Kriminalpsychol u Strafrechtsref 19: 8-17 Ja '28 8784

Stern, William. Meer Psychologie in het vooronderzoek; Beschouwingen naar aanleiding van twee gevallen van vrijspraak in zake zedemisdrijven. Tijdschr v d Politie 1(26): 466-74; (27): 486-91 N 14, 21 '28 8785

Stern, William. Über die Aussagepsychologie Sterns. Zeitsch f Sexualwissensch 14: 142-3 Jl '27 8786

Sträussler, E. Zwei forensische Gutachten als Beitrag zur Kenntnis der induzierten Psychosen. Wien med Wchnschr 78: 940-2 '28 8787

Strassmann, Georg. Beiträge zur Lehre von Kindesmord. Deut Zeitsch f d ges gerichtl Med 9: 546-64 Ap '27 8788

Strassmann, Georg. Beiträge zur Lehre von Kindesmord. Zentralbl f Gynäk 51: 20-47 '27 8789

Tesoro, Giorgio. La psicologia della testimonzia. 162p. Torino, Bocca, 1929 8790

Van Acker, C. La psychologie du témoignage véridique. J de Neurol et de Psychiat 30: 713-14 N '30 8791

Vecchio, G. del. La prova della verità nella diffamazione. Riv Pen di Dott. Legis e Giuris 105: 572-82 Je '27 8792

Voss, G. Zur Psychologie der ärztlichen Begutachtung. München med Wchnschr 77: 1553-4 S 5 '30 8793

Wassermann, Rudolf. Zur Psychologie der Aussage. Die Lehren des Magdeburger Falls Schröder. Monats f Kriminalpsychol u Strafrechtsref 18: 207-9 Ap '27 8794

WITNESSES

Authority to appear. Sol J 74: 807-8 D 6 '30 8795

Binding over witnesses conditionally. Just Peace 93: 23 Ja 12 '29 8796

Cautions to witnesses. Just Peace 94: 793-4 D 20 '30 8797

Criminal justice act and witnesses. L Times 163: 446-7 My 21 '27 8798

Harker, Oliver A. Compulsory attendance of non-resident witnesses in criminal cases. Ill L R 23: 195-9 Je '28 8799

Henson, William C. The unwilling witness. Ga Lawyer 1: 229-30 Mr '31 8800

Holding witnesses in bail. L Notes 33: 44 Je '29 8801

Mead, F. The accused as a witness—past, present and future. Just Peace 93: 603-4 S '28 8802

The missing witness. L Notes 32: 24-5 My '28 8803

P[almer], G[eorge] E[llis]. Compelling witness duty from absent nationals [Walsh act of 1926]. Mich L R 30: 137-42 N '31 **8804**

Rogers, Berto. Juror as witness. L Notes 34: 169-71 D '30 **8805**

Seelig, Ernst. Die Ergebnisse und Problemstellungen der Aussageforschung. Ergebn d ges Med 13: 401-50 '29 **8806**

Stern, W. Ueber psychologische Zeugenbegutachtung. Deut med Wchnschr 56: 1467-70 Ag 29 '30 **8807**

The super-expert witness. Sol J 73: 34 Ja 19 '29 **8808**

Time and distance. Sol J 73: 51 Ja 26 '29 **8809**

Uncalled witnesses. Sol J 73: 605 S 21 '29 **8810**

Williamson, A. F. Hostile witnesses. Crim L J India 28 pt1: 7-11 Ja '27 **8811**

Witness summons, discretion in granting. Just Peace 94: 756-7 D 6 '30 **8812**

Wolff, Kurt. Wiedererkennungs-Zeugen. Krimin Monatsh 1: 180-1 Ag '27 **8813**

COMPETENCY

Biggs, J. Crawford. Religious belief as qualification of a witness. N C L R 8: 31-43 D '29 **8814**

Bronaugh, Minor. Competency of husband or wife as witness in criminal case in federal court. L Notes 31: 108-12 S '27 **8815**

Carmichael, G. A. The policeman as a witness. Police "13-13" 2: 9- Jl '27 **8816**

Competency of husband and wife to testify against each other in criminal cases. Ga L R 1: 48 Je '28 **8817**

McIntosh, Andrew C. Incompetency of witness on account of religious belief. L Notes 33: 150-3 N '29 **8818**

EXAMINATION

Clark, John Holley, jr. Answer yes or no. N Am R 228: 85-90 Jl '29 **8819**

Cornelius, Asher Lynn. Cross examination of witnesses. 633p. Indianapolis, Bobbs-Merrill, 1929 **8820**

Cross-examination. Just Peace 93: 491-2 Ag 3 '29 **8821**

Friedmann, Fritz. Die Kunst der Verteidigung und der Forensischen Rede. 148p. Berlin, Pulvermacher, 1927 **8822**

Longenecker, Rolla R. Cross examination of the female witness. Case & Com 37: 2-6 Spring '31 **8823**

Mayo, Herbert. A note as to re-examination. Austral L J 4: 353-4 Mr '31 **8824**

Münsterberg, Hugo. On the witness stand. 269p. N. Y. Boardman, 1927 **8825**

Porterfield, Harold F. Making a witness one's own by cross-examination, impeachment. W Va L Q 34: 306-7 Ap '28 **8826**

Stephan, Leonard A. W. Cross-examination of adversary under the statute. Dakota L R 2: 156-60 Ap '28 **8827**

Stephens, Samuel J. Probate psychiatry—examination of testamentary capacity by a psychiatrist as a subscribing witness. Ill L R 25: 276-87 N '30 **8828**

W[alsh], J. H[erbert]. Cross-examination as to previous prosecution for, and conviction of crime, for purpose of affecting credibility. Geo L J 16: 487-9 Je '28 **8829**

Wellman, Francis Lewis. Art of cross examination. ed. rev. & enl. N.Y. Macmillan, 1927 **8830**

Zur Vernehmung von Kindern und Jugendlichen in Strafsachen: eine neue Verordnung des sächsischen Justizministeriums. Zeitsch f pädagog Psychol 29: 212-16 Ap '28 **8831**

IMPEACHMENT

Hall, C[larence] W[indley]. Impeachment by evidence of a witness's bad character. N C L R 5: 340-5 Je '27 **8832**

Pugliese, Sebastian C. Criminal conduct as instrument of testimonial impeachment in Pennsylvania. Temple L Q 4: 123-30 Mr '30 **8833**

JUVENILE

Beier. Ein Beitrag zur Psychologie der Kindesaussage. Krimin Monatsh 2: 59-61 Mr '28 **8834**

Busemann, A. Psychologische Beobachtungen anlässlich eines Sexualprozesses mit jugendlichen Zeuginnen. Zeitsch f ang Psychol 33: 388-404 Je '29 **8835**

Döring, Max. Eine wichtige Verordnung über die Vernehmung von Kindern und Jugendlichen in Strafsachen. Zeitsch f Sexualwissensch 15: 49-53 Ap '28 **8836**

Döring, Max. Die Vernehmung von Kindern und Jugendlichen in Strafsachen. Neue Bahnen 39: 131-3 Mr '28 **8837**

Döring, Max. Das Wiedererkennen von Personen durch Kinder. Neue Bahnen 38: 112-14 Mr '27 **8838**

Elwert. Jugendliche als Zeugen. Zentralbl f Jugendrecht u Jugendwohlfahrt 19: 169-72 '27 **8839**

Franzen, A. Die phantastische Kindesaussage. Deut Zeitsch f d ges gerichtl Med 10: 200 Ag '27 **8840**

Gross, J. Aussagepsychologische Untersuchungen an Kindern. Zeitsch f ang Psychol 37: 438-59 D '30 **8841**

Heiland, Gerhard. Vernehmung von Kindern und Jugendlichen in Strafsachen. Krimin Monatsh 3: 49-52 Mr '29 **8842**

Hentig. Jugendliche Zeugenaussagen (Ein Urteil). Monats f Kriminalpsychol u Strafrechtsref 21: 185-91 '30 **8843**

Hirschberg. Ein Fehlurteil auf Grund unwahrer Kinderaussagen. Monats f Kriminalpsychol u Strafrechtsref 19: 670-6 N '28 **8844**

Kleinschmidt. Ein Fall von suggestiver Kinderaussage. Krimin Monatsh 1: 54-5 Mr '27 **8845**

Marcuse, Max. Über die Glaubwürdigkeit sexueller Beschuldigungen durch Kinder und Jugendliche. Zeitsch f Sexualwissensch 17 (8): 463-86 Mr 31 '31 **8846**

Marx, A. M. Zur Bewertung der Zeugenaussagen von Kindern mit einem Vorschlage über die Aufnahme einschlägiger Zeugenprotokolle. Deut Zeitsch f d ges gerichtl Med 11: 225-52 Mr 15 '28 **8847**

Müller-Hess and Nau, Elisabeth. Die Bewertung von Aussagen Jugendlicher in Sittlichkeitsprozessen. Jahresk f ärztl Fortbild 21 (9): 48-72 S '30 **8848**

Plaut, Paul. Die Zeugenaussagen Jugendlicher Psychopathen. Ihre forensische Bedeutung. 84p. (Abh d gebiete der psychotherapie und medizin psychologie no8) Stuttgart, Enke, 1928 **8849**

Revesz, G. Beschuldigung eines Lehrers wegen unzüchtiger Handlung durch seine Schulerinnen. Zeitsch f ang Psychol 31: 385-409 '28 **8850**

Selz, Otto. Ein Schulbeispiel zur Frage der Würdigung jugendlicher Zeugenaussagen. Monats f Kriminalpsychol u Strafrechtsref 19: 641-58 N '28 **8851**

Stern, L. W. Zwei forensisch-psychologische gutachten über kindliche zeugen in sittlichkeitsprozessen. Zeitsch f ang Psychol 36: 151-73 '30 **8852**

Unsworn evidence of children. Sol J 72: 375 Je 9 '28 **8853**

Wartenberg. Kinderaussagen in der Praxis der Strafrichters. Krimin Monatsh 1: 220-1 O '27 **8854**

Das Wiedererkennen von Personen in Lichtbild durch jugendliche Zeugen. Arch f Krim 81: 163-7 S '27 **8855**

Witnesses of tender years. Just Peace 93: 451 Jl 13 '29 **8856**

Zillig, M. Experimentelle Untersuchungen über die Glaubwürdigkeit von Kindern. Zeitsch f Psychol 119: 311-71 Mr '31 **8857**

Zillig, M. Typisches Verhalten kindlicher Zeugen bei wiederholter Aussage. Zeitsch f Psychol 107: 366-410 '28 **8858**

TESTIMONY

Argyropoulos, Ap. La critique et la valeur du témoignage. 47p. Athènes, Imp. N. D. Franzeskaki, 1931 **8859**
In Greek language.

Foley, Francis C. Admission at second trial of testimony of missing witness—interpretation of Article 12 of the declaration of rights. Boston Univ L R 11: 550-3 N '31 **8860**

Gorphe, François. La critique du témoignage. ed.2. 470p. bibliog 427-64. Paris, Dalloz, 1927 **8861**

Halberstadt, G. La critique du témoignage. Ann Méd-Psychol s12 1: 32-9 Ja '28 **8862**

Hentig, H.v. Falsche uneidliche Aussage. Justiz 3: 156-65 '27 **8863**

Kafka, G. Ein aussageversuch mit kriminalbeamten. Zeitsch f ang Psychol 31: 173-201 S '28 **8864**

Kuraner, Alfred. The consistency of testimonial accuracy. J Crim L & Crimin 22: 406-14 S '31 **8865**

Monget, Maurice and Gelma, E. Erreur judiciaire due à une concordance de témoignages erronés. Ann de Méd Lég 7: 68-73 Ja '27 **8866**

Pasteau, E. G. La preuve en matière pénale, quelques considérations sur le témoignage. Etudes Crimin 4: 45-8 F '29 **8867**

Persons entitled to waive or claim privileges as to admission of testimony. Colum L R 30: 686-94 My '30 **8868**

Pessoa, Alberto. A prova testemunhal. Estudio de psicologia judiciaria. ed.3. 278p. Coimbra, Imp. da Universidad, 1931 **8869**

Pfahler, G. Rückeinstellung und aussage. Zeitsch f ang Psychol 35: 184-200 '30 **8870**

Plaut, Paul. Aussage und Umwelt in Sittlichkeitsprozessen. Heft 3 der Beiträge zur Massenpsychologie. 77p. Halle a.d.S., Carl Marhold, 1929 **8871**

Plaut, Paul. Der Zeuge und seine Aussage im Strafprozess. 315p. Leipzig, G. Thieme, 1931 **8872**

Plaut, Paul. Zur Zeugenaussage Erwachsener. Betrachtungen zum Husmann-Prozess. Zeitsch f ang Psychol 32: 321-42 Mr '29 **8873**

Probative force of negative testimony. Can B R 6: 295-6 Ap '28 **8874**

Salinger, F. Psychiatrische Begutachtung einer Zeugenaussage. Aerztl Sachverst-Zeit 33:114-17 My 1 '27 **8875**

Smith, Emory. The fallibility of eyewitness testimony. Am J Police Sci 1: 487-95 S '30 **8876**

Strassmann, G. Die Haftung des Arztes für Fehlgutachten. Deut Zeitsch f d ges gerichtl Med 14: 598-604 F 15 '30; same title: Med Klin 26: 337-8 Mr 7 '30 **8877**

Testimony and judgment. Just Peace 93: 391-2 Je 22 '29 **8878**

Weil, H. Aussagepsychologische Untersuchungen an integrierten Persönlichkeitstypen. Zeitsch f ang Psychol 37: 74-98 S '30 **8879**

Expert Testimony

Anderson, L. M. Expert testimony; its evils. Fla M A J 16: 218-19 N '29 **8880**

Antonini, G. and Bravetta, E. Perizia medico-legale sullo stato di mente di Renzo Pettine. Arch di Antrop Crim 48: 730-46 Jl '28 **8881**

Aschaffenburg, G. Der psychologische Sachverständige. Deut Zeitsch f d ges gerichtl Med 10: 149-54 Ag '27 **8882**

Bericht über eine Konferenz forensisch-psychologischer Sachverständiger. Erziehung 2: 714-16 '27 **8883**

Cassidy, Henry E. The attorney at law and the document examiner. Va L R 17: 800-8 Je '31 **8884**

Döring, Max. Die Praxis des kindespsycologischen Sachverständigen in Sexualprozessen bei den Leipziger Gerichten. Zeitsch f Sexualwissensch 14: 273-5 O '27 **8885**

Ebermayer. Der Arzt als Sachverständiger. München med Wchnschr 77: 1136-7 Jl 4 '30 **8886**

Expert evidence. Sol J 72: 260 Ap 21 '28 **8887**

Expert testimony. Notre Dame Law 3: 147-9 Ja '28; same title: Med-Leg J 45: 58-9 Mr '28 8888

Gross, Irwin Richard. The testimony and methods of psychiatrists at criminal trials. 134p. Thesis (J.D.) University of California, 1927 8889

Hellwig, A. Kriminalpsychologische Sachverständige. Deut med Wchnschr 56: 1489-90 '30 8890

Hellwig, A. Der psychologische Sachverständige im Gerichtsverfahren. Ind Psychotechn 7: 243-7 '30 8891

Hentig, H. v. Gesetzgeber und Sachverständnis. Monats f Kriminalpsychol u Strafrechtsref 19: 348-9 Je '28 8892

Höpler, E. Der Sachverständige im künftigen Strafverfahren. Beitr z gerichtl Med 9: 34-6 '29 8893

Illera, Cayetano Renjifo. Prueba pericial en materia criminal. Bogotá, 1928 8894

Kolle, Kurt. Ein "Hellseher" als "Sachverständiger." Monats f Kriminalpsychol u Strafrechtsref 18: 625-31 N '27 8895

Lafora, G. R. El peritaje psiquiátrico en el derecho penal. Siglo Méd 83: 597-600 Ap 20 '29 8896

Lobinger, C. S. The compensation of expert witnesses. Crim L J India 28 pt1: 13-15 Ja '27 8897

Marbe, Karl. Der Psycholog als gerichtlicher Sachverständiger. Arch f Krim 86: 1-14, 126-30, 208-19 F-Je '30 8898

Meier, Carl L. The x-ray in evidence, interpretation by expert witness. Univ Cin L R 2: 97-9 Ja '28 8899

Moll, A. Psychiater und Psychologe als gerichtliche Sachverständige. Monats f Psychiat u Neurol 64: 137-51 Jl '27 8900

Mügel, Leo. Der Sachverständige im Zivil- und Strafprozess. 48p. Köln, Paul Kuschbert, 1931 8901

Mueller, Oscar C. Expert: a plea for the adoption of a statute . . . to regulate expert testimony. 75p. Los Angeles, Saturday night pub. co. 1929 8902

New York (state). Crime commission. Special report to the Commission on psychiatric and expert testimony in criminal cases, December 15, 1929. 16p. Albany, 1930 8903

Palmer, L. J. Recent trends in giving of expert testimony. Psychiat Q 2: 465-7 O '28 8904

Palmieri, V. M. In attesa del nuovo codice di procedura penale. Riforma Med 45: 1541 N 9 '29 8905

Policemen as experts in drunkenness. Sol J 71: 197 Mr 12 '27 8906

Psychologen als Sachverständige vor Gericht. Aerztl Sachverst-Zeit 33: 214 Ag 1 '27 8907

Schläger. Zur Frage der Einholung von Sachverständigengutachten im Strafprozess. Med Klin 26: 758-60 My 16 '30 8908

Sellers, J. Clark. The expert. Int Assn Identif Proc 16: 82-6 '30 8909

Shea, William Dennis. Rules regulating the admissibility and use of expert testimony. 68p. Thesis (J.D.) University of California, 1927 8910

Smith, Emory. Unmasking the pseudo-expert. Am J Police Sci 1: 89-91 Ja '30; translation: Unberufene Sachverständige. Arch f Krim 87: 237-8 D '30 8911

Stern, William. Albert Moll und der psychologische Sachverständige. Krimin Monatsh 1: 138-41 Je '27 8912

Stern, William; Raecke, and Hentig, Hans v. Richter und Sachverständiger. Monats f Kriminalpsychol u Strafrechtsref 18: 590-5 O '27 8913

Vervaeck, Louis. Les conditions de l'expertise psychiatrique criminelle. R de Dr Pén et de Crimin 9: 685-94 Jl '29 8914

Villard, Henri. Le contrôle de l'expertise judiciaire en matière pénale. Paris, Libr. Gén. de droit et de jurisprudence, 1930 8915

Weber, W. Die Tätigkeit des psychologischen Sachverständigen vor Gericht, unter besonderer Berücksichtigung industrieller Verhältnisse. Ind Psychotechn 4: 273-83 '27 8916

Weiler, K. Wann entspricht ein Gutachten dem Willen des Gesetzgebers bzw. den Absichten des Vertrages? München med Wchnschr 77: 2028 N 21 '30 8917

Wiard, Seth. The cross-examination of expert witnesses. Am J Police Sci 2: 538-42 N '31 8918

Wiard, Seth. The preparation and presentation of expert testimony. Am J Police Sci 2: 143-7 Mr '31 8919

Withers, S. Story of first roentgen evidence. Radiology 17: 99-103 Jl '31 8920

MEDICAL JURISPRUDENCE

Almandos, Luis Reyna. El sistema Vucetich en América y la Conferencia de neurología, psiquiatría y medicina legal. R de Identif y Cienc Pen 3: 130-3 N '28 8921

American bar association. Medico-legal committee. Report. Am J Police Sci 1: 396-400 Jl '30 8922

Anales del Instituto de medicina legal. 1, 1928- 8923
Universidad nacional de Buenos Aires.

Archivo de medicina legal. Lisboa. 1, 1923- 8924

Archivos da Sociedade de medicina legale e criminologia de São Paulo. March 1928- 8925

Balthazard, V. Précis de médecine légale. ed.4 rev. 665p. Paris, Baillière, 1928 8926

Beltran, J. Ramon. La medicina legale nella Repubblica Argentina. Accad Med-Chir di Torino Gior 1929: 84-91 8927

Benassi, G. Osservazioni medico-legali sul progetto [di nuovo codice penale]. Studi Econ e Giurid Univ Cagliari 16: 109-30 '28 8928

Biancalani, Aldo. L'accertamento della causa della morte in medicina legale. (Istituto di medicina legale della r. Università di Firenze) 16p. Firenze, Giannini & Giovanelli, 1927 8929

Biancalani, A. and Costa, A. Sulle fratture craniche per colpi d'arma da fuoco. Arch di Antrop Crim 48: 499-547 My '28 8930

Bianchini, Giuseppe. La medicina legale nel presente e nell' avvenire. 24p. Siena, S. Bernardino, 1927 8931

Birnbaum, Karl, ed. Handwörterbuch der medizinischen Psychologie. 672p. Leipzig, Thieme, 1930 8932

Brend, William A. A handbook of medical jurisprudence and toxicology. ed.6 rev. 344p. London, Griffin, 1928 8933

Carrara, Mario. Il criterio antropologico nel giudizio medico legale. Arch di Antrop Crim 48: 30-44 Ja '28 8934

Carrara, Mario. La medicina legale e l'antropologia criminale in Egitto. Arch di Antrop Crim 50: 215-50 '29 8935

Chavigny. La chronologie en médecine légale. R Int de Crimin 2(1): 5-14 '30 8936

Chavigny and Simonin. La chronologie en médecine légale. Ann de Méd Lég 8: 117-25 Mr '28 8937

Chavigny, Paul. Le geste graphique en médecine légale en criminalistique. R Int de Crimin 3(3): 168-72 '31 8938

Clark, H. H. Medical jurisprudence. Sw Med 15: 453-8 O '31 8939

Conferencia latino americana de neurologia, psiquiatria y medicina legal. Actas de la primera Conferencia. . . 707p. Buenos Aires, Imp. de la Universidad, 1929 8940

Congrès de médecine légale de langue française. Compte rendu du XVe congrès. Ann de Méd Lég 10(7) Jl '30; 11: 1-37 Ja '31
Comptes rendus du XVIe congrès. Ann de Méd Lég 11: 193-354, 383-477, 558-77, 593-614, 637-65 Ap-N '31 8941

Dabrowski, W. Grzywo. L'Institut de médecine légale de Varsovie. Ann de Méd Lég 7: 357-62 Jl '27 8942

Desage. Le certificat médical et sa valeur judiciaire. Ann de Méd Lég 7: 180-4 Ap '27 8943

Deutsche Zeitschrift für die gesamte gerichtliche Medizin. Berlin, 1, 1922- 8944

Dewez. Empossonnement par le tortre stibié. R de Dr Pén et de Crimin 7: 853-86 Ag '27 8945

Fribourg-Blanc, A. and Durand, H. Corps étrangers méconnus chez les blessés du crâne. Ann de Méd Lég 8: 148-56 Mr '28 8946

Gesualdo, G. Il contenuto biologico e le applicazioni giuridiche della medicina legale militare. Arch di Antrop Crim 48: 241-58 Mr '28 8947

Glaister, John. Ein psychologisch bemerkenswerter Fall aus der gerichtlichen Medizin. Monats f Kriminalpsychol u Strafrechtsref 21: 20-2 '30 8948

Glaister, John. A text book of medical jurisprudence and toxicology. ed.5. Edinburgh, Livingstone, 1931 8949

Glaister, John. The teaching of forensic medicine. Brit M J (3479): 448-51 S 10 '27 8950

Glasser, O. First roentgen evidences. Radiology 17: 789-91 O '31 8951

Grosz, K. and Sträussler, E. Zur Frage der forensischen Bedeutung der Wagner-Jaureggschen Paralysebehandlung. Zeitsch f d Neurol u Psychiat 111: 485-94 '27 8952

Halberstadt. Contribution à l'étude médico-légale de la démence précoce. Ann de Méd Lég 7: 113-23 Mr '27 8953

Herzog, Alfred W. Medical jurisprudence. 1051p. Indianapolis, Bobbs-Merrill, 1931 8954

Hildebrand, Heinrich. Gerichtliche Medizin. Ein Leitfaden für Studierende und praktische Ärzte. 158p. Berlin, Schoetz, 1927 8955

Kleist, K. Aus unserer psychiatrischen Gutachterätigkeit; zur gutachtlichen Bedeutung der ungewöhnlichen autochthonen Psychosen, sogenannten Degenerationspsychosen. Allg Zeitsch f Psychiat 90: 446-65 Jl 4 '29 8956

Klemm, O. Über die Atmungssymptomatik bei Untersuchungsgefangenen. Neue Psychol Stud 5: 111-33 '29 8957

Kockel, R. Alte und neue Wege in der gerichtlichen Medizin. Deut Zeitsch f d ges gerichtl Med 11: 1-13 '27 8958

Kockel, R. Das erweiterte Institut für gerichtliche Medizin der Universität Leipzig. Arch f Krim 83: 206-7 O '28 8959

Krafft-Ebing, R. v. Psychopathia sexualis; a medico-forensic study embracing the antipathic sexual instinct. Authorized adaptation of the 12th German edition. Physicians & Surgeons, 1931 8960

Lacassagne, A. and Martin, Etienne. Précis de médecine légale. ed.3. 748p. Paris, Masson, 1927 8961

Laignel-Lavastine. Paul Zacchias. Paris Méd 2: i-vi Ag 1 '31 8962

Das Lettländische Institut für wissenschaftliche Gerichtsexpertise. Arch f Krim 81: 63 Jl '27 8963

Lorenzoni, M. Gefängnisärztliche Erfahrungen beim Landesgerichte für Strafsachen in Graz. Deut Zeitsch f d ges gerichtl Med 11: 193-201 '28 8964

Mazel, P. La preuve en médecine légale. Sa nature. Ses limites. Ses difficultés. J de Méd de Lyon 8: 583-8 '27 8965

Meixner, K. Umfang und Aufgaben der gerichtlichen Medizin. Wien Klin Wchnschr 41: 41-4 '28 8966

Menninger, Karl A. Medicolegal proposals of the American psychiatric association. J Crim L & Crimin 19: 367-77 N '28 8967

Minovici, Mina. Tratat complect de medecinâ legalâ, en legislatia si jurisprudenta romanâneascâ si streinâ. 2v. Bucuresti, Ateliere grefice Soced. 1930 8968

Modi, J. P. Medical jurisprudence and toxicology. ed.3. 760p. London, Butterworth, 1928 8969

Morrison. Certain contacts of medicine and the law. Can Med Assn J 24: 706-8 My '31 **8970**

Moser, Kurt. Zur Versorgungs- und Versicherungsrechtlichen Beurteilung und Begutachtung organischer Nervenkrankheiten. Arch f Psychiat 91: 411-50 '30 **8971**

Neureiter, F. v. Die für den Arzt und ärztlichen Sachverständigen wichtigen Bestimmungen des Entwurfes eines Allgemeinen Deutschen Strafgesetzbuches vom Jahre 1925. Wien Med Wchnschr 77: 959-61, 991-3, 1053-5 Jl 16-Ag 6 '27 **8972**

Ottolenghi, Salvatore. Lezioni di medicina legale. . . [1926-1927]. 176p. Roma, Sampaolesi, 1927 **8973**

Ottolenghi, Salvator. Medicina legale e polizia scientifica. Zacchia 6: 1-9 '27; same title: Arch di Antrop Crim 48: 45-52 Ja '28 **8974**

Perrando, [G.] Giacomo. La medicina legale italiana e il progetto del nuovo codice penale. Nuov Dir (7-8): 436-54 '29 **8975**

Perrando, G. G[iacomo]. I progressi della medicine legale nell'ultimo decennio. Rassegna Int di Clin e Terap 10: 1051-64 N '29 **8976**

Philippe, Marcel and Provent, Paul. Le XIVe congrès de médecine légale de langue française, Paris, 24-26 Juin 1929. Etudes Crimin 4: 239-40, 277-83 Jl, S '29 **8977**

Primera Conferencia Latino-americana de neurología, psiquiatría y medicina legal. R de Identif y Cienc Pen 2: 255-6 Jl '28 **8978**

Provent, Paul. Le XIIe Congrès de médecine légale. Etudes Crimin 2: 79-81 Jl '27 **8979**

Provent, Paul. Le XIIIe Congrès de médecine légale, 9 Octobre 1928. Etudes Crimin 4: 58-61 F '29 **8980**

Raitzin, A. El informe médico-legal: sus formas oral y escrita. R de Crimin, Psiquiat y Med Leg 15: 143-59 Mr '28 **8981**

Rehfeldt, Paul. Gerichtsaerztliche Tatbestandsfeststellungen im Dienste der Polizei. 134p. Berlin, Gruyter, 1927 **8982**

Repertorio bibliografico del Instituto de medicina legal de Paris. Bibl Nac de Crim y Cienc Afines Bol 1: 317-22 Ja '27 **8983**

Reuter, F. Alte und neue Wege in der gerichtlichen Medizin. Deut Zeitsch f d ges gerichtl Med 11: 14-35 '27 **8984**

Revista argentina de neurologia, psiquiatria y medicina legal. Buenos Aires. 1, 1927- **8985**

Riddell, George Allardice. Medico-legal problems. 100p. London, H. K. Lewis, 1929 **8986**

Robertson, W. G. Aitchison. Aids to forensic medicine and toxicology. ed.10. London, Bailliere, 1929 **8987**

Rojas, N. Decálogo médico legal. R de Crimin, Psiquiat y Med Leg 15: 257-66 My '28 **8988**

Romanese, R. Un nuovo criterio diagnostico desunto della presenza della incisura di uscita nelle ferite per arma da punta e taglio. Arch di Antrop Crim 47: 944-7 N '27 **8989**

Ryglicki, Stefan. Przyczynek do Zastosowania Promieni Roentgena w Medycynie Sadowej. Czasopismo Sadowo-Lekarskie (4): 244- '30 **8990**

Salinger, Fritz. Die forensische Bedeutung der Malariabehandlung der Paralyse. Monats f Kriminalpsychol u Strafrechtsref 19: 531-9 S '28 **8991**

Schackwitz, A. Seltenheiten aus der gerichtsärztlichen Praxis. Deut Zeitsch f d ges gerichtl Med 10: 31-53 Jl '27 **8992**

Scheffel, Carl. Medical jurisprudence. Philadelphia, Blakiston, 1931 **8993**

Schmidt, O. Beitrag zur chemischen Analyse von Schussverletzungen. (Nachweis von Quecksilber, Blei und Antimon) Deut Zeitsch f d ges gerichtl Med 18: 353-66 D 19 '31 **8994**

Schwarzacher, W. Aufgaben und Arbeitsweisen der gerichtlichen Medizin. Wien Klin Wchnschr 41: 1073-7 '28 **8995**

Simonin, Camille. Le diagnostic médico-légal de l'état d'ivresse. Etudes Crimin 3(3): 116-21 My '28 **8996**

Simonin, Camille. L'état d'ivresse, son importance judiciaire, son diagnostic médico-légal. 46p. Paris, Sirey, 1928? **8997**

Simonin, Camille. L'importance médico-judiciaire de l'alcoolisme aigu. Etudes Crimin 3(4-5): 158-66 bibliog (p165-6) S '28 **8998**

Simonin, C[amille]. La médecine légale et la médecine sociale des accidents d'automobiles. Ann de Méd Lég 11: 286-354 bibliog (p348-54) Ap '31 **8999**

Sklarz, Ernst. Medizinisch-Forensisches zum Reichsgesetz zur Bekämpfung der Geschlechtskrankheiten. Krimin Monatsh 1: 87-9 Ap '27 **9000**

Smith, Sydney Alfred. Forensic medicine. ed.3. 631p. London, Churchill, 1931 **9001**

Smith, Sydney [Alfred] and Glaister, John, jr. Recent advances in forensic medicine. 194p. Philadelphia, Blakiston, 1931 **9002**
Firearm injuries; identification of firearms; examination of powders and powder residues; examination of the weapon; examination of hairs; precipitin test for blood; spermato-precipitins; osteo-precipitins; musculo-precipitins; blood grouping; carbon monoxide in blood; spectroscopy; ultraviolet light; estimation of alcohol in blood and urine.

Szumlanski and Provent. Le XVe Congrès de médecine légale de langue française. Etudes Crimin 5: 207-14 Je '30 **9003**

Vogler. Gerichtliche Medizin und Psychiatrie. Psychiat-neurol Wchnschr 33(14): 158-61 Ap 4 '31 **9004**

Vorkastner, W. Über Werden und Wesen der gerichtlichen Medizin. Klin Wchnschr 10: 748-53 Ap 18 '31 **9005**

Webster, Ralph W. Legal medicine and toxicology. 862p. Philadelphia, Saunders, 1930 **9006**

Weeber, Richard. Das Psychobiogram und dessen Bedeutung für den Gerichtsarzt. Deut Zeitsch f d ges gerichtl Med 9: 618-21 Ap '27 9007

Wybauw, R. La mort subite ou la mort rapide par suite de la cessation du fonctionnement du coeur. R de Dr Pén et de Crimin 10: 763-84 bibliog (p784-8) '30 9008

Ziel, R. Gerichtliche Medizin und sozialhygienische Strömungen. Med Klin 25: 1608-9 O 11 '29 9009

MEDICAL WITNESS

Adams, E. Falls and pitfalls of medico-legal expert. M Times [N Y] 56: 317-25 D '28 9010

Bourland, O. M. The medical expert witness. Ark M Soc J 26: 220-2 Ap '30 9011

Bowers, P. E. Medical expert. Int Clin 3: 237-53 S '29 9012

Brown, W. E. jr. Medical expert testimony. M Soc N J J 25: 83-5 F '28 9013

[Burrows, Roland]. The medical practitioner and the administration of justice. L Times 165: 59-60 Ja 21 '28; same title: L J [London] ns65: 76-7 Ja 28 '28 9014

Edwards, G. H. Our medico legal status. Fla M Assn J 17: 579-82 Je '31 9015

Flesch, M. Aerztliches Gutachten und Rechtsspruch. Deut med Wchnschr 57: 1552-4 S 4 '31 9016

Giraud, Georges. El médico legista según los maestros. R de Crimin, Psiquiat y Med Leg 18: 129-42 Mr '31 9017

Goldmann, [Otto]. Gerichtsarzt und Untersuchungsrichter. Arch f Krim 83: 208-14 N '28 9018

Goldmann, Otto. Mord, Gerichtsarzt und Untersuchungsrichter. Monats f Kriminalpsychol u Strafrechtsref 19: 442-5 Jl '28 9019

Hamilton, A. M. Doctors in court. Roy Med-Chir Soc Glasgow Tr 24: 93-101 '30; same title: Glasgow M J 113: 225-34 My '30 9020

Herold, S. L. Medical expert testimony. New Orleans M & Surg J 81: 237-45 O '28 9021

Herzog, Alfred W. Medical expert testimony. Med-Leg J 44:4-5 Ja '27 9022

Horovitz, Samuel B. Method of handling cases which require medical testimony. Legal Aid R 25: 7-9 Ja '27 9023

Howell, Frank S. Some phases of medical jurisprudence. Neb St M J 14: 84-7 F '28 9024

Kennedy, F. The medical expert in the courts. Arch Neurol & Psychiat 17: 848-56 Je '27 9025

Kennedy, F. Rôle of medical expert in criminal trials. N Y Acad Med Bul 5: 608-13 Jl '29 9026

Leary, T. The doctor and the courts. Me M J 21: 188-92 N '30 9027

Lejbowitsch, J. Gerichtlich-medizinische Expertise. (Sammelheft 6) Moskau, Verlag des Volkskommisariats für Gesundheitswesen, 1927 9028

Lucier, A. A. Medical testimony. New England J Med 204:19-24 Ja 1 '31 9029

McCord, Carey P. The doctor in the dock. Forum 77: 867-79 Je '27 9030

McGovern, J. J. Medical expert testimony. Wis M J 27: 41-5 Ja '28 9031

Miloslavich, Edward L. Medical testimony. Marquette L R 12: 110-18 F '28 9032

Morgan, Edmund M. Expert medical testimony. Lawyer & Banker 21: 281-90 S '28 9033

Moss, L. Howard. The practising physician in court. 30p. Richmond Hill, N.Y. The Author, 1928; same title: Am B Assn J 15: 497-502 Ag '29 9034

Neuhaus, G. E. Medical expert in court. Neb M J 16: 46-8 F '31 9035

Peacock, R. The doctor and the law. M Soc N J J 28: 203-7 Mr '31 9036

Perdriau. Medical evidence. M J Austral 1: 187-93 F 14 '31 9037

Philbrook, W. C. Physician and professional testimony. Me M J 21: 192-6 N '30 9038

Porteous, W. A. Doctor in court. New Orleans M & Surg J 83: 61-71 Ag '30 9039

Rosen, J. R. Doctor on witness stand. M J & Rec 131: 337-40 Ap 2 '30 9040

Schlager. Die Haftung für Gutachten. Deut med Wchnschr 57: 1986-7 N 20 '31 9041

Schlager. Das Zeugnisverweigerungsrecht des Arztes. Med Klin 27: 229-30 F 6 '31 9042

Schorn. Der Gerichtsarzt. Monats f Kriminalpsychol u Strafrechtsref 19: 429-33 Jl '28 9043

Spear, Irving J. Medical expert testimony. Md S B Assn Rep 1930: 72-113 9044

Steiner, E. Der Arzt als Sachverständiger im Zivilund Strafprozess. Schweiz med Wchnschr 61: 1122-3 N 21 '31 9045

Taeusch, C. F. Should the doctor testify? Int J Ethics 38: 401-45 Jl '28 9046

Taft, Henry W. Opinion evidence of medical witnesses. Va L R 14: 81-99 D '27 9047

Trostler, I. S. Medical expert witness. Radiology 17: 807-15 O '31 9048

Wagner, A. F. Medical and other expert scientific testimony. Calif & W Med 30: 165-8 Mr '29 9049

Weatherly, L. A. Yesterday and to-day in our courts of law; a half century's experiences and opinions of a medical witness. M Press 129: 386, 413 My 7, 14 '30 9050

Williams, Edward Huntington. The doctor in court. 289p. Baltimore, Williams & Wilkins, 1929 9051

Zürcher, W. Die Aufgabe der ärztlichen Sachverständigen bei Verhandlungen gegen Jugendliche im Rahmen der öffentlichen Fürsorge für seelische abnorme Kinder. Allg Zeitsch f Psychiat 95: 145-71 Je 12 '31 9052

DENTAL JURISPRUDENCE

Brothers, Elmer DeWitt. Dental jurisprudence; an epitome of the law of dentistry and dental surgery. ed.2. 216p. St. Louis, Mosby, 1928 9053

Horn, Rudolf. Über die Bedeutung zahnärztlicher Sachverständigentatigkeit auf kriminalistischem Gebiete. Arch f Krim 88: 147-74 Mr '31 9054

Ivanhoe, H. Some questions pertaining to dental jurisprudence. Dent Dig 37: 539, 604 '31 9055

Misch, J. Forensische Zahnheilkunde. Fortschr d Zahnh 6: 1039-66 D '30 9056

HEARSAY AND MEMORY

Fee, George. Interpreter's statement as affected by hearsay rule. Univ Cin L R 1: 89-93 Ja '27 9057

Hutchins, Robert M. and Slesinger, Donald. Some observations on the law of evidence—Memory. Harv L R 41: 860-73 '28 9058

McCormick, Charles T. The borderland of hearsay. Yale L J 39: 489-504 F '30 9059

Morgan, Edmund M. The relation between hearsay and preserved memory. Harv L R 40: 712-32 Mr '27 9060

Wickes, Joseph A. Ancient documents and hearsay. Tex L R 8: 451-82 Je '30 9061

VERDICT

Curd, Thomas H. S. Elimination of general verdicts and instructions to juries. W Va L Q 33: 298-303 Ap '27 9062

Effect of acquittal. Sol J 73: 291 My 11 '29 9063

Freund, Arthur J. Power of a Missouri court to instruct the jury in a criminal case that it may return a general verdict of guilty and permit the court to fix the punishment. St Louis L R 13: 25-32 D '27 9064

Juries and verdicts. L Times 165: 27-8 Ja 14 '28 9065

Juries' verdicts. Sol J 72: 93 F 11 '28 9066

Jury verdicts as affecting tortured law. Scot L R 44: 126-30 Ap '28 9067

Majority verdicts. L Notes 34: 182 Ja '31 9068

Phelps, Edith M. ed. Three-fourths jury vote in criminal trials. Univ Debaters' Ann 14: 293-346 '27-'28 9069

Rex, F. comp. Notes on laws of states fixing the number of jurors necessary to render a verdict in jury trials. 7p. (typw) Chicago, Municipal reference library, 1927 9070

Riddell, William Renwick. Correction of erroneous verdicts. Tex L R 7: 335-44 Ap '29; same title: Geo L J 17: 323-8 Je '29 9071

Sachse. Die Abstimmung über die Schuldfrage im Strafgericht. Zeitsch f d ges Strafrechtswiss 49: 306-15 '29 9072

Shipp, Robert L. Verdicts by less than whole number of jurors. Fla St B Assn L J 21: 70 O '28 9073

Wilbur, Curtis D. Shall we continue to require a unanimous verdict? Pa B Assn Rep 34: 333-41 '28 9074

DIRECTED

Bennett, Roy E. Does motion for a directed verdict by both parties constitute a waiver of the jury? Rocky Mo L R 3: 67-75 N '30 9075

Carlin, Leo. Necessity of motion for new trial when verdict directed. W Va L Q 37: 76-81 D '30 9076

Lovejoy, A. B. The directed verdict. Ia St B Assn Proc 1930: 141-4 9077

SPECIAL

Coleman, Charles T. Advantages of special verdict. Am Jud Soc J 13: 122-3 D '29 9078

Crandall, C. W. Special verdict. Fla St B Assn L J 3: 64-7 Ap '30 9079

Staton, John W. The special verdict as an aid to the jury in civil cases. Am B Assn J 16: 192-7 Mr '30; same title: Am Jud Soc J 13: 176-82 Ap '30 9080

SENTENCE AND JUDGMENT

Adinolfi, Salvatore. Il riconoscimento della sentenza penale straniera nel progetto del codice penale. Rassegna Pen (1-2): 6-10 '29 9081

Altering sentences. Sol J 72: 216 Mr 31 '28 9082

Anderson, J. B. Foreign judgments in France and England. L J [London] ns66: 6-7, 43-4, 61-2 Jl 7-28 '28 9083

Aronson, Robert L. Conclusiveness upon indemnity insurer of a default of consent judgment rendered against its assured. St Louis L R 13: 143-50 Mr '28 9084

Attalla, Teodoro. Quattro recenti sentenze di assoluzione della Corte di appello di Firenze. 21p. Livorno, E. Pasquini, 1928 9085

Boucher, Paul. Effect of void sentence. N C L R 10: 71-2 D '31 9086

Coates, Albert. The convict's question. Pop Govt 1: 5-70 Ja '31 9087

Constitutional law, full faith and credit, collateral attack on sister state judgment obtained by fraud. Minn L R 11: 150-7 Ja '27 9088

A conviction discharged. Just Peace 94: 589-90 S 27 '30 9089

Costa, Stefano. Nuovo aspetto della questione sulla calcolabilità delle circostanze diminuenti nella sentenza di rinvio a giudizio. Riv Pen di Dott, Legis e Giuris (11): 466-72 '29 9090

Courts of resentence. L Notes 32: 162-3 D '28 9091

Definite sentences stop crime. Civic Alliance Bul (524) Ja 15 '27 9092

Degen, Richard. Neue Wege im Strafvollzug und in der Entlassenen für Sorge. Zeitwende 5: 385-96 My '29 9093

Delay in executing death sentence. L Notes 31: 141 N '27 9094

Donnedieu de Vabres, H. La valeur internationale des jugements repressifs d'après le mouvement législatif actuel. R de Dr Pén et de Crimin 10: 457-82 '30 9095

Donovan, William F. Sentenced to death. L Soc J 3: 10-14 N '30 9096

Edwards, A. S. Death sentence and psychological examinations. J Ap Psychol 15: 590-2 D '31 9097

Effect of English judgments in France. Sol J 72: 578 S 1 '28 9098

Execution before judgment. L Times 163: 535 Je 18 '27 9099

Exemplary sentence. Just Peace 93: 326 My 25 '29 9100

Fishman, Joseph Fulling. The short jail term; should it ever be imposed? Northwest Police J 7: 9-10 D '29 9101

Futility of petty sentences. Am B Assn J 15: 327 Je '29 9102

Glaser, S. La nullité absolue des jugements criminels. R de Dr Pén et de Crimin 8: 122-9 F '28; separate: 8p. Louvain, Pierre Mafrans, 1928 9103

Goeckel. Ist bei der Urteilsverkündung in Strafsachen die Anwesenheit der Staatsanwaltsschaft nötig? Arch f Rechtspfl in Sachsen, Thür u Anhalt 5: 165-8 '28 9104

Gov. Smith's recommendation about sentencing criminals. Mass L Q 13: 109 F '28 9105

Judgments in criminal appeals. Can B R 5: 429 Je '27 9106

Judicial finality of a criminal sentence. Harv L R 44: 967-71 Ap '31 9107

Judicial resentencing machinery suggested for New York by Association of grand jurors. Mass L Q 13: 100-3 Ag '28 9108

Kahn, R. English judgments in personam and in rem in Germany. J Comp Leg s3 9: 211-19 N '27 9109

Kleist, F. Erfahrungen eines Individualpsychologen im Strafvollzug. Arch f Psychiat 93: 331-2 '31 9110

Koppenfels. Rechtsmittelhäufigkeit und Rechtsmittelerfolg bei österreichischen Strafurteilen. Monats f Kriminalpsychol u Strafrechtsref 19: 444-5 Jl '28 9111

Lansden, D. V. Validity of sentence of banishment. Ill L R 26: 81-2 My '31; same title: J Crim L & Crimin 22: 121-2 My '31 9112

Loth, J. Un genre particulier de compensation pour crimes et offenses chez les Celtes insulaires. R Celtique 48 (1-4): 332-51 '31 9113

McCarty, Donovan D. Law of confession of judgment and warrants of attorney, Illinois. 516p. Chicago, Callaghan, 1930 9114

MacWilliams, Glenn. Salvaging the criminally unfit. Int Assn Identif, Calif Div Proc 15: 31-6 '30 9115

Mandatory laws as to sentence. L Notes 33: 43 Je '29 9116

Marsich, Piero. L'esecuzione penale. Saggio introduttivo. 93p. Padova, A. Milani, 1927 9117

Mimin, Pierre. Le style des jugements. 207p. Paris, Librairie des Juris-Classeurs, 1927 9118

New York (state). Crime commission. Subcommission on adjustment of sentences.
Report, February 28, 1927. 30p. Albany, 1927
Report, December 13, 1928. 15p. Albany, 1928
Report, February 28, 1929. 22p. Albany, 1929
Report, December 19, 1929. 20p. Albany, 1930 9119

Norvell, William E. jr. Extreme sentences for offenses mala prohibita. Am B Assn Rep 54: 570-82 '29 9120

Police statements affecting sentence. Just Peace 92: 807-8 D 15 '28 9121

Polke. Friesprüche trotz schwerwiegender Indizien. Krimin Monatsh 5: 81-5 Ap '31 9122

Polke. Scharfrichter und Hinrichtungen. Monats f Kriminalpsychol u Strafrechtsref 21: 273-81 My '30 9123

Popert, H. M. Folgen des Ausbleibens des Privatklägers und seines Anwalts im Verkündungstermin. Arch f Strafr u Strafproz 72: 164-74 My '28 9124

Quick justice. Just Peace 93: 561 S 7 '29 9125

Riddell, William Renwick. First legal execution for crime in Upper Canada. L Q R 45: 122-4 Ja '29; same title: Geo L J 17: 138-41 F '29 9126

Riddell, William Renwick. Judicial execution by burning at the stake in New York. Am B Assn J 15: 373-6 Je '29 1927

Right to be executed. Sol J 71: 887 N 19 '27 9128

Right to serve sentence. Sol J 71: 750 O 1 '27 9129

S., J. D. Judicial murder. Can B R 5: 329 My '27 9130

Schultze, Ernst. Amtlicher Entwurf eines Einführungsgesetzes zum Allgemeinen Deutschen Strafgesetzbuch und zum Strafvollzugsgesetz vom Standpunkte des Psychiaters mit Bemerkungen über den Entwurf eines Allgemeinen Deutschen Strafgesetzbuchs nach der ersten Lesung im Strafrechtsausschuss. Arch f Psychiat 93: 452-94 '31 9131

Sentencing of criminals by commission. L Notes 32: 25 My '28 9132

Short sentences. L Times 167: 322 Ap 20 '29; same title: Just Peace 93: 262-3 Ap 27 '29; 94: 533 Ag 23 '30 9133

Shumaker, W. A. Commissions to pronounce sentence. L Notes 31: 186-8 Ja '28 9134

Silva Riestra, Juan. El juicio oral en el procedimiento penal. R de Crimin, Psiquiat y Med Leg 16: 317-39 My '29 9135

Sokalski, W. Exécution des jugements répressifs étrangers. R Int de Dr Pén 6: 363-82 '29 **9136**

Wheeler, Thomas R. Changing decisions of the courts. Lincoln L R 2: 29-32 Ap '29 **9137**

When sentence begins to run. L Notes 31: 64 Jl '27 **9138**

Fines and Penalties

Combaldieu, Raoul. Du recouvrement de l'amende pénale. 233p. Toulouse, Imp. Cléder, 1929 **9139**

The contemptuous farthing. Sol J 72: 634 S 29 '28 **9140**

Enforcement of fines in Russia. Just Peace 91: 857 N 12 '27 **9141**

Fine without the option. Sol J 571-2 Ag 30 '30 **9142**

Fines and the changing value of money. Sol J 72: 734 N 3 '28 **9143**

Fines for breaches of probation orders. Just Peace 91: 969 D 17 '27 **9144**

Imprisonment for fines. Sol J 75: 319 My 16 '31 **9145**

Irrevocable fines. Just Peace 94: 82-3 F 8 '30 **9146**

Neymark, Edward. La peine d'amende. R de Dr Pén et de Crimin 8: 929-62, 1053-93 bibliog (p1093-4) '28; separate: 76p Louvain, Pierre Mafrans, 1929 **9147**

O'Brien, Harry T. Fines and penalties payable to the state. N Y St Assn Magistrates Proc 22: 8-14 '30 **9148**

Pitschel, Werner. Die Praxis in der Wahl der Geldstrafe. 43p. (Krimin Abh hrsg von Franz Exner, no8) Leipzig, Ernst Wiengandt, 1929 **9149**

Punishment by fine. L Notes 31: 123-4 O '27 **9150**

Rogers, Berto. Payment of fine in criminal case as affecting right to review conviction. L Notes 35: 31-3 My '31 **9151**

Stern, Max. Imprisonment for the nonpayment of fines in Chicago. Soc Serv R 5:459-67 S '31 **9152**

Restitution and Reparation

Florian, E. Per una più rigorosa disciplina dell'obbligazione di risarcimento del danno derivante da delitto penale. Scuola Pos ns8: 97-100 Mr '28 **9153**

Florian, E. Il risarcimento dei danni all'imputato, prosciolto, in ipotesi di reato perseguibile di officio e di non avvenuta costituzione di parte civile. Scuola Pos ns8: 457-8 S '28 **9154**

Florian, Eugenio. Una lacuna da colmare. L'obbligazione dei non-imputabili a risarcire i danni cagionati col delitto penale. Scuola Pos ns11: 289-90 Jl '31 **9155**

Maiorano, P. L'azione per la "riparazione pecuniaria." 83p. Terni, L'Economica, 1927 **9156**

Restitution by convicted criminals. L Notes 31: 124 O '27 **9157**

Sasserath, Simon. L'indemnité pour détention préventive non suivie de condamnation ou suivie d'une condamnation inférieure à la détention subie. Etudes Crimin 3: 94-9 My '28 **9158**

Siegert. Kann der Busseberechtigte nach Erlass des Urteils erster Instanz die Nebenklage erheben? Zeitsch f d ges Strafrechtswiss 49: 344-7 '29 **9159**

NEW TRIAL

Bistho[ven], R. Janssens de. Wiederaufnahme des Strafverfahrens in Belgien. Monats f Kriminalpsychol u Strafrechtsref 22: 513-36 S '31 **9160**

Desbois, H. De la reouverture de l'instruction sur charges nouvelles. Etudes Crimin 4: 177-88 Je '29 **9161**

Neumann, R. Über die Zulässigkeit einer Wiederaufnahme des Verfahrens bei rechtskraftigem Strafbefehlen. Arch f Strafr u Strafproz 72: 180-4 My '28 **9162**

New trials for newly discovered evidence. L Notes 31: 44 Je '27 **9163**

APPELLATE PROCEDURE

"A Solicitor." Quis custodiet? The right of appeal from courts of summary jurisdiction. Howard J 3: 15-26 '31 **9164**

Abstract of record, failure to condense evidence as ground for refusal to consider appeal. Ia L R 13: 471-2 Je '28 **9165**

Admission of evidence on appeal. Yale L J 36: 570-1 F '27 **9166**

Affidavits in appellate court of testimony given at trial. Harv L R 41: 394 Ja '28 **9167**

Aggrieved persons. Just Peace 93: 426-7 Jl 6 '27 **9168**

Allowed appeals. Just Peace 92: 411 Je 16 '28 **9169**

Anderson, W. D. The brief on appeal. Miss L J 2: 264-70 F '30 **9170**

Anglin, F. A. [Criminal appeal in Canada]. Can B R 5: 575-80 O '27 **9171**

Appeals from summary courts. Just Peace 95: 67-8 Ja 31 '31 **9172**

Atkin. Appeal in English law. Cambridge L J 3: 1-9 '27 **9173**

Barcus, George W. Appellate court procedure. Tex L R 7: 107-13 D '28 9174

Bates, Ruth E. Survey of appealed cases in Missouri in 1923-24. St Louis L R 15: 268-72 Ap '30 9175

Bishop, Edward T. Practice in the appellate department of the Superior court. Los Angeles B Assn Bul 6: 252-3 Ap 16 '31 9176

Blume, William Wirt. Problem of preserving excluded evidence in the appellate record. Minn L R 13: 169-80 F '29 9177

Bryan, George. Bill of exceptions, amended rule xxiv. Va L Reg ns13: 577-82 F '28 9178

Buchanan, George E. Appellate procedure in New York. N Y Univ L R 6: 428-44 My '29 9179

Butler, Edwin E. Reading dissenting opinion in argument to jury as cause of reversals. N C L R 10: 94-6 D '31 9180

Cameron, John. Working the Criminal appeal act. Scots L T 2: 127-9 Jl '27 9181

Chevallier, Yves. Essai sur la recevabilité et les effets de l'appel incident en matière pénale. Etudes Crimin 2: 67-72 Jl '27 9182

Clark, Samuel O. jr. English appellate procedure. Yale L J 39: 76-91 N '29 9183

Cook, Wayne, G. The rehearing evil. Ia L R 14: 36-62 D '29 9184

Cooper, F. E. Is the deciding of moot criminal cases a judicial function? Ore L R 7: 228-36 Ap '28 9185

Criminal appeal. L Times 164: 326 O 29 '27 9186

Dean, Claude M. Rules of appellate procedure in the federal courts. W Va B Assn Proc 1929: 92-100 9187

A delayed appeal. Sol J 72: 92-3 F 11 '28 9188

Doerr. Hat das Revisionsgericht die Zulässigkeit der vorausgegangenen Berufung von Amts wegen zu prüfen? Arch f Strafr u Strafproz 72: 91-3 Mr '28 9189

Does binding over constitute a conviction? Question of right of appeal? Just Peace 93: 450-1 Jl 13 '29 9190

Facilities for appeal. Sol J 73: 323-4 My 25 '29 9191

Fresh evidence on appeal. Sol J 72: 348-9 My 26 '28 9192

Graham, John M. Appellate court briefs and arguments. Ga L R 1: 26-30 D '27 9193

Harrison, W. B. Statutory requirements as to briefs in Alabama appellate courts. Ala L J 5: 12-20 N '29 9194

Hentig, Hans von. Wiederaufnahmerecht. (Die Wiederaufnahme des Strafverfahrens dogmatisch und rechtsvergleichend dargestellt). 291p. Heidelberg, Carl Winter, 1930 9195

Hicks, Edwin D. Moot appeals by the state in criminal case. Ore L R 7: 218-27 Ap '28 9196

Jessup, Henry Wynans. The presentation of appeals. N Y L R 7: 1-4 Ja '29 9197

Kesler, J[ohn] C. Appeal and error. N C L R 6: 85-7 D '27 9198

McCall, Frederick B. Appellate practice and procedure in North Carolina. N C L R 7: 130-49 F '29 9199

Miller, Justin. Appeals by the state in criminal cases. Yale L J 36: 486-512 F '27 9200

Molitoris and Hirschberg. Aufhebung eines Fehlurteils in einer Mordsache. Arch f Krim 82: 28-40 Ja '28 9201

Morgan, Jacob. What price success on appeal? Ind L J 3: 550-4 Ap '28 9202

Moss, John. Procedure relating to appeals under new Rating and valuation act, 1925. Just Peace 91: 187-90 Mr 12 '27 9203

O'Brien, Paul P. Manual of federal appellate procedure. 333p. San Francisco, The Author (Circuit court of appeals, Ninth circuit) 1929 9204

Pohle, Rudolf. Revision und neues Strafrecht. Leipz Rechtswiss Stud (56) 1-124 '30 9205

Ricot, Jean. Le pourvoi en cassation contre un arrêt de mise en liberté provisoire a-t-il un effet suspensif? Etudes Crimin 5: 45-7 F '30 9206

Riddell, William Renwick. Arguments in appellate courts. N Y L R 7: 115-17 Ap '29 9207

Right of appeal. Sol J 73: 549 Ag 24 '29 9208

Robertson, Ernest M. Setting aside verdict in criminal cases, interpretation of Art. VII, sec. 3c of Oregon constitution. Ore L R 6: 267-71 Ap '27 9209

Robertson, Reynolds. Appellate practice and procedure in the supreme court of the United States. N.Y. Prentice-Hall, 1928 9210

Sherrill, George Raymond. Criminal procedure in North Carolina as shown by criminal appeals since 1890. 173p. Chapel Hill, North Carolina university press, 1930 9211

Stating a case on refusal to commit for trial. Sol J 71: 497-8 Je 25 '27 9212

Statutory penalties to discourage frivolous appeals. Colum L R 28: 483-8 Ap '28 9213

Sunderland, Edson R. Problems of appellate procedure. Notre Dame Law 3: 50-69 D '27 9214

Sunderland, Edson R. Problems of appellate procedure. Tenn B Assn Proc 1927: 79-95 9215

Sunderland, Edson R. Simplification of appellate procedure. Univ Cin L R 3: 1-23 Ja '29 9216

Twenty years of criminal appeal. L Times 164: 153-4 Ag 27 '27 9217

Twenty-one years of criminal appeal. Just Peace 93: 200-1 Mr 30 '29 9218

Ware, Eugene Fitch (Ironquill, pseud). From court to court, setting forth the method of taking a case from a state court to the United States supreme court; ed.6 by Ralph S. Nelson. 223p. St. Paul, West, 1930 9219

REVIEW

Dodd, Walter F. Some problems of appellate review. Conf Jud Adm [Duluth] 1930: 21-7 9220

Gardiner, F. G. The South African system of automatic review in criminal cases. L Q R 44: 78-84 Ja '28 9221

Hinton, E. W. Necessity of assignment of error in motion for new trial as a basis for appellate review. Ill L R 26: 60-2 My '31 9222

Sunderland, Edson R. Problem of appellate review. Tex L R 5: 126-48 F '27 9223

REVERSALS

Aggeler, William T. Rarity of reversals in criminal cases. Los Angeles B Assn Bul 2: 18-19 Je 16 '27 9224

Mintz, Copal. Trial counsel misconduct as reversible error. St John's L R 4: 187-213 My '30 9225

Reversals in Illinois criminal cases. Harv L R 42: 566-70 F '29 9226

Rosenthal, James M. Reversible error in homicide cases in Massachusetts. Mass L Q 13: 106-20 My '28 9227

Vernier, C. G. and Selig, Philip. The reversal of criminal cases in the Supreme court of California. J Crim L & Crimin 20: 60-87 My '29 9228

SPECIFIC PROCEEDINGS

SUMMARY

Alcorn, Robert H. Disclosure of defense as an aid to summary judgments. Conn B J 2: 291-300 O '28 9229

Boesel, Frank T. Summary judgment procedure. Wis L R 6: 5-20 D '30 9230

Borms, V. Tayart de. Procédure sommaire devant les tribunaux de police. R de Dr Pén et de Crimin 7: 535-54 My '27; 8: 259-62 Mr '28 9231

Borms, V. Tayart de. La réforme de la procédure sommaire devant les tribunaux de police. R de Dr Pén et de Crimin 8: 80-4 Ja '28 9232

Clark, Charles E. The new summary judgment rule in Connecticut. Am B Assn J 15: 82-5 F '29 9233

Gardner, Arthur R. L. Summary jurisdiction in the metropolis: is there much wrong? Nation [London] 44: 348-50 D 8 '28 9234

Henkin, Leonard M. Motion for summary judgment in New York. N Y Univ L R 6: 59-70 N '28 9235

Remands. Sol J 73: 441 Jl 6 '29 9236

Right of address in summary proceedings. Just Peace 91: 683-4 S 17 '27 9237

Summary judgment procedure. Am Jud Soc J 12: 152-3, 157-8 F '29 9238

Summary trial of indictable offenses. Sol J 72: 92 F 11 '28; same title: Just Peace 94: 422-3 Jl 5 '30 9239

United States. Congress. House. Committee on judiciary. To provide for summary prosecution of petty offenses, report to accompany H. R. 9937. Washington, 1929 (71st Cong. 2d sess. H. Rep. 1732) 9240

INDEMNITY

Engell, Werner. Die Entschädigungs- und Wiedergutmachungspflicht des Staates gegenüber unschuldig Bestrafen und verhafteten. 133p. (Strafrechtl Abh no230) Breslau, Schletter, 1927 9241

Viti, A. Le indemnità giudiziarie. 58p. Firenze, M. Mozzon, 1928 9242

LAW ENFORCEMENT

Adie, David C. Allies of the court. N Y St Assn Magistrates Proc 20: 80-7 '28 9243

Albertsworth, E. F. Constitutional duties and inadequate enforcement machinery. Am B Assn J 17: 153-7 Mr '31 9244

American bar association. Section of criminal law and criminology. Report of Committee on lawless enforcement of law. Am J Police Sci 1: 575-93 N '30 9245

Andrews, Lincoln C. Prohibition enforcement as a phase of federal versus state jurisdiction in American life. Ann Am Acad 129: 77-87 Ja '27 9246

Association of the bar of the city of New York. Committee on criminal courts, law and procedure. Bulletin, 1, January 20, 1926- 9247

Baber, Roy Erwin. Factors in law enforcement. Soc Forces 8: 198-208 D '29 9248

Banton, Joab H. Criminal law and its enforcement. N Y St B Assn Proc 1927: 181-8 9249

Binkley, Robert C. The ethics of nullification. New Repub 58: 297-300 My 1 '29 9250

Black, Forrest Revere. Lawless enforcement of the law—the war psychosis. U S L R 64: 359-64 Jl '30 9251

Borah, William E. Civic righteousness; lawlessness the insidious disease of republics. Cent 114: 641-8 O '27 9252

Borah, William E. Obedience to law. 16p. Washington, Govt. Ptg. Off. February 18, 1929 9253

Brice, Charles R. Enforcement of the criminal law. N Mex St B Assn Proc 1930: 74-88 9254

Brodney, Spencer. American lawlessness a result of social conditions. Cur Hist 27: 332-4 D '27 9255

Bruce, Andrew. Why we are lawless. Ia St B Assn Proc 1929: 199-212; same title: Case & Com 35: 6-9 S '29 9256

Bugg, C. R. Spirit of lawlessness. New England J Med 201: 1044-8 N 21 '29 9257

Burgess, John W. Sanctity of law: wherein does it consist. 335p. N. Y. Ginn, 1927 9258

Cardozo, Benjamin N. Paradoxes of legal science. 142p. N. Y. Columbia university press, 1928 9259

Chamberlain, Joseph P. Legislative drafting and law enforcement. Am Lab Leg R 21: 235-43 Je '31 9260

Chavez, Dennis. Illegal methods of law enforcement. N Mex St B Assn Proc 1930: 39-47 9261

Coley, D. R. Law enforcement and law observance. Ala St B Assn Rep 1927: 94-6 9262

Coxe, Whitnell W. Government's responsibility for disrespect for law. Va St B Assn Rep 1929: 373-92 9263

Dickinson, John. Administrative justice and the supremacy of law in the United States. 403p. Cambridge, Harvard university press, 1927 9264

Dietrich, Frank S. Causes of disrespect for law. Id St B Proc 1929: 92-101 9265

Dobbins, Brantley W. Practical enforcement of the Wright law. Peace Offic Assn Calif Proc 9: 124-9 '29 9266

Dodd, William E. Our growing habit of lawlessness. Cent 116: 691-8 O '28; same title: R of R 78: 667-8 D '28 9267

Durant, William Crapo, ed. Law observance: shall the people of the United States uphold the Constitution. 573p. N. Y. Durant award office, 1929 9268

Ebermayer. Vorbildung und Berufslaufbahn der Organe der Strafrechtspflege. Deut Juristen-Zeit 33: 1142-6 S 1 '28 9269

The enforcement of laws against obscenity in New York. Colum L R 28: 950-7 N '28 9270

Estes, W. Lee. Law enforcement and the courts. Am B Assn Rep 54: 596-604 '29 9271

Finnegan, Richard J. Law enforcement and how. Welf Mag 18: 1551-65 D '27 9272

Hardee, Cary A. Law enforcement. Conf Gov'rs Proc 1929: 22-32, 37-45, 116-17, 134-46 9273

Hart, Hastings H. Law enforcement through self-restraint. Sci M 129: 35 F '27 9274

Hearst, W[illiam] R[andolph]. We need laws we can respect. 15p. San Francisco, Call-Bulletin, 1929 9275

Hopkins, Ernest Jerome. Lawless arm of the law. Atlan M 148: 279-87 S '31 9276

Indiana committee on observance and enforcement of law. Handbook, 1930. 24p. [Indianapolis] 1930 9277

Indiana committee on observance and enforcement of law. Report, January 5, 1931. 56p. [Indianapolis, 1931] 9278

Indiana conference on law observance and enforcement. [Proceedings] October 11-12, 1929. 144p. Indianapolis, State ptg. bd. 1929 9279

Johnsen, Julia Emily, comp. Selected articles on law enforcement. 411p. (Wilson's handbook ser 3 v4) N. Y. Wilson, 1930 9280

Johnson, George E. Q. Unified law enforcement; the factor of coordination in crime suppression. Police "13-13" 5: 7, 27 Ja '31 9281

Knight, John. Difficulties in enforcing criminal law. Cur Hist 27: 320-5 D '27 9282

Knott, Richard G. I am the law! and why do you not respect me? Outl 157: 15-17 Ja 7 '31 9283

Lawless enforcement of law: report of Committee to Section of criminal law and criminology of American bar association. Los Angeles B Assn Bul 6: 191-8 F 19; 223-9 Mr 15 '31 9284

Lawlessness in law enforcement. Chr Cent 48: 1061-3 Ag 26 '31 9285

Lile, William M. Judge-made law; an appreciation. Am B Assn Rep 1928: 587-99 9286

Limburg, Herbert R. Law enforcement in Germany and in the United States. Va L R 16: 659-88 My '30 9287

Llewellyn, Karl N. The experts on law enforcement. Survey 63: 571-2 F 15 '30 9288

McCraw, William. Law enforcement. Tex B Assn Proc 48: 228-34 '29 9289

McCreery, Donald C. Reign of law. Colo B Assn Rep 1928: 97-112 9290

Majesty of the law. New Repub 65: 341 F 11 '31 9291

National commission on law observance and enforcement. Problem of law enforcement; address by George W. Wickersham, April 16, 1931. 12p. Washington [1931] 9292

National commission on law observance and enforcement. Report on lawlessness in law enforcement. 347p. (Noll) Washington, June 25, 1931 9293

The third degree, by Zechariah Chafee, Jr., Walter H. Pollak, and Carl S. Stern. Unfairness in prosecutions, by Zechariah Chafee, Jr., Walter H. Pollak, and Carl S. Stern.

Nock, Albert Jay. Officialism and lawlessness. Harper's 160: 11-19 D '29 9294

Noonan, Thomas H. The importance of law enforcement. N Y St Assn Magistrates Proc 20: 76-80 '28 9295

O'Brien, Daniel J. Cooperation existing between the law enforcement officers of the United States and Canada. Int Assn Chiefs Police Proc 35: 26-8 '28 9296

Olson, Floyd B. Coordinating law enforcement agencies. Minn Munic 16: 15-18 Ja '31 9297

Persons, G. Ogden. Lawyers and their relation to law enforcement. Ga Lawyer 1: 225-6, 235-7 Mr '31 9298

Phillips, Clay A. Law and order. Ind Police N 1: 17-21 N '29 9299

Pound, Roscoe. Cooperation in enforcement of law. Am B Assn J 17: 9-14, 63-4 Ja '31 9300

Rogers, James Grafton. Some riddles of law observance. Rocky Mo L R 2: 1-15 N '29 9301

Sargent, John G. Importance of law observance. Pa B Assn Rep 1927: 308-22 9302

Sims, Henry Upson. Problem of law enforcement. Mo B Assn Proc 1929: 83-92 9303

Slavich, J. R. Program of the American legion on law and order. Int Assn Identif, Calif Div Proc 12: 22-4 '27 9304

Swaney, William B. Law enforcement. 23p. (mim) Charlottesville, Va. Institute of public affairs, August 15, 1929 9305

Thorpe, W. G. The law and law enforcement. Peace Offic Assn Calif Proc 10: 62-7 '30 9306

United States. Congress. House. Proposals to improve enforcement of criminal laws of the United States: message from the president of the United States transmitting comments upon the proposals to improve enforcement of the criminal laws of the United States. 27p. Washington, January 13, 1930 (71st Cong. 2d sess. H. Doc. no252) 9307

United States. President. Message . . . urging necessity of action by Congress upon recommendations made by him for more effective criminal law enforcement. 2p. Washington, April 28, 1930 (71st Cong. 2d sess. S Doc 136) 9308

VanOsdol, James A. Observance and enforcement of law. Ind Bul Char & Correc (190): 73-84 F '31 9309

Waite, John Barker. Punishing one in ten: our failure to enforce the law. Atlan M 139: 63-70 Ja '27 9310

Wilson, P. W. Criminal law enforcement in America and Europe. Cur Hist 27: 326-31 D '27 9311

Wright, R. H. Cooperation of law enforcement organizations. Los Angeles Chron 14: 15 Mr 31 '30 9312

Wyoming. Department of law enforcement. Biennial report, 1928/30. Cheyenne, 1930 9313

EXTRAORDINARY LEGAL REMEDIES

Caldwell, Harmon. Injunctions against crime. Ill L R 26: 259-81 N '31 9314

Hamley, Frederick G. Injunction to restrain threatened or impending criminal prosecutions. Wash L R 6: 131-8 Jl '31 9315

Lincoln, Alexander. Use of the federal padlock law in state courts. Mass L Q 14: 118-26 My '29 9316

McMurdy, Robert. The use of the injunction to destroy commercialized prostitution. J Crim L & Crimin 19: 513-17 F '29 9317

Williams, Nathan B. Forfeiture laws: [seizures in prohibition work]. Am B Assn J 16: 572-3 S '30 9318

REFORM OF CRIMINAL PROCEDURE

Altmann, L. Der Entwurf einer Strafprozessnovelle vom Jahre 1927. Jurist Bl 57: 43-5 '28 9319

Blanchard, O. S. Reforms in practice and procedure. Ore L R 6: 121-9 F '27 9320

Chamberlain, Joseph P. Legislative correction of criminal procedure. Am B Assn J 13: 653-5, 703-5 N, D '27 9321

Cook, Wayne G. Recent legislative changes in procedure. Ia L R 13: 47-60 D '27 9322

Criminal procedure reform. Ky L J 16: 248-9 Mr '28 9323

Enthoven, K. L. J. Herziening van het inlandsch strafprocesrecht zonder unificatie. Koloniale Stud 14: 278-88 O '30 9324

Evans, Evan A. Recommendations for reforms in criminal procedure. Ill L R 24: 112-18 My '29 9325

Feisenberger. Mit welchem Hauptzielen wird die Reform des Strafprozesses in Aussucht zu nehmen sein? Deut Juristen-Zeit 33: 1232-6 S 15 '28 9326

Goldschmidt, J. Mit welchem Hauptzielen wird de Reform des Strafverfahrens in Aussicht zu nehmen sein? Deut Juristen-Zeit 33: 1137-42 S 1 '28 9327

Grispigni, F. Sul progetto preliminare di un nuovo codice di procedura penale. Scuola Pos 38: 1-14 '30 9328

Harris, J. Suggested changes of criminal procedure. Id St B Proc 1930: 65-71 9329

Holbrook, Vinton A. Reforms in criminal procedure. L Notes 31: 128-30 O '27 9330

Keedy, Edwin R. The drafting of a code of criminal procedure. Am B Assn J 15: 7-11 Ja '29 9331

Lang. Vom künftigen Strafprozess. Leipz Zeitsch f Deut Recht 22: 289-95 '28 9332

Lobe, A. Zur Reform des Strafprozesses. Gerichtssaal 96: 1-4, 37-48; 97: 20-6 '28 9333

McGovern, Walter. Shall criminal procedure be "reformed"? Calif St B J 1: 139-41 F '27 9334

Miller, Justin. The compromise of criminal cases. S Calif L R 1: 1-3 N '27 9335

Panis, E. M. Simplification of criminal procedure needed. Police J [N Y] 17: 6 O '29 9336

Vecchio, Giuseppe del. Nell'attesa del nuovo codice di procedura penale: proposte, critiche e reforme degli institut vigenti. Riv Pen di Dott, Legis e Giuris 108: 201-19 S '28 9337

GERMANY

Schiffer, Eugen. Die deutsche Justiz. Grundzüge einer durchgreifenden Reform. 403p. Berlin, Lictmann, 1928 **9338**

Stämpfli, Franz. Das Bundesstrafverfahren nach dem Entwurf eines Bundesgesetzes über die Bundesstrafrechtspflege. Schweiz Zeitsch f Strafr 42: 328-59 '29 **9339**

POLAND

Glaser, Stefan. Neue Wege im Strafprozessrecht und die polnische Strafprozessreform. Zeitsch f d ges Strafrechtswiss 50 (4-5): 639-50 '30 **9340**

SCOTLAND

Mitchell, William. Criminal procedure reform: Scottish system. Contemp R 136: 766-70 D '29 **9341**

SWEDEN

Engströmer, Thore. Rättegångsreformen. Kort sammanfattning av processkommissionens betänkande. På offentligt uppdrag utaretad. 52p. Stockholm, Nord. Bokh. 1927 **9342**

Engströmer, Thore. Der schwedische Entwurf einer Prozessreform. Zeitsch f Ausländ u Int Privatrecht 3: 32-6 '29 **9343**

Sweden. Justitie Departmentet. Bebänkande augående ornande av vissa ekonomiska och organisatoriska förhållanden vid genomförande av den ifrågasatta rättengångsreform. 461p. Stockholm, Nord. Bokh. 1928 **9344**

Sweden. Justitie Departmentet. Städerna och rättegångsreform. 112p. Stockholm, Nord. Bokh. 1928 **9345**

UNITED STATES

CALIFORNIA

California. Commission for the reform of criminal procedure. Report, 1927. 43p. Sacramento, 1927 **9346**

Freedman, Nathan O. Comments on criminal procedure changes. Calif St B J 1: 153-4 F '27 **9347**

New plan of criminal procedure presented by the Committee of the Los Angeles bar association. J Delin 11: 309-19 D '27 **9348**

Randall, William G. and Ford, Tirey L. Some criticisms of proposed reform of criminal procedure. Calif S B J 1: 117-19 Ja '27 **9349**

Tuller, Walter K. California's new code of criminal procedure. Calif St B J 2: 4-6 Jl '27 **9350**

IOWA

Forrest, Leland S. Proposed changes in Iowa procedure. Ia L R 14: 161-71 F '29 **9351**

KENTUCKY

Willis, S. S. Some suggestions for improving practice and procedure in Kentucky. Ky St B Assn Proc 1927: 174-90 **9352**

NEW YORK

Medina, Harold R. Shall New York surrender leadership in procedural reform? Colum L R 29: 158-78 F '29 **9353**

NORTH CAROLINA

Coates, Albert. The revision and codification of criminal procedure in North Carolina. Am B Assn J 17: 134-5 F '31 **9354**

JUDICIAL ADMINISTRATION

GENERAL

American bar association. Report of Special committee on uniform judicial procedure. Rep 55: 521-62 '30 9355

Aumann, F. R. Judicial organization and procedure. Am Pol Sci R 25: 367-76 My '31 9356

Baceña, Francisco. Magistratura y justica. 419p. Madrid, Liberia Victoriano Suarez, 1928 9357

Clark, Alfred E. Is our judicial system responsible for our crime condition? Ore L R 10: 13-29 D '30 9358

Delfino, V. La criminalística y los progresos en la investigación judicial. Siglo Méd 85: 498-500 My 10 '30 9359

Dodd, Walter F. Notes on judicial organization and procedure. Am Pol Sci R 22: 936-53 N '28 9360

Henderson, O. J. Courts of foreign countries. Bul St Inst [Iowa] 32: 36-47 Ja '30 9361

Johnson, Sveinbjorn. The machinery of justice. Welf Mag 19: 183-93 F '28 9362

Larson, John A. and Hughes, M. Y. The efficacy of the present judicial system as a method for the determination of innocence or guilt. Police J [N Y] 14: 2 My '27 9363

Müller, H. Justiz and Verwaltung. Polizei 25: 332-4 My 20 '28 9364

Schorn, H. Die Verteilung der Strafsachen auf die erstinstanzlichen Strafgerichte (Amtsrichter und Schöffengericht). Monats f Kriminalpsychol u Strafrechtsref 18: 609-16 N '27 9365

Stevens, Truman S. The judicial task. Neb L Bul 8: 79-83 Jl '29 9366

Urteaga, H. La organización judicial en el Imperio de los Incas. R Hist [Peru] 9: 5-50 '28 9367

Wigmore, John Henry. A panorama of the world's legal systems. 3v. St Paul, West pub. co. 1929 9368

Willoughby, William Franklin. Principles of judicial administration. 662p. Washington, Brookings Institution, 1929 9369
Prevention of crime; office of prosecuting attorney; police; coroner; grand jury; court system in U.S.; judicial councils; municipal courts; justice of peace courts; juvenile and domestic relations courts; sentence; bail; legal aid.

CHINA

Judicial administration in China. Chinese Soc & Pol Sci R 14: 425-37 O '30 9370

EGYPT

Crabites, Pierre. The triumph of a judicial system. Temple L Q 4: 105-8 Mr '30 9371

EUROPE

Henning, Edward J. Observations of judicial procedure in European countries. Case & Com 35: 3-8 Je '29 9372

FRANCE

Monzie, A. de. Grandeur et servitude judiciaires. 205p. Paris, Editions Kra, 1931 9373

GERMANY

Simons, Walter C. Relation of the German judiciary to the executive and legislative branches. Am B Assn J 15: 762-7 D '29 9374

GREAT BRITAIN

Bromberg, Frederick G. English judicial procedure. Ala L J 2: 12-13 Ja '27 9375

HAWAII

Loo, Sau Ung. Administration of justice in Hawaii. Am Jud Soc J 12: 111-16 D '28 9376

ITALY

Alhadeff, V. L'ordinamento giuridico di Rodi e delle altre isole italiane dell'Egeo. 214p. Milano, Soc. An. Inst. Edit. Scient. 1927 9377

Verna, F. Il potere giudiziario nello stato Fascista. Proc Pen Ital 13: 105-17 '27 9378

JAPAN

Miyake, Masataro. The Japanese judiciary. Asiatic R 27: 306-10 Ap '31 9379

Miyake, Masataro. An outline of the Japanese judiciary and the administration of prisons in Japan. Japan Advertiser, Tokyo, 1930 Reprint 9380

Neville, Edwin L. Development of the new judiciary system in Japan. Trans-Pac 16: 5-6 F 4 '28 9381

TURKEY

Brinton, Jasper Y. Turkey's new system of laws and courts. Cur Hist 25: 498-503 Ja '27 9382

UNITED STATES

Daniel, A. T. United States Department of justice. N C L R 8: 340-4 Ap '30 9383

Farnum, George R. The Department of justice of the United States. L Soc J 1: 9-18 N '29 9384

Langeluttig, Albert. The Department of justice of the United States. 318p. Baltimore, Johns Hopkins press, 1927 9385
United States prisoners: pardons, prisons, paroles, probation; penal problems: employment, housing, probation, federal jails; detection of crime: secret service, prohibition unit, post office inspectors.

Outline of organisation of the United States government: legislative and judicial branches of the government (chart no2). U S Daily 4(72): 730 My 25 '29 9386

Potter, William W. Judicial power in the United States. Mich L R 27: 1-22, 167-90, 285-313 N '28-Ja '29 9387

United States. Department of justice. Register of the Department of justice and the courts of the United States. ed. 35. 112p. Washington, 1930 9388

INDIANA

Moll, Theophilus J. Re-arranging the Indiana judiciary. Ind L J 2: 247-54, 293-308 D '26, Ja '27 9389

MARYLAND

Reiblich, G. Kenneth. The study of judicial administration in the state of Maryland. 155p. Baltimore, Johns Hopkins press, 1929 9390

NORTH CAROLINA

North Carolina. Judicial conference. Minutes, December 31, 1929. 2p. [Raleigh] 1929 9391

North Carolina. Judicial conference. Report, 2, 1928. [Raleigh, 1928] 9392

OHIO

Ohio. Judicial council. Facts and the administration of justice. Interim statement, study of judicial administration in Ohio. 25p. (Bul no3) [Columbus, 1930] 9393

Ohio. Judicial council. A study of the administration of justice in Ohio by the Judicial council of Ohio, the Ohio state bar association, the Institute of law of the Johns Hopkins university. Statement of the immediate program. 7p. [Columbus, 1930] 9394

Study of judicial administration in Ohio. Am Jud Soc J 13: 140-1 F '30 9395

ASSOCIATIONS, CONGRESSES, ETC.

Chapin, Roger E. Illinois county and probate judges' association. Ill Conf Pub Welf Proc 1927: 55-6 9396

Conference on judicial administration, Duluth, 1930. Conference on judicial administration, July 8-9, 1930. 41p. Univ Minn Bul v34 no17 9397

Gleispach, W. Die Ausbildung der Organe der Strafrechtspflege und der Salzburger Deutsche Juristentag. Monats f Kriminalpsychol u Strafrechtsref 19: 733-7 D '28 9398

Gordon, James Gay, jr. Resolutions of 1928 Pennsylvania judicial conference. Temple L Q 2: 305-16 Jl '28 9399

New York state association of judges of children's courts. Proceedings, 5, 1927—7, 1929. Albany, New York (state) Department of correction, Division of probation, 1928-30 9400

New York state association of magistrates. Proceedings, 19, 1927—21, 1929. Albany, New York (state) Department of correction, Division of probation, 1928-31 9401

Pennsylvania. Judicial conference. Agenda containing reports of committees to be acted upon at the Third judicial conference, April 10-11, 1930. 47p. Philadelphia, 1930 9402

COURTS

GENERAL

Accuracy of court process. Sol J 75: 127 F 21 '31 9403

Altman, Harris. [Courts, place of holding in criminal cases]. Boston Univ L R 8: 145-8 Ap '28 9404

Amira, Karl. Das Femgerichtsbild des Soester Stadtarchivs. 15p. Leipzig, K. Hiersemann, 1927 9405

Bache, Louise Franklin. Publicity and the court. Nat Prob Assn Proc 1930: 251-9 9406

"Benthamite." Plain tales from the law courts. Fortn R 134: 50-8 Jl '30 9407

Bovensiepen. Die Organisation unserer Strafgerichte. Gesetz u Recht 28: 1-6 Ja 3 '27 9408

Bovensiepen. Die Organisation unserer Strafgerichte. Richter, Schöffen und Geschworenen. Polizei 24: 568-9 N 20 '27 9409

Butte, George C. Public policy and the courts. Tex B Assn Proc 1928: 90-107 9410

Caloyanni, Megalos A. La cour criminelle internationale. R Int de Dr Pén 5: 261-4 '28 9411

Caloyanni, Megalos A. An international criminal court. Grotius Soc, Problems of Peace and War 14: 69-79 '29 9412

Carey, Charles Henry. Why not trust the courts? Am Jud Soc J 12: 91-3 O '28 9413

Chamberlin, Henry Barrett. Concerning the criminal court. Crim Just [Chicago] 9: 5-6 Je '27 9414

Compere, Thomas. Befuddled justice; survey of the lower courts. Forum 84: 34-41 Jl '30 9415

Corrigan, Joseph E. The people's court. N Y St Assn Magistrates Proc 22: 77-81 '30 9416

Courts have power to defend themselves from harmful publicity. Am Jud Soc J 10: 133-8 F '27 9417

Dabney, Samuel B. Court organization: the superiority of the unit or collegiate system to the existing divided system. Tex L R 5: 377-91 Je '27 9418

Devices to avoid diversity jurisdiction. Harv L R 44: 97-100 N '30 9419

Gober, George F. Courts and the people. Ga L R 1: 15-23 Mr '27 9420

Howell, Edward Beach. Inefficient courts and the crime wave. R of R 75: 35-7 Ja '27 9421

Informing the public about the courts. Am Jud Soc J 10: 154-5 F '27 9422

An international criminal court. Just Peace 94: 183-4 Mr 22 '30 9423

Jacobson, Gabe. High-lights of the Great Sanhedrin. Miss L J 3: 261-8 My '31 9424

Kenner, Sumner. Power of courts to compel defendant in criminal case to submit to physical examination. Ind L J 4: 456-63 Ap '29 9425

Moley, Raymond. Our criminal court. Nat Prob Assn Proc 1930: 47-51 9426

Moley, Raymond. Our criminal courts. 294p. N.Y. Minton, 1930 9427

Mosher, Edgar S. Co-operation and the courts. N Y St Assn Magistrates Proc 22: 26-9 '30 9428

Nipper, Simon G. Courts. Mo B J 2: 8-9 Mr '31 9429

Norton, Thomas James. Our courts and free speech. Am B Assn J 13: 658-9 N '27 9430

Paul, W. J. Our courts. Mont B Assn Proc 1927: 91-103 9431

Pella, Vespasien V. La cour criminelle internationale. Projet de statut. R de Drept Pen 3-43 Mr '28; same title: R de Dr Pén et de Crimin 9: 172-206 '29 9432

Pella, Vespasien V. Rapport sur un projet de statut d'une cour criminelle internationale présenté au conseil de direction de l'A.I.D.P. R Int de Dr Pén 5: 265-307 '28 9433

Pound, Roscoe. Organization of courts. Am Jud Soc J 11: 69-83 O '27 9434

Rich, P. D. Slow, technical court procedure. Ga Lawyer 1: 179-80, 184, 193 D '30 9435

Roux, J.-A. A propos d'une cour de cassation internationale. R Int de Dr Pén 6(1): 12-17 '29 9436

Schnieper. Die Berichterstattung der Presse über strafgerichtliche Verhandlungen. Schweiz Ver f Straf- Gefängniswes u Schutzaufsicht Verh 8: 21-7 '28 9437

Talcott, Elizabeth H. Outline of our court system. Hartford, Conn. Connecticut League of women voters, 1928 9438

Thot, Ladislao. Creación de una corte ininternacional en lo criminal. R de Identif y Cienc Pen 6: 96-119 My '30 9439

Urch, Erwin J. Procedure in the courts of the Roman provincial governors. Class J 25: 93-101 N '29 9440

Wilson, Scott. Efficiency in our courts. Me St B Assn Proc 25: 21-38 '27 9441

Wolf, Conrad. The constitution and the courts. Ind L J 2: 659-72 Je '27 9442

Asia

Fioletoff, N. Mussulman courts in central Asia. Asiatic R 25: 727-33 O '29 9443
Summary of paper published in Novie Vostol v23-4.

Australia

Brennan, T. C. The high court and criminal appeals. Austral L J 3: 247-50 D '29 9444

High court of Australia. Austral L J 4: 160-72, 199-204 S '30 9445

Canada

Gravel, A. Saskatchewan surrogate courts. Can B R 6:339-55, 441-50, 530-6, 679-708 My-S '28 9446

MacDonald, A. A. Toronto non-jury. Can B R 5: 311-13 My '27 9447

Owen, Marjorie. The courts and the rum-running business. Can B R 8: 413-19 Je '30 9448

Popple, A. E. Central criminal courts, a suggested reform. Can B R 8: 498-9 S '30 9449

Riddell, William Renwick. Bar and the courts of the province of upper Canada, or Ontario. 251p. Toronto, Macmillan, 1928 9450

China

Heaton, Paul. The jurisdiction of American courts in China. Chinese Soc & Pol Sci R 12: 18-42 Ja '29 9451

Lockenour, Roy M. Chinese court system. Temple L Q 5: 253-9 Ja '31 9452

Egypt

Brinton, Jasper Yeates. Mixed courts of Egypt. 416p. New Haven, Yale university press, 1930 9453

Crabitès, Pierre. The mixed courts of Egypt. Va Q R 4: 546-53 O '28 9454

Goadby, F. M. Jurisdiction of the mixed courts in Egypt. J Comp Leg s3 11: 278-9 N '29 9455

Goodenough, Erwin R. The jurisprudence of the Jewish courts in Egypt. 268p. New Haven, Yale university press, 1929 9456

Mixed tribunals in Egypt. L Times 169: 173 F 22 '30 9457

France

Bouchardon, P. L'évolution de la cour d'Assises. Etudes Crimin 3: 12-19 Ja '28; same title: R de Dr Pén et de Crimin 8: 383-6 Ap '28 9458

Linn, William B. Flechier's memoirs: a court of extraordinary jurisdiction. Temple L Q 2: 95-107 Ja '28 9459

Perroud, J. Organization of the courts and the judicial bench in France. J Comp Leg s3 11: 1-18 F '29 9460

Woods, Damon C. The efficiency of French justice. Am B Assn J 15: 162-4 Mr '29 9461

Woods, Damon C. The French court of assizes. J Crim L & Crimin 22: 325-34 S '31 9462

Great Britain

Additional judges and the circuit system. L Times 165: 95-6 F 4 '28 9463

Blair, Paxton. The doctrine of forum non conveniens in Anglo-American law. Colum L R 29: 1-34 Ja '29 9464

Business in the King's Bench. L Times 164: 325-6 O 29 '27 9465

Carter, Albert Thomas. History of the English courts. ed.5. 183p. London, Butterworth, 1927 9466

The circuit system. L Times 170: 316 O 25 '30 9467

Courts of Birmingham: how English city gets efficient justice. Am Jud Soc J 11: 167-78 Ap '28 9468

Kingston, Charles. Bench and the dock. 290p. London, Stanley Paul, 1930 9469

Micklethwait, St. John. Circuit system. Sol J 74: 447-50 Jl 12 '30 9470

Montague, Richard W. Notes on English courts. Am Jud Soc J 14: 158-60 F '31 9471

Montmorency, J. E. G. de. The courts and criminal law. L Times 167: 463-4 Je 1 '29 9472

Odgers, Walter Blake. English courts of law. 88p. London, Sweet, 1929 9473
Extracts from ed.3 of his On the common law.

Parkes, Norman. British summary court in the Rhineland. 19th Cent 107: 526-34 Ap '30 9474

Wilson, Edward H. London courts compared with New York's. Am Jud Soc J 11: 118-19 D '27 9475

Woodbine, George E. Cases in new Curia Regis Rolls affecting old rules in English legal history. Yale L J 39: 505-13 F '30 9476

Hungary

Vodasz, E. La nouvelle procédure devant les Cours d'Assises en Hongrie. R Pénitent et de Dr Pén 51: 290-5 My '27 9477

India

High court of India. L Times 167: 138 F 16 '29 9478

Indian high courts. L Times 165: 496 Je 9 '28 9479

Macnair, J. C. H. The Indian civil service and the courts. Jurid R 40: 266-81 S '28 9480

Strangman, Thomas. Indian courts and characters. 213p. London, Heinemann, 1931 9481

United provinces of Agra and Oudh. Chief court of Oudh on criminal justice. Annual report, 1927- 9482

United provinces of Agra and Oudh. High court of judicature. Report, 1927- Allahabad 9483

Ireland

Irish Free state courts. L Notes 34: 96 Ag '30 9484

Law courts, Dublin. Irish L T 61: 100-1 Ap 23 '27 9485

Philippine Islands

Reforming the Philippine judiciary. Phil L J 8: 58-93 Ag '28 9486

Poland

Rappaport, Emil Stanislaw. Le problème de la Cour d'assises en Pologne. R Int de Dr Pén 8: 401-38 bibliog(p437-8) '31 9487

Russia

The legal system of the U. S. S. R. Soviet Union R 6: 39-40 Mr '28 9488
Special military courts; civil and criminal courts.

Scotland

Brown, A. R. Draft of suggested new table of fees for the sheriff court in Scotland. Scot L R 47: 73-84 Mr '31 9489

Companies Act. Jurisdiction in Sheriff court. Scot L R 45: 365-7 D '29 9490

M'Kechnie, Hector. Early sheriff court records. Scots L T 1929: 105-8 Ag 24 '29 9491

Scottish law officers. Sol J 73: 323 My 25 '29 9492

Wark, J. L. Business of the law courts. Scot L R 46: 73-8, 93-8, 153-8 My '30

Switzerland

Kinberg, O. La protection légale de l'aliéné devant un tribunal suédos. Acta Psychiat et Neurol 4: 341-88 '29 9494

Lüthi, Werner. Das Kriminalgerichtswesen der helvetischen Republik im Jahre 1789. 130p. (Abh zum schweizerischen Recht no61) Bern, Stämpfli, 1931 9495

Tunis

Rectenwald, G. Le tribunal criminel en Tunisie. J Débats 36 pt1: 271-3 F 15 '29

United States

Black, Forrest R. American conception of judicial control. Ky L J 16: 289-305 My '28 9497

Callendar, Clarence W. American courts, their organization and procedure. 284p. N.Y. McGraw-Hill, 1927 9498

Dodd, Walter F. Judicial organization and procedure. Am Pol Sci R 24: 416-25 My '30 9499

Dupriez, L. Le contrôle judiciaire de la constitutionnalité des lois aux Etats-Unis. Acad Sci Belg Bul Cl Lett s14 5(5): 166-89 '28 9500

McCormick, Charles T. Fusion of law and equity in United States courts. N C L R 6: 283-98 Ap '28 9501

McFarland, James G. Criticism, slander or contempt? S D B Assn Rep 1927: 141-52 9502

Martin, Clarence E. American judiciary and religious liberty. Va L Reg ns13: 641-65 Mr '28 9503

CALIFORNIA

Wood, John Perry. Business administration of the courts. Calif St B Assn Proc 1: 108-15 '28 9504

CONNECTICUT

Connecticut. [State attorneys and prosecuting attorneys]. Biennial report in relation to the criminal business of the courts, for the two years ended June 30, 1930. 44p. Hartford, 1930 9505

Webster, Arthur. Courts and procedural reform. Mich St B J 6: 191-201 Mr '27 9506

DISTRICT OF COLUMBIA

Clark, Charles E. Experiment in studying business of courts of a state. Am B Assn J 14: 318-19 Je '28 9507

FLORIDA

Whitfield, J. B. History of the third judicial circuit of the state of Florida. Fla St B Assn L J 4: 347-52 N '30 9508

GEORGIA

Grice, Warren. Half forgotten chapter in the judicial history of Georgia. Ga Lawyer 1: 68-9 Ag '30 9509

Stevens, Walter C. The court of ordinary. Ga Lawyer 1: 231-4, 238-9, 242-4 Mr '31 9510

Talley, J. N. The Southern circuit—a sketch. Ga B Assn Rep 1929: 177-221 9511

IDAHO

Budge, Alfred. Unification of courts. Id St B Proc 1929: 58-65 9512

Budge, Jesse R. Shall probate courts be abolished, probate jurisdiction vested in the district courts. Id St B Proc 1929: 81-8 9513

Merrill, A. L. A survey of Idaho judicial business. Id St B Proc 6: 29-35 '30 9514

ILLINOIS

Chamberlin, Henry Barrett. Concerning the criminal court. Crim Just [Chicago] 9: 5-6 Je '27 9515

Howe, Lawrence. Crime and the courts of Chicago. Nation [N Y] 131: 315-16 S 24 '30 9516

IOWA

The work of the courts. Ia L R 16: 125-33 D '30; 16: 289-94 F '31 9517

KENTUCKY

Hager, John F. Old circuit days in Kentucky. Am B Assn J 13: 542 S '27 9518

Porter, W. L. Sixty years at the bar in rural Kentucky. Ky St B Assn Proc 1929: 80-101 9519

Stickles, Arndt Mathis. Critical court struggle in Kentucky, 1819-1829. 122p. Bowling Green, Kentucky, College Heights bk. store, 1929 9520

MASSACHUSETTS

Rugg, Arthur P. General court of Massachusetts. Boston Univ L R 11: 1-21 Ja '31 9521

MISSISSIPPI

Butts, A. B. The court system of Mississippi. Miss L J 3: 97-125 N '30 9522

NEW JERSEY

Gudmundson, Gunnar G. Courts in New Jersey. 24p. Elizabeth, N.J. Thomas Jefferson High school, The Author, 1931 **9523**

NEW YORK

Improved conditions in New York courts. Am B Assn J 16: 545-7 S '30 **9524**

New York (state). Crime commission. Sub-commission on courts.
Report, February 28, 1927. 11p. Albany, 1927
Report, February 28, 1928. 26p. Albany, 1928
Report, February 28, 1929. 30p. Albany, 1929
Report, February 28, 1930. 28p. Albany, 1930 **9525**

OHIO

Aumann, F. R. Ohio tackles justice court problem. Am Jud Soc J 13: 25-7 Je '29 **9526**

OKLAHOMA

Bierer, A. G. C. Early day courts and lawyers. Okla St B Assn Proc 23: 193-205 '29-'30 **9527**

PENNSYLVANIA

Pennsylvania committee on penal affairs. The court and correctional system of the state of Pennsylvania, with a directory of judges and probation officers, parole officers and penal officials, state departments, state-wide agencies and institutions for custodial and protective care. 32p. [Philadelphia] September 1930 **9528**
Ed. 1, May 1927.

TENNESSEE

Williams, Samuel C. Records of our earliest courts. Tenn B Assn Proc 1927: 96-107 **9529**

TEXAS

Cook, M. L. Texas courts of exceptional jurisdiction and organization, constitutionality, small claims courts. Tex L R 9: 388-409 Ap '31 **9530**

Dabney, Samuel B. Court organization. Tex L R 5: 377-91 Je '27 **9531**

Dabney, Samuel B. Judicial situation in Texas. Tex B Assn Proc 48: 56-68 '29 **9532**

Williams, F. A. Suggestions for improving court procedure. Tex L R 5: 174-82 F '27 **9533**

WALES

Welsh in the courts of Wales. Sol J 71: 699-700 S 10 '27 **9534**

COURTS AND SOCIAL SERVICE

Bell, Marjorie. Courts and case work; reply to T. D. Eliot. Survey 61: 91-2 O 15 '28 **9535**
Juvenile courts acting in parental role.

Eliot, Thomas D. Case work for courts? rejoinder to M. Bell. Survey 61: 520-1 Ja 15 '29 **9536**

Eliot, Thomas D. Should courts do case work? Survey 60: 601-3 S 15 '28 **9537**

Foster, Edith. Possible contributions of social work agencies to courts and criminal institutions. 5p. (mim) (Wisconsin Conf Soc Wk, Pub no95) 1930 **9538**

Meyer, Charlotte. Literaturnachweise zur Frage der Sozialen Gerichtshilfe. Zeitsch f d ges Strafrechtswiss 50: 257-65 '30 **9539**

INFERIOR CRIMINAL COURTS

Kopp, Arthur W. Inferior courts of record in Wisconsin and their jurisdiction. Wis St B Assn Rep 1930: 10-32 **9540**

Lee, Henry James, ed. Inferior criminal courts act of the city of New York; also the domestic relations law and the Children's court act of the city of New York, with amendments, 1931. 127p. (Eagle library 46 no7 ser304) Brooklyn, Eagle pub co. 1931 **9541**

Mandl, J. P. The inferior courts. Calif St B J 3: 15-16 Jl '28 **9542**

Many justices but little justice. Am Jud Soc J 12: 44-5 Ag '28 **9543**
Survey of inferior courts of Allegheny county, Pa.

O'Sullivan, T. Jurisdiction of inferior courts where defendant is resident outside the state. Austral L J 4: 206-8 N '30 **9544**

Wright, G. Lytton. Jurisdiction of inferior courts where the defendant is resident outside the state. Austral L J 4: 113-16 Ag '30 **9545**

JUSTICE OF PEACE

Allen, William Kennedy Abbott. Justices acts of Queensland 1886-1924; with conspectus, annots, and supplementary forms. 500p. Sydney, Law bk. co. of Australasia, 1929 **9546**

Annales et journal spécial des justices de paix; recueil mensuel de législation, de doctrine et de jurisprudence. Paris, 1, 1784- **9547**

Appointment of justices. Just Peace 95: 83-4 F 7 '31 **9548**

Battle, Kemp D. North Carolina magistrates. N C L R 6: 349-54 Ap '28 **9549**

Baylies, Edwin. Bender's justices' manual of civil and criminal law and practice for justice of the peace in the state of New York. ed.7. 879p. Albany, Bender, 1928 **9550**

Butts, A. B. Justice of the peace, recent tendencies. Miss L J 1: 195-202 O '28; same title: Am Pol Sci R 22: 946-53 N '28 **9551**

Constant, Jean. De la compétence des juges de paix déchargés des affairs pénales en matière de Commissions rogatoires d'ordre répressif. R de Dr Pén et de Crimin 10: 48-54 '30 **9552**

Cottez, André. Traité de la compétence et de la procédure civiles des tribunaux de paix du Maroc. 303p. Paris, Librairie moderne de droit et de jurisprudence, 1927 **9553**

Gellért, Viktor. A békebiróság intézménye Franciaországban. Jogállam 28: 367-70 S '29 **9554**

Hall, Joseph Edward. Handbook of criminal law and procedure for peace officers. 72p. Caribou, Me. Caribou pub. co. 1931 **9555**

Hamele, Ottomar. In the J. P. court. Case & Com 37: 2-6 Summer '31 **9556**

Journal des juges de paix, juges suppléants et greffiers de paix. Paris, 1, 1905- **9557**

Journal des juges de paix, de leurs suppléants, des officiers du ministère public et des greffiers. Bruxelles, 1, 1892- **9558**

Justices as critics of the law. Just Peace 94: 641-2 O 18 '30 **9559**

"Justices' justice." Just Peace 94: 707-8 N 15 '30 **9560**

Justices of the peace. L Notes 31: 82 Ag '27 **9561**

Keebler, Robert S. Our justice of the peace courts—a problem in justice. Tenn L R 9: 1-21 D '30 **9562**

Lancaster, Lane W. Justice of the peace in Connecticut. Nat Munic R 19: 9-13 Ja '30 **9563**

Llewellyn-Jones, F. The French "Justice of the peace." Just Peace 91: 165-6, 224-5, 247-8 Mr 5-Ap 2 '27 **9564**

MacClamroch, James, jr. Discussion of justice of the peace courts in North Carolina. N C B Assn Proc 1930: 194-211 **9565**

Malcolm, Charles A. ed. The minutes of the justices of the peace for Lanarkshire, 1707-1723. 271p. Edinburgh, Constable, 1931 **9566**

Manning, J. W. In-justices of the peace. Nat Munic R 18: 225-7 Ap '29 **9567**

Milhaud, Léon. Les déclarations de nationalité devant le juge de paix. 134p. Paris, Librairie des Annales des Justices de paix, 1928 **9568**

Milhaud, Léon. La mission du juge de paix quant aux déclarations de nationalité. 132p. Paris, Librairie des Annales des justices de paix, 1927? **9569**

Milhaud, Léon. Les nouveaux traitements des juges de paix. J des Juges de Paix [Paris] 26: 241- Jl '30 **9570**

Milhaud, Léon. Le reclassement des justices de paix. J des Juges de Paix [Paris] 25: 445- D '29 **9571**

Milwaukee, Wis. [Justice of the peace]. Report *in* Annual report of Common council, 1927: 10-11; 1928: 14; 1929: 18 **9572**

New York board of trade, Inc. Proposal by Lloyd N. Scott to group justices and create specialized parts of the Supreme court, New York county. 6p. New York, February 11, 1930 **9573**

Power of justices to administer oaths. Just Peace 93: 342-4 Je 1 '29 **9574**

Putnam, Bertha H. Justices of the peace from 1558-1688. Inst Hist Res Bul 4: 144-56 F '27 **9575**

Putnam, B[ertha] H. Records of the keepers of the peace and their supervisors, 1307-27; with text of Assize rolls. Engl Hist R 45: 435-44 Jl '30 **9576**

Putnam, Bertha Haven. Transformation of the keepers of the peace into justices of the peace, 1327-1380. Royal Hist Soc [London] Tr s4 12: 19-48 '29 **9577**

Riddell, W. G. New Zealand justices' handbook. ed.2. London, Butterworth, 1929 **9578**

Rogers, Jesse La Fayette. The magistrate's manual and legal advisor, giving the mode of procedure before justices of the peace in Tennessee. ed.5. 781p. 1927; ed.6. 803p. revised by Giles L. Evans. Nashville, Marshall & Bruce co. 1931 **9579**

Simms, John T. Justices of the peace. W Va B Assn Proc 1930: 41-66 **9580**

Smith, Charles Samuel. Justices' guide; a guide to justices, commonwealth's attorneys, sheriffs, sergeants, constables, and attorneys who practice in justices' courts; being in the main a revision of Mayo's guide, first edition. 398p. Charlottesville, Va. Michie co. 1929 **9581**

Smith, Chester H. The justice of the peace system in the United States. Calif L R 15: 118-41 Ja '27 **9582**

Swackhamer, Gladys V. The advantages of cooperation between justices of the peace and a social agency. J Crim L & Crimin 20: 122-36 My '29 **9583**

Swan, Joseph Rockwell. Treatise on the laws of Ohio pertaining to the powers and duties of and practice and procedure before justices of the peace. 1010p. Cincinnati, Anderson, 1930 **9584**

T[horne], L[awrence] S. Jurisdiction in civil cases, effect on code provision relative to civil jurisdiction of sections pertaining to service of process, jurisdiction and venue distinguished. Va L R 16: 197-204 D '29 **9585**

Villamor, Ignacio. Development of justice of peace courts in Philippines. Phil L J 7: 398-404 Ap '28 **9586**

Warren, John H. Magisterial system. Socialist R 40-3 O '29 **9587**

Wigram, William Knox. Justices note book. ed.12 by John Edwin Mitchell and Joseph Smith. London, Stevens, 1931 **9588**

Willis, Hugh Evander. Are justice of the peace courts impartial tribunals? Ind L J 3: 654-7 My '28 **9589**

Zulueta, J[ose] C. Power to transfer a justice of the peace. Phil L J 9: 42-3 Jl '29 **9590**

MAGISTRATES'

Administrative changes in the magistrates' courts. City Club N Y Bul 8-9 O '31 9591

Brill, Jeannette G. The human drama as enacted in the magistrate's court. Brooklyn 11: 14, 42 Ja '30 9592

Coatsworth, Emerson. Model magistrate's court. Can B R 7: 377-84 Je '29 9593

Committee for the centralization of magistrates courts in Manhattan. Brief in support of centralizing the Magistrates' court in Manhattan. 15p. [New York] February 11, 1929 9594

Corrigan, Joseph E. The centralization of the Magistrates' courts of Manhattan; extracts from address. Pris Assn N Y Ann Rep 84: 81-6 '28 9595

Ervin, Spencer. How magistrates' courts defile justice. Nat Munic R 20: 573-6 O '31 9596

New York (state). Supreme court. Appellate division. First judicial department. In the matter of the investigation of the Magistrates' courts in the First judicial department and the magistrates thereof and of attorneys at law practicing in said courts. 4 pts. [Albany] June 1931 9597

Pfiffner, John M. Mayor's court and due process. Ia L R 12: 393-405 Je '27 9598

Popple, A. E. Magisterial courts, plea for a re-adjustment of their legal machinery. Can B R 5: 417-18 Je '27 9599

Prissaud, J. Les magistrats et les tribunaux d'Alsace. 47p. Paris, Boccard, 1927 9600

Spence, Kenneth M. The magistrate's courts and suggested remedies. Legal Aid R 1-7 Ap '30 9601

Wily, H. Jenner. Magistrates' courts practice and the imprisonment for debt limitation act, 1908 (and its amendments) with rules, regulations and forms. London, Butterworth, 1929 9602

Women's city club of New York and City club of New York. Magistrates' courts in the Borough of Manhattan, a study of some features. 11p. [New York] January 1929 9603

POLICE AND RECORDERS'

Caullet, Paul. Cours de police, administrative et judiciaire. 563p. Paris, Rousseau, 1928 9604

Civil jurisdiction of the police court. Sol J 74: 314-15 My 17 '30 9605

Crown proceedings in police courts. Sol J 71: 315 Ap 23 '27 9606

D., C. Judicial knowledge in the police courts. Scot L R 46: 328-9 N '30 9607

Gardner, Arthur R. L. Impressions of London police courts in the morning. Howard J 2: 318-21 Je '29 9608

Hamilton, Charles H. A study in crime in the recorders' court of North Carolina. Thesis (Ph.D.) University of North Carolina, 1928 9609

Harley, Herbert. Police court justice in England. Nat Munic R 18: 227-32 Ap '29 9610

Heinzen, Henrietta and Rypins, Rhoda K. Crime in San Francisco: a study of the police court docket, December 1924 through February 1925. J Crim L & Crimin 18: 75-91 My '27 9611

Metropolitan police courts. L Times 165: 27, 276 Ja 14, Mr 31 '28 9612

Orchard, H. Courtnay. The police court missionary's story. London, Town Mission, Walsall, 1931? 9613

Pascal, F. Le tribunal de simple police. Son ancienne et sa nouvelle compétence. 267p. Paris, Dalloz, 1928 9614

Pasquier, Antonin. Des pouvoirs correctionnels du tribunal de simple police. 163p. Thesis, Dijon, 1930 9615

Police courts and the public. L Times 164: 225 O 1 '27 9616

Potter, Hasloch. Inasmuch. The story of the police court mission, 1876-1926. 136p. London, Williams & Norgate, 1927 9617

Reform of police courts not impossible. Am Jud Soc J 13: 152-3 F '30 9618

Sunday courts. Just Peace 94: 50 Ja 25 '30 9619

Vignalou-Perer, B. Traité théorique et pratique de la compétence correctionnelle des tribunaux de simple police. 175p. Paris, Librairie des Juris-Classeurs, 1929 9620

MUNICIPAL

Hamlin, William M. The future of the city court. N Y St Assn Magistrates Proc 22: 88-92 '30 9621

Harley, Herbert. Administering justice in cities. Ann Am Acad 136: 87-94 Mr '28 9622

Maddox, Rolland. Municipal courts in Michigan, 1931. 41p. (mim) (Bull R-2) Ann Arbor, Michigan municipal league, October 1931 9623

BUFFALO

Falconer, Douglas P. Buffalo looks at its city court. N Y St Conf Prob Offic Proc 21: 165-71 '28 9624

CHICAGO

Chicago. Municipal court. Annual reports 19/22, 1924/1927; 23, 1929. [Chicago 1929-30] 9625

Morals courts; boys court; felony courts; domestic relations court; adult probation; jurors; bailiff's office; municipal psychopathic laboratory.

Gilbert, Hiram T[hornton]. The municipal court of Chicago. 599p. Chicago, 230 S. Clark st. The Author, 1928 9626

Moley, Raymond. The municipal court of Chicago. *In* Illinois association for criminal justice, Illinois crime survey, 393-425, 1929 9627

Reports concerning the criminal court. Crim Just [Chicago] (57): 12-44 Mr '29; (58): 17-52 My; (59): 3-55 D '30 9628

Des Moines

Des Moines. Municipal court. Annual report *in* Annual reports of City auditor, 20, 1927/28—23, 1930/31 **9629**

Milwaukee

Milwaukee. Criminal court. Annual report *in* Annual report of Common council, 1927: 10; 1928: 13-14; 1929: 17-18 **9630**

New York (city)

Great city court given management. Am Jud Soc J 12: 116-18 D '28 **9631**

Lauer, Edgar J. Municipal court of New York; successful results of the conciliation experiment. N Y L J 1279-80 D 11 '29 **9632**

Leary, Timothy A. Municipal court of the city of New York; rules controlling calendar practice, effective March 1, 1930. N Y L J 2609 F 24 '30 **9633**

New York (city). Court of special sessions. Annual reports 1927- New York [1927]- **9634**
Probation statistics; parole.

New York state association of magistrates. Report of Committee on city courts. Proc 22: 60-3 '30 **9635**

New York state association of magistrates. Report of Committee on village and rural courts. Proc 19: 125-31 '27; 22: 92-106 '30 **9636**

Philadelphia

Philadelphia. Bureau of municipal research. Auditing control and purchasing procedure, in the Municipal court of Philadelphia. 58p. Philadelphia, Thomas Skelton Harrison foundation, 1930 **9637**

Philadelphia. Bureau of municipal research. Central registration bureau of the Municipal court of Philadelphia. 92p. Philadelphia, Thomas Skelton Harrison foundation, 1930 **9638**

Philadelphia. Bureau of municipal research. Filing of social case records in the municipal court of Philadelphia. 51p. Philadelphia, 1930 **9639**

Philadelphia. Bureau of municipal research. History and functions of the Municipal court of Philadelphia. 102p. Philadelphia, Thomas Skelton Harrison foundation, 1930 **9640**

Philadelphia. Municipal court. Annual reports 14, 1927—18, 1931 [Philadelphia, 1928-32] **9641**
Criminal division; misdemeanants division; domestic relations division; juvenile division.

Survey of Philadelphia court: long deferred reports on municipal court are being published. Am Jud Soc J 14: 15-16 Je '30 **9642**

Portland

Portland, Ore. Municipal court. Annual report *in* Mayor's Message and annual report **9643**

San Francisco

San Francisco. City and county. Women's court. Report of Women's court, monthly, January 1927- **9644**

Toledo

Police court justice in Toledo: a survey of the municipal court. Toledo City J 13: 761-7 D 15 '28 **9645**

COURTS OF GENERAL JURISDICTION

Adams, Chester [D.]. Practice and procedure in Fayette county court. Ky L J 16: 149-58 Ja '28 **9646**

Bradshaw, William Leonard. Missouri county court; a study of the organization and functions of the county board of supervisors in Missouri. 210p. (Univ Mo Stud v6 no2) 1931 **9647**

Carpenter, Dunbar F. The superior court and the neck of the bottle again—1929 model. Mass L Q 14: 34-59 Ag '29 **9648**

Carpenter, Dunbar F. The Superior court, the neck of the bottle, the burden of luxurious litigation, some statistics, and a way out. Mass L Q 14: 1-21 F '29 **9649**

Cook, Wayne G. Classification of cities for superior court purposes. Ia L R 12: 138-62 F '27 **9650**

Cushman, Robert E. Public law in the state courts in 1926-27. Am Pol Sci R 21: 573-97 Ag '27 **9651**

Davenport, Wortham. Special organization of the district court in suits to restrain the enforcement of state statutes. Tex L R 8: 111-17 D '29 **9652**

Dvorak, R. W. Cook county's new criminal court. Crim Just [Chicago] (54): 4-5 S '27 **9653**

Hall, Eric E. and Hammett, Ralph W. Chicago, Ill. Cook county criminal court and jail. W Arch 38: 154-60 S '29 **9654**

Hudson, Fred G., jr. "Second circuit." La St B Assn Proc 29: 62-77 '29 **9655**

McCoy, Charles A. "First circuit." La St B Assn Proc 29: 57-62 '29 **9656**

New Hampshire. Legislature. Committee on crime. Report including survey of work of superior court for 1905-09 and 1921-25. Concord, 1927 **9657**

New Jersey. Judicial council. Report. . . on criminal actions in the courts of general jurisdiction in 1931. 59p. **9658**
Reprint from Third annual report of Judicial council.

Plucknett, Theodore F. T. New light on the old county court. Harv L R 42: 639-75 Mr '29 **9659**

Ruppenthal, J. C. The county courts of Kansas. Kan Offic 12: 5-8 Ja '29 **9660**

Tappaan, Claire S. Amelioration and acceleration of work of upper courts. Calif B Assn Proc 1927: 180-9 **9661**

MANUALS, RULES, ETC.

Bromberg, Frederick G. Constitutionality of the Alabama rules of court statute. Ala L J 4: 102-14 Ja '29 **9662**

District of Columbia. Supreme court. Rules of the Supreme court, adopted, 1924, with amendments to October 25, 1929. Washington, Law reporter ptg. co. 1929 **9663**

Ellis, W. H. The new rules. Fla St B Assn L J 4: 549-53 Mr '31 **9664**

Gorman, Michael James. Manual of county court practice in Ontario, comprising the County judges act, and the County courts act. ed.4. 257p. Toronto, Carswell, 1929 **9665**

Jones, Charles. County court guide; a practical manual of the ordinary procedure in these tribunals; ed.6 rev. by Prys Williams. 392p. London, E. Wilson, 1929 **9666**

Kleinschmidt, Rudolph August and Highley, Mont Frederick. Oklahoma form book and manual of pleading and practice, annotated. ed.6 rev. & enl. 1259p. Kansas City, Mo. Vernon, 1929 **9667**

New York (city). Children's court. Rules of practice and procedure, adopted June 13, 1929. 9p. [New York] 1931 **9668**

New York (state). Court of appeals. Rules of the court for the admission of attorneys and counselors-at-law, rules of the State board of law examiners, and rules of civil practice. 35p. Albany, State board of law examiners, 1927 **9669**

Pound, Roscoe. Regulating procedural details by rules of court. Am B Assn J 13 pt2: 12-14 Mr '27 **9670**

Proposed revision of the rules of the superior court. Mass L Q 15: 79 My '30 **9671**

Shelton, Thomas W. Philosophy of rules of court. Am B Assn J 13 pt2: 3-7 Mr '27 **9672**

Shelton, Thomas W. Progress of proposal to substitute rules of court for common law practice. Va L Reg ns12: 513- '27 **9673**

Stewart, James McCauley. Rules of court in Iowa. Ia L R 13: 398-425 Je '28 **9674**

Sunderland, Edson R. Expert control of legal procedure through rules of court. Am B Assn J 13 pt2: 2-3 Mr '27; same title: Am Jud Soc J 12: 24-6 Ap '28 **9675**

Sunderland, Edson R. The new Michigan court rules. Mich L R 29: 586-99 Mr '31 **9676**

Vermont. Supreme court. Rules of the Supreme court, County court and court of chancery of the state of Vermont, 1927. 185p. [Rutland, Vt.] Tuttle, 1927 **9677**

Whittier, Clarke B. Regulating procedure by rules of court. Am Jud Soc J 11: 15-19 Je '27 **9678**

APPELLATE COURTS

Andrews, William S. The decisions of the court of appeals in recent years, and how they have affected substantive law. Cornell L Q 12: 433-52 Je '27 **9679**

Cohen, Herman. The Court of criminal appeal. L J [London] ns65: 396-7 My 12 '28 **9680**

Court of criminal appeal, bail of appellant, power of justices to take recognizances. Just Peace 95: 154 Mr 7 '31 **9681**

A criminal appeal court for Northern Ireland. Sol J 74: 855 D 27 '30 **9682**

Dietzman, Richard Priest. Some epoch-making decisions of the Courts of appeals of Kentucky. Ky St B Assn Proc 1928: 90-107 **9683**

Dodd, Walter F. The problems of appellate courts. Am L Sch R 6: 681-93 Mr '30 **9684**

G., G. W. The Illinois appellate courts—are they satisfactory? Mich L R 27: 794-6 My '29 **9685**

Guest, C. W. Graham. Valuation appeal court, 1931. Scot L R 47: 113-21, 154-7 Ap, My '31 **9686**

Hewart. The English court of criminal appeal. Can B R 5: 568-72 O '27 **9687**

Hiscock, Frank H. Court of appeals of New York: some features of its organization and work. Cornell L Q 14: 131-40 F '29 **9688**

Howard, Pendleton. The English court of criminal appeal. Am B Assn J 17: 149-52 Mr '31 **9689**

J., G. G. Fact finding power of the appellate courts of California. Calif L R 16: 500-22 S '28 **9690**

Kenner, Sumner. Getting into the higher court. Ind L J 5: 267-78 Ja '30 **9691**

Knowles, C. M. The first twenty years of the Court of criminal appeal. Police J [London] 1: 218-28 Ap '28 **9692**

Leaño, Fernando. Is an intermediate court of appeals in the Philippines necessary? Phil L J 10: 131-7 O '30 **9693**

Perchard, James. Appellate courts and procedure. Rocky Mo L R 2: 60-3 N '29 **9694**

Power of appellate court to dispose of a case without remanding. Yale L J 38: 971-8 My '29 **9695**

[Sunderland, Edson R.]. Intermediate appellate courts: advantages of a single court of review. Am Jud Soc J 14: 54-8 Ag '30 **9696**

Sunderland, Edson R. The proper function of an appellate court. Ind L J 5: 483-506 Ap '30 9697

Thomas, Gus. Court of appeals. Ky St B Assn Proc 1930: 134-45 9698

Traeger, W[illiam] I. Courts of criminal appeal. Peace Offic Assn Calif Proc 10: 23-7 '30 9699

Waste, William H. Giving finality to decisions of the district court of appeal. Calif St B Assn Proc 1928: 92-100 9700

FINAL COURT OF APPEAL

Alip, Egmidio M. Philippine supreme court under fire. Phil L J 10: 141-5 O '30 9701

Alsberg, Max and Friedrich, Gero. Die strafprozessualen Entscheidungen der Oberlandesgerichte. 3v. Mannheim, Bensheimer, 1928 9702

Bales, Alonzo. How to relieve the congestion in the docket of the supreme court. Ind L J 4: 24-31 O '28 9703

Baudón, Héctor R. Función institucional de la Corte suprema de justicia. Colegio de Abogados, Buenos Aires R 7: 517-30 S '29 9704

Bickley, Howard L. Rules of the Supreme court. N Mex St B Assn Proc 1930: 26-39 9705

Brown, Armstead. Shall we have a supreme court of seven members? Fla St B Assn L J 3: 32-40 Ap '30 9706

California. Judicial council. Rules adopted regulating the business of the Supreme court, effective August 1, 1928. 16p. Sacramento, 1928 9707

[California. Judicial Council]. Rules of the Supreme court and district courts of appeal. 31p. Sacramento, 1928 9708

Chafee, Zechariah. Liberal trends in the supreme court. Cur Hist 35: 338-44 D '31 9709

D[empsey], F. K[enneth]. The supreme court. Geo L J 19: 350-6 Mr '31 9710

Final courts of appeal. L Times 164: 226 O 1 '27 9711

Fordham, Jeff B. Present supreme court, social legislation and the judicial process. W Va L Q 37: 167-208 F '31 9712

G., F. W. Brief history of the Supreme judicial court. Mass L Q 16: 1-16 S 5 '30 9713

Hankin, Gregory. United States supreme court problems. Am Jud Soc J 13: 92-4 O '29 9714

Hankin, Gregory. United States supreme court under new act [Act of Feb. 13, 1925]. Am Jud Soc J 12: 40-3 Ag '28 9715

Hankin, Gregory and Charlotte A. United States supreme court, 1928-29: a review of the work of the supreme court of the United States for October term, 1928. 321p. Washington, Legal research service, 1929 9716
Criminal cases, criminal cases—federal offenses.

How does our supreme court work. Phil L J 8: 281-5 Ja '29 9717

Illinois supreme court rebukes legislative interference with judicial functions. Am B Assn J 17: 209-10 Ap '31 9718

Lee, William E. Condition of the work in the supreme court and suggestions for expediting the determination of appeals. Id St B Proc 2/3: 103-5 '26-'27 9719

Mabasa, Wenceslao T. Constitutionality of the supreme court's sitting in divisions. Phil L J 10: 24-42 Jl '30 9720

McGowen, J. G. Mississippi supreme court. Miss L J 2: 61-9 Ag '29 9721

Malcolm, George A. Work of the supreme court and how it is performed. Phil L J 10: 173-83 N '30 9722

Marten, Amberson Barrington. Supreme court for federal India; with discussion. Asiatic R ns27: 243-79 Ap '31 9723

Mason, Charles W. Work of the supreme court. Okla St B Assn Proc 1930: 187-92 9724

Montgomery, H. F. The supreme court amendment. Tex L R 7: 416-20 Ap '29 9725

Parker, H. B. and McCormick, C. T. Does our supreme court need relief? N C L R 8: 487-9 Je '30 9726

Phelps, Esmond. Supreme court. La St B Assn Proc 29: 43-51 '29 9727

Powell, Ben H. Comparative review of the recent statute changing method of appointment of members of the commission of appeals of the supreme court and enlarging their duties. Tex L R 9: 190-207 F '31 9728

Prendergast, William A. Do the valuation rulings of the United States supreme court involve an unworkable or cumbersome plan? Am B Assn Rep 55: 760-71 '30 9729

Schochet, Nahman. Minnesota's first state supreme court (1858-65) and the introduction of the code of civil procedure. Minn L R 11: 93-128 Ja '27 9730

Schweppe, Alfred J. Possible methods of relieving the supreme court of the state of Washington. Wash L R 4: 1-14 F '29 9731

Sinco, V. G. Who should be appointed to the supreme court? Phil L J 10: 253-5 S '30 9732

State supreme courts. Austral L J 4: 152-5 S '30 9733

Supreme court of appeals. Can B R 8: 675-6 N '30 9734

Thompson, Floyd E. Practice in the supreme court of Illinois. Am B Assn J 13: 142-6 Mr '27 9735

Whittier, Clarke B. Supreme court of Washington exercised rule-making power. Am Jud Soc J 11: 187-8 Ap '28 9736

Williams, Samuel C. Genesis of the Tennessee supreme court. Tenn L R 66: 75-85 F '28 9737

Willis, Hugh Evander. Doctrine of the supremacy of the supreme court. Ind L J 6: 224-58 Ja '31 9738

FEDERAL COURTS

Albertsworth, E. F. The federal supreme court and the superstructure of the constitution. Am B Assn J 16: 565-71 S '30 9739

Apelt, Willibalt. Der neueste Gesetzentwurf über das Reichsverwaltungsgericht. Verwaltungsarch 36: 137-61 Ap '31 9740

Brown, Robert C. Jurisdiction of the federal courts based on diversity of citizenship. Univ Pa L R 78: 179-94 D '29 9741

Claybrook, J. N. Federal courts; from the articles on this subject in the Encyclopedia of the United States supreme court reports. 1178p. [Charlottesville, Va.] Michie, 1928 9742

Cochran, Ernest F. Some problems of procedure and suggested reforms. Am B Assn J 17: 495-502 Ag '31 9743

C[ullinan], E[dmund] P. Supreme court of the United States. Geo L J 18: 149-53 Ja '30 9744

Dawson, Charles I. Conflict of decisions between state and federal courts in Kentucky, and the remedy. Ky St B Assn Proc 1931: 140-60 9745

Dobie, Armistead Mason. Handbook of federal jurisdiction and procedure. 1151p. [St. Paul] West, 1928 9746

Effect of multiple incorporation on access to the federal courts. Harv L R 44: 1106-10 My '31 9747

Eggeman, Robert F. Federal court intervention in trials of prohibition officers. Notre Dame Law 5: 400-3 Ap '30 9748

Federal courts, jurisdiction, corporations. Lincoln L R 1: 7-8 Ap '28 9749

Fordham, J[efferson] B. Federal courts and the construction of uniform state laws. N C L R 7: 423-32 Je '29 9750

Foster, Rufus E. Diminishing the jurisdiction of the federal courts. Tex B Assn Proc 1928: 169-75 9751

Frankfurter, Felix. The business of the supreme court of the United States—a study in the federal judicial system. Harv L R 40: 431-68, 834-77, 1110-29 Ja-Je '27 9752

Frankfurter, Felix. Distribution of judicial power between courts of United States and courts of the states. N J B Assn Yrbk 1928: 99-128 9753

Frankfurter, Felix. Distribution of judicial power between United States and state courts. Cornell L Q 13: 499-530 Je '28 9754

Frankfurter, Felix. The federal courts. New Repub 58: 273-7 Ap 24 '29 9755

Frankfurter, Felix and Katz, Wilbur G. eds. Cases and other authorities on federal jurisdiction and procedure. 769p. Chicago, Callaghan, 1931 9756

Frankfurter, Felix and Landis, James M. The business of the supreme court: a study in the federal judicial system. 349p. N.Y. Macmillan, 1927 9757

Hall, Conner. Uniform law procedure in federal courts. W Va L Q 33: 131-8 F '27 9758

Hersman, Anne Bates. Intervention in federal courts. Am L R 61: 1-38, 161-93 Ja, Ap '27 9759

Hinton, E. W. Court rules for regulation of procedure in federal courts. Am B Assn J 13 pt2: 8 Mr '27 9760

Hughes, Charles Evans. The supreme court of the United States: its foundation, methods and achievements, an interpretation. 276p. N.Y. Columbia university press, 1928 9761

Humphrey, Edward P. Federal procedure. Ky St B Assn Proc 1930: 179-251 9762

Johnson, Raymond T. State law and federal courts. Ky L J 17: 354-69 My '29 9763

Katz, Wilbur Griffith. Federal legislative courts. Harv L R 43: 894-924 Ap '30 9764

Kerr, Charles. Thirty years war on the supreme court. Va L R 17: 629-52 My '31 9765

Marshall, Rembert. A study of the supreme court of the United States. Ga B Assn Proc 1930: 128-47 9766

Moore, R. Walton. Relieving the United States district courts. Va L R 13: 269-77 F '27 9767

Moschzisker, Robert von. Equity jurisdiction in the federal courts. Univ Pa L R 75: 287-301 F '27 9768

National commission on law observance and enforcement. Manual for field workers, study of business of federal courts. 43p. Washington, 1931 9769

National commission on law observance and enforcement. Progress report on the study of the federal courts. 120p. (No7) Washington, May 28, 1931 9770
Tentative analysis of criminal cases for district of Connecticut for 3 fiscal years ending June 30, 1930.

National study of law administration in the federal courts. Sch & Soc 33: 190 F 7 '31 9771

Newlin, Gurney E. Proposed limitations upon our federal courts. Am B Assn J 15: 401-6, 446-7 Jl '29 9772

Powell, Thomas Reed. Supreme court and state police power, 1922-1930. Va L R 17: 529-56, 653-75, 765-99 Ap-Je '31 9773

Practice of United States supreme court in remanding cases for further consideration. Harv L R 43: 940-4 Ap '30 9774

Robertson, Reynolds. Practice and procedure in the supreme court of the United States. rev.ed. 418p. N.Y. Prentice-Hall, 1929 9775

Saussy, F. T. Question of jurisdiction of the federal courts. Fla St B Assn L J 2: 70 Mr '29 9776

Shumaker, W. A. Federal courts and uniform laws. L Notes 31: 26-8 My '27 9777

Shumaker, W. A. Objections and exceptions in federal courts. L Notes 31: 164-6 D '27 9778

Sibley, Samuel H. Conflicts between state and federal courts. Ga Lawyer 1: 144-5, 161 N '30 9779

Stone, Harlan F. Fifty years' work of the United States supreme court. Am B Assn J 14: 428-36 Ag '28; Am B Assn Rep 53: 259-81 '28; same title: Ore L R 8: 248-68 Ap '29 9780

Tuttle, Charles H. Reforms in federal procedure. Am B Assn J 14: 37-42 Ja '28 9781

United States. Congress. House. Committee on judiciary. Judicial power and the power of Congress in its relations to the United States courts, H.R. bills nos 7759 and 8237. 50p. Washington, April 17, 1928 9782

United States. Congress. House. Committee on judiciary. To change procedure in the federal courts in certain cases: hearings February 7, 14, 1928 on H.R. 10639, H.R. 10548. 73p. Washington, 1928 9783

Van Devanter, Willis. The supreme court of the United States. Ind L J 5: 553-62 My '30 9784

Walsh, Thomas J. Reform of federal procedure. S D B Assn Rep 1927: 153-75 9785

Walsh, Thomas J. Reform of federal procedure. Tenn L R 6: 32-54 D '27 9786

Warren, Charles. Federal and state court interference. Harv L R 43: 345-78 Ja '30 9787

Watkins, William R. Non-conformity to state practice in law cases in federal courts. Am B Assn J 14: 341-2 Je '28 9788

Williams, Charles Parker. A treatise on federal practice, embracing jurisdiction, civil, criminal, appellate and admiralty procedure. ed.2. 1349p. St. Louis, Thomas law bk. co. 1927 9789

Willis, Hugh Evander. Some conflicting decisions of United States supreme court. Va L R 13: 155-74, 278-99 Ja, F '27 9790

Wooten, June P. Expediting business in federal courts. Lawyer & Banker 21: 102-7 Mr '28 9791

Wynne, T. D. Courts in relation to social progress. Ark B Assn Proc 33: 84-99 '30 9792

MILITARY LAW

Arnold, Frazer. The rationale of martial law. Am B Assn J 15: 550-3 S '29 9793

Bayle, C. Le projet de loi portant révision du code de justice militaire. R Pénitent et de Dr Pén 51: 173-236 My '27 9794

B[eekman], E. W. Onze militaire rechtspraak. Tijdschr v d Politie 1(21): 385-91 O 10 '28 9795

Court martial. Spectator 140: 556-7 Ap 14 '28 9796

Cuboni, G. Condanne militari e riabilitazione. Rassegna Pen (3): 260-4 '29 9797

Fairman, Charles. The law of martial rule. Am Pol Sci R 22: 591-616 Ag '28 9798

Grebe. Die wichtigsten Sonderbestimmungen des Militärstrafgesetzbuches. Leipz Zeitsch f Deut Recht 21: 1433-50 '27 9799

Grünewald. Gesetz zur Vereinfachung des Militärstrafrechts. Arch f Strafr u Strafproz 71: 5-11 Ja '27 9800

Guisan, F. Le champ d'application du code pénal militaire et la compétence des tribunaux militaires. Schweiz Zeitsch f Strafr 41: 250-73 '28 9801

Hentig, Hans v. Das neue französische Militärstrafrecht (Gesetz vom 9. März 1928). Monats f Kriminalpsychol u Strafrechtsref 19: 526-30 '28 9802

Izquierdo, Antonio. Organización del Ejército. Sus tribunales y jurisdicción. Leyes penales y procedimientos. 295p. Madrid, Reus, 1928 9803

Justice militaire. Insoumission. Desertion. 116p. Paris, Charles-Lavauzelle, 1928 9804

Lanza, Carlo. Criminalità militare. Responsibilità civile dello stato (Leggi di reclutamento). 69p. Torino, Bocca, 1927 9805

Lelewer, Georg. Grundriss des Militärstrafrechts. 152p. Wien, Staatsdruckerei, 1927 9806

Lévy-Ullmann. Le militaire de carrière exerce-t-il une fonction publique au sens de l'article 171 du code pénal complété par l'article 243 du nouveau code de justice militaire (9 mars 1928)? Etudes Crimin 5: 103-9 Ap '30 9807

Manzini, Vincenzo. Diritto penale militare. 354p. Padova, A. Milani, 1928 9808

Mattos, José Candido de Albuquerque Mello. Programma de diritto penal militar e respectivo processo. 41p. Rio-de-Janeiro, 1930 9809

Miller, J. F. Compton. Advocacy at courts-martial. Sol J 73: 182-3 Mr 23 '29 9810

Naval courts-martial. Nation [London] 42: 959-60 Mr 31 '28 9811

Le Poittevin, Gustave. [Courts-martial and their procedure]. Etudes Crimin 3: 121-4 '28 9812

Le Poittevin, Gustave. La justice militaire en temps de guerre. R de Dr Pén et de Crimin 8: 1010-25 N '28 9813

Le Poittevin, Gustave. Le nouveau code de justice militaire. R de Dr Pén et de Crimin 8: 466-76 '28; same title: Etudes Crimin 4: 2-8, 72-6 Ja, Mr '29 9814

Pouribas, N. Código de justicia militar vigente. 630p. Madrid, Reus, 1927 9815

Reggiani, R. Il codice penale militare. Vita Nova (6): 511-12 '29 9816

Rigby, William Cattron. Procedure of army courts-martial under the 1920 revision of the articles of war. Comm L Leag J 35: 141-3 Mr '30 9817

Trüssel, F. Das neue Militärstrafgesetz. Zeitsch des Bernischen Juristenvereins 64: 1-17 '28 9818

Austria

Lelewer, G. Ein gemeinsames Militärstrafgesetzbuch für Österreich und das Deutsche Reich. Gerichtssaal 97:44-59 '28 9819

Brazil

Carneiro, Mario Tiburcio Gomes. Codigos militares do Brasil e leis complementares. 550p. Rio-de-Janeiro, Francisco Alves, 1930 9820

France

Salerian-Saugy, Gh. La justice militaire des troupes suisses en France sous l'ancien régime. 163p. Paris, Jouve, 1927 9821

Hungary

Schultheiss, Emil. Kommentar zum ungarischen Militärstrafgesetzbuch. v.1 160p. Budapest, Zsigmond Politzer & Sohn, 1931 9822
(in ungarischer Sprache erschienen in)

Rumania

Provent, Paul. La réforme de la justice militaire en Roumanie. R Int de Dr Pén 4: 211-26 '27 9823

Switzerland

Kaegi, M. Das neue schweizerische Militärstrafgesetzbuch. Schweiz Juristen-Zeit 24: 93-8 '27 9824

Lenzlinger, Josef. Die schweizerische Militärstrafgerichtsbarkeit Systematisch dargestellt. 78p. Aarau, Sauerländer [1928] 9825

Otsuka, K. Suisu no shin gunkeihoten ni tsuite. Hogaku-Shirin 30: 110-20 N '28 9826

Overbeck, A. v. Das neue schweizerische Militärstrafgesetz. Gerichtssaal 97: 62-5 '28 9827

United States

A manual for courts-martial, U. S. Army... effective Apr. 1, 1928. 341p. Washington, Govt. Ptg. Off. 1927 9828

Wheless, Joseph. Military law and courts in the United States. Geo L J 15: 279-96 Mr '27 9829

SPECIAL COURTS

Beecroft, Eric Armour. Courts of specialized jurisdiction in Australia. Univ Pa L R 79: 1021-51 Je '31 9830

Grodsinsky, M. Die Kameradengerichte und Schlichtungskammern im Sovetrecht. Zeitsch f Ostrecht 4: 951-60 '30 9831

Lindsey, Ben B. The house of human welfare [suggested court to deal with the causes of crime]. Forum 78: 801-16 D '27 9832

Lucas, Georg. Justizreform. Zeitsch f d ges Staatswiss 85(3): 449-67 '28 9833

Wolaver, E. S. The merchant court. Am L Sch R 7: 238-43 My '31 9834

CONCILIATION

Aumann, F[rancis] R. The Des Moines conciliation court. Am Jud Soc J 12: 20-4 Je '28 9835

Aumann, Francis R. Des Moines tries the conciliation court. Nat Munic R 17: 211-13 Ap '28 9836

Holt, Emily. Justice without juries. Harper's 163: 92-102 D '31 9837

Lauer, Edgar J. Conciliation: a cure for the law's delay. Ann Am Acad 136: 54-9 Mr '28 9838

One year's operation of Des Moines conciliation court. M Lab R 27: 38-40 N '28 9839

Smith, Reginald Heber. Conciliation and legal aid an opportunity for pioneering. Ann Am Acad 136: 60-5 Mr '28 9840

Smith, Reginald Heber. The Danish conciliation system. Am Jud Soc J 11: 85-93 O '27 9841

DOMESTIC RELATIONS

Andreae, H. W. W. De rechtspraak der Gezinsrechtbanken in de Vereenigde Staten van N. Amerika. Maandbl v Berechting en Reclasseering 6: 211-23, 239-51, 293-8 Ag-O '27 9842

Aumann, F. R. Domestic relations courts in Ohio. Am Jud Soc J 15: 89-93 O '31 9843

Bringing the deserting husband to terms; a study of Allegheny county courts. Pen Affairs (16): 1-7 N '27 9844

Canadian council on child and family welfare. Family court. (Pub no53) Ottawa, 1930 9845

Condit, Jessie P. Some fundamental causes of family disruption. Nat Prob Assn Proc 1928: 89-101 9846

Day, L. B. The development of the family court. Ann Am Acad 136: 105-11 Mr '28 9847

Domestic courts. Just Peace 94: 562 S 13 '30 9848

Fagan, Bernard J. Training for families. Nat Prob Assn Proc 22: 161-7 '28 9849

Flexner, Bernard; Oppenheimer, Reuben, and Lenroot, Katharine F. The child, the family and the court: a study of the administration of justice in the field of domestic relations. 87p. (Pub no 193) Washington, U.S. Children's bureau, 1929 **9850**

Heilker, Helen. Domestic relations court of Cincinnati. Univ Cin L R 3: 458-61 N '29 **9851**

Hoffman, Charles W. The organization of domestic relations courts. Nat Prob Assn Proc 1928: 145-51 **9852**

Hoffman, C[harles] W. Problems of the family court. 10p. New York, National probation association, 1929 **9853**

De Jongh. Familie-verhoor. Maandbl v Ber en Reclasseer 7: 277-9 S '28 **9854**

Lenroot, Katharine F. The child, the family and the court. Nat Prob Assn Proc 1928: 102-23 **9855**

Madden, Joseph Warren. Cases on domestic relations. 742p. St. Paul, West pub. co. 1928 **9856**

Myers, Joseph. Courts of domestic relations. But St Inst [Iowa] 32: 61-3 Ja '30 **9857**

New Haven, N. J. Bureau of domestic rerations and the Juvenile court. Annual reports 4, 1928—7, 1931. New Haven, 1929-32 **9858**
Non-support statistics; commitment of women and girls; report on adult probation.

Oppenheimer, Reuben. Domestic relations courts; a study in Americana. Soc Serv R 4: 17-22 Mr '30 **9859**

Philadelphia. Bureau of municipal research. Domestic relations division of the municipal court of Philadelpha. 32p. Philadelphia, Thomas Skelton Harrison foundation, 1930 **9860**

Philadelphia. Municipal court. Domestic relations division. Annual reports *in* Annual reports of Municipal court, 14, 1927: 87-108; 15, 1928: 87-108; 16, 1929: 77-94; 17, 1930: 79-100; 18, 1931: 81-106 **9861**

Regan, Timothy W. Adventures in domestic relations. N Y St Conf Prob Offic Proc 21: 102-14 '28 **9862**

Shelly, Patrick J. The social and economic value of the family court. N Y St Conf Prob Offic Proc 20: 83-9 '27; same title: 7p. New York (state) Department of correction, Division of probation, 1929 **9863**

Why not a court of domestic relations? Sol J 72: 670-1 O 13 '28 **9864**

SMALL CLAIMS

Clark, Charles E. and O'Connell, Richard D. The working of the Hartford small claims court. Conn B J 3: 123-9 Ap '29 **9865**

Fernow, Fritz. Proposed small claims branch of the city court of Buffalo. Lincoln L R 2: 36-44 Ap '29 **9866**

Galbreth, R. Morgan. The small claims court. Los Angeles B Assn Bul 6: 113-14 D 14 '30 **9867**

Schramm, Gustav L. Piedpoudre courts: a study of the small claim litigant in the Pittsburgh district. 219p. Pittsburgh, Legal aid society, 1928 **9868**

Small claims courts. M Lab R 29: 121-2 Ag '29 **9869**

JUVENILE

General

Abbott, Grace. Case work responsibility of juvenile courts. Nat Prob Assn Proc 1929: 85-93; same title: Soc Serv R 3: 395-404 S '29 **9870**

Age limit for juvenile courts. Just Peace 94: 477 Jl 26 '30 **9871**

Ahlum, M. L. Juvenile courts and probation in the United States since 1925: a selected bibliography. 35p. (typw) Madison, Wisconsin university library school, June 1931 **9872**

Aichhorn, August. The juvenile court: is it a solution? R Int de l'Enf 9: 195-211 Mr '30 **9873**

Albó, Ramon. Seis años de vida del tribunal tutelar para niños. 310p. Barcelona, Artes. graficas, 1927 **9874**

Allen, Frederick H. Mental attitudes of adults in a juvenile court. Nat Prob Assn Proc 1929: 134-44; same title: J Crim L & Crimin 21: 201-11 Ag '30 **9875**

Alzate, M. A. Juvenile courts. Phila Pris R 4: 16-17 Je '28 **9876**

Appell, George C. Cheating our children. N Am R 226: 520-4 N '28 **9877**

Appell, George C. The Children's court. N Y St Assn Judges Proc 6: 53-61 '27 **9878**

Appell, George C. [The technique and form of the modern day children's court work]. N Y St Assn Judges Proc 6: 50-7 '28 **9879**

Bache, Louise Franklin. The juvenile court and John Smith. Child Welf 24: 411-13 Ap '30 **9880**

Bache, Louise Franklin. Standards for juvenile court and probation work. Pub Manage 13: 94-8 Mr '31 **9881**

Bartelme, Mary M. Twenty-five years ago and since. Nat Prob Assn Proc 25: 14-18 '31 **9882**

Berent, M. Jugendschutz im Strafgesetzentwurf. Zentralbl f Jugendrecht u Jugendwohlfahrt 18: 261-6 '27 **9883**

Bing, Lucia J. Juvenile courts. Ohio Welf Bul 7: 6-7 Mr '30 **9884**

Boole, Katharine L. The juvenile court: its origin, history and procedure. 128p. Thesis (J.D.) University of California, May 1928 **9885**

Boyd, T. Munford. The contribution which the juvenile court has to make to the success of law enforcement. Nat Conf Soc Wk Proc 55: 136-43 '28 **9886**

Breckenridge, Sophonisba P. Re-examination of the work of Children's courts. Nat Prob Assn Proc 1930: 52-65 **9887**

The child as defendant. Just Peace 91: 606-7 Ag 13 '27 **9888**

Children tried on indictment. Sol J 74: 511 Ag 2 '30 9889

Children's courts. L Times 170: 297 O 18 '30 9890

Children's magistrates. Just Peace 95: 50 Ja 24 '31 9891

Chute, Charles L. Juvenile court held an antidote for crime. Am City 42: 131 Mr '30 9892

Conti, U[go]. Il magistrato dei minorenni. Quel che si è fatto all'estero. Arch di Antrop Crim 48(5) '28 9893

Conti, Ugo. Les tribunaux pour enfants et les services auxiliaires. R Int de l'Enf 60: 439-54 D '30 9894

Courtney, Janet E. Children's courts. Fortn R ns121: 629-36 My '27 9895

Crane, H. W. Mental factors of particular importance for juvenile court consideration. Soc Forces 9: 216-19 D '30 9896

Criswell, W. S. Court and pre-court work with boys. Nat Prob Assn Proc 1928: 202-5 9897

Düring, Ernst v. and Stern, Ernst. Jugendfürsorge. v2. 116p. Breslau, Hirt, 1927 9898

Dugan, Daniel J. The children's court. N Y St Conf Prob Offic Proc 20: 117-25 '27 9899

Die Durchführung des Jugendgerichts gesetzes als Personenfrage. 128p. Berlin, Herbig, 1928 9900

Engelmann, Susanne. Nachwort zum Kranz-Prozess. Preuss Jahrb 33-6 Ap '28 9901

Enquête sur les tribunaux pour enfants. Comm Pénit Int Bul (3): 1-146 D '27 9902

Fagan, Bernard J. The child, its parents, and the community. N Y St Conf Prob Offic Proc 20: 164-70 9903

Francke. Die strafrechtliche Behandlung der über 18 Jahre alten Minderjährigen. Zeitsch f d ges Strafrechtswiss 47: 588-603 '27 9904

Frazer, Elizabeth. Give the juvenile courts a chance. Good Housekeeping 89: 46-7 Jl '29 9905

Frischauf, H. Geschichtspunkte zur Reform der Jugendgerichtsbarkeit. Wien med Wchnschr 78: 904 Jl 7 '28 9906

Furfey, P. H. The juvenile court movement. Thought 6: 207-27 S '31 9907

Gibson, Katherine. The juvenile court. Peace Offic 5: 17, 30 Ja '27 9908

Hiller, Francis H. New provisions for juvenile courts and probation. Probation 8: 1-2 Mr '30 9909

Hiller, Francis H. Summary of laws and decisions affecting juvenile courts and adult probation for the year ending Oct. 1, 1929. Nat Prob Assn Proc 1929: 234-41 9910

Hoffman, Charles W. The juvenile court; address before the Virginia institute of citizenship and government, May 1927. Univ Va Rec Ext Ser 11: 83-98 Je '27 9911

Individualizing the treatment of the child: 1, in case work responsibility of the juvenile court, by Netta Burt; 2, in an institution, by Ernest G. Alden. Ind Bul Char & Correc (190): 87-91 F '31 9912

Jongh, G. T. J. de. Kinderrecht. Haagsch Maandbl 4: 157-65 Ag '27 9913

Juvenile-court law. El Sch J 29: 642-4 My '29 9914

Juvenile court procedure. Just Peace 93: 214, 222 Ap 6 '29 9915

Juvenile courts. L Notes 33: 23-4 My '29 9916

Juvenile courts and metropolitan magistrates. L Times 167: 514 Je 22 '29 9917

Juvenile courts and privacy. Sol J 73: 100 F 16 '29 9918

Keltner, Sanford M. Are the juvenile courts facing a new problem? Ind L J 3: 651-3 My '28 9919

League of Nations. Child welfare committee. Organization of juvenile courts and the results obtained hitherto. 127p. Geneva, February 1, 1932 (C.975.M.540. 1931.IV) (1931.IV.13) Boston, World peace foundation, 1931 9920
In collaboration with the International prison commission.

Leendertz, A. C. Vijf jaren Kinderrechtspraak. Maandbl v Ber en Reclasseer 6: 303-11 N '27 9921

Lenroot, Katharine F. Progressive methods of care of children pending juvenile court hearing. Hosp Soc Serv R 15: 46-55 Ja '27 9922

Lindsey, Ben B. and Borough, Rube. The dangerous life. 450p. N. Y. Liveright, 1931 9923

Liszt, Elsa v. 10 Jahre Jugendgerichtsbarkeit, 1917-1927. 39p. Berlin, Herbig, 1927 9924

Liszt, E[lsa] v. and Scheidt. Der Jugendrichter als Einzelrichter für straffällige Minderjährige im Alter von 18-20 Jahren. Zentralbl f Jugendrecht u Jugendwohlfahrt 19: 13-14 '27 9925

Loewy, I. Eindrücke beim Jugendgericht. Int Zeitsch f Individualpsychol 5: 367-71 '31 9926

Luther, Friedrich. Jugendpsychologie und Jugendstrafrechtspflege mit Vorschlägen zu Reformen im Jugendgerichtsverfahren und Jugendstrafvollzug. Zeitsch f d ges Strafrechtswiss 51(1): 18-53 '31 9927

McDermott, Lillian P. Use of an advisory group in court work with girls. Nat Prob Assn Proc 1928: 235-9 9928

MacGill, Helen Gregory. Juvenile courts, successful and unsuccessful. Welf Mag 19: 584-90 My '28 9929

McGrath, William A. The juvenile court officer; shall he represent the police? Police "13-13" 5: 12-14, 28 My '30 9930

Matthews, H. M. Children's court and prevention of juvenile delinquency. R Int de L'Enf 9: 311-17 Ap '30 9931

Messerer, Richard. Probleme des Jugendstrafrechts. Deut Richter-Zeit 19(12): 459-63 '27 9932

Moran, Frederick A. New light on the juvenile court and probation. Nat Prob Assn Proc 1930: 66-75; same title: Nat Conf Soc Wk Proc 57: 70-80 '30 9933

Mosher, Charles L. Attendance problems and the children's court. N Y St Assn Judges Proc 5: 21-8 '27 9934

Müller. Zur Problematik des Jugendgerichts. Zentralbl f Jugendrecht u Jugendwohlfahrt 21(9): 330-4 D '29 9935

Müller, B. Die Entwicklung des Jugendrechts. Erziehung 2: 610-30 '27 9936

Murphy, J. Prentice. The juvenile court at the bar—a national challenge. Ann Am Acad 145: 80-97 S '29 9937

National probation association. A standard juvenile court law. rev. ed. 32p. New York, 1928 9938

National probation association. Standards for a progressive juvenile court; how does the juvenile court in your community measure up? Chart. New York, 1929 9939

Németh, P. Youth in danger. R Int de l'Enf 10: 3-14 Jl '30 9940

Nisot, Pierre. L'enfance délinquante et moralement abandonée. Les tribunaux pour enfants. 406p. Bruxelles, Dykmans [1927] 9941

Nutt, Alice Scott. Report on progress of the Children's bureau for uniform juvenile court statistics. Nat Prob Assn Proc 1928: 168-78 9942

Parker, William. Juvenile court work. Assn of Dir Poor & Char & Correc Proc 54: 82-90 '29 9943

Petraccone, G. La delinquenza dei minorenni e i suoi remedi. Scuola Pos ns7: 423-30 S '27 9944

Ricks, James Hoge. Juvenile courts and child welfare. Am Fed 38: 564-70 My '31 9945

Roubinovitch, J. La psychiatrie de l'enfance criminelle. Hyg Ment 22: 109-13 S '27 9946

S., W. L. Juvenile courts, jurisdiction. Can B R 5: 214-15 Mr '27 9947

Save the children international union. Enquiry into the auxiliary services of childrens courts made by the . . . Union through the Revue international de l'enfant, March 1930. 28p. (mim) Geneva, 1930 9948

Schnek. Kritische Bemerkungen zur Regierungsvorlage eines Jugendgerichtsgesetzes. Öster Anwalts-Zeit 4: 241-4 '27 9949

Schroeder, Paul L. and Bartelme, Phyllis. A mental health program as a juvenile court method of supervising the feebleminded. Am Assn Stud Feeblemind Proc 52: 37-58 '28 9950

Scott, Robert H. Modern science and the juvenile court. J Juv Res 14: 77-86 Ap '30 9951

Scott, W. L. The juvenile court in law and the juvenile court in action. 43p. (Pub no34) Ottawa, Canadian council on child welfare, 1927 9952

Shea, Edmund B. The Children's code and the juvenile court. Marquette L R 13: 208-18 Je '29 9953

Skorpil, R. Aus der Mappe eines Jugendrichters. Psychol Rundsch 3: 23-9 '31 9954

Solomonescu, G. Tribunalele de minori in Franta, Belgia si Germania. R de Drept Pen 44-56 Mr '28 9955

Source material: the Wellesley case and the juvenile court movement. Soc Serv R 4: 64-81 Mr '30 9956

Sousa, Tude Martins de. Jusqu'à quel âge doit s'étendre la compétence des tribunaux des mineurs? Bol do Inst de Crimin s8 15(2): 353-7 '31 9957

Stamm, Gladys Erna. Juvenile court as a possible administrative body. St Louis L R 16: 63-71 D '30 9958

S[tauffacher], C[asper] R. Prosecution of delinquent under criminal statutes. St Louis L R 14: 429-31 Jl '29 9959

Stooss, Carl. Die Beurteilung von Jugendlichen. Schweiz Zeitsch f Strafr 42: 34-7, 321-7 '29 9960

Torrance, Mary Fisher. Child prisoner at the bar. Parents' Mag 5: 22-3 Jl '30 9961

Wembridge, Eleanor Rowland. Sintach vs. Sapp. Survey 64: 148-50 My 1 '30 9962

AUSTRIA

Butschek, Franz. Zwei Jahre österreichisches Jugendgerichtsgesetz. Zeitsch f d ges Strafrechtswiss 51(6): 983-90 '31 9963

Grünhut, Max. Reichsdeutsche Bemerkungen zum österreichischen Jugendgerichtsgesetz. Monats f Kriminalpsychol u Strafrechtsref 20: 279-86 My '29 9964

Hückel-Rohm, H. Jugendgericht. Int Zeitsch f Individualpsychol 7: 432-5 '29 9965

Kadecka, Ferdinand. Das österreichische Jugendgerichtsgesetz (vom 18. Juli 1928) mit den Motiven und der Durchführungsverordnung. 238p. Wien, Manz, 1929 9966

Kraszna, Hermann. La nuova legge sul tribunale dei minori in Austria. Giustiz Pen 37 (3) ptl: 442-5 Mr '31 9967

Siegel, Otto. Der österreichische Regierungsentwurf eines Jugendgerichtsgesetzes. Monats f Kriminalpsychol u Strafrechtsref 20: 399-405 Jl '29 9968

Suchanek, V. Der neue Jugendgerichtsgesetzentwurf vom Jahre 1927. Zeitsch f Kinderschutz 19: 88-93 Je '27 9969

BELGIUM

Maus, I. L'enfant en danger moral et les services auxiliaires des tribunaux pour enfants. R Int de l'Enf 9: 99-115 F '30 9970

Maus, Isidore. L'office Belge de la protection de l'enfance. R de Dr Pén et de Crimin 7: 1-55 Ja '27 9971

CANADA

Juvenile courts in Canada. J Comp Leg s3 9: 135 F '27 9972

MacGill, H. G. Juvenile courts and their work in Canada. R Int de l'Enf 6: 678-83 O '28 9973

MacMurchy, Helen. The community looks at the court. Nat Prob Assn Proc 1929: 131-3; same title: Am Pris Assn Proc 59: 70-5 '29 9974

Toronto. Juvenile court. Report for the year 1927, 1928, 1929, 1930, 1931. [Toronto, 1927-31] 9975

Vancouver, B. C. Juvenile court and Civic juvenile detention home. Report of the Superintendent of the Detention home, Chief probation officer and clerk of the juvenile court 18, 1927—22, 1931. [Vancouver, 1928-32] 9976

EUROPE

[Stern, Leon]. How Europe's courts deal with children. Welf Mag 19: 839-42 Je '28 9977

FRANCE

Sadler, Ann. A Paris tribunal. Welf Mag 19: 1380-91 '28 9978

Spitzer, Olga. Le tribunal pour enfants et adolescents en France. R Int de l'Enf 52: 287-300 Ap '30 9979

GERMANY

Drewes, Paul. Das Reichsgesetz für Jugendwohlfahrt und das Jugendgerichtsgesetz. ed.2 rev. (Gutentagsche Sammlung deutscher Reichsgesetze no154) 496p. Berlin, Gruyter, 1928 9980

Franke, H. Die Wirksamkeit der Jugendgerichtshilfe in Deutschland. R Int de l'Enf 10: 16-29 Jl '30 9981

Haeckel, Heinrich. Jugendgerichtshilfe. 104p. (Schriftenr. d. Vereinigung f. Jugendgerichte u Jugendgerichtshilfe no 10) Berlin, Herbig, 1927 9982

Hartung, Fritz. Das Jugendgerichtsgesetz im Entwurf eines Einführungsgesetzes zum Allgemeinen Deutschen Strafgesetzbuch und zum Strafvollzugsgesetz. Zeitsch f d ges Strafrechtswiss 51 (6): 891-916 '31 9983

Lieck, Sophie. Juvenile courts in Germany. Just Peace 95: 319-20 My 16 '31 9984

Liszt, Elsa v. Probleme der Jugendgerichtsarbeit in Deutschland. R Int de l'Enf 8(46): 683-94 O '29 9985

Thót, Ladislao. Los tribunales para delincuentes jóvenes en Alemania. R de Crimin, Psiquiat y Med Leg 17: 519-26 S '30 9986

Weyl, Richard. Das deutsche Jugendrecht. 330p. Leipzig, Hirschfeld, 1927 9987

GREAT BRITAIN

Arenaza, C. de. Una audiencia en el tribunal de niños de Shoredich(Londres). R de Crimin, Psiquiat y Med Leg 15: 348-52 My '28 9988

Breach of probation order, young person bound over by juvenile court but now sixteen, by what court to be dealt with. Just Peace 95: 291 My 2 '31 9989

Brentford ("Jix"). What do we do with our bad boys? Sat Eve Post 202: 28, 114-17 Ja 11 '30 9990

Great Britain. Committee on the metropolitan police courts and juvenile courts. Report. 12p. London, H. M. Stationery Off. 1929 9991

Juvenile courts in Canada and in England. Just Peace 92: 766-7 N 24 '28 9992

MEXICO

Navarro, Berta. Cómo funciona el Tribunal para menores en México. Museo Soc Arg Bol 18: 261-4 My '30 9993

PERU

deParks, Mercedes Gallagher. Children's court work and reformatories in Peru. Pan Am Union Bul 65: 1134-9 N '31 9994

POLAND

Grzegorzewska, M. La protection des enfants moralement abandonnés en Pologne. R Int de l'Enf 9: 212-29 Mr '30 9995

SPAIN

Buettel, Mina. Jugendgerichte und Jugendkriminalität in Spanien. Zentralbl f Jugendrecht u Jugendwohlfahrt 21: 18-21 Ap '29 9996

García Molinas, F. Memoria del Tribunal tutelar para niños de Madrid. . .Ano 1926. 92p. Madrid, Tip. del Ref. del Príncipe de Asturias, 1927 9997

UNITED STATES

Lou, Herbert. Juvenile courts in the United States. 277p. Chapel Hill, University of North Carolina press, 1927 9998

United States. Children's bureau. Analysis and tabular summary of state laws relating to jurisdiction in children's cases and cases of domestic relations in the United States. 33p. (Chart no17) Washington, 1930 9999

Weiss, H. Ueber die Jugendgerichtsbarkeit in den Vereinigten Staaten Nordamerikas. Schweiz Zeitsch f Strafr 44: 160-85 '30 10000

CALIFORNIA

California. Laws, statutes, etc. Laws relating to the Department of social welfare, including juvenile court law. 62p. Sacramento, 1929 10001

Hiller, Francis H. Juvenile court of Los Angeles county, California; report of survey. 58p. Los Angeles, Rotary club, 1928 10002

San Francisco. Juvenile court. Statistics report: cases handled. . . 1927-1930. [San Francisco, 1927-30] 10003

Colorado

Inside annals of Denver juvenile court. Probation 6: 1- Ag '27 10004

Connecticut

Connecticut. Chief juvenile court probation officer. Connecticut children in court: annual report, 1931 10005

New London. Juvenile court. Report *in* Annual report of City manager 10006

District of Columbia

United States. President. Juvenile court of the District of Columbia: message from the President. . .transmitting a letter. . .submitting a report covering the work of the Juvenile court during the period, July 1, 1906 to June 30, 1926. 162p. Washington, 1927 (69th Cong. 2d sess. S Doc 236) 10007

pt1: Delinquent child and the law, study of development of legislation concerning delinquent children in District of Columbia with special reference to juvenile court [with bibliography] by Raymond W. Murray. pt2: Statistics of juvenile court of District of Columbia, 1906-1926.

United States. President. Message. . . transmitting a letter from the judge of the Juvenile court of the District of Columbia submitting a report, 1927-1931. Washington, 1929-32 10008

Florida

National probation association. Juvenile courts and probation in Florida. 50p. (Pub no3) [Tallahassee] State board of public welfare, February 1931 10009

Illinois

Cook county, Ill. Institute for juvenile research. Juvenile court branch. Report, December 1, 1926/November 30, 1927. [Chicago, 1927] 10010

Statistics of cases before juvenile court and probation.

Greenebaum, Betsy. Court of "another chance" where Judge Mary Bartelme presides. Woman Cit ns12: 12-14 Ag '27 10011

Illinois. Department of public welfare. Certified orphanages, child placing societies, juvenile probation officers, maternity hospitals and old people's homes, and juvenile court law. 37p. Springfield, March 31, 1928 10012

Millis, Savilla. The juvenile detention home in relation to juvenile court policy: study of the intake in the Cook county Chicago juvenile detention home. 96p. [Chicago, Citizens advisory committee on the Juvenile detention home of Cook county] 1927 10013

Iowa

Hiller, Francis H. and Gates, Charles A. Juvenile courts and probation in Iowa: report of a state wide survey. 88p. N. Y. National probation association, May 1930 10014

Kentucky

Adams, Chester D. Juvenile court administration in Kentucky. Ky L J 18: 264-71 Mr '30 10015

Massachusetts

Bell, Marjorie. A boy delinquent in the Boston juvenile court. Nat Prob Assn Proc 1928: 319-25 10016

Lenroot, Katharine F. Juvenile court standards. Does Massachusetts meet the test? Massachusetts civic league, January 17, 1929 10017

Michigan

Michigan. Laws, statutes, etc. Laws relating to juveniles. 119p. Lansing, 1930 10018

Minnesota

Minnesota. Hennepin county. Juvenile court. Report, 1926-1927-1928. 37p. Minneapolis, 1929 10019

Contains report of Hennepin county probation officer; Glen Lake Farm school for boys (county detention home).

Missouri

Rutnam, Walter. Study of the juvenile court of St. Louis. Thesis (M.A.) Washington university, 1931 10020

St. Louis. Juvenile court and probation office. Report. . . for the years 1925 to 1929, inclusive. 60p. St. Louis, 1930 10021

Court system; House of detention school; Industrial farm.

New Hampshire

Bell, Marjorie. Juvenile courts and probation in New Hampshire. 56p. N. Y. National probation association, 1930 10022

New Jersey

Potter, Ellen C. The juvenile court in New Jersey. Am Pris Assn Proc 60: 188-95 '30 10023

New York (state)

Buffalo. Children's court. Annual reports 16, 1927—19, 1930. Buffalo, 1928-31 10024

Charity organization society of the city of New York. Committee on criminal courts. The adolescent offender; a study of the age-limit of the Children's court. 85p. New York, 1928 10025

Colligan, Catherine I. The rural court and the clinic. Ment Hyg 14: 137-50 Ja '30 10026
Children's court, Clinton county, New York.

New York (city). Children's court. Annual reports, 1927—31. New York, 1928-32 10027
Statistical analysis of children arraigned; report of Probation bureau of children's court.

Westchester county. Children's court. Annual report, 1926. 56p. White Plains, 1927 10028

North Dakota

Harper, Fowler V. and Reinhardt, James M. Juvenile court problem in Grand Forks (N.D.) Univ N D Q J 20: 209-21 Spring '30 10029

Ohio

Aumann, F. R. The juvenile court movement in Ohio. J Crim L & Crimin 22: 556-65 N '31 10030

Cuyahoga county. Juvenile court. Annual reports 1, 1929—2, 1930. [Cleveland, 1929-30] 10031
Includes report on detention home.

Green, Howard Whipple. Analysis of 377 records of girls committed to the Girls industrial school by the juvenile court at Cleveland during a 6-year period, 1920-1925. 124p. Cleveland, Cleveland social hygiene association, 1929 10032

Oregon

Bell, Marjorie. The juvenile court of Multnomah county, Oregon: report of a survey. 43p. New York, National probation association, 1930 10033

Pennsylvania

Boys' club federation of America, New York city. Juvenile court cases, Pittsburgh, Pennsylvania, March 1, 1929-March 1, 1930. (spot map) 10034

Hiller, Francis H. The juvenile court of Allegheny county. 53p. New York, National probation association, 1927 10035

Mayer, Eward E. The juvenile court of Allegheny county—a psychiatric study. 14p. Pittsburgh, Juvenile court, 1930 10036
Analysis of 616 cases before the juvenile court.

Philadelphia. Bureau of municipal research. Juvenile division of the municipal court of Philadelphia. 163p. Philadelphia, Thomas Skelton Harrison foundation, 1930 10037

Philadelphia. Municipal court. Juvenile division. Annual report *in* Annual report of Municipal court 14, 1927: 1-85; 15, 1928: 1-86; 16, 1929: 1-76; 17, 1930: 1-78; 18, 1931: 1-80 10038

Stern, Leon. The work of the juvenile court of Allegheny county and the juvenile detention home. 128p. Philadelphia, Pennsylvania committee on penal affairs of the Public charities associations, January 1931 10039

Stern, Leon and Dunham, Arthur. The juvenile court of Lackawanna county, Pennsylvania, a survey. 98p. Philadelphia, Community welfare association of Scranton and Dunmore; Pennsylvania committee on penal affairs, April 1930 10040

Tennessee

Ringgold, Florida. Juvenile court problems of the smaller cities of Tennessee. Nat Prob Assn Proc 1928: 179-85 10041

Utah

National probation association. Juvenile courts in Utah: report of a state-wide survey. 79p. New York, 1929 10042

Utah. Juvenile court commission. Biennial reports, 1926/28-1928/30. [Salt Lake City, 1928-30] 10043

Utah. Laws, statutes, etc. Juvenile courts [law], approved March 19, 1931. 20p. [Salt Lake City, 1931] 10044

Washington

Seattle. Juvenile court. Annual reports, 1927—1930. Seattle 1927-31 10045

Detention of Juveniles

Arenaza, Carlos de. Establecimientos para detencion de menores Remand Home. R de Crimin, Psiquiat y Med Leg (93) My '29 10046

Chute, Charles L. A nation-wide study of juvenile detention. Probation 8: 1-2 Ja '30 10047

Cook county, Ill. Juvenile detention home. Report of the Superintendent *in* Report of Institute for juvenile research, Juvenile court branch, 1926/27: 95-116 10048

Dobbs, Harrison A. The problem of juvenile detention. Nat Prob Assn Proc 1930: 125-30 10049

Healy, William and Bronner, Augusta F. Juvenile detention homes. Ann Am Acad 151: 180-3 S '30 10050

Pennsylvania. Allegheny county. Juvenile detention home. Annual reports [1] 1929—[3] 1931. (mim) Pittsburgh, 1929-32 10051

Pierce, Paul R. Organization of the juvenile detention home school. Chic Sch J 11: 258-60 Mr '29 10052

Wills, Arnold L. Juvenile detention home standards. Nat Prob Assn Proc 25: 231-4 '31 10053

Willson, Elise. Detention facilities for juvenile court wards of Nebraska. Thesis (M.A.) University of Nebraska, 1931? 10054

Juvenile Court and School

Dolton, Isabella. The school and the juvenile court. Nat Prob Assn Proc 25: 48-60 '31 10055

Hammerschlag, Heinz Erich. Die Erziehungsmassregeln im Jugendgerichtsgesetz. 86p. (Strafrechtl Abh no222) Breslau, Schletter, 1927 10056

Hoyt, Guy M. The relation of the school to the juvenile court. Nat Prob Assn Proc 1929: 109-13 10057

Hyatt, Carl B. The school, the juvenile court and the social attitude. Nat Prob Assn Proc 25: 40-7 '31 10058

Vann, Harold K. The school and the juvenile court. Nat Prob Assn Proc 1929: 114-18 10059

Juvenile Court and Social Agencies

Baldwin, Ruth M. The working relationship of the family agency and the juvenile court. Minn St Conf & Inst Soc Wk Proc 38: 70-8 '30 10060

Foster, James H. The relation of children's courts to the state department of charities. N Y St Conf Prob Offic Proc 21: 141-5 '28 10061

Green, George T. Service clubs and the juvenile courts. Ill Conf Pub Welf Proc 1929: 26-9 10062

Healy, William. Resultados del functionamiento de los tribunales para menores. El desarrollo del sistema de la orientación del niño. Instit Int Am de Protec a la Infancia Bol 5: 220-8 O '31 10063

Wilson, Louis A. The relation of the children's court work to a state technical institution. N Y St Assn Judges Proc 6: 31-7 '28 10064

Juvenile Court and the Community

Brown, L. G. The court in the community. Ohio Welf Bul 5: 1-4 Ap '29 10065

Dobbs, Harrison A. The community views the court child. Minn St Conf & Inst Soc Wk Proc 35: 186-92 '27 10066

Lenroot, Katharine F. The place of the juvenile court in a community child welfare program. Minn St Bd Con Q 30: 42-8 S 12 '30 10067

GRAND JURY

Abolition of grand jury and waiver of jury trial. U S L R 65: 528-32 O '31 10068

Adams, J. G., jr. Quashing indictment for incompetent evidence before grand jury. N C L R 10: 75-7 D '31 10069

Alexander, Harold D. comp. Bender's handbook for grand jurors; their powers and duties. ed.10. 56p. Albany, M. Bender and co. 1927 10070

Appleton, Robert. The grand jury. On Guard 1: 10, 12 Jl '31 10071

Appleton, R[obert]. Secrecy of grand jury testimony. Panel 6: 6 S 1; 7-8 D '28 10072

Appleton, R[obert]. Special counsel for grand juries. Panel 8: 6 S '30 10073

Association of grand jurors of New York county. Panel. New York, v9 no1, January 1931- 10074

Chamberlin, Henry Barrett. Special grand juries in Illinois. J Crim L & Crimin 22: 163-70 Jl '31 10075

Charging the grand jury. Am L R 62: 630-8 Jl '28 10076

Crawford, Finla Goff. Criticisms of the grand jury. *In his* Readings on American government, 660-5. N.Y. Knopf, 1927 10077

Davis, Elmer Joseph. The grand jury . . . 1931. Chicago, Better government association, 1931 10078

Decision of grand jury, effect upon summary court. Just Peace 94: 729 N 22 '30 10079

Dodd, Charles J. The grand jury. St John's L R 3: 225-9 My '29 10080

Drawing of federal grand juries. L Notes 32: 3-4 Ap '28 10081

The grand jury. L Notes 32: 221 Mr '29 10082

The grand jury again. Just Peace 92: 21-2 Ja 14 '28 10083

The grand jury in Scotland. Sol J 74: 48 Ja 25 '30 10084

Improving the efficiency of our grand jury system. Panel 5: 1- Ap '27 10085

Light on grand jury procedure: research proves states best administer justice where grand jury is reserved for public scandal. Am Jud Soc J 15: 120-5 D '31 10086

Lindsay, John D. Grand jury as the people—a reply to Professor Moley. Panel 9: 13, 23 Mr '31 10087

Medalie, G. Z. Grand jury investigations. Panel 7: 5-7 Ja '29 10088

Minturn, J. F. Charging the grand jury. Am L R 62: 630-8 Jl '28 10089

Morse, Wayne L. A survey of the grand jury system. Ore L R 10: 101-60, 217-57, 295-365 F-Je '31 10090
Study of 7414 cases before the grand jury.

Nahum, Milton and Schatz, Louis M. The grand jury in Connecticut. Conn B J 5: 111-47 Ap '31 10091

Porter, H. F. J. Making the grand jury what it should be. Panel 5: 2-3 Ja '27 10092

San Francisco. City and county. Grand jury. Final report, 1927—1931 [San Francisco, 1927-31] 10093

Scott, Lloyd N. An auditing grand jury is suggested. Panel 9: 32 My '31 10094

Scragg, Harold A. The grand jury. Temple L Q 2: 317-29 Jl '28 10095

Shinn, Charles P. More about the grand jury. On Guard 1:5, 10 S '31 10096

Tuttle, C. H. The grand jury system: should it be abolished or strengthened? Panel 5: 2-3 O '27 10097

Ward, Hamilton. Powers of the grand jury and of the attorney general. Panel 8: 11-12 N '30 10098

Winfield, Charles H. The grand jury. ed.2. 87p. Newark, N.J. 1928 10099

COURT OFFICERS

Hellwig, Albert. Dürfen sich Organe der Strafrechtspflege der Hilfe sogenannter Kriminaltelepathen bedienen? Jurist Rundsch 4: 261-5 D 1 '28 10100

Levi, Nino. Il curatore del fallimento publico ufficiale. Riv d Dir Comm 28: 841-9 D '30 10101

Seelig, E. Die kriminologische Ausbildung der juristischen Organe der Strafrechtspflege. Monats f Kriminalpsychol u Strafrechtsref 19: 752-6 D '28 10102

JUDGES

Allen, Carleton Kemp. The judge as man of the world. L Q R 46: 151-8 Ap '30 10103

Alsberg, Max. Richter und Götter. Monats f Kriminalpsychol u Strafrechtsref 19: 147-51 Mr '28 10104

Alsberg, Max. Das Weltbild des Strafrichters. 31p. Mannheim, Bensheimer, 1930 10105

Assignment of federal judges. L Notes 33: 204-5 F '30 10106

Ball, Francis Elrington. The judges in Ireland, 1221-1921. 2v N.Y. Dutton, 1927 10107

Bendix, Ludwig. Richter-Götter und Verteidiger-Götter. Monats f Kriminalpsychol u Strafrechtsref 19: 346-8 Je '28 10108

Beradt, Martin. Der deutsche richter. 229p. Frankfort, Rütten & Loening, 1930 10109

Bouchardon, Pierre. Le magistrat. 125p. Paris, Hachette, 1927 10110

Bryson, Moore. Suggested plan for a rule making body. N C L R 8: 222-5 F '30 10111

Cann, George T. Charge of the court. Ga Lawyer 1: 91, 102-3 S '30 10112

Castellani, U. I magistrati per i minorenni e le opere ausiliatrici. Scuola Pos 38: 97-100 '30 10113

Cluysenaer, O. J. De na-academische strafrechtelyke opleiding voor de rechterlyke macht. Maandbl v Ber en Reclasseer 10: 217-23 Ag '31 10114

Concerning magistrates. Can B R 5: 681-2 N '27 10115

Conti, Ugo. Giudice penale unico o collegiale? Riv Pen di Dott, Legis e Giuris 10: 409-17 '29 10116

Corson, James C. Judges and statutory tenure in England in the seventeenth century. Jurid R 42: 136-49 Je '30 10117

County court judges. L Times 168: 428 N 23 '29 10118

Crane, Frederick E. Judge and jury. Am B Assn J 15: 201-4 Ap '29 10119

Crane, Frederick E. Part played by tradition in work of judiciary. Comm L J 36: 148 Mr '31 10120

Dalmazzo, Fanny. Il magistrato dei minorenni. Vita e Pensiero (11): 681-8 '29 10121

Dupeyron, Henry. Le juge unique et la réforme judiciaire. 207p. Paris, Dalloz, 1927 10122

Escobio, Felix. Pueden los jueces apartarse de la ley? Colegio de Abogados, Buenos Aires R 8: 233-8 My '30 10123

Ferro-Luzzi, G. Il magistrato dei minorenni. Pol Soc (6): 627-30 '29 10124

Gorphe, F. La conviction des juges. R de Dr Pén et de Crimin 11: 557-68 '31 10125

Green, Leon. Judge and jury. 429p. Kansas City, Mo. Vernon law bk. co. 1930 10126

Grünhut, M. Die Stellung des Richters im künftigen deutschen Strafrecht. Monats f Kriminalpsychol u Strafrechtsref 18: 13-22 Ja '27 10127

Gummersbach. Das Opfer als Richter. Monats f Kriminalpsychol u Strafrechtsref 19: 561-2 S '28 10128

Haller, Marguerite. Le principe de l'autorité de la chose jugée au criminel sur le civil en Alsace-Lorraine. Etudes Crimin 3: 99-102 My '28 10129

Hawkins, Daniel R. The judge and the court officer. N Y St Assn Magistrates Proc 22: 82-7 '30 10130

Hébraud, Pierre. L'autorité de la chose jugée au criminel sur le civil. Paris, Sirey, 1929 10131

Heilbronn, Brigitte. Freies pflichtmässiges Ermessen des Richters. 90p. (Strafrechtl Abh no253 begründet von Hans Bennecke) Breslau, Schletter, 1929 10132

Heimberger, Josef. Freiheit und Gebundenheit des Richters in weltlichem und kirchlichem Strafrecht. 23p. Frankfort, Englert & Schlosser, 1928 10133

Hellwig, Albert. Richter und Presse. Arch f Krim 87: 220-4 D '30 10134

Hendren, W. M. The chief justice of the United States. N C L R 8: 404-17 Je '30 10135

Höhn, Reinhard. Die Stellung des Strafrichters in den Gesetzen der französischen Revolutionszeit (1791-1810). 147p. (Beiträge zur Geschichte der deutschen Strafrechtspflege, no2, hrsg von Max Grünhut, und Eberhard Schmidt) Berlin, Gruyter, 1929 10136

Increase in justices' work. Just Peace 91: 204 Mr 19 '27 10137

Increase in number of new judges. Sol J 71: 933 D 10 '27 10138

Installation of judges in England and Scotland; judicial titles. Sol J 73: 17 Ja 12 '29 10139

Jessup, Henry K. Judicial office and bar's responsibility. Am B Assn J 13: 117-82 Ap '27 10140

Jofé, B. De l'application par le juge d'un état des lois pénales étrangères. R de Dr Pén et de Crimin 9: 753-68 '29 10141

Johnson, Walter Perry. Unprofitable expenditure of the time of judges in procedural routine. Calif St B Proc 1928: 104-8 10142

Jones, Walter B. Lights and shadows of the bench. Ala L J 5: 21-32 N '29 10143

Judges and magistrates. Sol J 72: 177 Mr 17 '28 10144

Judges and public affairs. L Times 164: 473-4 D 17 '27 10145

Judges and public service. Sol J 72: 21-2 Ja 14 '28 10146

Judges of the past. L Notes 33: 77-8 Jl '29 10147

Judges' titles. Scots L T 1929: 66-7 My 4 '29 10148

Judicial changes and government appointments. Scots L T 1929: 65 My 4 '29 10149

Judicial promotion in England and Scotland. Sol J 71: 813 O 22 '27 10150

Justices and search warrants. L Times 165: 48 Ja 21 '28 10151

Kavanaugh, Marcus. Judges and juries. Am L R 63: 307-12 Mr '29 10152

Kern, Eduard. Der gesetzliche Richter; herausgegeben von Heinrich Triepel, Erich Kaufmann, Rudolf Smend. 346p. Berlin, Liebmann, 1927 10153

Lambert, Ferdinando. La magistratura penale in Trani dal 1215. 15p. Trani, Paganelli, 1927 10154

Levy, Newman. The judges and the legislature. J Crim L & Crimin 19: 557-62 F '29 10155

Livingstone, John A. Rotation of superior court judges. N C L R 6: 110-17 D '27 10156

Ludwig, Carl. Richter und Strafvollzug. Schweiz Ver f Straf- Gefängniswes u Schutzaufsicht Verh ns10: 3-15 '30 10157

McCook, Philip J. Judge, jury and justice: two years of trial term. N Y L J 78: 2643-4 Mr 2 '28 10158

Magistrates and the law. Sol J 74: 617 S 20 '30 10159

Marshall, John. The federal judiciary. Va L R 16: 355-63 F '30 10160

Mignault, P. B. Indépendence des juges. Roy Soc Can Proc s1 3 sec21: 29-50 '27 10161

Modes of judicial address. Sol J 75: 19-20 Ja 10 '31 10162

Myer, J. M. The lawyer and the judge. Ga L R 1: 31-7 Mr '27 10163

Naegele, O. Menschenkenntnis und Selbsterkenntnis des Richters. Int Zeitsch f Individual Psychol 8: 181-8 '30 10164

Otis, Merrill E. Is a federal judge a human being? Mo B Assn Proc 1927: 127-33 10165

Parsons, Herbert C. The learned judge and the mental defective meet—what then? Am Assn Stud Feeblemind, Proc 51: 218-31 '27; same title: Ment Hyg 12: 25-37 Ja '28 10166

Penso, Girolamo. La partecipazione dei giudici popolari alla giustizia penale (a proposito del nuovo ordinamento delle Corti d'assise). Pensiero Giurid-Pen 3: 193-211 Jl '31 10167

Piggott, Theodore Caro. Outlaws I have known, and other reminiscences of an Indian judge. 310p. London, Blackwood, 1930 10168

Pound, Roscoe. American attitude toward the trial judge. S D St B Rep 1927: 103-16; same title: Mo B Assn Proc 1927: 138-49; Dakota L R 2: 5-16 F '28 10169

Pound, Roscoe. The judicial office in America. Va St B Assn Rep 1929: 406-21; same title: Boston Univ L R 10: 125-37 Ap '30 10170

Regueiferos, Erasmos; Revilla, Carlos; Sasserath, Simon; Fontigny, Arthur; Magnol; Jammont, Janusz; Agerman, Kazimierz Konstanty; Chiselitza, Cor; Opresco, Al; Clod, Georges; Solnar, Vladimir, and Dolenc, Metod. Le juge unique ou la collégialité du tribunal. R Int de Dr Pén 6(3-4): 402-73 '29 10171

Ricks, James Hoge. The judge and the probation officer. Nat Prob Assn Proc 1930: 214-17 10172

Riddell, William Renwick. Erring judges of the fourteenth century. Ill L R 21: 543-58 F '27 10173

Sanborn, John B. The trial judge's part in litigation. Conf Jud Adm [Duluth] Proc 1930: 3-12 10174

Sasserath, Simon and Fontigny, Arthur. Le juge unique en matière répressive. R de Dr Pén et de Crimin 9: 74-81 '29 10175

Schlesinger, Paul. Richter und gerichtete, von Sling (pseud). 380p. Berlin, Ullstein, c1929 10176

Schuind, Gaston. De l'influence de la chose jugée au criminel sur l'action civile. R de Dr Pén et de Crimin 10: 97-107 F '30 10177

The Scottish bench. Scot L R 45: 1-3 Ja '29 10178

Sears, Kenneth C. A Minnesota judgeship. Ill L R 26: 121-44 Je '31; same title: Mo B J 2: 7-10 Je '31 10179

Shelton, Thomas W. Federal judges and juries. Lawyer & Banker 24: 23-8 Ja '31 10180

Shelton, Thomas W. Hobbled justice—a talk with judges. Minn L R 13: 129-34 Ja '29 10181

Statutes of 1926 affecting justices. Just Peace 91: 163-4, 204-5 Mr 5, 19 '27 10182

Strother, D. J. G. Juries versus judges. W Va B Assn Proc 1929: 46-64 10183

Tierney, Leo. The trial judge. Ia St B Assn Proc 1927: 69-73 10184

V[otaw], A. H. Pennsylvania judges and district attorneys. Pris J 8: 1-8 Jl '28 10185

Weinberg, Siegfried. Der Alkohol vor dem Strafrichter. 36p. Berlin, Deutscher Arbeiter-Abstinenten-Bund, 1927 10186

Wigmore, John H. Why flatter our judiciary system. Ill L R 22: 170-2 Je '27 10187

Williams, Travis. The judiciary of Alabama. Ala L J 3: 187-91 Mr '28 10188

Powers

Andrews, C. O. Fundamentals of rule making power of courts. Fla St B Assn L J 2: 7-12 Ap '29 10189

A[rnold], T[hurman] W. Recent statutes on rule-making power of courts. W Va L Q 34: 84-9 D '27 10190

Boesel, Frank T. Rule-making power; discussion and report of committee on practice and procedure. Wis St B Assn Rep 1927: 234-59 10191

Bonnefoy, Gaston. La nouvelle compétence civile et pénale des juges de paix; texte et commentaire des décrets du 5 novembre et 28 décembre 1926. 182p. Paris, Librairie des Juris-Classeurs, 1928 10192

Bowen, Alfred W. When are three federal judges required? Minn L R 16: 1-42 D '31 10193

[Brown, Hugh Henry]. California needs rule-making power. Am Jud Soc J 13: 88-9 O '29 10194

Cicala, Salvatore. Poteri del giudice penale nella nuova codificazione. 15p. Roma, Libreria del Littorio, 1928 10195

Cook, Wayne G. Powers of court and judge—the distinction between the court and the judge in general. Ia L R 15: 141-61 F '30 10196

Dahm, Georg. Die Zunahme der Richtermacht im modernen Strafrecht. 23p. (Recht u Staat in Geschichte u Gegenwart 78) Tübingen, Mohr, 1931 10197

Drost, H[einrich]. Das Ermessen des Strafrichters. Zugleich ein Beitrag zu dem allgemeinen Problem Gesetz und Richteramt. 232p. Berlin, Carl Heymanns, 1930 10198

Gardner, Bunk. Province of the judge in the trial of jury cases. Ky St B Assn Proc 1927: 150-72 10199

Giblin, Vincent C. Advantages of the exercise by the supreme court of unrestricted rule-making power. Fla St B Assn L J 2: 13-15 Ap '29 10200

Gorphe, F. La fixation des faits de la cause par les juges. R Int de Crimin 3(2): 113-29 '31 10201

Hager, Beatrice. Brief digest of laws of Minnesota, Ohio and West Virginia relating to comment by judges on evidence and facts in the case, in criminal trials by jury. 4p. (typw) Madison, Wisconsin legislative library, January 1929 10202

Higgins, Joseph. Rule-making power of the supreme court of Tennessee. Tenn L R 8: 184-8 Ap '30 10203

H[oneck, S[tewart] G. Right of the trial judge to comment on the evidence. Marquette L R 12: 320-2 Je '28 10204

Hoyt, Frank. Judge's power to comment on testimony in his charge to the jury. Marquette L R 2: 67-72 F '27 10205

Ionesco-Dolj, I. and Solomonesco, Georges. De l'application par le juge d'un état des lois pénales étrangères. R Int de Dr Pén 6: 382-401 '29 10206

Jofé, B.; Garraud, Pierre, and Battaglini, Giulio. De l'application par le juge d'un état des lois pénales étrangères. R Int de Dr Pén 6(3-4): 310-62 '29 10207

Johnson, Kenneth M. Province of the judge in jury trials. Am Jud Soc J 12: 76-82 O '28 10208

Johnson, Sveinbjorn. Reform of legal procedure; rule-making power for courts. Ind L J 6: 383-96 Mr '31 10209

Lantz, Geo. D. Comment on evidence by judges. L Notes 30: 186-8 Ja '27 10210

Marvel, Josiah. The rule-making power of the courts. Ann Am Acad 136: 82-6 Mr '28; same title: Am Jud Soc J 12: 55-9 Ag '28; Boston Univ L R 9: 91-7 Ap '29 10211

Morgan, Edmund M. Functions of judge and jury in determination of preliminary questions of fact. Harv L R 43: 165-91 D '29 10212

Owen, W. C. Present status of rule-making power in Wisconsin. Wis St B Assn Rep 1927: 268-72 10213

Pound, Roscoe. Rule-making power of the courts. L Times 163: 144-6 F 12 '27 10214

Power of trial judge to increase verdict. N Y L R 5: 249-50, 361-2 Jl, S '27 10215

Randall, Frank H. Conciliation as a function of the judge. Ky L J 18: 330-40 My '30 10216

Recent statutes on rule-making power of courts. W Va L Q 34: 84 '27 10217

Rhode Island judicial council on the rule making power. Am B Assn J 16: 79-80 F '30 10218

Rosenwald, Robert E. Right of judicial comment on evidence in Missouri. St Louis L R 14: 221-58 Ap '29 10219

The rule-making power: a bibliography. Am B Assn J 16: 199-202 Mr '30 10220

Rule making power of the courts: [symposium]. Am B Assn J 13 pt2 Mr '27 10321

Rules-of-court statute held valid: Washington supreme court sustains constitutionality of act conferring power to regulate both civil and criminal procedure by rule-making power. Am Jud Soc J 12: 70-6 O '28 10222

Should a judge charging a jury be allowed to comment on the evidence? Mass L Q 14: 44-7 N '28 10223

Should court advise jury as to facts? Am Jud Soc J 13: 24-5 Je '29 10224

Shumaker, W. A. Comment on evidence by trial judges. L Notes 32: 5-7 Ap '28 10225

Shumaker, W. A. Validity of prohibition of comment on evidence by federal judge. L Notes 32: 125-7 O '28 10226

The three judge rule. Yale L J 38: 955-65 My '29 10227

Tolman, Edgar B. Justice and her ministers (includes brief discussion of legislative encroachment upon judicial prerogatives in matter of rule-making power). Conn B J 1: 194- Jl '27 10228

Tyler, Morris. Rule making power. Conn B J 4: 41-9 Ja '30 10229

Walker, Henry L. Judicial comment on the evidence in jury trials. Am B Assn J 15: 647-50 O '29 10230

Walsh, Thomas J. Rule-making power on law side of federal practice. Am B Assn J 13: 87-92 F '27 10231

Webster, Arthur. Practical use of rule-making power. Am Jud Soc J 10: 148-50 F '27 10232

Wisconsin takes long step forward: act conferring rule-making authority and creating advisory committee places responsibility on bench and bar. Am Jud Soc J 13: 71-2 O '29 10233

Selection

Additional expert opinion upon an age limit in the public service. N Y L R 28: 416-20 N '28 10234

The age of judges. Just Peace 91: 937 D 10 '27 10235

Alexander, Edward A. Movement for a better method of nominating judges. Panel 9: 11 Ja '31 10236

Alexander, Edward A. The nomination and promotion of worthy judges. Police J [N Y] 16: 28-9 Ja '29 10237

Animated discussion of the age limit for judges. N Y L R 6: 223-7 Je '28 10238

Aumann, Francis R. The selection, tenure, retirement and compensation of judges in Ohio. Univ Cin L R 5: 408-28 N '31 10239

Blindness as disqualification for judge. L Notes 33: 103-4 S '29 10240

Cannon, A. V. The Bar's duty in the selection of judges. Comm L J 36: 8-13 Ja '31 10241

Champlin, George M. The essential qualifications for a children's court judge. N Y St Conf Prob Offic Proc 21: 171-8 '28 10242

[Cleveland bar association]. Report recommends appointment of judges. Am Jud Soc J 10: 177-83 Ap '27 10243

Clostermann, Ludwig. Zur Ausbildung des Jugendrichters. Monats f Kriminalpsychol u Strafrechtsref 19: 607-11 O '28 10244

[Cohen, William N.]. "In the seats of the mighty": [selection of judges in New York city]. Los Angeles B Assn J 6: 246-9 Ap 16 '31 10245

Commonwealth club of California. Judicial elections. Trans 3(24) Je 14 '27 10246

Constitutional and statutory provisions bearing upon the retirement and pensioning of judges. N Y L R 6: 415-16 N '28 10247

Crane, M. M. Proposed constitutional amendment increasing supreme court judges to nine. Tex L R 5: 285-90 Ap '27 10248

Disqualification of a judge on the ground of bias. Harv L R 41: 78-82 N '27 10249

Donovan, William F. Election of judges. L Soc J 2: 12-13 Ag '30 10250

An elective judiciary. Sol J 71: 237 Mr 26 '27 10251

Expert opinion upon an age limit for judges. N Y L R 6: 375-8 O '28 10252

Extraordinary interest in the question of an age limit for federal judges. N Y L R 6: 260-4, 299-302 Jl, Ag '28 10253

Fight for non-political judiciary. Am B Assn J 13: 326-7 Je '27 10254

Haymond, Frank. Selection, tenure and removal of judges. W Va B Assn Proc 1930: 222-38 10255

Hinton, E. W. Selection of judges. Report of Cleveland bar association. Ill L R 21: 612-13 F '27; same title: N C L R 5: 378-9 Je '27 10256

Judicial pensions. Sol J 72: 17-18 O 27 '28 10257

Judicial referendums. Am B Assn J 13: 407-9 Jl '27 10258

Kales, Albert M. Methods of selecting and retiring judges. Am Jud Soc J 11: 133-45 F '28 10259

McKnight, A. H. How shall our judges be selected? Tex L R 6: 470-2 Je '28 10260

Marshall, John. Selection of federal judges. Kan St B Assn Proc 1929: 101-6 10261

Mitchell, William D. Appointment of federal judges. Am B Assn J 17: 568-74 S '31 10262

Monroe, Henry E. Commonwealth club plan for selection of judges. Calif St B Proc 2: 115-20 '29 10263

Overton, Eugene. Responsibility of bar in selection of judges. Calif St B J 1: 159-63, 176-8 Mr '27 10264

Retirement age of judges. Can B R 5: 283-4 Ap '27; 6: 50 Ja '28 10265

Ridgway, Thos. C. Selection of judicial candidates by the Los Angeles bar association. Calif St B J 1: 166-73 Mr '27 10266

Riquelme, Rafael Fontecilla. De quelles manières pourrait-on obtenir une meilleure spécialisation du juge pénal? R Int de Dr Pén 8: 450-7 '31 10267

San Francisco bar and election of judges. Am B Assn J 13: 356-8 Je '27 10268

Sears, Kenneth C. Appointment of federal district judges. Ill L R 25: 54-75 My '30; Comm L Leag J 35: 338-47 Jl '30 10269

Selecting judges in large cities. Am Jud Soc J 14: 155-8 F '31 10270

Selection of judges. L Notes 31: 41-2 Je '27; 32: 181 Ja '29 10271

Shartel, Burke. Federal judges—appointment, supervision and removal—some possibilities under the constitution. Mich L R 28: 485-529, 723-38, 870-909 Mr-My '30; same title: Am Jud Soc J 15: 21-30, 46-51, 79-89 Je-O '31 10272

Shartel, Burke. Pensions for judges. Mich L R 27: 134-66 D '28 10273

Should there be an age limit for federal judges? N Y L R 6: 185-6 My '28 10274

Simon, Jules. De quelles manières pourrait-on obtenir une meilleure spécialisation du juge pénal. R Int de Dr Pén 8: 443-50, 1029-35 '31 10275

Tilson, John Q. Qualifications of a judge. Conn B J 1: 87-93 Ap '27 10276

Trabue, Edmund F. The tenure of judges. Am L R 62: 321-66 My '28 10277

Trueman, W. H. Judicial appointments. Can B R 8: 1-7 Ja '30 10278

United States. Library of congress. List of references on the election versus appointment of judges. 8p. (typw) Washington, March 2, 1927 10279

Various ways of selecting judges. Am Jud Soc J 15: 38-41, 76-8 Ag, O '31 10280
Massachusetts, North Dakota, Louisiana, California, New York state.

When secrecy is best; Senate confirmation of nominations. World's Wk 59: 22 Jl '30 10281

CONDUCT

Cohen, William N. In the seats of the mighty: recent scandals about judges. Am Jud Soc J 14: 110-13 D '30 10282

Concerning the behaviour of judges. Can B R 6: 713-15 N '28 10283

Hart, Albert Bushnell. Corrupt judges and political bosses. Cur Hist 33: 180-2 N '30 10284

McGoldrick, Joseph. New York city: corruption as usual. New Repub 64: 226-8 O 15 '30 10285

McLellan, H. Gangs, bosses, and judges. R of R 82: 50-5 O '30 10286

R[eady], F[rancis] T. The judiciary and politics. Notre Dame Law 5: 327-9 Mr '30 10287

SALARIES

Bennett, R. B. Judicial salaries and tenure of office. Can B R 5: 272-8 Ap '27 10288

Committee on judges' salaries. Can B R 6: 289-90 Ap '28 10289

Compensation of judges. Calif St B J 1(8): 158, 178 Mr '27 10290

County court and other salaries. L Times 165: 158 F 25 '28 10291

Data on salaries of justices. Ala L J 3: 191-4 Mr '28 10292

Judicial salaries. L Times 165: 157-8 F 25 '28 10293

Judicial salaries. L Notes 34: 218-19 F '31 10294

Judicial salaries and pensions. Sol J 72: 405 Je 23 '28 10295

Judicial salaries in the United States. J Comp Leg s3 9: 267 N '27 10296

Osborn, O. O. Judicial salaries. Kan B Assn Proc 1930: 78-91 10297

Salaries of judges. N C L R 5: 187 F '27; same title: L Times 164: 171 S 3 '27 10298

Salaries of United States judges. Can B R 5: 138-9 F '27 10299

Salary basis for lower court judges. Ky L J 16: 250 Mr '28 10300

PROSECUTOR

Bartning, [Adolf]. Die Stellung des Verteidigers im Strafprozess. 20p. (Druckschriften [des] Deutsche[n] Anwaltverein[s] 18) Leipzig, Moser, 1929 10301

Binkley, W. E. The prosecuting attorney in Ohio—an obsolete officer. Nat Munic R 18: 569-73 S '29 10302

Davidson, Franklin G. The prosecuting attorney's office—do modern conditions create new duties for this office? Ind L J 4: 327-34 F '29 10303

Dills, Leslie H. Permissibility of comment on the defendant's failure to testify in his own behalf in criminal proceedings. Wash L R 3: 161-76 O '28 10304

Failure of accused to testify. Yale L J 37: 955-66 My '28 10305

Falck, C. Eine Neuordnung der Berliner Staatsanwaltschaft? Krimin Monatsh 2: 169-71 Ag '28 10306

Felstead, Sidney T. Sir Richard Muir: a memoir of a public prosecutor; edited by Lady Muir. London, John Lane, 1927 10307
Collection of "popular" descriptions of criminal trials for 30 years.

Friedersdorff, Ernst. Einführung in die staatsanwaltschaftliche Praxis. 252p. Berlin, Liebmann, 1927 10308

Functions of a district attorney. L Notes 33: 143-4 N '29 10309

Iowa abolishes rule prohibiting comment on accused's failure to testify. Ia L R 15: 113-20 D '29 10310

Jackson, Glen W. The prosecutor and the police. Mich Assn Chiefs Police Proc 6: 69-74 '29 10311

Kneer, August. Der Rechtsanwalt. Eine kulturgeschichtliche Studie. ed.2. 130p. Volksvereinsverlag G. m. b. H. 1928 10312

Love, William F. The prosecutor's part in law enforcement. N Y St Assn Magistrates Proc 20: 48-56 '28 10313

Mackay, Howard. New Jersey rule allowing comment upon defendant's silence. Panel 9: 35 My '31 10314

Merten. Strafbare Begünstigung durch Verteidiger. Krimin Monatsh 2: 11-15 Ja '28 10315

Moley, Raymond. The prosecutor and the plea of guilty. Am B Assn Rep 1928: 541-55 10316

Munro, Albert C. Functions of a prosecuting officer. Bi-M L R 11: 1-12 S '27 10317

National prosecuting attorneys' association. Minutes, March 23-24, 1931. 70p. (mim) Chicago, John A. Swanson, State's attorney, Cook county, 1931 10318

Oregon. Annual convention of district attorneys. Ore L R 6: 148-53 F '27 10319

Prosecuting attorneys' association of Michigan. [Constitution, organization, etc]. Mich St B J 8: 119-28 Ja '29 10320

The public prosecutor. L Notes 32: 124-5 O '28 10321

Rowland, Buford. District and prosecuting attorneys. Miss L J 3: 165 N '30 10322

Saint, Percy. Obligation of state attorney to safeguard accused. Lawyer & Banker 24: 85-7 Mr '31 10323

Schmidt, Albert. Die Stellung der Staatsanwaltschaft nach dem Entwurf eines Einführungsgesetzes zum allgemeinen deutschen Strafgesetzbuch. Jurist Rundsch 22: 245-9 N 15 '29 10324

Shall prosecutors conceal facts? Reply to M. Ernst. Nation 124: 628-30 Je 8 '27 10325

Stephan, F. Right of the prosecuting attorney to comment on the failure of the defendant to testify. Id St B Proc 2/3: 41-50 '26-'27 10326

Taylor, Franklin. Allow comment upon defendant's failure to testify. Panel 9:1 Ja '31 10327

What is wrong with the prosecutor? Am Jud Soc J 11: 67-8 O '27 10328

Wunderlich, Georg. Der belgische Justizstreik insbesondere die deutschen staatsanwaltschaften in Belgien (Zugleiche eine Studie zum Rechte der Okkupation). 135p. Berlin, Heymann, 1930 10329

BAR

Dunmore, Walter T. Cleveland's bar influence in judicial elections. Am Jud Soc J 12: 278-9 Ap '29 10330

Ebermayer. Fünf Jahre Oberreichsanwalt. Deut Juristen-Zeit 33: 33-8 '28 10331

Löwenstein, Siegfried. Das Recht des Anwalts im Entwurf eines allgemeinen deutschen Strafgesetzbuches. Jurist Wchnschr 56 (52-3): 3035-7 '27 10332

Kmoch, Hans. Die Kunst der Verteidigung. 116p. Berlin, Gruyter, 1927 10333

Marjoribanks, Edward. For the defence: the life of Sir Edward Marshall Hall. 471p. N.Y. Macmillan, 1929 10334

Ransom, William L. The lawyer today. Am B Assn J 16: 586-91 S '30 10335

ETHICS

[Ambulance chasing]. Panel 6: 5-6 F '28 10336

Carstarphen, F. A. Combat against ambulance chasing. Panel 5:3-5 O '27 10337

Chapman, Francis. Lectures on legal ethics. Temple L Q 3: 99-116, 289-97, 409-19 Mr-Ag '29 10338

Cooper, I. B. Barter and sale of patients and clients. Panel 6: 6-8 O '28 10339

Hart, John W. Ambulance chasing. Comm L J 36: 239-42 My '31 10340

Legal ethics; admission to the bar [bibliography]. Univ S Calif L Lib Bul 2(9): 2 O '31 10341

Nationwide war on "ambulance chasers." Am B Assn J 14: 561-4 N '28 10342

PUBLIC DEFENDER

Aumann, F. R. The public defender in the municipal court of Columbus. J Crim L & Crimin 21: 393-9 N '30 10343

Bachrach, Benj. C. The public defender of Cook county, Ill. Notre Dame Law 6: 322-31 Mr '31 10344

Bradway, John S. "Notes on the defender in criminal cases." Ann Am Acad 136: 19-28 Mr '28 10345

Canadian bar association. Report of special committee appointed to consider the question of the appointment of public defenders in criminal cases. Can B Assn Proc 14: 69-72 '29 10346

Cleveland bar opposes public defender plan. Am B Assn J 17: 141-2 Mr '31 10347

DeForrest, Robert G. The public defender in Connecticut. Conn B J 1: 330-5 O '27; same title: J Crim L & Crimin 18: 522-6 F '28 10348

Fox, Charles Edwin. A voluntary defender for Philadelphia. Pa B Assn Q 7: 11-16 Mr '31 10349

George, Charles E. The public defender. Lawyer & Banker 23: 127-34 My '30 10350

Goldman, Mayer C. Need for a public defender. Nation 128: 131-2 Ja 30 '29 10351

Goldman, Mayer C. Public defender. New Repub 61: 20, 200 N 27 '29, Ja 8 '30 10352

Kane, Francis Fisher. Public and voluntary defenders. Survey 65: 655-6 Mr 15 '31 10353

Miller, Justin. Guilty or not guilty? N Am R 227: 361-9 Mr '29 10354
Popular account of Los Angeles public defender system.

Mishkin, Charles. The public defender. Chic B Assn Rec 14: 98 F '31; same title: J Crim L & Crimin 22: 489-505 N '31 10355

New York (state) bar association. Report of Committee on public defenders, January 17, 1930. [Albany] 1930. 29p. 10356

Orfila, Ernest R. Public defender in the police courts. Ann Am Acad 136: 146-51 Mr '28 10357

Philadelphia. [Voluntary defender committee]. A voluntary defender in Philadelphia for defendants in the criminal courts accused of crime and unable to pay counsel fees. Statement of plan. . . . 7p. [Philadelphia] 1930 10358

Public defender. Just Peace 93: 310-12 My 18 '29; same title: Pris J 8: 12-17 Jl '28 10359

Public defender as an aid to criminal justice for the poor man. Am City 43: 97 Ag '30 10360

Rubin, Samuel. The public defender as aid to criminal justice. J Crim L & Crimin 18: 346-64 N '27; same title: Am L R 62: 385-408 My '28 10361

Shivers, Lyda Gordon. Office of public defender. Miss L J 2: 462-4 My '30 10362

The voluntary defender. Pris J 9: 6-13 Jl '29 10363

What about the public defender? Am City 44: 93 Ap '31 10364

Wigmore, John H. The public defender in our large cities. Ill L R 25: 687-9 F '31 10365

ATTORNEY GENERAL

Burrell, Almon W. The relation of the attorney-general's office to the courts. N Y St Assn Magistrates Proc 22: 71-7 '30 10366

Dejongh, Charles. Le procureur général servais. R de Dr Pén et de Crimin 8: 1002-9 '28 10367

Dodge, Arthur J. Origin and development of the office of the Attorney general. 80p. (H Doc 510) Washington, Govt. Ptg. Off. 1929 10368

ALABAMA

Alabama. Attorney general. Biennial report, 1926/28—1928/30 [Montgomery, 1929-31] 10369

Judicial statistics.

COLORADO

Colorado. Attorney general's office. Biennial reports, 1927/28—1929/30. Denver, 1929-31 10370

FLORIDA

Florida. Attorney general. Report, 1927/28—1929/30. Tallahassee, 1929-31 10371

HAWAII

Hawaii. Attorney general. Annual report, 1927/28- [Honolulu, 1928-] 10372

IDAHO

Idaho. Attorney general. Report, 1927/28—1929/30. [Boise, 1928-30] 10373

Report for 1930 has title Report and selected opinions.

ILLINOIS

Illinois. Attorney general. Report and opinions for the year: 1928-1931. [Springfield, 1928-31] 10374

INDIANA

Indiana. Attorney general. Report *in* Indiana Yearbook 1927: 252-3; 1928: 1103-4; 1929: 1051-3; 1930: 837-8; 1931: 377-95 10375

IOWA

Iowa. Attorney general. Biennial reports 17, 1927/28—18, 1929/30. Des Moines [1929-31] 10376

KANSAS

Kansas. Attorney general. Biennial reports, 1929/30. Topeka, 1931 10377

KENTUCKY

Kentucky. Attorney general. Opinions, 1929/30. Frankfort, 1930 10378

LOUISIANA

Louisiana. Attorney general. Statistical report, 1926/28—1928/30 [Baton Rouge, 1928-30] 10379

Louisiana. Attorney general. Statistical report (charges made, not trials) January 1, 1929- [Baton Rouge, 1929-] 10380

MARYLAND

Maryland. Attorney general. Annual report and official opinions of the attorney general of Maryland, 1929. 350p. [Baltimore, 1930] 10381

MASSACHUSETTS

Benton, Jay R. Massachusetts. Report of Attorney general for year ending November 30, 1926. Mass L Q 12 (1): 1-37 Ja '27 10382

Massachusetts. Attorney general. Report, 1927/28—1930/31 [Boston 1928-32] (Pub doc no12) 10383

MICHIGAN

Michigan. Attorney general. Biennial report, 1926/28—1930/32 [Lansing, 1928-32] 10384

MINNESOTA

Minnesota. Attorney general. Biennial report, 1927/28—1929/30 [St. Paul, 1929-31] 10385

MISSISSIPPI

Mississippi. Attorney general. Biennial report, 1929-31 [Jackson, 1931] 10386

Montana

Montana. Attorney general. Summary of reports of county attorneys, November 30, 1928—November 30, 1930. 1p. [Helena, 1930] **10387**

Nevada

Nevada. Attorney general. Biennial report, 1929/30- [Carson City, 1930] **10388**

New Hampshire

New Hampshire. Attorney general. Report, 1926/28—1930/32. Concord, 1928-32 **10389**

New Mexico

New Mexico. Attorney general. Opinions, 1929/30. [Santa Fe, 1930] **10390**

New York (state)

New York (state). Attorney general. Annual reports, 1928- [Albany, 1929-] **10391**

North Carolina

North Carolina. Attorney general. Biennial reports, 1926/28—1928/30 [Raleigh, 1928-30] **10392**

Warren, O. A. Office of attorney general in North Carolina. N C L R 8: 344-7 Ap '30 **10393**

North Dakota

North Dakota. Attorney general. Report, 1928/30—1930/32 [Bismarck, 1930-32] **10394**

Philippine Islands

Philippine Islands. Attorney general. Annual reports, 1928-31. Manila, 1929-32 **10395**

Porto Rico

Porto Rico. Attorney general. Report, 1926/27—1930/31. San Juan, 1927-31 **10396**

South Carolina

South Carolina. Attorney general. Annual report, 1929-31 [Columbia, 1930-32] **10397**
Fiscal year changed to end September 30 in 1930 report.

Texas

Texas. Attorney general. Biennial report, 1926/28—1928/30 [Austin, 1928-30] **10398**

Utah

Utah. Attorney general. Biennial report, 1926/28—1928/30 [Salt Lake City, 1928-30] **10399**

Vermont

Vermont. Attorney general. Biennial report, 1926/28—1930/32 [Montpelier, 1928-32] **10400**

Virginia

Virginia. Attorney general's office. Report, 1927/28—1930/31. Richmond, 1928-31 **10401**

West Virginia

West Virginia. Attorney general. Biennial report and official opinions 33, 1928/30. [Charleston, 1930] **10402**

Wyoming

Wyoming. Attorney general. Biennial report, 1928/30 [Cheyenne, 1930] **10403**

COURT RECORDS

Fowler, G. Herbert. Rolls from the office of the sheriff of Beds, and Bucks, 1332-34. 89p. (Quarto memoirs v3) Bedfordshire, Eng. Bedfordshire Hist. Rec. Soc. 1930 **10404**

Griswold, Erwin N. and Mitchell, William. Narrative record in federal equity appeals. Harv L R 42: 483-515 F '29 **10405**

Hentig, Hans v. Über die amtliche stenographische Aufnahme wichtiger Kriminalprozesse. Monats f Kriminalpsychol u Strafrechtsref 19: 559-60 S '28 **10406**

Rand, John L. Concerning the record of the Supreme court. Ore L R 7: 44-8 D '27 **10407**

Woodbine, George E. County court rolls and court records. Harv L R 43: 1083-110 My '30 **10408**

REFORM OF JUDICIAL ADMINISTRATION

Banton, Joab H. Would increase supreme court to supervise all courts. Panel 9: 25, 36 My '31 10409

Brown, Hugh Henry. Five points in judicial reform. Am Jud Soc J 12: 124-6 D '28 10410

Dabney, Samuel B. Judicial reconstruction. Tex L R 6: 302-26 Ap '28 10411

Detroit circuit court integrated: . . . improved judicial administration. Am Jud Soc J 14: 174-9 Ap '31 10412

Efficient criminal court machinery: Detroit's unified criminal court, the only one in the country. Am Jud Soc J 14: 180-8 Ap '31 10413

G., M. La nouvelle loi de réorganisation judiciaire questions relatives aux officiers ministériels. Lois Nouvelles 48(16): 305-11 O '29 10414

Gaucher, Maxime. La réforme judiciaire et les officiers ministériels. Lois Nouvelles 46(4): 81-95 F '27 10415

Jenkins, W. S. Ministry of justice in England. N C L R 8: 334-40 Ap '30 10416

Johnson, Kenneth M. The Lord Chancellor as a Minister of justice. Am Jud Soc J 13: 52-9 Ag '29 10417

Judicial reform has complete program: brief survey of development along all lines. Am Jud Soc J 12: 5-10 Je '28 10418

Kavanagh, Marcus A. Why the criminal law fails. Md St B Assn Rep 33: 149-79 '28 10419

Kelly, Amzi B. Suggested reform of the Philippine judiciary. Phil L J 9: 192-200 N '29 10420

Long, Huey P. Reform of the judiciary. La B Assn Proc 28: 79-96 '28 10421

McCall, Fred B. North Carolina judicial conference: recommendations of Conference for changes in judicial system have met with partial success at hand of legislature. Am B Assn J 15: 563-6 S '29 10422

McKee, Joseph V. Court and prison consolidation: a proposal to centralize the magistrates' courts, criminal courts, district attorney's office and city prisons in one building. Panel 9-10 Jl '30 10423

McKnight, A. H. Improving our court records. Tex L R 6: 180-2 F '28 10424

McKnight, A. H. Judicial reform in the forty-first legislature of Texas. Tex L R 7: 103-7 D '28 10425

McKnight, A. H. Program for judicial reform in Texas. Tex L R 7: 258-60 F '29 10426

Meng, C. Y. W. Judicial reform during the period of political tutelage. China W R 50: 310-12 O 26 '29 10427

Meng, C. Y. W. Modern judicial reform in China. China W R 55: 214, 235-7, 256-8, 281-3 Ja 10-24 '31 10428

Moody, Dan. Judicial reform. Tex B Assn Proc 1927: 64-72 10429

Neymark, Edward. La réforme judiciaire en Pologne. R de Dr Pén et de Crimin 9: 297-307 '29 10430

Parker, H. B.; Covington, A. M., and Benton, M. S. A Department of justice for North Carolina. N C L R 8: 348-52 Ap '30 10431

Popineau, Albert. La deuxième réforme judiciaire. Lois Nouvelles 48(17): 352-65 N '29 10432

Price, Lloyd E. Public attitude toward judicial reform. Tex L R 5: 182-4 F '27 10433

Provent, Paul. Quelques réflexions sur la réorganisation judiciaire au point de vue pénal. Etudes Crimin 5: 195-8, 267-72 Je, S '30 10434

Remedy proposed for justices' courts. Am Jud Soc J 11: 30-1 Je '27 10435

Rezneck, S. Statute of 1696: a pioneer measure in the reform of judicial procedure in England. J Mod Hist 2: 5-26 Mr '30 10436

Richaud, G. La réforme judiciaire. Lois Nouvelles 50 pt2(6): 1-8 Mr '31 10437

Schaffhauser, Emile. La suppression des tribunaux et des conséquences (essai di réforme judiciaire). Lois Nouvelles 46(1): 1-8 Ja '27 10438

Spirito, U. Le funzioni del giudice penale secondo il nuovo codice. Nuovi Stud di Dir Econ e Pol 1: 170-82 Mr '28 10439

Texas unifies trial courts; new act provides nine administrative districts for interchange of judges of district courts. Am Jud Soc J 11: 38-9 Ag '27 10440

White, Edward J. Reform of judicial procedure. *In his* Legal traditions and other papers, 50-70. St. Louis, Thomas law bk. co. 1927 10441

JUDICIAL COUNCILS

Arnold, Thurman. Judicial councils. W Va L Q 35: 193-238 Ap '29 10442

Budge, Alfred. The judicial council idea. Id St B Proc 1930: 21-5 10443

Compton, Rowena U. Bibliography on judicial councils. Index to Leg Per & L Lib J 24(1) Ja '31 10444

Experience with judicial councils. Am Jud Soc J 12: 83-91 O '28 10445

Feibelman, Herbert U. The judicial council. Fla St B Assn J 3: 59-60 S '29; same title: Ala L J 5: 52-5 N '29 10446

Give more power to judicial councils. L Notes 32: 224 Mr '29 10447

Givens, Raymond L. The judicial council. Id St B Proc 1929: 41-5 10448

Goodwin, Clarence M. For a national judicial commission. Am Jud Soc J 12: 172-4 Ap '29 10449

Grant, J. A. C. The judicial council movement. Am Pol Sci R 22: 936-46 N '28 10450

Hollzer, Harry A. Shall we lead or be driven? Am Jud Soc J 14: 78-83 O '30 10451

Judicial council and a forward look. Va L Reg ns13: 558-62 Ja '28 10452

Judicial council movement reviewed. Am Jud Soc J 13: 38-44 Ag '29 10453
Ohio, Oregon, Massachusetts, Washington, North Carolina, California, Rhode Island, North Dakota, Connecticut, Kansas, Virginia, Kentucky, Michigan, Texas, Illinois, Pennsylvania.

Judicial councils in theory and practice. Harv L R 42: 817-20 Ap '29 10454

[McClendon, James W.]. Powerful argument for judicial council. Am Jud Soc J 12: 45-53 Ag '28 10455

McClendon, James W. A review of the judicial council movement. Am Jud Soc J 14: 93-7 O '30 10456

Marvel, Josiah. Judicial councils and the rule-making power. Am B Assn J 14: 621 '28 10457

National conference of judicial councils. Am Jud Soc J 15: 110-13 D '31 10458

National conference of judicial councils: second annual meeting results in permanent organization. Am Jud Soc J 14: 77-8 O '30 10459

National union of judicial councils. Am Jud Soc J 13: 102-4 D '29 10460

Patteson, S. S. P. The judicial council. Va B Assn Rep 40: 103-12 '28 10461

Philips, Richard H. The judicial council. Conn B J 1: 124-38 Ap '27 10462

Ruppenthal, J. C. The work done by judicial councils. Am Jud Soc J 14: 17-30 Je; 58-61 Ag; 97-101 O '30; 15: 15-19 Je '31 10463

Shapiro, Joseph G. Judicial councils as a help to justice. Comm L J 36: 281-4 Je '31 10464

Sunderland, Edson R. The judicial council movement. Minn L R 15 sup17-24 D '30 10465

Taft, Henry W. Judicial councils. N Y St B Assn Proc 515-31 '29 10466

Unification of the judiciary: the nation's greatest need (with draft of model act pertaining to organization and structure of courts). Am Jud Soc J 11: 99-116 D '27 10467

California

California. Judicial council. Reports 1, 1927—3, 1929. Sacramento, 1927-29 10468

California judicial council in full swing. Am Jud Soc J 11: 9-12 Je '27 10469

California judicial councils work effectively. Am Jud Soc J 11: 155-7 F '28 10470

Hollzer, Harry A. Cooperation between the judicial council and the organized bar. Calif St B J 2: 98-9 N '27 10471

The judicial council amends the rules. Calif St B J 3: 92-3, 104-7 N '28 10472

The judicial council at work. Calif St B J 1: 138, 154-5 F '27 10473

Judicial council unifies California courts. Am Jud Soc J 12: 18-20 Je '28 10474

Kaufman, Joseph W. The judicial council in California. U S L R 65: 86-9 F '31 10475

McClendon, James W. Judicial council unified California courts. Am Jud Soc J 12: 18-19 Je '28 10476

Two state judicial councils created: California and North Dakota join list of progressive states. Am Jud Soc J 10: 171-2 Ap '27 10477

Waste, William H. One year of the judicial council. Calif St B J 2: 138-9 Ja '28 10478

Connecticut

Connecticut. Judicial council. Report 1, 1928- 10479

Jennings, Newell. Connecticut judicial council. Conn B J 3: 200-8 Jl '29 10480

Wheeler, George W. Address to Judicial council of Connecticut. Conn B J 1: 257-64 O '27 10481

Idaho

Brinck, Dana E. Idaho judicial council. Id L J 1: 111-17 My '31 10482

Idaho. Judicial council. Report, 1930 10483

Illinois

Brown, Gilson. What the local bar associations expect of the judicial advisory council. Ill St B Assn Proc 1931: 325-7 10484

Illinois. Judicial advisory council. Report of the Judicial advisory council of the state of Illinois and the Judicial advisory council of Cook county, January 1931. 42p. [Springfield, 1930] 10485

Indiana

Buschmann, C. Severin. Does Indiana need a judicial council? Ind L J 4: 254-9 Ja '29 10486

Iowa

Aumann, Francis R. The judicial council movement and Iowa. Ia L R 15: 425-33 Je '30 10487

Kansas

Kansas and Connecticut judicial councils. Am Jud Soc J 11: 8 Je '27 10488
Includes Connecticut act text.

Kansas. Judicial council. Annual reports 1, 1927—5, 1931 [Topeka, 1928-32] 10489

Ruppenthal, J. C. Kansas judicial council recommends legislation. Am B Assn J 15: 239-41 Ap '29 10490

Kentucky

A judicial council. Ky L J 15: 333-4 My '27 10491

Kentucky. Judicial council. Biennial report 1, 1929/30 [Frankfort, 1931] 10492

Kentucky. Judicial council. Organization, by-laws and rules of the Judicial council of Kentucky. 12p. January 8, 1929 10493

Ragland, George, jr. Kentucky judicial council. Ky L J 17: 372-81 My '29; same title: U S L R 63: 348-9 Jl '29 **10494**

Louisiana

White, R. F. Need of reorganization of appellate courts and for judicial council. Tulane L R 4: 409-11 Ap '30 **10495**

Massachusetts

Grinnell, Frank W. Report of Massachusetts judicial council. Am B Assn J 14: 20-2 Ja '28 **10496**

Judicial councils in Massachusetts and Connecticut report. Am B Assn J 15: 76-9 Ja '29 **10497**

Massachusetts. Judicial council. Reports, 1927-1931 [Boston 1927-31] **10498**

Third report of Judicial council of Massachusetts. Mass L Q 13: 142 N '27 **10499**

Michigan

Judicial council movement progresses: Michigan and Texas. Am Jud Soc J 13: 7-8 Je '29 **10500**

Michigan. Judicial council. First report, January 1931. 272p. Lansing, 1931 **10501**

Missouri

Atwood, Frank E. and White, Edward J. Work of special committees on judicial council. Mo B J 1: 3-4 Je '30 **10502**

New Jersey

A judicial council for New Jersey. Am Jud Soc J 14: 76 O '30 **10503**

New Jersey. Judicial council. Report to the governor, December 15, 1930. 21p. Supplement, April 15, 1931. 23p. Annual report 3, 1931 **10504**

Presents statistics on "criminal actions in the courts of general jurisprudence in 1931."

New York (state)

Merchants association of New York. Committee on judicial administration. The judicial council: a modern system of judicial administration which is in operation in twenty states; its applicability to New York state. 184p. New York, 1931 **10505**

North Dakota

McCleary, Glenn Avann. One year of the judicial council. Dakota L R 2: 295-302 D '28 **10506**

Ohio

Aumann, Francis R. The Ohio judicial council embarks on a survey of justice. Am Pol Sci R 24: 416-25 My '30 **10507**

Aumann, Francis R. The Ohio judicial council studies judicial administration. Ohio Soc Sci J 2: 44-57 My '30 **10508**

Ohio. Judicial council. First report . . to the General Assembly of Ohio convening January 5, 1931. 54p. Columbus, 1930 **10509**

Oregon

Oregon. Judicial council. Reports, 1928-1930. Ore L R Ap '29; Ap '30; Ap '31 **10510**

Oregon judicial council act not repealed. Am Jud Soc J 11: 1 Je '27 **10511**

Two judicial councils abolished [Oregon and North Carolina]; two new ones created [Utah and North Carolina]. Am Jud Soc J 15: 114 D '31 **10512**

Rhode Island

Rhode Island established judicial council [text of act adopted Apr. 21, 1927]. Am Jud Soc J 11: 117 D '27 **10513**

Texas

Concerning new judicial councils: progress in Texas and Pennsylvania. Am Jud Soc J 13: 77-8 O '28 **10514**

Virginia

Virginia acquires judicial council. Am Jud Soc J 12: 83-93 O '28 **10515**

Virginia. Judicial council. Report and minutes of meeting, April 30, 1929, August 1, 1929, October 29, 1929 **10516**

Washington

Faulknor, Judson F. Judicial council and the rule making power in the state of Washington. Id St B Proc 4: 43-53 '28 **10517**

Washington. Judicial council. Reports 1, 1927—2, 1928 **10518**

Wisconsin

Wisconsin. Board of circuit judges. Proceedings, 1927-30 **10519**

PUNISHMENT

GENERAL

Alexander-Katz, G. Die Bestrafung der Anmassung gewerblicher Schutzrechte. Jurist Rundsch 100-1 '28 10520

Allen, Devere. Would Jesus punish? World Tomorrow 12: 215-17 My '29 10521

Alternative punishments. Sol J 74: 809 D 6 '30 10522

Ammoun, Fouad. Les origines de la peine et le fondement du droit de punir. Gaz des Trib Libano-Syriens 4(1): 1143-50; (2): 33-40 Je, Jl '28 10523

Andrews, William. Bygone punishments. ed. 2. [311p.] London, Allan, 1931 10524

Barnes, Harry Elmer. Story of punishment: a record of man's inhumanity to man. 299p. Boston. Stratford, 1930 10525

Battaglini, Ernesto. In tema di tentativo penale. 12p. Città di Castello, "Leonardo da Vinci," 1930 10526
Extr: La Giustizia Penale.

Beccaria, C. B. Delitos y penas. Phil Pris R 3: 36-8 Ag '27 10527

Beltrán, J. R. Concepto psicoanalítico de la pena. Semana Méd 2: 1574-7 N 19 '31 10528

Bendix, Ludwig. Das Wort "strafbar." Monats f Kriminalpsychol u Strafrechtsref 18: 357-68 Jl '27 10529

Bernhard, Heinrich. Psychiatrie im Strafvollzug. Arbeiterwohlfahrt 4(3): 70-5 F '29; same title: Bl f Gefängniskunde 60: 70-6 '29 10530

Birkigt. Vergleichende Darstellung der für den Vollzug von Freiheitsstrafen geltenden einzelstaatlichen Bestimmungen. Bl f Gefängniskunde 58: 36-50 '27 10531

Blackburn, Burr. Shall social workers punish? Survey 60: 430-1 Jl 15 '28 10532

Brandstätter, H. Zur Frage nach dem Erfolg des heutigen Strafvollzuges. Bl f Gefängniskunde 61: 209-16 '30 10533

Bromberg, R. Du domaine de la peine et de la sanction administrative. R de Dr Pén et de Crimin 7: 387-93 Ap '27 10534

Burnstead, Eben W. Punishment for the armed criminal. Crim Just [Chicago] 9: 7 My '27 10535

Burnstead, Eben W. Punitive vs. the psychiatric treatment of criminals. Cur Hist 27: 399-400 D '27 10536

Campbell, C. Macfie. Crime and punishment: from the point of view of the psychopathologist. J Crim L & Crimin 19: 244-51 Ag '28 10537

Ceillier, A. La médecine au service de la justice. J de Méd de Paris 51: 465 My 21 '31 10538

Chamberlain, Joseph P. Punishment for crime: recidivism. Am B Assn J 14: 17-20, 67-70 Ja '28 10539

Chamberlain, Joseph P. Punishment of criminals. Am B Assn J 13: 12-14 Ja '27 10540

Child, Richard Washburn. The decline of authority. Vt B Assn Proc 1927: 56-64 10541

Cicala, Salvatore. La pena y la medida de seguridad en el congreso de Bruselas. Bibl Nac de Crim y Cienc Afines Bol 2: 396-400 Ap '28 10542

Civic welfare alliance. The second degree loophole in murder trials. 1p. (Bul no525) Boston, 1927 10543

Collin, F. Vergelding om verbetering. Ecrou 12: 403-20 O '31 10544

Contursi Lisi, Gaetano. I negatori del diritto di punire. Scuola Pos 11: 227-32 My '31 10545

Coutts, W. E. Del equivalente biológico en la applicación de las penas. Conf Latino Am de Neurol, Psiquiat y Med Leg Actas 2: 661-6 '29 10546

Craddock, Reginald. The ethics of punishment. Police J [London] 3: 550-9 O '30 10547

Crime and punishment; summary of a report of a special committee of the House. Outl 151: 253 F 13 '29 10548

Crime and punishment: a symposium. Cur Hist 27: 303-46, 399-400 D '27 10549

Crime and punishment in by-gone days. Just Peace 91: 463-4 Je 18 '27 10550

Cumulative punishments. Sol J 72: 651 O 6 '28 10551

Cutinelli, Francesco. Il diritto di punire nella concezione Fascista. 95p. Trani, Paganelli, 1928 10552

Daniel, Gerhard. Gefähliĉhkeit und Strafmass in Science der Positiven Kriminalistenschule. 51p. (Krimin Abh no4) Leipzig, Ernst Wiegandt, 1927 10553

Declining virtues, overdoing leniency. Just Peace 95: 146 Mr 7 '31 10554

Dehnow, F. Die Bestrafung geschlechtlicher Handlungen. Vererb u Geschlechtsleb 1927: 96-110 10555

Deterrent punishment. Just Peace 93: 749-50 N 30 '29 10556

Donnedieu de Vabres. La nouvelle proposition de loi relative à l'exécution des travaux forcés. R Pénitent et de Dr Pén 54: 107-36 Ap '30 10557

Double deaths. Va L R ns13: 756-9 Ap '28 10558

Effect of previous convictions. Just Peace 94: 526-8 Ag 23 '30 10559

Eichler, H. Neuzeitlicher Strafvollzug. Zeitsch f d ges Strafrechtswiss 47: 171-94 '27 10560

An eighteenth-century crime and punishment. Just Peace 93: 778 D 7 '29 10561

Ellger. Der Strafvollzug in Stufen und die Bestimmungen des amtlichen Entwurfs eines Strafvollzugsgesetzes. Bl f Gefängniskunde 58: 152-70 '27 10562

Ewing, Alfred C. The morality of punishment with some suggestions for a general theory of ethics. 233p. London, Kegan Paul, Trench, 1929 10563

Ewing, A[lfred] C. Punishment as a moral agency: an attempt to reconcile the retributive and the utilitarian view. Mind 36: 292-305 Jl '27 10564

Farrar, C. B. Zur Frage der Bestrafung eines Geschlechtsverkehrs "unter Anwendung hinterlistischer Kungstriffe." Monats f Kriminalpsychol u Strafrechtsref 21: 720-3 D '30 10565

Fenichel, Otto. The clinical aspect of the need for punishment. Int J Psycho-Analysis 9: 47-70 Ja '28 10566

Ferri, Enrique. Penas y medidas de seguridad. Bibl Nac de Crim y Cienc Afines Bol 1: 212-19 Ja '27 10567
Communicación al Congreso de la Asociación internacional de derecho penal de Bruselas, 1926.

Florian, Eugenio. Confluenza delle pene e delle misure di sicurezza. Scuola Pos (8-9): pt1a: 337- '30 10568

Florian, Eugenio. Pene e misure di sicurezza. Scuola Pos ns8: 193-9 My '28 10569

Frede. Aus der Praxis der Strafvollzugsreform. Monats f Kriminalpsychol u Strafrechtsref 20: 173-7 '29 10570

Frede, Lothar. Was soll aus dem Entwurf des Strafvollzugsgesetzes werden? Monats f Kriminalpsychol u Strafrechtsref 22: 161-5 Mr '31 10571

Glaser, Stefan. L'idée de la peine. R Pénitent et de Dr Pén 54(9-12): 493- '30; separate: 31p. Paris, Librairie des Juris-Classeurs, 1931 10572

Gleispach, W[enzeslaus]. Was ist Strafe? Einführungsrede. 19p. Wien, Holzhausen, 1929 10573

Gray, A. Herbert. The Christian view of the use of punishment. Howard J 2: 296-8 Je '29 10574

Harvey, A. B. Some problems of punishment. Queen's Q 35: 156-71 O '27 10575

Haun, Friedrich. Strafe für Psychopathen? Imago 267-302 '31; same title: 125p. Inaug. diss. München. Straubing, Druck der C. Attenkoferechen buchund kunstdruckerei, 1928 10576

Heintz, E. Der Strafzweck bei der richterlichen Strafbemessung mit besonderer Berücksichtigung der deutschen Entwürfe. Arch f Rechts u Wirtschaftsphilos 22: 259-88 '29 10577

Herbertz, R. Eine kriminalpsychologische Kernfrage. Individualisierung des Strafvollzuges. Christ u Wiss 5: 256-69 '29 10578

Hippel. [Address on the evolution of punishment]. Bl f Gefängniskunde 58: 1-3 '27 10579

Hirsch, Hans. Strafvollzug an Geisteskranken? 83p. (Würzburger Abh z dt. u ausländ. Prozessrecht 20) Leipzig, Hirschfeld, 1930 10580

Ingram, John L. Crime and its punishment in Virginia. Va St B Assn Rep 1930: 558-69 10581

Jiménez de Asúa, Luis. Pena privativa della libertà; unica o plurima? Giustiz Pen 37 pt1 (2): 177-83 F '31 10582

Junckerstorff, K. Der Strafvollzug im Lichte der geplanten Reform. Deut Spiegel 4: 1978-82 '27 10583

Kalischer, H. Leben und Selbstmord eines Zwangsdiebes; ein psychoanalytischer Beitrag zum Problem "Verbrechen und Strafe." Zeitsch f Psychoanal Päd 3: 363-79 '29 10584

Killick, Victor. Severity of punishment as a deterrent to crime. J Delin 11: 39-45 Mr '27 10585

Kimura, K. Gyokei no ue yori mitaru keibatsu no honshitsu. Hogaku-Shirin 30: 26-48, 61-91 O, N '28 10586

Kirchwey, George W. and Stearns, Albert Warren. Punishment versus treatment of offenders: the swing of the pendulum; the vision of the future. Nat Conf Soc Wk Proc 57: 87-106 '30 10587

Kössler, M. Zur Bestimmung des Strafgesetzentwurfes über das Absehen von Strafe bei besonders leichten Fällen. Öster Anwalts-Zeit 5: 40-2 '28 10588

Krebs, Otto. Strafvollzug. Arbeiterwohlfahrt 3: 33-40 '28 10589

Laird, John. Justifications of punishments. Monist 41: 352-75 Jl '31 10590

Lány, E. Sociální složky zločinosti a sociální zřetele ve výkonu trestu. Sociál R 11: 1-18 F '30 10591

Ledig. Philosophie der Strafzumessung. Deut Richterzeit 19: 428-31 '27 10592

Lehmann, Henri. Die Bestimmungen über Frauen im Entwurf eines Strafvollzugsgesetzes. Soz Praxis 37(12): 273-7 Mr 22 '28 10593

Leibbrand, Werner. Psychoanalyse und Strafreform. Psychiat-Neurol Wchnschr 31(49): 607-11 D 7 '29 10594

Let the punishment fit the crime. Arch Forum 54: 183-4 F '31 10595

Let the treatment fit the criminal. Outl 150: 1119 N 7 '28 10596

Lewin, Kurt. Die Psychologische Situation bei Lohn und Strafe. 67p. Leipzig, S. Hirzel, 1931 10597

Liepmann, M. Der Entwurf eines Strafvollzugsgesetzes. Leipz Zeitsch f Deut Recht 21: 1057-66 '27 10598

Liepmann, Moritz. Artikel "Jugendgefängnisse" und Strafvollzug" in Handwörterbuch der Rechtswissenschaft 3: 379-82; 5: 788-96. Berlin, Gruyter, 1928 10599

Lipkin, I. [The "careth" punishment]. Hamisphat 3: 9-16 '28 10600

Luz, Walter. Das Verbrechen in der Darstellung des Verbrechers. Ein Beitrag zur Naturgeschichte des kriminellen Menschen. 215p. (Monatsschrift für Kriminalpsychologie und Strafrechtsreform, Beiheft 2) Heidelberg, Carl Winter, 1927 10601

Lynd, Robert (Y.Y. pseud). In defence of punishment. New Statesman 32: 690-2 Mr 9 '29 10602

McCardie, H. A. (The problem of punishment). L Times 164: 318-19 O 22 '27 10603

Metzger, Karl. Die Verbrechen und ihre Straffolgen im Basler Recht des Spättern Mittelalters. I: Die Verbrechen und ihre Straffolgen im Allgemeinen. 144p. Basel, Helbing & Lichtenhan, 1931 10604

Mezger, Edmund. Strafzumessung im Entwurf. Zeitsch f d ges Strafrechtswiss 51(6): 855-77 '31 10605

Miller, Alfred J. Punishment or adjustment. N Y St Assn Magistrates Proc 21: 76-81 '29 10606

Morrison, A. C. L. Objects and conceptions of punishment. Just Peace 94: 304-6 My 10 '30 10607

Motta, Cándido. A funcção de punir. 121p. São Paulo [Universidad de São Paulo] 1928 10608

Multiple punishment under the double jeopardy rule. Colum L R 31: 291-7 F '31 10609

Nagler, J. Entwurf eines Strafvollzugsgesetzes. Gerichtssaal 95: 42-80 '27 10610

Nissen, H. Skjaerpet straff for sedelighedsforbrydelser? Nogen bemerkninger om den norske straffelovkomités forslag. Nord Tids f Straf 15: 19-35 Ja '27 10611

Originality in punishment. Sol J 73: 843 D 21 '29 10612

Penal servitude act, 1926. Just Peace 91: 522-3 Jl 9 '27 10613

Petrén, Alfred. Om förhållandet mellan straff och alkoholistvård. Nord Tids f Straf 17: 1-28 Ja '29 10614

Phelps, Harold A. Frequency of crime and punishment. J Crim L & Crimin 19: 165-80 Ag '28 10615

Polak, Leo. Zur sittlichen Rechtfertigung der Strafe. Kantstud 35: 59-76 '30 10616

Powers and limitations of Congress and the states in dealing with the punishment of crime. Cong Dig 6: 219-24 Ag '27 10617

Principles of punishment. Just Peace 93: 735-6 N 23 '29 10618

Proposed sentencing commission. Outl 147: 484 D 21 '27 10619

Provent, P. La répression pénale des actes immoraux commis sur les malades mentaux. Ann de Méd Lég 7: 193-207 Ap '27 10620

Punishing twice for the same offence. Just Peace 91: 653 S 3 '27 10621

Punishment and other penal terminology. J Crim L & Crimin 19: 1, 6-7 My '28 10622

The punishment of the responsible degenerate. L Notes 31: 224 Mr '28 10623

Pyle, W. H. The prevention of crime. Sch & Soc 30: 122-4 '29 10624

Rafacz, Jozef. Kara "chazby" w Sieradzkiem w XV wieku. Kwartalnik Hist 45: 16-24 '31 10625

Randall, Dorothy Jean. Possible penalties for crime [bibliography]. J Crim L & Crimin 20: 456-65 N '29 10626

Ricci, Corrado. La torre della gabbia. Nuov Antol s7 254 (1328): 150-65 Jl 16 '27 10627

Rosenberger, A. Die Zürcher Blutgerichtsordnung des XV Jahrhunderts. Zücher Taschenbuch 1927: 185-95 10628

Ross, W. D. The ethics of punishment. J Philos Stud 4: 205-11 '29 10629

Saldaña, Quintiliano. Peines et mesures de sureté. R Int de Dr Pén 4: 7-24 Ja '27; same title: R de Dr Pén et de Crimin 7: 418-34 '27; English translation by Caloyanni: R Int de Dr Pén 4: 24-42 '27; Spanish translation and extracts, by Jaime Masaveu: R Int de Dr Pén 4: 43-52 '27 10630

Saleilles, R. L'individualisation de la peine. Etude de criminalité sociale. ed. 3 with Gaston Morin. 288p. Paris, Alcan, 1927 10631

Sayre, Francis Bowes. Crime and punishment. Atlan M 141: 735-48 Je '28 10632

Schaefer. Strafvollzug und die Psychopathen. Bl f Gefängniskunde 59: 51-66 '28 10633

Schläger. Zeue Ziele der Strafvollstreckung. Bl f Gefängniskunde 60(3): 417-21 '29 10634

Schultz. Berechtigung und Ziel der Strafe. Leipz Zeitsch f Deut Recht 22: 295-300 '28 10635

Schultz. Besserungszweck der Strafe und freies richterliches Ermessen nach dem Strafgesetzentwurf. Deut Juristen-Zeit 32: 1442-6 '27 10636

Schwarz, F. Strafe, strafen, gestraft werden. Schweiz Zeitsch f ang Psychol 4: 98-102 '28 10637

Smith, Harold. To punish—or to reform. Welf Mag 19: 932-4 S '28 10638

Steinmetz S[ebald] Rudolf. Ethnologische Studien zur ersten Entwicklung der Strafe. ed.2 2v Groningen, P. Noordhoff, 1927 10639

Strube. Erziehungsgedanke und Stufenstrafvollzug. Kritik am Entwurf eines Strafvollzugsgesetzes. Bl f Gefängniskunde 58: 24-30 '27 10640

Stumpf. Abgrenzung des Begriffes der Freiheitsstrafe. Monats f Kriminalpsychol u Strafrechtsref 21: 14-19 Ja '30 10641

Temple, William. The ethics of punishment. Howard J 3: 12-18 S '30 10642

Thayer, W. N. jr. Certain defects in the determinate sentence system. Psychiat Q 460-2 O '28 10643

Tulin, Leon A. The role of penalties in criminal law. Yale L J 37: 1048-69 Je '28 10644

Turner, G. D. Punishment and prisons. Realist 90-102 Je '28 10645

Über die Bestrafung von Zuhältern. Monats f Kriminalpsychol u Strafrechtsref 18: 641-3 N '27 10646

Uneven punishment for crime. L Notes 33: 143 N '29 10647

Vaughn, J. and Diserens, C. M. Relative effects of various intensities of punishment on learning and efficiency. J Comp Psychol 10: 55-66 F '30 10648

Warner, Sam Bass. The theory of punishment. Ore L R 7: 119-26 F '28 10649

Way of science. Collier's 87: 78 F 14 '31 10650

[Weihofen], Henry. The purpose of punishment. Tenn L R 7: 145-76 Ap '29 10651

Weiss, Franz. Das Braunauer Blutbuch. 135p. (Sonderabdruck aus dem Jahrbuch des Deutschen Riesengebirgsvereins) Trautenau, "Heimat," 1927 10652

Why do we punish? Can B R 5: 682-3 N '27 10653

Wilson, Margaret (Mrs. G. D. Turner; Elizabeth West, Elderly Spinster). The crime of punishment. 318p. bibliog 313-14. London, Cape, 1931 10654

Wittels, Fritz. Die Welt ohne Zuchthaus. 286p. (Bücher des Werdenden v5) Stuttgart, Hippokrates-Verl. 1928 10655

Wroblewski, Bronislaw. Pénologie et sociologie des peines. R Int de Dr Pén 5: 116-52 '28 10656

Wunderer, R. Die Strafvorschriften für den Verkehr mit Kraftfahrzeugen. 95p. München, Stahl, 1927 10657

Zum Stufenvollzug. Monats f Kriminalpsychol u Strafrechtsref 18: 438-40 Ag '27 10658

AUSTRIA

Hentig, H. v. Mord und Strafmass in Österreich (1924-1926). Monats f Kriminalpsychol u Strafrechtsref 19: 676-7 N '28 10659

BELGIUM

Belym, Leon. Strafvollzugsreformen in Belgien. Monats f Kriminalpsychol u Strafrechtsref 18: 226-31 My '27; same title: R de Dr Pén et de Crimin 7: 1121-6 '27 10660

Heupgen, Paul. Les peines morales dans l'ancien droit pénal du Hainaut. R de Dr Pén et de Crimin 10: 630-41 '30 10661

CZECHOSLOVAKIA

Solnar, Vladimir. L'individualisation de la peine dans la nouvelle législation tchécoslovaque. Bul de Dr Tchecoslovaque 3(2-3): 43-53 My '31 10662

GERMANY

Behrle, Alfr. Die Stellung der deutschen Sozialisten zum Strafvollzug von 1870 bis zur Gegenwart. 182p. Berlin, Gruyter, 1931 10663

Cube, E. Neue Strömungen im deutschen Strafvollzug. Riga Zeitsch f Rechtswiss 2: 88-92 '28 10664

Exner, Franz. Studien über die Strafzumessungspraxis der deutschen Gerichte. 119p. (Krimin Abh no16) Leipzig, Wiegandt, 1931 10665

Frede, L. Der Stufenstrafvollzug in Thüringen und der Entwurf eines Reichsstrafvollzugsgesetzes. Arch f Rechtspfl in Sachsen, Thür u Anhalt 4: 244-64 '27 10666

Gentz, W. Das Strafvollzugsgesetz. Deut Zeitsch f d ges gerichtl Med 13: 124-39 F 28 '29 10667

Grohmann. Bemerkungen zum Entwurf zu einem Strafvollzugsgesetz. Arch f Krim 81: 220-9 D '27 10668

Hampe, Theodor. Crime and punishment in Germany, as illustrated by the Nuremberg malefactor's books; translated with an introduction based on Wm. Smith's Breef description of Norenberg (1594) by Malcolm Letts. 175p. N. Y. Dutton, 1929 10669

Herschmann, H. Der amtliche Entwurf eines deutschen Strafvollzugsgesetzes vom Jahre 1927. Zeitsch f d ges Neurol u Psychiat 110: 511-18 '27 10670

Hiller, Kurt. Sexualstrafrecht in Deutschland. Neue Generation 25: 92-8, 139-42 Mr, Ap '29 10671

Pfenninger, H. F. Die Reform des deutschen Strafvollzuges. Schweiz Ver f Straf- Gegängniswes u Schutzaufsicht Verh 8: 48-70 '28 10672

Reuter, F. Notzucht an einer Schwachsinnigen. Deut Med Wchnschr 56: 140-1 Ja 24 '30 10673

Schmidt, Eberhard. Kritisches zur Kritik am modernen Strafvollzuge. Monats f Kriminalpsychol u Strafrechtsref 22: 193-207 Ap '31 10674

Seelig, Ernst. Grundsätzliches zur Strafbemessung nach dem Entwurf 1925. Zugleich ein Beitrag zur Lehre von der Strafrechtsschuld und ihrer Beziehung zur Persönlichkeit. Monats f Kriminalpsychol u Strafrechtsref 18: 237-65 My '27 10675

Strube. Der neuzeitliche Strafvollzug im Lichte der Satzungen des Berliner Vereins zur Besserung der Strafgefangenen. Monats f Kriminalpsychol u Strafrechtsref 20: 65-75 F '29 10676

GREAT BRITAIN

Hentig, H. v. Aus dem englischen Strafvollzug. Monats f Kriminalpsychol u Strafrechtsref 18: 697-701 D '27 10677

Kohlmann, Richard. Zur Frage der Abschaffung der Todesstrafe in England. Der Bericht und die Vorschläge der Unterhauskommission. Zeitsch f d ges Strafrechtswiss 51(4): 593-7 '31 10678

INDIA

Kalff, S. De doodstraf in Indie. Vragen d Tijds 53: 335-53 '27 10679

ITALY

Jacobsen, J. H. Forbrydelsens Retsfølger efter det italienske Straffelovsudkast af 1921. Nord Tids f Straf 15: 281-306 O '27 10680

JAPAN

Plischke, R. Aus der Geschichte des japanischen Strafvollzuges. Bl f Gefängniskunde 59: 178-81 '28 10681

SWITZERLAND

Wagner, R. Über schweizerische Strafpraxis in Aufklärungszeitalter. Zeitsch des Bernischen Juristenvereins 63: 193-215, 241-57 '27 10682

UNITED STATES

The latest Baumes laws. Panel 5:2 My '27 10683

Mentor. Strafen und Strafvollzug in Amerika. Gegenwart 57: 241-2 N '28 10684

Wertenbaker, Thomas Jefferson. [Punishments in colonial America]. *In his* The first Americans, 1609-1690, 209-36. N. Y. Macmillan, 1927 10685

THEORIES OF PENAL TREATMENT

Amschl, Alfred. Pönologische Betrachtungen. 80p. (Abh aus dem juristisch-medizinischen Grenzgebiete, hrsg von Herschmann; E. Hopler; F. Neureiter) Wien, Hölder-Pichler-Tempsky, 1927 10686

Barnes, Harry Elmer. Evolution of penology in Pennsylvania; a study in American social history. 414p. Indianapolis, Bobbs, 1927 10687
Revision and elaboration of a historical study of the penal institutions and criminal law of Pennsylvania, undertaken for the Pennsylvania Commission to investigate penal systems in 1918.

Bates, Sanford. A program of protective penology [probation, prison and parole]. Ill Conf Pub Welf Proc 1929: 36-42; same title: Nat Soc Pen Inf N Y Bul 1: 7, 9-10 Je '30; Pris J 10: 16-18 O '30 10688

Bates, Sanford. Scientific penology. Pris J 10: 1-2 Ja '30 10689

Beringer, K. Strafgesetz und Strafvollzugsgesetz in der Sowjetunion. Monats f Kriminalpsychol u Strafrechtsref 20: 137-51 Mr '29 10690

Bromberg, R. Die niederländischen Gesetzbestimmungen gegen anomale Kriminelle. Monats f Kriminalpsychol u Strafrechtsref 18: 480-4 S '27 10691

Bumke. Europäische Strafrechtspflege in amerikanischer Beleuchtung. Jurist Wchnschr 56: 2665-7 '27 10692

Butler, F. O. Care and treatment of the defective delinquent. Am Assn Stud Feeblemind Proc 53: 52-7 '29 10693

Callahan, Jack. Colleges for crooks. Outl 158: 140-1 Je 3 '31 10694

Cass, E. R. The individual treatment of prisoners. Nat Soc Pen Inf N Y Bul 1: 5, 8 Je '30 10695

Chernin, Milton. History of California state administration in the field of penology. 237p. Thesis (M.A.) University of California, 1930 10696

Close, O. H. Method of dealing with delinquents. Int Assn Identif, Calif Div Proc 12: 81-6 '27 10697
Preston school, Calif.: equipment, organization, program, etc.

Commission pénale et pénitentiaire. Ensemble de règles pour le traitement des prisonniers. R Int de Dr Pén 8: 23-33 '31 10698

Criminal treatment of criminals. World Tomorrow 13: 245-6 Je '30 10699

Degen and Bumke. Der Entwurf eines Strafvollzugsgesetzes vom Standpunkte der Entlassenfürsorge aus. Monatsbl d deut Reichsverb f Gerichtshilfe 2: 93-120 '27 10700

Ducas, Georg B. Verbrechen und Strafe. Zeitsch f d ges Strafrechtswiss 49: 31-9 '29 10701

Enström, Henrik. Att straffa eller icke straffa det är frågan. 165p. Stockholm, Norstedt, 1928 10702

Foltin, E. M. Soll Sicherungsverwahrung der Besserung oder Unschädlichmachung dienen? Gerichtsaal 95: 142-56 '27 10703

Frede, Lothar. Die vom Reichsrat am Entwurf des Strafvollzugsgesetzes vorgenommenen Änderungen. Zeitsch f d ges Strafrechtswiss 48: 305-29 '28 10704

Frede, Lothar and Grünhut, Max, eds. Reform des Strafvollzuges. Kritische Beiträge zu dem Amtlichen Entwurf eines Strafvollzugsgesetzes. 264p. Leipzig, Gruyter, 1927 10705

Gillin, John Lewis. Taming the criminal: adventures in penology. 318p. chap. bibliogs. N. Y. Macmillan, 1931 10706
Japanese penal institutions; prison system of Ceylon; criminal tribes of India; Witzil, Swiss correctional colony; Belgium's adventures in redeeming men; penological experiments in England; prison systems in southern United States.

Hacker, Erwin. Gefängnisrecht im praktischen Strafvollzug. Bl f Gefängniskunde 60(3): 402-16 '29 10707

Hart, Hastings H. The new penology. Am Pris Assn Proc 1927: 116-32 10708

Hart, Hastings H. Progress in the treatment of the criminal. On Guard 1: 1, 10-11 N '31 10709

Hart, Hastings H. Recent progress in the treatment of the criminal. Am City 43: 113-14 S '30 10710

von Heydebrand und der Lasa, Ernst. Wissenschaft und Strafrecht. Umschau 33: 241-3 Mr 30 '29 10711

Hoffman. Die Neuregelung des Strafvollzuges vom Standpunkt des Sozialpädagogen. Soz Praxis 36: 1249-53 '27 10712

Imagination and reality. Just Peace 93: 562 S 7 '29 10713

Landauer, K. Das Strafvollzugsgesetz. Zeitsch f Psychoanal Päd 2: 33-8 '28 10714

Lawes, Lewis E. Dealing with criminals. N Am R 225: 321-30 Mr '28; same title: R of R 77: 310-11 Mr '28 10715

Loewenthal, Ernst. Soziale Tendenzen in der Strafrechtspflege. Monats f Kriminalpsychol u Strafrechtsref 21: 333-42 '30 10716

Nelson, Victor Folke. The new penology. Welf Mag 19: 216-23 F '28 10717

By an ex-convict who suggests we need a system which will turn out men who go straight after prison; Mutual welfare league.

Ott. Individualisierender Erziehungsstrafvollzug. Bl f Gefängniskunde 59: 92-5 '28 10718

Penn, W. F. Penology—its progress and future. Nat Conf Juv Agencies Proc 24: 71-9 '27 10719

Pound, Roscoe. The individualization of justice. Nat Prob Assn Proc 1930: 104-12 10720

Saldaña y Garcia Rubio, Quintiliano. Nueva penología (pensas y medidas de seguridad). 377p. bibliog 299-320. Madrid, Hernando, 1931 10721

Sauer, W. Die Strafe als Steigerung von Pflichten. Gerichtssaal 97: 27-43 '28 10722

Schäfer, Leopold and Hauptvogel, Fritz. Deutsche Gesetzentwürfe und Vorschriften über den Strafvollzug. 251p. Mannheim, Bensheimer, 1928 10723

Schlager. Der Entwurf des neuen Strafvollzugsgesetzes. Hanseat Rechts- u Gerichts-Zeitsch 11: 211-20 '28 10724

Thayer, Walter N. jr. New York's contributions to penology. Correction 1: 5-6 D '31 10725

Über den modernen Strafvollzug. Justiz 5: 588-92 Je '30 10726

JUVENILE PUNISHMENT

Bleidt. Der Strafvollzug an Minderjährigen nach dem amtlichen Entwurf eines Strafvollzugsgesetzes. Zeitsch f d ges Strafrechtswiss 48(2-3): 166-71 '28 10727

Foltin, Edgar M. Jugendstrafrecht. Prager Juris Zeitsch 10: 678-94 N 1 '30 10728

Hirsch, Max. Das Strafmündigkeitsalter der weiblichen Jugendlichen in Konstitutionsbiologischer Betrachtung. Zeitsch f d ges Strafrechtswiss 49: 441-51 '29 10729

Hull, Olive I. A resume of a study of state care of juvenile delinquents in Illinois. *In* Illinois. Committee on child welfare legislation, Report 1929: 197-308 10730

Juvenile penology; two styles. Commonweal 14: 172 Je 17 '31 10731

Kleist, Fritz. Jugendstrafvollzug und Heilpädagogik. Zeitsch f Kinderforsch 34(2): 213-17 Mr 20 '28 10732

Laforgue, R. Les mécanismes d'autopunition et leur influence sur le caractère de l'enfant. R Fr de Psychanal 3: 735-49 '29 10733

FORMS OF PUNISHMENT

Barberas y Fernandez, Antonio. Estudio medico-legal del garrote en Cuba. R de Med Leg de Cuba 6: 516-625 '27 10734

Black, Ernest G. Torture under English law. Univ Pa L R 75: 344-8 F '27 10735

Catalán, E. El destierro por hechicería en el Tucumán colonial. R de Crimin, Psiquiat y Med Leg 14: 6-29, 201-30 Ja, Mr '27 10736

Compensation as punishment. Just Peace 91: 888 N 19 '27 10737

Corporal punishment. Just Peace 93: 358, 458-9 Je, Jl 20 '29 10738

Ewald, O. Rechtskräftige Einziehung im Strafverfahren und Veräusserung. Zeitsch f d ges Strafrechtswiss 47: 194-206 '27 10739

Flogging. Comm & Fin Chron 131: 2749-51 N 1 '30 10740

Heald, Francis A. Reimbursement to victim as part of punishment for offender. Bul St Inst [Iowa] 32: 164-70 Jl '30 10741

History of imprisonment. L Times 165: 332-4 Ap 14 '28 10742

Jarotzky, H. v. Die Strafe der Einschliessung im neuen Strafrecht. Monats f Kriminalpsychol u Strafrechtsref 21: 480-93 '30 10743

Jewreinow, N[ikolaj]. Die Körperstrafen in der russischen Rechtspflege und Verwaltung. Beiträge zur Sittengeschichte d. vorrevolutionären Russland. 319p. Leipzig, Schneider, 1931 10744

Merten. Vereitelung der Strafvollstreckung durch Verbüssung der Freiheitsstrafe oder Zahlung der Geldstrafe durch einen anderen als den Verurteilten. Deut Polizei-Arch 6: 377-8 '27 **10745**

Plischke, Rudolf. Die Lebenslänglichen. Zeitsch f d ges Strafrechtswiss 50: 146-66 '30 **10746**

Shumaker, W. A. Life imprisonment for habitual offenders. L Notes 31: 106-8 S '27 **10747**

Thot, Ladislao. Del destierro y la deportación. R de Identif y Cienc Pen 1: 311-20 Mr '28 **10748**

Two years' imprisonment on summary conviction. Sol J 75: 977 Mr 21 '31 **10749**

Wolf, Erik. Witzwil und Regensdorf. Typische Formen des Strafvollzugs in der Schweiz. Monats f Kriminalpsychol u Strafrechtsref 18: 132-44 Mr '27 **10750**

CAPITAL PUNISHMENT

Adler, Felix. The ethical attitude toward the death penalty. Standard 14: 97-104 D '27 **10751**

Against capital punishment. Just Peace 94: 580 S 20 '30 **10752**

Aumonier, S. Does hanging deter the criminal? [3p] London, National committee for the abolition of the death penalty, 1928 **10753**

"B.2.15." Sentence of death. Howard J 2: 200-3 O '28 **10754**

Baldino, Ettore. Contro la pena di morte. 55p. Savona, Azienda ed. Savonese, 1927 **10755**

Baldwin, Celia. Story of Tom Tynan. Nation 124: 501-2 My 4 '27 **10756**

Barth. Der Kampf um die Todesstrafe. Deut Spiegel 4: 1736-40 '27 **10757**

Basler, Xenia. Thomas von Aquin und die Begründung der Todesstrafe aus der absoluten Überlegenheit des Staates über das Individuum. 41p. Diss. München, 1929. Freiburg (Schweiz), Divus Thomas-Verl. 1931 **10758**

Beiler, Irwin R. For the abolition of the death penalty; a needed clause in our social creed. Meth R 11: 219-28 Mr '28 **10759**

B[ierman], N[orman]. Validity of death penalty for robbery. St Louis L R 14: 80-1 D '28 **10760**

Brigance, William N. A life for a life. Indep 119: 200-2 Ag 27 '27 **10761**

Burnstead, Eben W. Case of capital punishment. Spectator [N Y] 119: 29 Ag 25 '27 **10762**

Burnstead, Eben W. Census and the death penalty. Crim Just [Chicago] 9: 11 Ap '27 **10763**

Calder, R. L. and Darrow, Clarence. Is capital punishment right? Forum 80: 321-32, 640, 955 S-D '28 **10764**

Calvert, E[ric] Roy. Against capital punishment. Howard J 2: 236-7 O '28 **10765**

Calvert, E[ric] Roy. The campaign against capital punishment. Howard J 2: 123-4 '27 **10766**

Calvert, Eric Roy. Capital punishment and world peace. World Tomorrow 12: 158-9 Ap '29 **10767**

Calvert, E[ric] Roy. Capital punishment in the twentieth century. ed.4. 210p. London, Putnam, 1930 **10768**

C[alvert], E[ric] R[oy]. Countries which have abolished the death penalty. 12p. London, National council for the abolition of the death penalty, 1928 **10769**

Calvert, Eric Roy. Death penalty enquiry: a review of the evidence before the Select committee on capital punishment, 1931. 116p. London, Victor Gollancz, 1931 **10770**

C[alvert], E[ric] R[oy]. Executions. 15p. London, National committee for the abolition of the death penalty, 1928 **10771**

Capital punishment. L Times 167: 50 Ja 19 '29; same title: Just Peace 93: 726-7 N 16 '29; Can B R 8: 532-3 S '30; Just Peace 94: 811-12 D 27 '30; Sol J 75: 34-5, 127 Ja 17, F 21 '31; L Times 171: 59-60, 83, 88 Ja 17-24 '31 **10772**

Capital punishment; an outline for debate [including bibliographical references]. World R 4: 72-5 O 17 '27 **10773**

Capital punishment is obsolete. Collier's 80: 54 S 10 '27 **10774**

Capital punishment—what the literati think of the death penalty. Pris J 8: 12-16 O '28 **10775**

Carnelutti, Francesco. La pena di morte nel diritto pubblico. Riv di Dir Pub Ammin in Italia 23: 349-56 Jl '31 **10776**

Cetti, Carlo. Della necessità di ristabilire la pena di morte per l'omicidio. 23p. Milano, Bolla, 1928 **10777**

Corsing, Fritz. Soll die Todesstrafe Gesetz bleiben? Ein Beitrage zu ihrer Entwicklungsgeschichte. 32p. Berlin, Metzner, 1930 **10778**

Craddock, Reginald. Capital punishment. 19th Cent 104: 806-17 D '28 **10779**

Craddock, Reginald. Capital punishment, rejoinder. 19th Cent 105: 286 F '29 **10780**

Cressman, Luther Sheeleigh. Goblins and death cells. Survey 59: 741-3 Mr 15 '28 **10781**

Darrow, Clarence. Capital punishment. 4p. N. Y. League to abolish capital punishment, 1929? **10782**

Death penalty. Outl 148: 183 F 1 '28; same title: Nation 127: 472 N 7 '28; Economist 111: 1164 D 20 '30 **10783**

Death penalty in the army. L Times 165: 300 Ap 7 '28 **10784**

Dehnow, Fritz. Das Für und Wider der Todesstrafe. 80p. Stuttgart, Püttmann, 1930 **10785**

Does the death penalty deter? Survey 64: 68 Ap 15 '30 **10786**

Duff, Charles. Handbook on hanging. 129p. Boston, Hale, 1929 **10787**

Duprat, Arturo Horacio. La pena de muerte. 39p. La Plata, 1929 **10788**

Enforce capital punishment. Civic Alliance Bul (530) Mr 1 '27 10789

Engelhardt, K. F. Todesstrafe und Gottesherrschaft. 28p. Kassel, Neuwerk-Verl. 1929 10790

Fackler, Hermann. Strafrechtsreform, insbesondere Abschaffung der Todesstrafe als Forderungen geistgemasser Menschenkunde. Drei 8: 848-55 F '29 10791

Fani, Vincenzo. La pena di morte nel nuovo codice penale. Riv Pen (9-10): 1001- '30 10792

Fischinger, Helmuth. Die Todesstrafe in Württemberg, 1840-1860. Monats f Kriminalpsychol u Strafrechtsref 19: 314-15 My '28 10793

Flesch, Max. Gehirn und Veranlagung des Verbrechers; Beitrage zur Aufhebung der Todesstrafe und zur Einführung eines Verwahrungsgesetzes, im Anschluss an die Besprechung interessanter Rechtsfälle. 151p. Berlin, Gruyter, 1929 10794

Florance, Howard. Shall the state take human life? Am R 75: 613-16 Je '27 10795

Forbes, Howard C. Death penalty from a scientific point of view. Sci M 25: 80-3 Jl '27 10796

Foveau de Courmelles. Guillotine et électrocution. Chron Méd 37: 86-90 Ap '30 10797

Frede. Todesstrafe und Sicherungsverwahrung. Monats f Kriminalpsychol u Strafrechtsref 19: 737-41 D '28 10798

Fuller, Edward. The child and the death penalty. Howard J 2: 111-14 '27 10799

G., F. W. Proposed resolve for a commission to study capital punishment. Mass L Q 16: 97-101 Ja '31 10800

Garofalo, R. La pena capitale. Dizion Pen 1: 18- '27 10801

Green, William McAllen. An ancient debate on capital punishment [in the Roman republic]. Class J 24: 267-75 Ja '29 10802

Greinwald, Sigisbert P. Für und wider die Todesstrafe. 103p. München, Seyfried, 1931 10803

Häberlin, Fritz. Zur der Frage Todesstrafe. Monats f Kriminalpsychol u Strafrechtsref 20: 618-21 O '29 10804

Hafter, Ernst. Todesstrafe. Europäische R 5: 201-7 Je '29 10805

Hall, Ibby. Guilt; victim of a grave judicial error. Outl 149: 183 My 30 '28 10806
Case in Berlin of unjust capital punishment of innocent victim.

Hall, John William. Capital punishment on trial. 35p. London, Howard league for penal reform, 1927 10807

Hall, W. G. Carlton. Capital punishment. Eng R 47: 566-71 N '28 10808

Hanna, Francis D. Penitentiary murderers are to hang. Crim Just [Chic] 9: 11-12 Jl '27 10809

Has capital punishment failed? Northwest Police J 5: 6-7 O '28 10810

Haustein, Hans. Strafrecht und Sodomie vor 2 Jahrhunderten. Zeitsch f Sexualwissensch 17: 98-105 Je 15 '30 10811

Hays, George W. The necessity for capital punishment. Scribner's 81: 577-82 Je '27 10812

Hedrick, Edwin. Hang the dog. Atlan M 140: 338-48 S '27 10813

Hentig, Hans v. Um die todesstrafe. Monats f Kriminalpsychol u Strafrechtsref 18: 322-4 '27 10814

H[erzog], A[lfred] W. Again capital punishment and the third degree. Med-Leg J 48: 4-5 Ja '31 10815

Herzog, Alfred W. On capital punishment, the right and wrong test. Med-Leg J 44: 129-35 S '27 10816

Hesse, M. Zur Kampf um die Todesstrafe. Natur & Gesell 14: 12-14 Ja '27 10817

Heymann, Robert. Fort mit der Todesstrafe. 84p. Berlin, Uhlmann, 1928 10818

Hollander, Bernard. Capital punishment. Engl R 47: 79-86 Jl '28 10819

Holters, E. Anleitung für die Bearbeitung von Kapitalverbrechen. Berlin, Weller, 1930 10820

Housman, Laurence. A substitute for capital punishment. Howard J 2: 193-6 O '28 10821

If not death, what? Outl 148: 223 F 8 '28 10822

Infliction of capital punishment. L Notes 31: 64-5 Jl '27 10823

Innerst, J. S. Capital punishment and lynching. Chr Cent 48: 381 Mr 18 '31 10824

Kansas. Governor. Message of Harry H. Woodring, Governor of the state of Kansas to the legislature of 1931 on capital punishment. [3]p. N. Y. American league to abolish capital punishment, inc. [1931] 10825

Kavanagh, Marcus A. and Lawes, Lewis A. Does the death penalty curb crime? Cur Hist 33: 356-66 D '30 10826

Kenworthy, J. M. Commonsense versus capital punishment. Criminologist [London] 1: 6-8 My 15 '27 10827

Kinskofer, Oskar. Der Tod des Schuldigen im Strafrecht. 80p. bibliog 79-80. Diss. Erlangen, 1930. Kulmbach, G. Schuhmann, 1930 10828

Kleerekooper, A. B. Weg met de doodstraf. 16p. Amsterdam, Ontwikkeling, 1927 10829

Klein, Felix Joseph. Tod als Strafe? Einige Gedanken über der Todesstrafe. 8p. Bonn, Selbstverl. 1929 10830

Kneer, A. Un die Todesstrafe. Soz Kultur 48: 9-12, 231-7 S, D '28 10831

Kornfeld, Paul. Die Todesstrafe. Tagebuch 12(21): 815-18 My 23 '31 10832

Lawes, Lewis E. A brief history of capital punishment. Is the death penalty necessary? The death penalty at Sing Sing; three articles. 15p. N.Y. American league to abolish capital punishment, 1927 10833

Lawes, Lewis E. Death penalty at Sing Sing; what the figures show. Survey 59: 69-70 O 15 '27 10834

Lawes, Lewis E. Who's afraid of the chair? Collier's 86: 10-11 Jl 12 '30; excerpts: R of R 82: 81-2 S '30 10835

Lawes, Lewis E. Why capital punishment? World's Wk 56: 316-22 Jl '28 10836

League to abolish capital punishment. Resolved, that capital punishment be abolished: debate, January 14, 1928. For the affirmative, Mr. Samuel Untermyer; for the negative, Senator Love. 30p. N.Y. 1928 10837

McIntosh, Andrew C. Manner of inflicting death penalty as cruel or unusual punishment. L Notes 34: 104-7 S '30 10838

Manzini, Vincenzo. La pena di morte nel nuovo diritto penale italiano. 12p. Padova, Antoniana, 1930 10839

Markall, William. While there is life. London, Gollancz, 1930? 10840

Marshall, J. E. Capital punishment. Q R 253: 74-84 Jl '29 10841

Martin, Stuart. Capital punishment. 288p. London, Hutchinson, 1930 10842

Melzer. Todesstrafe und Panzerkreuzer. Deutschl Erneuerung 13: 39-47 Ja '29 10843

Moley, Raymond. The convicts we kill. Survey 62: 610 S 15 '29 10844

Moore, Samuel H. Is capital punishment wrong? Welf Mag 19: 965-9 S '28 10845

Mungenast, Ernst Maritz. Der Mörder und der Staat. Die Todesstrafe im Urteil hervorragender Zeitgenossen. 94p. Stuttgart, Hädecke, 1928 10846

Parnisetti, Carlo. La pena capitale in Alessandria e la confraternità di S. Giovanni Decollato. Arch di Antrop Crim 47: 340-64 My '27 10847

Petersen, Werner. Die Abschaffung der Todesstrafe im Lichte der modernen Charakterforschung und Erblichkeitslehre. Deutschl Erneuerung 14(3): 150-4 Mr '30 10848

Phillips, George W. and Older, Fremont. Death penalty? Sunset 60: 18-21 Ja '28 10849

Polak, L. Vergeldende gerechtheid verbiedt de doodstraf. Mensch en Maatschappij 4: 353-70 Jl '28 10850

The question of capital punishment: powers and limitations of congress and the states; present federal and state laws dealing with capital crime; should capital punishment be retained? Cong Dig 6: 219-44 Ag '27 10851

Raven, Alice. Memoranda prepared for the select committee on capital punishment. Sociol R 23: 80-4 Jl '31 10852

Rosenfeld, Kurt. Fort mit der Todesstrafe. 31p. Berlin, Laub, 1927 10853

Ruesch, Arnold. Todesstrafe und Unfreiheit des Willens. 59p. Darmstadt, Otto Reichl Verl. 1927 10854

Sachs, Hanns. Does capital punishment exist? 20p. London, Pool, 1930 10855

Saved by five hours. Survey 65: 197 N 15 '30 10856

Schweigger, Maximilian. Abschaffung der Todesstrafe. Deutschl Erneuerung 13: 203-6 Ap '29 10857

Sellin, Thorsten. Todesstrafe in den Vereinigten Staaten. Monats f Kriminalpsychol u Strafrechtsref 21: 102-5 F '30 10858

Sir Samuel Romilly and the abolition of capital punishment. Soc Serv R 5: 276-96 Je '31 10859

Sohnrey, Helmut. Abschaffung der Todesstrafe? Stimmen aus der deutschen Volke. 88p. Berlin, Dt. Landbuchh. 1929 10860

Staub, H. Zum Kampf um die Todesstrafe. Psychoanal Beweg 3: 448-56 '31 10861

Stern, Samuel. Contre la peine de mort. Etudes Crimin 3(4-5): 144-9 S '26 10862

Suggested readings on capital punishment. Standard 14: 123 D '27 10863

Survival of barbarism. Nation 125: 240 S 14 '27 10864

Survival of savagery. Nation 124: 307 Mr 23 '27 10865

Tejera y Garcia, Diego Vicente. El hondo problema de la pena de muerte. 56p. Habana, "El Siglo XX," 1927 10866

Terrett, Courtenay. Warden Lawes and capital punishment. Outl 148: 250-1 F 15 '28 10867

To err is human. Nation 125: 620 D 7 '27 10868

Die Todesstrafe als Mordreiz. Monats f Kriminalpsychol u Strafrechtsref 19: 690-1 N '28 10869

United States. Library of Congress. Division of bibliography. Capital punishment: a bibliographical list. 23p. (mim) Washington, February 16, 1931 10870

del Val, Merry. Capital punishment; reply. 19th Cent 105: 143 Ja '29 10871

Vedrani, A. Documenti per la storia dell'opera di Kraepelin—l'abolizione della misura di pena. Gior di Psichiat Clin e Tecn Manic 55: 121-34 '27 10872

Viñas, A. Fundamentos del proyecto restableciendo la pena de muerte. R de Crimin, Psiquiat y Med Leg 14: 620-31 S '27 10873

Wells, Gabriel. On capital punishment. 11p. London, Heinemann, 1930 10874

Whitman, John H. A. Capital punishment and irresistible human impulses as defense. Notre Dame Law 5: 188-98 Ja '30 10875

Zisch, P. J. Lethal gas as a means of asphyxiating capital offenders. Med-Leg J 48: 25-7 Ja '31 10876

Zurkuhlen, H. Geschichtliches und Statistisches zum problem der Todesstrafe. Jahrb f Nationalökon u Statist s3 76(2): 255-68 Ag '29 10877

Zurkuhlen, H. Todesstrafe und Kriminalstatistik. Zeitsch f d ges Strafrechtswiss 50: 652-6 '30 10878

ALGERIA

Lemmonier, Henri. La "Dia" ou prix du sang en Algérie (à propos d'une exécution capitale). R Int de Dr Pén 4: 110-24 Ja '27 10879

Austria

Höpler, E. Mordkriminalität und Todesstrafe in Österreich in den Jahren 1874 bis 1927. Monats f Kriminalpsychol u Strafrechtsref 20: 449-511 Ag '29 **10880**

China

Abolition of execution by decapitation [in China]. China W R 48: 443 My 11 '29 **10881**

Denmark

Trommer, Harry. Todesurteile in Danemark in zwei Jahrzehnten. Monats f Kriminalpsychol u Strafrechtsref 20: 755-6 D '29 **10882**

Germany

Bloch. Die Todesstrafe im künftigen Strafrecht. Monats f Kriminalpsychol u Strafrechtsref 18: 45-7 Ja '27 **10883**

Exner, Franz. Mord und Todesstrafe in Sachsen 1855-1927. Monats f Kriminalpsychol u Strafrechtsref 20: 1-17 Ja '29 **10884**

Hentig, v. Hinrichtungen in Alt-Nürnberg. Monats f Kriminalpsychol u Strafrechtsref 19: 492-4 Ag '28 **10885**

Hentig, v. Die Todesstrafe in Sachsen. Monats f Kriminalpsychol u Strafrechtsref 20: 234-7 '29 **10886**

Land. Mord und Todesstrafe in Hamburg. Monats f Kriminalpsychol u Strafrechtsref 21: 129-48 Mr '30 **10887**

Great Britain

Capital punishment: memorandum of evidence submitted to the Select committee of the House of Commons on capital punishment, on behalf of the Executive committee of the Howard league for penal reform, July 1930. Howard J 3: 92-8 '31 **10888**

England considers capital punishment. R of R 83: 60 F '31 **10889**

Great Britain. House of Commons. Report from the Select committee on capital punishment: together with the proceedings of the committee, and the minutes of evidence, taken before the Select committee on capital punishment in 1929-1930. 681p. London, H. M. Stationery Off. 1931 **10890**

Hargrove, A. L. Britain and the death penalty. Howard J 3: 27-32 '31 **10891**

Kornitzer, Margaret. The problem of the death penalty in England today. Spectator [London] 144: 1001-2 Je 21 '30 **10892**

Reekie, I. H. Report on the Select committee on capital punishment. Howard J 3: 67-73 S '30 **10893**

Sarfatti, M. Verso l'abolizione della pena di morte in Inghilterra. Scuola Pos 39: 117-24 '31 **10894**

Italy

Mussolini abolished trial by jury in Italy. Capital punishment restored and prisoners must henceforth pay own expenses. Labor 11: 1 N 2 '29 **10895**

Meli, Vincenzo. Il ristabilimento della pena capitale in Italie. 154p. Roma, Mantegazza, 1928 **10896**

Rocco, Alfredo. La pena di morte del nuovo codice penale italiano. Gerarchia 10(11): 881-91 N '30 **10897**

Ruiz-Funes, M. La pena de muerte en Italia. R de Crimin, Psiquiat y Med Leg 14: 441-7, 563-87 Jl, S '27 **10898**

Turdera, Horacio. La pena de muerte en Italia. Bibl Nac de Crim y Cienc Afines Bol 1: 219-23 Ja '27 **10899**

Japan

The death penalty; question of abolition [in Japan]. Jap W Chron 681 Je 13 '29 **10900**

Netherlands

Van der Aa, J. Simon. Zur Frage der Todesstrafe. Monats f Kriminalpsychol u Strafrechtsref 20: 385-9 Jl '29 **10901**

Russia

Verax. Le code pénal soviétique: l'article de la mort. J Débats 38 pt1: 587-9 Ap 10 '30 **10902**

Spain

Ruiz-Funes, Mariano. Kurze Geschichte der Todesstrafe in Spanien. Monats f Kriminalpsychol u Strafrechtsref 20: 577-91, 641-54 '29; same title: 15, 14p. Heidelberg, Carl Winters, 1929 **10903**

Switzerland

Farbstein, D. [The abolition of the death penalty in Switzerland.] Hamishpat 3: 30-3 '28 **10904**

United States

IOWA

Saathoff, J. A. Capital punishment in Iowa. 97p. Thesis (M.A.) University of Iowa, 1927 **10905**

MASSACHUSETTS

Massachusetts council for the abolition of the death penalty. Abolish the death penalty. 31p. 1928 **10906**

MICHIGAN

Moving backward; Michigan senate votes to restore death penalty. Nation 128: 524 My 1 '29 **10907**

NEVADA

Nevada's gas house [lethal gas chamber of the prison at Carson City]. Outl 155: 255 Je 18 '30 **10908**

NEW YORK

New York kills again. Nation [NY] 126: 85 Ja 25 '28 **10909**

NORTH CAROLINA

Cleghorn, Sarah N. North Carolina has its doubts; review of capital punishment in North Carolina. World Tomorrow 12: 522-3 D '29 **10910**

North Carolina. State board of charities and public welfare. Capital punishment in North Carolina. 173p. (Spec Bul no10) Raleigh, 1929 **10911**

Statistics on convictions; prison population; county penal system; executive clemency; lynching and mob violence.

WISCONSIN

Holmes, F. L. Why Wisconsin does not hang men. Dearborn Indep 27: 1-2 My 28 '27 **10912**

EXECUTIONERS OF PUNISHMENT

Angstmann, Else. Der Henker in der Volksmeinung. 113p. Bonn, Fritz Klopp, 1928 **10913**

Bleackley, Horace William. Hangmen of England; how they hanged and whom they hanged; the life story of Jack Ketch through two centuries. 272p. London, Chapman, 1929 **10914**

Farga, Franz. Lord of the guillotine. Living Age 334: 532-5 Mr 15 '28 **10915**

Fessler. Der Scharfrichter in der Strafrechtspflege des deutschen Mittelalters. Deut Polizei-Arch 6: 4-6 Ja '27 **10916**

Gosselin, Louis Léon Théodore. The guillotine and its servants, by G. Lenôtre (pseud); translated by Mrs. Rodolph Stawell. 282p. London, Hutchinson [1929] **10917**

Keller, Albrecht, ed. A hangman's diary: being the journal of Master Franz Schmidt, public executioner of Nuremberg, 1573-1617; translated by C. Calvert and A. W. Gruner. 250p. London, Allan, 1928 **10918**

PROBATION

GENERAL

Anderson, Harry B. A federal judge's view of probation. Nat Prob Assn Proc 1928: 379-82 10919

Beley, J. Le système d'épreuve. 210p. Paris, Ed. et Publications Contemporaines, 1930 10920

Cassell, Rebecca. Rural probation. Nat Prob Assn Proc 25: 117-19 '31 10921

Chute, Charles L. Coordinating probation with institutional training. Nat Prob Assn Proc 23: 76-84 '29 10922

Chute, Charles L. The development and needs of probation service. J Crim L & Crimin 18: 514-21 F '28; same title: Nat Prob Assn Proc 22: 14-23 '28 10923

Chute, Charles L. The extension of probation in criminal courts. Ann Am Acad 136: 136-41 Mr '28 10924

Chute, Charles L. The need for state supervision in the development and coordination of probation and parole service. Nat Conf Juv Agencies Proc 27: 192-200 '30 10925

Chute, C[harles] L. Probation and the institutions. Probation 8: 3,5,6,8 N '29 10926

Chute, Charles L. Probation service today —progress or retrogression. Nat Prob Assn Proc 24: 89-93 '30 10927

Chute, Charles L. Progress and needs in probation work. Ohio Welf Bul 8: 32-6 Ja '31 10928

Chute, Charles D. Some essentials in probation work. N Y St Conf Prob Offic Proc 20: 170-6 '27 10929

Chute, Charles L. The state and probation. Minn St Bd Con Q 30: 4-9 N 25 '30; same title: Pris J 11: 5-7 Ap '31 10930

Chute, Charles L. State participation in probation work. Nat Prob Assn Proc 25: 169-79 '31 10931

Chute, Charles L. What should our probation standards be? J Soc Hyg 13: 86-92 F '27 10932

Cochran, Herbert G. Probation, its uses and potentialities. Nat Prob Assn Proc 23: 12-17 '29 10933

Cooley, Edwin J. Guideposts of probation. N Y St Conf Prob Offic Proc 20: 137-46 '27; same title: Family 8: 323-9 Ja '28 10934

Cooley, Edwin J. Probation and delinquency: the study and treatment of the individual delinquent. 530p. N.Y. 477 Madison ave. The Author, 1927 10935

Cooley, Edwin J. Probation and the delinquent child. 10p. National conference of juvenile agencies, 1928 10936

Cooley, Edwin J. Probation comes of age. N Y St Conf Prob Offic Proc 21: 179-91 '28 10937

Cooley, Edwin J. Probation: its status and prospects. Nat Conf Soc Wk Proc 21: 60-72 '27; same title: Hosp Soc Serv 16: 198-213 S '27 10938

Couchepin, A. Co-rapport . . . sur la droit d'établissement et patronage. Schweiz Ver f Straf- Gefängniswes u Schutzaufsicht Verh ns8: 105-17 '28 10939

Developments of a year in probation; reports from state secretaries and state representatives. Nat Prob Assn Proc 25: 144-68 '31 10940

Dutcher, Frederick L. Probation on trial. N Y St Conf Proc Offic Proc 21: 204-8 '28 10941

Emery, E. Van Norman. Mental diagnosis and probation. Nat Prob Assn Proc 23: 184-94 '29; same title: Ann Am Acad 149: 184-9 My '30 10942

Fifty years of probation. Survey 61: 220 N 15 '28 10943

Garvin, Edwin L. The growth of probation. Nat Prob Assn Proc 24: 209-13 '30 10944

Gerlach, Edgar M. The principles common to probation and institutional work. Nat Prob Assn Proc 25:235-40 '31 10945

Gillin, John L. Indeterminate probation and parole. J Juv Res 15: 1-6 '31 10946

Glueck, Sheldon. The status of probation. Ment Hyg 15: 290-8 Ap '31 10947

Goodell, C. J. The meaning of probation. San Francisco Bus 18: 17-18 Je 10 '29 10948

Halpern, Irving W. Practical problems in administering probation. Nat Prob Assn Proc 25: 105-16 '31 10949

Hiller, Francis H. The need for statewide probation. Minn St Conf & Inst Soc Wk Proc 38: 59-65 '30 10950

Hiller, Francis H. Summary of new legislation concerning probation and juvenile courts, 1930-1931. Nat Prob Assn Proc 25: 249-63 '31 10951

Hoey, Jane M. The place of probation service in the social work of a community. N Y St Conf Prob Offic Proc 21: 194-8 '28 10952

Hoffman, Charles W. The importance of probation. Nat Prob Assn Proc 22: 11-13 '28 10953

Hoffman, Charles W. Trends of probation. Am Pris Assn Proc 60: 286-98 '30; same title: Nat Prob Assn Proc 24: 76-88 '30 10954

Kawin, Irene. The relationships of probation to detention and the institution. Nat Prob Assn Proc 25: 221-30 '31 10955

Keck, Jay E. Is probation kin to social work? Ia St Conf Soc Wk Proc 30: 59-60 '29 10956

Address before Iowa probation association.

Kerbey, Wm. J.; Moran, Frederick A; Collins, Cornelius F.; Moley, Raymond, and McHugh, Rose J. Probation evaluated. Cath Char R 11: 159-67 My '27 10957

Lisman, F. J. Combinatie van voorwaardelijke en onvoorwaardelijke gevangenisstraf. Maandbl v Ber en Reclasseer 7: 107-9 Ap '28 10958

Lowrey, Sarah. Effective probation methods for the rural community. Minn St Conf & Inst Soc Wk Proc 36:169-75 '28 10959

Address before Minnesota state probation association.

Lowrey, Sarah. Rural probation. Nat Prob Assn Proc 25: 120-1 '31 10960

Lutz, A. Das Patronatssystem und die Verwahrungsfrage. Schweiz Ver f Straf-Gefängniswes u Schutzaufsicht Verh 8: 90-3 '28 10961

Michaelis. Zur Augsburger Tagung. Besprechung einiger Probleme. Bl f Gefängniskunde 59: 74-91 '28 10962

Miller, Justin. The law and probation. Am Pris Assn Proc 60: 298-308 '30; same title: Nat Prob Assn Proc 25: 74-90 '31 10963

Morrison, A. C. L. Probation—its growth and development. Just Peace 94: 397, 412-14 Je 21, 25 '30 10964

Murphy, Frank. Probation at the crossroads. Nat Prob Assn Proc 22: 24-36 '28 10965

National probation association. Books specially recommended: [bibliography on probation, juvenile court, delinquency, sociology and criminology, and psychology and psychiatry]. 2p. (typw) New York, 1929 10966

National probation association. The newer justice and the courts; annual report and proceedings, v21 1927. 307p. New York, 1928 10967

National probation association. The probation service of the United States courts. 15p. New York, 1928 10968

National probation association. Proving probation; proceedings, 1928. 413p. New York, 1929 10969

National probation association. Shall John have his ears clipped? 4p. New York, 1929? 10970

National probation association. The yearbook, 1930: probation, juvenile courts, domestic relations courts, crime prevention, etc. 358p. New York, 1930 10971

Our prison population. Lancet 214: 195-6 Ja 28 '28 10972

Paddon, Mary E. What probation needs. N Y St Conf Prob Offic Proc 20: 125-37 '27 10973

Palmer, Mrs. G. T. Probation—first line of defense. Ill Med J 58: 187-93 S '30 10974

Parsons, Herbert C[ollins]. Fifty years of probation. Nat Prob Assn Proc 22: 52-4 '28 10975

Parsons, Herbert Collins. The place of probation in public corrections. 10p. Boston, Massachusetts civic league, 1927 10976

Parsons, Herbert C. Probation: its aims, methods and limitations. Boston, Massachusetts civic league, 1929 10977

Patronato dei minorenni condannati condizionalmente. 27p. Roma, Mantellate, 1927 10978

Plischke, Rudolf. Historische Rückblicke ins 18. und 19. Jahrhundert zum Stufenstrafvollzug. Monats f Kriminalpsychol u Strafrechtsref 19: 417-29 Jl '28 10979

Plover, John. Probation. *In* Hiscock, Ira V. and others. A survey of health and welfare activities in Santa Barbara county, California, 102-10. American public health association, Committee on administrative practice, 1930 10980

Probation, monthly bulletin, 1, 1922- National probation association 10981

Probation and appeals. Sol J 75: 145 F 28 '31 10982

Probation in prison? Just Peace 95: 114 F 21 '31 10983

Probation plus whipping. Just Peace 92: 204 Mr 24 '28 10984

Ramsay, James P. Cooperation between the state and probation. Nat Prob Assn Proc 24: 230-3 '30 10985

Residence enforced on probation. Sol J 71: 261 Ap 2 '27 10986

Russell Sage foundation. Library. Probation: juvenile and adult. (Bul no89) New York, June 1928 10987

Saving the cost of gallows and prisons. Lit Dig 106: 18-19 Jl 26 '30 10988

Saylor, Anna L. The state and probation. Nat Prob Assn Proc 23: 43-9 '29; same title: 9p. N.Y. National probation association, 1930 10989

Scanlan, Michael J. Probation in the social work scheme. Nat Prob Assn Proc 24: 234-8 '30 10990

Sherman, Alfred L. Probation and parole. Vt B Assn Proc 1928: 143-8 10991

Shuford, Forrest H. Again, probation. Welf Mag 18: 1467-70 N '27 10992

Shumaker, W. A. Federal probation act. L Notes 31: 125-8 O '27 10993

Simon, T. Le service médical du "Service social de l'enfance en danger moral." Hyg Ment 23: 61-5 Mr '28 10994

Smyth, George W. Organizing a county probation department. Nat Prob Assn Proc 25: 91-104 '31 10995

Vial, Solon C. Protecting the family thru probation. Ind Bul Char & Correc (177): 535-7 D '29 10996

Volz, Edward P. Probation in the justices' court. N Y St Assn Magistrates Proc 20: 10-16 '28 10997

Woodrow, C. S. A plea for probation. Chief Constables' Assn Can Proc 25: 110-16 '29 10998

EUROPE

Trought, Thomas William. Probation in Europe. 255p. Oxford, Blackwell, 1927 **10999**

GERMANY

Haeckel, Heinrich. Jugendgerichtshilfe. 104p. (Schriftenr. d. Vereinigung f Jugendgerichten Jugendgerichtshilfen 10) Berlin, A. Herbig, 1927 **11000**

INDIA

Reclasseering en voorwaardelijke veroordeling in Indië. Maandbl v Ber en Reclasseer 7: 197-204 Jl '28 **11001**

MEXICO

Almaraz, José. Libertad preparatoria y condena condicional. R Int de Dr Pén 7: 383-6 French transl (p387-9) '30 **11002**

NEW ZEALAND

New Zealand. Chief probation officer. Offenders probation under Offenders probation act, 1920, and Crimes amendment act, 1910 (report on operation of) for the year 1930-31. Wellington, 1931 **11003**

SCOTLAND

Turnbull, Christine. Probation in Scotland. Howard J 3: 87-9 '31 **11004**

UNITED STATES

Bates, Sanford. Probation in the United States courts. Nat Prob Assn Proc 25: 69-73 '31 **11005**

Bates, Sanford. The status of federal probation. Nat Prob Assn Proc 24: 137-9 '30 **11006**

Chute, Charles L. The development of probation in federal courts. Nat Prob Assn Proc 23: 217-24 '29 **11007**

Cornil, P. La mise en probation aux Etats-Unis. R de Dr Pén et de Crimin 8: 724-6 Jl '28 **11008**

The federal probation system. Am L R 61: 246-62 Mr '27 **11009**

Is the probation plank in Mr. Hoover's prison relief plan practical? Pris J 9: 10-11 O '29 **11010**

McClintic, George W. Probation. Am B Assn J 17: 589-93 S '31 **11011**

McSweeney, Richard B. Federal probation. Nat Prob Assn Proc 24: 140-6 '30 **11012**

Moore, Joel R. The future of probation in the United States. Am Pris Assn Proc 60: 66-75 '30 **11013**

Recent developments in probation: roll call by states. Nat Prob Assn Proc 24: 301-14 '30 **11014**

United States. Congress. House. Committee on judiciary. Amend probation law, report to accompany H.R. 11801, February 22, 1929. 12p. Washington, 1929 (70th Cong. 2d sess. H Rep 2666) **11015**

Webster, Bethuel Matthew. The federal probation system. Am L R 61: 246-62 Mr '27 **11016**

ARKANSAS

Rector, Leonora. State aid and supervision of probation—reports from states: Arkansas. Nat Prob Assn Proc 25: 180-3 '31 **11017**

CALIFORNIA

Plover, John P. State aid and supervision of probation—reports from states: California. Nat Prob Assn Proc 25: 184-5 '31 **11018**

San Francisco. City and county. Probation department. Annual report, July 1, 1930/June 30, 1931. 13p. San Francisco, 1931 **11019**

CONNECTICUT

Godwin, Richard K. State aid and supervision of probation—reports from states: Connecticut. Nat Prob Assn Proc 25: 185-7 '31 **11020**

Stoeckel, Robbins B. A probation system for motor vehicle law violators. 4p. (Bul no80) Hartford, Connecticut. Department of motor vehicles, July 30, 1931 **11021**

ILLINOIS

Cook county, Ill. Chief probation officer. Annual report *in* Report of Institute for juvenile research, Juvenile court branch, 1926/27: 27-35 **11022**

Palmer, Mrs. George Thomas. Future of probation in Illinois. Ill Conf Pub Welf Proc 1929: 107 **11023**
Address before Illinois probation officers' association.

Palmer, Mrs. George Thomas. Probation in Illinois—plea for its extension. Welf Bul 21: 1, 5, 8-10 Ag, S '30 **11024**

Palmer, Mrs. George T[homas]. State aid and supervision of probation—reports from states: Illinois. Nat Prob Assn Proc 25: 187-91 '31 **11025**

INDIANA

Boys, Florence Riddick. Probation manual with digest of Indiana probation laws. 42p. [Pendleton] 1931 **11026**

Boys, Florence Riddick. State aid and supervision of probation—reports from states: Indiana. Nat Prob Assn Proc 25: 191-3 '31 **11027**

Boys, Florence Riddick. The state probation department. Ind Bul Char & Correc (200): 618-20 D '31 11028

Indiana probation news. v1 no1 November 1926- Indiana, State probation officer, Indianapolis 11029

Indiana. State probation department. Annual reports 7, 1927—11, 1931 [Indianapolis, 1927-31] 11030

Reprints from Yearbook.

New Indiana probation law. Probation 5: 4 Ap '27 11031

IOWA

Hiller, Francis H. The Iowa probation survey. Ia St Conf Soc Wk Proc 30: 57-8 '29 11032

MARYLAND

Hepbron, James M. Probation and penal treatment in Baltimore. J Crim L & Crimin 19: 64-74 My '28 11033

Hepbron, James M. Probation and penal treatment in Baltimore; being a study of the subsequent conduct of 305 probationers and a like number of convicts by the Criminal justice commission. 15p. Baltimore, Criminal justice commission, 1927 11034

MASSACHUSETTS

Carter, Albert Bradley. State aid and supervision of probation—reports from states: Massachusetts. Nat Prob Assn Proc 25: 193-7 '31 11035

Massachusetts. Board of probation. Annual report, 1930-1931. Boston, 1931-32 11036

Earlier reports issued by Commission on probation. No reports issued for 1928 and 1929 but material covered in 1930 report.

Massachusetts. Commission on probation. Annual report, 1927. 25p. Boston, 1928 11037

Later reports *see* Board of probation.

Massachusetts. Commission on probation. Probation manual. ed.5. 115p. Boston, January 1927 11038

MINNESOTA

Hennepin county. Probation officer. Report *in* Report of Juvenile court of Hennepin county, Minnesota, 1926-1927-1928: 12-27 [Minneapolis, 1929] 11039

Monachesi, Elio D. Prediction of outcome in probation cases in Minneapolis and St. Paul. Thesis (Ph.D.) University of Minnesota, 1931? 11040

Sutherland, E. H. Report of an investigation of probation in Minnesota. Minn St Conf & Inst Soc Wk Proc 35: 219-29 '27 11041

NEW JERSEY

Essex county. Probation department. Report of activities 24, December 31, 1927—27 1930. Newark, 1928-31 11042

NEW YORK

Cobb, W. Bruce. What the new probation laws mean: how they will affect Brooklyn. Brooklyn 6-7 Je 23 '28 11043

Esmond, Burton D. The new probation laws. N Y St Conf Prob Offic Proc 21: 151-60 '28 11044

Moran, Frederick A. The outlook for probation. Am Pris Assn Proc 54: 155-68 '29 11045

New York (state). Department of correction. Division of probation. Annual reports 21, 1927—22, 1928. Albany, 1928-32 11046

Earlier reports issued by State probation commission. Reports include statistics of probation officers and directory.

New York (state). Department of correction. Division of probation. Probation—do you want that. 8p. Albany, 1927 11047

New York (state). Department of correction. Division of probation. Program of the 22d annual conference held in Albany, November 19-22, 1929. 13p. Albany, 1929 11048

Owens, James S. State aid and supervision of probation—reports from states: New York. Nat Prob Assn Proc 25: 197-203 '31 11049

NORTH DAKOTA

MacGunigal, Margaret. State aid and supervision of probation—reports from states: North Dakota. Nat Prob Assn Proc 25: 204-5 '31 11050

OHIO

Ohio. Division of probation and parole. Laws of Ohio relative to probation, pardon and parole. 71p. (Department of public welfare, Pub no28) Columbus, July 1930 11051

Ohio. Division of probation and parole. Report *in* Annual report of the Department of public welfare 8, 1929: 108-13 11052

Report from April 15/December 31.

PENNSYLVANIA

Pennsylvania. Crime commission. Probation and the parole of offenders from local penal and correctional institutions; supplemental report. 30p. Philadelphia, 1929 11053

Worthington, George E. Criminal division probation in the municipal court of Philadelphia. 42p. Philadelphia, Bureau of municipal research, 1930 11054

Rhode Island

North, Donald C. State aid and supervision of probation—reports from states: Rhode Island. Nat Prob Assn Proc 25: 205-7 '31 11055

Rhode Island. State probation department. Report *in* Annual report of State public welfare commission 5, 1926/27: 178-89; 6, 1927/28: 163-77; 7, 1928/29: 68-71; 8, 1929/30: 22-4; 9, 1930/31: 29-38 11056

Utah

Robinson, B. H. State aid and supervision of probation—reports from states: Utah. Nat Prob Assn Proc 25: 207-8 '31 11057

Vermont

Beebe, Don C. H. State aid and supervision of probation—reports from states: Vermont. Nat Prob Assn Proc 25: 208-10 '31 11058

Wisconsin

Murphy, L. F. State aid and supervision of probation—reports from states: Wisconsin. Nat Prob Assn Proc 25: 211-20 '31 11059

Wisconsin. Probation department. Biennial report *in* Biennial report of State board of control 19, 1926/28: 94-102; 20, 1928/30: 1-9 11060

JUVENILE PROBATION

Birching and probation. Just Peace 93: 499 Ag 3 '29 11061

California. Department of social welfare. Annual report of juvenile probation, 1930/1931. 2p. (mim) [Sacramento, 1931] 11062

Clarry, E. The probation system and the juvenile delinquent; supervision and care of juvenile offenders. Soc & Ind R 3: 339-48 Ap '27 11063

[Coll, J. E.] Patronato nacional de menores. Memoria de la Comisión Honoraria de Superintendencia. Bibl Nac de Crim y Cienc Afines Bol 2: 448-97 Ap '28 11064

Connecticut. Department of public welfare. Connecticut juvenile probation. Bulletin no1 Ap 22, 1930- 11065

Futile probation. Sol J 73: 520 Ag 10 '29 11066

Johnson, Fred Robert. Probation for juveniles and adults; a study of principles and methods. 242p. N.Y. Century, 1928 11067

Llewellyn-Roberts. Le service social pour enfants anormaux au centre d'observation de neuropsychiatrie enfantile. Hyg Ment 23: 110-15 My '28 11068

[Muller, N.]. Jaarboek voor de reclasseering van volwassenen en kinderen. . . 1928. 46p. Eibergen, H. Heiner, 1928 11069

Reese, James B. Making juvenile probation successful. Cath Char R 14: 166-71 Je '30 11070

Rollet, H. Le patronage de l'enfance. Son origine. Ses débuts. Hyg Ment 23: 97-101 My '28 11071

Weiss, Hans. The child on probation. Nat Prob Assn Proc 23: 94-108 '29; same title: Nat Conf Soc Wk Proc 56: 163-71 '29 11072

Williams, Herbert D. The psychology of probation and work with delinquents. N Y St Conf Soc Wk Q Bul 34-45 O '30 11073

ADULT PROBATION

[Adult probation]. Minn St Bd Con Q 30(2) N 25 '30 11074

Chute, Charles L. Adult probation—present status and prospects. Nat Prob Assn Proc 21: 40-7 '27 11075

Doyle, John H. Adult probation, District court, Ramsey county, Minnesota. Minn St Bd Con Q 30: 40-2 N 25 '30 11076

Foley, Michael E. Probation of adult offenders. Ind Bul Char & Correc (193): 290-3 My '31 11077

[Georgia]. Development of adult probation service. *In* Georgia. Department of public welfare, Report 1927/28: 31-4 11078

Hannan, John J. A state system of adult probation [Minnesota]. Minn St Bd Con Q 30: 10-21 N 25 '30 11079

Hiller, Francis H. Adult probation laws of the United States. Nat Prob Assn Proc 24: 147-90 '30 11080

Hush, Howard R. Adult probation, District court, Hennepin county, Minnesota. Minn St Bd Con Q 30: 30-5 N 25 '30 11081

Leitch, Frances E. Reclaiming the woman offender. N Y St Conf Prob Offic Proc 20: 76-81 '27 11082

May, Carl L. Beneficial results of adult probation laws. 8p. American Legion, California, Penal institution commission, 1931? 11083

Pennsylvania. Allegheny county. Adult probation department. Annual report 18, 1927 [Pittsburgh, 1928] **11084**

Pennsylvania. Philadelphia county. Quarter sessions court. Probation department. Report . . . for adult offenders brought before the courts of Oyer and Terminer and Quarter sessions of Philadelphia county, 1925/27—1927/29. [Harrisburg, 1928-30] **11085**

Resche, F. E. Adult probation. District court, St. Louis county, Minnesota. Minn St Bd Con Q 30: 36-9 N 25 '30 **11086**

San Francisco. City and county. Adult probation department. Annual reports, 1927-1929/30. [San Francisco, 1928-31] **11087**

Vol, Brenton A. de. Adult probation. Ind Bul Char & Correc (190): 153-6 F '31 **11088**

Welch, J. R. The new adult probation law. Calif St B J 2: 49-51 S '27 **11089**

Zahm, Robert H. Adult probation problems. Nat Prob Assn Proc 23: 153-7 '29 **11090**

PROBATION OFFICERS

Bell, Marjorie. Meet Mr. Probation officer. Survey 63: 71-2 O 15 '29 **11091**

Brown, L. G. The probation officer's philosophy. Probation 9: 1-2, 5-6 O '30 **11092**

Colcord, Joanna C. The probation officer as a social worker. Probation 1-2, 6 N '30 **11093**

Curry, H. Ida. The relation of county agents to probation officers. N Y St Conf Prob Offic Proc 21: 146-51 '28 **11094**

Illinois probation officers' association **11095**

Meets and reports with Illinois conference on public welfare.

Mayo, Leonard W. The training and recruiting of probation officers. Nat Prob Assn Proc 24: 223-9 '30 **11096**

National probation association. Salaries of probation officers in cities of 20,000 or more population. 31p. (mim) New York [1931?] **11097**

New York (state) conference of probation officers. Proceedings *in* Annual report of New York (state) Department of correction, Division of probation 21, 1927—22, 1928 **11098**

Parsons, Philip A. How can we train for probation work? J Delin 11: 257-66 D '27 **11099**

Parsons, Philip A. Selection and training of probation officers. Nat Prob Assn Proc 22: 37-51 '28 **11100**

Parsons, Philip A. To-morrow's probation worker. Welf Mag 19: 175-82 F '28 **11101**

Pettit, Maurice L. The training course for probation workers at Notre Dame. Nat Prob Assn Proc 24: 218-22 '30 **11102**

Probation officers for women. Sol J 75: 239 Ap 11 '31 **11103**

United States. Congress. Senate. Committee on judiciary. Federal probation officers, report to accompany H.R.3975 [to amend sec. 726 and 727 of title 18, United States Code, with reference to federal probation officers] April 25, 1930. 2p. Washington, 1930 (71st Cong. 2d sess. S. Rep. 526) **11104**

INSTITUTIONAL TREATMENT

GENERAL

Ardisson, P. Sulla condizione giuridica delle persone detenute. Riv di Dir Peniten 1: 768-72 '30 11105

Ashe, Stanley P. [Penal institutions and the crime situation]. Assn of Dir Poor & Char & Correc Proc 56: 138-45 '31 11106

Bates, Sanford. Modern trends in the development of federal and state correctional programs. Am Pris Assn Proc 60: 377-91 '30 11107

Belym, Léon. Gefängnisse für junge Mütter und Kleinkinder. Monats f Kriminalpsychol u Strafrechtsref 22: 218-21 Ap '31 11108

B[ertrand], E. La stabilisation des traitements. Ecrou 8: 558-67 N '27 11109

Biesenthal. Aufsichtsbehörden. Bl f Gefängniskunde 59: 32-50 '28 11110

Bowen, A. L. The eleemosynary institution of the future. Am Pris Assn Proc 54: 89-94 '29 11111

Bozi, Alfred. Die Theorie der strafrechtlichen Erziehung. Monats f Kriminalpsychol u Strafrechtsref 18: 22-30 Ja '27 11112

Brandon, Rodney. Crime and public welfare; responsibilities of the state in the modern programme of correction. Police "13-13" 5: 8-10, 46 O '30 11113

Capobianco, Giuseppe Leonida. Impressioni e ricordi della prigionia di guerra in Austria. ed.2. 197p. Napoli, Federico & Ardia, 1928 11114

Davies, S. P. The state and its institution policy. Psychiat Q 4: 710-12 '30 11115

Delierneux, A. Essai de contribution au traitement des condamnés correctionnels adultes. R de Dr Pén et de Crimin 10: 976-91 '30; extract: 16p. Louvain, Pierre Mafrans, 1930 11116

Delos, J. La théorie de l'institution. Arch de Philos du Dr Cahier Double (1-2) '31 11117

Doll, Edgar A. Some principles of correctional treatment. J Crim L & Crimin 18: 197-206 Ag '28 11118

Ensemble de règles pour la traitement des prisonniers. R de Dr Pén et de Crimin 10: 67-77 '30 11119

Reprint from Bulletin de la Commission internationale pénale et pénitentiaire, October 1929.

Falcone, L. La correzione del delinquente e il personale carcerario. Riv di Dir Peniten 1: 773-9 '30 11120

Farnell, Frederic J. What can public welfare accomplish for state institutions? J Nerv & Ment Dis 72: 251-6 '30 11121

Fraser, Albert G. Team work that counts [cooperation between social agencies and institutions]. Pris J 10: 11-13 Jl '30 11122

Gómez, E. Programa de ciencia penal. Bibl Nac de Crim y Cienc Afines Bol 2: 377-81 Ap '28 11123

Grünhut, Max. Forderungen zum Strafvollzugsgesetz. Zeitsch f d ges Strafrechtswiss 51: 75-83 '31 11124

Hacker, Erwin. Die Zukunft der Freiheitsstrafe. Bl f Gefängniskunde 62(2): 346-57 '31 11125

Hodenberg. Verkehrsrechtsliche Probleme bei der Reform des Strafrechts und Strafprozesses. Jurist Wchnschr 58: 2793-6 O 5 '29 11126

Johnson, Kate Burr. [Case work in an institution]. Nat Conf Juv Agencies Proc 27: 27-32 '30 11127

Kieb, Raymond F. C. The reorganized Department of correction. N Y St Conf Prob Offic Proc 20: 156-64 '27 11128

Kinberg, O. Un système pénal édifé sur une base empirico-psychologique a-t-il besoin du concept de la responsabilité? Arch di Antrop Crim 50: 197-241 '30 11129

Klingaman, O. E. Some social problems. Bul St Inst [Iowa] 32: 224-31 O '30 11130

Koerber, Lenka v. Der Rechtsbrecher im Strafvollzug. Hilfe 37 (17): 427-8 S 1 '29 11131

League of Nations. Committee of experts for the progressive codification of international law. Communication of judicial and extra-judicial acts in penal matters and letters rogatory in penal matters. 33p. Geneva, 1927 11132

Ledig. Strafjustiz und Seelenforschung. Justiz 6: 90-6 N '30 11133

Makarewicz, Juliusz. Proceduralne watpliwości. Ruch Prawn i Ekon i Socjol 8: 311-47 '28 11134

Massari, E. La condizione giuridica delle persone detenute. Riv di Dir Peniten 1: 7-13 '30 11135

Mayer, Joseph. Bücher zur Gefängnisfürsorge und Strafvollzugsreform. Caritas ns8 (11): 475-8; (12): 513-15 '29 11136

Müller, Johannes. Über die Unterschiede von Gefängnisfürsorge Straffälligenpflege und Gerichtshilfe. Monats f Kriminalpsychol u Strafrechtsref 20: 597-606 O '29 11137

Musillami, G. Lo stato di detenzione e l'imposta sui selibi. Riv di Dir Peniten 1: 1379-85 '30 11138

Nagler, Johannes. Das Progressivsystem [im Strafvollzug]. Gerichtssaal 94 (5-6): 327-46 '27 11139

Ottolenghi, S. Il trattamento penale del delinquente nato. Scuola Pos 38: 15-21 '30; same title: Zacchia 9: 1-10 Ja '30 **11140**

Palevsky, Mary. An ideal program for an institution dealing with delinquents. Jewish Soc Serv Q 3: 24-34 Je '27 **11141**

Perkins, Clarence W. The opportunities and responsibilities of membership on institutional boards. Nat Conf Juv Agencies Proc 27: 110-19 '30 **11142**

Poller. Die Bestimmungen über die Sicherungsmassnahmen, die Haustrafen und das Beschwerderecht in den einzelnen Strafvollzugsordnungen. Bl f Gefängniskunde 58: 51-61 '27 **11143**

Potter, Ellen C. The influence of the mental hygiene movement on correctional institutions. Pris J 11: 1-3 Ja '31 **11144**

Preventive detention. Sol J 73: 535 Ag 17 '29 **11145**

Puglia, G. M. Il carcere preventivo. Scuola Pos 38: 142-52 '30 **11146**

Raabl-Werner, Heinrich von. Zur bevorstehenden Novellierung des Kriegsgefangenenrechtes. Preuss Jahrb 217: 36-57 Jl '29 **11147**

Reglamento del Instituto correccional de Meyères de Santa Fe. Bibl Nac de Crim y Cienc Afines Bol 3(3): 311- Ja '29 **11148**

Roux, J.-A. Observations présentées a la société des nations au sujet d'un ensemble de règles pour le traitement des prisonniers. R Int de Dr Pén 8: 6-22 '31 **11149**

Salinger, F. Die Verwahrung chronischer Trinker nach geltendem und zukünftigen Recht. Deut Zeitsch f d ges gerichtl Med 10: 408-18 S '27 **11150**

Santoro, Arturo. Il nuovo regolamento per gli istituti di prevenzione e di pena. Scuola Pos ns11: 390-5 Ag '31 **11151**

Schuind, Gaston. Considérations sur le problème pénal. R de Dr Pén et de Crimin 8: 529-38 Je '28 **11152**

Seggelke, Günther. Die Entstehung der Freiheitsstrafe. 153p. (Strafrechtl Abh no242, begr von Bennecke) Breslau, Schletter, 1928 **11153**

Sellin, Thorsten. Brief guide to penological literature. Ann Am Acad 157: 224-32 S '31 **11154**

Spallanzani, A. Osservazioni sulle carceri mandamentali. Riv di Dir Peniten 1: 248-64 '30 **11155**

Stern, Leon. Penal administration and the machinery of government. Pris J 7: 17-19 Jl '27 **11156**

Stoos[s], C. Die Trinkerheilanstalt. Monats f Kriminalpsychol u Strafrechtsref 22: 8-10 '31 **11157**

Stumpf. Diagnose der Strafgefangenen als Grundlage für ihre individuelle Behandlung. Eine kriminalpolitische Betrachtung von Werner Petrzilka. Bl f Gefängniskunde 61: 270-7 '30 **11158**

Thayer, Walter N. [jr.]. Institutional treatment for defective delinquents. N J Conf Soc Wk Proc 29: 23-9 '30 **11159**

Thayer, Walter N. jr. Institutions for defective delinquents. Pen Affairs (22): 4-12 My '30 **11160**

Thayer, W[alter] N. [jr.]. Needs of the state department of correction. Psychiat Q 4: 707-9 '30 **11161**

Toulemon, Andrée. Le progrès des institutions pénales. Essai de sociologie criminelle. 249p. Paris, Sirey, 1928 **11162**
Theory that institutions run the same life course as human beings is revivified in this work.

Tullio, B. di. Il medico criminalista nel moderno trattamento integrale scientifico della criminalità. Arch di Antrop Crim 48: 53-7 Ja '28 **11163**

Wilcox, Clair. State organization for penal administration. 56p. (mim) Philadelphia, Pennsylvania committee on penal affairs, July 1930; same title: J Crim L & Crimin 22: 51-98 My '31 **11164**

AUSTRALIA

Victoria. Inspector general of penal establishments. Penal establishments, gaols, and reformatory prisons: report and statistical tables, 1927-1930. Melbourne, Govt. Ptr. 1928-31 **11165**
Pentridge, Castlemaine, French Island, Beechwort, Geelong, Metropolitan (females), Metropolitan (males) reformatory prisons. Ballarat; Bendigo.

BELGIUM

Van Ranst, J. Organisation du dépot de mendicité a Merxplas; son évolution. R de Dr Pén et de Crimin 9: 20-38 Ja '29 **11166**

CANADA

Ontario. Inspector of prisons and public charities. Annual reports . . . upon prisons and reformatories 60, 1917—63, 1930. Toronto, 1928-31 **11167**
Gaols, Guelph reformatory, Mimico reformatory, Burwash farm, Fort Williams farm, Langstaff farm, Concord farm, Mercer reformatory, board of parole, extramural employment.

Ontario. Royal commission on public welfare. Report, 1930. 11p. Toronto, 1930 **11168**
Section VII: Corrective institutions.

Topping, C. W. Canadian penal institutions. 126p. Thesis (Ph.D.) Columbia university, 1929 **11169**
Sponsored by Canadian prisoners welfare association.

CHILE

Rojas, Jorge Gaete. Nuovo regime penale nel Cile. Arch di Antrop Crim 50: 59-61 Ja '30; translation: Nuevo régimen penal en Chile. R de Crimin e Med Leg 17: 204-6 Ap '30 **11170**

CZECHOSLOVAKIA

Juzova, M. A propos de la réforme du droit pénal de la jeunesse en Tchécoslovaquie. R Int de L'Enf 9: 142-3 F '30 11171

EUROPE

European penal problems. Outl 146: 524 Ag 24 '27 11172

National crime commission. European methods and ideas of penal treatment; a report submitted to the sub-committee of the commission on pardons, parole, probation, penal laws and institutional correction. 14p. New York, 1927 11173

Robinson, Louis N. Something more than locking and unlocking cell doors: report on European methods and ideas of penal treatment, prepared for the National crime commission. Am City 37: 285-9 S '27 11174

GERMANY

Blumenthal, Paul. Fürsorgerische Probleme im Strafrechts- und Gefängniswesen. Soz Praxis 40(14): 425-31 Ap 2 '31 11175

Carrière, R. Gründe der Überfüllung der Anstalten und Vorschläge zur Abhilfe-besonders für den Freistaat Sachsen. Allg Zeitsch f Psychiat 94: 130-72 Ja '31 11176

Haberland, Friedrich. Die Freiheitsstrafe in Hannover. 54p. (Strafrechtl Abh no293) Breslau, Schletter, 1931 11177

Haebler, Helma. Das Bildungs- und Unterrichtswesen im deutschen Strafvollzug. Praxis d Berufssch 9(39): 764-8 D 13 '29 11178

Wendt. Über die gegenwärtige und künftige Behandlung und Unterbringung der kriminellen Geisteskranken in Sachsen. Allg Zeitsch f Psychiat 85: 474-82 F '27 11179

GREAT BRITAIN

Doleisch von Dolsperg, Franz. Die Entstehung der Freiheitsstrafe unter besonderer Berücksichtigung der Auftretens moderner Freiheitsstrafe in England. 139p. (Strafrechtl Abh no244) Breslau, Schletter, 1928 11180

English penal methods. An outline of past and present methods of treating delinquency and of proposals for future reform. 36p. London, Friends Bk. Centre, 1928 11181

Foltin, Edgar M. Die Chronisch erhöht Gefährlichen; mit besonderer Berücksichtigung ihrer Behandlung im englischen Recht. 137p. bibliog 131-7. (Krimin Abh no3) Wien, Springer, 1927 11182

Lytton, Earl of. Moral hospitals. Howard J 2: 88-93 '27 11183

The Penal servitude act, 1927. Just Peace 91: 522-3 Jl 9 '27 11184

HAWAII

Hawaii. Governor. Annual report to Secretary of the Interior, 1927- Washington, Govt. Ptg. Off. 1928- 11185

Olinda prison camp, Maui; Kawailoa training school for girls; Waialee training school for boys; Territorial prison, Oahu; Waikia prison camp, Hilo; Kailua road camp, Keanae, Maui; Kahului fair camp, Maui; Territorial courts: domestic, federal, land; attorney general.

ITALY

Massari, Edoardo. Les origines et l'élaboration de la réforme pénale fasciste. R Pénitent de Pologne 4(1-2): 133-41 '29 11186

Novelli, Giovanni. L'esecuzione delle pene detentive nella nuova legislazione italiana. 45p. Roma, Mantellate, 1931 11187

Extr: Rivista di diritto penitenziario (2) 1931.

JAPAN

Gentz. Das japanische Strafvollzugsgesetz. Zeitsch d ges Strafrechtswiss 48: 372-80 '28 11188

NEW ZEALAND

Weldon, John L. Modern penal methods in New Zealand. Empire R 54: 28-32 Jl '31 11189

PHILIPPINE ISLANDS

Philippine Islands. Department of the interior. Office of the public welfare commissioner. Annual report of the Public welfare commissioner 11, 1931. Manila, Bureau of printing, 1932 11190

Training schools for boys and for girls; probation work; work for conditionally pardoned women prisoners.

POLAND

S[asserath], S. Notes sur la justice répressive en Pologne. R de Dr Pén et de Crimin 8: 72-3 Ja '28 11191

RUSSIA

Conforto, Giorgio. Positivismo e sistema penale sovietico. Europa Orient 10: 34-46, 90-103 Ja, Mr '30 11192

Pasche-Oserski, N. Strafe und Strafvollzug in der Sowjet-union. Neue Russland 5: 7-20 '28; same title: 107p. Berlin, Baumeister, 1929 11193

Perris, Corrado. La nuova teoria penale della Russia Sovietica. Scuola Pos 11: 1-21 Ja '31; same title: 23p. Milano, Vallardi, 1931 11194

Russia (RSFSR). Narodnyi komissariat i͡ustitsii. Spisok lits prigovorennykh uslovno k lisheni͡iu svobody, 1924- 11195

Zaitzeff, Leo. Das Strafrechtswesen im Sowjetstaate. Zeitsch f d ges Strafrechtsref 51(1): 1-18 '31 **11196**

SPAIN

Regolamento delle carceri spagnuole. Riv di Dir Peniten 1: 350-67 '30 **11197**

SWEDEN

Hagströmer, Sven. Riktlinjer för vinnande av viss koncentration inom det Svenska fångvårdsväsendet på offentligt uppdrag utarbetade och framlagda. 162p. (Statens offentliga utredningar 1931: 16) Stockholm, Justitiedepartementet, 1931 **11198**

SWITZERLAND

Beyli, Walter. Der aargauische Vorentwurf zu einem kantonalen Gesetz über die Versorgung von Gewohnheitsverbrechern und anderen gemeingefährlichen Personen. Schweiz Zeitsch f Strafr 40(4): 348-58 '27 **11199**

UNITED STATES

The American penal system. Pris J 11: 3-6 O '31 **11200**

American prison association. State and national penal and correctional institutions of the United States and Canada, March, 1929. New York, 1929 **11201**

Butler, Amos W. Prisoners and prisons: a report on federal penal and reformatory institutions, presented to a Special committee of the House of representatives, May 28, 1928. Ind Bul Char & Correc (175) O '29 **11202**

Conti, Ugo. Penal justice in the United States. Atlantica 7: 7-11 Je '29 **11203**

Indiana. Board of state charities. Report of federal penal and reformatory institutions. Ind Bul Char & Correc (171-2) Je-Jl '29 **11204**

Kellerhals, Hans. Amerikanische Strafanstalten. Monats f Kriminalpsychol u Strafrechtsref 19: 248-51 Ap '28 **11205**

Liepmann, M[oritz]. Amerikanische Gefängnisse und Erziehungsanstalten. Ein Reisebericht. 76p. (Hamburg. Schriften z. ges. Strafrechtswissenschaft no11) Mannheim, Bensheimer, 1927 **11206**

National commission on law observance and enforcement. Report on penal institutions, probation and parole. 344p. (No9) Washington, June 23, 1931 **11207**

Penal institutions; classification; labor and industry; education; parole; probation; Report of Advisory committee on penal institutions, probation and parole; Report on police jails and village lockups by Hastings H. Hart.

United States. Congress. House. Special committee on federal penal and reformatory institutions. Federal penal and reformatory institutions: hearings, January 7-15, 1929, pursuant to H. Res. 233, directing a committee to make a survey and report upon the care and employment of federal prisoners, agreed to May 28, 1928. 283p. Washington, 1929 (70th Cong. 2d sess.) **11208**

United States. Congress. House. Special committee on federal penal and reformatory institutions. Report on federal penal and reformatory institutions, report pursuant to H. Res. 233, January 31, 1929. 8p. Washington, 1929 (70th Cong. 2d sess. H Rp 2303) **11209**

CALIFORNIA

California. Governor's council. Minutes of monthly meetings: State department of penology, October 1929-December 1931. (mim) [Sacramento, 1929-31] **11210**

California. State department of social welfare. Mental hygiene survey of the state of California, by Frederick H. Allen, 1930. 177p. Sacramento, 1932 **11211**

Chap. viii: Mental hygiene problems of delinquency [institutional care of delinquents].

COLORADO

Moynihan, Charles J. Colorado penal institutions. Colo B Assn Proc 33: 206-23 '30 **11212**

CONNECTICUT

Connecticut. Commission on state institutions. Initial report of the commission on state institutions. 122p. (Pub doc no77) Hartford, 1927 **11213**

DISTRICT OF COLUMBIA

District of Columbia. Board of public welfare. Report of . . . Board . . . with report of charitable and correctional institutions and agencies, 1927- Washington, 1927- **11214**

Kober, George M. comp. Charitable and reformatory institutions in the District of Columbia: history and development of the public charitable and reformatory institutions and agencies in the District of Columbia. 375p. Washington, Govt. Ptg. Off. 1927 (69th Cong. 2d sess. S Doc 207) **11215**

GEORGIA

Georgia. Department of public welfare. Biennial report, 1927/28. Atlanta, 1929 **11216**

County jail work; criminal statistics; development of adult probation; work with delinquent children; juvenile courts.

ILLINOIS

Brandon, Rodney H. Correction in Illinois. Am Pris Assn Proc 60:75-9 '30 **11217**

Brandon, Rodney H. The new program of correction in Illinois. Int Assn Chiefs Police Proc 37: 177-85 '30 **11218**

Bruce, Andrew A. Penal administration in Illinois. J Crim L & Crimin 22: 483-6 N '31 11219

Illinois. Criminologist. Annual report 10, 1926/27—13, 1929/30. [Springfield] Department of public welfare, 1927-30 11220

INDIANA

Indiana. Board of state charities. Annual reports 39, 1928—41, 1930. Ind Bul Char & Correc (170) My '29; (182) My '30; (195) Jl '31 11221
Committee on penal and reformatory institutions.

Indiana. Joint purchasing committee of state institutions. Indiana's state institutions. 77p. Indianapolis, 1928 11222
Indiana boys school; Indiana girls school; Indiana state prison; Indiana reformatory; Indiana woman's prison; Indiana state farm.

IOWA

Iowa. Board of control of state institutions. Biennial reports 16, 1926/28—18, 1930/32. Des Moines, 1928-32 11223
Juvenile home, Toledo; Training school for boys, Eldora; Training school for girls, Mitchellville; State penitentiary, Fort Madison; Men's reformatory, Anamosa; Women's reformatory, Rockwell City.

Iowa. Board of control of state institutions. Bulletin of state institutions, v29, 1927- 11224

KANSAS

Kansas. Board of administration. Correctional institutions section. Biennial report 6, 1926/28 [Topeka, 1928] 11225

KENTUCKY

Kentucky. State board of charities and corrections. Biennial reports, 1925/27—1929/31. Frankfort, 1927-31 11226
Penal institutions and Houses of reform.

LOUISIANA

Louisiana. State board of charities and corrections. [Biennial] report 1925/27—1927/29. [Baton Rouge, 1928-30] 11227

MAINE

Maine. Department of public welfare. Biennial report 10, 1926/28—11, 1928/30 [Augusta] 1928-30 11228
County jails; juvenile delinquency.

MARYLAND

Maryland. Department of welfare. Laws relating to the penal and insane institutions. 77p. [Baltimore] 1927 11229

MASSACHUSETTS

Bates, Sanford. Massachusetts' Department of correction. Welf Mag 18: 640-5 My '27 11230

Massachusetts. Department of corrections. Annual reports 8, 1926/27—11, 1929/30 [Boston, 1927-30] 11231

Massachusetts. Department of public welfare. Manual of laws, including amendments to December 31, 1929. 148p. Boston, 1930 11232
Laws on Division of juvenile training.

MINNESOTA

Swendsen, C. J. A brief resume of Minnesota's institutional program for its handicapped wards. Minn St Conf & Inst Soc Wk Proc 35: 126-34 '27 11233
State prison; state reformatory; Boys' training school; Home school for girls.

MISSOURI

Kansas City public service institute. "Charities and corrections" Jackson county, Missouri; a survey of the welfare activities of the Jackson county government. 203p. (mim) Kansas City, Mo. March 1928 11234
Parole; probation; juvenile delinquency; reform schools.

Missouri. Department of penal institutions. Biennial report, 1926/28—1928/30. Jefferson City, 1929-31 11235
State penitentiary, Jefferson City; Reformatory, Boonville; State industrial home for girls, Chillicothe; State industrial home for Negro girls, Tipton.

Missouri. State board of charities and correction. Biennial report, 1927/28—1929/30. Jefferson City, 1929-31 11236
County jail inspection; juvenile court statistics.

Missouri. State survey commission. Penal and eleemosynary supporting data to the report of the . . . Commission, November 30, 1929, by P. E. Thomas and J. J. Sullivan. 44p. Jefferson City, 1929 11237
State penitentiary: Industrial home for girls; Industrial home for Negro girls; Reformatory.

NEW HAMPSHIRE

New Hampshire. State board of public welfare. Biennial reports 17, 1927/28—18, 1929/30. Manchester, Granite State press, 1928-30 11238
Statistics of county houses of correction and jails. Formerly State board of charities and correction.

NEW JERSEY

Atlantic City survey commission. Report of the survey of Atlantic county government. 119p. Atlantic City, December 1, 1930 11239
Atlantic county detention home; Probation office; Sheriff's office and county jail; county prosecutor's office.

Ellis, William J. Developments in connection with the New Jersey correctional system. Nat Soc Pen Inf N Y Bul 1: 5, 8 Ag '30 **11240**

Ellis, William J. The New Jersey plan: a central State department of institutions and agencies. Welf Mag 18: 78-90 Ja '27 **11241**

NEW YORK

Jewish board of guardians. Annual reports 7, 1927—10, 1930. New York city, 1928-31 **11242**

Hawthorne school; Cedar Knolls school; Lakeview home; the Shelter. Board is successor of Jewish protectory and aid society.

Kieb, Raymond F. C. The Department of correction. N Y St Assn Magistrates Proc 19: 85-90 '27 **11243**

New York (city). Department of correction. Report for the year 1927. 103p. New York, 1928 **11244**

City prison, Manhattan; City prison, Brooklyn; City prison, Queens; District prisons; Penitentiary, Welfare Island; Correction hospital, Welfare Island; Municipal farms, Rikers' Island; Reformatory prison, Hart's Island; New York city reformatory, New Hampton; Warwick honor camp; women's farm colony.

New York (state). Crime commission. Special report on penal institutions, 1930. 22p. Albany, 1930 **11245**

New York (state). Crime commission. Subcommission on penal institutions

Report, February 28, 1927. 16p. Albany, 1927

Report, February 18, 1928. 73p. Albany, 1928

Report, January 30, 1929. 23p. Albany, 1929

Report, 1930. 22p. Albany, 1930 **11246**

New York (state). State commission of correction. Annual reports 1, 1927—4, 1930 [Albany, 1928-31] **11247**

Prison population; cost of maintenance; probation and parole; federal prisoners; detention of juveniles; state prisons; reformatories; institution for defective delinquents; N.Y.C. institutions; N.Y.C. police stations; detention pens in Court houses; penitentiaries (county); county jails; special reports: delinquent youths; reports of inspection of state prisons: Auburn, Clinton, Great Meadow, Sing Sing; reformatories: Elmira, Albion state training school; N.Y.S. reformatory for women, Bedford Hills, Institution for defective delinquents, Napanoch; New York city institutions: N.Y. county penitentiary; correctional hospital, Welfare Island; Reformatory prison, Hart's Island; Municipal farm, Riker's Island; N.Y.C. reformatory, New Hampton; Women's farm colony, Greycourt; city prison, Manhattan; New York city police stations; county penitentiaries; county jails; city jails and county, town and village lockups; statistics.

OHIO

Kramer, Samuel A. The Norwood law and its effect upon the penal problem in Ohio. J Crim L & Crimin 21: 553-97 F '31 **11248**

Ohio. Department of public welfare. Law bulletin: laws relating to the Department of public welfare, benevolent, correctional and penal institutions, and kindred subjects. 361p. [Columbus] January 1, 1931 (Pub no32) **11249**

OKLAHOMA

Oklahoma. Laws, statutes, etc. Statutes governing the work of the Oklahoma state department of charities and corrections. 24p. [Oklahoma City] 1931 **11250**

Oklahoma. State commissioner of charities and corrections. Reports, 1927-1930. Oklahoma City, 1928-31 **11251**

PENNSYLVANIA

Pennsylvania. Commission on penal institutions. Report. Pris J 11: 6-12 Jl '31 **11252**

Pennsylvania. Commission on penal institutions. Report, May 1931. 41p. Harrisburg, 1931 **11253**

Pennsylvania. Department of welfare. Handbook of state institutions. 25p. (Bul no10 rev December 1927) Harrisburg, 1927 **11254**

Pennsylvania. Department of welfare. Bureau of restoration. Reports *in* Biennial reports of Secretary of welfare 1927/28: 72-86; 1929/30: 86-127 **11255**

List of county penal institutions in 1927/28; county prisons; Western penitentiary; Eastern penitentiary; Pennsylvania industrial reformatory.

Pennsylvania committee on penal affairs. Directory of correctional and penal resources of the state of Pennsylvania. 28p. Philadelphia, 1927 **11256**

Pennsylvania committee on penal affairs. Record of six years 1922-1928. 28p. Philadelphia, May 1928 **11257**

Pennsylvania committee on penal affairs. Weak spots in the penal system. Pen Affairs 15: 2-8 Je '27 **11258**

Philadelphia. Department of public welfare. Bureau of charities and correction. Annual report *in* Annual message of Mayor 1929: 439-77 **11259**

RHODE ISLAND

Rhode Island. Governor. Governor's message and report of Commission to investigate the state public welfare commission and all departments thereunder. 100p. Providence, 1929 **11260**

SOUTH DAKOTA

South Dakota. Board of charities and correction. Biennial reports 20, 1926/28—21, 1928/30 [Pierre, 1928-30] **11261**

TENNESSEE

Tennessee. Department of institutions. Biennial reports 1926/28—1928/30. Nashville, 1928-30 **11262**

VIRGINIA

Virginia. State department of public welfare. Annual reports 18, 1927—32, 1931. Richmond, 1927-31 11263
Summary of jail statistics.

WISCONSIN

Wisconsin conference of social work. Committee on crime and criminal justice. Report of conditions in Wisconsin penal, correctional, and charitable institutions, with recommendations. 17p. Madison, March, 1931 11264

Wisconsin. State board of control. Special report to the Governor . . . concerning appropriations in bill 477 S. as related to the service and housing requirements of the state charitable, curative, correctional, reformatory and penal institutions. [22]p. Madison, June 12, 1929 11265

WYOMING

Wyoming. State board of charities and reform. Biennial reports 1926/28—1928/30 [Cheyenne, 1928-30] 11266

ASSOCIATIONS, CONGRESSES, ETC.

American wardens' association 11267
Holds convention and reports as section of American prison association.

Die Augsburger Tagung des Vereins der deutschen Strafanstaltsbeamten. 19. Mitgliederversammlung (1-4, Juni 1927). Bl f Gefängniskunde 58: 97-389 '27 11268

Beringer, K. Versammlungsbericht. Die 19. Tagung der deutschen Strafanstaltsbeamten. Monats f Kriminalpsychol u Strafrechtsref 18: 443-8 Ag '27 11269

Bezirksvereins für Jugendschutz und Gefangenenfürsorge Freiburg i. Br. Jahresbericht. Bl f Gefängniskunde 59: 128-9 '28 11270

Bezirksvereins für Jugendschutz und Gefangenenfürsorge Mannheim. Tätigkeitsbericht. Bl f Gefängniskunde 59: 129-31 '28 11271

Central Howard association. Men whom men condemn: annual report 27, 1927. 31p. Chicago, 1928
The parting of the way: annual report 28, 1928. 32p. Chicago, 1929
Turning over a new leaf: annual report 29, 1929. 32p. Chicago, 1930 11272

Ceylon. Prisons department mutual provident fund co-operative society ltd. Report of the Honorary Secretary for the year ended 30th April, 1930. 3p. (typw) Colombo, 1931? 11273

Colorado prison association. Bulletin, v1, no1, December 1931- Denver, 1931- 11274

Colorado prison association. First annual Institute for the prevention and treatment of delinquency and crime: program, September 24, 1931. [Denver, 1931] 11275

Colorado prison association. Service report . . . for month of March, 1931. [4]p. (mim) [Denver, 1931] 11276

Colorado prison association. Summary of monthly service reports . . . from September 1, 1930 to March 1, 1931. [6]p. (mim) [Denver, 1931] 11277

Connecticut prison association. Report *in* Report of the Department of public welfare 1927/28: 42-3; 1929/30: 55-6 11278

County prison officials' association [of Pennsylvania]. Pris J 10: 23 Ja '30 11279

County prison officials' association [of Pennsylvania]. Third annual convention. Pris J 10: 3-27 Jl '30 11280

[County prison officials' association of Pennsylvania]. The wardens' association, second annual meeting. Pris J 9: 1-6 Jl '29 11281

[County prison officials' association of Pennsylvania]. The warden's conference. Pris J 8: 1-4 Ap '28 11282

Ferri, E. Le congrès pénitentiaire de Londres. R Int de Soc 35: 1-23 Ja '27 11283

Frede, Lothar and Sieverts, Rudolf. Die Beschlüsse der Internationalen Gefängnis-Kongresse 1872-1930. 139p. Eisenach, Thür. Gefängnisgesellschaft, 1931 11284

Gardner, Arthur R. L. The Howard league and its parents. II: The Howard association after 1901 and the Penal reform league. Howard J 3: 36-42 S '30 11285

Gefängnisgesellschaft für die Provinz Sachsen und Anhalt. Jahrbuch 43, 1927—47, 1931. Halle(Saale), Selbstverlag, 1927-31 11286

Grünhut, M. Bericht über die dritte Tagung der Arbeitsgemeinschaft für die Reform des Strafvollzuges. Monats f Kriminalpsychol u Strafrechtsref 18: 104-8 F '27 11287

Howard league. Just Peace 91: 796 O 22 '27 11288

Howard league for penal reform. Annual report 1927/28—1930/31. London, 1929-32? 11289

Jewish committee for personal service in state institutions. California, Annual report 6, 1927- San Francisco, 1927- 11290
Movement of Jewish population in state institutions.

Keimu Kyokwai [Japanese prison association]. Endowment act and regulations of the Japanese prison association. 8p. Tokyo, 1927 11291

Keimu Kyokwai [Japanese prison association]. Kei Sei, 1929-31. Tokyo, monthly 11292

Keimu Kyokwai [Japanese prison association]. Work of the Japanese prison association and its present status. 8p. Tokyo, 1927 11293

Lorion, Paul. La Société générale des prissons et de législation criminelle et la Howard League. R Pénitent et de Dr Pén 53: 50-85 Ja '29 11294

Lyon, F. Emory. The prison congress of 1926. J Crim L & Crimin 17: 487-9 F '27 **11295**

Massachusetts prison association. Constitution . . . amended January 10, 1928. 2p. (typw) **11296**

Missouri welfare league. Annual reports, 1927-1931. St. Louis, 1927-31 **11297**

Morrison, A. C. L. Voluntary workers and agencies. Just Peace 94: 477-9 Jl 26 '30 **11298**

Mossé, Armand. Le Congrès pénitentiaire de Prague. Etudes Crimin 5: 233-50 '30 **11299**

National committee on prisons and prison labor. Annual report, 1927-1929. New York, 1928-30 **11300**

National prisoners' aid association **11301**
Holds convention and reports with American prison association.

Pennsylvania prison society. Report for 1929. 12p. Philadelphia, 1930 **11302**

Prison association of New York. Annual reports 83, 1927—87, 1931. Albany, 1928-32 **11303**
Classification clinic, Sing Sing; Employment and relief bureau; Relief bureau for prisoners families.

Prison chaplain's association **11304**
Holds convention and reports with American prison association.

Resoluções approvadas pela Conferencia penal e penitenciaria Brasileira. Bol do Inst de Crimin s7 12(1): 309-22 '30 **11305**

Rheinish-Westfälischen Gefängnisgesellschaft. Jahresbericht 101, 1929. 121p. Düsseldorf, Selbstverlag, 1930 **11306**

Ryan, John H. The fifty-sixth annual prison congress: a review. Welf Mag 18: 86-9 Ja '27 **11307**

Sanches, Edgard. Discurso pronunciado na sessão solemne do Conselho Penitenciario do Estado em 13 de Maio de 1929. R de Cultura Jurid 1: 91-100 Ap '29 **11308**

Schlesischen Gefängnisgesellschaft in Breslau. Jahrbuch 10, 1927—13, 1930. Breslau [1928-31] **11309**

Schweizerischen Vereins für Straf-, Gefängniswesen und Schutzaufsicht. Verhandlungen, ns7, 1926—10, 1930. Aarau, Sauerländer, 1927-31 **11310**

Séance de la Société générale des prisons et de législation criminelle du 23 janvier 1931. R Pénitent et de Dr Pén 55:2-25 Ja '31 **11311**

Society for the friendless—historical statement, 1900-1931. First Friend 26: 1-3 Second & Third quarter '31 **11312**

Steffan prison association, Inc. Annual report, 1929. Philadelphia, 1929 **11313**
No reports for 1930 and 1931.

Tissier; Wattinne; Larnaude; Leclerq; Balthazard; Collard; Charpentier, and Zeyst. Séance commune de la Société de médecine légale et de la Société générale des prisons et de législation criminelle des 24 juin et 14 octobre 1929. R Pénitent et de Dr Pén 53:344-64 Ag '29 **11314**

Vereins der deutschen Strafanstaltsbeamten. Die Preussentagung . . . 20 Mitgliederversammlung vom 3.-7. Juni 1930 zu Kassel. Bl f Gefängniskunde 62(1): 3-329 '31 **11315**

Widmer, D. Ausserordentliche Vereinsversammlung vom 16. Juli 1928 in Olten. Schweiz Ver f Straf-, Gefängniswes u Schutzauf Verh ns9: 36-43 '29 **11316**

Women's prison association of New York. Annual reports 86, 1930—87, 1931. New York [1930-31] **11317**

AMERICAN PRISON ASSOCIATION

American prison association. Annual reports, 1927-31. New York [1928-32] **11318**

American prison association. The Congress bulletin, New York, v10, no1, December 1930 **11319**

American prison association. The declaration of principles of the 1870 Congress, revised and reaffirmed at the sixtieth annual congress. 11p. New York, October 10, 1930 **11320**

American prison association. Report of the Medical section. Proc 60: 196-223 '30 **11321**

American prison association. Report of the Women's committee. Proc 60: 175-95 '30 **11322**

Lyon, F. Emory. Ideals of the American prison association. J Crim L & Crimin 18: 327-30 N '27 **11323**

INTERNATIONAL PRISON CONGRESS

Bates, Sanford. [The Tenth International prison congress, Prague, August 25-30, 1930]. Am Pris Assn Proc 60: 308-20 '30 **11324**

Congrès pénal et pénitentiaire internationale de Prague. Actes. 4v. Berne, Staempfli, 1931 **11325**

Gardner, Arthur R. L. The Tenth International penal and penitentiary congress at Prague, 1930. Howard J 3: 83-5 '31 **11326**

Glueck, S. International prison congress of 1930, Prague. Ment Hyg 15: 775-90 O '31 **11327**

Goiccoechea, José Guallart L. de. El X Congreso penal y penitenciario internacional. R de Cultura 7: 1211-31 N '30 **11328**

International penal and penitentiary commission. Recueil de documents en matière pénale et pénitentiaire. Berne, March 1931- **11329**

La Du, Blanche L. The International prison conference. Minn St Bd Con Q 30: 50-60 S 12 '30 **11330**

Lehmann, Rudolf; Hauptvogel, Fritz; Ebermayer, Ludwig; Starke; Blumenthal, Paul, and Bumke, Erwin. Der zehnte Internationale Strafrechts- und Gefängniskongress in Prag 1930. Zeitsch f d ges Strafrechtswiss 51: 495-582 '31 **11331**

Lyon, F. Emory. Tenth International prison congress. J Crim L & Crimin 21: 499-504 F '31 **11332**

Novelli, Giovanni. Il decimo Congresso internazionale penale e penitenziario di Praga. 65p. Roma, Mantellate, 1930 **11333**
Extr: Rivista di diritto penitenziario, 1930.

Tenth International prison congress. Pris Assn N Y Ann Rep 86: 46-74 '30 **11334**
Includes Standard minimum rules for the treatment of prisoners.

Van der Aa, J. S. ed. International penitentiary congress, Proceedings, v11, 1925. 426p. Bern, Stämpfli, 1927 **11335**

PERIODICALS

Blätter für Gefängniskunde. Heidelberg, v58, 1927- **11336**
Zeitschrift des Verein der deutschen Strafanstaltsbeamten.

Correction. v1, no1, January 1931- New York (state) Department of correction, Elmira **11337**

Corrector. Chicago, v17, no1 July 1931- Chicago House of correction **11338**

L'Ecrou. Bruxelles, v8, no4, July-October 1927- **11339**
Organe de la Fédération des fonctionnaires et employés de prisons.

The First friend. v22, no3, Third quarter, 1927- **11340**
Official organ of the Society for the friendless [to promote the prevention and cure of crime].

National society of penal information, Inc. News bulletin. New York, v1, no1, April 1930- **11341**
v. 1 no3 lists federal and state prison news notes.

Penal affairs. Philadelphia, no21, December 1929- Pennsylvania committee on penal affairs **11342**

Prison journal. Philadelphia, v7, no1, January 1927- Pennsylvania prison society **11343**

Revue pénitentiaire et de droit pénal et Etudes criminologiques. Paris, 55, 1931- Société générale des prisons **11344**

Revue pénitentiaire de Pologne. Warszawa 3, 1928 **11345**

Rivista di diritto penitenziario. Roma, v1, January 1930- **11346**

ADMINISTRATION OF INSTITUTIONAL TREATMENT

PERSONNEL

Anderson, Nels. Man-handlers and man-breakers [prison officials]. Outl 150: 727-8 S 5 '28 **11347**

Bates, Sanford. Federal prison employees. Am Fed 37: 321-2 Mr '30 **11348**

Brown, Mrs. William J. Echoes from Switzerland. Tr Sch Bul 27: 170-1 F '31 **11349**

Gap between penal theory and administration. Am B Assn J 16: 211-12 Ap '30 **11350**

Hepbron, James M. The new director of Maryland prisons [Harold E. Donnell]. Nat Soc Pen Inf N Y Bul 1: 7-8 O '30 **11351**

Klemm, O. Erfahrungen bei einer Eignungsprüfung an Kriminalbeamten. Neue Psychol Stud 5: 3-22 '29 **11352**

Mulcahy, George F. A. Hints to correctional officers. 14p. Boston, Deer Island, Suffolk county house of correction, 1927 **11353**

National crime commission. Sub-committee on pardons, parole, probation, penal laws and institutional correction. Penal administration as related to job analysis, personnel and civil service. 57p. New York, 1929? **11354**

Personnel and penal administration. Good Govt 47(3) Mr '30 **11355**

Sanford Bates, new superintendent of federal prisons. Frat Order Police J 12: 6, 23 Je '29 **11356**

Stutsman, Jesse O. The prison staff. Ann Am Acad 157: 62-71 S '31 **11357**

Tischer, Albert. Von der Aufgabe des Strafanstaltslehrers. Bl f Gefängniskunde 60: 182-91 '29 **11358**

CHAPLAIN

Lancaster, R. V. Opportunities and embarrassments in the work of the chaplain. Am Pris Assn Proc 60: 341-4 '30 **11359**

Nadasting, F. Psychologische Erfahrungen aus der Gefängnisseelsorge. Zeitsch f Rel-Psychol 2: 62-73 '29 **11360**

GUARDS

[Examination questions for prison guards]. Ecrou 9: 186-95 Mr '28 **11361**

Fishman, Joseph Fulling. Death stalks the prison guard. On Guard 1: 2-3, 6 Ja '31 **11362**

Galston, Samuel H. What do they have to know? Keepers must undergo a rigid examination to determine their fitness for their work. On Guard 1: 6, 10-11 Je '31 **11363**

New York (city). Department of correction. Prison keepers council. On Guard v1, no1, January 1931- **11364**

PHYSICIANS

Gentz, W. Der Strafanstaltsarzt im Entwurf des Strafvollzugsgesetzes. Deut Zeitsch f d ges gerichtl Med 10: 214-34 Ag '27 **11365**

Hellstern, Erwin P. Strafanstaltsarzt und Strafvollzug. Monats f Kriminalpsychol u Strafrechtsref 19: 662-70 N '28 **11366**

Loudet, Osvaldo. El médico de la prisiones. R de Crimin, Psiquiat y Med Leg 15: 373-9 Jl '28; same title: Bibl Nac de Crim y Cienc Afines Bol 3(1): 3-7 Jl '28; R de Identif y Cienc Pen 3: 134-9 N '28 **11367**

MacMurchy, Helen. The doctor and what he may do for the prisoner. Am Pris Assn Proc 59: 349-54 '29 **11368**

Minnigerode, Lucy. Nursing in federal prisons. Am J Nursing 31: 1056-8 S '31 **11369**

Noble, Harold. The prison doctor. Bul St Inst [Iowa] 31: 100-2 Mr '29 **11370**

WARDEN

Espionage over prison wardens. L Notes 33: 5 Ap '29 **11371**

Fishman, Joseph Fulling. Old calamity. On Guard 1: 4-5, 8-11 O '31 **11372**

Kennedy, John B. Wages of sin; interview with L. E. Lawes. Collier's 85: 29 Ja 18 '30 **11373**

TRAINING

Bates, Sanford. Institutes and schools for prison officials. Nat Conf Soc Wk Proc 1931: 421-9 **11374**

Branham, V. C. The prison guard goes to school. Correction 1: 5-6 Ap '31 **11375**

Brucks. Fortbildungslehrgänge für Strafanstaltsbeamte in Preussen. Bl f Gefängniskunde 60(3): 422-6 '29 **11376**

Cox, Wm. B. Prison officers training school. Am Pris Assn Proc 60: 170-4 '30 **11377**

Hart, Hastings H. Training schools for prison officers; plans and syllabi of the United States training school for prison officers; the New York city keepers' training school; the British training school for prison officers. 70p. N. Y. Russell Sage foundation, 1930 **11378**

Lawes, Lewis E. The prison officers' school. Correction 1: 3-4 My '31 **11379**

Niles, William H. Keepers training school. On Guard 1: 4, 12 F '31 **11380**

Schmidt. Reform der Beamtenausbildung in der preussischen Strafanstaltsverwaltung. Bl f Gefängniskunde 62(2): 332-45 '31 **11381**

Sellin, Thorsten. Europe trains its prison personnel. Pris J 11: 7-8 O 31 **11382**

Steinmetz, Richard C. Training prison officers. Nat Soc Pen Inf N Y Bul 2: 10, 16 O '31 **11383**

Weidner. Ausbildung der Strafanstaltsbeamten. Ein Ausschnitt aus der praktischen Arbeit. Bl f Gefängniskunde 61: 225-36 '30 **11384**

Weissenrieder, Otto. Ausbildung und Prüfung der sächsischen Gefängnisfürsorger. Bl f Gefängniskunde 59: 96-102 '28 **11385**

ARCHITECTURE

Bates, Sanford. Architectural environment in relation to prisoners. J Crim L & Crimin 22: 536-44 N '31 **11386**

Bates, Sanford. Importance of architectural environment in the treatment of prisoners. Nat Conf Soc Wk Proc 1931: 105-15 **11387**

Bringhurst, G. K. Fin type radiation as used in public institutions. Heat & Ven 28: 72-4 Ap '31 **11388**

Callendar, John Hancock. Modern penology and prison design. Arch Forum 55: 381-6 S '31 **11389**

Caretti, C. V. La costruzione di un riformatorio. Riv di Dir Peniten 1: 295-321, 780-811 '30 **11390**

Davison, Robert L. Prison architecture. Arch Rec 67: 69-100 Ja '30; same title: Ann Am Acad 157: 33-9 S '31 **11391**

Durr, H. A. Combination steam and hot water systems heat Cook county court house and jail. Heating-Piping 3: 214-18 Mr '31 **11392**

Frede, Lothar and Perret, Alfred. Baupläne für eine moderne Strafanstalt. Monats f Kriminalpsychol u Strafrechtsref 22: 10-28 Ja '31 **11393**

Hentig, Hans v. Neue Bau-Probleme im Strafvollzug. Monats f Kriminalpsychol u Strafrechtsref 21: 281-91 My '30 **11394**

Hopkins, Alfred. Prisons and prison building. 140p. N. Y. Architectural bk. pub. co. 1929? **11395**

Hopkins, Alfred. Some recent plans for prisons of medium security. Nat Soc Pen Inf N Y Bul 2: 1-3, 5-8 O '31 **11396**

Items for sewage disposal and outfall for Attica state prison, N. Y. Eng N 105: 869-70 N 27 '30 **11397**

Jacoby. Die Gestaltung des Strafanstaltsgebäudes im modernen Strafvollzug. Monats f Kriminalpsychol u Strafrechtsref 21: 96-100 '30 **11398**

Jeremias. Der neue Schlafzellenbau der Landesstrafanstalt in Ludwigsburg. Bl f Gefängniskunde 60(2): 209-14 '29 **11399**

Lack of fire resistive material and fire protection cost 320 lives at Ohio state penitentiary. Safety Eng 59: 317-18 Je '30 **11400**

National committee on prisons and prison labor. Prison architecture. Arch Rec 77-91 Ja '30 **11401**

The new medium security prison [Wallkill, Ulster county, New York state]. Correction 1: 5-6 Ag '31 **11402**

Planning the fall of the Bastille. Pris J 11: 15-18 Jl '31 **11403**

Smith, J. Canadian inspector describes Headingly jail installation. Dom Eng 134: 43-5 Ja 24 '31 **11404**

Sullivan, Florence J. Facts relating to the removal of Sing Sing state prison from its present location. 8p. New York, 27 Cedar st. The Author, 1927 **11405**

Thot, Ladislao. Arquitectura penitenciaria; nota bibliográfica. R de Identif y Cienc Pen 6: 326-35 Jl '30 **11406**

DISCIPLINE

Belym, Léon. La crise du régime cellulaire. R de Dr Pén et de Crimin 11: 221-8, 325-58 '31 **11407**

Bernfeld, S. Die Formen der Disziplin in Erziehungsanstalten. Zeitsch f Kinderforsch 33: 367-90 O '27 **11408**

Bumke, Erwin. Die Regeln der Internationalen Kommission für die Behandlung der Gefangenen. Zeitsch f d ges Strafrechtswiss 51: 583-92 '31 **11409**

Canobbio, P. La disciplina nelle carceri. Riv di Dir Peniten 1: 278-87 '30 **11410**

Carrara, Mario. Trattamento individualissato di criminali in un penitenziario (Untermassfeld). Arch di Antrop Crim 50 (6): 901-26 N '30 **11411**

Cerberus on trial. Commonweal 11: 237-8 Ja 1 '30 **11412**

Cremona, G. Segregazione cellulare e pazzia. Arch di Antrop Crim 49: 773-801 N '29 **11413**
Analysis of statistical data of preventive and penal institutions for period 1909-23.

Dewan Bahadur P. Kesava Pillai. Treatment of prisoners: a plea for reform. Hindustan R 54: 133-7 F '30 **11414**

Egloffstein, Leo von. Rassenfragen im Gefängnis. Bl f Gefängniskunde 60(2): 198-209 '29 **11415**

Fishman, Joseph F. The Kangaroo court. On Guard 1: 4-5, 11-12 D '31 **11416**

Haskin, E. Réforme des règles sur le traitement des prisonniers en Prusse. R Int de Dr Pén 8: 244-70 '31 **11417**

Jacobi, Ludwig. Die Rechtsstellung der Strafgefangenen. Zeitsch f d ges Strafrechtswiss 50 (3): 376-405 '30 **11418**

Lawes, Lewis E. The importance of time-compensation as an aid to prison management; its historical background, and the testimony of prison administrators. Ossining, New York, Sing Sing, 1931 **11419**

League of Nations. Improvements in penal administration; standard minimum rules for the treatment of prisoners drawn up by the International prison commission. 6p. (1930.IV.10) Boston, World peace foundation, 1930 **11420**

Longhi, Silvio. Limiti e modalità del regime cellulare nel sistema penitenziario moderno. Riv Pen 1(8): 865-70 Ag '30 **11421**

Ottolenghi, S. L'assistenza del giudice nell'esecuzione della penal e i nuovi orizzonti della discipline carcerarie. Riv di Dir Peniten 1: 29-41 '30 **11422**

Poller. Ein Wort über unsere Hausstrafen. Ein Vorschlag zur Hebung der Disziplin in der Strafanstalt. Bl f Gefängniskunde 62: 427-9 '31 **11423**

Ribeiro, Carlos. Acção disciplinadora da vida carceraria sobre o caracter inicial do delinquente. R de Cultura Jurid 1: 149-52 Ap '29 **11424**
Conselho penitenciario, Pareceres.

Schläger. Die körperliche Durchsuchung im Strafprozess. Med Klin 26: 1278-9 Ag 22 '30 **11425**

Steckelings, Wilhelm. Die Schuldfrage im eignen Urteil des Rechtsbrechers: ein Beitrag zur Methodologie und Psychologie der Selbsterkenntnis sowie zu einer zu schaffenden Kriminalpädagogik. 189p. Paderborn, Ferdinand Schöningh, 1929 **11426**

Stevenson, Lilian. Mathilda Wrede of Finland, friend of prisoners. Howard J 3: 31-5 S '30 **11427**

Suitability for borstal discipline. Just Peace 95: 250-1 Ap 18 '31 **11428**

Thayer, Walter N. Jr. Rewarding prison inmates for good behavior. Correction 1: 3 F '31 **11429**

To spy or not to spy; espionage system introduced in federal prisons. Outl 151: 494-5 Mr 27 '29 **11430**

Tului, G. La segregazione cellulare. Riv di Dir Peniten 1: 71-5 '30 **11431**

Tului, G. Tra i segregati. Arch di Antrop Crim 47: 155-84 Mr '27 **11432**

Votaw, A. H. Discipline. Pris J 10: 7-9 O '30 **11433**

Wade, M. W. Bad men and good behavior. Cur Hist 27: 339-41 D '27 **11434**

RIOTS, ESCAPES, ETC.

Alger, George W. Behind the New York mutinies. Survey 62: 559-60 S 1 '29 **11435**

Alger, George W. The revolt of the convicts. Atlan M 145: 688-97 My '30 **11436**

Black, Jack. Why prisoners revolt. L I D M 8: 3-4 My '30 **11437**

Blocking the getaway. On Guard 1: 2-3, 5, 8-10 F '31 **11438**

Bloodiest prison mutiny [Colorado]. Lit Dig 103: 8-9 O 19 '29 **11439**

Booth, Maude Ballington. Prison riots and their causes. Am Pris Assn Proc 60: 109-17 '30 **11440**

Callahan, Jack. Let's riot. Scribner's 90: 387-90 O '31 **11441**

Carmody, Joseph J. Prison mutinies; causes of recent prison riot epidemic. Police "13-13" 4: 8-9 D '29 **11442**

Cornil, P. Révoltes dans les prisons américaines. R de Dr Pén et de Crimin 9: 933-4 Ag '29 **11443**

Desperation will out; mutinies in the state prisons of New York. Survey 63: 451-2 Ja 15 '30 **11444**

Esmond, Burton D. The effect of Baumes laws on prison outbreaks. N Y St Assn Magistrates Proc 21: 82-93 '29 **11445**

Fishman, Joseph Fulling. Causes of prison riots. On Guard 1: 1-2, 8-10 S '31 **11446**

Fishman, Joseph Fulling. Convict leaders: some interesting facts about those who instigate prison breaks. On Guard 1: 4-5, 12-13 Je '31 11447

Fishman, Joseph Fulling. Sleuths of the "stir": intelligent handling of every rumor and clue needed to thwart attempts of prisoners to make "getaway." On Guard 1: 6-7, 10-12 Ap '31 11448

Gernet, M. Psikhologia pobegov ie tyurem. Problemy Prestupnosti (4): 58-78 '29 11449

Hannan, John J. Prison rioting as result of idleness; distracted criminals turn to destructiveness. Nat Soc Pen Inf N Y Bul 1: 10 Ag '30 11450

Kugler, Michael. Die Meuterei und das Ausbrechen von Gefangenen de lege lata et ferenda. 68p. Diss. Erlangen, 1930. Babenhausen, J. Kreutzer, 1931 11451

Lane, Winthrop D. Illinois prison riots. Survey 66: 94 Ap 15 '31 11452

Lane, Winthrop D. Prisons at the breaking point. Survey 62: 557-8 S 1 '29 11453

Lane, Winthrop D. Prisons where trouble may come. Survey 64: 399-401 Ag 1 '30 11454

Löcker, Max. Die Befreiung von Gefangenen nach dem geltenden Recht und dem Entwurf zu einem Deutschen Strafgesetzbuch von 1927. 70p. bibliog vii-x. Diss. Erlangen, 1931. Kallmünz, Michael Lassleben, 1931 11455

Mackaye, Milton. Revolt in our prisons. Outl 153: 325-8 O 30 '29 11456

McLellan, H. Revolt among missing men. R of R 81: 54-60 F '30 11457
Riots at Dannemora, Auburn, and Leavenworth.

Mannheimer, Eugene. Thoughts on some recent prison outbreaks. Bul St Inst [Iowa] 32: 119-25 Mr '30 11458

Mutiny in Meerut jail. Lab M 12: 634-6 O '30 11459

Penitentiary riots; Joliet-Stateville. Welf Bul 22: 1, 3 Ap '31 11460

Phillip, Alban M. The prison breakers. 292p. N. Y. Holt, 1928 11461

Prison disorders. Commonweal 11: 211 D 25 '29 11462

Prison outbreaks. Pris Assn N Y Ann Rep 85: 17-29 '29 11463
Classification of prisoners; employment.

Prison outbreaks show urgency of prison reform. Am City 42: 106 Mr '30 11464

Responsibility for prison riots. Nat Soc Pen Inf N Y Bul 1: 3-4 D '30 11465

Riot at Auburn. Nation 129: 768 D 25 '29 11466

Rioting prisoners. Pris J 10: 1-2 Jl '30 11467

Riots and reforms. R of R 81: 59 Je '30 11468

Ryan, Paul C. Massachusetts troopers all set for possible riots in various prisons. State Trooper 13: 11, 22 D '31 11469

Two prison mutinies. New Repub 50: 302-3 Ag 7 '29 11470

United States. Congress. Senate. Committee on judiciary. Punishment for escaping prisoners, report to accompany H. R. 9021, January 24, 1929. 2p. Washington, 1929 (70th Cong. 2d sess. S. Rep. 1505) 11471

EDUCATION

Allen, Chester. Widening the horizon of the prison cell. Soc Forces 9: 76-9 O '30 11472

Asher, E. J. The training needs of reform school boys, experimentally determined. Je Delin 11: 151-8 S '27 11473
Study of 20 fourteen year old boys at Kentucky House of reform.

Beier, Lee C. Reformation as a science. Pris J 11: 9-11 O '31 11474

Bixby, F. Lovell. Objectives in prison education. Pris J 11: 11-13 Ap '31 11475

Black, Jack. The prison as character builder. Nat Conf Soc Wk Proc 56: 191-9 '29 11476

Brandstätter, H. Ein Beitrag zur Strafvollzugsbeamtenfrage. Monats f Kriminalpsychol u Strafrechtsref 22: 663-76 N '31 11477

Brandstätter, H. Die Erziehungsprobleme im Strafvollzug unter besonderer Berücksichtigung des Problems der pädagogischen Führerschaft. Monats f Kriminalpsychol u Strafrechtsref 20: 512-18 Ag '29 11478

British prisoners show marked effect of instruction. Sch Life 13: 51 N '27 11479

Castro, Pedro Barrontes. Education of prisoners in Peru. Pan-Am Union Bul 61: 679-84 Jl '27 11480

Close, O. H. What should be the training program of a correctional school? J Juv Res 15: 251-9 O '31 11481

Correspondence courses in the U.S.S.R. Soviet Union R 7: 41-2 Mr '29 11482

Cowles, Silvia. Arts and crafts in prison education. Howard J 3: 58-60 '31 11483

Cultural work among prisoners in U.S.S.R. Soviet Union R 7: 35 F '29 11484

Deggau, A. Pädagogische Fragen und Vorfragen zum erziehlichen Strafvollzug. Bl f Gefängniskunde 61: 217-24 '30 11485

Education in prison. Just Peace 95: 330 My 23 '31 11486

Education in San Quentin prison. Sch & Soc 33: 496 Ap 11 '31 11487

Frankhauser, Mary E. Ideal program for the education of adult prisoners. Am Lib Assn Bul 25: 142-3 Ap '31 11488

Frede, L. Educational system in penal institutions of Thuringia. Ment Hyg 14: 610-27 Jl '30 11489

Freden, Gustav and Robbins, C. L. The prison school. Sch & Soc 25: 577-82 My 14 '27 11490
Statistics of 36 schools.

Frederick, Joseph (pseud). Education in prison. Survey 57: 490-2 Ja 15 '27 11491

High school courses in the prison of California. Sch & Soc 31: 799 Je 14 '30 11492

Illinois. Southern Illinois penitentiary school, Menard. Annual report *In* Annual report of Department of public welfare 12, 1928/29: 255; 13, 1929/30: 326-8
School organized September 1927. 11493

Kent, Muriel. Education in prisons. Empire R (330): 65-71 Jl '28 11494

Kite, St. Alban. The New Jersey plan for the rehabilitation of offenders. Am Pris Assn Proc 60: 333-8 '30 11495

Klug, I[gnaz]. Kriminalpädagogik. 142p. Paderborn, Schöningh, 1930 11496

Kölblin. Erziehliche Einzelbehandlung im allgemeinen und progressiven Strafvollzug. Bl f Gefängniskunde 58: 170-97 '27 11497

Krebs. Der Erziehungsbeamte in der Strafanstalt. Zeitsch f d ges Strafrechtswiss 49: 65-83 '29 11498

Kuiper, A. D. De verzorging der godsdienstige behoeften der gevangenen. Maandbl v Ber en Reclasseer 7: 295-6 O '28 11499

Liepmann, M. American prisons and reformatory institutions; translated by Charles A. Fiertz. Ment Hyg 12: 225-315 Ap '28 11500

Lungwitz, Hans. Psychobiologische Erziehung der Strafgefangenen. Arch f Krim 84: 118-34 Ap '29 11501

MacCormick, A[ustin] H. Chair of education in prisons. Sch Life 16: 95-6 Ja '31 11502

MacCormick, Austin H. Education and the library in the prison. Am Pris Assn Proc 60: 35-49 '30 11503

MacCormick, Austin H. Education in penal institutions. Nat Conf Soc Wk Proc 1929: 200-12 11504

MacCormick, Austin H. Education in the prisons of tomorrow. Ann Am Acad 157: 72-7 S '31 11505

MacCormick, Austin H. Education of adult prisoners; a survey and a program. 456p. N. Y. National society of penal information, 1931 11506

MacCormick, Austin H. Light in dark places: adult education as a penal palliative. J Adult Educ 1: 129-41 '29 11507
San Quentin, California and Wisconsin prison education.

MacCormick, Austin H. Penal service calls for adult schooling. Pris J 10: 21-3 Ap '30 11508

MacCormick, Austin H. Rehabilitation through books. J Adult Educ 3: 433-7 O '31 11509

Masson, Harry. Education in Sing Sing prison. N Y St Educ 18: 160-2 O '30 11510

Monelli, G. La rieducazione dei corrigenti. Riv di Dir Peniten 1: 749-55 '30 11511

Moore, Sydney H. Re-making men [at Wakefield prison]. Congreg Q 25-31 Ja '27 11512

[Murray, S. R. G.]. Character building in prison. Howard J 3: 86-7 '31 11513

O'Hagan, Anne. Salvaging girls: is punishment or salvaging the better way with delinquents. Woman's J 13: 16-17 N '28 11514
New York (state) reformatory for women, Bedford Hills, theory of rehabilitation.

Penal service and adult education. Soc Serv R 4: 493-5 S '30 11515

Peterson, Clarence Stewart. Education training at the New Jersey reformatory. Nat Soc Pen Inf N Y Bul 2: 5 Je '31 11516

Porter, Rebecca N. World of forgotten men: extension work of the University of California among the prisoners at San Quentin. Survey 61: 738-40 Mr 1 '29; same title: R of R 79: 98- Ap '29 11517

Prison education in New York city. Sch & Soc 34: 144-5 Ag 1 '31 11518

Prison illiterates. Welf Mag 18: 375-6 Mr '27 11519

Prisoners at school. Survey 63: 479 Ja 15 '30 11520

Ruff, Walter. Erziehungsstrafvollzug und Kirche. Bl f Gefängniskunde 59(2): 182-215 '28 11521

Runkle, Fred C. High school education for the training school boy [Eldora]. Bul St Inst [Iowa] 32: 30-5 Ja '30 11522

Smith, Mary Byers. Girls' reading in correctional institutions. Wilson Bul 6: 113-26 O '31; [abstract]: Am Lib Assn Proc 53: 545-6 '31 11523

Stigers, E. M. World of forgotten men; reply. Survey 62: 375-6 Je 15 '29 11524
Types of education at San Quentin.

Taylor, Harold D. Educational activities—Illinois state reformatory. Nat Soc Pen Inf N Y Bul 2: 9, 16 O '31 11525

Todd, Hobart H. What should be the educational program of an institution. Nat Conf Juv Agencies Proc 24: 5-15 '27 11526

Varekamp, J. H. jr. De verzorging van de godsdienstige behoeften der gevangenen. Maandbl v Ber en Reclasseer 7: 272-7 S '28 11527

Vincent, W. D. Evaluation of educational elements in a corrective industrial training school. Nat Conf Juv Agencies Proc 24: 34-8 '27 11528

Wahlquist, John T. Education in the prisons of Utah. Sch & Soc 26: 45-6 Jl 9 '27 11529

Zeugner, Franz. Pestalozzis Stellung zur Kriminalpädagogik. Bl f Gefängniskunde 60(2): 172-81 '29 11530

Religious

Böse, Fritz. Der Kirchenraum der Landesstrafanstalten in Wolfenbüttel. Bl f Gefängniskunde 61: 77-9 '30 11531

Christianity and prisons. Pris J 10: 19-20 O '30 11532

Collins, Walter. Religion and social service: do they conflict in the rehabilitation of the prisoner? Am Pris Assn Proc 60: 238-41 '30 11533
Address before National prisoners' aid association.

Cowan, Thomas. Religion and social service: do they conflict in the rehabilitation of prisoners? Am Pris Assn Proc 60: 241-4 '30 11534
Address before National prisoners' aid association.

Lewis, Harry S. Faith as a force in prison work; rehabilitation of prisoners. On Guard 1: 2 My '31 11535

[Votaw, Albert H. and Stern, Leon]. Religious activities in the jails of Pennsylvania. Pris J 7: 7-11 Jl '27 11536

Wahl, Carl. Die Erziehung in der Strafanstalt vom Standpunkt des evangelischen Seelsorgers. Bl f Gefängniskunde 59: 67-73 '28 11537

EMPLOYMENT

American toy manufacturer, September 1930 is a prison labor number: Convict contracts for toys loom as large threat to toy makers; Sydney J. Rockwell. Prison made toys must go; Franklin Butler. Toy machinery in Michigan prison. 11538

Barred at ports, Soviet lumber may get in through courts. Bus W 13 F 18 '31 11539

Bennett, J. V. Prison industries. Am Pris Assn Proc 60: 135-43 '30 11540

Berger, Robert. Das Arbeitsrecht der Gefangenen. Arbeitsrecht 18: 19-26 Ja '31 11541

Bernus, Pierre. Les Soviets et l'europe officielle. J Débats 38 ptl: 302-3 F 20 '31 11542

Brandstätter, Heinz. Sozialpädagogische Betrachtungen zur Gefängnisarbeit. Monats f Kriminalpsychol u Strafrechtsref 21: 257-73 My '30 11543

Breen, Mary. Work in a woman's detention home [Detroit]. Am Pris Assn Proc 54: 229-36 '29 11544

Brook, H. M. Vocational training in state institutions. Bul St Inst [Iowa] 29: 93-9 Ap '27 11545

Buwalda, Imra Wann. The crime problem and prison industrialization: idleness the weak spot in our prison system. Tax Dig 9: 58-60 F '31 11546

Calvert, E. Roy. Prison labor abroad. Spectator 145: 331-3 S 13 '30 11547

Cass, Edward R. A general statement of the prison labor problem. 10p. Albany, J. B. Lyon co. 1928 11548

Cass, E[dward] R. Prison labor. Pris Assn N Y Ann Rep 83: 81-8 '27 11549

Cass, E[dward] R. Prison labor legislation and the health of prisoners. Nat Conf Soc Wk Proc 1931: 116-25 11550

Cialente, Amelio. Raggruppamento di delinquenti abituali e lavoro obbligatorio in colonia. Scuola Pos ns7: 154-8 Mr '27 11551

La concurrence des prisons. Ecrou 8: 393-6 Jl '27 11552

Finnell, Woolsey. Is prison labor economical on state highway construction? Am Rd Builders Assn Proc 1931: 441-5 11553

Fishman, Joseph. Employment in the county jails. 8p. (Pub no16) New Jersey, Department of institutions and agencies, 1928 11554

Franchi, B. Il lavoro all'aperto nel quadro dei problemi penitenziari. Arch di Antrop Crim 47: 46-73 Ja '27 11555

Gardiner, William Tudor. [Employment of prisoners]. Conf Gov'rs Proc 1929: 33-6 11556

Gill, Howard B. The prison labor problem. Ann Am Acad 157: 83-101 S '31 11557

Grant, W. W. jr. Obstacles to prison industrialization: prison expenditures heavy drain on taxpayer. Tax Dig 8: 360-2 O '30 11558

Hyneman, Charles S. The problem of providing incentive for prison labor. J Crim L & Crimin 17: 603-21 F '27 11559

Jackson, Henry Theodore. Prison labor. J Crim L & Crimin 18: 218-68 bibliog (p265-8) Ag '28 11560

Jaffray, Julia K. Work—the great reformer. Welf Mag 19: 614-19 My '28 11561

Karpoff, P. I. Die schöpferische Tätigkeit der Gefangenen. 82p. (Twortschesstwo sakljutschjönnich). Hrsg vom Volkskommissariat für Inneres. Moskau, 1929 11562

Kothe, A. Das Problem der Arbeit in den Gefangenenanstalten. Monats f Kriminalpsychol u Strafrechtsref 21: 342-8 '30 11563

Liszt, Eduard von. Korneuburg, seine Erziehungs- und Zwangsarbeitsanstalt. Bl f Gefängniskunde 60: 149-55 '29 11564

Mackall, Lawton. Working to beat crime. 2p. New York Herald Tribune, July 14, 1929, Reprint 11565

Mauro, G. B. de. Peine et travail. R Int de Dr Pén 6: 91-105 '29 11566

Mauro, G. B. de. Pena e lavoro. R de Identif y Cienc Pen 2: 197-210 Jl '28 11567

Memorandum regarding the use of convict labor in the construction of prisons. Pris J 9: 7-13 Ja '29 11568

National committee on prisons and prison labor. Report presented to the annual meeting, April 14, 1930. 26p. New York, 1930 11569

National committee on prisons and prison labor. Solution of the prison labor problem: summary of excerpts from the Governors' conference, 1923-1928. [9]p. New York, 1929 11670

National committee on prisons and prison labor. Committee on the care and training of delinquent women and girls. Industries for correctional institutions for women; report of a survey. 144p. New York, 1927 11571

National women's trade union league of America. Convict labor—loss or gain. Life & Lab Bul 5(4): 1-3 Mr '27 11572

No hard labour. Just Peace 93: 654 O 19 '29 11573

Novelli, G. Il lavoro dei detenuti. Riv di Dir Peniten 1: 469-552 '30 11574

Peirce, John M. The use of prison-made products by state and its political subdivisions. Pac Purchasor 12: 19-23 My '30 11575

Pennsylvania prison society. Memorandum regarding the use of convict labor in the construction of prisons. Pris J 9: 7-13 Ja '29 11576

Philippine Islands. Department of justice. Bureau of prisons. Catalogue of products of the Industrial division of Bilibid prison. 92p. (revised January 1930) Manila, 1930 11577

Appendix: Discipline above all, by Ramon Victorio.

Prison labor and the prison riots. L Notes 33: 204 F '30 11578

Prison problem as a business angle. Bus W 13 Ja 22 '30 11579

Rahne, Helmut. Die Gefangenenarbeit im Rahmen des Erziehungsstrafvollzuges. 98p. (Bl f Gefängniskunde, 62 supp '31) Heidelberg, Winter, 1931 11580

Report on prison-made goods. Ptr Ink 149: 132 O 10 '29 11581

Römer, A. Die Arbeit der Strafgefangenen in Beziehung zur Einzel- und Gesamtwirtschaft. Bl f Gefängniskunde 59(2): 153-62 '28 11582

Sagarna and Gomez. [Addresses on convict labor]. R de Crimin, Psiquiat y Med Leg 14: 371-8 My '27 11583

Scott, B. L. Manufacturers and labor advise on the development of prison industries. 7p. New York, National committee on prisons and prison labor, 1927 11584

Sommer, M. Der Resozialisierungswert der Arbeit nach dem amtlichen Entwurf eines Strafvollzugsgesetzes. Soz Praxis 36: 503-9 My 19 '27 11585

State to decide on prison goods. Bus W 10 O 12 '29 11586

Stoefs, A. Le travail des détenus. Ecrou 8: 59-69 Ja '27 11587

Stoefs, [A.]. Le travail des détenus. Rapport du Service central sur l'exercise 1925. With a criticism by E. B[ertrand]. Ecrou 8: 170-98 Mr '27 11588

Stone, Edna L. Recent references on convict labor. M Lab R 26: 199-203 My '28 11589

Supplementary to list in Monthly labor review, October 1925.

Whitin, E. Stagg. The employment of prisoners. Nat Soc Pen Inf N Y Bul 1: 3-4 Ag '30 11590

Whitin, E. S[tagg]. Labor for the benefit of the prisoner. 11p. New York, National committee on prisons and prison labor, 1930 11591

AUSTRALIA

Prisoners and afforestation: Western Australian scheme. Austral For J 10: 203-4 Ap '27 11592

GERMANY

Strube. Gefangenarbeitsfragen im Berliner Strafvollzugsamtsbezirk. Bl f Gefängniskunde 60(1): 46-64 '29 11593

GREECE

Rahne, Helmut. Die Aussenarbeit im Strafvollzug Griechenlands. Bl f Gefängniskunde 59(2): 163-77 '28 11594

ITALY

Ravizza, A. Il regime penitenziario e l'ordinamento del lavoro nella Tripolitania. Riv di Dir Peniten 1: 42-9 '30 11595

MEXICO

Gamio, Manuel. La implantación de nuevas industrias en los establecimientos penales. R Mexicana de Der Pen 1: 71-3 Jl '30 11596

RUSSIA

Forced and convict labor in lumber work in Russia (R.S.F.S.R.) M Lab R 30: 1276-7 Je '30 11597

Forced labor in Russia and elsewhere. World Tomorrow 14: 71 Mr '31 11598

Mokrinskii, S. Prinuditelnie rabote beg soderjania pod strajei v sovietskom prave. Problemy Prestupnosti 2: 212-32 '27 11599

Müller. Das Arbeitsproblem im russischen Strafvollzug. Bl f Gefängniskunde 62(2): 358-73 '31 11600

Soviet exiles are convicts, treasury agents will hold. Bus W 6 D 3 '30 11601

Wolfson, Martin. Convict labor in Russia. New Repub 64: 49-50 Ag 27 '30 11602

SUMATRA

Cohen, L. Poenale Sanctie. Tijdschr v h Onderwijs in d Aardrijkskunde 9: 241-6 D '31 11603

Consideration of abolition of compulsory labor in tobacco industry in Eastern Sumatra.

UNITED STATES

Cox, William B. Convict labor in the south. Am Pris Assn Proc 1928: 207-14 11604

Is prison labor on highway work economical? A study made possible by the cooperation of the highway departments and prison commissioners of the 48 states. Am City 43: 153-7 O '30 11605

National committee on prisons and prison labor. Institutional farms and farming; prepared for the Eastern-southern conference and New England conference on state institutional labor; preliminary edition. 16p. New York, 1931 11606

Prisoners released in flood district. Welf Mag 18: 971 Jl '27 11607

Robinson, Louis N. Should prisoners work? A study of the prison labor problem in the United States. 353p. bibliog 313-41. Philadelphia, John C. Winston, 1931 11608

United States. Bureau of foreign and domestic commerce. Prison industries. 132p. bibliog 110-32. Washington, 1929 (Dom Comm ser no27) 11609

United States. Bureau of labor statistics. Extent and character of convict labor. Bul (439): 67-80 Je '27 11610

United States. Congress. House. Committee on judiciary. Employment of federal prisoners, report to accompany H. R. 7412 [to provide for diversification of employment of federal prisoners, for their training and schooling in trades and occupations]. January 6, 1930. 5p. Washington, 1930 (71st Cong. 2d sess. H Rep 103) 11611

United States. Congress. House. Committee on labor. Prison-made merchandise: hearings on H. R. 7729 to divest goods, wares, and merchandise, manufactured, produced, or mined by convicts or prisoners of their interstate character in certain cases. 309p. Washington, 1928 11612

United States. Congress. House. Committee on rules. Interstate character of convict-made goods: hearings, March 30, 1928. 16p. Washington, 1928 11613

United States. Congress. Senate. Committee on interstate commerce. Convict labor, hearings on S. 1940, to divest goods, wares, and merchandise manufactured, produced or mined by convicts or prisoners of their interstate character in certain cases, February 7, 1928. 188p. Washington, 1928 11614

United States. Congress. Senate. Committee on interstate commerce. Divesting prison-made products of their interstate character in certain cases. 6p. (Rep no344) Washington, February 21, 1928 11615

United States lifts embargo on shipments of pulp wood from soviet Russia. Comm & Fin Chron 131: 868-9 Ag 9 '30 11616

Alabama

Alabama. Joint committee on Alabama School of trades and industries. Report, June 7, 1927. 8p. Montgomery, 1927 11617

California

California taxpayers' association, Inc. Report on prison labor in California. 41p. (mim) (Assn Rep no92) Los Angeles, 1930 11618

Peirce, John M. California state prison inmate occupations. Tax Dig 8: 239-44 Jl '30 11619

Peirce, John M. Occupations of California's prisoners. State Govt 5-9 S '30 11620

Peirce, John M. Prison made products in California. Tax Dig 8: 163-6 My '30 11621

Slack, E. S. Industries within the walls of San Quentin. Tax Dig 8: 157-9 My '30 11622

Traeger, W[m]. I. Our county prisoner problem. Los Angeles Chron 14: 15 F 28 '31 11623

Illinois

Illinois state federation of labor. Committee on convict labor. Report. Proc 49: 215-16 '31 11624

Massachusetts

Massachusetts. Department of correction. A descriptive list of the articles and materials for use in the public institutions. 52p. [Boston] September 1929 11625

New York

New York (state). Department of correction. Division of prison industries. Analysis of prison vs. competing free made goods. (Chart CPI-13) 11626

New York (state). Department of correction. Division of prison industries. Comparative analysis of inmate assignment and wage rates at four state prisons under executive orders of June 26 and August 29 covering classification and rates as of September 30, 1930 (Chart CPI-6) 11627

Oregon

Meyers, H. W. Prison labor in Oregon. Tax Dig 8: 209-11 Je '30 11628

Pennsylvania

Pennsylvania prison society. The prison labor problem: Pennsylvania's penitentiaries developing constructive work program for inmates. 7p. Philadelphia, 1930 11629

Scott, B. L. Pennsylvania's penitentiaries developing constructive work program for inmates. Pris J 10: 1-5 Ap '30 11630

Wisconsin

Wisconsin. Prison labor investigating committee. Report. . . July 1929. 23p. Madison, 1929 11631

Wisconsin clay men oppose starting of prison plant. Brick & Clay Rec 79: 109 Ag 11 '31 11632

Wyoming

Wyoming. State commission on prison labor. Report *in* Biennial report of State board of charities and reform 1928/30: 24-5 11633

Regulation

American federation of labor. Model amendments to solve prison labor competition; state legislatures have power to prohibit sale of penitentiary products from other states. 12p. Washington, 1930 11634

Business seeks relief from prison competition. Bus W 13 Jl 30 '30 11635

But what of the prisoners? Hawes-Cooper bill. Outl 151: 97 Ja 16 '29 11636

Convicts under workmen's compensation laws. M Lab R 28: 534-6 Mr '29 11637

Davis, Charles Hall. Hawes-Cooper act unconstitutional. Lawyer & Banker 23: 296-323 N '30 11638

Federal convict labor act of 1929; state convict labor legislation. M Lab R 28: 544-55 Mr '29 11639

Federal convict labor bill. Law & Lab 10: 137 Je '28 11640

Hawes, Harry B. Defying the laws of the states: how the Hawes-Cooper bill, now pending before the United States Senate, will end system of smuggling convict-made goods. 3p. [Washington] 1928 11641

Hawes, Harry B. The truth about prison employment, facts point to soundness of principle of convict-labor bill. 8p. (Speech . . . in the Senate of the United States, April 17, 1928) 11642

Laporte, Alphonse A. and Leuschner, Frederick D. Extending state jurisdiction by act of congress. Am B Assn J 15: 199-201 Ap '29 11643

Regulations regarding the importation of convict-made goods. M Lab R 32: 128-30 Ja '31 11644

State convict labor legislation. M Lab R 28: 126-7 Mr '29 11645

Statutes restricting the sale of convict-made goods. Harv L R 44: 846-50 Mr '31 11646

Treasury department regulations prohibiting importation into United States of convict made goods. Comm & Fin Chron 131: 3466-7 N 29 '30 11647

Two states lead the way to accident compensation for convicts. Am Lab Leg R 17: 269 D '27 11648

Types

Anderson, Nels. "Stir" slaves; the prison labor contractor; the state-use system. Outl 149: 492-4, 540-2, 615-17 Jl 25-Ag 15 '28 11649

Bagley, Edward C. R. Operation of state use law of Massachusetts. Am Pris Assn Proc 60: 130-5 '30 11650

Bates, Sanford. Industries in federal prisons; state use plan adopted by government. Nat Soc Pen Inf N Y Bul 2: 5-6 Ap '31 11651

Becker, W. Buchübertragungen in Blindenschrift als Gefangenenarbeit. Bl f Gefängniskunde 58: 62-3 '27 11652

Booth, Ernest. Texas chain gang. Am Mercury 12: 306-15 N '27 11653

Byrd, A. L. Concrete paving project manned with convict labor in Alabama. Am City 43: 135-6 D '30 11654

Cooper, C. W. Highway construction by convict labor. Am City 45: 65-6 D '31 11655

Ellis, Wm. J. Growing need and value of curative occupations in all types of institutions for mental cases and in penal and correctional institutions. Occup Therapy 9: 213-20 Ag '30 11656

Kent, Robert T. Making automobile license plates. Iron Age 119: 1653-7 Je 9 '27 11657

Minnesota. State prison. Catalog of Minnesota farm machinery and twine manufactured at the Minnesota state prison, Stillwater. 50p. [Stillwater, 1927] 11658

Minnesota. State prison. [Catalog of] Minnesota hay loaders, hay rakes, binders, mowers, twine [manufactured at the Minnesota state prison]. 26p. [Stillwater, 1931] 11659

National committee on prisons and prison labor. Eastern-southern conference on state institutional labor. 8p. New York, 1930 11660
Projected organization of state-use system.

North Carolina's chain gang problem. Outl 146: 427 Ag 3 '27 11661

Peirce, John M. Marketing prison made goods: state-use system most acceptable to labor and industry. Tax Dig 8: 410-14 N '30 11662

Schwartz, Isaac Herman. Welcome to our chain gang! New Repub 66: 200-2 Ap 8 '31 11663
County prisoners in Florida leased to private lumber firms.

Steiner, Jesse Frederick and Brown, Roy Melton. North Carolina chain gang; a study of county convict road work. 194p. Chapel Hill, University of North Carolina press, 1927 11664

Strief, J. Harry. Iowa prison industries. Welf Mag 18: 948-51 Jl '27; same title: Bul St Inst [Iowa] 29: 186-90 O '27; 30: 88-95 Je '28 11665
Contract, state-account and state-use systems.

Sullivan, J. J. Prison labor, Minnesota penitentiary pays its own way by prison industry. Tax Dig 8: 160-2 My '30 11666
State-account system.

Whitlock, Buford Danville. Making little ones out of big ones. Overland ns85: 143-4 My '27 11667
Rock quarries at Folsom, Calif.

Compensation

Milliken, Ben H. Four years' experience with convict wage. Calif Highw & Pub Wks 4: 3, 6-7 Ag '27 11668

Peirce, John M. Profit sharing in state prisons. Tax Dig 8: 379-82 O '30 11669

Seitz, Don C. California salvages sinners. Outl 146: 186 Je 8 '27 11670
"Convict pay law."

Wages of prisoners. Science ns65: sup12 Mr 4 '27 11671

Weyand, L. D. The Pennsylvania plan of wage payment to prisoners. J Crim L & Crimin 18: 277-83 Ag '27 11672

HEALTH

Alvarez, Walter C. and Stanley, L. L. Blood pressure in 6,000 prisoners and 400 prison guards; statistical analysis. Arch Int Med 46: 17-39 Jl '30 **11673**

Banerji, N. D. Basal metabolism of prisoners of district jail, Lucknow [United Provinces of Agra and Oudh]. Indian J M Res 19: 229-38 Jl '31 **11674**

Barringer, E. D. and others. Minimum standards for the prevention and treatment of venereal diseases in correctional institutions. 31p. New York, National committee on prisons and prison labor, 1927 **11675**

Claude, H. and Vervaeck, P. Mesures médico-administratives à l'égard des criminels anormaux. Ann de Méd Lég 7: 150-68 Mr '27 **11676**

Heger-Gilbert, F. Le service médical dans les prisons de Belgique. Bruxelles-Méd 7: 1361-73 Ag 21 '27 **11677**

Heger-Gilbert, [F]. Sur les services médicaux des prisons et le patronage des malades mentaux à Tournai. Scalpel 80: 626-32 '27 **11678**

Hellstern, Erwin P. Zur Gesundheitsfürsorge in den Strafanstalten Deutschlands. Monatsbl d deut Reichsverb f Gerichtshilfe 2: 55-64 '27 **11679**

Hoffman, George. Sanitation at Menard [Southern Illinois penitentiary]. Welf Mag 18: 745-8 Je '27 **11680**

Hoffman, George. The sick prisoner; method of care at Southern Illinois penitentiary. Welf Mag 18: 489-92 Ap '27 **11681**

Kätterer, O. Körperliche übungen in Strafanstalten und Anstalten für Jugendliche. Schweiz Ver f Straf-, Gefängniswes u Schutzauf Verh ns9: 20-36 '29 **11682**

Kernbach, M. Penitentiary medicine; medicolegal psychiatric and anthropologic consideration. Cluj Med 10: 427-9 S 1 '29 **11683**

Krishnamurty, C. Dysentery in central jail, Rajamandry, Madras presidency. Indian M Gaz 64: 679-81 D '29 **11684**

Maagk, W. Zahnärztlich-soziale Hygiene in der Krankenfürsorge und in Strafanstalten. Zeitsch f Schulgesundhpflg 40: 274-80 Je '27 **11685**

Magnus-Alsleben, E. Gefängnishaft als Ursache von Herzleiden und Diabetes? Gutachten. Deut Med Wchnschr 57: 637-9 Ap 10 '31 **11686**

Müller, Johannes. Die Schuldigen. Skizzen aus der Arbeit der Gefangenenfürsorge und Gerichtshilfe. 36p. Gera, Selbstverl. 1928 **11687**

Penitentiary health problems. Nation's Health 9: 55-6 Je '27 **11688**

Rector, Frank L. Health and medical service in American prisons and reformatories. 282p. New York, National society of penal information, 1929 **11689**

Reissner. Gefangenenfürsorge nach dem Entwurf eines Strafvollzugsgesetzes vom 9.9. 1927. Monats f Kriminalpsychol u Strafrechtsref 19: 209-23 Ap '28 **11690**

Sérieux, P. and Goulard, R. Le service médical au donjon de Vincennes (prison d'état). Soc Fr d'Hist de la Méd Bul 21: 419-35 N '27 **11691**

Spitta, O. Gesundheitliche Fürsorge für Gefangene. Arch f soz Hyg u Demog 4(5): 409-12 N '29 **11692**

Traeger, Wm. I. Health problems in L. A. county jail. Los Angeles Chron 14: 12 Ag 28 '31 **11693**

Treadway, W. L. Medical service in federal prisons. Pub Health Rep 45: 1361-7 Je 13 '30 **11694**

United States. Congress. House. Committee on judiciary. Public health service in federal prisons, report to accompany H. R. 9235, February 1, 1930. 1p. Washington, 1930 (70th Cong. 2d sess. H Rep 583) **11695**

Vervaeck, L. La prison envisagée au point de vue psychiatrique et médical. J de Neurol et de Psychiat 28: 647-58 '28 **11696**

Wolcott, H. B. Health as a factor in social rehabilitation of colony girl. Psychiat Q 5: 33-8 Ja '31 **11697**

Diet

Brewster, S. W. Uniform dietaries for prisons. Am Pris Assn Proc 60: 161-5 '30 **11698**

Henning. Die Ernährung der Gefangenen. Bl f Gefängniskunde 61: 237-46 '30 **11699**

Hirokawa, K. On food of prisoners in Chosen. Chosen M Assn J (93): 842-4 O 20 '28 **11700**

Howe, Paul E. and MacCormick, A. H. Study of diets of federal prisoners. Am J Pub Health 21: 993-8 S '31 **11701**

Menus for county prisons [Pennsylvania]. Pris J 9: 8-9 O '29 **11702**

Shido, T.; Kobayashi, M., and others. Über die im Gefängnis zu Dairen verabreichten Nahrungsmittel. J Orient Med 13: 29 S '30 **11703**

Care of Drug Addicts

Bennett, C. S. Hospitalization of narcotic addicts, U.S. penitentiary, Leavenworth, Kansas. Kansas M Soc J 30: 341-5 O '29 **11704**

"Guard Tower". "Doing your bit on a pill": narcotic problem in prisons. On Guard 1: 4-5, 8 My '31 **11705**

MacVean, Stuart N. The problem of drug addiction. On Guard 1: 5 Jl '31 **11706**

Morton, J. Hall. Alcoholics in prison. Howard J 2: 307-11 Je '29 **11707**

Nellans, C. T. and Massee, J. C. Management of drug addicts in United States penitentiary at Atlanta. Am M Assn J 92: 1153-5 Ap 6 '29 **11708**

Ryan, John. Always alert. On Guard 1: 4-5 N '31 **11709**

Sex

Belym, Léon. Aspects actuels de la criminalité sexuelle et perspectives de son traitement pénitentiaire. R de Dr Pén et de Crimin 7: 1015-44, 1174-95 N, D '27 11710

Bondy, Curt. "Geschlecht in Fesseln." Monats f Kriminalpsychol u Strafrechtsref 20: 166-9 '29 11711

Cleric, G. F. v. Geschlecht in Fesseln und Eros im Zuchthaus. Schweiz Juristen-Zeit 26: 61-5 S 1 '29 11712

Daniel, G. Zum Sexualproblem im Strafvollzug. Monats f Kriminalpsychol u Strafrechtsref 22: 422-3 Jl '31 11713
Consejo supremo de defensa y prevención social, Mexico.

Gentz, Werner. Das sexualproblem im Strafvollzuge. Zeitsch f d ges Strafrechtswiss 50(3): 406-27 '30 11714

[Gernet, Mikhail N.] (Michael Hernett). Das Geschlechtsleben im Kerker. Zeitsch f Sexualwissensch 15(5): 305-14 '29 11715

Hapke, E. Die sexualle Frage im Strafvollzug. Zeitsch f ang Psychol 34: 323-7 '29 11716

Hentig, H. v. Der Gefängniszuhälter. Monats f Kriminalpsychol u Strafrechtsref 19: 485-7 Ag '28 11717

Keil, G. W. Syphilis among state prisoners. Am M Assn J 94: 2084 Je 28 '30 11718

Plättner, Karl. Eros im Zuchthaus. Eine Beleuchtung der Geschlectsnot der Gefangenen. 225p. Berlin, Mopr, 1929 11719

Plischke, Rudolf. Zur Frage der Sexualnot der Gefangenen. Arch f Krim 84: 193-206 My '29 11720
Bibliographical footnotes.

Il problema della funzione sessuale negli istituti penitenziari. Riv di Dir Peniten 1: 1160-2 '30 11721

Riffel, P. Fürsorge für geschlechtskranke Gefangene. Bl f Gefängniskunde 61(1): 48-59 '30 11722

Rivarola, R. and Cirio, J. J. El tratàmiento de la sifilis en la penitenciaria nacional. Bibl Nac de Crim y Cienc Afines Bol 1: 298-301 Ja '27 11723

Scaglione, Giuseppe. Il problema della funzione sessuale negli istituti penitenziari. Rassegna di Stud Sess 10: 305-8 O '30 11724

Schmidt, P. W. Eine Untersuchung der Inassen der Strafanstalt Münster auf Geschlechtskrankheiten. Klin Wchnschr 7: 2010-11 O 14 '28 11725

Smythe, J. A. El problema sexual en las prisiones. Crón Méd [Lima] 47: 353 D '30; 48: 9, 49, 98, 132 Ja-Ap '31 11726

Souza, Oswaldo Devay de. Notulas sobre o problema sexual nas prisões. R de Cultura Jurid 1: 555-66 Jl '29 11727

Voigtländer, Else. Das Sexualproblem im Strafvollzug. Zeitsch f Sexualwissensch 14: 23 Ap '27 11728

Tuberculosis

Gonçalves, J. A mortalidade pela tuberculose na cadeia nacional de Lisboa. Med Contem 48: 275-7 Ag 3 '30 11729

Hellstern, Erwin P. Gesundheitsverhältnisse im Strafvollzug, unter besonderer Berücksichtigung der Tuberkulose. Arch f soz Hyg u Demog 2(5): 420-8 '27 11730

Kallweit, M. Tuberkulose in Strafanstalten. Zeitsch f Tuberk 53(6): 543-7 '29 11731

Koehler, F. Strafvollzug an tuberkulosen Strafgefangenen. Soz Praxis 39: 550-2 Je 5 '30 11732

Palmieri, V. M. Bekämpfung der Tuberkulose in italienischen Gefängnissen. Med Welt 3: 551 Ap 13 '29 11733

Palmieri, V. M. La lotta contro la tubercolosi nelle carceri. Riforma Med 45: 33 Ja 5 '29 11734

Pietrusky, F. Tuberkulose und Gefängniswesen. Zeitsch f Tuberk 47: 309-13 '27 11735

Putto, J. A. Tuberculosis in our penal institutions. Tegen de Tuberc 26: 185-92 N '30 11736

Scotti, E. La tubercolosi nelle carceri e la redenzione sociale. Riv Med 37: 145-8 O '29 11737

LIBRARIES

Fishman, Joseph Fuller. Intellectual stepchildren of the state [abstract]. Am Lib Assn Proc 53: 544-5 '31 11738

Kent, Muriel. Prison libraries. Lib R [Scotland] 7: 286-90 '28 11739

Leigh, Dawson M. Prison library: what it should mean. Lib J 55: 641 Ag '30 11740

Long, Harriet C. They read with a purpose in prison. Lib 33: 301 Je '28 11741

MacCormick, Austin H. The librarian goes to prison [abstract]. Am Lib Assn Proc 53: 543-4 '31 11742

MacCormick, A[ustin] H. The prison library. Lib J 56: 359-60 Ap 15 '31 11743

Massachusetts. Department of corrections. Concerning institution libraries in the Commonwealth. Q 3: 2 Ja '27 11744

Mulhauser, Roland, comp. Prison libraries; a selected bibliography. 4p. New York, Russell Sage foundation, 1930 11745

Ryan, John H. The institutional library. An important adjunct at the Illinois state reformatory. Welf Mag 18: 473-5 Ap '27 11746

CARE OF MENTALLY ABNORMAL

Aschaffenburg, G. Neue Aufgaben der praktischen Psychiatrie. Allg Zeitsch f Psychiat 86: 207-14 '27 11747

Ball, Robert Jaudon. General emotionality of prisoner. J Ap Psychol 15: 435-61 O '31 11748
Study of 135 cases at San Quentin, using Woodworth Personal data questionnaire.

Benon, R. Des psychoses pénitentiaires. Ann de Méd Lég 11: 20-31 Ja '31 **11749**

Berggrav, E[ivind]. Fångens själsliv. Iakttagelser och erfarenheter från straffängelset i Oslo. 182p. Uppsala, 1929 **11750**

Christian, Frank L. Segregation of psychopathic and mentally defective recidivists. Psychiat Q 3: 452-3 O '28 **11751**
Elmira, New York.

[Gernet, Mikhail N.] (M. N. Hernett). Tiorme. Ocherki Tioremmoi Psichologii. 263p. Leningrad, Yoridicheskoe Isdatelstvo, 1930 **11752**

Harding, John R. The place of psychiatry in the prison structure. Am Pris Assn Proc 60: 207-11 '30 **11753**

Herbertz. Das Seelenleben des Strafgefangenen. Psychol Rundsch 1: 2-3 '29 **11754**

Herschmann, H. Strafrechtliche Behandlung und Interbringung der geisteskranken und psychopathischen Verbrecher. Jahrb f Psychiat u Neurol 45: 221-75 '27 **11755**

Lazar, Erwin. Probleme der forensischen Jugendpsychiatrie. 72p. (Abh aus dem juristisch-medizinischen Grenzgebiete no5) Wien, Hölder-Pichler-Tempsky, 1927 **11756**
Problem in industrial schools and reformatories.

Loudet, Osvaldo. La ansiedad simple, obsesiva y delirante en los penados. R de Crimin, Psiquiat y Med Leg 17: 262-7 My '30; same title: R de Especialid 5: 1168-76 S '30; Semana Méd 2: 1658-61 N 27 '30 **11757**

Marco, A. de. Sopra un caso di psicosi amnesica isterica carceraria con emiplegia. Cervello 10: 177-92 Jl 15 '31 **11758**

Martin, Walter B. The development of psychoses in prison. J Crim L & Crimin 18: 404-15 bibliog (p414-15) N '27 **11759**

Menninger, Karl A. Psychiatry and the prisoner. Med-Leg J 44: 24-7 Ja '27 **11760**

Mursell, George Rex. Decrease in intelligence with increase in age among inmates of penal institutions; an examination of the curve of intelligence from mental maturity (15 years) to old age (75 years). J Juv Res 13: 197-203 Jl '29 **11761**

New York (state). Prison department. Dannemora state hospital. Medical superintendent. Annual reports 28, 1927 —31, 1930. [Albany, 1928-31] **11762**

Partridge, G. E. Psychopathic personalities among boys in training schools for delinquents. Am J Psychiat 8: 159-86 Jl '28 **11763**

Patini, Ettore. Sull'illegittimità clinica della "psicosi carceraria". Riv di Dir Peniten 2: 1193-1205 S '31 **11764**

Petrén, A. Fångvårdens sinnessjukavdelningar tillkommande uppgifter. Nord Tids f Straf 16: 38-52 Ja '28 **11765**

Pilcher, Ellen. Relation of mental disease to crime, including a special study of the State hospital for the criminal insane at Ionia, Michigan, a total survey of five criminal insane hospitals and studies of crimes committed by the criminal insane. J Crim L & Crimin 21: 212-46 Ag '30 **11766**
Ionia state hospital, Michigan; Central state hospital for the criminal insane, Waupun, Wis.; Bridgewater state hospital, State farm, Mass.; Lima state hospital, Ohio; Fairview state hospital for the criminal insane, Waymart, Pennsylvania.

Salinger, F. Über die Verurteilung von offenbar Geisteskranken. Allg Zeitsch f Psychiat 87: 228-38 '27 **11767**

Saporito, Filippo. La funzione sociale del manicomio criminale. Scuola Pos ns9: 191-207 My '29 **11768**

Schaefer. Psychotherapie und Strafvollzug. Zeitsch f d ges Strafrechtswiss 49: 98-107 '29 **11769**

Stearns, A. W. Psychiatry's part in proper care and treatment of prisoners. Am Pris Assn Proc 59: 250-6 '29; same title: New England J Med 201: 1238-40 D 19 '29 **11770**

Thayer, Walter N. jr. Six years' experience with the defective delinquent [at Napanoch]. Pen Affairs (17): 9-11 Ja '28 **11771**

Tullio, B. Di. La neuropsichiatria nelle carceri. Zacchia 6: 132-5 Jl '27 **11772**

Tullio, B. Di. Wesen und Verhütung der Gefängnispsychosen. Monats f Kriminalpsychol u Strafrechtsref 18: 616-21 N '27 **11773**

Vervaeck, L. La mise en vigeur de la loi hollandaise réglant le régime pénal des psychopathes. R de Dr Pén et de Crimin 9: 90-3 '29 **11774**

Vervaeck, L. Le traitement pénal et pénitentiaire des délinquants morbides. R de Dr Pén et de Crimin 7: 1116-20 N '27; same title: R de Crimin, Psiquiat y Med Leg 15: 108-14 Ja '28 **11775**

Webster, B. R. Psychoses among criminals. Psychiat Q 2: 136-43 Ap '28 **11776**
Study of 250 admissions to Dannemora state hospital.

Yeomans, Ruth F. Who are the "criminal insane"? Fifty patients committed to Boston state hospital under Sections 100 and 104, chapter 123 of General laws of Massachusetts. Ment Hyg 14: 672-96 Jl '30 **11777**

Young, H. T. P. Observations on the prison psychoses. J Ment Sci 73: 80-95 Ja '27 **11778**

RECREATION

Belym, L. Les récreations du détenu et le régime cellulaire au Congrès pénitentiaire de Prague. R de Dr Pén et de Crimin 11: 112-17 '31 **11779**

Etten, Henry van. La musique dans les prisons. Etudes Crimin 4: 213-16 Jl '29 **11780**

Henley, Homer. Prison music: a new road to reform. Atlan M 144: 69-76 Jl '29 11781

Lawes, Lewis E. Playing the game on Sing Sing's field. Correction 1: 9-10 D '31 11782
Football at Sing Sing.

Lowell, James R. Theatricals in the prison. Police J [N Y] 16: 24, 27 F '29 11783

Meloay, Ollie. Radio behind prison walls. Radio N 10: 10-11 Jl '28 11784

Stumpf. Musikalische Veranstaltungen in Strafanstalten. Bl f Gefängniskunde 62 (2): 413-20 '31 11785

Weidner. Der Film im Dienste des Strafvollzugs. Bl f Gefängniskunde 62(2): 396-9 '31 11786

INMATES, CONVICTS, ETC.

Alsberg, Henry G. Organize the prisoners. Nation 129: 493 O 30 '29 11787

Berggrav, Eivind. Die Seele des Gefangenen. Erfahrungen und Beobachtungen aus der Strafanstalt. 140p. Göttingen, Vandenhoeck & Rupprecht, 1929; translation: The prisoner's soul—and our own, by Laura Gravely. 182p. London, Dent, 1931? 11788

Bloodgood, Ruth Salter. Welfare of prisoners' families in Kentucky. 50p. (Pub no182) Washington, U.S. Children's bureau, 1928 11789

Brice, A. H. M. Look upon the prisoner. Studies in crime; edited by A. Cairns. 288p. London, Hutchinson, 1928 11790

Butler, Amos W. Prisoners and prisons. J Crim L & Crimin 20: 182-244 Ag '29 11791

Cantor, Nathaniel F. The prisoner and the law. Ann Am Acad 157: 23-32 S '31 11792

Chaplin, Ralph. Prison blight. Forum 83: 167-79 Mr '30 11793

A convict's insurance card. Sol J 73: 66 F 2 '29 11794

Don't let anybody tell you different, by culprit 49,068. Outl 145: 403-5 Mr 30 '27 11795

Duncan, Otis D. An analysis of the population of the Texas penitentiary from 1906 to 1924. Am J Sociol 36: 770-81 Mr '31 11796

Eaton, Gertrude. The need for an international charter for prisoners. Howard J 2: 93-7 '27 11797

Field, Henry E. The attitudes of prison inmates. Am J Orthopsychiat 1: 487-500 O '31 11798

Field, Henry E. The attitudes of prisoners as a factor in rehabilitation. Ann Am Acad 157: 150-63 S '31 11799

Fishman, Joseph Fulling. Some queer prison fish. On Guard 1: 2-3, 8-9 N '31 11800

[Gernet, Mikhail N.] (M. N. Hernett). "Im Kerker" (Wtjurjme). ed.2. 264p. Juristischer Verl. der Ukraine, 1930 11801

Giardini, Giovanni. A report on the Italian convict. Pittsburgh, Pa. Board of Trustees of the Western penitentiary, 1927 11802

Herbertz, R. Kurzgespräche mit Strafgefangenen. Psychol Rundsch 1: 373-6 '29; 2: 27-30 '30 11803

Herbertz, R. Das Seelenleben des Strafgefangenen. Psychol Rundsch 1: 41-5, 80-3 '29; same title: Schweiz Zeitsch f Strafr 44: 36-49 '30 11804

Historia clínica del Reo. R Mexicana d Der Pen 1: 100-21 Jl '30 11805

H[utton], T[homas] L. Convicts in federal prisons, service of process in divorce cases. Va L R 13: 664-7 Je '27 11806

Koerber, Lenka von. Menschen im Zuchthaus. 256p. Frankfurt, Sozietätsverl. 1930 11807

Krebs, A. Bericht über einen jungen Gefangenen. Zeitsch f Kinderforsch 37: 184-208 '30 11808

Lohsing, E. Die Fahrnisse der Untersuchungs- und Strafgefangenen. Oster Anwalts-Zeit 4: 351-4 '27 11809

McCann, Joseph A. Know thyself a fundamental precept: or the mental attitude of the prisoner. On Guard 1: 4-5 Mr '31 11810

Masterman, Lucy. Y. P's: young prisoners. Contemp R 135: 594-8 My '29 11811

Mead, Bennett. Progress and results of the federal census of prisoners in the United States. Am Pris Assn Proc 54: 168-76 '29 11812

The mentality of prisoners in Indiana. Lancet 216: 45 '29 11813

Moseley, Sydney Alexander. The convict of today. 237p. London, Palmer, 1927 11814

Most prison inmates convicted of robbery. East Underw 31: 40 Ja 24 '30 11815

Out of sight, out of mind. Outl 149: 571 Ag 8 '28 11816

"A Prisoner." The Prisoner speaks. Ann Am Acad 157: 137-49 S '31 11817

Prisoner no 4000-X. A criminal looks at crime and punishment. Scribner's 81: 86-9 Ja '27 11818

Prisoners in Indiana. Ind Bul Char & Correc (158) My '28 11819

Prisoners in Ohio. Ohio Cit (27-9): 1-22 D 10 '27 11820

Prisoners maintenance. Sol J 73: 458 Jl 13 '29 11821

Richmond, Frank C. Exalting the prisoner. Med-Leg J 46: 110-11 S '29 11822

Rosenquest, Carl M. The occupation status of the Texas convict. J Delin 11: 239-56 D '27 11823

Schumann, Curt. Wanderungen mit Gefangenen. Justiz 5(5): 307-16 F '30 11824

Senf, Paul. Den Gefangenen, dass sie los sein sollen. 19p. Elberfeld, Buchh d. Erziehungsvereins, 1927 (Stimmen aus d. chriftl. Gefangenenhilfe no6) 11825

Strasser, W. Sträfling und Presse. Schweiz Ver f Straf-, Gefängniswes u Schutzauf Verh ns10: 110-25 '30 11826

Tully, Jim. California holiday. Am Mercury 13: 22-9 Ja '28 11827

Whitin, E. Stagg. The transportation of prisoners in Greater New York. Panel 5, 12 Jl '30 11828

Wingler, Adolf. Anreden der Gefangenen. Monats f Kriminalpsychol u Strafrechtsref 19: 557-9 S '28 11829

CLASSIFICATION

Baker, A. T. The psychiatric clinic of Sing Sing prison. Psychiat Q 2: 464-5 O '28 11830
Classification and vocational training of convicts.

Barnes, Harry Elmer. Common sense and science in classifying and treating criminals. Am Pris Assn Proc 60: 369-76 '30 11831

Bixby, F. Lovell. Classification and prison building. Nat Soc Pen Inf N Y Bul 2: 1-2 Ap '31 11832

Bixby, F. Lovell. The classification committee as an administrative device. Nat Soc Pen Inf N Y Bul 2: 3-4 Je '31 11833

Bixby, F. Lovell. The relation of classification to penal administration. Am Pris Assn Proc 60: 391-6 '30 11834

Castellanos, Israel. Rudimentos de tecnica penitenciaria; la clasificacion de los reclusos. 30p. Habana, "El Universo," 1928 11835

Doll, Edgar A. The classification system at the New Jersey state prison. 7p. New York, National committee on prison labor, 1927 11836

Ellis, William J. Classification as the basis for institutional training, treatment and parole. Am Pris Assn Proc 54: 189-94 '29 11837

Ellis, William J. Classification as the basis for rehabilitation of prisoners. Nat Soc Pen Inf N Y Bul 2: 6-9 F '31 11838

Ellis, William J. The New Jersey plan of classification for correctional institutions. Hosp Soc Serv 24: 499-507 D '31 11839

Eysten, J. Wackie. Das Progressivverfahren in Holland. Monats f Kriminalpsychol u Strafrechtsref 22: 310-19 My '31 11840

Loudet, Osvaldo. La clasificación de los penados en el tratamiento penitenciario. R de Especialid 6: 413-16 Jl '31 11841

Maryland. Director of classification and psychiatric service. Report *in* Annual report of the Board of welfare 9, 1930/31: 19-22 11842

National committee on prisons and prison labor. Classification as a basis for training prisoners. [4]p. New York, 1929 11843

New Jersey. State department of institutions and agencies. Division of classification and parole. Memo on proposed classification of male correctional institutions in New Jersey. 6p. (mim) [Trenton] July 20, 1929 11844

New Jersey. State department of institutions and agencies. Division of classification and parole. A procedure for the classification of inmates in correctional institutions. 3p. (mim) [Trenton] 1929 11845

Prussia. Ministry of justice. The grade system of prison administration in Prussia; translated by C. M. Liepmann. 50p. (order of June 7, 1929) 11846

The grade system in prison administration in Prussia. Pris Assn N Y Ann Rep 86: 101-30 '30 11847

Schmidt, Eduard. Die Klassifizierung der Gefangenen in Holland vor 100 Jahren. Strafvollzug 21: 272-7 S '31 11848

Sears, Joseph D. Classification of prison inmates. Pris J 10: 8-10 Jl '30 11849

Steuk, G. Erziehungs- oder Stufenvollzug. Bl f Gefängniskunde 58: 31-5 '27 11850

Ybarra, T. R. New grade system in German prisons. Outl 153: 544 D 4 '29 11851

INMATE PUBLICATIONS

California state prison, San Quentin. The Bulletin 16 (1) August 1927 11852
Monthly devoted to educational work and edited and published by San Quentin agricultural club.

Colorado. Industrial school, Golden. The Industrial training school news 5(35-7) November 14, 1931- 11853

Connecticut. Prison, Wethersfield. The Monthly record 30(3) January 1, 1927- 11854

Illinois. School for boys, St. Charles. The Boy agriculturist 24 (12) December 1931- 11855

Kansas. Industrial reformatory, Hutchinson. Reformatory herald 18(2) February 1927- 11856

Maryland. Training school for boys, Loch Raven. Maryland school news 22(11) November 1931- 11857

Michigan. Boys vocational school, Lansing. The Vocational enterprise 34(1) January 1927- 11858

Michigan. State prison, Jackson. School news, 1927-? 11859

Minnesota. Prison, Stillwater. The Prison mirror 45 (20-3) December 1931- 11860

Minnesota. State reformatory, St. Cloud. The Reformatory pillar 29 (48-9) November 24, 1931- 11861

Minnesota. Training school for boys, Red Wing. The Riverside, August 1931- 11862

Montana. State industrial school, Miles City. The Boys' messenger 13 (11) January 1927- 11863

Nebraska. State industrial school for boys, Kearney. The Industrial school times 10 (5) May 1931- 11864

North Carolina. State's prison, Raleigh. The Prison news 2 (17) March 1, 1928- 11865

Philippine Islands. Bilibid prison. The Prisoners' review, January 1927- 11866

South Dakota. Penitentiary. Sioux Falls. The Messenger 10 (7-12) January-June 1928- 11867

United States. Penitentiary, Atlanta. Good words 20 (2) February 1931- 11868

Washington. State penitentiary, Walla Walla. Agenda 6 (3) September 1927- 11869

West Virginia. Penitentiary, Moundsville. Work and hope 11 (1) October 1929- 11870

SELF-GOVERNMENT

Cornil, P. Un essai de self government à la prison de Sing-Sing. R de Dr Pén et de Crimin 9: 537-41 '29 11871

Holler, Ernst. Über Selbstverwaltung Gefangener. Erziehung 5 (10-11): 608-20 Jl '30 11872

Experiences in Untermassfeld prison.

Krebs, Albert. Die Selbstverwaltung Gefangener in der Strafanstalt. Monats f Kriminalpsychol u Strafrechtsref 19: 152-65 Mr '28 11873

Liepmann, Clara Maria. Die Selbstverwaltung der Gefangenen. 226p. (Hamburg. Schriften z Ges Strafrechtswissenschaften no12, hrsg von M. Liepmann) Mannheim, Bensheimer, 1928 11874

WRITINGS OF INMATES

Bezsonov, Youri. Mes vingt-six prisons et mon évasion de Solovki; translated from Russian by E. Semenoff. 288p. Paris, Payot, 1928 11875

Chaplin, Ralph. Share my cell. Forum 82: 321-6 D '29 11876

Clark, Charles L. and Eubank, Earle Edward. Lockstep and corridor; thirty-five years of prison life. 177p. Cincinnati, University of Cincinnati press, 1927 11877

Debs, Eugene Victor. Walls and bars. 248p. Chicago, Socialist party, 1927 11878

DeFord, Miriam Allen. Shall prisoners write books? Nation 131: 495-7 N 5 '30 11879

Fuchs, Georg. Wir Zuchthäusler. Erinnerungen des Zellengefangenen Nr.2911. 312p. München, Langen, 1931 11880

Gowen, Emmett. Two years. Scribner's 90: 141-50 Ag '31 11881

How they get that way, by culprit 49,068. Outl 145: 368-70 Mr 23 '27 11882

Pride, Robert Edwin. The invisible power. 320p. Philadelphia, Scott pub. co. 1927 11883

Indictment of capital punishment, clothed in biography of "Slim" Ferguson, a murderer.

Prison poetry. On Guard 1: 4, 8 Ja '31 11884

Romanes, Alva. The great awakening [poems from the cellhouse]. 60p. San Francisco, Long pub. co. 1927 11885

Tasker, Robert Joyce. First day. Am Mercury 10: 292-9 Mr '27 11886

Tasker, Robert Joyce. Grimhaven. 241p. New York, Knopf, 1928 11887

Account of prison life in San Quentin.

EFFECTS OF INSTITUTIONAL TREATMENT

[Barber], E. H. What good do state prisons do? Int Assn Chiefs Police Proc 1927: 137-41; same title: Police J [N Y] 15: 16-17, 30 F '28 11888

Baughan, B. E. Beauty for ashes. New ways with criminals. Howard J 3: 85-91 S '30 11889

Black, Jack. Human nature under authority; prison as character builder. Nat Conf Soc Wk Proc 1929: 191-9 11890

Campbell, G. P. [How can a penal institution aid in lessening crime?] Mass Dept Correc Q 3: 3-4 Jl '27 11891

Dvorak, R. W. Does the reformatory help or harm? Crim Just [Chicago] 9: 1-4 Jl '27 11892

Fenn, Don Frank. The modern prison—a school of crime. Nat Police Offic 2: 1, 2 O '30 11893

Garrett, Paul W. The prison as a socializing agency. Ann Am Acad 157: 78-83 S '31 11894

Gehlke, C. E. Testing the work of the prison. Ann Am Acad 157: 121-30 S '31 11895

Glynn, John T. The making of criminals. Pris J 9: 19-20 O '29 11896

Gómez, Eusebio. La influencia del correccionalismo. Bibl Nac de Crim y Cienc Afines Bol 1: 209-12 Ja '27 11897

Heindl, R. Kann das Gefängnis den Sträfling bessern? Westerm Monatsh 142: 494-6 Jl '27 11898

Hentig. Mord und Selbstmord in der Strafanstalt. Monats f Kriminalpsychol u Strafrechtsref 19: 497-8 Ag '28 11899

Hentig, Hans v. Über den Einfluss der Sicherungsverwahrung auf die englische Kriminalität. Zeitsch f d ges Strafrechtswiss 49: 60-5 '29 11900

Hentig, Hans v. Zur Psychologie des Gefangenen. Schweiz Zeitsch f Strafr 44: 452-74 '30 11901

Innes, A. Mitchell. Martyrdom in our times; an introductory essay to prison and punishment. London, Athenaeum press, 1930? 11902

MacCormick, Austin H. Are prisons antisocial? Pris J 8: 11-14 Ja '28 11903

Martin, Etienne. Le rôle médico-social des prisons. J de Méd de Lyon 10: 715-23 N 20 '29 11904

Mondio, E. Sulle psicosi carcerarie. Ann di Neurol 42: 169-88 Jl '28 11905

Mulcahy, George F. A. How can a penal institution aid in lessening crime. 9p. Deer Isl. Boston, The Author, 1927 11906

National crime commission. Propagating crime through the jail and other institutions for short-term offenders; a report submitted to the Commission by the Subcommittee on pardons, paroles, probation, penal laws and institutional correction. New York, 1929 11907

Nofcier, W. L. The contribution of institutions to the cure of crime and delinquency. Nat Conf Juv Agencies Proc 27: 161-6 '30 11908

Phelps, Harold A. Effectiveness of life imprisonment as a repressive measure against murder in Rhode Island. Am Statist Assn J sup174-81 Mr '28 11909

Porot, A. L'assistance par le travail dans les asiles Hollandais. Hyg Ment 24: 41-54 F '29 11910

Prescott, Elizabeth B. Are we allowing the "it-never-has-been-done" complex of the institution to rob the individual? Nat Conf Juv Agencies Proc 24: 19-33 '27 11911

Reccord, Augustus Phineas. Can prison be made redemptive? Chr Cent 48: 116-18 S 9 '31 11912

Robinson, Louis N. Jails and workhouses breed crime. Am City 40: 126-8 Ap '29 11913

Smith, Harold. Speaking of reformatories. Welf Mag 19: 506-8 '28 11914

Sykes, M. Cready. Making beasts of men. Comm & Fin 19: 24 Ja 1 '30 11915

REFORM OF INSTITUTIONAL TREATMENT

Buffelan, Jean. La réforme pénitentiarie en Belgique et la loi de défense sociale du 9 avril 1930. 287p. Paris, Sirey, 1930 11916

Castellanos, Israel. Un plan para reforma el regimen penal cubano. 20p. Habana, "La Universal," 1927 11917

Chapman, John Jay. Thomas Mott Osborne. Harv Grad Mag 35: 465-76 Mr '27 11918

Cordova, Antonio. La riforma penale in Colombia. Riv Pen di Dott, Legis e Giuris 110: 5-32 Jl '29 11919

Crecchio, Giuseppe de. La riforma penitenziaria. Vita Ital 19: 176-84 Ag '31 11920

Eaton, Gertrude. International penal reform and the League of nations. Int Nursing R 5: 593-600 N '30 11921

Frede, L. Die Reform des Strafvollzuges in Thüringen. Schweiz Zeitsch f Strafr 44: 209-28, 305-26 '30 11922

Glaser, Stefan. Neue Richtungen im Strafrecht und die polnische Strafrechtsreform. Monats f Kriminalpsychol u Strafrechtsref 20: 193-207 Ap '29; separate: 14p. Heidelberg, Carl Winters, 1929 11923

Grant, William W. jr. What can be done to improve prison conditions. Am B Assn Rep 55: 575-8 '30 11924

"Guard Tower" (pseud). The lockstep, stripes and solitary; reforms in prison management. On Guard 1: 2-3, 10-11 Mr '31 11925

Hogarth, A. J. Prison reform in Jamaica. Howard J 3: 52-5 S '30 11926

Kern. Der Einfluss der Strafrechtsreform auf Gerichtsverfassung und Strafverfahren. Jurist Wchnschr 58: 2670-2 S 28 '29 11927

Méndes de Almeida, Candido. Reforma do regimen penal—as penitenciárias agricolas e a pena indeterminada. Rio de Janeiro, 1931 11928

Morrison, A. C. L. Rise of the idea of reform, and its appearance in prison administration. Just Peace 94: 333-4 My 24 '30 11929

National committee on prisons and prison labor. Abolish the county jails and establish in their stead farms under state control. New York, 1929 11930

Nelson, Victor Folke. Beatae memoriae to Tom Brown, 1859-1926. Welf Mag 19: 30-1 Ja '28 11931

Nelson, Victor Folke. Is honesty abnormal? An exclusive interview with Thomas Mott Osborne. Welf Mag 19: 26-9 Ja '28 11932

Neymark, Edward. Reforma wieziennictwa polskiego. Ruch Prawn i Ekon i Socjol 8(3): 272-5 '28 11933

Neymark, Edward. La réforme pénitentiaire en Pologne. Etudes Crimin 3: 135-8 S '28; same title: R de Dr Pén et de Crimin 9: 663-8 '29 11934

Penal reform and the public. Just Peace 93: 519-20 Ag 17 '29 11935

Pollitz. Ein Versuch einer Gefängnisreform in der Türkei. Monats f Kriminalpsychol u Strafrechtsref 19: 32-41 Ja '28 11936

Practical measure for prison reform. L Notes 33: 104-5 S '29 11937

Prison conditions must be remedied. Chr Cent 46: 1077 S 4 '29 11938

Prison reform. Soviet Union R 7: 195 D '29 11939

Progress of prison reform. Just Peace 93: 726 N 16 '29 11940

Robinson, Louis N. A plan for remedying evil conditions in the local penal institutions. Am City 40: 108-10 My '29 11941

Rowe, John G. John Howard; prison reformer and philanthropist. 128p. London, Epworth press, 1927 **11942**

Saporito, Filippo. La riforma penale (Riflessione di un biologo). Scuola Pos ns7: 144-53 Mr '27 **11943**

Sellin, Thorsten. Dom Jean Mabillon—a reformer of the seventeenth century. J Crim L & Crimin 17: 581-602 bibliog (p601-2) F '27 **11944**

Sellin, Thorsten. Prison reform in Europe. Pris J 11: 19-23 Jl '31 **11945**

S[hawcross], H. W. Parliament and penal reform. Howard J 2: 124-7 '27 **11946**

Society of friends. Penal reform committee. Penal reform: an outline of past and present methods of treating delinquency and of proposals for future reform. 36p. London, Friends' bk. centre, 1928 **11947**

Stern, S. M. Proposed prison reforms; a resumé of the findings of the New York state commission to investigate the prisons. On Guard 1-9 Mr '31 **11948**

Tannenbaum, Frank. The ordeal of Thomas Mott Osborne. Survey 65: 614-16, 323-5 Mr 1 '31 **11949**

Tannenbaum, Frank. Vision that came to Thomas Mott Osborne. Survey 65: 6-11, 156-8, 614-16 O 1 '30-Mr 1 '31 **11950**

United States. Library of congress. Prison reform: recent references. 5p. (typw) Washington, December 12, 1927 **11951**

Victorio, R[amon]. Prison reform in the Philippines. Manila [Bureau of prisons] 1927 **11952**

Watkin, V. E. Penal reform and the League of Nations. Howard J 3: 80-2 S '30 **11953**

Yen, Ching-Yueh. Penal reform and criminology in China. J Crim L & Crimin 22: 576-8 N '31 **11954**

TYPES OF INSTITUTIONAL TREATMENT

PRISONS

About our prisons. Inf Serv [1-2] Jl 11 '31 **11955**

American prison association. Responsibility for prison conditions. 3p. New York, October 16, 1930 **11956**

American prisons [bibliography]. Welf Mag 19: 859-60 Je '28 **11957**

As to prisons. Commonweal 12: 63 My 21 '30 **11958**

Barr, A. J. Let tomorrow come. 269p. New York, Norton, 1929 **11959**

Barthès, L. Etude sur la décentralisation pénitentiaire. R Pénitent et de Dr Pén 51: 281-90 My '27 **11960**

Barton, George. Mass in the penitentiary. Commonweal 6: 398-9 Ag 31 '27 **11961**

Bates, Sanford. Prison administration. Ann Am Acad 157: 53-61 S '31 **11962**

Bates, Sanford. The prison of the future. Ment Hyg 14: 628-42 Jl '30 **11963**

Bertsch, Albert. Durchs Gitterfenster. Helles und Dunkles aus dem Zuchthaus. ed.2. 116p. Stuttgart, Steinkopf, 1927 **11964**

Bondy, Curt and Frede, Lothar. Gefängniskunde [Literaturübersicht]. Zeitsch f d ges Strafrechtswiss 51(4): 624-62 '31 **11965**

Bruzin. La réorganisation judiciaire et pénitentiaire. R Pénitent et de Dr Pén 51: 11-45, 48-93 Ja, Ap '27 **11966**

Le budget des prisons devant la chambre. Ecrou 9: 234-42 My '28 **11967**

Byers, Joseph P. Obstacles to proper prison control. Am Pris Assn Proc 60: 265-78 '30 **11968**

Cass, E. R. Responsibility for prison conditions. J Crim L & Crimin 22: 586-8 N '31 **11969**

Caton, A. R. Impressions of Eastern prisons. Howard J 2: 211-13 O '28 **11970**

Charpentier, Clément. Les conséquences de la réforme judiciaire au point de vue pénitentiaire. R Pénitent et de Dr Pén 53: 245-54 Je '29 **11971**

Chisolm, B. Ogden. About prisons. Welf Mag 18: 1083-6 Ag '27 **11972**

Colorado prison association. Prisons and prisoners; whither and why. 22p. Denver [1929] **11973**

The criminal's world, a prison governor on prison life. Just Peace 92: 194 Mr 17 '28 **11974**

Deutsche Liga für Menschrenrechte. Das Zuchthaus—die politische Waffe. 8 Jahre politische Justiz. 284p. Berlin, Hensel, 1927 **11975**

Diaz de Ceballos, Alfonso. Legislación de prisiones. Obra ajustada al programa para las oposiciones a aspirantes a ayudantes del cuerpo de prisiones. 232p. Madrid, Reus, 1929 **11976**

The dread of prison. Just Peace 94: 738 N 29 '30 **11977**

Egloffstein, Leo von. Kriminalistik im Gefängnis. Bl f Gefängniskunde 60(3): 367-76 '29 **11978**

Ellis, William J. Public control and supervision of prisons. Ann Am Acad 157: 40-52 S '31 **11979**

A European view of prisons. Ohio Cit (30-1) Je 4 '30 **11980**

Failure of terrorism in the prisons. Am City 42: 94 Ja '30 **11981**

Finkey, Franz von. Die Fortschritte im Gefängniswesen während der letzten hundert Jahre. 43p. Budapest, Ausgabe der ungar. Akademie der Wissenschaften, 1930 **11982**
In ungarischer Sprache erschienen in.

Fisher, John S. [The problem of prisons and prison management]. Pris J 10: 6-8 Jl '30 11893

Foreign prisons. Just Peace 95: 82 F 7 '31 11984

Frede, Lothar. Prison administration. Pris J 10: 5-6 O '30 11985

Grant, Wm. W. jr. A legislator looks at prison. State Govt 3: 14-16 My '30 11986

Higgins, Henry A. Visiting a penal institution. 12p. Boston, Massachusetts prison association, 1930 (No71) 11987

Higgins, Henry A. What we see when we visit a penal institution. Am Pris Assn Proc 60: 323-32 '30 11988
Address before National prisoners' aid association.

Howard, John. The state of the prisons. London, Dent, 1929 11989
First reprint since 4th ed. in 1792.

Imprisonment in 1925-26. Brit M J (3457): 680-1 Ap 9 '27 11990

Kelly, Martin C. The prison on wheels. On Guard 1: 3 Je '31 11991

Kirchwey, G[eorge] W. American prison in twentieth century. M Times [N Y] 58: 279-88 S '30 11992

Kirchwey, George W. The prison's place in the penal system. Ann Am Acad 157: 13-22 S '31 11993

Lawes, Lewis E. Prisons. Nat Soc Pen Inf N Y Bul 2: 3 D '31 11994

Lewisohn, Adolph. What should we do with criminals. R of R 84: 65 S '31 11995

Lowrey, Edward G. Black and white stripes in the red, white and blue. World's Wk 59: 32-5 S '30 11996

Lynd, Robert (Y.Y.pseud). Charms of gaol. New Statesman 32: 786-7 Mr 30 '29 11997

McIver, John J. Prison Sunday. Homiletic R 98: 314-15 O '29 11998

Makowski, Waclaw. Le rôle de l'organisation pénitentiaire dans le futur code pénal. R Pénitent de Pologne (3-4): 336-'29 11999

Martínez, A. Fernández. De la funcion penitenciaria. Bibl Nac de Crim y Cienc Afines Bol 223-5 Ja '27 12000

Moore, Frank. Fitting the prison to its problem. Am Pris Assn Proc 59: 375-82 '29; same title: First Friend 25:1-2 Second quarter '30 12001

Morris, Anna Wharton. The key note. Nat Soc Pen Inf N Y Bul 1: 1-2 Ag '30 12002

Mossé, Armand. Introduction à la science pénitentiaire. Etudes Crimin 3: 177-86 N '28; 4: 10-18 Ja '29 12003

Mossé, Armand. Variétés pénitentiaires. Asiles et prisons. Le congrès de Prague. L'enseignement religieux dans les prisons. 109p. Paris, Sirey, 1931 12004

Murphy, Patrick Charles. Shadows of the gallows. 192p. Caldwell, Idaho, Caxton ptrs. ltd. 1928 12005

Navarro de Palencia, Alvaro. Sociologia criminal. Obra ajustada al programa para las oposiciones a aspirantes a ayudantes del cuerpo de prisiones. 186p. Madrid, Reus, 1929 12006

Neumiller, Charles L. Prison and parole system. Inst Assn Identif, Calif Div Proc 14: 46-50 '29 12007

Neymark, Edward. La science pénitentiaire contemporaine. R de Dr Pén et de Crimin 10: 789-800, 1117-32, 1236-42 '30 12008

Oželis, K. New methods in prisons. Medicina[Kaunas] 12: 569-83 S '31 12009

Parrella, A. Fascino e suggestione in regime penitenziario. Riv di Dir Peniten 1: 1299-307 '30 12010

Patterson, Richard C. Problems of prison administration. Panel 5-6 Mr '30; same title: Police J [N Y] 17: 8-9 O '30 12011

Prison or institution? Sol J 74: 618 S 20 '30 12012

Prison Sunday. Pris J 11: 13-24 O '31 12013

The prison system. L Times 164: 403 N 26 '27 12014

Prisons. Outl 158: 421-2 Ag 5 '31 12015

Reile. Die Gefangenkartei. Krimin Monatsh 4: 85-6 Ap '30 12016

Reiss, Alfons. Gedanken zur Gefangenenfürsorge. Bl f Gefängniskunde 58(1): 1-23 '27 12017

Report on prisons. Outl 157: 8-9 Ja 7 '31 12018

Reps, Albert. Die Methoden der Gefängnisfürsorge. Bl f Gefängniskunde 61(1): 8-48 '30 12019

Scott, B. L. [The purpose of the prison]. Assn of Dir Poor & Char & Correc Proc 56: 145-51 '31 12020

Sears, Joseph D. A prison program. 18p. New York, National committee on prisons and prison labor, 1930 12021

Sellin, Thorsten. The historical background of our prisons. Ann Am Acad 157: 1-5 S '31 12022

Shepherd, William G. Guests of the people. Collier's 79: 8-9 F 26 '27 12023

Smith, Edward Henry. You can escape. 364p. New York, Macmillan, 1929 12024

Some impressions of prisons. Just Peace 94: 334-5 My 24 '30 12025

Springer, Gertrude. Brains instead of prison walls: review of report of commission to investigate prison administration and construction. Survey 65: 657-8 Mr 15 '31 12026

Stearns, A. Warren. A scientific program for prisons. Ann Am Acad 157: 117-20 S '31 12027

Sutherland, Edwin H. and Sellin, Thorsten, eds. Prisons of tomorrow. Ann Am Acad v157 S '31 12028

Tesauro, A. La natura e la funzione del diritto penitenziario. Riv di Dir Peniten 1: 237-47 '30 12029

Thayer, Walter N. jr. and Sellin, Thorsten. The prison in the twentieth century. Nat Conf Soc Wk Proc 57: 107-32 '30 12030

Veiller, Lawrence. Prisons—or men's clubs—which? Worlds Wk 54: 86-95 My '27 12031

Victorio, R[amon]. Our prisons—as educational and vocational institutions. Manila [Bureau of prisons] 1927 12032

Waddell, G. L. Early floating prisons. Nat Repub 18: 20-1 O '30 12033

What makes a prison. Panel 5: 2-3 Je '27 12034

Whitin, E. Stagg. An analysis of the prison problem. J Crim L & Crimin 20: 519-32 F '30 12035

Whitin, E. S[tagg]. Prison legislation in 1900. Am B Assn J 17: 303-5 My '31 12036

AFGHANISTAN

Stratil-Sauer, G. Prisoner in Afghanistan. Asia 29: 644-50 Ag '29 12037

ARGENTINE

El cinquentenario de la penitenciaria nacional [Argentine]. R de Crimin, Psiquiat y Med Leg 14: 354-70 My '27 12038

Goméz, E. [The administration of the National penitentiary of Argentine]. Bibl Nac de Crim y Cienc Afines Bol 2: 443-7 Ap '28 12039

Proyecto de reglamento para la Carcel penitenciaria de Tucuman. Bibl Nac de Crim y Cienc Afines Bol 3(3): 287- Ja '29 12040

Román, Miguel Figueroa. Organización carcelaria—la penitenciaria de Tucuman. R de Crimin, Psiquiat y Med Leg 16: 169-205 Ap '29 12041

BELGIUM

Delierneux, A. jr. Evolution of the prison system in Belgium. Ann Am Acad 157: 180-96 S '31 12042

Gillin, John L. New prison methods in Belgium. Sociol & Soc Res 14: 503-15 Jl '30 12043

Notice sur l'organisation des prisons en Belgique [Louvain, Gand, Merxplas]. R de Dr Pén et de Crimin 9: 1041-71 '29 12044

Ordres de service de la prison centrale de Louvain. Ecrou 9: 33-71, 129-66, 260-300, 394-422 Ja-Jl '28 12045

Les prisons de Liège et la Compagnie de Charité. Ecrou 8: 133-47 Mr '27 12046

Rabinowicz, Leon. La lutte moderne contre le crime. 285p. Bruxelles, Larcier, 1930 12047
Evolution of prison treatment in Belgium.

Rabinowicz. Le rôle de la Belgique dans la lutte contre le crime. R de Dr Pén et de Crimin 10: 616-30 '30 12048

Stefanescu, G. B. Regimul penitenciaru lui central din Louvain-Belgia. R de Drept Pen (5-6): 241- '30 12049

[Vandervelde, Emile]. Las reformas del derecho penal y de las instituciones penitenciarias en Bélgica. Museo Soc Arg Bol 16: 266-70 S '28 12050

BRAZIL

Britto, Lemos. Les prisons du Brésil. 15p. Rio de Janeiro, Imp. Nacional, 1930 12051

Jiménez de Asúa, Luis. La maravillosa penitenciaria de São Paulo. R de Crimin Psiquiat y Med Leg 16: 67-70 Ja '29 12052

Lima, Estacio de. Tatuagens e tatuados da penitenciaria da Bahia. R de Cultura Jurid 1: 326-80 Jl '29 12053

Mendes de Almeida and others. Le régime pénitentiaire au Brésil et le Congrès international de Prague. R Pénitent et de Dr Pén 54: 373-94 S '30 12054

Price, W. Cecil. A prison de luxe; making murderers comfortable. Police J [London] 4: 418-24 Jl '31 12055
State penitentiary of São Paulo, Brazil.

Reeth, Emile Van. Une visite à la prison de São Paulo. R de Dr Pén et de Crimin 10: 269-71 '30 12056

CANADA

Canada. Superintendent of penitentiaries. Annual reports, 1927—31. Ottawa, 1928-32 12057
Kingston, St. Vincent de Paul, Dorchester, British Columbia, Manitoba, Saskatchewan. Dominion parole officers' report.

CHINA

Chih-hsiang, Hoh. Existing conditions in Chekiang first prison. China W R 53: 289 Jl 26 '30 12058

Gull, Beatrix Manico. Life in a Chinese prison. Fortn R 300-9 Mr '27 12059

In a Canton prison. Trans-Pac 16: 7 O 13 '28 12060

Powell, J. B. Voice from the Shanghai settlement prison. China W R 50: 257-8 O 19 '29 12061

Yen, Ching-Yueh. What are the Chinese prisons after all? China W R 55: 387 F 14 '31 12062

CONGO

Le régime pénitentiaire au Congo. Ecrou 8: 374-8 Jl '27 12063

CUBA

Colvin, F. H. There's one good prison! The Presidio modelo on the Isle of Pines. New Repub 68: 236 O 14 '31 12064

Vervaeck, Louis. La prison modèle de Cuba. R de Dr Pén et de Crimin 9: 1101-4 '29 12065

Vervaeck, Louis. La rèforme du régime pénitentiaire de la république de Cuba. R de Dr Pén et de Crimin 9: 1098-9 '29 12066

CZECHOSLOVAKIA

Czechoslovakia. Ministry of justice. The prison system in the Czechoslovak republic. 82p. Prague, 1930 12067
Mens prison at Plzen; mens prison and provisional penal institute at Leopoldov; Mens prison at Kartouzy, Ilava, Mírov (for invalid prisoners); womens prison at Repy; reformatory and penal institution at Mikulov; Komenský institute at Kosice; provincial penal settlements and reformatories; prison statistics.

Stefanescu, G. B. Organizarea penitenciarelor din Republica Cecoslovaca. R de Drept Pen (7-8): 396- '30 12068

DENMARK

Calvert, E. Roy. Prisons in Denmark. Howard J 2: 301-6 Je '29 12069

Osborne, Lithgow. The Danish prison system. Nat Soc Pen Inf N Y Bul 1: 1, 3-4 O '30 12070

DUTCH EAST INDIES

Hymans, H. M. Le régime pénitentiaires aux Indes nëerlandaises. R Int de Dr Pén 5: 156-64 '28 12071

EUROPE

Cass, E. R. Foreign observations and comments. J Crim L & Crimin 22: 414-22 S '31 12072

Cass, E. R. Penal systems of Europe and America. On Guard 1: 3-4 Jl '31 12073

Sellin, Thorsten. Prison tendencies in Europe. R de Identif y Cienc Pen 6: 134-9 My '30; same title: J Crim L & Crimin 21: 485-98 F '31 12074

Wilkins, Harold T. Exploring Europe's torture dungeons. Pop Mech 55: 450-4 Mr '31 12075

FRANCE

Albert-Lambert, Jacqueline. Leçons de puericulture à Fresnes. Illustration 87 (4513): 215 Ag 31 '29 12076

France. Ministère de l'intérieur (administration pénitentiaire). Rapport présenté par l'Inspection générale des Services administratifs. 245p. Melun, Imp. Administrative, 1927 12077

Groen, H. A. French prisoners must wear masks. Police J [N Y] 17: 14 Ja '30 12078

Latude, Jean Henri Masers de and Linguet, Simon Nicolas Henri. Memoirs of the Bastille; translated by J. Mills Whitham and S. F. Mills Whitham. 220p. New York, Brentano's, 1927 12079

Mossé, Armand. Les prisons et les institutions d'éducation corrective. rev.ed. 456p. Paris, Sirey, 1929 12080

Prudhomme, Henri. Les prisons de la Seine en 1926 d'après le rapport de l'Inspection générale des services administratives. R Pénitent et de Dr Pén 51: 320-36 My '27 12081

GERMANY

Bumke, Erwin, ed. Deutsches Gefängniswesen. Ein Handbuch. 536p. Berlin, Franz Vahlen, 1928 12082

[Bumke, Erwin, ed.]. Strafvollzug in Preussen. Herausgegeben vom Preussischen Justizministerium. 293p. Mannheim, Bensheimer, 1928 12083

Gefängnisgesellschaft für die Provinz Sachsen und Anhalt. Der Strafvollzug in Stufen. Jahrbuch, 46, 1930. 126p. Halle (Saale), Selbstverlag, 1931 12084

Gefängnisse in Thüringen: berichte über die Reform des Strafvollzugs. 134p. Weimar, Panses, 1930 12085

Hentig, Hans von. Germany's prison system. Ann Am Acad 157: 174-9 S '31 12086

Klein. Zwei neue bedeutsame Bücher aus der deutschen Gefängnisliteratur. Bl f Gefängniskunde 60: 8-37 '29 12087

Rahne, Helmut. The progressive system in Prussia. Howard J 3: 47-52 S '30 12088

Schunck, Fritz. Das Gefängniswesen des ehemaligen Herzogtums Zweibrücken. Bl f Gefängniskunde 60: 305-63 '29 12089

Der Strafvollzug im Thüringischen Landesgefängnis Ichtershausen. 43p. Ichtershausen, Thür. Landesgef. [1927] 12090

GREAT BRITAIN

Begbie, Harold. Punishment and personality. 126p. London, Mills & Boon, 1927 12091

Brentford, "Jix". English prisons, what they are like. Sat Eve Post 202: 29-30 D 14 '29 12092

Craven, Cicely M. The Prison commissioners' report, 1928. Howard J 3: 62-5 S '30 12093

Craven, Cicely M. The Prison commissioners' report for 1929. Howard J 3: 42-7 '31 12094

C[raven], C[icely] M. The report of the Prison commissioners, 1925-26. Howard J 2: 119-23 '27 12095

Craven, Cicely M. The report of the Prison commissioners for 1926. Howard J 2: 219-23 O '28 12096

English prison system. Pris Assn N Y Ann Rep 86: 84-100 '30 12097

The establishment of "penitentiary houses." Soc Serv R 5: 74-93 Mr '31 12098

Gardner, Arthur R. L. Outline history of English prison system, 1775-1926. Just Peace 91: 363-4, 383-4, 403-4 My 14-28 '27 12099

Great Britain. Commissioners of prisons and the Directors of convict prisons. Report . . . for the year 1925-26- London, 1927- 12100

Hauptvogel, Fritz. Aufzeichnungen über das Gefängniswesen Englands. Ein Reisebericht. Bl f Gefängniskunde 62 sonderheft 5-219 '31 12101

Local prisons; convict prisons; Borstal; preventive detention prisons; Wormwood Scrubs; Holloway; Brixton; Feltham; Aylesbury; Broadmoor; Parkhurst; Camp Hill; Dartmoor; Wakefield.

Hauptvogel, Fritz. Die Sicherungsverwahrung der Gewohnheitsverbrecher in England und ihr Vollzug. Zeitsch f d ges Strafrechtswiss 51(4): 480-95 '31 12102

Camp Hill prison.

Kent, Beatrice. Prisons and prisoners in England. Hosp Soc Serv 16: 23-8 Jl '27 12103

Mountain, T. Whyte. Life in London's great prisons. 180p. London, Methuen, 1930 12104

Wormwood Scrubs; Wandsworth.

O'Donoghue, Edwards Geoffrey. Bridewell hospital, palace, prison and schools from the death of Elizabeth to modern times. 314p. London, Lane, 1929 **12105**

Paterson, Alexander. English prisons. Ann Am Acad 157: 164-73 S '31 **12106**

Pocock, Sydney J. The prison and the prisoner. 143p. London, Alston Rivers, 1930 **12107**
Wormwood Scrubs prison.

Prisons of the future. Spectator 143: 760-1 N 23 '29 **12108**

Sutherland, E. H. and Ruch, S. K. Study of the decrease in the English prison population. New York, Bureau of social hygiene, 1931 **12109**
Only copy available at Bureau of social hygiene.

Turner, G. D. Five years of progress in prison administration. Contemp R 138: 200-8 Ag '30 **12110**

Turner, G. D. Holloway zoo. Spectator [London] 145: 521-2, 634, 670 O 18-N 8 '30 **12111**

Warden (pseud). "His Majesty's guests"; secrets of the cells. 256p. London, Jarrolds, 1929 **12112**

Wilson, Margaret. The crime of punishment. Soc Serv R 5: 1-9 Mr '31 **12113**

Wyndham, Horace. Prison visiting in England. Cath World 125: 676-9 Ag '27 **12114**

GREECE

Scouriotis, P. L'organisation pénitentiaire en Grèce. R Pénitent de Pologne 4: 199-208 Ja '29 **12115**

HUNGARY

Hankinson, Frederick. The convict prison at Vacz, Hungary. Howard J 3: 83-4 S '30 **12116**

Szöllösy, Oskar. Ungarisches Gefängniswesen. 389p. Budapest, Verl. des Verfassers, 1930 **12117**
Published in Hungarian.

INDIA

Andrews, C. F. Meerut trial. New Repub 61: 72 D 11 '29 **12118**

Ceylon. Inspector-general of prisons. Administration report, 1929—1930. Colombo, Govt. press, 1930-31 **12119**
Welikada prison and Hulftsdorf prison; Bogambara prison; Kandy and Old Remand prison; Mahara prison; Jaffna prison; prisons at Anuradhapura, Galle, Negombo, Badulla and Batticaloa.

Durai, J. Chinna. Indian prisons. J Comp Leg s3 11: 245-9 N '29; same title: Indian R 32: 418-22 Jl '31 **12120**

Hamilton, W. G. Imprisonment and detention in India. Asiatic R ns26: 421-44 Jl '30 **12121**

Prison administration in India. Near East & India 37: 542 My 15 '30 **12122**

IRELAND

Craven, Cicely M. Irish Free State: report of the general prisons board, 1926-27. Howard J 2: 223-4 O '28 **12123**

Irish Free State. Department of justice. Annual report on prisons, 1928- **12124**
Continues reports of General prisons board.

Irish Free State. General prisons board. Annual report 4, 1927/28// **12125**
Continues in part Ireland. General prisons board. Report; Continued as Department of justice.

North Ireland. Ministry of home affairs. Report on the administration of Home office services, 1927- **12126**
Includes reports on penal and correctional institutions. . ., police administration and criminal statistics.

ITALY

Barilli, Bruno. Sulla soglia d'un ergastolo. Nuov Antol s7 265 (1374): 437-41 Je 16 '29 **12127**

Collin, F. Il progetto di codice penale italiano da un punto di vista penitenziario. Riv di Dir Peniten 1: 1098-117 '30 **12128**

Lussu, Emilio. Flight from Lipari. Atlan M 146: 31-42 Jl '30 **12129**

Novelli, Giovanni. The prison program of Italy. Ann Am Acad 157: 208-20 S '31 **12130**

Palopoli, Nicola. Le nouveau code pénal italien et la reorganisation des établissements de peine. R de Dr Pén et de Crimin 11: 1128-35 '31 **12131**

Palopoli, Nicolás. El nuevo código penal italiano y la reorganización de los establecimientos penales. R de Crimin Psiquiat y Med Leg 18: 393-400 Jl '31 **12132**

Rosselli, Carlo. My escape. Contemp R 139: 604-13 My '31 **12133**

Saporito, F. L'isola di Pianosa e i suoi stabilimenti penitenziari. Riv di Dir Peniten 1: 960-73 '30 **12134**

JAMAICA

Jamaica. Prisons office, Kingston. Report *in* Annual general report of Jamaica, 1927: 41-66; 1928: 59-87; 1929: 91-138; 1930: 81-110 **12135**
Includes Government industrial school, Stony Hill.

JAPAN

Gillin, John Lewis. Japan's prison system. Soc Forces 7: 177-89 D '28 **12136**

Metcalf, J. W. In a Japanese prison. Trans-Pac 16: 5 Ap 28 '28 **12137**

Miyake, Masataro. Japanese prisons. Trans-Pac 18: 5-6 Jl 24 '30; same title: Asiatic R ns27: 496-502 Jl '31 **12138**

Vervaeck, Louis. L'organisation du régime pénitentiaire au Japon. R de Dr Pén et de Crimin 9: 1168 '29 **12139**

MEXICO

Almaraz, José. Mexico's prisons in the light of its new penal code. Ann Am Acad 157: 221-4 S '31 **12140**

Powell, Rachel Hopper. Visit to La Penitenciaria del D.F., Mexico City. Nat Soc Pen Inf N Y Bul 2: 1-2 D '31 **12141**

NETHERLANDS

Hallema, Anne. Haarlemsche gevangenissen. 112p. Haarlem, De Erven F. Bohn, 1928 **12142**

Weber, Franz. Zur neuren Entwicklung der niederländischen Gefängniswesens. Bl f Gefängniskunde 58: 69-73 '27 **12143**

NEW SOUTH WALES

New South Wales. Comptroller-general of prisons. Report, 1927/29—1929/30. Sydney, 1930-31 **12144**

Parramatta; Goulburn; Bathurst; Maitland; Albury; Broken Hill; Grafton; Tamworth; Emu Plains prison farm; Prisoners' afforestation camp; Tuncurry; Mila; Mount Mitchell; Shaftesbury institution.

NEW ZEALAND

New Zealand. Prisons department. Reports, 1929-1930. Wellington, 1930-31 **12145**

Auckland prison; Jautu prison; New Plymouth prison; Paparua prison; Waikune prison (road construction camp); Erua; Wanganui prison; Rangipo prison; Wellington prison; Wi Tako prison; Heretaunga; Addington reformatory prison (women); Invercargill Borstal institution; Waikeria Borstal institution (Te Awamutu); Point Halswell Borstal institution.

NORWAY

Skattum, H. Fra fengsels-og tvangsarbeidsvesenet i Norge i året 1926. Nord Tids f Straf 15: 150-3 Ap '27 **12146**

PERU

Escuela penitenciaria de Lima. R de Crimin Psiquiat y Med Leg 14: 540-1 Jl '27 **12147**

PHILIPPINE ISLANDS

Philippine Islands. Bureau of prisons. Report *in* Annual report of Governor general **12148**

Prisons in the Philippines. Pris J 7: 10-11 Ap '27 **12149**

POLAND

Car, Stanislaw. Le dixième anniversaire du système pénitentiaire polonais. R Pénitent de Pologne 4: 45-58 English transl (p58-73) Ja '29 **12150**

Neymark, Edward. Le dixième anniversaire du système pénitentiaire en Pologne. R de Identif y Cienc Pen 3: 70-95 N '28; translation: Le dixième anniversaire du système pénitentiaire en Pologne. L'état actuel du système pénitentiaire en Pologne. R Int de Dr Pén 6(1): 66-90 '29 **12151**

Neymark, Edward. The prisons in Poland. J Crim L & Crimin 19: 399-407 N '28 **12152**

Neymark, Edouard. The prisons of Poland. Howard J 2: 321-7 Je '29 **12153**

RUMANIA

Barbusse, Henri. True tales of Rumania; recent atrocities. Living Age 333: 707-11 O 15 '27 **12154**

Sasserath, Simon. Le régime pénitentiaire en Roumanie et la prison d'Aiud. R de Dr Pén et de Crimin 9: 924-8 Ag '29 **12155**

RUSSIA

Cederholm, Boris. Dans les prisons de l'U.S.S.R. 1924-26; transl by Hélène Iswolsky. R Deux Mondes 57: 622-53, 851-78; 48: 186-206 O 1-N 1 '28; same title: ed.4. 413p. Paris, Tallandier, 1928 **12156**

Chirvindt, E. Les prisons en U.R.S.S. 63p. Paris, Bur. d'édit. de diffusion, 1927 **12157**

Douillet, Joseph. Ce que j'ai vu, entendu et vécu dans les oubliettes du Gépéou. Correspondant 310: 736-51 Mr 10 '28 **12158**

El regimen de las prisiones en la Rusia Sovietica. Bibl Nac de Crim y Cienc Afines Bol 3(3): 318- Ja '29 **12159**

Giddy, O. C. H. Our Russian interlude in the Gulf of Finland on August 18, 1919. Blackwood 228: 1-23 Jl '30 **12160**

Guiboud-Ribaud, P. Le régime pénitentiaire et les prisons en U.R.S.S. Etudes Crimin 3: 138-44 S '28 **12161**

Müller, W. Persönliche Eindrücke aus russischen Gefängnissen. Monats f Kriminalpsychol u Strafrechtsref 22: 207-23 Ap '31 **12162**

Shirvindt, Eusevii Gustavovich. Sovetskoe penitentsiarnoe pravo. 276p. Moskva, 1927 **12163**

Schirwindt, E[milian]. Gefängnisse in der Sowjetunion. 35p. Berlin, Verl. f. Literatur u Politik, 1927 **12164**

Schlesinger. Russische Gefängnisse. Bl f Gefängniskunde 60(2): 156-71 '29 **12165**

Soviet death corridors. Lit Dig 109: 16 My 2 '31 **12166**

Soviet prisons. Soviet Union R 8: 165-6 N '30 **12167**

Stuart, Esmé. Prisons and prisoners in 1793 and 1923. Chr Q R 111: 78-95 O '30 **12168**

Vervaeck, [Louis]. L'organisation pénitentiaire des Soviets. R de Dr Pén et de Crimin 7: 370 '27 **12169**

SCANDINAVIA

Almquist, Viktor. Scandinavian prisons. Ann Am Acad 157: 197-207 S '31 **12170**

SCOTLAND

Anderson, Marjorie. Annual report of the prisons department for Scotland. Howard J 3: 65-6 S '30 12171

Crawford, Mary A. Report of the prison commissioners for Scotland, 1927. Howard J 2: 224-6 O '28 12172

Great Britain. Prisons department for Scotland. Annual reports, 1926- Edinburgh, H. M. Stationery Off. 1927- 12173

Scotland. Prison commission. Annual report, for the year 1927. 98p. (Cmd3092) Edinburgh, H. M. Stationery Off. 1928 12174

SPAIN

Aumonier, Stacy. A prison in Spain. Fortn R ns124: 243-9 Ag '28; same title: Living Age 335: 111-12 O '28 12175

Baar, A. Het penitentiaire recht in Spanje. Tijds v Straf 37: 321-59 '27 12176

Cadalso y Manzano, Fernando. Iniciativas penitenciarias en España. 33p. Madrid, Imp. Julio Cosano [1927] 12177

Cadalso y Manzano, Fernando. Systèmes pénaux et pénitentiaires en Espagne, au XVIe siècle; transl by Henri Prudhomme. R Int de Dr Pén 4: 252-62; Spanish transl (p263-73) '27 12178

Cadalso [y Manzano], Fernando. Tratadistas de derecho penal y de sistemos penitenciarios en España en el siglo XVI. R Int de Dr Pen 5: 68-82 French transl (p83-98) by Henri Prudhomme '28 12179

Regolamento del penitenziario di Cordoba. Riv di Dir Peniten 1: 114-23 '30 12180

SWEDEN

Palmstierna. Svartsjö: an open-air prison in Sweden. Howard J 2: 99-100 '27 12181

SWITZERLAND

Almquist, V. El sistema penitenciario y la organizacion de las prisiones en Suecia. R de Crimin Psiquiat y Med Leg 15: 311-23 My '28 12182

UNITED STATES

Adams, Hancock. Improving federal prisons. Nat Repub 18: 14-15 Ag '30 12183

Bullen, Percy S. America's overcrowded prisons. Living Age 338: 503 Je 15 '30 12184

Calvert, E. Roy. American prisons. Howard J 3: 42-7 S '30; same title: Nat Soc Pen Inf N Y Bul 1: 1-2 D '30 12185

Cass, E. R. American prisons today; a survey. Ann Am Acad 157: 6-12 S '31; excerpts: R of R 84: 76-7 N '31 12186

Crowded federal prisons. Survey 163: 563 F 15 '30 12187

Foltin, Edgar M. Amerikanisches Gefängniswesen. 276p. Reichenberg, Geb. Stiepel, 1930 12188

Freudenthal, Berthold. Tagebücher . . . über seine amerikanisch-englische Studienreise. Bl f Gefängniskunde 61: 133-96 '30 12189

Garrett, Paul W. and MacCormick, Austin H. eds. Handbook of American prisons and reformatories, 1929. 1035p. New York, National society of penal information, 1929 12190

Federal institutions: civil, army, naval; state institutions; capital punishment.

Groff, Sam. Stone walls don't make a prison (McNeil Island federal penitentiary). Northwest Police J 7: 12, 98 Je '30 12191

Hart, Albert Bushnell. American prison methods attacked. Cur Hist 32: 117-19 Ap '30 12192

MacCormick, Austin H. The new federal penal program. Nat Soc Pen Inf N Y Bul 1: 3 Je '30 12193

A new federal penitentiary [Union county, Pa.]. Pris J 10: 10-11 O '30 12194

Shepherd, William G. Look out, the hash is sour! Collier's 85: 10-11 F 22 '30 12195

Stevenson, Charles. Ending federal prison scandal. Cur Hist 34: 555-60 Jl '31 12196

United States. Bureau of prisons. Federal offenders, 1930-1931. Fort Leavenworth, Kansas, U.S. Penitentiary annex press [1931] 12197

Review of work of Federal bureau of prisons, 1930/31. Brings together annual report of Attorney general, director of Bureau of prisons and the Board of parole, and reports of federal prisons and reformatories.

United States. Bureau of prisons. Letter to President of the United States [regarding condition of federal prisons] by Sanford Bates. 15p. (mim) Washington, 1931 12198

United States. Congress. House. Committee on judiciary. Establishing 2 institutions for confinement of United States prisoners, report to accompany H.R. 6807, January 6, 1930. 2p. Washington, 1930 (71st Cong. 2d sess. H. Rep. 101) 12199

United States. Congress. House. Committee on judiciary. To reorganize administration of federal prisons, to authorize Attorney general to contract for care of United States prisoners, to establish federal jails, report to accompany H.R 7832, January 6, 1930. 3p. Washington, 1930 (71st Cong. 2d sess. H. Rep. 106) 12200

United States. Congress. House. Committee on rules. Federal prison bill, hearings on H. Res. 17, March 15, 1928. 17p. Washington, 1928 12201

United States. Congress. House. Special committee on federal penal and reformatory institutions. Hearings . . . pursuant to H. Res. 233 . . . directing a committee to make a survey and report upon the care and employment of federal prisoners, agreed to May 28, 1928, January 7, 1929 to January 15, 1929. 283p. Washington, 1929 12202

Wells, Hulet M. Travelogue of hell [Leavenworth]. World Tomorrow 14: 246-9 Ag '31 12203

Alabama

Alabama. Convict department. [Quadrennial report] *in* Quadrennial report of State board of administration, 1926/30: 26-87 **12204**

Alabama. County convict department. Report *in* Quadrennial report of State board of administration, 1926/30: 88-153 **12205**

Alabama. Prison inspector. Report of the State prison inspector, 1926/28—1928/30. Montgomery, 1929-30 **12206**

Arkansas

Arkansas. State penitentiary, Little Rock. Report, 1926/28—1928/30. Little Rock, 1928-30 **12207**
Convict farm (colored), Cummins; Convict farm (white), Tucker; Report on parole law; statistics.

California

California. State board of prison directors. Biennial report, 1926/28—1928/30. Sacramento, 1928-30 **12208**
Folsom and San Quentin.

Gregoraci, Giuseppe. Nelle prigioni americane. Riv Pen (3-4): 360- '30 **12209**
San Quentin, Calif.

Peirce, John M. The penal system of California; the prison as an agency to criminal reform. Tax Dig 9: 316-19 S '31 **12210**

Tully, Jim. Two time losers. Am Mercury 13: 311-19 Mr '28 **12211**

Colorado

Colorado. Penitentiary, Canon City. Biennial report 26, 1926/28—27, 1928/30. [Canon City] 1929-31 **12212**

Colorado tries a new strategy. Chr Cent 148: 125 Ja 28 '31 **12213**

Connecticut

Connecticut. State prison, Wethersfield. Biennial reports, 1926/28—1928/30. (Pub doc no4) Hartford, 1928-30; [summary]: Report of the Department of public welfare, 1926/28: 37-41; 1928/30: 51-4 **12214**

It's the system. Survey 65: 552 F 15 '31 **12215**

District of Columbia

Detroit bureau of governmental research. Observations on the prisons of the District of Columbia. (mim) (Rep no115) Detroit, March 1930 **12216**

Florida

Florida. Department of agriculture. Prison division. Biennial reports 20, 1927/28—21, 1929/30. [Tallahassee, 1929-31] **12217**
General laws governing care and maintenance of state and county prisoners.

Georgia

Georgia. Prison commission. Biennial reports 2, 1927/28—3, 1929/30. [Atlanta, 1929-31] **12218**

Idaho

Idaho. Penitentiary, Boise. Biennial report, 1926/28—1928/30. [Boise, 1928-31] **12219**

Illinois

Bowen, A. L. Ten years ago and today; the changing world leaves its impression on Joliet state prison. Welf Mag 19: 575-84 My '28 **12220**

Do you know? [S. Illinois penitentiary, Menard]. Welf Mag 18: 385-7 Mr '27 **12221**

Illinois. Department of public welfare. Division of prisons. Report, July 25, 1929/June 30, 1930 *in* Annual report of Department of public welfare 13, 1929/30: 19-24 **12222**

Illinois. Joint legislative commission on prisons, probation and parole. Report, December 1931. 48p. Springfield, 1931 **12223**
Survey of European prisons: Dartmoor, Wakefield, Wormwood Scrubs, Borstal institution at Rochesterkent, Eng.; Haarlem prison, Amsterdam, Amsterdam prison; Tegal prison near Berlin; Moabit prison near Berlin; Criminal insane hospital, Tournal, Belg.; Fresne prison near Paris; Mt. Joy prison near Dublin.

[Illinois. Legislative committee on management of Joliet penitentiary]. Report, May 28, 1931. Welf Mag 22: 1, 4-6 Je '31 **12224**

Illinois. Southern Illinois penitentiary, Menard. Report *in* Annual report of Department of public welfare 10, 1926/27: 260-9; 11, 1927/28: 316-23; 12, 1928/29: 252-4; 13, 1929/30: 318-28 **12225**

Illinois. State penitentiary, Joliet. Report *in* Annual report of Department of public welfare 10, 1926/27: 253-6; 11, 1927/28: 304-11; 12, 1928/29: 239-42 **12226**

Little; Thon; McCaskrin; Igoe, and Bray. The Joliet (Illinois) legislative investigation. J Crim L & Crimin 22: 254-63 Jl '31 **12227**

Model prison. Nation 132: 343-4 Ap 1 '31 **12228**

Indiana

Indiana. State prison, Michigan City. Annual reports, 1926/27—1930/31. [Michigan City, 1928-31] **12229**

Indiana. State prison, Michigan City. Special census report. . . September 30, 1927. 19p. [Michigan City] 1927 **12230**

Iowa

Iowa. State penitentiary, Fort Madison. Biennial reports 43, 1926/28—44, 1928/30. [Fort Madison] 1928-30 **12231**

Kansas

Kansas. State penitentiary, Lansing. Biennial reports 26, 1926/28—27, 1928/30. Topeka, 1928-30; *also in* Biennial report of Board of administration, Correctional institutions section 6, 1926/28—7, 1928/30 **12232**

The Kansas state penitentiary. Peace Offic 5: 48, 50 My '27 **12233**

Kentucky

Kentucky, State penitentiary, Eddyville. Reports *in* Biennial reports of the State board of charities and corrections, 1925/27—1929/31 **12234**

Maryland

Maryland. Penitentiary, Baltimore. Annual report *in* Report of Board of welfare 5, 1927: 23-63; 6, 1928: 19-61; 7, 1929: 13-60; 8, 1930: 15-66; 9, 1931: 25-76 **12235**

Maryland. Superintendent of prisons. Report *in* Annual report of Board of welfare 9, 1930/31: 12-17 **12236**

Massachusetts

Gill, Howard B. The Norfolk state prison colony at Massachusetts. J Crim L & Crimin 22: 107-12 My '31 **12237**

Massachusetts. State prison, Charlestown. Annual report *in* Annual report of Commissioner of correction 1927: 14-26; 1929: 12-27 **12238**

Massachusetts. State prison colony, Norfolk. Annual report 1, 1929 *in* Annual report of Commissioner of correction 10, 1929: 27-33 **12239**

Michigan

Jackson, Harry H. The Michigan state prison, 1837-1928. 80p. Jackson, Michigan state prison printing off. 1928 **12240**

Jackson, Harry H. The new prison at Jackson, Michigan; its plan of construction and program of treatment. Am Pris Assn Proc 60: 278-85 '30 **12241**

Michigan. State prison, Jackson. Statistical report: monthly, February 1929- Jackson, 1929- **12242**

Minnesota

Minnesota. State prison, Stillwater. Biennial report 25, 1926/28—26, 1928/30. Stillwater, 1928-30; [summary]: *in* Biennial report of the State board of control 14, 1926/28: 144-7; 15, 1928/30: 168-71 **12243**

General rules governing the discipline of the institution.

Minnesota. State prison, Stillwater. Handbook . . . July 1928. 29p. [Stillwater, 1928]; Handbook . . . May 1930. 30p. [Stillwater, 1930] **12244**

Mississippi

Mississippi. State penitentiary, Jackson. Biennial report of Board of trustees, superintendent and other officers, 1925/27—1929/31. Jackson, 1927-31 **12245**

Missouri

Hart, Hastings H. The Missouri state penitentiary, July 1929. 10p. (mim) St. Louis, Missouri welfare league, 1929 **12246**

Montana

Montana. State prison, Deer Lodge. Biennial report 26, 1926/28—27, 1928/30. [Helena, 1928-30] **12247**

Nebraska

Nebraska. State penitentiary, Lincoln. Biennial report of the Warden, 1925/27—1929/31. [Lincoln, 1927-31] **12248**

Nevada

Nevada. State prison, Carson City. Report *in* Biennial report of the Superintendent of Nevada state police and Warden of the State penitentiary, 1926/28. Carson City, 1929 **12249**

New Hampshire

New Hampshire. State prison. Report of Officers *in* Report of Purchasing agent and state institutions, 1926/28—1928/30. Concord, 1928-30; *also in* Biennial report of State board of charities and corrections 17, 1926/28: 52 **12250**

New Mexico

New Mexico. State penitentiary, Santa Fe. Report of Board of commissioners and Superintendent 15, 1926/27—19, 1930/31. Santa Fe [1927-31] **12251**

New York

Kirchwey, George W. Delinquency [Sing Sing]. Minn St Bd Con Q 29(1): 38-47 S 13 '29 **12252**

Lawes, Lewis E. Life and death in Sing Sing; with a foreword by Adolph Lewisohn. 267p. N.Y. Doubleday, 1928; same title: World's Wk 56: 50-63, 159-70, 316-22, 395-9, 550-6, 675-81 My-O '28 **12253**

Lewis, H. MacLean. Physical conditions and public services. Regional survey of New York and its environs, v8. New York, 1929 **12254**

New York (state). Auburn prison, Auburn. Report *in* Annual report of Commissioner of correction 1927: 130-93 **12255**

New York (state). Clinton prison, Dannemora. Report *in* Annual report of Commissioner of correction 1927: 229-81 12256

New York (state). Commission of correction. Report of inspection of Auburn. 10p. (mim) [Albany, 1929] 12257

New York (state). Commission of correction. Report of inspection of Clinton, Dannemora. 11p. (mim) [Albany, 1929] 12258

New York (state). Commission of correction. Report of inspection of Great Meadow, Comstock. 9p. (mim) [Albany, 1930] 12259

New York (state). Commission to investigate prison administration and construction. Report, presented to the Legislature, February 15, 1931. 107p. [Albany, 1931] 12260

Addendum 1. Preliminary report, December 22, 1930. 27p. [Albany, 1930]
Addendum 2. Supplemental report, the classification of the prison inmates of New York state. 69p. [Albany, 1931]
Addendum 3. Report upon conditions affecting safety to life with respect to fire, by the National board of fire underwriters. 134p. [Albany] February 3, 1931

New York (state). Department of public works. Report on conditions, Attica state prison and answers to the four questions in letter dated November 22, 1929, from . . . Governor Roosevelt . . . requesting an investigation. 10p. [Albany] 1930 12261

New York (state). Great Meadow prison, Comstock. Report *in* Annual report of Commissioner of correction 1927: 285-319 12262

New York (state). Sing Sing prison, Ossining. Annual report *in* Annual report of Commissioner of correction 1927: 17-127 12263

Sullivan, Florence J. Sing Sing: capital punishment and "honest-graft." 111p. New York, Connolly press, 1928 12264

The Token system in the Tombs prison. Panel 5:2 Je '27 12265

North Carolina

[North Carolina]. State prison advisory commission. Report of sub-committee of State prison advisory commission, 1930. [Raleigh, 1930] 12266

North Carolina. State's prison, Raleigh. Biennial report, 1926/28—1928/30. Raleigh, 1928-30 12267

North Carolina. Subcommittee on North Carolina's prison problem. Report . . . *in* Biennial report of State's prison 1928/30: 10-21 12268

North Dakota

North Dakota. State penitentiary, Bismarck. Biennial reports *in* Annual reports of Board of administration 9/10, 1926-28: 337-415; 11/12, 1928-30: 465-526 12269

Ohio

Cox, William B. Ohio [penitentiary fire, Columbus]. Nat Soc Pen Inf N Y Bul 1: 1, 4- Je '30 12270

Fire at Columbus. Outl 155: 12 My 7 '30 12271

Kennedy, John B. Big smudge. Collier's 87: 14-15 F 7 '31 12272

Ohio. Penitentiary, Columbus. Report *in* Annual report of Department of public welfare 6, 1927: 403-16; 7, 1928: 381-93; 8, 1929: 497-511 12273

Ohio inspection bureau. Report on the Ohio state penitentiary fire, Columbus, Ohio, April 21, 1930. [7p]. Columbus, 1930 12274

Ohio prison catastrophe. Comm & Fin Chron 130: 3059-61 My 3 '30 12275

Ohio's prison holocaust. World's Wk 59: 19 Jl '30 12276

Oklahoma

Oklahoma. State penitentiary, McAlester. Report *in* Annual report of State commissioner of charities and corrections 1927: 85-8; 1928: 37-44; 1929: 17-21; 1930: 83-4 12277

Oregon

Oregon. State penitentiary, Salem. Biennial reports 14, 1926/28—15, 1928/30. Salem, 1929-31; *also in* Biennial report of State board of control 9, 1928/30: 111-32 12278

Pennsylvania

Lewis, Orlando F. Eastern penitentiary history. Pris J 8: 18-22 O '28; 9: 4-6 Ja '29 12279

Pennsylvania. Eastern state penitentiary, Philadelphia. Annual reports, 1926/27—1928/29. [Philadelphia, 1927-29] 12280

Pennsylvania. State penitentiary, Philadelphia. The new eastern state penitentiary, Graterford, Pennsylvania. [23]p. [Philadelphia, 1929] 12281

Pennsylvania's prisons. Survey 58: 209 My 15 '27 12282

Rhode Island

Rhode Island. State prison and Providence county jail, Howard. Annual reports, 1927-1929; December 1, 1929/ June 30, 1930; 1930/31. [Providence, 1928-31]; statistical reports *in* Annual report of State public welfare commission 5, 1927: 24-8; 6, 1928: 84-90; 7, 1929: 49-50; 8, 1930: 106-19 12283

South Carolina

South Carolina. Penitentiary, Columbia. Annual report of Board of directors and Superintendent, 1927-1930. [Columbia, 1928-31] 12284

South Dakota

Muchow, Arthur H. Our prison problem. Int Assn Identif Proc 16: 78-81 '30 **12285**

South Dakota. Penitentiary, Sioux Falls. Biennial report *in* Biennial report of State board of charities and corrections 19, 1926/28: 35-71; 20, 1928/30: 40-80 **12286**

South Dakota. Penitentiary, Sioux Falls. Condensed summary report, 1918-1926. 20p. Sioux Falls, 1927 **12287**

South Dakota. Penitentiary, Sioux Falls. Interesting facts concerning South Dakota penitentiary, 1918-1928. 26p. Sioux Falls, 1928 **12288**

South Dakota. Penitentiary, Sioux Falls. A visit to the South Dakota penitentiary, with comprehensive data regarding the different departments and activities of the state's penal institution, May 1, 1928, by G. T. Jameson. 24p. [Sioux Falls] 1928 **12289**

Tennessee

Tennessee. Brushy Mountain penitentiary, Petros. Biennial reports *in* Biennial reports of Department of institutions 1926/28: 319-49; 1928/30: 331-64 **12290**

Tennessee. State penitentiary, Nashville. Biennial reports *in* Biennial reports of Department of institutions 1926/28: 353-84; 1928/30: 367-95 **12291**

Texas

Texas. Prison board. Annual reports of the . . . Board of the Texas prison system, 1928—1931. [Austin, 1929-32] **12292**

Utah

Utah. State building commission. Joint report of Utah state building commission and Board of corrections concerning the Utah state prison. 14p. [Salt Lake City] January 1931 **12293**

Utah. State prison, Salt Lake City. Biennial reports, 1926/28—1928/30. [Salt Lake City, 1928-30] **12294**

Vermont

Vermont. State prison and House of correction for men, Windsor. Biennial reports *in* Biennial reports of Department of public welfare 1926/28: 61-78; 1928/30: 57-86 **12295**

Virginia

Virginia. Penitentiary, Richmond. Annual report of Board of directors, 1926/27—1929/30; [summary]: Annual reports of State department of public welfare 18, 1926/27: 20; 19, 1927/28: 21; 20, 1928/29: 26; 21, 1929/30: 22; 22, 1930/31: 20 **12296**
Includes State convict road force.

Washington

Washington. State penitentiary, Walla Walla. Biennial report *in* Biennial report of Department of business control 4, 1926/28: 124-58; 5, 1928/30: 36-47 **12297**
Statistics: education, labor, parole, indeterminate sentence.

West Virginia

West Virginia. Penitentiary. Triennial statistics report, 1927/30. [Charleston, 1930] **12298**

Wisconsin

Wisconsin. State prison, Waupun. Biennial report 23, 1926/28—24, 1928/30. [Waupun, 1928-30]; *also in* Biennial report of State board of control 19, 1926/28: 520-47; 20, 1928/30: 441-66 **12299**

Wyoming

Wyoming. State penitentiary, Rawlins. Biennial reports *in* Biennial reports of State board of charities and reform 1926/28: 47-56; 1928/30: 75-87 **12300**

REFORMATORIES

Glynn, John T. What price reformatories. Police J [N Y] 15: 18-19 My '28 **12301**

Lekkerker, E. C. Uit Amerikaansche Reformatories. Maandbl v Ber en Reclasseer 7: 4-9, 76-81, 204-10 Ja-Jl '28 **12302**

Neelands, C. F. Reformatory methods in Ontario. Am Pris Assn Proc 59: 317-27 '29 **12303**

Selling, Lowell Sinn. Pseudo family. Am J Sociol 37: 247-53 S '31 **12304A**

ALABAMA

Alabama. Joint committee on state training schools for girls and other institutions of like character. Report, June 21, 1927. 8p. Montgomery, 1927 **12304B**

COLORADO

Colorado. Reformatory, Buena Vista. Biennial report of the State board of corrections and warden, 1926/28—December 1, 1928/ June 30, 1931. Denver, 1928-31 **12305**

CONNECTICUT

Connecticut. House of the good shepherd, Hartford. Reports *in* Reports of Department of public welfare 1926/28: 65-7; 1928/30: 79-81 **12306**

Connecticut. Long Lane Farm, Middleton. Annual reports 58/59, 1927/28—60/61, 1929/30. (Pub doc no21) Hartford, 1928-30; *also in* Report of Department of public welfare, 1927/28: 62-4; 1929/30: 76-8 **12307**

Connecticut. Reformatory, Chesire. Report of the Directors, 1926/28—1930/32. [Hartford, 1928-32]; [summary]: Report of the Department of public welfare 1926/28: 50-3; 1928/30: 64-7 **12308**

Erskine, George C. Connecticut reformatory. Conn B J 2: 18-21 Ja '28 **12309**

DISTRICT OF COLUMBIA

District of Columbia. Reformatory, Lorton, Va. Reports *in* Reports of the Board of public welfare 1927: 38-40; 1928: 42-6; 1929: 42-4; 1930: 32-4; 1931: 44-7 **12310**

ILLINOIS

Illinois. State reformatory, Pontiac. Reports *in* Annual reports of Department of public welfare 10, 1926/27: 270-5; 11, 1927/28: 324-31; 12, 1928/29: 243-8; 13, 1929/30: 331-58 **12311**

INDIANA

Indiana. Reformatory, Pendleton. Annual reports, 1926/27—1930/31. [Pendleton, 1927-31] **12312**

IOWA

Eardley, M. T. My observations at the Men's reformatory. Bul St Inst [Iowa] 31: 158-61 Jl '29 **12313**

Iowa. Men's reformatory, Anamosa. Report *in* Biennial report of Board of control of state institutions 16, 1926/28; 17, 1928/30 **12314**

KANSAS

Kansas. Industrial reformatory, Hutchinson. Biennial report 17, 1926/28—18, 1928/30. Topeka, 1928/30; *also in* Biennial report of the Board of administration, Correctional institutions section 6, 1926/28—7, 1928/30 **12315**

Kansas. Training school, Winfield. Biennial report 25, 1928/30. [Winfield, 1930] **12316**

The Kansas state industrial reformatory [Hutchinson]. Peace Offic 5: 14-16 D '27 **12317**

KENTUCKY

Kentucky. State reformatory, Frankfort. Report *in* Biennial reports of the State board of charities and corrections, 1925/27—1929/31 **12318**

MASSACHUSETTS

Glueck, Sheldon. Facts about the inmates of an American reformatory [Massachusetts reformatory]. Am Pris Assn Proc 54: 28-49 '29 **12319**

Massachusetts. Reformatory, Concord Junction. Annual report *in* Annual report of Commissioner of correction 1927: 27-48; 1929: 34-53 **12320**

MINNESOTA

Minnesota. Reformatory, St. Cloud. Biennial reports, 1926/28—1928/30. [St. Cloud, 1929-30]; *also in* Biennial report of State board of control 14, 1926/28: 136-40; 15, 1928/30: 159-64 **12321**

MISSOURI

Hart, Hastings H. and Bates, Carol. Missouri reformatory, Boonville, July 1929. 12p. (mim) St. Louis, Missouri welfare league, 1929? **12322**

NEBRASKA

Nebraska. State reformatory for men, Lincoln. Biennial report of the Superintendent 7, 1925/27—8, 1927/29. [Lincoln, 1927-29] **12323**

NEW JERSEY

New Jersey. State reformatory, Rahway. Annual report of the Board of managers, 1926/27. Rahway, 1927 **12324**

NEW YORK (STATE)

Allen, F. C. Handbook of the New York state reformatory at Elmira. 140p. New York, New York state reformatory at Elmira, 1927 **12325**

New York (city). Reformatory for misdemeanants, New Hampton farms, Orange county. Report *in* Annual report of Department of correction 1927: 84-90 **12326**

New York (city). Reformatory prison, Hart's Island. Report *in* Report of Department of correction 1927: 77-84 **12327**

OHIO

Ohio. State reformatory, Mansfield. Reports *in* Reports of Department of public welfare 6, 1927: 425-33; 7, 1928: 403-18; 8, 1929: 521-30 **12328**

United States. Congress. House. Committee on judiciary. To remove age limits of persons who may be confined at Industrial reformatory at Chillicothe, Ohio, report to accompany H.R. 12249, May 3, 1928. 2p. Washington, 1928 (70th Cong. 1st sess. H. Rep. 1498) **12389**

OKLAHOMA

Oklahoma. State reformatory, Granite. Report *in* Reports of Commission of charities and corrections 1927: 80-5; 1928: 45-8; 1929: 23-6; 1930: 78-82 **12330**

PENNSYLVANIA

Pennsylvania. Industrial reformatory, Huntingdon. Biennial report 20, 1927/28. 62p. Huntingdon, 1928 **12331**

RHODE ISLAND

Rhode Island. Reformatory for men. Statistical report *in* Annual report of State public welfare commission 5, 1926/27: 35-6 12332

WASHINGTON

Washington. State reformatory. Biennial reports *in* Reports of Department of business control 4, 1926/28: 159-70; 5, 1928/30: 53-62 12333

WISCONSIN

Wisconsin. State reformatory, Green Bay. Biennial reports 16, 1926/28—17, 1928/30. [Madison, 1928-30]; *also in* Biennial reports of State board of control 19, 1926/28: 494-517; 20, 1928/30: 415-40 12334

JAILS

American prison association. Committee on jails. Report. Proc 59: 218-38 '29 12335

Bertrand, E. Voyage autour de la geole. Ecrou 8: 483-543 N '27 12336

Buckler, Helen. Attack the county jail. Good Housekeeping 91: 48-9 Ag '30; same title: R of R 82: 83-4 S '30 12337

California. University. Bureau of public administration. County jails: selected bibliography. 2p. (typw) Berkeley, June 22, 1929 12338

County court house and jails; views and plans. Arch Forum 55: 273-96 S '31 12339

The county jails. Ind Bul Char & Correc (149): 230-3 Je '27 12340

Fewer jails and more asylums. L Notes 31: 184-5 Ja '28 12341

Fitzgerald, W. J. Should county jails become state prisons? Peace Offic Assn Calif Proc 9: 73-6 '29 12342

Griffin, S. C. County jails. Ohio Welf Bul 7: 10-11 Mr '30 12343

Hart, Hastings H. Do these conditions exist in your local police station, county jail, or workhouse? Am City 41: 111-12 O '29 12344

Hart, Hastings H. The rural jail. Nat Conf Soc Wk Proc 1927: 152-7 12345

Hart, Hastings [H.]. Some county jails. (Pub 16) Trenton, New Jersey Department of institutions and agencies, 1928 12346

Haynes, Tom H. County jails and workhouses. Am City 39: 140-1 Ag '28 21347

Haynes, Tom H. County jails and workhouses; making the best of a necessary evil. Police J [N Y] 16: 17-18 D '28 12348

Jail and the child. Probation 8: 1-2 Ap '30 12349

Jails 130 years ago and now. Pris J 11: 26-7 Ap '31 12350

Johnston, E. Pauline. Jails. Bul St Inst [Iowa] 31: 173-8 Jl '29 12351

Lathrop, Charles Newton. Menace of our jails. Miss R World 51: 555-8 Jl '28 12352

Local jail with all its iniquitous horrors must go. Am City 38: 143 Ja '28 12353

Local jails. L Notes 32: 223 Mr '29 12354

Mangold, George B. and Hardy, Sophie. County jails. *In their* Building a better San Jose: a social survey, 138-45. San Jose, Community Chest, 1930 12355

Mills, Robert. Model jail of the olden time. 12p. Russell Sage foundation, Department of delinquency and penology, Pam D P 2. New York, 1929 12356

Designs for a "debtors' gaol and workhouse for felons" for Burlington county, state of New Jersey, summarized by George J. Giger.

National committee on prisons and prison labor. The county jail. 19p. New York, 1929 12357

Prison association of New York. The county jail must go. New York, 1928 12358

Rationalize the gaol industry. Can Forum 11: 6 O '30 12359

Robinson, Louis N. The relation of jails to county and state. J Crim L & Crimin 20: 396-420 N '29 12360

Thirty-two million dollars for jails. Playground 24: 298 Ag '30 12361

A top floor jail. Welf Mag 18: 76-7 Mr '27 12362

Tully, Jim. Jailbirds. Am Mercury 15: 65-71 S '28 12363

CANADA

Canada. Alberta. Provincial gaol, Fort Saskatchewan. Reports *in* Annual reports of Department of public works 1927/28: 27-31; 1928/29: 28-31; 1929/30: 29-33; 1930/31: 30-4 12364

Canada. Alberta. Provincial gaol, Lethbridge. Reports *in* Annual reports of Department of Public works 1927/28: 32-6; 1928/29: 32-5; 1929/30: 34-6; 1930/31: 35-7 12365

Topping, C. W. The passing of the county jail in Canada. Am Pris Assn Proc 59: 238-50 '29 12366

COSTA RICA

Costa Rica. Secretaria de seguridad publica. Memoria . . . correspondiente al año 1927. San José, Imp. Nacional, 1928 12367

Police, jail for men, jail for women, San José; jail at Heredia; police of Puntarenas; jail at Puntarenas; jail at Limon; jail at San Ramon; jail at Santa Cruz.

GERMANY

Jarotzky, H. v. "Fort mit dem Zuchthaus." Ein Beitrag zur Reform des Strafrechts. Monats f Kriminalpsychol u Strafrechtsref 22: 84-104 F '31 12368

INDIA

Barker, F. A. Imprisonment. 191p. Madras, Christian Literature society for India, 1930 **12369**

Bihar and Orissa. Inspector general of prisons. Administration report on the jails of Bihar and Orissa, 1927-1930. Patna, Govt. Ptr. 1928-31 **12370**

Judicial statistics; prison discipline; costs; employment; vital statistics; jailors.

Northwest frontier province. Jail department. Administration report on the jails of the North-west frontier province, Peshawar **12371**

United provinces of Agra and Oudh. Report on the condition and management of jails for the year ending December 31, 1927- **12372**

UNITED STATES

Liepmann, M. American jails condemned. Justice 1: 52 O '28 **12373**

United States. Bureau of prisons. Federal prisoners in jails, 1929-30; a supplement to the annual report of the Federal penal and correctional institutions. 57p. Washington, 1931 **12374**

ALABAMA

Andrews, Glenn. A comparative statement relative to certain conditions obtaining in the county jails in the state of Alabama. 18p. Montgomery, Ala. State prison inspector, 1928 **12375**

Andrews, Glenn. Law governing inspection of jails in Alabama. Am Pris Assn Proc 60: 157-61 '30 **12376**

County jails [report] *in* Report of State prison inspector 1926/28: 9-33; 1928/30: 9-156 **12377**

CALIFORNIA

County jails. *In* Biennial report of California. Department of social welfare 2, 1928/30: 46-7, 49-52 **12378**

CONNECTICUT

Connecticut. Returns of county commissioners in relation to jails and the receipts and expenditures of the several counties, state of Connecticut, for the two years ended September 30, 1930. 68p. (Pub doc no14) Hartford, 1930 **12379**

County jail reports *in* Report of the Connecticut Department of public welfare 1927/28: 43-9; 1929/30: 56-63 **12380**

Hartford county; Tolland county; Middlesex county; Litchfield county; Windham county; Fairfield county; New London county; New Haven county.

DISTRICT OF COLUMBIA

District of Columbia. Asylum and jail, Washington. Report *in* Report of Board of public welfare 1927: 30-3; 1928: 32-6; 1929: 53-5; 1930: 44-6; 1931: 48-50 **12381**

GEORGIA

County jail work *in* Report of Georgia Department of public welfare 1927/28: 11-21 **12382**

Georgia. State department of public welfare. Humanizing Georgia's county jails; a handbook of standards and information. ed.2. 78p. Atlanta, 1927 **12383**

ILLINOIS

Delaney, John F. Cook county's new criminal court building and county jail. Justice 1: 21, 23 O '28 **12384**

Fisher, E. F. Cleaning up the old Cook county jail. Crim Just [Chicago] 9: 5-6 My '27 **12385**

Hopkins, Albert A. Chicago gets a new jail; Cook county jail. Sci Am 143: 48-9 Jl '30 **12386**

The inspection of county homes and jails. Welf Bul 21: 4 F '30 **12387**

Loomis, Frank D. Jails for more than custody, Cook county. Survey 62: 125-7 Ap 15 '29 **12388**

Robertson, A. F. What Fogarty's report shows: interesting facts, concerning the jail population in Cook county, Illinois, disclosed in annual report. Crim Just [Chicago] 9:6 My '27 **12389**

MARYLAND

Baltimore. Board of visitors to the city jail. Annual report . . . to the mayor and city council, 1928-1931. Baltimore, 1929-32 **12390**

Prisoners' aid association of Maryland report of work at Baltimore city jail.

Baltimore. City jail. Report *in* Mayor's message, May 9, 1927, together with a summary of the operations of the city departments and commissions for the years 1923-1927. 229p. Baltimore, 1927 **12391**

Maryland. Board of welfare. Annual report of the inspection of the county jails of Maryland 3, 1927—7, 1931. [Baltimore, 1927-31] **12392**

NEW YORK

Albany county's new jail. Correction 1: 5-6 S '31 **12393**

Fishman, Joseph F. What New York city is doing in its jails. Am Pris Assn Proc 54: 219-25 '29 **12394**

OHIO

Ohio federation of women's clubs. Department of public welfare. Report of the survey of the Ohio jails, by Irma Gerkins. 1928? **12395**

Pennsylvania

Jail or boarding houses. Pris J 8:6 O '28 **12396**

Pennsylvania committee on penal affairs. What shall be done about Pennsylvania jails: what Berks and Delaware counties are doing. Pen Affairs (21) D '29 **12397**

Rhode Island

County jail report *in* Annual report of State public welfare commission 6, 1927/28—10, 1930/31 **12398**
Bristol county; Kent county; Newport county; Providence county; Washington county.

Utah

Smith, T. O. Salt Lake county jail: an analysis of its intake and administration. Thesis (M.A.) University of Utah, 1931? **12399**

Wisconsin

Statistics of county jails *in* Biennial report of Wisconsin State board of control 19, 1927/28 **12400**

CORRECTIONAL FARMS AND WORKHOUSES

Bondy, Curt. Arbeitshaus und Bewahrungsanstalt. Zeitsch f ges Strafrechtswiss 50(4-5): 524-38 '30 **12401**

Hannan, W. E. Compilation and digest of the laws of the various states relating to state and county penal farms. 69p. Albany, New York (state). Library. Legislative reference section, February 1928 **12402**

Hart, Myrtle Grace. Farm colonies for misdemeanants: bibliography. J Crim L & Crimin 17: 626-39 F '27 **12403**

Miller, F. Selskochozyaistvennia kolonii dlia zakliuchenneck (K voprosu o borbe s derevenski prestupnostiu). Problemy Prestupnosti 2: 159-89 '27 **12404**

Ploss, Rudolf. Das Arbeitshaus. 100p. (Leipz rechtswissensch Stud. 35) Leipzig, Weicher, 1928 **12405**

Verzeichnis der deutschen Arbeitshäuser und der in denselben eingerichteten gewerblichen Betriebe und der Betriebsformen. 12p. (Bl f Gefängniskunde v58 sup) Heidelberg, Winter, 1927 **12406**

Delaware

New Castle county workhouse. Board of trustees. Reports, 1927/28—1929/30. [Wilmington, 1929-31] **12407**
Serves as Wilmington city jail, county workhouse and State prison.

Prisoners as guests [New Castle county workhouse]. Pris J 9: 16-18 O '29 **12408**

District of Columbia

District of Columbia. Workhouse, Occoquan, Va. Report *in* Report of Board of public welfare 1927: 34-7; 1928: 37-41; 1929: 40-1; 1930: 30-1; 1931: 41-3 **12409**

Illinois

Illinois. State farm, Vandalia. Report *in* Annual report of Department of public welfare 10, 1926/27: 276-7; 11, 1927/28: 332-5; 12, 1928/29: 236-8; 13, 1929/30: 361-3 **12410**

Indiana

Indiana. State farm, Greencastle. Annual reports 13, 1926/27—17, 1930/31. [Indianapolis, 1928-31] **12411**

Maryland

Maryland. State penal farm, Hagerstown. Annual report, no. 1 *in* Annual report of Board of welfare 9, 1931: 130-7 **12412**

Massachusetts

Massachusetts. State farm, Bridgewater. Report *in* Annual report of Commissioner of correction 1927: 65-87; 1929: 72-98 **12413**

Minnesota

Taxpayers' league of St. Louis county, Inc. Report, St. Louis county work farm. 76p. (mim) Duluth, Minn. June 1930 **12414**

New Hampshire

County farms report *in* New Hampshire State board of charities and correction, Biennial report 17, 1926/28—18, 1928/30 **12415**
County farms: Rockingham county farm; Strafford county; Belknap county; Carroll county; Merrimack county; Hillsborough county; Cheshire county; Sullivan county; Grafton county; Coos county.
County jails: Rockingham county; Portsmouth county; Hillsborough county.

New Jersey

Inglis, William. Where convicts will not run away. R of R 84: 62-6 S '31 **12416**
New Jersey state farm.

New York

County farm report *in* Annual report of Erie county Commissioner of charities and correction 1927: 84-6; 1928: 84-6; 1929: 62-3; 1930: 58-61; 1931: 45-8 **12417**

New York (city). Municipal farm, Rikers Island. Report *in* Annual report of Department of correction 1927: 72-7 **12418**

New York (city). Penitentiary and workhouse, Welfare Island, Manhattan. Report *in* Report of Department of correction 1927: 50-72 **12419**

Great prison city rising from ashes on Rikers Island. Gas Logic 3-4 O '31 **12420**

Porter, H. F. J. The Rikers Island penitentiary. Panel 9-10 Jl '30 **12421**

Ohio

Ohio. London prison farm, London. Report *in* Annual report of Department of public welfare 6, 1927: 417-24; 7, 1928: 395-401; 8, 1929: 512-20 **12422**

Sherrill, C. O. Cincinnati's city workhouse. Nat Munic R 18: 525-8 Ag '29 **12423**

Pennsylvania

Allegheny county workhouse and inebriate asylum, Blawnox. Annual reports 58, 1927—60, 1929. Blawnox, 1928-30 **12424**

Farm colony for Philadelphia boys. Sch & Soc 26: 583-4 N 5 '27 **12425**

Farm prisons. Pris J 9: 25 Ja '29 **12426**

Gilfillan, Alexander. County farm and workhouse. Assn of Dir Poor & Char & Correc Proc 54: 41-9 '29 **12427**
Allegheny county workhouse and inebriate asylum.

Montgomery county prison farm. Pris J 10: 14 Jl '30 **12428**

Morton, Eleanor. Prison farms. Pris J 10: 11-12 Ja '30 **12429**

Pennsylvania. Department of welfare. Institutional farms, September 15, 1927/April 1, 1929. 26p. (Bul no40) Harrisburg, 1929 **12430**

Pennsylvania prison association. The industrial prison farm movement makes progress in Pennsylvania; educational program bringing results as county officials study conditions. 6p. Philadelphia, 1930 **12431**

The prison farm movement. Pris J 11: 22-3 Ja '31 **12432**

Trembath, William J. The workhouse. Assn of Dir Poor & Char & Correc Proc 54: 36-41 '29 **12433**
Detention of deserting husbands.

Virginia

Virginia. State farm and farm for defective misdemeanants, State Farm, P.O. Report *in* Report of State department of public welfare 18, 1927: 20-1; 19, 1928: 22-3; 20, 1929: 27-8; 21, 1930: 23-4; 22, 1931: 22 **12434**

COUNTY PRISONS

Efficiency estimate of county prisons [Pennsylvania]. Pris J 10: 5-7 Ap '30 **12435**

The Holmesburg (Philadelphia) county prison. Pris J 10: 23-5 Ja '30 **12436**

Hopkins, Alfred. Building a county penal institution. Pris J 10: 17-24 Jl '30 **12437**

New York. Erie county, Penitentiary, Wende. Report *in* Annual report of Commissioner of charities and corrections 1927: 11-22; 1928: 11-22; 1929: 11-22; 1930: 11-22; 1931: 11-21 **12438**

Pennsylvania. Department of welfare. Bureau of restoration. Adequacy of the county prisons, 1929. 6p. (Bul 44-1930) Harrisburg, 1930 **12439**

Pennsylvania. Philadelphia county prison. Summary of activities of the Board of inspectors, Philadelphia county prison, during the year 1929, and the improvements during that period. [Philadelphia, 1930] **12440**

Philadelphia county prison. Pris J 9: 1-4 Ap '29 **12441**

Schaeffer, Paul N. The administration of a county prison [Berks county, Pa.]. Pris J 10: 15-16 Jl '30 **12442**

Scott, B. L. Making the prison an asset to the county. Pris J 10: 1-4 O '30 **12443**

Shillinglaw, James McC. Albany county penitentiary. Correction 1: 7 S '31 **12444**

Stern, Leon. The county prison of Allegheny county; with an analysis of detention and prison farm plans. 58p. Philadelphia, Pennsylvania committee on penal affairs, 1930 **12445**

HOUSES OF CORRECTION

Bitter, Margarethe. Das Zucht und Arbeitshaus sowie das Criminalinstitut des Reichsgrafen F. L. Schenk von Castell zu Oberdischingen im Kreise Schwaben, von 1789-1808. 80p. Murnau, J. Fürst, 1930 **12446**

Jahresbericht der Strafanstalt Witzwil für 1927 [summary]. Bl f Gefängniskunde 59: 232-4 '28 **12447**

Mohr, Christian. Die Strafanstalt als Erziehungsanstalt. 231p. Celle, Verl. der Christlichen Gefangenenhilfe, 1929 **12448**

Outievski, B. Les maisons de correction et de travail en Russie. R Mondiale 192: 404-8 Ag 15 '29 **12449**

Pietsch, Günter. Das Zuchtsauswesen Alt-Danzigs. 83p. Diss. Göttingen. Danzig, Kafemann, 1931 **12450**

Maryland

Maryland. House of correction, Jessups. Annual report *in* Annual report of Board of welfare 5, 1927: 67-96; 6, 1928: 64-96; 7, 1929: 62-98; 8, 1930: 68-107; 9, 1931: 79-128 **12451**

Michigan

Detroit. Bureau of governmental research. The Detroit house of correction: organization of a welfare department. 31p. (mim) (No125) Detroit, August 1931 **12452**

Detroit. House of correction. Annual reports 67, 1927—69, 1929. [Detroit, 1927-29]; reports also *in* Annual reports of common council 12453

O'Hara, John P. New Detroit House of correction and plan of segregation. Am Pris Assn Proc 60: 125-30 '30 12454

Pennsylvania

Philadelphia. House of correction. Annual report *in* Annual message of Mayor 1929: 439-77 12455

Union of House of correction with county prison [Holmesburg]. Pris J 8: 8-9 O '28 12456

Wisconsin

Milwaukee county. House of correction, Milwaukee. Annual report *in* Biennial report of State board of control 20, 1928/30: 500-1 12457

INSTITUTIONS FOR JUVENILES

Bastin, H. V. City and county versus state institutions for dependent, defective and delinquent children. Nat Conf Juv Agencies Proc 27: 139-49 '30 12458

Bentley, Herbert. Child offenders and industrial schools. Child [London] 17: 169-71 Mr '27 12459

Chamberlin, H. E. When should the institution be prescribed for the problem children? Nat Conf Soc Wk Proc 1928: 383-9 12460

Correctional institutions for girls. J Soc Hyg 15: 542-7 D '29 12461

Delierneux, Adolphe. Serait-il désirable de donner aux tribunaux ordinaires le pouvoir de placer les jeunes délinquants dans une institution ou un quartier spécial? R de Dr Pén et de Crimin 11: 628-37 '31 12462

Dobbs, Harrison A. Institutional care for delinquent children: a new appraisal. Ann Am Acad 151: 173-9 S '30 12463

Faulkner, Leon C. Institutional management and the juvenile offender. Am Pris Assn Proc 59: 365-9 '29 12464

Flanagan, E. J. Practical aspects of the pre-delinquent child in the institution. Minn St Conf & Inst Soc Wk Proc 37: 139-43 '29 12465

Frankel, Emil and Heyer, Helen E. Juvenile delinquents enter state institutions —1930: statistical summary of admissions and discharges for the year ending June 30, 1930. 17p. (mim) Trenton, New Jersey Department of institutions and agencies, October 1931 12466

Hapke, E. Jugendstrafvollzug. Zeitsch f Kinderforsch 36: 135-41 '30 12467

Hoerst, Wilhelm. Fürsorgeerziehung krimineller Jugendlicher über 16 Jahre in England. Zentralbl f Jugendrecht u Jugendwohlfahrt 21: 301-05, 351-6 D 29, Ja '30 12468

The imprisonment of youthful offenders. Just Peace 92: 675-6 D 1 '28 12469

Jacubson, V. Lisbenie svobode v sistme mer borde s detskoi prestupnosti. Problemy Prestupnosti 2: 268-80 '27 12470

Juveniles in prison. Commonweal 14: 293 Jl '31 12471

Kleist, F. Jugend hinter Gittern. Im Jugendgefängnis. 219p. Jena, Zwing, 1931 12472

Krog, O. S. von. Institutions and schools of other states [training schools for boys]. Bul St Inst [Iowa] 30: 82-7 Je '28 12473

Prison for a boy. Sol J 74: 541 Ag 16 '30 12474

Proyecto de ley sobre el plan general de construccion de establecimientos para menores. Bibl Nac de Crim y Cienc Afines Bol 3(3): 274- Ja '29 12475

Stiffler, M. L. The place of the institution for the pre-delinquent child. Minn St Conf & Inst Soc Wk Proc 37: 133-7 '29 12476

Argentina

Creacion de un reformatorio para menores delincuentes en Mendoza. Bibl Nac de Crim y Cienc Afines Bol 1: 233-5 Ja '27 12477

Fernández, Francisco J. Los reformatorios de menores de Santa Fé y Rosario. Museo Soc Arg Bol 18: 324-34, 385-94 Je, Jl '30 12478

Paz Anchorena, José M. Las instituciones oficiales y privadas en la prevención y protección a la infancia desvalida y delinquente. Museo Soc Arg Bol 19 (112-14): 448-60 O '31 12479

Australia

Prior, Percy B. Australia's unfortunate girl. Welf Mag 18: 1147-51 S '27 12480

Canada

British Columbia. Provincial industrial school for boys, Port Coquitlam. Annual reports 23, 1926/27—27, 1930/31. Victoria, 1928-31 12481

Halifax industrial school, Halifax. Annual reports 66, 1929—68, 1931. [Halifax, 1929-31] 12482

Manitoba industrial training school, Portage La Prairie. Boys in trouble: a review of the work of the Manitoba industrial training school for boys over a five-year period from July 15, 1926—July 5, 1931. 23p. 1931? 12483

New Brunswick. Boys' industrial home, East Saint John. Report of the Superintendent 35, 1928—38, 1931. [East Saint John, 1928-31] 12484

Germany

Barandun. Das Jugendgefängnis in Wittlich. Schweiz Ver f Straf-, Gefängniswes u Schutzauf Verh 8: 70-88 '28 12485

Sommer, W. Schloss Heiligenstedten. Howard J 2: 196-9 O '28 12486

Great Britain

Borstal cases: criminal tendencies. Just Peace 95: 146 Mr 7 '31 12487

Borstal in 1930. Just Peace 94: 614 O 4 '30 12488

Borstal system. Sch & Soc 26: 360-1 Ag 27 '27 12489

Exner, Franz. Das Borstal-system. Monats f Kriminalpsychol u Strafrechtsref 21: 473-80 '30 12490

Home Office schools, an exhibition of work. Just Peace 95: 339-40 My 23 '31 12491

The imprisonment of young offenders in England. Sch & Soc 25: 490 Ap 23 '27 12492

Johnstone, J. D. Home office schools. Police J [London] 4: 273-84 Ap '31 12493

Morrison, A. C. L. Home office schools. Just Peace 94: 364-6 Je 7 '30 12494

Morrison, A. C. L. Impressions of Borstal. Just Peace 94: 350-1 My 31 '30 12495

Hawaii

Hawaii. Board of industrial schools. Report . . . for the period July 1, 1929/December 31, 1930. 36p. Honolulu, 1931 12496

Maunawili training school for girls; Waialee training school for boys.

Italy

Sellin, Thorsten. The House of correction for boys in the hospice of Saint Michael in Rome. J Crim L & Crimin 20: 533-53 F '30 12497

Vidoni, G. Relazione su la "Sezione per delinquente minorenni" nelle carceri giudiziarie di Genova. Arch di Antrop Crim 47: 74-80 Ja '27 12498

Watkin, V. E. Italian farm colony for delinquent boys [Ligurian farm colony]. Howard J 2: 106-8 '27 12499

Russia

Drake, M. The Gorki colony for delinquent children and adolescents in Russia. Howard J 3: 79-80 S '30 12500

Spain

Las Heras, José De. La juventud delincuente en España y su tratamiento reformador. 150p. Alcalà de Henares, Imp. de la Escuela Ind. de Jòvenes, 1927 12501

United States

Reeves, Margaret. Training schools for delinquent girls. 455p. bibliog 437-40. New York, Russell Sage foundation, 1929 12502

United States. Bureau of education. Industrial schools for delinquents, 1926-27. 22p. (Bul 1928 no10) Washington, 1928 12503

United States. Bureau of the census. Children under institutional care, 1923: statistics of dependent, neglected and delinquent children in institutions and under the supervision of other agencies for the care of children, with a section on adults in certain types of institutions. 381p. Washington, 1927 12504

California

Begun in idealism, ended in politics; El Retiro school for problem girls. Survey 59: 83-4 O 15 '27 12505

California. Preston school of industry, Waterman. Biennial report *in* Biennial report of Department of institutions 4, 1926/28: 53-79; 5, 1928/30: 100-30 12506

California. Ventura school for girls, Ventura. Report *in* Biennial report of Department of institutions 4, 1926/28: 94-103; 5, 1928/30: 131-57 12507

California. Whittier state school for boys, Whittier. Report *in* Biennial report of Department of institutions 4, 1926/28: 80-93; 5, 1928/30: 158-74 12508

Knox, Elmer E. Follow-up of 103 Whittier state school boys ten years after admission. J Juv Res 12: 261-9 S '28 12509

Nelles, Fred C. Work at Whittier state school. J Delin 11: 69-71 Je '27 12510

Scudder, Kenyon J. The contagion of a good environment [Whittier state school]. J Juv Res 13: 258-61 O '29 12511

Shepard, John B. The physical education program at Whittier state school. J Delin 11: 88-99 Je '27 12512

Sullivan, Ellen B. Age, intelligence, and educational achievement of boys entering Whittier state school. J Delin 11: 23-38 Mr '27 12513

Colorado

Colorado. Industrial school for boys, Golden. Biennial reports 24, 1927/28—25, 1929/30. [Golden, 1928-31] 12514

Colorado. State industrial school for girls, Mt. Morrison. Biennial report, 1926/28—1929/31. Denver, 1929-31 12515

Connecticut

Connecticut. School for boys, Meriden. Report *in* Report of Department of public welfare 1926/28: 58-61; 1928/30: 72-4 12516

DELAWARE

Delaware. Industrial school for colored girls, Marshallton. Report, 1928—[1930]. [Marshallton, 1929-30] **12517**

Delaware. Industrial school for girls, Claymont. Biennial report, 1928/30. 26p. [Claymont, 1930] **12518**

DISTRICT OF COLUMBIA

District of Columbia. District training school. Report *in* Report of Board of public welfare 1927: 72-4; 1928: 93-5; 1929: 109-12; 1930: 82-5; 1931: 96-100 **12519**

District of Columbia. Industrial home school, Washington. Report *in* Report of Board of public welfare 1927: 80-3; 1928: 99-101; 1929: 117-20; 1930: 90-3; 1931: 106-10 **12520**

District of Columbia. Industrial home school for colored children. Annual report *in* Report of Board of public welfare 1927: 75-9; 1928: 96-8; 1929: 113-16; 1930: 86-9; 1931: 101-5 **12521**

District of Columbia. National training school for boys, Bladensburg Road. Report *in* Report of Board of public welfare 1927: 41-2; 1928: 47-9; 1929: 56-7; 1931: 9, 19, 24 **12522**

District of Columbia. National training school for girls. Report *in* Report of Board of public welfare 1927: 43-7; 1928: 50-3; 1929: 58-61; 1930: 47-50; 1931: 51-5 **12523**

(colored) Conduit Road, Washington. (white) Muirkirk, Md.

FLORIDA

Florida. Dade county home for delinquent girls and indigents, Miami. Report *in* Dade county, Board of county commissioners, Your Dade county taxes, where they go, what they do, 7-9. Miami, January 1931 **12524**

Florida. Industrial school for boys, Marianna. Biennial report of the Superintendent to the Board of commissioners of state institutions, 1928/30. General information to December 31, 1930. 34p. [Marianna, 1931] **12525**

GEORGIA

Georgia. Training school for boys, Milledgeville. Biennial reports, 1925/27—1929/31. Milledgeville, 1927-31 **12526**

Georgia. Training school for girls, Atlanta. Biennial report of the Board of managers, 1927/28—1929/30. [Atlanta, 1929-31] **12527**

IDAHO

Idaho. Industrial training school, St. Anthony. Biennial report 14, 1929/30. [Boise, 1931] **12528**

ILLINOIS

Cook county. Chicago and Cook county school for boys, Riverside. Report of the Superintendent, 1926/27—1929/30. [Riverside, 1927-30] **12529**

Byron, Wright. Out at St. Charles! Welf Mag 18: 1053-5 Ag '27 **12530A**

Erlewine, Ella. Training the delinquent girl [State training school, Geneva]. Welf Mag 18: 749-58 Jl '27 **12530B**

Hanna, Francis D. Trying to help the boys go straight. Crim Just [Chicago] (54): 14-15 S '27 **12531**

Illinois. St. Charles school for boys, St. Charles. Report *in* Annual report of Department of public welfare 10, 1926/27: 240-8; 11, 1927/28: 296-303; 12, 1928/29: 197-200; 13, 1929/30: 292-300 **12532**

Illinois. State training school for girls, Geneva. Report *in* Annual report of Department of public welfare 10, 1926/27: 249-52; 11, 1927/28: 288-95; 12, 1928/29: 201-6; 13, 1929/30: 301-16 **12533**

INDIANA

Indiana. Boys' school, Plainfield. Annual report 61, 1926/27—65, 1930/31. Indianapolis, 1928-31 **12534**

Indiana. Girls' school, Indianapolis. Annual report 21, 1926/27—25, 1930/31. Indianapolis, 1928-32 **12535**

IOWA

Gray, R. E. Physical and mental condition of boys received at the Training school for boys, Eldora. Bul St Inst [Iowa] 33: 51-4 Ja '31 **12536**

Iowa. Training school for boys, Eldora. Biennial report 31, 1926/28. 80p. [Eldora, 1928] **12537**

Iowa. Training school for girls, Mitchellville. Biennial report of the Superintendent 31, 1926/28—32, 1928/30. [Mitchellville, 1928-30] **12538**

31st report of Superintendent is also 12th biennial report of the State agent of the Training school for girls.

KANSAS

Kansas. Boys' industrial school, Topeka. Biennial report 24, 1926/28—25, 1928/30. Topeka, 1928-30; *also in* Biennial report of Board of administration, Correctional institutions section **12539**

Kansas. Girls' industrial school, Beloit. Biennial report 20, 1926/28—21, 1928/30. Topeka, 1928/30; *also in* Biennial report of Board of administration, Correctional institutions section **12540**

KENTUCKY

Kentucky. State house of reform, Greendale. Report *in* Biennial report of State board of charities and corrections, 1925/27—1929/31 **12541**

Kentucky. State school for girls, Greendale. Report *in* Biennial report of State board of charities and corrections, 1925/27—1929/31 **12542**

MARYLAND

Maryland. House of reformation for colored boys, Cheltenham. Biennial report of the Board of Managers, 1926/28—1928/30. [Cheltenham, 1928-30] **12543**

Maryland. Training school for boys, Loch Raven. Biennial report 69, 1926/28—70, 1928/30. Loch Raven, 1928-30 **12544**

Maryland. Training school for boys, Loch Raven. Dedicatory exercises commemorating the one hundredth anniversary of the founding, May 28, 1931. 31p. [Loch Raven, 1931] **12545**

MASSACHUSETTS

County training schools report *in* Annual report of Massachusetts Department of public welfare **12546**

Essex county training school, Lawrence; Hampden county training school, Springfield; Middlesex county training school, North Chelmsford; Norfolk, Bristol and Plymouth union training school, Walpole; Worcester county training school, Oakdale.

Massachusetts. Department of public welfare. Division of juvenile training. Trustees of Massachusetts training schools. Report, 1927-1931. Boston 1928-31 (Pub doc no93) **12547**

Lyman school for boys; Industrial school for boys; Industrial school for girls; parole.

Massachusetts. Industrial school for boys, Shirley. Report *in* Annual report of Department ol public welfare 11, 1929/30: 41-3 **12548**

Massachusetts. Industrial school for girls, Lancaster. Report *in* Annual report of Department of public welfare 8, 1926/27: 45-6; 9, 1927/28: 39-40; 10, 1928/29: 42-3; 11, 1929/30: 43-5 **12549**

Massachusetts. Lyman school for boys, Westborough. Report *in* Annual report of Department of public welfare 8, 1926/27: 42-3; 9, 1927/28: 37-8; 10, 1928/29: 40-1; 11, 1929/30: 40-1 **12550**

MINNESOTA

Minnesota. Hennepin county. Glen Lake farm school for boys. Report *in* Report of Juvenile court of Hennepin county, Minnesota 1926-1927-1928: 32-4 **12551**

Minnesota. Hennepin county home school for girls, Minneapolis. Report *in* Report of Juvenile court of Hennepin county, Minnesota 1926-1927-1928: 30-1 **12552**

Minnesota. Home school for girls, Sauk Center. Biennial report *in* Biennial report of State board of control 14, 1926/28: 131-6; 15, 1928/30: 153-8 **12553**

Minnesota. Training school for boys, Red Wing. Minnesota training school for boys, Red Wing, and Home school for girls, Sauk Center; reports of Superintendents to the State board of control, 1926/28—1928/30. [Red Wing, 1928-30] **12554**

MISSISSIPPI

Mississippi. Industrial and training school, Columbia. Biennial report of Board of trustees and Superintendent of training school 6, 1925/27—8, 1929/31. [Columbia] 1927-31 **12555**

MISSOURI

Hart, Hastings H. Industrial home for girls—Chillicothe, July 1929. 7p. (mim) St. Louis, Missouri welfare league, 1929? **12556**

Hart, Hastings H. Industrial home for Negro girls—Tipton, July 1929. 4p. (mim) St. Louis, Missouri welfare league, 1929? **12557**

Missouri. Industrial home for Negro girls, Tipton. Report *in* Biennial report of Department of penal institutions 1927/28: 209-31; 1929/30: 272-94 **12558**

Missouri. Intermediate reformatory, Algoa. Report *in* Biennial report of Department of penal institutions 1929/30: 131-69 **12559**

Missouri. Reformatory for boys, Boonville. Report *in* Biennial report of Department of penal institutions 1927/28: 153-72; 1929/30: 173-232 **12560**

Missouri. State industrial home for girls, Chillicothe. Report *in* Biennial report of Department of penal institutions 1927/28: 175-206; 1929/30: 235-70 **12561**

MONTANA

Montana. State industrial school, Miles City. Annual report 20, 1927—23, 1931. [Miles City, 1927-31] **12562**

NEBRASKA

Nebraska. Girls' training school, Geneva. Biennial report, 1925/27—1927/29. [Geneva, 1927-29] **12563**

Nebraska. Industrial home (girls), Milford. Biennial report of the Superintendent, 1927/29—1929/31. [Milford, 1929-31] **12564**

Nebraska. State industrial school for boys, Kearney. Biennial report of the Superintendent, 1927/29. [Kearney, 1929] **12565**

NEW HAMPSHIRE

New Hampshire. Industrial school, Manchester. Report of superintendent *in* Report of Purchasing agent and state institutions 1926/28—1928/30; *also in* Biennial report of State board of charities and corrections, 1926/28 **12566**

NEW MEXICO

New Mexico. Industrial school, Springer. Report of the Board of trustees and superintendent, 1929/30. [Springer, 1930] **12567**

NEW YORK

New York (city). Society for the reformation of juvenile delinquents, Randall's Island. Annual report 104, 1927/28. [New York, 1928] 12568

New York (state). Agricultural and industrial schools, Industry. Annual report 79, 1927—82, 1930. [Industry, 1927-30] 12569

New York (state). Children's village, Dobbs Ferry. Annual report 76, 1927. [Dobbs Ferry, 1927] 12570

New York (state). Executive department. Division of the budget. Report on the affairs of the Society for the reformation of juvenile delinquents relating to the House of refuge, Randall's Island, New York city. 70p. [New York, 1928] 12571

New York (state). Rome state school, Rome. Annual report 33, 1926/27—37, 1930/31. Rome, 1927-31 12572

New York (state). Training school for girls, Hudson. Annual report of the Superintendent, 1926/27—1927/28. [Albany, 1927-28] 12573

NORTH CAROLINA

North Carolina. Eastern Carolina industrial school for boys, Rocky Mount. Biennial report 1, 1926/28—2, 1928/30. [Rocky Mount, 1928-30] 12574

North Carolina. Morrison training school for Negro boys, Hoffman. Biennial report *in* Biennial report of the North Carolina charitable, penal and correctional institutions of the State board of charities and public welfare, Division of institutions 1930/32: 345-66 12575

North Carolina. School for Negro girls, Efland. Biennial report *in* Biennial report of the North Carolina charitable, penal and correctional institutions of the State board of charities and public welfare, Division of institutions 1930/32: 395-8 12576

NORTH DAKOTA

North Dakota. State training school, Mandan. Biennial report 13, 1926/28—14, 1928/30. [Mandan, 1928-30]; *also in* Annual report of Board of administration 9/10, 1926/28: 309-34; 11/12, 1928/30: 433-63 12577

OHIO

Ohio. Boys' industrial school, Lancaster. Annual report *in* Annual report of Department of public welfare 6, 1927: 385-96; 7, 1928: 359-74; 8, 1929: 470-86 12578

Ohio. Girls' industrial school, Delaware. Annual report *in* Annual report of Department of public welfare 6, 1927: 397-402; 7, 1928: 375-80; 8, 1929: 487-96 12579

OKLAHOMA

Oklahoma. Industrial home for colored girls, Taft. Report *in* Report of State commissioner of charities and corrections 1929: 35-6; 1930: 24-9 12580

Oklahoma. State industrial school for white girls, Tecumseh. Report *in* Report of State commissioner of charities and corrections 1927: 36-8; 1928: 49-55; 1929: 27-32; 1930: 13-19 12581

Oklahoma. State training school for Negro boys, Boley. Report *in* Report of State commissioner of charities and corrections 1927: 38-9; 1928: 64-6; 1929: 44; 1930: 30 12582

Oklahoma. State training school for white boys, Pauls Valley. Annual report *in* Report of State commissioner of charities and corrections 1927: 32-6; 1928: 57-61; 1929: 37-43; 1930: 20-3 12583

OREGON

Oregon. State industrial school for girls, Salem. Report *in* Biennial report of State board of control 9, 1928/30: 195-202 12584

Oregon. State training school for boys, Woodburn. Report *in* Biennial report of State board of control 9, 1928/30: 143-52 12585

PENNSYLVANIA

Branson, J. Howard. Huntingdon [Pennsylvania reformatory for boys]. Pris J 8: 10 O '28 12586A

Elliott, Mabel Agnes. Correctional education and the delinquent girl: a follow-up study of one hundred and ten Sleighton Farm girls. 112p. Harrisburg, Department of Public welfare, 1928 12586B

Pennsylvania. Girls' department of the Glen Mills schools (Sleighton Farm), Darlington. Annual report, 1927. [Darlington, 1928] 12587

Pennsylvania. Girls' department of the Glen Mills schools (Sleighton Farm), Darlington. The new spirit of an old farm [annual report], 1928, by Leigh Mitchell Hodges 12588

Pennsylvania. Glen Mills schools. Annual report of the Board of managers 100, 1927—103, 1930/31. [Philadelphia, 1928-31] 12589

RHODE ISLAND

Rhode Island. Oaklawn school for girls, Howard. Annual report, 1930/31. 12p. [Providence, 1931]; *also in* Annual report of State public welfare commission 5, 1926/27: 135-7; 6, 1927/28: 107-11; 1928/29: 15-21; 8, 1929/30: 77-87 12590

Rhode Island. Sockanosset school for boys, Howard. Annual report, 1930/31. 35p. [Howard, 1931]; *also in* Annual report of State public welfare commission 5, 1926/27: 37-55; 6, 1927/28: 13-33; 7, 1928/29: 22-9; 8, 1929/30: 88-105 12591

SOUTH CAROLINA

South Carolina. Dr. John de la Howe industrial school, Willington. Annual report of the Board of trustees 10, 1927—13, 1930. [Willington, 1928-31] 12592

SOUTH DAKOTA

South Dakota. Training school, Plankinton. Report *in* Biennial report of Board of charities and corrections 20, 1926/28: 22-34; 21, 1928/30: 28-37 12593

TENNESSEE

Tennessee. Training and agricultural school for boys, Nashville. Biennial report *in* Biennial report of Department of institutions 1926/28: 249-71; 1928/30: 261-85 12594

Tennessee. Vocational school for colored girls. Biennial report *in* Biennial report of Department of institutions 1926/28: 291-8; 1928/30: 305-12 12595

Tennessee. Vocational school for girls, Tullahoma. Biennial report *in* Biennial report of Department of institutions 1926/28: 275-87; 1928/30: 289-302 12596

TEXAS

Texas. Girls' training school, Gainesville. Biennial report, 1928/29. (typw) [Gainesville, 1929] 12597

UTAH

Utah. State industrial school, Ogden. Biennial report 16, 1926/28—17, 1928/30. [Ogden, 1928-30] 12598

VERMONT

Vermont. Industrial school, Vergennes. Report *in* Biennial report of Department of public welfare 1926/28: 93-102; 1928/30: 103-12 12599

VIRGINIA

Virginia. Home and industrial school for girls, Bon Air. Report *in* Annual report of State department of public welfare 18, 1927: 28-9; 19, 1928: 27; 20, 1929: 32; 21, 1930: 29; 22, 1931: 27 12600

Virginia. Industrial school for boys, Maidens. Report *in* Annual report of State department of public welfare 18, 1927: 28; 19, 1928: 27; 20, 1929: 31-2; 21, 1930: 28; 22, 1931: 26-7 12601

Virginia. Industrial school for colored girls, Peaks Turnout. Annual report 12, 1926/27—16, 1930/31. [Richmond, 1927-31] 12602

Virginia. Manual labor school for colored boys, Hanover. Report *in* Annual report of State department of public welfare 18, 1927: 29; 19, 1928: 28; 20, 1929: 32-3; 21, 1930: 29-30; 22, 1931: 27-8 12603

WASHINGTON

Washington. State school for girls, Grand Mound. Report *in* Biennial report of Department of business control 4, 1926/28: 184-91; 5, 1928/30: 51-2 12604

Washington. State training school for boys, Chehalis. Report *in* Biennial report of Department of business control 4, 1926/28: 176-83; 5, 1928/30: 48-50 12605

WISCONSIN

Wisconsin. Industrial school for boys, Waukesha. Report *in* Biennial report of State board of control 19, 1926/28: 434-52; 20, 1928/30: 355-73 12606

Wisconsin. Industrial school for girls, Milwaukee. Report *in* Biennial report of State board of control 19, 1926/28: 454-72; 1928/30: 376-400 12607

WYOMING

Wyoming. Girls industrial institute, Sheridan. Report *in* Biennal report of Board of charities and reform 1926/28: 92-100; 1928/30: 123-34 12608

Wyoming. Industrial institute, Worland. Report *in* Biennial report of Board of charities and reform 1926/28: 63-9; 1928/30: 88-95 12609

CHILDREN'S REPUBLICS

Bazeley, E. T. Homer Lane and the Little commonwealth. 200p. New York, Allen, 1928 12610

Bruner, Earle D. A laboratory study in democracy; the agitator and other types. 262p. New York, Doubleday, 1927 12611

Children's republics. R Int de l'Enf 3: 168-72 Mr '27 12612

Crane, Annie L. Commonwealth for delinquent boys at Albion, Michigan. World Today 55: 24-6 D '29 12613

Junior citizens of the George Junior republic, Freeville, N.Y. (2) July 1925- 12614

Junior republic (California, George junior republic) Chino, Calif. 1, 1911- 12615

INSTITUTIONS FOR WOMEN

Alsen, Ola. Die Tochter Lots. Aufzeichnungen aus einem Frauengefängnis. 294p. Leipzig, Ernst Oldenburg, 1931? 12616

Biha. Im Frauengefängnis von Belgrad. Neue Generation 23: 367-70 N '27 12617

Booth, Ernest. Ladies in durance vile. Am Mercury 22: 392-402 Ap '31 12618

Boucard, Robert. Les dessous des prisons de femmes. Comment elles vivent, expient, se pervertissent. 255p. Paris, Les Edit. Documentaires, 1930 12619

Buckler, Helen. Women's prisons. Good Housekeeping 92: 26-7 F '31 12620

Carco, Francis Carcopino. Prisons de femmes. 269p. Paris, Les Edit. de France, 1930 12621

Growdon, Clarence H. The mental status of reformatory women. J Crim L & Crimin 22: 196-220 Jl '31 12622

Hentig, H. v. and Albrecht. Strafanstalten für junge Mütter. Monats f Kriminalpsychol u Strafrechtsref 18: 374-6 Jl '27 12623

Johnston, E. Pauline. Women's reformatories. Bul St Inst [Iowa] 30: 78-81 Je '28 12624

Koerber, L. von. Frauenerfahrungen aus der strafgefangenenfürsorge. Westerm Monatsh 146: 577-80 Ag '29 12625

Lathrop, Florence B. Organizing a women's reformatory on an educational basis. Thesis (M.A.) Harvard university, 1931? **12626**

Monahan, Florence. Administration of a reformatory for women. Am Pris Assn Proc 59: 369-75 '29 **12627**

Monahan, Florence. Clothing for inmates in state institutions. Minn St Bd Con Q 29: 17-19 F 25 '30 **12628**

Picton, Werner and Harold. The women's prison in Berlin. Howard J 3: 77-9 '31 **12629**

Potter, Ellen C. How shall we plan for children of unmarried mothers in correctional institutions? Hosp Soc Serv 23: 403-12 Ap '31 **12630**

Reuss, Maria. Der Strafvollzug an Frauen, vor, in und nach dem Kriege unter Berücksichtigung der Wechselwirkungen zwischen Verwaltungs- und Fürsorgearbeit. 62p. München, Reinhardt, 1927 **12631**

Snow, Edgar. Hard lot of women prisoners in Hon Sanso. China W R 55: 255 Ja 17 '31 **12632**

Wittpenn, H. Otto. Some European institutions for women. N J Conf Soc Wk Proc 29: 36-8 '30 **12633**

Woollcombe, Joan. Life in a woman's prison. Spectator 142: 1002-3 Je 29 '29 **12634**

Zaglits, Carla. Holloway: das Londoner Frauengefängnis. Zeitsch f Kinderschutz 23: 26-8 F '31 **12635**

UNITED STATES

Hazard, Helen H. Women prisoners; the United States government undertakes a new project [Federal industrial institution, Alderson, W.Va.]. Howard J 2: 298-301 Je '29 **12636**

Lekkerkerker, Eugenia C. Reformatories for women in the United States. 615p. bibliog 582-604. Groningen, Wolters, 1931 **12637**

CALIFORNIA

Buwalda, Imra Wann. The California institution for women. Calif Conf Soc Wk Q Bul 12: 31-4 F '29 **12638**

McDougall, George B. California institution for women. Calif Highw & Pub Wks 8: 2-4 S '30 **12639**

CONNECTICUT

Connecticut. State farm for women, East Lyme. Biennial report of the Board of directors, 1926/28—1928/30. (Pub doc no67) Hartford, 1928-30; *also in* Report of Department of public welfare 1926/28: 54-7; 1928/30: 68-71 **12640**

Rogers, Helen Worthington. A history of the movement to establish a state reformatory for women in Connecticut. J Crim L & Crimin 19: 518-41 bibliog (p541) F '29 **12641**

DELAWARE

Delaware. Women's prison, Greenbank. Report, 1, *in* Report of New Castle county workhouse, 1929/30 **12642**

ILLINOIS

Beatty, Florence Northridge. The woman's prison [Joliet, Ill.]. Welf 18: 921-6 Jl '27 **12643**

Illinois. State reformatory for women, Dwight. Report, April 10, 1930/June 30, 1930 *in* Annual report of Department of public welfare 13, 1929/30: 359-60 **12644**

Illinois. Women's prison, Joliet. Report *in* Annual report of Department of public welfare 10, 1926/27: 257-9; 11, 1927/28: 312-15; 12, 1928/29: 249-51; 13, 1929/30: 329-30 **12645**

INDIANA

Indiana. Women's prison, Indianapolis. Annual report 56, 1926/27—60, 1930/31. [Indianapolis, 1927-31] **12646**
Includes report of Correctional department.

IOWA

Iowa. Women's reformatory, Rockwell City. *See* Iowa Men's reformatory **12647**

KANSAS

Kansas. Industrial farm for women, Lansing. Biennial report 6, 1926/28—7, 1928/30. [Lansing] 1928-30; *also in* Biennial report of Board of administration, Correctional institutions section 6, 1926/28—7, 1928/30 **12648**

MASSACHUSETTS

Massachusetts. Reformatory for women, Framingham. Report *in* Annual report of Commissioner of correction 1927: 48-61; 1929: 53-67 **12649**

MINNESOTA

Minnesota. Reformatory for women, Shakopee. Biennial report 4, 1926/28—5, 1928/30. Shakopee [1928-30]; *also in* Biennial report of the State board of control 14, 1926/28: 141-3; 15, 1928/30: 165-7 **12650**

MISSOURI

Hart, Hastings H. Women's department, Missouri penitentiary, State farm no. 1, Jefferson City, Mo. 4p. (mim) St. Louis, Missouri welfare league, 1929? **12651**

NEBRASKA

Nebraska. State reformatory for women, York. Biennial report of the Superintendent, 1927/29. [York, 1929] **12652**

NEW YORK

New York (city). Woman's municipal farm, Greycourt. Report *in* Report of Department of correction 1927: 90-2 12653

New York (state). Albion state training school, Albion. Report *in* Report of Commissioner of correction 1927: 397-414 12654

1931 transformed into Institution for mentally defective women.

New York (state). State prison for women, Auburn. Report *in* Report of Commissioner of correction 1927: 197-225 12655

NORTH CAROLINA

North Carolina. Industrial farm colony for women, Kinston. Report *in* Biennial report of North Carolina charitable, penal and correctional institutions of the State board of charities and public welfare, Division of institutions 1930/32: 401-24 12656

Opened April 3, 1929; no printed report covering April 3, 1929/June 30, 1930.

North Carolina. State home and industrial school for girls and women, Samarcand. Biennial report of the Board of directors 6, 1928/30. [Samarcand, 1930] 12657

North Carolina. Stonewall Jackson manual training and industrial school, Concord. Biennial report of the Superintendent 10, 1926/28—11, 1928/30. [Concord, 1928-30] 12658

OHIO

Ohio. Reformatory for women, Marysville. Report *in* Report of Department of public welfare 6, 1927: 435-46; 7, 1928: 418-28; 8, 1929: 531-42 12659

PENNSYLVANIA

Pennsylvania. Industrial home for women, Muncy. Report of the Board of trustees and the Superintendent, 1928/30. 25p. [Muncy, 1930] 12660

Weaver, William M. A visit to Muncy. Pris J 8: 11 O '28 12661

Wilson, Franklin R. [The Women's reformatory, Muncy, Pa.]. Assn of Dir Poor & Char & Correc Proc 55: 178-87 '30 12662

RHODE ISLAND

Rhode Island. Reformatory for women, Howard. Report *in* Annual report of State public welfare commission 5, 1927: 151-8; 6, 1928: 112-21; 7, 1929: 52-5; 8, 1930: 130-4 12663

VERMONT

Cleghorn, Sarah and [Fisher], Dorothy Canfield. Miss Ross' girls. Survey 66: 429-33 Ag 1 '31 12664

Riverside, the Vermont state prison and House of correction for women, Rutland, Vt.; data on earnings of the laundry.

Ross, Lena C. Riverside—the women's reformatory at Rutland. Vt Highw 14-18 Je '30 12665

Vermont. State prison and House of correction for women, Rutland. Report *in* Biennial report of the Department of public welfare 1926/28: 81-9; 1928/30: 89-99 12666

WISCONSIN

Wisconsin. Industrial home for women, Taycheedah. Report *in* Biennial report of State board of control 19, 1926/28: 474-92; 20, 1928/30: 401-14 12667

Reports also issued as separates.

DETENTION HOMES

Best we knew how; new Women's house of detention, New York. Survey 66: 86 Ap 15 '31 12668

Mingos, Howard. Jail for a lady; new house of detention. Outl 156: 422 N 12 '30 12669

Philadelphia. Woman's misdemeanants' House of detention. Report *in* Annual report of Municipal court 14, 1927: 151-3; 15, 1928: 151-3; 16, 1928: 137-9; 17, 1930: 143-4; 18, 1931: 153-60 12670

Votaw, Albert H. The unconvicted prisoner. Pris J 8: 1-5 O '28 12671

Walls of steel for security; detention quarters of the Cuyahoga county criminal court building, Cleveland. Arch Forum 54: 637-40 My '31 12672

The Women's detention home of Cleveland. Policewoman's Int Bul 4:2 Mr '28 12673

INSTITUTIONS FOR CRIMINAL INSANE

Moseley, Sydney A. The truth about Broadmoor. Fortn R ns121: 89-98 Ja '27 12674

UNITED STATES

Harms, Mary. Institutional care of the criminal insane in the United States. Ment Hyg 15: 135-54 Ja '31 12675

United States. Congress. House. Committee on judiciary. To establish a hospital for defective delinquents: report to accompany H. R. 7410, January 6, 1930. 2p. Washington, 1930 (71st Cong. 2d sess. H. Rep. 102) 12676

INDIANA

Indiana. Hospital for insane criminals, Michigan City 12677

Adjoins State prison and under same management.

KENTUCKY

Kentucky. Central state hospital [for criminal insane], Lakeland. Report *in* Biennial report of the State board of charities and corrections, 1925/27—1929/31 12678

MASSACHUSETTS

Massachusetts. Department for defective delinquents. Report of agent *in* Annual report of Commissioner of correction 8, 1926/27: 74-87; 10, 1928/29: 84-91 12679

NEW YORK

New York (state). Dannemora state hospital, Dannemora. Annual report, 1927-1930. Dannemora, 1927-30; *also in* Annual report of Commissioner of correction 1927: 367-96 12680

New York (state). Matteawan state hospital, Beacon. Report *in* Annual report of Commissioner of correction 1927: 323-64 12681

OHIO

Ohio. Lima state hospital for criminal insane, Lima. Report *in* Annual report of Department of public welfare 6, 1927: 221-43; 7, 1928: 179-206; 8, 1929: 263-99 12682

PENAL COLONIES

Allison-Booth, William Edwin. Devil's Island: revelations of the penal settlements in French Guiana. 235p. London, Putnam, 1930; same under title: Hell's outpost; the true story of Devil's Island by a man who exiled himself there. 271p. New York, Minton, 1931 12683

Barker, F. A. The Andaman Islands and the transportation system in India. Howard J 3: 36-41 '31 12684

Batzler-Heim, Georg. The horrors of Cayenne; the experiences of a German as a French bagno-convict; transl by Beatrice Marshall; edited by Karl Bartz. New York, Constable, 1930; Richard R. Smith, 1931 12685

Beyli, Walter. Verwahrung und Arbeitskolonie. Schweiz Zeitsch f Strafr 41: 225-9 '28 12686

[Cairns, Elizabeth]. A criminal colony in India. Pris J 7: 34 Ja '27 12687

Cayenne. Just Peace 95: 130 F 28 '31 12688

The convict colony in French Guiana. Howard J 3: 65-76 '31 12689

Gorky, Maxim. The labor colonies of the OGPU. Soviet Union R 9: 185-7 S '31 12690

Translated from Moscow *Izvestia,* July 14, 1931.

Le Goupils, Marc. Sous les niaoulis: souvenirs d'un planteur calédonien (1898-1904). R Deux Mondes 111-43 S '27 12691

Halliburton, Richard. De profundis; French Guiana, the dry guillotine. Ladies Home J 46: 30-1 N '29; same title: R of R 80: 86-8 D '29 12692

Niles, Blair. Desperate escapes [Devil's Island]. Forum 78: 836-47 D '27 12693

Nitti, Francesco Fausto. Escape: the personal narrative of a political prisoner who was rescued from Lipari, the Fascist "Devil's Island." 267p. New York, Putnam, 1930 12694

Péan, Charles. Terre de Bagne. 254p. Paris, La Renaissance Moderne, 1930? 12695

Rashleigh, Ralph (pseud). Adventures of an outlaw; the memoirs of R. Rashleigh, a penal exile in Australia, 1825-44. 349p. New York, Cape, 1929 12696

Valdes, Manuel Menendez. French justice; transl by D. Pound. 256p. London, Faber & Faber, 1930? 12697

Vaughn, Herbert S. Convict ship. Edinb R 249: 145-59 Ja '29 12698

PRISON CAMPS

Dieudonné, Eugène. Waldlager im Bagno. Tagebuch 11: 1196-8 Jl 26 '30 12699

Massachusetts. Prison camp and hospital, West Rutland. Report *in* Annual report of Commissioner of correction 8, 1927: 62-5; 10, 1929: 67-71 12700

Prison road camps in California. Pris J 7: 11 Jl '27 12701

United States. Congress. House. Committee on judiciary. To establish federal prison camps, report to accompany H.R. 11285, May 18, 1928. 4p. Washington, 1928 (70th Cong. 1st sess. H. Rep. 1735) 12702

Virginia. State convict road force. Report *in* Report of State department of public welfare 18, 1927: 21; 19, 1928: 22; 20, 1929: 27; 21, 1930: 23; 22, 1931: 21; *also in* Annual report of Board of directors of the penitentiary 12703

PARDON, PAROLE AND INDETERMINATE SENTENCE

PARDON

GENERAL

American prison association. Committee on pardon and parole. Round table meeting [report]. Proc 60: 224-37 '30 12704

Barnett, James D. The grounds for pardon. Am L R 61: 694-750 S '27 12705

Barnett, James D. The grounds of pardon. J Crim L & Crimin 17: 490-530 F '27; same title: Ore L R 6: 204-40 Ap '27 12706

Davis, Fred H. Function of the pardon board as a part of our legal system. Fla St B Assn L J 4: 467-71 F '31 12707

Dürr. Die neuen bayerischen Begnadigungsvorschriften vom 31. Dez. 1927. Deut Juristen-Zeit 33: 284-6 '28 12708

A free pardon. Just Peace 94: 510 Ag 16 '30; Irish L T 64: 214-15 S 6 '30 12709

Fricke, S. Die Zuständigkeit in Gnadensachen im Reiche und in Preussen. Jurist Wchnschr 57: 390-2 '28 12710

Hentig, H. v. Zur Psychologie der Begnadigung. Monats f Kriminalpsychol u Strafrechtsref 19: 355-6 Je '28 12711

Lord, B. Thorn. Power to revoke pardon for fraud. L Notes 34: 148-51 N '30 12712

Pardons for "lifers": should they or should they not be granted? Northwest Police J 7: 18, 40-1 Ja '30 12713

Ramos, Aurelio C. Pardoning power of Mayor of city of Manila. Phil L J 7: 297-315 F '28 12714

Rice, Wm. G. jr. Power of pardon. Wis St B Assn Rep 1927: 36-55 12715

Schoetensack. Verfahren in Begnadigungssachen in Bayern. Gerichtssaal 97: 65-106 '28 12716

Stoke, Harold W. Review of the pardoning power. Ky L J 16: 34-42 N '27 12717

UNITED STATES

Neal, Ann and Hager, Beatrice. Summary of the provisions of the constitution and statutes of the several states relating to pardons. 22p. Madison, Wisconsin Legislative reference library, January 1929; same title: J Crim L & Crimin 20: 364-96 N '29 12718

CONNECTICUT

Cohen, George H. Is a pardon possible under Connecticut law? Conn B J 5: 148-54 Ap '31 12719

ILLINOIS

Illinois. Department of public welfare. Division of pardons and paroles. Rules and laws governing the Division of pardons and paroles of the Department of public welfare of the state of Illinois, for the pardon, reprieve, commutation, or parole of prisoners. 32p. [Springfield, 1928] 12720

IOWA

Iowa. Governor. Report . . . of pardons, suspensions and commutations of sentence and remissions of fines, January 1, 1927/December 31, 1928—January 1, 1929/December 31, 1930. Des Moines, 1929-31 12721

MASSACHUSETTS

Lattin, Norman D. The pardoning power in Massachusetts. Boston Univ L R 11: 505-25 N '31 12722

WYOMING

Wyoming. State board of pardons. Report *in* Biennial report of State board of charities and reform 1926/28: 57-60; 1928/30: 20-3 12723

AMNESTY

Carnevale, E. L'amnistia e gli speciali adattamenti del diritto. Scuola Pos 35: 289-95 '27 12724

Decusară, E. C. Résultats des recherches statistiques sur les effets de la loi d'amnestie. Bul Statist României 1: 125-9 Ja '30 12725

Dimitriu, V. M. Legea amnistiei. R de Drept Pen 37-40 Ja '28 12726

Garofalo, Raffaele. Criminalità e amnistìa in Italia. Nuov Antol 259: 49-61 My 1 '28 12727

Mari, A. Amnistia e diserzione. Riv Pen 105: 461-5 My '27 12728

Sterk, Gertrud. Ausgestaltung und Resultate des bedingten Straferlasses im Kanton St. Gallen. 117p. Diss. Bern, 1931. St. Gallen [Fehr in Komm.] 1931 12729

COMMUTATION

California. Governor. Reprieves, commutations and pardons by Governor C. C. Young, 1929-30, communicated to the Legislature, pursuant to the provisions of the constitution . . . and statutes of the state of California, on January 5, 1931. 48p. Sacramento, 1931 12730

Frangen, Heinrich. Gnadenwesen und Strafmilderung in Preussen. 105p. Köln, Schmidt, 1927 12731

Harno, Albert J. Power of executive to commute death sentence to life imprisonment. Ill L R 22: 442-4 D '27 12732

The President's power of commutation. N Y L R 5: 399-404 N '27 12733

EXECUTIVE CLEMENCY

Burlingham, Charles C. The independence of the executive practice of clemency: the New York practice. Mass L Q 12: 13-14 My '27 12734

Reprint from Boston Herald, April 29, 1927.

Griffin, Edwin G. Executive clemency. Ann Am Acad 136: 142-5 Mr '28 12735

Hale, Richard W. The independence of the executive practice of clemency: the practice of the English home office. Mass L Q 12: 1-12 My '27 12736

Ohio. Board of clemency. Annual report 6, 1929—7, 1930. Columbus, 1929-30; *also in* Annual report of Department of public welfare 12737

PAROLE AND INDETERMINATE SENTENCE

GENERAL

Alegre, Pedro J. Libertad provisoria y liberación condicional. R de Identif y Cienc Pen 4: 265-74 Jl '29 12738

Bellini, U. Condanna e liberazione condizionali. Riv di Dir Peniten 1: 265-77 '30 12739

Bondy, Curt. Zur unbestimmten Verurteilung bei Minderjährigen. Monats f Kriminalpsychol u Strafrechtsref 22: 135-40 Mr '31 12740

Borden, Howard G. Factors for predicting parole success. J Crim L & Crimin 19: 328-36 N '28 12741

Bramer, John Philip. A treatise giving the history, organization, and administration of parole. New York, Irving press, 1927 12742

Britto, Lemos. La mise en liberté des condamnés. 17p. Rio-de-Janeiro, 1930 12743

Bruce, Andrew A.; Burgess, E. W., and Harno, Albert J. The probation and parole system. *In* Illinois association for criminal justice, Illinois crime survey, 427-574, 1929 12744

Bruère, Robert W. Five minutes for parole. Survey 57: 488-9 Ja 15 '27 12745

Burgess, Ernest W. Is prediction feasible in social work? An inquiry based upon a sociological study of parole records. Soc Forces 7: 533-45 Je '29 12746

Cass, E. R. Digest of indeterminate sentence laws and parole rules. 29p. New York, Prison association of New York, 1927 12747

Catalano, Joseph. A preliminary study of parolees of the Western penitentiary in relation to parole violation. Thesis (M.A.) University of Pittsburgh, 1931 12748

Chicago. Municipal reference library. Parole and the indeterminate sentence. 280p. [Chicago] 1928 12749

Civic welfare alliance. Definite sentences stop crime. 1p. (Bul no524) Boston, January 15, 1927 12750

Close, O. H. and Erskine, George C. When is an individual eligible for parole from an institution. Am Pris Assn Proc 60: 224-9 '30 12751

Cosby, Sara V. To parole or not to parole. Welf Mag 18: 441-5 Ap '27 12752

Eichhorn, W. H. The indeterminate sentence and parole law. Ind Bul Char & Correc (193): 285-9 My '31 12753

Enquête sur les conditions dans lesquelles s'effectue la mise en liberté des condamnés a une peine privative de liberté. R Int de Dr Pén 7: 27-116 '30 12754

Belgium by Gillard and Delierneux; Spain by Cuello Calon; France by Armand Mossé and Léon Barthes; Great Britain by Howard league for penal reform; Greece by Panaghis Scouriotis; Italy by D'Amelio; Luxemburg by Ensch; Poland by E. Neymark; Portugal by A. Charula Pessanha; Rumania by Glod; Sweden by Thyrén; Switzerland by Mercier-Dufour; Czechoslovakia by Emil Lány.

Filho, Aloysio de Carvalho. Sentença indeterminada. 105p. Bahia, Livraria e papelaria Catilina, 1929 12755

Gardikas, Konstantin. Condemnatio sine praefinitione temporis. 220p. Athens, 1927 12756

In Greek.

Give parole a trial. Survey 63: 693 Mr 15 '30 12757

Goldsmith, Irving I. The parole commission, its plans and purposes. N Y St Conf Soc Wk Q Bul 2: 14-19 Jl '31 12758

Hafter, E. Bedingter Straferlass. Schweiz Zeitsch f Strafr 40: 200-2 '27 12759

History and theory of parole. Pris J 7: 14-16 O '27 12760

How the evils of parole can be eliminated. World's Wk 53: 472-3 Mr '27 12761

Hulbert, Harold S. Psychiatrist as member of parole board. J Crim L & Crimin 22: 487-8 N '31 12762

Hyde, L[aurance] M. Indeterminate sentence laws. Mo B J 2: 14-15 S '31 12763

Indeterminate sentence. L Notes 34: 102 S '30 12764

The indeterminate sentence and parole law. Ind Bul Char & Correc (149): 216-18 Je '27 12765

Indeterminate sentences. Sol J 72: 588-9 S 8 '28 12766

Jiménez de Asúa, Luis. Nueva juventud de la sentencia indeterminada. R Gen de Leg y Juris 152: 390-5 Ap '28 12767

Kelso, Robert Wilson. How to predict behavior on parole. Survey 61: 373-4 D 15 '28 12768

Kidd, A[lexander] M[arsden]. The indeterminate sentence—probation and parole. Commonwealth club Calif Tr 23: 404-16 D 11 '28 12769

La Du, Blanche L. Parole: its administration. Am Pris Assn Proc 1927: 76-85 12770

Lambert, June, comp. Digest of provisions in state laws relating to time prisoners become eligible for parole. Albany, New York (state). Library. Legislative reference section, 1931 12771

Lang, R. A. The underprivileged youth: his training and supervision of parole. Am Pris Assn Proc 1927: 302-11 12772

Lawes, Lewis E. Does prediction conflict with individualization? Soc Forces 7: 546-9 Je '29 12773

Lawler, R. H. Abuses of the parole system. Chief Constables' Assn Can Proc 26: 37-42 '30 12774

Libonati, M. La liberazione condizionale. Riv di Dir Peniten 1: 756-67 '30 12775

Lyon, F. Emory. The place of private agencies in parole work. Am Pris Assn Proc 60: 338-40 '30 12776

Martz, E. W. A phase of unsuccessful parole from state schools. Psychiat Q 5: 506-10 Jl '31 12777

Mauro, G. B. de. La peine a temps indéterminé. R de Pén et de Crimin 9: 225-37 '29 12778
Traduction de Gino Cutore di San Carlo.

Miller, Justin. Strengths and weaknesses of our parole laws. Am Pris Assn Proc 60: 353-61 '30 12779

Morgan, W. M. The indeterminate sentence law. Id St B Proc 2/3: 106-17 '26-'27 12780

Ohio. Department of public welfare. Duties of parole officers. 15p. (Publ no30) [Columbus] December 1, 1930 12781

Pope, James H. The parole system in misdemeanor cases. Los Angeles B Assn Bul 6: 243-5 Ap 16 '31 12782

Popenoe, Paul. Success on parole after sterilization. Am Assn Stud Feeblemind Proc 51: 86-103 '27 12783
Study of 182 males and 423 females paroled from California institutions.

Roux, J.-A. La crise de la liberation. R Int de Dr Pén 7 (1): 15-27 '30; same title: R de Dr Pén et de Crimin 10: 273-80 '30 12784

Spinelli, G. La libertà provvisoria e la riabilitazione. 10p. Bari, Cressati, 1927 12785

Sutherland, E. H. Prognose von Erfolg oder Fehlschlag bei Bewahrungsfrist. Monats f Kriminalpsychol u Strafrechtsref 21: 507-13 Ag '30 12786

Swearingen, Henry Chapman. Some problems of parole. Am Pris Assn Proc 54: 194-208 '29 12787

Swendsen, C. J. Chances for convicts to make good: indeterminate sentence and parole system. Nat Soc Pen Inf N Y Bul 1: 9 Ag '30 12788

Swendsen, C. J. Paths of the handicapped: of the paroled prisoners. Minn St Bd Con Q 29: 32-6 S 13 '29 12789

Veiller, Lawrence. Turning the criminals loose. World's Wk 53: 546-55 Mr '27 12790

Vold, George B. Do parole prediction tables work in practice? Am Sociol Soc Proc 25: 136-8 '30 12791

Vold, George B. Factors entering into the success or failure of Minnesota men on parole. Am Sociol Soc Proc 24: 167-9 '29; same title: J Educ Soc 3: 370-1 F '30 12792

Vold, George B. Some possibilities in the predicting of success or failure on parole. Minn St Conf & Inst Soc Wk Proc 38: 115-25 '30 12793

Votaw, A. H. The economic value of parole. Pris J 7: 20-1 Ja '27 12794

Wells, Maie Lounsbury. The institution—and then? Welf 19: 79-84 Ja '28 12795

Who will make good on parole? Survey 61: 237-8 N 15 '28 12796

Wilcox, Clair. The open door. Ann Am Acad 157: 102-12 S '31 12797

Wilcox, Clair. Parole: principles and practice. J Crim L & Crimin 20: 345-54 N '29 12798

Witmer, Helen Leland. The history, theory and results of parole. J Crim L & Crimin 18: 24-64 My '27 12799

Witmer, Helen Leland. Some factors in success or failure on parole. J Crim L & Crimin 18: 384-403 N '27 12800

Zahdi, M. I. De la sentence indéterminée ou de l'indétermination dans la sentence. 299p. Paris, Libr. Gén. de Droit et de Jurispr. 1927 12801

Argentina

Chanetón, J. Adolfo. Función social del patronate del liberados. R de Crimin Psiquiat y Med Leg 18: 195-202 Mr '31; same title: R de Identif y Cienc Pen 8: 287-96 My '31 12802

Australia

Victoria. Indeterminate sentences board. Annual report, 1927—1931. Melbourne, Govt. Ptr. 1927-31 12803
Parole statistics; ages and offenses of reformatory inmates; intelligence tests; causes of delinquency; education; Pentridge reformatory; Castlemaine reformatory; McLeod Settlement; French Island; Beechworth; Geelong reformatory; Coburg reformatory (females); probation.

Belgium

Delierneux. Enquête international sur les conditions dans lesquelles s'effectue la mise en liberté des condamnés à une peine privative de liberté. R Int de Dr Pén 7: 30-41 '30 12804

Gilliard. Réponse à l'enquête sur les conditions de mise en liberté des détenus, condamnés à une peine privative de liberté. R Int de Dr Pén 7: 28-30 '30 12805

Canada

Coatsworth, Emerson. The indeterminate sentence and parole in Ontario. Am Pris Assn Proc 54: 208-18 '29; same title: Can B R 8: 269-77 Ap '30 12806

Manitoba and parole. Can Police Bul 13: 5-7 Mr '28 12807

Germany

Dohna, Alexander. Auf dem Wege zum unbestimmten Strafurteil. Zeitsch f d ges Strafrechtswiss 51(4): 449-55 '31 12808

Reps. Bemerkungen zu der preussischen Verordnung über den Strafvollzug in Stufen. Vom 7. Juni 1929. Monats f Kriminalpsychol u Strafrechtsref 21: 291-6 My '30 12809

Great Britain

Witmer, Helen Leland. The development of parole in England. J Crim L & Crimin 18: 24-64 My '27 12810

Phillippine Islands

Nieva, Antonio S. Study of the parole law of the Philippines. Phil L J 9: 255-76 Ja '30 12811

Russia

Tsheltrow-Bebutow, M. A. Indeterminate sentence and Soviet penal law. J Crim L & Crimin 19: 408-10 N '28 12812

United States

A resume of the indeterminate sentence laws and parole rules of the United States. Am Pris Assn Proc 59: 177-86 '29 12813

Sheppard, J. Stanley. Supervision of federal parolees. Am Pris Assn Proc 60: 231-3 '30 12814

Smith, P. B. Supervision of federal parolees. Am Pris Assn Proc 60: 233-7 '30 12815

United States. Congress. House. Committee on judiciary. To amend act providing for parole of United States prisoners, approved June 25, 1910, as amended [so as to create single Board of parole], report to accompany H.R. 7413, January 6, 1930. 4p. Washington, 1930 (71st Cong. 2d sess. H. Rep. 104) 12816

ARKANSAS

Arkansas. State parole officer. Report *in* Report of State penitentiary 1926/28: 1-4; 1928/30: 9-10 12817

CALIFORNIA

Lang, R. A. The underprivileged youth, his training and supervision on parole [Preston school of industry]. Nat Conf Juv Agencies Proc 24: 39-50 '27 12818

Whyte, Ed. H. The parole system in California. Tax Dig 8: 267-8 Ag '30 12819

ILLINOIS

Bruce, Andrew Alexander and others. The working of the indeterminate sentence law and the parole system in Illinois. 277p. Springfield, Sup't of Docs. 1928 12820

Clabaugh, Hinton G. Special report and recommendations, parole system of Illinois. Springfield, Ill. Board of pardons and paroles, March 4, 1927 12821

Dearborn, Henry, jr. Clabaugh tells of parole in Illinois. Crim Just [Chicago] (51): 3-4 My '27 12822

Illinois. Department of public welfare. Division of supervision of parolees. Report *in* Annual report of Department of public welfare 13, 1929/30: 147-52 12823

Tibbitts, Clark. Success or failure on parole can be predicted; a study of the records of 3,000 youths from the Illinois state reformatory. J Crim L & Crimin 22: 11-50 My '31 12824

MARYLAND

Maryland. Parole commissioner, Baltimore. Report for years 1927 and 1928; 1929 and 1930. [Baltimore, 1929-31] 12825

MASSACHUSETTS

Massachusetts. Board of parole. Report *in* Annual report of Commissioner of correction 8, 1927: 7-10 12826

MICHIGAN

Michigan. Executive office. Division of pardons. Indeterminate sentence law of 1905 (with amendments) and rules adopted by the Governor and the Commissioner of pardons and paroles concerning applications for clemency and the conduct of prisoners on parole. 37p. Lansing, 1928 12827

Michigan. Executive office. Division of pardons. Report of the Commissioner of pardons and paroles for . . . 1927 and 1928. 196p. Lansing, 1929 12828

Michigan. Executive office. Division of pardons and paroles. Special report of the Commissioner of pardons and paroles, January 7, 1928. 35p. Lansing, 1928 **12829**

MINNESOTA

Minnesota. Board of parole. Biennial report 9, 1926/28—10, 1928/30. [Stillwater, 1929-31] **12830**
State prison, Stillwater; State reformatory, St. Cloud; State reformatory for women, Shakopee.

The Parole board of Minnesota. Pris J 7: 17-20 Ap '27 **12831**

Vold, George Bryan. Prediction methods and parole; a study of the factors involved in the violation or non-violation of parole in a group of Minnesota adult males. 138p. Minneapolis, Sociological press, 1931 **12832**
Study of 1192 men paroled 1922-1927.

NEW JERSEY

Lane, Winthrop D. Parole procedure in New Jersey. J Crim L & Crimin 22: 375-405 S '31 **12833**

NEW YORK

Catholic charities of the Archdiocese of New York. Report, 1927—31. New York, 1927-31 **12834**
Protective care: parole of men and women; institutions for delinquent women and girls.

Convicts and ex-convicts. Governor Roosevelt's special committee on paroles. Commonweal 11: 461-2 F 26 '30 **12835**

Fagan, Bernard J. New parole law and organization in New York state. Am Pris Assn Proc 60: 361-7 '30 **12836**

Goldsmith, Irving I. State board of parole; duties of new agency outlined and history traced. N Y St B Assn Bul 2-32 Ja '31 **12837**

Hanscom, Frank I. Ideals and objectives of the new parole board. N Y St Assn Magistrates Proc 22: 64-71 '30 **12838**

Lewisohn, Sam A. Parole. N Y St Conf Soc Wk Q Bul 11-13 Jl '31 **12839**

New York (city). Parole commission. Annual report, 1927. 22p. New York, 1928 **12840**
No reports for 1928, 1929, 1930.

New York (state). Board of parole for state prisons. Report *in* Annual report of Commissioner of correction 1927: 417-21 **12841**

New York (state). Executive department. Division of parole. Annual report 1, July 1/December 31, 1930—2, January/December 1931. [Albany, 1931-32] **12842**

New York (state). Special committee on the parole problem. Report, January 24, 1930. 37p. New York, 1930 **12843**

PENNSYLVANIA

Dearborn, Henry, jr. Parole in the keystone state. Crim Just [Chicago] (52): 16 Je '27 **12844**

Pennsylvania state parole commission. Pris J 7: 13-17 Ap '27 **12845**

Pennsylvania. State parole commission. Report to the Legislature, 1927. 2pts. Philadelphia, 1927 **12846**

Wilcox, Clair. Parole of adults from state penal institutions in Pennsylvania and in other commonwealths. 259p. Philadelphia, University of Pennsylvania, 1927 **12847**

SOUTH DAKOTA

South Dakota. State parole officer. Report *in* Biennial report of Board of charities and correction 20, 1926/28: 162-6; 21, 1928/30: 178-82 **12848**

UTAH

Thomas, George and Jensen, Adolph Ladru. Study of the indeterminate sentence, probation and parole in Utah. 120p. (Bul v21 no7) Salt Lake City, University of Utah, 1931 **12849**

WASHINGTON

Washington. Parole department. Report *in* Biennial report of business control 4, 1926/28: 16; 5, 1928/30: 11 **12850**

WISCONSIN

Wisconsin. Parole department. Biennial report *in* Biennial report of State board of control 19, 1926/28: 462-7 **12851**

CRIME PREVENTION

GENERAL

Additon, Henrietta. The prevention of crime and delinquency. J Soc Hyg 17: 200-8 Ap '31 12852

Adler, Alfred. Prevention and change. Police J [N Y] 17: 5-7, 23- My '30 12853

Adler, Herman M. The work of institutions in the prevention of delinquency. J Juv Res 15: 18-27 '31 12854

Allen, Stephen H. Prevention rather than punishment for crimes. Am B Assn J 17: 260-2 Ap '31 12855

American prison association. Report of Committee on prevention. Proc 59: 83-101 '29 12856

Arnold, Frazer. Practical measure of crime prevention. Mo B Assn Proc 1929: 171-8; same title: Comm L J 36: 292-3 Je '31 12857

Balderston, J. L. This business of crime prevention. Northwest Police J 7: 13, 93 Ap '30 12858

Basuino, Francis M. Crime prevention a public problem. Police J [N Y] 18: 15 Ja '31 12859

Bayle, E. L'effort international contre les malfaiteurs cosmopolites. R de Gendarm (12) N 15 '29 12860

Böhrsch, Norbert. Der Freiheitsentzug als sichernde Massnahme im tschechoslowakischen Strafgesetzentwurf. Monats f Kriminalpsychol u Strafrechtsref 18: 476-80 S '27 12861

Broughton, J. M. Crime—its prevention and cure. Police J [N Y] 16: 10- N '28 12862

Butcher, William Lewis. Some methods of preventing crime. Pub Manage 13: 93-4 Mr '31 12863

Calder, R. L. Crime prevention. First Friend 24: 1-2, 4-6 Fourth Quarter '29 12864A

Ceylon discharged prisoners' aid association. The movement for the prevention of crime. 27p. Colombo, The Association, 1930 12864B

Comité d'études et d'action pour la diminution du crime. Etudes Crimin 4: 240-1 Jl '29 12865

Compulsory reporting of gunshot wounds. Am M Assn J 88: 404 F 5 '27 12866

Davis, M. K. Recent action in Bombay City for the prevention and right treatment of juvenile delinquency. Shield 7: 147-52 '31 12867

Davis, Watson. Nation-wide campaign to reduce crime. Cur Hist 27: 303-8 D '27 12868

Delaquis, Ernst. Die erste internationale Tagung der Vertreter der Zentralstellen zur Bekämpfung der Geldfälschung. Krimin Monatsh 5: 73-5 Ap '31 12869

Dow, Grove Samuel. Crime and its prevention. 327p. Ann Arbor, Mich. Edwards bros. 1927 12870

Elliott, J. L. Constructive program for crime prevention. Ref Shelf 6(3): 175-9 Ag '29 12871

Elliott, John L. Crime prevention. Neighborhood 4: 213-19 S '31 12872

Elliott, John L. A program of crime prevention. Standard [N Y] 13: 257-64 My '27 12873

Ellis, William J. Classification as an aid in crime prevention. Police J [N Y] 17: 10- O '30 12874

Fenn, Frank. Prevention of juvenile delinquency. Minn St Conf & Inst Soc Wk Proc 38: 166-74 '30 12875

Address before Minnesota and northwest association of policewomen.

Fenton, Norman. A state program for the prevention of delinquency. J Juv Res 13: 285-92 '29 12876

Fraser, John D. Crime prevention. Peace Offic Assn Calif Proc 10: 31-4 '30 12877

Gand, M. Guide juridique et pratique pour la lutte contre la license des rues. 72p. Paris, Giraudon, 1927 12878

Gates, Charles A. An approach to crime prevention. Am Pris Assn Proc 59: 94-102 '29 12879

Giannitrapani, Alfredo. Giovani delinquenti. Studio di prevenzione penale. 207p. Palermo, Sandron, 1928 12880

Giesen, A. H. v. d. De wetsontwerpen houdende nadere voorzieningen. Tijdschr v d Politie 1: 89-98 My 9 '28 12881

Herzog, Alfred W. What can we do to diminish crime? Med-Leg J 46: 105-8 S '29 12882

Hopkins, Albert A. Foiling the burglar. Sci Am 141: 50-2, 148-50, 226-8 Jl-S '29 12883

Human elements in preventing delinquency. Playground 22: 226 Jl '28 12884

Jenkins, F[rederick] W[arren]. Crime prevention and crime repression; a selected bibliography. (Lib Bul no81) New York, Russell Sage foundation, February 1927 12885

Kell, S. J. Crime prevention. W Va M J 26: 19-20 Ja '30 12886

Kinberg, Olaf. Über die relative Bedeutung der Generalprävention und der Spezialprävention. Monats f Kriminalpsychol u Strafrechtsref 21: 468-73 Ag '30 12887

Kinley, David. The importance of prevention. Ill Conf Pub Welf Proc 1927: 53-5; same title: Welf Mag 18: 1634-7 D '27 12888

Kolle, K. Heilung von verbrecherischer Veranlagung. Zentralbl f Psychotherap 3: 648-9 '30 12889

Investigation at Kiel, 1929.

A lesson in crime prevention. L Notes 31: 224 Mr '28 12890

Loudon, Anne L. The work of the visiting teacher. Minn St Conf & Inst Soc Wk Proc 37: 237-42 '29 12891

Loveland, R. P. Place of science in treatment of criminals and in prevention of crime. New England J Med 205: 1190-5 D 17 '31 12892

McNamara, Thomas J. Crime elimination. N Y St Assn Magistrates Proc 20: 56-62 '28 12893

Matheson, Duncan. Crime prevention. J Crim L & Crimin 18: 121-3 My '27 12894

Michael, H. B. Modern burglary and robbery protection methods. Am J Police Sci 2: 20-9 Ja '31 12895

Miller, Justin. Preventive justice and the law. Nat Prob Assn Proc 1929: 18-33 12896

Mukerji, Suresh Chandra. The prevention of offenses. 759p. Calcutta, Art press [1927] 12897

National economic league. Crime: its prevention and punishment, by Thomas C. T. Crain, and others. 35p. (Consensus v15 no1) Boston, 1930 12898

Parsons, Philip Archibald. Measures looking to crime prevention. Am City 37: 35-7 Jl '27 12899

Pigeon, Helen D. Seventh International anti-crime conference, Nelson, British Columbia. Police J [N Y] 15: 14- Jl '27 12900

Proskauer, Joseph M. Delinquency—its cure. Pris J 10: 5-10 Ja '30 12901

Public interest in crime prevention. L Notes 31: 163-4 D '27 12902

Pyle, W. H. The prevention of crime. Sch & Soc 30: 122-4 '29 12903

Ramos, Juan P. La defensa social contra el delito. R de Crimin Psiquiat y Med Leg 16: 273-88 My '29 12904

Saunders, Albert J. Reclaiming criminals in Sholapur, India. Sociol & Soc Res 12: 61-4 S '27 12905

de Saussure, R. Prophylaxie du crime et de la délinquance dans la jeunesse. Hyg Ment 26: 101-16 My '31 12906

Shumaker, W. A. Preventive justice. L Notes 32: 185-7 Ja '29 12907

Smith, Bruce. A municipal program for combating crime. Nat Munic R 17: 33-40 Ja '28; same title: Am City 38: 100-2 Ja '28 12908

Steigerthal. Gemeinsame Aufgaben von Strafrechts- und Wohlfahrtspflege bei der Behandlung asozialer Personen. Monats f Kriminalpsychol u Strafrechtsref 18: 369-74 Jl '27 12909

Stevenson, George S. Science and crime prevention. J Juv Res 14: 22-6 Ja '30 12910

Stooss, C. Freie Schutzmassregeln gegen Verbrechen. Schweiz Zeitsch f Strafr 41: 192-5 '28 12911

Stooss, Carl. Die kriminalpolitische Bedeutung der sichernden Massnahmen. Monats f Kriminalpsychol u Strafrechtsref 19: 544-6 S '28 12912

Veratti, N. La profilassi del delitto. Arch di Antrop Crim 48: 1030-6 '28 12913

Vervaeck, L. L'internement des aliénés criminels. R de Dr Pén et de Crimin 7: 452-5 Ap '27 12914

Vollmer, August. Coordinated effort to prevent crime. J Crim L & Crimin 19: 196-210 Ag '28 12915

Wickersham, George W. Prevention and punishment of crime; the practice and the theory. Am Pris Assn Proc 60: 100-17 '30 12916

BELGIUM

Lambert, H. Orientation nouvelle de la répression en Belgique. Ecrou 12: 185-96, 334-43 Ap, Jl '31 12917

Rabinowicz, Léon. El papel de Bélgica en la lucha contra la criminalidad. R de Crimin Psiquiat y Med Leg 17: 453-62 Jl '30 12918

Ranst, J. Van. Organisation du dépot de mendicité a Merxplas—son évolution. R de Dr Pén et de Crimin 9: 20-38 '29 12919

DENMARK

Goll, Aug. Sicherungsmassnahmen in Dänemark. Monats f Kriminalpsychol u Strafrechtsref 18: 484-502 S '27 12920

GERMANY

Krauss, Friedrich S. Wider die Unzuchtschnüffler der deutschen Justiz. 55p. Basel, Reber [1928] 12921

ITALY

Ciaccio, Enrico. Le misure di sicurezza nel diritto italiano. Scuola Pos ns7: 242-9 My '27 12922

NETHERLANDS

Veenstra, S. L. La lutte contre la criminalité. En Hollande. Monde Nouv 11: (3): 173-6; (9): 638-43 My, N '29 12923

RUSSIA

Sapir, Boris. Der Kampf mit dem Verbrechtum in der Sowjetrepublik. Monats f Kriminalpsychol u Strafrechtsref 21: 693-5 '30 12924

SPAIN

Saldaña, Quintiliano. La lutte contre les criminels en Espagne. Pensiero Giurid-Pen 2(2): 140- '30; same title: Monde Nouv 12(5): 323-31 Jl '30 12925

UNION OF SOUTH AFRICA

Gray, G. D. The prevention of juvenile crime. Police J [N Y] 18: 18, 23 Mr '31 12926

UNITED STATES

Kirchwey, George W. The movement for the repression of crime in the United States. 7p. Philadelphia, All-Philadelphia conference on social work, 1927 **12927**

Lenroot, Katharine F. The scope and significance of the White house conference as a factor in national program of prevention. Nat Conf Juv Agencies Proc 27: 178-84 '30 **12928**

National commission on law observance and enforcement. Report on the enforcement of the deportation laws of the United States. 179p. (No5) Washington, May 27, 1931 **12929**

New York (state). Crime commission. A special report on the National conference at Washington on the reduction of crime. 20p. Albany, 1928 **12930**

CALIFORNIA

Fenton, Norman. A state program for the prevention of delinquency. J Juv Res 13: 285-92 O '29 **12931**

CONNECTICUT

Hartford. Juvenile commission. Annual report, 1926/27—1930/31. Hartford [1927-31] **12932**

ILLINOIS

Chicago. Crime commission. Organizing a crime prevention program. Crim Just [Chicago] 6-7 Mr '29 **12933**

Eliot, Thomas D. The prevention of delinquency in Evanston. Welf Mag 18: 232-4 F '27 **12934**

MASSACHUSETTS

Massachusetts. Advisory council on crime prevention. Report *in* Annual report of Commissioner of correction 1927: 12-14 **12935**

Stearns, A. W. Program for control of crime in the state of Massachusetts. New England J Med 204: 529-32 Mr 12 '31 **12936**

MISSOURI

Missouri welfare league. Prevention of delinquency; reduction of crime; and treatment of offenders in Missouri, 1929. 13p. (mim) St. Louis [1929] **12937**

NEW YORK

New York (city). Police department. Crime prevention bureau. Report, 1930-1931. New York, 1931-[32] **12938**

Socialization of the New York police department [Crime prevention bureau]. J Soc Hyg 16: 544-6 D '30 **12939**

Thrasher, Frederic M. Nipping the buds of crime. Survey 65: 317-18 D 15 '30 **12940**

Summary of report of sub-commission of Crime commission of New York.

PENNSYLVANIA

Pennsylvania committee on penal affairs. What the 1929 legislature did to prevent crime. Pen Affairs (20) Je '29 **12941**

AFTERCARE AND CRIME PREVENTION

Arenaza, Carlos de. La readaptación social del menor delincuente. Museo Soc Arg Bol 19 (112-14): 471-91 O '31 **12942**

Brants. Pro juventute in de bank der verdachten. Maandbl v Ber en Reclasseer 7: 325-9 N '28 **12943**

Burgess, E. W. Predicting success or failure upon release from state institutions. J Juv Res 13: 270-84 '29 **12944**

Butler, Amos W. What the courts, the prisons, the employer and the public should know of the prisoner. Ind Bul Char & Correc (187): 421-8 N '30; same under title: What the courts, the prisons, the employer and the public should know of the released prisoner. J Crim L & Crimin 21: 504-12 F '31 **12945**

Civil rights of former convicts. M Lab R 25: 296 Ag '27 **12946**

Discharged convicts report, 1928. Just Peace 92: 540 Ag 11 '28 **12947**

Draper, D. C. What should be done to prevent men returning to prison. Am Pris Assn Proc 59: 354-61 '29 **12948**

Faltlhauser, V. Psychiatrische Schutzaufsicht und psychische Hygiene. Zeitsch f Psychis Hyg 20-8 '29 **12949**

Feld. Fürsorge für Rechtsbrecher in der Schweiz. Deut Zeitsch f Wohlfahrts-pfl 4: 12-19 '28 **12950**

Fliegel, M. O. A. Die Strafentlassenenpflege im Freistaat Sachsen. 56p. Dresden, Sächs. Schutzverein f. Strafentl. 1927 **12951**

Foltin, Edgar M. Bedeutung und Anwendungsgebeit der Schutzaufsicht gegenüber Erwachsenen. Monats f Kriminalpsychol u Strafrechtsref 18: 289-301 Je '27 **12952**

Fraser, Albert G. After prison what? Pris J 9: 16-24 Jl '29 **12953**

Fraser, A[lbert] G. The value of case records. Am Pris Assn Proc 54: 75-83 '29; same title: Pris J 9: 1-7 O '29 **12954**

Address before National prisoners' aid association.

Giacobini, J. Institución del peritaje médico-legal del liberado en el procedimiento criminal. R de Crimin Psiquiat y Med Leg 14: 30-3 Ja '27 **12955**

Hoffman, George. Reconstructing for society. Welf Mag 18: 202-6 F '27 **12956**

Hülsmann, H. J. Verbond der Vereenigingen pro juventute. Maandbl v Ber en Reclasseer 7: 322-5 N '28 **12957**

Hughes, W. S. What should be done to insure the future good citizenship of those sentenced to the penitentiary. Am Pris Assn Proc 59: 361-5 '29 **12958**

Jaquays, Emily. What is our mental attitude to the delinquent girl? Soc Welf [Toronto] 9: 378- Mr '27 **12959**

Kidman, John. Work among delinquents and their dependents in Canada. Am Pris Assn Proc 59: 327-37 '29 **12960**
Prisoners aid association in Montreal.

"Kolonien" en "Marine" en Reclasseering. Maandbl v Ber en Reclasseer 6: 51-2 F '27 **12961**

Krebs, O. Strafentlassenenfürsorge. Arbeiterwohlfahrt 3: 225-34 '28 **12962**

Kronfeld, A. Über seelische Selbstumstellung eines jugendlichen Gewohnheitsverbrechers. Int Zeitsch f Individualpsychol 8: 177-81 '30 **12963**

Lambert, June, comp. Digest of the laws of various states relating to the care of insane criminals after the expiration of the term of sentence. 6p. Albany, New York (state). Library. Legislative reference section, February 1930 **12964**

Lawes, Lewis E. Life of an ex-convict. World's Wk 56: 675-81 O '28 **12965**

Lending a hand to former prisoners. Welf Mag 18: 1517-18 N '27 **12966**

Levin, B. Borgerlig Oprejsning efter Regeneringens Forslag af 1928 til Borgerlig Straffelov. Nord Tids f Straf 16: 365 '28 **12967**

Lutz, A. Einige Gedanken und Vorschläge über Zusammenarbeit in der Schutzaufsicht und Entlassenenfürsorge. Schweiz Ver f Straf-, Gefängniswes u Schutzauf Verh 8: 28-35 '28 **12968**

McConnell, J. Paul. The after-prison life of paroled prisoners. Thesis (Ph.D.) University of North Carolina, 1931? **12969**

May, Carl L. What should be done to rehabilitate the criminal? Los Angeles B Assn Bul 2: 12-14 Ja 20 '27 **12970**

Maynard, Lawrance. First day out. Am Mercury 21: 35-41 S '30 **12971**

M[uller, N.]. Een bevriend vijand. Maandbl v Ber en Reclasseer 7: 329-36 N '28 **12972**

Muller, N. ed. Jaarboek voor de reclasseering van volwassenen en kinderen, 1925-1926. 59p. Eibergen (Holland), H. Reinen, 1927 **12973**

Murphy, M. J. The discharged prisoner. Welf Mag 18: 31-2 Ja '27 **12974**

New York (state). Westchester county penitentiary committee . . . concerned with providing employment for prisoners released from the . . . penitentiary. Report, December 1, 1930/May 31, 1931. 8p. June 1931 **12975**

Noetzel. Die Rückkehr des Rechtsbrechers in die Gesellschaft. Deut Richterzeit 20: 18-21 '28 **12976**

Over de organisatie van de reclasseering in de groote steden. Maandbl v Ber en Reclasseer 7: 185-7 Je '28 **12977**

Le patronage. Ecrou 9: 223-34 My '28 **12978**

Preventive hechtenis en reclasseering. Maandbl v Ber en Reclasseer 7: 236-8 Ag '28 **12979**

Rahne, H. Gefangenenfürsorge in England. Monatsbl d deut Reichsverb f Gerichtshilfe 2: 73-7 '27 **12980**

Rapporten en patronaat door de particuliere instellingen, contrôle door de Rijksambtenaren. Maandbl v Ber en Reclasseer 6: 105-11 Ap '27 **12981**

Rickett, A. Compton. Her stigma. 312p. London, Herbert Jenkins, 1928 **12982**

Root, William T. The ex-prisoner in the community. 16p. Pen Affairs (18) Je '28 **12983**

Schmidmüller, Martin. Die Entlassenenfürsorge. Versuch einer planmässigen Darstellung der Grundsätze der Entlassenenfürsorge mit besonderer Berücksichtigung der Grundsätze für den Vollzug von Freiheitsstrafen vom 7.6. 1923, des Entwurfes eines Strafvollzugsgesetzes vom 9.9.1927 und des Entwurfes eines Allgemeinen Deutschen Strafgesetzbuchs vom 14.5. 1927. 87p. Diss. Erlangen, 1931. Ebersberg, Karl Schmidle, 1931 **12984**

Scott, B. L. The discharged prisoner. Ann Am Acad 157: 113-16 S '31 **12985**

Second annual report of the department of released prisoners. Pris J 7: 22-3 Ja '27 **12986**

Spinetto, A. Patronato de liberados. R de Crimin, Psiquiat y Med Leg 14: 632-49 S '27 **12987**

Stahl, Adolf. Grenzfragen zwischen Strafrecht, Seelsorge und Fürsorge. 56p. Berlin-Dahlem, Wichern, 1928 **12988**

Taak en toekomst van de Kinderreclasseering. Maandbl v Ber en Reclasseer 7: 288-95 O '28 **12989**

Ten dollars and make good, by 20,803. Outl 147: 403 N 30 '27 **12990**

Thieme, R. Erfahrungen eines Übergangsheims für Strafentlassene. [Saxony] Monats f Kriminalpsychol u Strafrechtsref 22: 347-50 My '31 **12991**

Turner, G. D. Aid for prisoners on discharge. Police J [London] 3: 11-19 Ja '30 **12992**

Varekamp, J. H. Een nieuwe Reclasseeringsinstelling? Maandbl v Ber en Reclasseer 7: 297-301 O '28 **12993**

Vervaeck, L. L'activité de la section post-pénitentiaire de l'office de réadaptation sociale de Bruxelles en 1928. R de Dr Pén et de Crimin 9: 1095-7 '29 **12994**

Weber, Gerhard. Die Strafentlassenenpflege. Versuch einer Grundlegung mit besonderer Berücksichtigung der volkswirtschaftlichen Bedeutung strafentlassenenpflegerischer Tätigkeit. Bl f Gefängniskunde 59: 271-345 '28 **12995**

Willems, Eugène. Le service social des cas individuels en Belgique. R de Dr Pén et de Crimin 8: 884-90 Ag '28 12996

Willer, H. Die Entlassenenfürsorge in Deutschland unter Berücksichtigung der Entwürfe zu einem Straf- und Strafvollzugsgesetz. Deut Zeitsch f d ges gerichtl Med 11: 423-51 '28 12997

Work for ex-prisoners. Just Peace 93: 214 Ap 6 '29 12998

Wüllner, J. Gedanken zur Neuregelung der Strafentlassenenfürsorge. Freie Wohlfahrtspfl 5(9): 414-20; (10): 449-54 D '30, Ja '31 12999

X. Stufenvollzug und Übergangsheime. (Gedanken eines Strafentlassenen). Monats f Kriminalpsychol u Strafrechtsref 21: 34-6 '30 13000

SOCIETIES FOR AIDING DISCHARGED PRISONERS

Aargauischer Verein für Schutzaufsicht und Entlassenenfürsorge. Jahresbericht, 1927-1931. Aarau, Selbstverlag, 1928-32 13001

Ceylon discharged prisoners' aid association. Annual report and statements of accounts, 1929/30—1930/31. Colombo, 1930-31 13002

Deutschen Reichsverbands für Gerichtshilfe. Gefangenen- und Entlassenen-Fürsorge, Satzung. Bl f Gefängniskunde 59: 125-7 '28 13003

Inglis, William. Gangsters help them stop crime. Nation's Bus 18: 132- Ja '30 13004
Alpheus Geer founder of Marshall Stillman movement service club, New York.

Just, A. Die Stellung der Gefängnis-Gesellschaften in der Straffälligenfürsorge. Freie Wohlfahrtspfl 1: 456-63 '27 13005

Massachusetts society for aiding discharged prisoners. Annual report 81, 1926/27—85, 1930/31. Boston, State House, 1927-31 13006

Pennsylvania prison society. Department of released prisoners. Report. Pris J 7: 22-8 Ja '27; 8: 24-39 Ja '28; 9: 28-38 Ja '29; 10: 13-17 Ap '30; 11: 15-21 Ap '31 13007

Prisoners' aid association. Sophia Little home, Edgewood, R.I. Fifty years of service. 15p. Edgewood, R.I. January 30, 1931 13008

Prisoners' aid society, Essex county, N.J. [Annual appeal] 1917-1930. President, T. W. Dennison, Montclair, N.J. 13009

St. Giles Christian mission: annual meeting. L Times 163: 499 Je 4 '27 13010

Scott, B. L. A modern program for Prisoners' aid associations. Am Pris Assn Proc 60: 30-5 '30 13011

COMMUNITY RESPONSIBILITY

Austin, James, jr. Can courts prevent crime? Welf Mag 19: 767-71 Je '28 13012

Binford, Jessie F. Community responsibility for delinquency. Nat Prob Assn Proc 1928: 124-34; same title: Welf Mag 19: 143-8 F '28 13013

Butler, Smedley D. Wipe out the gangsters! proposal for an anti-crime legion. Forum 86: sup17-18 O '31 13014

Cain, Mrs. Ira L. Challenge of youth to the community. Child Welf 23: 303-5 F '29 13015

Carstens, C. C. A community plan in prevention of delinquency. Am Pris Assn Proc 60: 90-8 '30 13016

Dennis, Charles Henry. Newspapers and crime prevention. 12p. (Reprints no28) Chicago, Chicago daily news, 1927 13017

Fenton, Norman. Community planning and the problem child. Sch & Soc 34: 387-92 S 19 '31 13018

Gallagher, Hubert R. Crime prevention as a municipal function. 66p. Syracuse, Syracuse university, School of citizenship and public affairs, 1930 13019

Gerk, Joseph A. Environment as a remedy for crime. Int Assn Chiefs Police Proc 1927: 35-7; same title: Police J [N Y] 15: 5 S '27; Detective 42-3 D '27 13020

Hanna, Francis D. Fixing community responsibility. Crim Just [Chicago] (49): 10-12 Mr '27 13021

Jameson, Samuel Haig. Social responsibility and juvenile delinquency. J Juv Res 15: 7-17 Ja '31 13022

New York (state). Crime commission. Sub-commission on causes and effects of crime. Crime and the community; a study of trends in crime prevention, January 15, 1930. 292p. bibliog 290-2. Albany, 1930 13023

Neymark, Edward. La cooperación de la sociedad en la supresión del crimen. R de Identif y Cienc Pen 4: 230-51 Jl '29; translation: La coopération de la société a la lutte contre la criminalité. R de Dr Pén et de Crimin 9: 969-93 '29 13024
Address before Congrès Panaméricain des sciences pénales, Buenos Aires, 1929.

Odiorne, Helena W. The library as a social agency. Soc Sci Monog 1: 34-41 Ja '31 13025

Shulman, Harry M. Social agencies and crime prevention. J Crim L & Crimin 22: 545-55 N '31 13026

CONTROL OF DRUGS

Bee, R. V. Narcosan—the new drug cure. Police J [N Y] 16: 5 O '28 13027

Brewster, S. W. Narcotic educational work. Int Assn Chiefs Police Proc 1927: 182-8 13028

California. State narcotic committee. Report on drug addiction. 41p. Sacramento, 1927 13029

California. State narcotic committee. The trend of drug addiction in California. 34p. Sacramento, 1931 13030

Detroit community fund. A farm cure for drug addicts: the story of an unique human experiment. (Community fund news no68) Detroit, July 1928 13031

Narcotic educational association of Michigan.

Egypt. Central narcotics intelligence bureau. Annual report for the year 1931. 163p. Cairo, Govt. press, 1932 13032

Entwurf eines Gesetzes über den Verkehr mit Betäubungsmitteln [Opiumgesetz]. 11p. (Reichstag. 4. Wahlperiode. 1928. Drucks. 1386) Berlin, Heymann, 1929 13033

Gavit, John Palmer. Uncle Sam scores one on opium. Survey 57: 485-6 Ja 15 '27 13034

Hurley, James D. The narcotic problem: federal control. Cornell L Q 13: 627-30 Je '28 13035

LaMotte, Ellen N. Drug "limitation" in the United States. Nation 128: 543-4 My 1 '29 13036

Sharman, C. H. L. Narcotic control in Canada. Police J [London] 3: 535-49 O '30 13037

Sharman, C. H. L. The new narcotic act. Chief Constables Assn Can Proc 25: 75-85 '29 13038

Treadway, Walter L. Drug addiction—some epidemiological features and individual characteristics. Am Pris Assn Proc 59: 49-61 '29 13039

United States. Congress. House. Committee on judiciary. Authorizing Commissioner of prohibition to pay for information concerning violations of narcotic laws, report to accompany H. R. 16874, February 24, 1929. 1p. Washington, 1929 (70th Cong. 2d sess. H. Rep. 2722) 13040

United States. Congress. House. Committee on judiciary. Enforcement of the narcotic laws: hearings on H.R. 16874 and H.R. 16875, February 11, 1929. 25p. Washington, 1929 13041

United States. Congress. House. Committee on judiciary. Establishment of two federal narcotic farms: hearings on H.R. 12781 and H.R. 13645, April 26-28, 1928. 235p. Washington, 1928 13042

United States. Federal narcotics control board. The Narcotic drugs import and export act, as amended and the regulations thereunder, April 1928. 16p. Washington, 1928 13043

United States. Public health service. State laws relating to the control of narcotic drugs and the treatment of drug addiction. 330p. Washington, 1931 13044

World conference on narcotic education. Draft for discussion of a uniform state narcotic defense law. 11p. Washington [1927] 13045

EDUCATION

Beltrán, J. R. La reeducatión de los delincuentes inimputables. Semana Méd 2: 841-3 S 19 '29 13046

Bonaventura, Enzo. L'educazione dei fanciulli anormali psichici e la prevenzione delle delinquenza. Rassegna di Stud Sess 10: 285-96 O '30 13047

Brown, S. Guidance and character training of children. M R of R 33: 430-5 S '27 13048

Crime prevention through moral and religious education. Miss R 54: 109-12 F '31 13049

National commission on crime prevention through moral and religious education.

Foerster, A. Prophylaktische Erziehung von Kindern trunksüchtiger Eltern und heilpädagogische Beeinflussung jugendlicher Alkoholiker. Vjsch f Wiss Päd 3: 522-8 '27 13050

Hodann, M. Sexualpädagogik, Erziehungshygiene und Gesundheitspolitik. 254p. Rudolstadt, Greifenverl. 1928 13051

Kloss, Heinz. Pflegeberufe lediger Frauen als Aufgabe präventiver Kriminalpolitik. Monats f Kriminalpsychol u Strafrechtsref 18: 679-82 D '27 13052

Knox, Margaret. School, the maladjusted child, and the visiting teacher. El Sch J 28: 176-80 N '27 13053

Lommen, Georgiana. Educating for desirable attitudes in conduct. J Educ Meth 6: 291-6 Mr '27 13054

Máday, S. v. Die Heilerziehung der geistig abnormen Kinder vom Standpunkte des Arztes, des Pädagogen und des Sozialpolitikers. Wien Med Wchnschr 77: 1751-3 '27 13055

Matheson, Duncan. Character building and crime prevention. Int Assn Chiefs Police Proc 1927: 119-21; same title: Detective 42:8 Je '27 13056

Miller, Joseph. Educational guidance leading to a better social adjustment. Psychol Clin 18: 39-43 Mr '29 13057

Shulman, Harry M. Crime prevention and the public schools. J Educ Soc 4: 69-81 O '30 13058

EUGENICS: STERILIZATION

Adam, Frantz. Erotisme et réactions sexuelles délictueuses chez des sujets congénitalement stériles ou accidentellement stérilisés. Ann de Méd Leg 9: 15-17 Ja '29 13059

Aikman, K. B. Multiplication of the less fit. Edinb R 250: 82-92 Jl '29 13060

Aronoff, Jacob Broches. The constitutionality of asexualization legislation in the United States. St John's L R 1: 146-74 My '27 13061

Barth. Kastration und Geschlechtsleben. Krimin Monatsh 5: 57-9 Mr '30 13062

Bibliographia eugenica. Eugen N sup125 Mr '27 13063

Binney, Cecil. The law as to sterilization. 24p. London, Eugenics society, 1930 13064

Boeters. Die Kastration von Sexualverbrechern. Münch med Wchnschr 77: 369-70 '30 13065

Brief list of references to books and periodicals relating to the sterilization of criminal insane and similar defectives. J Crim L & Crimin 19: 97-8 My '28 13066

Brown, Frederick W. Eugenic sterilization in the United States. Ann Am Acad 149 pt3: 22-35 My '30 13067

Bruehl, Charles Paul. Birth control and eugenics in the light of fundamental ethical principles. 256p. N.Y. Wagner, 1928 13068

Chamberlain, Joseph P. Eugenics in legislatures and courts. Am B Assn J 15: 165-9 Mr '29 13069

Cunningham, Simon W[arren, II]. Corporations: sterilization statutes. [87]p. Thesis (J.D.) University of California, May 1930 13070

[Cunningham, Simon Warren, II]. Sterilization of defectives. Calif L R 17: 270-6 Mr '29 13071

Dansk Kommissionsudkast til en Lov om Sterilisation. Nord Tids f Straf 15: 36-40 Ja '27 13072

Dight, C. F. Application of eugenic measures for prevention of crime and race betterment. M World 45: 399-401 N '27 13073

Dight, C. F. Sterilization procedure and its success in California institutions. Lancet ns47: 462-3 O 1 '27 13074

La esterilización en Estados Unidos. Colegio de Abogados, Buenos Aires R 7(2): 123-39 '27 13075

Eugenics society. Committee for legalizing eugenic sterilization. Eugenic sterilization. ed.2. 40p. London, 1930 13076

Fitzpatrick, Frank. Crime and heredity; sterilization of criminals as a crime preventive. Police "13-13" 5: 10-12 Ja '30 13077

Fraeb, Walter Martin. Zur Frage der Sicherungsverwahrung, Sterilisation und Kastration der Sexualverbrecher. Arch f Krim 85: 109-30 O '29 13078

Fürth, Henriette. Die Regelung der Nachkommenschaft als eugenisches Problem. Schriften zur Psychologie und Soziologie von Sexualität und Verbrechen. 143p. Stuttgart, Püttmann, 1929 13079

Gallichan, Walter M. Sterilization of the unfit. 192p. London, Laurie, 1929 13080

Gosney, Ezra Seymour and Popenoe, Paul Bowman. Sterilization for human betterment; a summary of results of 6,000 operations in California, 1909-1929. 220p. New York, Macmillan, 1929 13081

Haack, O. Dänische Kommissions-Vorlage betreffend die Sterilisation. Monats f Kriminalpsychol u Strafrechtsref 18: 268-81 '27 13082

Haack, Olaf. Danske Sterilisationslov. Nord Tids f Straf 17 (4): 300-4 '29 13083

Hannan, W. E. comp. Digest of the laws of the various states relating to the sterilization of the feeble-minded insane and habitual criminals. 41p. Albany, New York (state). Library. Legislative reference section, 1929 13084

Hirschfeld, M. Kastration bei Sittlichkeitsverbrechern. Zeitsch f Sexualwiss 15: 54-5 Ap '28 13085

Höpler, E. Sterilisierung und Strafrecht. Arch f Rassen- u Gesell-Biol 25: 197-216 Jl 27 '31 13086

Human betterment foundation. Sterilization of criminals and defectives. Pasadena, Calif. Pacific Southwest bldg. foundation, 1930 13087

Johnson, Gardiner B. C. The constitutionality of eugenical sterilization. Thesis (J.D.) University of California, May 1928 13088

Kankeleit, Otto. Die Unfruchtbarmachung aus rassenhygienischen und sozialen Gründen. 112p. bibliog 97-112. München, Lehmanns, 1929 13089

Klinkenberg, F. Zur Frage der Unfruchtbarmachung geistig Minderwertiger insbesondere nach eugenischen Gesichtspunkten. Allg Zeitsch f Psychiat 87: 410-38 '27 13090

Krüger. Sterilisation von Männern durch Kastration zur Verhütung von Sittlichkeitsdelikten. Krimin Monatsh 4: 256-7 N '30 13091

Landman, J. H. History of human sterilization in the United States—theory, statute, adjudication. Ill L R 23: 463-80 Ja '29; same title: Am L R 63: 48-71 Ja '29; Med-Leg J 46: 40-52 Mr '29 13092

Laughlin, Harry Hamilton. The legal status of eugenical sterilization: history and analysis of litigation under the Virginia sterilization statute, which led to a decision of the Supreme court of the United States upholding the statute. 83p. (Sup to Annual report, 1929) Chicago, Municipal court, 1929 13093

Laughlin, Harry H[amilton]. The legalisation of voluntary eugenical sterilization. Eugen R 19: 12-18 Ap '27 13094

Ley, Aug. Sur la stérilisation des dégénérés. J de Neurol et de Psychiat 31: 696-700 N '31 13095

Macpherson, John. Futility of sterilising mental defectives. 19th Cent 106: 805-12 D '29 13096

Mayer, Joseph. Gesetzliche Unfruchtbarmachung Geisteskranker. 466p. Freiburg, Herder, 1927 13097

Meltzer. Der derseitige Stand der Frage der Unfruchtbarmachung Minderwertiger. Psychiat-Neurol Wchnschr 29: 517-23, 527-33 '27 13098

Moll, Albert. Sterilisierung und Verbrechen. Krimin Monatsh 3: 121-6 Je '29 13099

Montavon, William Frederick. Eugenic sterilization in the laws of the United States. 32p. Washington, National Catholic welfare conference, 1930 13100

Moore, Eldon. Sterilization of the unfit. 19th Cent 105: 499-511 Ap '29 13101

Moser, G. Sterilisierung und Verbrechen. Zeitsch f Sexualwissensch 16: 340-6 '29 13102

Muret, M. De la stérilisation humaine. Schweiz Zeitsch f Gesundheitspfl 7: 328-39 '27 13103

The new Iowa statute on sterilization of defectives. Ia L R 15: 238-44 F '30 13104

North Carolina statute: not a eugenical sterilization law. Eugen N 12: 44-5 Ap '27 13105

Oswald, Frances. Eugenic sterilization in the United States. Am J Sociol 36: 65-73 Jl '30 13106

P.-W. La loi de défense social envisagée au point de vue eugénique. R de Dr Pén et de Crimin 8: 617-18 Je '28 13107

Petren, Alfred. Det Svenska Förslaget till Steriliseringslag jämta nogra reflexioner i ämnet. Nord Tids f Straf 18: 129-38 '30 13108

Popenoe, Paul. Eugenic sterilization in California. J Soc Hyg 13: 257-68, 321-30, 468-77 My-N '27; same title: J Hered 19: 405-11 S '28 13109

Popenoe, Paul. Eugenic sterilization in California: effects of vasectomy on the sexual life. J Abnorm & Soc Psychol 24: 251-68 O '29 13110

Raynaud, E. La castration pénale. Mercure Fr 211: 681-7 My 1; 212: 506-7, 668-73 Je 1, 15 '29 13111

Rex, Frederick, comp. Brief list of references . . . relating to the sterilization of criminal insane and similar defectives. 2p. (typw) Chicago, Municipal reference library, 1927 13112

Rodewald. Die Unfruchtbarmachung geistig Minderwertiger im Lichte der Medizin und des Rechts. Monats f Kriminalpsychol u Strafrechtsref 22: 705-20 D '31 13113

Ruddy, Clarence J. Compulsory sterilization: an unwarranted extension of the powers of government. Notre Dame Law 3: 1-16 O '27 13114

Ryan, John A. Human sterilization. 9p. Washington, National Catholic welfare conference, 1927 13115

Schreiber, Georges. La sterilisation humaine aux Etats-Unis. R Anthrop 39: 260-81 Jl '29 13116

Shipley, Maynard. Sterilization of defectives. Am Mercury 15: 454-7 D '28 13117

Spampinato, Loris. La sterilizzazione dei delinquenti in rapporto ai problemi demografici. Rassegna di Stud Sess 10: 153-76 Jl '30 13118

Sterilization in California. Eugen N 12: 28-9 Mr '27 13119

Törnell, Gottfrid. Betänkande med förslag till steriliseringslag. Svenska Läk-tidning 34: 977-81 Ag 23 '29 13120

Tredgold, A. F. A note on the sterilization of mental defectives. Ment Welf 11: 9-14 Ja '30 13121

United States Supreme court upholds sterilization. Am J Pub Health 17: 773-4 Jl '27 13122

Wassermann. Ist die Sterilisierung von Männern durch Kastration als Mittel zur Verhinderung von Sittlichkeitsverbrechen angebracht und zulässig? Arch f Krim 86: 199-207 Je '30 13123

Watkins, Harvey M. Selective sterilization. Assn of Dir Poor & Char & Correc Proc 55: 106-17 '30 13124

Whitney, E. A. Eugenic sterilization of the mentally unfit. M J & Rec 129: 696-8 Je 19 '29 13125

Whitney, Leon F. Eugenical sterilization. Am J Nursing 27: 741-3 S '27 13126

Wildenskov, H. O. The question of sterilization in Denmark. Ment Welf 8: 74-8 Jl 15 '27 13127

JUVENILE PROTECTIVE WORK

Additon, Henrietta Silvia. City planning for girls. 150p. (Soc Serv Monog 5) Chicago, University of Chicago press, 1928 13128

Allen, Whitcomb H. Safeguarding the child in the community. N Y St Conf Prob Offic Proc 20: 111-15 '27 13129

Arenaza, Carlos de. La readaptacion social del menor delincuente. Museo Soc Arg Bol 19: 471-91 O '31 13130

Beer, Jos. Etude comparative des projets de loi relatifs à la protection morale de l'enfance. R de Dr Pén et de Crimin 7: 587-96 Je '27 13131

Boardman, Rhea K. The young offender and the adult. Nat Prob Assn Proc 1928: 135-44 13132

Borchardt. Der Kampf gegen die Verwahrlosung der Jugend. Gesetz u Recht 28: 193-5 Jl 1 '27 13133

Brazão, Arnaldo. Protecção aos menores delincuentes; marcha evolutiva da legislação Portuguesa. Bol do Inst de Crim s8 15(2): 339-51 '31 13134

Catalan, Emilio. Necesidad de organizar el patronato de menores en la República Argentina. R de Crimin Psiquiat y Med Leg 15: 647-69 N '28 13135

Coll, Jorge Eduardo. Proteccion de la infancia desamparada. R de Der Pen 2(2): 167-91 S 30 '30 13136

Comité de défense des enfants traduits en justice de Paris. R Pénitent et de Dr Pén 55: 66-91 Ja '31 13137

Le VIIe Congrès international de la protection de l'enfance. (Paris, 8 Juillet 1928) Etudes Crimin 4: 27-31 Ja '29 13138

Delfino, Victor. La protection des mineurs dans la République Argentine. R de Dr Pén et de Crimin 7: 665-9 Je '27 13139

Fuller, T. O. The Negro boy. Nat Prob Assn Proc 1928: 342-51 13140

Goguel, S. La protection de l'enfance abandonée et criminelle après la guerre, en Russie et dans les autres pays d'Europe et d'Amérique. Bul Int de la Protec de l'Enf 56: 143-68 F 28 '27 13141

Hellwig, A. Jugendschutz gegen Schundliteratur. 407p. Berlin, Stilke, 1927 13142

Heuyer, G. Mesures de protection en faveur de l'enfance en danger moral. Paris Méd 2: 427-30 N 17 '28 13143

Jiménez de Asúa, Luis. El tratamiento de los menores abandonados y delincuentes en el Brasil. R de Crimin Psiquiat y Med Leg 16: 70-7 Ja '29 13144

Juvenile protective association of Chicago. Annual report, 1927—1930. Chicago, 1928-31 13145

Lea-Plaza, Hugo. Protección social de los niños anormales y delincuentes. Museo Soc Arg Bol 18: 164-9 Mr '30 13146

Martens, Elise H. Berkeley's coordinated program of child adjustment. Sch Life 16: 23-4, 56-8 O, N '30 13147

Maus, Isidore. L'application de la loi du 15 Mai 1912 sur la protection de l'enfance de 1913 à 1926. R de Dr Pén et de Crimin 8: 162-76 F '28 13148

National anti-weapon association. Will your child become a gunman? 3p. Washington, D.C. 1931 13149

Paz Anchorena, José M. Las instituciones oficiales y privadas en la prevencion y proteccion a la infancia desvalida y delincuente. Museo Soc Arg Bol 19: 448-60 O '31 13150

Prevention of juvenile delinquents. Sol J 71: 967-8 D 17 '27 13151

Schumacker, G. C. The prevention of the problem child. Pub Health Nurse 19: 187-9 Ap '27 13152

Smith, J. P. Our boys and girls. Chief Constables' Assn Can Proc 25: 47-50 '29 13153

Sortor, Addie F. Placement of the girl in industry. Nat Prob Assn Proc 1928: 232-5 13154

Thót, Ladislao. Las obras de Don Bosco y la prevención de la criminalidad juvenil. R de Crimin Psiquiat y Med Leg 17: 401-5 Jl '30 13155

Turning the good boys into bad. Am City 41: 128 Ag '29 13156
Summary of recommendations of New York state crime commission report.

Wilkinson, Mildred Rumbold. Juvenile protection work of Congress of parents and teachers. Sch Life 12: 91 Ja '27 13157

Woods, Elizabeth L. The school and delinquency: every school a clinic. Nat Conf Soc Wk Proc 1929: 213-21 13158

Wright, Donald C. Prevention of juvenile crime. Police J [London] 3: 601-10 O '30 13159

Zwanck, Alberto. El servicio social en la asistencia de la infancia abandonada y delincuente. Museo Soc Arg Bol 19: 442-7 O '31 13160

MENTAL HYGIENE WORK

Adler, Herman M. Mental hygiene in a research clinic. National research council, Anthropology and psychology division, Child development committee, Second conference on research in child development [Proceedings] 1927: 78-90 13161

Adler, Herman M. What psychiatry can do to prevent crime. Ind Bul Char & Correc (167): 32-9 F '29; same title: Policewoman's Int Bul 5: 4-5 My '29; Police J [N Y] 17: 19-20 S '29 13162

Allen, Elizabeth. Mental hygiene in two schools. Pub Health Nurse 19: 430-4 '27 13163

Böhme, A. Psychotherapie, Psychoanalyse und Kastration im Dienste der vorbeugenden Verbrechensbekämpfung. München med Wchnschr 77: 1580-4, 369-70 '30 13164

Branham, V. C. Suggestions for a practical program of prevention for New York state exclusive of New York city. Psychiat Q 4: 675-89 '30 13165
Program drawn up by Executive committee of New York state commission on mental hygiene.

Byers, Mrs. Joseph P. The community significance of a proper mental hygiene and child welfare program. Nat Conf Juv Agencies Proc 27: 97-109 '30 13166

Fenton, Norman. Mental hygiene and juvenile research. Sierra Educ N 25: 34 N '29 13167

Fenton, Norman. A state program of preventive mental hygiene. Los Angeles Sch J 13: 18 '30 13168

Gillespie, R. D. The service of psychiatry in the prevention and treatment of crime. Howard J 3: 22-8 S '30 13169

National committee for mental hygiene. Weekly bibliography of current literature on mental hygiene and related subjects, listing articles appearing in approximately one hundred medical, psychological and sociological journals. New York, 1, January 5, 1925- 13170

Orbison, Thomas. The prevention of crimes in mental deviates. J Delin 11: 100-5 Je '27 13171

Starke, E. Individualpsychologie und Verbrechenstherapie. Int Zeitsch f Individualpsychol 6: 96-9 '28 13172

Stiffler, M. L. A mental hygiene program. Minn St Conf & Inst Soc Wk Proc 35: 215-19 '27 13173

POLICE WORK

Crime prevention work by American police departments. Am City 36: 387-9 Mr '27 13174

Dain, J. H. The Norwich Lad's club: welfare work by the police. Police J [London] 2: 387-96 Jl '29 13175

French, H. E. Crime prevention program for municipal police departments. Conf Mayors N Y Proc 1927: 133-9 13176

The functions and organization of a police unit doing protective work with women and children. Pub Personnel Stud 5: 245-53 D '27 13177

Janke, Kurt. Die polizeiliche Schutzhaft Minderjähriger. Zentralbl f Jugendrecht u Jugendwohlfahrt 23 (9): 307-16 D '31 13178

Killick, Victor W. What the Los Angeles county sheriff's office is doing in crime prevention work. Inst Police Adm Proc 1929: 89-95 13179

Lossing, Elizabeth. Pre-delinquency angle of police work. Inst Police Adm Proc 1929: 100-2 13180

Nebel, Richard W. The juvenile offender; police problems in the field of crime prevention among juveniles. Police "13-13" 5: 13-15 N '30 13181

O'Brien, Raymond J. The cop and the boy. Police "13-13" 5: 16-17 D '30 13182

Palitzsch. System der Verbrechensbekämpfung. Krimin Monatsh 1: 164-71 Ag '27 13183

Peterson, Leroy. The police and boys' work. Welf 19: 38-60 Ja '28; same title: Northwest Police J 7: 43-7 Ja '30 13184

Pigeon, Helen D. Crime prevention by policewomen. Policewomen Int Bul 5(42) Ja '29 13185

Read, George M. The importance of a socialized police force in the program of prevention. Nat Conf Juv Agencies Proc 27: 33-41 '30 13186

Russell, William F. The prevention of juvenile crime. Police J [London] 4: 60-7 Ja '31 13187

Sirks, A. H. The police and dangerous drugs. Police J [London] 3: 560-72 O '30 13188

What can police do to prevent boys from becoming gangsters? State Trooper 10: 23 My '29 13189

CONTROL OF PROSTITUTION

Baltra Gacitua, R. Proyecto reglamentación de la prostitución. Cong de Méd y Cir Nav y Mil de Chile 1929: 664-74 13190

Bénech, J. La fiche médico-sociale du dispensaire de salubrité publique de la ville de Nancy. Ann d Mal Vén 24: 707-12 Jl '29 13191

Borms, V. Tayart de. De la réglementation de la prostitution suivant les idées de feu Jules le Jeune. R de Dr Pén et de Crimin 9: 1-18 '29 13192

Bruck, F. War die geringe Zahl der kontrollierten Puellae publicae ein berechtigter Grund, die polizeiliche Kontrolle aufzuheben? München med Wchnschr 75: 739 Ap 27 '28 13193

Carle. Le controle sanitaire de la prostitution. R Int de Crimin 2(1): 36-41 '30 13194

Carle, M. Law against prostitution in United States. Urol & Cutan R 34: 164 Mr '30 13195

Carle, M. and Lacassagne, J. Le dernier projet de loi sur la prostitution vu par des médecins. Ann d Mal Vén 23: 821-34 N '28 13196

Carle, M. and Lacassagne, J. Prostitution et prophylaxie antivénérienne à propos d'un nouveau projet de loi. J de Méd de Lyon 9: 291-4 My 20 '28 13197

Carrera, J. L. Jalone deficientes de la lucha antivenérea en Buenos Aires. Prensa Méd Arg 17: 923-30 N 30 '30 13198

Cuenca y Lamas, B. La inspección sanitaria de la prostitución. Lo que es y lo que debe ser. Cons Nac de Hig Bol 25: 189-219 Mr '31 13199

Deguy. La prostitution. Prophylax Antivén 3: 579-85 S '31 13200

Düring, E. v. Bekämpfung der Prostitution? Monats f Harnkrankh u Sex Hyg 1(1): 15-19 '27 13201

Fiaux, L. La nouvelle réglementation de la Bulgarie. Abolition des maisons dites de tolérance (1929). Prophylax Antivén 3: 165-73 Mr '31 13202

Fuchs, Malvy. Die neue Sittlichkeitsverordnung in Ungarn. Neue Generation 24: 29-30 Ja '28 13203

Goodman, H. Experiences with repression and regulation of prostitution with emphasis on medical aspects. M Times [N Y] 56: 150-7 Je '28 13204

Hanauer, W. Was wird aus der Prostitution in Deutschland nach dem 1. Oktober 1927? Dermat Wchnschr 85: 1447-59 O 15 '27 13205

Heiland, G. Die Bekämpfung der Prostitution. Polizei 24: 546-8 N 20 '27 13206

Ichok, G. L'action législative contre la prostitution et les maladies vénériennes en Allemagne et en France. Presse Méd 36: 651-3 My 23 '28 13207

Ichok, G. La réglementation de la prostitution et la lutte antivénérienne en Bulgarie. R d'Hyg 53: 756-64 O '31 13208

König, Andreas. Die Reglementierung der Prostitution in Ungarn. Zeitsch f Sexualwissensch 15: 59-60 Ap '28 13209

Lesser, F. Ein Jahr Reichsgesetz zur Bekämpfung der Geschlechtskrankheiten. Zur Wohnungsregelung der Prostituierten. Med Klin 24: 1534-6 S 28 '28 13210

The licensing laws and "reputed prostitutes." Shield s3 6: 204-8 N '30 13211

La lutte contre la réglementation de la prostitution. 28p. Genève, Fédération abolitionniste international, 1931 13212

Mallard, H. Le contrôle de la prostitution. Prog Méd 1126-31 Je 20 '31 13213

Martell, P. Polizei und Sittenkontrolle. Arch f Soz Hyg u Demog 2: 465-8 Jl '27 13214

Mazzeo, M. La profilassi celtica e le discussioni sul "regolamentarismo" e l'"abolizionismo." Morgagni 69: 841-63 My 29 '27 13215

Melcher. Polizei und Prostitution. Deut Gesell z Bekämpf d Geschlechtskrankh Mitt 27: 441-53 N '29; same title: Polizei 26 (22): 557-62 N 20 '29 13216

Miner, C. E. Repression versus segregation in Chicago. J Soc Hyg 17: 283-7 My '31 13217

Penlington, J. N. The licensed women of Japan. Cur Hist 34: 887-91 S '31 13218

von Pezold. Zur Emanzipation der Prostituierten. Deut med Wchnschr 57: 19-20 Ja 2 '31 13219

von Pezold. Zur Frage der Kasernierung der Prostituierten. Deut med Wchnschr 57: 1631-3 S 18 '31 13220

Protecting the community from commercialized vice. Soc Hyg N 2: 1-4 Ap 30 '27 13221

Raymond, Neveu. La lutte antivénérienne en France et dans les colonies. Rassegna di Stud Sess 7: 201-8 '27 13222

Rothig, Friede. Fortschritt oder Rückschritt in der Prostitutionsbekämpfung? Freie Wohlfahrtspfl 6(5): 209-18 Ag '31 13223

Schäfer, L. Prostitution und Rechtsprechung. Deut Gesell z Bekämpf d Geschlechtskrankh Mitt 27: 412-31 N '29 13224

Sorge, Wolfgang. Japan gegen die Prostitution. Zeitsch f Sexualwissensch 15: 353-4 O '28 13225

Thiroux, A. De l'opportunité de la surveillance des moeurs dans les colonies françaises. R de Méd et d'Hyg Trop 23: 17-22 Ja '31 13226

Uenoda, S. System of licensed vice aimed to abolish secret prostitutes. Trans-Pac 19: 4 Jl 23; 4- Jl 30 '31 13227

White, C. What law enforcement means to us; the problem of prostitution. J Soc Hyg 17: 393-402 O '31 13228

von Zwehl, Hans. Das erste Vierteljahr ohne Sittenpolizei. Neue Generation 24: 118-21 Ap '28 13229

Zwiller, Y. M. La question du maintien des maisons de tolérance. R Fr de Dermat et de Vén 3: 555-62 N '27 13230

RECREATIONAL WORK

Big brother movement. Annual report 22, 1927—23, 1928. [New York, 1928-29] 13231

Big sisters, Inc. Annual report 16, 1927—19, 1930. New York [1928-31] 13232

Big sisters, Inc. What big sister work means and how we do it. 12p. New York, 1929? 13233

Butler, Burridge D. Boys' clubs and crime. R of R 79: 74 Ap '29 13234

Crime and recreation; the value of neighborhood social clubs. Playground 23: 183-4 Je '29 13235

Doyle, Clyde. The Long Beach coordinate recreation program. J Juv Res 14: 171-5 Jl '30 13236

Eliminating bad boys by good playgrounds. Am City 39: 149 O '28 13237

Girls' service league of America. Annual report 19, 1927—[22] 1930. New York [1927-30] 13238

Before 1922 titled: New York (city) probation and protective association.

Hiller, Francis H. The working of county dance hall ordinances in Wisconsin. J Soc Hyg 13: 1-11 Ja '27 13239

Jan, H. Der Schutz der Jugend vor Schund- und Schmutzschriften. Bayr Verwaltungs-Bl 75: 257-61 '27 13240

Juvenile crime study reveals urgent need for more recreation. Am City 39: 157 Jl '28 13241

Kites, marbles and crime. Playground 22: 362 S '28 13242

Lies, Eugene T. Why not more play? Welf Mag 18: 415-20 Ap '27 13243

New York (city). Police department. Crime prevention bureau. Recreational facilities, provided by the city and state governments and private agency. 16p. 1931 13244

Pettit, M. L. An experiment in the use of recreation in treating delinquents. Nat Prob Assn Proc 25: 61-8 '31 13245

Recreation as a preventive of delinquency. Playground 23: 405-6 S '29 13246

Reed, Dorothy. Play a vital force in checking delinquency. Playground 22: 199-200 Jl '28 13247

Ricks, James Hoge. Striking at the roots. Playground 21: 189 Jl '27 13248

Shulman, H. [M.]. Questions which recreation workers should face with reference to the reduction of delinquency: summary of discussion, 17th recreation congress. Playground 24: 492-4 D '30 13249

Stringham, Frank D. Parks and open spaces are best cure for crime. Calif Leag Munic Official Prog 1927: 17-18 13250

Sutherland, Frances. Camp fire girls. Minn St Conf & Inst Soc Wk Proc 35: 208-10 '27 13251

Todd, Ethel N. and Sheley, Cora B. Girl scouting; Geneva training school for girls believes its training invaluable. Welf Mag 18: 1077-9 Ag '27 13252

Williams, Herbert D. Philosophy of Big brother and big sister service. Minn St Conf & Inst Soc Wk Proc 38: 179-86 '30 13253

RELIGION

Aronson, David. The church as a factor in the prevention of delinquency. Minn St Conf & Inst Soc Wk Proc 36: 198-201 '28 13254

Blessing, Joseph Marx. Can the church check crime? Meth R 114: 58-64 Ja '31 13255

Hering, Ambrose. The church as a factor in the prevention of delinquency. Minn St Conf & Inst Soc Wk Proc 36: 201-3 '28 13256

Miner, John R. Do the churches prevent crime? Am J Police Sci 2: 468-72 N '31 13257

Pratt, Grace E. The church as a factor in the prevention of delinquency. Minn St Conf & Inst Soc Wk Proc 36: 205-8 '28 13258

PROHIBITION

Addams, Jane. A decade of prohibition. Survey 63: 5-10 O 1 '29 13259

After repeal, more crime or less? Scribner's 89: 258-66 Mr '31 13260

Association against the prohibition amendment. Prohibition enforcement; its effect on courts and prisons. 32p. December 1930 13261

Association against the prohibition amendment. Reforming America with a shot gun; a study of prohibition killings. 44p. November 1929 13262

Association against the prohibition amendment. Scandals of prohibition enforcement. 34p. (No4) March 1, 1929 13263

Auerbach, J. S. An indictment of prohibition. 94p. New York, Harper, 1930 13264

Beman, Lamar Taney, comp. Prohibition: modification of the Volstead law. 154p. New York, H.W. Wilson, 1927 13265

Black, Forrest R. The expansion of criminal equity under prohibition. Wis L R 5: 412-25 Ap '30 13266

Bruce, William Cabell. What substitute for prohibition? Cur Hist 31(3): 463-8 D '29 13267

Bruère, Martha Bensley. Does prohibition work? 329p. New York, Harper, 1927 13268

Butler, N. M. Problems of the eighteenth amendment. Am L R 62: 193-214 Mr '28 13269

Caton, Cuthbert B. Effect of national prohibition on state criminal jurisdiction. Cornell L Q 14: 492-6 Je '29 13270

Citizens' committee of one thousand. Youth commission. Will youth accept the law? 15p. 1931 13271

Dorr, Rheta Childe. Drink: coercion or control. 330p. New York, Stokes, 1929 13272

Edwards, Elvin N. Curbing the nuisance speakeasy in Nassau county, New York. Panel 9: 30 My '31 13273

Fellner, Wilhelm. Das amerikanische Alkoholverbot vom Standpunkte der Volkswirtschaftslehre. 136p. Berlin, Christians, 1929 13274

Forrester, J. J. Ten years of prohibition. Cur Hist 33: 807-13 Mr '31 13275

Grohmann. Der Wert der Alkoholabstinenz für Verbrecherische. Monatsbl d deut Reichsver f Gerichtshilfe 2: 167-74 '27 13276

Jaques, Ernst. Die Bekämpfung des Alkoholismus als Aufgabe der Öffentlichen Wohlfahrtspflege. 100p. Berlin, Neulandverl. 1931 13277

Kaesehagen. Massnahmen zur Bekämpfung des Alkoholmissbrauchs. Volkswohlfahrt 11(4): 155-62 F 15 '30 **13278**

Kjerluff, Johnny. Alkoholforbudet i de Forenede Stater. Spiritusfloden over Amerika. 32p. København, Landsforeningen, 1929 **13279**

Lang, O. Der Vorbeugungsgedanke in der Strafrechtspflege. Beziehungen zum Alkohol. Schweiz Zeitsch f Gesundheitspfl 7: 232-8 '27 **13280**

McAdoo, William G. Challenge: liquor and lawlessness versus constitutional government. 304p. New York, Century, 1928 **13281**

McBain, Howard L[ee]. Prohibition: legal and illegal. 171p. New York, Macmillan, 1928 **13282**

Nicholson, Dorothy C. and Graves, Richard P. Selective bibliography on the operation of the eighteenth amendment. 47p. (mim) Berkeley, University of California, Bureau of public administration, June 1931 **13283**

Schmölders, Günter. Die Prohibition in den Vereinigten Staaten Triebkräfte u Auswirkungen d. amerikan. Alkoholverbots. 266p. Leipzig, Hirschfeld, 1930 **13284**

Seggelke, Gunter. Die Strafrechtliche Bekämpfung des Alkoholismus. Arch f Strafr u Strafproz 74: 359- N '30 **13285**

Social science research council. Sources of information concerning the operation of the 18th amendment: a report of a Special advisory committee of the Social science research council. 70p. New York, April 1928 **13286**

Thomas, Norman. The "unholy union" of prohibition and politics. Cur Hist 31: 58-63 O '29 **13287**

United States. Library of congress. Brief list of references on prohibition in the United States. 13p. (mim) Washington, October 28, 1927 **13288**

United States. Library of congress. List of references on the modification or repeal of the eighteenth amendment. 16p. (mim) Washington, December 2, 1930 **13289**

United States. Library of congress. Prohibition: a list of recent books. 4p. (mim) Washington, October 2, 1928 **13290**

Vervaeck, L. Quelques chiffres récents relatifs à la prohibition de l'alcool en Amérique et à ses resultats. R de Dr Pén et de Crimin 7: 1130-1 N '27 **13291**

Willig, Samuel. Violation of eighteenth amendment and the Volstead act as elements of crime in New York. Cornell L Q 12: 509-13 Je '27 **13292**

INDEX

C

G

J

K

L

M

N

O

Q

R

S

U

V

W

X

Y

Z